AMERICAN

FOREIGN POLICY

THEORETICAL ESSAYS

SIXTH EDITION

G. JOHN IKENBERRY

EDITOR

PRINCETON UNIVERSITY

WADSWORTH
CENGAGE Learning

Australia • Brazil • Japan • Korea • Mexico • Singapore • Spain • United Kingdom • United States

WADSWORTH
CENGAGE Learning

American Foreign Policy: Theoretical Essays, Sixth Edition

G. John Ikenberry

Senior Publisher: Suzanne Jeans

Executive Editor: Carolyn Merrill

Development Editor: Anne Prucha

Assistant Editor: Katie Hayes

Editorial Assistant: Angela Hodge

Senior Marketing Manager: Amy Whitaker

Marketing Coordinator: Josh Hendrick

Marketing Communications Manager: Heather Baxley

Content Project Manager: Jessica Rasile

Art Director: Linda Helcher

Print Buyer: Linda Hsu

Senior Rights Acquisition Account Manager-Text: Katie Huha

Production Service/Compositor: MPS Limited, A Macmillan Company

Photo Manager: Jennifer Meyer Dare

Cover Designer: Grannan Graphic Design, Ltd.

Cover Image: ©mstay

For product information and technology assistance, contact us at **Cengage Learning Customer & Sales Support, 1-800-354-9706**

For permission to use material from this text or product, submit all requests online at **www.cengage.com/permissions.** Further permissions questions can be emailed to **permissionrequest@cengage.com.**

Library of Congress Control Number: 2009932855

ISBN-13: 978-0-547-19828-6

ISBN-10: 0-547-19828-0

Wadsworth
20 Channel Center Street
Boston, MA 02210
USA

Cengage Learning is a leading provider of customized learning solutions with office locations around the globe, including Singapore, the United Kingdom, Australia, Mexico, Brazil and Japan. Locate your local office at **international.cengage.com/region**

Cengage Learning products are represented in Canada by Nelson Education, Ltd.

For your course and learning solutions, visit **www.cengage.com.**

Purchase any of our products at your local college store or at our preferred online store **www.CengageBrain.com.**

Printed in the United States of America
1 2 3 4 5 6 7 14 13 12 11 10

Contents

ᔓPART FOURᔓ

National Values, Democratic Institutions, and Foreign Policy
219

ᔓPART FIVEᔓ

Public Opinion, Policy Legitimacy, and Sectional Conflict
301

ᕈᕐPART SIXᕈᕐ
Bureaucratic Politics and Organizational Culture 401

ᕈᕐPART SEVENᕈᕐ
Perceptions, Personality, and Social Psychology 479

ᕈᕐPART EIGHTᕈᕐ
American Foreign Policy After the Bush Administration 551

Preface

The purpose of this book is to provide students with representative statements of the major, contending explanations of American foreign policy. The idea is to showcase the variety of theoretical perspectives that scholars have pursued in attempting to make sense of policy. I have gathered these essays together in the hope that students will become more familiar with the avenues of inquiry that are available and the debates they engender. Left only to the textbook or the occasional popular book on the subject, students and teachers alike can all too easily overlook the very real controversies at the heart of the study of American foreign policy: What political, economic, and cultural forces shape policy? What is the realm of choice and what is the realm of necessity in making policy? What type of language and level of analysis are most useful in our search to explain policy? My hope is that after reading the essays in this volume, the student can achieve more clarity in answering these questions.

The theoretical traditions that these essays represent are long standing. Scholars over many generations have worked within and drawn on many of them, although the specific formulations presented in most of the essays are quite original. Because the effort is to present theoretical approaches and not analysis of current foreign policy events, the essays themselves range in vintage as widely as they range in content. This is a virtue; it reinforces the notion that scholarly endeavor springs from theoretical traditions. We build upon some and react to others. Through this process we create new traditions.

In the Introduction to the volume, I present an overview of the problem of explanation in foreign policy. The problem in the study of American foreign policy is that we have too many ways of explaining policy—we have an overabundance of theory. In this essay I explore some of the methods whereby students can deal with this problem of overdetermination. Part One, The Problem of Explanation, presents discussions of analytic choice in the study of foreign policy. These essays help us develop a set of tools to explore more specific types of explanation. Each of the following parts represents an alternative route to explanation. Taken together, the book provides a sort of compendium of maps for the study of foreign policy. It is the readers who must judge which map is most useful.

Many of the categories of explanation and some of the essays that are presented here were used in a course I taught for many years at Princeton University. After returning to Princeton in 2004, I am again teaching American foreign policy, organizing my course around debates about theories and explanation. Over the years this course was taught by and passed along to several professors. Its organization, with a focus on theories and explanation, was given shape by Miles Kahler and Kenneth Oye as well as by me. Its original inspiration, if oral history is correct, came from James Kurth when he taught Government 179, Comparative Foreign Policy, at Harvard. As it turns out, the teaching of American foreign policy also has its traditions.

G. JOHN IKENBERRY
Princeton University
June 2009

Introduction

G. John Ikenberry

Few areas of American political life have attracted more commentators, critics, and interpreters than United States foreign policy. Popular views of the proper direction and aims of American foreign policy are as ubiquitous and wide ranging as the policies themselves. The end of the Cold War has only widened and intensified the public debate. 9/11 and the American wars in Afghanistan and Iraq have also intensified the debate on the sources of American action abroad. Scholarly analysis of American foreign policy is no less diverse. Schools of thought that claim to explain the sources and purposes of foreign policy are scattered across the academic landscape. This is scarcely surprising. The foreign policy of the United States covers so much history and so many events that it seems capable of sustaining many interpretations, even contradictory ones, at the same time. Scholars are drawn to the study of foreign policy in efforts to develop powerful and satisfying accounts of the forces that shape policy. Yet very little agreement can be found over what those forces are and how they operate. The student of foreign policy is left with an array of historical cases and lots of theories. What is to be done?

Confronted with this predicament, happily, we can make some headway. We can begin by clarifying what exactly these theories seek to explain. A more precise understanding of the claims that a theoretical approach makes allows us to judge its plausibility; we put ourselves in a position to accept or reject the claims in the light of the historical evidence. This volume is organized so as to allow this process of clarification to take place. We are confronted with important and divergent approaches to American foreign policy. Presented with a sort of theoretical menu, we can see what each has to offer. What specifically is each theoretical approach attempting to explain? What are the forces and mechanisms at work? What explicit or implicit models of individual and state action are embedded within each approach? How generalizable are the claims? What unacknowledged normative claims linger below the surface concerning how American foreign policy is best conducted?

Coming to grips with the range of explanations for American foreign policy still leaves us with an overabundance of theory, but we can make headway here as well. In some cases we are confronted with competing explanations for policy—different theories that claim to explain the same events. In circumstances such as these we need to know how to evaluate the alternatives; we need standards of judgment as we sort through the theoretical options. Which types of theories provide the most powerful and robust explanations?

In other cases we are confronted with theories that are lodged at different levels of explanation. The theories are trained on different aspects of foreign policy and are not in direct competition. Here we need to know how to provide layered analysis and to judge which levels are most enduring and fundamental. In both these cases we need a sort of methodology of choice, or a theory of theories, that provides guidance in how to deploy our analysis.

In this introduction I discuss each of these tasks—the clarification of theories and the methodology of choice. We begin this exercise with a sober appreciation of the problems of

1

finding definitive answers to our questions. We must be willing to manage the ambiguity that is inherent in attempting to understand a seemingly unmanageable array of history that we loosely group together as American foreign policy. But the exercise is essential. Precisely because everybody has an opinion on foreign policy, we need to probe more deeply the theoretical assumptions that lie beneath the surface. At the very least we will come to a better understanding of the largely implicit theoretical commitments we often make in the heat of political debate. But we just might advance even further and cut through the welter of opinion to stake out a more systematic and reasoned set of views on American foreign policy. The absence of a systematic and reasoned set of views on foreign policy is often the first criticism we level at our political leaders. We should demand no less of ourselves.

VARIETIES OF THEORY AND LEVELS OF ANALYSIS

Part of the problem in clarifying and comparing alternative explanations of American foreign policy is that these explanations do not always seek to explain the same events. Foreign policy can be found, among other places, in the decisions of a president or secretary of state, in the policies of a government, or in the broad patterns of the nation's history. In explaining the American intervention in Vietnam, are we interested in understanding President Johnson's fateful 1965 decision to send combat troops to South Vietnam or in the larger sequence of American policy and the doctrine of containment that stretched over five administrations? Are we interested in explaining specific decisions of a single individual, sequences of decisions that stretch over many years, or the policy outcomes of entire government bodies, such as Congress or the executive branch? The types of policy outcomes or decisions that we seek to explain may well influence what theoretical bodies of literature we want to draw on. At the same time, what appear to be contradictory theoretical claims by different scholars may actually simply arise from differences in their choice of subject matter.

Levels of Analysis

In clarifying the range of foreign policy outcomes and the range of theoretical explanations, many scholars have invoked the notion of levels of analysis. Kenneth Waltz, concerning himself with international politics and not foreign policy as such, has specified three "images" of international politics: the individual, the state, and the state system.[1] Each image captures a different level of causation in international relations. The first image is the individual; as a source of behavior in international politics, it brings with it the idiosyncratic features and beliefs that constitute all individuals. How do you explain why a nation goes to war? You look at the ambitions and personalities of its leaders. The second image focuses on the characteristics of the nation-state, its culture, society, and political institutions. How do you explain why a nation goes to war? You look at the forces that grow out of its democratic or authoritarian or socialist institutions. The third image is the international system. At this systemic level the concern is with the enduring patterns and structures of power within the state system. How do you explain why a nation goes to war? You look at the competitive nature of the state system and the changing balance of power. Waltz argues that this level is the most powerful as a guide to understanding international politics. The systemic level identifies the forces within which individuals and states operate; it generates constraints and imperatives by which all individuals and states, regardless of their uniquenesses, must abide.

In another classic statement of the problem, J. David Singer also distinguishes levels of analysis. In assessing the levels' descriptive, explanatory, and predictive capabilities, Singer finds that the international system level is the most comprehensive and most capable of predictive generalizations. Yet in moving to a systemic model, such theory loses the richness and specificity of analysis on the national level. At the international level states take on a certain sameness as the analysis deemphasizes national autonomy and independence of choices.[2] In the end Singer argues for a balance of systemic and national-level analysis; an exclusive preoccupation with one or the other risks an exaggeration of either similarities or differences in states.

In a further refinement Robert Jervis distinguishes among four levels of analysis: the level of decision making; the level of bureaucracy; the nature of the state and the workings of domestic politics; and the international environment.[3] Apart from the decision-making level, which delineates the realm of choice for the actor, the other levels locate features of the actor's setting. Analysis at each of these levels makes a claim: that if we know enough about the setting in which foreign policy is made—bureaucratic, national, or international—we can explain and predict the actor's behavior. Yet the emphasis on one of these variables seems to diminish the importance of the others. The importance of the international setting as a force that shapes foreign policy, for example, suggests an image of foreign policy officials relatively unconstrained by their own bureaucracy or domestic political system. Likewise, if bureaucracy plays a serious role in shaping policy, this has implications for the claims we might make about the role of political parties or public opinion. Specifying levels of analysis immediately reveals the theoretical tensions.

There is no uniform method for the classification of types of theories or variables. The organization of this book goes further than the authors just discussed by distinguishing between types of variables or levels of analysis. Several of the sections, such as those concerning economic and cultural determinants of foreign policy, fall rather easily into Waltz's second image or Jervis's national level of analysis. The categorization of variables into levels of analysis is at least initially simply a matter of theoretical housekeeping. For our purposes the levels-of-analysis exercise organizes into manageable parts the various elements of social reality that bear on the making of foreign policy.

International and Domestic Structures

Running through the discussion of levels of analysis is the issue of the primacy of one level over the others. In this there is some controversy. Kenneth Waltz, as we have noted, gives pride of place to forces that operate at the international level. An anarchic state system and a prevailing distribution of power are unrelenting forces that operate on states. To begin one's analysis with more particularistic national or individual variables is to risk missing common international forces that impose their constraints on many states. Political culture or public opinion, for example, may influence foreign policy in specific cases and at the margin, but it is the basic structure of the international system that sets the terms of the conduct of foreign policy over the long run. J. David Singer is not as insistent on leaving explanations at the international level. Theorists of foreign policy are in effect caught between Scilla and Charybdis; a proper theoretical understanding of foreign policy must avoid the dangers that emerge when we move too far in either a national or systemic direction.

There is reason to be skeptical of the strongest claims of systemic analysis that the structure of the international system *determines* foreign policy; indeed, most of the controversy is really over how theoretically privileged this level of analysis should be. Most scholars who stress the importance of systemic forces argue that it sets constraints on foreign policy rather than shaping policy in any more direct sense; it is a necessary but not sufficient component of our analysis. Waltz's theory of international politics is just that: a theory that seeks to explain recurring patterns of behavior within the international system. As Waltz notes, to explain how any single nation-state will respond to the constraints imposed by the international structure requires a theory of foreign policy.[4] The international system influences but does not determine foreign policy.

Yet even if the international system (characterized by its competitive nature and prevailing distribution of power) manifests imperatives and constraints, it is still necessary to understand how and to what extent those imperatives and constraints operate. How does a state (or how do individuals within it) perceive and act on forces generated within a competitive state system? The international system may well create incentives for political leaders to protect their national autonomy and security, but many foreign policy outcomes are consistent with this demand. Statesmen may be pressed to attend to the nation's survival and well-being, but the international setting does not provide unambiguous clues about how best to do so. In the same way, the specification of international constraints may leave a wide range of options open to state officials. Constraints may be more or less confining, and so we need to know under what conditions they are more and under what conditions they are less confining. A focus on constraints tells us what is not possible. If constraints are very tight, we may have most of the story. If they are loose, we are left with little guidance concerning what is still possible.[5]

If the international setting does not provide enough explanatory power, we might want to turn to national-level variables. Here we are interested in such factors as the social and economic structure of the nation and the character of its domestic politics. The variety of domestic variables that may impinge on foreign policy is huge, and many of them are organized in the sections of this book. Some theories argue for the importance of the nation's culture, its economic and class structure, or its ruling political institutions. Some make strong claims that a particular variable determines foreign policy in conjunction with other variables. When we move to this level of analysis, the types of variables that may impinge on foreign policy proliferate.

In each case we are confronted with the same issues as those that arose in our discussion of systemic theory. Each approach makes a claim about the constraints and imperatives that are imposed by a particular set of characteristics in the decision maker's domestic setting. States with the same critical domestic feature should pursue similar sorts of foreign policy when they are in similar sorts of international situations (and also act similarly when confronted with significantly different situations); states that differ in this critical domestic feature should also differ in their foreign policy, even if they are confronted with similar sorts of international situations.[6] It is here that national-level theories of foreign policy are put to the test. Revisionist historians argue that the Cold War had its roots in the expansive behavior of American capitalist society. Critics of this position argue that United States policy toward the Soviet Union was motivated by geopolitical circumstances that would have been felt and acted on by American political leaders regardless of the nation's internal economic or political characteristics. History makes it very difficult to settle this controversy, but the theoretical issues at stake are clear.

Theories of foreign policy that stress the importance of domestic setting make the implicit claim that if different leaders were present in the same domestic circumstances, they would make the same choices. The stronger the claim made about the role of domestic setting, the less it is necessary to know about the activities and beliefs of the actual individuals who make decisions. But again we are confronted with theoretical challenges. Unless one takes an extreme position, the theory characterizes the domestic sources of foreign policy as constraints and imperatives that more or less shape policy. In what way do political leaders feel the pressures and constraints of culture, class, or political institutions? What are the mechanisms? How do they operate? Under what conditions can they be ignored or transformed? If a particular type of domestic structure, such as class structure, is only loosely constraining, we may need to consider several sets of structures and entertain the possibility that they interact with one another. Bureaucratic politics may be magnified by the play of societal pressures, or it may insulate political leaders from the larger society. Political culture and ideals may manifest themselves most profoundly in the institutions of government that in turn help to influence the course of foreign policy.

Choice and Decision Making

When we have exhausted the explanatory power of a state's domestic and international setting, we are left with the decision makers themselves. The theories we have discussed to this point are *structural* theories. That is, they are theories that make predictions about foreign policy outcomes without reference to the cognition and actions of the actors themselves. According to these theories, setting, of whatever type, shapes policy. In their strongest form structural theories that stress domestic and international setting leave little or no room for individual beliefs, perceptions, or choices. Individuals are theoretically fungible. Substitute one individual for another, and if the setting remains the same, so too does foreign policy.

If structural theories do not satisfactorily explain foreign policy, we can turn to *decision-making* explanations of policy. Here we are interested in theories that explain policy in terms of the reasons, beliefs, and processes by which individuals make choices. Domestic and international structures may constrain and propel foreign policy, but when they leave room for meaningful choice, we need theories of individual and group decision making.[7]

The autonomy of the decision-making level remains a matter of some controversy. This issue is implicit when students of American foreign policy debate various historical "what-ifs." If Franklin Roosevelt had lived, would he have been able to prevent or moderate postwar hostilities between the United States and the Soviet Union beyond the talents of an inexperienced Harry Truman? If John F. Kennedy had not been killed in Dallas, would the tragedy of Vietnam have been avoided? Alternatively, in both these cases were the evolving geopolitical circumstances or shifting international currents leading these presidents in the same direction as their successors? In the most important episodes of postwar American foreign policy, when policy was made that lasted a generation, did individuals make a difference or were they swept up in larger historical forces? These are questions about the role of the individual in history. They are questions as stimulating as they are frustrating, and we cannot provide definitive answers to them. Nonetheless, if we are prepared to grant our foreign policy leaders a realm of choice, we must equip ourselves with a means to understand their decisions.

Several literatures probe the workings of foreign policy decision making. One group of theories focuses on the manner in which government bureaucracy shapes the content of policy. The claims of this type of explanation are fourfold: The de facto power to make foreign policy is divided across the executive establishment; the various "players" in the decision-making process have different goals and interests, largely determined by their bureaucratic position ("Where a person stands depends on when he sits"); decision making is a process of bargaining and compromise; and consequently, policy is a "resultant"—it is the product of a political rather than an analytical process. The seminal statement of this approach is provided by Graham Allison, and it is included in this volume along with major statements of critique.

The implication of this body of theory, if it is to be truly taken seriously, is that policy emerges not in response to the external setting of the actors charged with making decisions but rather from within the organizations of the state itself. It is the bureaucratic interests of government officials and the distribution of power within the state that determine the substantive content of policy. If, however, those interests and configurations of power are only a reflection of larger social interests and powers, the bureaucratic approach to explanation is substantially reduced in theoretical importance. We may want to know about the details of decision making within the "black box" of government, but that process is trivial as a guide to the forces that shape policy. Alternatively, bureaucratic politics and organizational process may be decisive sources of policy in the foreign policy backwaters—in areas of least significance. We must be prepared to differentiate policies as we search for explanations.

The decision-making level has also been approached by other scholars who focus on the beliefs and cognition of top leaders. As is the case with the bureaucratic politics approach, the attention to beliefs and perceptions assumes a realm of choice in policy making. The importance of cognitive variables may emerge in several situations. We may want to focus on this aspect of decision making if there are cases in which consistent differences exist between decision makers' perceptions and reality. These may be cases of major foreign policy blunders, when officials misjudge their position or that of their adversary. Such cases may provide evidence of the role of domestic constraints or pressures, but it is equally plausible that the officials were conducting policy with an inappropriate set of beliefs. Alternatively, we may want to probe the role of perceptions and beliefs when officials placed in the same situation behave differently. In these cases officials may bring to office very different sets of beliefs about the world.[8] These types of beliefs and cognitive frameworks are explored in Part Seven of this book.

Provided with these various levels of analysis and theoretical approaches, we can explore their utility in the study of foreign policy. We can begin to appreciate the various levels of social structure and decision making that may bear on policy. At the same time it is easy to see that we are supplied with an overabundance of theory. We need further guidance in making theoretical choices. It is not enough simply to pick some theoretical approach and run with it. We need guidance in how to proceed when different approaches seem to provide equally plausible explanations—to better understand when a particular level of analysis or type of variable is most suitable in rendering an account of foreign policy. We turn to these issues now.

THE PROBLEM OF THE OVERSUPPLY OF THEORY

Of the various approaches to foreign policy in this volume, each promises to explain some aspects of American foreign policy, and at each level there is seemingly great promise. The international system can be brought to bear in explaining almost all foreign policy. Internationally generated pressures of various sorts find their way into all facets of policy making. Foreign policy also elicits strong views from many segments of society, and some types of foreign policy serve to advantage and disadvantage various societal groups. Thus, even if direct pressure by these groups is not apparent, an underlying set of societal interests may still account for patterns of outcomes. Finally, political leaders and the bureaucracy have a hand in shaping foreign policy simply by virtue of their location and formal powers. Indeed, to no one's surprise, these officials find it easy to rationalize their actions in terms of national or "state" interests. It is clear that we are left not with an absence of adequate explanations of foreign policy but with an oversupply. As James Kurth puts the issue, "[t]he problem with questions about the making of military policy, and also about the making of foreign policy, is not that there are no answers but that there are too many answers."[9] How are we to proceed?

It may not be possible to settle these theoretical controversies—to decide which theory or level of analysis is most important. But we can put ourselves in a situation to judge the merits of various approaches to foreign policy. When we are confronted with competing and seemingly coequal explanations of foreign policy, we can turn to three methods by which to adjudicate the claims: empirical, aesthetic, and analytical.

The most obvious attempt to solve the problem of overdetermination is to turn the problem into an *empirical* problem. If we are confronted, for example, with a structural account and a decision-making account of an episode in American foreign policy, we may want to investigate the recollections of the government officials themselves to see what they perceived to be their realm of choice. Stanley Hoffmann provides a structural account of American policy in the early postwar period: "When the nature of Soviet power and policy and the crumbling of British strength became obvious, the United States simply had to fill the vacuum. President Truman's freedom of choice was strictly limited; it concerned the moment and the manner in which America's taking up the challenge would be demonstrated. Even in this respect the margin of choice was narrowed by the development of the crisis in Greece in 1947 . . . Rarely has freedom been more clearly the recognition of necessity, and statesmanship the imaginative exploitation of necessity."[10] This systemic argument about the forces that drove American policy (and the various bureaucratic, economic, and cultural accounts that compete against it) can be clarified by investigating the range of options that officials themselves entertained.

There are inherent limits, however, to empirical solutions to theoretical problems. Government officials may seek to rationalize their decisions by arguing that the imperatives of geopolitics left them no choice; or they may take credit for making a choice where none really existed. Even more problematic, the theories themselves point to different types of evidence, each with its own biases. In explaining why President Kennedy chose a policy of blockade during the Cuban missile crisis, we can find evidence to support a variety of explanations. We could point to the president's individual characteristics, to political pressures of the upcoming midterm election in 1962, or to the international balance of power. There is evidence that would seem to suit each type of explanation. Adjudication of the claims of various theories by strict reference to the historical "facts" runs into the same problem we have with the theories themselves: There is an overabundance, not a paucity, of empirical evidence. Empirical investigations may give us some help, but they do not resolve the problems of the oversupply of theory.

A second approach to the problem of competing explanations could be called the *aesthetic* solution. Competing theories are judged in terms of basic standards of theoretical rigor. These standards, as Harry Eckstein argues, include regularity (does a theory involve claims to "rule-fulness" with statements of causation and probability?); reliability and validity (does the theory provide a set of conditions that if repeated would produce the same outcome?); foreknowledge (does the theory provide statements of anticipated outcomes in areas currently unknown?); and parsimony (how wide a range and number of phenomena can the theory order and how simple are the theoretical constructs it uses to do so?).[11]

From the standpoint of these elements of rigor, the theories in this volume present different strengths and weaknesses. Systemic theory, with its attention to international structural variables, is attractive for its parsimony. If we want to explain general characteristics of American foreign policy over long stretches of time, this is a good place to begin. Yet international-level theory, as we have already noted, posits constraints and imperatives on actors; it does not provide the basis for predicting specific outcomes. Systemic theory may still provide the most powerful explanation of foreign policy in some circumstances, yet its parsimony is often purchased at the price of less specificity in the outcomes it can explain. Other structural theories that specify the setting within which actors make decisions also suffer from problems of this sort. Theories that rely on political culture or ideology, although they are less parsimonious than systemic theory, also tend to have a huge variety of outcomes that are consistent with their predictions. Theories that are lodged at the decision-making level rely on variables that tend to come and go with the individuals themselves; patterns and regularities in foreign policy are tied closely to sets of intervening conditions. At the same time, decision-making theories may be able to capture more of the richness and critical detail of foreign policy.

It is clear that no one theory or set of variables can be the most important in all situations. Consequently, our efforts are probably not best served by seeking to find one approach that triumphs over the rest. The importance of a set of variables varies with the cases we are seeking to understand. This leads to a final method for dealing with the problem of the oversupply of theory—what we can call the *analytical* approach. Here the effort is not to choose between the contending explanations as such, but to draw on each in various ways. This can be done in two ways. One approach is eclectic. In this we simply pick and choose from the various approaches in fashioning plausible accounts of American foreign policy. This approach appears reasonable at first glance, particularly because the types of policies we might wish to explain vary so enormously. Nonetheless, this ad hoc approach has flaws, as James Kurth criticizes: "It is intellectually unsatisfying and even self-abnegating. Further, it suffers from what might be called the nth+1 problem. Given n theories, the simply eclectic will accept them all and equally, for he has no standards with which to discriminate among them. But suppose someone offers another explanation, the nth+1 theory. The simply eclectic must accept this theory too. And the same is true for the nth+2, nth+3 . . . "[12]

The analytical solution, however, does not need to be eclectic. Rather than simply picking and choosing elements of the various approaches, this approach can involve the development of more overarching propositions that bring the various theories together in comprehensive ways. In effect what this final approach attempts to do is to develop "metatheory" that incorporates the several types of variables into larger-scale frameworks. An exercise of this sort is all the more useful when we note that many of the theories are not strictly speaking alternative and coequal. The explanatory usefulness of a variable, as we have argued, may depend on the level of generality in which we wish to locate our analysis. The international system may influence the general contours of American foreign policy, but domestic and decision-making variables are necessary to explain more specific aspects. Or it may be, as Robert Jervis argues, that the importance of variables at each level may vary with the stages of decision: "domestic politics may dictate that a given event be made the occasion for a change in policy; bargaining within the bureaucracy may explain what options are presented to the national leaders; the decision maker's predisposition could account for the choice that was made; and the interests and routines of the bureaucracies could explain the way the decision was implemented."[13]

Another way to make sense of the multitude of variables and levels is to pose their significance as conditional propositions. Thus, we can argue that systemic-level variables are most important during times of international crisis. It is at these moments that government officials are most attentive to the constraints and opportunities of the international system and most willing to ignore domestic political pressures. In the absence of a foreign policy crisis, domestic politics or the working of bureaucracy are more likely to come into play. One can also develop contingent propositions that relate variables to different types of foreign policy issues. Foreign economic policy may be subject to greater domestic pressures than military policy.[14] Doubtless there are many other ways to develop contingent propositions of this sort that link sets of variables with divergent aspects of American foreign policy. In the end we are still left with an overabundance of theory, but we now have methods with which to cope with the many possibilities.

CONCLUSION

The choices we make about how to probe the workings of American foreign policy carry with them normative implications. This is not evident at first glance. Discussions of theory, and even more so "metatheory," seem to be far removed from our own views about the conduct of foreign policy. Yet the link exists. James Kurth observes that the conclusions we draw on the theory of foreign policy tell us, when we turn to policy advocacy, what needs to be reformed. If we conclude that high levels of military spending and an expansionary foreign policy are rooted in the very nature of the American capitalist system, as Marxists and others have argued, the agenda for change is profound indeed. If such policies are propelled by more transient sets of institutions or ruling coalitions, reform would lead in a different direction. Our theories give us guidance when we want to talk about improving American foreign policy.

Those who argue that the international system is an overpowering force in shaping foreign policy are faced with their own moral questions. If foreign policy officials are the faithful stewards of the balance of power, who is to be judged accountable? Robert Jervis poses this issue:

> When all people would respond the same way to a given situation, it is hard to praise or blame the decision maker. Thus, those accused of war crimes will argue that their behavior did not differ from others who found themselves in the same circumstance. And the prosecution will charge, as it did against Tojo and his colleagues, that "These defendants were not automatons; they were not replaceable cogs in a machine. . . . It was theirs to choose whether their nation would lead an honored life . . . or . . . would become a symbol of evil throughout the world. They made their choice. For this choice they must bear the guilt."[15]

Our theories tell us who should be held accountable in the conduct of foreign policy. Is the president in control or is he the hostage of a massive federal bureaucracy? Do our democratic institutions shape foreign policy or is it guided by the hidden hand of class interests?

We may have to live with the fact that our answers to these questions are not definitive. The drawing of satisfying theoretical conclusions about the sources and purposes of American foreign policy is a complicated affair; we are left with a certain amount of theoretical ambiguity. We can remember Albert Einstein's advice that "if you wish to describe truth, leave elegance to the tailor." At the very least we can begin by being more theoretically self-conscious about our arguments and opinions. This book seeks to array the relevant literatures so as to allow such a process to go forward.

NOTES

1. Kenneth N. Waltz, *Man, the State, and War* (New York: Columbia University Press, 1959).
2. J. David Singer, "The Level-of-Analysis Problem in International Relations," in Klaus Knorr and Sidney Verba, eds., *The International System: Theoretical Essays* (Princeton: Princeton University Press, 1961).
3. Robert Jervis, *Perception and Misperception in International Politics* (Princeton: Princeton University Press, 1976), Chapter 1.
4. Kenneth N. Waltz, *Theory of International Politics* (Reading, Mass.: Addison-Wesley, 1979). Chapter 6, "Anarchic Orders and Balances of Power," reprinted in this book as Chapter 3.
5. For a very insightful discussion of the nature of constraints and determinants see Arthur A. Stein, "Structure, Purpose, Process, and Analysis of Foreign Policy: The Growth of Soviet Power and the Role of Ideology," in Roman Kolkowicz, ed., *The Roots of Soviet Power: Domestic Determinants of Foreign and Defense Policy* (Boulder: Westview Press, 1989).
6. See Jervis, *Perception and Misperception in International Politics*, p. 22.
7. See Stein, "Structure, Purpose, Process, and the Analysis of Foreign Policy."
8. Jervis, *Perception and Misperception in International Politics*, p. 29.
9. James R. Kurth, "A Widening Gyre: The Logic of American Weapons Procurement," *Public Policy* XIX (Summer 1971).
10. Stanley Hoffmann, "Restraints and Choices in American Foreign Policy," in Stanley Hoffmann, *The State of War: Essays on the Theory and Practice of International Politics* (Praeger Publishers, 1965).
11. Harry Eckstein, "Case Study and Theory in Political Science," in Nelson Polsby and Fred Greenstein, eds., *Handbook of Political Science* (Reading, Mass.: Addison- Wesley, 1975), vol. 2, p. 88. See also Alexander George, "Case Studies and Theory Development," in Paul Lauren, ed., *Diplomacy: New Approaches in Theory, History, and Policy* (New York: Free Press, 1979), pp. 43–68; and Alexander George and Tim McKeown, "Case Studies and Theories of Organizational Decision Making," in Robert Coulan and Richard Smith, eds., *Advances in Information Processing in Organizations* (Greenwich, CT: JAI Press, 1985), pp. 43–68. For a critique of the case study method, see Olav Njolstad, "Learning from History? Case Studies and the Limits of Theory Building," in Njolstad, ed., *Arms Races: Technological and Political Dynamics* (Beverly Hills, CA: Sage, 1990), pp. 220–46. For discussion of the scientific method as it relates to the study of Soviet foreign policy, see Jack Snyder, "Richness and Rigor, and Relevance in the Study of Soviet Foreign Policy," *International Security*, vol. 9, no. 3 (Winter 1984/85).
12. James R. Kurth, "United States Policies and Latin American Politics: Competing Theories and Comparative Analyses," unpublished paper, 1972.
13. Jervis, *Perception and Misperception in International Politics*, p. 17.
14. See Barry B. Hughes, *The Domestic Context of American Foreign Policy* (San Francisco: W.H. Freeman and Company, 1978), Chapter 7.
15. Jervis, *Perception and Misperception in International Politics*, pp. 15–16.

↪ PART ONE ↩

The Problem
of Explanation

The following two essays examine the general analytical problems of explaining foreign policy. The problem of explanation is not that there are no answers but that there are too many answers. The ability to arrive at determinate causal explanations of foreign policy is elusive. The authors argue, nonetheless, that progress can be made. They argue that it is important to tackle particular foreign policy puzzles—why the United States intervened abroad militarily or worked to create a new international institution, for example—armed with multiple explanatory lenses. Explaining American foreign policy involves a battle of explanations. The first step in the process is to clarify the various models or lenses that are relevant to a particular foreign policy episode. Explanations themselves often involve not proving one model or lens right and the others wrong—but showing how various models or lenses reveal different aspects of the puzzle.

Ole Holsti is interested in facilitating exchange between diplomatic historians and political scientists, which he does by offering a map of the various schools of thought in the professional study of international relations and foreign policy. Holsti's survey begins by examining theories of the international system: classical realism and its modern variations, global society and complex interdependence, and Marxism. Holsti moves on to examine various models of foreign policy decision making: bureaucratic politics, group dynamics, and individual decision making. Holsti argues that systemic and decision-making approaches each have advantages and limitations, and a satisfying explanation may need to work within both traditions. At the same time, it is important to clearly specify the outcome that one wants to explain; this also determines which model is most useful.

W. Michael Reisman is concerned with a more narrow question: how to make sense of the complex, ambivalent, and shifting relationship that the United States has had over the last century with multilateral institutions. He identifies four roles that the United States fulfills when it supports or resists involvement in international institutions. Each role reflects a different impulse or motivation behind American policy—visionary ideals, power politics, institutional routines, and domestic pressure politics. Reisman shows us how a proper understanding of the American encounter with global institutions requires a variety of analytical models.

Models of International Relations and Foreign Policy

Ole R. Holsti

Universities and professional associations usually are organized in ways that tend to separate scholars in adjoining disciplines and perhaps even to promote stereotypes of each other and their scholarly endeavors. The seemingly natural areas of scholarly convergence between diplomatic historians and political scientists who focus on international relations have been underexploited, but there are also a few welcome signs that this may be changing. These include recent essays suggesting ways in which the two disciplines can contribute to each other; a number of prize- winning dissertations, later turned into books, by political scientists during the past decade that effectively combine political science theories and historical research and materials; collaborative efforts among scholars in the two disciplines; and the appearance of such interdisciplinary journals as *International Security* that provide an outlet for historians and political scientists with common interests.[1]

This essay is an effort to contribute further to an exchange of ideas between the two disciplines by describing some of the theories, approaches, and "models" that political scientists have used in their research on international relations during recent decades. A brief essay cannot do justice to the entire range of models that may be found in the current literature, if only because the period has witnessed a proliferation of approaches. But perhaps the models described here, when combined with citations to some representative works, will provide diplomatic historians with a useful, if sketchy, road map toward some of the more prominent landmarks in a neighboring discipline.

Because "classical realism" is the most venerable and persisting model of international relations, it provides a good starting point and baseline for comparison with competing models. Robert Gilpin may have been engaging in hyperbole when he questioned whether our understanding of international relations has advanced significantly since Thucydides, but one must acknowledge that the latter's analysis of the Peloponnesian War includes concepts that are not foreign to contemporary students of balance-of-power politics.[2]

Following a discussion of classical realism, an examination of "modern realism" will identify the continuities and differences between the two approaches. The essay then turns to several models that challenge one or more core premises of both classical and modern realism. The first two challengers focus on the system level: Global-Society/Complex-Interdependence models and Marxist/World-System/Dependency models. Subsequent sections discuss several "decision-making" models, all of which share a skepticism about the adequacy of theories that

Ole R. Holsti, "Models of International Relations and Foreign Policy," *Diplomatic History, 13, 1* (Winter 1989), pp. 15–43. Reprinted by permission of Blackwell Publishing.

focus on the structure of the international system while neglecting political processes within units that comprise the system.

Three limitations should be stated at the outset. Each of the three systemic and three decision-making approaches described below is a composite of several models; limitations of space have made it necessary to focus on the common denominators rather than on subtle differences among them. This discussion will also avoid purely methodological issues and debates; for example, what Stanley Hoffmann calls "the battle of the literates versus the numerates."[3] Finally, efforts of some political scientists to develop "formal" or mathematical approaches to international relations are neglected here; such abstract, often ahistorical models are likely to be of limited interest to historians.[4] With these caveats, let me turn now to classical realism, the first of the systemic models to be discussed in this essay.

There have always been Americans, such as Alexander Hamilton, who viewed international relations from a realist perspective, but its contemporary intellectual roots are largely European. Three important figures of the interwar period probably had the greatest impact on American scholarship: the historian E. H. Carr, the geographer Nicholas Spykman, and the political theorist Hans J. Morgenthau. Other Europeans who have contributed significantly to realist thought include John Herz, Hedley Bull, Raymond Aron, and Martin Wight, while notable Americans of this school include scholars Arnold Wolfers and Norman Graebner, as well as diplomat George F. Kennan, journalist Walter Lippmann, and theologian Reinhold Niebuhr.[5]

Although realists do not constitute a homogeneous school—any more than do any of the others discussed in this essay—most of them share at least five core premises about international relations. To begin with, they view as central questions the causes of war and the conditions of peace. They also regard the structure of the international system as a necessary if not always sufficient explanation for many aspects of international relations. According to classical realists, "structural anarchy," or the absence of a central authority to settle disputes, is the essential feature of the contemporary system, and it gives rise to the "security dilemma": in a self-help system one nation's search for security often leaves its current and potential adversaries insecure, any nation that strives for absolute security leaves all others in the system absolutely insecure, and it can provide a powerful incentive for arms races and other types of hostile interactions. Consequently, the question of *relative* capabilities is a crucial factor. Efforts to deal with this central element of the international system constitute the driving force behind the relations of units within the system; those that fail to cope will not survive. Thus, unlike "idealists" or "liberal internationalists," classical realists view conflict as a natural state of affairs rather than a consequence that can be attributed to historical circumstances, evil leaders, flawed sociopolitical systems, or inadequate international understanding and education.[6]

A third premise that unites classical realists is their focus on geographically based groups as the central actors in the international system. During other periods the major entities may have been city states or empires, but at least since the Treaties of Westphalia (1648), states have been the dominant units. Classical realists also agree that state behavior is rational. The assumption behind this fourth premise is that states are guided by the logic of the "national interest," usually defined in terms of survival, security, power, and relative capabilities. To Morgenthau, for example, "rational foreign policy minimizes risks and maximizes benefits." Although the national interest may vary according to specific circumstances, the similarity of motives among nations permits the analyst to reconstruct the logic of policymakers in their pursuit of national interests—what Morgenthau called the "rational hypothesis"—and to avoid the fallacies of "concern with motives and concern with ideological preferences."[7]

Finally, the nation-state can also be conceptualized as a *unitary* actor. Because the central problems for states are starkly defined by the nature of the international system, their actions are primarily a response to external rather than domestic political forces. At best, the latter provide very weak explanations for external policy. According to Stephen Krasner, for example, the state "can be treated as an autonomous actor pursuing goals associated with power and the general interest of the society."[8] However, classical realists sometimes use domestic politics as a residual category to explain deviations from rational policies.

Realism has been the dominant model of international relations during at least the past five decades, perhaps in part because it seemed to provide a useful framework for understanding World War II and the Cold War. Nevertheless, the classical versions articulated by Morgenthau and others have received a good deal of critical scrutiny. The critics have included scholars who accept the basic premises of realism but who found that in at least four important respects these theories lacked sufficient precision and rigor.

Classical realism usually has been grounded in a pessimistic theory of human nature, either a theological version (e.g., St. Augustine and Reinhold Niebuhr), or a secular one (e.g., Machiavelli, Hobbes, and Morgenthau). Egoism and self-interested behavior are not limited to a few evil or misguided leaders, as the idealists would have it, but are basic to *homo politicus* and thus are at the core of a realist theory. But according to its critics, because human nature, if it means anything, is a constant rather than a variable, it is an unsatisfactory explanation for the full range of international relations. If human nature explains war and conflict, what accounts for peace and cooperation? In order to avoid this problem, most modern realists have turned their attention from human nature to the structure of the international system to explain state behavior.

In addition, critics have noted a lack of precision and even contradictions in the way classical realists use such concepts as "power," "national interest," and "balance of power."[9] They also see possible contradictions between the central descriptive and prescriptive elements of classical realism. On the one hand, nations and their leaders "think and act in terms of interests defined as power," but, on the other, statesmen are urged to exercise prudence and self-restraint, as well as to recognize the legitimate national interests of other nations.[10] Power plays a central role in classical realism, but the correlation between the relative power balance and political outcomes is often less than compelling, suggesting the need to enrich analyses with other variables. Moreover, the distinction between "power as capabilities" and "useable options" is especially important in the nuclear age.

While classical realists have typically looked to history and political science for insights and evidence, the search for greater precision has led many modern realists to look elsewhere for appropriate models, analogies, metaphors, and insights. The discipline of choice is often economics, from which modern realists have borrowed a number of tools and concepts, including rational choice, expected utility, theories of firms and markets, bargaining theory, and game theory. Contrary to the assertion of some critics, however, modern realists *share* rather than reject the core premises of their classical predecessors.[11]

The quest for precision has yielded a rich harvest of theories and models, and a somewhat less bountiful crop of supporting empirical applications. Drawing in part on game theory, Morton Kaplan described several types of international systems—for example, balance-of-power, loose bipolar, tight bipolar, universal, hierarchical, and a unit-veto system in which any action requires the unanimous approval of all its members. He then outlined the essential rules that constitute these systems. For example, the rules for a balance-of-power system are:

"(1) increase capabilities, but negotiate rather than fight; (2) fight rather than fail to increase capabilities; (3) stop fighting rather than eliminate an essential actor; (4) oppose any coalition or single actor that tends to assume a position of predominance within the system; (5) constrain actors who subscribe to supranational organizational principles; and (6) permit defeated or constrained essential actors to re-enter the system."[12] Richard Rosecrance, J. David Singer, Karl Deutsch, Bruce Russett, and many others, although not necessarily realists, also have developed models which seek to understand international relations by virtue of system-level explanations. Andrew M. Scott's survey of the literature, which yielded a catalogue of propositions about the international system, also illustrates the quest for greater precision in systemic models.[13]

Kenneth Waltz's *Theory of International Politics,* the most prominent effort to develop a rigorous and parsimonious model of "modern" or "structural" realism, has tended to define the terms of a vigorous debate during the past decade. It follows and builds upon another enormously influential book in which Waltz developed the Rousseauian position that a theory of war must include the system level (what he called the "third image") and not just first (theories of human nature) or second (state attributes) images. Why war? Because there is nothing in the system to prevent it.[14]

Theory of International Relations is grounded in analogies from microeconomics; international politics and foreign policy are analogous to markets and firms. Oligopoly theory is used to illuminate the dynamics of interdependent choice in a self-help anarchical system. Waltz explicitly limits his attention to a structural theory of international systems, eschewing the task of linking it to a theory of foreign policy. Indeed, he doubts that the two can be joined in a single theory and he is highly critical of many system-level analysts, including Morton Kaplan, Stanley Hoffmann, Richard Rosecrance, Karl Deutsch and J. David Singer, and others, charging them with various errors, including "reductionism"; that is, defining the system in terms of the attributes or interactions of the units.

In order to avoid reductionism and to gain rigor and parsimony, Waltz erects his theory on the foundations of three core propositions that define the structure of the international system. The first concentrates on the principles by which the system is ordered. The contemporary system is anarchic and decentralized rather than hierarchical; although they differ in many respects, each unit is formally equal.[15] A second defining proposition is the character of the units. An anarchic system is composed of similar sovereign units and therefore the functions that they perform are also similar rather than different; for example, all have the task of providing for their own security. In contrast, a hierarchical system would be characterized by some type of division of labor, as is the case in domestic politics. Finally, there is a distribution of capabilities among units in the system. Although capabilities are a unit-level attribute, the distribution of capabilities is a system-level concept.[16]

A change in any of these elements constitutes a change in system structure. The first element of structure as defined by Waltz is a quasi-constant because the ordering principle rarely changes, and the second element drops out of the analysis because the functions of units are similar as long as the system remains anarchic. Thus, the last of the three attributes, the distribution of capabilities, plays the central role in Waltz's model.

Waltz uses his theory to deduce the central characteristics of international relations. These include some non-obvious propositions about the contemporary international system. For example, with respect to system stability (defined as maintenance of its anarchic character and no consequential variation in the number of major actors) he concludes that: because the present bipolar system reduces uncertainty, it is more stable than alternative structures; interdependence has declined rather than increased during the twentieth century, a tendency that has actually contributed to stability; and the proliferation of nuclear weapons may contribute to rather than erode system stability.[17]

Unlike some system-level models, Waltz's effort to bring rigor and parsimony to realism has stimulated a good deal of further research, but it has not escaped controversy and criticism.[18] Leaving aside highly charged polemics—for example, that Waltz and his supporters are guilty of engaging in a "totalitarian project of global proportions"—most of the vigorous debate has centered on four alleged deficiencies relating to interests and preferences, system change, misallocation of variables between the system and unit levels, and an inability to explain outcomes.[19]

Specifically, a spare structural approach suffers from an inability to identify completely the nature and sources of interests and preferences because these are unlikely to derive solely from the structure of the system. Ideology or domestic considerations may often be at least as important. Consequently, the model is also unable to specify adequately how interests and preferences may change. The three defining characteristics of system structure are too general, moreover, and thus they are not sufficiently sensitive to specify the sources and dynamics of system change. The critics buttress their claim that the model is too static by pointing to Waltz's assertion that there has only been a single structural change in the international system during the past three centuries.

Another drawback is the restrictive definition of system properties, which leads Waltz to misplace, and therefore neglect, elements of international relations that properly belong at the system level. Critics have focused on his treatment of the destructiveness of nuclear weapons and interdependence. Waltz labels these as unit-level properties, whereas some of his critics assert that they are in fact attributes of the system.

Finally, the distribution of capabilities explains outcomes in international affairs only in the most general way, falling short of answering the questions that are of central interest to many analysts. For example, the distribution of power at the end of World War II would have enabled one to predict the rivalry that emerged between the United States and the Soviet Union, but it would have been inadequate for explaining the pattern of relations between these two nations— the Cold War rather than withdrawal into isolationism by either or both, a division of the world into spheres of influence, or World War III.[20] In order to do so, it is necessary to explore political processes *within* states—at minimum within the United States and the USSR—as well as *between* them.

Robert Gilpin shares with Waltz the core assumptions of modern realism, but his study of *War and Change in World Politics* also attempts to cope with some of the criticism leveled at Waltz's theory by focusing on the dynamics of system change. Drawing upon both economic and sociological theory, his model is based on five core propositions. The first is that the international system is stable—in a state equilibrium—if no state believes that it is profitable to attempt to change it. Second, a state will attempt to change the status quo of the international system if the expected benefits outweigh the costs; that is, if there is an expected net gain for the revisionist state. Related to this is the proposition that a state will seek change through territorial, political, and economic expansion until the marginal costs of further change equal or exceed the marginal benefits. Moreover, when an equilibrium between the costs and benefits of further change and expansion is reached, the economic costs of maintaining the status quo (expenditures for military forces, support for allies, etc.) tend to rise faster than the resources needed to do so. An equilibrium exists when no powerful state believes that a change in the system would yield additional net benefits. Finally, if the resulting disequilibrium between the existing governance of the international system and the redistribution of power is not resolved, the system will be changed and a new equilibrium reflecting the distribution of relative capabilities will be established.[21]

Unlike Waltz, Gilpin includes state-level processes in order to explain change. Differential economic growth rates among nations—a structural-systemic level variable—play a vital role in his explanation for the rise and decline of great powers, but his model also includes propositions about the law of diminishing returns on investments, the impact of affluence on martial spirits and on the ratio of consumption to investment, and structural change in the economy.[22] Table 1.1 summarizes some key elements of realism. It also contrasts them to two other system-level models of international relations—the Global-Society/Complex-Interdependence and the Marxist/World-System/Dependency models, to which we now turn our attention.

Just as there are variants of realism, there are several Global Society/Complex-Interdependence (GS/CI) models, but this discussion focuses on two common denominators; they all challenge the first and third core propositions of realism identified earlier, asserting that inordinate attention to the war/peace issue and the nation-state renders it an increasingly anachronistic model of global relations.[23] The agenda of critical problems confronting states has been vastly expanded during the twentieth century. Attention to the issues of war and peace is by no means misdirected, according to proponents of a GS/CI perspective, but concerns for welfare, modernization, the environment, and the like are today no less potent sources of motivation and action. The diffusion of knowledge and technology, combined with the globalization of communications, has vastly increased popular expectations. The resulting demands have outstripped resources and the ability of existing institutions—notably the sovereign nation-state—to cope effectively with them. Interdependence arises from an inability of even the most powerful states to cope, or to do so unilaterally or at acceptable levels of cost and risk, with issues ranging from trade to AIDS, and immigration to environmental threats.

Paralleling the widening agenda of critical issues is the expansion of actors whose behavior can have a significant impact beyond national boundaries; indeed, the cumulative effects of their actions can have profound consequences for the international system. Thus, although nation-states continue to be important international actors, they possess a declining ability to control their own destinies. The aggregate effect of actions by multitudes of non-state actors can have potent effects that transcend political boundaries. These may include such powerful or highly visible non-state organizations as Exxon, the Organization of Petroleum Exporting Countries, or the Palestine Liberation Organization. On the other hand, the cumulative effects of decisions by less powerful or less visible actors may also have profound international consequences. For example, decisions by thousands of individuals, mutual funds, banks, pension funds, and other financial institutions to sell securities on 19 October 1987 not only resulted in an unprecedented "crash" on Wall Street, but also within hours its consequences were felt throughout the entire global financial system. Governments might take such actions as loosening credit or even closing exchanges, but they were largely unable to contain the effects of the panic.

The widening agenda of critical issues, most of which lack a purely national solution, has also led to creation of new actors that transcend political boundaries; for example, international organizations, transnational organizations, non-government organizations, multinational

Table 1.1 THREE MODELS OF THE INTERNATIONAL SYSTEM

	Realism	Global Society	Marxism
Type of model	Classical: descriptive and normative Modern: deductive	Descriptive and normative	Descriptive and normative
Central problems	Causes of war Conditions of peace	Broad agenda of social, economic, and environmental issues arising from gap between demands and resources	Inequality of exploitation Uneven development
Conception of current international system	Structural anarchy	Global society Complex interdependence (structure varies by issue-area)	World capitalist system
Key actors	Geographically based units (tribes, city-states, nation-states, etc.)	Highly permeable nation-states *plus* a broad range of onstate actors, including IOs, IGOs, NGOs, and individuals	Classes and their agents
Central motivations	National interest Security Power	Human needs and wants	Class interests
Loyalties	To geographically based groups (from tribes to nation-states)	Loyalties to nation-state declining To emerging global values and institutions that transcend those of the nation-state and/or to sub-national groups	To class values and interests that transcend those of the nation-state
Central processes	Search for security and survival	Aggregate effects of decisions by national and nonnational actors How units (not limited to nation-states) cope with a growing agenda of threats and opportunities arising from human wants	Modes of production and exchange International division of labor in a world capitalist system
Likelihood of system transformation	Low (basic structural element of system have revealed an ability to persist despite many other kinds of changes)	High in the direction of the model (owing to the rapid pace of techno-logical change, etc.)	High in the direction of the model (owing to inherent contradiction within the world capitalist system)
Sources of theory, insights, and evidence	Politics History Economics (especially "modern" realists)	Broad range of social sciences Natural and technological sciences	Marxist-Leninist theory (several variants)

corporations, and the like. Thus, not only does an exclusive focus on the war/peace issue fail to capture the complexities of contemporary international life but it also blinds the analyst to the institutions, processes, and norms that permit cooperation and significantly mitigate some features of an anarchic system. In short, according to GS/CI perspectives, an adequate understanding of the emergent global system must recognize that no single model is likely to be sufficient for all issues, and that if it restricts attention to the manner in which states deal with traditional security concerns, it is more likely to obfuscate than clarify the realities of contemporary world affairs.

The GS/CI models have several important virtues. They recognize that international behavior and outcomes arise from a multiplicity of motives, not merely security, at least if security is defined solely in military or strategic terms. They also alert us to the fact that important international processes and conditions originate not only in the actions of nation-states but also in the aggregated behavior of other actors. These models not only enable the analyst to deal with a broader agenda of critical issues but, more importantly, they force one to contemplate a much richer menu of demands, processes, and outcomes than would be derived from power-centered realist models. Stated differently, GS/CI models are more sensitive to the possibility that politics of trade, currency, immigration, health, the environment, and the like may significantly and systematically differ from those typically associated with security issues.

On the other hand, some GS/CI analysts underestimate the potency of nationalism and the durability of the nation-state. Two decades ago one of them wrote that "the nation is declining in its importance as a political unit to which allegiances are attached."[24] Objectively, nationalism may be an anachronism but, for better or worse, powerful loyalties are still attached to nation-states. The suggestion that, because even some well-established nations have experienced independence movements among ethnic, cultural, or religious minorities, the sovereign territorial state may be in decline is not wholly persuasive. Indeed, that evidence perhaps points to precisely the opposite conclusion: In virtually every region of the world there are groups which seek to create or restore geographically based entities in which its members may enjoy the status and privileges associated with sovereign territorial statehood. Evidence from Poland to Palestine, Spain to Sri Lanka, Estonia to Eritrea, Armenia to Afghanistan, and elsewhere seems to indicate that obituaries for nationalism may be somewhat premature.

The notion that such powerful non-national actors as major multinational corporations (MNC) will soon transcend the nation-state seems equally premature. International drug rings do appear capable of dominating such states as Colombia and Panama. However, the pattern of outcomes in confrontations between MNCs and states, including cases involving major expropriations of corporate properties, indicate that even relatively weak nations are not always the hapless pawns of the MNCs. Case studies by Joseph Grieco and Gary Gereffi, among others, indicate that MNC-state relations yield a wide variety of outcomes.[25]

Underlying the GS/CI critique of realist models is the view that the latter are too wedded to the past and are thus incapable of dealing adequately with change. At least for the present, however, even if global dynamics arise from multiple sources (including non-state actors), the actions of nation-states and their agents would appear to remain the major sources of change in the international system. However, the last group of systemic models to be considered, the Marxist/World-System/Dependency (M/WS/D) models, downplays the role of the nation-state even further.

As in other parts of this essay, many of the distinctions among M/WS/D models are lost by treating them together and by focusing on their common features, but in the brief description possible here only common denominators will be presented. These models challenge both the war/peace and state-centered features of realism, but they do so in ways that differ sharply from challenges of GS/CI models.[26] Rather than focusing on war and peace, these models direct attention to quite different issues, including uneven development, poverty, and exploitation within and between nations. These conditions, arising from the dynamics of the modes of production and exchange, are basic and they must be incorporated into any analysis of intra- and inter-nation conflict.

At a superficial level, according to adherents of these models, what exists today may be described as an international system—a system of nation-states. More fundamentally, however, the key groups within and between nations are classes and their agents: As Immanuel Wallerstein put it, "in the nineteenth and twentieth centuries there has been only one world system in existence, the world capitalist world-economy."[27] The "world capitalist system" is characterized by a highly unequal division of labor between the periphery and core. Those at the periphery are essentially the drawers of water and the hewers of wood, whereas the latter appropriate the surplus of the entire world economy. This critical feature of the world system not only gives rise to and perpetuates a widening rather than narrowing gap between the wealthy core and poor periphery but also to a dependency relationship from which the latter are unable to break loose. Moreover, the class structure within the core, characterized by a growing gap between capital and labor, is faithfully reproduced in the periphery so that elites there share with their counterparts in the core an interest in perpetuating the system. Thus, in contrast to realist theories, M/WS/D models encompass and integrate theories of both the global and domestic arenas.

M/WS/D models have been subjected to trenchant critiques.[28] The state, nationalism, security dilemmas, and related concerns essentially drop out of these analyses; they are at the theoretical periphery rather than at the core: "Capitalism was from the beginning an affair of the world-economy," Wallerstein asserts, "not of nation-states."[29] A virtue of many M/WS/D models is that they take a long historical perspective on world affairs rather than merely focusing on contemporary issues. However, by neglecting nation-states and the dynamics arising from their efforts to deal with security in an anarchical system—or at best relegating these actors and motivations to a minor role—M/WS/D models lose much of their appeal. Models of world affairs during the past few centuries that fail to give the nation-state a central role seem as deficient as analyses of *Hamlet* that neglect the central character and his motivations.

Second, the concept of "world capitalist system" is central to these models, but its relevance for the late twentieth century can be questioned. Whether this term accurately describes the world of the 1880s could be debated, but its declining analytical utility or even descriptive accuracy for international affairs of the 1980s seems clear. Thus, one can question Wallerstein's assertion that "there are today no socialist systems in the world economy any more than there are feudal systems because there is only *one world system*. It is a world-economy and it is *by definition capitalist* in form."[30] Where within a system so defined do we locate the USSR or Eastern Europe? This area includes enough "rich" industrial nations that it hardly seems to belong in the periphery. Yet to place these states in the core of a "world capitalist system" would require terminological and conceptual gymnastics of a high order. Does it increase our analytical capabilities to describe the USSR and East European countries as "state capitalists?" Where do we locate China in this conception of the system? How do we explain dynamics within the "periphery," or the differences between rapid-growth Asian nations such as South Korea, Taiwan, or Singapore, and their slow-growth neighbors in Bangladesh, North Korea, and the Philippines? The inclusion of a third structural position—the "semi-periphery"—does not wholly answer these questions.

Third, M/WS/D models have considerable difficulty in explaining relations between non-capitalist nations—for example, between the USSR and its East European neighbors or China—much less outright conflict between them. Indeed, advocates of these models usually have restricted their attention to West–South relations, eschewing analyses of East–East or East–South relations. Does one gain greater and more general analytical power by using the lenses and language of Marxism or of realism to describe relations between dominant and lesser nations; for example, the USSR and Eastern Europe, the USSR and India or other Third World nations, China and Vietnam, India and Sri Lanka, or Vietnam and Kampuchea? Are these relationships better described and understood in terms of such M/WS/D categories as "class" or such realist ones as "relative capabilities?"

Finally, the earlier observations about the persistence of nationalism as an element of international relations seem equally appropriate here. Perhaps national loyalties can be dismissed as prime examples of "false consciousness," but even in areas that have experienced almost two generations of one-party Communist rule, as in Poland, evidence that feelings of solidarity with workers in the Soviet Union or other nations have replaced nationalist sentiments among Polish workers is in short supply.

Many advocates of realism recognize that it cannot offer fine-grained analyses of foreign policy behavior and, as noted earlier, Waltz denies that it is desirable or even possible to combine theories of international relations and foreign policy. Decision-making models challenge the premises that it is fruitful to conceptualize the nation as a unitary rational actor whose behavior can adequately be explained by reference to the system structure—the second, fourth, and fifth realist propositions identified earlier—because individuals, groups, and organizations acting in the name of the state are also sensitive to pressures and constraints other than international ones, including elite maintenance, electoral politics, public opinion, pressure group activities, ideological preferences, and bureaucratic politics. Such core concepts as "the national interest" are not defined solely by the international system, much less by its structure alone, but they are also likely to reflect elements within the domestic political arena. Thus, rather than assuming with the realists that the state can be conceptualized as a "black box"—that the domestic political processes are both hard to comprehend and quite unnecessary for explaining its external behavior—decision-making analysts believe one must indeed take these internal processes into account, with special attention directed at decision-makers and their "definitions of the situation."[31] To reconstruct how nations deal with each other, it is necessary to view the situation through the eyes of those who act in the name of the nation-state: decision makers, and the group and bureaucratic-organizational contexts within which they act. Table 1.2 provides an overview of three major types of decision-making models that form the subject for the remainder of this essay, beginning with bureaucratic-organizational models.[32]

Traditional models of complex organizations and bureaucracy emphasized the positive contributions to be expected from a division of labor, hierarchy, and centralization, coupled with expertise, rationality, and obedience. Such models assumed that clear boundaries should be maintained between politics and decision making, on the one hand, and administration and implementation on the other. Following pioneering works by Chester I. Barnard, Herbert Simon, James G. March and Simon, and others, more recent theories depict organizations quite differently.[33] The central premise is that decision making in bureaucratic organizations is not constrained only by the legal and formal norms that are intended to enhance the rational and eliminate the capricious aspects of bureaucratic behavior. Rather, all (or most) complex organizations are seen as generating serious "information pathologies."[34] There is an *emphasis* upon

Table 1.2 THREE MODELS OF DECISION MAKING

	Bureaucratic politics	Group dynamics	Individual decision making
Conceptualization of decision making Premises	Decision making as the result of bargaining within bureaucratic organizations Central organizational values are imperfectly internalized Organizational behavior is political behavior Structure and SOPs affect substance and quality of decisions	Decision making as the product of group interaction Most decisions are made by small elite groups Group is different than the sum of its members Group dynamics affect substance and quality of decisions	Decision making as the result of individual choice Importance of subjective appraisal (definition of the situation) and cognative processes (information processing, etc.)
Constraints on rational decision making	Imperfect information, resulting from: centralization, hierarchy, and specialization Organizational inertia Conflict between individual and organizational utilities Bureaucratic politics and bargaining dominate decision making and implementation of decisions	Groups may be more effective for some tasks, less for others Pressures for conformity Risk-taking propensity of groups (controversial) Quality of leadership "Groupthink"	Cognitive limits on rationality Information processing distorted by cognitive consistency dynamics (unmotivated biases) Systematic and motivated biases in causal analysis Individual differences in abilities related to decision making (e.g., problem-solving ability, tolerance of ambiguity, defensiveness and anxiety, information seeking, etc.)
Sources of theory, insights, and evidence	Organization theory Sociology of bureaucracies Bureaucratic politics	Social psychology Sociology of small groups	Cognitive dissonance Cognitive psychology Dynamic psychology

rather than a denial of the political character of bureaucracies, as well as on other "informal" aspects of organizational behavior. Complex organizations are composed of individuals and units with conflicting perceptions, values, and interests that may arise from parochial self-interest ("what is best for my bureau is also best for my career"), and also from different perceptions of issues arising ineluctably from a division of labor ("where you stand depends on where you sit"). Organizational norms and memories, prior policy commitments, normal organizational inertia routines, and standard operating procedures may shape and perhaps distort the structuring of problems, channeling of information, use of expertise, and implementation of executive decisions. The consequences of bureaucratic politics within the executive branch or within the government as a whole may significantly constrain the manner in which issues are defined, the range of options that may be considered, and the manner in which executive decisions are implemented by subordinates. Consequently, organizational decision making is essentially political in character, dominated by bargaining for resources, roles and missions, and by compromise rather than analysis.[35]

Perhaps owing to the dominant position of the realist perspective, most students of foreign policy have only recently incorporated bureaucratic-organizational models and insights into their analyses. An ample literature of case studies on budgeting, weapons acquisitions, military doctrine, and similar situations confirms that foreign and defense policy bureaucracies rarely conform to the Weberian "ideal type" of rational organization.[36] Some analysts assert that crises may provide the motivation and means for reducing some of the non-rational aspects of bureaucratic behavior: crises are likely to push decisions to the top of the organization where a higher quality of intelligence is available; information is more likely to enter the top of the hierarchy directly, reducing the distorting effects of information processing through several levels of the organization; and broader, less parochial values may be invoked. Short decision time in crises reduces the opportunities for decision making by bargaining, logrolling, incrementalism, lowest-common-denominator values, "muddling through," and the like.[37]

However, even studies of international crises from a bureaucratic-organizational perspective are not uniformly sanguine about decision making in such circumstances. Graham T. Allison's analysis of the Cuban missile crisis identified several critical bureaucratic malfunctions concerning dispersal of American aircraft in Florida, the location of the naval blockade, and grounding of weather reconnaissance flights from Alaska that might stray over the Soviet Union. Richard Neustadt's study of two crises involving the United States and Great Britain revealed significant misperceptions of each other's interests and policy processes. And an examination of three American nuclear alerts found substantial gaps in understanding and communication between policymakers and the military leaders who were responsible for implementing the alerts.[38]

Critics of some organizational-bureaucratic models and the studies employing them have directed their attention to several points.[39] They point out, for instance, that the emphasis on bureaucratic bargaining fails to differentiate adequately between the positions of the participants. In the American system, the president is not just another player in a complex bureaucratic game. Not only must he ultimately decide but he also selects who the other players will be, a process that may be crucial in shaping the ultimate decisions. If General Matthew Ridgway and Attorney General Robert Kennedy played key roles in the American decisions not to intervene in Indochina in 1954 or not to bomb Cuba in 1962, it was because Presidents Eisenhower and Kennedy chose to accept their advice rather than that of other officials. Also, the conception of bureaucratic bargaining tends to emphasize its non-rational elements to the exclusion of genuine intellectual differences that may be rooted in broader concerns—including disagreements on what national interests, if any, are at stake in a situation—rather than narrow parochial interests. Indeed, properly managed, decision processes that promote and legitimize "multiple advocacy" among officials may facilitate high-quality decisions.[40]

These models may be especially useful for understanding the slippage between executive decisions and foreign policy actions that may arise during implementation, but they may be less valuable for explaining the decisions themselves. Allison's study of the Cuban missile crisis does not indicate an especially strong correlation between bureaucratic roles and evaluations of the situation or policy recommendations, as predicted by his "Model III" (bureaucratic politics), and recently published transcripts of deliberations during the crisis do not offer more supporting evidence for that model.[41] On the other hand, Allison does present some compelling evidence concerning policy implementation that casts considerable doubt on the adequacy of "Model I" (the traditional realist conception of the unitary rational actor).

Another decision-making model used by some political scientists supplements bureaucratic-organizational models by narrowing the field of view to top policymakers. This approach lends itself well to investigations of foreign policy decisions, which are usually made in a small-group context. Some analysts have drawn upon sociology and social psychology to assess the impact of various types of group dynamics on decision making.[42] Underlying these models are the premises that the group is not merely the sum of its members (thus decisions emerging from the group are likely to be different than what a simple aggregation of individual preference and abilities might suggest), and that group dynamics, the interactions among its members, can have a significant impact on the substance and quality of decisions.

Groups often perform better than individuals in coping with complex tasks owing to diverse perspectives and talents, an effective division of labor, and high-quality debates centering on evaluations of the situation and policy recommendations for dealing with it. Groups may also provide decision makers with emotional and other types of support that may facilitate coping with complex problems. On the other hand, they may exert pressures for conformity to group norms, thereby inhibiting the search for information and policy options or cutting it off prematurely, ruling out the legitimacy of some options, curtailing independent evaluation, and suppressing some forms of intragroup conflict that might serve to clarify goals, values, and options. Classic experiments by the psychologist Solomon Asch revealed the extent to which group members will suppress their beliefs and judgments when faced with a majority adhering to the contrary view, even a counterfactual one.[43]

Drawing upon a series of historical case studies, social psychologist Irving L. Janis has identified a different variant of group dynamics, which he labels "groupthink" to distinguish it from the more familiar type of conformity pressure on "deviant" members of the group.[44] Janis challenges the conventional wisdom that strong cohesion among the members of a group invariably enhances performance. Under certain conditions, strong cohesion can markedly degrade the group's performance in decision making. Thus, the members of a cohesive group may, as a means of dealing with the stresses of having to cope with consequential problems and in order to bolster self-esteem, increase the frequency and intensity of face-to-face interaction. This results in a greater identification with the group and less competition within it. The group dynamics of what Janis calls "concurrence seeking" may displace or erode reality testing and sound information processing and judgment. As a consequence, groups may be afflicted by unwarranted feelings of optimism and invulnerability, stereotyped images of adversaries, and inattention to warnings. Janis's analyses of both "successful" (the Marshall Plan, the Cuban missile crisis) and "unsuccessful" (Munich Conference of 1938, Pearl Harbor, the Bay of Pigs invasion) cases indicate that "groupthink" or other decision-making pathologies are not inevitable, and he develops some guidelines for avoiding them.[45]

Still other decision-making analysts focus on the individual. Many approaches to the policymaker emphasize the gap between the demands of the classical model of rational decision making and the substantial body of theory and evidence about various constraints that come into play in even relatively simple choice situations.[46] The more recent perspectives, drawing upon cognitive psychology, go well beyond some of the earlier formulations that drew upon psychodynamic theories to identify various types of psychopathologies among political leaders: paranoia, authoritarianism, the displacement of private motives on public objects, etc.[47] These more recent efforts to include information-processing behavior of the individual decision maker in foreign policy analyses have been directed at the cognitive and motivational constraints that, in varying degrees, affect the decision-making performance of "normal" rather than pathological subjects. Thus, attention is directed to all leaders, not merely those, such as Hitler or Stalin, who display evidence of clinical abnormalities.

The major challenges to the classical model have focused in various ways on limited human capabilities for performing the tasks required by objectively rational decision making. The cognitive constraints on rationality include limits on the individual's capacity to receive, process, and assimilate information about the situation; an inability to identify the entire set of policy alternatives; fragmentary knowledge about the consequences of each option; and an inability to order preferences on a single utility scale.[48] These have given rise to several competing conceptions of the decision maker and his or her strategies for dealing with complexity, uncertainty, incomplete or contradictory information, and, paradoxically, information overload. They variously characterize the decision maker as a problem solver, naive or intuitive scientist, cognitive balancer, dissonance avoider, information seeker, cybernetic information processor, and reluctant decision maker.

Three of these conceptions seem especially relevant for foreign policy analysis. The first views the decision maker as a "bounded rationalist" who seeks satisfactory rather than optimal solutions. As Herbert Simon has put it, "the capacity of the human mind for formulating and solving complex problems is very small compared with the size of the problem whose solution is required for objectively rational behavior in the real world—or even a reasonable approximation of such objective rationality."[49] Moreover, it is not practical for the decision maker to seek optimal choices; for example, because of the costs of searching for information. Related to this is the more recent concept of the individual as a "cognitive miser," one who seeks to simplify complex problems and to find shortcuts to problem solving and decision making.

Another approach is to look at the decision maker as an "error prone intuitive scientist" who is likely to commit a broad range of inferential mistakes. Thus, rather than emphasizing the limits on search, information processing, and the like, this conception views the decision maker as the victim of flawed heuristics or decision rules who uses data poorly. There are tendencies to underuse rate data in making judgments, believe in the "law of small numbers," underuse diagnostic information, overweight low probabilities and underweight high ones, and violate other requirements of consistency and coherence. These deviations from classical decision theory are traced to the psychological principles that govern perceptions of problems and evaluations of options.[50]

The final perspective I will mention emphasizes the forces that dominate the policymaker, forces that will not or cannot be controlled.[51] Decision makers are not merely rational calculators; important decisions generate conflict, and a reluctance to make irrevocable choices often results in behavior that reduces the quality of decisions. These models direct the analyst's attention to policymakers' belief systems, images of relevant actors, perceptions, information-processing strategies, heuristics, certain personality traits (ability to tolerate ambiguity, cognitive complexity, etc.), and their impact on decision-making performance.

Despite this diversity of perspectives and the difficulty of choosing between cognitive and motivational models, there has been some convergence on several types of constraints that may affect decision processes.[52] One involves the consequences of efforts to achieve cognitive consistency on perceptions and information processing. Several kinds of systematic bias have been identified in both experimental and historical studies. Policymakers have a propensity to assimilate and interpret information in ways that conform to rather than challenge existing beliefs, preferences, hopes, and expectations. Frequently they deny the need to confront tradeoffs between values by persuading themselves that an option will satisfy all of them. And, finally, they indulge in rationalizations to bolster the selected option while denigrating those that were not selected.

An extensive literature on styles of attribution has revealed several types of systematic bias in causal analysis. Perhaps the most important for foreign policy analysis is the basic attribution error—a tendency to explain the adversary's behavior in terms of his characteristics (for example, inherent aggressiveness or hostility) rather than in terms of the context or situation, while attributing one's own behavior to the latter (for example, legitimate security needs arising from a dangerous and uncertain environment) rather than to the former. A somewhat related type of double standard has been noted by George Kennan: "Now is it our view that we should take account only of their [Soviet] capabilities, disregarding their intentions, but we should expect them to take account only for our supposed intentions, disregarding our capabilities?"[53]

Analysts also have illustrated the important effect on decisions of policymakers' assumptions about order and predictability in the environment. Whereas a policymaker may have an acute appreciation of the disorderly environment in which he or she operates (arising, for example, from domestic political processes), there is a tendency to assume that others, especially adversaries, are free of such constraints. Graham T. Allison, Robert Jervis, and others have demonstrated that decision makers tend to believe that the realist "unitary rational actor" is the appropriate representation of the opponent's decision processes and, thus, whatever happens is the direct result of deliberate choices. For example, the hypothesis that the Soviet destruction of KAL flight 007 may have resulted from intelligence failures or bureaucratic foulups, rather than from a calculated decision to murder civilian passengers, was either not given serious consideration or it was suppressed for strategic reasons.[54]

Drawing upon a very substantial experimental literature, several models linking crisis-induced stress to decision processes have been developed and used in foreign policy studies.[55] Irving L. Janis and Leon Mann have developed a more general conflict-theory model which conceives of man as a "reluctant decision-maker" and focuses upon "when, how and why psychological stress generated by decisional conflict imposes limitations on the rationality of a person's decisions."[56] One may employ five strategies for coping with a situation requiring a decision: unconflicted adherence to existing policy, unconflicted change, defensive avoidance, hypervigilance, and vigilant decision making. The first four strategies are likely to yield low-quality decisions owing to an incomplete search for information, appraisal of the situation and options, and contingency planning, whereas the vigilant decision making characterized by a more adequate performance of vital tasks is more likely to result in a high-quality choice. The factors that will affect the employment of decision styles are information about risks, expectations of finding a better option, and time for adequate search and deliberation.

A final approach we should consider attempts to show the impact of personal traits on decision making. There is no shortage of typologies that are intended to link leadership traits to decision-making behavior, but systematic research demonstrating such links is in much shorter supply. Still, some efforts have borne fruit. Margaret G. Hermann has developed a scheme for analyzing leaders' public statements of unquestioned authorship for eight variables: nationalism, belief in one's ability to control the environment, need for power, need for affiliation, ability to differentiate environments, distrust of others, self-confidence, and task emphasis. The scheme has been tested with impressive results on a broad range of contemporary leaders.[57] Alexander L. George has reformulated Nathan Leites's concept of "operational code" into five philosophical and five instrumental beliefs that are intended to describe politically relevant core beliefs, stimulating a number of empirical studies and, more recently, further significant conceptual revisions.[58] Finally, several psychologists have developed and tested the concept of "integrative complexity," defined as the ability to make subtle distinction along multiple dimensions, flexibility, and the integration of large amounts of diverse information to make coherent judgments.[59] A standard content-analysis technique has been used for research on documentary materials generated by top decision makers in a wide range of international crises, including World War I, Cuba (1962), Morocco (1911), Berlin (1948–49 and 1961), Korea, and the Middle East wars of 1948, 1956, 1967, and 1973.[60]

Decision-making approaches clearly permit the analyst to overcome many limitations of the systemic models described earlier, but not without costs. The three decision-making models described here impose increasingly heavy data burdens on the analyst. Moreover, there is a danger that adding levels of analysis may result in an undisciplined proliferation of categories and variables with at least two adverse consequences: it may become increasingly difficult to determine which are more or less important; and ad hoc explanations for individual cases erode the possibilities for broader generalizations across cases. However, several well-designed, multicase, decision-making studies indicate that these and other traps are not unavoidable.[61]

The study of international relations and foreign policy has always been a somewhat eclectic undertaking, with extensive borrowing from disciplines other than political science and history.[62] At the most general level, the primary differences today tend to be between two broad approaches. Analysts of the first school focus on the structure of the international system, often borrowing from economics for models, analogies, insights, and metaphors, with an emphasis on *rational preferences and strategy* and how these tend to be shaped and constrained by the structure of the international system. Decision-making analysts, meanwhile, display a concern for domestic political processes and tend to borrow from social psychology and psychology in order to understand better the *limits and barriers* to information processing and rational choice.

At the risk of ending on a platitude, it seems clear that for many purposes both approaches are necessary and neither is sufficient. Neglect of the system structure and its constraints may result in analyses that depict policymakers as relatively free agents with an almost unrestricted menu of choices, limited only by the scope of their ambitions and the resources at their disposal. At worst, this type of analysis can degenerate into Manichean explanations that depict foreign policies of the "bad guys" as the external manifestation of inherently flawed leaders or domestic structures, whereas the "good guys" only react from necessity. Radical right explanations of the Cold War often depict Soviet foreign policies as driven by inherently aggressive totalitarian communism and the United States as its blameless victim; radical left explanations tend to be structurally similar, with the roles of aggressor and victim reversed.[63]

Conversely, neglect of foreign policy decision making not only leaves one unable to explain the dynamics of international relations, but many important aspects of a nation's external behavior will be inexplicable. Advocates of the realist model have often argued its superiority for understanding the "high" politics of deterrence, containment, alliances, crises, and wars, if not necessarily for "low" politics. But there are several rejoinders to this line of reasoning. First, the low politics of trade, currencies, and other issues that are almost always highly sensitive to domestic pressures are becoming an increasingly important element of international relations. Second, the growing literature on the putative domain *par excellence* of realism, including deterrence, crises, and wars, raises substantial doubts about the universal validity of the realist model even for these issues.[64] Finally, exclusive reliance on realist models and their assumptions of rationality may lead to unwarranted complacency about dangers in the international system. Nuclear weapons and other features of the system have no doubt contributed to the "long peace" between major powers.[65] At the same time, however, a narrow focus on power balances, "correlations of forces," and other features of the international system will result in neglect of dangers—for example, the command, communication, control, intelligence problem, or inadequate information processing—that can only be identified and analyzed by a decision-making perspective.[66]

At a very general level, this conclusion parallels that drawn three decades ago by the foremost contemporary proponent of modern realism: the "third image" (system structure) is necessary for understanding the context of international behavior, whereas the first and second images (decision makers and domestic political processes) are needed to understand dynamics within the system.[67] But to acknowledge the existence of various levels of analysis is not enough. *What* the investigator wants to explain and the *level of specificity and comprehensiveness* to be sought should determine which level(s) of analysis are relevant and necessary. In this connection, it is essential to distinguish two different dependent variables: foreign policy decisions by states, on the one hand, and the outcomes of policy and interactions between two or more states, on the other. If the goal is to understand the former—foreign policy decisions—Harold and Margaret Sprout's notion of "psychological milieu" is relevant and sufficient; that is, the objective structural variables influence the decisions via the decision maker's perception and evaluation of those "outside" variables.[68] However, if the goal is to explain outcomes, the "psychological milieu" is quite inadequate; the objective factors, if misperceived or misjudged by the decision maker, will influence the outcome. Political scientists studying international relations are increasingly disciplining their use of multiple levels of analysis in studying outcomes that cannot be adequately explained via only a single level of analysis.[69]

Which of these models and approaches are likely to be of interest and utility to the diplomatic historian? Clearly there is no one answer; political scientists are unable to agree on a single multilevel approach to international relations and foreign policy; thus they are hardly in a position to offer a single recommendation to historians. In the absence of the often-sought but always-elusive unified theory of human behavior that could provide a model for all seasons and all reasons, one must ask at least one further question: A model for what purpose? For example, in some circumstances, such as research on major international crises, it may be important to obtain systematic evidence on the beliefs and other intellectual baggage that key policymakers bring to their deliberations. Some of the approaches described above should prove very helpful in this respect. Conversely, there are many other research problems for which the historian would quite properly decide that this type of analysis requires far more effort than could possibly be justified by the benefits to be gained.

Of the systemic approaches described here, little needs to be said about classical realism because its main features, as well as its strengths and weaknesses, are familiar to most diplomatic historians. Those who focus on security issues can hardly neglect its central premises and concepts. On the other hand, modern or structural realism of the Waltz variety is likely to have rather limited appeal to historians, especially if they take seriously his doubts about being able to incorporate foreign policy into it. It may perhaps serve to raise consciousness about the importance of the systemic context within which international relations take place, but that may not be a major gain—after all, such concepts as "balance of power" have long been a standard part of the diplomatic historian's vocabulary. Gilpin's richer approach, which employs both system- and state-level variables to explain international dynamics, may well have greater appeal. It has already been noted that there are some interesting parallels between Gilpin's *War and Change in World Politics* and Paul Kennedy's recent *The Rise and Fall of the Great Powers.*

The Global-Society/Complex-Interdependence models will be helpful to historians with an interest in evolution of the international system and with the growing disjuncture between demands on states and their ability to meet them—the "sovereignty gap." One need not be very venturesome to predict that this gap will grow rather than narrow in the future. Historians of all kinds of international and transnational organizations are also likely to find useful concepts and insights in these models.

It is much less clear that the Marxist/World-System/Dependency models will provide useful new insights to historians. They will no doubt continue to be employed, but for reasons other than demonstrated empirical utility. If one has difficulty in accepting certain assumptions as *true by definition*—for example, that there has been and is today a single "world capitalist system"—then the kinds of analyses that follow are likely to seem seriously flawed. Most diplomatic historians also would have difficulty in accepting models that relegate the state to a secondary role. Until proponents of these models demonstrate a greater willingness to test them against a broader range of cases, including East–South and East–East relations, their applicability would appear to be limited at best. Finally, whereas proponents of GS/CI models can point with considerable justification to current events and trends that would appear to make them more rather than less relevant in the future, supporters of the M/WS/D models have a much more difficult task in this respect.

Although the three decision-making models sometimes include jargon that may be jarring to the historian, many of the underlying concepts are familiar. Much of diplomatic history has traditionally focused on the decisions, actions, and interactions of national leaders who operate in group contexts, such as cabinets or ad hoc advisory groups, and who draw upon the resources of such bureaucracies as foreign and defense ministries or the armed forces. The three types of models described above typically draw heavily upon psychology, social psychology, organizational theory, and other social sciences; thus for the historian they open some important windows to highly relevant developments in these fields. For example, theories and concepts of "information processing" by individuals, groups, and organizations should prove very useful to diplomatic historians.

Decision-making models may also appeal to diplomatic historians for another important reason. Political scientists who are accustomed to working with fairly accessible information such as figures on gross national products, defense budgets, battle casualties, alliance commitments, United Nations votes, trade and investments, and the like, often feel that the data requirements of decision-making models are excessive. This is precisely the area in which the historian has a decided comparative advantage, for the relevant data are usually to be found in the paper trails— more recently, also in the electronic trails—left by policymakers, and they are most likely to be unearthed by archival research. Thus, perhaps the appropriate point on which to conclude this essay is to reverse the question posed earlier: Ask not only what can the political scientist contribute to the diplomatic historian but ask also what can the diplomatic historian contribute to the political scientist. At the very least political scientists could learn a great deal about the validity of their own models if historians would use them and offer critical assessments of their strengths and limitations.

NOTES

1. See, for example, John Lewis Gaddis, "Expanding the Data Base: Historians, Political Scientists, and the Enrichment of Security Studies," *International Security* 12 (Summer 1987): 3–21; John English, "The Second Time Around: Political Scientists Writing History," *Canadian Historical Review* 57 (March 1986): 1–16; Jack S. Levy, "Domestic Politics and War," *Journal of Interdisciplinary History* 18 (Spring 1988): 653–73; Joseph S. Nye, Jr., "International Security Studies," in *American Defense Annual, 1988–1989,* ed. Joseph Kruzel (Lexington, MA, 1988), 231–43; Deborah Larson, *Origins of Containment: A Psychological Explanation* (Princeton, 1985); Timothy Lomperis, *The War Everyone Lost–And Won: America's Intervention in Viet Nam's Twin Struggles* (Washington, 1987); Barry Posen, *The Sources of Military Doctrine: France, Britain, and Germany between the World Wars* (Ithaca, 1984); Paul Gordon Lauren, ed., *Diplomacy: New Approaches to History, Theory, and Policy* (New York, 1979); and Richard R. Neustadt and Ernest R. May, *Thinking in Time: The Use of History for Decision-Makers* (New York, 1986). Many other examples could be cited.
2. Robert Gilpin, *Change and War in World Politics* (Cambridge, England, 1981).
3. Stanley Hoffmann, "An American Social Science: International Relations," *Daedalus* 106 (Summer 1977): 54.
4. The British meteorologist Lewis Fry Richardson is generally regarded as the pioneer of mathematical approaches to international relations. See his *Statistics of Deadly Quarrels* (Pittsburgh, 1960); and his *Arms and Insecurity: A Mathematical Study of the Causes and Origins of War* (Chicago, 1960). These are summarized for nonmathematicians in Anatol Rapport, "L. F. Richardson's Mathematical Theory of War," *Journal of Conflict Resolution* 1 (September 1957): 249–99. For a more recent effort see Bruce Bueno de Mesquita, *The War Trap* (New Haven, 1981); and idem, "The War Trap Revisited: A Revised Expected Utility Model," *American Political Science Review* 79 (March 1985): 156–77.
5. Among the works that best represent their realist perspectives are E. H. Carr, *Twenty Years' Crisis* (London, 1939); Nicholas Spykman, *America's Strategy in World Politics: The United States and Balance of Power* (New York, 1942); Hans J. Morgenthau, *Politics among Nations: The Struggle for Power and Peace,* 5th ed. (New York, 1973); John Herz, *International Politics in the Atomic Age* (New York, 1959); Hedley Bull, *The Anarchical Society: A Study of Order in World Politics* (London, 1977); Raymond Aron, *Peace and War* (Garden City, NY, 1966); Martin Wight, "The Balance of Power and International Order," in *The Bases of International Order: Essays in Honor of C. A. W. Manning,* ed. Alan James (London, 1973); Arnold Wolfers, *Discord and Collaboration* (Baltimore, 1962); Norman A. Graebner, *America as a World Power: A Realist Appraisal from Wilson to Reagan* (Wilmington, DE, 1984); George F. Kennan, *American Diplomacy, 1900–1950* (Chicago, 1951); Walter Lippmann, *U.S. Foreign Policy: Shield*

of the Republic (Boston, 1943); and Reinhold Niebuhr, *The Children of Light and the Children of Darkness* (New York, 1945).

6. For useful comparisons of realism and liberalism see Joseph Grieco, "Anarchy and the Limits of Cooperation: A Realist Critique of the Newest Liberal Institutionalism," *International Organization* 42 (Summer 1988): 485–507; and Joseph S. Nye, Jr., "Neorealism and Neoliberalism," *World Politics* 40 (January 1988): 235–51.

7. Morgenthau, *Politics*, 7, 5.

8. Stephen D. Krasner, *Defending the National Interest: Raw Materials Investment and U.S. Foreign Policy* (Princeton, 1978), 33. Krasner's study compares realist, interest-group liberal, and Marxist theories.

9. Inis L. Claude, *Power and International Relations* (New York, 1962); James S. Rosenau, "National Interest," *International Encyclopedia of the Social Sciences,* vol. 11 (New York, 1968), 34–40; Alexander L. George and Robert Keohane, "The Concept of National Interests: Uses and Limitations," in *Presidential Decision-Making in Foreign Policy: The Effective Use of Information and Advice,* ed. Alexander George (Boulder, 1980); Ernst B. Haas, "The Balance of Power: Prescription, Concept, or Propaganda?" *World Politics* 5 (July 1953): 442–77; Dina A. Zinnes, "An Analytical Study of the Balance of Power," *Journal of Peace Research* 4, no. 3 (1967): 270–88.

10. Morgenthau, *Politics*, 5.

11. Richard K. Ashley, "The Poverty of Neorealism," *International Organization* 38 (Spring 1984): 225–86.

12. Morton Kaplan, *System and Process in International Politics* (New York, 1957).

13. Richard Rosecrance, *Action and Reaction in International Politics* (Boston, 1963); idem, "Bipolarity, Multipolarity, and the Future," *Journal of Conflict Resolution* 10 (September 1966): 314–27; Kenneth Waltz, "The Stability of a Bipolar World," *Daedalus* 93 (Summer 1964): 881–909; J. David Singer, "Inter-Nation Influence: A Formal Model," *American Political Science Review* 57 (June 1963): 420–30; Bruce M. Russett, "Toward a Model of Competitive International Politics," *Journal of Politics* 25 (May 1963): 226–47; Karl W. Deutsch and J. David Singer, "Multipolar Power Systems and International Stability," *World Politics* 16 (April 1964): 390–406; Andrew Scott, *The Functioning of the International Political System* (New York, 1967).

14. Kenneth Waltz, *Theory of International Politics* (Reading, MA, 1979); idem, *Man, the State, and War* (New York, 1959).

15. Because Waltz strives for a universal theory that is not limited to any era, he uses the term "unit" to refer to the constituent members of the system. In the contemporary system these are states, but in order to reflect Waltz's intent more faithfully, the term "unit" is used here.

16. Waltz, *Theory*, 82–101.

17. Waltz, "The Myth of National Interdependence," in *The International Corporation,* ed. Charles P. Kindleberger (Cambridge, MA, 1970); Waltz, "The Spread of Nuclear Weapons: More May Be Better," *Adelphi Papers,* no. 171 (1981).

18. Joseph M. Grieco, *Cooperation Among Nations: Europe, America, and Non-Tariff Barriers to Trade* (Ithaca: Cornell University Press, 1990); Stephen M. Walt, *The Origin of Alliances* (Ithaca, 1987). The best single source for the various dimensions of the debate is Robert Keohane, ed., *Neorealism and Its Critics* (New York, 1986).

19. Ashley, "Poverty," 228.

20. I am grateful to Alexander George for this example.

21. Gilpin, *War and Change*, 10–11.

22. *Ibid.*, Chap. 4. Gilpin's thesis appears similar in a number of respects to Paul Kennedy, *The Rise and Fall of the Great Powers: Economic Change and Military Conflict from 1500 to 2000* (New York, 1987).

23. Robert Keohane and Joseph S. Nye, Jr., *Power and Interdependence: World Politics in Transition* (Boston, 1977); Edward Morse, *Modernization and the Transformation of International Relations*

(New York, 1967); James N. Rosenau, *The Study of Global Interdependence* (London, 1980); Richard Mansbach and John Vasquez, *In Search of Theory: A New Paradigm for Global Politics* (New York, 1981); Andrew M. Scott, *The Dynamics of Interdependence* (Chapel Hill, 1982); James N. Rosenau, *Turbulence in World Politics: A Theory of Change and Continuity* (Princeton: Princeton University Press, 1990).

24. Rosenau, "National Interest," 39. A more recent statement of this view may be found in Richard Rosecrance, *The Rise of the Trading State* (New York, 1986). See also John H. Herz, "The Rise and Demise of the Territorial State," *World Politics* 9 (July 1957): 473–93; and his reconsideration in "The Territorial State Revisited: Reflections on the Future of the Nation-State," *Polity* 1 (Fall 1968): 12–34.

25. Joseph Grieco, *Between Dependence and Autonomy: India's Experience with the International Computer Industry* (Berkeley, 1984); Gary Gereffi, *The Pharmaceutical Industry and Dependency in the Third World* (Princeton, 1983).

26. John Galtung, "A Structural Theory of Imperialism," *Journal of Peace Research* 8, no. 2 (1971): 81–117; James Cockroft, André Gunder Frank, and Dale L. Johnson, *Dependence and Under-Development* (New York, 1972); Immanuel Wallerstein, *The Modern World-System* (New York, 1974); idem, "The Rise and Future Demise of the World Capitalist System: Concepts for Comparative Analysis," *Comparative Studies in Society and History* 16 (September 1974): 387–415; Christopher Chase-Dunn, "Comparative Research on World System Characteristics," *International Studies Quarterly* 23 (December 1979): 601–23; idem, "Interstate System and Capitalist World Economy: One Logic or Two?" *ibid.* 25 (March 1981): 19–42; J. Kubalkova and A. A. Cruickshank, *Marxism and International Relations* (Oxford, 1985). Debates among advocates of these models are illustrated in Robert A. Denemark and Kenneth O. Thomas, "The Brenner-Wallerstein Debates," *International Studies Quarterly* 32 (March 1988): 47–66.

27. Wallerstein, "Rise and Future Demise," 390.

28. Tony Smith, "The Underdevelopment of Development Literature: The Case of Dependency Theory," *World Politics* 31 (January 1979): 247–88; Aristide R. Zolberg, "Origins of the Modern World System," *ibid.* 33 (January 1981): 253–81.

29. Wallerstein, "Rise and Future Demise," 401.

30. *Ibid.*, 412 (emphasis added).

31. Richard C. Snyder, H. W. Bruck, and Burton Sapin, eds., *Foreign Policy Decision-Making* (New York, 1962).

32. There are also models that link types of polities with foreign policy. Two of the more prominent twentieth-century versions—the Leninist and Wilsonian—have been effectively criticized by Waltz in *Man, the State, and War.* Although space limitations preclude a discussion here, for some recent and interesting research along these lines see, among others, Rudolph J. Rummel, "Libertarianism and International Violence," *Journal of Conflict Resolution* 27 (March 1983): 27–71; Michael Doyle, "Liberalism and World Politics," *American Political Science Review* 80 (December 1986): 1151–70; and Doyle, "Kant, Liberal Legacies, and Foreign Affairs," *Philosophy and Public Affairs* 12 (Winter 1983): 205–35.

33. Chester Barnard, *Functions of the Executive* (Cambridge, MA, 1938); Herbert Simon, *Administrative Behavior: A Study of Decision-Making Processes in Administrative Organization* (New York, 1957); James G. March and Herbert Simon, *Organizations* (New York, 1958).

34. Harold Wilensky, *Organizational Intelligence: Knowledge and Policy in Government and Industry* (New York, 1967).

35. Henry A. Kissinger, "Domestic Structure and Foreign Policy," *Daedalus* 95 (Spring 1966): 503–29; Graham T. Allison, *Essence of Decision: Explaining the Cuban Missile Crisis* (Boston, 1971); Graham T. Allison and Morton Halperin, "Bureaucratic Politics: A Paradigm and Some Policy Implications," *World Politics* 24 (Supplement 1972): 40–79; Morton Halperin, *Bureaucratic Politics and Foreign Policy* (Washington, 1974).

36. The literature is huge. See, for example, Samuel R. Williamson, Jr., *The Politics of Grand Strategy: Britain and France Prepare for War, 1904–1914* (Cambridge, MA, 1969); Paul Gordon Lauren, *Diplomats and Bureaucrats: The First Institutional Responses to Twentieth-Century Diplomacy in France and Germany* (Stanford, 1975); and Posen, *Sources of Military Doctrine.*

37. Wilensky, *Organizational Intelligence;* Theodore J. Lowi, *The End of Liberalism: Ideology, Policy, and the Crisis of Public Authority* (New York, 1969); Sidney Verba, "Assumptions of Rationality and Non-Rationality in Models of the International System," *World Politics* 14 (October 1961): 93–117.

38. Charles F. Hermann, "Some Consequences of Crises which Limit the Viability of Organizations," *Administrative Science Quarterly* 8 (June 1963): 61–82; Allison, *Essence;* Richard Neustadt, *Alliance Politics* (New York, 1970); Scott Sagan, "Nuclear Alerts and Crisis Management," *International Security* 9 (Spring 1985): 99–139.

39. Robert Rothstein, *Planning, Prediction, and Policy-Making in Foreign Affairs: Theory and Practice* (Boston, 1972); Stephen D. Krasner, "Are Bureaucracies Important? (Or Allison Wonderland)" *Foreign Policy* 7 (Summer 1972): 159–70; Robert J. Art, "Bureaucratic Politics and American Foreign Policy: A Critique," *Policy Sciences* 4 (December 1973): 467–90; Desmond J. Ball, "The Blind Men and the Elephant: A Critique of Bureaucratic Politics Theory," *Australian Outlook* 28 (April 1974): 71–92; Amos Perlmutter, "Presidential Political Center and Foreign Policy: A Critique of the Revisionist and Bureaucratic-Political Orientations," *World Politics* 27 (October 1974): 87–106.

40. Alexander L. George, "The Case for Multiple Advocacy in Making Foreign Policy," *American Political Science Review* 66 (September 1972): 751–85, 791–95.

41. David A. Welch and James G. Blight, "The Eleventh Hour of the Cuban Missile Crisis: An Introduction to the ExComm Transcripts," *International Security* 12 (Winter 1987/88): 5–29; McGeorge Bundy and James G. Blight, "October 27, 1962: Transcripts of the Meetings of the ExComm," *ibid.,* 30–92.

42. Joseph de Rivera, *The Psychological Dimension of Foreign Policy* (Columbus, OH, 1968); Glenn D. Paige, *The Korean Decision, June 24–30, 1950* (New York, 1968); Irving L. Janis, *Victims of Groupthink: A Psychological Study of Foreign Policy Decisions and Fiascos* (Boston, 1972); idem, *Groupthink: Psychological Studies of Policy Decisions and Fiascos* (Boston, 1982); Margaret G. Hermann, Charles F. Hermann, and Joe D. Hagan, "How Decision Units Shape Foreign Policy Behavior," in *New Directions in the Study of Foreign Policy,* ed. Charles F. Hermann, Charles W. Kegley, and James N. Rosenau (London, 1987); Charles F. Hermann and Margaret Hermann, "Who Makes Foreign Policy Decisions and How: An Initial Test of a Model" (Paper presented at the annual meeting of the American Political Science Association, Chicago, 1987); Philip D. Stewart, Margaret G. Hermann, and Charles F. Hermann, "The Politburo and Foreign Policy: Toward a Model of Soviet Decision Making" (Paper presented at the annual meeting of the International Society of Political Psychology, Amsterdam, 1986).

43. Leon Festinger, "A Theory of Social Comparison Processes," and Solomon Asch, "Opinions and Social Pressure," in *Small Groups: Studies in Social Interaction,* ed. A. Paul Hare, Edgar F. Borgatta, and Robert F. Bales (New York, 1965); Asch, "Effects of Group Pressures upon Modification and Distortion of Judgment," in *Group Dynamics: Research and Theory,* ed. Dorwin Cartwright and A. Zander (Evanston, IL, 1953).

44. Janis, *Victims;* idem, *Groupthink.* See also Philip Tetlock, "Identifying Victims of Groupthink from Public Statements of Decision Makers," *Journal of Personality and Social Psychology* 37 (August 1979): 1314–24; and the critique in Lloyd Etheredge, *Can Governments Learn? American Foreign Policy and Central American Revolutions* (New York, 1985), 112–14.

45. Janis, *Groupthink,* 260–76.

46. For a review of the vast literature see Robert Abelson and A. Levi, "Decision Making and Decision Theory," in *Handbook of Social Psychology,* 3d ed., vol. 1, ed. Gardner Lindzey and Elliot Aronson (New York, 1985). The relevance of psychological models and evidence for international relations is most fully discussed in Robert Jervis, *Perception and Misperception in International Politics*

(Princeton, 1976); John Steinbruner, *The Cybernetic Theory of Decision: New Dimensions of Political Analysis* (Princeton, 1974); and Robert Axelrod, ed., *The Structure of Decision: The Cognitive Maps of Political Elites* (Princeton, 1976).

47. See, for example, Harold Lasswell, *Psychopathology and Politics* (Chicago, 1931).
48. March and Simon, *Organizations,* 113.
49. Simon, *Administrative Behavior,* 198.
50. Amos Tversky and Daniel Kahneman, "The Framing of Decisions and the Psychology of Choice," *Science* 211 (30 January 1981): 453–58; Kahneman and Tversky, "On the Psychology of Prediction," *Psychological Review* 80 (July 1973): 237–51; Kahneman, Paul Slovic, and Tversky, *Judgment under Uncertainty: Heuristics and Biases* (Cambridge, England, 1982).
51. Irving L. Janis and Leon Mann, *Decision Making: A Psychological Analysis of Conflict, Choice, and Commitment* (New York, 1977); Miriam Steiner, "The Search for Order in a Disorderly World: Worldviews and Prescriptive Decision Paradigms," *International Organization* 37 (Summer 1983): 373–414; Richard Ned Lebow, *Between Peace and War* (Baltimore, 1981).
52. Donald Kinder and J. R. Weiss, "In Lieu of Rationality: Psychological Perspectives on Foreign Policy," *Journal of Conflict Resolution* 22 (December 1978): 707–35; Ole R. Holsti, "Foreign Policy Formation Viewed Cognitively," in Axelrod, *Structure of Decision.*
53. George F. Kennan, *The Cloud of Danger: Current Realities of American Foreign Policy* (Boston, 1978), 87–88.
54. Allison, *Essence;* Jervis, *Perception;* Seymour M. Hersh, *The Target Is Destroyed: What Really Happened to Flight 007 and What America Knew about It* (New York, 1986).
55. Charles F. Hermann, International Crises: Insights from Behavioral Research (New York, 1972); Margaret G. Hermann and Charles F. Hermann, "Maintaining the Quality of Decision-Making in Foreign Policy Crises," in Report of the Commission on the Organization of the Government for the Conduct of Foreign Policy, vol. 2 (Washington, 1975); Margaret G. Hermann, "Indicators of Stress in Policy-Makers during Foreign Policy Crises," *Political Psychology* 1 (March 1979): 27–46; Ole R. Holsti, *Crisis, Escalation, War* (Montreal, 1972); Ole R. Holsti and Alexander L. George, "The Effects of Stress on the Performance of Foreign Policy-Makers," *Political Science Annual,* vol. 6 (Indianapolis, 1975); Lebow, *Between Peace and War.*
56. Janis and Mann, *Decision Making,* 3.
57. Margaret G. Hermann, "Explaining Foreign Policy Behavior Using Personal Characteristics of Political Leaders," *International Studies Quarterly* 24 (March 1980): 7–46; idem, "Personality and Foreign Policy Decision Making," in *Perceptions, Beliefs, and Foreign Policy Decision Making,* ed. Donald Sylvan and Steve Chan (New York, 1984).
58. Nathan Leites, *The Operational Code of the Politburo* (New York, 1951); Alexander L. George, "The 'Operational Code': A Neglected Approach to the Study of Political Leaders and Decision-Making," *International Studies Quarterly* 13 (June 1969): 190–222; Stephen G. Walker, "The Interface between Beliefs and Behavior: Henry Kissinger's Operational Code and the Vietnam War," *Journal of Conflict Resolution* 21 (March 1977): 129–68; idem, "The Motivational Foundations of Political Belief Systems: A Re-Analysis of the Operational Code Construct," *International Studies Quarterly* 27 (June 1983): 179–202; idem, "Parts and Wholes: American Foreign Policy Makers as 'Structured' Individuals" (Paper presented at the annual meeting of the International Society of Political Psychology, Secaucus, New Jersey, 1988).
59. Integrative simplicity, on the other hand, is characterized by simple responses, gross distinctions, rigidity, and restricted information usage.
60. Peter Suedfeld and Philip Tetlock, "Integrative Complexity of Communications in International Crises," *Journal of Conflict Resolution* 21 (March 1977): 169–86; Suedfeld, Tetlock, and C. Romirez, "War, Peace, and Integrative Complexity: UN Speeches on the Middle East Problem, 1947–1976," *ibid.* (September 1977): 427–42; Theodore D. Raphael, "Integrative Complexity Theory and Forecasting International Crises: Berlin 1946–1962," *ibid.* 26 (September 1982):

423–50; Tetlock, "Integrative Complexity of American and Soviet Foreign Policy Rhetoric: A Time Series Analysis," *Journal of Personality and Social Psychology* 49 (December 1985): 1565–85.

61. Alexander L. George and Richard Smoke, *Deterrence in American Foreign Policy: Theory and Practice* (New York, 1974); Smoke, *Escalation* (Cambridge, MA, 1977); Glenn H. Snyder and Paul Diesing, *Conflict among Nations: Bargaining, Decision Making, and System Structure in International Crises* (Princeton, 1977); Michael Brecher and Barbara Geist, *Decisions in Crisis: Israel, 1967 and 1973* (Berkeley, 1980); Lebow, *Between Peace and War*. Useful discussions on conducting theoretically relevant case studies may be found in Harry Eckstein, "Case Study and Theory in Political Science," in *Handbook of Political Science*, ed. Fred I. Greenstein and Nelson W. Polsby (Reading, MA, 1975), 7: 79–138; and Alexander L. George, "Case Studies and Theory Development: The Method of Structured, Focused Comparison," in *Diplomacy: New Approaches in History, Theory, and Policy*, ed. Paul Gordon Lauren (New York, 1979), 43–68.

62. The classic overview of the field and the disciplines that have contributed to it is Quincy Wright, *The Study of International Relations* (New York, 1955).

63. Ole R. Holsti, "The Study of International Politics Makes Strange Bedfellows: Theories of the Radical Right and the Radical Left," *American Political Science Review* 68 (March 1974): 217–42.

64. In addition to the literature on war, crises, and deterrence already cited see Richard Betts, *Nuclear Blackmail and Nuclear Balance* (Washington, 1987); Robert Jervis, Richard Ned Lebow, and Janice G. Stein, *Psychology and Deterrence* (Baltimore, 1985); Lebow, *Nuclear Crisis Management: A Dangerous Illusion* (Ithaca, 1987); and Ole R. Holsti, "Crisis Decision-Making," and Jack S. Levy, "The Causes of War: A Review of Theories and Evidence," in *Behavior, Society, and Nuclear War*, vol. 1, ed. Philip E. Tetlock et al. (New York, 1989).

65. John Lewis Gaddis, "The Long Peace: Elements of Stability in the Postwar International System," *International Security* 10 (Spring 1986): 99–142.

66. Paul Bracken, *Command and Control of Nuclear Forces* (New Haven, 1983); Bruce Blair, *Strategic Command and Control: Redefining the Nuclear Threat* (Washington, 1985); John D. Steinbruner, "Nuclear Decapitation," *Foreign Policy* 45 (Winter 1981–82): 16–28; Sagan, "Nuclear Alerts"; Alexander L. George, *Presidential Decision-Making in Foreign Policy: The Effective Use of Information and Advice* (Boulder, 1980).

67. Waltz, *Man, the State, and War*, 238.

68. Harold and Margaret Sprout, "Environmental Factors in the Study of International Politics," *Journal of Conflict Resolution* 1 (December 1957): 309–28.

69. See, for example, David B. Yoffie, *Power and Protectionism: Strategies of the Newly Industrializing Countries* (New York, 1983); John Odell, *U.S. International Monetary Policy: Markets, Power, and Ideas as Sources of Change* (Princeton, 1982); Jack Snyder, *The Ideology of the Offensive: Military Decision Making and the Disaster of 1914* (Ithaca, 1984); Vinod K. Aggarwal, *Liberal Protectionism: The International Politics of Organized Textile Trade* (Berkeley, 1985); Larson, *Origins of Containment*; Posen, *Sources of Military Doctrine*; and Walt, *Alliances*.

✑

The United States and International Institutions

W. Michael Reisman

Each state that elects to participate in a multilateral institution realises a different constellation of costs and benefits, but some denominators are common. Each state sacrifices a measure of (often theoretical) freedom of action in the area of regulation, in return for a package of benefits that is expected to include comparable restraints on the actions of others. Each expects to gain an amplification of national power in the pursuit of specific objectives when the multilateral institution which it joins becomes the vehicle for action that might otherwise have been undertaken (if at all) unilaterally.

For small and very small states, multilateral institutions may become the major avenues for diplomacy, far outstripping bilateral relations and offering the most prized diplomatic posts. The small states' votes in these institutions may become their most formidable and possibly their only base of power, and their representatives may acquire a degree of influence far beyond what they might expect as ambassadors in a bilateral relationship. The larger the state and the greater its power, the more will bilateral diplomacy be preferred over multilateral, and the more measured will be the attitude towards multilateral institutions. But no state can afford to be oblivious to multilateral institutions: world-wide communications and the movement of persons, goods and services have created interdependencies, to the point where the apparatus of even the most effective states can no longer adequately and economically achieve their objectives without the authority and material support available only through external alignments.

In this, as in other areas of international life, the United States is like other states and yet is also quite different from them. Although it is the most powerful state in the international arena, the U.S. has helped to conceive, and today participates in, a wide variety of multilateral institutions, each of which is marked by some sort of formal, rule-based decision-making process that, in many ways, proves more constricting for American action than would the unilateral exercise of its power. The U.S. espouses multilateralism as a virtue. Like every other state, it also seeks to use multilateral institutions as instruments for achieving its own policies.

In apparent contrast to other members, the U.S. is able, by virtue of its power—at least in the short run—to suspend or to modify institutional rules in particular cases, absorb whatever political and diplomatic costs ensue, and accomplish its objectives unilaterally. When this happens, other member-states often attribute cynicism and hypocrisy to American declarations of support for multilateral diplomacy and international law, and assume America's avowed support for multilateralism to be no more than a fig leaf for opportunism.

This conclusion simplifies a much more complex relationship that, on the one hand, puts the U.S. among the most avid supporters of multilateral institutions, and yet, in different

W. Michael Reisman is McDougal Professor of Law, Yale Law School. *Survival 41–4*, Winter 1999–2000, pp. 62–80.

circumstances, pits it against the members and administration of some of those same institutions. The relationship is most dramatic with the UN, but applies in varying degree to every institution to which the U.S. is party. In some ways, U.S. behaviour with respect to the international institutions in which it participates is indistinguishable from the foreign-policy techniques of other states or state groupings.[1] In other critical ways, the modes in which the U.S. relates to multilateral institutions and to endeavours within areas of their formal competence are both more complex and more distinctive than would first appear, and are driven by factors different from those frequently assumed by many commentators. America's complex relations with multilateral international institutions is best understood in terms of four international political roles which it continuously and simultaneously plays (and in some instances is called upon to play) in contemporary world politics:

- *A prophetic and reformist role.* For more than a century, the U.S. has seen its destiny as linked to the reform of international politics, an impulse that arises from many strands in American political and civic culture. This sense of mission has led it to conceive and support the establishment of international institutions endowed with formal decision-making procedures, in which, as in its domestic experience, law and legal symbols figure prominently.
- An *infra-organisational role.* Within the organisational politics of each institution, the U.S. sometimes—but less often than its power would allow—operates in ways characteristic of all states in multilateral institutions. Yet U.S. behaviour is magnified by virtue of its preponderant power, and is aggravated by the apparent inconsistency of actions taken in pursuit of specific interests with its prophetic and reformist role.
- *A custodial role.* The United States functions as the ultimate custodian of international order, the actor of last resort in matters of fundamental importance to contemporary international politics. The custodial role may involve usurping ordinary decision-making procedures in order to vouchsafe the fundamental goals of the larger system which the institution is supposed to serve. The custodial role sometimes requires the U.S. to resist organic institutional developments which it may have initiated or previously supported, even though they are natural outgrowths of its reformist role, or to act extra-legally or supra-legally with respect to those same institutions when an urgent issue of minimum world public order is at stake. The custodial role may generate acute connects with other members of the institution, especially when military action is required and when the coalition leader is constrained to favour its own view of efficiency or institutional amelioration over prescribed coalition procedures, a choice which brings stress to the coalition. In a government marked by rule of law, the custodial role may also exacerbate tensions between internal governmental participants, for whom rule-of-law is their core ideology, and those charged with external responsibilities.
- *A domestic-pressure reactive role.* The foreign-policy establishment of the United States, itself a complex organism that incorporates government officials and private persons, frequently identifies what many of its members consider to be a national interest. But as a complex constitutional system and a robustly effective democracy, the U.S. acting externally must respond to the demands—whether intermittent or persistent—of internal constituencies, which are sometimes generated, refracted, or amplified by the mass media. The transfer of foreign-affairs power from a specialist professional class to a much wider slice of the community is characteristic of modern

democracies, but is particularly advanced in the U.S.. The dynamic that operates here sometimes moves what the specialists would characterise as a micro-issue or marginal issue to centre stage, and often 'localises'—in this context a preferable term to its pejorative counterpart 'parochialises'—perspective and evaluation, at least from the alternative perspective of the foreign-policy specialist.

Each of these roles has its own internal dynamic. Some are uniquely American and deeply rooted in the U.S. national experience or derive from its power; others are shared, in varying degree, by different states. But in the case of the U.S., their effects on the institution concerned are greatly magnified by its predominant power in contemporary world politics. On occasion all four roles are performed harmoniously, such as during the 1991 Gulf War. But the intersection of these roles in particular cases may lead to inconsistent and sometimes conflicting US behaviour. Such situations can cause the United States to conduct its international institutional diplomacy less efficiently and more abrasively than intended, to the point where the inherent dynamics of some of the roles may undermine the performance of others and generate periodic crises in relations with multilateral institutions and in the institutions themselves.

THE U.S. AS REFORMER

Since the late nineteenth century, the focus of U.S. foreign policy and, as a critical part of it, discussions among intellectuals, church groups, and popular movements, has shifted from the choice of a role *within* an existing system to a role of innovative architect and redesigner *of* that system, engaged in increasingly ambitious projects to change radically the structure of and, as a result, behaviour within that system. The creation of the Permanent Court of Arbitration, the precursor of the Permanent and now International Court of Justice, was largely an American initiative at the 1899 Hague Peace Conference (which had actually been convened by the Tsar in the hope of securing an interim arms control agreement that would retard the development of comparative German and Austro-Hungarian advantages).[2] The notion that an international court could transform the historically violent and destructive methods of conflict resolution into orderly judicial procedures had deep roots in the 'Peace Movement', a popular, religious-based mass movement in the United States that took shape in the nineteenth century. The League of Nations, as a mechanism for and guarantor of collective security, was, of course, President Woodrow Wilson's pet project. (US membership in the League was blocked in the Senate, largely because of the ailing Wilson's mishandling of the matter rather than because of an essential antipathy to an active foreign policy.) The International Labor Organization was largely an American invention. The basic ideas for the United Nations, the World Bank and many of the specialised agencies were also largely conceived and pushed by the U.S. during the Second World War.

Thus, one of the distinctive characteristics of U.S. participation in international politics for the past century has been the desire to engage in major international social engineering, expecting that, if properly done, initiatives involving the design and creation of new institutions would transform the essential nature and procedures of those politics. It is fair to call this energetic bully-pulpitism a 'prophetic role' in the non-religious sense in which the Oxford English Dictionary uses the term: 'the accredited spokesman, proclaimer, or preacher of some principle, cause or movement'. The particular content of the policies for restructuring international politics has varied from period to period, but the common objective has been to change world politics so that they take on the character of what Americans believe their own politics to be. The symbol of law is extremely important. Law is to play as large a role in international politics as Americans believe it plays in their own domestic processes, and judicial institutions (that is to say, institutions *applying law* as opposed to third-party procedures which simply resolve disputes) are deemed central. Over time, the deep belief that the savagery of international and domestic politics can be tamed and transformed has prevailed, along with the belief that these can be significantly improved by new patterns of institutional collaboration, and that it is wholly appropriate for the U.S. to take the lead, indeed to press vigorously for those changes if necessary.

This is not a narrow or arcané litist interest, protectively couched in inaccessible specialist jargon. Analysis of public opinion over time demonstrates consistent strong popular support for such international programmes. Nor has it been merely a popular amusement for the rank-and-file. For most of the twentieth century, the United States has probably been the only country in the world in which significant numbers of serious and accomplished businessmen, clergy, politicians and diplomats—the sort of people who consider their time very 'valuable'—have met publicly and privately over extended periods of time to collaborate in the production of plans for new institutional arrangements to effect the transformation of the world or particular regions. This practice was conducted with great seriousness during the Second World War and has been pursued continuously since then.[3] And not for modest projects: the targets have included matters as varied as the restructuring of the global economy, the control of the diffusion of the most destructive weapons, the redesign of the UN, the reorganisation of the world health system, 'nation-building' within particular states or, most ambitiously, the international human-rights programme, which in essence seeks to change the technique of governance everywhere so that it comports with what is taken to be a Western ideal.

Dramatic U.S. behaviour that is interpreted as 'anti-institutional' or 'organisation-bashing' should be viewed in terms of this prophetic and reformist role. When the U.S. withdraws from an international institution—for example, the International Labor Organization—or when it withholds funds from an institution—for example, the UN—it does not signal a fit of pique nor a withdrawal into isolationism. On the contrary, in the U.S. view it is corrective, contingent behaviour designed to secure precise adjustments which the institution in question must undertake as the condition for U.S. re-entry or repayment.[4] Part of the angry reaction that these acts precipitate among other members has less to do with the gravamen—the particular pathology in the organisation concerned—and more to do with the fact that, precisely because its power and wealth are necessary for the institution's optimal operation, the U.S. can arrogate to itself the right to demand corrections in such a fashion. The angry reaction may make the reform initiative less effective or more costly than would a suave diplomatic approach, but because both action and reaction here are driven by their own forces, the collision between them seems inevitable.

Some observers would say that, whether consciously or not, the policies which the U.S. pursues in these macro-social reform initiatives are designed to enhance and sustain American power and interests. Although avowedly altruistic behaviour usually has a core of self-interest, claims that the U.S., in its reformist role, is exclusively pursuing its own self-interest are grotesquely exaggerated. While the values espoused are—not surprisingly—essentially American and hence congenial to Americans (and indeed to many others), quite a few of the policies and institutional arrangements that have been pursued—for example, free trade—are, if the theory is correct, supposed to 'level the playing field', something one would not expect a superpower to seek. Others—for example, democracy and human rights—give no real gains to U.S. power, limit the ambit of operation of some executive agencies, put the U.S. on the defensive when it finds itself constrained to support, to paraphrase Franklin D. Roosevelt, one of 'our SOBs', and often vex relations with governments that are important and sometimes vital to American foreign relations. Demands for the achievement everywhere of multi-cultural and nonracial societies, values that are central to the American political experiment, promise no particular gains for the U.S., and often embroil it in conflicts in which 'national interests', as foreign-policy specialists might define them, are not really engaged and in which prospects for meaningful achievement of goals are slim.

Prior to the Second World War, these kinds of American initiatives were viewed by many as romantic, quixotic, idealistic, irritating or ridiculous. Since that war, and certainly since the end of the Cold War, they are also viewed as policies to be reckoned with, precisely because the United States, unlike other states that intermittently seek the bully pulpit for prophetic and reformist purposes, is the major international actor, and disposes of the power and money to press these programmes vigorously.

THE INFRA-ORGANISATIONAL FACTOR

The prophet who envisions a new religion, institution, or organisation and who is concerned about his historical image would do well to time the moment of its creation with his own bodily ascent to heaven. If he does not, his prophetic mantle will become more and more tattered as he tries to participate in his creation and is sucked ever deeper into the gritty quotidian politics inherent in every working institution. This virtual iron law of status decay is particularly painful when the founder-prophet is a state and the institution concerned is a multilateral inter-governmental one. And it is uniquely problematic for the U.S..

In international institutions—the constant celebration of the supposedly preeminent authority of the institution notwithstanding—the actual assignment of each state's representative is to pursue that state's particular objectives and to reinforce the powers of the international institution only insofar as it contributes to that end. From the standpoint of government officials charged with the conduct of their country's external affairs, a multilateral institution is an instrument of policy to be wielded, like other instruments, in the pursuit of national interest. The personnel of governments who decide on and implement national policies within and through the international institutions identify with their states; though some may harbour secret loyalties to more inclusive identities, their public commitments, supported by oath and often reinforced by promises of material and symbolic rewards and threats of severe criminal sanctions, continue to be to their own states. Within the state, there may be official programmes—in schools, churches and the media—extolling this multilateral institution or that, but primary loyalty to the state continues to be demanded and policed.

Thus, rhetoric notwithstanding, national officials are not romantic about international institutions. They better than anyone know that the institutions are created by the agreements of individuals who occupy high positions in governments; that the highest-level personnel in the institutions are selected by high government representatives and, in effect, often serve at their pleasure; that the national personnel who create and maintain multilateral institutions select the managerial level of multilateral institutions and, as in most selection processes, seek to replicate their own values as best they can; that the monetary resources of such institutions depend upon continuing contributions by governments; and that the capacities of these institutions to engage in coercive action—the *ultima ratio* of politics—depend upon provision of the necessary resources by governments.

Understood in this context, the extent to which the U.S. defers to and defends established institutional and bureaucratic decision procedures and does not use its power to influence decisions that would favour its or its nationals' interests is remarkable. Nonetheless, a significant amount of day-to-day American behaviour *within* a multilateral organisation is likely to be driven by the same sorts of interests that motivate other member-states—that is, after all, one of the functions of diplomacy in these institutions. But while observers and commentators may be understanding about the vigorous insistence on the satisfaction of minimum security or economic concerns voiced by, let us say, Ireland, Israel, Italy or some other smaller state, and view it as perfectly normal (indeed as normative international institutional behaviour), they are prone to be very critical when the U.S. insists on positions within an organisation that accommodate its own interests. Partly because of its self-assumed prophetic role, the U.S. is held to a higher standard.

As in all law, legal arrangements are created within political processes, and necessarily incorporate the values and demands of the most politically relevant actors. It should come as no surprise, therefore, that in their constitutions and prescribed procedures, international institutions reflect the relative power positions of the states that formed them. Politics is, at its most elemental, the pursuit of values by means of power, and those who have more power are hardly likely to create institutions that minimise that power and discriminate against their own values. But the constitution of each organisation must still incorporate divergent interests, so the life of every political institution is marked by a constant testing and stressing of legal and other power arrangements, by those who feel themselves prejudiced by them, in search of changes they believe will benefit them.

Once a decision procedure has been established within an institution, the U.S., like every other state, does defend its rights under it. All members of these institutions struggle to hold on to the power they have, or to acquire more: in a power arena, power is the coin of exchange and actors quite naturally seek to preserve or expand their 'monetary reserves'. Multilateral international institutions, despite their legal character, continue to be arenas of the larger power process. In the UN, where organisational power is essentially assigned to a Security Council in which five states have permanent membership with a veto right over decisions they oppose, there is a constant struggle between small and mid-sized powers, on the one hand, who seek to change the charter system, and the permanent members who seek to preserve their status and 'acquired rights', on the other. While the struggle often pits emotive symbols such as 'democracy' and 'equality' against equally emotive symbols such as 'fidelity to law', it is essentially a struggle for power. The same state that insists on 'democracy' in this context is likely to insist on its 'sovereign rights' *vis-à-vis* a smaller state in another, and to resist indignantly as an unlawful interference in its domestic jurisdiction any examination of the absence of democracy in its internal processes. The technique of international institutional diplomacy is to clothe frequent claims of special interest in the signs and symbols of common interest. Happily, the very multiplicity of actors with diverse interests acts, in the aggregate, as some restraint on the pursuit of special interest, while the constant reiteration by all of the symbols of common interest helps to reinforce the authority that undergirds the institution.

Once an institution is established, however, its internal power process may become quite different from the surrounding power arena. Institutions acquire lives of their own, they engage employees who devote their lives to them, and they generate affirmative attitudes and even loyalties in different sectors within and outside, not least in parts of the media, the neural system of modern mass society. And although every organisation is created by and reflects a political power process, once an organisation is established, the formulation of its procedures in the language of the law brings the lawyers into play, inevitably introducing a complex calculus of legal values that henceforth influences how it will operate. Elements such as these are, in their own way, bases of power which introduce new factors into the international power process.

Consider the UN Charter, which has created organs besides the Security Council. In many of them, power is distributed quite differently than it is in the Security Council, whose permanent members have most of the population, wealth and power of the world community and which, as a result, more accurately mirrors the composition and dynamics of 'the real world'. From time to time, these other organs may be mobilised by coalitions of smaller opposing states attempting to change the allocation of power within the institution. When this happens, the more powerful and organisationally endowed states react in ways that preserve their power. Take the International Court of Justice, the UN's principal judicial organ. It has a broadly defined competence.[5] None of its 15 members, a collegium which is always likely to include the nominees of the permanent members of the Security Council, has a veto. So one can envision initiatives to change the UN structure, that would surely be vetoed in the Security Council, producing a different and veto-proof outcome in the Court.[6] Although implementation of a judgement of the Court will ultimately depend on the discretion of the Security Council, the mere authority of a judgement or opinion as to what the law is may have a significant political valence in some contexts.[7]

When the International Court sought to go beyond its conventional ambit and to condemn the U.S. for its activities in support of one side in the Nicaraguan civil war,[8] the U.S. withdrew its declaration of jurisdiction to the optional clause of the Court's statute.[9] But this particular response was not unique to the United States. A decade earlier, the Court, on the basis of only arguable jurisdiction, had subjected France's nuclear-weapons testing programme to its review,[10] whereupon France withdrew its declaration of jurisdiction.[11]

As a major architect of the UN Charter and a permanent member of the Security Council, one would expect the United States to behave conservatively when initiatives to reduce its power are pressed in the United Nations. But on occasion the U.S. has sought to expand the power of the General Assembly, at the expense of the Security Council, precisely because it wished to use the authority of a multilateral institution rather than 'go it alone'. After the eruption of the 1950–53 Korean War, for example, the U.S. conceived the so-called 'Uniting For Peace' Resolution.[12] This resolution purported to authorise the General Assembly to exercise some of the powers of the Security Council with regard to peace and security when the Council was blocked. The theme was the 'democratisation' of the UN. At the time the U.S. was confident that it would always be able to marshal a majority in the Assembly. Fifteen years later, at the end of the Six Day War when the Soviet Union indicated that it planned to convene the Assembly under 'Uniting for Peace', the United States resisted in the name of fidelity to the Charter. Thereafter, with the rise of an independent Non-Aligned Movement in the Assembly, both the U.S. and the Soviet Union became adherents to the principle of fidelity to the text of the Charter. In the run-up to the March–June 1999 military action in Kosovo, when the U.S. unsuccessfully explored the possibility of a Security Council authorisation, it probably could have marshalled a majority in the Assembly under the 'Uniting For Peace' resolution. Presumably, it eschewed this option because of the precedential implications of a constitutional change, enhancing the power of the Assembly *vis-à-vis* the Council, that would have persisted long after that event.

The infra-organisational role of the U.S. often generates tension with its own closest and most powerful allies. This occurs not because these allies do not understand the multiple roles the U.S. plays, but because, in pursuing their own policies, they find in the conflicts of the various American roles opportunities to enhance their own positions. The two democratic permanent members of the Security Council that often cooperate with the U.S. in the performance of custodial functions compete nonetheless for power and the manifold advantages it offers. Sometimes they take advantage of unpopular positions that the American perception of its roles and responsibilities forces it to defend. The 1998 diplomatic conference in Rome that produced a statute for an International Criminal Court (ICC) provides an interesting example. France, like the U.S., did not initially support the ICC, for parallel and in some cases converging reasons. But when it became apparent in Rome that there would be a statute, France effected a dramatic *volte face*, and announced its support for the project. In the tumultuous moments of the final vote, the French ambassador stood and clapped enthusiastically, as the American delegation sat in gloom.

The custodial role of the U.S. is perceived as conflicting with the ICC as it was structured by the Rome Conference, because it may obstruct or raise the cost of the performance of certain critical custodial functions. Yet, without the active support of the U.S., it is difficult to see how the Criminal Court can achieve its objectives. That does not mean that its existence and operation, however ineffective in terms of its manifest goals, will not affect the international political process. Once the ICC seemed inevitable, a major power like France could calculate that while the operation of the new court would complicate the discharge of American functions, it could also provide new opportunities to France for competition with the U.S.. As a party to the statute of the ICC, France could participate in the selection of the judges and critical staff of the Court and, even more important, play a major parliamentary-diplomatic role in the Assembly of States, the ultimate control mechanism of the ICC. Since one of the latent functions of the ICC is to reduce the power of the Security Council, France can thus benefit from the existence of the Criminal Court at the expense of the U.S., serving as the indispensable link between Council and Court, while remaining confident that, when circumstances require it, the United States will still function as the custodian of world order.

THE U.S. AS CUSTODIAN

As the strongest power in the world community, the U.S. is called upon to play an additional and unique role: that of the ultimate custodian of the fundamental goals of the multilateral institutions that it has helped to establish, when these institutions prove unable to act. And they often prove unable to act, because one of the sad facts of international life is that multilateral institutions have certain inherent defects that arise from the very nature of international politics. International institutions are created by the states that elect to participate in them for the purpose of achieving their common and particular objectives. The institutions testify, by their very existence, to a shared perception of certain common interests, sufficient at least to create them, and they may have great appeal for sectors or strata of the rank-and-file if they promise to enhance values which they seek. But no matter how romanticised the institutions may be, any honest appraisal should locate them clearly in the reality of an international politics still dominated by actors operating largely from national perspectives. Those actors create institutions that require their agreement for decision and action, but they are subsequently unlikely to agree on many of the most fundamental issues that call for decision.

The most avid proponents of multilateralism tend to believe that international institutional paralysis results from transient factors: the Cold War, the North-South division, the Palestine problem and so on. Solve the relevant transient problem and the institutions will be able to function as planned. But when the transient problem is resolved or recedes because it has ceased to be important, the institutions still suffer paralysis at the moment they are most needed. The reason is as apparent as the seating system in any international institution: despite a certain homogenisation of global culture, the elites (and many of the rank-and-file) of these states continue to operate with identifications, demands and matter-of-fact assumptions about past and future that are significantly different from those held by their counterparts in other states. They perceive events and value outcomes differently. In the aggregate, they have different interests and those differences become painfully apparent when multilateral institutions have to make fundamental decisions about world order. As currently structured, the institutions often prove unable to act, whether because of a veto right or a requirement of consensus. But a change of procedure will not resolve the problem, for the obstacles to action are reflections of the international political process itself. So the alternatives for a state that is able to act unilaterally are to do nothing, because unilateral action would be 'against the law', or to act alone, if necessary, to preserve the system in ways that might be deemed inconsistent with the law. For the U.S., for all the centrality of law to its national experience, the answer has been as simple as it is ineluctable, whether domestically or internationally. In Justice Oliver Wendell Holmes' pithy apophthegm, 'a constitution is not a suicide pact'.

The word 'custodian' is used advisedly, because the emphasis here is on a role that requires the incumbent to act in the best interests of those in its custody—as the custodian sees it. In this respect, the term is different from 'leadership', which American politicians frequently use to describe the national role, as well as from 'hegemony', which is used just as frequently by critics of the U.S. role. Nor is the term synonymous with 'the world's policeman', a controversial term in U.S. domestic politics, for it implies that, like the domestic 'cop on the beat' American military power will be deployed for each and every infraction—from border wars to *coups d'etat* to human-rights violations—when the UN is unable or unwilling to repair them. These and similar events may have great political or moral importance, but the custodian of the system is concerned with threats to the system as such, not infractions within it.

The U.S. is acutely aware of its status in world politics, and its officials perforce plan for contingencies in which it will be called upon to act as custodian. But in moments of crisis, the initial invocation of the custodial role is likely to come from other beleaguered or otherwise involved states, who urgently remind the U.S. of its 'responsibilities'. American reactions to many of these calls may appear inconsistent, and the internal debate within the U.S. about the appropriate response may suggest deep internal divisions about custodianship. In fact, the United States has been rather consistent in fulfilling the custodial role, but the divergence between insiders and outsiders with regards to its 'when, why and how' underlines another aggravating factor in the performance of this role: it is the custodian who ultimately decides when, why, and how to act.

The custodial role conflicts with the formally prescribed procedures of multilateral institutions in a number of ways. The custodian guarantees the ultimate goals of the system, but without explicit authority and outside the processes or procedures that have been established within each institution for making decisions. If they were followed in these instances, there would be no decision. In the UN, the ultimate goal is the maintenance of minimum world order, a concept that originally meant the protection of the territory of states from aggression, but has now been extended to include the policing of selected activities within states if their foreseeable consequences threaten minimum world order. In the economic agencies, the ultimate goal is the maintenance of the international economic and financial infrastructure that undergirds the science-based and technological civilisation of key parts of the world. This goal may require the salvaging of distressed national economies or their 'restructuring', usually in ways that are costly and painful in the domestic politics of those undergoing the transformation.

In circumstances where the ultimate goals are gravely at issue, but the processes and procedures of the institutions that have been established to secure them are unlikely to produce the decisions that are called for, the custodian, frequently with the support of other significant actors, may have to act outside the established legal framework of the institution in order to secure the international goals at stake. This supra-legal or extra-legal action is justified as 'lawful' rather than 'legal'—that is to say, in conformity with the ultimate goals of the system or institution in question, if not with the procedures that have been prescribed to achieve them. Sometimes these actions can still be 'legalised' by adroit manipulation of key elastic terms in the constitutive instruments of the institution. For example, unilateral action inconsistent with the authority assigned to the Security Council to respond to acts of aggression, breaches of the peace and threats to the peace may be 'legalised' by an expansive reading of the 'inherent right of self-defence' in another article of the Charter. Despite the fact that the UN Charter reserves the powers to maintain minimum order to the Security Council, where action otherwise supported by a majority could still be vetoed by a Permanent Member, the 'Uniting for Peace' resolution purported to self-authorise the General Assembly to exercise its newly discovered 'secondary competence'.

In the performance of custodial functions, there are real advantages to conducting operations through a multilateral institution. It is clear that U.S. policy-makers prefer that route, when it is possible, for reasons of both efficiency and ideology. It is in this context that one must understand the affirmation of a conditional commitment by the Clinton administration (and, indeed, preceding administrations): 'multilateral when we can, unilateral when we must'. Unfortunately, it is not always possible to do things through multilateral institutions. To wield the not-inconsiderable authority available in Chapter VII of the UN Charter, the United States must win the acquiescence, within the Security Council, of two other advanced industrial democracies, one unstable government in an uncertain transition, and one unapologetic dictatorship, any one of whom may veto Council action, or impose unacceptable costs or conditions, as its price for consent. To go to the General Assembly under 'Uniting for Peace' may afford authority for a particular action, but reduces, precedentially, the exclusive power of the Security Council, in which the U.S. enjoys a veto. That would conflict with the infra-organisational role considered above and could, moreover, compromise future custodial operations. Hence, in the Kosovo action, President Bill Clinton repeatedly stated that the United States and NATO were operating on behalf of 'the world-community'. As an empirical matter, they probably were. Yet the alliance did not go to the basic institution of the world community to receive an explicit authorisation.

The perceptions that are a critical part of the custodial role are frequently different from those of other friendly members of the institutions concerned. In the Siberian-pipeline controversy of the 1980s, the U.S., as ultimate guarantor of security in Europe *vis-à-vis* the Soviet Union, tried to exercise a custodial role with respect to an incipient arrangement that it felt would increase Western Europe's dependence and vulnerability to Soviet economic pressure.[13]

The European governments felt that the matter was simply one of economic utility. To Europeans, American behaviour, including its insistence on the stringent application of its import-export controls, represented a violation of the norms and ethics of multilateral trade institutions, driven by crude and imperfectly concealed self-interest. From the American perspective, its own actions were driven by the imperatives of custodianship of the security of the free world, which it had preserved twice before in the century, at the cost of considerable blood and treasure, a responsibility which it hoped to avert a third time by prudently restraining the formation of economic dependencies on the adversary.

During the Cold War, a similar dynamic operated within the Coordinating Committee on Multilateral Export Controls (COCOM) with regard to sales of dual-use materials to explicit or latent adversaries. The United States, as the ultimate custodian of security, was more likely to view the sales in terms of urgent security, of which it was the guarantor, while its allies and partners in COCOM would incline to view them as simply economic.[14] For example, since the U.S. submarine leg of the nuclear triad was the ultimate deterrent to nuclear war, the sale by a Japanese company to the Soviet Union of technology that permitted Soviet submarines to substantially reduce the radial area of their noise—and hence the ability of the U.S. navy to locate them—was viewed gravely by the U.S. Department of Defense; some circles in other parts of the alliance considered this a hysterical overreaction. Currently, the tension between custodial responsibilities and economic interests of other friendly states continues with respect to nuclear proliferation and the spread of missile technology.

The custodial role may lead to actions that are apparently incompatible with the prophetic role, in immediate cases as well as prospectively. In an immediate case, such as the 1990 Iraqi invasion of Kuwait, the U.S. made it clear that it would expel Iraq, acting unilaterally if necessary, should the Security Council fail to provide authorisation. In the 1999 Kosovo crisis, the U.S., through NATO, acted without explicit Security Council authorisation. Given the distribution of power in the larger arena, a decision by the United States to proceed puts pressure on recalcitrant members of the institution to go along by bartering the institutional authority which they can dispense; thus they may retain some influence over actions that will, in any case, inevitably follow. Yet even when other members of the institution concerned get on board, it is clear that exercise of the custodial role is still challenging the institutional procedures that the U.S. itself had worked to establish, and committed itself to follow, and is leaving in its wake a residuum of resentment.

In some circumstances, evolutions within institutions the U.S. has helped to establish have required it to adjust its relationship in order to protect its custodial role. Thus, after the jurisdictional decision by the International Court of Justice in the Nicaragua case, the U.S. denounced its optional declaration to the jurisdiction of the Court. The action caused real anguish in many quarters of the Executive Branch where there had been a strong commitment and prior leadership with respect to the expansion of international adjudication as a mode of international dispute resolution. Yet it was plain that new alignments within the Court on critical substantive matters, coupled with a new approach to jurisdiction, made American subjection to the Court's appraisal at the initiative of virtually any member of the UN incompatible with the future performance of its custodial responsibilities.

Because the executive agencies of the U.S. are acutely aware of the custodial role they may be called upon to perform, their personnel look at incipient changes in multilateral institutions in terms of the impact on custodial performance in a variety of future scenarios. This sometimes results in national positions that are inconsistent with developments within those institutions, as well as with prior positions taken by the U.S.. Thus the 1997 Land Mines Convention was opposed by elements within the Executive Branch of the U.S. who believed that such weapons were indispensable to the performance of certain international security functions that would remain a U.S. responsibility for several decades. The International Criminal Court was initially espoused by the U.S. and supported with funds and personnel— indeed more than by any other state—in its early incarnation as the Former Yugoslav and Rwanda Tribunals, and in the draft proposed by the International Law Commission. Washington ultimately opposed the court, however, because the instrument that emerged from the 1998 Rome Conference was viewed as likely to obstruct the custodial role the U.S. could expect to be called upon to perform militarily.

The custodial role would be more compatible with the prophetic and reformist role if the institutional modalities the U.S. helped put into place were not so legalistic. But precisely because the emphasis on law is so strong in the reformist role of the U.S., immediate or prospective custodial actions are often viewed by many, within the U.S. as well as beyond, not simply as violations of the legal procedures of the institutions, but as violations of the prophetic role itself.

THE INFLUENCE OF DOMESTIC PRESSURE

In international political and legal analysis, states are frequently regarded as monads. But, obviously, internal political dynamics play a considerable role in determining external political behaviour. Even in democracies, the internal factor may vary according to the constitutional structure: in the Westminster model, for example, the Executive can wield considerably more foreign-affairs power than can its counterpart in a republican, constitutional model, such as that found in the U.S.. A unitary as opposed to federal system minimises the internal diffusion of power.

The internal politics of the United States are a critical and insufficiently appreciated dimension of American relations to multilateral institutions, with a profound influence on the content of decisions and their modes of implementation. The U.S. is a robust, federated democracy, whose constitutional structure, unlike the Westminster model, distributes competence among three branches. These three branches check and balance each other in different ways in virtually all areas, including foreign affairs. In a federal system, state law and administration is often the direct target of international-treaty activity. As a practical political matter, the U.S. federal government may find that its room for international manoeuvre is quite limited in many negotiations by values and policies of state and local officials.

The political-party system in the U.S. makes the legislative branch particularly diverse in its foreign-policy conceptions. The now golden age of a 'bipartisan' foreign policy did not depend upon consensus, but upon political parties with sufficient internal discipline to enable party leaders to enforce a position, once adopted, on all the members. That discipline derived, in no small part, from the party leaders' capacity to grant or withhold funds for local elections. That discipline is gone, and with it the relatively easy possibility of a president striking a foreign-policy deal with the congressional leadership of the opposition party, knowing that Congress will then implement it. Moreover, the proliferation of mass media now greatly enhances the capacity of each member of Congress to address the public directly. The competitive structure of the media means that more dramatic and simple presentations are often more likely to gain attention. While many in the U.S. lament an apparent nadir of civility in federal politics, the problems that relate to foreign policy are structural and are likely to persist, even if civility returns.

The representative character of the American system means that relatively small pressure groups that focus on a single issue—whether they are a small industry, a region or an ethnic or religious group whose members happen to be distributed strategically in electoral districts—may amplify their power and sometimes have a significant influence on the formation of policy. If they are unsuccessful in one branch, there is always another. Nor can internal bureaucratic politics be ignored: in some cases, the policies espoused by these groups may be resisted by groups, within the Executive, that have a different view of a particular national interest. With all these internal forces operating, the notion of an objectively verifiable 'national interest' is difficult to apply to U.S. politics. American scholars use the term 'foreign-policy process' in order to describe more accurately the way American external policy is formed. It is important to bear this in mind if one is to understand why, for example, the U.S. is on the one hand a critical supporter of UNICEF, a highly respected multilateral institution dedicated to the protection of children, and yet is often a fierce opponent of dissemination of birth-control information and technology, a policy with some obvious connections to the achievement of UNICEF's mission. (No one who wishes to understand American political behaviour should underestimate the passions engaged in the controversy over legalised abortion.) Or why the U.S. can so anger or confound its friends in multilateral institutions on matters concerning Cuba, Israel or, for that matter, China.

The impact of the internal constitutional factor on American participation in institutions created to prescribe and apply human-rights norms is particularly ironic. Human rights have been a critical part of the vision and politics of America and of its international prophetic and reformist role; moreover, the U.S. has been a central, indispensable initiator and sustainer of many of the international supervisory mechanisms of the modern programmes for the international protection of human rights. Yet it is not a party to the American Convention on Human Rights, despite the fact that it has been the major financial supporter of the Commission and Court, the oversight mechanisms of this regional human-rights system. And while it was the primary mover of the Universal Declaration of Human Rights, it only became party to the Covenant on Civil and Political Rights in 1992, and then quickly became embroiled in controversy with its oversight body. Some incline to personalise this conflict and to blame particular senators or representatives, but the problem is not personalities. Even though the U.S. generally meets or exceeds the international standard and has effective internal mechanisms for correcting abuses, there seems to be a unique lack of fit between the way the U.S. is structured and the international human-rights institutions.

When domestic politics within a large state create stresses in the relations with the international multilateral institutions in which it participates, there is a tendency to see the domestic influences as some sort of moral failure, especially if one assumes that multilateral institutions are essentially 'progressive' while states are always regressive atavisms. That assumption should be examined carefully. For all the mutations it has undergone, the state as an institution has been a remarkably efficient response to individual need for security. There always have been and still are cogent reasons why people organise themselves in exclusive rather than ever-more inclusive groups.

The reasons why people tend to respect and value their own communities are greatly reinforced in democracies, especially with respect to decisions about war and peace. The moral premise of democracy is that those who are affected by decisions should participate in making them. The political and possibly empirical premise of democracy is that people, with their mix of abilities, education and experience, will more often decide what is best for them than will aristocrats, autocrats, *soi disant* philosopher kings and sundry pundits, and armchair strategists. There may have been a time in the past when these premises did not apply with full force to foreign affairs, and they may not apply to the application of certain military technologies such as naval movements or electronic interventions or covert operations. But with a more efficient democracy, and a vigilant media which legitimises itself by 'exposing' such actions, politicians in the great modern democracies must increasingly accept the fact that they are bound in a sometimes unstated but nonetheless clearly understood compact with their constituents. This compact holds that leaders will not engage the people in conflicts that threaten significant consumption of blood and treasure unless a compelling case can be made that urgent national interests need to be protected, and no less costly method is feasible. A case for elective military action can still be successfully made, but it will depend on a fragile quotient of the modalities and the costs likely to be incurred.

In democratic societies, multilateral institutions may provoke complex and inconsistent reactions in many sectors of the public. The *raison d'etre* of the state is to provide security and the conditions for welfare, while remaining responsive to individual demands. Paradoxically, the more that multilateral international institutions attract loyalty and operate effectively, the more they are likely to generate anxieties and deep and contradictory reactions in both the leadership and rank-and-file of precisely those states that are perceived as democratic and effective—a reaction demonstrated by the often ambivalent popular responses to the evolving European Union.[15] These feelings are likely to be further aggravated by the perception of loss of power which membership in each institution engenders: citizens in stronger states will always feel that they have not received a measure commensurate with the responsibility and the costs that their states' power in the larger arena actually imposes on them; citizens of weaker states, insisting on the international norm of the 'equality of states', will always bemoan the asymmetrical distribution of power in the institution concerned.[16]

CONCLUSION

Sophisticated observers appreciate that the foreign policy of the government of every state is subject to conflicting forces and pressures. The United States is exceptional, not so much in the diversity of forces that operate on it in the formation of its international policy, as in the four roles it plays, each of which is magnified by its relative size and power. Tensions between the prophetic reformist, infra-organisational and custodial roles are all rendered more acute by the political uncertainties endemic to a large, federated democracy. The formation of foreign policy is therefore influenced by the comparative intensities of internal demands, and shifts in those demands are bound to aggravate other members of the institutions and organisations in which the U.S. participates. The lack of congruence between the aspirations and powers of comprehensive security organisations such as the UN means that the U.S. will feel compelled and will be called upon to act as custodian in exigent circumstances, and the four roles it plays mean that it will sometimes perform the custodial role in ways that displease some other states and actors in the international political system. There may be spikes of greater tension—as occurred after the passage of the General Assembly's 'Zionism is racism' resolution—or periods of greater harmony—as occurred after the Gulf War—but the essential pattern of the relationship will persist.[17]

Because making real decisions ineluctably indulges some and deprives others, it is inevitable that some actors in the international political process will resent the US—with varying degrees of intensity. That commonplace aside, many students of foreign affairs believe that the United States sometimes underuses multilateral institutions and needlessly aggravates its partners—in the issue of its unpaid UN dues, for example. They may be right, but it should be clear from the analysis of the four roles that reactions of other states to these aggravations are a relatively small part of the anger and tension that often attends—and will continue to attend—American relations with multilateral international institutions. More members of Congress—and the Executive—may become more sensitive to the feelings of other states, may better appreciate that multilateral institutions are useful tools of policy, may pay dues on time and appreciate that even a larger share of them is a pittance for the infra-institutional influence they bring. But the tensions between the U.S. and other members of international institutions are systemic and, in that respect, tragic. Considering the way world politics now work, there appears to be no escape from them.

One can imagine alternative futures in which the international political predominance of the U.S. is neutralised. Such a future could result, for example, from a more tightly organised Europe with a coherent foreign policy and an adequately funded effective military instrument to implement it, if need be; or by alignments of Russia and China that challenge the U.S.. If these developments were to occur, they could change American relationships to multilateral institutions. It is doubtful, however, that either of these hypothetical futures promises a better system of international order for the people of the world than the fragile and imperfect one we now have. In any case, such projections seem idle, for the more probable future is one in which the United States continues to be paramount and, because of its character and the multiplicity of its roles, continues to stir controversy in its complex relationships with international institutions.

ACKNOWLEDGMENTS

Mahnoush Arsanjani, Allan Gerson and Andrew Willard read drafts of this paper and made valuable criticisms and comments.

NOTES

1. To cite one example, the EU has its problems with the Appellate Body of the World Trade Organization (WTO), just as Japan and the U.S. have theirs; if one substitutes 'animal hormones' for 'alcohol' or 'bananas', the attacks on the WTO are equivalent in terms of intensity of vitriol and apparent disregard for the viability and future of the institution.
2. See Geoffrey Best, 'Peace Conferences and The Century of Total War. The 1899 Hague Conference and What Came After', *International Affairs,* vol. 75 (1999) pp. 619, 622.
3. See, for example, Dorothy B. Robins, *Experiment in Democracy: The Story of U.S. Citizen Organizations in Forging the Charter of the United Nations* (New York: Parkside Press, 1971); on the role of private groups in pressing for human rights instruments, see Michael Reisman, 'Private International Declaration Initiatives', in *La Déclaration universelle des droits de l'homme 1948–49* (Paris: La Documentation Française, 1998), pp. 79–116.
4. Paradoxically, when the United States suspends payment of its dues, it often continues to make large voluntary contributions to programmes conducted by the institutions in question.

5. Article 36(1) of the Statute of the International Court of Justice provides that the 'jurisdiction of the Court comprises all cases which the parties refer to it and all matters specially provided for in the Charter of the United Nations or in treaties of convention in force'.

6. For an examination of this, see Michael Reisman, 'The Constitutional Crisis in the United Nations', *American Journal of International Law,* vol. 87 (1993), p. 83.

7. UN Charter Article 94(2).

8. *Military and Paramilitary Activities in and against Nicaragua (Nicaragua v. U.S.), Jurisdiction and Admissibility,* 1984 ICJ Reports, p. 392 (Judgement of November 26).

9. In a letter dated 4 October 1985, the U.S. notified the Secretary General of the United Nations that it was terminating its declaration of jurisdiction, effective six months from 7 October 1985. For text and details, see *American Journal of International Law,* vol. 80 (1986), pp. 163–65.

10. *Nuclear Tests Case (Australia v. France), Request for the Indication of Interim Measures,* 1973 ICJ Reports, p. 99.

11. Letter of 2 January 1974, terminating the French declaration of acceptance of compulsory jurisdiction of 16 May 1966: 562 United Nations Treaty Series, No. 8196.

12. GA Resolution 377 (V), UN GAOR, 5th Session, Supp. No. 20 at 10, UN Doc. A/1775 (1950); repr. in 1950 UN Year Book, p. 193.

13. See Patrick J. DeSouza, 'The Soviet Gas Pipeline Incident: Extension of Collective Security Responsibilities to Peacetime Commercial Trade', in Michael Reisman and Andrew Willard, *International Incidents: The Law that Counts in World Politics* (Princeton, NJ: Princeton University Press, 1988), pp. 85–114.

14. See the examination of U.S. export-control regimes from this perspective in Michael Reisman and William Araiza, 'National Reports: United States of America', in Karl M. Meesen, (ed.) *International Law of Export Control, Jurisdictional Issues* (London: Graham & Trotman, 1992), p. 163.

15. Robert A. Dahl, *Democracy and its Critics* (New Haven and London: Yale University Press, 1989) p. 319.

16. United Nations Charter Article 2(1).

17. GA Resolution 3379, 30 UNGAOR Supp. (No. 34) at 83–84, UN Doc. A/10034 (1975); repealed by GA Resolution 46/86 UNGAOR 46th Sess. 74th plen. mtg. at 1, UN Doc A/Res/46/86 (1992).

✌ PART TWO ✌

International Sources
of Foreign Policy

Pride of place is often given to systemic explanations of foreign policy. It is here that the structural forces of the international system shape and constrain the choices of foreign policy officials. What are the characteristics of the international system, and how does the international system actually influence foreign policy? Scholars continue to debate these questions. The most consistent advocates of systemic explanations are Realist scholars who focus on the distribution of power and the enduring competitive nature of international politics.

Kenneth Waltz produces one of the most influential Realist analyses of international politics. In this chapter from his influential book, *Theory of International Politics*, Waltz details the essential organizational characteristics of the international system—organizational characteristics he calls anarchy. Waltz insists on fundamental distinctions between the organizing principles of domestic politics and those of international politics. Domestic politics is the realm of specialization and hierarchy. International politics takes place in a self-help system with inherent limits on the level of integration and specialization. With the anarchic nature of the international system properly understood, Waltz is able to describe recurrent types of strategies that states pursue to safeguard their security. In particular, states act to promote or ensure a balance of power. Waltz does not present a theory of foreign policy; rather he argues that the anarchic system and the distribution of power produce a certain sameness in the behavior of states. The international system does not directly shape the foreign policy of states, but it does present powerful constraints and imperatives in terms of which states are likely to abide.

Melvyn Leffler is a diplomatic historian who is interested in discovering the fundamental strategic and economic factors that shaped the American concept of national security after World War II. In effect, this essay probes the actual experience of government officials who sought to interpret and respond to the emerging postwar international structure. Leffler finds American defense planners and other officials preoccupied with preserving the geopolitical balance of power in Europe and Asia but the perceived threat to that balance came less from Soviet military capability as from the communist exploitation of widespread social and economic disarray and turmoil. The essay reveals the bureaucratic and intellectual complexities that confronted postwar planners as they attempted to create and implement an American concept of national security.

Robert Kagan seeks to provide a structural explanation for recent conflicts between the United States and Europe. In this portrait, the United States is a global power that operates in a world of anarchy and power politics while an inward-looking Europe seemingly remains secure within its own continent. The United States is powerful but also worried by threats that loom around the globe. Europe is weak but is satisfied by the democratic peace that prevails within its region. Kagan argues that these differences in circumstances create different strategic orientations toward the use of force, international law, and the organization of world politics. Power and weakness produce different foreign policy dispositions—and these differences fuel conflict between the two old Western partners.

Robert Jervis explores the implications of a unipolar distribution of power for American foreign policy. In previous decades, the United States has found itself in various sorts of balance of power systems. During the Cold War, it operated within a bipolar distribution of power. How do the constraints and opportunities facing American foreign policy shift with the rise of post-Cold War unipolarity? Jervis offers a variety of answers. A unipolar distribution of power provides extraordinary opportunities for the United States to define and pursue its interests—and it can allow ideologies wider sway in the conduct of foreign policy. But Jervis also argues that unipolarity seems to make the unipolar state not content and happy with the status quo but worried and uncertain—stimulating an ambitious agenda for the transformation of international order. Untangling the structural influences of the unipolar distribution of power from the specific characteristics of the unipolar polity and its leaders' ideas is the ongoing challenge.

∽

Anarchic Orders and Balances of Power

Kenneth Waltz

I

VIOLENCE AT HOME AND ABROAD

The state among states, it is often said, conducts its affairs in the brooding shadow of violence. Because some states may at any time use force, all states must be prepared to do so—or live at the mercy of their militarily more vigorous neighbors. Among states the state of nature is a state of war. This is meant not in the sense that war constantly occurs but in the sense that with

Kenneth Waltz, "Anarchic Orders and Balances of Power," from *Theory of International Politics.* p. 102–108. Reprinted by permission of The McGraw-Hill Companies.

each state deciding for itself whether or not to use force, war may at any time break out. Whether in the family, the community, or the world at large, contact without at least occasional conflict is inconceivable; and the hope that in the absence of an agent to manage or to manipulate conflicting parties the use of force will always be avoided cannot be realistically entertained. Among men as among states, anarchy, or the absence of government, is associated with the occurrence of violence.

The threat of violence and the recurrent use of force are said to distinguish international from national affairs. But in the history of the world surely most rulers have had to bear in mind that their subjects might use force to resist or overthrow them. If the absence of government is associated with the threat of violence, so also is its presence. A haphazard list of national tragedies illustrates the point all too well. The most destructive wars of the hundred years following the defeat of Napoleon took place not among states but *within* them. Estimates of deaths in China's Taiping Rebellion, which began in 1851 and lasted thirteen years, range as high as twenty million. In the American Civil War some six hundred thousand people lost their lives. In more recent history, forced collectivization and Stalin's purges eliminated five million Russians, and Hitler exterminated six million Jews. In some Latin American countries coups d'état and rebellions have been normal features of national life. Between 1948 and 1957, for example, two hundred thousand Colombians were killed in civil strife. In the middle 1970s most inhabitants of Idi Amin's Uganda must have felt their lives becoming nasty, brutish, and short, quite as in Thomas Hobbes's state of nature. If such cases constitute aberrations, they are uncomfortably common ones. We easily lose sight of the fact that struggles to achieve and maintain power, to establish order, and to contrive a kind of justice within states may be bloodier than wars among them.

If anarchy is identified with chaos, destruction, and death, then the distinction between anarchy and government does not tell us much. Which is more precarious: the life of a state among states, or of a government in relation to its subjects? The answer varies with time and place. Among some states at some times, the actual or expected occurrence of violence is low. Within some states at some times, the actual or expected occurrence of violence is high. The use of force or the constant fear of its use are not sufficient grounds for distinguishing international from domestic affairs. If the possible and the actual use of force mark both national and international orders, then no durable distinction between the two realms can be drawn in terms of the use or the nonuse of force. No human order is proof against violence.

To discover qualitative differences between internal and external affairs one must look for a criterion other than the occurrence of violence. The distinction between international and national realms of politics is not found in the use or the nonuse of force but in their different structures. But if the dangers of being violently attacked are greater, say, in taking an evening stroll through downtown Detroit than they are in picnicking along the French and German border, what practical difference does the difference of structure make? Nationally as internationally, contact generates conflict and at times issues in violence. The difference between national and international politics lies not in the use of force but in the different modes of organization for doing something about it. A government, ruling by some standard of legitimacy, arrogates to itself the right to use force—that is, to apply a variety of sanctions to control the use of force by its subjects. If some use private force, others may appeal to the government. A government has no monopoly on the use of force, as is all too evident. An effective government, however, has a monopoly on the *legitimate* use of force, and legitimate here means that public agents are organized to prevent and to counter the private use of force. Citizens need not prepare to defend themselves. Public agencies do that. A national system is not one of self-help. The international system is.

INTERDEPENDENCE AND INTEGRATION

The political significance of interdependence varies depending on whether a realm is organized, with relations of authority specified and established, or remains formally unorganized. Insofar as a realm is formally organized, its units are free to specialize, to pursue their own interests without concern for developing the means of maintaining their identity and preserving their security in the presence of others. They are free to specialize because they have no reason to fear the increased interdependence that goes with specialization. If those who specialize most benefit most, then competition in specialization ensues. Goods are manufactured, grain is produced, law and order are maintained, commerce is conducted, and financial services are provided by people who ever more narrowly specialize. In simple economic terms the cobbler depends on the tailor for his pants and the tailor on the cobbler for his shoes, and each would be ill-clad without the services of the other. In simple political terms Kansas depends on Washington for protection and regulation and Washington depends on Kansas for beef and wheat. In saying that in such situations interdependence is close, one need not maintain that the one part could not learn to live without the other. One need only say that the cost of breaking the interdependent relation would be high. Persons and institutions depend heavily on one another because of the different tasks they perform and the different goods they produce and exchange. The parts of a polity bind themselves together by their differences.[1]

Differences between national and international structures are reflected in the ways the units of each system define their ends and develop the means for reaching them. In anarchic realms like units coact. In hierarchic realms unlike units interact. In an anarchic realm, the units are functionally similar and tend to remain so. Like units work to maintain a measure of independence and may even strive for autarchy. In a hierarchic realm the units are differentiated and they tend to increase the extent of their specialization. Differentiated units become closely interdependent, the more closely so as their specialization proceeds. Because of the difference of structure, interdependence within and interdependence among nations are two distinct concepts. So as to follow the logicians' admonition to keep a single meaning for a given term throughout one's discourse, I shall use *integration* to describe the condition within nations and *interdependence* to describe the condition among them.

Although states are like units functionally, they differ vastly in their capabilities. Out of such differences something of a division of labor develops. The division of labor across nations, however, is slight in comparison with the highly articulated division of labor within them. Integration draws the parts of a nation closely together. Interdependence among nations leaves them loosely connected. Although the integration of nations is often talked about, it seldom takes place. Nations could mutually enrich themselves by further dividing not just the labor that goes into the production of goods but also some of the other tasks they perform, such as political management and military defense. Why does their integration not take place? The structure of international politics limits the cooperation of states in two ways.

In a self-help system each of the units spends a portion of its effort, not in forwarding its own good, but in providing the means of protecting itself against others. Specialization in a system of divided labor works to everyone's advantage, though not equally so. Inequality in the expected distribution of the increased product works strongly against extension of the division of labor internationally. When faced with the possibility of cooperating for mutual gain, states that feel insecure must ask how the gain will be divided. They are compelled to ask not "Will both of us gain?" but "Who will gain more?" If an expected gain is to be divided, say, in the ratio of two to one, one state may use its disproportionate gain to implement a policy intended to damage or destroy the other. Even the prospect of large absolute gains for both parties does not elicit their cooperation so long as each fears how the other will use its increased capabilities. Notice that the impediments to collaboration may not lie in the character and the immediate intention of either party. Instead, the condition of insecurity—at the least the uncertainty of each about the other's future intentions and actions—works against their cooperation.

In any self-help system, units worry about their survival, and the worry conditions their behavior. Oligopolistic markets limit the cooperation of firms in much the way that international political structures limit the cooperation of states. Within rules laid down by governments, whether firms survive and prosper depends on their own efforts. Firms need not protect themselves physically against assaults from other firms. They are free to concentrate on their economic interests. As economic entities, however, they live in a self-help world. All want to increase profits. If they run undue risks in the effort to do so, they must expect to suffer the consequences. As William Fellner[2] says, it is "impossible to maximize joint gains without the collusive handling of all relevant variables." And this can be accomplished only by "complete disarmament of the firms in relation to each other." But firms cannot sensibly disarm even to increase their profits. This statement qualifies rather than contradicts the assumption that firms aim at maximum profits. To maximize profits tomorrow as well as today, firms first have to survive. Pooling all resources implies, again as Fellner puts it, "discounting the future possibilities of all participating firms." But the future cannot be discounted. The relative strength of firms changes over time in ways that cannot be foreseen. Firms are constrained to strike a compromise between maximizing their profits and minimizing the danger of their own demise. Each of two firms may be better off if one of them accepts compensation from the other in return for withdrawing from some part of the market. But a firm that accepts smaller markets in exchange for larger profits will be gravely disadvantaged if, for example, a price war should break out as part of a renewed struggle for markets. If possible, one must resist accepting smaller markets in return for larger profits. "It is," Fellner insists, "not advisable to disarm in relation to one's rivals." Why not? Because "the potentiality of renewed warfare always exists." Fellner's reasoning is much like the reasoning that led Lenin to believe that capitalist countries would never be able to cooperate for their mutual enrichment in one vast imperialist enterprise. Like nations, oligopolistic firms must be more concerned with relative strength than with absolute advantage.

A state worries about a division of possible gains that may favor others more than itself. That is the first way in which the structure of international politics limits the cooperation of states. A state also worries lest it become dependent on others through cooperative endeavors and exchanges of goods and services. That is the second way in which the structure of international politics limits the cooperation of states. The more a state specializes, the more it relies on others to supply the materials and goods that it is not producing. The larger a state's imports and exports, the more it depends on others. The world's well-being would be increased if an ever more elaborate division of labor were developed, but states would thereby place themselves in situations of ever closer interdependence. Some states may not resist that. For small and ill-endowed states the costs of doing so are excessively high. But states that can resist becoming ever more enmeshed with others ordinarily do so in either or both of two ways. States that are heavily dependent or closely interdependent worry about securing that which they depend on. The high interdependence of states means that the states in question experience or are subject to the common vulnerability that high interdependence entails. Like other organizations, states seek to control what they depend on or to lessen the extent of their dependency. This simple thought explains quite a bit of the behavior of states: their imperial thrusts to widen the scope of their control and their autarchic strivings toward greater self-sufficiency.

Structures encourage certain behaviors and penalize those who do not respond to the encouragement. Nationally, many lament the extreme development of the division of labor, a development that results in the allocation of ever narrower tasks to individuals. And yet specialization proceeds, and its extent is a measure of the development of societies. In a formally organized realm a premium is put on each unit's being able to specialize in order to increase its value to others in a system of divided labor. The domestic imperative is "specialize!" Internationally, many lament the resources states spend unproductively for their own defense and the opportunities they miss to enhance the welfare of their people through cooperation with other states. And yet the ways of states change little. In an unorganized realm each unit's incentive is to put itself in a position to be able to take care of itself, since no one else can be counted on to do so. The international imperative is "take care of yourself!" Some leaders of nations may understand that the well-being of all of them would increase through their participation in a fuller division of labor. But to act on the idea would be to act on a domestic imperative, an imperative that does not run internationally. What one might want to do in the absence of structural constraints is different from what one is encouraged to do in their presence. States do not willingly place themselves in situations of increased dependence. In a self-help system considerations of security subordinate economic gain to political interest.

What each state does for itself is much like what all of the others are doing. They are denied the advantages that a full division of labor, political as well as economic, would provide. Defense spending, moreover, is unproductive for all and unavoidable for most. Rather than increased well-being, their reward is in the maintenance of their autonomy. States compete, but not by contributing their individual efforts to the joint production of goods for their mutual benefit. Here is a second big difference between international-political and economic systems.

STRUCTURES AND STRATEGIES

That motives and outcomes may well be disjoined should now be easily seen. Structures cause actions to have consequences they were not intended to have. Surely most of the actors will notice that, and at least some of them will be able to figure out why. They may develop a pretty good sense of just how structures work their effects. Will they not then be able to achieve their original ends by appropriately adjusting their strategies? Unfortunately, they often cannot. To show why this is so I shall give only a few examples; once the point is made, the reader will easily think of others.

If shortage of a commodity is expected, all are collectively better off if they buy less of it in order to moderate price increases and to distribute shortages equitably. But because some will be better off if they lay in extra supplies quickly, all have a strong incentive to do so. If one expects others to make a run on a bank, one's prudent course is to run faster than they do even while knowing that if few others run, the bank will remain solvent, and if many run, it will fail. In such cases pursuit of individual interest produces collective results that nobody wants, yet individuals by behaving differently will hurt themselves without altering outcomes. These two much-used examples establish the main point. Some courses of action I cannot sensibly follow unless you do too, and you and I cannot sensibly follow them unless we are pretty sure that many others will as well. Let us go more deeply into the problem by considering two further examples in some detail.

Each of many persons may choose to drive a private car rather than take a train. Cars offer flexibility in scheduling and in choice of destination; yet at times, in bad weather for example, railway passenger service is a much-wanted convenience. Each of many persons may shop in supermarkets rather than at corner grocery stores. The stocks of supermarkets are larger, and their prices lower; yet at times the corner grocery store, offering, say, credit and delivery service, is a much-wanted convenience. The result of most people usually driving their own cars and shopping at supermarkets is to reduce passenger service and to decrease the number of corner grocery stores. These results may not be what most people want. They may be willing to pay to prevent services from disappearing. And yet individuals can do nothing to affect the outcomes. Increased patronage *would* do it, but not increased patronage by me and the few others I might persuade to follow my example.

We may well notice that our behavior produces unwanted outcomes, but we are also likely to see that such instances as these are examples of what Alfred E. Kahn describes as large changes that are brought about by the accumulation of small decisions. In such situations people are victims of the "tyranny of small decisions," a phrase suggesting that "if one hundred consumers choose option x, and this causes the market to make decision X (where X equals 100 x), it is not necessarily true that those same consumers would have voted for that outcome if that large decision had ever been presented for their explicit consideration."[3] If the market does not present the large question for decision, then individuals are doomed to making decisions that are sensible within their narrow contexts even though they know all the while that in making such decisions they are bringing about a result that most of them do not want. Either that or they organize to overcome some of the effects of the market by changing its structure—for example by bringing consumer units roughly up to the size of the units that are making producers' decisions. This nicely makes the point: So long as one leaves the structure unaffected, it is not possible for changes in the intentions and the actions of particular actors to produce desirable outcomes or to avoid undesirable ones. Structures may be changed, as just mentioned, by changing the distribution of capabilities across units. Structures may also be changed by imposing requirements where previously people had to decide for themselves. If some merchants sell on Sunday, others may have to do so in order to remain competitive even though most prefer a six-day week. Most are able to do as they please only if all are required to keep comparable hours. The only remedies for strong structural effects are structural changes.

Structural constraints cannot be wished away, although many fail to understand this. In every age and place the units of self-help systems—nations, corporations, or whatever—are told that the greater good, along with their own, requires them to act for the sake of the system and not for their own narrowly defined advantage. In the 1950s, as fear of the world's destruction in nuclear war grew, some concluded that the alternative to world destruction was world disarmament. In the 1970s, with the rapid growth of population, poverty, and pollution, some concluded, as one political scientist put it, that "states must meet the needs of the political ecosystem in its global dimensions or court annihilation."[4] The international interest must be served; and if that means anything at all, it means that national interests are subordinate to it. The problems are found at the global level. Solutions to the problems continue to depend on national policies.

What are the conditions that would make nations more or less willing to obey the injunctions that are so often laid on them? How can they resolve the tension between pursuing their own interests and acting for the sake of the system? No one has shown how that can be done, although many wring their hands and plead for rational behavior. The very problem, however, is that rational behavior, given structural constraints, does not lead to the wanted results. With each country constrained to take care of itself, no one can take care of the system.

A strong sense of peril and doom may lead to a clear definition of ends that must be achieved. Their achievement is not thereby made possible. The possibility of effective action depends on the ability to provide necessary means. It depends even more so on the existence of conditions that permit nations and other organizations to follow appropriate policies and strategies. World-shaking problems cry for global solutions, but there is no global agency to provide them. Necessities do not create possibilities. Wishing that final causes were efficient ones does not make them so.

Great tasks can be accomplished only by agents of great capability. That is why states, and especially the major ones, are called on to do what is necessary for the world's survival. But states have to do whatever they think necessary for their own preservation, since no one can be relied on to do it for them. Why the advice to place the international interest above national interests is meaningless can be explained precisely in terms of the distinction between micro and macro theories. Among economists the distinction is well understood. Among political scientists it is not. As I have explained, a microeconomic theory is a theory of the market built up from assumptions about the behavior of individuals. The theory shows how the actions and interactions of the units form and affect the market and how the market in turn affects them. A macro theory is a theory about the national economy built on supply, income, and demand as systemwide aggregates. The theory shows how these and other aggregates are interconnected and indicates how changes in one or some of them affect others and the performance of the economy. In economics, both micro and macro theories deal with large realms. The difference between them is found not in the size of the objects of study, but in the way the objects of study are approached and the theory to explain them is constructed. A macro theory of international politics would show how the international system is moved by systemwide aggregates. One can imagine what some of them might be—amount of world GNP, amount of world imports and exports, of deaths in war, of everybody's defense spending, and of migration, for example. The theory would look something like a macroeconomic theory in the style of John Maynard Keynes, although it is hard to see how the international aggregates would make much sense and how changes in one or some of them would produce changes in others. I am not saying that such a theory cannot be constructed, but only that I cannot see how to do it in any way that might be useful. The decisive point, anyway, is that a macro theory of international politics would lack the practical implications of macroeconomic theory. National governments can manipulate systemwide economic variables. No agencies with comparable capabilities exist internationally. Who would act on the possibilities of adjustment that a macro theory of international politics might reveal? Even were such a theory available, we would still be stuck with nations as the only agents capable of acting to solve global problems. We would still have to revert to a micropolitical approach in order to examine the conditions that make benign and effective action by states separately and collectively more or less likely.

Some have hoped that changes in the awareness and purpose, in the organization and ideology, of states would change the quality of international life. Over the centuries states have changed in many ways, but the quality of international life has remained much the same.

States may seek reasonable and worthy ends, but they cannot figure out how to reach them. The problem is not in their stupidity or ill will, although one does not want to claim that those qualities are lacking. The depth of the difficulty is not understood until one realizes that intelligence and goodwill cannot discover and act on adequate programs. Early in this century Winston Churchill observed that the British-German naval race promised disaster *and* that Britain had no realistic choice other than to run it. States facing global problems are like individual consumers trapped by the "tyranny of small decisions." States, like consumers, can get out of the trap only by changing the structure of their field of activity. The message bears repeating: The only remedy for a strong structural effect is a structural change.

THE VIRTUES OF ANARCHY

To achieve their objectives and maintain their security, units in a condition of anarchy—be they people, corporations, states, or whatever—must rely on the means they can generate and the arrangements they can make for themselves. Self-help is necessarily the principle of action in an anarchic order. A self-help situation is one of high risk—of bankruptcy in the economic realm and of war in a world of free states. It is also one in which organizational costs are low. Within an economy or within an international order, risks may be avoided or lessened by moving from a situation of coordinate action to one of super- and subordination, that is, by erecting agencies with effective authority and extending a system of rules. Government emerges where the functions of regulation and management themselves become distinct and specialized tasks. The costs of maintaining a hierarchic order are frequently ignored by those who deplore its absence. Organizations have at least two aims: to get something done and to maintain themselves as organizations. Many of their activities are directed toward the second purpose. The leaders of organizations, and political leaders preeminently, are not masters of the matters their organizations deal with. They have become leaders not by being experts on one thing or another but by excelling in the organizational arts—in maintaining control of a group's members, in eliciting predictable and satisfactory efforts from them, in holding a group together. In making political decisions the first and most important concern is not to achieve the aims the members of an organization may have but to secure the continuity and health of the organization itself.[5]

Along with the advantages of hierarchic orders go the costs. In hierarchic orders, moreover, the means of control become an object of struggle. Substantive issues become entwined with efforts to influence or control the controllers. The hierarchic ordering of politics adds one to the already numerous objects of struggle, and the object added is at a new order of magnitude.

If the risks of war are unbearably high, can they be reduced by organizing to manage the affairs of nations? At a minimum management requires controlling the military forces that are at the disposal of states. Within nations, organizations have to work to maintain themselves. As organizations, nations, in working to maintain themselves, sometimes have to use force against dissident elements and areas. As hierarchical systems, governments nationally or globally are disrupted by the defection of major parts. In a society of states with little coherence, attempts at world government would founder on the inability of an emerging central authority to mobilize the resources needed to create and maintain the unity of the system by regulating and managing its parts. The prospect of world government would be an invitation to prepare for world civil war. This calls to mind Milovan Djilas's reminiscence of World War II.[6] According to him, he and many Russian soldiers in their wartime discussions came to believe that human struggles would acquire their ultimate bitterness if all men were subject to the same social system, "for the system would be untenable as such and various sects would undertake the reckless destruction of the human race for the sake of its greater 'happiness.'"[7] States cannot entrust managerial powers to a central agency unless that agency is able to protect its client states. The more powerful the clients and the more the power of each of them appears as a threat to the others, the greater the power lodged in the center must be. The greater the power of the center, the stronger the incentive for states to engage in a struggle to control it.

States, like people, are insecure in proportion to the extent of their freedom. If freedom is wanted, insecurity must be accepted. Organizations that establish relations of authority and control may increase security as they decrease freedom. If might does not make right, whether among people or states, then some institution or agency has intervened to lift them out of nature's realm. The more influential the agency, the stronger the desire to control it becomes. In contrast, units in an anarchic order act for their own sakes and not for the sake of preserving an organization and furthering their fortunes within it. Force is used for one's own interest. In the absence of organization, people or states are free to leave one another alone. Even when they do not do so, they are better able, in the absence of the politics of the organization, to concentrate on the politics of the problem and to aim for a minimum agreement that will permit their separate existence rather than a maximum agreement for the sake of maintaining unity. If might decides, then bloody struggles over right can more easily be avoided.

Nationally, the force of a government is exercised in the name of right and justice. Internationally, the force of a state is employed for the sake of its own protection and advantage. Rebels challenge a government's claim to authority; they question the rightfulness of its rule. Wars among states cannot settle questions of authority and right; they can only determine the allocation of gains and losses among contenders and settle for a time the question of who is the stronger. Nationally, relations of authority are established. Internationally, only relations of strength result. Nationally, private force used against a government threatens the political system. Force used by a state—a public body—is, from the international perspective, the private use of force; but there is no government to overthrow and no governmental apparatus to capture. Short of a drive toward world hegemony, the private use of force does not threaten the system of international politics, only some of its members. War pits some states against others in a struggle among similarly constituted entities. The power of the strong may deter the weak from asserting their claims, not because the weak recognize a kind of rightfulness of rule on the part of the strong, but simply because it is not sensible to tangle with them. Conversely, the weak may enjoy considerable freedom of action if they are so far removed in their capabilities from the strong that the latter are not much bothered by their actions or much concerned by marginal increases in their capabilities.

National politics is the realm of authority, of administration, and of law. International politics is the realm of power, of struggle, and of accommodation. The international realm is preeminently a political one. The national realm is variously described as being hierarchic, vertical, centralized, heterogeneous, directed, and contrived; the international realm, as being anarchic, horizontal, decentralized, homogeneous, undirected, and mutually adaptive. The more centralized the order, the nearer to the top the locus of decisions ascends. Internationally, decisions are made at the bottom level, there being scarcely any other. In the vertical-horizontal dichotomy, international structures assume the prone position. Adjustments are made internationally, but they are made without a formal or authoritative adjuster. Adjustment and accommodation proceed by mutual adaptation. Action and reaction, and reaction to the reaction, proceed by a piecemeal process. The parties feel each other out, so to speak, and define a situation simultaneously with its development. Among coordinate units adjustment is achieved and accommodations arrived at by the exchange of "considerations," in a condition, as Chester Barnard put it, "in which the duty of command and the desire to obey are essentially absent."[8] Where the contest is over considerations, the parties seek to maintain or improve their positions by maneuvering, by bargaining, or by fighting. The manner and intensity of the competition are determined by the desires and the abilities of parties that are at once separate and interacting.

Whether or not by force, each state plots the course it thinks will best serve its interests. If force is used by one state or its use is expected, the recourse of other states is to use force or be prepared to use it singly or in combination. No appeal can be made to a higher entity clothed with the authority and equipped with the ability to act on its own initiative. Under such conditions the possibility that force will be used by one or another of the parties looms always as a threat in the background. In politics force is said to be the ultima ratio. In international politics force serves not only as the ultima ratio but indeed as the first and constant one. To limit force to being the ultima ratio of politics implies, in the words of Ortega y Gasset, "the previous submission of force to methods of reason."[9] The constant possibility that force will be used limits manipulations, moderates demands, and serves as an incentive for the settlement of disputes. One who knows that pressing too hard may lead to war has strong reason to consider whether possible gains are worth the risks entailed. The threat of force internationally is comparable to the role of the strike in labor and management bargaining. "The few strikes that take place are in a sense," as Livernash has said, "the cost of the strike option which produces settlements in the large mass of negotiations."[10] Even if workers seldom strike, their doing so is always a possibility. The possibility of industrial disputes leading to long and costly strikes encourages labor and management to face difficult issues, to try to understand each other's problems, and to work hard to find accommodations. The possibility that conflicts among nations may lead to long and costly wars has similarly sobering effects.

ANARCHY AND HIERARCHY

I have described anarchies and hierarchies as though every political order were of one type or the other. Many, and I suppose most, political scientists who write of structures allow for a greater and sometimes for a bewildering variety of types. Anarchy is seen as one end of a continuum whose other end is marked by the presence of a legitimate and competent government. International politics is then described as being flecked with particles of government and alloyed with elements of community—supranational organizations whether universal or regional, alliances, multinational corporations, networks of trade, and whatnot. International political systems are thought of as being more or less anarchic.

Those who view the world as a modified anarchy do so, it seems, for two reasons. First, anarchy is taken to mean not just the absence of government but also the presence of disorder and chaos. Since world politics, although not reliably peaceful, falls short of unrelieved chaos, students are inclined to see a lessening of anarchy in each outbreak of peace. Since world politics, although not formally organized, is not entirely without institutions and orderly procedures, students are inclined to see a lessening of anarchy when alliances form, when transactions across national borders increase, and when international agencies multiply. Such views confuse structure with process, and I have drawn attention to that error often enough.

Second, the two simple categories of anarchy and hierarchy do not seem to accommodate the infinite social variety our senses record. Why insist on reducing the types of structure to two instead of allowing for a greater variety? Anarchies are ordered by the juxtaposition of similar units, but those similar units are not identical. Some specialization by function develops among them. Hierarchies are ordered by the social division of labor among units specializing in different tasks, but the resemblance of units does not vanish. Much duplication of effort continues. All societies are organized segmentally or hierarchically in greater or lesser degree. Why not, then, define additional social types according to the mixture of organizing principles they embody? One might conceive some societies approaching the purely anarchic, of others approaching purely hierarchic, and of still others reflecting specified mixes of the two organizational types. In anarchies the exact likeness of units and the determination of relations by capability alone would describe a realm wholly of politics and power with none of the interaction of units guided by administration and conditioned by authority. In hierarchies the complete differentiation of parts and the full specification of their functions would produce a realm wholly of authority and administration with none of the interaction of parts affected by politics and power. Although such pure orders do not exist, to distinguish realms by their organizing principles is nevertheless proper and important.

Increasing the number of categories would bring the classification of societies closer to reality. But that would be to move away from a theory claiming explanatory power to a less theoretical system promising greater descriptive accuracy. One who wishes to explain rather than to describe should resist moving in that direction if resistance is reasonable. Is it? What does one gain by insisting on two types when admitting three or four would still be to simplify boldly? One gains clarity and economy of concepts. A new concept should be introduced only to cover matters that existing concepts do not reach. If some societies are neither anarchic nor hierarchic, if their structures are defined by some third ordering principle, then we would have to define a third system. All societies are mixed. Elements in them represent both of the ordering principles. That does not mean that some societies are ordered according to a third principle. Usually one can easily identify the principle by which a society is ordered. The appearance of anarchic sectors within hierarchies does not alter and should not obscure the ordering principle of the larger system, for those sectors are anarchic only within limits. The attributes and behavior of the units populating those sectors within the larger system differ, moreover, from what they would be and how they would behave outside of it. Firms in oligopolistic markets again are perfect examples of this. They struggle against one another, but because they need not prepare to defend themselves physically, they can afford to specialize and to participate more fully in the division of economic labor than states can. Nor do the states that populate an anarchic world find it impossible to work with one another, to make agreements limiting their arms, and to cooperate in establishing organizations. Hierarchic elements within international structures limit and restrain the exercise of sovereignty but only in ways strongly conditioned by the anarchy of the larger system. The anarchy of that order strongly affects the likelihood of cooperation, the extent of arms agreements, and the jurisdiction of international organizations.

But what about borderline cases, societies that are neither clearly anarchic nor clearly hierarchic? Do they not represent a third type? To say that there are borderline cases is not to say that at the border a third type of system appears. All categories have borders, and if we have any categories at all, we have borderline cases. Clarity of concepts does not eliminate difficulties of classification. Was China from the 1920s to the 1940s a hierarchic or an anarchic realm? Nominally a nation, China looked more like a number of separate states existing alongside one another. Mao Tse-tung in 1930, like Bolshevik leaders earlier, thought that striking a revolutionary spark would "start a prairie fire." Revolutionary flames would spread across China, if not throughout the world. Because the interdependence of China's provinces, like the interdependence of nations, was insufficiently close, the flames failed to spread. So nearly autonomous were China's provinces that the effects of war in one part of the country were only weakly registered in other parts. Battles in the Hunan hills, far from sparking a national revolution, were hardly noticed in neighboring provinces. The interaction of largely self-sufficient provinces was slight and sporadic. Dependent neither on one another economically nor on the nation's center politically, they were not subject to the close interdependence characteristic of organized and integrated polities.

As a practical matter observers may disagree in their answers to such questions as just when did China break down into anarchy, or whether the countries of western Europe are slowly becoming one state or stubbornly remaining nine. The point of theoretical importance is that our expectations about the fate of those areas differ widely depending on which answer to the structural question becomes the right one. Structures defined according to two distinct ordering principles help to explain important aspects of social and political behavior. That is shown in various ways in the following pages. This section has explained why two and only two types of structure are needed to cover societies of all sorts.

II

How can a theory of international politics be constructed? Just as any theory must be. First, one must conceive of international politics as a bounded realm or domain; second, one must discover some lawlike regularities within it; and third, one must develop a way of explaining the observed regularities. . . . Political structures account for some recurrent aspects of the behavior of states and for certain repeated and enduring patterns. Wherever agents and agencies are coupled by force and competition rather than by authority and law, we expect to find such behaviors and outcomes. They are closely identified with the approach to politics suggested by the rubric realpolitik. The elements of realpolitik, exhaustively listed, are these: the ruler's, and later the state's, interest provides the spring of action; the necessities of policy arise from the unregulated competition of states; calculation based on these necessities can discover the policies that will best serve a state's interests; success is the ultimate test of policy, and success is defined as preserving and strengthening the state. Ever since Machiavelli, interest and necessity—and raison d'état, the phrase that comprehends them—have remained the key concepts of realpolitik. From Machiavelli through Meinecke and Morgenthau the elements of the approach and the reasoning remain constant. Machiavelli stands so clearly as the exponent of realpolitik that one easily slips into thinking that he developed the closely associated idea of balance of power as well. Although he did not, his conviction that politics can be explained in its own terms established the ground on which balance-of-power theory can be built.

Realpolitik indicates the methods by which foreign policy is conducted and provides a rationale for them. Structural constraints explain why the methods are repeatedly used despite differences in the persons and states who use them. Balance-of-power theory purports to explain the result that such methods produce. Rather, that is what the theory should do. If there is any distinctively political theory of international politics, balance-of-power theory is it. And yet one cannot find a statement of the theory that is generally accepted.

Carefully surveying the copious balance-of-power literature, Ernst Haas discovered eight distinct meanings of the term, and Martin Wight found nine. Hans Morgenthau, in his profound historical and analytic treatment of the subject, makes use of four different definitions.[11] Balance of power is seen by some as being akin to a law of nature; by others, as simply an outrage. Some view it as a guide to statesmen; others as a cloak that disguises their imperialist policies. Some believe that a balance of power is the best guarantee of the security of states and the peace of the world; others, that it has ruined states by causing most of the wars they have fought.

To believe that one can cut through such confusion may seem quixotic. I shall nevertheless try. It will help to hark back to several basic propositions about theory. (1) A theory contains at least one theoretical assumption. Such assumptions are not factual. One therefore cannot legitimately ask if they are true, but only if they are useful. (2) Theories must be evaluated in terms of what they claim to explain. Balance-of-power theory claims to explain the results of states' actions under given conditions, and those results may not be foreshadowed in any of the actors' motives or be contained as objectives in their policies. (3) Theory, as a general explanatory system, cannot account for particularities.

Most of the confusions in balance-of-power theory, and criticisms of it, derive from misunderstanding these three points. A balance-of-power theory, properly stated, begins with assumptions about states: They are unitary actors who at a minimum seek their own preservation and at a maximum drive for universal domination. States, or those who act for them, try in more or less sensible ways to use the means available in order to achieve the ends in view. Those means fall into two categories: internal efforts (moves to increase economic capability, to increase military strength, to develop clever strategies) and external efforts (moves to strengthen and enlarge one's own alliance or to weaken and shrink an opposing one). The external game of alignment and realignment requires three or more players, and it is usually said that balance-of-power systems require at least that number. The statement is false, for in a two-power system the politics of balance continue, but the way to compensate for an incipient external disequilibrium is primarily by intensifying one's internal efforts. To the assumptions of the theory we then add the condition for its operation: that two or more states coexist in a self-help system, one with no superior agent to come to the aid of states that may be weakening or to deny to any of them the use of whatever instruments they think will serve their purposes. The theory, then, is built up from the assumed motivations of states and the actions that correspond to them. It describes the constraints that arise from the system that those actions produce, and it indicates the expected outcome: namely, the formation of balances of power. Balance-of-power theory is micro theory precisely in the economist's sense. The system, like a market in economics, is made by the actions and interactions of its units, and the theory is based on assumptions about their behavior.

A self-help system is one in which those who do not help themselves or who do so less effectively than others will fail to prosper, will lay themselves open to dangers, will suffer. Fear of such unwanted consequences stimulates states to behave in ways that tend toward the creation of balances of power. Notice that the theory requires no assumptions of rationality or of constancy of will on the part of all of the actors. The theory says simply that if some do relatively well, others will emulate them or fall by the wayside. Obviously, the system won't work if all states lose interest in preserving themselves. It will, however, continue to work if some states do while others do not choose to lose their political identities, say, through amalgamation. Nor need it be assumed that all of the competing states are striving relentlessly to increase their power.

The possibility that force may be used by some states to weaken or destroy others does, however, make it difficult for them to break out of the competitive system.

The meaning and importance of the theory are made clear by examining prevalent misconceptions of it. Recall our first proposition about theory. A theory contains assumptions that are theoretical, not factual. One of the most common misunderstandings of balance-of-power theory centers on this point. The theory is criticized because its assumptions are erroneous. The following statement can stand for a host of others:

> If nations were in fact unchanging units with no permanent ties to each other, and if all were motivated primarily by a drive to maximize their power, except for a single balancer whose aim was to prevent any nation from achieving preponderant power, a balance of power might in fact result. But we have seen that these assumptions are not correct, and since the assumptions of the theory are wrong, the conclusions are also in error.[12]

The author's incidental error is that he has compounded a sentence some parts of which are loosely stated assumptions of the theory and other parts not. His basic error lies in misunderstanding what an assumption is. From previous discussion we know that assumptions are neither true nor false and that they are essential for the construction of theory. We can freely admit that states are in fact not unitary purposive actors. States pursue many goals, which are often vaguely formulated and inconsistent. They fluctuate with the changing currents of domestic politics, are prey to the vagaries of a shifting cast of political leaders, and are influenced by the outcomes of bureaucratic struggles. But all of this has always been known, and it tells us nothing about the merits of balance-of-power theory.

A further confusion relates to our second proposition about theory. Balance-of-power theory claims to explain a result (the recurrent formation of balances of power) which may not accord with the intentions of any of the units whose actions combine to produce that result. To contrive and maintain a balance may be the aim of one or more states, but then again it may not be. According to the theory, balances of power tend to form whether some or all states consciously aim to establish and maintain a balance, or whether some or all states aim for universal domination. Yet many, and perhaps most, statements of balance-of-power theory attribute the maintenance of a balance to the separate states as a motive. David Hume, in his classic essay "Of the Balance of Power," offers "the maxim of preserving the balance of power" as a constant rule of prudent politics.[13] So it may be, but it has proved to be an unfortunately short step from the belief that a high regard for preserving a balance is at the heart of wise statesmanship to the belief that states must follow the maxim if a balance of power is to be maintained. This is apparent in the first of Morgenthau's four definitions of the term: namely, "a policy aimed at a certain state of affairs." The reasoning then easily becomes tautological. If a balance of power is to be maintained, the policies of states must aim to uphold it. If a balance of power is in fact maintained, we can conclude that their aim was accurate. If a balance of power is not produced, we can say that the theory's assumption is erroneous. Finally, and this completes the drift toward the reification of a concept, if the purpose of states is to uphold a balance, the purpose of the balance is "to maintain the stability of the system without destroying the multiplicity of the elements composing it." Reification has obviously occurred where one reads, for example, of the balance operating "successfully" and of the difficulty that nations have in applying it.

Reification is often merely the loose use of language or the employment of metaphor to make one's prose more pleasing. In this case, however, the theory has been drastically distorted, and not only by introducing the notion that if a balance is to be formed, somebody must want it and must work for it. The further distortion of the theory arises when rules are derived from the results of states' actions and then illogically prescribed to the actors as duties. A possible effect is turned into a necessary cause in the form of a stipulated rule. Thus, it is said, "the balance of power" can "impose its restraints upon the power aspirations of nations" only if they first "restrain themselves by accepting the system of the balance of power as the common framework of their endeavors." Only if states recognize "the same rules of the game" and play "for the same limited stakes" can the balance of power fulfill "its functions for international stability and national independence."[14]

The closely related errors that fall under our second proposition about theory are, as we have seen, twin traits of the field of international politics: namely, to assume a necessary correspondence of motive and result and to infer rules for the actors from the observed results of their action. . . . In a purely competitive economy, everyone's striving to make a profit drives the profit rate downward. Let the competition continue long enough under static conditions, and everyone's profit will be zero. To infer from that result that everyone, or anyone, is seeking to minimize profit, and that the competitors must adopt that goal as a rule in order for the system to work, would be absurd. And yet in international politics one frequently finds that rules inferred from the results of the interactions of states are prescribed to the actors and are said to be a condition of the system's maintenance. Such errors, often made, are also often pointed out, though seemingly to no avail. S. F. Nadel has put the matter simply: "an orderliness abstracted from behaviour cannot guide behaviour."[15]

Analytic reasoning applied where a systems approach is needed leads to the laying down of all sorts of conditions as prerequisites to balances of power forming and tending toward equilibrium and as general preconditions of world stability and peace. Some require that the number of great powers exceed two; others that a major power be willing to play the role of balancer. Some require that military technology not change radically or rapidly; others that the major states abide by arbitrarily specified rules. But balances of power form in the absence of the "necessary" conditions, and since 1945 the world has been stable, and the world of major powers remarkably peaceful, even though international conditions have not conformed to theorists' stipulations. Balance-of-power politics prevail wherever two and only two requirements are met: that the order be anarchic and that it be populated by units wishing to survive.

For those who believe that if a result is to be produced, someone or everyone must want it and must work for it, it follows that explanation turns ultimately on what the separate states are like. If that is true, then theories at the national level or lower will sufficiently explain international politics. If, for example, the equilibrium of a balance is maintained through states abiding by rules, then one needs an explanation of how agreement on the rules is achieved and maintained. One does not need a balance-of-power theory, for balances would result from a certain kind of behavior explained perhaps by a theory about national psychology or bureaucratic politics. A balance-of-power theory could not be constructed because it would have nothing to explain. If the good or bad motives of states result in their maintaining balances or disrupting them, then the notion of a balance of power becomes merely a framework organizing one's account of what happened, and that is indeed its customary use. A construction that starts out to be a theory ends up as a set of categories. Categories then multiply rapidly to cover events that the embryo theory had not contemplated. The quest for explanatory power turns into a search for descriptive adequacy.

Finally, and related to our third proposition about theory in general, balance-of-power theory is often criticized because it does not explain the particular policies of states. True, the theory does not tell us why state X made a certain move last Tuesday. To expect it to do so would be like expecting the theory of universal gravitation to explain the wayward path of a falling leaf. A theory at one level of generality cannot answer questions about matters at a different level of generality. Failure to notice this is one error on which the criticism rests. Another is to mistake a theory of international politics for a theory of foreign policy. Confusion about the explanatory claims made by a properly stated balance-of-power theory is rooted in the uncertainty of the distinction drawn between national and international politics or in the denials that the distinction should be made. For those who deny the distinction, for those who devise explanations that are entirely in terms of interacting units, explanations of international politics *are* explanations of foreign policy, and explanations of foreign policy *are* explanations of international politics. Others mix their explanatory claims and confuse the problem of understanding international politics with the problem of understanding foreign policy. Morgenthau, for example, believes that problems of predicting foreign policy and of developing theories about it make international-political theories difficult, if not impossible, to contrive.[16] But the difficulties of explaining foreign policy work against contriving theories of international politics only if the latter reduces to the former. Graham Allison betrays a similar confusion. His three "models" purport to offer alternative approaches to the study of international politics. Only model I, however, is an approach to the study of international politics. Models II and III are approaches to the study of foreign policy. Offering the bureaucratic-politics approach as an alternative to the state-as-an-actor approach is like saying that a theory of the firm is an alternative to a theory of the market, a mistake no competent economist would make.[17] If Morgenthau and Allison were economists and their thinking continued to follow the same pattern, they would have to argue that the uncertainties of corporate policy work against the development of market theory. They have confused and merged two quite different matters.

Any theory covers some matters and leaves other matters aside. Balance-of-power theory is a theory about the results produced by the uncoordinated actions of states. The theory makes assumptions about the interests and motives of states, rather than explaining them. What it does explain are the constraints that confine all states. The clear perception of constraints provides many clues to the expected reactions of states, but by itself the theory cannot explain those reactions. They depend not only on international constraints but also on the characteristics of states. How will a particular state react? To answer that question we need not only a theory of the market, so to speak, but also a theory about the firms that compose it. What will a state have to react to? Balance-of-power theory can give general and useful answers to that question. The theory explains why a certain similarity of behavior is expected from similarly situated states. The expected behavior is similar, not identical. To explain the expected differences in national responses, a theory would have to show how the different internal structures of states affect their external policies and actions. A theory of foreign policy would not predict the detailed content of policy but instead would lead to different expectations about the tendencies and styles of different countries' policies. Because the national and the international levels are linked, theories of both types, if they are any good, tell us some things, but not the same things, about behavior and outcomes at both levels. . . .

III

. . . Before subjecting a theory to tests, one asks whether the theory is internally consistent and whether it tells us some things of interest that we would not know in its absence. That the theory meets those requirements does not mean that it can survive tests. Many people prefer tests that, if flunked, falsify a theory. Some people, following Karl Popper,[18] insist that theories are tested only by attempting to falsify them. Confirmations do not count because among other reasons confirming cases may be offered as proof, while consciously or not, cases likely to confound the theory are avoided. This difficulty, I suggest later, is lessened by choosing hard cases—situations, for example, in which parties have strong reasons to behave contrary to the predictions of one's theory. Confirmations are also rejected because numerous tests that appear to confirm a theory are negated by one falsifying instance. . . . However, [there is] the possibility of devising tests that confirm. If a theory depicts a domain and displays its organization and the connections among its parts, then we can compare features of the observed domain with the picture the theory has limned.[19] We can ask whether expected behaviors and outcomes are repeatedly found where the conditions contemplated by the theory obtain.

Structural theories, moreover, gain plausibility if similarities of behavior are observed across realms that are different in substance but similar in structure, and if differences of behavior are observed where realms are similar in substance but different in structure. This special advantage is won: International-political theory gains credibility from the confirmation of certain theories in economics, sociology, anthropology, and other such nonpolitical fields.

Testing theories, of course, always means inferring expectations, or hypotheses, from them and testing those expectations. Testing theories is a difficult and subtle task, made so by the interdependence of fact and theory, by the elusive relation between reality and theory as an instrument for its apprehension. Questions of truth and falsity are somehow involved, but so are questions of usefulness and uselessness. In the end one sticks with the theory that reveals most, even if its validity is suspect. I shall say more about the acceptance and rejection of theories elsewhere. Here I say only enough to make the relevance of a few examples of theory testing clear. Others can then easily be thought of. . . .

Tests are easy to think up, once one has a theory to test, but they are hard to carry through. Given the difficulty of testing any theory and the added difficulty of testing theories in such nonexperimental fields as international politics, we should exploit all of the ways of testing I have mentioned—by trying to falsify, by devising hard confirmatory tests, by comparing features of the real and the theoretical worlds, by comparing behaviors in realms of similar and of different structure. Any good theory raises many expectations. Multiplying hypotheses and varying tests are all the more important because the results of testing theories are necessarily problematic. That a single hypothesis appears to hold true may not be very impressive. A theory becomes plausible if many hypotheses inferred from it are successfully subjected to tests.

Knowing a little bit more about testing, we can now ask whether expectations drawn from our theory can survive subjection to tests. What will some of the expectations be? Two that are closely related arise in the above discussion. According to the theory, balances of power recurrently form, and states tend to emulate the successful policies of others. Can these expectations be subjected to tests? In principle the answer is yes. Within a given arena and over a number of years, we should find the military power of weaker and smaller states or groupings of states growing more rapidly, or shrinking more slowly, than that of stronger and larger ones. And we should find widespread imitation among competing states. In practice to check such expectations against historical observations is difficult.

Two problems are paramount. First, though balance-of-power theory offers some predictions, the predictions are indeterminate. Because only a loosely defined and inconstant condition of balance is predicted, it is difficult to say that any given distribution of power falsi-fies the theory. The theory, moreover, does not lead one to expect that emulation among states will proceed to the point where competitors become identical. What will be imitated, and how quickly and closely? Because the theory does not give precise answers, falsification again is difficult. Second, although states may be disposed to react to international constraints and incentives in accordance with the theory's expectations, the policies and actions of states are also shaped by their internal conditions. The failure of balances to form, and the failure of some states to conform to the successful practices of other states, can too easily be explained away by pointing to effects produced by forces that lie outside of the theory's purview.

In the absence of theoretical refinements that fix expectations with certainty and in detail, what can we do? As I have just suggested . . . we should make tests ever more difficult. If we observe outcomes that the theory leads us to expect even though strong forces work against them, the theory will begin to command belief. To confirm the theory one should not look mainly to the eighteenth-century heyday of the balance of power when great powers in con-venient numbers interacted and were presumably able to adjust to a shifting distribution of power by changing partners with a grace made possible by the absence of ideological and other cleavages. Instead one should seek confirmation through observation of difficult cases. One should, for example, look for instances of states allying in accordance with the expecta-tions the theory gives rise to even though they have strong reasons not to cooperate with one another. The alliance of France and Russia, made formal in 1894, is one such instance. . . . One should, for example, look for instances of states making internal efforts to strengthen themselves, however distasteful or difficult such efforts might be. The United States and the Soviet Union following World War II provide such instances: the United States by rearming despite having demonstrated a strong wish not to by dismantling the most powerful military machine the world had ever known; the Soviet Union by maintaining about three million men under arms while striving to acquire a costly new military technology despite the terrible destruction she had suffered in war.

These examples tend to confirm the theory. We find states forming balances of power whether or not they wish to. They also show the difficulties of testing. Germany and Austria-Hungary formed their Dual Alliance in 1879. Since detailed inferences cannot be drawn from the theory, we cannot say just when other states are expected to counter this move. France and Russia waited until 1894. Does this show the theory false by suggesting that states may or may not be brought into balance? We should neither quickly conclude that it does nor lightly chalk the delayed response off to "friction." Instead, we should examine diplomacy and policy in the fifteen-year interval to see whether the theory serves to explain and broadly predict the actions and reactions of states and to see whether the delay is out of accord with the theory. Careful judgment is needed. For this historians' accounts serve better than the historical summary I might provide.

The theory leads us to expect states to behave in ways that result in balances forming. To infer that expectation from the theory is not impressive if balancing is a universal pattern of political behavior, as is sometimes claimed. It is not. Whether political actors balance each other or climb on the bandwagon depends on the system's structure. Political parties, when choosing their presidential candidates, dramatically illustrate both points. When nomination time approaches and no one is established as the party's strong favorite, a number of would-be leaders contend. Some of them form coalitions to check the progress of others. The maneuvering and balancing of would-be leaders when the party lacks one is like the external behavior of states. But this is the pattern only during the leaderless period. As soon as someone looks like the winner, nearly all jump on the bandwagon rather than continuing to build coalitions intended to prevent anyone from winning the prize of power. Bandwagoning, not balancing, becomes the characteristic behavior.

Bandwagoning and balancing behavior are in sharp contrast. Internally, losing candidates throw in their lots with the winner. Everyone wants someone to win; the members of a party want a leader established even while they disagree on who it should be. In a competition for the position of leader, bandwagoning is sensible behavior where gains are possible even for the losers and where losing does not place their security in jeopardy. Externally, states work harder to increase their own strength, or they combine with others if they are falling behind. In a competition for the position of leader, balancing is sensible behavior where the victory of one coalition over another leaves weaker members of the winning coalition at the mercy of the stronger ones. Nobody wants anyone else to win; none of the great powers wants one of their number to emerge as the leader.

If two coalitions form and one of them weakens, perhaps because of the political disorder of a member, we expect the extent of the other coalition's military preparation to slacken or its unity to lessen. The classic example of the latter effect is the breaking apart of a war-winning coalition in or just after the moment of victory. We do not expect the strong to combine with the strong in order to increase the extent of their power over others, but rather to square off and look for allies who might help them. In anarchy security is the highest end. Only if survival is assured can states safely seek such other goals as tranquility, profit, and power. Because power is a means and not an end, states prefer to join the weaker of two coalitions. They cannot let power, a possibly useful means, become the end they pursue. The goal the system encourages them to seek is security. Increased power may or may not serve that end. Given two coalitions, for example, the greater success of one in drawing members to it may tempt the other to risk preventive war, hoping for victory through surprise before disparities widen. If states wished to maximize power, they would join the stronger side, and we would see not balances forming but a world hegemony forged. This does not happen because balancing, not bandwagoning, is the behavior induced by the system. The first concern of states is not to maximize power but to maintain their positions in the system.

Secondary states, if they are free to choose, flock to the weaker side; for it is the stronger side that threatens them. On the weaker side they are both more appreciated and safer, provided, of course, that the coalition they join achieves enough defensive or deterrent strength to dissuade adversaries from attacking. Thus Thucydides records that in the Peloponnesian War the lesser city states of Greece cast the stronger Athens as the tyrant and the weaker Sparta as their liberator.[20] According to Werner Jaeger, Thucydides thought this "perfectly natural in the circumstances," but saw "that the parts of tyrant and liberator did not correspond with any permanent moral quality in these states but were simply masks which would one day be interchanged to the astonishment of the beholder when the balance of power was altered."[21] This shows a nice sense of how the placement of states affects their behavior and even colors their characters. It also supports the proposition that states balance power rather than maximize it. States can seldom afford to make maximizing power their goal. International politics is too serious a business for that.

The theory depicts international politics as a competitive realm. Do states develop the characteristics that competitors are expected to display? The question poses another test for the theory. The fate of each state depends on its responses to what other states do. The possibility that conflict will be conducted by force leads to competition in the arts and the instruments of force. Competition produces a tendency toward the sameness of the competitors. Thus Bismarck's startling victories over Austria in 1866 and over France in 1870 quickly led the major continental powers (and Japan) to imitate the Prussian military staff system, and the failure of Britain and the United States to follow the pattern simply indicated that they were outside the immediate arena of competition. Contending states imitate the military innovations contrived by the country of greatest capability and ingenuity. And so the weapons of major contenders, and even their strategies, begin to look much the same all over the world. Thus at the turn of the century Admiral Alfred von Tirpitz argued successfully for building a battleship fleet on the grounds that Germany could challenge Britain at sea only with a naval doctrine and weapons similar to hers.[22]

The effects of competition are not confined narrowly to the military realm. Socialization to the system should also occur. Does it? Again, because we can almost always find confirming examples if we look hard, we try to find cases that are unlikely to lend credence to the theory. One should look for instances of states conforming to common international practices even though for internal reasons they would prefer not to. The behavior of the Soviet Union in its early years is one such instance. The Bolsheviks in the early years of their power preached international revolution and flouted the conventions of diplomacy. They were saying, in effect, "we will not be socialized to this system." The attitude was well expressed by Trotsky, who, when asked what he would do as foreign minister, replied, "I will issue some revolutionary proclamations to the peoples and then close up the joint."[23] In a competitive arena, however, one party may need the assistance of others. Refusal to play the political game may risk one's own destruction. The pressures of competition were rapidly felt and reflected in the Soviet Union's diplomacy. Thus Lenin, sending foreign minister Chicherin to the Genoa Conference of 1922, bade him farewell with this caution: "Avoid big words."[24] Chicherin, who personified the carefully tailored traditional diplomat rather than the simply uniformed revolutionary, was to refrain from inflammatory rhetoric for the sake of working deals. These he successfully completed with that other pariah power and ideological enemy, Germany.

The close juxtaposition of states promotes their sameness through the disadvantages that arise from a failure to conform to successful practices. It is this sameness, an effect of the system, that is so often attributed to the acceptance of so-called rules of state behavior. Chiliastic rulers occasionally come to power. In power, most of them quickly change their ways. They can refuse to do so and yet hope to survive only if they rule countries little affected by the competition of states. The socialization of nonconformist states proceeds at a pace that is set by the extent of their involvement in the system. And that is another testable statement.

The theory leads to many expectations about behaviors and outcomes. From the theory one predicts that states will engage in balancing behavior whether or not balanced power is the end of their acts. From the theory one predicts a strong tendency toward balance in the system. The expectation is not that a balance, once achieved, will be maintained, but that a balance, once disrupted, will be restored in one way or another. Balances of power recurrently form. Since the theory depicts international politics as a competitive system, one predicts more specifically that states will display characteristics common to competitors: namely, that they will imitate each other and become socialized to their system. . . .

NOTES

1. E. Durkheim, *The Division of Labor in Society* (New York: Free Press, 1964).
2. W. Fellner, *Competition among the Few* (New York: Knopf), pp. 35, 132, 177, 199, 217–18.
3. A. Kahn, "The tyranny of small decisions: market failures, imperfections, and the limits of econometrics." In Bruce M. Russett (ed.), *Economic Theories of International Relations* (Chicago: Markham, 1968), p. 523.
4. R. W. Sterling, *Macropolitics: International Relations in a Global Society* (New York: Knopf), p. 336.
5. P. Diesing, *Reason in Society* (Urbana: University of Illinois Press, 1962), pp. 198–204. A. Downs, *Inside Bureaucracy* (Boston: Little, Brown, 1967), pp. 262–70.
6. M. Djilas, *Conversations with Stalin* (New York: Harcourt, Brace and World, 1962), p. 50.
7. C. Barnard, "On planning for world government," in Barnard (ed.), *Organization and Management* (Cambridge: Harvard University Press, 1948), pp. 148–52. M. Polanyi, "The growth of thought in society," *Economica,* vol. 8, 1941, pp. 428–56.
8. C. Barnard, "On planning for world government," in Barnard (ed.), *Organization and Management* (Cambridge: Harvard University Press, 1948), pp. 150–51.
9. Quoted in C. Johnson, *Revolutionary Change* (Boston: Little, Brown, 1966), p. 13.
10. E. R. Livernash, "The relation of power to the structure and process of collective bargaining," in Bruce M. Russett (ed.), *Economic Theories of International Politics* (Chicago: Markham, 1968), p. 430.
11. E. Haas, "The balance of power: prescription, concept, or propaganda?" *World Politics,* vol. 5, 1953. M. Wight, "The balance of power," in H. Butterfield and Martin Wight (eds.), *Diplomatic Investigations: Essays in the Theory of International Politics* (London: Allen and Unwin, 1966). H. Morgenthau, *Politics Among Nations,* 5th ed. (New York: Knopf, 1953).
12. A. F. K. Organski, *World Politics,* 2nd ed. (New York: Knopf, 1968), p. 292.
13. D. Hume, "Of the balance of power," in Charles W. Hendel (ed.), *David Hume's Political Essays* (Indianapolis: Bobbs-Merrill, 1953), pp. 142–44.
14. H. Morgenthau, *Politics Among Nations,* 5th ed. (New York: Knopf, 1973), pp. 167–74, 202–207, 219–20.
15. S. F. Nadel, *The Theory of Social Structure* (Glencoe, Ill.: Free Press, 1957), p. 148. E. Durkheim, *The Division of Labor in Society* (New York: Free Press, 1964), pp. 386, 418. M. Shubik, *Strategy and Market Structure* (New York: Wiley, 1959), pp. 11, 32.
16. H. Morgenthau, *Truth and Power* (New York: Praeger, 1970), pp. 253–58.
17. G. T. Allison, *Essence of Decision* (Boston: Little, Brown, 1971), and Morton Halperin, "Bureaucratic politics: a paradigm and some policy implications," *World Politics,* vol. 24, 1972.
18. K. Popper, *The Logic of Scientific Discovery* (New York: Basic Books, 1959), Chapter 1.
19. E. E. Harris, *Hypothesis and Perception* (London: Allen and Unwin, 1970).
20. Thucydides, *History of the Peloponnesian War* (New York: Modern Library, Random House, 1951), Book 5, Chapter 17.
21. W. Jaeger, *Paideia: The Ideals of Greek Culture,* vol. 1 (New York: Oxford University Press), 1939.
22. R. J. Art, "The influence of foreign policy on seapower: new weapons and Weltpolitik in Wilhelminian Germany," *Sage Professional Paper in International Studies,* vol. 2. (Beverly Hills: Sage Publications, 1973), p. 16.
23. T. H. Von Laue, "Soviet Diplomacy: G. V. Chicherin, People's Commissar for Foreign Affairs 1918–1930." In Gordon A. Craig and Felix Gilbert (eds.), *The Diplomats, 1919–1939,* vol. 1 (New York: Atheneum, 1963), p. 235.
24. B. Moore, Jr., *Soviet Politics: The Dilemma of Power* (Cambridge: Harvard University Press, 1950), p. 204.

The American Conception of National Security and the Beginnings of the Cold War, 1945–1948*

Melvyn P. Leffler

In an interview with Henry Kissinger in 1978 on "The Lessons of the Past," Walter Laqueur observed that during World War II "few if any people thought . . . of the structure of peace that would follow the war except perhaps in the most general terms of friendship, mutual trust, and the other noble sentiments mentioned in wartime programmatic speeches about the United Nations and related topics." Kissinger concurred, noting that no statesman, except perhaps Winston Churchill, "gave any attention to what would happen after the war." Americans, Kissinger stressed, "were determined that we were going to base the postwar period on good faith and getting along with everybody."[1]

That two such astute and knowledgeable observers of international politics were so uninformed about American planning at the end of the Second World War is testimony to the enduring mythology of American idealism and innocence in the world of Realpolitik. It also reflects the state of scholarship on the interrelated areas of strategy, economy, and diplomacy. Despite the publication of several excellent overviews of the origins of the Cold War, despite the outpouring of incisive monographs on American foreign policy in many areas of the world, and despite some first-rate studies on the evolution of strategic thinking and the defense establishment, no comprehensive account yet exists of how American defense officials defined national security interests in the aftermath of World War II. Until recently, the absence of such a study was understandable, for scholars had limited access to records pertaining to national security, strategic thinking, and war planning. But in recent years documents relating to the early years of the Cold War have been declassified in massive numbers.

This documentation now makes it possible to analyze in greater depth the perceptions, apprehensions, and objectives of those defense officials most concerned with defining and defending the nation's security and strategic interests.[2] This essay seeks neither to explain the process of decision making on any particular issue nor to dissect the domestic political considerations and fiscal

---

*The extensive footnotes of the original article have been heavily redacted in this reprint. Interested readers should consult the original publication for the excellent detailed literature review and original research that Professor Leffler provides there.

Melvyn P. Leffler, "The American Conception of National Security and the Beginnings of the Cold War, 1945-1948," *American Historical Review*, Vol. 89, no. 2 (April 1984) pp. 346–381. Copyright © 1984 American Historical Association. Reprinted by permission of the author and University of Chicago Press.

constraints that narrowed the options available to policy makers. Furthermore, it does not pretend to discern the motivations and objectives of the Soviet Union. Rather, the goal here is to elucidate the fundamental strategic and economic considerations that shaped the definition of American national security interests in the postwar world. Several of these considerations—especially as they related to overseas bases, air transit rights, and a strategic sphere of influence in Latin America—initially were the logical result of technological developments and geostrategic experiences rather than directly related to postwar Soviet behavior. But American defense officials also considered the preservation of a favorable balance of power in Eurasia as fundamental to U.S. national security. This objective impelled defense analysts and intelligence officers to appraise and reappraise the intentions and capabilities of the Soviet Union. Rather modest estimates of the Soviets' ability to wage war against the United States generated the widespread assumption that the Soviets would refrain from military aggression and seek to avoid war. Nevertheless, American defense officials remained greatly preoccupied with the geopolitical balance of power in Europe and Asia, because that balance seemed endangered by communist exploitation of postwar economic dislocation and social and political unrest. Indeed, American assessments of the Soviet threat were less a consequence of expanding Soviet military capabilities and of Soviet diplomatic demands than a result of growing apprehension about the vulnerability of American strategic and economic interests in a world of unprecedented turmoil and upheaval. Viewed from this perspective, the Cold War assumed many of its most enduring characteristics during 1947–48, when American officials sought to cope with an array of challenges by implementing their own concepts of national security.

American officials first began to think seriously about the nation's postwar security during 1943–44. Military planners devised elaborate plans for an overseas base system. Many of these plans explicitly contemplated the breakdown of the wartime coalition. But, even when strategic planners postulated good postwar relations among the Allies, their plans called for an extensive system of bases. These bases were defined as the nation's strategic frontier. Beyond this frontier the United States would be able to use force to counter any threats or frustrate any overt acts of aggression. Within the strategic frontier, American military predominance had to remain inviolate. Although plans for an overseas base system went through many revisions, they always presupposed American hegemony over the Atlantic and Pacific oceans. These plans received President Franklin D. Roosevelt's endorsement in early 1944. After his death, army and navy planners presented their views to President Harry S. Truman, and Army Chief of Staff George C. Marshall discussed them extensively with Secretary of State James C. Byrnes.

Two strategic considerations influenced the development of an overseas base system. The first was the need for defense in depth. Since attacks against the United States could only emanate from Europe and Asia, the Joint Chiefs of Staff concluded as early as November 1943 that the United States must encircle the Western Hemisphere with a defensive ring of outlying bases. In the Pacific this ring had to include the Aleutians, the Philippines, Okinawa, and the former Japanese mandates. Recognizing the magnitude of this strategic frontier, Admiral William E. Leahy, chief of staff to the president, explained to Truman that the joint chiefs were not thinking of the immediate future when, admittedly, no prospective naval power could challenge American predominance in the Pacific. Instead, they were contemplating the long term, when the United States might require wartime access to the resources of southeast Asia as well as "a firm line of communications from the West Coast to the Asiatic mainland, plus denial of this line in time of war to any potential enemy."[3] In the Atlantic, strategic planners maintained that their minimum requirements included a West African zone, with primary bases in the Azores or Canary Islands. Leahy went even further, insisting on primary bases in West Africa itself—for example, at Dakar or Casablanca. The object of these defensive bases was to enable the United States to possess complete control of the Atlantic and Pacific oceans and keep hostile powers far from American territory.[4]

Defense in depth was especially important in light of the Pearl Harbor experience, the advance of technology, and the development of the atomic bomb. According to the Joint Chiefs of Staff, "Experience in the recent war demonstrated conclusively that the defense of a nation, if it is to be effective, must begin beyond its frontiers. The advent of the atomic bomb reemphasizes this requirement. The farther away from our own vital areas we can hold our enemy through the possession of advanced bases . . . , the greater are our chances of surviving successfully an attack by atomic weapons and of destroying the enemy which employs them against us." Believing that atomic weapons would increase the incentive to aggression by enhancing the advantage of surprise, military planners never ceased to extol the utility of forward bases from which American aircraft could seek to intercept attacks against the United States.[5]

The second strategic consideration that influenced the plan for a comprehensive overseas base system was the need to project American power quickly and effectively against any potential adversary. In conducting an overall examination of requirements for base rights in September 1945, the Joint War Plans Committee stressed that World War II demonstrated the futility of a strategy of static defense. The United States had to be able to take "timely" offensive action against the adversary's capacity and will to wage war. New weapons demanded that advance bases be established in "areas well removed from the United States, so as to project our operations, with new weapons or otherwise, nearer the enemy." Scientists, like Vannevar Bush, argued that, "regardless of the potentialities of these new weapons [atomic energy and guided missiles], they should not influence the number, location, or extent of strategic bases now considered essential." The basic strategic concept underlying all American war plans called for an air offensive against a prospective enemy from overseas bases. Delays in the development of the B-36, the first intercontinental bomber, only accentuated the need for these bases.

In October 1945 the civilian leaders of the War and Navy departments carefully reviewed the emerging strategic concepts and base requirements of the military planners. Secretary of the Navy James Forrestal and Secretary of War Robert P. Patterson discussed them with Admiral Leahy, the Joint Chiefs of Staff, and Secretary of State Byrnes. The civilian secretaries fully endorsed the concept of a far-flung system of bases in the Atlantic and Pacific oceans that would enhance the offensive capabilities of the United States. Having expended so much blood and effort capturing Japanese-held islands, defense officials, like Forrestal, naturally wished to devise a base system in the Pacific to facilitate the projection of American influence and power. The Philippines were the key to southeast Asia, Okinawa to the Yellow Sea, the Sea of Japan, and the industrial heartland of northeast Asia. From these bases on America's "strategic frontier," the United States could preserve its access to vital raw materials in Asia, deny these resources to a prospective enemy, help preserve peace and stability in troubled areas, safeguard critical sea lanes, and, if necessary, conduct an air offensive against the industrial infrastructure of any Asiatic power, including the Soviet Union.

Control of the Atlantic and Pacific oceans through overseas bases was considered indispensable to the nation's security regardless of what might happen to the wartime coalition. So was control over polar air routes. Admiral Leahy criticized a Joint Strategic Survey Committee report of early 1943 that omitted Iceland and Greenland as primary base requirements. When General S. D. Embick, the senior member of that committee, continued to question the desirability of a base in Iceland, lest it antagonize the Russians, he was overruled by Assistant Secretary of War John McCloy. McCloy charged that Embick had "a rather restricted concept of what is necessary for national defense." The first postwar base system approved by both the Joint Chiefs of Staff and the civilian secretaries in October 1945 included Iceland as a primary base area. The Joint War Plans Committee explained that American bases must control the air in the Arctic, prevent the establishment of enemy military facilities there, and support America's own striking forces. Once Soviet-American relations began to deteriorate, Greenland also was designated as a primary base for American heavy bombers and fighters because of its close proximity to the industrial heartland of the potential enemy. As the United States sought rights for bases along the Polar route in 1946 and 1947, moreover, American defense officials also hoped to thwart Soviet efforts to acquire similar rights at Spitzbergen and Bear Island.

In the immediate postwar years American ambitions for an elaborate base system encountered many problems. Budgetary constraints compelled military planners to drop plans for many secondary and subsidiary bases, particularly in the South Pacific and Caribbean. These sacrifices merely increased the importance of those bases that lay closer to a potential adversary. By early 1948, the joint chiefs were willing to forego base rights in such places as Surinam, Curacoa-Aruba, Cayenne, Nounea, and Vivi-Levu if "joint" or "participating" rights could be acquired or preserved in Karachi, Tripoli, Algiers, Casablanca, Dharan, and Monrovia. Budgetary constraints, then, limited the depth of the base system but not the breadth of American ambitions. Furthermore, the governments of Panama, Iceland, Denmark, Portugal, France, and Saudi Arabia often rejected or abolished the exclusive rights the United States wanted and sometimes limited the number of American personnel on such bases. Washington, therefore, negotiated a variety of arrangements to meet the objections of host governments. By early 1948, for example, the base in Iceland was operated by a civilian company under contract to the United States Air Force; in the Azores, the base was manned by a detachment of Portuguese military personnel operating under the Portuguese flag, but an air force detachment serviced the American aircraft using the base. In Port Lyautey, the base was under the command of the French navy, but under a secret agreement an American naval team took care of American aircraft on the base. In Saudi Arabia, the Dharan air strip was cared for by 300 U.S. personnel and was capable of handling B–29s. Because these arrangements were not altogether satisfactory, in mid-1948 Secretary of Defense Forrestal and Secretary of the Army Kenneth Royall advocated using American economic and military assistance as levers to acquire more permanent and comprehensive base rights, particularly in Greenland and North Africa.

Less well known than the American effort to establish a base system, but integral to the policymakers' conception of national security, was the attempt to secure military air transit and landing rights. Military planners wanted such rights at critical locations not only in the Western Hemisphere but also in North Africa, the Middle East, India, and southeast Asia. To this end they delineated a route from Casablanca through Algiers, Tripoli, Cairo, Dharan, Karachi, Delhi, Calcutta, Rangoon, Bangkok, and Saigon to Manila. In closing out the African–Middle East theater at the conclusion of the war, General H. W. Aurand, under explicit instructions from the secretary of war, made preparations for permanent rights at seven airfields in North Africa and Saudi Arabia. According to a study by the Joint Chiefs of Staff, "Military air transit rights for the United States along the North African–Indian route were most desirable in order to provide access to and familiarity with bases from which offensive and defensive action might be conducted in the event of a major war, and to provide an alternate route to China and to United States Far Eastern bases." In other words, such rights would permit the rapid augmentation of American bases in wartime as well as the rapid movement of American air units from the eastern to the western flank of the U.S. base system. In order to maintain these airfields in a state of readiness, the United States would have to rely on private airlines, which had to be persuaded to locate their operations in areas designated essential to military air transit rights. In this way, airports "in being" outside the formal American base system would be available for military operations in times of crisis and war. Assistant Secretary McCloy informed the State Department at the beginning of 1945 that a "strong United States air transport system, international in scope and readily adapted to military use, is vital to our air power and future national security." Even earlier, the joint chiefs had agreed not to include South American air bases in their strategic plans so long as it was understood that commercial fields in that region would be developed with a view to subsequent military use.[6]

In Latin America, American requirements for effective national security went far beyond air transit rights. In a report written in January 1945 at Assistant Secretary McCloy's behest, the War Department urged American collaboration with Latin American armed forces to insure the defense of the Panama Canal and the Western Hemisphere. Six areas within Latin America were considered of special significance either for strategic reasons or for their raw materials: the Panama Canal and approaches within one thousand miles; the Straits of Magellan; northeast Brazil; Mexico; the river Plate estuary and approaches within five hundred miles; and Mollendo, Peru-Antofagasta, and Chile. These areas were so "important," Secretary of War Patterson explained to Secretary of State Marshall in early 1947, "that the threat of attack on any of them would force the United States to come to their defense, even though it were not certain that attack on the United States itself would follow." The resources of these areas were essential to the United States, because "it is imperative that our war potential be enhanced . . . during any national emergency."[7]

While paying lip service to the United Nations and worrying about the impact of regional agreements in the Western Hemisphere on Soviet actions and American influence in Europe, the Joint Chiefs of Staff insisted that in practice non-American forces had to be kept out of the Western Hemisphere and the Monroe Doctrine had to be kept inviolate. "The Western Hemisphere is a distinct military entity, the integrity of which is a fundamental postulate of our security in the event of another world war."[8] Developments in aviation, rockets, guided missiles, and atomic energy had made "the solidarity of the Hemisphere and its united support of the principles of the Monroe Doctrine" more important than before. Patterson told Marshall that effective implementation of the Monroe Doctrine now meant "that we not only refuse to tolerate foreign colonization, control, or the extension of a foreign political system to our hemisphere, but we take alarm from the appearance on the continent of foreign ideologies, commercial exploitation, cartel arrangements, or other symptoms of increased non-hemispheric influence. . . . The basic consideration has always been an overriding apprehension lest a base be established in this area by a potentially hostile foreign power." The United States, Patterson insisted, must have "a stable, secure, and friendly flank to the South, not confused by enemy penetration, political, economic, or military."[9]

The need to predominate throughout the Western Hemisphere was not a result of deteriorating Soviet-American relations but a natural evolution of the Monroe Doctrine, accentuated by Axis aggression and new technological imperatives.[10] Patterson, Forrestal, and Army Chief of Staff Dwight D. Eisenhower initially were impelled less by reports of Soviet espionage, propaganda, and infiltration in Latin America than by accounts of British efforts to sell cruisers and aircraft to Chile and Ecuador; Swedish sales of anti-aircraft artillery to Argentina;

and French offers to build cruisers and destroyers for both Argentina and Brazil. To foreclose all foreign influence and to insure United States strategic hegemony, military officers and the civilian secretaries of the War and Navy departments argued for an extensive system of United States bases, expansion of commercial airline facilities throughout Latin America, negotiation of a regional defense pact, curtailment of all foreign military aid and foreign military sales, training of Latin American military officers in the United States, outfitting of Latin American armies with U.S. military equipment, and implementation of a comprehensive military assistance program.[11]

The military assistance program, as embodied in the Inter-American Military Cooperation Act, generated the most interagency discord. Latin American experts in the State Department maintained that military assistance would stimulate regional conflicts, dissipate Latin American financial resources, and divert attention from economic and social issues. Before leaving office, Byrnes forcefully presented the State Department position to Forrestal and Patterson. Instead of dwelling on the consequences of military assistance for Latin America, Byrnes maintained that such a program would be too costly for the United States, would focus attention on a region where American interests were relatively unchallenged, and would undermine more important American initiatives elsewhere on the globe. "Greece and Turkey are our outposts," he declared.[12]

The secretary of state clearly did not think that Congress would authorize funds for Latin America as well as for Greece and Turkey. Although Truman favored military assistance to Latin America, competing demands for American resources in 1947 and 1948 forced both military planners and U.S. senators to give priority to Western Europe and the Near East. In June 1948 the Inter-American Military Cooperation Act died in the Senate. But this signified no diminution in American national security imperatives; indeed, it underscored Byrnes's statement of December 1946 that the "outposts" of the nation's security lay in the heart of Eurasia.[13]

From the closing days of World War II, American defense officials believed that they could not allow any prospective adversary to control the Eurasian land mass. This was the lesson taught by two world wars. Strategic thinkers and military analysts insisted that any power or powers attempting to dominate Eurasia must be regarded as potentially hostile to the United States. Their acute awareness of the importance of Eurasia made Marshall, Thomas Handy, George A. Lincoln, and other officers wary of the expansion of Soviet influence there. Cognizant of the growth in Soviet strength, General John Deane, head of the United States military mission in Moscow, urged a tougher stand against Soviet demands even before World War II had ended. While acknowledging that the increase in Soviet power stemmed primarily from the defeat of Germany and Japan, postwar assessments of the Joint Chiefs of Staff emphasized the importance of deterring further Soviet aggrandizement in Eurasia. Concern over the consequences of Russian domination of Eurasia helps explain why in July 1945 the joint chiefs decided to oppose a Soviet request for bases in the Dardanelles; why during March and April 1946 they supported a firm stand against Russia in Iran, Turkey, and Tripolitania; and why in the summer of 1946 Clark Clifford and George Elsey, two White House aides, argued that Soviet incorporation of any parts of Western Europe, the Middle East, China, or Japan into a communist orbit was incompatible with American national security.

Yet defense officials were not eager to sever the wartime coalition. In early 1944 Admiral Leahy noted the "phenomenal development" of Soviet power but still hoped for Soviet-American cooperation. When members of the Joint Postwar Committee met with their colleagues on the Joint Planning Staff in April 1945, Major General G. V. Strong argued against using U.S. installations in Alaska for staging expeditionary forces, lest such a move exacerbate Russo-American relations. A few months later Eisenhower, Lincoln, and other officers advised against creating a central economic authority for Western Europe that might appear to be an anti-Soviet bloc.[14] The American objective, after all, was to avoid Soviet hegemony over Eurasia. By aggravating Soviet fears, the United States might foster what it wished to avoid. American self-restraint, however, might be reciprocated by the Soviets, providing time for Western Europe to recover and for the British to reassert some influence on the Continent.[15] Therefore, many defense officials in 1945 hoped to avoid an open rift with the Soviet Union. But at the same time they were determined to prevent the Eurasian land mass from falling under Soviet and communist influence.

Studies by the Joint Chiefs of Staff stressed that, if Eurasia came under Soviet domination, either through military conquest or political and economic "assimilation," America's only potential adversary would fall heir to enormous natural resources, industrial potential, and manpower. By the autumn of 1945, military planners already were worrying that Soviet control over much of Eastern Europe and its raw materials would abet Russia's economic recovery, enhance its war-making capacity, and deny important foodstuffs, oil, and minerals to Western Europe. By the early months of 1946, Secretary Patterson and his subordinates in the War Department believed that Soviet control of the Ruhr-Rhineland industrial complex would constitute an extreme threat. Even more dangerous was the prospect of Soviet predominance over the rest of Western Europe, especially France. Strategically, this would undermine the impact of any prospective American naval blockade and would allow Soviet military planners to achieve defense in depth. The latter possibility had enormous military significance, because American war plans relied so heavily on air power and strategic bombing, the efficacy of which might be reduced substantially if the Soviets acquired outlying bases in Western Europe and the Middle East or if they "neutralized" bases in Great Britain.[16]

Economic considerations also made defense officials determined to retain American access to Eurasia as well as to deny Soviet predominance over it. Stimson, Patterson, McCloy, and Assistant Secretary Howard C. Peterson agreed with Forrestal that long-term American prosperity required open markets, unhindered access to raw materials, and the rehabilitation of much—if not all—of Eurasia along liberal capitalist lines. In late 1944 and 1945, Stimson protested the prospective industrial emasculation of Germany, lest it undermine American economic well being, set back recovery throughout Europe, and unleash forces of anarchy and revolution. Stimson and his subordinates in the Operations Division of the army also worried that the spread of Soviet power in northeast Asia would constrain the functioning of the free enterprise system and jeopardize American economic interests. A report prepared by the staff of the Moscow embassy and revised in mid-1946 by Ambassador (and former General) Walter Bedell Smith emphasized that "Soviet power is by nature so jealous that it has already operated to segregate from world economy almost all of the areas in which it has been established." While Forrestal and the navy sought to contain Soviet influence in the Near East and to retain American access to Middle East oil, Patterson and the War Department focused on preventing famine in occupied areas, forestalling communist revolution, circumscribing Soviet influence, resuscitating trade, and preserving traditional American markets especially in Western Europe. But American economic interests in Eurasia were not limited to Western Europe, Germany, and the Middle East. Military planners and intelligence officers in both the army and navy expressed considerable interest in the raw materials of southeast Asia, and, as already shown, one of the purposes of the bases they wanted was to maintain access to those resources and deny them to a prospective enemy.[17]

While civilian officials and military strategists feared the loss of Eurasia, they did not expect the Soviet Union to attempt its military conquest. In the early Cold War years, there was nearly universal agreement that the Soviets, while eager to expand their influence, desired to avoid a military engagement. In October 1945, for example, the Joint Intelligence Staff predicted that the Soviet Union would seek to avoid war for five to ten years. In April 1946, while Soviet troops still remained in Iran, General Lincoln, the army's principal war planner, concurred with Byrnes's view that the Soviets did not want war. In May, when there was deep concern about a possible communist uprising in France, military intelligence doubted the Kremlin would instigate a coup, lest it ignite a full scale war. At a high-level meeting at the White House in June, Eisenhower stated that he did not think the Soviets wanted war; only Forrestal dissented. In August, when the Soviet note to Turkey on the Dardanelles provoked consternation in American policy-making circles, General Hoyt Vandenberg, director of central intelligence, informed President Truman that there were no signs of unusual Soviet troop movements or supply build-ups. In March 1947, while the Truman Doctrine was being discussed in Congress, the director of army intelligence maintained that the factors operating to discourage Soviet aggression continued to be decisive. In September 1947, the CIA concluded that the Soviets would not seek to conquer Western Europe for several reasons: they would recognize their inability to control hostile populations; they would fear triggering a war with the United States that could not be won; and they would prefer to gain hegemony by political and economic means. In October 1947, the Joint Intelligence Staff maintained that for three years at least the Soviet Union would take no action that would precipitate a military conflict.

Even the ominous developments during the first half of 1948 did not alter these assessments. Despite his alarmist cable of March 5, designed to galvanize congressional support for increased defense expenditures, General Lucius Clay, the American military governor in Germany, did not believe war imminent. A few days later, the CIA concluded that the communist takeover in Czechoslovakia would not increase Soviet capabilities significantly and reflected no alteration in Soviet tactics. On March 16, the CIA reported to the president, "The weight of logic, as well as evidence, also leads to the conclusion that the Soviets will not resort to military force within the next sixty days." While this assessment was far from reassuring, army and navy intelligence experts concurred that the Soviets still wanted to avoid war; the question was whether war would erupt as a result of "miscalculation" by either the United States or Russia. After talking to Foreign Minister V. M. Molotov in June, Ambassador Smith concluded that Soviet leaders would not resort to active hostilities. During the Berlin blockade, army intelligence reported few signs of Soviet preparations for war; naval intelligence maintained that the Soviets desired to avoid war yet consolidate their position in East Germany. In October 1948, the Military Intelligence Division of the army endorsed a British appraisal that "all the evidence available indicates that the Soviet Union is not preparing to go to war in the near future." In December Acting Secretary of State Robert Lovett summed up the long-standing American perspective when he emphasized that he saw "no evidence that Soviet intentions run toward launching a sudden military attack on the western nations at this time. It would not be in character with the tradition or mentality of the Soviet leaders to resort to such a measure unless they felt themselves either politically extremely weak, or militarily extremely strong."

Although American defense officials recognized that the Soviets had substantial military assets, they remained confident that the Soviet Union did not feel extremely strong. Military analysts studying Russian capabilities noted that the Soviets were rapidly mechanizing infantry units and enhancing their firepower and mobility. It was estimated during the winter of 1946–47 that the Soviets could mobilize six million troops in thirty days and twelve million in six months, providing sufficient manpower to overrun all important parts of Eurasia. The Soviets were also believed to be utilizing German scientists and German technological know-how to improve their submarine force, develop rockets and missiles, and acquire knowledge about the atomic bomb. During 1947 and 1948, it was reported as well that the Soviets were making rapid progress in the development of high performance jet fighters and already possessed several hundred intermediate range bombers comparable to the American B-29.

Even so, American military analysts were most impressed with Soviet weaknesses and vulnerabilities. The Soviets had no long-range strategic air force, no atomic bomb, and meager air defenses. Moreover, the Soviet navy was considered ineffective except for its submarine forces. The Joint Logistic Plans Committee and the Military Intelligence Division of the War Department estimated that the Soviet Union would require approximately fifteen years to overcome wartime losses in manpower and industry, ten years to redress the shortage of technicians, five to ten years to develop a strategic air force, fifteen to twenty-five years to construct a modern navy, ten years to refurbish military transport, ten years (or less) to quell resistance in occupied areas, fifteen to twenty years to establish a military infrastructure in the Far East, three to ten years to acquire the atomic bomb, and an unspecified number of years to remove the vulnerability of the Soviet rail-net and petroleum industry to long-range bombing.[18] For several years at least, the Soviet capability for sustained attack against North America would be very limited. In January 1946 the Joint Intelligence Staff concluded that "the offensive capabilities of the United States are manifestly superior to those of the U.S.S.R. and any war between the U.S. and the U.S.S.R. would be far more costly to the Soviet Union than to the United States."[19]

Key American officials like Lovett, Clifford, Eisenhower, Bedell Smith and Budget Director James Webb were cognizant of prevailing Soviet weaknesses and potential American strength. Despite Soviet superiority in manpower, General Eisenhower and Admiral Forrest E. Sherman doubted that Russia could mount a surprise attack, and General Lincoln, Admiral Cato Glover, and Secretaries Patterson and Forrestal believed that Soviet forces would encounter acute logistical problems in trying to overrun Eurasia—especially in the Near East, Spain, and Italy. Even Forrestal doubted reports of accelerating Soviet air capabilities. American experts believed that most Soviet planes were obsolescent, that the Soviets had insufficient airfields and aviation gas to use their new planes, and that these planes had serious problems in their instrumentation and construction.

In general, improvements in specific areas of the Soviet military establishment did not mean that overall Soviet capabilities were improving at an alarming rate. In July 1947, the Military Intelligence Division concluded, "While there has been a slight overall improvement in the Soviet war potential, Soviet strength for total war is not sufficiently great to make a military attack against the United States anything but a most hazardous gamble." This view prevailed in 1946 and 1947, even though the American nuclear arsenal was extremely small and the American strategic bombing force of limited size. In the spring of 1948 the Joint Intelligence Committee at the American embassy in Moscow explained why the United States ultimately would emerge victorious should a war erupt in the immediate future. The Soviets could not win because of their "inability to carry the war to U.S. territory. After the occupation of Europe, the U.S.S.R. would be forced to assume the defensive and await attacks by U.S. forces which should succeed primarily because of the ability of the U.S. to outproduce the U.S.S.R. in materials of war."[20]

Awareness of Soviet economic shortcomings played a key role in the American interpretation of Soviet capabilities. Intelligence reports predicted that Soviet leaders would invest a disproportionate share of Russian resources in capital goods industries. But, even if such Herculean efforts enjoyed some success, the Soviets still would not reach the pre–World War II levels of the United States within fifteen to twenty years. Technologically, the Soviets were behind in the critical areas of aircraft manufacturing, electronics, and oil refining. And, despite Russia's concerted attempts to catch up and to surpass the United States, American intelligence experts soon started reporting that Soviet reconstruction was lagging behind Soviet ambitions, especially in the electronics, transportation, aircraft, construction machinery, nonferrous metals, and shipping industries. Accordingly, throughout the years 1945–48 American military analysts and intelligence experts believed that Soviet transportation bottlenecks, industrial shortcomings, technological backwardness, and agricultural problems would discourage military adventurism.

If American Defense Officials did not Expect a Soviet military attack, why, then, were they so fearful of losing control of Eurasia? The answer rests less in American assessments of Soviet military capabilities and short-term military intentions than in appraisals of economic and political conditions throughout Europe and Asia. Army officials in particular, because of their occupation roles in Germany, Japan, Austria, and Korea, were aware of the postwar plight of these areas. Key military men—Generals Clay, Douglas MacArthur, John Hilldring, and Oliver P. Echols and Colonel Charles H. Bonesteel—became alarmed by the prospects of famine, disease, anarchy, and revolution. They recognized that communist parties could exploit the distress and that the Russians could capitalize upon it to spread Soviet influence. As early as June 1945, Rear Admiral Ellery Stone, the American commissioner in Italy, wrote that wartime devastation had created fertile soil for the growth of communism in Italy and the enlargement of the Soviet sphere. MacArthur also feared that, if the Japanese economy remained emasculated and reforms were not undertaken, communism would spread. Clay, too, was acutely aware that German communists were depicting themselves and their beliefs as their country's only hope of salvation. In the spring of 1946 military planners, working on contingency plans for the emergency withdrawal of American troops from Germany, should war with Russia unexpectedly occur, also took note of the economic turmoil and political instability in neighboring countries, especially France. Sensitivity to the geopolitical dimensions of the socioeconomic crisis of the postwar era impelled Chief of Staff Eisenhower to give high priority in the army budget to assistance for occupied areas.

Civilian officials in the War, Navy, and State departments shared these concerns. In the autumn of 1945, McCloy warned Patterson that the stakes in Germany were immense and economic recovery had to be expedited. During the first half of 1946 Secretary Patterson and Assistant Secretary Peterson continually pressed the State Department to tackle the problems beleaguering occupation authorities in Germany and pleaded for State Department support and assistance in getting the Truman administration to provide additional relief to the devastated areas of Europe. On Peterson's urging, Acheson wrote Truman in April 1946, "We have now reached the most critical period of the world food crisis. We must either immediately greatly increase the exports of grain from the United States or expect general disorder and political upheaval to develop in [most of Eurasia]."[21] Forrestal had already pressed for a reassessment of occupation policies in Germany and Japan. In May, Clay suspended reparation payments in order to effect an accord on German economic unity. In June, Patterson began to support the merger of the American and British zones. The man most responsible for this latter undertaking was William Draper, Forrestal's former partner in Dillon, Read, and Co., and Clay's chief economic assistant. Draper firmly believed that "economic collapse in either [France or Germany] with probable political break-down and rise of communism would seriously threaten American objectives in Europe and in the world."[22]

American defense officials, military analysts, and intelligence officers were extremely sensitive to the political ferment, social turmoil, and economic upheaval throughout postwar Europe and Asia. In their initial postwar studies, the Joint Chiefs of Staff carefully noted the multiplicity of problems that could breed conflict and provide opportunities for Soviet expansion. In the spring of 1946 army planners, including General Lincoln, were keenly aware that conflict was most likely to arise from local disputes (for example, in Venezia-Giulia) or from indigenous unrest (for example, in France), perhaps even against the will of Moscow. A key War Department document submitted to the State-War-Navy Coordinating Committee in April 1946 skirted the issue of Soviet military capabilities and argued that the Soviet Union's strength emanated from totalitarian control over its satellites, from local communist parties, and from worldwide chaotic political and economic conditions. In October 1946 the Joint Planning Staff stressed that for the next ten years the major factor influencing world political developments would be the East-West ideological conflict taking place in an impoverished and strife-torn Europe and a vacuum of indigenous power in Asia. "The greatest danger to the security of the United States," the CIA concluded in mid-1947, "is the possibility of economic collapse in Western Europe and the consequent accession to power of Communist elements."[23]

In brief, during 1946 and 1947, defense officials witnessed a dramatic unravelling of the geopolitical foundations and socioeconomic structure of international affairs. Britain's economic weakness and withdrawal from the eastern Mediterranean, India's independence movement, civil war in China, nationalist insurgencies in Indo-China and the Dutch East Indies, Zionist claims to Palestine and Arab resentment, German and Japanese economic paralysis, communist inroads in France and Italy—all were ominous developments. Defense officials recognized that the Soviet Union had not created these circumstances but believed that Soviet leaders would exploit them. Should communists take power, even without direct Russian intervention, the Soviet Union, it was assumed, would gain predominant control of the resources of these areas because of the postulated subservience of communist parties everywhere to the Kremlin. Should nationalist uprisings persist, communists seize power in underdeveloped countries, and Arabs revolt against American support of a Jewish state, the petroleum and raw materials of critical areas might be denied the West. The imminent possibility existed that, even without Soviet military aggression, the resources of Eurasia could fall under Russian control. With these resources, the Soviet Union would be able to overcome its chronic economic weaknesses, achieve defense in depth, and challenge American power—perhaps even by military force.

In this frightening postwar environment American assessments of Soviet long-term intentions were transformed. When World War II ended, military planners initially looked upon Soviet aims in foreign affairs as arising from the Kremlin's view of power politics, Soviet strategic imperatives, historical Russian ambitions, and Soviet reactions to moves by the United States and Great Britain. American intelligence analysts and strategic planners most frequently discussed Soviet actions in Eastern Europe, the Balkans, the Near East, and Manchuria as efforts to establish an effective security system. Despite enormous Soviet gains during the war, many assessments noted that, in fact, the Soviets had not yet achieved a safe security zone, especially on their southern periphery. While Forrestal, Deane, and most of the planners in the army's Operations Division possessed a skeptical, perhaps even sinister, view of Soviet intentions, the still prevailing outlook at the end of 1945 was to dismiss the role of ideology in Soviet foreign policy yet emphasize Soviet distrust of foreigners; to stress Soviet expansionism but acknowledge the possibility of accommodation; to abhor Soviet domination of Eastern Europe but discuss Soviet policies elsewhere in terms of power and influence; and to dwell upon the Soviet preoccupation with security yet acknowledge doubt about ultimate Soviet intentions.

This orientation changed rapidly during 1946. In January, the Joint War Plans Committee observed that "the long-term objective [of the Soviet Union] is deemed to be establishment of predominant influence over the Eurasian land mass and the strategic approaches thereto." Reports of the new military attach . . . in Moscow went further, claiming that "the ultimate aim of Soviet foreign policy seems to be the dominance of Soviet influence throughout the world" and "the final aim . . . is the destruction of the capitalist system." Soon thereafter, Kennan's "long telegram" was widely distributed among defense officials, on whom it had considerable impact. Particularly suggestive was his view that Soviet leaders needed the theme of capitalist encirclement to justify their autocratic rule. Also influential were Kennan's convictions that the Soviet leaders aimed to shatter the international authority of the United States and were beyond reason and conciliation.

During the spring and summer of 1946, defense officials found these notions persuasive as an interpretation of Soviet intentions because of the volatile international situation, the revival of ideological fervor within the Soviet Union, and the domestic political atmosphere and legislative constraints in the United States. President Truman wished to stop "babying the Soviets," and his predilection for a tougher posture probably led his subordinates to be less inclined to give the Soviets the benefit of any doubt when assessing Russian intentions.[24] Forrestal believed the Soviet communist threat had become more serious than the Nazi challenge of the 1930s; General John E. Hull, director of the Operations Division, asserted that the Soviets were "constitutionally incapable of being conciliated"; and Clark Clifford and George Elsey considered Soviet fears "absurd." A key subcommittee of the State-War-Navy Coordinating Committee declared that Soviet suspicions were "not susceptible of removal," and in July 1946 the Joint Chiefs of Staff declared the Soviet objective to be "world domination." By late 1946 it was commonplace for intelligence reports and military assessments to state, without any real analysis, that the "ultimate aim of Soviet foreign policy is Russian domination of a communist world."[25] There was, of course, plentiful evidence for this appraisal of Soviet ambitions—the Soviet consolidation of a sphere of influence in Eastern Europe; the incendiary situation in Venezia Giulia; Soviet violation of the agreement to withdraw troops from Iran; Soviet relinquishment of Japanese arms to the Chinese communists; the Soviet mode of extracting reparations from the Russian zone in Germany; Soviet diplomatic overtures for bases in the Dardanelles, Tripolitania, and the Dodecanese; Soviet requests for a role in the occupation of Japan; and the Kremlin's renewed emphasis on Marxist-Leninist doctrine, the vulnerability of capitalist economies, and the inevitability of conflict.

Yet these assessments did not seriously grapple with contradictory evidence. While emphasizing Soviet military capabilities, strategic ambitions, and diplomatic intransigence, reports like the Clifford-Elsey memorandum of September 1946 and the Joint Chiefs of Staff report 1696 (upon which the Clifford-Elsey memorandum heavily relied) disregarded numerous signs of Soviet weakness, moderation, and circumspection. During 1946 and 1947 intelligence analysts described the withdrawal of Russian troops from northern Norway, Manchuria, Bornholm, and Iran (from the latter under pressure, of course). Numerous intelligence sources reported the reduction of Russian troops in Eastern Europe and the extensive demobilization going on within the Soviet Union. In October 1947 the Joint Intelligence Committee forecast a Soviet army troop strength during 1948 and 1949 of less than two million men. Soviet military expenditures appeared to moderate. Other reports dealt with the inadequacies of Soviet transportation and bridging equipment for the conduct of offensive operations in Eastern Europe. And, as already noted, assessments of the Soviet economy revealed persistent problems likely to restrict Soviet adventurism.

Experience suggested that the Soviet Union was by no means uniformly hostile or unwilling to negotiate with the United States. In April 1946, a few days after a State-War-Navy subcommittee issued an alarming political estimate of Soviet policy (for use in American military estimates), Ambassador Smith reminded the State Department that the Soviet press was not unalterably critical of the United States, that the Russians had withdrawn from Bornholm, that Stalin had given a moderate speech on the United Nations, and that Soviet demobilization continued apace. The next month General Lincoln, who had accompanied Byrnes to Paris for the meeting of the council of foreign ministers, acknowledged that the Soviets had been willing to make numerous concessions regarding Tripolitania, the Dodecanese, and Italian reparations. In the spring of 1946, General Echols, General Clay, and Secretary Patterson again maintained that the French constituted the major impediment to an agreement on united control of Germany. At the same time the Soviets ceased pressing for territorial adjustments with Turkey. After the diplomatic exchanges over the Dardanelles in the late summer of 1946 the Soviets did not again ask for either a revision of the Montreux Convention or the acquisition of bases in the Dardanelles. In early 1947 central intelligence delineated more than a half-dozen instances of Soviet moderation or concessions. In April the Military Intelligence Division noted that the Soviets had limited their involvement in the Middle East, diminished their ideological rhetoric, and given only moderate support to Chinese communists. In the months preceding the Truman Doctrine, Soviet behavior—as noted by American military officials and intelligence analysts—hardly justified the inflammatory rhetoric Acheson and Truman used to secure congressional support for aid to Greece and Turkey. Perhaps this is why General Marshall, as secretary of state, refrained from such language himself and preferred to focus on the socioeconomic aspects of the unfolding crisis.

In their overall assessments of Soviet long-term intentions, however, military planners dismissed all evidence of Soviet moderation, circumspection, and restraint. In fact, as 1946 progressed, these planners seemed to spend less time analyzing Soviet intentions and more time estimating Soviet capabilities.[26] Having accepted the notion that the two powers were locked in an ideological struggle of indefinite duration and conscious of the rapid demobilization of American forces and the constraints on American defense expenditures, they no longer explored ways of accommodating a potential adversary's legitimate strategic requirements or pondered how American initiatives might influence the Soviet Union's definition of its objectives.[27] Information not confirming prevailing assumptions either was ignored in overall assessments of Soviet intentions or was used to illustrate that the Soviets were shifting tactics but not altering objectives. Reflective of the emerging mentality was a report from the Joint Chiefs of Staff to the president in July 1946 that deleted sections from previous studies that had outlined Soviet weaknesses. A memorandum sent by Secretary Patterson to the president at the same time was designed by General Lauris Norstad, director of the War Department's Plans and Operations Division, to answer questions about relations with the Soviet Union "without ambiguity." Truman, Clark Clifford observed many years later, liked things in black and white.

During 1946 and early 1947, the conjunction of Soviet ideological fervor and socioeconomic turmoil throughout Eurasia contributed to the growth of a myopic view of Soviet long-term policy objectives and to enormous apprehension lest the Soviet Union gain control of all the resources of Eurasia, thereby endangering the national security of the United States. American assessments of Soviet short-term military intentions had not altered; Soviet military capabilities had not significantly increased, and Soviet foreign policy positions had not greatly shifted. But defense officials were acutely aware of America's own rapidly diminishing capabilities, of Britain's declining military strength, of the appeal of communist doctrine to most of the under-developed world, and of the opportunities open to communist parties throughout most of Eurasia as a result of prevailing socioeconomic conditions. War Department papers, studies of the joint chiefs, and intelligence analyses repeatedly described the restiveness of colonial peoples that had sapped British and French strength, the opportunities for communist parties in France, Italy, and even Spain to capitalize upon indigenous conditions, and the ability of the Chinese communists to defeat the nationalists and make the resources and manpower of Manchuria and North China available to the Soviet Union. In this turbulent international arena, the survival of liberal ideals and capitalist institutions was anything but assured. "We could point to the economic benefits of Capitalism," commented one important War Department paper in April 1946, "but these benefits are concentrated rather than widespread, and, at present, are genuinely suspect throughout Europe and in many other parts of the world."[28]

In this environment, there was indeed no room for ambiguity or compromise. Action was imperative—action aimed at safeguarding those areas of Eurasia not already within the Soviet sphere. Even before Kennan's "long telegram" arrived in Washington the joint chiefs adopted the position that "collaboration with the Soviet Union should stop short not only of compromise of principle but also of expansion of Russian influence in Europe and in the Far East."[29] During the spring and summer of 1946, General Lincoln and Admiral Richard L. Conolly, commander of American naval forces in the eastern Atlantic and Mediterranean, worked tirelessly to stiffen Byrnes's views, avert American diplomatic concessions, and put the squeeze on the Russians.[30] "The United States," army planners explained, "must be able to prevent, by force if necessary, Russian domination of either Europe or Asia to the extent that the resources of either continent could be mobilized against the United States." Which countries in Eurasia were worth fighting over remained unclear during 1946. But army and navy officials as well as the joint chiefs advocated a far-reaching program of foreign economic assistance coupled with the refurbishment of American military forces.[31]

During late 1946 and early 1947, the Truman administration assumed the initiative by creating German Bizonia, providing military assistance to Greece and Turkey, allocating massive economic aid to Western Europe, and reassessing economic policy toward Japan. These initiatives were aimed primarily at tackling the internal sources of unrest upon which communist parties capitalized and at rehabilitating the industrial heartlands of Eurasia. American defense officials supported these actions and acquiesced in the decision to give priority to economic aid rather than rearmament. Service officers working on foreign assistance programs of the State-War-Navy Coordinating Committee supported economic aid, showed sensitivity to the socioeconomic sources of unrest, and recognized that economic aid was likely to be the most efficacious means of preserving a favorable balance of power in Eurasia. Because they judged American military power to be superior and war to be unlikely, Forrestal, Lovett, and Webb insisted that military spending not interfere with the implementation of the Marshall Plan, rehabilitation of Germany, and revival of Japan. "In the necessarily delicate apportioning of our available resources," wrote Assistant Secretary of War Peterson, "the time element permits present emphasis on strengthening the economic and social dikes against Soviet communism rather than upon preparing for a possibly eventual, but not yet inevitable, war."[32]

Yet if war should unexpectedly occur, the United States had to have the capability to inflict incalculable damage upon the Soviet Union. Accordingly, Truman shelved (after some serious consideration) proposals for international control of atomic energy. The Baruch Plan, as it evolved in the spring and summer of 1946, was heavily influenced by defense officials and service officers who wished to avoid any significant compromise with the Soviet Union. They sought to perpetuate America's nuclear monopoly as long as possible in order to counterbalance Soviet conventional strength, deter Soviet adventurism, and bolster American negotiating leverage. When negotiations at the United Nations for international control of atomic energy languished for lack of agreement on its implementation, the way was clear for the Truman administration gradually to adopt a strategy based on air power and atomic weapons. This strategy was initially designed to destroy the adversary's will and capability to wage war by annihilating Russian industrial, petroleum, and urban centers. After completing their study of the 1946 Bikini atomic tests, the Joint Chiefs of Staff in July 1947 called for an enlargement of the nuclear arsenal. While Truman and Forrestal insisted on limiting military expenditures, government officials moved vigorously to solve problems in the production of plutonium, to improve nuclear cores and assembly devices, and to increase the number of aircraft capable of delivering atomic bombs. After much initial postwar disorganization, the General Advisory Committee to the Atomic Energy Commission could finally report to the president at the end of 1947 that "great progress" had been made in the atomic program. From June 30, 1947, to June 30, 1948, the number of bombs in the stockpile increased from thirteen to fifty. Although at the time of the Berlin crisis the United States was not prepared to launch a strategic air offensive against the Soviet Union, substantial progress had been made in the development of the nation's air-atomic capabilities. By the end of 1948, the United States had at least eighteen nuclear-capable B-50s, four B-36s, and almost three times as many nuclear-capable B-29s as had been available at the end of 1947.

During late 1947 and early 1948, the administration also responded to pleas of the Joint Chiefs of Staff to augment the overseas base system and to acquire bases in closer proximity to the Soviet Union. Negotiations were conducted with the British to gain access to bases in the Middle East and an agreement was concluded for the acquisition of air facilities in Libya. Admiral Conolly made a secret deal with the French to secure air and communication rights and to stockpile oil, aviation gas, and ammunition in North Africa. Plans also were discussed for postoccupation bases in Japan, and considerable progress was made in refurbishing and constructing airfields in Turkey. During 1948 the Turks also received one hundred eighty F-47 fighter-bombers, thirty B-26 bombers, and eighty-one C-47 cargo planes. The F-47s and B-26s, capable of reaching the vital Ploesti and Baku oil fields, were more likely to be used to slow down a Soviet advance through Turkey or Iran, thereby affording time to activate a strategic air offensive from prospective bases in the Cairo-Suez area.

Despite these developments, the joint chiefs and military planners grew increasingly uneasy with the budgetary constraints under which they operated. They realized that American initiatives, however necessary, placed the Soviet Union on the defensive, created an incendiary situation, and made war more likely—though still improbable. In July 1947, intelligence analysts in the War Department maintained that the Truman Doctrine and the Marshall Plan had resulted in a more aggressive Soviet attitude toward the United States and had intensified tensions. "These tensions have caused a sharper line of demarcation between West and East tending to magnify the significance of conflicting points of view, and reducing the possibility of agreement on any point." Intelligence officers understood that the Soviets would perceive American efforts to build strategic highways, construct airfields, and transfer fighter bombers to Turkey as a threat to Soviet security and to the oilfields in the Caucuses. The latter, noted the director of naval intelligence, "lie within easy air striking range of countries on her southern flank, and the Soviet leaders will be particularly sensitive to any political threat from this area, however remote." Intelligence analysts also recognized that the Soviets would view the Marshall Plan as a threat to Soviet control in Eastern Europe as well as a death-knell to communist attempts to capture power peacefully in Western Europe. And defense officials were well aware that the Soviets would react angrily to plans for currency reform in German Trizonia and to preparations for a West German republic. "The whole Berlin crisis," army planners informed Eisenhower, "has arisen as a result of . . . actions on the part of the Western Powers." In sum, the Soviet clampdown in Eastern Europe and the attempt to blockade Berlin did not come as shocks to defense officials, who anticipated hostile and defensive Soviet reactions to American initiatives.

The real consternation of the Joint Chiefs of Staff and other high-ranking civilian and military officials in the defense agencies stemmed from their growing conviction that the United States was undertaking actions and assuming commitments that now required greater military capabilities. Recognizing that American initiatives, aimed at safeguarding Eurasia from further communist inroads, might be perceived as endangering Soviet interests, it was all the more important to be ready for any eventuality. Indeed, to the extent that anxieties about the prospects of war escalated in March and April 1948, these fears did not stem from estimates that the Soviets were planning further aggressive action after the communist seizure of power in Czechoslovakia but from apprehensions that ongoing American initiatives might provoke an attack. On March 14 General S. J. Chamberlin, director of army intelligence, warned the chief of staff that "actions taken by this country in opposition to the spread of Communism . . . may decide the question of the outbreak of war and of its timing." The critical question explicitly faced by the intelligence agencies and by the highest policy makers was whether passage of the Selective Service Act, or of universal military training, or of additional appropriations for the air force, or of a military assistance program to Western European countries, or of a resolution endorsing American support for West European Union would trigger a Soviet attack. Chamberlin judged, for example, that the Soviets would not go to war just to make Europe communist but would resort to war if they felt threatened. The great imponderable, of course, was what, in the Soviet view, would constitute a security threat justifying war.

Recognizing the need to move ahead with planned initiatives but fearing Soviet countermeasures, the newly formed staff of the National Security Council undertook its first comprehensive assessment of American foreign policy. During March 1948, after consulting with representatives of the army, navy, air force, State Department, CIA, and National Security Resources Board, the National Security Council staff produced NSC 7, "The Position of the United States with Respect to Soviet-Dominated World Communism." This study began with the commonplace assumption that the communist goal was "world conquest." The study then went on to express the omnipresent theme behind all conceptions of American national security in the immediate postwar years. "Between the United States and the USSR there are in Europe and Asia areas of great potential power which if added to the existing strength of the Soviet world would enable the latter to become so superior in manpower, resources, and territory that the prospect for the survival of the United States as a free nation would be slight." Accordingly, the study called, first, for the strengthening of the military potential of the United States and, second, for the arming of the non-Soviet world, particularly Western Europe. Although this staff study was never formally approved, the national security bureaucracy worked during the spring and summer of 1948 for West European unity, military assistance to friendly nations, currency reform in Trizonia, revitalization of the Ruhr, and the founding of the Federal Republic of Germany.

The priority accorded to Western Europe did not mean that officials ignored the rest of Eurasia. Indeed, the sustained economic rejuvenation of Western Europe made access to Middle Eastern oil more important than ever. Marshall, Lovett, Forrestal, and other defense officials, including the joint chiefs, feared that American support of Israel might jeopardize relations with Arab nations and drive them into the hands of the Soviet Union. Although Truman accepted the partition of Palestine and recognized Israel, the United States maintained an embargo on arms shipments and sought to avoid too close an identification with the Zionist state lest the flow of oil to the West be jeopardized. At the same time, the Truman administration moved swiftly in June 1948 to resuscitate the Japanese economy. Additional funds were requested from Congress to procure imports of raw materials for Japanese industry so that Japanese exports might also be increased. Shortly thereafter, Draper, Tracy S. Voorhees, and other army officials came to believe that a rehabilitated Japan would need the markets and raw materials of Southeast Asia. They undertook a comprehensive examination of the efficacy and utility of a Marshall Plan for Asia. Integrating Japan and Southeast Asia into a viable regional economy, invulnerable to communist subversion and firmly ensconced in the Western community, assumed growing significance, especially in view of the prospect of a communist triumph in China. But communist victories in China did not dissuade policymakers from supporting, for strategic as well as domestic political considerations, the appropriation of hundreds of millions of dollars in additional aid to the Chinese nationalists in the spring of 1948. And the American commitment to preserve the integrity of South Korea actually increased, despite the planned withdrawal of occupation forces.

The problem with all of these undertakings, however, was that they cost large sums, expanded the nation's formal and informal commitments, and necessitated larger military capabilities. Yet on March 24, 1948, just as NSC 7 was being finished, Truman's Council of Economic Advisors warned that accelerating expenditures might compel the president "to set aside free market practices—and substitute a rather comprehensive set of controls." Truman was appalled by this possibility and carefully limited the sums allocated for a build-up of American forces. Key advisers, like Webb, Marshall, Lovett, and Clifford, supported this approach because they perceived too much fat in the military budget, expected the Soviets to rely on political tactics rather than military aggression, postulated latent U.S. military superiority over the Soviet Union, and assumed that the atomic bomb constituted a decisive, if perhaps short-term, trump card. For many American policy makers, moreover, the Iranian crisis of 1946, the Greek civil war, and the ongoing Berlin airlift seemed to demonstrate that Russia would back down when confronted with American determination, even if the United States did not have superior forces-in-being.

As secretary of defense, however, Forrestal was beleaguered by pressures emanating from the armed services for a build-up of American military forces and by his own apprehensions over prospective Soviet actions. He anguished over the excruciatingly difficult choices that had to be made between the imperatives of foreign economic aid, overseas military assistance, domestic rearmament, and fiscal orthodoxy. In May, June, and July 1948, he and his assistants carefully pondered intelligence reports on Soviet intentions and requested a special State Department study on how to plan American defense expenditures in view of prospective Soviet policies. He also studied carefully the conclusions of an exhaustive study of the navy's contribution to national security undertaken by the General Board of the navy under the direct supervision of Captain Arleigh Burke. Still not satisfied, Forrestal asked the president to permit the National Security Council to conduct another comprehensive examination of American policy objectives. Forrestal clearly hoped that this reassessment would show that a larger proportion of resources should be allocated to the military establishment.

The Policy Planning Staff of the Department of State prepared the initial study that Forrestal requested and Truman authorized. Extensively redrafted it reappeared in November 1948 as NSC 20/4 and was adopted as the definitive statement of American foreign policy. Significantly, this paper reiterated the longstanding estimate that the Soviet Union was not likely to resort to war to achieve its objectives. But war could erupt as a result of "Soviet miscalculation of the determination of the United States to use all the means at its command to safeguard its security, through Soviet misinterpretation of our intentions, and through U.S. miscalculation of Soviet reactions to measures which we might take." Immediately following this appraisal of the prospects of war, the National Security Council restated its conception of American national security: "Soviet domination of the potential power of Eurasia, whether achieved by armed aggression or by political and subversive means, would be strategically and politically unacceptable to the United States."[33]

Yet NSC 20/4 did not call for a larger military budget. With no expectation that war was imminent, the report emphasized the importance of safeguarding the domestic economy and left unresolved the extent to which resources should be devoted to military preparations. NSC 20/4 also stressed "that Soviet political warfare might seriously weaken the relative position of the United States, enhance Soviet strength and either lead to our ultimate defeat short of war, or force us into war under dangerously unfavorable conditions." Accordingly, the National Security Council vaguely but stridently propounded the importance of reducing Soviet power and influence on the periphery of the Russian homeland and of strengthening the pro-American orientation of non-Soviet nations.[34]

Language of this sort, which did not define clear priorities and which projected American interests almost everywhere on the globe, exasperated the joint chiefs and other military officers. They, too, believed that the United States should resist communist aggression everywhere, "an overall commitment which in itself is all-inclusive." But to undertake this goal in a responsible and effective fashion it was necessary "to bring our military strength to a level commensurate with the distinct possibility of global warfare." The Joint Chiefs of Staff still did not think the Soviets wanted war. But, given the long-term intentions attributed to the Soviet Union and given America's own aims, the chances for war, though still small, were growing.

Particularly worrisome were studies during 1948 suggesting that, should war occur, the United States would have difficulty implementing basic strategic undertakings. Although the armed services fought bitterly over the division of funds, they concurred fully on one subject— the $15 billion ceiling on military spending set by Truman was inadequate. In November 1948, military planners argued that the $14.4 billion budget would jeopardize American military operations by constricting the speed and magnitude of the strategic air offensive, curtailing conventional bombing operations against the Soviet Union, reducing America's ability to provide naval assistance to Mediterranean allies, undermining the nation's ability to control Middle East oil at the onset of a conflict, and weakening initial overall offensive capabilities. On November 9, the joint chiefs informed the secretary of defense that the existing budget for fiscal 1950 was "insufficient to implement national policy in any probable war situation that can be foreseen."

From the viewpoint of the national military establishment, the deficiency of forces-in-being was just one of several problems. Forrestal told Marshall that he was more concerned about the absence of sufficient strength to support international negotiations than he was about the availability of forces to combat overt acts of aggression, which were unlikely in any case. During 1948, the joint chiefs also grew increasingly agitated over the widening gap between American commitments and interests on the one hand and American military capabilities on the other. In November, the Joint Chiefs of Staff submitted to the National Security Council a comprehensive list of the formal and informal commitments that already had been incurred by the United States government. According to the joint chiefs, "current United States commitments involving the use or distinctly possible use of armed forces are very greatly in excess of our present ability to fulfill them either promptly or effectively." Limited capabilities meant that the use of American forces in any specific situation—for example, in Greece, Berlin, or Palestine—threatened to emasculate the nation's ability to respond elsewhere.[35]

Having Conceived of American National Security in terms of Western control and of American access to the resources of Eurasia outside the Soviet sphere, American defense officials now considered it imperative to develop American military capabilities to meet a host of contingencies that might emanate from further Soviet encroachments or from indigenous communist unrest. Such contingencies were sure to arise because American strategy depended so heavily on the rebuilding of Germany and Japan, Russia's traditional enemies, as well as on air power, atomic weapons, and bases on the Soviet periphery. Such contingencies also were predictable because American strategy depended so heavily on the restoration of stability in Eurasia, a situation increasingly unlikely in an era of nationalist turmoil, social unrest, and rising economic expectations. Although the desire of the national military establishment for large increments in defense expenditures did not prevail in the tight budgetary environment and presidential election year of 1948, the mode of thinking about national security that subsequently accelerated the arms race and precipitated military interventionism in Asia was already widespread among defense officials.

Indeed, the dynamics of the Cold War after 1948 are easier to comprehend when one grasps the breadth of the American conception of national security that had emerged between 1945 and 1948. This conception included a strategic sphere of influence within the Western Hemisphere, domination of the Atlantic and Pacific oceans, an extensive system of outlying bases to enlarge the strategic frontier and project American power, an even more extensive system of transit rights to facilitate the conversion of commercial air bases to military use, access to the resources and markets of most of Eurasia, denial of those resources to a prospective enemy, and the maintenance of nuclear superiority. Not every one of these ingredients, it must be emphasized, was considered vital. Hence, American officials could acquiesce, however grudgingly, to a Soviet sphere in Eastern Europe and could avoid direct intervention in China.

But cumulative challenges to these concepts of national security were certain to provoke a firm American response. This occurred initially in 1947–48 when decisions were made in favor of the Truman Doctrine, Marshall Plan, military assistance, Atlantic alliance, and German and Japanese rehabilitation. Soon thereafter, the "loss" of China, the Soviet detonation of an atomic bomb, and the North Korean attack on South Korea intensified the perception of threat to prevailing concepts of national security. The Truman administration responded with military assistance to southeast Asia, a decision to build the hydrogen bomb, direct military intervention in Korea, a commitment to station troops permanently in Europe, expansion of the American alliance system, and a massive rearmament program in the United States. Postulating a long-term Soviet intention to gain world domination, the American conception of national security, based on geopolitical and economic imperatives, could not allow for additional losses in Eurasia, could not risk a challenge to its nuclear supremacy, and could not permit any infringement on its ability to defend in depth or to project American force from areas in close proximity to the Soviet homeland.

To say this is neither to exculpate the Soviet government for its inhumane treatment of its own citizens nor to suggest that Soviet foreign policy was idle or benign. Indeed, Soviet behavior in Eastern Europe was often deplorable; the Soviets sought opportunities in the Dardanelles, northern Iran, and Manchuria; the Soviets hoped to orient Germany and Austria toward the East; and the Soviets sometimes endeavored to use communist parties to expand Soviet influence in areas beyond the periphery of Russian military power. But, then again, the Soviet Union had lost twenty million dead during the war, had experienced the destruction of seventeen hundred towns, thirty-one thousand factories, and one hundred thousand collective farms, and had witnessed the devastation of the rural economy with the Nazi slaughter of twenty million hogs and seventeen million head of cattle. What is remarkable is that after 1946 these monumental losses received so little attention when American defense analysts studied the motives and intentions of Soviet policy; indeed, defense officials did little to analyze the threat perceived by the Soviets. Yet these same officials had absolutely no doubt that the wartime experiences and sacrifices of the United States, though much less devastating than those of Soviet Russia, demonstrated the need for and entitled the United States to oversee the resuscitation of the industrial heartlands of Germany and Japan, establish a viable balance of power in Eurasia, and militarily dominate the Eurasian rimlands, thereby safeguarding American access to raw materials and control over all sea and air approaches to North America.

To suggest a double standard is important only insofar as it raises fundamental questions about the conceptualization and implementation of American national security policy. If Soviet policy was aggressive, bellicose, and ideological, perhaps America's reliance on overseas bases, air power, atomic weapons, military alliances, and the rehabilitation of Germany and Japan was the best course to follow, even if the effect may have been to exacerbate Soviet anxieties and suspicions. But even when one attributes the worst intentions to the Soviet Union, one might still ask whether American presuppositions and apprehensions about the benefits that would accrue to the Soviet Union as a result of Communist (and even revolutionary nationalist) gains anywhere in Eurasia tended to simplify international realities, magnify the breadth of American interests, engender commitments beyond American capabilities, and dissipate the nation's strength and credibility. And, perhaps even more importantly, if Soviet foreign policies tended to be opportunist, reactive, nationalistic, and contradictory, as some recent writers have claimed and as some contemporary analysts suggested, then one might also wonder whether America's own conception of national security tended, perhaps unintentionally, to engender anxieties and to provoke countermeasures from a proud, suspicious, insecure, and cruel government that was at the same time legitimately apprehensive about the long-term implications arising from the rehabilitation of traditional enemies and the development of foreign bases on the periphery of the Soviet homeland. To raise such issues anew seems essential if we are to unravel the complex origins of the Cold War.

NOTES

1. Kissinger, *For the Record: Selected Statements,* 1977–1980 (Boston, 1980), 123–24.
2. I use the term "defense officials" broadly in this essay to include civilian appointees and military officers in the departments of the Army, Navy, and Air Force, in the office of the secretary of defense, in the armed services, in the intelligence agencies, and on the staff of the National Security Council. While purposefully avoiding a systematic analysis of career diplomats in the Department of State, who have received much attention elsewhere, the conclusions I draw here are based on a consideration of the views of high-ranking officials in the State Department, including James F. Byrnes, Dean Acheson, George C. Marshall, and Robert Lovett.
3. For Leahy's explanation, see JCS, "Strategic Areas and Trusteeships in the Pacific," October 10, 18, 1946, RG 218, ser. CCS 360 (12-9-42), JCS 1619/15, 19; JCS, "United States Military Requirements for Air Bases," November 2, 1943; JCS, "Overall Examination of United States Requirements for Military Bases and Base Rights," October 25, 1945, *ibid.,* JCS 570/40.
4. JCS, "United States Military Requirements for Air Bases," November 2, 1943; JCS, Minutes of the 71st meeting, March 30, 1943, RG 218, ser. CCS 360 (12-9-42); Leahy, Memorandum for the President, November 15, 1943, *ibid.;* Nimitz, Memorandum, October 16, 1946, *ibid.,* JCS 1619/16; and Joint Planning Staff [hereafter, JPS], "Basis for the Formulation of a Post-War Military Policy," August 20, 1945, RG 218, ser. CCS 381 (5-13-45), JPS 633/6.
5. JCS, "Statement of Effect of Atomic Weapons on National Security and Military Organization," March 29, 1946, RG 165, ser. ABC 471.6 Atom (8–17–45), JCS 477/10. Also see JCS, "Guidance as to the Military Implications of a United Nations Commission on Atomic Energy," January 12, 1946, *ibid.,* JCS 1567/26; and JCS, "Over-All Effect of Atomic Bomb on Warfare and Military Organization," October 30, 1945, *ibid.,* JCS 1477/1.
6. JPS, "Over-All Examination of Requirements for Transit Air Bases . . . ," January 20, 1946, RG 218, ser. CCS 360 (10-9-42), JPS 781/1; and McCloy, Memorandum to the Department of State, January 31, 1945, RG 165, OPD 336 (top secret). Also see JPS, "Over-All Examination of Requirements for Transit Air Bases," January 8, 1946; and, for the joint chiefs' view on South American air fields, see JCS, Minutes of the 69th meeting, March 23, 1943, RG 218, CCS 360 (12-9-42).
7. P&O, "The Strategic Importance of Inter-American Military Cooperation" [January 20, 1947], RG 319, 092 (top secret). Also see H. A. Craig, "Summary," January 5, 1945, RG 107, Records of the Assistant Secretary of War for Air, Establishment of Air Fields and Air Bases, box 216 (Latin America); and War Department, "Comprehensive Statement" [January 1945], *ibid.*
8. JCS, "Foreign Policy of the United States," February 10, 1946, RG 218, ser. CCS 092 United States (12-21-45), JCS 1592/2; and JCS to the Secretary of the Navy and Secretary of War, September 19, 1945, *ibid.,* ser. CCS 092 (9-10-45), JCS 1507/2. For JCS views on the Western Hemisphere, also see JCS to the Secretary of the Navy and Secretary of War, February 11, 1945, *ibid.,* ser. CCS 092 (1-18-45); JCS, "International Organization for the Enforcement of World Peace and Security," April 14, 1945, *ibid.,* ser. CCS 092 (4-14-45), JCS 1311; and JCS, "Guidance as to Command and Control of the Armed Forces to be Placed at the Disposal of the Security Council of the United Nations," May 26, 1946, *ibid.,* JCS 1670/5.
9. For Patterson's views, see P&O, "Strategic Importance of Inter-American Military Cooperation" [January 20, 1947]; and Patterson to Byrnes, December 18, 1946, RG 107, RPPP, safe file, box 3.

10. This evaluation accords with the views of Chester J. Pach, Jr.; see his "The Containment of United States Military Aid to Latin America, 1944–1949," *Diplomatic History,* 6 (1982):232–34.

11. See, for example, Craig, "Summary," January 5, 1945; JPS, "Military Arrangements Deriving from the Act of Chapultepec Pertaining to Bases," January 14, 1946, RG 218, ser. CCS 092 (9-10-45), JPS 761/3; Patterson to Byrnes, December 18, 1946; and P&O, "Strategic Importance of Inter-American Military Cooperation" [January 20, 1947].

12. Minutes of the meeting of the Secretaries of State, War, and the Navy, December 18, 1946, April 23, May 1, 1947, RG 107, RPPP, safe file, box 3; and M. B. Ridgway, Memorandum for the Assistant Secretary of War, February 1947, *ibid.,* HCPP, 092 (classified).

13. Pach, "Military Aid to Latin America," 235–43.

14. Leahy, excerpt from letter, May 16, 1944, RG 59, lot 54D394 (Records of the Office of European Affairs), box 17. For Strong's opinion, see JPS, Minutes of the 199th meeting, April 25, 1945, RG 218, ser. CCS 334 (3-28-45); and, for the views of Eisenhower and Lincoln, see Lincoln, Memorandum for Hull, June 24, 1945, USMA, GLP, War Dept. files; and Leahy, Memorandum for the President [late June 1945], *ibid.*

15. For the emphasis on expediting recovery in Western Europe, see, for example, McCloy, Memorandum for Matthew J. Connelly, April 26, 1945, HTL, HSTP, PSF, box 178; and, for the role of Britain, see, for example, Joint Intelligence Staff [hereafter, JIS], "British Capabilities and Intentions," December 5, 1945, RG 218, ser. CCS 000.1 Great Britain (5-10-45), JIS 161/4.

16. See, for example, JIS, "Military Capabilities of Great Britain and France," November 13, 1945, RG 218, ser. CCS 000.1 Great Britain (5-10-45), JIS 211/1; JIS, "Areas Vital to Soviet War Effort," February 12, 1946, *ibid.,* ser. CCS 092 (3-27-45), JIS 226/2; and JIS, "Supplemental Information Relative to Northern and Western Europe," April 18, 1947, *ibid.,* JIS 275/1.

17. Strategy Section, OPD, "Post-War Base Requirements in the Philippines," April 23, 1945; JCS, "Strategic Areas and Trusteeships in the Pacific," October 18, 1946; MID, "Positive U.S. Action Required to Restore Normal Conditions in Southeast Asia," July 3, 1947, RG 319, P&O, 092 (top secret); and Lauris Norstad to the Director of Intelligence, July 10, 1947, *ibid.*

18. JLPC, "Russian Capabilities," November 15, 1945; and MID, "Intelligence Estimate of the World Situation for the Next Five Years," August 21, 1946, RG 319, P&O, 350.05 (top secret). For a contemporary analysis of the Soviet transport network, also see Paul Wohl, "Transport in the Development of Soviet Policy," *Foreign Affairs,* 24 (1946): 466–83.

19. JIS, "Soviet Post-War Military Policies and Capabilities," January 15, 1946, RG 218, ser. CCS 092 USSR (3-27-45), JIS 80/24; MID, "Ability of Potential Enemies to Attack the Continental United States," August 8, 1946; and P&O, "Estimate of the Situation Pertaining to the Northeast Approaches to the United States," August 12, 1946, RG 319, P&O, 381 (top secret).

20. MID, "Estimate of the Possibility of War between the United States and the USSR Today from a Comparison with the Situation as It Existed in September 1946," July 21, 1947, RG 319, P&O, 350.05 (top secret); and JIC, Moscow Embassy, "Soviet Intentions," April 1, 1948.

21. Acheson to Truman, April 30, 1946, RG 107, HCPP, general subject file, box 1. Also see McCloy to Patterson, November 24, 1945, *ibid.,* RPPP, safe file, box 4. For pressure on the State Department, see Patterson to Byrnes, December 10, 1945, RG 165, Civil Affairs Division [hereafter, CAD], ser. 014 Germany; Patterson to Byrnes, February 25, 1946; OPD and CAD, "Analysis of Certain Political Problems Confronting Military Occupation Authorities in Germany," April 10, 1946, RG 107, HCPP, 091 Germany (classified); and "Combined Food Board" file, spring 1946, *ibid.,* HCPP, general subject file, box 1.

22. William Draper, Memorandum [early 1947], RG 107, HCPP, 091 Germany (classified); and Forrestal to Acheson, January 14, 1946, ML, JFP, box 68. For Clay's initiative, see Smith, *Papers of General Lucius D. Clay,* 1:203–04, 213–14, 218–23; John F. Gimbel, *The American Occupation of Germany: Politics and the Military, 1945–1949* (Stanford, 1968), 35–91; John H. Backer, *The Decision to Divide Germany: American Foreign Policy in Transition* (Durham, N.C., 1978), 137–48; and Bruce Kuklick, *American Policy and the Division of Germany: The Clash with Russia over Reparations* (Ithaca,

N.Y., 1972), 205–35. For Patterson's concerns and his support of Bizonia, see Patterson to Byrnes, June 11, 1946, RG 107, HCPP, 091 Germany (classified); Patterson to Truman, November 20, 1946, *ibid.*, RPPP, safe file, box 4; Minutes of the War Council meeting, December 5, 1946, *ibid.*, box 7; and Patterson to Palmer Hoyt, December 27, 1946, *ibid.*, box 4. For the merger of the zones, also see *FRUS, 1946,* 5:579–659; Smith, *Papers of General Lucius D. Clay,* 1:245, 248–49; and, for Draper's importance, also see Carolyn Eisenberg, "U.S. Social Policy in Post-War Germany: The Conservative Restoration," paper delivered at the Seventy-Fourth Annual Meeting of the Organization of American Historians, held in April 1981, in Detroit.

23. CIA, "Review of the World Situation as It Relates to the Security of the United States," September 26, 1947. Also see, for example, JCS, "Strategic Concept and Plan for the Employment of United States Armed Forces," Appendix A, September 19, 1945; JPS, Minutes of the 249th and 250th meetings; Lincoln to Wood, May 22, 1946, RG 165, ser. ABC 381 (9-1-45); [Giffin (?)] "U.S. Policy with Respect to Russia" [early April 1946], *ibid.,* ser. ABC 336 (8-22-43); JPS, "Estimate of Probable Developments in the World Political Situation up to 1956," October 31, 1946, RG 218, ser. CCS 092 (10-9-46), JPS 814/1; MID, "World Political Developments Affecting the Security of the United States during the Next Ten Years," April 14, 1947, RG 319, P&O, 350.05 (top secret).

24. Robert L. Messer, *The End of an Alliance: James F. Byrnes, Roosevelt, Truman, and the Origins of the Cold War* (Chapel Hill, N.C., 1982), 152–94, and "Paths Not Taken," 297–319.

25. Forrestal to Clarence Dillon, April 11, 1946, ML, JFP, box 11; Hull to Theater Commanders, March 21, 1946, RG 165, ser. ABC 336 (8-22-43); for the Clifford-Elsey viewpoint, see Krock, *Memoirs: Sixty Years on the Firing Line,* 428; and SWNCC, "Resume of Soviet Capabilities and Possible Intentions," August 29, 1946, NHC, SPD, ser. 5, box 106, A8. For the SWNCC estimate, see JCS, "Political Estimate of Soviet Policy for Use in Connection with Military Studies," April 5, 1946, RG 218, ser. CCS 092 USSR (3-27-45), JCS 1641/4; and JCS "Presidential Request for Certain Facts and Information Regarding the Soviet Union," July 25, 1946. Some of the most thoughtful studies on Soviet intentions, like that of the Joint Intelligence Staff in early January 1946 (JIS 80/20), were withdrawn from consideration. See the evolution of studies and reports in RG 218, ser. CCS 092 USSR (3-27-45), sects. 5–7.

26. Both the quantity and the quality of JCS studies on Soviet intentions seem to have declined during 1946. In "Military Position of the United States in Light of Russian Policy" (January 8, 1946), strategic planners of the Joint War Plans Committee maintained that it was more important to focus on Soviet capabilities than on Soviet intentions. During a key discussion at the White House, Admiral Leahy also was eager to dismiss abstract evaluations of Russian psychology and to focus on Russian capabilities; S. W. D., Memorandum for the Record, June 12, 1946. My assessment of the quality of JCS studies is based primarily on my analysis of the materials in RG 218, ser. CCS 092 USSR (3-27-45); ser. CCS 381 USSR (3-2-46); RG 319, P&O, 350.05 (top secret); and NHC, SPD, central files, 1946–48, A8.

27. During 1946 it became a fundamental tenet of American policy makers that Soviet policy objectives were a function of developments within the Soviet Union and not related to American actions. See, for example, Kennan's "long telegram," in *FRUS, 1946,* 4:696–709; JCS, "Political Estimate of Soviet Policy," April 5, 1946; JCS, "Presidential Request," July 25, 1946; and the Clifford/Elsey memorandum, in Krock, *Memoirs,* esp. 427–36.

28. [Giffin] "U.S. Policy with Respect to Russia" [early April 1946]. Also see Giffin, Draft of Proposed Comments for Assistant Secretary of War on "Foreign Policy," [early February 1946]; MID. "Intelligence Estimate," June 25, 1946; JPS, "Estimate of Probable Developments in the World Political Situation," October 31, 1946, RG 218, ser. CCS 092 (10-9-46), JPS 814/1; Special Ad Hoc Committee of SWNCC, "Study on U.S. Assistance to France," April 9, 1947, RG 165, ser. ABC 400.336 France (3-20-47); MID, "World Political Developments," April 14, 1947; JWPC, "The Soviet Threat against the Iberian Peninsula and the Means Required to Meet It," May 8, 1947, RG 218, ser. CCS 381 USSR (3-2-46), JWPC 465/1; and CIA. "Review of the World Situation," September 26, 1947.

29. JCS, "Foreign Policy of the United States," February 10, 1946.
30. Lincoln to Hull [April 1946], RG 59, Office of European Affairs, box 17; Lincoln, Memorandum for the Record, April 16, 1946; Lincoln to Hull, April 16, 1946, RG 165, ser. ABC 092 USSR (11-15-44); Lincoln to Cohen, June 22, 1946, *ibid.*, ABC 381 (9-1-45); Richard L. Conolly, oral history (Columbia, 1960), 293–304; Lincoln, Memorandum for Chief of Staff, May 20, 1946; and Lincoln, Memorandum for Norstad, July 23, 1946, USMA, GLP, War Department files.
31. Giffin, "Draft of Proposed Comments" [early February 1946]. Also see, for example, JCS, "Foreign Policy of the United States," February 10, 1946; [Giffin] "U.S. Policy with Respect to Russia" [early April 1946]; JCS, "Political Estimate of Soviet Policy," April 5, 1946; and Sherman, Memorandum for Forrestal, March 17, 1946, ML, JFP, box 24.
32. Peterson, as quoted in Chief of Staff, Memorandum [July 1947], RG 165, ser. ABC 471.6 Atom (8-17-45). Also see, for example, Lovett diaries, December 16, 1947, January 5, 15, 1948; Baruch to Forrestal, February 7, 1948, ML, JFP, box 78; Forrestal to Baruch, February 10, 1948, *ibid.*; and Excerpt of Phone Conversation between Forrestal and C. E. Wilson, April 2, 1948, *ibid.*, box 48.
33. NCS 20/1 and 20/4 may be found in Gaddis and Etzold, *Containment*, 173–211 (the quotations appear on page 208). Also see *FRUS, 1948*, 1:589–93, 599–601, 609–11, 615–24, 662–69.
34. Gaddis and Etzold, *Containment*, 209–10.
35. For the position of the JCS, see NSC 35, "Existing International Commitments," November 17, 1948, *FRUS, 1948*, 1:656–62. For Forrestal's view, see *ibid.*, 644–46. For background, see William A. Knowlton, Memorandum for the Chief of Staff, October 21, 1948, RG 319, P&O, 092 (top secret); for the reference to Greece, see JCS, "The Position of the United States with Respect to Greece," April 13, 1948, RG 218, ser. CCS 092 Greece (12-30-47), JCS 1826/8.

$$\mathcal{S}$$

Power and Weakness: Why the United States and Europe See the World Differently

Robert Kagan

It is time to stop pretending that Europeans and Americans share a common view of the world, or even that they occupy the same world. On the all-important question of power—the efficacy of power, the morality of power, the desirability of power—American and European perspectives are diverging. Europe is turning away from power, or to put it a little differently, it is moving beyond power into a self-contained world of laws and rules and transnational negotiation and cooperation. It is entering a post-historical paradise of peace and relative prosperity, the realization of Kant's "Perpetual Peace." The United States, meanwhile, remains mired in history, exercising power in the anarchic Hobbesian world where international laws and rules are unreliable and where true security and the defense

Robert Kagan, "Power and Weakness," *Policy Review*, June/July 2002. Reprinted by permission.

and promotion of a liberal order still depend on the possession and use of military might. That is why on major strategic and international questions today, Americans are from Mars and Europeans are from Venus: They agree on little and understand one another less and less. And this state of affairs is not transitory—the product of one American election or one catastrophic event. The reasons for the transatlantic divide are deep, long in development, and likely to endure. When it comes to setting national priorities, determining threats, defining challenges, and fashioning and implementing foreign and defense policies, the United States and Europe have parted ways.

It is easier to see the contrast as an American living in Europe. Europeans are more conscious of the growing differences, perhaps because they fear them more. European intellectuals are nearly unanimous in the conviction that Americans and Europeans no longer share a common "strategic culture." The European caricature at its most extreme depicts an America dominated by a "culture of death," its warlike temperament the natural product of a violent society where every man has a gun and the death penalty reigns. But even those who do not make this crude link agree there are profound differences in the way the United States and Europe conduct foreign policy.

The United States, they argue, resorts to force more quickly and, compared with Europe, is less patient with diplomacy. Americans generally see the world divided between good and evil, between friends and enemies, while Europeans see a more complex picture. When confronting real or potential adversaries, Americans generally favor policies of coercion rather than persuasion, emphasizing punitive sanctions over inducements to better behavior, the stick over the carrot. Americans tend to seek finality in international affairs: They want problems solved, threats eliminated. And, of course, Americans increasingly tend toward unilateralism in international affairs. They are less inclined to act through international institutions such as the United Nations, less inclined to work cooperatively with other nations to pursue common goals, more skeptical about international law, and more willing to operate outside its strictures when they deem it necessary, or even merely useful.[1]

Europeans insist they approach problems with greater nuance and sophistication. They try to influence others through subtlety and indirection. They are more tolerant of failure, more patient when solutions don't come quickly. They generally favor peaceful responses to problems, preferring negotiation, diplomacy, and persuasion to coercion. They are quicker to appeal to international law, international conventions, and international opinion to adjudicate disputes. They try to use commercial and economic ties to bind nations together. They often emphasize process over result, believing that ultimately process can become substance.

This European dual portrait is a caricature, of course, with its share of exaggerations and oversimplifications. One cannot generalize about Europeans: Britons may have a more "American" view of power than many of their fellow Europeans on the continent. And there are differing perspectives within nations on both sides of the Atlantic. In the U.S., Democrats often seem more "European" than Republicans; Secretary of State Colin Powell may appear more "European" than Secretary of Defense Donald Rumsfeld. Many Americans, especially among the intellectual elite, are as uncomfortable with the "hard" quality of American foreign policy as any European; and some Europeans value power as much as any American.

Nevertheless, the caricatures do capture an essential truth: The United States and Europe are fundamentally different today. Powell and Rumsfeld have more in common than do Powell and Hubert Védrine or even Jack Straw. When it comes to the use of force, mainstream American Democrats have more in common with Republicans than they do with most

European Socialists and Social Democrats. During the 1990s even American liberals were more willing to resort to force and were more Manichean in their perception of the world than most of their European counterparts. The Clinton administration bombed Iraq, as well as Afghanistan and Sudan. European governments, it is safe to say, would not have done so. Whether they would have bombed even Belgrade in 1999, had the U.S. not forced their hand, is an interesting question.[2]

What is the source of these differing strategic perspectives? The question has received too little attention in recent years, either because foreign policy intellectuals and policymakers on both sides of the Atlantic have denied the existence of a genuine difference or because those who have pointed to the difference, especially in Europe, have been more interested in assailing the United States than in understanding why the United States acts as it does—or, for that matter, why Europe acts as it does. It is past time to move beyond the denial and the insults and to face the problem head-on.

Despite what many Europeans and some Americans believe, these differences in strategic culture do not spring naturally from the national characters of Americans and Europeans. After all, what Europeans now consider their more peaceful strategic culture is, historically speaking, quite new. It represents an evolution away from the very different strategic culture that dominated Europe for hundreds of years and at least until World War I. The European governments—and peoples—who enthusiastically launched themselves into that continental war believed in *machtpolitik*. While the roots of the present European worldview, like the roots of the European Union itself, can be traced back to the Enlightenment, Europe's great-power politics for the past 300 years did not follow the visionary designs of the philosophies and the physiocrats.

As for the United States, there is nothing timeless about the present heavy reliance on force as a tool of international relations, nor about the tilt toward unilateralism and away from a devotion to international law. Americans are children of the Enlightenment, too, and in the early years of the republic were more faithful apostles of its creed. America's eighteenth - and early nineteenth-century statesmen sounded much like the European statesmen of today, extolling the virtues of commerce as the soothing balm of international strife and appealing to international law and international opinion over brute force. The young United States wielded power against weaker peoples on the North American continent, but when it came to dealing with the European giants, it claimed to abjure power and assailed as atavistic the power politics of the eighteenth- and nineteenth-century European empires.

Two centuries later, Americans and Europeans have traded places—and perspectives. Partly this is because in those 200 years, but especially in recent decades, the power equation has shifted dramatically: When the United States was weak, it practiced the strategies of indirection, the strategies of weakness; now that the United States is powerful, it behaves as powerful nations do. When the European great powers were strong, they believed in strength and martial glory. Now, they see the world through the eyes of weaker powers. These very different points of view, weak versus strong, have naturally produced differing strategic judgments, differing assessments of threats and of the proper means of addressing threats, and even differing calculations of interest.

But this is only part; of the answer. For along with these natural consequences of the transatlantic power gap, there has also opened a broad ideological gap. Europe, because of its unique historical experience of the past half-century—culminating in the past decade with the creation of the European Union—has developed a set of ideals and principles regarding the utility and morality of power different from the ideals and principles of Americans, who have not shared that experience. If the strategic chasm between the United States and Europe appears greater than ever today, and grows still wider at a worrying pace, it is because these material and ideological differences reinforce one another. The divisive trend they together produce may be impossible to reverse.

THE POWER GAP: PERCEPTION AND REALITY

Europe has been militarily weak for a long time, but until fairly recently its weakness had been obscured. World War II all but destroyed European nations as global powers, and their postwar inability to project sufficient force overseas to maintain colonial empires in Asia, Africa, and the Middle East forced them to retreat on a massive scale after more than five centuries of imperial dominance—perhaps the most significant retrenchment of global influence in human history. For a half-century after World War II, however, this weakness was masked by the unique geopolitical circumstances of the Cold War. Dwarfed by the two superpowers on its flanks, a weakened Europe nevertheless served as the central strategic theater of the world-wide struggle between communism and democratic capitalism. Its sole but vital strategic mission was to defend its own territory against any Soviet offensive, at least until the Americans arrived. Although shorn of most traditional measures of great-power status, Europe remained the geopolitical pivot, and this, along with lingering habits of world leadership, allowed Europeans to retain international influence well beyond what their sheer military capabilities might have afforded.

Europe lost this strategic centrality after the Cold War ended, but it took a few more years for the lingering mirage of European global power to fade. During the 1990s, war in the Balkans kept both Europeans and Americans focused on the strategic importance of the continent and on the continuing relevance of NATO. The enlargement of NATO to include former Warsaw Pact nations and the consolidation of the Cold War victory kept Europe in the forefront of the strategic discussion.

Then there was the early promise of the "new Europe." By bonding together into a single political and economic unit—the historic accomplishment of the Maastricht treaty in 1992—Many hoped to recapture Europe's old greatness but in a new political form. "Europe" would be the next superpower, not only economically and politically, but also militarily. It would handle crises on the European continent, such as the ethnic conflicts in the Balkans, and it would re-emerge as a global player. In the 1990s Europeans could confidently assert that the power of a unified Europe would restore, finally, the global "multipolarity" that had been destroyed by the Cold War and its aftermath. And most Americans, with mixed emotions, agreed that superpower Europe was the future. Harvard University's Samuel P. Huntington predicted that the coalescing of the European Union would be "the single most important move" in a worldwide reaction against American hegemony and would produce a "truly multipolar" twenty-first century.[3]

But European pretensions and American apprehensions proved unfounded. The 1990s witnessed not the rise of a European superpower but the decline of Europe into relative weakness. The Balkan conflict at the beginning of the decade revealed European military incapacity and political disarray; the Kosovo conflict at decade's end exposed a transatlantic gap in military technology and the ability to wage modern warfare that would only widen in subsequent years. Outside of Europe, the disparity by the close of the 1990s was even more starkly apparent as it became clear that the ability of European powers, individually or collectively, to project decisive force into regions of conflict beyond the continent was negligible. Europeans could provide peacekeeping forces in the Balkans—indeed, they could and eventually did provide the vast bulk of those forces in Bosnia and Kosovo. But they lacked the wherewithal to introduce and sustain a fighting force in potentially hostile territory, even in Europe. Under the best of circumstances, the European role was limited to filling out peacekeeping forces after the United States had, largely on its own, carried out the decisive phases of a military mission and stabilized the situation. As some Europeans put it, the real division of labor consisted of the United States "making the dinner" and the Europeans "doing the dishes."

This inadequacy should have come as no surprise, since these were the limitations that had forced Europe to retract its global influence in the first place. Those Americans and Europeans who proposed that Europe expand its strategic role beyond the continent set an unreasonable goal. During the Cold War, Europe's strategic role had been to defend itself. It was unrealistic to expect a return to international great-power status, unless European peoples were willing to shift significant resources from social programs to military programs.

Clearly they were not. Not only were Europeans unwilling to pay to project force beyond Europe. After the Cold War, they would not pay for sufficient force to conduct even minor military actions on the continent without American help. Nor did it seem to matter whether European publics were being asked to spend money to strengthen NATO or an independent European foreign and defense policy. Their answer was the same. Rather than viewing the collapse of the Soviet Union as an opportunity to flex global muscles, Europeans took it as an opportunity to cash in on a sizable peace dividend. Average European defense budgets gradually fell below 2 percent of GDP. Despite talk of establishing Europe as a global superpower, therefore, European military capabilities steadily fell behind those of the United States throughout the 1990s.

The end of the Cold War had a very different effect on the other side of the Atlantic. For although Americans looked for a peace dividend, too, and defense budgets declined or remained flat during most of the 1990s, defense spending still remained above 3 percent of GDP. Fast on the heels of the Soviet empire's demise came Iraq's invasion of Kuwait and the largest American military action in a quarter-century. Thereafter American administrations cut the Cold War force, but not as dramatically as might have been expected. By historical standards, America's military power and particularly its ability to project that power to all corners of the globe remained unprecedented.

Meanwhile, the very fact of the Soviet empire's collapse vastly increased America's strength relative to the rest of the world. The sizable American military arsenal, once barely sufficient to balance Soviet power, was now deployed in a world without a single formidable adversary. This "unipolar moment" had an entirely natural and predictable consequence: It made the United States more willing to use force abroad. With the, check of Soviet power removed, the United States was free to intervene practically wherever and whenever it chose—a fact reflected in the proliferation of overseas military interventions that began during the first Bush administration with the invasion of Panama in 1989, the Persian Gulf War in 1991, and the humanitarian intervention in Somalia in 1992, continuing during the Clinton years with interventions in Haiti, Bosnia, and Kosovo. While American politicians talked of pulling back from the world, the reality was an America intervening abroad more frequently than it had throughout most of the Cold War. Thanks to new technologies, the United States was also freer to use force around the world in more limited ways through air and missile strikes, which it did with increasing frequency.

How could this growing transatlantic power gap fail to create a difference in strategic perceptions? Even during the Cold War, American military predominance and Europe's relative weakness had produced important and sometimes serious disagreements. Gaullism, *Ostpolitik,* and the various movements for European independence and unity were manifestations not only of a European desire for honor and freedom of action. They also reflected a European conviction that America's approach to the Cold War was too confrontational, too militaristic, and too dangerous. Europeans believed they knew better how to deal with the Soviets: through engagement and seduction, through commercial and political ties, through patience and forbearance. It was a legitimate view, shared by many Americans. But it also reflected Europe's weakness relative to the United States, the fewer military options at Europe's disposal, and its greater vulnerability to a powerful Soviet Union. It may have reflected, too, Europe's memory of continental war. Americans, when they were not themselves engaged in the subtleties of detente, viewed the European approach as a form of appeasement, a return to the fearful mentality of the 1930s. But appeasement is never a dirty word to those whose genuine weakness offers few appealing alternatives. For them, it is a policy of sophistication.

The end of the Cold War, by widening the power gap, exacerbated the disagreements. Although transatlantic tensions are now widely assumed to have begun with the inauguration of George W. Bush in January 2001, they were already evident during the Clinton administration and may even be traced back to the administration of George H. W. Bush. By 1992, mutual recriminations were rife over Bosnia, where the United States refused to act and Europe could not act. It was during the Clinton years that Europeans began complaining about being lectured by the "hectoring hegemon." This was also the period in which Védrine coined the term *hyperpuissance* to describe an American behemoth too worryingly powerful to be designated merely a superpower. (Perhaps he was responding to then-Secretary of State Madeleine Albright's insistence that the United States was the world's "indispensable nation.") It was also during the 1990s that the transatlantic disagreement over American plans for missile defense emerged and many Europeans began grumbling about the American propensity to choose force and punishment over diplomacy and persuasion.

The Clinton administration, meanwhile, though relatively timid and restrained itself, grew angry and impatient with European timidity, especially the unwillingness to confront Saddam Hussein. The split in the alliance over Iraq didn't begin with the 2000 election but in 1997, when the Clinton administration tried to increase the pressure on Baghdad and found itself at odds with France and (to a lesser extent) Great Britain in the United Nations Security Council. Even the war in Kosovo was marked by nervousness among some allies— especially Italy, Greece, and Germany—that the United States was too uncompromisingly militaristic in its approach. And while Europeans and Americans ultimately stood together in the confrontation with Belgrade, the Kosovo war produced in Europe less satisfaction at the successful prosecution of the war than unease at America's apparent omnipotence. That apprehension would only increase in the wake of American military action after September 11, 2001.

THE PSYCHOLOGY OF POWER AND WEAKNESS

Today's transatlantic problem, in short, is not a George Bush problem. It is a power problem. American military strength has produced a propensity to use that strength. Europe's military weakness has produced a perfectly understandable aversion to the exercise of military power. Indeed, it has produced a powerful European interest in inhabiting a world where strength doesn't matter, where international law and international institutions predominate, where unilateral action by powerful nations is forbidden, where all nations regardless of their strength have equal rights and are equally protected by commonly agreed-upon international rules of behavior. Europeans have a deep interest in devaluing and eventually eradicating the brutal laws of an anarchic, Hobbesian world where power is the ultimate determinant of national security and success.

This is no reproach. It is what weaker powers have wanted from time immemorial. It was what Americans wanted in the eighteenth and early nineteenth centuries, when the brutality of a European system of power politics run by the global giants of France, Britain, and Russia left Americans constantly vulnerable to imperial thrashing. It was what the other small powers of Europe wanted in those years, too, only to be sneered at by Bourbon kings and other powerful monarchs, who spoke instead of *raison d'état*. The great proponent of international law on the high seas in the eighteenth century was the United States; the great opponent was Britain's navy, the "Mistress of the Seas." In an anarchic world, small powers always fear they will be victims. Great powers, on the other hand, often fear rules that may constrain them more than they fear the anarchy in which their power brings security and prosperity.

This natural and historic disagreement between the stronger and the weaker manifests itself in today's transatlantic dispute over the question of unilateralism. Europeans generally believe their objection to American unilateralism is proof of their greater commitment to certain ideals concerning world order. They are less willing to acknowledge that their hostility to unilateralism is also self-interested. Europeans fear American unilateralism. They fear it perpetuates a Hobbesian world in which they may become increasingly vulnerable. The United States may be a relatively benign hegemon, but insofar as its actions delay the arrival of a world order more conducive to the safety of weaker powers, it is objectively dangerous.

This is one reason why in recent years a principal objective of European foreign policy has become, as one European observer puts it, the "multilateralising" of the United States.[4] It is not that Europeans are teaming up against the American hegemon, as Huntington and many realist theorists would have it, by creating a countervailing power. After all, Europeans are not increasing their power. Their tactics, like their goal, are the tactics of the weak. They hope to constrain American power without wielding power themselves. In what may be the ultimate feat of subtlety and indirection, they want to control the behemoth by appealing to its conscience.

It is a sound strategy, as far as it goes. The United States *is* a behemoth with a conscience. It is not Louis XIV's France or George III's England. Americans do not argue, even to themselves, that their actions may be justified by *raison d'état*. Americans have never accepted the principles of Europe's old order, never embraced the Machiavellian perspective. The United States is a liberal, progressive society through and through, and to the extent that Americans believe in power, they believe it must be a means of advancing the principles of a liberal civilization and a liberal world order. Americans even share Europe's aspirations for a more orderly world system based not on power but on rules—after all, they were striving for such a world when Europeans were still extolling the laws of *machtpolitik*.

But while these common ideals and aspirations shape foreign policies on both sides of the Atlantic, they cannot completely negate the very different perspectives from which Europeans and Americans view the world and the role of power in international affairs. Europeans oppose unilateralism in part because they have no capacity for unilateralism. Polls consistently show that Americans support multilateral action in principle—they even support acting under the rubric of the United Nations—but the fact remains that the United States can act unilaterally, and has done so many times with reasonable success. For Europeans, the appeal to multilateralism and international law has a real practical payoff and little cost. For Americans, who stand to lose at least some freedom of action, support for universal rules of behavior really is a matter of idealism.

Even when Americans and Europeans can agree on the kind of world order they would strive to build, however, they increasingly disagree about what constitutes a threat to that international endeavor. Indeed, Europeans and Americans differ most these days in their evaluation of what constitutes a tolerable versus an intolerable threat. This, too, is consistent with the disparity of power.

Europeans often argue that Americans have an unreasonable demand for "perfect" security, the product of living for centuries shielded behind two oceans.[5] Europeans claim they know what it is like to live with danger, to exist side-by-side with evil, since they've done it for centuries. Hence their greater tolerance for such threats as may be posed by Saddam Hussein's Iraq or the ayatollahs' Iran. Americans, they claim, make far too much of the dangers these regimes pose.

Even before September 11, this argument rang a bit hollow. The United States in its formative decades lived in a state of substantial insecurity, surrounded by hostile European empires, at constant risk of being torn apart by centrifugal forces that were encouraged by threats from without: National insecurity formed the core of Washington's Farewell Address. As for the Europeans' supposed tolerance for insecurity and evil, it can be overstated. For the better part of three centuries, European Catholics and Protestants more often preferred to kill than to tolerate each other; nor have the past two centuries shown all that much mutual tolerance between Frenchmen and Germans.

Some Europeans argue that precisely because Europe has suffered so much, it has a higher tolerance for suffering than America and therefore a higher tolerance for threats. More likely the opposite is true. The memory of their horrendous suffering in World War I made the British and French publics more fearful of Nazi Germany, not more tolerant, and this attitude contributed significantly to the appeasement of the 1930s.

A better explanation of Europe's greater tolerance for threats is, once again, Europe's relative weakness. Tolerance is also very much a realistic response in that Europe, precisely because it is weak, actually faces fewer threats than the far more powerful United States.

The psychology of weakness is easy enough to understand. A man armed only with a knife may decide that a bear prowling the forest is a tolerable danger, inasmuch as the alternative—hunting the bear armed only with a knife—is actually riskier than lying low and hoping the bear never attacks. The same man armed with a rifle, however, will likely make a different calculation of what constitutes a tolerable risk. Why should he risk being mauled to death if he doesn't need to?

This perfectly normal human psychology is helping to drive a wedge between the United States and Europe today. Europeans have concluded, reasonably enough, that the threat posed by Saddam Hussein is more tolerable for them than the risk of removing him. But Americans, being stronger, have reasonably enough developed a lower threshold of tolerance for Saddam and his weapons of mass destruction, especially after September 11. Europeans like to say that Americans are obsessed with fixing problems, but it is generally true that those with a greater capacity to fix problems are more likely to try to fix them than those who have no such capability. Americans can imagine successfully invading Iraq and toppling Saddam, and therefore more than 70 percent of Americans apparently favor such action. Europeans, not surprisingly, find the prospect both unimaginable and frightening.

The incapacity to respond to threats leads not only to tolerance but sometimes to denial. It's normal to try to put out of one's mind that which one can do nothing about. According to one student of European opinion, even the very focus on "threats" differentiates American policymakers from their European counterparts. Americans, writes Steven Everts, talk about foreign "threats" such as "the proliferation of weapons of mass destruction, terrorism, and 'rogue states.'" But Europeans look at "challenges," such as "ethnic conflict, migration, organized crime, poverty, and environmental degradation." As Everts notes, however, the key difference is less a matter of culture and philosophy than of capability. Europeans "are most worried about issues . . . that have a greater change of being solved by political engagement and huge sums of money." In other words, Europeans focus on issues—"challenges"—where European strengths come into play but not on those "threats" where European weakness makes solutions elusive. If Europe's strategic culture today places less value on power and military strength and more value on such soft-power tools as economics and trade, isn't it partly because Europe is militarily weak and economically strong? Americans are quicker to acknowledge the existence of threats, even to perceive them where others may not see any, because they can conceive of doing something to meet those threats.

The differing threat perceptions in the United States and Europe are not just matters of psychology, however. They are also grounded in a practical reality that is another product of the disparity of power. For Iraq and other "rogue" states objectively do *not* pose the same level of threat to Europeans as they do to the United States. There is, first of all, the American security guarantee that Europeans enjoy and have enjoyed for six decades, ever since the United States took upon itself the burden of maintaining order in far-flung regions of the world—from the Korean Peninsula to the Persian Gulf—from which European power had largely withdrawn. Europeans generally believe, whether or not they admit it to themselves, that were Iraq ever to emerge as a real and present danger, as opposed to merely a potential danger, then the United States would do something about it—as it did in 1991. If during the Cold War Europe by necessity made a major contribution to its own defense, today Europeans enjoy an unparalleled measure of "free security" because most of the likely threats are in regions outside Europe, where only the United States can project effective force. In a very practical sense—that is, when it comes to actual strategic planning—neither Iraq nor Iran nor North Korea nor any other "rogue" state in the world is primarily a European problem. Nor, certainly, is China. Both Europeans and Americans agree that these are primarily American problems.

In the Persian Gulf, in the Middle East, and in most other regions of the world (including Europe), the United States plays the role of ultimate enforcer. "You are so powerful," Europeans often say to Americans. "So why do you feel so threatened?" But it is precisely America's great power that makes it the primary target, and often the only target. Europeans are understandably content that it should remain so.

Americans are "cowboys," Europeans love to say. And there is truth in this. The United States does act as an international sheriff, self-appointed perhaps but widely welcomed nevertheless, trying to enforce some peace and justice in what Americans see as a lawless world where outlaws need to be deterred or destroyed, and often through the muzzle of a gun. Europe, by this old West analogy, is more like a saloonkeeper. Outlaws shoot sheriffs, not saloonkeepers. In fact, from the saloonkeeper's point of view, the sheriff trying to impose order by force can sometimes be more threatening than the outlaws who, at least for the time being, may just want a drink.

When Europeans took to the streets by the millions after September 11, most Americans believed it was out of a sense of shared danger and common interest: The Europeans knew they could be next. But Europeans by and large did not feel that way and still don't. Europeans do not really believe they are next. They may be secondary targets—because they are allied with the U.S.—but they are not the primary target, because they no longer play the imperial role in the Middle East that might have engendered the same antagonism against them as is aimed at the United States. When Europeans wept and waved American flags after September 11, it was out of genuine human sympathy, sorrow, and affection for Americans. For better or for worse, European displays of solidarity were a product more of fellow-feeling than self-interest.

THE ORIGINS OF MODERN EUROPEAN FOREIGN POLICY

Important as the power gap may be in shaping the respective strategic cultures of the United States and Europe, it is only one part of the story. Europe in the past half-century has developed a genuinely different perspective on the role of power in international relations, a perspective that springs directly from its unique historical experience since the end of World War II. It is a perspective that Americans do not share and cannot share, inasmuch as the formative historical experiences on their side of the Atlantic have not been the same.

Consider again the qualities that make up the European strategic culture: the emphasis on negotiation, diplomacy, and commercial ties, on international law over the use of force, on seduction over coercion, on multilateralism over unilateralism. It is true that these are not traditionally European approaches to international relations when viewed from a long historical perspective. But they are a product of more recent European history. The modern European strategic culture represents a conscious rejection of the European past, a rejection of the evils of European *machtpolitik*. It is a reflection of Europeans' ardent and understandable desire never to return to that past. Who knows better than Europeans the dangers that arise from unbridled power politics, from an excessive reliance on military force, from policies produced by national egoism and ambition, even from balance of power and *raison d'état*? As German Foreign Minister Joschka Fischer put it in a speech outlining his vision of the European future at Humboldt University in Berlin (May 12, 2000), "The core of the concept of Europe after 1945 was and still is a rejection of the European balance-of-power principle and the hegemonic ambitions of individual states that had emerged following the Peace of Westphalia in 1648." The European Union is itself the product of an awful century of European warfare.

Of course, it was the "hegemonic ambitions" of one nation in particular that European integration was, meant to contain. And it is the integration and taming of Germany that is the great accomplishment of Europe—viewed historically, perhaps the greatest feat of international politics ever achieved. Some Europeans recall, as Fischer does, the central role played by the United States in solving the "German problem." Fewer like to recall that the military destruction of Nazi Germany was the prerequisite for the European peace that followed. Most Europeans believe that it was the transformation of European politics, the deliberate abandonment and rejection of centuries of *machtpolitik*, that in the end made possible the "new order." The Europeans, who invented power politics, turned themselves into born-again idealists by an act of will, leaving behind them what Fischer called "the old system of balance with its continued national orientation, constraints of coalition, traditional interest-led politics and the permanent danger of nationalist ideologies and confrontations."

Fischer stands near one end of the spectrum of European idealism. But this is not really a right-left issue in Europe. Fischer's principal contention—that Europe has moved beyond the old system of power politics and discovered a new system for preserving peace in international relations—is widely shared across Europe. As senior British diplomat Robert Cooper recently wrote in the *Observer* (April 7, 2002), Europe today lives in a "postmodern system" that does not rest on a balance of power but on "the rejection of force" and on "self-enforced rules of behavior." In the "postmodern world," writes Cooper, *"raison d'état* and the amorality of Machiavelli's theories of statecraft . . . have been replaced by a moral consciousness" in international affairs.

American realists might scoff at this idealism. George F. Kennan assumed only his naive fellow Americans succumbed to such "Wilsonian" legalistic and moralistic fancies, not those war-tested, historically minded European Machiavels. But, really, why shouldn't Europeans be idealistic about international affairs, at least as they are conducted in Europe's "postmodern system"? Within the confines of Europe, the age-old laws of international relations have been repealed. Europeans have stepped out of the Hobbesian world of anarchy into the Kantian world of perpetual peace. European life during the more than five decades since the end of World War II has been shaped not by the brutal laws of power politics but by the unfolding of a geopolitical fantasy, a miracle of world-historical importance: The German lion has laid down with the French lamb. The conflict that ravaged Europe ever since the violent birth of Germany in the nineteenth century has been put to rest.

The means by which this miracle has been achieved have understandably acquired something of a sacred mystique for Europeans, especially since the end of the Cold War. Diplomacy, negotiations, patience, the forging of economic ties, political engagement, the use of inducements rather than sanctions, the taking of small steps and tempering ambitions for success—these were the tools of Franco-German rapprochement and hence the tools that made European integration possible. Integration was not to be based on military deterrence or the balance of power. Quite the contrary. The miracle came from the rejection of military power and of its utility as an instrument of international affairs—at least within the confines of Europe. During the Cold War, few Europeans doubted the need for military power to deter the Soviet Union. But within Europe the rules were different.

Collective security was provided from without, meanwhile, by the *deus ex machina* of the United States operating through the military structures of NATO. Within this wall of security, Europeans pursued their new order, freed from the brutal laws and even the mentality of power politics. This evolution from the old to the new began in Europe during the Cold War. But the end of the Cold War, by removing even the external danger of the Soviet Union, allowed Europe's new order, and its new idealism, to blossom fully. Freed from the requirements of any military deterrence, internal or external, Europeans became still more confident that their way of settling international problems now had universal application.

"The genius of the founding fathers," European Commission President Romano Prodi commented in a speech at the Institute d'Etudes Politiques in Paris (May 29, 2001), "lay in translating extremely high political ambitions . . . into a series of more specific, almost technical decisions. This indirect approach made further action possible. Rapprochement took place gradually. From confrontation we moved to willingness to cooperate in the economic sphere and then on to integration." This is what many Europeans believe they have to offer the world: not power, but the transcendence of power. The "essence" of the European Union, writes Everts, is "all about subjecting inter-state relations to the rule of law," and Europe's experience of successful multilateral governance has in turn produced an ambition to convert the world. Europe "has a role to play in world 'governance,'" says Prodi, a role based on replicating the European experience on a global scale. In Europe "the rule of law has replaced the crude interplay of power . . . power politics have lost their influence." And by "making a success of integration we are demonstrating to the world that it is possible to create a method for peace."

No doubt there are Britons, Germans, French, and others who would frown on such exuberant idealism. But many Europeans, including many in positions of power, routinely apply Europe's experience to the rest of the world. For is not the general European critique of the American approach to "rogue" regimes based on this special European insight? Iraq, Iran, North Korea, Libya—these states may be dangerous and unpleasant, even evil. But might not an "indirect approach" work again, as it did in Europe? Might it not be possible once more to move from confrontation to rapprochement, beginning with cooperation in the economic sphere and then moving on to peaceful integration? Could not the formula that worked in Europe work again with Iran or even Iraq? A great many Europeans insist that it can.

The transmission of the European miracle to the rest of the world has become Europe's new *mission civilisatrice*. Just as Americans have always believed that they had discovered the secret to human happiness and wished to export it to the rest of the world, so the Europeans have a new mission born of their own discovery of perpetual peace.

Thus we arrive at what may be the most important reason for the divergence in views between Europe and the United States. America's power, and its willingness to exercise that power—unilaterally if necessary—represents a threat to Europe's new sense of mission. Perhaps the greatest threat. American policymakers find It hard to believe, but leading officials and politicians in Europe worry more about how the United States might handle or mishandle the problem of Iraq—by undertaking unilateral and extralegal military action— than they worry about Iraq itself and Saddam Hussein's weapons of mass destruction. And while it is true that they fear such action might destabilize the Middle East and lead to the unnecessary loss of life, there is a deeper concern.[6] Such American action represents an assault on the essence of "postmodern" Europe. It is an assault on Europe's new ideals, a denial of their universal validity, much as the monarchies of eighteenth- and nineteenth-century Europe were an assault on American republican ideals. Americans ought to be the first to understand that a threat to one's beliefs can be as frightening as a threat to one's physical security.

As Americans have for two centuries, Europeans speak with great confidence of the superiority of their global understanding, the wisdom they have to offer other nations about conflict resolution, and their way of addressing international problems. But just as in the first decade of the American republic, there is a hint of insecurity in the European claim to "success," an evident need to have their success affirmed and their views accepted by other nations, particularly by the mighty United States. After all, to deny the validity of the new European idealism is to raise profound doubts about the viability of the European project. If international problems cannot, in fact, be settled the European way, wouldn't that suggest that Europe itself may eventually fall short of a solution, with all the horrors this implies?

And, of course, it is precisely this fear that still hangs over Europeans, even as Europe moves forward. Europeans, and particularly the French and Germans, are not entirely sure that the problem once known as the "German problem" really has been solved. As their various and often very different proposals for the future constitution of Europe suggest, the French are still not confident they can trust the Germans, and the Germans are still not sure they can trust themselves. This fear can at times hinder progress toward deeper integration, but it also propels the European project forward despite innumerable obstacles. The European project must succeed, for how else to overcome what Fischer, in his Humboldt University speech, called "the risks and temptations objectively inherent in Germany's dimensions and central situation"? Those historic German "temptations" play at the back of many a European mind. And every time Europe contemplates the use of military force, or is forced to do so by the United States, there is no avoiding at least momentary consideration of what effect such a military action might have on the "German question."

Perhaps it is not just coincidence that the amazing progress toward European integration in recent years has been accompanied not by the emergence of a European superpower but, on the contrary, by a diminishing of European military capabilities relative to the United States. Turning Europe into a global superpower capable of balancing the power of the United States may have been one of the original selling points of the European Union—an independent European foreign and defense policy was supposed to be one of the most important byproducts of European integration. But, in truth, the ambition for European "power" is something of an anachronism. It is an atavistic impulse, inconsistent with the ideals of postmodern Europe, whose very existence depends on the rejection of power politics. Whatever its architects may have intended, European integration has proved to be the enemy of European military power and, indeed, of an important European global role.

This phenomenon has manifested itself not only in flat or declining European defense budgets, but in other ways, too, even in the realm of "soft" power. European leaders talk of Europe's essential role in the world. Prodi yearns "to make our voice heard, to make our actions count." And it is true that Europeans spend a great deal of money on foreign aid— more per capita, they like to point out, than does the United States. Europeans engage in overseas military missions, so long as the missions are mostly limited to peacekeeping. But while the EU periodically dips its fingers into troubled international waters in the Middle East or the Korean Peninsula, the truth is that EU foreign policy is probably the most anemic of all the products of European integration. As Charles Grant, a sympathetic observer of the EU, recently noted, few European leaders "are giving it much time or energy."[7] EU foreign policy initiatives tend to be short-lived and are rarely backed by sustained agreement on the part of the various European powers. That is one reason they are so easily rebuffed, as was the case in March 2002 when Israeli Prime Minister Ariel Sharon blocked EU foreign policy chief Javier Solana from meeting with Yasser Arafat (only to turn around the next day and allow a much lower-ranking American negotiator to meet with the Palestinian leader).

It is obvious, moreover, that issues outside of Europe don't attract nearly as much interest among Europeans as purely European issues do. This has surprised and frustrated Americans on all sides of the political and strategic debate: Recall the profound disappointment of American liberals when Europeans failed to mount an effective protest against Bush's withdrawal from the ABM treaty. But given the enormous and difficult agenda of integration, this European tendency to look inward is understandable. EU enlargement, the revision of the common economic and agricultural policies, the question of national sovereignty versus supranational governance, the so-called democracy deficit, the jostling of the large European powers, the dissatisfaction of the smaller powers, the establishment of a new European constitution—all of these present serious and unavoidable challenges. The difficulties of moving forward might seem insuperable were it not for the progress the project of European integration has already demonstrated.

American policies that are unwelcome on substance—on a missile defense system and the ABM treaty, belligerence toward Iraq, support for Israel—are all the more unwelcome because for Europe, they are a distraction. Europeans often point to American insularity and parochialism. But Europeans themselves have turned intensely introspective. As Dominique Moisi noted in the *Financial Times* (March 11, 2002), the recent French presidential campaign saw "no reference . . . to the events of September 11 and their far-reaching consequences." No one asked, "What should be the role of France and Europe in the new configuration of forces created after September 11? How should France reappraise its military budget and doctrine to take account of the need to maintain some kind; of parity between Europe and the United States, or at least between France and the UK?" The Middle East conflict became an issue in the campaign because of France's large Arab and Muslim population, as the high vote for Le Pen demonstrated. But Le Pen is not a foreign policy hawk. And as Moisi noted, "for most French voters in 2002, security has little to do with abstract and distant geopolitics. Rather, it is a question of which politician can best protect them from the crime and violence plaguing the streets and suburbs of their cities."

Can Europe change course and assume a larger role on the world stage? There has been no shortage of European leaders urging it to do so. Nor is the weakness of EU foreign policy today necessarily proof that it must be weak tomorrow, given the EU's record of overcoming weaknesses in other areas. And yet the political will to demand more power for Europe appears to be lacking, and for the very good reason that Europe does not see a mission for itself that requires power. Its mission is to oppose power. It is revealing that the argument most often advanced by Europeans for augmenting their military strength these days is not that it will allow Europe to expand its strategic purview. It is merely to rein in and "multilateralize" the United States. "America," writes the pro-American British scholar Timothy Garton Ash in the *New York Times* (April 9, 2002), "has too much power for anyone's good, including its own." Therefore Europe must amass power, but for no other reason than to save the world and the United States from the dangers inherent in the present lopsided situation.

Whether that particular mission is a worthy one or not, it seems unlikely to rouse European passions. Even Védrine has stopped talking about counterbalancing the United States. Now he shrugs and declares there "is no reason for the Europeans to match a country that can fight four wars at once." It was one thing for Europe in the 1990s to increase its collective expenditures on defense from $150 billion per year to $180 billion when the United States was spending $280 billion per year. But now the United States is heading toward spending as much as $500 billion per year, and Europe has not the slightest intention of keeping up. European analysts lament the continent's "strategic irrelevance." NATO Secretary General George Robertson has taken to calling Europe a "military pygmy" in an effort to shame Europeans into spending more and doing so more wisely. But who honestly believes Europeans will fundamentally change their way of doing business? They have many reasons not to.

THE U.S. RESPONSE

In thinking about the divergence of their own views and Europeans', Americans must not lose sight of the main point: The new Europe is indeed a blessed miracle and a reason for enormous celebration—on both sides of the Atlantic. For Europeans, it is the realization of a long and improbable dream: a continent free from nationalist strife and blood feuds, from military competition and arms races. War between the major European powers is almost unimaginable. After centuries of misery, not only for Europeans but also for those pulled into their conflicts—as Americans were twice in the past century—the new Europe really has emerged as a paradise. It is something to be cherished and guarded, not least by Americans, who have shed blood on Europe's soil and would shed more should the new Europe ever fail.

Nor should we forget that the Europe of today is very much the product of American foreign policy stretching back over six decades. European integration was an American project, too, after World War II. And so, recall, was European weakness. When the Cold War dawned, Americans such as Dean Acheson hoped to create in Europe a powerful partner against the Soviet Union. But that was not the only American vision of Europe underlying U.S. policies during the twentieth century. Predating it was Franklin Delano Roosevelt's vision of a Europe that had been rendered, in effect, strategically irrelevant. As the historian John Lamberton Harper has put it, he wanted "to bring about a radical reduction in the weight of Europe" and thereby make possible "the retirement of Europe from world politics."[8]

Americans who came-of age during the Cold War have always thought of Europe almost exclusively in Achesonian terms—as the essential bulwark of freedom in the struggle against Soviet tyranny. But Americans of Roosevelt's era had a different view. In the late 1930s the common conviction of Americans was that "the European system was basically rotten, that war was endemic on that continent, and the Europeans had only themselves to blame for their plight."[9] By the early 1940s Europe appeared to be nothing more than the overheated incubator of world wars that cost America dearly. During World War II Americans like Roosevelt, looking backward rather than forward, believed no greater service could be performed than to take Europe out of the global strategic picture once and for all. "After Germany is disarmed," FDR pointedly asked, "what is the reason for France having a big military establishment?" Charles DeGaulle found such questions "disquieting for Europe and for France." Even though the United States pursued Acheson's vision during the Cold War, there was always a part of American policy that reflected Roosevelt's vision, too. Eisenhower undermining Britain and France at Suez was only the most blatant of many American efforts to cut Europe down to size and reduce its already weakened global influence.

But the more important American contribution to Europe's current world-apart status stemmed not from anti-European but from pro-European impulses. It was a commitment to Europe, not hostility to Europe, that led the United States in the immediate postwar years to keep troops on the continent and to create NATO. The presence of American forces as a security guarantee in Europe was, as it was intended to be, the critical ingredient to begin the process of European integration.

Europe's evolution to its present state occurred under the mantle of the U.S. security guarantee and could not have occurred without it. Not only did the United States for almost half a century supply a shield against such external threats as the Soviet Union and such internal threats as may have been posed by ethnic conflict in places like the Balkans. More important, the United States was the key to the solution of the German problem and perhaps still is. Germany's Fischer, in the Humboldt University speech, noted two "historic decisions" that made the new Europe possible: "the USA's decision to stay in Europe" and "France's and Germany's commitment to the principle of integration, beginning with economic links." But of course the latter could never have occurred without the former. France's willingness to risk the reintegration of Germany into Europe—and France was, to say the least, highly dubious— depended on the promise of continued American involvement in Europe as a guarantee against any resurgence of German militarism. Nor were postwar Germans unaware that their own future in Europe depended on the calming presence of the American military.

The United States, in short, solved the Kantian paradox for the Europeans. Kant had argued that the only solution to the immoral horrors of the Hobbesian world was the creation of a world government. But he also feared that the "state of universal peace" made possible by world government would be an even greater threat to human freedom than the Hobbesian international order, inasmuch as such a government, with its monopoly of power, would become "the most horrible despotism."[10] How nations could achieve perpetual peace without destroying human freedom was a problem Kant could not solve. But for Europe the problem was solved by the United States. By providing security from outside, the United States has rendered it unnecessary for Europe's supranational government to provide it. Europeans did not need power to achieve peace and they do not need power to preserve it.

The current situation abounds in ironies. Europe's rejection of power politics, its devaluing of military force as a tool of international relations, have depended on the presence of American military forces on European soil. Europe's new Kantian order could flourish only under the umbrella of American power exercised according to the rules of the old Hobbesian order. American power made it possible for Europeans to believe that power was *no* longer important. And now, in the final irony, the fact that United States military power has solved the European problem, especially the "German problem," allows Europeans today to believe that American military power, and the "strategic culture" that has created and sustained it, are outmoded and dangerous.

Most Europeans do not see the great paradox: that their passage into post-history has depended on the United States not making the same passage. Because Europe has neither the will nor the ability to guard its own paradise and keep it from being overrun, spiritually as well as physically, by a world that has yet to accept the rule of "moral consciousness," it has become dependent on America's willingness to use its military might to deter or defeat those around the world who still believe in power politics.

Some Europeans do understand the conundrum. Some Britons, not surprisingly, understand it best. Thus Robert Cooper writes of the need to address the hard truth that although "within the postmodern world [i.e., the Europe of today], there are no security threats in the traditional sense," nevertheless, throughout the rest of the world—what Cooper calls the "modern and pre-modern zones"—threats abound. If the postmodern world does not protect itself, it can be destroyed. But how does Europe protect itself without discarding the very ideals and principles that undergird its pacific system?

"The challenge to the postmodern world," Cooper argues, "is to get used to the idea of double standards." Among themselves, Europeans may "operate on the basis of laws and open cooperative security." But when dealing with the world outside Europe, "we need to revert to the rougher methods of an earlier era—force, preemptive attack, deception, whatever is necessary." This is Cooper's principle for safeguarding society: "Among ourselves, we keep the law but when we are operating in the jungle, we must also use the laws of the jungle."

Cooper's argument is directed at Europe, and it is appropriately coupled with a call for Europeans to cease neglecting their defenses, "both physical and psychological." But what Cooper really describes is not Europe's future but America's present. For it is the United States that has had the difficult task of navigating between these two worlds, trying to abide by, defend, and further the laws of advanced civilized society while simultaneously employing military force against those who refuse to abide by those rules. The United States is already operating according to Cooper's double standard, and for the very reasons he suggests. American leaders, too, believe that global security and a liberal order—as well as Europe's "postmodern" paradise—cannot long survive unless the United States does use its power in the dangerous, Hobbesian world that still flourishes outside Europe.

What this means is that although the United States has played the critical role in bringing Europe into this Kantian paradise, and still plays a key role in making that paradise possible, it cannot enter this paradise itself. It mans the walls but cannot walk through the gate. The United States, with all its vast power, remains stuck in history, left to deal with the Saddams and the ayatollahs, the Kim Jong Ils and the Jiang Zemins, leaving the happy benefits to others.

AN ACCEPTABLE DIVISION?

Is this situation tolerable for the United States? In many ways, it is. Contrary to what many believe, the United States can shoulder the burden of maintaining global security without much help from Europe. The United States spends a little over 3 percent of its GDP on defense .today. Were Americans to increase that to 4 percent—meaning a defense budget in excess of $500 billion per year—it would still represent a smaller percentage of national wealth than Americans spent on defense throughout mosf of the past half-century. Even Paul Kennedy, who invented the term "imperial overstretch" in the late 1980s (when the United States was spending around 7 percent of its GDP on defense), believes the United States can sustain its current military spending levels and its current global dominance far into the future. Can the United States handle the rest of the world without much help from Europe? The answer is that it already does. The United States has maintained strategic stability in Asia with no help from Europe. In the Gulf War, European help was token; so it has been more recently in Afghanistan, where Europeans are once again "doing the dishes" Saddam. Europe has had little to offer the United States in strategic military terms since the end of the Cold War—except, of course, that most valuable of strategic assets, a Europe at peace.

The United States can manage, therefore, at least in material terms. Nor can one argue that the American people are unwilling to shoulder this global burden, since they have done so for a decade already. After September 11, they seem willing to continue doing so for a long time to come. Americans apparently feel no resentment at not being able to enter a "postmodern" Utopia. There is no evidence most Americans desire to. Partly because they are so powerful, they take pride in their nation's military power and their nation's special role in the world.

Americans have no experience that would lead them to embrace fully the ideals and principles that now animate Europe. Indeed, Americans derive their understanding of the world from a very different set of experiences. In the first half of the twentieth century, Americans had a flirtation with a certain kind of internationalist idealism. Wilson's "war to end all wars" was followed a decade later by an American secretary of state putting his signature to a treaty outlawing war. FDR in the 1930s put his faith in non-aggression pacts and asked merely that Hitler promise not to attack a list of countries Roosevelt presented to him. But then came Munich and Pearl Harbor, and then, after a fleeting moment of renewed idealism, the plunge into the Cold War. The "lesson of Munich" came to dominate American strategic thought, and although it was supplanted for a time by the "lesson of Vietnam," today it remains the dominant paradigm. While a small segment of the American elite still yearns for "global governance" and eschews military force, Americans from Madeleine Albright to Donald Rumsfeld, from Brent Scowcroft to Anthony Lake, still remember Munich, figuratively if not literally. And for younger generations of Americans who do not remember Munich or Pearl Harbor, there is now September 11. After September 11, even many American globalizers demand blood.

Americans are idealists, but they have no experience of promoting ideals successfully without power. Certainly, they have no experience of successful supranational governance; little to make them place their faith in international law and international institutions, much as they might wish to; and even less to let them travel, with the Europeans, beyond power. Americans, as good children of the Enlightenment, still believe in the perfectibility of man, and they retain hope for the perfectibility of the world. But they remain realists in the limited sense that they still believe in the necessity of power in a world that remains far from perfection. Such law as there may be to regulate international behavior, they believe, exists because a power like the United States defends it by force of arms. In other words, just as Europeans claim, Americans can still sometimes see themselves in heroic terms—as Gary Cooper at high noon. They will defend the townspeople, whether the townspeople want them to or not.

The problem lies neither in American will or capability, then, but precisely in the inherent moral tension of the current international situation. As is so often the case in human affairs, the real question is one of intangibles—of fears, passions, and beliefs. The problem is that the United States must sometimes play by the rules of a Hobbesian world, even though in doing so it violates European norms. It must refuse to abide by certain international conventions that may constrain its ability to fight effectively in Robert Cooper's jungle. It must support arms control, but not always for itself. It must live by a double standard. And it must sometimes act unilaterally, not out of a passion for unilateralism but, given a weak Europe that has moved beyond power, because the United States has no choice *but* to act unilaterally.

Few Europeans admit, as Cooper does implicitly, that such American behavior may redound to the greater benefit of the civilized world, that American power, even employed under a double standard, may be the best means of advancing human progress—and perhaps the only means. Instead, many Europeans today have come to consider the United States itself to be the outlaw, a rogue colossus. Europeans have complained about President Bush's "unilateralism," but they are coming to the deeper realization that the problem is not Bush or any American president. It is systemic. And it is incurable.

Given that the United States is unlikely to reduce its power and that Europe is unlikely to increase more than marginally its own power or the will to use what power it has, the future seems certain to be one of increased transatlantic tension. The danger—if it is a danger—is that the United States and Europe will become positively estranged. Europeans will become more shrill in their attacks on the United States. The United States will become less inclined to listen, or perhaps even to care. The day could come, if it has not already, when Americans will no more heed the pronouncements of the EU than they do the pronouncements of ASEAN or the Andean Pact.

To those of us who came of age in the Cold War, the strategic decoupling of Europe and the United States seems frightening. DeGaulle, when confronted by FDR's vision of a world where Europe was irrelevant, recoiled and suggested that this vision "risked endangering the Western world." If Western Europe was to be considered a "secondary matter" by the United States, would not FDR only "weaken the very cause he meant to serve—that of civilization?" Western Europe, DeGaulle insisted, was "essential to the West. Nothing can replace the value, the power, the shining example of the ancient peoples." Typically, DeGaulle insisted this was "true of France above all." But leaving aside French *amour propre,* did not DeGaulle have a point? If Americans were to decide that Europe was no more than an irritating irrelevancy, would American society gradually become unmoored from what we now call the West? It is not a risk to be taken lightly, on either side of the Atlantic.

So what is to be done? The obvious answer is that Europe should follow the course that Cooper, Ash, Robertson, and others recommend and build up its military capabilities, even if only marginally. There is not much ground for hope that this will happen. But, then, who knows? Maybe concern about America's overweening power really will create some energy in Europe. Perhaps the atavistic impulses that still swirl in the hearts of Germans, Britons, and Frenchmen—the memory of power, international influence, and national ambition—can still be played upon. Some Britons still remember empire; some Frenchmen still yearn for *la gloire;* some Germans still want their place in the sun. These urges are now mostly channeled into the grand European project, but they could find more traditional expression. Whether this is to be hoped for or feared is another question. It would be better still if Europeans could move beyond fear and anger at the rogue colossus and remember, again, the vital necessity of having a strong America—or the world and especially for Europe.

Americans can help. It is true that the Bush administration came into office with a chip on its shoulder. It was hostile to the new Europe—as to a lesser extent was the Clinton administration—seeing it not so much as an ally but as an albatross. Even after September 11, when the Europeans offered their very limited military capabilities in the fight in Afghanistan, the United States resisted, fearing that European cooperation was a ruse to tie America down. The Bush administration viewed NATO's historic decision to aid the United States under Article V less as a boon than as a booby trap. An opportunity to draw Europe into common battle out in the Hobbesian world, even in a minor role, was thereby unnecessarily lost.

Americans are powerful enough that they need not fear Europeans, even when bearing gifts. Rather than viewing the United States as a Gulliver tied down by Lilliputian threads, American leaders should realize that they are hardly constrained at all, that Europe is not really capable of constraining the United States. If the United States could move past the anxiety engendered by this inaccurate sense of constraint, it could begin to show more understanding for the sensibilities of others, a little generosity of spirit. It could pay its respects to multilateralism and the rule of law and try to build some international political capital for those moments when multilateralism is impossible and unilateral action unavoidable. It could, in short, take more care to show what the founders called a "decent respect for the opinion of mankind."

These are small steps, and they will not address the deep problems that beset the transatlantic relationship today. But, after all, it is more than a cliché that the United States and Europe share a set of common Western beliefs. Their aspirations for humanity are much the same, even if their vast disparity of power has now put them in very different places. Perhaps it is not too naively optimistic to believe that a little common understanding could still go a long way.

NOTES

1. One representative French observer describes "a U.S. mindset" that "tends to emphasize military, technical and unilateral solutions to international problems, possibly at the expense of co-operative and political ones." See Gilles Andreani, "The Disarray of U.S. Non-Proliferation Policy," *Survival* (Winter 1999–2000).
2. The case of Bosnia in the early 1990s stands out as an instance where some Europeans, chiefly British Prime Minister Tony Blair, were at times more forceful in advocating military action than first the Bush and then the Clinton administration. (Blair was also an early advocate of using air power and even ground troops in the Kosovo crisis.) And Europeans had forces on the ground in Bosnia when the United States did not, although in a un peacekeeping role that proved ineffective when challenged.
3. Samuel P. Huntington, "The Lonely Superpower," Foreign Affairs (March–April 1999).
4. Steven Everts, "Unilateral America, Lightweight Europe?: Managing Divergence in Transatlantic Foreign Policy," Centre for European Reform working paper (February 2001).
5. For that matter, this is also the view commonly found in American textbooks.
6. The common American argument that European policy toward Iraq and Iran is dictated by financial considerations is only partly right. Are Europeans greedier than Americans? Do American corporations not influence American policy in Asia and Latin America, as well as in the Middle East? The difference is that American strategic judgments sometimes conflict with and override financial interests. For the reasons suggested in this essay, that conflict is much less common for Europeans.
7. Charles Grant, "A European View of ESDP," Centre for European Policy Studies working paper (April 2001).
8. John Lamberton Harper, *American Visions of Europe: Franklin D. Roosevelt, George F. Kennan, and Dean G, Acheson* (Cambridge University Press, 1996), 3. The following discussion of the differing American perspectives on Europe owes much to Harper's fine book.
9. William L. Langer and S. Everett Gleason, *The Challenge to Isolation, 1937–1940* (Harper Bros., 1952), 14.
10. See Thomas L. Pangle and Peter J. Ahrensdorf, *Justice Among Nations: On the Moral Basis of Power and Peace* (University Press of Kansas, 1999), 200–201.

The Remaking of a Unipolar World

Robert Jervis

Common sense and most, academic thinking argue that a hegemon's prime objective should seek to maintain the prevailing international system, but that is not the world in which we live today. Measured in any conceivable way, the United States has a greater share of world power than any other country in history. Whether it is referred to as the world leader by those who approve of its policies or an empire by those who oppose them, it is a hegemon in today's unipolar world order. The irony is that Washington seeks to change the rules of that order. Why?

Positioned at the top of the hierarchy, the hegemon should want to maintain and solidify it. Even though it may have to pay a disproportionate share of the costs, including heavy UN dues and a high defense budget, such burdens are difficult to shirk and represent a small price to pay for the international order that: provides the hegemon with so many benefits. Other states may appear to get a better deal by prospering within the international system without having to pay the high price; western Europe, for example, can free ride on U.S. efforts in many spheres while still complaining about. U.S. dominance. Yet, enormous U.S. power brings unprecedented benefits, ranging from the key role of the U.S. dollar in world finance to the centrality of the English language throughout the world to Washington's ability to block most political initiatives that would bring it harm.

The current international system, although not necessarily perfect, is certainly satisfactory, partly because the United States has played such a large role in establishing it. No state can have a greater stake in the prevailing order than the hegemon, nor can any state have greater power to maintain the system. The United States should then be a very conservative state in its foreign relations; with its power and dominance thus assured, it should be the quintessential status quo power. It makes a puzzle of Washington's current behavior, which is anything but conservative. In the fierce debate over the merits of its post-September 11 foreign policy, insufficient attention has been paid to the odd fact that the United States, with all its power and stake in the system, is behaving more like a revolutionary state than one committed to preserving the arrangements that seem to have suited it well.

THE POST-COLD WAR CONSERVATIVE IMPULSE

U.S. policy from the end of the Cold War to the September 11 attacks, defined by some as dull and characterized by frequent if small military interventions, sought to bolster the international system. This conservative stance was endorsed by perhaps the most famous statement of

Robert Jervis, "The Remaking of a Unipolar World," *The Washington Quarterly*, 29:3, pp. 7–19. © 2006 by The Center for Strategic and International Studies and the Massachusetts Institute of Technology. Reprinted by permission.

the George H. W. Bush administration: the 1992 draft Defense Guidance, written under the direction of Paul Woltowitz for then-Secretary of Defense Dick Cheney. Because either bipolarity or multipolarity would recapitulate the history of world politics and threaten U.S. interests by producing great conflict if not major wars, the draft argued that the United States should ensure that no peer competitor would arise. Accordingly, Washington had to maintain a military force so modern and potent that no one could consider challenging it. It also had to handle a range of problems that were important to other states so that they would not need to develop their own robust military capabilities. The thrust of the argument was that the United States should do what was necessary to maintain the trajectory of world politics, and although the bellicose tone of the document had to be modified once it was leaked to the press, it stands as the standard conservative position.

Under President Bill Clinton, some critics argued that the United States was confusing foreign policy with missionary work while others decried its passivity in the face of world poverty, genocide in Rwanda, and growing autocracy in Russia, yet neither critique gained great traction. For most people, there were no pressing reasons for more dramatic action. Many international politics experts agreed, especially those of a realist stripe, and argued that the United States should follow a policy of selective engagement and maintain a role as an offshore balancer.

The first President Bush and Clinton had the same basic idea: support the status quo and intervene only to prevent or reverse destabilizing shocks such as Iraq's invasion of Kuwait or Serbia's brutalities in Europe's backyard. Such interventions could be short lived, and few other problems were severe enough to merit this kind of attention. In fact, most changes in world politics could be tolerated because they were not great enough to threaten the fundamentals of the unipolar system. Thus, when the United States did intervene, it was playing an essentially conservative role.

A NEW BEGINNING: HEGEMONIC REVISIONISM

Although the 1992 Defense Guidance was drafted by neoconservatives and is often seen as foreshadowing current U.S. policy, the contrast between the two is actually quite severe. Three linked elements that have become central to contemporary U.S. foreign policy had little place in the draft document almost a decade earlier. First, current doctrine emphasizes that peace and cooperation can exist only when all important states are democratic. Because a country's foreign policy reflects the nature of its domestic regime, states that rule by law and express the interests of their people will conduct benign foreign policies, and tyrannies will inflict misery abroad as well as at home.

Second, a vital instrument to preserve world order is what the administration calls preemption but is actually prevention, including preventive war. In extreme cases such as Iraq, the United States has justified the use of force by arguing that even though Saddam Hussein did not have weapons of mass destruction (WMD) programs, he would have developed them when conditions were propitious. It was better for the United States to act rather than wait for this to occur. This may be a political and psychological rationalization, but the argument does have a strong logic to it, especially if deterrence cannot cope with dedicated adversaries, most notably terrorists. When defense is also inadequate, the United States must use preventive measures.

Preventive actions, however, even if effective in the short run, will only be a stopgap if international politics were to proceed on its normal trajectory. To bring lasting peace, stability, and prosperity, the system must not simply be preserved, as the Defense Guidance advocated; it must be transformed.

Although the second element in this trilogy can perhaps be squared with a conservative view of the role of the hegemon, the other two cannot. Together, the three argue that even if the status quo is in some sense satisfactory, it is an illusion to believe that it can be maintained. One way or another, world politics will change drastically. The questions are who will change it and whether it will be for better or worse. In a way that should shock Henry Kissinger and other students of the order established by the Congress of Vienna, U.S. foreign policy should be more closely modeled after Napoleon than after Talleyrand and Metternich, The United States simply cannot maintain its hegemonic position through the policies advocated by realists and followed before September 11, 2001, so current doctrine argues that the United States must instead be a revolutionary power.

THE LIMITED EXPLANATORY POWER OF SEPTEMBER 11

The most simple and obvious explanation for this strategic shift is the September 11 attacks. Few analysts have dissented from the administration's claim that radical measures are required to confront the threat of terrorism, even if they disagree with many of its policies. For George W. Bush, the change has been even more drastic as the September 11 attacks greatly heightened his sense of threat and strengthened his belief that there is a tight link between tyrants and terrorists. Although Bush and his colleagues may have cynically exaggerated the ties between Saddam and Al Qaeda, they do appear to believe that only nondemocratic regimes, if not all nondemocratic regimes, will sponsor terrorism and that without state backing, terrorism will disappear. Combined with the belief that terrorism constitutes a fundamental threat to the rest of the world, this leads to the conclusion that the world can only be safe if all countries are transformed into democracies. Although cynics may see these beliefs as mere rationalizations for policies arrived at on other grounds, they are likely sincerely held and are partly responsible for the revolutionary U.S. policy.

This is not to say that the beliefs are well founded. As Gregory Cause has written, the connection between tyrants and terrorists is tenuous at best.[1] The Palestinian semistate is democratic, but will it abandon its use of terrorism? The extent of Pakistan's sponsorship of terrorism in Kashmir and India has not ebbed and flowed with the extent to which Pakistan has been democratic. Iran sponsors some terrorism and yet is much more democratic than Saudi Arabia, which does not. Aside from killing their vocal opponents who have gone into exile, most nondemocracies shun terrorism, especially because terrorists are difficult to control.

The more fundamental claim that terrorism is such a threat that it requires transformation of the international system must also be questioned. Unless they use nuclear weapons or deadly contagious diseases, terrorists cannot inflict great damage.[2] As terrible as the September 11 attacks were, fewer people were killed on that day than die in automobile accidents in one month. Acquiring nuclear weapons and even infectious biological agents, which of course could kill the terrorists' friends as well as their enemies, is extraordinary difficult. Although significant prophylactic efforts are necessary, there is a great disproportion between the threat and the remedies that Washington proposes. The threat looms large to the United States in part because, unlike the countries of western Europe, it had not experienced a successful terrorist attack of this scale in the past, and the visual image of the twin towers burning and collapsing has been etched vividly and indelibly on the American psyche. Terrorism also seems so threatening because U.S. hegemony and the dramatic decline in international war that may be a product of it mean that many of the threats that had been so prominent: previously have now disappeared. There is little else to compare it to today. Psychologically if not logically, small threats appear to be in the same class with fundamental challenges such as the Cold War.

Herein lies the paradox. On one hand, many scholars deny that the terrorist threat, requires the United States to transform the world. On the other hand, it is not only Bush and a neoconservative cabal who believe that it does but also a significant segment of elite opinion, including some who opposed the war in Iraq as a counterproductive digression. The September 11 attacks are part of the explanation for why many U.S. citizens feel that a heterogeneous world is unsafe, bur this conclusion does not follow ineluctably from these events. Something more deeply rooted is involved.

THE HEGEMON'S SECURITY DILEMMA

The United States believes itself caught in a version of the familiar security dilemma. To make itself secure, it must impinge on the security of nondemocracies. Despite the intrinsic value it places on democracy, it might be willing to live in a mixed world if it were a safe one. Yet, such safety could not be guaranteed because nondemocracies will always threaten the United States. Although the current world system is unipolar, the situation resembles that of the Cold War, when the United States and the Soviet Union were mutually threatening and threatened because their contrasting ideologies and domestic regimes made each an inherent menace to the other. Ironically, the fact: that the United States is a hegemon feeds its revolutionary impulse. Hope as well as fear, opportunity as well as threat are at work.

The Power to Change

The fact that the United States lacks a peer competitor means that it can turn its focus elsewhere. Furthermore, with the disintegration of the USSR, Bush's 2002 national security doctrine is correct to assert that "[t]he great struggles of the twentieth century between liberty and totalitarianism ended with a decisive victory for the forces of freedom—and a single sustainable model for national success: freedom, democracy, and free enterprise."[3] Because almost all countries pay lip service to democratic values, U.S. leaders can readily believe that now is the best time for the United States to remake the system in its own image.

The key is to lead other states and societies to become liberal democracies and respect individual rights, the law, and their neighbors. All instruments are to be deployed to this end: military power, covert: action, nongovernmental organizations, and diplomacy, which is to be reorganized to support a "transformational" program.[4] Although Bush recently has avoided calling for the overthrow of regimes in North Korea and Iran, the logic of his policy clearly points in that: direction. Even the most effective antiproliferation policies leave room for cheating. The only way to ensure that the mullahs of Iran or the dictator of North Korea do not acquire nuclear weapons is to remove them from power.

One can disagree with the theory that democracies are benign or note Bush's hypocrisy, as well as that of previous U.S. presidents, because they have attacked democratic governments that follow unacceptable policies, such as Hugo Chavez's Venezuela or the Palestinian government under Hamas. More importantly in this context, one can argue that the U.S.

stance is mere rhetoric, as it was in the past. Yet, all signs indicate that Bush and many of his colleagues believe in what they say, and even critics have been surprised (some horrified and others heartened) by the unprecedented extent to which Washington has pressed friendly and probably unstable regimes such as Egypt and Saudi Arabia to democratize, even if it has not used the most extreme instruments at its disposal.

Bush's stance is both pessimistic in its assertion that standard tools of international politics are insufficient to tame tyrannical regimes and optimistic in its argument that democracies will be well behaved internationally and will accept U.S. leadership. Optimism is also prominent in his belief that, with U.S. assistance, democracy can be brought to all other countries. According to the Bush administration, this form of government will thrive when the artificially imposed barriers to it from old autocratic regimes are removed. Democracy does not require demanding preconditions and the prior transformation of society.

Remaking the System in the Hegemon's Image

The other side of this coin is that as long as many countries are undemocratic, democracies elsewhere, including the United States, cannot be secure. President Woodrow Wilson wanted to make the world safe for democracy. Bush extends and reverses this, arguing that only in a world of democracies can the United States be safe. The ringing cry in his second inaugural address that "[t]he survival of liberty in our land increasingly depends on the success of liberty in other lands; the best hope for peace in our world is the expansion of freedom in all the world"[5] echoed then-Secretary of State Dean Acheson's statement in 1950 that "[w]e are children of freedom. We cannot be safe except in an environment of freedom."[6] Throughout the Cold War, the United States vacillated between accepting a heterogeneous world and believing that the USSR would be a threat as long as it was Communist. President Ronald Reagan took Acheson's position to heart, although perhaps only when it appeared that the Soviet system might indeed be brought down without triggering a war.

The U.S. position in the world is without precedent, but the basic impulses animating it are not. Having established order within its large sphere, a hegemon will find itself threatened by whatever is beyond its reach. The very extent of the hegemon's influence means that all sorts of geographic and ideological disturbances can threaten it. Frontiers can be expanded, but doing so just recreates them. Despite the fact that or perhaps because it lacked what would now be referred to as peer competitors, the Roman empire was never able to establish stable frontiers, and although the United Kingdom in the nineteenth century was able to develop tolerable working relationships with European states, its empire expanded beyond the original intention in part because of the inability to control and limit its holdings in Africa and Asia. Having established trading outposts, it was driven to further expansion not only by competition with other European states, but by the difficulties of establishing local order.[7] For the United States, the frontier is ideological rather than geographic, but the basic point is the same: preservation of a desirable and ordered zone requires taming or subduing areas and ideologies of potential disturbance.

Hegemony thus also ironically magnifies the sense of threat. The very fact that the United States has interests throughout the world leads to the fear that undesired changes in one area could undermine its interests elsewhere. Most changes will harm the United States if they do not improve its situation. Furthermore, U.S. hegemony means that even those who share its values and interests have incentives to free ride on its efforts, knowing that Washington cannot shirk its role. Thus, although the United States has few intrinsic interests in the borderlands around China and Japan is strong enough to carry much of the weight in this region, U.S. fears about the rise of China follow a certain logic. Unless China becomes a benign democracy, increases in its regional influence will diminish that of the United States. Although China cannot become a peer competitor in the foreseeable future, even those who are not paranoid believe that China will intrude on the U.S. order because the latter extends to China's doorstep. Disturbances that would be dismissed in a multipolar or bipolar world loom much larger for the hegemon because it is present in all corners of the globe and everything seems interconnected. It is a truism of realism that increases in national power bring increases in interests. It is not only with aggressors that the appetite grows with the eating.

Hegemonic Power and International Law

The U.S. rejection of international law in general and the International Criminal Court (ICC) in particular demonstrates why its stance is not and cannot be conservative. At first glance, one would think the United States would seek to strengthen many legal restraints.[8] Because it is developed by the most powerful actors, international law limits the changes that are likely to accompany shifting power relations, greatly reduces the costs the hegemon has to pay for inducing others to comply, and is thus generally conservative. Yet, whereas a legal system applies the same rules to all actors, a hegemonic system is quite differentiated, with the hegemon having a role distinct from that of other states.

Seen in this light, the Bush administration's claim that other states cannot adopt the doctrine of preventive war and its rejection of the ICC make a great deal of sense. Only the hegemon can nip problems, including others' problems, in the bud, and the very fact that it acts preventively means that others need not and must not do so. Hegemony similarly requires the use of military force in a way that exposes the hegemon to ICC action. It will be the hegemon's forces that are engaged in the most difficult activities, and its status makes it the obvious target for those with multiple motives ranging from jealousy to domestic policy to regional aspirations that can be furthered by embarrassing it. Given the difficulties of the task it has taken on, it is unlikely that the hegemon can live by any set of rules that cannot encompass all the unforeseen circumstances in which it may have to act. If the United States is to transform the system, it cannot adopt the egalitarian and collegial model so favored by standard liberal theories of international cooperation.

AMERICAN MISSIONARY ZEAL AND ITS PRESIDENT

Besides the systemic factors leading today's hegemon to change rather than preserve the system, other elements besides September 11 are also at work: Bush's personal religious outlook and personality and U.S. political culture.

Bush's Religious Conviction

Coming into office, and indeed as late as September 10, 2001, the president did not have deeply rooted views about foreign policy. Those that he did have had inclined him toward a traditional if assertive realist policy, as summarized by the 1992 draft Defense Guidance. Yet, after the September 11 attacks, he adopted the new stance with extraordinary speed and within days became committed to preventive action and spreading democracy around the world. Part of the explanation for this shift lies in his personality, especially his attraction to certainty and grand gestures and, to an even greater extent, the religious conviction that permeates his way of thinking.[9]

Growing out of the way in which turning to Christ enabled him to break with his aimless and alcoholic past, Bush is prone to look for missions that give his life and his country meaning, to see the world in terms of good and evil, and to believe in the possibility and efficacy of transformations. When early in his administration he said that he was "tired of swatting flies"[10] as a counterterrorism policy, Bush was indicating his predilection toward more sweeping solutions, brushing aside the question of whether these might prove excessively costly and even counterproductive. This way of thinking was reinforced by the terrorist attacks, which led Bush to feel that he had now found his mission. He sees himself and his country as involved in a struggle against evil. An associate of the president reports that, after the September 11 attacks, Bush thought "[t]his is what I was put on this earth for."[11] As a born-again Christian, he is strongly attracted to the idea of transforming people, societies, and world politics. Bush's predisposition here converges with strands of neoconservative thinking that see the need for the United States to undertake ambitious foreign policy missions to maintain its domestic political and moral health, as well as the related belief in the possibility of international progress through converting people to correct ideas and ideals.[12] Incrementalism and accepting the ways things are cannot save souls or bring lasting peace.

The American Political Culture

People who lack Bush's personal history and beliefs may reach similar conclusions. Vice President Cheney and Secretary of Defense Donald Rumsfeld, to name only the two most obvious cases, helped shape the Bush doctrine, although their personalities are very different from his. Yet, as Americans, they are influenced by the strands of the U.S. tradition that feed a transformationalist approach. As Harvard political theorist Louis Hartz brilliantly argued 50 years ago, as a society founded by a middle-class fragment, the United States has had great difficulties understanding societies that are not liberal, has misunderstood revolutionary impulses, and has expected its own model to be readily replicated.[13] Often incorrectly reviled as conservative if not apologetic, this perspective remains powerful and penetrating. Under current circumstances, it helps explain the combination of fear and optimism that character-izes the United States, but few of its allies. Therefore, a heterogeneous world is a dangerous one, values that Americans hold dear are instinctively shared by others even if they do not know it, and once the heavy hand of oppression is lifted, other countries will become liberal democracies.

Throughout the Cold War, U.S. leaders stressed that the United States was a revolution-ary power.[14] This was partly a rhetorical device to counter the impression that the Soviet Union stood for progressive change while the United States stood in its way, but the message was not entirely fictional. The United States had never been happy with a world of nondemo-cratic states. It has always had deep reservations about traditional power politics and is much more prone than the Europeans to believe that a country's foreign policy is strongly influenced by its domestic arrangements. Both critics and defenders of U.S. foreign policy often noted its distinctively reformist characteristics.

A second and related tradition is Wilsonianism. Wilson thought that the United States could spread democracy abroad and that these regimes would be inherently peace loving and cooperative. Although these views were not uniquely American—Wilson was in part influenced by the writings of British liberal reformers—they have deep resonance within the U.S. polity. It was one reason why Reagan did not feel inhibited to label the Soviet Union an evil empire and confidently push for ending the Communist system.

Even when it was not seeking such grand a goal, the United States was prone to react to setbacks and obstacles during the Cold War not through midcourse corrections, but: rather by seeking bold initiatives, such as unifying Europe, modernizing the Third World, or overruling British and French resistance and pushing for German unity in 1989–1990.[15] Some of these moves succeeded and others failed, but they were not the sort of system-maintaining prudent policies that one expects from a status quo state. Rather than deal with specific difficulties on their own terms, ameliorating them or designing around them, the United States sought far-reaching changes.

THE IMPLICATIONS OF A REVISIONIST HEGEMON

For better or for worse, then, a variety of systemic, national, and individual reasons explain why the United States is a revisionist hegemon seeking a new and better international system rather than a status quo power continuing the order in which it now wields significant power and exercises great influence. Bush and his colleagues fervently believe that transformation can succeed. In February 2002, the president responded to a question about the predictable French criticisms of his policy by saying that "history has given us a unique opportunity to defend freedom. And we're going to seize the moment and do it."[16] A month later he declared, "We understand history has called us into action, and we are not going to miss that opportunity to make the world more peaceful and more free."[17] This is an opportunity because not only does the United States have great power, but spreading democracy is in everyone's interest, except the few remaining dictators, and people all over the world want to be free.

This is a marvelous story, but each of its aspects is flawed. U.S. power, although great, is far from unlimited. Indeed, the very fact of its great-power means that even those sympathetic to it will worry with good reason that their interests may be neglected. Foot dragging if not active resistance is to be expected, and not only by France. This is particularly troublesome because widespread and active support from a very broad coalition could help spread democracy by showing that it is not merely a cover for U.S. power. More importantly, although Bush is undoubtedly correct that: few people want to be ruled by dictators, establishing a working democracy is difficult. Most would agree with Bush that, over the long run, democracy would prevail, but there is very little in historical experience or social science theory to lead one to expect these transformations to be quick or easy.

Furthermore, if the required effort is to be sustained over a prolonged period, commitment is required in the United States, across society and the political system. Yet, this seems unlikely. Everyone wants to see democracies established abroad, but if the effort runs into trouble, involves high costs, and produces instability and anti-American regimes, it is not likely to be domestically sustainable. The U.S. political system was not constructed to support. an active foreign policy, much as Bush wishes that it were.

Although the Bush experiment is not likely to succeed, some of the transformationalist impulse will continue because of its deep roots in the United States' worldview as well as its hegemony. How to balance what is desirable with the constraints of an intractable world will be the challenge for Bush's successors.

NOTES

1. F. Gregory Gause III, "Can Democracy Stop Terrorism?" *Foreign Affairs* 84, no. 5 (September/ October 2005): 62–76.

2. For a good discussion, see John Mueller, "Six Rather Unusual Propositions About Terrorism," *Terrorism and Political Violence* 17, no. 4 (January 2005): 487–505.

3. "The National Security Strategy of the United States of America," September 2002, p. iii, http:// www.whitehouse.gov/nsc/nss/2002/nss.pdf.

4. On the latter, see Condoleezza Rice, "Transformational Diplomacy," Washington, D.C., January 18, 2006, http://www.state.gov/sccretary/rm/2006/59306.htm. See also Condoleezza Rice, "Remarks on Foreign Assistance," Washington, D.C., January 19, 2006, http://www.state.gov/secretary/rin/2006/59408.htm.

5. Office of the Press Secretary, The White House, "President Sworn-In [sic] to Second Term," January 20, 2005, http://www.whitehouse.gov/news/releases/2005/01/ 20050120-l.html.

6. John Lewis Gaddis, *Strategies of Containment*, rev. and ext. ed. (New York: Oxford University Press, 2005), p. 106.

7. John Galbraith, "The 'Turbulent' Frontier as a Factor in British Expansion," *Comparative Studies in Society and History* 2, no. 1 (January 1960): 34–48.

8. See, for example, John lkenberry, *After Victory: Institutions, Strategic Restraint, and the Rebuilding of Order After Major Wars* (Princeton, N.J.: Princeton University Press, 2001).

9. For a very perceptive account written shortly after the attacks, see Frank Bruni, "For President, a Mission and a Role in History," *New York Times*, September 22, 2001, p. 1. See also Steve Erickson, "George Bush and the Treacherous Country," LA Weekly, February 13, 2004, pp. 28–33.

10. Quoted in The 9/11 *Commission Report* (New York: W.W. Norton, 2004), p. 202.

11. Quoted in James Harding, "Growing Divide Between the Bushes," *Financial Times*, March 20, 2003, p. 4.

12. See Michael Williams, "What Is the National Interest? The Neoconservative Challenge in IR Theory," *European Journal of International Relations* 11, no. 3 (September 200.5): .307–337; Michael Boyle, "Utopianism and the Bush Foreign Policy," *Cambridge Review of International Affairs* 17, no. 1 (April 2004): 81–103.

13. Louis Hartz, *The Liberal Tradition in America* (New York: Harcourt, Brace, and World, 1955).

14. See "Harry Truman: 7th State of the Union Address," http://www.theamericanpresidency.us/ 195.3hst.htm; "President Gerald R. Ford's Address in Helsinki Before the Conference on Security and Cooperation in Europe," August 1, 1975, http://www.fordlibraTynuiseurn.gov/ library/ speeches/750459.htm; "Ronald Reagan Speeches: Address to the British Parliament (June 8, 1982)," http://millercenter.virginia.edu/sc.ripps/diglibrary/prezspeec.hes/ reagan/rwr_1982_0608.html.

15. Steven Sestanovich, "American Maximalism," *National Interest*, no. 79 (Spring 2005): 13–23. See also John Lewis Gaddis, *Surprise, Security, and the American Experience* (Cambridge: Harvard University Press, 2004).

16. Office of the Press Secretary, The White House, "President Bush, Prime Minister Koizumi Hold Press Conference," February 18, 2002, http://www.whit.ehouse.gov/ news/relcases/2002/02/20020218. html.

17. Office of the Press Secretary, The White House, "President, Vice President Discuss the Middle East," March 21, 2002, http://www.whitehouse.gov/news/releases/2002/ 03/20020321-6.html.

҉ PART THREE ҉

Capitalism, Class, and Foreign Policy

American foreign policy is conducted in the leading capitalist society. Accordingly, an important theoretical tradition has investigated the linkages between capitalism, economic interests, and foreign policy. The earliest scholarship in this area emerged in the years immediately preceding and after World War I, when Marxists and other writers probed the economic and class determinants of European imperialism and war. In the United States the tradition was invigorated again during the Vietnam War as scholars provided radical critiques of American foreign policy. Some writers have focused on the underlying structures of capitalist society and the general pattern of imperialist foreign policy. Here the linkages between capitalism and policy are deep and structural: Governmental officials, whether they know it or not, act to protect and advance the interest of capitalism as a whole. The limited range of foreign policy options are generated by the system itself. Others adopt a more narrow instrumental perspective and focus on particular capitalist elites and particular policies. In this approach it is the capitalists themselves who act within the institutions of government to advance their own class interests.

Jeff Frieden, working primarily within the instrumentalist tradition, provides an interpretation of the historic shift during the interwar period in American foreign economic policy from nationalism to internationalism. After World War I, Frieden argues, many U.S. banks and corporations saw opportunities in overseas expansion and attempted to push American policy in an internationalist direction. Other U.S. corporations saw international competition as a threat and supported the prevailing isolationist stance of government. Throughout the 1920s and early 1930s the two coalitions struggled to dominate foreign economic policy, each attaching themselves to different parts of the governmental apparatus. The standoff ended with the triumph of the internationalist wing of American capitalism, a victory made possible by the crisis of the 1930s and the destruction of foreign economic competition following World War II. Historic shifts in American foreign policy make sense, Frieden argues, only when related to the underlying struggles among competing class factions.

Fred Block is interested in the 1950 rearmament decision and its similarities with the expansion of military spending at the end of the Carter administration. Adopting a neo-Marxist perspective, Block argues that interstate "threats" can be used by state officials seeking to justify increased military spending and an expansionary foreign policy to stabilize and protect the national economy and an open world capitalist system. Block examines the historic planning document from the Truman administration, NSC-68, from this perspective. Foreign policy officials, according to Block, sought military rearmament as a way to meet critical economic objectives but felt compelled to justify increased military spending in the context of a more dramatic and sweeping "militarization" of American foreign policy.

James Shoch traces the rise of domestic interest groups that have resisted America's post-Cold War commitment to economic globalization and the building of international institutions intended to manage an open world economy. These groups include left-leaning labor and environmental movements and right-leaning Republican nationalists. Shoch seeks to explain why these resistance groups failed to block the approval of the North American Free Trade Agreement in the early Clinton administration but succeeded in winning battles with free trade advocates in 1997 and 1998. Shoch surveys the domestic political struggles over trade policy in the 1990s and shows how antiglobalization groups—most importantly, organized labor—slowly gathered strength, marshaling human and financial resources to lobby against trade liberalization measures.

A. G. Hopkins takes up the question of how capitalism and nationalism act on American foreign policy, looking in particular at the Bush administration's intervention in Iraq. Classical theories of imperialism—which stress the direct role of economic interests in expansionist state policies—are not very helpful in explaining the decision to use force in Iraq. Neither oil companies nor domestic economic interest groups advocated invasion. But Hopkins argues that globalization and rapid economic growth generated anxieties and worries within American society, fueling a conservative political revival organized around the themes of "family, faith, and flag." It was upon this foundation of conservative patriotism and assertive nationalism that neoconservatives could draw in making their case for war. Hopkins argues that over the longer term, American society is becoming increasingly divided between new globalized interests and insular national interests—a divide that will feed a contest between a foreign policy of internationalism and a "fortress America" orientation.

᠔

Sectoral Conflict and U.S. Foreign Economic Policy, 1914–1940

Jeff Frieden

The period from 1914 to 1940 is one of the most crucial and enigmatic in modern world history and in the history of modern U.S. foreign policy. World War I catapulted the United States into international economic and political leadership, yet in the aftermath of the war, despite grandiose Wilsonian plans, the United States quickly lapsed into relative disregard for events abroad: it did not join the League of Nations, disavowed responsibility for European reconstruction, would not participate openly in many international economic conferences, and

Jeffry A. Frieden, "Sectoral Conflicts and U.S. Foreign Economic Policy:1914–1940,"*International Organization,* 42:1 (Winter, 1988), pp. 59–90. © 1988 by the World Peace Foundation and the Massachusetts Institute of Technology. Reprinted by permission of MIT Press Journals.

restored high levels of tariff protection for the domestic market. Only in the late 1930s and 1940s, after twenty years of bitter battles over foreign policy, did the United States move to center stage of world politics and economics: it built the United Nations and a string of regional alliances, underwrote the rebuilding of Western Europe, almost single-handedly constructed a global monetary and financial system, and led the world in commercial liberalization.

This article examines the peculiar evolution of U.S. foreign economic policy in the interwar years and focuses on the role of domestic socioeconomic and political groups in determining foreign policy. The American interwar experience powerfully demonstrates that the country's international position and economic evolution do not sufficiently explain its foreign policy. Indeed, although the contours of the international system and the place of the United States in it changed dramatically during and after World War I, these changes had a very different impact on different sectors of American society. World War I dramatically strengthened the overseas economic interests of many major U.S. banks and corporations, who fought hard for more political involvement by the United States in world affairs. Yet domestically oriented economic groups remained extremely powerful within the United States and sought to maintain a relatively isolated America. Through the 1920s and early 1930s, the two broad coalitions battled to dominate foreign economic policy. The result was an uneasy stand-off in which the two camps entrenched themselves in different portions of the state apparatus, so that policy often ran on two tracks and was sometimes internally contradictory. Only the crisis of the 1930s and the eventual destruction of most of America's overseas competitors led to an "internationalist" victory that allowed for the construction of the American-led post–World War II international political economy.

THE PROBLEM

To virtually all observers then and since, at the end of World War I the United States seemed to dominate the international political economy. It had financed the victorious war effort and provided most of the war matériel that went into it; its industry was by far the world's largest and most productive. Despite its traditional economic insulation, the sheer size of the U.S. economy made the country the world's largest trading power. The center of world finance had shifted from London to New York. The United States clearly had the military, industrial, and financial capacity to impose its will on Europe. Yet after World War I the United States, in the current arcane iconography of the field, did not play the part of international economic hegemon, arbiter, and bank roller of the world economic order. The United States was capable of hegemonic action, and President Woodrow Wilson had hegemonic plans, but they were defeated. The problem was not in Europe, for although the British and French were stronger in 1919 than they would be in 1946, they could hardly have stood in the way of American hegemony. Indeed, European complaints about the United States after World War I were in much the opposite direction: the Europeans bitterly protested America's *refusal* to accept the responsibilities of leadership. The Europeans charged that the United States was stingy with its government finance, hostile in its trade policy, scandalous in its refusal to join the League of Nations, unwilling to get involved in overseeing and smoothing Europe's squabbles. The British and French tried for years to entice and cajole a reluctant America into leadership. America would not be budged, at least until 1940.

The world's most powerful nation pursued a contradictory and shifting set of foreign economic policies. The country both asserted and rejected world leadership, simultaneously initiated and blocked efforts at European stabilization, and began such major cooperative ventures as the League of Nations and the Dawes Plan only to limit its participation in these American initiatives in ultimately fatal ways. The analytical problem bedevils both economic determinists and political Realists. For those who believe in the primacy of international power politics, it is difficult to explain why a United States able to reconstruct the world political system was unwilling to do so. For those who look at economic affairs first and foremost, America's unchallenged position as the world's leading capital exporter should have accelerated the trend towards trade liberalization and international monetary leadership begun before World War I; instead, the pendulum swung back towards protectionism and little public U.S. government involvement in international monetary issues.

The relevant international relations literature, faced with such analytical anomalies, generally falls back on vague reference to domestic constraints in explaining U.S. foreign economic policy in the interwar period. Charles Kindleberger, whose comparison of the era with the Pax Britannica and Pax Americana is the foundation stone for most international relations thinking on the interwar years, cites E. H. Carr approvingly to the effect that "in 1918, world leadership was offered, by almost universal consent, to the United States . . . [and] was declined," and concludes that "the one country capable of leadership [i.e. the United States] was bemused by domestic concerns and stood aside."[1]

Seen from the perspective of American domestic politics, however, the problem is quite reversed. In the context of traditional American apathy or even hostility toward world affairs, the interwar years saw an amazing flurry of global activity by the country's political, economic, and cultural leaders. Against the backdrop of the long-standing indifference of most of the American political system to events abroad, the level of overseas involvement in the 1920s and 1930s appears both startling and unprecedented.[2]

The contradictory role of the United States in the interwar period can be traced to the extremely uneven distribution of international economic interests within American society. America's international economic position did change during and after World War I, yet overseas assets were accumulated by a very concentrated set of economic actors. This left most of the U.S. economy indifferent to foreign economic affairs, while some of the country's leading economic sectors were both deeply involved and deeply concerned with the international economy. American foreign policy was thus torn between insularity and internationalism; the segments of the foreign-policy bureaucracy that reflected internationally oriented interests tried to use American power to reorganize the world's political economy, while portions of the government tied to domestically oriented sectors insisted on limiting America's international role. The crisis of the 1930s dissolved many of the entrenched interests that had kept policy stalemated and allowed a new group of political leaders to reconstitute a more coherent set of policies.

This article builds on the work of historians investigating the interwar period[3] and on the contributions of other social scientists concerned with the relationship between the international and domestic political economies. The work of Charles Kindleberger and Peter Gourevitch, among many others, has shown the importance of sectoral economic interests in explaining domestic politics and foreign-policy making in advanced industrial societies. Both Gourevitch and Thomas Ferguson have used a sectoral approach to elucidate domestic and international events in the 1930s. The present article is thus an attempt to build on existing sectoral interpretations of modern political economies and an extension of the approach to problems in international relations.[4]

THE ARGUMENT SUMMARIZED

Between 1900 and 1920 the United States went from a position of relative international economic insignificance to one of predominance. A major international borrower and host of foreign direct investment before 1900, by 1920 the United States was the world's leading new lender and foreign direct investor. The development of American overseas investments was in itself unsurprising, and in this the United States simply repeated the experience of other developed countries. Yet the rapidity of the country's shift from a major capital importer and raw-materials exporter to the leading exporter of capital, largely because of the peculiarities of the international economy in the ten years after 1914, was quite extraordinary. Even as a few major American economic actors were catapulted into global economic leadership, most of the economy remained as inward-looking as ever. This division in American economic orientation was at the root of the foreign-policy problems of the 1920s and 1930s.

As American industry and finance matured and the country became richer in capital, many large American corporations and banks looked abroad for markets and investment opportunities. United States overseas investment thus grew gradually from the 1890s until the eve of World War I. As Table 3.1 indicates, American foreign direct investment was

Table 3.1 INDICATORS OF THE IMPORTANCE OF U.S. FOREIGN INVESTMENT, 1900–1939 (IN MILLIONS OF DOLLARS AND PERCENT)

	1900	1912	1922	1929	1933	1939
1. U.S. foreign direct investment	751	2,476	5,050	7,850	7,000[e]	6,750
2. Domestic corporate and agricultural wealth[a]	37,275	75,100	131,904	150,326	109,375	119,324
3. Row 1 as a percent of Row 2	2.0%	3.3%	3.8%	5.2%	6.4%	5.7%
4. U.S. foreign bondholdings[b]	159[d]	623	4,000	7,375	5,048[f]	2,600[g]
5. U.S. holdings of non-government bonds[c]	5,151	14,524	23,687	38,099	37,748	32,502
6. 4/5, percent	3.1%	4.3%	16.9%	19.4%	13.4%	8.0%

[a] Net reproducible tangible wealth of U.S. corporations and agriculture.

[b] Due to the different sources used, figures here conflict with those in Table 3.4; those of Table 3.4 are probably more reliable, but to ensure comparability Goldsmith's figures are used throughout the table.

[c] Excludes only holdings of securities issued by U.S. federal, state, or local governments.

[d] Includes stocks (for 1900 only).

[e] Author's estimates.

[f] Figures are for 1934, from Foreign Bondholders Protective Council, *Annual Report for 1934* (Washington, D.C.: FBPC, 1935), p. 224. This includes only bonds being serviced; a more reasonable measure would include the market value of bonds in default. If this averaged 30% of par value, figures for 1933–34 would be $5,954 million and 15.8% for rows 4 and 6, respectively.

[g] Figures for 1939 holdings of foreign bonds are from Goldsmith and are probably understated.

Source: Foreign investment: Raymond Goldsmith, *A Study of Saving in the United States,* vol. 1 (Princeton, N.J.: Princeton University Press, 1955), p. 1093.

Domestic data: Raymond Goldsmith, Robert Lipsey, and Morris Mendelson, *Studies in the National Balance Sheet of the United States,* vol. 2 (Princeton, N.J.: Princeton University Press, 1963), pp. 72–83.

appreciable by 1900; it was concentrated in raw materials extraction and agriculture in the Caribbean basin. By 1912 foreign direct investment was quite substantial and overseas lending had become of some importance; the focus was still the Caribbean area.

The gradual expansion of American overseas investment, especially overseas lending, was given a tremendous shove by World War I. The war forced several belligerent countries to borrow heavily from the United States, and previous borrowers from European capital markets now turned to the United States to satisfy their needs for capital. As Table 3.1 shows, American holdings of foreign bonds soared from less than 5 percent of total American holdings of nongovernment bonds in 1912 to nearly 17 percent in 1922. Foreign direct investment also grew rapidly as European preoccupation with war and reconstruction cleared the way for many American corporations to expand further into the Third World and after the war ended in Europe itself. The 1920s saw a continuation of the wartime increase in overseas American lending and investment. American overseas investment in industrial production—especially manufacturing and utilities—and petroleum grew particularly rapidly.

By 1929 American overseas private assets—direct and portfolio investments, along with other assorted long- and short-term assets—were $21 billion. Overseas investments in 1929 were equivalent to over one-fifth of the country's gross national product, a level that was reached again only in 1981.[5]

Although America's overseas investments were substantial by the 1920s, they were very unevenly distributed among important sectors of the U.S. economy. Tables 3.2 and 3.3 illustrate that while overseas investment was extremely important for the financial community and some industrial sectors, most other sectors' foreign assets were insignificant. American foreign investments in mining and petroleum were considerable, both absolutely and relative to capital invested in corresponding activities within the United States. Foreign investment was also of great relative importance to corporations in machinery and equipment (especially electrical appliances), motor vehicles, rubber products, and chemicals. Yet these sectors, which accounted for well over half of all overseas investment in manufacturing, represented barely one-fifth of the country's manufacturing plant; far more American industries were quite uninvolved in overseas production.

Although only a few industries had major foreign operations, foreign lending was a favorite activity on Wall Street. As Table 3.3 shows, between 1919 and 1929 new foreign capital issues in New York averaged over a billion dollars a year, over one-sixth of all issues (excluding federal, state, and local securities); in a couple of years the proportion approached one-third. The United States was the world's principal long-term lender, and foreign lending was very important to American finance.

The reasons for the uneven pattern of overseas investment are fairly straight forward. It is not surprising that a capital-starved world would turn for loans to the capital-rich United States, especially to the Northeastern financial powerhouses. Foreign direct investment, on the other hand, responded to more specific incentives. Tariff barriers, which proliferated after World War I, forced former or prospective exporters to locate production facilities in overseas markets; often the advantages of local production were great even in the absence of tariffs. Foreign direct investment was thus largely confined to firms with specific technological, managerial, or marketing advantages, such as motor vehicles, electric appliances and utilities, and petroleum, as well as in the extraction of resources available more readily abroad. There was little overseas investment by industries producing such relatively standardized goods as steel, clothing, and footwear; they generally had little exporting experience and few advantages over

Table 3.2 FOREIGN DIRECT INVESTMENT AND BOOK VALUE OF FIXED CAPITAL OF SELECTED U.S. INDUSTRIES, 1929 (IN MILLIONS OF DOLLARS AND PERCENT)

Sector	A Foreign direct investment	B Book value of fixed capital	A/B in percent
Mining and petroleum[a,b]	$2,278	$12,886	17.7%
Public utilities, transport, and communications	1,625	41,728[c]	3.9%
Manufacturing	1,534	23,672	6.5%
Machinery and equipment	444	1,907	23.3%
Motor vehicles	184	1,232	14.9%
Rubber products	60	434	13.8%
Chemicals	130	1,497	8.7%
Foodstuffs	222	4,001	5.5%
Lumber and products	69	2,001	3.4%
Metals and products	150	4,788	3.1%
Textiles and products	71	2,932	2.4%
Stone, clay and glass products	23	1,451	1.6%
Leather and products	4	269	1.3%
Agriculture[d]	875	51,033	1.5%

[a] Figures for total manufacturing do not include petroleum refining, which is included under "Mining and petroleum."

[b] Figures for domestic mining and petroleum-invested capital are for the book value of capital including land but excluding working capital.

[c] Value of plant and equipment.

[d] Domestic invested capital is reproducible tangible assets of agricultural sector.

Source: Foreign direct investment: U.S. Department of Commerce, *American Direct Investments in Foreign Countries* (Washington, D.C.: GPO, 1930), pp. 29–36.

Domestic fixed capital: Daniel Creamer, Sergei Dobrovolsky, and Israel Borenstein, *Capital in Manufacturing and Mining* (Princeton, N.J.: Princeton University Press, 1960), pp. 248–51, 317–18; Melville J. Ulmer, *Capital in Transportation, Communications and Public Utilities* (Princeton, N.J.: Princeton University Press, 1960), pp. 235–37; Raymond Goldsmith, Robert Lipsey, and Morris Mendelson, *Studies in the National Balance Sheet of the United States* vol. 2 (Princeton, N.J.: Princeton University Press, 1963), pp. 78–79.

firms in their lines of business abroad. Thus the major money-center investment and commercial banks were highly international, as were the more technologically advanced manufacturing and extractive industries; traditional labor-intensive industries, which were by far the majority, were little involved in foreign investment.

American industrial export interests were similar to its foreign investments. The major industrial sectors with overseas investments were also the country's leading industrial exporters, as product-cycle theory would predict.[6] Refiners of copper and petroleum and producers of machinery and equipment, motor vehicles, chemicals, and processed food were all major exporters as well as major foreign investors. The only important exceptions to the general congruence of trade and asset diversification were the steel industry and some agricultural interests, especially in the South. Neither steel producers nor, of course, cotton and tobacco farmers had many overseas investments. To a large extent, then, the trade and foreign investment line-ups were complementary.[7]

Table 3.3   NEW CORPORATE AND FOREIGN CAPITAL ISSUES IN NEW YORK,
1919–1929 (IN MILLIONS OF DOLLARS AND PERCENT)

	A All corporate issues	B Foreign issues	B/A in percent
1919	$2,742	$771	28.1%
1920	2,967	603	20.3%
1921	2,391	692	28.9%
1922	2,775	863	31.1%
1923	2,853	498	17.5%
1924	3,831	1,217	31.8%
1925	6,219	1,316	21.2%
1926	8,628	1,288	14.9%
1927	9,936	1,577	15.9%
1928	9,894	1,489	15.0%
1929	11,604	706	6.1%
Total, 1919–1929	63,840	11,020	17.3%
Annual average, 1919–1929	5,804	1,002	17.3%

Source: United States Department of Commerce, *Handbook of American Underwriting of Foreign Securities* (Washington, D.C.: GPO, 1930), pp. 32–37.

Sectors with major overseas investment interests would be expected to have a different foreign economic and political outlook than sectors with little or no international production or sales. Internationally oriented banks and corporations would be generally favorable to freer trade, the former to allow debtors to earn foreign exchange and the latter both because intra-firm trade was important to them and because they tended to fear retaliation. Internationally oriented sectors could also be expected to support an extension of American diplomatic commitments abroad, both specifically to safeguard their investments and more generally to provide an international environment conducive to foreign economic growth. Those sectors that sold but did not invest abroad would be sympathetic to American attempts to stabilize foreign markets but might oppose international initiatives that reinforced competing producers overseas. Economic sectors with few foreign assets or sales could be anticipated to support protectionist policies in their industries because they were not importing from overseas subsidiaries, tended to be less competitive, and had few worries about retaliation. Such sectors would be unsupportive of major American international involvement that might strengthen real or potential competitors of U.S. industry.

Two broad blocs on foreign economic policy did indeed emerge after World War I, and their preferences were more or less as might have been predicted. One group of economic interests was "internationalist": it supported American entry into the League of Nations, U.S. financing of European reconstruction, commercial liberalization, and international monetary and financial cooperation. The other cluster of economic interests was the "isolationists": it opposed the league and American financing of Europe, called for renewed trade protection, and was indifferent or hostile to global financial and monetary accords.[8] The two sets of policy preferences were competing rather than complementary, and although there were some actors in a middle ground, the extreme unevenness of American overseas economic expansion meant that preferences tended to harden in their opposition.

The central dilemma of U.S. foreign economic policy for fifteen years after World War I was the great economic strength of two opposing sets of economic and political actors, neither of which was powerful enough to vanquish the other. Among the consequences of interest to the analyst of international relations is that the state *did not* undertake to impose a foreign policy derived from America's international position upon recalcitrant domestic actors; instead, the central state apparatus found itself torn between conflicting interests. The various economic interests entrenched themselves in the political arena and found allies within the government bureaucracy, so that domestic sociopolitical strife was carried out *within* the state apparatus. The Federal Reserve System and the State Department were dominated by economic internationalists, whether of the Wilsonian or Republican variants; the majority of the Congress and the powerful Commerce Department were more closely aligned with the economic nationalists who might support limited measures to encourage American exports but stopped there.

The result was a foreign policy that was eminently contradictory and volatile. The same administration encouraged foreign lending and trade protection against the goods of the borrowers, worked for international monetary cooperation and sought to sabotage it, struggled to reinforce European reconstruction and impeded it at crucial junctures. This was not due to policy stupidity but to the underlying differences in international outlook of powerful domestic socioeconomic groups. The period is thus a useful and illuminating illustration of the interaction of international and domestic sources of foreign policy.

Although it concentrates on the analytical issues of the 1920s and early 1930s, the article shows how after 1933 the world crisis served to thaw some of the policy paralysis that had characterized the postwar Republican administrations. The international and domestic crises both changed the relative strength of important social actors and allowed policy makers to reformulate their relationship to these social actors.

The remainder of this article analyzes the development of American foreign economic policy from 1914 to 1940 in the light of the preceding considerations. The analysis focuses on the interests and activities of America's international bankers. The nation's international financiers were both the most internationally oriented group of economic actors in the United States at the time (as they are today) and the most powerful and prominent members of the internationalist coalition. Their trajectory demonstrates the general lines of the approach taken here quite well, and also clarifies the role of the differentiated state apparatus in the evolution of U.S. foreign economic policy after World War I. The article does not present a complete account of the period in question—this would require a much more detailed discussion of, among other things, overseas events, America's economic nationalists, and institutional and bureaucratic developments—but it does discuss enough of the era to show how a fuller analysis could be developed.

THE EMERGENCE OF AMERICAN ECONOMIC INTERNATIONALISM, 1914–1933

For fifty years before World War I, the American political economy was oriented to the needs of domestic industry. The war accelerated a process already under way, the expansion of international investments by one segment of the U.S. business community. Along with this economic change came the development of a new set of political interests that challenged the previous pattern of foreign economic policy. In the fifteen years after World War I, the economic internationalists developed great, if quite private, influence over foreign policy but lost many public political battles. Until the Depression, American foreign economic policy was divided between measures to support "nationalist" industries and most of agriculture and those preferred by "internationalist" banks, industries, and some export agriculture.

From the Civil War until the early 1900s, however, the country's foreign economic policy was clearly designed to serve domestic industry, mostly home production for the home market and some exportation. The strategy adopted had a number of aims and evolved over time, as David Lake has demonstrated.[9] Raw materials available overseas needed to be developed and imported. Industrial goods, especially the products of basic industry, needed to find overseas markets. American tariffs on raw materials might come down, but the American market was essentially closed to industrial goods.

In this picture America's embryonic international bankers played a subsidiary but important role. They financed overseas raw materials developments and facilitated the transport and sale of raw materials to American industry. They lent dollars to overseas consumers of America's basic industrial products—railways, railroad and subway cars, mining equipment, ships. And of course they financed much of the domestic expansion and merger activity of the industrial combines.

World War I was a turning point in the evolution of American international economic interests. During the war and the period immediately following it, New York became the world's center for long-term lending. American financial supremacy drew America's internationally oriented business people and politicians into world leadership during the war and in the postwar reconstruction of Europe, a role that was to be severely hampered by the strength of economic nationalists within the United States.

The outbreak of hostilities caused financial chaos on European money markets. Panic was only narrowly averted in New York, but by early 1915 the New York market had been stabilized and was the only fully functioning major capital market in the world. Originally the Wilson administration had indicated that it considered the extension of all but short-term loans to the warring powers by American financiers "inconsistent with the true spirit of neutrality." But as the fighting continued, the belligerents began to place major orders in the United States to supply their industries and compensate for their lagging agricultures. American munitions exports went from $40 million in 1914 to nearly $1.3 billion in 1916; all merchandise exports increased from $2.4 billion in 1914 to $5.5 billion in 1916, from about 6 percent to about 12 percent of gross national product. Because imports remained near prewar levels, between 1914 and 1917 the United States averaged an astounding annual trade surplus of $2.5 billion, more than five times the immediate prewar average.[10]

The Allies, who accounted for most of this export expansion (the Central Powers were effectively blockaded), financed some of their American purchases by selling back to United States investors about $2 billion in American securities between the beginning of the war and U.S. entry. This was insufficient, of course, and soon the Wilson administration reversed its earlier financial neutrality. In October 1915, J. P. Morgan and Co. underwrote a $500 million loan to the English and French governments. Because of the opposition of neutralists and anti-Russian, German-American, and Irish-American forces, Morgan was only able to secure the full amount with some difficulty.[11]

Despite widespread hostility to their efforts, the New York bankers continued to finance the Allies. In addition, their long-standing ties with the big industrial combines placed the bankers well to arrange for Allied purchases and shipping. Thus Morgan acted during the war as the purchasing agent in the United States for the British and French, and in the three-year period up to June 1917 these purchases amounted to over one-quarter of all American exports.[12]

The Allies' financial requirements increased as the war dragged on, as did American sympathy for the Allied cause. Morgan led a series of syndicates in a further $250 million loan to England in August 1916, another of $300 million in October 1916, a $250 million issue in January 1917; France floated a $100 million bond in March 1917. All told, between January 1915 and 5 April 1917 the Allies borrowed about $2.6 billion: Great Britain and France $2.11 billion, Canada and Australia $405 million, Russia and Italy $75 million.[13]

Upon American entry into the war, private lending to the belligerents essentially ceased. Instead, between May 1917 and April 1919 the U.S. government issued four Liberty Loans and one postwar Victory Loan and used the proceeds to lend the Allies $9.6 billion.[14] American banks also took the opportunity to establish or drastically expand their branches in France to service the hordes of arriving American troops.[15]

Private lending resumed almost as soon as wartime conditions ended, as Table 3.3 indicates. Especially after the 1924 Dawes Plan, which symbolized for many the economic stabilization of Europe, lending boomed. As can be seen in Table 3.4 in the early 1920s American lending also shifted away from the wartime allies and toward "non-traditional borrowers": Germany, Canada, Italy, smaller Western European countries, the more commercially important countries of South America, and the Dutch East Indies. United States banks also expanded their branch network overseas from 26 in 1914 to 154 in 1926. As we have mentioned, direct investment abroad by American corporations also rose very rapidly, from $2.7 billion in 1914 to $7.9 billion in 1929.

The rapid overseas expansion of United States businesses after 1914 led to the maturation of an outward-looking internationalist perspective, especially on the part of the international bankers. The leaders of American finance took a new, broader view of the world in which they had invested and decided that as Woodrow Wilson said in 1916, "We have got to finance the world in some important degree, and those who finance the world must understand it and rule it with their spirits and with their minds."[16]

Apart from the general expansion of their lending, the bankers' customers had changed. No longer were the loans going to specific raw-materials projects or railroad development. The new debtors of the 1920s were more advanced nations; many of them, like Germany, were major competitors of U.S. industry. Concern about American tariffs on manufactured goods was thus logical. The debtors were also usually governments, and the close ties the bankers were building with, for example, Central and Eastern European regimes made them especially interested in European economic reconstruction and political harmony. The major international bankers, then, wanted a more internationalist foreign policy for the United States, lower tariffs, and American aid for a European settlement.

The financiers acted on their beliefs, and the postwar period saw the construction of formal and informal institutions and networks that have ever since been at the center of the American foreign policy establishment. The Council on Foreign Relations was formed right after the war: John W. Davis, Morgan's chief counsel and later a Democratic candidate for president, was the council's first president; Alexander Hemphill, chairman of the Guaranty Trust Co., headed the council's finance committee. Thomas W. Lamont of J. P. Morgan and Co. played an active role in the council and brought the founding editor of the council's journal, *Foreign Affairs*, to the job (he was editor of Lamont's *New York Evening Post*). Otto Kahn and Paul Warburg of the investment bank Kuhn, Loeb were founding directors, as was Paul

Table 3.4 AMERICAN PORTFOLIO OF FOREIGN SECURITIES, 1914–1935 (IN MILLIONS OF DOLLARS; EXCLUDES INTERGOVERNMENT WAR DEBTS)

	1914	1919	1924	1929	1935
Europe	196	1,491	1,946	3,473	2,586
Austria	1	0	27	72	57
Belgium	0	12	181	214	152
Czechoslovakia	—	0	32	32	30
Denmark	0	15	89	165	135
Finland	—	0	29	63	32
France	10	343	449	343	158
Germany	23	2	132	1,019	829
Great Britain	122	891	414	287	42
Hungary	—	0	9	63	57
Italy	0	38	41	365	271
Netherlands	0	0	99	62	132
Norway	3	5	97	185	151
Poland	0	0	30	132	97
Russia	29	127	104	104	104
Sweden	5	20	66	196	213
Switzerland	0	35	116	49	0
Yugoslavia	0	0	18	50	47
Other Europe[a]	3	3	13	72	79
Canada	179	729	1,551	2,003	1,965
South America	43	113	464	1,294	1,241
Argentina	26	58	188	370	344
Bolivia	8	10	38	62	59
Brazil	6	41	146	325	320
Chile	1	1	53	238	237
Colombia	0	1	15	167	146
Peru	2	0	9	77	74
Uruguay	0	2	15	45	51
Venezuela	0	0	0	10	10
Caribbean Region	310	305	390	430	434
Cuba	35	33	76	95	115
Dominican Republic	5	6	15	19	16
Haiti	0	0	17	15	10
Mexico	266	265	270	266	261
Central America	4	2	12	35	32
Asia	217	227	519	926	772
Australia	0	1	24	241	253
China	7	20	23	23	21
Dutch East Indies	0	0	150	175	25
Japan	184	166	234	387	384
Philippines	26	40	88	100	89
Other and international	0	0	0	18	29
Total	945	2,862	4,870	8,144	7,026

Source: Adapted from Cleona Lewis, *America's Stake in International Investments* (Washington, D.C.: Brookings Institution, 1938), pp. 654–55.

[a] In descending order of financial importance in 1929: Greece, Bulgaria, Rumania, Luxemburg, Ireland, Estonia, Danzig, and Lithuania.

Cravath, the firm's lawyer. Norman H. Davis, another founding director, was a Wall Street banker who served as assistant secretary of the treasury and undersecretary of state under Wilson; he worked closely with Lamont and financier Bernard Baruch in defining the postwar economic settlement in Europe.[17]

The council was the most important such organization, but the internationalist segment of the American business community, headed by the international bankers, also worked with other similar groups. The Foreign Policy Association, the Carnegie Endowment for International Peace (founded 1908), the League of Nations Association, and many others brought scholars, bankers, journalists, politicians, and government officials together in the pursuit of internationalism. In addition to consultation, coordination, and research, the internationalist network aimed to convince average Americans, in the words of the chairman of the Foreign Policy Association, "that their stake in the restoration of normal economic conditions in Europe is in reality as direct and vital as that of the international banker."[18]

More direct was the initiation during World War I of a system of close cooperation between foreign-policy makers, especially those concerned with foreign economic policy, and America's international bankers. It was common for important figures in American international financial circles to serve on policy advisory bodies and sometimes to rotate through positions in government, usually at the State Department and the Federal Reserve Bank of New York. Indeed, during and after the war the State Department and the Federal Reserve Bank of New York established durable working relations with the New York bankers. On every significant foreign policy initiative of the 1920s—from the Versailles Treaty itself to war debts and reparations, to the tariff issue, to the Dawes and Young Plans, to the boom in foreign borrowing and the establishment of the Bank for International Settlements—the international bankers worked together with the like-minded internationalists of the State Department and the Federal Reserve Bank of New York in the evolution of policy.

The financial and other internationalists faced the opposition of extremely powerful forces of economic nationalism in the United States. Senior Morgan partner Thomas Lamont decried "the failure of the American people to understand that the United States of America held a new position in the world" and later reflected on the unfortunate fact that "America entered upon the new decade of the 1920s in full panoply of wealth and power, but possessing little ambition to realize her vast potentialities for strengthening the world in stability and peace."[19]

The stumbling block was the existence of a considerable anti-internationalist political bloc with support from business people who had little interest in foreign affairs, worried about foreign competition, and opposed the export of American capital. The Commerce Department of Herbert Hoover, the prime mover of U.S. economic policy in the 1920s, was closely linked and deeply committed to American domestic industry. In foreign economic affairs its principal concern was thus to promote industrial exports and primary imports, not overseas lending and manufacturing investment. America's domestic industrialists could, like Hoover, agree on some things with the bankers. They all favored expanding American exports, and some kinds of imports. Yet there was little sympathy in domestically oriented industry for freer trade insofar as it meant manufactured imports. Domestic industrialists were also unhappy with American bank loans to foreign competitors, and some of them were wary of capital exports in general. As Hoover put it, "a billion dollars spent upon American railways will give more employment to our people, more advance to our industry, more assistance to our farmers, than twice that sum expended outside the frontiers of the United States."[20]

The United States faced a bewildering array of foreign-policy problems in the 1920s, and in virtually every case the tension between internationalists and nationalists defined the discussion and outcome. There is no need to describe these debates at length, for there is an ample literature on them.[21] Three broad problems—European reconstruction, trade policy, and capital exports—were of special importance, and later I shall summarize the major issues involved in these debates and note the common pattern. In virtually every case internationalist financiers and their allies in the State Department and the Federal Reserve faced the opposition of nationalist forces in Congress and other segments of the executive. The internationalists were almost always defeated, forced to compromise, or forced to adopt some form of semiofficial arrangement that kept the process out of the public eye.

European Reconstruction and War Debts

The general desire of the United States international bankers was for the rapid reconstruction of Europe. Private funds might be used for this purpose, but the financial shakiness of the potential borrowers (especially in Central Europe) made U.S. government involvement preferable. Inasmuch as the debts owed the U.S. government by the Allies were an obstacle to European reconstruction, especially since they encouraged the French to demand larger reparations payments from the Germans, the American financiers favored partial or total cancellation of official war debts.[22] All of this required American leadership: the United States government should help the Europeans back onto the gold standard, arrange for a government-backed bankers' consortium to restore Europe's shattered currencies, regularize and encourage American private capital exports to Europe, force the Europeans to negotiate a reduction of Germany's reparations burden in return for war debts leniency, and combat economic nationalism on the Continent.

This leadership was not forthcoming. Talk of war debt cancellation was quashed by economic nationalists in the cabinet and in Congress, for whom war-debt forgiveness represented a levy on American taxpayers, who would be called upon to make up the Treasury's loss, in favor of the country's European competitors. Although some refunding and reduction did occur, the bankers were forced to retreat. Government-backed loans to the Europeans were also vetoed, as was any official American involvement in the reparations tangle. Only in monetary matters, where the bankers' house organ, the Federal Reserve Bank of New York, was given fairly free rein, was limited progress made.[23]

Opposition to the bankers' plans solidified under President Warren Harding in the early 1920s. Congress and much of the executive branch were intran-sigent on the war debts and reparations issues. Herbert Hoover's Commerce Department was not generally favorable to financial schemes that might strengthen overseas competitors of American industry or that might allow foreign raw materials producers to raise prices to American manufacturers.[24] Morgan partner Thomas Lamont bitterly blasted "ill-advised steps for the collection of that debt, every penny, principal and interest," while Lamont's New York Evening Post editorialized: "We cannot emphasize too often the mischief for the European situation to-day wrought by Herbert Hoover's assertion that 95 percent of America's claims on the continent are good."[25]

It was not for lack of trying that the bankers were unable to secure government involvement. Benjamin Strong at the Federal Reserve Bank of New York played a major role in European reconstruction planning and implementation. As he said when proposing central-bank cooperation for exchange stabilization to an October 1921 meeting of the Board of Governors of the Federal Reserve System, "whether we want to or not we are going to take some part in this situation abroad. We probably won't do it politically, but we have to do it financially and economically." The governors, far more sympathetic to the desperate straits of European finances than the administration, were strongly in favor, as Governor Norris of Philadelphia indicated:

> I think the three great opportunities that we have had to accomplish the stabilization of foreign exchange were, first, to go into the League of Nations; second, to make a readjustment of our tariff . . . and the third was to empower the Secretary of the Treasury to deal in an intelligent way with the refunding of foreign obligations. . . . But because we have lost those three it does not follow, of course, that we ought to throw aside and discard all others . . . [and] it seems to me that the proposition you have suggested is one that undoubtedly has merit and may reasonably be expected to accomplish some results.[26]

Yet a month later the executive branch refused to allow a central bank conference that Strong and Montagu Norman of the Bank of England had proposed. Strong wrote to Norman at the time, "between the lines I read that there would in fact be no objection if the matter were undertaken privately and without government support or responsibility." Thus when the League of Nations's Financial Committee was supervising an Austrian stabilization program in 1922–1923, the New York bankers were regularly consulted to ensure that the program would meet with the approval of U.S. financial markets—which it did when the U.S. portion of the stabilization loan was floated in June 1923.[27]

Nevertheless, for all intents and purposes the bankers' plans for an American-supervised economic settlement in Europe were foiled. As the Central European economies collapsed in 1923 and 1924, the administration attempted to balance the financiers' insistence on American involvement against equally insistent nationalist demands that the United States stay out of Europe. The State Department, anxious to use American influence and finance to stabilize Europe, began the process that would lead to the Dawes Plan in April 1924. The arrangement worked out was ingenious: negotiations were entrusted to an unofficial delegation of American business people, headed by internationally minded Chicago banker Charles G. Dawes and Owen D. Young, chairman of the board of General Electric. The prominent internationalist bankers and business people at the center of the negotiations consulted closely, if surreptitiously, with the State Department and the Federal Reserve Bank of New York.[28]

The Dawes Plan called for foreign supervision of German public finances, with reparations payments overseen by an American with discreet ties to Morgan's. The German currency was stabilized and investor confidence in Germany restored with a $200 million bond flotation, of which J. P. Morgan and Co. managed $110 million in New York.[29] All things considered, the plan was a reasonable compromise: it used American financial supremacy to settle (at least temporarily) a major European wrangle without committing the U.S. government directly. The only open government involvement was an encouragement to American investors to subscribe to the Dawes loan, and indeed Morgan received over a billion dollars in applications, ten times the amount of the loan. The settlement satisfied most internationalists and most nationalists in the United States temporarily, and even this was quite a feat.[30]

Free Trade and the Tariff

Fundamental domestic differences over U.S. trade policy were harder to paper over. Indeed, the future of America's traditional protectionism was perhaps the most contentious issue in American politics in the 1920s. During World War I, the administration had apparently committed itself to low and flexible tariffs, in line with the bankers' preferences. When the United States became a major lender, foreign borrowers had to be permitted freer access to the U.S. market or loans could not be serviced. Tariff barriers, argued the bankers, were a cause of useless trade rivalries and war. As Morgan partner Dwight Morrow put it, "leadership in world trade is not a thing to be sought by any nation to the exclusion of all others."[31]

But in Congress those American economic actors who demanded protection from foreign imports had the upper hand. In 1921 Congress passed a restrictive Emergency Tariff Act that was followed in 1922 by the Fordney–McCumber tariff.[32] This act had provisions that attempted to satisfy both protectionist industrialists and farmers, and less successfully, internationalist bankers, investors, and traders. The compromise was generally unsatisfactory to both factions, and controversy on the tariff raged throughout the 1920s. Few doubted that traditional American protectionism had returned, and the French Finance Ministry called Fordney–McCumber "the first heavy blow directed against any hope of effectively restoring a world trading system."[33]

Such financiers as Otto Kahn looked with dismay on the continued strength of protectionist sentiment:

> Having become a creditor nation, we have got now to fit ourselves into the role of a creditor nation. We shall have to make up our minds to be more hospitable to imports. We shall have to outgrow gradually certain inherited and no longer applicable views and preconceptions and adapt our economic policies to the changed positions which have resulted from the late war.[34]

Supervision of Foreign Loans

In the early 1920s opposition to the export of American capital mounted. Domestic industrial interests were concerned that the loans were strengthening foreign competitors, especially in Germany, and reducing the capital available to domestic producers. They were also concerned that loans to raw-materials producers might be used to organize producers' cartels that would raise prices charged to U.S. industry. Hoover and Treasury Secretary Andrew Mellon thus wanted to make new loans contingent on the use of at least part of them for the purchase of American goods, or to a commitment by the borrowers to allow American suppliers to bid on ensuing contracts; they also opposed lending to nations disinclined to service their war debts to the U.S. government and lending that might reinforce the position of suppliers to or competitors with American industry. The bankers, of course, along with Benjamin Strong of the Federal Reserve Bank of New York, opposed any government controls; Secretary of State Charles E. Hughes leaned towards their position.

In 1921 President Harding, Hoover, Hughes, and Mellon met with the leading New York bankers and reached an agreement that the banks would notify the Department of State of all foreign loans and give the department the opportunity to object. Formalized in 1922, the policy was applied as sparingly as possible by a State Department that supported the bankers. Even so, in a number of instances Hoover was able to override the bankers; two prominent successes were blocked loans to a French—German potash cartel and to Brazilian coffee growers. The commerce secretary warned "the American banking community" that "the commissions which might be collected on floating such loans would be no compensation" for the "justifiable criticism . . . from the American potash and coffee consumers when [they] become aware that American capital was being placed at the disposal of these agencies through which prices were being held against our own people." Hoover also threatened to form a pool to break a British rubber cartel, complained about American lending to the German steel trust, and he and Mellon succeeded in stopping several loans for reasons related to war debts or other foreign policy objectives.[35]

Here, again, the conflict between the international interests of financiers and the national concerns of many American business people and politicians clashed. Once more, the outcome was indecisive; the State Department succeeded in blunting most of Hoover's attacks on foreign lending he regarded as excessive, yet pressure never let up.

The deadlock between internationalism and nationalism that formed in the early 1920s remained in place throughout the Coolidge and Hoover administrations. Foreign economic policy retained much of its ambiguity, with government departments and the international bankers cooperating and colliding, depending on the issue and the department involved. Internationalist bankers and business people complained bitterly of the Commerce Department's attempts to restrict their activities and to penalize their overseas clients. As Owen Young wrote to Hoover in 1926, "I am sincerely troubled by our national program, which is demanding amounts from our debtors up to the breaking point, and at the same time excluding their goods from our American markets, except for those few raw materials which we must have."[36]

Although a wide range of issues in American foreign economic policy remained unsolved, the financiers fought continually to implement some form of European economic reconstruction. After the Dawes Plan gave Germany, and by implication other Central European borrowers, the stamp of approval of international finance, loans to Europe exploded. Between 1925 and 1930 Americans lent a total of $5.3 billion to foreigners; $1.3 billion went to Canada, $1.6 billion to Latin America, and $305 million to Japan. Virtually all of the rest—$2.6 billion—went to Europe, as follows: Germany $1.2 billion (47 percent of the European total), Italy $345 million (13 percent), Eastern and Southeastern Europe $386 million (15 percent), and Scandinavia $385 million (15 percent); the remainder was scattered across a number of lesser borrowers.[37]

The United States had become the world's leading capital exporter, its bankers often acting as leaders in international financial consortia. By far the most important borrower was Germany; by 1929 American portfolio investment there had gone from nearly nothing to over a billion dollars (see Table 3.4). Germany and Central European prosperity, deemed essential to the political and economic stabilization of Europe, depended largely on injections of United States capital. Between 1925 and 1928 foreigners provided 39 percent of all long-term borrowing by the German public sector and 70 percent of all long-term private borrowing; half of the foreign lending was from America.[38]

Yet it was clear to the financiers that European economic expansion was precarious, and the fundamental division of American foreign economic policy made it more so. The bankers and their allies in the State Department and the Federal Reserve System did what they could to solidify their tenuous attempts at international economic leadership. The curious and often awkward modus vivendi that evolved was illustrated by the financial stabilization programs arranged in a series of European nations between late 1926 and late 1928. In Belgium, Poland, Italy, and Rumania, cooperative central-bank credits—generally put together by the Bank of England and the Federal Reserve Bank of New York—were extended in conjunction with longer-term private loans, of which American banks typically provided at least half. The private bankers were closely involved in the negotiations leading up to the stabilization agreements.[39]

In early 1929 the international bankers who had put together the Dawes Plan—including many who had participated in the financial stabilization programs of the late 1920s—came together again to attempt a further regularization of international financial matters. The United States was represented (unofficially, of course, as at the Dawes Conference) by Owen Young and J. P. Morgan; Thomas Lamont was Morgan's alternate. After dealing with German issues, the conference established the Bank for International Settlements (BIS) to accept continuing German reparations (renamed *annuities*) payments, and more broadly, to manage the international financial system. The BIS, which was the product of the American financiers, was to promote financial stability and take finance out of the hands of unreliable politicians. Indeed, it was founded in such a way as to make congressional approval unnecessary and congressional oversight impossible.[40]

The BIS, however, was powerless to counter the effects of the Great Depression. In May 1931, the Kreditanstalt failure triggered panic throughout Central Europe. President Hoover recognized the inevitable and in late June 1931 declared a moratorium on the payment of war debts in an attempt to stave off, in Treasury Undersecretary Ogden Mills's words, "a major catastrophe of incalculable consequences to the credit structure of the world and to the economic future of all nations."[41] Nevertheless, in 1932 defaults began in Hungary, Greece, Bulgaria, Austria, Yugoslavia, Sweden, and Denmark; in 1933 Germany and Rumania joined the list. By the end of 1934 over 40 percent of American loans to Europe were in default.[42] In the interim, of course, the United States substantially raised tariffs, even though, as Morgan's Thomas Lamont recalled, "I almost went down on my knees to beg Herbert Hoover to veto the asinine Hawley-Smoot Tariff."[43]

The contradictory nature of American foreign economic policy in the 1920s was much noted by financiers and scholars at the time. On the one hand, there was a massive outflow of private capital to Europe, while on the other, European exports to the United States, necessary to debt service, were severely restricted. To top it off, the Harding-Coolidge-Hoover administrations insisted on considering the Allies' war debts to the U.S. government as binding commercial obligations, which further restricted Europe's capacity to service American commercial debts.[44] The reason for this vacillation was that two powerful sets of interests, economic nationalists and economic internationalists, were fighting for power within the United States, and the battle raged through the 1920s and into the 1930s.

The degree to which the contradictions of U.S. foreign economic policy were recognized by the general public is indicated in Franklin Delano Roosevelt's August 1932 campaign-speech explanation of American foreign lending in *Alice in Wonderland* style:

A puzzled, somewhat skeptical Alice asked the Republican leadership some simple questions:
"Will not the printing and selling of more stocks and bonds, the building of new plants, and the increase of efficiency produce more goods than we can buy?"
"No," shouted Humpty Dumpty. "The more we produce the more we can buy."
"What if we produce a surplus?"
"Oh, we can sell it to foreign consumers."
"How can the foreigners pay for it?"
"Why, we will lend them money."
"I see," said little Alice, "they will buy our surplus with our money. Of course these foreigners will pay us back by selling us their goods?"
"Oh, not at all," said Humpty Dumpty. "We set up a high wall called the tariff."
"And," said Alice at last, "how will the foreigners pay off these loans?"
"That is easy," said Humpty Dumpty. "Did you ever hear of a moratorium?"
And so, at last, my friends, we have reached the heart of the magic formula of 1928.[45]

From 1914 on, major overseas investors, led by the international banks, rapidly extended their influence abroad and at home. Yet the battle for control of the state was undecided; instead of a unitary foreign-policy making apparatus with a coherent strategy, the United States had a foreign economic policy in the 1920s and early 1930s that was dualistic and irrational, in the sense that its various parts were in direct conflict with one another.[46] The political ambiguity of American foreign policy left American financial and other internationalists alone with their grandiose plans in a devastated world, determined that they would not again be defeated by forces that did not share their world vision.

THE RISE OF AMERICAN ECONOMIC INTERNATIONALISM, 1933–1940

Just as the shock of World War I dramatically accelerated the extension of American international economic interests, the shock of the 1930s accelerated the demise of America's economic nationalists. During the first two Roosevelt administrations, economic internationalism gradually and haltingly came to dominate U.S. foreign policy, even as policy making became ever more protected from the economic nationalists who continued to dominate the legislature. Faced with international and domestic economic crises of unprecedented depth and scope, the Roosevelt administration, after a brief attempt to rebuild international economic cooperation, retreated into domestic New Deal reforms, then slowly reemerged in the mid- and late-1930s with a series of international economic initiatives that foreshadowed the postwar Bretton Woods system.

The Depression, indeed, had a devastating impact on the traditional economic and political base of the economic nationalists. Industrial production did not regain its 1929 peak until World War II, and in the interim few regarded industry as the dynamo it had been. Agriculture was even more devastated. The banking system, of course, was also hard-hit, but most of the failures were of smaller banks. The big internationally oriented banks remained active both at home and abroad, although their economic and political influence was reduced both by the Depression itself and by Depression-era banking reforms. Table 3.1 demonstrates the continuing importance of international economic interests. Foreign direct investment, as a percentage of total corporate and agricultural invested capital, climbed through the 1930s, largely due to domestic deflation. Foreign bondholdings, of course, dropped because of defaults; this certainly harmed the bondholders but had little effect on the big investment and commercial banks themselves. In any case, holdings of foreign bonds remained substantial, and international bankers continued to hope that pre-1930 levels of lending could be restored.

When Roosevelt took office in March 1933, he hoped to reconcile two major goals: to stabilize international economic relations and to resolve the country's pressing domestic economic problems. Britain had gone off the gold standard in 1931 to devalue the pound and improve Britain's trade position; it had also moved towards trade protection within the empire. By 1933 international monetary, financial, and trade relations were in shambles. At the same time the United States was in the midst of a serious banking crisis, and the agricultural depression that had begun in the late 1920s was deepening. Roosevelt made no secret of the fact that his first priority was domestic, not international, stability.

The administration went into the international economic conference, which began in London in June 1933, willing to discuss some form of monetary cooperation with the British and French but determined that these discussions should not interfere with domestic economic measures. As it turned out, the participants in the London conference were unable to reconcile national economic priorities with internationalism. Early in July Roosevelt effectively wrecked the conference and any hopes for international currency stabilization, saying that "what is to be the value of the dollar in terms of foreign currencies is and cannot be our immediate concern."[47]

With the collapse of international cooperative efforts Roosevelt turned his attention to the domestic economy. In October the U.S. began devaluing the dollar's gold value from $20.67 to $35 an ounce. Although the devaluation was not quite the success its proponents had expected, it did mark the administration's disenchantment with internationally negotiated attempts at stabilization.[48]

Many international bankers approved of Roosevelt's domestic banking decisions and of the dollar devaluation. Yet as 1933 wore on, they were alarmed by his more unorthodox positions. Hostility between the administration and the financiers continued despite the attempts of Roosevelt and some of the bankers to call a truce, and in late 1933 and 1934, a number of financiers and policy makers close to the financial community left the administration or denounced it.[49]

The first two years of the Roosevelt administration were in fact characterized by divisions within the administration and the banking community, as well as a great deal of policy experimentation. Within the administration a running battle was waged between Wilsonian Democrat Cordell Hull as secretary of state, Assistant Secretary Francis Sayre (an international lawyer and Wilson's son-in-law) and other free-trade internationalists on the one hand, and such economic nationalists as Presidential Foreign Trade Advisor and first President of the Export-Import Bank George Peek on the other.[50] To add to the confusion, Treasury Secretary Henry Morgenthau, Roosevelt's closest adviser on economic affairs, was both fascinated by and ignorant of international financial matters.

The nearly desperate economic crisis made the early Roosevelt administration willing to consider politically and ideologically unorthodox policies.[51] Indeed, much of the bankers' distrust of FDR in 1933–1934 stemmed from the belief that he was embracing the notion of national self-sufficiency—economic nationalism with feeling—that was becoming so popular at the time and was often laced with semifascist ideology. For his part, Roosevelt was seriously concerned with the Depression's effect on the nation's social fabric and was convinced that the British and French were insurmountable obstacles to a stabilization agreement that would allow for American economic recovery. Alarmed by the domestic political situation and thoroughly disenchanted with the British and French, Roosevelt enacted emergency measures to stabilize the system. Some financiers approved; most did not.

After the first frenzied phase of crisis management, however, the administration did indeed begin to move in a cautiously internationalist direction. In June 1934 Congress passed Hull's Reciprocal Trade Agreements Act, which was broadly understood as a move towards freer trade. By 1934, too, the value of the dollar had been essentially fixed at $35 an ounce, indicating a renewed commitment to currency stability. In spring 1935 Roosevelt began cooperating with the French (over British objections) to stabilize the franc and pushed for English, American, and French collaboration for exchange-rate stability.[52] In late 1935 George Peek resigned in disgust over Roosevelt's drift to internationalism.

The financiers responded optimistically, if cautiously, to the administration's international initiatives. Early in 1936 Leon Fraser of the First National Bank of New York expressed his general approval of administration policy and his wish that this policy might become whole-hearted:

> . . . [A]fter a period of painful trial and harmful error, the authorities have seemingly reached three conclusions, each vital to monetary stabilization at home and abroad. First, they have in fact, but in silence, rejected the proposed elastic dollar and have relinked the dollar to gold instead of to some commodity index. Second, they have been, and are, practising the gold standard internationally, sub-ject to certain qualifications deemed to be necessary because of the present chaos. Third, as the log-ical next step, they stand ready to participate with other countries in the restoration of foreign exchange stabilization . . . Excellent—but a more affirmative stand will become necessary, a more explicit recognition of the responsibility which the advocacy of stabilization implies, and some assur-ances of a readiness to discharge these responsibilities in order to maintain the reestablished order.[53]

The commitment Fraser sought was indeed forthcoming. Through the summer of 1936 the administration, the British, and the French moved slowly towards a "gentlemen's agreement" to restore their currencies' convertibility to gold and commit themselves to mutual consultations and intervention to avoid exchange-rate fluctuations. On 25 September 1936, the three govern-ments agreed on a scheme embodying these commitments, with a dollar effectively linked to gold. The Tripartite Agreement—soon joined by Belgium, Switzerland, and the Netherlands—was a step towards rebuilding international economic cooperation. As one scholar has noted, "the Tripartite system may be seen as the beginning of an historical evolution that would issue after World War II in a global dollar standard."[54] For the first time the United States participated openly and prominently in leading the way towards international monetary cooperation, and the symbolic importance was more significant than any real accomplishments of the agreement.

By 1937, one prominent banker was able to name three developments that had given hope to those whose greatest fear was economic nationalism:

> First, the tripartite monetary agreement of last September was a challenge to the application of economic nationalism in monetary affairs. Second, our bilateral trade negotiations are a challenge to economic nationalism in trade affairs . . . Third, some progress is being made in the direction of the re-creation of a normal international capital market in the Western hemisphere by the recent and current negotiations with South America.[55]

Yet the developing internationalism was hardly the same as the bankers' gold-standard liberal orthodoxy. The new system compromised more with domestic countercyclical demand management and with the imperatives of the embryonic "welfare state."[56] Many of the finan-ciers indeed realized that a return to the classical gold standard was unthinkable and with Leon Fraser in 1936 looked forward merely to "a union of what was best in the old gold stan-dard, corrected on the basis of experience to date, and of what seems practicable in some of the doctrines of 'managed currencies.'"[57] Yet during the late New Deal, the foreign exchange cooperation of the Trilateral Agreement, the tentative attempts at trade liberalization (by 1939 the reciprocal trade agreements covered 30 percent of American exports and 60 percent of imports[58]) and newfound moderation towards errant debtors all indicated a less ambiguous internationalist course than at any time since Wilson.

THE EPISODE CONSIDERED

Economic nationalism reigned supreme in the U.S. political economy from 1860 until World War I, while since World War II, economic internationalism has dominated; the period considered here marks the transition from a protected home market to full participation in and leadership of world investment and trade. As such, it is of great interest to those who would draw more general conclusions about the origins of state policy in the international arena. The era involved open conflict over the levers of foreign economic policy. In the midst of this conflict the state was unable to derive and implement a unitary foreign economic policy; faced with a fundamentally divided set of domestic economic interests in foreign economic policy, the state and its policies were also divided. Each grouping of economic interests concentrated its forces where it was strongest: economic internationalists built ties with the State Department and the Federal Reserve System, while economic nationalists concentrated their efforts on Congress and a congenial Commerce Department. As socioeconomic interests were split, so too were policy makers and foreign economic policy itself.

The Depression and eventually World War II weakened the economic nationalists and allowed the state to reshape both policies and policy networks. By the late 1930s, economic nationalists were isolated or ignored, and most relevant decisions were placed within the purview of relatively internationalist bureaucracies. As economic internationalism was consolidated, the foreign-policy bureaucracy came to reflect this tendency—even as, in pre-World War I days, the apparatus had been unshakably nationalist in economic affairs.

The evidence examined here provides little support for theories that regard nation-states as rational, unitary actors in the international system. The most serious challenge of the interwar period is to "statist" assertions that foreign-policy makers represent a national interest that they are able to define and defend.[59] By extension, interwar American foreign-policy making calls into question systemic-level approaches that attempt to derive national foreign policies solely from the position of the nation-state in the international structure.[60]

The national interest is not a blank slate upon which the international system writes at will; it is internally determined by the socioeconomic evolution of the nation in question. Some nations aim primarily to expand their primary exports, others to restrict manufactured imports, still others to protect their overseas investments. These goals are set by the constraints and opportunities that various domestic economic interests face in the world arena and by the underlying strength of the various socioeconomic groups. The ability to pursue these "national interests" successfully, and the best strategy to do so, may similarly be determined by international conditions, but the interests themselves are domestically derived and expressed within the domestic political economy. A nation dominated by agro-exporters may respond to a world depression with redoubled efforts to expand exports, while a nation dominated by domestically oriented industry may respond to the same events with a spurt of industrial protectionism.

Nonetheless, underlying socioeconomic interests are mediated through a set of political institutions that can alter their relative influence. Although the relative importance of American overseas investment to the U.S. economy was roughly equal in the 1920s and 1970s, the institutional setting in the first period was far less suited to the concerns of overseas investors than it was in the second period. By the same token, policy makers can at times take the initiative in reformulating the institutional setting and the policies it has produced, as the Roosevelt administration did in the 1930s.

Indeed, one of the questions this survey of interwar American policy raises is the role of major crises in precipitating changes in political institutions, and in policy makers' room to maneuver. The Depression and World War II removed many of the institutional, coalitional, and ideological ties that had bound policy makers in the 1920s. In the United States the result was the defeat of economic nationalism, but of course the crisis had very different effects elsewhere. It would be comforting to regard the victory of economic internationalism in the United States in the 1930s and 1940s as predetermined by the country's previous evolution and experiences, but this is far too facile a solution to a complex problem. A fuller explanation of the forces underlying American foreign-policy making in the 1930s and 1940s is clearly needed, and indeed it is the logical next step for the historians who have added so much to our understanding of the 1919–1933 period or for their followers.

More generally, the interwar period in American foreign economic policy is a fascinating and extreme case of a broader problem, the conflict between domestic and international interests in modern political economies. Virtually all nations have some economic actors for whom the international economy represents primarily opportunities and others for whom it is mostly threats. This tension is especially evident in major capital exporters, since the needs of holders of overseas assets may well conflict with the desires of domestic groups. The twentieth century is full of examples in which the international-domestic divide has been central to political developments in advanced industrial societies: Britain and Germany in the interwar years are perhaps the best-known examples.[61] The American interwar experience is thus an important example of conflict between internationally oriented and domestically based interests. The conditions under which such interaction leads to major sociopolitical clashes or is overcome, and under which the foreign-policy outcome is aggressively nationalistic or internationally cooperative, or some mix of the two, are obviously of great interest to analysts of international politics.

CONCLUSION

This essay has used the evolution of U.S. foreign economic policy from 1914 to 1940 as a benchmark against which to examine the role of international and domestic determinants in the making of foreign economic policy. We have argued that the foreign economic policy of the United States in the interwar period was the result of domestic political struggle between domestic economic actors with conflicting interests in the international economy, and thus different foreign economic policy preferences. After World War I many U.S. banks and corporations saw great opportunities for overseas expansion, and fought for U.S. foreign economic policy to be assertively "internationalist." Other U.S. corporations saw the world economy primarily as a competitive threat and fought for protection and "isolationism." The evolution of the international political and economic environment, the reaction of domestic actors to this evolution, and the unfolding of domestic political struggle combined to determine U.S. foreign economic policy. This essay's effort to specify the interplay of international and domestic forces in the making of foreign policy, raises real questions about approaches that ignore domestic determinants of foreign policy. Between 1914 and 1940 at least, the foreign economic policy of the United States simply cannot be understood without a careful analysis of conflict among the disparate socioeconomic and political forces at work inside the United States itself. Such domestic forces deserve careful, rigorous, and systematic study.

NOTES

1. Charles Kindleberger, *The World in Depression 1929–1939* (Berkeley: University of California Press, 1973), pp. 297–99. The Carr citation is from his *The Twenty Years Crisis, 1919–1930* (London: Macmillan, 1939), p. 234. A popular British satirical history of the 1930s, under the heading, "A Bad Thing," summarized the results of the Great War somewhat more succinctly: "America was thus clearly top nation, and History came to an end." Walter Sellar and Robert Yeatman, *1066 And All That* (New York: Dutton, 1931), p. 115.

2. Robert Dallek, *The American Style of Foreign Policy* (New York: Knopf, 1983) is a good survey of traditional American insularity.

3. The historical literature on the period is so enormous that it is feasible only to cite the most recent important additions. Two review essays and a forum are a good start: Kathleen Burk, "Economic Diplomacy Between the Wars," *Historical Journal* 24 (December 1981), pp. 1003–15; Jon Jacobson, "Is There a New International History of the 1920s?" *American Historical Review* 88 (June 1983), pp. 617–45; and Charles Maier, Stephen Schuker, and Charles Kindleberger, "The Two Postwar Eras and the Conditions for Stability in Twentieth-Century Western Europe," *American Historical Review* 86 (April 1981). Other important works include Denise Artaud, *La question des dettes inter-alliées et la reconstruction de l'Europe* (Paris: Champion, 1979); Frank Costigliola, *Awkward Dominion: American Political, Economic, and Cultural Relations with Europe 1919–1933* (Ithaca, N.Y.: Cornell University Press, 1984); Michael J. Hogan, *Informal Entente: The Private Structure of Cooperation in Anglo-American Economic Diplomacy, 1918–1928* (Columbia: University of Missouri Press, 1977); Melvyn Leffler, *The Elusive Quest: America's Pursuit of European Stability and French Security, 1919–1933* (Chapel Hill: University of North Carolina Press, 1979); William McNeil, *American Money and the Weimar Republic* (New York: Columbia University Press, 1986); Stephen Shucker, *The End of French Predominance in Europe* (Chapel Hill: University of North Carolina Press, 1976); and Dan Silverman, *Reconstructing Europe after the Great War* (Cambridge: Harvard University Press, 1982). Many of the leading scholars in the field summarize their views in Gustav Schmidt, ed., *Konstellationen Internationaler Politik 1924–1932* (Bochum, W. Ger.: Studienverlag Dr. N. Brockmeyer, 1983).

4. Charles Kindleberger, "Group Behavior and International Trade," *Journal of Political Economy* 59 (February 1951), pp. 30–46; Peter Gourevitch, "International Trade, Domestic Coalitions, and Liberty: Comparative Responses to the Crisis of 1873–1896," *Journal of Interdisciplinary History* 8 (Autumn 1977), pp. 281–313; Peter Gourevitch, "Breaking with Orthodoxy: the Politics of Economic Policy Responses to the Depression of the 1930s," *International Organization* 38 (Winter 1984), pp. 95–129; Thomas Ferguson, "From Normalcy to New Deal: Industrial Structure, Party Competition, and American Public Policy in the Great Depression," *International Organization* 38 (Winter 1984), pp. 41–94.

5. For figures on U.S. foreign private assets see Raymond Goldsmith, *A Study of Savings in the United States*, vol. 1 (Princeton, N.J.: Princeton University Press, 1955), p. 1093.

6. The classical explanation of the process is Raymond Vernon, "International Investment and International Trade in the Product Cycle," *Quarterly Journal of Economics* 80 (May 1966), pp. 190–207.

7. On agricultural and industrial trade preferences in the 1920s, see Barry Eichengreen, "The Political Economy of the Smoot-Hawley Tariff," Discussion Paper No. 1244, Harvard Institute for Economic Research, May 1986.

8. Opposition to the league was indeed led by a prominent nationalist Massachusetts senator whose adamant insistence on protecting manufactured goods while allowing the free import of inputs was ably captured by "Mr. Dooley," who noted that "Hinnery Cabin Lodge pleaded f'r freedom f'r th' skins iv cows" in ways that "wud melt th' heart iv th' coldest mannyfacthrer iv button shoes." Cited in John A. Garraty, *Henry Cabot Lodge* (New York: Knopf, 1953), p. 268; the book contains ample, and somewhat weightier, evidence of Lodge's economic nationalism.

9. David Lake, "The State and American Trade Strategy in the Pre-Hegemonic Era," *International Organization* 42 (Winter 1988).

10. George Edwards, *The Evolution of Finance Capitalism* (London: Longmans, 1938), pp. 204–5, and U.S. Department of Commerce, *Historical Statistics of the United States* (Washington: GPO, 1960), pp. 139, 537. The definitive work on the period is Kathleen Burk, *Britain, America and the Sinews of War, 1914–1918* (Boston: Allen & Unwin, 1985). See also David Kennedy, *Over Here: The First World War and American Society* (New York: Oxford University Press, 1980); John T. Madden,

Marcus Nadler, and Harry C. Sauvain, *America's Experience as a Creditor Nation* (New York: Prentice-Hall, 1937), pp. 44–46; Alexander Dana Noyes, *The War Period of American Finance* (New York: Putnam, 1926), pp. 113–18; William J. Schultz and M. R. Caine, *Financial Development of the United States* (New York: Prentice-Hall, 1937), 503–4.

11. Harold Nicolson, *Dwight Morrow* (New York: Macmillan, 1935), pp. 171–75.

12. Cleona Lewis, *America's Stake in International Investments* (Washington, D.C.: Brookings Institution, 1938), p. 352. See for a discussion of the experience Roberta A. Dayer, "Strange Bedfellows: J. P. Morgan and Co., Whitehall, and the Wilson Administration During World War I," *Business History* 18 (July 1976), pp. 127–51.

13. Lewis, *America's Stake*, p. 355; Nicolson, *Dwight Morrow*, pp. 177–82; Vincent P. Carosso, *Investment Banking in America: A History* (Cambridge, Mass.: Harvard University Press, 1970), pp. 205–14. For a thoughtful survey of the political effects, see John Milton Cooper, Jr., "The Command of Gold Reversed: American Loans to Britain, 1915–1917," *Pacific Historical Review* 45 (May 1976), pp. 209–30.

14. This is Lewis's figure; *America's Stake*, p. 362. Others give different amounts. See for example Noyes, *The War Period*, pp. 162–93; Schultz and Caine, *Financial Development*, pp. 525, 533–42; Hiram Motherwell, *The Imperial Dollar* (New York: Brentano's, 1929), p. 85.

15. Charles Kindleberger, "Origins of United States Direct Investment in France," *Business History Review* 48 (Autumn 1974), p. 390.

16. Scott Nearing and Joseph Freeman, *Dollar Diplomacy* (New York: Huebsch, 1925), p. 273.

17. Lawrence H. Shoup and William Minter, *Imperial Brain Trust: The Council on Foreign Relations and United States Foreign Policy* (New York: Monthly Review, 1977), pp. 11–28.

18. Cited in Frank Costigliola, "United States–European Relations and the Effort to Shape American Public Opinion, 1921–1933," in Schmidt, ed., *Konstellationen Internationaler Politik*, p. 43. See also Costigliola, *Awkward Dominion*, pp. 56–75 and 140–66, and Robert A. Divine, *Second Chance: The Triumph of Internationalism in America During World War II* (New York: Atheneum, 1972), pp. 6–23.

19. Thomas W. Lamont, *Across World Frontiers* (New York: Harcourt, Brace, 1951), pp. 215, 217–18.

20. Jacob Viner, "Political Aspects of International Finance," *Journal of Business of the University of Chicago* 1 (April 1928), p. 146.

21. See, in addition to works cited above, Paul P. Abrahams, *The Foreign Expansion of American Finance and its Relationship to the Foreign Economic Policies of the United States, 1907–1921* (New York: Arno, 1976); Herbert Feis, *The Diplomacy of the Dollar: First Era 1919–1932* (Baltimore: Johns Hopkins University Press, 1950); Joan Hoff Wilson, *American Business and Foreign Policy, 1920–1933* (Lexington: University Press of Kentucky, 1971); Frank Costigliola, "The United States and the Reconstruction of Germany in the 1920s," *Business History Review* 50 (Winter 1976), pp. 477–502; and Frank Costigliola, "Anglo-American Financial Rivalry in the 1920s," *Journal of Economic History* 38 (December 1977), pp. 911–34. Because the issues are so widely treated, citations will only be given where necessary to confirm a specific fact, controversial interpretation, or direct quotation.

22. On these issues see the articles by Thomas Lamont, James Sheldon, and Arthur J. Rosenthal in *Annals of the American Academy of Political and Social Science* 88 (March 1920), pp. 114–38.

23. See especially Abrahams, *Foreign Expansion of American Finance;* and Costigliola, "Anglo-American Financial Rivalry," pp. 914–20. For an interesting view of one aspect of the war debts tangle, see Robert A. Dayer, "The British War Debts to the United States and the Anglo-Japanese Alliance, 1920–1923," *Pacific Historical Review* 45 (November 1976), pp. S69–95.

24. Joseph Brandes, *Herbert Hoover and Economic Diplomacy* (Pittsburgh: University of Pittsburgh Press, 1962), pp. 170–96; and Melvyn Leffler, "The Origins of Republican War Debt Policy, 1921–1923," *Journal of American History* 59 (December 1972), pp. 585–601.

25. Cited in Silverman, *Reconstructing Europe,* pp. 157 and 189.

26. Cited in U.S. Congress, House of Representatives, Committee on Banking and Currency, Subcommittee on Domestic Finance, *Federal Reserve Structure and the Development of Monetary Policy, 1915–1935: Staff Report* (Washington, D.C.: GPO, 1971), p. 62. I am grateful to Jane D'Arista for bringing these and other documents to my attention.

27. Hogan, *Informal Entente,* pp. 62–66.

28. See, for example, Stephen V. O. Clarke, *Central Bank Cooperation 1924–1931* (New York: Federal Reserve Bank of New York, 1967), pp. 46–57, and Charles G. Dawes, *A Journal of Reparations* (London: Macmillan, 1939), pp. 262–64, for evidence of just how central the bankers were.

29. The agent-general, S. Parker Gilbert, was a close associate of Morgan partner Russell Leffingwell. Costigliola, "The United States and the Reconstruction of Germany," pp. 485–94; Feis, *Diplomacy of the Dollar,* pp. 40–43; Leffler, *Elusive Quest,* pp. 90–112; Nearing and Freeman, *Dollar Diplomacy,* pp. 221–32; Nicolson, *Dwight Morrow,* pp. 272–78; Schuker, *French Predominance in Europe,* pp. 284–89.

30. For Lamont's optimism, see *Proceedings of the Academy of Political Science* 11 (January 1925), pp. 325–32.

31. Nicolson, *Dwight Morrow,* pp. 191–92.

32. Wilson, *American Business,* pp. 70–75.

33. Cited in Silverman, *Reconstructing Europe,* p. 239.

34. Mary Jane Maltz, *The Many Lives of Otto Kahn* (New York: Macmillan, 1963), pp. 204–5. For the similar views of Norman H. Davis, see *Proceedings of the Academy of Political Science* 12 (January 1928), pp. 867–74. See also Wilson, *American Business,* pp. 65–100.

35. Hoover is cited in Joseph Brandes, "Product Diplomacy: Herbert Hoover's Anti-Monopoly Campaign at Home and Abroad," in Ellis Hawley, ed., *Herbert Hoover as Secretary of Commerce* (Iowa City: University of Iowa Press, 1981), p. 193. See also H. B. Elliston, "State Department Supervision of Foreign Loans," in Charles P. Howland, ed., *Survey of American Foreign Relations 1928* (New Haven, Conn.: Yale University Press for the Council on Foreign Relations, 1928), pp. 183–201; John Foster Dulles, "Our Foreign Loan Policy," *Foreign Affairs* 5 (October 1926), pp. 33–48; Brandes, *Herbert Hoover,* pp. 151–96; Feis, *Diplomacy of the Dollar,* pp. 7–17; Leffler, *Elusive Quest,* pp. 58–64.

36. David Burner, *Herbert Hoover: A Public Life* (New York: Alfred A. Knopf, 1979), p. 186.

37. These are recalculated from Lewis, *America's Stake,* pp. 619–29; her aggregate figures are inexplicably inconsistent.

38. McNeil, *American Money,* p. 282.

39. See Richard H. Meyer, *Banker's Diplomacy* (New York: Columbia University Press, 1970).

40. Frank Costigliola, "The Other Side of Isolationism: The Establishment of the First World Bank, 1929–1930." *Journal of American History* 59 (December 1972), and Harold James, *The Reichsbank and Public Finance in Germany 1924–1933* (Frankfurt: Knapp, 1985), pp. 57–94. On BIS attempts at international financial cooperation from 1930 to 1931, see William A. Brown, Jr., *The International Gold Standard Reinterpreted, 1914–1934,* vol. 2 (New York: National Bureau of Economic Research, 1940), pp. 1035–47. For the views of New York bankers see the articles by Shepard Morgan of Chase and Jackson Reynolds of the First National Bank of New York in *Proceedings of the Academy of Political Science* 14 (January 1931), pp. 215–34, and Shepard Morgan, "Constructive Functions of the International Bank," *Foreign Affairs* 9 (July 1931), pp. 580–91. For an excellent overview of this period, see Clarke, *Central Bank Cooperation.*

41. Cited in Leffler, *Elusive Quest,* p. 238. On German-American financial relations after 1930, see Harold James, *The German Slump: Politics and Economics 1924–1936* (Oxford: Clarendon Press, 1986), pp. 398–413.

42. Lewis, *America's Stake,* pp. 400–1; Foreign Bondholders Protective Council, *Annual Report for 1934* (New York: FBPC, 1934), pp. 218–24.

43. Burner, *Herbert Hoover,* p. 298.

44. M. E. Falkus, "United States Economic Policy and the 'Dollar Gap' in the 1920s," *Economic History Review* 24 (November 1972), pp. 599–623, argues that America's enormous balance-of-trade surplus in the 1920s was due more to the structure and composition of U.S. industry and trade than to trade barriers. Whether this is true or not, the fact remains, as Falkus recognizes, that contemporaries on both sides of the tariff wall *perceived* U.S. tariffs to be of major significance in limiting European exports.

45. Feis, *Diplomacy of the Dollar*, p. 14.

46. These conclusions about American foreign policy in the 1920s differ a bit from those of some of the historians upon whose work my analysis is based. Leffler and Costigliola, especially, stress what they see as the unity of American policy, although both emphasize the importance of domestic constraints on this policy. In my view both scholars, despite their innovations, are too wedded to a modified Open-Door interpretation that overstates the unity and purposiveness of U.S. economic interests, and this methodological overlay colors their conclusions. I believe that the evidence, even as presented by them, warrants my analytical conclusions.

47. Stephen V. O. Clarke, *The Reconstruction of the International Monetary System: The Attempts of 1922 and 1933*, Princeton Studies in International Finance No. 33 (Princeton, N.J.: International Finance Section, Department of Economics, 1973), pp. 19–39; James R. Moore, "Sources of New Deal Economic Policy: The International Dimension," *Journal of American History* 61 (December 1974), pp. 728–44.

48. See especially John Morton Blum, *Roosevelt and Morgenthau* (Boston: Houghton Mifflin, 1970), pp. 45–53, and Ferguson, "Normalcy to New Deal," pp. 82–85. For a sympathetic European view of Roosevelt's policy, see Paul Einzig, *Bankers, Statesmen and Economists* (London: Macmillan, 1935), pp. 121–57.

49. See Blum, *Roosevelt and Morgenthau*, pp. 40–42, and for an interesting example Irving S. Mitchelman, "A Banker in the New Deal: James P. Warburg," *International Review of the History of Banking* 8 (1974), pp. 35–59. For an excellent survey of the period, see Albert Romasco, *The Politics of Recovery: Roosevelt's New Deal* (New York: Oxford University Press, 1983).

50. For details of the Hull-Peek controversy, see Frederick C. Adams, *Economic Diplomacy: The Export-Import Bank and American Foreign Policy 1934–1939* (Columbia: University of Missouri Press, 1976), pp. 81–93 and Robert Dallek, *Franklin D. Roosevelt and American Foreign Policy 1932–1945* (New York: Oxford University Press, 1979), pp. 84–85, 91–93.

51. For a discussion of the impact of crisis on ideologies and institutions, see Judith Goldstein, "Ideas, Institutions and American Trade Policy," *International Organization* 42 (Winter 1988).

52. Blum, *Roosevelt and Morgenthau*, pp. 64–67; Stephen V. O. Clarke, *Exchange Rate Stabilization in the Mid-1930s: Negotiating the Tripartite Agreement*, Princeton Studies in International Finance No. 41 (Princeton, N.J.: International Finance Section, Department of Economics, 1977), pp. 8–21.

53. *Proceedings of the Academy of Political Science* 17 (May 1936), p. 107.

54. Harold van B. Cleveland, "The International Monetary System in the Inter-War Period," in Benjamin Rowland, ed., *Balance of Power or Hegemony: The Interwar Monetary System* (New York: NYU Press, 1976), p. 51. For a lengthier explanation of the ways in which the Tripartite Agreement marked the turning point in the evolution of U.S. economic internationalism, see Charles Kindleberger, *The World in Depression 1929–1939* (Berkeley: University of California Press, 1973), pp. 257–61. See also Blum, *Roosevelt and Morgenthau*, pp. 76–88; and Clarke, *Exchange Rate Stabilization*, pp. 25–58.

55. Robert B. Warren, "The International Movement of Capital," *Proceedings of the Academy of Political Science* 17 (May 1937), p. 71.

56. John G. Ruggie, "International Regimes, Transactions, and Change: Embedded Liberalism in the Postwar Economic Order," *International Organization* 36 (Spring 1982), pp. 379–415, discusses the order that emerged.

57. *Proceedings of the Academy of Political Science* 17 (May 1936), p. 113.
58. Herbert Feis, *The Changing Pattern of International Economic Affairs* (New York: Harper, 1940), p. 95. Stephen Schuker has, in personal communication, insisted that it was not until 1942 or 1943 that Roosevelt moved away from extreme economic nationalism. He marshals important evidence and convincing arguments to this effect, but the account presented here reflects current scholarly consensus. If, as he has done in the past, Schuker can disprove the conventional wisdom, this analysis of U.S. foreign economic policy in the late 1930s would, of course, need to be revised in the light of new data.
59. See, for example, Stephen D. Krasner, *Defending the National Interest* (Princeton, N.J.: Princeton University Press, 1978).
60. As, for example, David A. Lake, "International Economic Structures and American Foreign Policy, 1887–1934," *World Politics* 35 (July 1983), pp. 517–43.
61. For a survey of each see Frank Longstreth, "The City, Industry and the State," in Colin Crouch, ed., *State and Economy in Contemporary Capitalism* (London: Croom Helm, 1979), and David Abraham, *The Collapse of the Weimar Republic* (Princeton, N.J.: Princeton University Press, 1981). On a related issue see Paul Kennedy, "Strategy *versus* Finance, in Twentieth-Century Britain," in his *Strategy and Diplomacy 1870–1945* (London: Allen & Unwin, 1983).

꩜

Economic Instability and Military Strength: The Paradoxes of the 1950 Rearmament Decision

Fred Block

The crisis created by the Soviet invasion of Afghanistan at the end of 1979 bears a striking resemblance to the events almost thirty years before when North Korean forces invaded South Korea and began the Korean War. In both situations, the invasions were widely seen as proof of the Soviet Unions' commitment to a policy of global conquest, and each invasion precipitated an effort by the administration in Washington to increase dramatically U.S. levels of military spending and military preparedness. To be sure, the events in Korea gave rise to direct U.S. military involvement and the loss of thousands of American lives, while it appears likely that U.S. involvement in Afghanistan will be limited to covert support for the various groups resisting the Soviet-backed regime. Yet despite this difference, there is another even more important similarity: in both situations, the invasion precipitated a shift in U.S. policy that appeared to have been in preparation for some time before. The Carter administration had been gradually shifting toward a more anti-Soviet foreign policy and toward support for increased military spending. Similarly, pressures had been building up for some time for the

Fred Block, "Economic Instability and Military Strength: The Paradoxes of the 1950 Rearmament Decision," *Politics and Society*, 10:1, 1980, pp. 35–58. Copyright © 1980 by Sage Publications. Reprinted by permission.

administration to overcome the weaknesses of the all-volunteer army by restoring the draft. Hence, a number of the post-Afghanistan policy initiatives of the Carter administration had the quality of initiatives that were waiting for a crisis to justify them, rather than being direct responses to a sudden change in the global political military situation.

While the evidence is still not completely in for the Carter administration's recent policy shifts, the documents are available to indicate that this is precisely what happened with the Truman administration and the Korean invasion.[1] Months before the outbreak of the Korean War, the Truman administration had approved a document called NSC (National Security Council)-68, which called for a massive rearmament effort by the United States and Western Europe as the only means to resist Soviet expansion. Despite the worsening of Soviet-American relations in the period from 1947-49, U.S. defense spending had remained in the vicinity of $15 billion a year. The drafters of NSC-68 proposed a rearmament effort that would bring the level of defense spending to $40 billion a year.[2] But given the mood at the time, which included the widespread view that the Soviets were trying to fool the U.S. into spending its way to national bankruptcy, there was no way to gain public and Congressional support for NSC-68. Instead, the Truman administration bided its time, until the coming of the Korean War, particularly the Chinese involvement in the war, created a changed national mood in which the implementation of NSC-68 became possible. As a result, levels of military spending rose dramatically, far in excess of the immediate requirements of the Korean War, so that by 1954, after the Korean truce, military spending was at $41.1 billion a year.[3]

The similarity between the two crises is more than accidental. In a number of important respects, the period of the Korean War rearmament continues to influence the making of U.S. foreign policy. In order to understand these connections, it is necessary to examine more closely the politics of the 1950 rearmament decision. The present paper will do this through a careful analysis of NSC-68 itself and of related documents published in the State Department's *Foreign Relations of the United States* series. This will necessarily fall far short of a full discussion of the complexities of the rearmament decision; such a project would require extensive archival research and probably several book-length manuscripts. My purpose here is more limited—to highlight a number of key aspects of NSC-68 that are important for understanding the concrete legacy it has left for contemporary U.S. policy makers.

THE LOGIC OF NSC-68

The document NSC-68 (which was only declassifed in 1975) is a lengthy and careful review of the global situation. It examines the structure of the U.S.–Soviet conflict, outlines the options available to the U.S., and advocates the particular option of extensive rearmament.[4] The scope of the document is broad—it includes the international military situation, the problems of the world economy, and the morale of Western societies. The document grew out of a review of the world situation begun by Truman in late 1949, in the aftermath of the "fall" of China and the first Soviet atomic explosion. One of the key precipitants of the study was the debate over the desirability of U.S. actions to develop the hydrogen bomb and the compatibility of such an effort with the rest of the national defense effort, but the study moved far beyond that specific issue to a broader review of U.S. strategy.

The document bears many of the marks of a bureaucratic product, such as the frequent resort to lists of factors without specifying their relative importance. This device serves as an attempt at bureaucratic log-rolling to gain support among a variety of different agencies.

Nevertheless, the document has a high level of internal coherence, indicating that a small number of people were responsible for the actual drafting, so that it is possible to identify a single major logic at work in the document. In short, the document is not simply a hodge-podge of different agency viewpoints. It is a serious effort to develop a coherent strategy.

Ironically, the task of understanding this logic is made easier by some of the current academic discussions about the capitalist world system. It is ironic because it seems that academic discourse, or at least neo-Marxist academic discourse, is only now catching up to the analysis of policy makers thirty years ago. In the debates generated by Immanuel Wallerstein's work on the capitalist world system,[5] a number of writers have insisted on the need to recognize the analytic distinction between the world market and the competitive state system.[6] International competition, in other words, occurs both in the world market and in the international state system. These two types of competition overlap in a variety of ways, and often success in one realm is translated into success in the other, as when an economically powerful nation is able to afford a strong military or when political–military strength results in economic gains. Wallerstein's critics suggest that the analytic distinction must be constantly borne in mind, first, because it is needed to explain those important instances where success in one realm has negative consequences in the other, and second, without the distinction, it is too easy to slip into an economic determinism in which the dynamics of political–military rivalry are not given then-due in historical explanation.[7]

In the following passage that appears near the beginning of NSC-68, the drafters of the document show that they clearly understood the distinction between objectives in the international economic realm and objectives in the competitive state system:

> Our overall policy at the present time may be described as one designed to foster a world environment in which the American system can survive and flourish. It therefore rejects the concept of isolation and affirms the necessity of our positive participation in the world community.
>
> This broad intention embraces two subsidiary policies. One is a policy which we would probably pursue even if there were no Soviet threat. It is a policy of attempting to develop a healthy international community. The other is the policy of containing the Soviet system. These two policies are closely interrelated and interact on one another. Nevertheless, the distinction between them is basically valid and contributes to a clearer understanding of what we are trying to do.[8]

For the drafters of NSC-68, a healthy international community meant the restoration of an open world economy in which goods and capital were able to flow across national boundaries in response to market forces. The underlying assumptions linking such an international community to the survival of the American system were spelled out with brutal clarity by Dean Acheson (secretary of state at the time of NSC-68) in Congressional testimony in 1944 that has often been quoted:

> We cannot go through another ten years like the ten years at the end of the Twenties and the beginning of the Thirties, without having the most far-reaching consequences upon our economic and social system . . . . When we look at that problem we may say it is a problem of markets. You don't have a problem of production. The United States has unlimited creative energy. The important thing is markets. We have to see that what the country produces is used and is sold under financial arrangements which make its production possible . . . . You must look to foreign markets.
>
> If you wish to control the entire trade and income of the United States, which means the life of the people, you could probably fix it so that everything produced here would be consumed here, but that would completely change our constitution, our relations of property, human liberty, our very

conceptions of law. And nobody contemplates that. Therefore, you find you must look to other markets and those markets are abroad . . . .[9]

Acheson's testimony highlights the close connection between the stability of the domestic U.S. economy in the postwar period and the organization of the international economy. In light of the enormous productiveness of U.S. industry and agriculture and market-imposed limits on domestic purchasing power, the U.S. appeared to face a return to economic depression unless some solution could be found to the problem of creating adequate demand. The solution that required the least change in existing institutions and that had the support of the largest industrial firms and banks was an international one. The United States would run an export surplus for a period of years, exporting substantially more to the rest of the world than it imported.[10] This export surplus would be financed by a dramatic increase in U.S. foreign investment, as U.S. business took advantage of profitable opportunities abroad. This solution would provide markets for U.S. surpluses of agricultural and industrial commodities, supplementing domestic demand with foreign demand, and it would maximize the opportunities available for U.S. business. But its viability depended upon the restoration of a stable international monetary order with a high level of openness to market forces. Without such a stable and open international order, the U.S. would not be able to find markets abroad for its products, nor would overseas investment opportunities be attractive to U.S. firms, since there would be little guarantee that profits could be repatriated. In sum, U.S. policy makers shared the realistic assessment that the strength of the domestic economy was inseparable from the task of stabilizing the international monetary order—creating "a healthy international community."[11]

The drafters of NSC-68 recognized that the creation of an international economic order that was consistent with U.S. economic strength was a problem distinct from the rivalry with the Soviet Union in the international state system. There were nevertheless significant overlaps between the two realms. First, nations that came under Soviet political–military influence were unlikely to cooperate with the U.S. in creating an open world economy. Second, the failure of the U.S. to create a stable international economic order and prevent the return to depression conditions would likely bring to power in Europe leftist regimes that would be more sympathetic to the Soviet Union.[12] Nevertheless, the drafters insisted that the distinction between the two policy areas "is basically valid and contributes to a clearer understanding of what we are trying to do."

This assertion seems strangely out of place. The thrust of the document is to forget the distinction by defining the U.S. global position strictly in political–military terms. The rhetoric of NSC-68 repeatedly proclaims the existence of a political–military conflict that threatens the very existence of the West, so that economic questions pale in comparison. On the first page of NSC-68, the drafters write:

. . . the Soviet Union, unlike previous aspirants to hegemony, is animated by a new fanatic faith, antithetical to our own, and seeks to impose its absolute authority over the rest of the world. Conflict has, therefore, become endemic and is waged, on the part of the Soviet Union, by violent or non-violent methods in accordance with the dictates of expediency . . . Any substantial further extension of the area under the domination of the Kremlin would raise the possibility that no coalition adequate to confront the Kremlin with greater strength could be assembled. It is in this context that this Republic and its citizens in the ascendancy of their strength stand in their deepest peril.[13]

And the document's final paragraph begins:

> The whole success of the proposed program hangs ultimately on the recognition by this Government, the American people, and all free peoples, that the cold war is in fact a real war in which the survival of the free world is at stake.[14]

There was good reason for this rhetoric; the drafters of NSC-68 believed that a rearmament policy would solve the problems in both the political–military realm and the economic realm and that a rearmament policy could be sold only through an emphasis on a military threat. More specifically, the drafters were afraid that only in the context of a full militarization of foreign policy would Congress be induced to provide the funds necessary to achieve the critical economic policy objectives.

As we shall see, confusing the distinction between political–military and economic objectives was a tactical expedient designed to solve immediate problems. The brief reference to the importance of the distinction makes sense as a reminder of the sleight of hand that the drafters were performing because they wanted to keep in mind the distinction for long-term strategic purposes. They were aware, in short, of the dangers to a dominant power of overemphasizing one competitive realm at the expense of the other, and they did not want the current expedient to become long-term policy.

THE CONTEXT: INTERNATIONAL ECONOMIC INSTABILITY

To understand why the drafters resorted to this expedient, it is necessary to examine both the international economic context and the international military context. The key economic problem for the United States in the postwar period was that the U.S. enthusiasm for an open world economy was shared by only a tiny fraction of the Western European population, since even many European capitalists were skeptical of the American design.[15] Behind this skepticism lay two concrete realities of Europe's postwar situation: strong inflationary pressures and a deterioration of Europe's international payments position. The inflation was rooted in intense struggles over inadequate supplies of goods. The war had impaired the capacity of the European economies to produce civilian goods, and the end of the war generated tremendous demands on the existing civilian capacity. Capitalists wanted resources to rebuild their plants, while workers wanted more goods and social services as compensation for the long years of war and depression. The results of this conflict were intense inflationary pressures.

No matter whether inflation was held in check by price controls or allowed free reign, the inflationary pressures made any movement toward economic liberalism impractical. In fact, in the immediate postwar years, the movement was entirely in the direction of increased controls over international economic transactions. Exchange controls were carried over from the war to minimize the flow of capital into more stable currencies. Quantitative restrictions were placed on imports so that strong domestic demand would not lead to disastrous trade deficits. Governments also negotiated a series of bilateral trading agreements that made it possible to continue more international trade under conditions where domestic prices were largely irrelevant. Finally, state trading—government centralization of trade in certain commodities—was increasingly resorted to, which also had the effect of severing domestic prices from international prices.

Since the U.S. and Canada did not suffer from the same inflationary pressures, any effort by the Europeans toward international economic liberalization would have led to disastrous outflows of hard currency to these two nations, which had both ample supplies of goods and far more stable currencies. Such an outcome would have been very serious since Europe's international economic position had already deteriorated dramatically from prewar patterns. Before the war, Western Europe was able to finance a trade deficit of some $2.1 billion a year with its earnings from invisibles—shipping, banking, and returns on foreign investments— largely in the Third World. By 1947, Western Europe was running a deficit on those invisibles of some $0.6 billion. The shift occurred because of the liquidation of foreign investments, the accumulation of overseas debts, and the costs of ongoing military efforts in Vietnam, Indonesia, and Malaya. This shift meant that the prewar triangular pattern, in which Europe financed its deficit with the United States with surpluses earned in Asia, could not continue. Since Europe's currency reserves had also declined sharply, there was no obvious way that Europe could finance its Hade deficit with the U.S. In the short term, Western Europe had little to export, and in the long term, U.S. protectionism made it unlikely that Western Europe could pay for its dollar imports with exports to the U.S.

The nightmare for U.S. policy makers was that this situation might lead Europe to insulate itself permanently from the U.S. economy. If Europe could not finance its deficit with the U.S., nor risk an economic liberalization that would include the U.S., the Europeans might erect a system of controls that would sharply restrict U.S. exports to Europe. Such controls would also restrict U.S. investment in Europe, since exchange controls would cast doubt on the ability of firms to repatriate profits earned on European investments. Furthermore, if Europe continued down that course, trade between Europe and its former colonies in Asia and Africa would be organized along bilateral lines that would discourage U.S. penetration of those areas. The prospect was of U.S. economic activity largely restricted to the Western hemisphere, leading perhaps to the fundamental institutional changes that Acheson had warned of in 1944.

By 1947 it was clear that without a major American initiative that nightmare would become a reality. Western Europe's imports from the U.S. had already begun to decline because of the lack of means to finance them, and Europe's economic controls appeared likely to harden into a permanent arrangement. It was in this context that the Marshall Plan was devised. The plan represented a multifaceted attack on the various obstacles to Western European participation in an open world economy.

Most obviously, the Marshall Plan provided a means to finance continued Western European imports from the United States at a level of $4 to 5 billion a year. This postponed any chance that Western Europe would close itself off to U.S. exports, and it reversed the decline in the level of U.S. exports. However, the policy makers were keenly aware that Congress was unlikely to approve Marshall Aid for more than a limited number of years. As it was, Congressional resistance to what was widely perceived as a giveaway of U.S. dollars was only overcome through the deliberate creation and exaggeration of Cold War tensions by the Truman administration.[16] From the start, therefore, the problem was how to avoid a reassertion of Western Europe's need to restrict its economic links to the United States once Marshall Aid ended.

The proposed solution was to use the period of the Marshall Plan to strengthen the Western European economies to the point where they could successfully compete in an open world economy. Most immediately this meant squeezing the inflation out of those economies through a combination of deflationary economic policies and political maneuvers designed to weaken the union movements. Additional policies were needed to achieve the long-term goal;

great emphasis was placed on encouraging productive investment to strengthen Western Europe's export capacity. Recognizing that the small size of the different European economies could result in needless duplication of capacity, U.S. policy makers supported Western European regionalism as a means to increase the efficiency of new investments. Support for regionalism also made possible a gradualist program of economic liberalization. Since it was impractical to expect nations to move directly from bilateral trading arrangements to full participation in an open world economy, liberalization within Western Europe could he an intermediary step on the road to full liberalization. Finally, Western European regionalism gave legitimacy to the controversial U.S. goal of restoring Germany's industrial strength, which was seen by U.S. policy as indispensable for Western Europe's future participation in an open world economy.[17]

In a number of respects the Marshall Plan was a brilliant success, It provided a temporary solution to the dollar problem, halted the movement toward economic closure, and shifted the European political climate in a pro-American direction. It was also successful in weakening the left and in slowing inflation. Nevertheless, its long-term goals remained elusive. To make Western Europe's economy self-supporting in dollars in an open world economy required major structural changes in the pattern of world trade, which could not be accomplished in a four-year period. It was simply too large a task to alter the practices of European businessmen, to develop efficient mechanisms for planning investments within nations, to achieve a high level of economic coordination across nations, and to overcome Congressional protectionism to expand U.S. markets for European exports. By 1949 it was already clear that when the Marshall Plan came to an end in 1951 the United States would be faced with the same danger—the progressive insulation of the European economies.

But there were also a number of factors that made these concerns even more immediate during the course of 1949. First, there was the continuing possibility that Congress would sharply reduce Marshall Plan appropriations for the third or fourth years of the plan, precipitating a more immediate crisis. Second, Great Britain experienced a serious foreign exchange crisis during 1949. It had been the hope of U.S. policy makers that Great Britain and the British pound would provide a bridge between the U.S. and Western Europe in the constructing of an open world economy. To this end, the U.S. had pressured Britain in 1947 to dismantle many of its exchange controls, so that the pound could again play a role in financing international trade. The results of the experiment were disastrous, and exchange controls were quickly reimposed. Yet in 1949, even with controls and Marshall Plan aid, Great Britain was running an insupportable dollar deficit. The Commonwealth ministers responded by increasing their restrictions on dollar imports and threatened even more severe restrictions if more dollar aid were not forthcoming. And this pressure by Britain for a greater share of Marshall Aid came at a time when there were already fierce conflicts over the distribution of the aid—conflicts that threatened the continuation of European-American cooperation. Third, the U.S. economy slipped into recession in late 1948. Unemployment averaged 5.9 percent during 1949 and reached a peak of 7.6 percent in February of 1950. Since this was the first postwar recession, there was little reason to assume that recovery would occur automatically. It was just as plausible to see the economic downturn as a prelude to the return of the Great Depression. Hence, when U.S. exports began to drop in the second half of 1949, anxiety increased that international factors would intensify deflationary pressures at home. Finally, there were indications of economic slowdown in Western Europe during 1949. While these slowdowns generally originated in deliberate anti-inflationary policies, their continuation could further reduce demand for U.S. exports.

In short, it was relatively easy during the second half of 1949 to construct apocalyptic scenarios in which Britain's problems and economic stagnation on the Continent served to reduce U.S. exports. This reduction, coming on top of a U.S. recession caused by lagging industrial investment, could push the U.S. economy into a downward spiral.

THE CONTEXT: MILITARY STRENGTH

At the same time, the United States faced serious problems in its political–military competition with the Soviet Union. The successful Soviet atomic test came sooner than U.S. policy makers had anticipated, and it meant the loss of the self-confidence that the atomic monopoly had given the U.S.[18] Furthermore, during 1949, there was mounting pressure within Europe for direct negotiations between the United States and the Soviet Union to reduce global tensions. The primary issue to be negotiated was the future of Germany.[19] It was a central tenet of U.S. policy that an economically restored West Germany be strongly oriented toward the West. It was feared by U.S. policy makers that in light of West Germany's strategic location and its economic strength, its neutralization would shift the balance of power in Europe strongly in favor of the Soviets. Without West Germany as an anti-Soviet bulwark—politically, economically, and militarily—France, Italy, and Great Britain would necessarily move closer to the Soviets. This was the threatened "Finlandization" of Western Europe. Just as Finland maintained its independence but was forced to accommodate itself to the Soviet Union in certain areas of policy, so U.S. policy makers feared that all of Western Europe would be Finlandized if Germany were neutralized.

U.S. policy makers believed that if a general European settlement were negotiated during 1949-50, it would be impossible for the U.S. to resist the neutralization of Germany. The problem was that neutralization was an obvious logical solution and it was attractive to those many Europeans who found the idea of an economically and militarily revived Germany abhorrent. Hence, U.S. policy was to avoid negotiation while actively working to incorporate West Germany into a pro Western alliance. To justify this policy, Dean Acheson used the concept "negotiation from strength" to mean that the United States was eager to negotiate a general European settlement but was only willing to do so when it could come into negotiations from a position of strength.

NSC-68 proposed to create that strength through a massive rearmament effort that would triple U.S. military spending, while also rearming the other members of the Western Alliance. The latter effort would require both dramatic increases in military spending, particularly in France and Britain, and greatly increased U.S. military and economic aid to Western Europe. This rearmament effort was justified by an analysis that stressed the Kremlin's expansionary ambitions and insisted that only through such an effort could liberty and freedom be preserved.

While the rhetoric stressed the political–military necessity of rearmament, it is also clear from the document that rearmament was seen as a solution to the economic weakness of the West. The necessity of continued aid to support Western Europe's rearmament would provide a continuing means to overcome Western Europe's dollar shortage—both immediately and after the Marshall Plan. The advantages of linking aid to rearmament are spelled out in a State Department memo, written in late 1950, that argues for incorporating all aid to Europe into one bill:

It seems desirable, therefore, if it is feasible, to deal with the European problem in one title. We have been furnishing three kinds of assistance to these areas, (a) military end items, (b) economic aid in support of the military effort abroad [for example, support for the French in Indochina], (c) aid to achieve European economic recovery. The advantages of combining all of these types of aid in one title are as follows. (1) Congress is more likely to be sympathetic toward a program based upon military security than one in which part of the justification is based on continued economic recovery. (2) The three types of assistance are in effect closely interrelated. Maximum flexibility is needed between funds available for procuring U.S. manufactured end-use items and for the production of such items abroad. *The distinction between aid in support of foreign military effort abroad and aid for economic recovery is largely artificial.*[20]

Furthermore, the rearmament effort was intended to respond to the weakness of demand in both the U.S. and the Western European economies. In NSC-68's assessment of the West's over-all economic situation, the drafters write:

. . . there are grounds for predicting that the United States and other free nations will within a period of a few years at most experience a decline in economic activity of serious proportions unless more positive governmental programs are developed than are now available.[21]

This is supplemented by another passage that argues:

With a high level of economic activity, the United States could soon attain a gross national product of $300 billion per year, as was pointed out in the President's Economic Report (January 1950). Progress in this direction would permit, and might itself be aided by, a build-up of the economic and military strength of the United States and the free world; furthermore, if a dynamic expansion of the economy were achieved, the necessary build-up could be accomplished without a decrease in the national standard of living because the required resources could be attained by siphoning off a part of the annual increment in the gross national product.[22]

These passages indicate that the drafters were influenced by Keynesian thought and saw military spending as a way to bolster economic activity. For the United States, rearmament could lead to such a great increase in economic activity that it would be possible to have both guns and butter—a continually rising standard of living. For Western Europe, rearmament would boost economic activity to prevent destabilizing unemployment,[23] and it would expand West Germany's Western markets. The latter was critical in order to reinforce West Germany's pro-Western orientation.

The logic of NSC-68 therefore was to accomplish both objectives of U.S. foreign policy—the containment of the Soviet Union and the creation of an open world economy—through rearmament. Military spending would strengthen the Western Alliance, including West Germany, by adding military interdependence to a precarious economic interdependence, and it would provide the strength that was seen as a precondition for negotiating with the Soviets. At the same time, rearmament would overcome the economic weakness of the West by providing a means to finance Europe's dollar deficit and a means to bolster economic demand.

CRITICISMS AND CONTRADICTIONS

NSC-68's strategy of solving economic problems through military means depended on a rather simple transposition. Instead of honestly confronting the weaknesses of liberal capitalism and the enormous difficulties of creating an open world economy, the drafters chose to transpose Western economic weakness into Soviet military strength. To be sure, the West's economic weakness did greatly enhance the Soviet Union's global strategic position, but this source of strength had nothing to do with Soviet military capacities. The drafters believed, however, that they could provide a justification for rearmament policies by vastly exaggerating Soviet military strength. These rearmament measures would, in turn, strengthen the West militarily and, as we have seen, provide solutions to some of the West's most pressing economic problems. And the success of such a policy would make further use of this transposition unnecessary because the main source of Western weakness would be overcome. In sum, the heart of NSC-68 was the use, as a short-term expedient, of a rhetoric that subordinated all other considerations to the direct confrontation with the Soviet military challenge.

There were voices that objected strenuously to this strategy. No less a figure than George Kennan, an increasingly marginal figure in Acheson's State Department, developed a careful critique of the logic that led to NSC-68, In a memo to Acheson in February of 1950, Kennan sought to show how the logic underlying the Marshall Plan was fundamentally different from the logic of those favoring rearmament:

> Because the Russian attack, ideologically speaking, was a global one, challenging the ultimate validity of the entire non-communist outlook on life, predicting its failure, and playing on the force of that prediction as a main device in the conduct of the cold war, it could be countered only by a movement on our part equally comprehensive, designed to prove the validity of liberal institutions, to confound the predictions of their failure, to prove that a society not beholden to Russian communism could still "work." In this way, the task of combating communism became as broad as the whole great range of our responsibilities as a world power, and came to embrace all those things which would have had to be done anyway—even in the absence of a communist threat—to assure the preservation and advance of civilization. That Moscow might be refuted, it was necessary that some thing else should succeed. Thus Moscow's threat gave great urgency to the solution of all those bitter problems of adjustment which in any event would have plagued and tested the countries of the non-communist world in the wake of these two tremendous and destructive world conflicts. And it was not enough, in the face of this fact, to treat the communist attack as purely an outside one, to be dealt with only by direct counter-action. Such an approach was sometimes necessary; but primarily *communism had to be viewed as a crisis of our own civilization, and the principal antidote lay in overcoming the weaknesses of our own institutions.*[24]

For Kennan, the Marshall Plan succeeded because it simultaneously countered the Soviet Union and strengthened liberal institutions in the West. He could not see how the rearmament policy—predicated on the assumption that the threat was strictly external—could solve the problems posed by "the weaknesses of our own institutions." While Kennan could see clearly the transposition involved in the rearmament policy and warn of its limitations, he himself lacked a serious policy alternative. In this period, he campaigned for an economic merger between the United States and Great Britain as a way to bolster Britain's economy and make it an effective bridge between the U.S. and Western Europe.[25] The immense impracticality of this alternative suggests both the enormous seriousness of the West's economic problems and the difficulty of devising a solution that did not rest on the militarization of foreign policy.

In fact, rearmament became official policy largely because of the absence of coherent alternatives. This can be seen by focusing on one particular aspect of the policy—the mechanisms for financing Western Europe's dollar deficit. The rearmament policy provided a number of different ways to funnel dollars into Western European hands. First, dollar aid to support the rearmament effort was far more popular with Congress than simple economic aid, but it could easily be used for many of the same purposes. Second, the stationing of large numbers of U.S. troops in Western Europe and elsewhere added to the outflow of dollars. Finally, off-shore procurement of military goods provided an additional form of dollar aid. The U.S. could, for example, buy weapons for France from Great Britain and thus provide Britain with much needed dollars. Together these mechanisms accounted for a substantial and flexible outflow of dollars.

Those attempting to develop an alternative policy to rearmament had to figure a comparable way to provide enough dollars to Western Europe to finance current deficits and discourage any attempts at increased European protectionism. They had only three means available—increased private investment in Europe, increased imports of European goods, or increased government aid. The first was impractical because political and economic instability in Western Europe acted as a major disincentive for business investment. Furthermore, resort to major private (or even public) loans to underwrite European currency stabilization had been discredited by the disastrous experience of the interwar years. Increasing Europe's ability to earn dollars through exports quickly ran into the problem of Congressional protectionism—a powerful force that was unlikely to compromise in the midst of a domestic economic downturn. Finally, any scheme for government aid had to involve some procedure for disarming Congressional skepticism, which is what Kennan sought to do with his improbable idea of a merger between the United States and Great Britain. This skepticism had made it increasingly difficult for the Truman administration to gain Congressional approval for Marshall Plan aid with each passing year. In order to gain such approval, the administration had constantly promised the Congress that the Marshall Plan would succeed in making Western Europe self-sufficient by the program's end. Thus, to preserve the Marshall Plan for its four years, the administration had to bargain away its chance to ask for any continuation of the program.[26] In sum, the seriousness of the problem is indicated by the unlikelihood that even the full militarization of foreign policy could have succeeded in overcoming Congressional resistance to additional aid for Europe, had it not been for the crisis atmosphere created by the Chinese entrance into the Korean War.

The architects of NSC-68 succeeded not because they had a compelling view of the long-term needs of U.S. capitalism, but because they put together a policy that provided solutions to a number of immediate and pressing problems. And moreover, they were provided with an opportunity—in the form of the Korean War—that made their proposals politically practical. The strength of their proposals was that they tended to minimize immediate risks, in contrast, for example, to efforts to reform Western institutions that might have greater long-term benefits but less chance of immediate success. But while the rearmament policy made sense as a five-year plan, its critical flaw was that it biased policy makers toward the militarization of foreign policy for the generation to follow.[27]

THE LEGACY OF NSC-68

Even thirty years later, the legacy of NSC-68 weighs heavily on U.S. foreign policy. It was NSC-68's success in solving short-term problems of U.S. foreign policy that elevated militarization of foreign policy into a paradigmatic solution to foreign policy difficulties. To be sure, the militarization of foreign policy, and the accompanying adoption of Manichean imagery that holds a foreign enemy responsible for all problems, is a temptation with an ancient lineage. The successes that came in the wake of the Truman administration's surrender to this temptation served to make this policy choice even more attractive. Hence, both John Kennedy and Jimmy Carter, when faced with serious obstacles to successful domestic policy initiatives and deteriorating relations within the Western Alliance, moved in the direction of the militarization of foreign policy, opting for increased defense budgets and more belligerent anti-Communist rhetoric. If such tactics succeeded for Truman—both in terms of his own popularity and in easing the economic and political problems of U.S. foreign policy—then surely they might work once again.

Yet the continuing appeal of the paradigm of militarization of foreign policy cannot be explained simply in terms of its earlier success; there are three distinctive structures, created in substantial part by NSC-68, that act to prevent American policy makers from straying too far from the logic of militarization. These structures are the Western military alliance, the military–industrial complex, and the "loss of China" complex.

The Western Alliance

As we have seen, a key component of the strategy of NSC-68 was to overcome Western Europe's tendency to pursue an independent economic course by binding Western Europe to the U.S. with military ties. With the passage of time, this dimension of U.S. policy has become progressively more important, since Western Europe's greater economic power creates multiple interest conflicts between it and the United States. The principal means by which the U.S. has acted to dampen these conflicts and to discourage Western Europe from pursuing the independent policy has been to remind Western Europe of its dependence on the U.S. defense commitment. The great risk for U.S. policy of detente with the Soviet Union is that it would act to sharply reduce Western Europe's fear of the Soviet Union, leading to a weakening of the Western Alliance and increased conflict between the U.S. and Western European governments over such issues as trade, international monetary arrangements, and energy. In this context, periodic resorts to militarization and the revival of Cold War tension between the U.S. and the Soviet Union generate pressures to bring Western Europe back into line.[28]

The Military–Industrial Complex

The rearmament proposed by NSC-68 led to the creation of a large sector of the economy devoted to military production. This sector accounted for a considerable percentage of total corporate profits and total employment in the economy. Once in place, this military–industrial complex tended to be self-perpetuating, since the corporations involved and their employees exerted strong pressure for continuing high levels of military spending. This pressure was effectively transmitted through Congress, as individual senators and representatives acted to maintain stable or increasing levels of employment in their districts. This pressure has been sufficient to prevent any sharp decreases in military spending, except in the immediate aftermath of the Korean and Vietnam Wars.

There have been, however, two periods, 1954-60 and 1971-77, in which the level of military spending remained roughly stable, so that defense spending declined considerably as a percentage of GNP. Yet in the latter part of each of these periods, there was mounting pressure for dramatic new increases in military spending. The pressure derives directly from the military–industrial complex, which stands to gain from higher levels of spending. And in both periods a strong intellectual case could be made for higher levels of defense spending because of the dynamics of a competitive arms race. By the late fifties, for example, the Soviet Union was finally developing the military capacities that the advocates of rearmament in 1950 had foreseen as an immediate threat to the U.S. That the Soviets developed those capacities largely in response to the American rearmament was irrelevant to the case for increased military spending in the early sixties. Similarly, by the late seventies, defense analysts could point with alarm to the Soviet gains that had been made in response to increased American military spending of the sixties.[29] While politicians might be able to resist these pressures for a new round of escalated military spending for a number of years out of a fear of too much stimulus to the economy or out of a commitment to civilian spending, it is difficult to resist the tide indefinitely. The forces for rearmament are persistent and well organized, and the instability of international politics seems bound to provide them with an opportunity to prevail.

Moreover, the structure of the military–industrial complex itself seems to give plausibility to these demands for periodic jumps in the level of military spending. In order to solidify the corporate–government alliance that is at the heart of the military–industrial complex, it was necessary to assure business especially high levels of profits as an exchange for the loss of business autonomy that results from having the government as one's only market for certain goods. This meant institutionalizing certain practices, such as the cost-plus contracts, that guarantee generous corporate profits. The results of such arrangements are that a high degree of waste has been built into the system of military procurement.[30] Added to this is the special attractiveness in military development of unusually large or exotic weapon systems—an attractiveness that derives from the interagency and intercorporate rivalries within the military–industrial complex.

Taken together, these two factors operate against efficient and effective use of military spending at any level. As long as one takes these two factors as given, then a plausible case can always be made that current levels of military preparedness are inadequate and that billions more should be spent both to produce new generations of more basic military weapons and to bring to fruition the large and elaborate systems that are still on the drawing boards.

The "Loss of China" Complex

The final structure is the one that goes furthest to explain why the paradigm of militarization operates so much more strongly on Democratic presidents than on Republicans. The loss-of-China complex operates as a structure precisely because its rests on the special dynamics of the two-party system in the U.S. Here, too, the implementation of NSC-68 created a structure that still shapes policy.

While NSC-68 itself remained classified, its implementation required that the Truman administration adopt in its public rhetoric the Manichean imagery of a world divided between Communist evil and the Western forces of good. This imagery included the notion of a tipping point—any further increase in Communist power anywhere in the world might effectively tip the balance, so that the forces of good would no longer be able to resist the global spread of tyranny.[31] This imagery, of course, had largely been monopolized by the extreme anti-Communist right-wing. In adopting it, the Truman administration gave enormous legitimacy to this extreme anti-Communist viewpoint. In short, by making the defeat of Soviet expansionism the only question of American foreign policy, the Truman administration made itself quite vulnerable to those who felt that insufficient effort had been expended in saving China from the Communists. Within the Manichean framework, the risk of the U.S. being bogged down in a major land war in Asia was certainly less than the dangers involved in increasing the Communist empire by hundreds of millions of Chinese.

Added to this vulnerability was the standard dynamic of a two-party system in which parties out of office move away from the political center. Hence, the position of McCarthy and his allies in the right-wing of the Republican party was enhanced in a period where the normal drift of the party was to the right. The result was the mobilization of large sectors of public opinion against the Truman administration for being soft on communism at precisely the point at which the administration was launching a hard-line anti-Communist foreign policy. Thus Acheson, one of the major architects of NSC-68, was excoriated by McCarthy and others for a host of crimes ranging from his defense of Alger Hiss to the loss of China.[32]

This right-wing attack was doubly costly for the leading figures of the Democratic party. It exposed some of them to a humiliating personal attack that forced them to defend themselves against charges of treason, and it played an important role in the Democratic electoral defeat in 1952. While Eisenhower's victory that year was hardly in doubt, the extent of the Republican landslide certainly owed a good deal to the rhetoric that charged the Democrats with "twenty years of treason."

The lesson that Democratic politicians and policy makers derived from this trauma was not the obvious one. They might well have recognized that adopting the right wing's rhetoric is a dangerous tactic, since the right wing will always be able to find fault with the lack of Democratic party single-mindedness in combating Communism. However, once the genie had been let out of the bottle—once the Democratic party had endorsed the Manichean world view—it was risky for Democratic leaders to repudiate it openly. Instead, the Democrats derived a different lesson—the necessity of avoiding situations where one could be held responsible for the loss of one or another country. The Democrats felt that right-wing charges of insufficient anti-Communist vigilance only became a serious threat when the right-wing could point to a specific country that had been allowed to enter the Communist empire as a result of inaction by a Democratic administration.

The resulting loss-of-China complex explains a great deal of the variation in U.S. imperial foreign policy over the past thirty years. Republican administrations have been far freer to develop a strategy of intervention that took account of the actual specifics of the situation. Hence, Eisenhower was able to decide against American intervention in Vietnam after the defeat of the French at Dienbienphu, since he had little reason to fear a concerted attack on his administration for losing North Vietnam. The Democrats could hardly be persuasive in launching such an attack, and the right wing of the Republican party was a minor threat with the Republican party in office. This meant that Eisenhower could pursue interventions, such as those in Iran, Guatemala, and Lebanon, where the military costs were slight and avoid those that might sap U.S. strength.

In contrast, the loss-of-China complex was a key factor in the Kennedy–Johnson period, making it difficult for those administrations to develop a rational policy of intervention.[33] The resurgence of the Republican right-wing that resulted in the Goldwater nomination in 1964 made the Democrats extremely wary of giving the Republicans an issue that would expand their appeal. This fear operated as a major determinant of the Vietnam policy, since South Vietnam was clearly a prime candidate for the China role. To avoid this danger the Democratic administrations stressed military toughness and gradually escalated the war effort. The key turning point came around 1966 as it became clear that it would take a huge American military effort to defeat the Communist forces and that even such a massive effort might fail. It was at this point that a number of proposals for strategic retreat emerged within high-level policy circles, such as the Gavin plan for a U.S. retreat to coastal enclaves.

The Johnson administration steadfastly resisted such proposals, pursuing instead its policy of continuing escalation, despite severe costs for the domestic economy, further deterioration of the U.S. balance of payments, and growing domestic disorder. The administration's stubbornness was rooted in the anxiety that any policy other than continued escalation was too risky in that it might lead to the collapse of the Saigon government and a Communist victory.[34] Domestic considerations, in short, forced the administration to pursue an extremely dangerous policy rather than take the reasonable risks involved in a strategic retreat that counted on U.S. air power to prevent a Communist military victory. Ironically, it was precisely the latter policy that the Republican administration pursued. It hardly bears repeating that the long-term consequences of the Johnson administration's refusal to make that strategic retreat were enormous for the U.S. global position. It was precisely the ineffectiveness of the U.S. escalation from 1966 to 1968 that created the image of the U.S. as a helpless giant—an image that was important for OPEC's defiance of the U.S. in the seventies. Furthermore, the prolongation of the war undermined the strength of the U.S. army itself and created a popular backlash within the U.S. against an interventionist foreign policy. Finally, the post-1966 escalation rapidly accelerated the tendency toward declining U.S. industrial competitiveness and permanent inflation.

While the Carter administration has avoided direct military intervention in Afghanistan, its definition of the Soviet invasion of that country as the greatest threat since World War II clearly reflects its terror of being held responsible for another strategic loss. Once again, the right wing of the Republican party is dominant and holds the prospect of gaining an electoral victory if it can effectively hang the treason label on the Carter administration. In recognition of this, the Carter administration has sought to undercut the Republicans by borrowing both their rhetoric and their foreign policy—rearmament, revival of the Cold War, and a return to conscription. The Carter, administration hopes that by moving quickly to a militarization of foreign policy it can cover itself with the flag before the Republicans have the chance to focus public attention on responsibility for the loss of Afghanistan. Short of directly opposing the right's Manichean world view, this is the only real strategy open to Carter. It is, however, a strategy with considerable risks, since we know that the Republicans' right was successful in attacking the Truman administration just when that administration had fully accepted the militarization of foreign policy. The right's ultimate resource is that it can argue that any specific policy moves are "too little and too late" given the seriousness of the danger—a seriousness that even the Democrats have been forced to acknowledge.

CONCLUSION

It is the combined weight of these three structural realities—each of which was set in motion by NSC-68—that continues to push American foreign policy toward militarization. The tragedy of this is that militarization of foreign policy is an ineffective response to the real dangers posed by Soviet strength. The periodic injections of higher levels of military spending into the American economy have deleterious economic side effects that more than outweigh their marginal contributions to enhanced military security. Further, the resort to militarization of foreign policy consistently involves a diversion for U.S. policy makers from the more difficult tasks of developing diplomatic strategies for responding to the Soviet Union. Just as Truman, at the beginning of the Cold War, relied on the still-secret A-bomb as a substitute for diplomatic skill,[35] so American policy makers have continued to succumb to the fantasy that there exists a technological escape from the problems of great power competition. Finally, in the area where the Soviet threat is perceived to be most serious—the Persian Gulf—the danger arises not from the great strength of the Soviet army, but from the weakness of the feudal regimes with which the U.S. is allied. George Kennan's observation is as true now as it was in 1950: "communism [has] to be viewed as a crisis of our own civilization, and the principal antidote [lies] in overcoming the weaknesses of our own institutions."

NOTES

1. For an analysis of the forces leading up to the Carter policy shifts, see Michael T. Klare, "Resurgent Militarism," Institute for Policy Studies, *Issue Paper*, 1978.
2. Because of internal conflicts within the administration, the drafters of NSC-68 studiously avoided putting a specific dollar figure in the document. However, the $40 billion figure was used privately by the drafters. On this point, and for a useful overview of the rearmament decision that also emphasizes the parallels with contemporary debates, *see* Samuel Wells, Jr., "Sounding the Tocsin: NSC 68 and the Soviet Threat," *International Security* (Fall 1979), pp. 116–58.
3. U.S., Department of Commerce, *The National Income and Product Accounts of the United States, 1929–74* (Washington; Government Printing Office), pp. 96–97.
4. For NSC-63, see U.S., Department of Sate, *Foreign Relations of the United States 1950* (Washington: Government Printing Office, 1977), 1: 235–92 (hereafter referred to as *FRUS 1950*).
5. *The Modern World System; Capitalist Agriculture and the Origins of the European World-Economy in the Sixteenth Century* (New York; Academic Press, 1974) and *The Capitalist World Economy* (Cambridge: Cambridge University Press, 1979).
6. See, particularly, Theda Skocpol, "Wallerstein's World System: A Theoretical and Historical Critique," *American Journal of Sociology* 82 (March 1977): 1075–90; and Aristide R. Zolberg, "Origins of die Modem World System: A Missing Link" (Paper presented at the American Political Science Association meetings, August 1979).
7. One key use of the analytic distinction is to grasp the process by which an imperial power overinvests in political–military competition, resulting in domestic economic decline.
8. *FRUS* 1950,1: 252.
9. Acheson's testimony before the Special Subcommittee on Postwar Economic Policy and Planning of the House of Representatives is cited in William Appleman Williams, *The Tragedy of American Diplomacy* (New York: Dell, 1962), pp. 235–36.
10. This argument is developed at greater length in Fred Block, *The Origins of International Economic Disorder* (Berkeley: University of California Press, 1977), csp. pp. 33–42.
11. The emphasis on an open world economy also had important ideological dimensions since U.S. policy makers tended to see a close St between free markets, political liberty, and international peace. These connections are spelled out in Stephen Kramer, "United States Commercial and Monetary Policy: Unraveling the Paradox of External Strength and Internal Weakness," in *Between Power and Plenty*, ed. Peter Katzenstein (Madison: University of Wisconsin Press, 1978), pp. 51–88.
12. A high State Department official wrote in early 1950 of the need to persuade the Soviet Union *"that there will be at least in the near future NO capitalist economic crisis of major proportions. It is of vital importance that we demonstrate domestically, in Western Europe and in the Western world generally, that a free economy is able to produce and distribute generously and continuously. A serious economic depression would obviously be an enormous boon to the Soviets." FRUS 1950, 1: 159* (emphasis in original).
13. Ibid., pp. 237–38.
14. Ibid., p.292
15. The next section draws heavily on Block, *Origins*, pp. 70–122.

16. Richard Freeman, *The Truman Doctrine and the Origins of McCarthyism* (New York: Knopf, 1972), chap. 6.
17. The indispensability derived from West Germany's industrial superiority, which was critical if Western Europe was to improve its over-ail trade balance with the rest of the world.
18. In reality, the atomic monopoly was still effective, since the USSR did not develop the means to deliver a nuclear attack on the U.S. until after 1955. Wells, "Sounding the Tocsin," pp. 153–54.
19. On the problem of Germany, sec Coral Bell, *Negotiation from Strength* (New York: Knopf, 1963).
20. *FRUS 1950*,1: 409 (emphasis added).
21. Ibid., p. 261.
22. Ibid., p. 258.
23. For evidence of State Department concern with excess industrial capacity in Western Europe and with military spending as a means to stimulate those economies, *see FRUS* 1950, 3: 36–40, 45–48.
24. *FRUS* 1950, 1: 163–64 (emphasis added). Note that Kennan also clearly distinguishes between political–military rivalry with the Soviet Union on the one hand and the tasks of organizing the world economy on the other.
25. R. B. Manderson-Jones, *The Special Relationship* (London: Weidenfield and Nicolson, 1972), pp. 61–63.
26. On Congressional fears about the length of the program, sec William Adams Brown, Jr., and Redvers Opie, *American Foreign Assistance* (Washington: Brookings, 1953), pp. 148–49, 172–76.
27. By militarization of foreign policy I mean the effort to achieve foreign-policy goal through an almost exclusive reliance on military means—from rearmament to actual warfare. Militarization implies a neglect of diplomatic strategies and a failure to balance military concerns with an awareness of the economic costs of particular policies.
28. For an extended discussion of this thesis, see Mary Kaldor, *The Disintegrating West* (New York: Hill & Wang; 1978).
29. For an account of this history, see Alan Wolfe, *The Rise and Fall of the "Soviet Threat"* (Washington: Institute for Policy Studies, 1979).
30. For the classic descriptions of military waste, see Seymour Melman, *Our Depleted Society* (New York: Delta, 1965); and idem, *The Permanent War Economy* (New York: Simon & Schuster, 1974).
31. The tipping point idea is contained in the passage from the first page of NSC-68, quoted above.
32. Freeman, *Truman Doctrine*, pp. 347–60.
33. Political memory operated even more powerfully here because many of the key foreign-policy makers in the Kennedy-Johnson years had served formative apprenticeships in the Truman administration during the rearmament period. Secretary of State Rusk had served in Achcson's State Department and was recommended to Kennedy by Acheson. See Arthur M. Schiesinger, Jr., *A Thousand Days* (Greenwich, Conn.: Fawcett, 1965), pp. 136, 286–91. A more recent example of these continuities was the emergence of Clark Clifford, a veteran of the Truman administration, as a spokesman for the Carter administration's hard-line response to the Soviet invasion of Afghanistan.
34. Daniel Ellsberg makes this argument about the importance of the China analogy at length in *Papers on the War* (New York: Simon and Schuster, 1972), pp. 86–131. Ellsberg was assigned by his superior in the Defense Department the task of imagining alternative ways that "we might come to 'lose Indochina,'" but, he was warned, "you should be clear that you could be signing the death warrant to your career by having anything to do with calculations and decisions like these. A lot of people were ruined for less." Ibid., p. 88.
35. See Martin Sherwin, *A World Destroyed* (New York: Vintage, 1977), chap. 9. *Politics & Society* 10, no, 1 (1980): pp. 35–58.

ॐ

Contesting Globalization: Organized Labor, NAFTA, and the 1997 and 1998 Fast-Track Fights

James Shoch

INTRODUCTION

Since the late 1970s or early 1980s and for the third time in the past 100 years, the world has witnessed a major wave of economic "globalization"—of trade, production, and finance,[1] In an ever-widening debate, many scholars have argued that globalization both constrains sovereign states from pursuing autonomous national economic policies and thwarts resistance by domestic actors to the adverse consequences of globalization.[2]

One such allegedly constraining process is the globalization of trade. First, the expansion of world trade is said to undermine popular support for and thus the option of protectionism by raising the aggregate efficiency, price, and employment costs of market closure and retaliatory trade wars, especially for countries with relatively small and relatively open economies.

Second, the globalization of trade is said to have shifted the balance of domestic interest group forces against protectionism and toward support for free trade. On one hand, the growth of trade has structurally strengthened the economic position and therefore also the political influence of trade-dependent, pro-free-trade business interests, including exporters, importers, intermediate goods users, and multinational corporations (MNCs).[3] On the other hand, globalization, especially if accompanied for whatever reasons by initial steps toward trade liberalization, eventually either erodes the position of import-competing sectors of business and labor or forces them to abandon protectionism in favor of strategies of industrial restructuring, the outsourcing of supply, and the off-shoring of production.[4]

These globalization-induced domestic political changes have in turn facilitated global institutions—the "internationalization" or "hollowing out" of the national state[5]—intended to liberalize, and thus further expand, the growth of world trade. At the regional level, the past fifteen years have seen the initiation of Europe's Single Market program, the negotiation and approval of the North American Free Trade Agreement (NAFTA), and the formation of the Asia-Pacific Economic Cooperation forum (APEC). At the global level, the Uruguay Round of the General Agreement on Tariffs and Trade (GATT) was concluded with an agreement that created the new World Trade Organization (WTO).

James Shoch, "Contesting Globalization: Organized Labor, NAFTA, and the 1997 and 1998 Fast-Track Fights," Politics and Society 28:1, March 2000, pp. 119–150. Copyright © 2000 Sage Publications. Reprinted by permission.

Contesting Globalization

While "hyperglobalist" scholars see the logic of globalization and its constraints as inexorable, other "antiglobalist" analysts insist both that the extent of globalization has been exaggerated and that considerable policy autonomy and space for opposition remain available to national governments and domestic political actors, especially in nations such as the United States with relatively large and relatively closed economies.

Analysts of this persuasion believe that the aggregate welfare costs to the United States of a limited dose of protectionism or the opportunity costs of a failure to further liberalize trade are likely to be rather small. Similarly, the structurally conditioned balance of strength between trade-dependent and import-sensitive interests is thought likely to evolve slowly enough such that strategically resourceful economic nationalist forces—perhaps more predisposed toward collective action than globalization's "winners" and especially if aided by sympathetic allies—may be able to win protection or at least block or slow the further progress of trade liberalization.

In fact, there has been substantial resistance in the United States—on the Left from the labor and environmental movements and their Democratic supporters and on the Right from conservative Republican nationalists—to both economic globalization and the formation and strengthening of international institutions intended to manage global economic processes. Such resistance has been most significant in the sphere of trade policy, where the Clinton administration had to overcome stiff congressional opposition to pass the NAFTA agreement and, to a lesser extent, the GATT accord.

The 1997 and 1998 Fast-Track Fights

It is true that as pitched as the NAFTA and GATT battles may have been, the supporters of globalization eventually prevailed, Yet in 1997 and 1998, globalization critics won two major battles on a trade policy issue of high priority for economic and political internationalists that should give pause to those who insist that the logic of globalization is an inevitable one. In November 1997, opponents defeated Bill Clinton's business-backed attempt to regain "fast-track" trade negotiating authority, which requires that trade liberalization agreements be awarded quick up-or-down votes in Congress without amendments that can unhinge such pacts and which Clinton needed to begin negotiating new free-trade agreements with developing nations in Latin America and Asia. And ten months later, in September 1998, fast-track opponents won a second, albeit less significant, victory when they beat back yet another proposal, this one Republican sponsored. The 1997 outcome was unprecedented; it was the first time that a president had been denied such negotiating authority since the advent of the fast-track procedure in 1974. In fact, this was the first time that a trade liberalization proposal had been rejected in the entire post-World War II era.

How can we explain why globalization skeptics, having failed to defeat NAFTA, were able to win the 1997 and 1998 struggles over fast track, especially at a time when the structurally determined balance of political forces appeared still to be shifting against them? To answer this question, I will first analyze the fight over NAFTA. I will then contrast this with the 1997 fast-track battle. Finally, I will conclude the narrative with a much briefer discussion of the 1998 fast-track fight.

Analytically, I will argue that a number of factors together explain the contrast between NAFTA's approval and the defeat of the 1997 and 1998 fast-track proposals, including a shift in public and to a lesser extent expert opinion, weaker and less effective business and presidential efforts on behalf of fast track, and growing Republican doubts about free trade. Most important, though, was rising Democratic opposition to further trade liberalization, which in turn was due mainly to the improved ability of the leading free-trade opponent and a core Democratic constituency—organized labor—to marshal and mobilize its human and financial resources. Capitalizing on its successes in the 1996 elections, labor effectively used "inside" and "outside" lobbying tactics—that is, Washington lobbying, coalition building, issue advertising, grassroots mobilization, and so on—to pressure reelection-minded congressmembers, especially Democrats, to oppose fast track. Particularly important in the 1997 fight, however, was a shift in the structure of campaign finance following the 1994 congressional elections, which rendered the Democrats relatively more dependent on labor for campaign funds, a dependence that labor was effectively able to exploit during the fast-track battle. In the 1998 fast-track fight, however, labor's grassroots organizing around both the issue itself and the fast-approaching midterm elections appears to have played a more important role than did union money in sending the Republican proposal down to defeat.

In short, I will argue that globalization proponents who were surprised by the defeat of the 1997 and 1998 fast-track proposals underestimated labor's political strength by focusing too heavily on the secular structural changes that have undoubtedly eroded labor's social weight while neglecting the heightened effectiveness of labor's structurally enabled agency and strategies.

I will end with a brief discussion of the likely contours of future trade conflicts in the wake of the recent "battle in Seattle," and the collapse in that city of the WTO meeting intended to launch a new round of international trade negotiations. Despite the Seattle events, I will suggest that there are reasons to think that labor may well not be able to simply block any and all new trade liberalization proposals and, beyond this, that labor should not try to stop all such proposals. Rather, new "counterhegemonic" strategies of accommodation and compromise with the forces of globalization and liberalization are in order.

THE NAFTA BATTLE[6]

In early 1991, responding to a proposal from Mexican president Carlos Salinas de Gortari and pursuing a number of economic and political goals of his own, President George Bush notified Congress of his intent to negotiate a regional free-trade agreement with Mexico and Canada. To facilitate these negotiations, on March I, Bush sent a request for a two-year extension of his fast-track authority to Congress.

The battle lines that emerged that spring over Bush's fast-track request had actually been forming for some months.[7] On the pro-NAFTA side first were competitive agricultural exporters and high-technology and other manufacturing exporters seeking to realize economies of scale.[8] The strongest business proponents of fast track and an eventual deal, however, were U.S.-based multinational corporations that, more than trade liberalization, sought the liberalization of Mexico's investment rules. These firms anticipated that NAFTA would enable them to more easily tap Mexico's vast pool of cheap labor to improve their international competitiveness vis-à-vis their European and especially their Japanese rivals.[9] At the same time, corporations could use the increased threat of flight to Mexico to force workers in their American plants to make wage and work rule concessions, still further reducing their costs and boosting their competitiveness and profits.[10]

On the anti-NAFTA side, various labor-intensive, import-competing agricultural and industrial interests strongly opposed an agreement, fearing a wave of cheap imports.

The most concerted opposition to a regional trade pact, however, was mounted by the American labor movement. For labor, as for U.S. multinational business interests, NAFTA was more an investment than a trade issue. Industrial unions were worried that by liberalizing not just trade but also investment rules, such an agreement would intensify both the actual and threatened flight of manufacturing capital to Mexico in search of cheap labor, thus eliminating U.S. jobs and undercutting American workers' bargaining power and wages.[11]

Initially joining labor in its opposition to an agreement were environmentalists who worried that pollution-intensive firms would also relocate manufacturing operations to northern Mexico to take advantage of mat country's weakly enforced environmental laws, thus both exacerbating pollution problems along the border and eroding U.S. environmental standards.

To defuse opposition to the proposed pact, on May 1, Bush produced an "action plan" committing himself to an agreement that cushioned workers and upheld environmental standards. While the plan was not sufficient to change labor's position on fast track, it did help him win the support of key environmental groups as well as the endorsement of the congressional Democratic leadership. With this new support in hand, White House and business lobbyists were able to outgun their labor adversaries. In mid-May, both the House and Senate defeated resolutions to disallow fast-track authority.

The Main Event

NAFTA was completed in August 1992, in time for George Bush to try to use the treaty during the general election phase of the presidential campaign to woo Hispanic voters and business interests in Texas and California. His opponent, Bill Clinton, was a free-trading "New Democrat" who sought to reconstitute his party's coalition to include the expanding suburbanized middle class and internationally oriented business interests but who also hoped to avoid alienating organized labor, a core Democratic constituency. Thus, Clinton straddled the NAFTA issue until early October, when in an effort to bridge the divide within his party, he finally endorsed the pact under the condition that side agreements be negotiated to deal with labor standards—including laws on worker health and safety, child labor, the rights of unions to organize, and so on—the environment, and the threat of sudden import surges. While labor was critical of Clinton's NAFTA endorsement, it did have hopes that the side agreements would guarantee the effective enforcement of Mexican labor and environmental laws, thus reducing the incentives for U.S. manufacturers to relocate plants to that country.

At first it appeared that labor's hopes might be realized. After some early waffling that produced an outcry from congressional Democrats, in May 1993, the new Clinton administration presented proposals to Mexican and Canadian negotiators calling for the formation of independent commissions that would have had the power to ensure that the countries enforced their own labor and environmental laws. These proposals, however, met with strong opposition from business, congressional Republicans, and the Mexican and Canadian governments. With labor on the sidelines refusing to involve itself in the negotiating process, the Clinton administration backed away from its proposals and in August agreed instead to a much weaker set of enforcement procedures, especially with respect to labor standards.

Appalled by the labor side agreements, the AFL-CIO formally came out in opposition to the treaty, and labor escalated its battle against the pact at both the grassroots and in

Washington. State and local union affiliates mounted a grassroots mobilization against the agreement that was unprecedented in recent memory. At the same time, the AFL-CIO funded a TV, radio, and print media blitz against the pact. Finally, individual unions threatened to withhold campaign contributions from congressmembers who voted for the treaty. Joining labor in what was widely termed an "unholy alliance" of "strange bedfellows" against the pact were some environmentalists, human rights activists, the grassroots Citizens Trade Campaign, Ross Perot, Jerry Brown, Pat Buchanan, Jesse Jackson, and Ralph Nader.

With a big jump on its pro-NAFTA opponents and with public opinion still substantially opposed to the treaty in the fall, this labor-led coalition was able to enlist the support of an impressive number of members of Congress, including key Democratic leaders such as House Majority Leader Richard Gephardt (D-MO) and House Whip David Bonior (D-MI). For a time it appeared that labor might actually win this crucial battle over the U.S. orientation toward the emerging global economy.

This, of course, was before the pro-NAFTA forces had fully swung into action. The moribund USA*NAFTA, a business coalition supporting the agreement, was revived and began to lobby intensively. The elite media regularly editorialized in support of the treaty, often citing the views of leading members of the economics profession. Republican congressional leaders, once assured that Bill Clinton was committed to the fight, worked hard to win GOP support for the pact. The moderates and free traders of the Democratic Leadership Council, convinced that the Democrats' future lay in the growing high-tech, middle-class suburbs rather than in the declining industrial cities, saw NAFTA as a defining issue for their party and threw themselves into the struggle for the treaty's approval.

Most important, after some initial hesitation, Bill Clinton engaged himself fully in the fight. Clinton both attempted to win over public opinion on the issue and furiously lobbied members of Congress, especially Democrats, with promises of trade relief and other favors and with persuasive pleas to resist isolationism and the crippling of his wider efforts on behalf of trade liberalization.

The eleventh-hour efforts of Clinton and other NAFTA supporters paid off, and in mid-November 1993, the treaty was approved by the House and Senate by votes of 234–200 and 61–38, respectively. Three-quarters of House Republicans supported the deal, as did 40 percent of House Democrats. More than three-quarters of Senate Republicans backed the treaty, along with half of Senate Democrats.

Labor's Role

Though defeated, organized labor had a significant influence on the NAFTA vote. In House and Senate voting on the treaty, various studies have shown that the higher the percentage of blue-collar workers and union members in a representative or senator's district or state, the more likely he or she was to vote against NAFTA. In addition, the bigger was labor's share of a legislator's total campaign contributions, again the more likely he or she was to oppose the treaty.[12]

Unfortunately for organized labor, structural shifts in the economy and other factors had been eroding the movement's social and political strength for years, leaving it with too little influence to defeat NAFTA.[13] First, the decline of the northern, urban industrial workforce, along with other factors, led to a drop in union membership. Combined with the growth of the new high-technology and white-collar workforce in the suburbs and the Sunbelt, this produced a relative decline in labor's electoral influence. Second, as we shall see in more detail below, labor's decline limited the funds it could contribute to congressional campaigns, while the amount donated by corporate political action committees exploded, especially during the 1980s. This benefited the pro-business, pro-free-trade Republicans while forcing Democratic congress-members to themselves become relatively more reliant on business for campaign funding.

Since the early 1970s, these trends together had limited labor's influence on many issues, including trade policy.[14] With the post-World War II decline of the American economy relative to its reconstructed West European and Japanese rivals and the later onset of the crisis of Fordism, in the late 1960s, organized labor, largely representing unskilled and low-end semiskilled workers in labor-intensive, import-competing industries, began to abandon its earlier support for free trade.[15] Backed by northern industrial state Democrats, much of labor now opposed further trade liberalization initiatives while calling instead for legislation to slow the rising tide of imports.

Labor's efforts in the 1970s went unrewarded. Early in the decade, Congress refused to consider the union-backed Burke–Hartke bill, which would have imposed across-the-board import curbs. Labor also failed to prevent passage of the liberalizing *Trade Reform Act of 1974* (which introduced the fast-track procedure) and the *Trade Agreements Act of 1979*. In all these fights, labor was defeated by the concerted efforts of free-trading Presidents Nixon and Carter, import-export and multinational business interests, and congressional Republicans, often from export-dependent farm and Sunbelt states, which had become ideologically aligned with and politically reliant on these internationally oriented interests.

Labor did not fare much better in the 1980s when the competitive weaknesses of American industry were compounded by the grossly overvalued dollar, leading to new demands for both import curbs and action to pry open closed foreign and especially Japanese markets. In 1982 and 1983, labor could not even get the Republican-controlled Senate to take up the twice House-passed "domestic content" bill intended to help the beleaguered auto industry.[16] Labor suffered another defeat in 1984 when it failed to seize an opportunity to amend or block a provision in the Senate version of what became the *Trade and Tariff Act of 1984* that continued the Generalized System of Preferences (GSP) for developing countries, an arrangement that labor had long opposed.

Labor was more successful in its efforts to shape the huge *Omnibus Trade and Competitiveness Act of 1988*.[17] The final version of the bill contained a number of provisions supported by labor, including the "Super 301" law, which required the United States Trade Representative (USTR) to identify countries that consistently erected barriers to U.S. exports and to initiate steps to remove those barriers.[18] On balance, however, labor was quite disappointed with the trade bill. Under business, Republican, and presidential pressure, various labor-backed provisions were dropped or watered down. In particular, the provision in early House drafts of the bill most strongly supported by labor—the so-called "Gephardt amendment,"[19] which would have required the use of quotas and tariffs to penalize countries such as Japan that ran large chronic surpluses with the United States—was replaced in the final draft by the Senate's weaker "Super 301" plank.

In 1993, the trends that had limited labor's influence in earlier trade fights again limited the movement's impact during the NAFTA debate, including on the Democrats. Labor's diminished political clout, the business mobilization in support of the pact, and Clinton's success in neutralizing public opinion on the issue and in winning Democratic support for the treaty, particularly from moderate and conservative southerners, with his deals and persuasion,[20] together allowed the pro-NAFTA forces to carry the day.

Four years later, however, the 1997 fast-track battle would break the mold of all previous trade struggles.

THE FAST-TRACK FIGHTS: LABOR WINS TWO BIG ONES[21]

In the fall of 1997, another trade policy battle royal was fought as the Clinton administration sought to revive the process of American trade liberalization, which had ground to a halt since the congressional approval of the Uruguay Round GATT treaty in late 1994.[22] Hoping to strengthen his legacy as a champion of liberal trade during his second term, Clinton requested new fast-track authority with the immediate aim of expanding NAFTA to include Chile. But his broader ambition was to negotiate still other free-trade agreements with developing nations in Latin America and Asia.

In 1994, the Clinton administration, looking toward an agreement with Chile, had actually already sought such new fast-track authority in its draft of the Uruguay Round implementing legislation. But anxious to heal the rift with labor resulting from the NAFTA fight before the 1996 presidential campaign, USTR Mickey Kantor proposed that labor and environmental standards be explicitly included as negotiating goals. Both the business community and its Republican congressional allies were militantly opposed to the inclusion of such standards. Rather than jeopardize the approval of the GATT agreement, the Clinton administration decided to remove the fast-track provision from the implementing legislation. The introduction of a new fast-track proposal was postponed until after the election.

Clinton Tries Again, but Labor Carries the Day

Having secured his reelection, in early 1997 Clinton set out again to win new fast-track authority.[23] This time, the administration was willing to consider a "clean" bill (i.e., one that ruled out the inclusion of labor and environmental issues in the core of any new trade agreements) to gain business and GOP support.

The new White House strategy was based on the calculation that the labor movement would not make trade a top priority in 1997. New AFL-CIO president John Sweeney, formerly president of the Service Employees International Union (SEIU), and his close advisers all came out of the service and public sectors, and thus they tended to care less about trade than did the industrial unions.

In the end, however, the administration's calculations with respect to labor's intentions proved to be mistaken. Under pressure from the industrial unions, Sweeney eventually overcame his reservations about opposing the renewal of Clinton's fast-track authority, and at its annual February meeting, the AFL-CIO denounced any NAFTA expansion agreement that did not include provisions to raise foreign wages and labor standards.[24]

Presidential election politics now once again intruded into the debate. Aligning himself with labor, potential presidential hopeful and "Old" Democrat Richard Gephardt circulated a twelve-page letter attaching a wide range of labor, environmental, and political conditions to any new free-trade agreements. Vice President and "New" Democrat Al Gore had been a strong supporter of Bill Clinton's trade liberalization program. But hoping to avoid a politically damaging fight with organized labor that might boost Gephardt's candidacy, Gore urged at least a delay in the submission of the fast-track proposal to Congress to allow him more time to strengthen his ties to labor.

White House officials had no wish to jeopardize Gore's presidential chances. Nor did they wish to further offend congressional liberals as they pursued Clinton's top priority—a balanced budget. Thus, in mid-May, the White House decided to postpone delivery of its fast-track proposal until the fall.

Clinton finally unveiled his fast-track plan on September 16. In the proposal, the White House attempted to find a middle ground between Democrats and Republicans. Labor and environmental standards were included among the "negotiating objectives" set out in the bill. But such issues were to be included in trade pacts only if they were "directly related to trade." Also, the enforcement of such standards was assigned to multilateral trade institutions such as the World Trade Organization, which had in the past been hostile to linking labor standards and trade. Commercial issues, however, such as intellectual property, trade in services, and agriculture, were to be addressed in core trade agreements, where sanctions could be used to enforce them.

Clinton's plan initially satisfied no one. Labor and its Democratic allies attacked the proposal for not placing enough emphasis on the inclusion of strong labor and environmental standards in future trade accords, while business and Republican critics were angry that the plan called for any attention at all to labor and environmental issues.

By the time of the October 1 markup of the bill by the pro-free-trade Senate Finance Committee, the White House, convinced that the fate of its fast-track proposal lay in Republican rather than Democratic hands, had agreed to weaken the measure's labor and environmental provisions enough to mollify most GOP concerns. Thus, the bill was passed by the committee with only one opposing vote. A week later, after another round of negotiations with the administration, the House Ways and Means Committee approved a similar version of the bill. But heralding the partisan battle to come, only four of the panel's sixteen Democratic members voted in favor of the measure.

During the next two months, another NAFTA-like battle was waged between the supporters and opponents of further trade liberalization. As in that earlier contest, by the end of the struggle, the pro-fast-track coalition—again including internationally oriented business interests, the elite media, the economics profession, the Republican congressional leadership, the Democratic Leadership Council, and, of course, Bill Clinton—was fighting hard for passage of the bill. On the other side of the trenches, organized labor, environmental and citizens groups, and liberal congressional Democrats were just as strenuously opposing the measure for its neglect of labor and environmental issues. These liberal forces were again joined on the barricades by conservative Republican nationalists concerned about the alleged threat to U.S. "sovereignty."

While the traditionally pro-free-trade Senate would have passed its version of the, fast-track bill,[25] this time in the House, labor and its allies emerged victorious. After votes on the fast-track bill were delayed twice, Clinton was forced to withdraw his proposal when it became clear that he lacked the votes in the House to pass it. A number of tallies suggested that the measure would have gotten the support of about 70 to 75 percent of House Republicans but only 21 percent of House Democrats.[26]

Explaining Labor's Victory

Following so soon after NAFTA's approval, how can the defeat of Clinton's fast-track proposal be explained? The secularly deteriorating structural position of organized labor had certainly not improved since 1993. Unions today represent only 14 percent of all U.S. workers, down from 35 percent in the 1950s, And despite the AFL-CIO's heightened commitment to organizing following the election of its new president, John Sweeney, in late 1995, union membership is still down in both relative and absolute terms since early 1996.[27] In addition, in late 1997, economic growth was strong, unemployment was low, Bill Clinton's popularity was high, and the generally pro-free-trade Republican party was in control of both houses of Congress. What other factors had changed to permit labor's fast-track victory?

First, whereas by the end of the NAFTA fight, public opinion on the treaty had been evenly split, by late 1997 the American public was solidly opposed to renewing Clinton's fast-track authority. This was due in large part to the widespread belief, shared by many in Congress, that NAFTA had been a failure. Much of the public believed that (1) with the trade deficit with Mexico rising, NAFTA had cost U.S. jobs; (2) jobs gained from increased exports were no better than those lost to imports or foreign investment; (3) competition from Mexico was undermining American workers' bargaining power and wages; and (4) NAFTA had eroded U.S. environmental quality. Such perceptions fueled a more general concern—or "globalphobia," as it was termed—that globalization and trade liberalization were adversely affecting American jobs, living standards, and quality of life.[28]

Still, the role of public opinion in stopping fast track should not be exaggerated. Government officials have often pursued free-trade policies even when those policies were unpopular.[29] This is especially likely to occur when the public's preferences are not intense, as appears to have been the case on fast track, which voters found less salient than NAFTA. Had public opinion as a whole played a predominant role in the demise of fast track, more than 25 to 30 percent of House Republicans should have opposed it.

Second, expert opinion had also shifted to some degree since the NAFTA fight. A number of studies questioned the degree to which NAFTA had benefited the country or different groups within the population,[30] while still other analyses argued more broadly that globalization had negatively affected the wages of certain sectors of the labor force as well as the distribution of income.[31] Again, though, most trade and other experts strongly supported the fast-track bill.

Third, business support for fast track was both slower in mobilizing and less enthusiastic than had been the case for NAFTA, whose benefits to business were clearer than were those expected to result from the more procedural fast-track bill. In June, Americans Lead on Trade, a coalition of about 550 umbrella business organizations, trade associations, and companies, was formed to build support for the renewal of fast-track authority.[32] But fearing that Clinton's fast-track proposal might include unacceptable labor and environmental provisions, the coalition refused to endorse the measure until it saw the final Senate and House language, and thus it really did not start working the bill until late October. Nonetheless, the business push for fast track during the last weeks of the fight was substantial.

Fourth, conservative economic nationalist influences, both electoral and ideological, contributed to the decision of a substantial bloc of Republicans to oppose fast track. Once the party of protectionism, after World War II the Republicans had gradually entered into a bipartisan consensus on liberal trade. But following the end of the cold war, working- and lower-middle-class "Reagan Democrats" began to look toward populist and economic nationalist, though not liberal, solutions to the emerging problems of job loss and wage stagnation. Their mounting anger fueled the presidential campaigns of both Pat Buchanan and Ross Perot in 1992 and 1996. They also propelled a wave of radical populist Republicans into the House in the 1994 elections, helping the GOP to capture control of Congress. These firebrands in many cases replaced marginal Democrats, especially in the South, whose support for NAFTA and free trade more generally had alienated blue-collar voters. Thus, more than half of the ninety-one Republicans first elected to the House in 1994 and 1996 opposed the fast-track bill.[33]

In the end, though, the overall impact of conservative economic nationalist influences on the preferences of House Republicans, and thus also the role of these influences in the defeat of fast track, was relatively limited. Fully 70 to 75 percent of the House GOP members supported the fast-track bill, close to the same proportion that had backed NAFTA in 1993. For all their sound and fury, the populist and nationalist bloc of House Republicans did not actively mobilize against the measure, while the House Republican leadership energetically threw itself into the fight for fast track.

Anti-Fast-Track Influences on the Democrats

A number of factors contributed to the defeat of fast track primarily through their influence on the Democrats, whose overwhelming opposition to the measure ultimately doomed it, Whereas 60 percent of House Democrats had voted against NAFTA in 1993, 79 percent of party members opposed fast track in 1997.

To an important extent, the more unified Democratic opposition to fast track in 1997 was an artifact of the more homogeneously liberal composition of the House Democratic caucus.[34] A substantial number of moderate and conservative, mostly southern and suburban pro-NAFTA Democrats retired or were defeated in the Democratic rout of 1994 and in the subsequent 1996 election.[35] Surviving Democratic incumbents, on the other hand, were more likely to come from liberal urban or labor-dominated districts where opposition to free trade was strongest.[36] In addition, in 1996, the Democrats won a number of new seats, mostly in liberal northern districts. Only 23 percent of these new Democratic members planned to vote for fast track. Thus, due to electoral shifts, the House Democratic caucus in 1997 was smaller but more consistently liberal than it had been in 1993.

This explanation of heightened Democratic cohesion on fast track is incomplete, however. It cannot explain why, among the ranks of Democratic fast-track opponents, were both seventeen former NAFTA supporters and some newly elected nonsouthern moderates.[37] Included in these two groups were half of the forty-one members of the moderate New Democratic Caucus who sympathized with the views of the Democratic Leadership Council. What explains the opposition to fast track among these Democrats who might have been expected to support Clinton's proposal?

First, Clinton's efforts on behalf of fast track were less concerted and effective than they had been during the NAFTA battle, when he had been able to win over a substantial number of undecided and wavering Democratic moderates.[38] Not wanting to call attention to the intra-Democratic split over the issue or to unduly offend labor, whose support Al Gore would need in the 2000 presidential campaign, Clinton never took his case to an anxious public that remained highly skeptical of the value of liberalized trade. Instead, Clinton relied exclusively on an "inside-the-beltway" strategy, promising congressmembers a flurry of last-minute concessions in return for their votes. But his deal making did not work this time since his credibility had been diminished by his failure to deliver on most of the promises he had made during the NAFTA fight.[39]

Clinton had also antagonized House Democrats in other ways, perhaps most importantly with the balanced budget deal that he had struck with the Republicans the previous summer. Many Democrats believed that the concessions on taxes and spending that Clinton had made to reach such an agreement had undermined his ability to create the "social compact" that he had repeatedly promised for those displaced by economic change.[40]

Nonetheless, toward the end of the controversy, Clinton worked hard to win the fast-track battle.

Labor's Decisive Role: Laying the Groundwork in the 1996 Elections

I would argue that the most important factor underlying the Democrats' solid opposition to fast track was the structurally enabled "agency" of organized labor. Reflecting on the political significance of labor's victory, Thomas Edsall went so far as to suggest that the "unions' formidable efforts to block the 'fast track' trade bill shows that organized labor has more influence than at any time since 1968, when it nearly elected a president."[41]

As we shall see in a moment, during the fast-track fight, labor employed a wide range of strategies.[42] But to an important extent, the key to labor's victory was its extensive prior involvement in the 1996 congressional elections. This effort left labor with both an impressive grassroots organizing infrastructure and substantial leverage on congressional Democrats during the fast-track battle the following year.

Shortly after the Republican takeover of Congress in 1994, labor launched a concerted campaign—"Labor 96"—to help the Democrats recapture control of at least the House of Representatives.[43] Individual unions provided tens of thousands of volunteers who educated, registered, and turned out voters to the polls in support of labor-backed candidates. Beyond this, after replacing the quiescent leadership team headed by Lane Kirkland, the AFL-CIO under new president John Sweeney waged an independent, $35 million campaign on behalf of Democratic candidates that included a grassroots field effort in 120 congressional districts directed by 135 full-time political coordinators and a multimedia issue advocacy campaign. In addition, union political action committees (PACs) increased their campaign spending on behalf of their endorsed candidates to better able those candidates to reach and persuade uninformed or inattentive voters.

Labor's intensified efforts in 1996 were effective. In the 1992 presidential and congressional elections, exit polls showed that 19 percent of the electorate was from union households. Two years later, angered by their loss to Clinton on NAFTA, union activists largely sat out the midterm elections. The result was a decline in the union share of the turnout to only 14 percent. But in 1996, turnout among union households jumped to 23 percent of the electorate. In addition, while 40 percent of union members had voted for Republican congressional candidates in 1994, this figure dropped to 35 percent in 1996.

Labor's campaign contributions also played an important role in the 1996 elections. Business as usual substantially outspent labor in PAC and individual contributions, this time by a margin of 7 to 1.[44] But with business PACs shifting their contributions toward the Republicans following the GOP takeover of Congress in 1994, the Democrats were left more dependent on labor money to finance their 1996 campaigns. In House races, for example, labor PAC contributions, which totaled roughly 36 percent of all PAC donations to Democratic candidates in 1994, rose to about 48 percent in 1996.[45] Thus, union money helped keep Democratic candidates at least competitive with their Republican rivals in 1996.

Labor's education, registration, and turnout efforts, together with its PAC contributions, paid real dividends in the 1996 elections. Democratic House candidates defeated 45 of the 105 Republicans targeted by the AFL-CIO.

The Labor Mobilization against Fast Track and Its Effects

During the fast-track fight a year later, labor sought both to build and capitalize on its efforts in the 1996 elections.[46] First, labor employed a number of "outside" lobbying tactics.[47] Relying on "Labor '96" coordinators who remained in place in many congressional districts, the AFL-CIO mounted an exceptionally effective grassroots and advertising offensive against fast track in targeted districts, while several federation affiliates—especially the Teamsters, the Steelworkers, and the Union of Needle, Industrial, and Textile Employees (UNITE)— undertook their own independent anti-fast-track activities. And it was not just the industrial unions that waged the battle. The previous summer, the industrial unions had backed up their public-sector colleagues in the fight over the balanced budget. Now those same public-sector unions repaid their debt by throwing themselves into the fast-track fight.

Union members opposed to fast track sent hundreds of thousands of letters and postcards to their representatives, placed more than 10,000 phone calls to Congress, made hundreds of visits to congressional district offices, distributed thousands of anti-fast-track videos and booklets, and held dozens of teach-ins and rallied on trade. Meanwhile, the AFL-CIO spent about $2 million on TV and radio ads in twenty key congressional districts.

Labor also actively engaged in "inside" lobbying within the Washington Beltway. Labor lobbyists regularly met with and pressed House members—mostly Democrats, but also some Republicans—to oppose fast track. Labor also enlisted the active support of key House leaders, especially Minority Leader Richard Gephardt and Minority Whip David Bonior, who worked hard to convince undecided Democrats to come out against Clinton's proposal. Finally, union staff members also participated actively in the weekly strategy meetings of the Citizens' Trade Campaign, a broad anti-fast-track coalition of labor, environmental, consumer safety, and civil rights organizations.

In waging its anti-fast-track campaign, labor learned from its unsuccessful fight against NAFTA four years earlier. Attempting to combat the charge that it was acting as a narrow "special interest" in defense only of its own members, labor rejected the protectionist label and instead acknowledged the inevitability and even the desirability of global economic integration. But as AFL-CIO president John Sweeney explained, "The question is not . . . whether we are internationalists, but what values our internationalism serves."[48]

Thus, labor and its liberal Democratic allies framed their opposition to Clinton's "clean" fast-rack proposal as part of a wider, more positive argument that globalization had to be managed in the general interest of the country and indeed the, world as a whole rather than just the big exporters and multinational corporations. This meant "rules for—not resistance to—globalization," as Richard Gephardt put it.[49] More specifically, labor and its supporters called for labor and environmental standards in developing nations to be raised to simultaneously improve living conditions in those poverty-ridden countries, create an expanding middle class that could buy American products, and prevent a corporate "race to the bottom" that would erode U.S. jobs, wages, and environmental quality.[50]

In pursuit of these goals, during the fast-track fight, labor sought to build what, following Karl Polanyi, might be termed a broad *protective countermovement* to limit globalization's various adverse and disruptive effects.[51] More concretely, to turn public opinion against fast track, labor cooperated more actively and fully with environmental, human rights, consumer safety, and other groups than had been the case during the anti-NAFTA campaign, stressing a wide range of both labor and nonlabor concerns. "We didn't just want to talk to union members," said Steven Trossman, an anti-fast-track strategist with the Teamsters. "We wanted to talk to a broader audience to say this is bad for families, even if your job is not on the line."[52]

Labor's various outside and inside lobbying activities were productive. Labor's grassroots mobilization and issue advocacy advertising efforts contributed to the movement of public opinion against Clinton's proposal and conveyed information on the public's preferences on the issue to congressmembers. At the same time, labor's inside lobbying efforts reinforced the message from the grassroots, while also perhaps playing some role in altering legislators' personal preferences on the issue.

But labor's campaign did more than convey information on different aspects of the fast-track issue to House members. Labor leaders also exerted more forceful pressure by bluntly warning that lawmakers who supported fast track could not expect either union manpower or money for their 1998 campaigns, even if that meant that some Democrats might lose.[53]

This labor pressure had its desired effect. As noted earlier, informal tallies indicated that 79 percent of House Democrats would have opposed Clinton's fast-track bill had it come to a vote. Many Democrats, including moderate members of the New Democratic Caucus, feared that their support for fast track would lead union activists to sit out the 1998 campaign, as many had done in 1994. Thanks largely to labor's mobilization in 1996, the Democrats had benefited from a significant increase in the union vote that year, and many party members were reluctant to risk another depressed labor turnout in 1998 by backing the fast-track bill.[54]

The Crucial Role of Labor Money

I would argue, however, that even more important in convincing Democrats to oppose fast track than the possible loss of union manpower in the 1998 elections was the threatened loss of union money. While studies of the effects of campaign spending by individual PACs on congressional voting have been inconclusive, it has been demonstrated that broad aggregations of corporate or labor PAC contributions can produce voting effects on issues of general concern to business or labor.[55] In particular, business and labor PAC spending does seem to have significant effects on congressional voting on trade issues.[56] In the specific case of the fast-track fight, the force of labor's threats to reduce or withdraw contributions to Democratic incumbents who voted for Clinton's proposal stemmed from a recent and substantial shift in the sources of Democratic campaign finance.

Beginning in the mid-1970s, business PACs dramatically proliferated, and their total spending on congressional campaigns exploded.[57] At the same time, hoping to scale back the New Deal social welfare and regulatory state, these PACs abandoned their traditional, access-oriented strategy of donating to candidates of both parties and instead shifted the bulk of their contributions to Republican candidates in the 1978, 1980, and 1982 congressional elections.

Since the number of union PACs grew only slowly during this period and because these PACs also regularly ran up against campaign contribution limits, congressional Democrats were left desperately short of funds to conduct their increasingly media and consultant-intensive campaigns. To regain lost corporate support, the Democrats were forced to adopt more business-friendly and less labor-responsive policy positions, including on trade issues such as NAFTA.[58] This policy shift, along with the Democrats' retention of control of the House of Representatives in the 1982 elections and their recapture of the Senate in 1986, produced a partial shift of business campaign contributions back to the Democrats.[59] Thanks to this new influx of business money, from 1982 to 1992, the business share of House Democrats' total PAC receipts[60] jumped from 41 to 54 percent, while labor's share fell from 43 to 33 percent.

The 1994 elections, however, produced yet another shift in the structure of campaign finance, also with corresponding policy consequences.[61] After the Republican takeover of Congress, business PACs, pressured by the new GOP congressional leadership, again reduced their contributions to the Democrats while substantially increasing their donations to the now majority Republicans. Meanwhile, labor PACs increased their contributions to Democratic candidates.[62] Thus, as noted earlier, union PAC contributions, which totaled roughly 36 percent of all PAC donations to Democratic House candidates in 1994, rose to about 48 percent in 1996. Still more important, Democratic challengers who won Republican-held seats in 1996 received more than 60 percent of their PAC contributions from labor.[63]

This renewed Democratic dependence on organized labor for campaign funds was further compounded by the fundraising scandals stemming from the 1996 election. Abandoned by many of its major donors, the Democratic National Committee was $15 million in debt, leaving it unable to aid party candidates with soft money.[64]

The Democrats' desperate need for union money heightened the credibility of labor's threat to withhold funds from fast-track supporters in the 1998 midterm elections and thus decisively contributed to the defeat of Clinton's proposal.[65] "Labor has obviously increased its influence in the Democratic Party since we've become the minority and the business community is either less engaged or less influential with us than ever before," said one senior House Democrat.[66] A House Democratic leadership aide observed, "Your average House Democrat is thinking, 'The DNC is broke, Clinton is helping Gore, Big Business is with the Republicans, all we've got is labor.'"[67] "This is a $200,000 vote for me," another Democrat reportedly told a Clinton aide, explaining why he might not vote for fast track even though he had voted for NAFTA.[68]

It is important to be clear that during the fast-track fight, labor's financial clout gave the movement influence with Democrats of various ideological stripes, not just pro-union liberals. With business turning away from the Democrats, even the moderates of the New Democratic Caucus were badly in need of money for their 1998 campaigns. Looking to labor for help, half of them opposed the fast-track bill, to the dismay of the leaders of the Democratic Leadership Council.[69] "The business community really has to think very hard about ignoring House Democrats," complained DLC President Al From.[70]

Thus, despite its continued long-term decline, by converting and strategically deploying its structurally generated human and especially its financial resources in a temporarily favorable political conjuncture, organized labor was able to win a major battle against the forces of globalization and free trade. At least in this instance, labor's structurally enabled agency triumphed over the structural constraints that so often limit the movement's advance.

1998: The Lines Are Drawn Again

Chastened by his defeat at labor's hands, Bill Clinton had no plans to introduce another fast-track proposal until after the 1998 and perhaps even the 2000 elections, in both of which Democratic candidates, including likely presidential aspirant Al Gore, would need labor votes, money, and volunteers. In fact, looking ahead to the 2000 campaign in which Clinton hoped to pass his mantle on to his vice president, both Clinton and Gore spent much of 1998 working to repair their ties to the liberal-labor wing of the Democratic Party.[71]

Thus, it was Republican Speaker of the House Newt Gingrich who in late June surprised observers by announcing a late September vote on a new fast-track proposal containing no strong labor and environmental provisions.[72] Gingrich's motives appear to have been partisan. First, the Speaker hoped to exploit differences on trade among labor, House Democrats, and the White House just before the fall midterm congressional elections. Second, Gingrich wanted to show business that the GOP cared as much about the corporate agenda as it did about the concerns of social conservatives whose strength within the party had recently appeared to be growing. Finally, Gingrich hoped to mend political fences with farmers to make up for phasing out the farm subsidies that once cushioned price drops.

Most House Republicans backed their leader's bill, determined to hold Democrats accountable in the upcoming elections for blocking fast track's passage. In particular, the Republicans hoped to spotlight the Democrats' alleged subservience to labor in regions with concentrations of export-dependent agricultural interests.[73]

The great majority of House Democrats opposed the GOP measure, due once again mainly to pressure from organized labor.[74] On one hand, labor vociferously attacked and mobilized against the bill. At the same time, concerned to prevent the election of a filibuster-proof Republican Senate, labor mounted another major effort in support of Democratic candidates in the upcoming congressional races. This time, though, labor found itself massively outspent by business. Labor also faced the threat of a low turnout of its members, who along with other Americans had become increasingly alienated from politics by a succession of scandals. Thus, labor now decided that its route to greater congressional influence lay not primarily in its campaign contributions, which for the most part had already been collected anyway, or even in a media "air war," but rather in a full-scale, get-out-the-vote "ground war."[75]

Labor's strategy paid off almost immediately on fast track. Desperate to retain the support of grassroots union activists to avoid another depressed turnout of their core labor base in the elections now only six weeks away, both traditional union supporters and other more moderate Democrats opposed Gingrich's fast-track measure.

On September 25, the House decisively defeated the Republican fast-track bill by a vote of 180-243, a substantially greater margin than the one by which Clinton's fast-track proposal had been rejected the year before. Only 29 Democrats, or about 15 percent, voted for the measure this time, while 171 opposed it. On the Republican side, 151 members, or about 70 percent, voted for it, and 71 voted against it. Labor had won yet another major trade policy victory.

LOOKING AHEAD: THE "BATTLE IN SEATTLE" AND BEYOND

In early December 1999, Bill Clinton made one more attempt to further establish his legacy as a champion of free trade when he journeyed to Seattle to try to convince delegates to the WTO meeting to launch a new "Millennium Round" of international trade negotiations. The talks collapsed, however, amidst dramatic, well-organized street protests by anti-WTO activists, who built upon their experiences in the NAFTA and fast-track fights.

In fact, inside the meeting hall, the discussions fell apart in good measure because Clinton was attending to another element of his legacy: the vindication of his presidency through the election of his vice president, Al Gore, as his successor in the 2000 election.

Once again the key to understanding this development was organized labor, whose support Gore would need in both the primaries and the general election. Labor had been angered in mid-November when, shortly after the AFL-CIO had endorsed Gore, the administration, to facilitate China's entry into the WTO, negotiated a trade pact with Beijing that the unions worried would lead to a surge of cheap textile and other imports. Now labor came in force to Seattle, joining environmental, human rights, and other activists, to demand that any new international trade agreements include core labor standards.

Concerned that a negotiating agenda that made no reference to worker rights would out-rage labor and damage Gore's prospects (and might also intensify labor opposition to China's entrance into the WTO),[76] Clinton proposed that the WTO establish a working group on international labor standards and even suggested that the organization might need to use sanc-tions to enforce compliance with such standards. The developing nations took great offense at these ideas, seeing in them a thinly veiled protectionist attempt by the U.S. to exclude their goods from American markets. Thus, the WTO talks collapsed.

What will the post-Seattle future hold? This spring or summer will see a furious congres-sional battle over Clinton's last free-trade initiative: the permanent normalization of trade relations with China, which is necessary if the U.S. is to receive the market-opening conces-sions China has made to get into the WTO.[77] The issue is of immense importance to the American business community, which, led by the Business Roundtable and the U.S. Chamber of Commerce, is planning to spend more than $10 million on a massive personal, grassroots, and media lobbying campaign.

On the other side of the trenches, fearing that the entrance of China into the WTO will prevent that body from ever giving serious considerations to worker rights, organized labor, along with its allies, is planning to unleash one of its most intensive lobbying campaigns ever, to pressure lawmakers to reject permanent normal trading relations with Beijing. After again helping congressional Democrats to make important gains in the 1998 elections,[78] labor has been planning a stepped-up grassroots campaign for this year's races.[79] Labor will once again make it clear to its Democratic allies that members who back the unions on China may well lose labor support in November. As of this writing, this fight is too close to call.

The Long Run

What about the longer term? Will trade liberalization remain stalled, or will we eventually see the negotiation and ratification of new regional or multilateral trade agreements? On one hand, it is possible that aggressive organizing efforts will allow labor to offset the structural changes that have eroded the movement's social and political weight in the past several decades. Recent organizing successes among home health care workers in Los Angeles, textile workers in North Carolina, public employees in Puerto Rico, graduate student teaching assistants at the University of California, computer programmers in Washington state, and doctors in Pennsylvania provide some evidence for this scenario.[80] It is also possible that the strong dollar and economic weak-ness overseas may continue to widen the U.S. trade deficit, raise unemployment in particular industries, generate new demands for protection, and intensify public "globalphobia."[81] In such circumstances, a revitalized labor movement and its allies, with public opinion at their backs and supported by liberal congressional Democrats and some Republican nationalists, might well be able to continue to prevent or block new presidential trade liberalization initiatives that lack strong labor and environmental standard provisions. Alternatively, labor and its allies may even be able to force the inclusion of such provisions in new trade legislation.

On the other hand, developments may transpire that will make it more difficult for labor to continue to win such victories. First, structural economic changes may continue to erode organized labor's numbers and resources. Second, if domestic economic growth remains steady and unemployment low, and the value of the dollar declines while overseas growth picks up, thus reducing the trade deficit, popular opposition to trade liberalization may recede, further depriving labor of the ally of public opinion. Finally, stunned by its 1997 fast-track defeat, the business community has begun to reorient its trade and wider political strategies in ways that could eventually help revive both Democratic and popular support for free trade. This last point is worth a longer discussion.

Many corporate leaders now believe that business made a mistake in so dramatically shifting its support from Democratic to Republican incumbents after the 1994 midterm elections. These leaders worry that the Republicans have become too strongly influenced by social conservatives, small business populists, and economic nationalists hostile to the interests of big multinational companies, especially with regard to trade policy. They also recognize that business will need at least some Democratic allies if it hopes to win on issues such as fast track in the future, but this requires that labor's current position of strength within the party be weakened or offset. Thus, a range of business interests has urged corporate and PAC officials to resume their support of and contributions to both political parties.[82]

To encourage this business reorientation, the New Democratic Network PAC, philosophically aligned though not formally affiliated with the Democratic Leadership Council, was formed in mid-1996. The PAC's aim is to help push the Democratic Party in a moderate, pro-business, and pro-free-trade direction by raising more corporate money for ideologically sympathetic Democratic candidates, thus weaning the party away from its heavy dependence on labor union contributions.[83]

There is evidence that business has in fact begun to rebalance its financial support for the parties, once again reducing the Democrats' dependence on labor money. In the 1997–1998 election cycle, the share of House Democrats' PAC money that came from labor fell to 43.6 percent, down from 48.4 percent two years earlier.[84]

And in the first half of 1999, with business now also beginning to hedge its bets against a possible Democratic takeover of the House, the National Republican Campaign Committee and the Democratic Congressional Campaign Committee split donations from business 50–50. This is in sharp contrast to the 1998 election, when the NRCC collected 63 percent of the business money.[85]

Second, beginning in early 1998, a number of major business organizations—including the Business Roundtable, Big Business's premiere lobbying organization; the Emergency Committee for American Trade, a lobbying group representing 53 multinational corporations; and the U.S. Chamber of Commerce—have undertaken or are planning to launch grassroots education and lobbying campaigns in targeted congressional districts and elsewhere to persuade American voters and their representatives of the merits of free trade.[86]

It is possible that continuing labor weakness, the shift of some business campaign contributions back to the Democrats, and the success of business's new outside lobbying efforts in strengthening popular support for free trade may together moderate Democratic opposition to further trade liberalization. This, in turn, may allow free traders to win approval of new trade liberalization legislation containing no serious labor and environmental standards provisions.

A Path for Labor

In weighing these two scenarios, I would argue that in the long run, labor is not likely to have sufficient strength to block all future liberalizing trade agreements. Beyond this, I would maintain that labor should not try to block all such agreements. As longtime United Electrical

Workers staffmember Lance Campa has explained, while shifting trade flows hurt many workers, many others gain from trade, and many more could benefit from a liberal trading order accompanied by strong labor standards to protect workers' rights. Compa also argues that if trade agreements are simply blocked, economic integration will proceed anyway, leaving no international scrutiny on labor rights. Thus, Compa concludes that rather than oppose such accords outright, labor should instead engage in the fight for worker rights on many fronts[87] while remaining ready to compromise for incremental advances. This could include support for a modified fast-track bill or acceptance of a free-trade agreement containing only modest gains for labor rights.[88]

In its efforts to achieve such compromises, labor would be wise to continue its recent emphasis on the grassroots mobilization of its membership since the redirection of corporate campaign funds back to congressional Democrats is once again likely to dilute the influence of labor's own financial contributions.

To counter business's new offensive on behalf of free trade, the labor movement will also need to strengthen its already substantial commitment to coalition politics. As we have seen, labor has built effective coalitions with a wide range of organizations in the NAFTA and especially the 1997 fast-track fights and will do so again in the upcoming China battle. Since John Sweeney's installation as AFL-CIO president in late 1995, unions have also forged other promising alliances, especially with churches and community organizations in successful "living-wage" campaigns in more than thirty cities and with students on dozens of college campuses in fights against American-owned foreign sweatshops.[89]

Labor's task now, as suggested earlier, is to continue to build a broader and more durable "protective countermovement" against globalization's harmful consequences. This, in turn, will be more easily accomplished if labor is able to oppose capital's accumulation strategies with its own nonprotectionist, counter-hegemonic vision for organizing the global economy that incorporates the concerns of environmentalists, human rights advocates, and others. Such a vision would involve a "grand compromise" with capital and at least the more democratic developing countries in which these nations agree to enforceable labor and environmental standards in exchange for guaranteed commitments of long-term development aid and debt relief.[90] In fact, there are indications that the AFL-CIO is thinking seriously about such a "progressive internationalist" alternative program.[91]

If such a program and movement can be developed, labor and its allies may be able to strike an accommodation with the globalist adversaries at home and with developing countries abroad that is adapted to the new era we have entered. In such circumstances, the 1997 fast-track fight may prove to have been a turning point in the struggle over the shape of the emerging global economy.

NOTES

1. The first wave of globalization took place during the fifty years or so that ended in world war. The second wave occurred in the 1950s and 1960s. Richard Higgott, "Economics, Politics and (International) Political Economy: The Need for a Balanced Diet in an Era of Globalisation," *New Political Economy* 4, no. 1 (1999).
2. At this point in the debate on globalization and its consequences, the literature has simply become too vast to cite in any detail. But for a comprehensive recent discussion, see David Held, Anthony McGrew, David Goldblatt, and Jonathan Perraton, *Global Transformations: Politics, Economics and Culture* (Stanford, CA: Stanford University Press, 1999).

3. Helen Milner, *Resisting Protectionism: Global Industries and the Politics of International Trade* (Princeton, NJ: Princeton University Press, 1988); I. M. Destler and John S. Odell, *Anti-Protection: Changing Forces in United States Trade Politics* (Washington, DC: Institute for International Economics, 1987).

4. See Michael Lusztig, "The Limits of Rent Seeking: Why Protectionists Become Free Traders," *Review of International Political Economy* 5, no. 1 (1998): 38-63; Oona A. Hathaway, "Positive Feedback: The Impact of Trade Liberalization on Industry Demands for Protection," *International Organization* 52, no. 3 (1998): 575-612.

5. Terms suggested by Robert Cox and Bob Jessop, respectively. Robert W. Cox, *Production, Power, and World Order: Social Forces in the Making of History* (New York: Columbia University Press, 1987); Bob Jessop, "Post-Fordism and the State," in Ash Amin, ed., *Post-Fordism: A Reader* (Cambridge, MA: Blackwell, 1994).

6. For two extremely useful overviews and analyses, see Frederick W. Mayer, *Interpreting NAFTA: The Nature of Politics and the Art of Political Analysis* (New York: Columbia University Press, 1998); George W. Grayson, *The North American Free Trade Agreement: Regional Community and the New World Order* (Lanham, MD: University Press of America, 1995).

7. For the next two paragraphs, see Mayer, *Interpreting NAFTA*, 69-77; William P. Avery, "Domestic Interests in NAFTA Bargaining," *Political Science Quarterly* 113, no. 2 (1998): 281-305.

8. On general patterns of business support for NAFTA, see Ronald W. Cox, "Corporate Coalitions and Industrial Restructuring: Explaining Regional Trade Agreements," *Competition & Change* 1 (1995): 13-30.

9. As Sandra Masur, director of Public Policy Analysis for Eastman Kodak and leader of the influential Business Roundtable's efforts onbehalf of NAFTA, explained, American business supported NAFTA because "U.S. manufacturing must pursue joint production [with Mexico] to keep costs down and compete against European and Japanese competitors who pursue similar strategies." Sandra Masur, "The North American Free Trade Agreement: Why It's in the Interest of U.S. Business," *Columbia Journal of World Business* 26, no. 2 (1991): 101. According to a 1992 Roper poll, 40 percent of some 450 U.S. corporate executives said it was "very" or "somewhat" likely that their companies would "shift some production to Mexico to Mexico . . . if NAFTA is ratified." For large companies, the figure was 55 percent. Samuel Bowles and Mehrene Larudee, "Nafta: Friend or Foe?" *New York Times* (15 November 1993).

10. In the same 1992 Roper poll, 24 percent of the executives surveyed admitted that it was either very or somewhat likely that "Nafta will be used by [their] company as a bar gaining chip to keep wages down in the U.S." Bowles and Larudee, "Nafta: Friend or Foe?"

    On NAFTA as an element of a strategy of industrial restructuring at labor's expense, see Mark E. Rupert, "(Re)Politicizing the Global Economy: Liberal Common Sense and Ideological Struggle in the U.S. NAFTA Debate," *Review of International Political Economy* 2, no. 4 (1995): 658-92; Kim Moody, "NAFTA and the Corporate Redesign of America," *Latin American Perspectives* 22, no. 1 (1995): 95-115.

11. On a theoretical note, in a study of labor's influence on congressional voting on NAFTA in 1993, John Conybeare and Mark Zinkula suggest that large sectors of labor can be expected to support protectionism or to oppose trade liberalization, regardless of whether a "Stolper-Samuelson" or a "specific-factors" model of trade policy preference formation is assumed. According to Stolper-Samuelson theories, which assume that factors of production—broadly defined as capital, labor, and land—are perfectly mobile, owners of abundant factors will support free trade, while owners of scarce factors will back protectionism. Thus, in an advanced country such as the United States, in which labor is the scarce factor of production, labor as a whole should support protectionism. On the other hand, according to specific-factors models, which assume that production factors are immobile or sector specific, thus leading business and labor preferences to be determined at the industry or sector level, most workers should also support protectionism since a dis proportionate share of the workforce is

employed in labor-intensive, import-competing industries. See John A. C. Conybeare and Mark Zinkula, "Who Voted against NAFTA? Trade Unions versus Free Trade," *World Economy* 19, no. 1 (1996): 2-3.

In fact, labor opposition to NAFTA was stronger than either set of models would predict. Both Stolper-Samuelson and specific-factors models assume that capital is geographically immobile. But even if production factors are immobile across different industrial sectors, as assumed in specific-factors models, capital is often internationally mobile while labor is not. Consequently, labor feared that by increasing both the reality and the threat of a manufacturing capital flight to low-wage Mexico, NAFTA would have negative domestic employment and wage effects well beyond those created by an increase in imports produced by Mexican-owned firms. Robert C. Feenstra, "Integration of Trade and Disintegration of Production in the Global Economy," *Journal of Economic Perspectives* 12, no. 4 (1998); 31-50.

12. Thus, in the House, those members who relied most heavily on campaign contributions from union political action committees—all Democrats—cast lopsided votes against NAFTA. More specifically, in districts where Democratic members got 20 percent of more of their total campaign contributions from labor PACs, 77 percent of those members opposed the treaty. But those Democrats who received more money from business PACs than labor PACs split on the issue, voting against the treaty by a narrow 82-88 margin. Jon Healey and Thomas H. Moore, "Clinton Forms New Coalition to Win NAFTA Approval," *CQ Weekly* (20 November 1997): 3183.

Statistical studies that find significant labor effects on either House or Senate NAFTA voting include Conybeare and Zinkula, "Who Voted against NAFTA?"; Sharyn O'Halloran, "Comment," in Susan Collins, ed., *Imports, Exports, and the American Worker* (Washington, D.C.: Brookings Institution, 1998); Leo H. Kahane, "Congressional Voting Patterns on NAFTA: An Empirical Interpretation," *American Journal of Economics and Sociology* 5, no. 4 (1996): 394-409; Janet M. Box-Steffensmeir, Laura W, Arnold, and Christopher J. S. Zorn, "The Strategic Timing of Position Taking in Congress: A Study of the North American Free Trade Agreement," *American Political Science Review* 91, no. 2 (1997): 324-38; Eric M. Uslaner, "Let the Chips Fall Where They May? Executive and Constituency Influences on Congressional Voting on NAFTA," *Legislative Studies Quarterly* 23, no. 3 (1998): 347-71; Jeffrey W. Steagall and Ken Jennings, "Unions, PAC Contributions, and the NAFTA Vote, *Journal of Labor Research* 17, no. 3 (1996): 515-21; Robert E. Baldwin and Christopher S. Magee, "Is Trade Policy for Sale? Congressional Voting on Recent Trade Bills," NBER Working Papers Series No. 6376 (1998).

13. In his provocative new book, Taylor Dark disputes the widely shared view that labor's political influence declined during the post-World War II era, but I think he over-, states his case. See Taylor Dark, *The Unions and the Democrats: An Enduring Alliance* (Ithaca, NY: Cornell University Press, 1999).

14. For the next four paragraphs, see I. M. Destler, "Trade Politics and Labor Issues: 1953-95," in Collins, ed., *Imports, Exports, and the American Worker*.

15. Alan V. Deardorff and Robert M. Stern, "American Labor's Stake in International Trade," in Walter S. Adams, ed., *Tariffs, Quotas, and Trade: The Politics of Protectionism* (San Francisco: Institute for Contemporary Studies, 1979); Paul Midford, "International Trade and Domestic Politics: Improving on Rogowski's Model of Political Alignments," *International Organization* 47, no. 4 (1993): 538-39, 555-57.

16. By curbing the import of cars and car parts and encouraging foreign countries to produce in the United States by limiting the amount of imported parts and labor permitted in cars sold in this country.

17. For a thorough analysis of this bill and the politics surrounding it, see Susan C. Schwab, *Trade-Offs: Negotiating the Omnibus Trade and Competitiveness Act* (Boston: Harvard Business School Press, 1994).

18. The bill also contained a tougher and expedited unfair trade practices procedure, including the designation of violations of workers' rights as unfair trade practices, and an expanded training and

adjustment assistance program. A measure requiring that advance notification be given of plant closures involving 100 or more workers, originally included in the bill, was eventually passed as a freestanding piece of legislation.

19. Sponsored by Rep. Richard Gephardt (D-MO).

20. On Clinton's success in both moving public opinion and in winning over Democratic legislators, see Uslaner, "Let the Chips Fall Where They May?"; Eric M. Uslaner, "Trade Winds: NAFTA and the Rational Public," *Political Behavior* 20, no. 4 (1998): 341-60; C. Don Livingston and Kenneth Wink, "The Passage of the North American Free Trade Agreement in the U.S. House of Representatives: Presidential Leadership or Presidential Luck?" *Presidential Studies Quarterly* 27, no. 1 (1997): 52-70.

21. For additional discussion of the events covered in this section through the summer of 1997, see I. M. Destler, *Renewing Fast-Track Legislation* (Washington, D.C.: Institute for International Economics, 1997), 16-27; I. M. Destler, "Congress and Foreign Trade," in Robert A. Pastor and Rafael Fernandez de Castro, eds., *The Controversial Pivot: The U.S. Congress and North America* (Washington, DC: Brookings Institution, 1998), 127-39.

22. Because of the complexity of the GATT agreement and the resulting uncertainty as to its effects, the accord did not evoke the visceral responses that NAFTA had from U.S. workers, for whom the flight of manufacturing capital to Mexico had constituted a palpable threat, Consequently, labor largely sat out the fight over the approval of the less controversial GATT deal, and the agreement was eventually passed with substantial bipartisan majorities. Thus, I will not discuss it here.

23. For the next five paragraphs, see Aaron Bernstein, "NAFTA: A New Union-Busting Weapon?" *Business Week* (27 January 1997): 4; Paul Blustein, "Fast-Track Trade Plan Pits White House against Top Congressional Democrats," *The Washington Post* (22 March 1997): All; John Maggs, "Trading Places," *The New Republic* (14 April 1997): 15-16; Robert S. Greenberger, "Clinton to Delay Fast-Track Trade Bill until Fall," *The Wall Street Journal* (23 May 1997): A2; Dan Balz, "The Battle to Seize the Heart and Soul of the Democrats," *The Washington Post National Weekly Edition* (9 June 1997): 11-12; David Corn, "Dick Gephardt: Working-Class Hero, On-the-Make Pol or Both?" The Nation (7 July 1997): 11-16; Jonathan Cohn, "Hard Labor," *The New Republic* (6 October 1997): 21-26.

24. The industrial unions' resolve was heightened by the findings of a study conducted for the U.S., Canadian, and Mexican governments by Cornell University labor economist Kate Bronfenbrenner. The three-year survey, which the U.S. Labor Department initially sat on, found that 60 percent of union organizing efforts in manufacturing after NAFTA were met by management threats to close the factories, compared with 29 percent before NAFTA. Kate Bronfenbrenner, *Final Report: The Effects of Plant Closings or the Threat of Plant Closings on the Right of Workers to Organize* (Ithaca: New York State School of Industrial and Labor Relations, Cornell University, 1997).

25. In early November, the Senate voted 69-31 in favor of a cloture resolution to defeat an attempted filibuster and allow consideration of the fast-track bill. Given the substantial size of many states, protectionist interests are more easily counterbalanced by pro-free-trade interests than is the case in smaller House districts. In addition, states with low levels of unionization are overrepresented in the Senate, again predisposing the upper chamber toward free trade. On the latter point, see Daniel Wirls, "The Consequences of Equal Representation: The Bicameral Politics of NAFTA in the 103rd Congress," *Congress & the Presidency* 25, no. 2 (1998): 129-45.

26. Forty-three Democrats and 160 to 170 Republicans would have voted for fast track. For these estimates, see Claude E. Barfield, "Politics of Trade and Fast Track in the United States" (paper presented at the First Academic Colloquium of the Americas, University of Costa Rica, March 1998, AEI Speeches [Online]. Available: http://www.aei.org/sp/ spbarfld.htm).

27. Although unions did gain a net 100,000 new members in 1998.

28. A July *Wall Street Journal*/NRC News poll showed that 42 percent of Americans believed that NAFTA had a negative impact on the United States—up from 35 percent in mid-1994—while only

32 percent believed it had had a positive impact. Respondents also opposed granting Clinton new fast-track authority by a 62 to 32 percent margin. Other polls also showed that the public was generally skeptical of free trade and by a wide margin supported the use of trade agreements to protect the environment and raise living standards.

For polling results on NAFTA and fast track, see Julie Kosterlitz, "Muddy Track," *The National Journal* (9 August 1997): 1595; William Schneider, "Democrats Battling Over Their Future," *The National Journal* (13 September 1997): 1810. For more general surveys of public opinion on trade and trade policy, see Alan Tonelson, "Public Opinion Demands Fixes to Trade Policy," *The Seattle Post-Intelligencer* (30 April 1997): A13; The Public Perspective (August/September 1997): 36-37.

29. On this point, see Christoph Scherrer, *Free Trade Elites and Fair Trade Masses: Why Has Public Opinion Mattered So Little?* (Berlin: John F. Kennedy-Institut fur Norda- merikastudien, 1994), Working Paper No. 65.

30. For discussion of these studies, see Kosterlitz, "Muddy Track"; Diane E. Lewis, "Report Hits NAFTA on Jobs," *Boston Globe* (27 June 1997): Dl; "The NAFTA Effect: When Neighbors Embrace," *The Economist* (5 July 1997): 21-23.

31. See especially William Greider, *One World Ready or Not: The Manic Logic of Global Capitalism* (New York: Simon & Schuster, 1997); Dani Rodrik, *Has Globalization Gone Too Far?* (Washington, DC: Institute for International Economics, 1997); George Soros, "The Capitalist Threat," The Atlantic (February 1997): 47-58.

32. Amy Borrus, "Business Is in a Hurry for Fast-Track," *Business Week* (15 September 1997): 38-39; Peter H. Stone, "Business Pushes for Fast-Track," *The National Journal* (27 September 1997): 1903-4.

33. On the rise of Republican populism and economic nationalism, see John B. Judis, "The Tariff Party," *The New Republic* (30 March 1992): 23-25; John B. Judis, "White Squall," *The New Republic* (11 March 1996): 26-30; Ben Wildavksy, "Going Nativist?" *The National Journal* (27 May 1995): 1278-81; David Frum, *Dead Right* (New York: Basic Books, 1995), 136-41. On the role of this group in the fast-track fight, see Peter Beinart, "The Nationalist Revolt," *The New Republic* (1 December 1997): 22-26.

34. On these points see Barfield, "Politics of Trade," from which most of the accompanying statistics are taken, See also Beinart, "The Nationalist Revolt"; James A. Barnes and Richard E. Cohen, "Divided Democrats," *The National Journal* (15 November 1997): 2304-7.

35. Southern House Democrats had been much more supportive of NAFTA than were their colleagues in the rest of the country, backing the deal 53-32, while the rest of the caucus opposed it by almost a 3 to 1 margin. Since 1991, however, the number of white Democratic House members from the thirteen southern states had declined from 79 to only 42.

36. Overall, whereas 40 percent of all House Democrats voted for NAFTA, 54 percent of those party members who were in the House in 1993 but not in 1997 voted for the accord, while only 30 percent of those who were House members in both years voted for the deal.

37. Only 20 percent of Democrats who were members of the House in both 1993 and 1997 planned to vote for fast track, a drop of 10 percent compared with the support for NAFTA within this group. Barfield, "Politics of Trade."

38. For the points in this paragraph, see Barnes and Cohen, "Divided Democrats"; Julie Kosterlitz, "The Pinstripers Ignored 'Ordinary Americans,'" *The National Journal* (1 November 1997): 2191-92; Michael Frisby and Bob Davis, "Missing in Action: As Trade Vote Looms, Clinton Is Hurt by Lack of Steady Supporters," *The Wall Street Journal* (6 November 1997): Al.

39. John Maggs, "Before and NAFTA," *The New Republic* (I September 1997): 11-12; Nancy Dunne, "Clinton Goes to the Wire to Save Fast-Track," *The Financial Times* (7 November 1997): 7.

40. E. J. Dionne, Jr., "Why the Democrats Bolted," *The Washington Post* (14 November 1997): A27.

41. Thomas B. Edsall, "Big Labor Flexes Its Muscle Once Again," *The Washington Post National Weekly Edition* (24 November 1997): 11.

42. For recent overviews of the literature on interest group behavior, see Frank R. Baumgartner and Beth L. Leech, *Basic Interests: The Importance of Groups in Politics and Political Science* (Princeton, NJ: Princeton University Press, 1998); John R. Wright, *Inter est Groups and Congress: Lobbying, Contributions, and Influence* (Boston: Allyn & Bacon, 1996); Allan J. Cigler and Burdett A. Loomis, *Interest Group Politics*, 5th ed. (Washington, DC: CQ Press, 1998); Paul S. Herrnson, Ronald G. Shaiko, and Clyde Wil cox, eds., *The Interest Group Connection: Electioneering, Lobbying and Policymaking in Washington* (Chatham, NJ: Chatham House, 1998).

43. On labor's electoral efforts in 1996, see Dark, *Unions and the Democrats*, 184-87; Barnes and Cohen, "Divided Democrats"; Elizabeth Drew, *Whatever It Takes: The Real Struggle for Political Power in America* (New York; Penguin, 1998), 69-77, 246-47; SteveRosenthal, "Building to Win, Building to Last," in Jo-Ann Mort, ed., *Not Your Father'sUnion Movement: Inside the AFL-CIO* (New York: Verso, 1998), 99-111; Robin Gerber,"Building to Win, Building to Last: The AFL-CIO COPE Takes on the Republican Congress," in Robert Biersack, Paul S. Herrnson, and Clyde Wilcox, eds., *After the Revolution: PACs and Lobbies in the Republican Congress* (Boston: Allyn & Bacon, 1999).

   More generally on interest group involvement electoral campaigns, see Mark J. Rozell and Clyde Wilcox, *Interest Groups in American Campaigns: The New Face of Electioneering* (Washington, DC: CQ Press, 1999); Paul Herrnson, "Interest Groups, PACs, and Campaigns," in Herrnson, Shaiko, and Wilcox, eds., *The Interest Group Connection*.

44. The margin rises to a staggering 23 to 1 if "soft" money contributions to political parties are included.

45. For these and subsequent PAC contribution figures, see Harold W. Stanley and Richard G. Niemi, *Vital Statistics on American Politics 1997-1998* (Washington, DC: CQ Press, 1998), 101-3.

46. For a detailed account of the labor mobilization against fast track, see David Glenn, "Fast Track Derailed," in Mort, ed., *Not Your Father's Union Movement*. See also Dark, *Unions and the Democrats*, 199; Kosterlitz, "Muddy Track"; Darrell West and Burdett A. Loomis, *The Sound of Money* (New York: Norton, 1999), 5-7; Jill Abramson with Steven Greenhouse, "The Trade Bill: Labor," *New York Times* (12 November 1997): Al; Glenn Burkins, "Labor Fights against Fast-Track Measure," *The Wall Street Journal* (16 September 1997): A24; Frank Swoboda, "Labor Plans Ads, Lobbying on Trade Pacts," *The Washington Post* (11 September 1997): A6; Harold Meyerson, "No Brainer, No Votes," *The LA Weekly* (14-20 November 1997): 11.

47. On "outside" lobbying by interest groups, see West and Loomis, *The Sound of Money*, Ken Kollman, *Outside Lobbying: Public Opinion and Interest Group Strategies* (Princeton, NJ: Princeton University Press, 1998).

48. Glenn, "Fast Track Derailed," 199.

49. Corn, "Dick Gephardt: Working-Class Hero."

50. Julie Kosterlitz, "The Wages of Trade," *The National Journal* (18 October 1997): 2076-79.

51. Karl Polanyi, *The Great Transformation* (New York: Rhinehart, 1944).

52. For example, unions held demonstrations with Friends of the Earth and the Sierra club in half a dozen cities to call attention to NAFTA's environmental effects on Mexican border towns. Abramson with Greenhouse, "The Trade Bill." See also Glenn, "Fast Track Derailed"; Beinart, "The Nationalist Revolt."

53. "Labor is practicing the politics of intimidation either with outright threats or implied threats . . . that labor will withdraw any campaign support, either financial or otherwise" to fast-track support-ers, said California Rep. Calvin M. Dooley, chairman of the New Democratic Coalition. Ronald Brownstein, "Trade Is Still the Exception to Clinton's Rule," *Los Angeles Times* (7 November 1997): A24. While such labor warnings were mostly targeted at Democrats, union lobbyists also pressured some two dozen northeastern and midwestern Republicans.

54. Many lawmakers who opposed fast track had studied what happened to several dozen Democratic congress members who voted for NAFTA in 1993 and then lost to Republicans in 1994, partly because alienated union members stayed away from the polls. Abramson with Greenhouse, 'The Trade Bill."

55. For studies that find evidence of labor PAC influence on congressional voting onlabor issues, see Gregory M. Saltzman, "Congressional Voting on Labor Issues: The Roleof PACs," *Industrial and Labor Relations Review* 40, no. 2 (1987): 163-79; Allen Wilhite and John Theilman, "Labor PAC Contributions and Labor Legislation: A Simultaneous Logit Approach," *Public Choice* 53, no. 3 (1987): 267-76; Woodrow Jones, Jr. and Robert K.Keiser, "Issue Visibility and the Effects of PAC Money," *Social Science Quarterly* 68, no. 1(1987): 170-76; Alan Neustadtl, "Interest Group PACsmanship: An Analysis of Campaign Contributions, Issue Visibility, and Legislative Impact," Social Forces 69, no. 2 (1990):549-64.

   For reviews of the wider literature on the effects of PAC spending on congressional voting behavior, see Baumgartner and Leech, Basic Instincts; Wright, *Interest Groups and Congress;* Thomas Gais, *Improper Influence: Campaign Finance Law, Political Interest Groups, and the Problem of Equality* (Ann Arbor; University of Michigan Press, 1996).

56. See the studies of congressional voting on NAFTA cited in note 12 above. For other studies that find PAC effects on congressional trade voting, see Cletus C. Coughlin, "Domestic Content Legislation: House Voting and the Economic Theory of Regulation," *Economic Inquiry* 23, no. 3 (1985): 437-48; Suzanne C. Tosini and Edward Tower, "The Textile Bill of 1985: The Determinants of Congressional Voting Patterns," *Public Choice* 54, no. 1 (1987): 19-25; Stephen V. Marks, "Economic Interests and Voting on the Omnibus TradeBill of 1987," *Public Choice* 75, no. 1 (1993): 21-42; Stanley D. Nollen and Dennis P. Quinn, "Free Trade, Fair Trade, Strategic Trade, and Protectionism in the U.S. Congress, 1987-88," *International Organization* 48, no. 3 (1994): 491-525.

57. For general discussions of PACs and their strategies, see Gais, *Improper Influence;* Theodore J. Eismeier and Philip H. Pollock III, *Business, Money, and the Rise of Corporate PACs in American Elections* (New York: Quorum, 1988); Frank J. Sorauf, Inside Campaign Finance: Myths and Realities (New Haven, CT: Yale University Press, 1992); Dan Clawson, Alan Neustadt, and Mark Weller, *Dollars and Votes: How Business Campaign Contribution Subvert Democracy* (Philadelphia, PA: Temple University Press, 1998).

58. Gais, *Improper Influence,* 167-69; Eismeier and Pollock, *Business, Money, and the Rise of Corporate PACs in American Elections;* Clawson, Neustadtl, and Weller, *Dollars and Votes,* 150-57; Brooks Jackson, *Honest Graft: Big Money and the American Political Process* (New York: Knopf, 1988).

59. In 1982, business PACs gave only about 40 percent of their contributions in House races to Democrats. By 1992, this had jumped to almost 57 percent.

   On the advantage in the receipt of corporate PAC contributions enjoyed by members of the House majority party, see Thomas J. Rudolph, "Corporate and Labor PAC Contributions in House Elections: Measuring the Effects of Majority Party Status," *Journal of Politics* 61, no. 1 (1999): 195-206; Gary W. Cox and Eric Magar, "How Much Is Majority Status in the U.S. Congress Worth?" *American Political Science Review* 93, no. 2 (1999): 299-309.

60. Including contributions from both "corporate" and "trade, membership, and health" PACs.

61. See Cohen, "Dems Feel the Squeeze"; Cohen and Barnes, "Divided Democrats"; Beinart, "The Nationalist Revolt"; Abramson with Greenhouse, "The Trade Bill"; Edsall, "Big Labor Flexes Its Muscle Once Again"; Meyerson, "No-Brainer, No Votes."

62. While business PACs gave $47.5 million to House Democrats in 1994, that figure had dropped to $33 million in 1996. Meanwhile, labor PACs increased their contributions to Democrats from $32.5 million in 1994 to $37.3 million in 1996.

63. The figure for all Democratic challengers, including both winners and losers, was 71 percent.

64. As the fast-track vote approached, Democrats took note of a recent special election in Staten Island where a strong Democratic candidate lost because the Republicans were able to spend $800,000 on soft-money-funded ads, while the Democratic Party lacked the funds to reply.

65. Martha Gibson and Stephen Carter demonstrate that as in NAFTA voting, the larger was labor's share of a member's total PAC contributions, the more likely the member was to oppose fast track.

This time, though, the Democrats' heightened dependence on labor money spelled defeat for Clinton's proposal. Martha L. Gibson and Stephen Carter, "The Politicization of Fast Track" (paper presented at the meeting of the American Political Science Association, Boston, September 1998).

66. Brownstein, "Trade Is Still the Exception to Clinton's Rule."

67. Barnes and Cohen, "Divided Democrats," 2306.

68. John F. Harris, "Clinton Hits 'Fast-Track' Opponents," *The Washington Post* (28 October 1997): A4.

69. Peter Beinart, "Why the Center Can't Hold," *Time* (24 November 1997): 52.

70. Abramson with Greenhouse, "The Trade Bill."

71. See Steven Greenhouse, "Two Feuding Democratic Voices Call a Truce," *New York Times* (9 August 1998): 20; John Judis, "New Labor, New Democrats—New Alliance?" *The American Prospect* (September-October 1998): 12-14.

72. On the late summer and fall 1998 fast-track fight, see Paul Magnusson, "Newt May Have Put Fast-Track on an Even Slower Boat," *Business Week* (13 July 1998): 49; David Hosansky, "Tenuous Bipartisan Alliance on Trade Succumbs to Election-Year Tensions," *CQ Weekly* (1 August 1998): 2072; Julie Kosterlitz, "A Vote the Dems Would Like to Trade In," *The National Journal* (12 September 1998): 2108; David Hosansky, "House Vote Signals,a Key Reversal of U.S. Support for Free Trade," *CQ Weekly* (26 September 1998): 2603-4.

73. Juliet Eilperin, "House Defeats Fast-Track Trade Authority," *The Washington Post* (26 September 1998): A10; Jonathan Peterson, "Democrats Call House Defeat of Fast-Track Trade Bill Bid to Humiliate Them," *Los Angeles Times* (26 September 1998): A18.

74. Bill Clinton also opposed the Republicans' attempt to put Democrats on the spot before the November elections, especially after it became clear that he would need Democratic support to fend off impeachment over the Monica Lewinsky scandal.

75. While spending only about $5 million on TV ads in 1998, labor spent $ 18 million on a tightly targeted "GOTV" effort coordinated by 400 field activists, up from 135 in 1996, and focused on 8 Senate races and 45 tight House races, down from more than 100 two years earlier. Aaron Bernstein and Richard S. Dunham, "Unions: Laboring Mightily to Avert a Nightmare in November," *Business Week* (19 October 1998): 53; Steven Greenhouse, "Republicans Credit Labor for Success by Democrats," *New York Times* (6 November 1998): A28; Aaron Bernstein, "Labor Helps Turn the Tide—The Old Fashioned Way," *Business Week* (16 November 1998): 45; David Magleby and Marianne Holt, "The Long Shadow of Soft Money and Issue Advocacy Ads," *Campaigns & Elections* (May 1999): 22-27.

76. "The only thing worse than no agreement," one administration official said, "was the agreement it looked like we might get." Joseph Kahn and David E. Sanger, "Impasse on Trade Delivers a Stinging Blow to Clinton," *New York Times* (5 December 1999): AI.

77. Less Dramatic fights will be fought over bills to lower U.S. tariffs and quotas on goods from sub-Saharan Africa, the Caribbean, and Central America, and possibly over continued U.S. participation in the WTO (which the AFL-CIO does not oppose). For much of the information in this paragraph and the next, see "Trade Winds Swirling Over China Vote," *The National Journal* (12 December 1999): 3618-20.

78. Twenty-four percent of those turning out came from union households, and according to an AFL-CIO poll, 71 percent of union members voted Democratic in a year that saw the party pick up five House seats.

79. Kirk Victor and Eliza Newlin Carney, "Labor's Political Muscle," *The National Journal* (4 September 1999): 2478-82.

80. James L. Tyson, "In High-Tech Age, Unions Can Score," *Christian Science Monitor* (20 July 1999): 1; Julie Kosterlitz, "Searching for New Labor," *The National Journal* (4 September 1999): 2470-77; Paul Buhle and Steve Fraser, "A New Day for Labor," *The Nation* (20 September 1999): 7-8. More generally, see Mort, ed., *Not Your Father's Union Movement.*

81. A highly publicized poll released in November 1999 by the Program on International Policy Attitudes at the University of Maryland found that 72 percent of the U.S. public believed that too little attention is paid in trade talks to "working Americans," and 78 percent thought that the WTO should pay more attention to labor and environmental standards. Mark Suzman, "Trade: Clinton Links Environment to Trade Deals," *The Financial Times* (17 November 1999): 6.

82. "Some Republicans aren't going to be there on trade issues," said Dan Schnur, a California GOP consultant. "Ultimately, business is going to form relationships with elements of both parties." Richard S. Dunham and Amy Borrus, "Still the Party of Big Business?" *Business Week* (14 September 1998): 150-60. Business interests calling for renewed support for the Democrats included the Business-Industry Political Action Committee, a corporate lobbying coalition; the U.S. Chamber of Commerce; and the editorialists at *Business Week*. See "There's More Than One Party of Business," *Business Week* (4 May 1988): 182; Richard S. Dunham, "Is the GOP the Only Party of Business?" *Business Week* (4 May 1998): 154; Thomas B. Edsall, "Giving Republicans the Business," The Washington Post National Weekly Edition (22 June 1998): 10; "Building the Chamber's Clout," Business Week (22 March 1999): 51.

83. Eliza Newlin Carney, "What? A Smiling 'New Democrat?'" *The National Journal* (6 December 1997): 2476-77.

84. Norman J. Ornstein, Thomas E. Mann, and Michael Malbin, *Vital Statistics on Congress, 1999-2000* (Washington, DC: AEI Press, 2000), 106.

85. The figures are taken from a report prepared by the Center for Responsive Politics. Susan B. Glasser and Juliet Eilperin, "GOP Scrambles to Counter Business's Aid to Democrats," *Washington Post* (10 November 1999): A6.

86. See Julie Kosterlitz, "Trade Crusade," *The National Journal* (9 May 1998):1054-57; Bob Davis, "CEOs, Stymied in Capital on Trade, Lobby Hinterland," *The Wall Street Journal* (15 June 1998): A30; Michael Phillips and Helenc Cooper, "Business Launches Free Trade Offensive," *The Wall Street Journal* (29 November 1999): A2.

87. Including filing complaints under U.S. trade laws with labor rights provisions and under the NAFTA side agreements, working with European Union colleagues under the EU Works Council Directive, bringing cases to the International Labor Organization, and pressing for corporate codes of conduct, filing lawsuits, and other mechanisms.

88. Lance Compa, "Free Trade, Fair Trade, and the Battle for Labor Rights" (paper presented at the conference on "The Revival of the Labor Movement?" School of Industrial and Labor Relations, Cornell University, Ithaca, NY, October 1998). See also Lance Compa, "A Fast Track for Labor," *The American Prospect* (September-October 1998): 60-64.

89. Buhle and Fraser, "A New Day for Labor."

90. In an important recent study of 93 nations, Dani Rodrik shows that democracies pay higher wages than autocracies for a given level of manufacturing productivity. This suggests that more democratic developing countries might eventually be persuaded to agree to modest international labor standards, since they are at a competitive disadvantage with respect to more repressive developing countries in which wages are lower. Dani Rodrik, "Democracies Pay Higher Wages," *Quarterly Journal of Economics* 114, no, 3 (1999): 707-38. For a useful discussion of Rodrik's findings, see Aaron Bernstein, "Labor Standards: Try a Little Democracy," *Business Week* (13 December 1999): 42-43.

91. See the sketch of elements of such a program by Thomas I. Palley, assistant director of public policy for the AFL-CIO, in "How to Say No to the IMF," *The Nation* (21 June 1999): 21 -22. For a fuller argument, see Thomas I. Palley, *Plenty of Nothing; The Downsizing of the American Dream and the Case for Structural Keynesianism* (Princeton, NJ: Princeton University Press, 1998). See also Jeff Faux, "A New Grand Bargain," *The American Prospect* (17 January 2000): 20.

ༀ

Capitalism, Nationalism, and the New American Empire

A. G. Hopkins

This article draws on Pareto's theory of elites to explore the relationship between American capitalism and American nationalism, and to connect the invasion of Iraq to classical theories of imperialism. Globalisation has changed the structure of the American economy and promoted interests that have an increased stake in free trade. Neither these interests nor the oil companies advocated intervention in Iraq. Globalisation also accelerated the decline of older industries that were inclined to be protectionist, but these were not prominent advocates of the invasion either. Winners and losers, however, were both deeply affected by the wider consequences of rapid economic change, which generated uncertainty about the direction society was taking and concern about its moral foundations. These anxieties prepared the way for a conservative revival based on family, faith, and flag that enabled the neoconservatives to transform conservative patriotism into assertive nationalism after 9/11. In the short term, the invasion of Iraq was a manifestation of national unity. Placed in a longer perspective, it reveals a growing divergence between new globalised interests, which rely on cross-border negotiation, and insular nationalist interests, which seek to rebuild fortress America.

Empires are once again big business. The United States is said to be building one in the Middle East, or at least making the attempt, and the word itself has become obligatory for titles of books dealing with contemporary international relations. Readers can now be colonised by *Irresistible Empires, Accidental Empires, Resurrected Empires* and *Incoherent Empires*—to name just a few of the species.[1] If they seek spiritual uplift they can turn to *Jesus and Empire: The Kingdom of God and the New World Disorder;*[2] if they are looking in the opposite direction, they can observe *Reproducing Empire: Race, Sex, Science and US Imperialism in Puerto Rico,*[3] which closely follows *Naked Empire,*[4] involves an *Empire of Debt*[5] and results, naturally enough, in *Sorrows of Empire.*[6] It all ends in tears, but then it always has done, as the *Complete Idiot's Guide to the Roman Empire* confirms.[7]

The outpouring of books on empire is readily explained as a reaction to the events of 9/11. Before then, the study of empires was scarcely a fashionable subject, unless the aim was to denounce them, in which case the term imperialism was preferred. The new literature has now transformed the historiography of the subject by placing empire at the centre of public debate, thus making it fashionable and, in some interpretations, desirable too. The result is that there is nowa plenitude of information on every aspect of America's supposed new empire—from the ideological roots of neo-conservatism to military strategy by way of the inner workings of the Pentagon, the CIA and the White House. Even the luckless Iraqis are now familiar to us as Sunnis, Shi'ites, and Kurds, and of course as generalised insurgents.

A.G. Hopkins, "Capitalism, Nationalism and the New American Empire," *The Journal of Imperial and Commonwealth History* 35:1, March 2007, pp. 95–117. Reprinted by permission of Taylor & Francis Group, http://www.informaworld.com.

Indeed, the weight of information on Iraq alone is now so great that it is producing both reader fatigue and author fatigue. As repetition and diminishing returns set in, some of the latest books are beginning to look ahead, though not, it has to be said, to a golden age of perpetual peace. On the contrary, we are now being warned of *The Next Attack* and frightened by *China's Plan to Dominate Asia and the World*.[8] If there is no rest for the wicked, the just must be permanently alert.

Indications that commentators on current affairs may be moving on, with customary enthusiasm, to imminent future catastrophes suggest that historians can now begin to grapple with the immediate past, freshly turned from the present, though few have yet done so.[9] Studies of the new American empire have been written almost exclusively by nonhistorians who have taken their historical bearings from two main sources: Paul Kennedy's *The Rise and Fall of the Great Powers*, which is cited chiefly for its use of the now familiar phrase 'imperial overstretch', and Niall Ferguson's *Colossus: The Price of America's Empire*, which recommends the extension of American power while expressing concern that Americans might lack the stamina needed to carry the accompanying imperial burden. Caution in entering this subject is understandable: historians like to see the dust settle before they try to discern patterns in the past, and the American venture in Iraq has yet to be concluded.[10] Accordingly there is a case for suggesting that historians ought to begin to place the episode in a much broader context, while acknowledging that the perspective is still compressed and the source materials limited.

I

Most of the now innumerable books on this subject deal with the unfolding issues of the day and lack a wider focus. The much smaller number that seeks to place current events in a larger perspective occupy a range of positions, though the most distinctive, including many of the most influential, are those placed on the right and left of the political spectrum. The literature on the right, associated mainly with the neo-conservatives but not confined to them, has promoted a vision of a democratic and pacific world order, which the United States is destined to bring into being through the exercise of its supreme power, including its military power.[11] According to this view, the invasion of Iraq was intended to be the first of a series of decisive interventions that would enable the United States to realise its providential mission. The literature on the left has advanced an alternative vision of a more equitable society, which will arise after the contradictions inherent in the capitalism have conspired to bring the system down.[12] From this perspective, imperialism expresses the growing power of giant monopolies and world finance at a particular stage in the development of late capitalism. The invasion of Iraq can be seen, and has been seen, as a measure taken to incorporate the economy, essentially its oil resources, into the world capitalist system.[13]

These opposed positions have the merit of painting big pictures that enable us to place Iraq in a global framework. But they have the disadvantage of fitting the invasion of Iraq into predetermined designs, and they also suffer from significant empirical deficiencies. The radical right makes its policy recommendations on behalf of a national entity, the United States, and is cast in an idealist, political mould that fails to relate foreign policy to the domestic socioeconomic order. The radical left engages with internal developments but is hampered by the fact that an analysis based on class loses explanatory power in a country where politics is not primarily a function of class conflict.[14] Nevertheless, commentators on the right have identified one of the most important elements in understanding the foreign policy of imperial

America: political nationalism. Commentators on the left have identified the other: capitalism. What is lacking is a means of fitting them together.

One way of joining the two is by returning to a neglected classic: Vilfredo Pareto's theory of elites. Pareto formulated his theory in 1901,[15] partly in response to Marx's emphasis on class relationships and partly in reaction to the way that Italy's democratic institutions had functioned since unification in the 1860s. Pareto's disillusion with the mass of the electorate, which he thought was easily manipulated and inclined to act irrationally, led him to emphasise the importance of sentiments in determining human actions. From this starting point he moved on to consider the character of govferning elites and the strategies they used to perpetuate their dominance. The two most important types of elite are those he referred to as lions and foxes.[16] Lions are conservatives who possess 'the persistence of aggregates' and stand for tradition and the use of force, if necessary, to uphold it. Foxes are innovators who have the 'instinct for combining' and promote their interests by persuasion and guile.[17] When lions predominate, the government is more inclined to favour coercive means; when foxes are in control, negotiation and co-option are the preferred techniques. Pareto then described how elites tend to exaggerate their dominant characteristics by recruiting like-minded members and by drawing strength from external influences: war and depression favour lions; peace and prosperity help foxes. The conditions that produce success, however, also prepare the way for failure. Uneven recruitment eventually creates an imbalance in the resources needed for governing. Lions have insufficient skill in negotiation; foxes are less adept at the use of force. The resulting unstable equilibrium is resolved by transferring dominance from one group to another, whether by the ballot box or through revolution. The ensuing circulation of elites is the motor of the political system.

Pareto's interest in ruling elites was shared by notable contemporaries, such as Mosca, Michels and Sorel, which suggests that he had identified an issue that was widely applicable to the Europe of the day. His insights into the history of elites also extended well beyond his own time. His anthropomorphic references to lions and foxes drew on an Italian tradition reaching back to Machiavelli, whose princes were either warriors in the heroic mould of Achilles or confidence tricksters possessed of cunning and subtlety.[18] Pareto's younger compatriot, Antonio Gramsci, pursued the question of how ruling classes maintained their dominance by developing his concept of moral hegemony, which is now as well-known as Pareto himself is neglected.

A further connection can be made between Pareto's ideas and the classical theories of imperialism. Pareto himself was not concerned to make the link;[19] studies of the new American empire have not done so either. Taking this step, however, makes it possible to place the actions of the United States in Iraq in a much longer perspective, and thus to begin to make it a subject of history. Radical theories of imperialism, as formulated by Cobden, Hobson and Veblen, emphasised the role of noncapitalist elites in promoting war and imperialism, and the contrasting commitment of the bulk of business interests in maintaining peace.[20] The danger, as they saw it, was that militant elements, supported by special interests (such as the armaments industry) and driven along by irrational nationalist fervour, would take control and destroy the modern capitalist system. The foxes might fail to tame the lions; they might also be drawn into aggressive behaviour. Schumpeter, writing in 1919, took this interpretation to its highest stage by arguing that capitalism was indeed inherently pacific and that imperialism was the product of atavistic forces that had outlived their usefulness but were still able to influence policy.[21] Three years earlier, Lenin had produced a theory of imperialism that emphasised the opposite view, namely that the bourgeois order would be driven to war by contradictions in the capitalist system.[22] Foxes, so to speak, were really lions in disguise.

These now distant writers formulated the basic arguments that have resurfaced today in two sharply opposed claims: on the one hand, the view that the invasion of Iraq had non-economic causes, whether strategic, political or even personal; on the other, the notion that capitalism is driven by economic imperatives that produce war, conquest and destruction. Pareto's discussion of elites builds a bridge between the two.[23] The connection made here, briefly put, suggests that the decision to invade Iraq can be seen as marking a historic divergence between the rapid development of capitalism and the lagging development of the nation state. Profound changes in the structure of the economy of the United States in the late twentieth century created important new interests that depend on maintaining amicable relations with the wider world and call for largely fox-like attitudes. The nation-state, on the other hand, represents a constellation of embedded, lion-like interests, ranging from declining industries to populist nationalism, which incline towards a mixture of defensive isolationism at home and assertive action abroad. The two interests are not as estranged as this summary statement suggests because they share an underlying ideology of conservative patriotism that is capable, given the right circumstances, of overlaying their differences. Foxes had no direct interest in occupying Iraq, but they were co-opted by the lions in the administration, who succeeded in the aftermath of 9/11 in transforming domestic patriotism into forceful nationalism.

II

The capitalist element in the story can be followed by tracing the evolution of the military–industrial complex—a term launched by President Eisenhower in his Farewell Address and revived today by the debate over the causes of the Iraq war.[24] Eisenhower's concern was that the expansion of the military–industrial complex would lead to what he called 'unwarranted influence' in the 'councils of government'. Although an old lion himself, Eisenhower feared that an excessive growth in the number of lions would lead to the 'disastrous rise of misplaced power' that would 'endanger our liberties or democratic processes'. Eisenhower's remedy—in fact his main message—was to urge that government policies should result from balanced deliberation. Sound judgement at home called for 'an alert and knowledgeable citizenry'; sound judgment abroad involved diplomacy as well as force. 'The conference table,' Eisenhower said, 'though scarred by many frustrations, cannot be abandoned for the certain agony of the battlefield.' In other words, balance could be achieved only if fox-like qualities of persuasion and flexibility were incorporated into government policies to a degree that would rein in the assertive tendencies of the lion-like interests who managed the military-industrial complex.

Eisenhower's thoughts were his own, but they undoubtedly reflected a much wider preoccupation of the time. A few years earlier, C, Wright Mills had published an account of what he called *The Power Elite*, a study that was widely discussed at the time and is regarded now as a modern classic. Mills did not use the term 'military–industrial complex', nor, curiously, did he make use of Pareto, though he was influenced by Veblen, and saw himself as updating his theory of the leisure class.[25] Nevertheless, Mills produced the most comprehensive study of the elites of the day, and what he called the 'warlords' and their business associates featured prominently in it. Mills used the term 'power elite' to refer a cluster of elites—economic, political and military—who came together in 'often uneasy coincidence' to run the country.[26] Competition among elites in the 'higher circles' was conducted within a framework set by shared values derived from common educational and social backgrounds. Their grip on power had grown as a result of the rise of the large corporation, the expansion of government (during the Roosevelt years and in the course of the Second World War) and 'the development of a permanent military establishment'.[27] In Mills's view, the citizenry at large were being steadily excluded from the decision-making processes that affected their lives, and the notion that imbalances in power would correct themselves automatically no longer held.

Mills's discussion of what he called 'the theory of balance' echoes Pareto's notion of equilibrium and connects even more readily to Eisenhower's emphasis on the need for a counterweight to the military–industrial complex. Unlike Pareto, however, Mills did not offer an account of how elites would transform themselves. Indeed, his analysis suggested that the power elite was able to contain its internal differences and present a generally united front to the rest of society. The result, in his rather bleak assessment, was government by a plutocratic oligarchy consisting of both lions and foxes.

Mills's study has been much discussed and his conclusions and wider judgements have been both assaulted and defended.[28] But his general picture of the changes that had taken place during the previous half century is still regarded as being broadly accurate. As the United States became united, so the 'command posts' of power, as Mills called them, had shifted from local societies to the national stage. As institutional hierarchies, private and public, had grown, so too had the power of those who directed them. As clusters of national elites distanced themselves from the population at large, transparency and accountability were reduced and the gap between rulers and ruled grew ever wider. These views were shared by many writers on the radical left whose work became particularly influential in the 1960s and 1970s. For example, William Appleman Williams, one of the most prominent historians of the time, regarded American foreign policy as an imperial policy driven primarily by internal forces that were bound up with the rise of state and corporate capitalism and the expansion of the military interest.[29]

This line of thinking has been applied to the invasion of Iraq where, so it has been held, oil was the primary motive and the military–industrial complex the main agent.[30] This claim needs careful evaluation. There is no doubt of the continuing importance of the complex, though it is not easily measured, either today or in the 1950s.[31] The best proxy is probably annual defence expenditure, which ran at about 5–6 percent of GDP during the era of the Cold War, dropped to about 3.5 percent in the 1990s and is now back up to about 5 percent. But of course the GDP is much larger now than it was in the 1950s, and annual expenditure in (constant) dollars is correspondingly greater.[32] This sum, which is currently over $400bn., is greater than that spent on defence by the rest of the world as a whole. Illustrative evidence of links between armaments firms, the military and Congress is also readily available, as are stunning examples of pork barrel politics, including one where the Air Force requested five C-130 aircraft and was voted funds for 256.[33] Bringing home the bacon is particularly important for localities where employment has become dependent on defence contracts: Boeing in Seattle and Lockheed Martin in Bethesda (Maryland) are well-known examples, but there are many other centres, scattered across the United States, that would suffer if the defence budget were cut significantly.

At the same time, it is important to recognise that the composition of the military–industrial complex has changed considerably since the 1950s. On the military side, the most significant development has been the introduction of precision-guided weapons, which have reduced the need for a huge air force and cut the demand for manpower in the army.

One consequence has been a fall in employment in the old, metal-working industries and a corresponding increase in links between new, 'high-tech' industries and defence.[34] Military research programmes fund the development of semiconductors, software and sensors; military contractors buy back the resulting products cheaply because they have also been mass-produced for the consumer market. A second consequence has been the decline of the tradition of the 'citizen–soldier' and the creation of a professional army that is increasingly removed from the wider society it is contracted to represent.[35] The Constitution remains unaltered, but the abolition of the draft has in practice diminished a powerful check on the use of the military.

By the end of the twentieth century, the industrial component of the military–industrial complex had also changed.[36] The new, 'high-tech' industries that helped to produce precision weapons were part of a much broader trend representing a shift away from long-established industries. Textiles and steel are in the final stages of a protracted and painful decline; the motor vehicle industry is in serious difficulties, too, as the desperate state of General Motors' finances demonstrates.[37] Manufacturing accounted for about 30 percent of GDP in 1953 but only around 15 percent in 2000 and ceased to generate new jobs after 1980.[38] The complement to this trend has been the expansion of the service economy, assisted by new digital information technology, in response to the demand for education, health care, entertainment and financial, legal and personal services: in 1948 its share of GDP stood at 45 percent; by 2000 it had reached 66 percent.[39]

These developments were accompanied by increasing integration with the outside world, and by a shift in economic gravity within the United States from the north east to the south and west.[40] Commodity exports grew from about 4 percent of GDP in 1950 to around 15 percent in 2000; imports moved in parallel fashion until 1976, since when they have risen rapidly, thus producing a persistent and swelling deficit in the balance of trade. Exported services, on the other hand, not only expanded but also generated a growing surplus, though this was insufficient to close the gap on the current account, which was met by borrowing from abroad. Foreign holdings of United States treasury securities and corporate stocks and bonds have increased rapidly since the 1980s, as has foreign direct investment in the United States. There was a corresponding, though slightly greater, growth in American investment overseas as multinational corporations shifted operations abroad—a phenomenon known today as outsourcing. The American economy still consists of a vast internal market, especially if Canada and Mexico (its NAFTA partners) are included, but over the last 30 years it has also been joined more firmly to other parts of the world, especially to Western Europe, Japan and China.[41] This new orientation has been made possible by reduced trade barriers, deregulation and greater financial integration, and carries with it a general commitment to free trade.[42] Agriculture and the older industries, on the other hand, are more inclined to support protection because they fear foreign competition.[43] The foxes promote globalisation; the lions seek shelter.

III

Evidently, the relationship between the economy and the American presence abroad is far more complicated today than it was in the 1950s, when Williams advanced the view that the chief purpose of foreign policy was to secure markets for manufacturers.[44] It is hard to sustain this argument today and harder still to relate it to the invasion of Iraq. The limited information currently available suggests that the military–industrial complex played a minor part in the decision to go to war in 2003. The best evidence concerns the military itself, which was determined above all to avoid another Vietnam experience.[45] From the 1970s onwards the chiefs of staff tried to steer clear of marginal wars, guerrillas and potential quagmires. These priorities were reinforced by President Bush's secretary of state, Colin Powell, who wanted to ensure that future wars were limited to those that were absolutely necessary and clearly winnable.[46] Even in these cases; the Powell Doctrine held that the army ought not to be deployed unless it had overwhelming force and a defined exit strategy. Powell's aim was to create an army that was highly valued, well funded and rarely deployed, and to erect barriers that would prevent politicians from misusing the massive military power at their disposal. The lions had not lost their appetites, but they had learned by experience when to hunt and when to conserve their energies.[47]

With regard to the industrial component, it has yet to be argued that industries linked to defence agitated for war. The old defence industries undoubtedly lost ground to new 'high-tech' firms, but the trend would not have been altered by successful war-mongering, and might even have accentuated it. A number of specialised 'high-tech' companies were closely involved with the military, but the overwhelming interest of the industry as a whole lay in the civilian market both at home and abroad. Moreover, many of the new suppliers were small, scattered and not as readily mobilised for political purposes as the older, giant corporations, while the significant (and little publicised) participation of foreign-owned companies in defence contracts meant that the new industries could not easily present themselves as being part of the national interest, even if they wished to do so.[48]

This leaves firms that were linked to the military–industrial complex without being confined by it, the most important, of course, being the great oil companies and their close associates.[49] It is self-evident that the American presence in the Middle East is dominated by oil (and Israel), and that the oil companies have a permanent interest in ensuring that supplies flow through them at required levels and appropriate prices.[50] It is also well-known that President Bush and his some of his senior associates have lose ties to the oil industry.[51] Moreover, there is no doubt that the development of oil in the Middle East and the political involvement of foreign powers in the region are closely related.[52] This was true of the period of British dominance; it applies equally to the extension of the American presence from the 1940s.[53] Added to this, some commentators have claimed that the oil companies were keen to secure Iraq's rich oil reserves at a time when demand was beginning to outstrip supply.[54] Taken together, these arguments have led to the widespread belief that the invasion of Iraq was prompted primarily by the desire to control its oil resources.[55]

The case is attractive. Foxes, too, can bite when threatened, and the oil companies have been involved in various political interventions in the past. But the evidence relating to the invasion of 2003 is at present circumstantial and will remain so until the records are available. Meanwhile, there are grounds for an alternative view. In the first place, there was no immediate supply crisis in the years immediately before the invasion, and prices since the first Gulf War had followed the normal course of supply and demand.[56] The question of long-term reserves had long been debated within the oil industry, and had produced judgements and strategies other than resorting to war, which risked massive disruption to plant as well as threatening to destabilise the region as a whole.[57] Above all, the oil companies had long accepted that the days of gun-boat diplomacy had come to an end. By the 1970s, the demise of the Western empires, combined with the rising value of oil exports, had shifted power to the independent states of the Gulf.[58] The oil companies came to terms with this development by reaching an accommodation with the various authoritarian regimes in the region. There is no indication in 2003 that they wished to abandon the relationships they had carefully built up since the formation of OPEC in 1960 and, more particularly, the oil crisis of 1973.

On the contrary, it is now known that the oil industry opposed the administration's plan, devised shortly before the invasion in March 2003, to privatise the oil fields and to destroy the OPEC cartel by selling Iraq's oil above the quota allocated.[59] The oil companies defeated the scheme and devised an alternative in 2004 calling for the formation of a state-owned oil company that would support OPEC. Philip Carroll, the former CEO of Shell Oil USA who took control of Iraq's oil production for the American government after the invasion, made a revealing (and rare) public comment on the episode: 'Many neoconservatives are people who have certain ideological beliefs about markets, about democracy, about this, that and the other. International oil companies, without exception, are very pragmatic commercial organizations. They don't have a theology.'[60] Shortly after the invasion, the Chairman of PFC Energy, one of the leading advisory companies to the industry, offered the following judgement: 'I don't think we went there for the oil and I don't think we went there for the things the White House said we went there for either. The main reason was to consolidate our position as a superpower.'[61] The interest of the oil companies lay in upholding the political *status quo* while negotiating contracts for new investments once the sanctions imposed by the United Nations Security Council were removed.[62] They were well aware that the stability of the Middle East was precarious, that their own presence as foreign firms was a sensitive matter and that, accordingly, discretion—not valour—was called for.[63]

IV

The lions in this affair were not the pride of the military–industrial complex but an alliance of assorted political idealists, commonly known as neoconservatives, and assertive nationalists, whose influence has now been subjected to detailed scrutiny.[64] The word 'nationalist' is appropriate here, even though discussion of America's role in the world since 9/11 has referred almost exclusively to 'patriotism', presumably because this term is thought to be untainted and free from dangers of excess. In the present context, however, it is useful to draw a distinction between the two while also recognising the link between them. Patriots have an affiliation to what is and what has been; nationalists have an additional sense of destiny that is shaped to a greater extent by relations with the outside world.[65] The neoconservatives were nationalists who wished to realise a messianic mission abroad. They traced their intellectual lineage to Wilsonian idealism and they endorsed in particular Wilson's vision of spreading democracy throughout the world. But they disowned important elements of his programme, such as multilateralism and disarmament, and advocated instead unilateral action and the expansion of the military. Their allies were nationalist realists who agreed on the need for an assertive foreign policy but took a more pragmatic view of how to advance America's interests abroad.

The resurgence of the militant right has now been traced from its beginnings in the 1960s, through its defeat of the isolationist wing of the nationalist movement in the 1990s,[66] and on to its triumph following the election of President Bush in 2000, when its representatives were elevated to powerful positions in the administration.[67] The conventional wisdom of the 1960s, which held that the right was a marginal deviation from a liberal, progressive norm, has been replaced by a much improved understanding of the centrality of conservative values to American life, a corresponding appreciation of the breadth of their appeal to differing socioeconomic groups and regions, and a greater awareness of the continuing significance of patriotic sentiment and display in sustaining the unity of the nation.[68] However, there instill a missing link in the story. While some of the most valuable studies place the neoconservatives and their nationalist allies in a wider political and intellectual setting, their rise has yet to be joined to the transformation of the American economy during the past 25 years. By taking this step, we can also make a final connection, via Pareto, to the classic theories of imperialism.

Neoconservatives and nationalists have contributed little to the discussion of economic policy apart from general endorsements of free markets, low taxes and minimal government.[69] They are strong supporters of capitalism but they also have reservations about a consumer society that elevates the power of the market and individual gratification above the national interest and threatens the moral order that underpins it. They agree, too, that liberty turned to license in the 1960s and 1970s, leading to the decay of traditional values and a drift towards a godless society. In these circumstances they looked to a refurbished Republican Party to uphold true American values, and founded a new set of think tanks to produce the requisite policies.[70] The disaffection of the neoconservatives in particular was enhanced during the Clinton years by the growing conviction that prosperity had distracted the United States from its historic mission of spreading freedom and democracy, and that by promoting globalisation the administration had embraced a weak foreign policy that was a further symptom of moral decline.[71] The nationalists who did not regard themselves as being neoconservatives had a less messianic outlook and were ambivalent about the free trading implications of globalisation, but concurred that American interests abroad needed to be represented more assertively.[72] Following the collapse of the Soviet Union, the United States had become the undisputed supreme power. It had the means to impress itself on the world, but not, so it seemed, the will. Caged lions could only watch as foxes gambled with America's future.

Nevertheless, the neoconservative and nationalist alliance was determined not to allow a unique opportunity to pass. As is now well-known, its leading figures devised a plan for a decisive and awe-inspiring demonstration of American power, and they also selected a recipient: Saddam Hussein.[73] The aim was to remake the Middle East, beginning with Iraq, on the heroic assumption that installing democratic forms of government would produce states that were both pacific and friendly to the United States.[74] A new Iraq also held out the prospect of repositioning the United States in the Middle East by extracting it from the now tainted authoritarian regime of Saudi Arabia.[75] The election of George W. Bush in 2000 was a move in the right direction because it delivered a president who had no expertise in foreign affairs and who was open to the influence of those who claimed that they did, especially if the argument was capable of being expressed in clear-cut moral terms, which it was. 9/11 presented the opportunity that the neoconservatives had long waited for. It was the mother of all wake-up calls, rallying the nation to its duty and setting the stage for a display of martial virtues that would redirect the country and reshape the world. A huge professional army stood ready. Success in the first Gulf War had boosted its reputation; its ethos, which emphasised discipline and order and a commitment to defend American values, if need be, to the death, embodied all the qualities that civil society seemed to have abandoned.[76] Spreading democracy abroad was the international arm of a policy that was also designed to rehabilitate society at home. The lions had been lionised. The only problem was that they did not want to fight.

Fight they did, however, and for two main reasons. After 9/11, the relatively small group of neoconservatives and nationalist activists was able to sound an alarm that rang throughout the United States. In the first place, their call resonated with long-standing and deeply held conservative beliefs embodied in the notion of American exceptionalism, which held that the United States was the ultimate custodian of liberty and democracy and had a duty to defend them against assailants at home and abroad.[77] The events of 9/11 ensured that there would be a rapid and widespread response to an appeal to rally round the flag and to launch what was called, briefly, a 'crusade' against terrorism. Equally, it was an opportunity to undertake at home the moral rearmament that the right-wing alliance thought was so badly needed.

The second reason why 9/11 stirred up the forces of popular nationalism lies in more recent history. Globalisation, as we have seen, had caused the United States to be increasingly integrated with the rest of the world in the second half of the twentieth century, and especially from the 1980s. In doing so, it had set in train a process of uneven development that amplified socioeconomic disparities within the country. Although average incomes have grown during the last 20 years, median incomes have been flat or declining.[78] This divergence has been reflected in the rapid increase in inequality between the top 1 percent and the bottom 90 percent of income-earners and in gathering worries about the prospects for upward mobility. Those who gained, such as the new rich in California's high-tech industries, favoured globalisation and in general had little economic incentive to adopt a nationalist approach to geopolitical issues.[79] Those who suffered either lost their jobs in the older industries or faced new uncertainties, as companies moved to short-term contracts and cut benefits in an attempt to stay competitive.[80] Anxiety about employment prospects caused by outsourcing was intensified by substantial inflows of immigrants, especially from Mexico and Central America.

Economic change was accompanied by growing sociocultural anxieties. The old, Anglo-Saxon assimilationist model of society no longer held, but multiculturalism, intensified by expanding immigration, raised doubts about what it was to be American, and increased geographical and social mobility shifted established boundaries, including those governing relations between men and women.[81] These swirling uncertainties help to explain the rise and politicisation of evangelical faiths, which provided material support for those who were losing their place and spiritual guidance for those who were losing their way.[82] The evangelicals propounded an assertive form of Christianity that fitted into secular patriotism and provided validation for it.[83] This programme appealed to at least some of those who were well on their way to realising the American dream of permanent affluence, as well as to those made susceptible by failure. Success in a highly individualistic consumer society imperilled a sense of community and raised questions about the sources of moral authority. Conservative values, stiffened by evangelical teaching, provided unambiguous and reassuring answers.[84] Increasingly, too, they found expression in the Republican Party. As the Republicans improved their position in the southern states in the closing decades of the twentieth century, so the south infused the party with its own style of tradition, religion and patriotism.[85]

In other circumstances, this mix of economic discontent and social unease might have been channelled into class conflict; in the United States it was grouped in support of the traditional values represented by faith, family and flag. The trauma of 9/11 called for national solidarity, which was achieved by promoting shared values and endowing them with an appeal that took the form of a renewed commitment to freedom and democracy, and so rose above party and special interests. Republicans were more successful than Democrats in presenting themselves as guardians of the homeland and in basing their manifesto on fundamental moral values. They succeeded, too, in turning public opinion against the 'liberal elite' by characterising it as being weak on defence and strong on big government.[86] The neoconservative and nationalist alliance succeeded in implementing its assertive foreign policy not only because it was well entrenched in the corridors of power but also because, in the aftermath of 9/11, it was able to convert conservative patriotism across the United States into assertive nationalism. The warfare state was to supplant the welfare state; martial qualities would stiffen the moral fibre of the nation at home and promote a powerful yet benign *imperium* abroad.[87]

V

Machiavelli wrote his masterpiece, *The Prince*, at a time when the Italian states were torn by internal dissension and beset by external enemies.[88] In his estimation, exceptional circumstances called for an exceptional leader who, by combining the force of lions and the cunning of foxes, would restore internal order and scare off foreign predators. Pareto, writing at a time when, as he saw it, Italy was squandering the opportunities presented by unification, concluded that the state was suffering from the excesses of a plutocratic elite of foxes and needed to be rebalanced by adding lion-like discipline and the weight of traditional values. The United States is neither Renaissance Florence nor Italy after the Risorgimento, but it has been beset by external enemies, and it is also under considerable internal socioeconomic strain. Arguably, too, it is characterised by what Pareto termed a 'demagogic plutocracy', in which huge wealth is a necessary qualification for governing, and the exercise of power relies heavily on purchasing support and manipulating the core ideologies associated with American exceptionalism.[89] Here Pareto's emphasis on the power of sentiment rather than reason in influencing behaviour is highly relevant to understanding the fear generated by the threat of alien invasion and the heavy stress placed on moral values in restoring social stability—both of which featured so prominently in the presidential election of 2004.

Influential explanations of America's role as a world power have either emphasised its benign, selfless motives in spreading freedom and democracy or focused on its malign consequences as an agent of capitalism in crisis. The first view treats ideology as an unproblematic and transparent influence that is largely removed from economic considerations. The second view regards ideology as masking the fundamental economic forces of an industrial order wrestling with ever deepening contradictions. The argument put here has tried to draw these two lines of thought together by investigating the relationship between the ideology of patriotism-turned-nationalism and the transformation of the American economy in the second half of the twentieth century. The governing elite has been placed at the centre of the enquiry because it directed the traffic at the intersection of nationalism and capitalism. Giving prominence to human agency provides a means of animating otherwise impersonal forces. It also underlines the importance of relating America's presence abroad to developments at home rather than relying on the assumption that foreign policy is determined by the workings of an abstraction beyond its shores called the international regime.[90]

This line of enquiry leads to the conclusion that American imperialism, as illustrated by the invasion of Iraq, was the product of nationalism rather than of capitalism. On current evidence, neither the military–industrial complex nor Big Oil was pushing for war. Nevertheless, an understanding of the evolution of the capitalist system in the United States is still central to the analysis of the forces favouring invasion, despite the fact that specific interests connected to defence and oil were not directly implicated. In the second half of the twentieth century American capitalism experienced profound changes that led to greater integration with the outside world, The most important of these ties were with Europe, the Far East and the other members of NAFTA. None of these regions was a suitable candidate for empire-building or even for the bullying brand of diplomacy advocated by warrior–commentators. The success of the new American capitalism rested instead on promoting fox-like qualities of innovation, guile and persuasion that were needed to manage business relationships across cultures and countries. These qualities were also manifested in the attitude of the oil companies, which decided from the 1970s to work with rather than against nationalists in the Middle East.

The progressive globalisation of the economy, however, also generated economic and social dislocation. An important consequence was the creation of a sense of uncertainty about cultural identity and moral purpose that encompassed those who were gaining from economic change as well as to those who were suffering from it. The main difference was that the winners held to a patriotic conservatism that was consistent with globalisation and free trade, whereas the losers were more inclined to turn to isolationist and protectionist forms of nationalism. The sense that society was drifting from its anchorage lay behind the conservative revival that began as a reaction to what were seen to be liberal excesses in the 1960s and 1970s, and gathered strength in the 1980s from anxieties generated by the character and pace of economic development and the rapidity of social change. In Pareto's terms, the fox-like character of the dominant elite and the morality it endorsed inspired a movement to restore traditional lion-like values. But when these values were extended to the conservative foreign policies advanced in the 1990s, one isolationist and the other assertive, they departed from the developing, international interests of American capitalism; when patriotism was converted into nationalism following the shock of 9/11, the disjunction was complete.

The argument put here that the developing interests of American capitalism were at variance with the decision to go to war suggests that, in this instance at least, Marxist and radical-left interpretations of imperialism have limited explanatory power. Notwithstanding the business connections of senior members of the administration, the military–industrial complex was not agitating for war, still less for the creation of a new formal empire. Schumpeter's view that imperialism was the product of noncapitalist forces seems, on this occasion, to be closer to the mark, though the elites who directed policy in the United States cannot be regarded simply as atavistic residues because the conservative values they represented fitted the capitalist society from which they sprang.

The contest between these interpretations, however, needs to be related to time and place. Economic explanations of imperialism have greater purchasing power where there is a close fit between the development of capitalism and the direction of overseas expansion. This was the case, so it has been argued, with the growth of the British empire in the nineteenth century.[91] 'International trade was characterised by the exchange of manufactures from the metropole for raw materials from the colonies and semi-colonies; expansion was managed by an elite of lions and foxes who had enough in common to ensure both cohesion and continuity. Economic integration does not necessarily bring peace, as Cobden and many subsequent commentators assumed, and it is evident that the frontiers of finance and trade were often moved on in the nineteenth century by political and military action. If this interpretation holds, then Schumpeter's view that capitalism was invariably a pacific force also needs modification. What can be said is that the particular type of integration associated with contemporary globalisation makes open conflict among the powers concerned a highly costly and counterproductive exercise. The main lines of capitalist development today join countries in the advanced and rapidly advancing countries of the world. These relationships do not lend themselves to colonial ventures, which are either irrelevant or impossible. Elsewhere, as the United States has so painfully discovered in Iraq, foreign occupation, however benign its intent, provokes intense resentment and determined resistance that draws its inspiration, in a postcolonial era, from the right of self-determination that President Wilson himself did so much to promote. The implication of this argument is clear: empire is indeed art anachronism in the twenty-first century, despite the renewed call to arms that has been sounded in recent years.[92]

As the disjunction between nationalism and capitalism clearly shows, the United States has globalised the world but not itself. The economy is becoming international; politics remains local. The divorce was well illustrated in 2006 by the debate over the attempt by a Dubai company to buy the management business of six major ports in the United States, and by the larger controversy over immigration.[93] In both cases, the administration was caught on its own barbed wire: economic advantage pointed towards globalisation, but fear of foreign invaders, stirred up in the aftermath of 9/ 11, called for the rebuilding of fortress America.[94] These conflicting interests were replicated on a much larger scale in the invasion of Iraq, which represented the triumph of combative nationalism over economic internationalism and caused the United States to attempt to found an empire and, momentarily at least, to lose a role.

ACKNOWLEDGMENTS

Different (and preliminary) versions of this essay were delivered as the J. Jean Hecht Lecture at St. John's University, New York, the Andrew Appleby Memorial Lecture at San Diego State University, and at a seminar for the British Studies Group at the University of Chicago. I am grateful to all three institutions for opportunities to develop the ideas presented here, and to other colleagues, notably Peter Cain, George Forgie, Mark Lawrence and Mark Metzler, for their comments on earlier drafts.

NOTES

1. de Grazia, *Irresistible Empire;* Gorenberg, *The Accidental Empire;* Khalidi, *Resurrecting Empire;* Mann, *Incoherent Empire.*
2. Horsley, *Jesus and Empire.*
3. Briggs, *Reproducing Empire.*
4. Eland, *The Empire has no Clothes;* Goodkind, *Naked Empire.*
5. Bonner and Wiggin, *Empire of Debt.*
6. Johnson, *Sorrows of Empire.*
7. Nelson, *Complete Idiot's Guide.*
8. Benjamin and Simon, *The Next Attack;* Mosher, *Hegemon.*
9. The *Journal of American History* produced a special issue in 2002, 89, No.2; *Daedalus* followed suit in 2005, 134, No.2.
10. The special issue on Iraq in *Current History,* 105 (2006), provides an accessible survey.
11. The literature is now huge. Dorrien, *Imperial Designs* provides a valuable introduction and numerous further references.
12. Representative commentary can be found in the *Monthly Review, New Left Review* and the *Socialist Register,* especially, Panitch and Leys (eds), *New Imperial Challenge* and *The Empire Reloaded.*
13. For example, Foster, 'Imperial America', 11-12.
14. Lipset and Marks, *It Didn't Happen Here.*

15. The most penetrating of several introductions to Pareto's theory of elites remains Pareto, *Sociological Writings*.
16. It need hardly be said that this is a simplification of Pareto's complex typology. Pareto identified a total of six elements, which he called 'residues', each with various sub-classes. Residues represented the more or less permanent springs of human action, and were found, notably, in tendencies to conserve (lions) and innovate (foxes). Derivations, in Pareto's terminology, refer to attitudes and beliefs that people express. These may reflect or conceal underlying residues.
17. Combination is a direct translation of *combinazioni*, which means 'inventive cunning, foresight, and guile'. See Powers, *Vilfredo Pareto*, 73.
18. '[T]he lion cannot defend himself from traps, and the fox cannot defend himself from wolves. It is therefore necessary to be a fox to recognize traps and a lion to frighten the wolves.' Machiavelli, *The Prince*, 75.
19. Pareto was opposed to nearly all 'isms' (including imperialism), which he saw as devices to manipulate the mass of the people.
20. See Cain, *Hobson and Imperialism* and 'Capitalism, Internationalism'. Hobson's theory is commonly over-summarised as an example of the influence of financial interests, but he also laid great emphasis on the role of what he called 'pride and pugnacity'.
21. Schumpeter, *Imperialism*.
22. Lenin, *Imperialism*.
23. It is unnecessary for present purposes to explore here the complexities that Pareto added to his theory over the years. These have been much discussed by sociologists and political scientists and lead in many different directions.
24. 17 Jan. 1961, Public Papers of the Presidents, Dwight D. Eisenhower, 1035-40, readily available on the World Wide Web.
25. *Theory of the Leisure Class*. Mills wrote an introduction to the Mentor edition of Veblen's study (1953) that drew a connection between *The Theory of the Leisure Class* and his own work, *The Power Elite*, which was to appear three years later. Mills referred to Pareto very briefly in ch. 1, ns 3-4; Mosca is mentioned on 172, n.7 in the 2000 ed.
26. Mills, *Power Elite*, 278.
27. Ibid., 19.
28. Ibid., 380-81 for a brief guide to the literature produced since 1956.
29. See especially *The Tragedy of American Diplomacy*.
30. Representative examples include: Paul, 'Oil Companies in Iraq'; Everest, *Oil, Power and Empire*.
31. Johnson, *Sorrows of Empire*, Bacevich, *New American Militarism*, and Priest, *The Mission*, document the military side. As yet, there is no full study of the industrial component.
32. Hartung, 'Eisenhower's Warning', 1-2, In real terms the expenditure projected for 2006 is greater than in any year of the Cold War except 1952. See Benjamin, 'Pentagon Papers'.
33. Hartung, 'Eisenhower's Warning'; Flake, 'Earmarked Men'.
34. Huber, 'Military–Industrial Complex', 1.
35. Bacevich, *New American Militarism*, 26-28.
36. The most recent compilation is Kozmetsky and Yue's comprehensive study, *Economic Transformation*.
37. Peters, 'GM Loss'.
38. Kozmetsky and Yue, *Economic Tramfortnation*, 470. The figures for the goods-producing sector as a whole (manufacturing, agriculture, fishing, forestry, mining and construction) were 44 percent in 1948 and 23 percent in 2000. Ibid., 297.
39. Ibid., 297, 468, 471-75; Bosworth and Triplet!, *Productivity in the U.S. Services Sector*.
40. Kozmetsky and Yue, *Economic Transformation*, 272-85.
41. This development is not confined to the outsourcing of manufacturing jobs. Wal-Mart is expanding abroad rapidly: it has 56 stores in China and intends to hire an extra 150,000 Chinese employees during the next five years. See BBC News, 20 March 2006.

42. Cox and Skidmore-Hess, *U.S. Politics and the Global Economy.*

43. Bergstrom, 'The United States'; Smitka, 'Foreign Policy'; Goodman, Spar, and Yoffie, 'Foreign Direct Investment'.

44. Williams, *Tragedy of American Diplomacy.*

45. Bacevich, *New American Militarism*, ch. 2. General Anthony Zinni, former head of the U.S. Central command, claims that the invasion of Iraq was a war that the politicians, not the military, wanted; 'I can't speak for all generals, certainly. But I know we felt that this situation was contained. Saddam was effectively contained. The no-fly, no-drive zones. The sanctions that were imposed on him.' CBS News, '60 Minutes', 21 May 2004.

46. Secretary of State, 2001-05, and before that Chairman of the Joint Chiefs of Staff, 1989-93 and National Security Advisor, 1987-89. Powell's well-known disagreements with the hawkish Vice-President, Dick Cheney, are recorded by Woodward in *Plan of Attack.*

47. Opposition to the war in Iraq was openly expressed in 2006 by a number of newly-retired senior officers. Shane, 'Generals Break with Tradition'.

48. At the latest count, no fewer than 98 foreign-owned firms had agreements with the Pentagon to have access to classified government defence programmes. See McCarthy, 'Foreign Firms a Mainstay'. Procurement has also been globalised. The army uses Italian-made Berettas; police forces in the USA, as well as in Iraq, are armed with pistols manufactured by Glock, an Austrian company.

49. The leading associates are Halliburton, which is the largest oil-services company in the United States, and Bechtel, which holds most of the reconstruction contracts for Iraq. On the distribution of the spoils see, among many possible illustrations, Weisman and Reddy, 'Spending on Iraq'. There is no reliable information about whether these firms favoured the invasion or, if they did, what influence their representations had on the decision.

50. Two sober and well-informed assessments, written shortly before the invasion, are; Graham-Brown and Toensing, 'Why Another War?'; Cable (former Chief Economist for Shell Oil), 'Economic Fallout'.

51. President Bush and his father both owned oil companies in Texas; Vice President Dick Cheney is the former CEO of Halliburton; Secretary of State Condoleezza Rice is a former director of Chevron Texaco.

52. The literature is vast. An accessible guide is Yergin, *The Prize.*

53. For example, Heiss, *Empire and Nationhood;* Vitalis 'Black Gold'. Stoff has shown in *Oil, War, and American Security* how the administration came to rely on the oil companies to represent national interests in the Middle East in the period 1941-47.

54. Simmons, *Twilight in the Desert.* The starting point for this literature is the concept of Hubbert's Peak, on which see the concise survey by Semple, 'The End of Oil'. An extension of this argument, which cannot be discussed here, holds that the invasion was motivated by the need to ensure that Iraq continued to price its oil in dollars. The case has been put by Clark, *Petrodollar Warfare.* The issue is clearly important for the future of the dollar as the world's premier currency, but there is no evidence that it motivated the invasion of Iraq.

55. See n. 30.

56. WTRG Economics. A balanced guide is Retort, 'Blood for Oil?'

57. For the alternative, optimistic view of energy supplies, see Yergin, 'It's Not the End'.

58. Especially Vitalis, 'The Closing of the Arabian Oil Frontier'.

59. Palast, 'Secret Plans'.

60. Ibid. The full transcript is at <http://www.gregpalast.com> .

61. Vahan Zanoyan, quoted in O'Brien, 'Just What Does America Want'. It is of course possible that these claims are merely covers for the real, oil-based motive, but the case has to be demonstrated, not simply inferred. It is also worth noting that Lee Raymond, the chief executive of the Exxon Mobil, the world's largest oil company, until 2006, held consistently to a long-term political and economic strategy in the Middle East. See Bartiromo, 'Lee Raymond'.

62. Graham-Brown and Toensing, 'Why Another War?', 15. On sanctions, see Graham-Brown, *Sanctioning Saddam.*

63. This conclusion agrees with that of Yergin, 'The Fight over Iraq's Oil'. On the disastrous consequences of the invasion on oil production, see Negus, 'Oil Ministry the Key'. While high oil prices benefit the oil companies in the short term, they also increase the power of producers to adjust the gains in their favour. See Mouawad, 'As Profits Surge'.

64. In President Bush's administration, the former included Paul Wolfowitz and Richard Perle; the latter Dick Cheney and Donald Rumsfeld. The categories can only be approximate because they overlapped and the attitudes of individuals evolved. Full accounts of all the leading figures can be found in Dorrien, *Imperial Designs*, and Mann, *Rise of the Vulcans*.

65. According to Irving Kristol, one the founding figures of American neo-conservatism: 'Patriotism springs from love of the nation's past; nationalism arises out of hope for the nation's future, distinctive greatness.' Quoted in Lieven, *America Right or Wrong*, 6.

66. Buchanan, *Where the Right Went Wrong*, ch. 2.

67. Valuable recent accounts include: Micklethwaite and Wooldridge, *The Right Nation;* Halper and Clarke, *America Alone;* Lieven, *America Right or Wrong;* Mann, *Rise of the Vulcans;* Dorrien, *Imperial Designs.*

68. This point is well made by McGirr's important study, *Suburban Warriors,* especially 6-19 and ch. 4.

69. The neo-conservatives had been strong advocates of tax cuts and welfare reform in the 1980s, but their rise to prominence in the 1990s was associated almost exclusively with their developing interest in an assertive foreign policy. See Feldman, *The Neoconservative Revolution;* Boot, 'What the Heck'.

70. The most prominent think tanks are the Heritage Foundation, which was founded in 1973, principally to reduce government regulation of business, and the American Enterprise Institute, which was formed in 1943 but did not expand until the 1970s. The universities, considered to be the last bastions of liberalism, were not converted; they were simply bypassed. These developments are dealt with by Micklethwait and Wooldridge, *Right Nation,* and Halper and Clarke, *America Alone.*

71. See the perceptive essay by Robin, 'How 9/11 Unified Conservatives'.

72. The two groups came together in the Project for a New American Century, a Washington think tank founded in 1997.

73. There is now a large literature detailing the influence of the neo-conservatives and nationalists on foreign policy since 2001. See especially Halper and Clarke, *America Alone;* Mann, *Rise of the Vulcans;* Lieven, *America Right or Wrong;* Daalder and Lindsay, *America Unbound;* Woodward, *Plan of Attack;* Bamford, *Pretext for War;* Packer, *Assassins' Gate;* Gordon and Trainor, *Cobra II.* As it became clear that the invasion of Iraq was both a blunder and a quagmire, the hawks started to break ranks. By 2005 their influence was slipping, and in 2006 they began to blame President Bush for mismanaging their (still unimpeachable) plan for transforming the Middle East. The most highly publicised defection was that of Francis Fukuyama, *America at the Crossroads.*

74. The proposition (derived from Kant) that democratic societies were also pacific, or, more precisely that they did not fight one another, has generated a huge industry among political scientists during the past 20 years and provided much of the intellectual basis for promoting democracy throughout the world. The latest study, published (unfortunately) after the decision to promote democracy in Iraq by force, argues that, while mature democracies may not fight one another, new democracies can and sometimes do. See Mansfield and Snyder, *Electing to fight.*

75. Johnson, *Sorrows of Empire,* 236-43, after reviewing other explanations, including the need for bil, 227-36. This is not to deny the importance of contract-hunting after the decision to invade Iraq had been taken. See, for example, Klein, 'Baghdad Year Zero'.

76. Bacevich, *New American Militarism,* provides an extensive treatment of this theme.

77. Liberty was present 'at the creation'; democracy was added in the twentieth century. On the relation between ideology and foreign policy see Hunt, *Ideology and U.S. Foreign Policy,* and Stephanson, *Manifest Destiny.*

78. The trend dates from the 1980s. See Lee, 'Wage Inequality'. Recent data are summarised by Luce, 'Out on a Limb'.

79. In 2006 big business (including oil) and finance opposed proposals that would have checked the flow of investment into the USA. See Kirchgaessner, 'Business Lobby'.
80. Uchitelle, *Disposable American*; Levy, 'New Corporate Outsourcing'.
81. The war of 1898 (so it has been argued) also gave expression to gender politics. See Hoganson, *Fighting for American Manhood*.
82. Entry points to what is now a large literature include: Halper and Clarke, *America Alone*, Ch.6; Lieven, *America Right or Wrong*, ch. 4, Phillips, *American Theocracy*, offers an appropriately apocalyptic account of the dangers of excessive religiosity.
83. On the perfect union, see Blumenthal, 'Credo of Joel Osteen'.
84. McGirr's analysis of Orange County in *Suburban Warriors* complements Frank's widely publicised book, *What's the Matter with Kansas?* Although the communities studied had widely different economic circumstances, they shared a common socio-cultural outlook, which derived from the fact that the majority of the new conservatives in Orange County had migrated from the mid-west. See also n. 87.
85. Kevin Phillips has studied this phenomenon in a series of books, the most recent being *American Theocracy* (especially chs 5-6), See also Trubowitz, *Defining the National Interest*, ch. 4.
86. Frank's account of this process in *What's the Matter with Kansas?* shows how 'market populism' enabled business interests, which favoured the cheap labour that came with immigration, to win the support of wage-earners (and voters), even though such policies affected them adversely.
87. Widely publicised examples of muscular, military approaches to the problems of the world include: Boot, *Savage Wars of Peace*; Kagan, *Of Paradise and Power*; and Frum and Perle, *An End to Evil*.
88. Plague and the French both descended on Florence 1494.
89. We await a new C. Wright Mills to deal with these issues in the case of the United States. Mean while, valuable information has been put together by Phillips, *Wealth and Democracy* and *American Dynasty*.
90. Trubowitz, *Defining the National Interest*, provides a powerful analysis of the role of (regional) domestic forces in shaping foreign policy.
91. Cain and Hopkins, *British Imperialism*.
92. Kinzer, *Overthrow*, catalogues a series of interventions and their consequences.
93. Gross, 'Globalization Offered Two Ways'. 'Uncle Sam Says Yes', 67, notes that America's huge external deficit points to the wisdom of adopting a friendly attitude towards foreign investors, On immigration see, Pew Research Center, 'America's Immigration Quandary'; Maddox, 'U.S. Immigration'.
94. And protectionist talk was amplified. See Stelzer, 'America Puts Security before Free Trade'. Signs of a revival of isolationist sentiment were already present, as a Pew survey in the fall of 2005 showed. See Bortin, 'Survey Shows a Revival of Isolationism'.

REFERENCES

Bacevich, Andrew J. *The New American Militarism*. Oxford: Oxford University Press, 2005.

Bamford, James. *A Pretext for War: 9/11, Iraq and the Abuse of America's Intelligence Agencies*. New York: Doubleday, 2004.

Bartiromo, Maria. 'Lee Raymond: Exit Interview'. *Business Week* 20 Feb. 2006.

BBC News, 20 March 2006. Available at: <http://news.bbc.uk/go/pr/fr/-/2/hi/business/4824786.stm>.

Benjamin, Daniel. 'The Pentagon Papers'. *Washington Post* 14 May 2006. Benjamin, Daniel, and Steven Simon. *The Next Attack: The Failure of the War on Terror and a Strategy for Getting it Right*. New York: Times Books, 2005.

Bergstrom, Fred C. 'The United States and the World Economy'. *Annals of the American Academy of Political and Social Science* 460 (1982): 11–20.

Blumenthal, Ralph. 'Credo of Joel Osteen, Pastor of Lakewood Church: Eliminate the Negative, Accentuate Prosperity'. *New York Times* 30 March 2006.

Bonner, William, and Addison Wiggin. *Empire of Debt: The Rise and Fall of an Epic Financial Crisis.* Hoboken, NJ: Wiley, 2005.

Boot, Max. *The Savage Wars of Peace: Small Wars and the Rise of American Power.* New York: Basic Books, 2002.

———. 'What the Heck is a Neocon?' *Wall Street Journal* 30 Dec. 2002.

Bortin, Meg. 'Survey Shows a Revival of Isolationism among Americans'. *New York Times* 17 Nov. 2005.

Bosworth, Barry P., and Jack E Triplett. *Productivity in the U.S. Services Sector: New Sources of Economic Growth.* Washington, DC: Brookings Institute, 2004.

Briggs, Laura. *Reproducing Empire: Race, Sex, Science and U.S. Imperialism in Puerto Rico.* Berkeley, CA: University of California Press, 2002.

Buchanan, Patrick J, *Where the Right Went Wrong: How Neoconservatives Subverted the Reagan Revolution and Hijacked the Bush Presidency.* New York: Thomas Dunne, 2004.

Cable, Vincent. 'Economic Fallout from a War in Iraq'. *The World Today* Feb. 2003.

Cain, Peter. 'Capitalism, Internationalism, and Imperialism in the Thought of Richard Cobden'. *British Journal of International Studies* 3 (1979): 229-47.

———. Hobson *and Imperialism: Radicalism, New Liberalism and Finance, 1887-1938.* Oxford: Oxford University Press, 2002.

Cain, P. J. and Hopkins, A. G. *British Imperialism, 1688-2000.* London: Longman, 2002.

CBS News, '60 Minutes'. 21 May 2004. Available at: <http://www.cbsnews.com/stories/2004/05/21/60minutes/printable618896.shtml>.

Clark, William R. *Petrodollar Warfare: Oil, Iraq and the Future of the Dollar.* Gabriola Island, BC: New Society Publishers, 2005.

Cox, Ronald W., and Daniel Skidmore-Hess. *U.S. Politics and the Global Economy: Corporate Power, Conservative Shift.* Boulder, CO: Lynne Rienner, 1999.

Daalder, Ivo H., and James M. Lindsay. *America Unbound: The Bush Revolution in Foreign Policy.* Washington, DC: Brookings Institute, 2004.

Dorrien, Gary. *Imperial Designs: Neoconservatism and the New Pax Americana.* New York: Routledge, 2004.

Eland, Ivan. *The Empire Has No Clothes: U.S. Foreign Policy Exposed.* Oakland, CA: Independent Institute, 2004.

Everest, Larry. *Oil, Power and Empire: Iraq and the U.S. Global Agenda.* Monroe, ME: Common Courage Press, 2004.

Feldman, Murray. *The Neoconservative Revolution: Jewish Intellectuals and the Shaping of Public Policy.* Cambridge; Cambridge University Press, 2005.

Flake, Jeff. 'Earmarked Men'. *New York Times* 9 Feb. 2006.

Foster, John Bellamy. 'Imperial America and War'. *Monthly Review* 55 (2003); 11-12.

Frank, Thomas. *What's the Matter with Kansas? How Conservatives Won the Heart of America.* New York: Metropolitan Press, 2004.

Frum, David, and Richard Perle. *An End to Evil: How to Win the War on Terror.* New York: Random House, 2004.

Fukuyama, Francis. *America at the Crossroads: Democracy, Power, and the Neocomervative Legacy.* New Haven, CT: Yale University Press, 2006.

Goodkind, Terry. *Naked Empire.* New York: Tor, 2003.

Goodman, John B., Debora Spar and David Yofiie. 'Foreign Direct Investment and the Demand for Protection in the United States'. *International Organization* 50 (1996): 565-91.

Gordon, Michael R., and Bernard E. Trainor. *Cobra II: The Inside Story of the Invasion and Occupation of Iraq.* New York: Pantheon, 2006.

Gorenberg, Gershom. *The Accidental Empire: Israel and the Birth of the Settlements, 1967-1977.* New York: Times Books, 2006.

Graham-Brown, Sarah. *Sanctioning Saddam: The Politics of Intervention in Iraq.* London: I, B. Tauris, 1999.

Graham-Brown, Sarah, and Chris Toensing. 'Why Another War? A Background on the Iraq Crisis'. *Middle East Research & Information Project* Dec. 2002.

Grazia, Victoria de. *Irresistible Empire: America's Advance through Twentieth-Century Europe.* Cambridge, MA: Belknap Press, 2005.

Gross, Daniel. 'Globalization Offered Two Ways: A la Carte and Prix Fixe'. *New York Times* 12 March 2006.

Halper, Stefan, and Jonathan Clarke. *America Alone: The Neo-Conservalives and the Global Order.* Cambridge: Cambridge University Press, 2004.

Hartung, William D. 'Eisenhower's Warning: The Military–Industrial Complex Forty Years Later'. *World Policy Journal* 18 (2001): 1-2.

Heiss, Mary Ann. *Empire and Nationhood: The United States, Great Britain, and Iranian Oil, 1950–1954.* New York: Columbia University Press, 1997.

Hoganson, Kristin L. *Fighting for American Manhood: How Gender Politics Provoked the Spanish American and Philippine-American Wars.* New Haven, CT: Yale University Press, 1998.

Horsley, Richard A. *Jesus and Empire: The Kingdom of God and the New World Disorder.* Augsburg, Minneapolis. MN: Fortress Press, 2003.

Huber, Peter. 'Military–Industrial Complex, 2003'. *Forbes Global* 5 Dec. 2003: 1.

Hunt, Michael H, *Ideology and U.S. Foreign Policy.* New Haven, CT: Yale University Press, 1987.

Johnson, Chalmers A. *The Sorrows of Empire: Militarism, Secrecy and the End of the Republic.* New York: Metropolitan Books, 2004.

Kagan, Robert. *Of Paradise and Power: America and Europe in the New World Order.* New York: Knopf, 2003.

Kennedy, Paul M. *The Rise and Fall of the Great Powers: Economic Change and Military Conflict from 1500 to 2000.* New York: Random House, 1989.

Khalidi, Rashid. *Resurrecting Empire: Western Footprints and America's Perilous Path in the Middle East.* Boston, MA: Beacon Press, 2004.

Kinzer, Stephen. *Overthrow: America's Century of Regime Change from Hawaii to Iraq.* New York: Times Books, 2006.

Kirchgaessner, Stephanie. 'Business Lobby Targets Senate on Review of Foreign Deals'. *Financial Times* 24 March 2006.

Klein, Naomi, 'Baghdad Year Zero: Pillaging Iraq in Pursuit of a Neo-Con Utopia'. *Harper's* Sept. 2004: 1-22.

Kozmetsky, George, and Piyu Yue. *The Economic Transformation of the United States, 1950-2000.* West Lafayette, IN: Purdue University Press, 2005.

Lee, David S. 'Wage Inequality in the United States during the 1980s: Rising Dispersion or Falling Minimum Wages?' *Quarterly Journal of Economics* 114 (1999): 977-1023.

Lenin, V. I. *Imperialism, the Highest Stage of Capitalism: A Popular Outline.* New York: International Publishers, 1969, 1939.

Levy, Clifford J. 'The New Corporate Outsourcing'. *New York Times* 29 Jan. 2006.

Lieven, Anatol. *America Right or Wrong: An Anatomy of American Nationalism.* New York: Oxford University Press, 2004.

Lipset, Seymour Martin, and Gary Marks, *It Didn't Happen Here: Why Socialism Failed in the United States.* New York: Norton, 2005.

Luce, Edward. 'Out on a Limb: Why Blue-Collar Americans see their Future as Precarious'. *Financial Times* 3 May 2006.

Machiavelli, Niccolo. *The Prince,* in *The Prince and Other Writings,* edited by Wayne A. Rebhorn. New York: Barnes & Noble, 2003.

Maddox, Bronwen. 'U.S. Immigration is a New Mass Movement'. *The Times* 28 March 2006.

Mann, Jim. *Rise of the Vulcans: The History of Bush's War Cabinet.* New York: Viking, 2004.

Mann, Michael. *Incoherent Empire.* London: Verso, 2003.

Mansfield, Edward D., and Jack Snyder. *Electing to Fight: Why Emerging Democracies Go to War.* Cambridge, MA: MIT Press, 2005.

McCarthy, Ellen. 'Foreign Firms a Mainstay of Pentagon Contracting'. *Washington Post* 18 March 2006.

McGirr, Lisa. *Suburban Warriors: The Origins of the New American Right.* Princeton, NJ: Princeton University Press, 2001.

Micklethwaite, John, and Adrian Wooldridge. *The Right Nation: Conservative Power in America.* New York: Penguin, 2004.

Mills, C. Wright. *The Power Elite.* New York: Oxford University Press, 1956.

Mosher, Steven W *Hegemon: China's Plan to Dominate Asia and the World.* San Francisco, CA: Encounter Books, 2000.

Mouawad, Jad. 'As Profits Surge, Oil Giants Find Hurdles Abroad'. *New York Times* 6 May 2006.

Negus, Steve. 'Oil Ministry the Key to Unlocking Paralysis in Iraq'. *Financial Times* 6 May 2006.

Nelson, Eric D, *The Complete Idiot's Guide to the Roman Empire.* Indianapolis, IN: Alpha, 2001.

O'Brien, Timothy L. 'Just What does America Want to do with Iraq's Oil?' *New York Times* 8 June 2003.

Packer, George. *The Assassins' Gate: America in Iraq.* New York: Farrar, Straus & Giroux, 2005.

Palast, Greg. 'Secret Plans for Iraq's Oil'. BBC News, 17 March 2003. Available at: <http://news.bbc.co.uk/2/hi/programmes/newsnight/4354269.s>.

Panitch, Leo, and Colin Leys (eds). *The New Imperial Challenge.* London: Merlin Press, 2003.

———. (eds). *The Empire Reloaded.* London: Merlin Press, 2004.

Pareto, Vilfredo. *Sociological Writings,* edited by S. E. Finer. New York: Praeger, 1966.

Paul, James A. 'Oil Companies in Iraq: A Century of Rivalry and War'. *Global Policy Forum* Nov. 2003.

Peters, Jeremy W. 'GM Loss for 2005 is Steeper'. *New York Times* 17 March 2006.

Pew Research Center. 'America's Immigration Quandary'. 30 March 2006.

Phillips, Kevin. *Wealth and Democracy: A Political History of the American Rich.* New York: Broadway Books, 2002.

———. *American Dynasty: Aristocracy, Fortune and the Politics of Deceit in the House of Bush.* New York; Viking, 2004.

———. *American Theocracy: The Peril and Politics of Radical Religion, Oil and Borrowed Money in the Twenty-First Century.* New York: Viking, 2006.

Powers, Charles II. *Vilfredo Pareto.* Newbury Park, CA: Sage, 1987.

Priest, Dana. *The Mission: Waging War and Keeping Peace with America's Military.* New York: Norton, 2003.

Retort. 'Blood for Oil?' *London Review of Books* 21 April 2005.

Robin, Corey. 'How 9/11 Unified Conservatives in Pursuit of Empire'. *Washington Post* 2 May 2004.

Schumpeter, Joseph A. *Imperialism and Social Classes: Two Essays.* New York: Meridian Books, 1955.

Semple, Robert. 'The End of Oil'. *New fork Times* 1 March 2006.

Shane, Scott. 'Generals Break with Tradition over Rumsfeld'. *New York Times* 15 April 2006.

Simmons, Matthew R. *Twilight in the Desert: The Coming Oil Shock and the World Economy.* Hoboken, NJ: Wiles, 2005.

Smitka, Michael. 'Foreign Policy and the U.S. Automotive Industry'. *Business and Economic History* 28 (1999): 277-85.

Stelzer, Irwin. 'America Puts Security before Free Trade'. *The Times* 19 March 2006.

Stephanson, Anders. *Manifest Destiny: American Expansionism and the Empire of Right.* New York: Hill & Wang, 1995.

Stoff, Michael B. *Oil, War, and American Security: The Search for National Policy on Foreign Oil, 1941-1947.* New Haven, CT: Yale University Press, 1980.

Trubowitz, Peter. *Defining the National Interest: Conflict and Change in U.S. Foreign Policy.* Chicago, IL: University of Chicago Press, 1998.

Uchitelle, Louis. *The Disposable American: Layoffs and their Consequences.* New York: Knopf, 2006.

'Uncle Sam Says Yes'. *The Economist* 6-12 May 2006.

Veblen, Thorstein. *Tlie Theory of the Leisure Class.* New York: Mentor Edition, New American Library, 1953.

Vitalis, Robert. 'The Closing of the Arabian Oil Frontier and the Future of the Saudi-American Relations'. *Middle East Report* 204 (1997): 15-21.

———. 'Black Gold, White Crude: An Essay on American Exceptionalism, Hierarchy, and Hegemony in the Gulf. *Diplomatic History* 26 (2002): 185-213.

Weisman, Jonathan, and Anitha Reddy. 'Spending on Iraq Sets off Gold Rush'. *Washington Post* 9 Oct. 2003.

Williams, William Appleman. *The Tragedy of American Diplomacy.* 2nd ed. New York: Dell, 1972.

Woodward, Bob. *Plan of Attack.* New York: Simon & Schuster, 2004.

WTRG Economics. Available at: <http://www.wtrg.com/prices.htm>.

Yergin, Daniel, *The Prize: The Epic Quest for Oil, Money, and Power.* New York: Simon & Schuster, 1991.

———. 'The 'Fight over Iraq's Oil'. BBC News, 14 March 2003. Available at: <http://news.bbc.co.uk/1 /hi/business/2847905.s>.

———. 'It's Not the End of the Oil Age'. *Washington Post* 31 July 2005.

❧ PART FOUR ❧

National Values, Democratic Institutions, and Foreign Policy

A distinctive set of values imbues American political culture and gives shape to its political institutions. These values and institutions in turn leave their mark on American foreign policy. In different ways the essays in this section attempt to give meaning to this set of relationships. Samuel Huntington provides the most encompassing examination. Arguing that there is an uneasy relationship between American values and American political institutions, Huntington contends that this gap in normative orientation and practice presents a dynamic of change that can be felt in foreign policy. The pull of American values is manifest in two ways: in attitudes about the institutions that make American foreign policy and in attitudes about changing the institutions and policies of other societies to conform with American values. Huntington argues that in both these areas American history is marked by efforts to close the gap between values of institutions, but that these efforts always embody tensions. The promotion of American liberty abroad often carries with it the need to expand the powers of American government, which in turn conflicts with domestic values of liberty. These tensions present an inevitable "promise of disharmony."

Michael Mastanduno examines the old orthodoxy that democracies—such as America's—are "decidedly inferior" in the conduct of foreign policy. Do democratic institutions inhibit coherent and effective foreign policy by being more responsive to interest groups than to the imperatives of international politics? Mastanduno finds the American experience to be decidedly mixed and concludes that there are as many advantages and virtues to decentralized and pluralistic institutions in the conduct of foreign policy as there are dangers and liabilities. The old conventional wisdom needs to be rethought.

Jonathan Monten offers a portrait of American efforts at democracy promotion; during the George W. Bush administration these efforts became a central component of national security policy and its "war on terrorism." Monten argues that the United States has pursued two contending approaches to the long-term promotion of democracy: "exemplarism," or leadership by example, and "vindicationism," or the direct application of American power, including the use of coercive force. Looking back at the 20th century, Monten suggests that exemplarism has been the dominant American approach to democracy promotion, while the Bush administration has pursued a strategy of vindicationism. In explaining the activist Bush approach, Monten points to America's preeminent power position and the presence of a nationalist domestic ideology.

✣

American Ideals Versus American Institutions

Samuel P. Huntington

Throughout the history of the United States a broad consensus has existed among the American people in support of liberal, democratic, individualistic, and egalitarian values. These political values and ideals constitute what Gunnar Myrdal termed "the American Creed," and they have provided the core of American national identity since the eighteenth century. Also throughout American history, political institutions have reflected these values but have always fallen short of realizing them in a satisfactory manner. A gap has always existed between the ideals in which Americans believed and the institutions that embodied their practice. This gap between ideals and institutional practice has generated continuing disharmony between the normative and existential dimensions of American politics. Being human, Americans have never been able to live up to their ideals; being Americans, they have also been unable to abandon them. They have instead existed in a state of national cognitive dissonance, which they have attempted to relieve through various combinations of moralism, cynicism, complacency, and hypocrisy. The "burr under the saddle," as Robert Penn Warren called it, and the efforts to remove that burr have been central features of American politics, defining its dynamics and shape, since at least the eighteenth century and perhaps before. The question now is: Will the gap between ideals and institutional practices and the responses to it continue to play the same role in American politics in the future that they have in the past? Or are there changes taking place or likely to take place in American political ideals, political institutions, and the relation between them that will make their future significantly different from their past?

Three possibilities exist. The relation between ideals and institutions, first, could continue essentially unchanged; second, it could be altered by developments within American society; or third, it could be altered by developments outside American society and by American involvements abroad. Developments within American society or changes in the international environment could alter the relation between American political ideals and institutions in four ways: the content of the ideals could change; the scope of agreement on the ideals could change; the nature of American political institutions could more closely approximate American ideals, thereby reducing the gap between them; or American political institutions could be significantly altered in an illiberal, undemocratic, anti-individualistic direction; or some combination of these developments could take place.

Samuel P. Huntington, "American Ideals Versus American Institutions," *Political Science Quarterly*, Vol. 97, No. 1 (Spring 1982). Reprinted with permission.

HISTORY VERSUS PROGRESS?

At various periods in their history Americans have attempted to eliminate or reduce the gap between ideals and institutions by moralistic efforts to reform their institutions and practices so as to make them conform to the ideals of the American Creed. These periods include the Revolutionary years of the 1760s and 1770s, the Jacksonian surge of reforms in the 1820s and 1830s, the Progressive era from the 1890s to 1914, and the latest resurgence of moralistic reform in the 1960s and early 1970s. These four periods have much in common, and almost always the proponents of reform have failed to realize their goals completely. The relative success of reform, however, has varied significantly: in particular the goals of reform have tended to be more widely achieved in the early periods than in the later ones. In the earlier periods the affirmation of the goals of liberty, equality, democracy, and popular sovereignty was directed at the destruction or modification of traditional political and economic institutions; in the later periods, it was directed at the elimination or modification of modern political and economic institutions that had emerged in the course of historical development. In the earlier periods, in short, history and progress (in the sense of realizing American ideals) went hand in hand; in the later periods the achievement of American ideals involved more the restoration of the past than the realization of the future, and progress and history worked increasingly at cross purposes.

The revolutionaries of the 1770s were the first to articulate the American Creed on a national basis and were generally successful in effecting major changes in American institutions: the overthrow of British imperial power, the end of monarchy, the widespread acceptance of government based on popular consent, the extension of the suffrage, an end to what remained of feudal practices and privileges, and the substitution of a politics of opinion for a politics of status. In part the articulation of their goals was conservative; the rights asserted were justified by reference to common law and the rights of Englishmen. But the formulation and public proclamation of those rights was also a revolutionary event in terms of political theory and political debate.

In the Jacksonian years the American ideology was still new, fresh, and directed toward the elimination of the political restrictions on democracy, the broadening of popular participation in government, the abolition of status and the weakening of specialization—that is, of both ascriptive and achievement norms—in the public service, and the destruction of the Bank of the United States and other manifestations of the "money power," so as to open wide the doors of economic opportunity. "Originally a fight against political privilege, the Jacksonian movement . . . broadened into a fight against economic privilege, rallying to its support a host of 'rural capitalists and village entrepreneurs.'"[1] Except for the role of blacks and women in American society, the Jacksonian reforms did complete the virtual elimination of traditional institutions and practices, either inherited from a colonial past or concocted by the Federalist commercial oligarchy, which deviated from liberal–democratic values. All this was progressive in the broad sense, but it too carried with it elements of conservatism. The paradox of the Jacksonians was that even as they cleared away obstacles to the development of laissez-faire capitalism, they also looked back politically to ideals of rural republican simplicity.[2] Restoration, not revolution, was their message.

The institutional changes of the Jacksonian years did not, of course, bring political reality fully into accord with Jacksonian principle. Neither property nor power was equally distributed. In the major cities a small number of very wealthy people, most of whom had inherited their position, controlled large amounts of property.[3] As is generally the case, however, income was much more equally distributed than wealth, and both wealth and income were far more evenly distributed in the rural areas, where 90 percent of the population lived, than in the urban areas. In addition there were high levels of social and political equality, which never failed to impress European visitors, whether critical or sympathetic. All in all, money, status, and power were probably more equally distributed among white males in Jacksonian America than at any other time before or since. The other central values of the American Creed—liberty, individualism, democracy—were in many respects even more markedly embodied in American institutions at that time.

For these reasons, Gordon Wood argued, the Jacksonian generation "has often seemed to be the most 'American' of all generations." This "Middle Period" in American history has been appropriately labeled because

> many of the developments of the first two centuries of our history seem to be anticipations of this period, while many of the subsequent developments taking us to the present seem to be recessions from it. In the traditional sense of what it has meant to be distinctly American, this Middle Period of 1820–1860 marks the apogee in the overall trajectory of American history. Americans in that era of individualism, institutional weakness, and boundlessness experienced "freedom" as they rarely have since; power, whether expressed economically, socially, or politically, was as fragmented and diffused as at any time in our history.[4]

After the democratization of government and before the development of industry, the Middle Period is the time when the United States could least well be characterized as a disharmonic society. It was a period when Americans themselves believed that they had "fulfilled the main principles of liberty" and hence were exempt from "further epochal change."[5] All that was needed was to remain true to the achievements of the past.

In the Middle Period, in short, American dream and American reality came close to joining hands even though they were shortly to be parted. The gap between American ideals and institutions was clearly present in Jacksonian America but outside the South probably less so than at any other time in American history. The inequality of social hierarchy and political aristocracy had faded; the inequality of industrial wealth and organizational hierarchy had yet to emerge. Primogeniture was gone; universal (white male) suffrage had arrived; the Standard Oil trust was still in the future.

In the Middle Period and the years following, the only major institutional legacy that was grossly contradictory to the American Creed was slavery and the heritage of slavery, the remnants of which were still being removed a hundred years after the Civil War. With respect to the role of blacks, the creed played a continuingly progressive role, furnishing the basis for challenging the patterns of racial discrimination and segregation that ran so blatantly against the proposition that all men are created equal. Hence, in analyzing the American dilemma in the 1930s, Gunnar Myrdal could take an essentially optimistic attitude toward its eventual resolution. He could see hope in America because his attention was focused on the one area of inequality in American life that was clearly an anachronistic holdover from the past.

More generally, the Middle Period marked a turning point in the nature of progress in America. Prior to that time "progress" in terms of the realization of American ideals of liberty and equality did not conflict with "historical development" in terms of the improvement of economic well-being and security. After the Middle Period, however, progress and history began to diverge. Progress in terms of the "realization of the democratic ideal," in Herbert Croly's phrase, often ran counter to historical trends toward large-scale organization, hierarchy, specialization, and inequality in power and wealth that seemed essential to material improvement. Political progress involves a return to first principles; politically Americans move forward by looking backward, reconsecrating themselves to the ideals of the past as guidelines for the future. Historical development involves pragmatic responses to the increasing scale and complexity of society and economy and demands increasing interaction, both cooperative and competitive, with other societies.

This distinctive character of the Middle Period and its inappropriateness as a foretaste of things to come are well reflected in the observations of the most celebrated foreign observer of the Jacksonian scene. Tocqueville was in a sense half right and half wrong in the two over-arching empirical propositions (one static, one dynamic) that he advanced about equality in America. The most distinctive aspect of American society, he argued, is "the general equality of condition among the people." This "is the fundamental fact from which all others seem to be derived and the central point at which all my observations constantly terminated." Second, the tendency toward equality in American and European society constitutes an "irresistible revolution"; the "gradual development of the principle of equality" is a "providential fact"; it is "lasting, it constantly eludes all human interference, and all events as well as all men contribute to its progress."[6] Like other European observers before and since, Tocqueville tended to confuse the values and ideals of Americans with social and political reality. His descriptive hypothesis, nonetheless, still rings true. By and large American society of the Middle Period was characterized by a widespread equality of condition, particularly in comparison to conditions in Europe. Tocqueville's historical projection, in contrast, clearly does not hold up in terms of the distribution of wealth and only in limited respects in terms of the distribution of political power.

In attempting to sum up the diversity and yet common purpose of the Jacksonian age, Joseph L. Blau employs a striking metaphor: "As one drives out of any large city on a major highway, he is bound to see a large signpost, with arrows pointing him to many possible destinations. These arrows have but one thing in common; all alike point away from the city he has just left. Let this stand as a symbol of Jacksonians. Though they pointed to many different possible American futures, all alike pointed away from an America of privilege and monopoly."[7] The Jacksonians were, however, more accurate in pointing to where America should go in terms of its democratic values and ideals than they were in pointing to the actual direction of economic and political development. Industrialization following the Civil War brought into existence new inequalities in wealth, more blatant corruptions of the political process, and new forms of "privilege and monopoly" undreamed of in the Jacksonian years. This divorce of history from progress had two consequences for the reaffirmation of American political values in the Progressive period.

First, during both the revolutionary and Jacksonian years, the articulation of American political ideals was couched to some degree in conservative and backward-looking terms, as a reaffirmation of rights that had previously existed and as an effort to reorder political life in terms of principles whose legitimacy had been previously established. During the Progressive era the backward-looking characteristics of the ideals and vision that were invoked stood out much more sharply. As Richard Hofstadter suggested, the Founding Fathers "dreamed of and planned for a long-term future," the Middle Period generations were absorbed with the present, and the Progressives consciously and explicitly looked to the past: "Beginning with the time of [William Jennings] Bryan, the dominant American ideal has been steadily fixed on bygone institutions and conditions. In early twentieth-century progressivism this backward-looking vision reached the dimension of a major paradox. Such heroes of the progressive revival as Bryan, [Robert M.] La Follette, and [Woodrow] Wilson proclaimed that they were trying to undo the mischief of the past forty years and re-create the old nation of limited and decentralized power, genuine competition, democratic opportunity, and enterprise."[8] The Progressives were reaffirming the old ideals in opposition to large-scale new organizations—economic and political—which were organizing and giving shape to the twentieth century. This was most manifest in William Jennings Bryan, who was, as Croly said, basically "a Democrat of the Middle Period." Bryan, according to Walter Lippmann, "thought he was fighting the plutocracy" but in actuality "was fighting something much deeper than that; he was fighting the larger scale of human life." Bryan was thus a "genuine conservative" who stood for "the popular tradition of America," whereas his enemies were trying to destroy that tradition.[9] But he was also a radical attempting to apply and to realize the ideals of the American Revolution. Bryan was, in fact, just as radical as William Lloyd Garrison, but Garrison was moving with history and Bryan against it. In a similar vein Woodrow Wilson also reacted to the growth of large-scale economic organization with the call to "restore" American politics to their former pristine, individualistic strength and vigor. To achieve this goal Wilson was willing to employ governmental power, thereby, as Lippmann pointed out, creating the inner contradiction that was at the heart of the Progressive outlook. Among the Progressives Theodore Roosevelt was most explicit in arguing that large-scale economic organizations had to be accepted; nonetheless he too held to much of the older ideal; his argument was couched in pragmatic rather than ideological terms: "This is the age of combination, and any effort to prevent all combination will be not only useless, but in the end vicious, because of the contempt for the law which the failure to enforce law inevitably produces."[10]

Second, the reaffirmation of American ideals at the turn of the century could not be as effective as the Revolutionary and Jacksonian affirmations in realizing those ideals in practice. At the extreme Bryan became the Don Quixote of American politics, battling for a vision of American society that could never be realized again. In the Revolutionary and Jacksonian periods the institutional reforms had been substantial and effective. In the Progressive period both economic and political reforms could at best be described as only partly successful. The antitrust laws and other efforts to curb the power of big business made a difference in the development of American business—as any comparison with Europe will demonstrate—but they clearly did not stop or reverse the tendencies toward combination and oligopoly. In the political sphere the introduction of primaries did not bring an end to political machines and bossism, and according to some may even have strengthened them. In Congress the attack on "Czar" Joseph Cannon established the dominance of the seniority system; paternalistic autocracy in effect gave way to gerontocratic oligarchy. The efforts to make government more responsible encouraged the growth of presidential power. That institutional changes were made is indisputable, but so is the fact that by and large they were substantially less successful than the changes of the Revolutionary and Jacksonian years in realizing the hopes and goals of their proponents.

The passion of the 1960s and 1970s was in some respects ideologically purer than the theories of the Progressives. Perhaps for this reason it was also somewhat more effective in eroding political authority. Yet outside of race relations its more specific reforms were little more successful than those of the Progressives. Economic power was assaulted but remained concentrated. Presidential authority was weakened but rebounded. The military and intelligence agencies declined in money, matériel, and morale in the 1970s but were reestablishing themselves on all three fronts by the early 1980s. It seemed likely that the institutional structure and the distribution of power in American society and politics in 1985 would not differ greatly from what they had been in 1960. With the important exception of race relations the gap between ideals and institutions of the early 1980s duplicated that of the early 1960s.

This changing record of success from one creedal passion period to the next reflected the changing nature of reform. In the earlier periods reform generally involved the dismantling of social, political, and economic institutions responsible for the ideals-versus-institutions gap. The disharmony of American politics was thought to be—and in considerable measure was—man-made. Remove the artificial restraints, and society and politics would naturally move in the direction in which they morally should move. In later creedal passion periods, beginning with the Progressive era, this assumption of *natural* congruence of ideal and reality was displaced by the idea of *contrived* congruence. Consciously designed governmental policy and action was necessary to reduce the gap. In the post-World War II period, for instance, "for the first time in American history, equality became a major object of governmental policy."[11] The Progressives created antitrust offices and regulatory commissions to combat monopoly power and promote competition. The reformers of the 1960s brought into existence an "imperial judiciary" in order to eliminate racial segregation and inequalities. To a much greater degree than in the earlier periods, in order to realize American values the reformers of the later periods had to create institutional mechanisms that threatened those values.

In a broader context the actual course of institutional development is the product of the complex interaction of social, political, economic, and ideological forces. In the United States any centralization of power produced by the expansion of governmental bureaucracy is mitigated by pluralistic forces that disperse power among bureaucratic agencies, congressional committees, and interest groups and that undermine efforts to subordinate lower-ranking executive officials to higher-ranking ones. Yet an increasingly sophisticated economy and active involvement in world affairs seem likely to create stronger needs for hierarchy, bureaucracy, centralization of power, expertise, big government specifically, and big organizations generally. In some way or another society will respond to these needs while still attempting to realize the values of the American Creed to which they are so contradictory. If history is against progress, for how long will progress resist history?

Acute tension between the requisites of development and the norms of ideology played a central role in the evolution of the People's Republic of China during its first quarter-century. China can avoid this conflict for as long as its leaders agree on the priority of development over revolution. In the United States, in contrast, no group of leaders can suppress by fiat the liberal values that have defined the nation's identity. The conflict between developmental need and ideological norm that characterized Mao's China in the 1960s and 1970s is likely to be duplicated in the American future unless other forces change, dilute, or eliminate the central ideals of the American Creed.

What is the probability of this happening? Do such forces exist? Several possibilities suggest themselves. First, the core values of the creed are products of the seventeenth and eighteenth centuries. Their roots lie in the English and American revolutionary experiences, in seventeenth-century Protestant moralism and eighteenth-century liberal rationalism. The historical dynamism and appeal of these ideals could naturally begin to fade after two centuries, particularly as those ideals come to be seen as increasingly irrelevant in a complex modern economy and a threatening international environment. In addition, to the extent that those ideals derive from Protestant sources, they must also be weakened by trends toward secularism that exist even in the United States. Each of the four creedal passion periods was preceded or accompanied by a religious "great awakening." These movements of religious reform and revival, however, have successively played less central roles in American society, that of the 1950s being very marginal in its impact compared to that of the 1740s. As religious passion weakens, how likely is the United States to sustain a firm commitment to its traditional values? Would an America without its Protestant core still be America?

Second, the social, economic, and cultural changes associated with the transition from industrial to postindustrial society could also give rise to new political values that would displace the traditional liberal values associated with bourgeois society and the rise of industrialism. In the 1960s and 1970s in both Europe and America social scientists found evidence of the increasing prevalence of "postbourgeois" or "postmaterialist" values, particularly among younger cohorts. In a somewhat similar vein George Lodge foresaw the displacement of Lockean individualistic ideology in the United States by a "communitarian" ideology, resembling in many aspects the traditional Japanese collectivist approach.[12]

Third, as Hofstadter and others argued, the early twentieth-century immigration of Orthodox, Catholics, and Jews from central, eastern, and southern Europe introduced a different "ethic" into American cities. In the late twentieth century the United States experienced its third major wave of postindependence immigration, composed largely of Puerto Ricans, Mexicans, Cubans, and others from Latin America and the Caribbean. Like their predecessors, the more recent immigrants could well introduce into American society political and social values markedly in contrast with those of Lockean liberalism. In these circumstances the consensus on this type of liberalism could very likely be either disrupted or diluted.

Fourth, the historical function of the creed in defining national identity could conceivably become less significant, and widespread belief in that creed could consequently become less essential to the continued existence of the United States as a nation. Having been in existence as a functioning national society and political entity for over two hundred years, the United States may have less need of these ideals to define its national identity in the future. History, tradition, custom, culture, and a sense of shared experience such as other major nations have developed over the centuries could also come to define American identity, and the role of abstract ideals and values might be reduced. The *ideational* basis of national identity would be replaced by an *organic* one. "American exceptionalism" would wither. The United States would cease to be "a nation with the soul of a church" and would become a nation with the soul of a nation.

Some or all of these four factors could alter American political values so as to reduce the gap between these values and the reality of American institutional practice. Yet the likelihood of this occurring does not seem very high. Despite their seventeenth- and eighteenth-century origins American values and ideals have demonstrated tremendous persistence and resiliency in the twentieth century. Defined vaguely and abstractly, these ideals have been relatively easily adapted to the needs of successive generations. The constant social change in the United States indeed underlies their permanence. Rising social, economic, and ethnic groups need to reinvoke and to reinvigorate those values in order to promote their own access to the rewards of American society. The shift in emphasis among values manifested by younger cohorts in the 1960s and 1970s does not necessarily mean the end of the traditional pattern. In many respects the articulation of these values was, as it had been in the past, a protest against the perceived emergence of new centers of power. The yearning for "belonging and intellectual and esthetic self-fulfillment" found to exist among the younger cohorts of the 1960s and 1970s[13] could in fact be interpreted as "a romantic, Luddite reaction against the bureaucratic and technologi-cal tendencies of postindustrialism." This confrontation between ideology and institutions easily fits into the well-established American pattern. Indeed, insofar as "the postindustrial society is more highly educated and more participatory than American society in the past and insofar as American political institutions will be more bureaucratic and hierarchical than before, the conflict between ideology and institutions could be more intense than it has ever been."[14]

Similarly, the broader and longer-term impact of the Latin immigration of the 1950s, 1960s, and 1970s could reinforce the central role of the American Creed both as a way of legitimizing claims to political, economic, and social equality and also as the indispensable element in defining national identity. The children and grandchildren of the European immi-grants of the early twentieth century in due course became ardent adherents to traditional American middle-class values. In addition, the more culturally pluralistic the nation becomes, particularly if cultural pluralism encompasses linguistic pluralism, the more essential the political values of the creed become in defining what it is that Americans have in common. At some point traditional American ideals—liberty, equality, individualism, democracy—may lose their appeal and join the ideas of racial inequality, the divine right of kings, and the dictator-ship of the proletariat on the ideological scrap heap of history. There is, however, little to suggest that this will be a twentieth-century happening.

If the gap between ideals and institutions remains a central feature of American politics, the question then becomes: What changes, if any, may occur in the traditional pattern of responses to this gap? Three broad possibilities exist. First, the previous pattern of response could continue. If the periodicity of the past prevails, a major sustained creedal passion period will occur in the second and third decades of the twenty-first century. In the interim moralism, cynicism, complacency, and hypocrisy will all be invoked by different Americans in different ways in their efforts to live with the gap. The tensions resulting from the gap will remain and perhaps increase in intensity, but their consequences will not be significantly more serious than they have been in the past. Second, the cycle of response could stabilize to a greater degree than it has in the past. Americans could acquire a greater understanding of their case of cognitive dissonance and through this understanding come to live with their dilemma on somewhat easier terms than they have in the past, in due course evolving a more complex but also more coherent and constant response to this problem. Third, the oscillations among the responses could intensify in such a way as to threaten to destroy both ideals and institutions.

In terms of the future stability of the American political system, the first possibility may be the most likely and the second the most hopeful, but the third is clearly the most danger-ous. Let us focus on the third.

Lacking any concept of the state, lacking for most of its history both the centralized authority and the bureaucratic apparatus of the European state, the American polity has his-torically been a weak polity. It was designed to be so, and traditional inheritance and social environment combined for years to support the framers' intentions. In the twentieth century foreign threats and domestic economic and social needs have generated pressures to develop stronger, more authoritative decision-making and decision-implementing institutions. Yet the continued presence of deeply felt moralistic sentiments among major groups in American society could continue to ensure weak and divided government, devoid of authority and unable to deal satisfactorily with the economic, social, and foreign challenges confronting the nation. Intensification of this conflict between history and progress could give rise to increasing frustration and increasingly violent oscillations between moralism and cynicism. American moralism ensures that government will never be truly efficacious; the realities of power ensure that government will never be truly democratic.

This situation could lead to a two-phase dialectic involving intensified efforts to reform government followed by intensified frustration when those efforts produce not progress in a liberal–democratic direction but obstacles to meeting perceived functional needs. The weakening of government in an effort to reform it could lead eventually to strong demands for the replacement of the weakened and ineffective institutions by more authoritarian structures more effectively designed to meet historical needs. Given the perversity of reform, moralistic extremism in the pursuit of liberal democracy could generate a strong tide toward authoritarian efficiency. "The truth is that," as Plato observed, "in the constitution of society . . . any excess brings about an equally violent reaction. So the only outcome of too much freedom is likely to be excessive subjection in the state or in the individual; which means that the culmination of liberty in democracy is precisely what prepares the way for the cruelest extreme of servitude under a despot."[15]

American political ideals are a useful instrument not only for those who wish to improve American political institutions but also for those who wish to destroy them. Liberal reformers, because they believe in the ideals, attempt to change institutions to approximate those ideals more closely. The enemies of liberalism, because they oppose both liberal ideals and liberal institutions, attempt to use the former to undermine the latter. For them the gap between ideals and institutions is a made-to-order opportunity. The effectiveness of liberal–democratic institutions can be discredited by highlighting their shortcomings compared to the ideals on which they are supposedly modeled. This is a common response of foreigners critical of the American polity, but this approach is not limited to liberalism's foreign enemies. The leading theorists of the American Southern Enlightenment, for instance, took great delight in describing the inequality and repression of the Northern "wage slave" system not because they believed in equality and liberty for all workers but because they wished to discredit the economy that was threatening the future of slavery in the South. "Their obvious purpose [was] to belabor the North rather than to redeem it."[16]

Those who have battered liberal institutions with the stick of liberal ideals have, however, more often been on the left than on the right. There is a reason for this, which is well illustrated by the attitudes of conservatives, liberals, and revolutionaries toward political equality. Traditional conservatives oppose equality. They may perceive American political institutions as embodying more equality than they think desirable. In this case they normally opt out of American society in favor of either internal or external emigration. Traditional conservatives may also perceive and take comfort in the realities of power and inequality that exist in the United States behind the facade and rhetoric of equality. Liberal defenders of American institutions embrace the hypocritical response: they believe that inequality does not exist and that it should not exist. Both the perceptive conservatives and the liberal hypocrites are thus in some sense standpatters, satisfied with the status quo, but only because they have very different perceptions of what that status quo is and very different views about whether equality is good or bad. The ability of traditional conservatives and liberal hypocrites to cooperate in defense of the status quo is hence very limited: neither will buy the others' arguments. In addition, articulate traditional conservatives have been few and far between on the American political landscape, in large part because their values are so contrary to those of the American Creed (see Table 4.1).

Table 4.1   POLITICAL BELIEFS AND POLITICAL EQUALITY

	Traditional conservative	Liberal		Marxist revolutionary
		Hypocrite	Moralist	
Perception of political equality	Does not exist	Does exist	Does not exist	Does not exist
Judgment on political equality	Bad	Good	Good	Good
	Standpatters		Radicals	

On the other side of the political spectrum a very different situation exists. Like hypo-critical liberals, moralist liberals believe that inequality is bad. Unlike the hypocrites, however, they perceive that inequality exists in American institutions and hence vigorously devote themselves to reform in an effort to eliminate it. To their left, however, the Marxist revolution-aries have views and beliefs that on the surface at least, coincide with those of moralistic liberals. Marxist revolutionaries hold inequality to be bad, see it as pervasive in existing institutions, and attack it and the institutions vigorously. At a deeper and more philosophical level Marxist revolutionaries may believe in the necessity of the violent overthrow of the capitalist order, the dictatorship of the proletariat, and a disciplined Leninist party as the revolutionary vanguard. If they blatantly articulate these beliefs, they are relegated to the outermost fringes of American politics and foreswear any meaningful ideological or political influence. It is, moreover, in the best Leninist tradition to see reform as the potential catalyst of revolution.[17] Consequently, major incentives exist for Marxist revolutionaries to emphasize not what divides them from the liberal consensus but what unites them with liberal reformers, that is, their perception of inequality and their belief in equality. With this common commitment to reform, liberal mor-alists and Marxist revolutionaries can cooperate in their attack on existing institutions, even though in the long run one group wants to make them work better and the other wants to overthrow them.

The role of Marxism in the consensus of society of America thus differs significantly from its role in the ideologically pluralistic societies of Western Europe. There the differences between liberal and Marxist goals and appeals are sharply delineated, the two philosophies are embraced by different constituencies and parties, and the conflict between them is unceasing. In the United States the prevalence of liberalism means a consensus on the standards by which the institutions of society should be judged, and Marxism has no choice but to employ those standards in its own cause. Philosophical differences are blurred as reform liberalism and revolutionary Marxism blend into a nondescript but politically relevant radicalism that serves the immediate interests of both. This convergence, moreover, exists at the individual as well as the societal level: particular individuals bring together in their own minds elements of both liberal reformism and revolutionary Marxism. American radicals easily perceive the gap between American ideals and American institutions; they do not easily perceive the conflict between reform liberalism and revolutionary Marxism. With shared immediate goals, these two sets of philosophically distinct ideas often coexist in the same mind.

This common ground of liberal reformer and revolutionary Marxist in favor of radical change contrasts with the distance between the liberal hypocrite and the traditional conservative.

The hypocrite can defend American institutions only by claiming they are something that they are not. The conservative can defend them only by articulating values that most Americans abhor. The Marxist subscribes to the liberal consensus in order to subvert liberal institutions; the conservative rejects the liberal consensus in order to defend those institutions. The combined effect of both is to strengthen the attack on the established order. For paradoxically, the conservative who defends American institutions with conservative arguments (that they are good because they institutionalize political inequality) weakens those institutions at least as much as the radical who attacks them for the same reason. The net impact of the difficulties and divisions among the standpatters and the converging unity of the liberal and Marxist radicals is to enhance the threat to American political institutions posed by those political ideas whose continued vitality is indispensable to their survival.

Two things are thus clear. American political institutions are more open, liberal, and democratic than those of any other major society now or in the past. If Americans ever abandon or destroy these institutions, they are likely to do so in the name of their liberal–democratic ideals. Inoculated against the appeal of foreign ideas, America has only to fear its own.

AMERICA VERSUS THE WORLD?

The gap between ideals and institutions poses two significant issues with respect to the relations between the United States and the rest of the world. First, what are the implications of the gap for American institutions and processes concerned with foreign relations and national security? To what extent should those institutions and processes conform to American liberal, individualistic, democratic values? Second, what are the implications of the gap for American policy toward other societies? To what extent should the United States attempt to make the institutions and policies of other societies conform to American values? For much of its history when it was relatively isolated from the rest of the world, as it was between 1815 and 1914, the United States did not have to grapple seriously with these problems. In the mid-twentieth century, however, the United States became deeply, complexly, and seemingly inextricably involved with the other countries of the world. That involvement brought to the fore and gave new significance and urgency to these two long-standing and closely related issues. These issues are closely related because efforts to reduce the ideal-versus-institutions gap in the institutions and processes of American foreign relations reduce the ability of the United States to exercise power in international affairs, including its ability to reduce that gap between American values and foreign institutions and policies. Conversely, efforts to encourage foreign institutions and practices to conform to American ideals require the expansion of American power and thus make it more difficult for American institutions and policies to conform to those ideals.

Foreign-Policy Institutions

The relation of its institutions and processes concerned with foreign relations to the ideals and values of its political ideology is a more serious problem for the United States than for most other societies. The differences between the United States and Western Europe in this respect are particularly marked. First, the ideological pluralism of Western European societies does not provide a single set of political principles by which to judge foreign-policy institutions and practices. Those, as well as other institutions and practices, benefit in terms of legitimacy as a result of varied strands of conservative, liberal, Christian Democratic, and Marxist political thought that have existed in Western European societies. Second and more important, in most European societies at least an embryonic national community and in large measure a national state existed before the emergence of ideologies. So also did the need to conduct foreign relations and to protect the security of the national community and the state. National security bureaucracies, military forces, foreign offices, intelligence services, internal security, and police systems were all in existence when ideologies emerged in the eighteenth and nineteenth centuries. Although the ideologies undoubtedly had some implications for and posed some demands on these institutions, their proponents tended to recognize the prior claims of these institutions reflecting the needs of the national community in a world of competing national communities. European democratic regimes thus accept a security apparatus that exists in large part outside the normal process of democratic politics and that represents and defends the continuing interests of the community and the state irrespective of the ideologies that may from one time to another dominate its politics.

In Europe, ideology—or rather ideologies—thus followed upon and developed within the context of an existing national community and state. In America ideology in the form of the principles of the American Creed existed before the formation of a national community and political system. These principles defined the identity of the community when there were no institutions for dealing with the other countries of the world. It was assumed that the foreign-policy institutions, like other political institutions, would reflect the basic values of the preexisting and overwhelmingly preponderant ideology. Yet precisely these institutions— foreign and intelligence services, military and police forces—have functional imperatives that conflict most sharply and dramatically with the liberal–democratic values of the American Creed. The essence of the creed is opposition to power and to concentrated authority. This leads to efforts to minimize the resources of power (such as arms), to restrict the effectiveness of specialized bureaucratic hierarchies, and to limit the authority of the executive in the conduct of foreign policy. This conflict manifests itself dramatically in the perennial issue concerning the role of standing armies and professional military forces in a liberal society. For much of its history the United States was able to avoid the full implications of this conflict because its geographic position permitted it to follow a policy of extirpation—that is, almost abolishing military forces and relegating those that did exist to the distant social and geographic extremities of society.[18] Similarly, the United States did not seem to need and did not have an intelligence service, a professional foreign service, or a national police force.

In the twentieth century the impossibility of sustained isolation led the United States to develop all these institutions. Much more so than those in Western Europe, however, these institutions have coexisted in uneasy and fundamentally incompatible ways with the values of the prevailing ideology. This incompatibility became acute after World War II, when the country's global role and responsibilities made it necessary for the government to develop and to maintain such institutions on a large scale and to accord them a central role in its foreign policy. During the 1950s and early 1960s Americans tended to be blissfully complacent and to ignore the broad gap between ideals and institutions that this created in the foreign-policy and defense sectors of their national life. At the same time, various theories—such as Kennan's ideal of the detached professional diplomat and Huntington's concept of "objective civilian control"—were developed to justify the insulation of these institutions from the political demands of a liberal society.[19] In the end, however, the liberal imperatives could not be avoided, and the late 1960s and 1970s saw overwhelming political pressure to make foreign-policy and security institutions conform to the requirements of the liberal ideology. In a powerful outburst of creedal passion, Americans embarked on crusades against the CIA and FBI, defense spending, the use of military force abroad, the military-industrial complex, and the imperial presidency (to use Arthur Schlesinger, Jr.'s phrase), attempting to expose, weaken, dismantle, or abolish the institutions that protected their liberal society against foreign threats. They reacted with outraged moralistic self-criticism to their government engaging in the type of activities—deception, violence, abuse of individual rights—to protect their society that other countries accept as a matter of course.

This penchant of Americans for challenging and undermining the authority of their political institutions, including those concerned with the foreign relations and security of the country, produces mixed and confused reactions on the part of Europeans and other non-Americans. Their initial reaction to a Pentagon Papers case, Watergate, or investigation of the CIA is often one of surprise, amazement, bewilderment. "What are you Americans up to and why are you doing this to yourselves?" A second reaction, which often follows the first, is grudging admiration for a society that takes its principles so seriously and has such effective procedures for attempting to realize them. This is often accompanied by somewhat envious and wistful comments on the contrast between this situation and the paramountcy of state authority in their own country. Finally, a third reaction often follows, expressing deep concern about the impact that the creedal upheaval will have on the ability of the United States to conduct its foreign policy and to protect its friends and allies.

This last concern over whether its liberal values will permit the United States to maintain the material resources, governmental institutions, and political will to defend its interests in the world becomes more relevant not just as a result of the inextricable involvement of the United States in world affairs but also because of the changes in the countries with which the United States will be primarily involved. During the first part of the twentieth century American external relations were largely focused on Western Europe, where in most countries significant political groups held political values similar to American values. Even more important, lodged deeply in the consciousness of Western European statesmen and intellectuals was the thought, impregnated there by Tocqueville if by no one else, that American political values in some measure embodied the wave of the future, that what America believed in would at some point be what the entire civilized world would believe in. This sympathy, partial or latent as it may have been, nonetheless gave the United States a diplomatic resource of some significance. European societies might resent American moral or moralistic loftiness, but both they and the Americans knew that the moral values set forth by the United States (sincerely or hypocritically) would have a resonance in their own societies and could at times be linked up with internal social and political movements that would be impossible for them to ignore.

In the mid-twentieth century the widespread belief in democratic values among younger Germans and to a lesser degree among younger Japanese provided some support for the convergence thesis. At a more general level, however, the sense that America was the future of Europe weakened considerably. More important, in the late twentieth century the countries with which the United States was having increasing interactions, both competitive and cooperative, were the Soviet Union, China, and Japan. The partial sense of identification and of future convergence that existed between the United States and Europe are absent in American relations with these three countries. Like the United States, these countries have a substantial degree of consensus or homogeneity in social and political values and ideology. The content of each country's consensus, however, differs significantly from that of the United States. In all three societies the stress in one form or another is on the pervasiveness of inequality in human relationships, the "sanctity of authority,"[20] the subordination of the individual to the group and the state, the dubious legitimacy of dissent or challenges to the powers that be. Japan, to be sure, developed a working democracy after World War II, but its long-standing values stressing hierarchy, vertical ranking, and submissiveness leave some degree of disharmony that has resemblances to but is just the reverse of what prevails in American society. The dominant ideas in all three countries stand in dramatic contrast to American ideas of openness, liberalism, equality, individual rights, and freedom to dissent. In the Soviet Union, China, and Japan the prevailing political values and social norms reinforce the authority of the central political institutions of society and enhance the ability of these nations to compete with other societies. In the United States the prevailing norms, insofar as Americans take them seriously, undermine and weaken the power and authority of government and detract, at times seriously, from its ability to compete internationally. In the small world of the West Americans were beguiling cousins; in the larger world that includes the East Americans often seem naïve strangers. Given the disharmonic element in the American political system—the continuing challenge, latent or overt, that lies in the American mind to the authority of American government—how well will the United States be able to conduct its affairs in this league of powers to whose historical traditions basic American values are almost entirely alien?

Foreign-Policy Goals

In the eyes of most Americans not only should their foreign-policy institutions be structured and function so as to reflect liberal values, but American foreign policy should also be substantively directed to the promotion of those values in the external environment. This gives a distinctive cast to the American role in the world. In a famous phrase Viscount Palmerston once said that Britain did not have permanent friends or enemies, it only had permanent interests. Like Britain and other countries, the United States also has interests, defined in terms of power, wealth, and security, some of which are sufficiently enduring as to be thought of as permanent. As a founded society, however, the United States also has distinctive political principles and values that define its national identity. These principles provide a second set of goals and a second set of standards—in addition to those of national interest—by which to shape the goals and judge the success of American foreign policy.

This heritage, this transposition of the ideals-versus-institutions gap into foreign policy, again distinguishes the United States from other societies. Western European states clearly do not reject the relevance of morality and political ideology to the conduct of foreign policy. They do, however, see the goal of foreign policy as the advancement of the major and continuing security and economic interests of their state. Political principles provide limits and parameters to foreign policy but not to its goals. As a result European public debate over morality versus power in foreign policy has except in rare instances not played the role that it has in the United States. That issue does come up with the foreign policy of Communist states and has been discussed at length, in terms of the conflict of ideology and national interest, in analyses of Soviet foreign policy. The conflict has been less significant there than in the United States for three reasons. First, an authoritarian political system precludes public discussion of the issue. Since the 1920s debate of Trotsky versus Stalin over permanent revolution there has been no overt domestic criticism concerning whether Soviet foreign policy is at one time either too power-oriented or at another time too ideologically oriented. Second, Marxist-Leninist ideology distinguishes between basic doctrine on the one hand and strategy and tactics on the other. The former does not change; the latter is adapted to specific historical circumstances. The twists and turns in the party line can always be justified as ideologically necessary at that particular point in time to achieve the long-run goals of communism, even though those shifts may in fact be motivated primarily by national interests. American political values, in contrast, are usually thought of as universally valid, and pragmatism is seen not as a means of implementing these values in particular circumstances but rather as a means of abandoning them. Third, Soviet leaders and the leaders of other Communist states that pursue their own foreign policies can and do, when they wish, simply ignore ideology when they desire to pursue particular national interest goals.

For most Americans, however, foreign-policy goals should reflect not only the security interests of the nation and the economic interests of key groups within the nation but also the political values and principles that define American identity. If these values do define foreign-policy goals, then that policy is morally justified, the opponents of that policy at home and abroad are morally illegitimate, and all efforts must be directed toward overcoming the opponents and achieving the goals. The prevailing American approach to foreign policy thus has been not that of Stephen Decatur ("Our country, right or wrong!") but that of Carl Schurz ("Our country, right or wrong! When right, to be kept right; when wrong, to be put right!"). To Americans, achieving this convergence between self-interest and morality has appeared as no easy task. Hence the recurring tendencies in American history, either to retreat to minimum relations with the rest of the world and thus avoid the problem of reconciling the pursuit of self-interest with the adherence to principle in a corrupt and hostile environment, or the opposite solution, to set forth on a crusade to purify the world, to bring it into accordance with American principles and in the process to expand American power and thus protect the national interest.

This practice of judging the behavior of one's country and one's government by external standards of right and wrong has been responsible for the often substantial opposition to the wars in which the United States has engaged. The United States will only respond with unanimity to a war in which both national security and political principle are clearly at stake. In the two hundred years after the Revolution, only one war, World War II, met this criterion, and this was the only war to which there was no significant domestic opposition articulated in terms of the extent to which the goals of the war and the way in which it was conducted deviated from the basic principles of the American Creed. In this sense World War II was for the United States the "perfect war"; every other war has been an imperfect war in that certain elements of the American public have objected to it because it did not seem to accord with American principles. As strange as it may seem to people of other societies, Americans have had no trouble conceiving of their government waging an un-American war.

The extent to which the American liberal creed prevails over power considerations can lead to hypocritical and rather absolutist positions on policy. As Seymour Martin Lipset pointed out, if wars should only be fought for moral purposes, then the opponents against which they are fought must be morally evil and hence total war must be waged against them and unconditional surrender exacted from them. If a war is not morally legitimate, then the leaders conducting it must be morally evil and opposition to it in virtually any form is not only morally justified but morally obligatory. It is no coincidence that the country that has most tended to think of wars as crusades is also the country with the strongest record of conscientious objection to war.[21]

The effort to use American foreign policy to promote American values abroad raises a central issue. There is a clear difference between political action to make American political practices conform to American political values and political action to make *foreign* political practices conform to American values. Americans can legitimately attempt to reduce the gap between American institutions and American values, but can they legitimately attempt to reduce the gap between other people's institutions and American values? The answer is not self-evident.

The argument for a negative response to this question can be made on at least four grounds. First, it is morally wrong for the United States to attempt to shape the institutions of other societies. Those institutions should reflect the values and behavior of the people in those societies. To intrude from outside is either imperialism or colonialism, each of which also violates American values. Second, it is difficult practically and in most cases impossible for the United States to influence significantly the institutional development of other societies. The task is simply beyond American knowledge, skill, and resources. To attempt to do so will often be counterproductive. Third, any effort to shape the domestic institutions of other societies needlessly irritates and antagonizes other governments and hence will complicate and often endanger the achievement of other more important foreign-policy goals, particularly in the areas of national security and economic well-being. Fourth, to influence the political development of other societies would require an enormous expansion of the military power and economic resources of the American government. This in turn would pose dangers to the operation of democratic government within the United States.

A yes answer to this question can, on the other hand, also be justified on four grounds. First, if other people's institutions pose direct threats to the viability of American institutions and values in the United States, an American effort to change those institutions would be justifiable in terms of self-defense. Whether or not foreign institutions do pose such a direct threat in any given circumstance is, however, not easily determined. Even in the case of Nazi Germany in 1940 there were widely differing opinions in the United States. After World War II opinion was also divided on whether Soviet institutions, as distinct from Soviet policies, threatened the United States.

Second, the direct-threat argument can be generalized to the proposition that authoritarian regimes in any form and on any continent pose a potential threat to the viability of liberal institutions and values in the United States. A liberal–democratic system, it can be argued, can only be secure in a world system of similarly constituted states. In the past this argument did not play a central role because of the extent to which the United States was geographically isolated from differently constituted states. The world is, however, becoming smaller. Given the increasing interactions among societies and the emergence of transnational institutions operating in many societies, the pressures toward convergence among political systems are likely to become more intense. Interdependence may be incompatible with coexistence. In this case the world, like the United States in the nineteenth century or Western Europe in the twentieth century, will not be able to exist half-slave and half-free. Hence the survival of democratic institutions and values at home will depend upon their adoption abroad.

Third, American efforts to make other people's institutions conform to American values would be justified to the extent that the other people supported those values. Such support has historically been much more prevalent in Western Europe and Latin America than it has in Asia and Africa, but some support undoubtedly exists in almost every society for liberty, equality, democracy, and the rights of the individual. Americans could well feel justified in supporting and helping those individuals, groups, and institutions in other societies who share their belief in these values. At the same time it would also be appropriate for them to be aware that those values could be realized in other societies through institutions significantly different from those that exist in the United States.

Fourth, American efforts to make other people's institutions conform to American values could be justified on the grounds that those values are universally valid and universally applicable, whether or not most people in other societies believe in them. For Americans not to believe in the universal validity of American values could indeed lead to a moral relativism: liberty and democracy are not inherently better than any other political values; they just happen to be those that for historical and cultural reasons prevail in the United States. This relativistic position runs counter to the strong elements of moral absolutism and messianism that are part of American history and culture, and hence the argument for moral relativism may not wash in the United States for relativistic reasons. In addition the argument can be made that some element of belief in the universal validity of a set of political ideals is necessary to arouse the energy, support, and passion to defend those ideals and the institutions modeled on them in American society.

Historically Americans have generally believed in the universal validity of their values. At the end of World War II, when Americans forced Germany and Japan to be free, they did not stop to ask if liberty and democracy were what the German and Japanese people wanted. Americans implicitly assumed that their values were valid and applicable and that they would at the very least be morally negligent if they did not insist that Germany and Japan adopt political institutions reflecting those values. Belief in the universal validity of those values obviously reinforces and reflects those hypocritical elements of the American tradition that stress the United States's role as a redeemer nation and lead it to attempt to impose its values and often its institutions on other societies. These tendencies may, however, be constrained by a recognition that although American values may be universally valid, they need not be universally and totally applicable at all times and in all places.

Americans expect their institutions and policies that are devoted to external relations to reflect liberal standards and principles. So also in large measure do non-Americans. Both American citizens and others hold the United States to standards that they do not generally apply to other countries. People expect France, for instance, to pursue its national self-interests—economic, military, and political—with cold disregard for ideologies and values. But their expectations with respect to the United States are very different: people accept with a shrug actions on the part of France that would generate surprise, consternation, and outrage if perpetrated by the United States. "Europe accepts the idea that America is a country with a difference, from whom it is reasonable to demand an exceptionally altruistic standard of behaviour; it feels perfectly justified in pouring obloquy on shortcomings from this ideal; and also, perhaps inevitably, it seems to enjoy every example of a fall from grace which contemporary America provides."[22]

This double standard is implicit acknowledgment of the seriousness with which Americans attempt to translate their principles into practice. It also provides a ready weapon to foreign critics of the United States, just as it does to domestic ones. For much of its history, racial injustice, economic inequality, and political and religious intolerance were familiar elements in the American landscape, and the contrast between them and the articulated ideals of the American Creed furnished abundant ammunition to generations of European critics. "Anti-Americanism is in this form a protest, not against Americanism, but against its apparent failure."[23] This may be true on the surface. But it is also possible that failure—that is, the persistence of the ideals-versus-institutions gap in American institutions and policies—furnishes the excuse and the opportunity for hostile foreign protest and that the true target of the protest is Americanism itself.

POWER AND LIBERTY: THE MYTH OF AMERICAN REPRESSION

The pattern of American involvement in world affairs has often been interpreted as the outcome of these conflicting pulls of national interest and power on the one hand and political morality and principles on the other. Various scholars have phrased the dichotomy in various ways: self-interest versus ideals, power versus morality, realism versus utopianism, pragmatism versus principle, historical realism versus rationalist idealism, Washington versus Wilson.[24] Almost all, however, have assumed the dichotomy to be real and have traced the relative importance over the years of national interest and morality in shaping American foreign policy. It is, for instance, argued that during the Federalist years realism or power considerations were generally preponderant, whereas during the first four decades of the twentieth century moral considerations and principles came to be uppermost in the minds of American policy makers. After World War II a significant group of writers and thinkers on foreign policy—including Reinhold Niebuhr, George Kennan, Hans Morgenthau, Walter Lippmann, and Robert Osgood—expounded a "new realism" and criticized the moralistic, legalistic, "utopian" Wilsonian approaches, which they claimed had previously prevailed in the conduct of American foreign relations. The new realism reached its apotheosis in the central role played by the balance of power in the theory and practice of Henry Kissinger. A nation's foreign policy, he said, "should be directed toward affecting the foreign policy" of other societies; it should not be "the principal goal of American foreign policy to transform the domestic structures of societies with which we deal."[25]

In the 1970s, however, the new realism of the 1950s and 1960s was challenged by a "new moralism." The pendulum that had swung in one direction after World War II swung far over to the other side. This shift was one of the most significant consequences of American involvement in Vietnam, Watergate, and the democratic surge and creedal passion of the 1960s. It represented the displacement onto the external world of the moralism that had been earlier directed inward against American institutions. It thus represented the first signs of a return to the hypocritical response to the gap between American values and American institutions. The new moralism manifested itself first in congressional action, with the addition to the foreign assistance act of Title IX in 1966 and human rights conditions in the early 1970s. In 1976 Jimmy Carter vigorously criticized President Ford for believing "that there is little room for morality in foreign affairs, and that we must put self-interest above principle."[26] As president, Carter moved human rights to a central position in American foreign relations.

The lines between the moralists and the realists were thus clearly drawn, but on one point they were agreed: they both believed that the conflict between morality and self-interest, or ideals and realism, was a real one. In some respects it was. In other respects, particularly when it was formulated in terms of a conflict between liberty and power, it was not. As so defined, the dichotomy was false. It did not reflect an accurate understanding of the real choices confronting American policy makers in dealing with the external world. It derived rather from the transposition of the assumptions of the antipower ethic to American relations with the rest of the world. From the earliest years of their society Americans have perceived a conflict between imperatives of governmental power and the liberty and rights of the individual. Because power and liberty are antithetical at home, they are also assumed to be antithetical abroad. Hence the pursuit of power by the American government abroad must threaten liberty abroad even as a similar pursuit of power at home would threaten liberty there. The contradiction in American society between American power and American liberty at home is projected into a contradiction between American power and foreign liberty abroad.

During the 1960s and 1970s this belief led many intellectuals to propagate what can perhaps best be termed the myth of American repression—that is, the view that American involvement in the politics of other societies is almost invariably hostile to liberty and supportive of repression in those societies. The United States, as Hans Morgenthau put it, is "repression's friend": "With unfailing consistency, we have since the end of the Second World War intervened on behalf of conservative and fascist repression against revolution and radical reform. In an age when societies are in a revolutionary or prerevolutionary stage, we have become the foremost counterrevolutionary status quo power on earth. Such a policy can only lead to moral and political disaster."[27] This statement, like the arguments generally of those intellectuals supporting the myth of American repression, suffers from two basic deficiencies.

First, it confuses support for the left with opposition to repression. In this respect, it represents another manifestation of the extent to which similarity in immediate objectives can blur the line between liberals and revolutionaries. Yet those who support "revolution and radical reform" in other countries seldom have any greater concern for liberty and human dignity than those who support "conservative and fascist repression." In fact, if it is a choice between rightist and Communist dictatorships, there are at least three good reasons in terms of liberty to prefer the former to the latter. First, the suppression of liberty in right-wing authoritarian regimes is almost always less pervasive than it is in left-wing totalitarian ones. In the 1960s and 1970s, for instance, infringements of human rights in South Korea received extensive coverage in the American media, in part because there were in South Korea journalists, church groups, intellectuals, and opposition political leaders who could call attention to those infringements. The absence of comparable reports about the infringements of human rights in North Korea was evidence not of the absence of repression in that country but of its totality. Right-wing dictatorships moreover are, the record shows, less permanent than left-wing dictatorships; Portugal, Spain, and Greece are but three examples of right-wing dictatorships that were replaced by democratic regimes. As of 1980, however, no Communist system had been replaced by a democratic regime. Third, as a result of the global competition between the United States and the Soviet Union, right-wing regimes are normally more susceptible to American and other Western influence than left-wing dictatorships, and such influence is overwhelmingly on the side of liberty.

This last point leads to the other central fallacy of the myth of American repression as elaborated by Morgenthau and others. Their picture of the world of the 1960s and 1970s was dominated by the image of an America that was overwhelmingly powerful and overwhelmingly repressive. In effect they held an updated belief in the "illusion of American omnipotence" that attributed the evil in other societies to the machinations of the Pentagon, the CIA, and American business. Their image of America was, however, defective in both dimensions. During the 1960s and 1970s American power relative to that of other governments and societies declined significantly. By the mid-1970s the ability of the United States to influence what was going on in other societies was but a pale shadow of what it had been a quarter-century earlier. When it had an effect, however, the overall effect of American power on other societies was to further liberty, pluralism, and democracy. The conflict between American power and American principles virtually disappears when it is applied to the American impact on other societies. In that case, the very factors that give rise to the consciousness of a gap between ideal and reality also limit in practice the extent of that gap. The United States is in practice the freest, most liberal, most democratic country in the world, with far better institutionalized protections for the rights of its citizens than any other society. As a consequence, any increase in the power or influence of the United States in world affairs generally results—not inevitably, but far more often than not—in the promotion of liberty and human rights in the world. The expansion of American power is not synonymous with the expansion of liberty, but a significant correlation exists between the rise and fall of American power in the world and the rise and fall of liberty and democracy in the world.

The single biggest extension of democratic liberties in the history of the world came at the end of World War II, when stable democratic regimes were inaugurated in defeated Axis countries: Germany, Japan, Italy, and, as a former part of Germany, Austria. In the early 1980s these countries had a population of over two hundred million and included the third and fourth largest economies in the world. The imposition of democracy on these countries was almost entirely the work of the United States. In Germany and Japan in particular the United States government played a major role in designing democratic institutions. As a result of American determination and power the former Axis countries were "forced to be free."[28] Conversely, the modest steps taken toward democracy and liberty in Poland, Czechoslovakia, and Hungary were quickly reversed and Stalinist repression instituted once it became clear that the United States was not able to project its power into Eastern Europe. If World War II had ended in something less than total victory, or if the United States had played a less significant role in bringing about the victory (as was indeed the case east of the Elbe), these transitions to democracy in central Europe and eastern Asia would not have occurred. But— with the partial exception of South Korea—where American armies marched, democracy followed in their train.

The stability of democracy in these countries during the quarter-century after World War II reflected in large part the extent to which the institutions and practices imposed by the United States found a favorable social and political climate in which to take root. The continued American political, economic, and military presence in Western Europe and eastern Asia was, however, also indispensable to this democratic success. At any time after World War II the withdrawal of American military guarantees and military forces from these areas would have had a most unsettling and perhaps devastating effect on the future of democracy in central Europe and Japan.

In the early years of the cold war, American influence was employed to ensure the continuation of democratic government in Italy and to promote free elections in Greece. In both cases, the United States had twin interests in the domestic politics of these countries: to create a system of stable democratic government and to ensure the exclusion of Communist parties from power. Since in both cases the Communist parties did not have the support of anything remotely resembling a majority of the population, the problem of what to do if a party committed to abolishing democracy gains power through democratic means was happily avoided. With American support, democracy survived in Italy and was sustained for a time in Greece. In addition, the American victory in World War II provided the stimulus in Turkey for one of the rarest events in political history: the peaceful self-transformation of an authoritarian one-party system into a democratic competitive party system.

In Latin America, the rise and fall of democratic regimes also coincided with the rise and fall of American influence. In the second and third decades of this century, American intervention in Nicaragua, Haiti, and the Dominican Republic produced the freest elections and the most open political competition in the history of those countries. In these countries, as in others in Central America and the Caribbean, American influence in support of free elections was usually exerted in response to the protests of opposition groups against the repressive actions of their own governments and as a result of American fears that revolution or civil war would occur if significant political and social forces were denied equal opportunity to participate in the political process. The American aim, as Theodore Wright made clear in his comprehensive study, was to "promote political stability by supporting free elections" rather than by strengthening military dictatorships. In its interventions in eight Caribbean and Central American countries between 1900 and 1933 the United States acted on the assumption that "the only way both to prevent revolutions and to determine whether they are justified if they do break out is to guarantee free elections."[29] In Cuba the effect of the Platt Amendment and American interventions was "to pluralize the Cuban political system" by fostering "the rise and entrenchment of opposition groups" and by multiplying "the sources of political power so that no single group, not even the government, could impose its will on society or the economy for very long. . . . The spirit and practices of liberalism—competitive and unregulated political, economic, religious, and social life—overwhelmed a pluralized Cuba."[30] The interventions by United States Marines in Haiti, Nicaragua, the Dominican Republic, and elsewhere in these years often bore striking resemblances to the interventions by federal marshals in the conduct of elections in the American South in the 1960s: registering voters, protecting against electoral violence, ensuring a free vote and an honest count.

Direct intervention by the American government in Central America and the Caribbean came to at least a temporary end in the early 1930s. Without exception the result was a shift in the direction of more dictatorial regimes. It had taken American power to impose even the most modest aspects of democracy in these societies. When American intervention ended, democracy ended. For the Caribbean and Central America, the era of the Good Neighbor was also the era of the bad tyrant. The efforts of the United States to be the former give a variety of unsavory local characters—Trujillo, Somoza, Batista—the opportunity to be the latter.

In the years after World War II, American attention and activity were primarily directed toward Europe and Asia. Latin America was by and large neglected. This situation began to change toward the later 1950s, and it dramatically shifted after Castro's seizure of power in Cuba. In the early 1960s Latin America became the focus of large-scale economic aid programs, military training and assistance programs, propaganda efforts, and repeated attention by the president and other high-level American officials. Under the Alliance for Progress, American power was to be used to promote and sustain democratic government and greater social equity in the rest of the Western Hemisphere. This high point in the exercise of United States power in Latin America coincided with the high point of democracy in Latin America. This period witnessed the Twilight of the Tyrants: it was the age in which at one point all but one of the ten South American countries (Paraguay) had some semblance of democratic government.[31]

Obviously the greater prevalence of democratic regimes during these years was not exclusively a product of United States policy and power. Yet the latter certainly played a role. The democratic governments that had emerged in Colombia and Venezuela in the late 1950s were carefully nurtured with money and praise. Strenuous efforts were made to head off the attempts of both left-wing guerrillas and right-wing military officers to overthrow Betancourt in Venezuela and to ensure the orderly transition to an elected successor for the first time in the history of that country. After thirty years in which "the U.S. government was less interested and involved in Dominican affairs" than at any other time in history—a period coinciding with Trujillo's domination of the Dominican Republic—American opposition to that dictator slowly mounted in the late 1950s. After his assassination in 1961 "the United States engaged in the most massive intervention in the internal affairs of a Latin American state since the inauguration of the Good Neighbor Policy."[32] The United States prevented a return to power by Trujillo's family members, launched programs to promote economic and social welfare, and acted to ensure democratic liberties and competitive elections. The latter, held in December 1962, resulted in the election of Juan Bosch as president. When the military moved against Bosch the following year, American officials first tried to head off the coup and then, after its success, attempted to induce the junta to return quickly to constitutional procedures. But by that point American "leverage and influence [with the new government] were severely limited," and the only concession the United States was able to exact in return for recognition was a promise to hold elections in 1965.[33]

Following the military coup in Peru in July 1962, the United States was able to use its power more effectively to bring about a return to democratic government. The American ambassador was recalled; diplomatic relations were suspended; and $81 million in aid was canceled. Nine other Latin American countries were induced to break relations with the military junta—an achievement that could only have occurred at a time when the United States seemed to be poised on the brink of dispensing billions of dollars of largesse about the continent.[34] The result was that new elections were held the following year, and Belaunde was freely chosen president. Six years later, however, when Belaunde was overthrown by a coup, the United States was in no position to reverse the coup or even to prevent the military government that came to power from nationalizing major property holdings of American nationals. The power and the will that had been there in the early 1960s had evaporated by the late 1960s, and with it the possibility of holding Peru to a democratic path. Through a somewhat more complex process, a decline in the American role also helped produce similar results in Chile. In the 1964 Chilean elections, the United States exerted all the influence it could on behalf of Eduardo Frei and made a significant and possibly decisive contribution to his defeat of Salvador Allende. In the 1970 election, the American government did not make any comparable effort to defeat Allende, who won the popular election by a narrow margin. At that point, the United States tried to induce the Chilean Congress to refuse to confirm his victory and to promote a military coup to prevent him from taking office. Both these efforts violated the norms of Chilean politics and American morality, and both were unsuccessful. If on the other hand the United States had been as active in the popular election of 1970 as it had been in that of 1964, the destruction of Chilean democracy in 1973 might have been avoided.

All in all the decline in the role of the United States in Latin America in the late 1960s and early 1970s coincided with the spread of authoritarian regimes in that area. With this decline went a decline in the standards of democratic morality and human rights that the United States could attempt to apply to the governments of the region. In the early 1960s in Latin America (as in the 1910s and 1920s in the Caribbean and Central America), the goal of the United States was democratic competition and free elections. By the mid-1970s that goal had been lowered from the fostering of democratic government to attempting to induce authoritarian governments not to infringe too blatantly on the rights of their citizens.

A similar relationship between American power and democratic government prevailed in Asia. There too the peak of American power was reached in the early and mid-1960s, and there too the decline in this power was followed by a decline in democracy and liberty. American influence had been most pervasive in the Philippines, which for a quarter-century after World War II had the most open, democratic system (apart from Japan) in east and southeast Asia. After the admittedly fraudulent election of 1949 and in the face of the rising threat to the Philippine government posed by the Huk insurgency, American military and economic assistance was greatly increased. Direct American intervention in Philippine politics then played a decisive role not only in promoting Ramon Magsaysay into the presidency but also in assuring that the 1951 congressional elections and 1953 presidential election were open elections "free from fraud and intimidation."[35] In the next three elections the Philippines met the sternest test of democracy: incumbent presidents were defeated for reelection. In subsequent years, however, the American presence and influence in the Philippines declined, and with it one support for Philippine democracy. When President Marcos instituted his martial law regime in 1972, American influence in southeast Asia was clearly on the wane, and the United States held few effective levers with which to affect the course of Philippine politics. In perhaps even more direct fashion, the high point of democracy and political liberty in Vietnam also coincided with the high point of American influence there. The only free national election in the history of that country took place in 1967, when the American military intervention was at its peak. In Vietnam, as in Latin America, American intervention had a pluralizing effect on politics, limiting the government and encouraging and strengthening its political opposition. The defeat of the United States in Vietnam and the exclusion of American power from Indochina were followed in three countries by the imposition of regimes of almost total repression.

The American relationship with South Korea took a similar course. In the late 1940s, under the sponsorship of the United States, U.N.-observed elections inaugurated the government of the Republic of Korea and brought Syngman Rhee to power. During the Korean War (1950–1953) and then in the mid-1950s, when American economic assistance was at its peak, a moderately democratic system was maintained, despite the fact that South Korea was almost literally in a state of siege. In 1956 Rhee won reelection by only a close margin and the opposition party won the vice-presidency and swept the urban centers.

In the late 1950s, however, as American economic assistance to Korea declined, the Rhee regime swung in an increasingly authoritarian direction. The 1960 vice-presidential election was blatantly fraudulent; students and others protested vigorously; and as the army sat on the sidelines, Rhee was forced out of power. A democratic regime under the leadership of John M. Chang came into office but found it difficult to exercise authority and to maintain order. In May 1961 this regime was overthrown by a military coup despite the strong endorsement of the Chang government by the American embassy and military command. During the next two years, the United States exerted sustained pressure on the military government to hold elections and return power to a civilian regime. A bitter struggle took place within the military over this issue; in the end President Park Chung Hee, with American backing and support, overcame the opposition within the military junta, and reasonably open elections were held in October 1963, in which Park was elected president with a 43 percent plurality of the vote. In the struggle with the hard-line groups in the military, one reporter observed, "the prestige and word of the United States have been put to a grinding test"; by insisting on the holding of elections, however, the United States "emerged from this stage of the crisis with a sort of stunned respect from South Koreans for its determination—from those who eagerly backed United States pressures on the military regime and even from officers who were vehemently opposed to it."[36] Thirteen years later, however, the United States was no longer in a position to have the same impact on Korean politics. "You can't talk pure Jefferson to these guys," one American official said. "You've got to have a threat of some kind or they won't listen. . . . There aren't many levers left to pull around here. We just try to keep the civil rights issue before the eyes of Korean authorities on all levels and hope it has some effect."[37] By 1980 American power in Korea had been reduced to the point where there was no question, as there was in 1961 and 1962, of pressuring a new military leadership to hold prompt and fair elections. The issue was simply whether the United States had enough influence to induce the Korean government not to execute Korea's leading opposition political figure, Kim Dae Jung, and even with respect to that, one Korean official observed, "the United States has no leverage."[38] Over the years, as American influence in Korea went down, repression in Korea went up.

The positive impact of American power on liberty in other societies is in part the result of the conscious choices by presidents such as Kennedy and Carter to give high priority to the promotion of democracy and human rights. Even without such conscious choice, however, the presence or exercise of American power in a foreign area usually has a similar thrust. The new moralists of the 1970s maintained that the United States has "no alternative" but to act in terms of the moral and political values that define the essence of its being. The new moralists clearly intended this claim to have at least a normative meaning. But in fact it also describes a historical necessity. Despite the reluctance or inability of those imbued with the myth of American repression to recognize it, the impact of the United States on the world has in large part been what the new moralists say it has to be. The nature of the United States has left it little or no choice but to stand out among nations as the proponent of liberty and democracy. Clearly, the impact of no other country in world affairs has been as heavily weighted in favor of liberty and democracy as has that of the United States.

Power tends to corrupt, and absolute power corrupts absolutely. American power is no exception; clearly it has been used for good purposes and bad in terms of liberty, democracy, and human rights. But also in terms of these values, American power is far less likely to be misused or corrupted than the power of any other major government. This is so for two reasons. First, because American leaders and decision makers are inevitably the products of their culture, they are themselves generally committed to liberal and democratic values. This does not mean that some leaders may not at times take actions that run counter to those values. Obviously this happens: sensibilities are dulled; perceived security needs may dictate other actions; expediency prevails; the immediate end justifies setting aside the larger purpose. But American policy makers are more likely than those of any other country to be sensitive to these trade-offs and to be more reluctant to sacrifice liberal–democratic values. Second, the institutional pluralism and dispersion of power in the American political system impose constraints—unmatched in any other society—on the ability of officials to abuse power and also to ensure that those transgressions that do occur will almost inevitably become public knowledge. The American press is extraordinarily free, strong, and vigorous in its exposure of bad policies and corrupt officials. The American Congress has powers of investigation, legislation, and financial control unequaled by any other national legislature. The ability of American officials to violate the values of their society is therefore highly limited, and the extent to which the press is filled with accounts of how officials have violated those values is evidence not that such behavior is more widespread than it is in other societies but that it is less tolerated than in other societies. The belief that the United States can do no wrong in terms of the values of liberty and democracy is clearly as erroneous abroad as it is at home. But so, alas, is the belief— far more prevalent in American intellectual circles in the 1970s—that the United States could never do right in terms of those values. American power is far more likely to be used to support those values than to counter them, and it is far more likely to be employed on behalf of those values than is the power of any other major country.

The point is often made that there is a direct relation between the health of liberty in the United States and the health of liberty in other societies. Disease in one is likely to infect the other. Thus, on the one hand, Richard Ullman argued that "the quality of political life in the United States is indeed affected by the quality of political life in other societies. The extinction of political liberties in Chile, or their extension in Portugal or Czechoslovakia, has a subtle but nonetheless important effect on political liberties within the United States." Conversely, he also goes on to say, "just as the level of political freedom in other societies affects our own society, so the quality of our own political life has an important impact abroad."[39] This particular point is often elaborated into what is sometimes referred to as the clean hands doctrine—that the United States cannot effectively promote liberty in other countries so long as there are significant violations of liberty within its borders. Let the United States rely on the power of example and "first put our house in order," as Hoffmann phrased it. "Like charity, well-ordered crusades begin at home."[40]

Both these arguments—that of the corrupting environment and that of the shining example—are partial truths. By any observable measure the state of liberty in countries like Chile or Czechoslovakia has in itself no impact on the state of liberty in the United States. Similarly, foreigners usually recognize what Americans tend to forget—that the United States is the most open, free, and democratic society in the world. Hence any particular improvement in the state of liberty in the United States is unlikely to be seen as having much relevance to their societies. Yet these arguments do have an element of truth in them when one additional variable is added to the equation. This element is power.

The impact that the state of liberty in other societies has on liberty in the United States depends upon the power of those other societies and their ability to exercise that power with respect to the United States. What happens in Chile or even Czechoslovakia does not affect the state of liberty in the United States because those are small, weak, and distant countries. But the disappearance of liberty in Britain or France or Japan would have consequences for the health of liberty in the United States, because they are large and important countries intimately involved with the United States. Conversely, the impact of the state of liberty in the United States on other societies depends not upon changes in American liberty (which foreigners will inevitably view as marginal) but rather upon the power and immediacy of the United States to the country in question. The power of example works only when it is an example of power. If the United States plays a strong, confident, preeminent role on the world stage, other nations will be impressed by its power and will attempt to emulate its liberty in the belief that liberty may be the source of power. This point was made quite persuasively in 1946 by Turkey's future premier, Adnan Menderes, in explaining why his country had to shift to democracy:

> The difficulties encountered during the war years uncovered and showed the weak points created by the one-party system in the structure of the country. The hope in the miracles of [the] one-party system vanished, as the one-party system countries were defeated everywhere. Thus, the one-party mentality was destroyed in the turmoil of blood and fire of the second World War. No country can remain unaffected by the great international events and the contemporary dominating ideological currents. This influence was felt in our country too.[41]

In short, no one copies a loser.

The future of liberty in the world is thus intimately linked to the future of American power. Yet the double thrust of the new moralism was paradoxically to advocate the expansion of global liberty and simultaneously to effect a reduction in American power. The relative decline in American power in the 1970s has many sources. One of them assuredly was the democratic surge (of which the new moralism was one element) in the United States in the 1960s and early 1970s. The strong recommitment to democratic, liberal, and populist values that occurred during these years eventually generated efforts to limit, constrain, and reduce American military, political, and economic power abroad. The intense and sustained attacks by the media, by intellectuals, and by congressmen on the military establishment, intelligence agencies, diplomatic officials, and political leadership of the United States inevitably had that effect. The decline in American power abroad weakened the support for liberty and democracy abroad. American democracy and foreign democracy may be inversely related. Due to the mediating effects of power their relationship appears to be just the opposite of that hypothesized by Ullman.

The promotion of liberty abroad thus requires the expansion of American power; the operation of liberty at home involves the limitation of American power. The need in attempting to achieve democratic goals both abroad and at home is to recognize the existence of this contradiction and to assess the trade-offs between these two goals. There is, for instance, an inherent contradiction between welcoming the end of American hegemony in the Western Hemisphere and at the same time deploring the intensification of repression in Latin America. It is also paradoxical that in the 1970s those congressmen who were most insistent on the need to promote human rights abroad were often most active in reducing the American power that could help achieve that result. In key votes in the Ninety-fourth Congress, for instance, 132 congressmen consistently voted in favor of human rights amendments to foreign aid legislation. Seventy-eight of those 132 representatives also consistently voted against a larger military establishment, and another 28 consistent supporters of human rights split their votes on the military establishment. Only 26 of the 132 congressmen consistently voted in favor of both human rights and the military power whose development could help make those rights a reality.

The new realism of the 1940s and 1950s coincided with the expansion of American power in the world and the resulting expansion of American-sponsored liberty and democracy in the world. The new moralism of the 1970s coincided with the relative decline in American power and the concomitant erosion of liberty and democracy around the globe. By limiting American power the new moralism promoted that decline. In some measure, too, the new moralism was a consequence of the decline. The new moralism's concern with human rights throughout the world clearly reflected the erosion in global liberty and democratic values. Paradoxically, the United States thus became more preoccupied with ways of defending human rights as its power to defend human rights diminished. Enactment of Title IX to the foreign assistance act in 1966, a major congressional effort to promote democratic values abroad, came at the mid-point in the steady decline in American foreign economic assistance. Similarly, the various restrictions that Congress wrote into the foreign assistance acts in the 1970s coincided with the general replacement of military aid by military sales. When American power was clearly predominant, such legislative provisions and caveats were superfluous: no Harkin Amendment was necessary to convey the message of the superiority of liberty. The message was there for all to see in the troop deployments, carrier task forces, foreign-aid missions, and intelligence operatives. When these faded from the scene, in order to promote liberty and human rights Congress found it necessary to write more and more explicit conditions and requirements into legislation. These legislative provisions were in effect an effort to compensate for the decline of American power. In terms of narrowing the ideals-versus-institutions gap abroad, they were no substitute for the presence of American power.

Contrary to the views of both "realists" and "moralists," the contradiction arising from America's role in the world is not primarily that of power and self-interest versus liberty and morality in American foreign policy. It is rather the contradiction between enhancing liberty at home by curbing the power of the American government and enhancing liberty abroad by expanding that power.

THE PROMISE OF DISAPPOINTMENT

The term *American exceptionalism* has been used to refer to a variety of characteristics that have historically distinguished the United States from European societies—characteristics such as its relative lack of economic suffering, social conflict, political trauma, and military defeat. "The standing armies, the monarchies, the aristocracies, the huge debts, the crushing taxation, the old inveterate abuses, which flourish in Europe," William Clarke argued in 1881, "can take no root in the New World. The continent of America is consecrated to simple humanity, and its institutions exist for the progress and happiness of the whole people." Yet, as Henry Fairlie pointed out in 1975, "there now *are* standing armies of America; there now *is* something that, from time to time, looks very like a monarchy; there now *is* a permitted degree of inherited wealth that is creating some of the elements of an aristocracy; there now *is* taxation that is crushing."[42] In the same year Daniel Bell came to a similar conclusion by a different path. The "end of American exceptionalism," he argued, is to be seen in "the end of empire, the weakening of power, the loss of faith in the nation's future. . . . Internal tensions have multiplied and there are deep structural crises, political and cultural, that may prove more intractable to solution than the domestic economic problems."[43]

In the late twentieth century, the United States surely seemed to confront many evils and problems that were common to other societies but that it had previously avoided. These developments, however, affected only the incidental elements of American exceptionalism, those of power, wealth, and security. They did not change American political values and they only intensified the gap between political ideals and political institutions that is crucial to American national identity. They thus did not affect the historically most exceptional aspect of the United States, an aspect eloquently summed up and defended by a Yugoslav dissident.

> The United States is not a state like France, China, England, etc., and it would be a great tragedy if someday the United States became such a state. What is the difference? First of all, the United States is not a national state, but a multinational state. Second, the United States was founded by people who valued individual freedom more highly than their own country.
>
> And so the United States is primarily a state of freedom. And this is what is most important. Whole peoples from other countries can say, Our homeland is Germany, Russia, or whatever; only Americans can say, My homeland is freedom.[44]

Americans have said this throughout their history and have lived throughout their history in the inescapable presence of liberal ideals, semiliberal institutions, and the gap between the two. The United States has no meaning, no identity, no political culture or even history apart from its ideals of liberty and democracy and the continuing efforts of Americans to realize those ideals. Every society has its own distinctive form of tension that characterizes its existence as a society. The tension between liberal ideal and institutional reality is America's distinguishing cleavage. It defines both the agony and the promise of American politics. If that tension disappears, the United States of America as we have known it will no longer exist.

The continued existence of the United States means that Americans will continue to suffer from cognitive dissonance. They will continue to attempt to come to terms with that dissonance through some combination of moralism, cynicism, complacency, and hypocrisy. The greatest danger to the gap between ideals and institutions would come when any substantial portion of the American population carried to an extreme any one of these responses. An excess of moralism, hypocrisy, cynicism, or complacency could destroy the American system. A totally complacent toleration of the ideals-versus-institutions gap could lead to the corruption and decay of American liberal–democratic institutions. Uncritical hypocrisy, blind to the existence of the gap and fervent in its commitment to American principles, could lead to imperialistic expansion, ending in either military or political disaster abroad or the undermining of democracy at home. Cynical acceptance of the gap could lead to a gradual abandonment of American ideals and their replacement either by a Thrasymachusian might-makes-right morality or by some other set of political beliefs. Finally, intense moralism could lead Americans to destroy the freest institutions on earth because they believed they deserved something better.

To maintain their ideals and institutions, Americans have no recourse but to temper and balance their responses to the gap between the two. The threats to the future of the American condition can be reduced to the extent that Americans:

- continue to believe in their liberal, democratic, and individualistic ideals and also recognize the extent to which their institutions and behavior fall short of these ideals;
- feel guilty about the existence of the gap but take comfort from the fact that American political institutions are more liberal and democratic than those of any other human society past or present;
- attempt to reduce the gap between institutions and ideals but accept the fact that the imperfections of human nature mean the gap can never be eliminated;
- believe in the universal validity of American ideals but also understand their limited applicability to other societies;
- support the maintenance of American power necessary to protect and promote liberal ideals and institutions in the world arena, but recognize the dangers such power could pose to liberal ideals and institutions at home.

Critics say that America is a lie because its reality falls so far short of its ideals. They are wrong. America is not a lie; it is a disappointment. But it can be a disappointment only because it is also a hope.

NOTES

1. Richard Hofstadter, *The American Political Tradition* (New York: Alfred A. Knopf, 1951), pp. 65–66.
2. Marvin Meyers, *The Jacksonian Persuasion: Politics and Belief* (Stanford, Calif.: Stanford University Press, 1957), p. 8.

3. See Edward Pessen, "The Egalitarian Myth and the American Social Reality: Wealth, Mobility, and Equality in the 'Era of the Common Man,'" *American Historical Review* 76 (October 1971): 989–1034, and idem, *Riches, Class, and Power before the Civil War* (Lexington, Mass.: D. C. Heath, 1973). For critical discussions of Pessen's evidence and argument see Whitman Ridgway, "Measuring Wealth and Power in Ante-Bellum America: A Review Essay," *Historical Methods Newsletter* 8 (March 1975): 74–78, and Robert E. Gallman, "Professor Pessen on the 'Egalitarian Myth,'" *Social Science History* 2 (Winter 1978): 194–207. For Pessen's response, see his "On a Recent Cliometric Attempt to Resurrect the Myth of Antebellum Egalitarianism," *Social Science History* 3 (Winter 1979): 208–27.

4. Gordon S. Wood, *History Book Club Review* (June 1975): 16–17, commenting on Rush Welter's, *The Mind of America: 1820–1860* (New York: Columbia University Press, 1975).

5. Welter, *The Mind of America: 1820–1860*, pp. 7–10.

6. Alexis de Tocqueville, *Democracy in America,* 2 vols., ed. Phillips Bradley (New York: Vintage Books, 1954), 1:6–17.

7. Joseph L. Blau, ed., *Social Theories of Jacksonian Democracy* (New York: Liberal Arts Press, 1954), pp. xxvii–xxviii.

8. Hofstadter, *American Political Tradition,* p. vi.

9. Herbert Croly, *The Promise of American Life* (New York: Macmillan, 1909), p. 156; and Walter Lippmann, *Drift and Mastery* (Englewood Cliffs, N.J.: Prentice-Hall, 1961), pp. 81–82.

10. Hofstadter, *American Political Tradition,* p. 223.

11. J. R. Pole, *The Pursuit of Equality in American History* (Berkeley: University of California Press, 1978), p. 326.

12. See Ronald Inglehart, *The Silent Revolution: Changing Values and Political Styles among Western Publics* (Princeton, N.J.: Princeton University Press, 1977), and George C. Lodge, *The New American Ideology* (New York: Alfred A. Knopf, 1975).

13. Ronald Inglehart, "The Silent Revolution in Europe: Intergenerational Change in Post-Industrial Societies," *American Political Science Review* 65 (December 1971): 991–1017.

14. Samuel P. Huntington, "Postindustrial Politics: How Benign Will It Be?" *Comparative Politics* 6 (January 1974): 188–89.

15. Plato, *The Republic,* trans. Francis MacDonald Cornford (New York: Oxford University Press, 1945), p. 290.

16. Louis Hartz, *The Liberal Tradition in America* (New York: Harcourt, Brace, 1955), p. 181.

17. Samuel P. Huntington, *Political Order in Changing Societies* (New Haven, Conn.: Yale University Press, 1968), pp. 362–69.

18. See Samuel P. Huntington, *The Soldier and the State: The Theory and Politics of Civil-Military Relations* (Cambridge: Harvard University Press, 1957), esp. pp. 143–57.

19. George F. Kennan, *American Diplomacy 1900–1950* (Chicago, Ill.: University of Chicago Press, 1951), pp. 93–94; and Huntington, *The Soldier and the State,* pp. 80–97.

20. Lucian W. Pye, *The Spirit of Chinese Politics* (Cambridge, Mass.: MIT Press, 1968), p. 91.

21. Seymour Martin Lipset, "The Banality of Revolt," *Saturday Review,* 18 July 1970, p. 26.

22. Peregrine Worsthorne, "America—Conscience or Shield?" *Encounter,* no. 14 (November 1954): 5.

23. Henry Fairlie, "Anti-Americanism at Home and Abroad," *Commentary* 60 (December 1975): 35.

24. See for example Hans J. Morgenthau, *In Defense of the National Interest* (New York: Alfred A. Knopf, 1951), and idem, "Another 'Great Debate': The National Interest of the United States," *American Political Science Review* 46 (December 1952): 961–88; Reinhold Niebuhr, *Christian Realism and Political Problems* (New York: Charles Scribner's Sons, 1953), and idem, *The Irony of American History* (New York: Charles Scribner's Sons, 1952); Kennan, *American Diplomacy 1900–1950;* Robert E. Osgood, *Ideals and Self-Interest in America's Foreign Relations* (Chicago, Ill.: University of Chicago

Press, 1953); and Richard H. Ullman, "Washington versus Wilson," *Foreign Policy,* no. 21 (Winter 1975–76): 97–124.

25. Henry A. Kissinger, quoted in Raymond Gastil, "Affirming American Ideals in Foreign Policy," *Freedom at Issue,* no. 38 (November–December 1976):12.

26. Jimmy Carter, address, B'nai B'rith convention, Washington, D.C., 8 September 1976.

27. Hans J. Morgenthau, "Repression's Friend," *New York Times,* 10 October 1974.

28. See John D. Montgomery, *Forced To Be Free: The Artificial Revolution in Germany and Japan* (Chicago, Ill.: University of Chicago Press, 1957).

29. Theodore P. Wright, *American Support of Free Elections Abroad* (Washington, D.C.: Public Affairs Press, 1964), pp. 137–38.

30. Jorge I. Dominguez, *Cuba: Order and Revolution* (Cambridge: Harvard University Press, 1978), p. 13.

31. See Tad Szulc, *The Twilight of the Tyrants* (New York: Henry Holt, 1959).

32. Jerome Slater, *Intervention and Negotiation* (New York: Harper & Row, 1970), p. 7.

33. Abraham F. Lowenthal, *The Dominican Intervention* (Cambridge: Harvard University Press, 1972), p. 16.

34. Jerome Levinson and Juan de Onis, *The Alliance that Lost Its Way* (Chicago, Ill.: Quadrangle Books, 1970), pp. 81–82.

35. H. Bradford Westerfield, *The Instruments of America's Foreign Policy* (New York: Thomas Y. Crowell, 1963), p. 416.

36. A. M. Rosenthal, *New York Times,* 8 April 1963.

37. Quoted by Andrew H. Malcolm, *New York Times,* 11 June 1976.

38. *The Economist,* 30 August 1980, pp. 27–28.

39. Ullman, "Washington versus Wilson," pp. 117, 123.

40. Stanley Hoffmann, "No Choice, No Illusions," *Foreign Policy,* no. 25 (Winter 1976–77): 127.

41. Adnan Menderes, *Cumhuriyef,* 18 July 1946, quoted in Kemal H. Karpat, *Turkey's Politics* (Princeton, N.J.: Princeton University Press, 1959), p. 140, n. 10.

42. Fairlie, "Anti-Americanism at Home and Abroad," p. 34, quoting William Clarke, 1881.

43. Daniel Bell, "The End of American Exceptionalism," in *The American Commonwealth 1976,* eds. Nathan Glazer and Irving Kristol (New York: Basic Books, 1976), p. 197.

44. Mihajlo Mihajlov, "Prospects for the Post-Tito Era," *New America* 17 (January 1980): 7.

꙳ᴥ

The United States Political System and International Leadership: A "Decidedly Inferior" Form of Government?

Michael Mastanduno

INTRODUCTION: THE DEMOCRATIC DILEMMA

The framers of the U.S. Constitution created, by conscious design, a constrained government. They were more concerned to avoid the abuse of political power than to create circumstances under which it could be easily exercised. Thus, instead of concentrating power they sought to disperse it, and created the familiar system of "checks and balances" to assure that no part of government accumulated enough influence to threaten the integrity of democracy.

Foreign policy did not constitute an exception to this principle, and the framers assured that the Executive and Congress shared power and decision-making authority. Indeed, in enumerating the powers of each branch they were arguably more generous to the legislature than to the president. On the crucial issue of war-making authority, for example, the president was named Commander-in-Chief, but Congress was given the authority to raise and support an army, provide and maintain a navy, and most importantly, to commit the nation to armed struggle by declaring war. The president, with the advice and consent of the Senate, was granted appointment and treaty-making powers. However, the all-important power to collect taxes and appropriate funds was given to the Congress, as was the equally crucial authority to regulate the commerce of the United States with other countries.

The design of a constrained government and the sharing of foreign policy authority created a dilemma, the core of which remains with the United States to this day. On the one hand, the dispersal of political power has the *internal advantage* of helping to promote and protect American democracy. On the other hand, the dispersal of power has an *external disadvantage*, in that it poses a potential constraint on the ability of the United States to conduct effective foreign policy.[1] To survive or flourish in an international system characterized by anarchy, or the lack of a central governing authority, often requires speed, secrecy, and decisiveness in foreign policy decision-making. Governments must be able to seize opportunities, respond to threats and challenges, and make and honor commitments. They must pursue a set of core objectives with consistency, and at the same time manage conflicts among these objectives,

Michael Mastanduno, "The United States Political System and International Leadership: A 'Decidedly Inferior' Form of Government?" Paper prepared for background and discussion at the Dartmouth College-International House of Japan Conference. "The United States and Japan on the Eve of the 21st Century: Prospects for Joint Leadership," held at Dartmouth College, June 27–29, 1994. Reprinted with permission.

make tactical compromises where necessary, and adjust to changing international circumstances. These qualities are more likely to be maximized in more centralized, rather than decentralized, political systems. Alexis de Tocqueville, in his classic appraisal of the United States, recognized this dilemma in concluding that "especially in their conduct of foreign relations, democracies appear to me decidedly inferior to other governments." They "obey impulse rather than prudence," have a propensity to "abandon a mature design for the gratification of a momentary passion," and in general are deficient in the qualities demanded by effective foreign policy.[2]

America's early statesmen were similarly cognizant of the so-called democratic dilemma, and they found a way to resolve it in the *substance* of U.S. foreign policy. By adopting an isolationist foreign policy, they reasoned, the internal benefits of democratic governance would be preserved while the external disadvantages would be minimized. If decentralized, deliberative government handicapped the United States in the age-old game of European power politics, the United States could choose not to play. Geography facilitated and reinforced this choice, since the Atlantic ocean provided a physical barrier that could not be overcome easily by the technologies of the day. The classic statement of the new nation's strategy was articulated by Washington in his Farewell Address, as he admonished his fellow citizens to "steer clear of permanent alliances" and counseled that "[t]he great rule of conduct for us in regard to foreign nations is . . . to have with them as little *political* connection as possible."[3]

The isolationist solution to the democratic dilemma was feasible for over one hundred years, but by the early part of the twentieth century, as U.S. economic power and political influence increased rapidly, strains were apparent. A return to isolationism following U.S. involvement in World War I resulted in an unmitigated disaster for world politics and the global economy. U.S. officials drew the appropriate lessons, and following World War II they abandoned isolationism and sought to exercise international leadership.[4] In the postwar era, U.S. officials were forced to confront directly the dilemma that had been so deftly avoided in earlier times.

DOMESTIC CONSTRAINTS AND U.S. LEADERSHIP

The view that the U.S. political system is "decidedly inferior," or a significant constraint on the ability of the United States to lead internationally approaches conventional wisdom among students and practitioners of U.S. foreign policy. George Kennan once made an unflattering comparison between the foreign policy of American democracy and the behavior of a dinosaur with a huge body and pin-sized brain: the beast is slow to rouse, but when it finally recognizes threats to its interests, it flails about indiscriminantly, wrecking its native habitat while attempting to destroy its adversary.[5] Theodore Lowi has claimed that America's decentralized decision-making system creates incentives for leaders to adopt foreign policy strategies that compromise effectiveness, such as the inflation of foreign policy threats and the "overselling" of foreign policy opportunities. He argues that the domestic political system is an "anachronism in foreign affairs," and that it is "the system itself that has so often made our international relations so inimical to our own best interests."[6] In the context of international political economy, Stephen Krasner has popularized the conception of the United States as a "weak state" whose domestic institutions placed it at a considerable disadvantage in the conduct of commercial diplomacy—a disadvantage only offset by the fact that the United States has been extraordinarily powerful internationally.[7] In a 1984 book entitled *Our Own Worst Enemy*, I. M. Destler, Leslie Gelb, and (current Clinton National Security Advisor) Anthony Lake contended that "not only our government but our whole society has been undergoing a systemic breakdown when attempting to foster a coherent, consistent approach to the world."[8] More recently, the distinguished columnist David Broder, reflecting on the first year experience of the Clinton administration, argued that the "decayed condition of our vital institutions" has "damaged the capacity of our system to develop and sustain coherent policy."[9]

What is it about the U.S. political system that so handicaps foreign policy and international leadership? The answer is found in an analysis of the relationship between Executive and Congress: of the institutions of and relationships within the Executive: and of the role played by interest groups and the media in the foreign policy process.

Executive vs. Congress

The power-sharing arrangements stipulated by the U.S. Constitution invite the president and Congress to conduct an ongoing struggle over the control of foreign policy. For the first two decades after World War II, however, that struggle was held in abeyance. The two branches worked out an arrangement in which Congress delegated authority and deferred politically to the Executive, on the grounds that only the presidency possessed the institutional resources, intelligence capability, and decision-making qualities—speed, steadiness, resolve, and flexibility—required to conduct the cold war effectively and lead a global coalition in the struggle against the Soviet Union and communism. The eagerness of Congress to defer might also be attributed to its desire to atone for its contributions to the foreign policy disasters of the interwar period, such as the Smoot-Hawley tariff and the failure of the Versailles Treaty and the League of Nations. In any event, Congress took a secondary and in some cases peripheral role as presidents confronted the Soviet Union in a series of cold war crises, intervened covertly and overtly in the third world, and enmeshed the United States in an array of entangling alliances around the globe. In commercial policy, Congress delegated tariff-cutting authority to the president and passed export control legislation enabling him to restrict trade to any destination for reasons of national security or foreign policy. The great symbol of congressional acquiescence was the Tonkin Gulf Resolution of 1964, which President Johnson took as a green light to expand dramatically America's role in the Vietnam war.

The Vietnam experience shattered this interbranch arrangement and renewed the foreign policy struggle. Out of that debacle emerged the "new" Congress of the 1970s, 1980s, and 1990s—a Congress that was more assertive politically, less inclined to defer to an "imperial" presidency that had squandered U.S. international leadership, and in possession of greater resources and expertise in foreign affairs. Members of Congress have sought to reclaim or expand their authority over the direct use of force, covert intervention, weapons sales, intelligence oversight, trade policy, economic and security assistance, and numerous other aspects of the substance and process of foreign policy. They have increased the size of their personal and committee staffs and have strengthened the capacity of and their reliance upon collective resources such as the General Accounting Office, Congressional Budget Office, and Office of Technology Assessment. Members of Congress are now less reliant on the Executive for sources of foreign policy information and expertise, and possess the administrative resources to facilitate involvement—and potentially to contest the Executive—across a range of foreign policy issues.

Unfortunately, the new Congress has become less coherent institutionally as it has become more assertive. Reforms undertaken in the aftermath of Watergate and Vietnam created greater decentralization, with less emphasis on seniority and with the erosion of committee discipline. As a result, there are now 535 would-be secretaries of state (or commerce, or defense), each with more resources and political influence at his or her disposal. At the same time, these representatives remain beholden to their local constituencies and retain their tendency to approach foreign affairs from a more parochial, as opposed to national, perspective. In short, the Executive shares power with a Congress whose individual members demand and play a greater role in foreign policy, but without necessarily coordinating their initiatives or framing them in terms of a consistent national strategy. As a former member of the Senate, John Tower, has noted, "Five hundred and thirty-five Congressmen with different philosophies, regional interests, and objectives in mind cannot forge a unified foreign policy that reflects the interests of the United States as a whole."[10]

There are numerous examples of the Executive and newly-assertive Congress working at cross-purposes, to the detriment of coherent foreign policy and effective international leadership. With the passage of the Jackson–Vanik Amendment to the Trade Act of 1974, Congress made its mark on foreign policy by linking most-favored-nation (MFN) status to the human rights practices of communist countries. Unfortunately, the Nixon administration had already completed a trade agreement with the Soviet Union and committed itself to granting MFN without any explicit human rights conditions attached. The Amendment made the United States appear unreliable, and helped to destroy the detente strategy of Nixon and Kissinger.[11] Congress and the Executive clashed later in the decade over the SALT II Treaty, and once again the United States came across as an unreliable negotiating partner.

During the 1980s, the Reagan administration and Congress could not agree on the utility or desirability of aiding the Nicaraguan contras. The result was incoherent policy and the sending of mixed signals to allies and adversaries. The administration's foreign policy was ultimately driven into crisis as executive officials sought in frustration and poor judgment to evade congressional prohibitions through extra-legal means. In trade policy, the exposure of members of Congress to protectionist interests and their tendency to blame foreigners for the U.S. trade deficit led to initiatives—most notably the Super 301 provision of the Omnibus Trade and Competitiveness Act of 1988—that significantly complicated the task of the Executive as it attempted to move forward multilateral negotiations to liberalize international trade.[12]

Relations Within the Executive

One important reason the Executive is presumed to enjoy a "comparative advantage" over the Congress in the conduct of foreign policy is that the president has at his disposal an enormous bureaucratic machine to assist in the formulation and implementation of policy. The foreign policy bureaucracy was expanded greatly after World War II to provide the necessary resources and expertise to wage the cold war. State Department personnel multiplied in Washington and abroad, and the National Security Act of 1947 led to the development of parallel institutions—a permanent Department of Defense led by civilians, and a centralized intelligence establishment under the direction of the CIA.[13] In addition, postwar presidents could draw upon the foreign policy resources of the Commerce Department, the Treasury, the Department of Labor, the Office of the U.S. Trade Representative, and numerous other more specialized offices and agencies.

This very structure that provides advantages, however, also poses a potential constraint on foreign policy. Bureaucracies obviously are not passive instruments; they develop and defend their own institutional interests. Their interests come into conflict because they share jurisdiction over so many areas of U.S. foreign policy, and not surprisingly they compete with each other to control the agenda and the substance of policy. In the absence of central direction, the result is often stalemate or vacillation in foreign policy. The turbulent postwar history of U.S. export control policy, in which the Defense, Commerce, and State Departments have struggled over whether to liberalize or restrict trade in advanced technology often without clear guidance from the White House serves as an apt example.[14]

The president obviously needs to control and coordinate the various parts of the foreign policy bureaucracy, and in 1947 Congress provided the institutional means through the creation of the National Security Council (NSC). Eventually, this solution created new problems, as the staff of the NSC transcended its coordinating role and became yet another combatant in the inter-agency struggle to control foreign policy. This process began with President Kennedy, who desired an activist National Security Advisor to offset the inherent incrementalism of the State Department, and reached its zenith under President Nixon, whose National Security Advisor Henry Kissinger sought to neutralize the State Department and to run foreign policy directly from the White House with the assistance of a small staff.[15] The Nixon-Kissinger system produced significant accomplishments—the opening to China, detente with the Soviet Union, extrication from the Vietnam war—but also caused significant problems. Important issues were left unattended until they reached crisis proportions (e.g., international economic policy and the eventual "Nixon shocks" of August 1971), and the overall foreign policy was difficult to legitimate since much of it was conducted in behind-the-scenes negotiations by officials who were neither elected by the public nor accountable to members of Congress.[16]

The problem took a new form during the 1970s and 1980s, as secretaries of state and national security advisors battled to control U.S. foreign policy. During the Carter administration, Cyrus Vance and Zbigniew Brzezinski clashed over arms control, human rights, and policy towards Africa. Their debates were often public, exacerbating the incoherence and lack of direction in U.S. policy. During the Reagan administration, Alexander Haig and William Clark engaged in similar struggles over intervention in Lebanon and the U.S. response to energy trade between the Soviet Union and Western Europe. Although public conflict between the State Department and White House was more muted during Reagan's second term, the NSC staff contributed prominently to the turmoil in U.S. foreign policy created by the Iran-Contra initiatives. Congressional and other critics expressed concern that the NSC staff had moved beyond its traditional coordinating function and had usurped "operational control" of U.S. policy from other executive departments. In fact, the Reagan NSC was continuing, in more extreme fashion, the tradition of NSC control established during the Kennedy administration.[17]

The overall point should be clear. The Executive has been plagued to a significant degree by the same institutional weaknesses attributed to Congress—parochial interests, decentralization, and the lack of effective coordination. Even in the absence of congressional "interference," foreign policy by the Executive may tend to lack consistency or direction. With both branches engaged, the problems are multiplied.

The difficulties raised by the NSC in security policy are also found in foreign economic policy. There, too, interagency struggles are commonplace, usually involving the Departments of State, Treasury, Commerce, and Labor, the Council of Economic Advisors (CEA), the Office of Management and Budget, and several other agencies. The Office of the U.S. Trade

Representative (USTR), lodged within the White House, takes on the job of coordinating agency positions and interests in trade policy. Like the NSC, however, USTR is a player as well as a coordinator, with its own set of institutional interests. USTR officials have clashed in recent years with their counterparts in Treasury over the Europe 1992 project, and with officials at the State Department, CEA, and OMB over U.S. trade policy toward Japan.

Two other issues that bear on the ability of the Executive to conduct effective foreign policy are worthy of note. First, although U.S. economic policy and security policy are each plagued by problems of coordination, the problems are far more profound when one considers the need for coordination *across* the two types of policies. As Destler has argued, the economic and security decision-making "complexes" within the executive are self-contained units and almost totally separate from each other in their day to day operations.[18] A President who focuses on one side of the foreign policy house may find it difficult to master or mobilize effectively the bureaucracy on the other side. Bill Clinton has devoted considerable energies to economic policy, and his foreign policy has been criticized as half-hearted, incoherent, and lacking in leadership.[19] In contrast, George Bush sought to master security policy, and often found himself handcuffed in economic policy—as demonstrated by this ill-fated trip to Japan in January 1992.

Issues that fall at the intersection of the two policy complexes are often handled poorly. The FSX dispute provides a clear example: the security complex (the State and Defense Departments) negotiated that agreement with Japan in isolation from the economic complex (the Commerce Department and USTR). The former believed the agreement was in the national security interest, while the latter saw it as violating the national economic interest. The resulting bureaucratic battle and decision to reconsider the agreement left America's most important Pacific ally to question the reliability and credibility of its alliance partner. In post-cold war foreign policy, as economic and security issues becoming increasingly intertwined and the United States grows more concerned about "economic security," the institutional divide between the two spheres of policy-making is likely to prove more troublesome. The latest institutional innovation—Clinton's creation of a National Economic Council to mirror the National Security Council and to coordinate economic policy—may reinforce rather than rectify the divide.

Second, the U.S. government has appropriately been called a "government of strangers."[20] The political appointments of each new administration reach far down into the executive bureaucracy. Although this has the advantage of enabling a new administration to put a distinctive stamp on policy, it leaves the United States with a deficit in experience and institutional memory, particularly in contrast to states characterized by "permanent government" such as Japan. Former U.S. negotiators often lament the disadvantage posed to U.S. commercial diplomacy by the fact that Japanese (and other negotiators) often have greater experience and knowledge of the United States than U.S. officials have of foreign countries.[21]

Interest Groups and the Media

Not only is the U.S. government fragmented and decentralized: it also affords ready access to private actors seeking to manipulate government policy to serve their particular interests. If, for government officials, the rule of bureaucratic politics is "where you stand depends on where you sit," the rule of interest group politics is "which way you lean depends on who is pushing you." A former U.S. Senator, Charles Mathias, noted recently in an assessment of U.S. Middle East policy that "as a result of the activities of the [Israeli] lobby,

Congressional conviction has been measurably reinforced by the knowledge that political sanctions will be applied to any who fail to deliver."[22]

Interest groups hoping to influence U.S. foreign policy have a variety of channels through which to exert political pressure. They can "push" on members of the House and Senate, on the White House, and on the different agencies of the Executive. The decentralized structure also enables interest groups to play off one branch of government or agency against another, and thereby enhance their potential influence. This point has not been lost on U.S. firms seeking protection or market access abroad—the rule is if the State Department is unsympathetic, try Commerce or USTR; if the Executive as a whole is unresponsive, try the Congress, which may be able to solve your problem by itself, or at least can help to pressure the executive. In trade with Japan, the dogged determination of firms such as Motorola or Toys R Us to "work the system" has been rewarded by special negotiating efforts by U.S. government officials to achieve market access.

The U.S. government often responds more readily to principles that pragmatism, and thus the more powerful or skillful interest groups, can "capture" foreign policy by appealing to broad principles that transcend their narrow self-interest. During the cold war, firms frequently exploited the fear of communism to prod the government to use foreign policy to serve their corporate interests. The interventions in Guatemala in 1954 and Iran in 1953, in the interest of United Fruit and U.S. oil companies, respectively, serve as prominent examples.[23] Others have appealed more recently to "national security" or "fair trade" to bolster their case for protection or special treatment. The machine tool industry's efforts were rewarded by the Reagan administration's negotiation of a voluntary restraint agreement in 1986, and in that same year the semiconductor industry obtained a commitment to market access through the by now infamous U.S.–Japan Semiconductor Arrangement.

Interest groups do not always push in the same direction, and, since the government tends to be receptive, the result can be immobility or stalemate in foreign policy. Jeff Frieden has traced the ambivalence of the United States government toward international economic leadership during the interwar years to the conflict at the societal level between nationalist and internationalist coalitions.[24] Domestically-oriented industry and agriculture "captured" Congress and the Commerce Department, while internationally-oriented industry and finance held sway over the State and Treasury Departments. U.S. foreign policy, reflecting the industry group struggle, bounced back and forth incoherently between engagement and insularity. A similar problem appears to have plagued the Clinton administration's China policy prior to the May 1994 decision to delink trade and human rights. While Secretary of State Christopher lectured the Chinese on their human rights practices, high Commerce officials and large U.S. firms such as General Electric and AT&T conducted their own diplomacy to strengthen economic ties. Industry officials complained publicly that their economic interests were being jeopardized by the State Department, while State contended that its credibility and leverage as an enforcer of U.S. human rights principles had been undermined by the activities of Commerce and U.S. firms. The United States failed to speak with one voice, affording China the opportunity to exploit the divisions.[25]

It is important to note that access to the U.S. political system is readily available not only to domestic groups, but to *foreign* interest groups and governments as well. Foreign lobbying, of course, takes place in all countries and is a standard feature of international relations. The U.S. system is distinctive, however, in that it is especially accommodating to foreign influence. The same multiple channels of influence that are open to domestic groups are open to foreigners as well. And, since political appointments penetrate deeply into the government structure and high officials frequently stay in government for short periods of time and then return to lucrative careers in the private sector, there is a readily available stream of influential individuals for hire by foreign (as well as domestic) interests.

Over the past several years, as U.S.–Japanese economic frictions have intensified, Japanese lobbying efforts in the United States have become particularly contentious. Critics contend that Japanese firms and foundations have undertaken a systematic financial campaign to tip the U.S. political debate in a direction more sympathetic to Japan's point of view, by generously endowing universities and think tanks, and by hiring influential former officials of the U.S. government.[26] There is ample evidence to support this view of a Japanese corporate effort: whether and to what extent that effort has been successful is less certain. Where Japanese firms have succeeded (e.g., in the Toshiba incident of 1987, or in keeping semiconductors off the Super 301 list in 1989), they have done so not by overturning a U.S. consensus on their own, but by throwing support behind one side or another in an on-going U.S. political debate either within the U.S. Executive or between the Executive and Congress.[27] This reinforces the main point—the decentralized and fragmented U.S. system allows ready access to powerful and skilled interest groups, whether they be domestic or foreign.

Like the role of Congress, the role of the *media* in foreign policy was affected profoundly by Vietnam and Watergate. Prior to those events, the media tended to act as a conduit for the executive's foreign policy by interpreting, amplifying, and often supporting official positions. After Vietnam, it became far more assertive and adversarial. Some argue that the media played a dominant role in the war itself, in that its critical stance helped to turn the U.S. public against the war effort.[28]

The new, more assertive media, like the new Congress, helps to preserve the integrity of American democracy. It provides a check on the imperial tendencies of the presidency by subjecting official policy to critical scrutiny and by assuring that voices other than that of the president and his inner circle are heard. Yet what is good for democracy may not necessarily be good for foreign policy. Although the media by itself hardly can be held responsible for incoherence in U.S. foreign policy, it clearly exacerbates any lack of coherence by consistently publicizing and dwelling on disputes among high officials and the contradictions and failures of administration policy. As David Broder has noted:

> Reporters are instinctively fight promoters. Consensus-building is not our forte—or our job. Carrying through policy requires sustained effort. The press in all its forms is episodic. We flit from topic to topic. We hate repetition. Our attitude toward institutions is cavalier.[29]

The media do not simply react to official initiatives, but increasingly have the power to help set the foreign policy agenda by shaping the public and official response to foreign events. Television has replaced print as the principal source of news information for Americans, and one consequence, in the words of Lloyd Cutler, is that foreign policy has been placed "on deadline."[30] Government officials react to the pressure of publicity, and the result is often hasty, ill-conceived policies that play to the immediate impulses of the public rather than to the long-term interests of the country. U.S. policy toward Somalia provides a striking example: the Bush administration's last minute decision to send the U.S. military on a humanitarian mission was driven in part by the strong public reaction to the images of starving children conveyed by evening news programs. Similarly, the Clinton administration's subsequent and rather abrupt decision to abandon the military commitment was influenced by the visceral public reaction of outrage to the image of captured U.S. service personnel being dragged through the streets of Mogadishu. At the time, Secretary of State Christopher and other high officials cautioned against conducting "foreign policy by CNN," but that is precisely what the administration seemed to be doing.

LEADERSHIP IN SPITE OF DOMESTIC CONSTRAINTS?

The post-Vietnam Congress is assertive yet ineffective in foreign policy. The Executive has problems coordinating policy even within its own institutional setting, much less with the Congress. Domestic and foreign interest groups have easy access to government and can distort policy to suit their needs. The media prey on the incoherence of it all and distort policy further through their control of the information that reaches the public most quickly and directly.

This institutional landscape poses a forbidding constraint on the exercise of U.S. leadership. Or does it? In this section I argue, contrary to the conventional wisdom, that the extent to which the domestic political system frustrates or constrains U.S. leadership has been significantly exaggerated. First, the overall record of postwar U.S. foreign policy has been reasonably strong in terms of consistency, flexibility, and the ability to achieve major objectives.[31] Second, the record also indicates that the President has the means and capability to manage domestic constraints and minimize their detrimental impact on leadership. Third, the President can actually turn the domestic system into an asset, or source of strength, in the conduct of foreign policy and the exercise of leadership. A final point, made in a concluding section, is that power and purpose are at least as important as the structure of the domestic political system in determining the effectiveness of U.S. leadership.

The Postwar Record

"International leadership" was defined earlier as the ability to develop and sustain foreign policies that significantly affect the structure and substance of international relations and that contribute significantly to the solution of collective problems or the realization of collective opportunities. One way to approach the question of leadership capacity is to examine the performance record of the United States in the era in which it sought to exercise leadership. Notwithstanding the democratic dilemma and constraints of the domestic system, the postwar U.S. record is quite strong. U.S. officials managed to develop and pursue a set of policies that had a profound impact on the international system. They pursued these policies with consistency over an extended period of time and across administrations, and achieved a large measure of success. Moreover, U.S. policy has been flexible in adjusting to changes in the international environment, and in responding to crises that threaten core foreign policy objectives.

An obvious example of a foreign policy pursued with consistency and systemic effect was containment of the Soviet Union. From Kennan's long telegram in 1946 to the collapse of the Berlin Wall in 1989 (and the subsequent collapse of the Soviet Union itself), U.S. officials across nine administrations led the non-communist world in an effort to prevent the expansion of Soviet political and military influence. As Gaddis notes, different administrations may have pursued different "strategies" of containment.[32] Yet all agreed on the priority of the core objective of containment, irrespective of whether the party in power was Democratic or Republican, whether Congress was assertive or acquiescent, or whether the era was pre- or post-Vietnam. Deviations from containment were sometimes initiated but never pursued seriously as policy alternatives. In this category one might place the Eisenhower/Dulles exploration of rollback, the Carter administration's interest in shifting foreign policy from an "East–West" to a "North–South" emphasis, and the Reagan administration's half-hearted attempt at rollback symbolized by the Reagan Doctrine. The basic objective of containment remained intact and for the most part achieved success.

A corollary to containment was the formation and maintenance of a set of security alliances with non-Communist powers. Here, too, U.S. officials pursued a policy consistently over time that had a major impact on the international system. Notwithstanding discontent over burden-sharing, several major crises (e.g., Suez in 1956, the pipeline in 1982), and occasional domestic attempts to reconsider the core policy (e.g., the Mansfield Amendment), America's basic alliance commitments were not called into question, and in fact thus far have outlived the cold war.

Another core, postwar objective of the United States has been the creation and expansion of an open world economy and multilateral trading system. That objective has been pursued across administrations and has been institutionalized in international institutions such as the IMF and the GATT. The United States has remained the prime mover in the GATT as that institution first took on the tariff barriers that developed during the war and depression years, then attacked non-tariff barriers, and most recently has accepted the challenge of bringing excluded sectors and issues (e.g., agriculture, textiles, services) into the multilateral regime. As U.S. power has declined in relative terms, domestic pressure has built for protection and a reconsideration of the GATT commitment. U.S. officials have tried to resist the pressure, have not abandoned GATT, and instead have worked to strengthen its efficacy and credibility.

Other examples of core U.S. foreign policy objectives pursued with consistency and effectiveness might include the maintenance of a "zone of peace" that incorporated the aggressors of the last major war, and decolonization and the integration of less developed countries into the liberal world economy.[33] The main point should be clear—in terms of the main policies and objectives of postwar U.S. leadership, pursued over the long term, the domestic political system did *not* result in uncertainty, incoherence, or vacillation. Either the domestic constraints were modest, or executive officials apparently found ways to overcome them quite consistently.

The U.S. record also indicates a reasonable degree of *flexibility* in responding to structural changes in the global environment. The Nixon administration's opening to China, in the interest of exploiting the Sino–Soviet split, reversed decades of ideological hostility that was deeply embedded in public and elite sentiment. The opening was not a one-shot deal, as the commitment normalizing relations with China has been sustained through the Ford, Carter, Reagan, Bush, and Clinton administrations. Second, when faced during the early decades of the cold war with the choice between support for democracy or for anti-communist authoritarianism, U.S. officials consistently chose the latter. After Vietnam, U.S. officials began to rethink this approach, and gradually a "prodemocracy" emphasis came to replace uncritical support for right-wing dictators as a core foreign policy objective. The end of the cold war obviously has accelerated this development, but the initial thrust was quite apparent in both the Carter and Reagan administrations. In international monetary policy, the United States moved during the 1970s from supporting a fixed to a floating exchange rate system when it was clear (due in large part to America's own economic policies) that the fixed system was no longer viable. With the glaring exception of the first Reagan administration, U.S. officials have sought in the floating system to coordinate exchange rate and macroeconomic policies with other advanced industrial states in order to recapture the stability and predictability in international economic transactions achieved in the era of fixed rates.[34]

Finally, the democratic dilemma suggests that the nature of the domestic political system will make it difficult for the United States to respond with the necessary speed, secrecy, and decisiveness in times of foreign policy crisis. Again, the record suggests otherwise. Whether one considers threats to national security such as the Cuban Missile Crisis, threats to alliance stability such as the Suez crisis of 1956 or the 1973 Middle East war, or threats to international economic stability such as the Mexican debt crisis of 1982 or the extreme pressures for protection that accompanied record U.S. trade deficits during the mid-1980s, the domestic political system did not prevent U.S. officials from responding quickly and decisively to preserve core foreign policy objectives.

Managing Domestic Constraints

An important reason for the strength of the U.S. postwar record is that an administration with a clear sense of foreign policy purpose has the wherewithal to manage and deflect the potentially detrimental constraints of the domestic political system. Administration officials have at their disposal a variety of instruments and techniques. They can mobilize previously uninvolved domestic actors to support their preferred positions on a given issue. They can appeal to national security and exploit the "rally around the flag" effect as a way to centralize power and gain public support. They can enlist the support of international actors. They can bind the United States to pursue certain policies through international commitments, and then use the existence of those commitments to overcome domestic opposition to the policies. In short, administration officials can exploit their unique position at the intersection of the domestic system and the international system to further their objectives in each arena.[35] Several examples are useful to illustrate these points.

During the Korean war, the Truman and Eisenhower administrations had a severe disagreement with Congress over West European and Japanese trade with Communist countries.[36] Executive officials wanted to curtail that trade, yet recognized that it would be politically difficult and economically costly for America's allies to sever it altogether. To demand and expect full compliance would likely do more damage to the alliance than to the Communist bloc, and thus executive officials were willing to compromise and tolerate some level of continued East–West trade. Congress was unwilling to compromise, believing that with U.S. soldiers dying in Korea it was incumbent upon America's allies, who were receiving U.S. financial assistance, to abandon their Eastern trade. To enforce this preference, members of Congress passed a controversial law (known as the Battle Act), which required America's allies to give up either their Eastern trade or their American economic and military aid.

Executive officials, caught between their domestic constraint and their interest in maintaining alliance cohesion, responded creatively. They lobbied for a loophole in the law that would allow exceptions to be made on national security grounds, and they negotiated a change in the alliance export control regime (CoCom) that enabled the allies to comply with the letter of the law without necessarily having to sever their trade completely. The Executive, not Congress, ultimately controlled negotiations with other noncommunist states, and used that control to deflect congressional pressure and to achieve its objectives—to maintain as comprehensive an embargo as possible while preserving alliance cohesion.

A second example concerns the critical ability to commit the nation's armed forces to overseas conflict. After Vietnam, Congress sought to reassert its constitutional prerogative in this area with the passage of the War Powers Resolution in 1973. The Resolution helped to restore Congress' appropriate role, but also had the potential to frustrate the credibility and effectiveness of U.S. military statecraft. By imposing specific time limits on the deployment of U.S. troops and other requirements, the Resolution gives America's adversaries the opportunity to exploit divisions between the Executive and Congress when the former contemplates or threatens the use of force.[37]

Since 1973, Presidents have responded to these requirements in a way that allows Congress some role, but without compromising their ability to use force as necessary to further national or collective goals. As a matter of principle, no President has been willing to concede the constitutionality of the Resolution, but most have been willing to placate Congress by observing in practice at least some of its provisions some of the time. Presidents have been prepared to neglect the consultation or time limit provisions of the Resolution if they believed that to be necessary to protect national security or maintain diplomatic discretion. Even in the case where Congress played its most prominent role, the Persian Gulf conflict, the Bush administration devoted far more energy to gaining international support than to gaining congressional approval. The latter was sought and obtained very late in the process, after an international coalition had been mobilized and an ultimatum delivered to Saddam Hussein.

Third, throughout the postwar era successive administrations have had to defend the liberal trading order against interest groups and members of Congress more inclined toward economic nationalism and protectionism. Executive officials have relied upon delegations of authority from Congress to engage in international negotiations, have channeled demands for protection into the executive bureaucracy, and have cut special deals for interests (e.g., agriculture, textiles) too powerful politically to ignore.[38] Perhaps the most distinctive tactic adopted during the 1980s was the effort to "externalize" the demand for protection at home by focusing on market access abroad. This tactic was employed by the Reagan administration in 1985, as it mobilized export interests by initiating the Uruguay Round, utilizing Section 301 of U.S. trade law, and providing export subsidies in competition for agricultural markets.

The Bush administration similarly adopted a strategy for deflecting illiberal interests. By 1989, large and persistent bilateral trade deficits generated open hostility toward Japan and demands for "managed trade." The administration utilized Super 301, but more sparingly than Congress preferred. It compensated by working with Japan to launch the Structural Impediments Initiative, an ambitious attempt to get at the root causes of market access problems, and a plausible alternative to managed trade. In the face of intense congressional and industry scrutiny, the administration brought both Super 301 and SII negotiations to completion in the middle of 1990, deflecting congressional pressure and leaving Executive officials to focus full attention of their primary trade policy priority—the completion of the Uruguay Round and strengthening of GATT.

These examples suggest that even though Congress and interest groups play a prominent role, the result is not necessarily stalemate, ineffective policy, and the abdication of U.S. leadership. It may require time, effort, and the expense of political capital, but a determined President with a sense of foreign policy purpose can manage the constraints of the domestic political system.

The Domestic System as an Asset to Leadership

Foreign policy officials can do more than merely manage constraints or "limit the damage" of the domestic political system. That system itself can actually be an asset, which Presidents can use to further international leadership.

For example, the pressure exerted by Congress on the Executive can be transformed by the Executive into bargaining leverage. As Pastor has noted, "a president who is sensitive to the public mood that stimulates congressional concern can turn Congress into an incomparable bargaining asset in international negotiations."[39] Congressional pressure helps the Executive to negotiate more forcefully, by lending credibility to Executive demands while allowing Executive officials to appear moderate and reasonable. This dynamic is most readily apparent in trade policy, and is all-too-familiar to Japanese negotiators. U.S. negotiators hoping to open Japanese or other foreign markets have been able to claim, in effect, with a reasonable degree of plausibility, that "it's best for you to make a deal with us now, for if you wait, Congress will be far more unreasonable and harder on you than we are being." This tactic has also proven useful to presidents in other areas, such as the promotion of human rights.[40] The intense concern of Congress in this area and its willingness to tie U.S. economic and military assistance conditionally to the human rights record of foreign governments has given executive officials the potential to extract concessions in this area while still maintaining a focus on broader geopolitical and security concerns.

Presidents are also subject to the constraint of public opinion, but this, too, can actually be an asset to international leadership. The need for public support creates incentives for executive officials to develop policies that can command a public consensus—or that reflect one already in existence. Foreign policies and international commitments that reflect a public consensus are more likely to be sustained over the long run than are those which do not.

Until recently, the conventional view among political scientists and policy analysts was that on matters of foreign policy, public opinion tended to be impulsive, erratic, and ill-informed. Foreign policy required public consensus, but the public was moodish, unpredictable, and incapable of sound judgment—creating yet one more constraint on effective international leadership. Presidents, by implication, needed to "find a way around" public opinion. However, recent work by Shapiro and Page, among others, has challenged this view and developed what is, from the perspective of international leadership, a far more optimistic view of the public's role in and impact on foreign policy.[41] They find, tracing through decades of survey data, that public opinion on foreign policy issues is "coherent, consistent, and reflective of values that endure over long periods of time."[42] Public opinion is stable and constructive: it signals quite clearly the kind of policies and initiatives that are (or are not likely) to command enduring support. For example, a strong aversion to the direct use of military force—unless there is a clear threat to U.S. interests and no viable alternative—runs through decades of survey data, and was only reinforced by the Vietnam experience. On the other hand, since 1942 there has been high and stable support for an active U.S. role in world affairs, including support for the significant presence of U.S. troops in Europe and Asia. Surveys conducted through the 1970s and 1980s suggest some public sympathy for protectionism: yet, when questions were framed to emphasize reciprocity and the opportunities for U.S. exports, the postwar public consensus in favor of free trade resurfaced.

Although stable, public opinion is not immutable. Shapiro and Page find that public opinion "responds to new information and to objective changes in ways that are regular, predictable, and generally sensible."[43] The collective public is responsive to and can be educated by a President willing to devote the political energy and lay the groundwork for new or changed foreign policy priorities. The postwar shift in public opinion from isolationism to internationalism, and the more recent shift from viewing the Soviet Union as an "unfriendly enemy" to viewing Russia as a country worthy of economic assistance (despite the general and enduring aversion of the public to foreign aid) illustrate the point. The upshot of this revisionist view is that instead of something to be feared or evaded, the impact of public opinion on foreign policy should be welcomed and cultivated by executive officials.

Similarly, an administration with a sensitivity to public opinion can turn the media into an asset as well. One does not have to believe that U.S. public support for the Persian Gulf war was the result of a conspiracy between George Bush and the "punditocracy," to appreciate that the President did use the media effectively to convey his belief that Saddam Hussein represented a profound threat to U.S. interests and to the values of the international community.[44] Yet, administrations can miss opportunities as well. With regard to Japan, the Bush administration worked hard to defend liberal policies against economic nationalism, but did not always speak forcefully at the public level in favor of this preference. The rhetorical ground was left to the critics of administration policy, who were more inclined, for example, to depict Japanese foreign investment as part of a "Japanese invasion" than as an important contributor to the revitalization of the U.S. economy.

A crucial component of leadership is the ability to enter into and sustain international commitments. The United States has made a host of such commitments in the postwar era, and recently Peter Cowhey has argued that the structure of the U.S. political system actually helps U.S. officials to sustain them.[45] He finds that in systems where power is divided, once international commitments are made they are hard to reverse, since reversal requires the acquiescence of more than one center of power. Moreover, the fact that the U.S. system is open and transparent makes it easier for America's negotiating partners to monitor U.S. compliance with commitments. Since the willingness of other states to maintain commitments depends in part on their assessment of whether the United States will keep to the bargain, the transparency of the U.S. political system helps to increase the prospects for enduring international cooperation. Ironically, the "foreign penetration" of the U.S. political system, viewed by some as a weakness or threat, may actually enhance leadership by helping others to track U.S. adherence to international commitments.[46]

CONCLUSION: POWER, PURPOSE, AND LEADERSHIP

The postwar U.S. leadership record, the fact that administrations have techniques to manage domestic constraints, and the fact that the domestic system can actually be turned to international advantage all suggest that as the United States enters the post-cold war era, the foreign policy process need not be viewed as a serious impediment to the exercise of U.S. leadership. The domestic process, however, is only one possible determinant of international leadership. Two other important ones are international power and foreign policy purpose. Although widely debated of late, the United States retains sufficient international power to lead in a post-cold war world. Whether the United States also possesses the foreign policy purpose, however, is more uncertain.

Is the United States a great power in decline? If "power" is defined in terms of relative position over time, and operationalized as control over economic resources, the answer seems clear. The U.S. share of world trade, of financial reserves, and of global output of commodities such as steel and petroleum decreased sharply between 1950 and the 1980s. During the 1980s, the United States shifted from creditor to debtor status as its international financial position deteriorated sharply and rapidly. At the same time, it faced serious competition in world markets and a challenge to its pre-eminence in advanced technology from Japan.[47]

In absolute terms, however, the United States just as clearly remains a dominant power. Its economy remained the largest in terms of GNP, and its market is either the largest or second largest, depending on whether one aggregates the members of the European Union. U.S. productivity stagnated after 1973 but recently has rebounded, and although the United States does not lead in every sector, across manufacturing as a whole it retains its position as the most productive of the advanced industrial states.[48] Widespread concern during the mid-1980s that the United States was "deindustrializing" seems to have abated, and by the early 1990s attention was focused instead on the striking export performance of U.S. firms. A favorable exchange rate, generous amounts of foreign investment, and a concerted effort by U.S. firms to cut costs and improve quality all seemed to contribute to the renewed prowess of U.S. firms in international competition.[49]

Equally important, economic is not the sole form of international power. With the collapse of the Soviet Union, the United States is unambiguously the world's leading military power and is increasingly dominant in the production (and export) of sophisticated weaponry.[50] The United States also possesses the "soft" power resources of culture and ideology; as Russett and Nye argue, to the extent American values (e.g., anti-authoritarianism, liberal economies, individual rights) have become widespread, the United States has been able to retain control over international outcomes without having to exercise overt power over others.[51]

The point is not that United States enjoys complete mastery over international outcomes, or that it will always prevail in international disputes. It never enjoyed that degree of influence, even at the peak of its postwar power. Rather, the point is that despite its relative decline, the United States clearly retains sufficient power to contemplate seriously a leadership role internationally.

The United States may possess the power—does it also possess the foreign policy purpose? The cold war era was distinctive in that it witnessed the combination of U.S. power and purpose. The elements of U.S. foreign policy purpose are well-known: containment of the Soviet Union, permanent alliances with non-Communist states, a willingness to intervene using direct force if necessary to prevent Communist takeovers, and the pursuit of multilateralism in the international economy. With the end of the cold war, the U.S. purpose is no longer clear. There is no central enemy, and despite the best efforts of some officials, a collection of "nasty little states" such as Iraq and North Korea cannot substitute for the big nasty one. There is no consensus on when the United States should intervene, and for what reason. There is both support for, and suspicion of, joining with the United Nations in collective security efforts. The consensus in favor of economic liberalism and multilateralism has been challenged by advocates of industrial policy, managed trade, aggressive unilateralism, regionalism, and by those who view "geo-economic competition" as the principal source of great power rivalry in the years ahead.

The absence of foreign policy purpose is largely a function of the fact that the cold war ended rather abruptly and the adjustment to a new order is still taking place. Yet the problem has been exacerbated by the Clinton administration, which has been strikingly unsuccessful at providing purpose to U.S. policy. It has been noted often that President Clinton seems to wish for the world to stay still while he handles domestic problems, and that the world is clearly not cooperating. The *Economist* recently editorialized that Clinton's "undisguised disinterest in foreign policy, together with his administration's utter absence of a framework for thinking about America's place in the world, have convinced many of America's friends that their worst nightmare may be coming true: a one-superpower world in which the superpower does not have the faintest idea how to perform its central role of preserving peace through preserving the balance of power."[52]

In the absence of clear purpose, foreign policy tends to be reactive, episodic, and direction-less. And this is precisely the context within which the potentially *negative* aspects of the U.S. political system weigh most heavily on foreign policy. When there is a lack of consensus at the top, bureaucratic battles within the executive develop and usually become public, as evidenced by the struggles between Brzezinski and Vance during the Carter years over how to deal with the Soviet Union. When the executive is perceived as weak or uncertain, Congress attempts to fill the void, even though it is institutionally incapable of doing so. When neither the executive nor Congress provide direction, the media and to some extent interest groups tend to fill the void, and the administration finds itself—as in recent policy toward Somalia, Bosnia, and NAFTA—catching up with and reacting to events rather than setting the foreign policy agenda, domestically and internationally.

In these circumstances, it is tempting to find fault with the process, and to retreat into the logic of the democratic dilemma. That, however, is to mistake the symptom for the cause. International leadership requires purpose, and when it exists, the system can be made to work.

NOTES

1. See, for example, John W. Spanier and Eric M. Uslaner, *American Foreign Policy Making and the Democratic Dilemmas* (New York: Macmillan Publishing Company, 6th ed., 1994), pp. 17–23.
2. Alexis De Tocqueville, *Democracy in America,* vol. I. trans. by Henry Reeve (Boston: John Allyn, 1882), pp. 299–300.
3. Washington is quoted in *ibid.*, pp. 296–97, emphasis in original.
4. By "international leadership" I mean the ability of a country to develop and sustain foreign policies that have a profound effect on the structure and substance of international relations. I would also include the ability to identify common problems and opportunities, and to take the initiative in mobi-lizing resources and coalitions to address them.
5. Kennan is quoted in Robert Pastor, "The President Versus Congress," in Robert J. Art and Seyom Brown, eds., *U.S. Foreign Policy: The Search for a New Role* (New York: Macmillan, 1993), p. 12. Pastor's essay is one of a small handful in the literature that challenges the conventional wisdom directly and effectively.
6. See Lowi, "Making Democracy Safe for the World: On Fighting the Next War," in G. John Ikenberry, ed., *American Foreign Policy: Theoretical Essays* (New York: HarperCollins, 1989), pp. 258–292, quotations at 288.
7. See Krasner, "United States Commercial and Monetary Policy: Unravelling the Paradox of External Strength and Internal Weakness," in Peter Katzenstein, ed., *Between Power and Plenty* (Madison: University of Wisconsin Press, 1978), pp. 51–88: *Defending the National Interest* (Princeton: Princeton University Press, 1978); and "Domestic Constraints on International Economic Leverage," in Klaus Knorr and Frank Trager, *Economic Issues and National Security* (Lawrence: University of Kansas Press, 1977), pp. 160–181.
8. Destler, Gelb, and Lake, *Our Own Worst Enemy: The Unmaking of American Foreign Policy* (New York: Simon and Schuster, 1984), p. 11.
9. Broder, "Can We Govern? Our Weakened Political System Sets Us Up For Failure," in *The Washington Post* (National Weekly Edition), January 31, 1994, p. 23.
10. Tower is quoted in James M. McCormick, *American Foreign Policy and Process,* 2nd ed. (Itasca, Illinois: F. E. Peacock Publishers, 1992), p. 341.

11. The Soviets abrogated the trade agreement after the Jackson–Vanik Amendment passed. See Paula Stern, *Water's Edge: Domestic Politics and the Making of Foreign Economic Policy* (Westport, Conn.: Greenwood Press, 1979).

12. Most of the world trading community viewed Super 301 as contrary to the spirit and possibly the letter of GATT, at a time when the United States was seeking to strengthen GATT and international adherence to it. See, for example, Jagdish Bhagwati, *Aggressive Unilateralism: America's 301 Trade Policy and the World Trading System* (Ann Arbor: University of Michigan Press, 1990).

13. See James A. Nathan and James K. Oliver, *Foreign Policy Making and the American Political System*, 2nd ed. (Boston: Little, Brown, 1987), pp. 24–25.

14. See Michael Mastanduno, *Economic Containment: CoCom and the Politics of East–West Trade* (Ithaca: Cornell University Press, 1992).

15. See Henry A. Kissinger, *White House Years* (Boston: Little, Brown, 1979).

16. Alexander L. George, "Domestic Constraints on Regime Change in U.S. Foreign Policy: The Need for Policy Legitimacy," in Ikenberry, ed., *American Foreign Policy*, pp. 583–608.

17. See John Canham-Clyne, "Business as Usual: Iran-Contra and the National Security State," in Eugene R. Wittkopf, ed., *The Domestic Sources of American Foreign Policy*, 2nd ed. (New York: St. Martin's, 1994), pp. 236–246, at 240–241.

18. I. M. Destler, "A Government Divided: The Security Complex and the Economic Complex," in David A. Deese, ed., *The New Politics of American Foreign Policy* (New York: St. Martin's, 1994), pp. 132–147.

19. For example, Dan Williams and Ann Devroy, "Buckling Under the Weight of the World: The White House Appears Weak and Wavering in Foreign Affairs," *Washington Post*, National Weekly Edition, May 2, 1994, p. 14.

20. Hugh Heclo, *A Government of Strangers* (Washington, D.C.: The Brookings Institution, 1976).

21. For example, Clyde V. Prestowitz, Jr., *Trading Places: How We Are Giving Our Future to Japan and How to Reclaim It*, 2nd ed. (New York: Basic Books, 1989).

22. See Mitchell G. Bard, "The Influence of Ethnic Interest Groups on American Middle East Policy," in Wittkopf, ed., *The Domestic Sources of American Foreign Policy*, pp. 79, 86.

23. See Krasner, *Defending the National Interest*.

24. Jeff Frieden, "Sectoral Conflict and U.S. Foreign Economic Policy, 1914–1940," in Ikenberry, ed., *American Foreign Policy*, pp. 133–161.

25. See Robert S. Greenberger, "Cacophony of Voices Drowns Out Message From U.S. to China," *Wall Street Journal*, March 22, 1994, p. A1.

26. The most prominent articulation of this argument is Pat Choate, *Agents of Influence: How Japanese Lobbyists in the United States Manipulate America's Political and Economic System* (New York: Knopf, 1990).

27. See John B. Judis, "The Japanese Megaphone: Foreign Influences on Foreign Policy-making," in Wittkopf, ed., *The Domestic Sources of American Foreign Policy*, p. 102.

28. See, for example, Spanier and Uslaner, *American Foreign Policy and the Democratic Dilemmas*, pp. 233–36.

29. Broder, "Can We Govern?," p. 23.

30. Lloyd Cutler, "Foreign Policy on Deadline." *Foreign Policy*, no. 56 (Fall 1984), pp. 113–128.

31. In his assessment of the interbranch relationship, Robert Pastor similarly argues that the U.S. performance record has been better than it is usually given credit for in terms of consistency and flexibility. See Pastor, "The President Versus Congress," pp. 16–22.

32. John Lewis Gaddis, *Strategies of Containment: A Critical Appraisal of Postwar American National Security Policy* (New York: Oxford University Press, 1982).

33. See Bruce Russett, "The Mysterious Case of Vanishing Hegemony; or, Is Mark Twain Really Dead?," *International Organization*, vol. 39, no. 2 (Spring 1985), pp. 207–231.

34. See John Odell, *U.S. International Monetary Policy* (Princeton: Princeton University Press, 1982), and Yoichi Funabashi, *From the Plaza to the Louvre* (Washington, D.C.: Institute for International Economics, 1989).

35. For an elaboration and illustration of these arguments, see John Ikenberry, David Lake, and Michael Mastanduno, eds., *The State and American Foreign Economic Policy* (Ithaca: Cornell University Press, 1988).

36. For full discussion, see Mastanduno, *Economic Containment*, Ch. 3.

37. A good discussion is McCormick, *American Foreign Policy and Process*, pp. 313–325.

38. See I. M. Destler, *U.S. Trade Politics: System Under Stress* (Washington, D.C.: Institute for International Economics, 1986).

39. Pastor, "The President versus Congress," p. 16.

40. *Ibid.*, p. 17.

41. See, for example, Robert Y. Shapiro and Benjamin J. Page, "Foreign Policy and Public Opinion," and Thomas W. Graham, "Public Opinion and U.S. Foreign Policy Decision-Making," in Deese, ed., *The New Politics of American Foreign Policy*, pp. 190–235. The shifting consensus in the literature is reviewed by Ole Holsti, "Public Opinion and Foreign Policy: Challenges to the Almond-Lippmann Consensus," *International Studies Quarterly*, vol. 36, no. 4 (December 1992), pp. 439–466.

42. Shapiro and Page, "Foreign Policy and Public Opinion," p. 217.

43. *Ibid.*, p. 226.

44. See Eric Alterman, "Operation Pundit Storm: The Media, Political Commentary, and Foreign Policy," in Wittkopf, *The Domestic Sources of American Foreign Policy*, pp. 120–131.

45. Peter Cowhey, "Domestic Institutions and the Credibility of International Commitments: Japan and the United States," *International Organization*, vol. 47, no. 2 (Spring 1993), pp. 299–326.

46. *Ibid.*, p. 314. Interestingly, Cowhey finds in comparative terms that the Japanese political system is less well-equipped for international leadership. The electoral system rewards private rather than public goods, reducing incentives for leaders to make international commitments; the parliamentary system makes it easier to reverse commitments; and the system is less transparent, making Japanese compliance with agreements harder to monitor.

47. The "declinist" argument has been made most forcefully by Robert Gilpin, *U.S. Power and the Multinational Corporation* (New York: Basic Books, 1975) and *The Political Economy of International Relations* (Princeton: Princeton University Press, 1987); Robert Keohane and Joseph Nye, *Power and Interdependence* (Boston: Little, Brown, 1977); and Paul Kennedy, *The Rise and Fall of the Great Powers* (New York: Random House, 1987).

48. A well-publicized report by McKinsey and Company in 1993 documented the overall superiority of the United States in manufacturing productivity relative to its primary competitors, Japan and Germany. See Sylvia Nasar, "The American Economy, Back on Top," *New York Times*, February 27, 1994, Sec. 3, pp. 1, 6, and "Why US is Indeed Productive," *New York Times*, October 22, 1993, p. D1.

49. See "Who's Sharper Now?," and "Ready to Take on the World," *The Economist*, January 15, 1994, pp. 15, 65–66.

50. Ethan Kapstein, "America's Arms-Trade Monopoly," *Foreign Affairs*, vol. 73, no. 3 (May/June 1994), pp. 13–19.

51. Russett, "The Mysterious Case of Vanishing Hegemony," pp. 228–230, and Joseph Nye, *Bound to Lead* (New York: Basic Books, 1990).

52. "Cornered by His Past," June 4, 1994, pp. 13–14.

✌

The Roots of the Bush Doctrine: Power, Nationalism, and Democracy Promotion in U.S. Strategy

Jonathan Monten

The promotion of democracy is central to the George W. Bush administration's prosecution of both the war on terrorism and its overall grand strategy, in which it is assumed that U.S. political and security interests are advanced by the spread of liberal political institutions and values abroad. In an approach variously characterized as "democratic realism," "national security liberalism," "democratic globalism," and "messianic universalism," the Bush administration's national security policy has centered on the direct application of U.S. military and political power to promote democracy in strategic areas. In a summer 2004 interview, Bush expressed his "deep desire to spread liberty around the world as a way to help secure [the United States] in the long-run."[1] According to Bush, "As in Europe, as in Asia, as in every region of the world, the advance of freedom leads to peace."[2] This generic statement of cause and effect is also applied specifically to terrorism: "democracy and reform will make [Middle Eastern states] stronger and more stable, and make the world more secure by undermining terrorism at its source."[3] More broadly, the Bush administration proposes a liberal international order grounded in U.S. military and political power; as its 2002 National Security Strategy (NSS) contends, the unparalleled U.S. position of primacy creates a "moment of opportunity to extend the benefits of freedom across the globe . . . [the United States] will actively work to bring the hope of democracy, development, free markets, and free trade to every corner of the world." This view appears to be contingent on the belief that U.S. power is "the sole pillar upholding a liberal world order that is conducive to the principles [the United States] believes in."[4]

Although a radical departure in many other respects, the current U.S. grand strategy's privileging of liberalism and democracy falls squarely within the mainstream of American diplomatic traditions. For reasons unique to the American political experience, U.S. nationalism—that is, the factors that define and differentiate the United States as a self-contained political community—has historically been defined in terms of both adherence to a set of liberal, universal political ideals and a perceived obligation to spread those norms internationally. The concept of the United States as agent of historical transformation and liberal change in the international system therefore informs almost the entire history of U.S. foreign policy. As Jeanne Kirkpatrick has observed, no modern idea "holds greater sway in the minds of educated Americans than the belief that it is possible to democratize governments anytime, anywhere, and under any circumstances."[5] Or as Thomas Paine wrote to George Washington in the

Jonathan Monten, "The Roots of the Bush Doctrine: Power, Nationalism, and Democracy Promotion in U.S. Strategy," International Security, Vol. 29, No. 4 (Spring 2005), pp. 112–156. Reprinted by permission.

dedication of *The Rights of Man,* the United States was founded to see "the New World regenerate the Old."[6] Democracy promotion is not just another foreign policy instrument or idealist diversion; it is central to U.S. political identity and sense of national purpose.

Although grounded in the same nationalist premise of liberal exceptionalism, two contending schools have developed with respect to the long-term promotion of democratic change. One perspective—which, following historian H.W. Brands, may be termed "exemplarism"—conceives of the United States as founded in separation from Old World politics and the balance of power system. It suggests that U.S. institutions and values should be perfected and preserved, often but not exclusively through isolation. The United States exerts influence on the world through the force of its example; an activist foreign policy may even corrupt liberal practices at home, undermining the potency of the U.S. model. A second perspective—"vindicationism"—shares this "city-on-a-hill" identity but argues that the United States must move beyond example and undertake active measures to spread its universal political values and institutions.[7] Henry Kissinger observes these "two contradictory attitudes" in how the United States conceives of its international role: America as both beacon and crusader.[8] Anthony Smith, a British historian of nationalism, recognizes this same dichotomy in more general terms, drawing a distinction between "covenanted peoples" who "turn inward away from the profane world" and "missionary peoples" who "seek to expand into and transform the world."[9]

Both exemplarism and vindicationism follow from a foreign policy nationalism that regards the United States as an instrument of democratic change in the international system. Given this broad agreement on moral and strategic objectives—Americans are all, or at least historically have been, liberal exceptionalists—the debate has been over the policy means with which to prosecute that mission. One is a strategy organized around the concept of the United States as exemplar, the other around the United States as missionary and evangelist. At stake between them are a series of normative and causal claims about the nature of international politics and the capacity of U.S. power to produce major social and political change abroad; they are in effect competing theories of democracy promotion.

Although these contending approaches have coexisted throughout U.S. political history, they have also prevailed at different times. Students of U.S. history generally agree on the direction of change: whereas the first few generations of U.S. political leaders believed that the United States was exceptional for the example it set, vindicationism largely prevailed in the twentieth century, culminating in a Bush doctrine in which the active—and even coercive—promotion of democracy is a central component of U.S. grand strategy. The central puzzle addressed in this article is: what explains this shift in democracy-promotion strategy, from the concept of the United States as example to the concept of the United States as mission? What explains the long-term shift from exemplarism to vindicationism? Whence this peculiarly American faith in what has been called "global social engineering," or the belief in the capacity of U.S. power to effect major social and political change abroad?

It could be argued that broad variation in the U.S. approach to democracy promotion is explained entirely by power. Political realism predicts that, due to the incentives and pressures created by the international political environment, the expansion and contraction of a state's political interests tend to correspond with changes in relative power. In fact, the broad change from exemplarism to vindicationism correlates with a massive increase in relative power; as the United States acquired the capability to use intervention as a mechanism of democratic change, it exercised it. This hypothesis is advanced independent of variation at the domestic level; its conceptual implication is that ideology and nationalist ideas are either epiphenomenal of material structure, or cannot account for any variation independent of changes in a state's relative power position. But is early exemplarism explained entirely by the fact U.S. political leaders presided over a weak and disunited state, and now inapplicable to the conduct of U.S. hegemony? To appropriate Robert Kagan's pithy formulation, is exemplarism just a "weapon of the weak?"[10]

My argument is that periods of activist democracy promotion can be explained by both the expansion of material capabilities and the presence of a nationalist domestic ideology that favors vindicationism over exemplarism. While power is an important factor, long-term variation in the United States' democracy-promotion strategy also turns on subtle but significant ideational shifts in the doctrine of liberal exceptionalism. The founders, grounded in a political-realist and Calvinist view of politics, were skeptical toward the capacity of the United States to effect democratic change abroad, distrusted the concentration of power necessary to implement an activist foreign policy, and resolved to limit the U.S. liberal mission to demonstrating the success of an experiment in self-government. The character of liberal exceptionalism began to shift in the late nineteenth century. Various reform movements such as Progressivism and the Social Gospel, both political reactions to post-Civil War industrialization and modernization, produced a different set of normative and instrumental beliefs about the nature of progress and the efficacy of U.S. power to create a more perfect social and political order.

If persuasive, this argument contributes to two sets of debates, one theoretical and one substantive. Theoretically, it conceptualizes "nationalism"—which, in the U.S. case, is inextricably linked with a liberal-exceptionalist ideology and identity—both as a source of political preferences and as an intervening variable that mediates how states respond to the incentives and constraints created by the international political environment. A "neoclassical" line of realist argumentation contends that the mechanisms by which the effects of relative power are translated into state behavior are not as smooth or determinate as structural realist theories assume, and must be supplemented with unit-level variables.[11] U.S. democracy promotion illustrates the utility of this approach: if, according to Kenneth Waltz, "international political theory deals with the pressures of structure on states and not how states will respond to those pressures,"[12] my argument privileges ideological changes in the doctrine of liberal exceptionalism as a domestic political process that determines the latter, shaping how states respond to external constraints and incentives. With respect to the Bush Doctrine, if relative power shapes the basic parameters of a state's foreign policy, unipolarity has created a permissive environment in which an aggressive ideology of democracy promotion can flourish. Power and ideas are not mutually exclusive explanations, but interact to produce foreign policy outcomes of interest.

Empirically, neoconservatism is situated within a long tradition of vindicationism. Treatments of neoconservatism are usually descriptive, often alarmist, and occasionally conspiratorial. My argument treats neoconservatism not as a momentary aberration, but as consistent with a history of nationalist ideologies rooted in liberal exceptionalism, and specifically emerging from a late nineteenth-century Progressive and Social Gospel understanding of political progress and the capacity of American power to effect democratic change in the international system.

The first section of this article introduces the basic realist hypotheses about state behavior that are relevant to understanding variation in U.S. democracy-promotion behavior. The second section examines the sources of liberal exceptionalism as the defining feature of American nationalism. The third section develops the two competing perspectives on democracy promotion more fully, and the fourth explains why the founders resolved the democracy-promotion debate in favor of exemplarism. The fifth and sixth sections investigate this long-term shift by looking at two cases, the 1890s and the Bush Doctrine. Both the 1890s and Bush administration will be compared along the following dimensions: the expansion of material power, the political effects of such expansion, and the presence of a prevailing vindicationist ideology.

POLITICAL REALISM AND STATE BEHAVIOR

Political realism advances a number of general propositions about the impact of relative power on foreign policy behavior. These arguments are important because they propose a series of testable hypotheses applicable to U.S. democracy promotion and because they form a tradition of political philosophy from which U.S. political leaders, and especially the country's founders, have drawn. Two arguments are of particular interest.

First, a key realist hypothesis since Thucydides has been that states expand in the absence of countervailing power; unbalanced power will act without moderation, and states not subject to external restraint tend to observe few limits on their behavior. Political agents, according to Thucydides' Athenians, are "under an innate compulsion to rule when empowered."[13] Modern realism thus argues that states balance against extreme asymmetries in power; under conditions of anarchy, imbalanced power creates the possibility for aggressive behavior, regardless of the domestic character or benign intent of the leading state.[14]

Second, realism advances the hypothesis that states' definitions of their interests—both political and strategic—tend to expand as a consequence of increasing relative power. According to Gideon Rose, the "central empirical prediction" of classical realism is that "the relative material power resources countries possess will shape the magnitude and ambition . . . of their foreign policies: as their relative power rises states will seek more influence abroad, and as it falls their actions and ambitions will be scaled back accordingly."[15]

Realism has offered a number of different causal logics to explain why political interests expand commensurate with relative power. In Robert Gilpin's account of international change, states pursue a "bundle" of security and welfare objectives, finding an optimum position on a set of indifference curves. Because the indifference curve selected by a state is in part a function of its capabilities, an increase in relative power "stimulates" a state to demand a larger bundle of these objectives.[16] Other scholars have argued that states are "influence-maximizing": because of the inherent uncertainty in international politics, they seek to maximize control over their external environments.[17] A final causal story is that hegemonic states tend to acquire a greater stake in world order, leading inexorably to an expansion of their political and security interests and commitments. As a corollary, because of these wide-ranging commitments, powerful states tend to identify their own national interests as necessarily consistent with public, international interests.[18]

Relative power is a necessary, but not sufficient, condition for explaining variation in the United States' democracy-promotion strategy. The capability to project political and military power is clearly a precondition to actively promoting democracy abroad, but not all states with this capability necessarily pursue a policy of democracy promotion. Realism can explain the broad contours of political expansion, but it cannot capture within the terms of the factors it privileges variation in the specific content of interests or policy choice. Realist behavioral expectations are overly general; they follow from a positional logic, independent of the properties or intentions unique to states. The conceptual frame of nationalism and national identity help to explain why the United States defines its political interests in terms of democracy promotion.[19]

EXCEPTIONALISM AND U.S. FOREIGN POLICY

U.S. national political identity is expressed in foreign policy primarily through the idea of "exceptionalism."[20] Historically, this doctrine has referred to "the perception that the United States differs qualitatively from other developed nations, because of its unique origins, national credo, historical evolution, and distinctive political and religious institutions."[21] Most broadly, it has referred to the distinctive qualities that follow from a U.S. political community uniquely defined by a set of universal, liberal–democratic values. Writing in *U.S. News & World Report*, Michael Barone accurately captured the logic of U.S. exceptionalism: "Every nation is unique, but America is the most unique."[22]

This tradition of liberal exceptionalism is expressed internationally in terms of a kind of foreign policy nationalism, or a belief that U.S. foreign policy should substantively reflect the liberal political values that define the United States as a national political community and meaningfully distinguish it from others.[23] Distinct from traditional great powers, U.S. political identity has been organized around a particular conception of the national purpose, expressed in foreign policy as the belief that Americans are "a chosen people," an elect nation guided by a "special providence" to demonstrate the viability and spread of the democratic institutions and values that inform the American experiment.[24]

What explains this historical interest in the internal political organization of other states? Many national communities have conceptualized themselves as superior or endowed with a mandate to enlighten an otherwise unregenerate world.[25] Nonetheless, because of the ideational—as opposed to organic—origins of U.S. political identity, U.S. nationalism has historically been defined in terms of both an adherence to the set of universal political values that constitute the "American Creed"—in most accounts, constitutionalism, individualism, democracy, and egalitarianism—and a perceived obligation to promote those values in its external relations.[26] By this argument, U.S. interest in democracy promotion originated not only in the instrumental maximization of some material interest, but in a moral commitment to the universal political values that define the United States as a self-contained political community.[27] This core, nationalist belief in a special mandate to promote liberal–democratic values and institutions abroad largely derives from three sources: Calvinism, the Enlightenment, and most important, functional or historical necessity.

Calvinism and Mission

The first source of the U.S. self-perception of mission is seventeenth-century Calvinism. The Calvinist influence was confined primarily to the Puritans in New England, but was also manifest in settler communities in Pennsylvania, New York, and New Jersey.[28] Although a minority of the total colonial population, the Puritans exerted a disproportionate political and cultural influence on early American life, reasserted through subsequent, periodic revivals and "great awakenings." According to Samuel Huntington, the Puritan influence "reinforced republican and democratic tendencies in the eighteenth century and provided the underlying ethical and moral basis for American ideas on politics and society."[29]

Puritanism imbued U.S. nationalism with the belief that the United States was a chosen instrument of God, divinely appointed to introduce a government and society on the American continent in which individuals would possess the liberties God had granted them. The first Puritan settlers believed they were commissioned by God for a special purpose; as John Winthrop wrote in 1630, "The work we have in hand, it is by mutual consent through a special overruling Providence . . . to seek out a place of cohabitation and consorting under a due form of government both civil and ecclesiastical."[30] The conviction of religious mission and providential mandate, later secularized, provided a core tenet of U.S. national identity and sense of purpose. Biblical metaphor was common; as Herman Melville later wrote, "We Americans are a peculiar, chosen people, the Israel of our times; we bear the ark of the liberties of the world."[31]

The geographic isolation of the United States appeared to be further evidence of God's special partiality for Americans; and the concept of separation, and its implicit rejection of Europe, became a major theme in the formation of a U.S. national identity organized around liberal exceptionalism. The physical fact of separation appeared to impose a qualitative political and moral distinction between the Old and New Worlds; by virtue of its geographic position and possibly, it was thought, some higher design, the United States was removed from the corrupting politics of the European balance of power system, with its attendant ambition, aggrandizement, and amorality. Although elevated to the level of timeless grand-strategic doctrine under Washington and Alexander Hamilton, to the Puritans American isolation was not strategic but virtuous.

The Enlightenment and Universalism

The second major source of the U.S. moral commitment to democracy promotion was the influence of the eighteenth-century Enlightenment. Through an Enlightenment faith in a common rationality, a cosmopolitan spirit, and the universal constancy of human nature, many of the liberal norms that came to define U.S. national identity were framed in absolute and universal terms. Early American leaders such as Thomas Paine, Thomas Jefferson, and Benjamin Franklin regarded themselves as "children of the Age of Reason." Among the generation of U.S. revolutionaries, the belief was widespread that, as Jefferson wrote, they had acted "not for ourselves, but for the whole human race," suggesting that the political ideas that motivated the revolution were universal and exportable.[32] Enlightenment thought also contributed a specific set of political principles to the American Creed, including the belief in constitutionalism and a government limited by the rule of law, individualism, egalitarianism, and the Lockean social contract. Because these basic political values were considered universally valid and applicable, they inevitably provided a set of standards by which U.S. foreign policy could be evaluated, and goals toward which it was substantively oriented.

Functional or Historical Necessity

The functional demands of creating a cohesive, national state from the early American colonies were the third source of democracy promotion. In addition to their philosophical origins in Enlightenment rationalism, framing the political–cultural norms that defined U.S. national identity in universal terms served an important functional purpose. The early American colonies lacked the factors that often served as sources of cohesion in other nation–states: ethnic solidarity, a distinct language, a common history, a church, a monarchy, or a military or aristocratic caste. In addition to lacking what Anthony Smith has termed a dominant or latent *ethnie,* an early commitment to religious pluralism precluded defining national identity exclusively in terms of traditional Protestantism.

Consequently, in an oft-noted distinction, U.S. national identity became defined in civic and ideational (or "creedal")—and not ethnic or organic—terms.[33] Civic ideology and institutions, and not a latent *ethnie*, were necessary to provide a source of political cohesion and national consciousness, both unifying the United States as a self-contained political community and meaning fully differentiating it from others. Functionally, a set of universally framed political ideas were necessary to unite a regionally, ethnically, and religiously diverse state, providing the social cohesion and sense of national purpose necessary for consensual, liberal–democratic politics.[34] According to Gunnar Myrdal, these "general ideals" formed "the cement in the structure of this great and disparate nation."[35] Because of the historical unifying function of defining U.S. nationalism in terms of both universal political norms and a perceived national purpose to spread those norms, American national identity is inextricably linked with the liberal-exceptionalism premise of the United States as an agent of democratic change, that is, a promoter of democracy.

TWO SCHOOLS OF DEMOCRACY PROMOTION

As two sides of liberal exceptionalism, exemplarism and vindicationism are in effect competing sets of interrelated causal beliefs that aggregate into coherent doctrines relating liberalism to U.S. power, each privileging different mechanisms to achieve international democratic change. "Causal beliefs" can be defined as logical propositions held by policymakers about relations of cause and effect.[36] According to Judith Goldstein and Robert Keohane, they often serve as "road maps" for decisionmakers under conditions in which there is incomplete information about both the range of possible policy options and the likely effects of those policies.[37] Similarly, Barry Posen and Stephen Walt conceptualize "grand strategies" as aggregations of hypotheses on how to "cause" one's security; as a subset, exemplarism and vindicationism represent underlying causal logics, that, if implicitly, advance competing theories of how best to "cause" the promotion and consolidation of democracy abroad.[38]

Exemplarism

Exemplarists argue that the United States should promote democracy by offering a benign model of a successful liberal–democratic state. The United States should focus on perfecting its own domestic political and social order, and close the gap between the ideals of the American Creed and the actual performance of U.S. political institutions. By this logic, the mechanism of change in international politics is the moral force of the U.S. example. Exemplarism appears to be a more passive and less ambitious approach to democracy promotion. Nonetheless, it advances the overtly strategic claim that the United States can "better serve the cause of universal democracy by setting an example rather than by imposing a model."[39]

Two corollary arguments tend to be grouped with the nationalist concept of mission as example. First, exemplarism makes the causal claim that an activist foreign policy undermines liberal domestic political culture and institutions. The external pressures generated by international political and security competition tend to concentrate power in the state, as the processes and mechanisms of creating military power—those institutions that connect the state to its society and enable it to transform societal resources into military capabilities—are also those that tend to promote strong, centralized states.[40] Because of its geographic insularity and the absence of immediate military threats, the United States was able to avoid these state-centralizing tendencies in its early political development, and a national political community developed around a set of liberal–democratic principles that necessarily conflicted with the functional, state-centralizing requirements of security and foreign policy institutions. Consequently, exemplarists acknowledge a paradox in which those security and power-creating institutions necessary to project power and advance liberalism abroad are precisely those that threaten liberalism and the American Creed at home, undermining the attraction of the U.S. example.

A second corollary is that improving the quality of the U.S. domestic political and social order, in addition to the intrinsic value of reducing the gap between the American Creed in principle and in practice, serves the strategic purpose of strengthening the attraction of the U.S. liberal example. Exemplarists have historically been more skeptical toward U.S. institutions, or at least more cognizant of the capacity for reform and improvement. Rather than spreading U.S. institutions abroad, exemplarists counsel the somewhat indirect foreign policy strategy of strengthening them at home. The United States has a strategic interest in preserving and improving its own institutions, making its example more compelling.

Exemplarism also contains a claim about the efficacy of democracy promotion and the limits to U.S. power. Exemplarists have been comparatively skeptical toward the U.S. capacity to produce liberal change in the world. Because democracy is fragile and difficult to propagate, the ability of the U.S. government to directly promote and consolidate democratic institutions is limited and constrained.

Vindicationism

Alternatively, vindicationists argue that the United States must move beyond example and undertake active measures to spread its universal values. It must, in Brands's phrasing, actively use its power to "vindicate the right" in an otherwise illiberal world.[41] The exemplarist expectation that other states will emulate the U.S. example is viewed as at best inefficient and at worst Utopian; the United States should expedite this process of democratization, through intervention and force if necessary. Those advocating the concept of the United States as evangelic also tend to be more optimistic about the quality of democracy at home: U.S. institutions, if flawed, are comparatively superior and fit for export.

Vindicationism also contains an underlying claim about the efficacy of U.S. power to produce democratic change. According to this school, the expansion of U.S. power tends to correlate positively with the expansion of democracy internationally Huntington, for example, argues that "any increase in the power or influence of the U.S. in world affairs generally results . . . in the promotion of liberty and human rights in the world."[42] Vindicationists are comparatively less concerned about the potential for abuse inherent in any missionary exercise. American power is less likely to be misused or corrupted than that of any other government, both because American leaders are generally committed to liberal–democratic values and because of the constraints impose by the American political system's institutional dispersion of power.[43]

Two central philosophical issues—a Puritan sense of mission and a belief in progressive change—underlie these two positions.

Calvinism

Exemplarism and vindicationism share a Puritan sense of mission, but are rooted in different aspects of the early American Calvinist ethos. These coexisting Puritan traditions have historically offered distinct perspectives on the character of American political life and the precise nature of its moral obligation to the world.

One aspect of Calvinism stresses the innate imperfection and weakness of the human character, as well as the "awful precariousness of human existence."[44] The human condition is conceived as an endless and immutable process of trials, tests, and probations. Harriet Beecher

Stowe captured this Calvinist ethos as it permeated early New England: "The underlying foundation of life . . . in New England, was one of profound, unutterable, and therefore unuttered melancholy, which regarded human existence itself as a ghastly risk, and, in the case of the vast majority of human beings, inconceivable misfortune."[45] This Puritan tradition resulted in what political scientists would now recognize as a realist view of human nature; according to John Winthrop, the Puritan settlers "were not of those that dream of perfection in this world."[46]

Two political implications derive from the mind-set that Americans were not exempt from the universal imperfection of human character and striving. First, early American leaders took a historically conscious and pragmatic view of the American life. The U.S. polity was understood as an inherently problematic and precarious experiment, and its mission was thus limited to testing the hypothesis that an experiment in constitutional self-government could actually succeed. The United States was at best an example to emulate; hence the focus should be on perfecting and improving the domestic political order, and not attempting to spread those institutions through divine mandate. This Calvinist tradition regarded the United States as "involved in a test case which would determine whether men could live on Earth according to the will of the Lord,"[47] or whether, in its later secular variation, "a new nation, conceived in liberty, and dedicated to the proposition that all men are created equal . . . can long endure."[48]

A second political implication was that U.S. interests and motives were not exceptional in their purity or benevolence. Americans were not immune from potential corruption and temptation; according to George Washington, no nation, including the United States, can be "trusted farther than it is bound by its interest."[49] The U.S. mission is to provide an experiment to be emulated; to attempt to act on a more general basis invites a potential abuse of power and private interest.

The second broad Calvinist tradition, from which vindicationism draws, is less pragmatic and more millennialist. In this interpretation, Americans are an elect people, more immediate to God than others, chosen to redeem an otherwise unregenerate world. Arthur Schlesinger traces the distinction between these two competing traditions to Augustine, who compared the idea of "providential history"—the rise and decline of groups within history—to "redemptive history"—the journey of the elect to salvation beyond history.[50] To some the United States clearly resided in the latter, chosen to actively lead the world toward a millennium of liberty. According to early American minister Increase Mather, "God hath covenanted with his people . . . without a doubt, the Lord Jesus hath a peculiar respect unto this place, and for this people."[51] "God has still greater blessings in store for this vine which his own right hand hath planted," sermonized Ezra Stiles in 1783, and "the Lord shall have made his American Israel high above all nations which he hath made."[52]

Whereas the first tradition regarded the United States as a precarious historical experiment, it was through this tradition that Americans began to conceive of themselves as, according to American theologian Reinhold Niebuhr, "tutors to mankind in its pilgrimage to perfection."[53] Again, certain political conclusions follow from this view. The United States conceives of itself not as within history but outside of it, exempt from the political and historical factors that bear on other nations, and most notably that of European balance of power iniquities. Its redemptive mission allows it to act benevolently on behalf of common interests. The intentions of the United States are benign, and its political heart is pure. Power can be exercised without risk of abuse, and the United States can assume for itself the public and international interest, beyond its private ones. It is this Calvinist tradition that lends vindicationism its missionary, evangelic edge; not only are Americans the new Israelites, according to Melville, but the "political messiah has come," and "he has come in us."[54]

Progress and the Efficacy of U.S. Power

Divergent exemplarist and vindicationist propositions about the U.S. capacity to effect political change abroad are also rooted in contending underlying claims about progress and the essential character of political life. Exemplarism, drawing on a long political realist tradition, is fundamentally "pessimistic" about the capacity to produce progressive (small-p) change.[55] The prevalence of power and political struggle are believed to limit and condition human progress and the capacity to qualitatively change history. In his account of the rise and collapse of the Greek moral and civilizational order, for example, Thucydides wrote that "the plain truth is that both past events and those at some future time, in accordance with human nature, will recur in similar or comparable ways."[56] The fundamental conservatism of exemplarism with respect to the capacity of the United States to actively promote democratic change abroad derives from this realist skepticism about the possibilities of achieving a radically better world.

Vindicationism, in contrast, is comparatively "optimistic" about the essential nature of politics. Its adherents implicitly assume that the character of social and political life is basically harmonious, and any difficulties are momentary and superficial. Qualitative changes can be achieved through purposive, assertive action. According to Russell Nye, the U.S. "doctrine of progress," derived from an enlightenment faith in universal reason, holds that "if the obstacles to man's advancement are removed, and the flaws in his institutions corrected, progress will be swift and sure; otherwise it will be slow and uncertain."[57] Although fundamentally optimistic, progress requires the exercising of political agency. Vindicationism and exemplarism therefore reach different conclusions about the efficacy of U.S. power and the limits to its capacity to compel or effect significant social and political change.

THE FOUNDERS: AN EARLY EXEMPLARIST CONSENSUS

There is substantial evidence that the founders regarded the American Revolution and their subsequent political system as a liberal–democratic model and precedent for others. Consistent with a prevailing enlightenment universalism, the American Revolution was viewed as exerting a moral influence through the sheer force of example. As the Continental Congress expressed in 1789, the success of the revolution granted "the cause of liberty . . . a dignity and luster it has never yet enjoyed, and an example will be set which cannot have but the most favorable influence on mankind."[58]

Why did the founders reject any nascent vindicationist ambition and embrace a wider democratic agenda? Their belief in the exceptional character of the United States and its revolution was tempered by a number of factors, all squarely within—and to a large degree came to define—the U.S. exemplarist tradition; a skepticism toward the capacity of the United States to promote democracy abroad, rooted in a fundamentally realist worldview; a Calvinist conception of the U.S. exceptionalist mission as problematic and experimental; and a fear of the corrupting impact of an activist foreign policy on fledgling republican institutions.

The Efficacy of Democracy Promotion

The founders' views on politics and human nature were influenced by a profound political realism and a particular interpretation of Calvinism, both of which conditioned their expectations about the U.S. liberal mission and the likelihood of promoting democracy abroad. The founders constructed a system of government around a fundamentally pessimistic view of human nature. This underlying worldview was succinctly stated by Washington: "A small knowledge of human nature will convince us that with far the greatest part of mankind, interest is the governing principle . . . no institution not built on the presumptive truth of this maxim can succeed."[59] John Adams was similarly skeptical about the prospects of changing an otherwise depraved human nature; tyranny is rooted in "passions of men" that are "fixed and timeless."[60] This view of human nature was complemented by intense suspicion of power. According to Bernard Bailyn, the founders believed the essential attribute of power was its "aggressiveness: its endlessly propulsive tendency to expand itself beyond its legitimate boundaries," and thus organized a system of government around its institutional dispersion.[61]

Thus, like the first Calvinist tradition, the founders' understanding of U.S. democracy was grounded in a worldview that stressed the inherent fragility of republican institutions and the experimental nature of the U.S. polity, and not a teleological mission to expedite the inevitable triumph of liberalism. According to Schlesinger, the founders maintained "an intense conviction of the improbability of their undertaking."[62] A certain foreign policy humility followed: the United States was not viewed as immune to the laws of power and interest that, according to Washington and American philosophical descendents of Calvin, govern the behavior of both individuals and states. Consequently, U.S. ambition was limited to testing the historical experiment, both secular and religious, their political community represented.

This skepticism about the viability and difficulty in propagating democracy both at home and abroad was reinforced by a number of other factors. The study of the classics was widespread among the first generation of U.S. leaders; they were well aware of the fate of democracy in ancient history, from the Thirty Tyrants overthrowing democracy in Athens to Caesar subverting the Roman republic.[63] Moreover, the violent degeneration of the revolution in France and the failure to consolidate democratic change in Latin America following various anticolonial movements corroborated pessimism about democratic change and the limits of U.S. influence.[64]

Democracy Promotion at Home

The second broad set of arguments advanced by the founders in favor of exemplarism involved concern for the domestic effects of a vindicationist foreign policy. Originally, this included the fear that active international engagement would produce domestic disunity and factions, undermining and even corrupting U.S. political institutions. As John Jay warned in *Federalist* 3, political disunity was an invitation for foreign influence to subvert the integrity of domestic affairs. Fear of foreign subversion and the corrupting influence of Old World power politics, even if incurred in advocacy of liberal causes, was seemingly confirmed by the Citizen Genet and Randolph affairs, in which the French attempted to influence American public opinion and support the 1794 Whiskey Rebellion in Pennsylvania, respectively.[65] Intervention in the politics of other states thus risked foreign powers "inflaming" factions within the United States.

As U.S. institutions stabilized and the fear of faction correspondingly subsided, the founders' exemplarism was motivated by a second domestic concern: that an activist foreign policy would concentrate power within the state and executive in particular, especially with respect to the centralizing effects of crises and the use of force. True to exemplarist form, they explicitly recognized that the foreign policy and security institutions necessary to project power in the service of liberal ends were precisely those that undermined liberal government at home. Having denounced standing armies as "engines of despotism" in *Federalist 8,* for example, Hamilton continued that security threats "compel nations the most attached to liberty . . . to institutions which have a tendency to destroy their civil and political rights."[66]

For these reasons, the first generation of U.S. political leaders resolved the debate over the nature of U.S. liberal exceptionalism in favor of the concept of the United States as an example, a tradition largely continued throughout the early nineteenth century. Vindicationism was largely in defeat for the remainder of the century. What accounts for the turn away from this early nationalist legacy, from example to mission, almost a century later, beginning in the 1890s? Why did the millennial displace the exemplarist as the premise of national purpose? Had the founders not controlled a weak, disunited, and consolidating state contending with the European great powers, would they have opted for vindicationism as a democracy-promotion strategy? Is variation in democracy promotion contingent on these dimensions of state power, independent of ideational change?

CASE 1: THE 1890s

The 1890s is widely acknowledged as representing a major shift in U.S. foreign policy.[67] During this decade the United States emerged as a great power; commensurate with a spectacular growth in material power in the decades after the Civil War, the United States acquired the capabilities to project military power overseas in the form of a modern navy, began to exert political influence beyond its immediate hemisphere, and initiated a program of territorial annexation, culminating in the 1898 Spanish–American War and the subsequent colonial interest in the Philippines, Puerto Rico, Guam, the Hawaiian islands, and the Cuban protectorate. The period also witnessed the first attempt to export democracy, directly to the Philippines and indirectly through a humanitarian interest in liberating Cuba from an imperial European power. Although not the height of U.S. vindicationism, the 1890s was the first period in which the nationalist concept of the United States as mission had a major influence on the conduct of foreign policy.

A number of explanations have been advanced to account for the grand-strategic change and expansion of the period: geopolitical interest, commercial expansion, social and cultural change, bureaucratic and institutional politics, and shifting regional alignment.[68] Although all are posited as explanations for broad strategic adjustment and the emergence of the United States as a great power, they do not advance competing accounts of the specific political outcome in question: the broad shift from exemplarism to vindicationism evident in the ostensibly humanitarian reasons for the war with Spain, and the subsequent attempt to export democracy to the Philippines. Rising U.S. power led to a more assertive foreign policy, but what accounts for the centrality of democracy promotion to this period of U.S. expansion?

The argument in this section is that the vindicationist character of imperialism and political expansion in the 1890s is explained by the confluence of a tremendous expansion of material power and the Progressive movement, which produced subtle but significant changes in the nationalist ideology of liberal exceptionalism. This coalition of reform movements, representing a political reaction to post-Civil War industrialization and modernization, produced underlying ideational changes in prevailing beliefs toward the nature of progress in political life, the U.S. liberal-exceptionalist mission, the efficacy of social and political reform, and the role of the federal government and political power as an instrument of change.

Material Expansion

In the decades between the Civil War and World War I, the United States engaged in a sustained period of economic growth and industrialization. By virtually any significant economic measure, the United States had by the 1890s established itself as a major industrial power. Between 1865 and 1898, coal production increased 800 percent, steel 523 percent, railway track mileage 567 percent, and agricultural production 256 percent. The rapidly expanding iron and steel industry, stimulated by railroad growth, became the foundation of an industrial U.S. economy. The U.S. population more than doubled, augmented by the influx of immigration and the rise of major urban centers, primarily in the North and East.[69] U.S. economic growth was even more dramatic in relative terms. By 1885 the United States surpassed Britain in total world share of manufacturing output and steel production. The United States outpaced Britain in energy production, often identified as a key measure of industrial power, by 1890, and by 1900 surpassed Germany, France, Austria–Hungary, Russia, Japan, and Italy combined.[70] In terms of material resources, the Gilded Age established the United States as a great power.

The Political Effects of Rising Power

The rapid increase in relative material power accounts for the broad contours of U.S. grand-strategic adjustment in the 1890s. Realism expects that the relative power possessed by a state will shape the magnitude of its political interests abroad. U.S. expansion in the 1890s is largely consistent with this empirical prediction: the United States expanded its international political, security, and economic interests in a manner commensurate with its newfound great power status. George Kennan's observation that many influential policymakers "simply liked the smell of empire and felt an urge to range themselves among the colonial powers of the time . . . to bask in the sunshine of recognition as one of the great imperial powers of the world" confirms this basic realist logic.[71]

U.S. strategic adjustment was also a consequence of more specific strategic concerns motivated by the security dilemma and international political competition. Policymakers believed that if the United States failed to expand its security and political position in the Philippines and the Caribbean, other great powers would.[72] Beginning in the 1890s, influential figures such as Alfred Mahan, Theodore Roosevelt, and Henry Cabot Lodge argued that technological and political changes had rendered an insular, continental approach to national security obsolete. "Where formerly we had only commercial interests," stated John Basset Moore, a U.S. government official in the late 1890s, "we now have territorial and political interests as well."[73] Contrary to a previously regional strategic orientation, the United States began to develop an interest in the balance of power in regions outside its immediate hemisphere.

Although relative power can account for an increasingly assertive U.S. grand strategy, it cannot capture the liberal character of its political expansion in the 1890s, and particularly with its acquisition and management of the Philippines. The rise of vindicationism correlates with material expansion—the capability to project power is clearly a precondition to actively promoting democracy abroad—but the underlying ideational shift it represents is not entirely reducible to power. Changes in nationalist ideology intervene between relative power and how the United States manages the interests that power is intended to secure. Therefore, as Tony Smith argues, a realist "lust for power" largely explains "the American conquest of the

Philippines in the first place," but an imperial state that defines its national identity in terms of universal liberal values "had no choice thereafter but to govern with a serious commitment to the islands's democratization"[74]

A Vindicationist Idealogy: Progressivism

During this period of U.S. material expansion, a vindicationist ideology emerged in the form of Progressivism, a loose set of reform movements that developed in response to the changing social and economic conditions associated with post-Civil War industrialization and urbanization. Its general theme was to restore the economic individualism, political democracy, and civic purity that had been undermined by the United States' transition from a predominantly agrarian society to a modern, urban, industrial nation. These values were believed to have been destroyed by factors associated with modern life: large and unaccountable corporations, corrupt political machines, urban poverty and vice, and social conflict. In this broader sense, Progressivism was not confined to a single political party or president, but dominated the politics of the period, producing a change in "the whole tone of American political life."[75] Although the Progressive reform movement reached its height from approximately 1902 to 1917, many of its key ideas emerged in the antecedent decade. With the exception of certain leaders such as Robert LaFollette, Jane Addams, and William Borah, Progressives tended to support an activist foreign policy informed by liberal–democratic ideals, and the movement culminated—and ultimately declined—with Woodrow Wilson and the vindicationist manner with which he prosecuted U.S. involvement in World War I.[76]

For Progressivism, the reform impulse at home and abroad were linked. There are four dimensions to the nexus between Progressivism and vindi-cationism. First, Progressives represented a subtle but important shift in how progress itself was understood. The founders were generally pessimistic toward politics and human nature, and elevated this pessimism to an organizing principle of government. To the extent that Enlightenment thinkers such as Jefferson and Paine believed in progress, it was a passive, general optimism about the inevitability of improvement in the political condition: away from recurrent political struggles of the Old World, and toward a politics based on law and universal reason.

Progressive reformers assumed, in contrast, that progress could be expedited with the positive, purposive action of political agents, and especially government. Progress was no longer a remote historical process, but accessible and subject to manipulation. If the illiberal obstacles to improvement were removed and the flaws in political and social institutions corrected—whether through science, education, government, or human association—then rational progress could be hastened. Man was no longer a helpless sinner in the hands of a Calvinist (or political-realist) God, but had the capacity to effect a more perfect social and political order.

Progressive views on progress were augmented by the concurrent rise of the Social Gospel, or the movement to apply Christian teaching to resolving contemporary social and economic problems.[77] The Social Gospel's belief in the capacity to achieve an improved or more perfect social order complemented changes in secular liberalism's concept of progress; like millennial Calvinism, "the very heart of the social gospel," according to Washington Gladden, one of its chief exponents, was the message that the "kingdom [was] a possibility within history."[78]

Even after its sixteenth-century cultural hegemony, the Puritan tradition continued to influence U.S. political culture through periodic religious revivals and Great Awakenings, which focused on reforming both the individual and society. Although confined mostly to New England, eclectic reform groups flourished in the antebellum period, including abolitionists, suffragists, Sabbatarians, and advocates of temperance and public health.[79] These movements accelerated substantially after 1880; like other progressive reformers, the Social Gospel movement responded to the social pressures of poverty, vice, crime, and general dislocation generated by industrialization and urbanization.[80]

Religious reform movements reinforced vindicationist democracy promotion in a number of key ways. The Social Gospel argued for the efficacy of social reform and the U.S. capacity to bring about a more perfectly ordered system of social and political relations. This American idea of progress can be traced as much to the religious thought of Social Gospel reform as a secular liberal tradition; as Timothy Smith writes, "Insofar as perfectionist optimism is a spiritual inheritance in America, John Wesley, George Whitefield, and Samuel Hopkins more than Benjamin Franklin or Jean Jacques Rousseau were its progenitors."[81]

Second, and perhaps more important, the Social Gospel suggested that power wielded by Americans was inherently virtuous and benign. Progressives believed themselves to be, according to Arthur Link, "custodians of the spirit of righteousness, of the spirit of equal-handed justice, of the spirit of hope which believes in the perfectablity of the law with the perfectibility of human life itself."[82] This Protestant tradition advanced a view of power that sharply contrasted with that of the founders, which stressed that the United States was not exempt from the lessons of history and the corrupting influence of power. Because the United States was an agent of progressive historical change, it was a benign custodian of power. As Albert Beveridge, a leading Progressive who campaigned for the regulation of child labor, trusts, and the railroads, stated: "God has marked the American people as His chosen Nation to finally lead in the regeneration of the world."[83] While the exceptionalist sense of mission has previously been limited to example and experiment, these two reform movements produced a faith in progress and the American capacity to effect liberal change abroad.

Third, Progressivism privileged an activist federal government as the instrument of liberal change. Instead of the state being limited to the negative, laissez-faire functions of preserving a basic legal and political order in which individuals can compete and pursue self-interest freely, Progressives advanced the Hamiltonian concept of positive government, directing national power on behalf of liberal ends both domestically and internationally[84] Progressivism and vindicationist imperialism were grounded in the same philosophy of government: a strong, efficient, central government asserting the national interest both at home and abroad.[85] Domestically, the national government shattered monopolies, corporate abuse, and political machines, extending political and economic democracy against the contending forces of strict construction, limited government, and states' rights. Internationally, the Hamiltonian state challenged authoritarianism and colonialism, advancing the U.S. democratic mission against the contending forces of isolationism and exemplarism. Herbert Croly, whose *The Promise of American Life* became an influential Progressive work, made the link between the positive national state and liberal exceptionalist mission explicit: "Not until the Spanish War was a condition of public feeling created which made it possible to revive Hamiltonianism. That war . . . represented both the national idea and the spirit of reform."[86] For Croly, vindicationism abroad and reform at home were connected: U.S. democratic leadership "constituted a beneficial and a necessary stimulus to the better realization of the Promise of our domestic life."[87]

Finally, Progressives argued that the order, efficiency, and rationality they applied to domestic problems could be projected internationally. Progressivism was largely an attempt to rationalize the social and political world; early Progressive philosophers such as John Dewey and Lester Frank Ward developed a concept of "social engineering," in which social problems and sources of illiberalism were resolved through the application of reason and good government. These same techniques were thought to be applicable internationally. In a 1900 speech, President William McKinley asked: "Is it not possible that seventy-five million of American freemen are unable to establish liberty and justice and good government in our new possessions?"[88] Similarly, Roosevelt argued that "our proper conduct toward the tropic islands we have wrested from Spain" follows from the same "civic honesty, civic cleanliness, [and] civic good sense" with which domestic affairs are administered.[89] For Roosevelt, U.S. imperialism was the international expression of Progressive order and rationality; imperialism served as the functional equivalent of civic order in international politics, ensuring that "each part of the world should be prosperous and well-policed."[90]

It may seem counterintuitive to identify progressive vindicationism as a primary feature of the McKinley presidency; he and his closest adviser, Ohio industrialist Mark Hanna, were largely pro-business and conservative on the defining economic issue of the era, the gold standard, and by many historical accounts were pressured into war by congressional and popular opinion. This argument is misleading in three respects. First, many of the key figures within the McKinley administration—especially Roosevelt—were strongly motivated by Progressive ideas. Second, the sensationalist journalism largely responsible for creating popular and political pressure on McKinley was the direct predecessor to the Progressive, "muckraking" journalism in the early 1900s; both were motivated by reform impulses. Finally, McKinley and Hanna may have been pursuing conservative and business interests, but were compelled to do so in the context of constraints established by a liberal-exceptionalist political culture. Having acquired the Philippines, McKinley was forced to justify its acquisition and manage the territory in a manner consistent with vindicationist democracy promotion.[91]

Progressivism was not the exclusive cause of foreign policy change in the 1890s, but the ideational changes associated with the Progressive movement, in conjunction with growing U.S. power, produced a gradual shift away from the exemplarist consensus of the early nineteenth century and toward a more assertive vindicationism. Material power broadly accounts for U.S. foreign policy expansion, but a belief, both secular and religious, in liberal progress and the United States as an agent of that progress produced what Kennan decscribed as an "overweening confidence in our strength and our ability to solve problems."[92]

Why did vindicationism prevail over exemplarism? Why did the U.S. government not concur with Carl Schurz, a German revolutionary turned U.S. senator, that if the United States "deliberately resists the temptation of conquest, it will achieve the grandest triumph of the democratic idea that history knows of. . .its voice will be heard in the council of nations with more sincere respect and more deference than ever"?[93] Part of the explanation is power: due to the pressures of the international political system, states rarely decline opportunities to expand in the absence of countervailing force. As realism predicts, powerful states are generally not content with doctrines of moral example. The second part of the causal story is ideational: the Progressive reform movement, a political reaction to industrialization and modernization, produced an underlying shift in how the United States understood national power, progress, and liberal exceptionalism. The combination of ideology and power meant the United States could now use its foreign policy to produce democratic change.

CASE 2: THE BUSH DOCTRINE

The Bush administration represents the perfect vindicationist storm: internationally, it commands overwhelming, unbalanced power; domestically, its dominant policymaking coalition conceptualizes the United States through the exceptionalist prism of liberal evangelism, and not liberal exemplarism. Although there are clear ideological divisions within the administration, there also appears to be convergence on an irreducible set of normative and causal ideas about liberalism and power in international politics, an essential set of beliefs from which policy choices follow.[94] After the terrorist attacks of September 11, 2001, the Bush administration increasingly defined U.S. security requirements in terms of the U.S. capacity to influence the domestic political structures and societies of failed and threatening states. Vindicationism has thus been elevated to one of the central organizing principles of post September 11 grand strategy, and, as evidenced by two regional wars in Afghanistan and Iraq, is a major element of the U.S. response to the strategic threat posed by international terrorism.

That what can informally be called the "Bush Doctrine"—for our purposes an operationalization of neoconservatism—defines U.S. security interests in terms of the expansion of U.S.-style liberalism is not unique, and its nationalist vision of the United States as a redeeming force in international politics provides an essential point of continuity with preceding generations of grand strategy. Where the Bush Doctrine and its underlying neoconservative disposition diverge from tradition, however, is in the particular vehemence with which it adheres to a vindicationist framework for democracy promotion, in which the aggressive use of U.S. power is employed as the primary instrument of liberal change. The United States' nationalist obligation to the world is discharged, and its security and political interests defended, through the policy mechanism of mission, and not example.

Like the 1890s, the foreign policy outcome in question is not broad grand-strategic change, but the centrality of vindicationism to the Bush administration's approach to security policy and grand strategy. In this section I argue that the convergence of unipolarity and key ideological dimensions of neoconservatism have produced a particularly aggressive iteration of vindicationist democracy promotion. This case builds on the previous section in two ways. First, the same explanatory model is applied to both cases, providing further evidence that variation in U.S. democracy-promotion strategy is a function of both a system-level causal factor (relative power) and a domestic level factor (the nature of U.S. nationalism). Second, the actual ideological content of neoconservatism contains significant parallels with earlier waves of vindicationist thought and the Progressive movement, including a broad optimism about progress in international politics, a belief in the benign and virtuous nature of U.S. power, and a belief that the United States has the capacity to effectively promote liberal change abroad. These assumptions are augmented by a series of causal suppositions about the exercise of power and the importance of resolve in international politics.

Material Expansion

Like imperialism in 1898, the Bush Doctrine follows a period of enormous material expansion. The United States was widely believed to be in relative decline in the mid-to-late 1980s, and many observers expected the end of the Cold War to result in a multipolar international system with rising centers of power in Asia and Europe.[95] Instead, the United States ended the 1990s at the top of a unipolar distribution of power, commanding a greater share of world capabilities than any state in modern international history. U.S. economic dominance is surpassed only by its own position immediately following World War II. U.S. military dominance is even more asymmetrical: U.S. defense spending in 2003 was more than the combined defense spending of the next twenty-five military powers, many of which are U.S. allies, and it conducts approximately 80 percent of the world's military research and development. The United States dominates across most of the quantitative dimensions of power traditionally used by political scientists to measure polarity, as well as in many qualitative, information-age measures. The extent of current U.S. preponderance is difficult to overstate: it is the only state with global power projection capabilities, and the post–September 11 exercise of U.S. military force has made these asymmetries in power—somewhat latent during the 1990s—even more apparent.[96]

The Political Effects of Unipolarity

U.S. behavior under the Bush Doctrine broadly corroborates the basic realist hypothesis that variation in political expansion is a function of relative changes in material capabilities. Particularly since September 11, the United States has engaged in a massive projection of power and an extension of its political and security interests abroad, as well as published an official strategy document in which it proposes to maintain its position of primacy by adding to its margin of superiority and dissuading peer competitors. Realism suggests that this outcome follows inexorably from the U.S. unipolar position; states rarely observe voluntary restraint on their behavior in the absence of counter vailing power. According to Robert Jervis, for example, "The forceful and unilateral exercise of U.S. power is not simply the by-product of September 11. . . It is the logical outcome of the current unrivaled U.S. position in the international system."[97] The contingent effects of September 11 may account for the specific direction of U.S. policy and the timing of political expansion, but realism generally expects that under the permissive conditions of unipolarity, a doctrine sanctioning the aggressive use of power is likely. Although occurring in a widely different international environment than the 1890s, the expansionary political effects of structural change are similar. As was also the case with the 1890s, however, realism cannot capture the liberal character of this expansion. Realism is a necessary, but not sufficient, condition in explaining the contemporary rise of U.S. vindicationism.

A Vindicationist Ideology; Neoconservatism

Neoconservatism emerged in the mid-1970s as a faction of Cold War anti-communism disillusioned with détente and the post-Vietnam distrust of U.S. power, although many of its central strategic ideas can be traced to early Cold War debates over rollback and strategic superiority. Over time, neoconservatism has come to embody a distinctive and somewhat coherent set of causal and normative beliefs organized around the assertion of U.S. military strength, resolve, and political values.

Although occasionally dismissed as temporary or aberrant, neoconservatism falls squarely within the vindicationist wing of U.S. nationalism. The Bush administration clearly subscribes to the nationalist premise of the United States as a force for democracy; much in the way Pericles described Athens as a "school for Hellas," Bush contends that the United States represents the "single sustainable model for national success: freedom, democracy, and free enterprise."[98] In this view, democracy promotion is inextricably linked with national identity; as Bush stated in his acceptance speech at the 2004 Republican Convention, "Our nation's founding commitment is still our deepest commitment: In our world, and here at home, we will extend the frontiers of freedom."[99] Bush has been consistently forceful in his belief that "the United States is the beacon for freedom in the world," and that he has "a responsibility to promote freedom that is as solemn as the responsibility [to protect] the American people, because the two go hand-in-hand."[100]

Like missionary Calvinism, like Progressivism, and like the Social Gospel, neoconservatism appeals to what Walter Lippman identified as the "persistent evangel in Americanism."[101] There are three core dimensions to the administration's missionary take on liberal exceptionalism, from which a vindicationist policy follows: liberal optimism, a belief that U.S. power is inherently benign, and a belief that the exercise of U.S. power and leadership can effectively promote democratic change. In conjunction, these ideas constitute the reconservative "theory" of democracy promotion.

Liberal Optimism

Consistent with the history of vindicationist thought in the United States, neoconservatism contains an underlying view of progress that is fundamentally optimistic about the possibilities for liberal political change in the international system. Although often couched in the language of security and threat, the neoconservative view of democracy promotion implicitly suggests that the essential character of political life is harmonious, and that qualitative improvement in a political and social order can be achieved through purposive, assertive action.

Progressivism assumed that liberal rationality spread when illiberal obstructions were removed. Similarly, principal Bush administration policymakers presuppose that, far from being a product of rare or unusually favorable conditions, democracy is spontaneous and natural in the absence of some artificial obstacle, such as self-serving elites or a subversive, violent minority. Part of the optimistic tone struck by the Bush administration is directly traceable to the personal and political style of Ronald Reagan; as one editorial eulogized upon his death, "Optimism is ultimately what the Gipper was all about."[102] Reaganesque optimism about the spread of American ideals is evident in the 2002 National Security Strategy's statement that American power can be used to create "conditions in which all nations and all societies can choose for themselves the rewards and challenges of political and economic liberty." States can be compelled to embrace liberalism because it is unlikely that, given a choice, any competing political model would be freely chosen. As the National Security Strategy continues, "No people on earth yearn to be oppressed, aspire to servitude, or eagerly await the midnight knock of the secret police."[103] The implication of this view of progress—rooted in Progressivism and the Social Gospel—is that any obstruction to this default position can be resolved through the application of political power, and that liberal institutions can therefore be advanced at little to moderate cost.

This liberal optimism is reinforced by a belief that the political values and institutions that have traditionally defined U.S. national identity are universal and exportable. Bush has consistently and conspicuously employed a diplomatic language of right and wrong; the "values of freedom are right and true for every person, in every society." This univeralist belief creates certain expectations about the viability of a program of active democracy promotion: if "the self-evident truths of our founding are true for us, they are true for all," then it follows for the Bush administration that "freedom is stirring in the Middle East and no one should bet against it."[104]

The widely recognized inadequacy in postwar planning in Iraq is evidence of an underlying Progressive faith in progress and liberal rationality. The assumption that democracy is a universal system, and therefore spontaneous in the absence of some specific illiberal obstruction, resulted in the belief that military victory in Iraq was the equivalent of democratization. Fundamentally optimistic assumptions about Iraq underpinned initial Bush administration planning for troop levels to be reduced from about 140,000 to 30,000 within six months of the invasion, and its initial expectation that a functioning interim Iraqi government would be established within thirty to sixty days.[105] Administration planners appeared to believe that the ousting of Saddam Hussein would itself provide the conditions in which democracy could begin to emerge in Iraq; as Bush told Australian Prime Minister John Howard in April 2003, "The psychology inside Iraq is that Saddam has his fingers around the throat of the Iraqi people and he has two fingers left and we are prying them loose."[106] According to Penn Kemble, a former director of the U.S. Information Agency, "The distinction between liberation and democratization. . .was an idea never understood by the administration."[107] This misunderstanding followed directly from a liberal optimism about the possibilities of democratic change.

The Benign Nature of U.S. Power

Like Progressivism, neoconservatism is motivated by the belief that U.S. Power is an inherently benign and redeeming force in international politics, and regards U.S. foreign policy as exceptional in character. Apart from traditional great powers, U.S. foreign policy is believed to be based on a "distinctly American internationalism that reflects the union of our values and our national interests."[108] Echoing the neoconservatives of the 1970s, Bush argued in his West Point commencement speech that "wherever we carry it, the American flag will stand not only for our power, but for our freedom. Our nation's cause has always been larger than our nation's defense."[109] Charles Krauthammer concurs that "the American claim to benignity is not mere self-congratulation. We have a track record."[110] These arguments would not surprise Niebuhr, who observed that the United States is almost perpetually "inclined to pretend that our power is exercised by a peculiarly virtuous nation."[111]

Although Bush contends that the United States has no "utopia to establish," and can thus be trusted to wield power without constraint in international politics, these arguments are grounded in the millennialist—as opposed to pragmatic—side of the sixteenth-century Calvinist legacy discussed above. The United States is conceived of as a favored, elect people, mandated with a redemptive mission and thus exempt from the lessons of history and immune from the political factors that bear on and corrupt other states. Bush employs classic millennial language, informed by Puritanism and the Social Gospel tradition: "Today, humanity holds in its hands the opportunity to further freedom's triumph over all these foes. The United States welcomes our responsibility in this great mission."[112] This rhetoric is similar to the missionary Calvinism of the Social Gospel, for example Josiah Strong's 1886 *Our Country.* [113]

Two political implications follow from the vindicationist belief that the United States is, as Melville wrote, a "political messiah" in international politics. First, U.S. power can be exercised without risk of abuse or domination. Its intentions are benign. As an agent of liberal change, it acts benevolently on behalf of common and universal interests, and can thus assume international interests beyond its private ones. Rather than view excess power as corrupting, the neoconservatives follow in the tradition of Progressivism and the Social Gospel in their belief that the United States can be trusted to benignly, virtuously, and without risk of abuse exercise power on behalf of liberal ends.

In addition, it follows that the United States can legitimately reject constraints—whether legal, negotiated, or imposed through countervailing power—on its own behavior and freedom of action. This belief stems not only from a strategic judgment about the constraining effects of rules and institutions, but from a set of normative ideas that follow from a liberal exceptionalist sense of mission.

The neoconservative claim to benevolence in part derives from the tendency to conflate U.S. national interests with what are asserted to be common, international interests. It is common for hegemonic states, necessarily having a greater stake in world order, to identify their national interests as consistent with international ones.[114] This dynamic, however, can be a function of ideology as well as power. Neoconservatism assumes that when the United States acts in its own interests, it necessarily serves the interests of the international system. It is therefore not only legitimate but virtuous for the United States to deploy its power on behalf of nationally defined goals. According to Condoleezza Rice, for example, "America's pursuit of the national interest will create conditions that promote freedom, markets, and peace. Its pursuit of national interests after World War II led to a more prosperous and democratic world. This can happen again."[115] Lest this conflation of private and public interests appear self-serving, Robert Kagan and William Kristol assure Americans that "their support for pre-eminence is as much a boost for international justice as any people are capable of giving."[116]

In the diplomacy preceding the Iraq war, the Bush administration's belief that it was acting on behalf of international, and not exclusively national, interests strongly shaped its approach to the United Nations and the Security Council process. Key U.S. decisionmakers perceived their actions as defending the credibility of the United Nations. As Rice argued in early 2003, "It isn't American credibility on the line, it is the credibility of everybody that this gangster can yet again beat the international system." Regarding the weapons of mass destruction (WMD) inspections process, Rice believed that allowing Iraq to "play volleyball with the international community this way will come back to haunt us someday. That is the reason [to invade]. . .Iraq is critical to reestablishing the bona fides of the Security Council."[117] The United States as sumed for the UN the defense of its credibility, and thus empowered itself to pursue those interests at its unilateral discretion, not constrained by the with holding of consent by the organization itself.

Neoconservatives therefore operate in the absence of the ideational factors that traditionally temper liberal exceptionalism, resulting in a lack of humility in exercising power. An entirely different set of assumptions, supported by political realism, Calvinism, and a reading of the classics, informed the founders' worldview that that the political world is governed by interest and power, that the United States is not exempt from these motives, and that the sobering lessons of history bear on the United States as well as nondemocratic states.

The Efficacy of American Power

Neoconservatism contends that U.S. power can be effective deployed as an instrument of liberal change in the international system. This belief in turn relies on a series of causal suppositions—that is, assumptions about relations of cause and effect—about the operation of power and coercive force in international politics. Two assumptions in particular underlie the Bush administration belief that the exercise of power can be an effective mechanism of liberal change: that band wagoning is more common than balancing, and that technological change and a preponderance of U.S. military power allow the United States to overcome previous constraints on vindicationist democracy promotion. These two assumptions are couched within neoconservatism's traditional agenda of restoring the U.S. will to use its power on behalf of its political values. The neoconservative "theory" of democracy promotion is thus that the assertion of U.S. power and leadership can effectively produce democratic change abroad.

Neoconservatism as grand-strategic perspective has historically been organized around the basic premise that the assertion of power is an effective means to some policy end; put simply, strength works. This expectation is implicitly based on the causal logic of bandwagoning. According to Jervis, one property of a political system is the interconnection of its parts: trends in one part of the system "feed back" to others. In international politics, balancing is a kind of negative feedback—disequilibria in power are restored through balancing. In a positive feedback system, the accumulation or projection of power is accelerated or reinforced as other states "bandwagon" with the forceful or leading state. Within the administration, Bush in particular has consistently articulated a strongly held personal belief that exercising leadership, projecting power, and demonstrating resolve generates "positive feedback" at all levels of politics. To borrow Norman Ornstein's phrase, Bush acts on the causal belief that "winners win": by demonstrating leadership and acquiring a reputation for success, in both domestic and international politics, others will follow.[118] For example, Bush observed to Britain's prime minister, Tony Blair, upon Blair's victory in a key parliamentary vote on Iraq, that "not only did you win, but public opinion shifted because you're leading. . .that is why the vote happened the way it happened. It's the willingness of someone to lead."[119]

The causal logic of bandwagoning is central to how neoconservatism understands the mechanics of power in international politics, and thus the efficacy of U.S. power in promoting democracy. Implicit in the logic of the 2002 National Security Strategy, for example, is the assumption that states will bandwagon, and not balance, against the projection of U.S. military and political power on behalf of liberal ends.[120] Although the NSS uses language consistent with the concept of the balance of power, it in actuality employs a bandwagoning logic: the stated intent of the NSS is to use "a position of unparalleled military strength" to "maintain a balance of power that favors freedom," suggesting that the exercising of U.S. primacy will attract a bandwagon of support that creates an imbalance of power in favor of the United States and liberal change.[121]

All levels of the administration's Iraq policy, war planning, and assessments of success were infused with the underlying assumption that decisive U.S. leadership and the assertion of power would generate a bandwagon of support in favor of U.S. policy goals. In Bob Woodward's *Plan of Attack,* Bush posits the causal claim that "confident action will yield positive results [and] provides a kind of slipstream into which reluctant nations and leaders can get behind."[122] Internationally, this assumption shaped the administration's expectations about the effects of the military action on postconflict support. If winners truly do win in international politics, broad international support–both political and material—would be forthcoming following a successful U.S. military operation, even from those states that had not initially supported, or even actively opposed, the direction of U.S. policy. In one account, the Bush administration expected four divisions of foreign troops—both from NATO and Arab states—to assist with peacekeeping and stabilization operations.[123] A 2003 planning document entitled "U.S. and Coalition Objectives," written by Defense Undersecretary for Policy Douglas Feith, suggested that the administration also expected to obtain international participation in the reconstruction effort, as well as the "political support of the international community."[124] Assumptions about the political effects of exercising power shaped the Bush administration's belief that the U.S. action could effectively produce a stable democratic outcome in Iraq.

Bandwagoning assumptions also generated the expectation that U.S. military power would produce a benign form of the domino dynamic in the region itself: the demonstration effect of regime change in Iraq would embolden liberals and deter authoritarians throughout the Middle East.[125] As Bush argued, a "free Iraq can be an example of reform and progress to all the Middle East."[126] In his June 2004 commencement speech to the Air Force Academy, Bush advanced a clear empirical prediction based on the causal logic of band-wagoning: "Freedom's advance in the Middle East will have another very practical effect. The terrorist movement feeds on the appearance of inevitability. It claims to rise on the currents of history, using past American withdrawals from Somalia and Beirut to sustain this myth. . . .The success of free and stable governments in Afghanistan and Iraq and elsewhere will shatter the myth and discredit the radicals."[127]

Weapons of mass destruction-related concessions by Libya were construed as apparent confirmation of the positive feedback in credibility that follows from a regional demonstration of power. In his 2004 State of the Union address, Bush stated that "nine months of intense negotiations succeeded with Libya, while twelve years of diplomacy with Iraq did not. . . .Words must be credible, and no one can now doubt the word of America."[128] Similarly, Max Boot argues that newfound post-Iraq credibility "helps explain [Libyan leader] Muammar Qaddafi's sudden willingness to give up his WMD arsenal. . . .and the Iranian mullahs willingness to accept greater international scrutiny of their nuclear program."[129]

Key administration decisionmakers also appeared to believe the positive results of demonstrating resolve (i.e., a bandwagoning dynamic) would operate within Iraq itself, increasing the likelihood and accelerating the pace of democratization. In Woodward's account of the war planning process, major figures in the Bush administration assumed that "the Iraqis would join in if it looked like the U.S. was coming. . . . the first steps toward war and demonstration of resolve would make winning the war that much easier. And as they all knew, little was more appealing to President Bush than showing resolve."[130] Hence the appeal of a "shock and awe" strategy, in which it was assumed that the overwhelming display of U.S. military power would create domestic conditions in Iraq conducive to democratization.[131]

Beliefs about the political effects of exercising power were augmented by the notion that U.S. technological superiority made military power a usable and low-cost instrument of democratic change. As Bush declared in his infamous "mission accomplished" speech, "we have witnessed the arrival of a new era. In the past, military power was used to end a regime by breaking a nation. Today, we have the greater power to free a nation by breaking a dangerous and aggressive regime."[132] The campaign in Afghanistan demonstrated the effectiveness of the U.S. military in projecting the power necessary to rapidly and decisively overthrow a weak regime, and in a manner that corroborated Defense Secretary Donald Rumsfeld's agenda of transforming the military such that it relied less on heavy weaponry and ground troops and more on technology, intelligence, and special operations forces.

After Afghanistan, similar assumptions about technology and military power continued to shape the Iraq war planning process. The "off the shelf" war plan in December 2001—known as Op Plan 1003—assumed a scenario similar to the Persian Gulf War, and called for a force level of 500,000 to be built up over approximately six months. Both Tommy Franks, commander in chief of United States Central Command, and Rumsfeld agreed that a mass army strategy was unnecessary; Rumsfeld observed that he was "not sure that much force is needed given what we've learned coming out of Afghanistan."[133] The expectation that a minimum of military force would be needed to accomplish U.S. political objectives in Iraq made the use of force a more attractive policy option.

Neoconservative views on the efficacy of U.S. power in promoting democratic change are embedded in a broader post-Vietnam agenda of restoring the faith of the United States in its capacity to usefully project power and reversing the perception, both domestically and internationally, of U.S. weakness and failure of will. The neoconservatism of the 1970s argued that detente and the failure in Vietnam resulted from, and in turn contributed to, the belief that there were clear limits to U.S. power, resulting in a retrenchment that prominent neoconservative writer Norman Podhoretz characterized as "Finlandization from within" and a "culture of appeasement."[134] Perception of decline and constraint were paralleled by academic debates over the usability of power and the structural diffusion of military and economic capabilities from bipolararity to multipolarity, and resulted in a gradual drift toward exemplarism that, particularly as practiced by President Jimmy Carter's administration in the late 1970s, neoconservatives regarded as a failure of will and resolve.[135] Neoconservatives argued that this psychology about U.S. power and the use of force continued throughout the 1990s, culminating in President Bill Clinton's risk aversion, reluctance to take casualties, and overreliance on airpower.[136]

However, the confluence of primacy, acute threat, and the political environment created by September 11 provided an opportunity in which U.S. power could again be rendered usable. The military actions in Afghanistan and Iraq and the ensuing democracy-promotion program, in addition to their immediate security motivations, were driven in part by the neoconservative desire to restore U.S. strength and credibility, domestically by reversing popular reluctance about the use of force, and internationally by reversing perceptions of U.S. weakness and failure of will. Figures within the Bush administration were cognizant of this purpose in using force in Iraq. Bush's speeches rhetorically emphasized action and will: "The only path to safety is the path of action. This nation will act."[137] Within the Bush cabinet, Rumsfeld in particular "was insistent upon boots on the ground to change the psychology of how Americans viewed war."[138] As a result, Max Boot argues that the Afghan invasion "provided a vital boost for U.S. security, not only by routing the terrorist network, but also by dispelling the myth of U.S. weakness," and the Iraq invasion "will be another vital step towards restoring a healthy fear of U.S. power."[139]

Like progressivism, the result of these ideological dimensions in conjunction—liberal optimism, the virtue of U.S. power, and the capacity of U.S. power to effect democratic change—place contemporary neoconservatism squarely in the vindicationist tradition of U.S. liberal exceptionalism. To the extent these ideas represent the dominant policymaking coalition within the Bush administration, U.S. national security policy favors mission over example as the primary means of extending democracy to strategic areas.

An Exemplarist Opposition?

Is there a viable policy alternative to the contemporary dominance of vindicationism, or does exemplarism no longer have any relevance to U.S. foreign policy in an age of unipolarity? Some historical elements of the exemplarist position are absent and not likely to return. The military, despite the Iraq prison scandal, remains one of the most trusted public institutions in the United States,[140] and in the absence of a viable isolationist political faction, the necessity of a foreign policy bureaucracy to manage international engagement is no longer questioned.

Nonetheless, certain exemplarist themes are reemerging. The traditional tension between the functional requirements of security and military institutions and liberal distrust of concentrated authority remain, a dilemma as acute as ever in the war on international terrorism and the domestic security issues it raises. For example, in her rejection of the assertion of presidential authority to designate and detain "enemy combatants" indefinitely, Supreme Court Justice Sandra Day O'Connor employed classic exemplarist arguments: "A state of war is not a blank check for the president when it comes to the rights of the nation's citizens. . . .. We must preserve our commitment at home to the principles for which we fight abroad."[141]

A second dimension of the exemplarist critique is skepticism about the capacity of U.S. power to promote and consolidate democratic change abroad. Although the Iraq debate has been dominated by the issues of preemption, systemic intelligence failure, and strategic miscalculation, arguments have also been advanced against the coercive promotion of democracy. Not surprisingly, much of this critique has come from the political Right in the United States. Exemplarism has traditionally contained a deeply conservative belief that progress and democratic change are fragile and difficult to consolidate. The conservative focus on culture, incrementalism, and the organic nature of political change suggests a pessimistic view toward the efficacy of liberal statebuilding: that societies are unable to democratize by force, that beliefs are slow to change, and that the demand for effective public institutions cannot be compelled externally.

Interestingly, some of the most well known statements of this exemplarist view were articulated by earlier generations of neoconservative thinkers. For example, Jeane Kirkpatrick, an ambassador to the United Nations in the Reagan administration, argued that democracy is the result of a complex set of conditions that can be achieved only through a process of political evolution, and that attempts to change political systems by force not only often fail to achieve their objectives, but frequently produce unintended consequences that undermine their benign intentions.[142] Writing in the context of the late Cold War, Kirkpatrick provided as damning a critique of Bush-style vindicationism as any contemporary observer: "The political temptation . . . in believing that [our] intelligence and exemplary motives equip [us] to reorder the institutions, the lives, and even the characters of almost everyone—this is the totalitarian temptation."[143] In unwitting exemplarist fashion, Kansas Republican Senator Pat Roberts emphatically updated this view: "Liberty cannot be laid down like so much AstroTurf."[144]

Why does this set of exemplarist ideas not gain more political traction? Like the 1890s, the answer is a combination of power and nationalism. There are powerful structural incentives for the United States to expand in the absence of countervailing restraint. But although realism can account for a more assertive U.S. grand strategy under the Bush administration, it cannot account for the liberal character of that assertion. Contemporary American vindicationism is a function of both unipolarity and a series of ideological commitments about democracy promotion that follow from the neoconservative brand of liberal exceptionalism, in which it is contended that U.S. power can effectively be deployed as an agent of democratic change in international politics.

UNDERSTANDING DEMOCRACY PROMOTION IN U.S FOREIGN POLICY

Despite what the recent public debate over Iraq might lead one to believe, democracy promotion is not a new idea in U.S. foreign policy; in fact, it is probably the oldest. This article developed a model to explain variation in U.S. democracy-promotion policy, and used two cases to illustrate the argument: the 1890s and the Bush administration.

This history of U.S. democracy promotion illustates the explanatory payoff to be gained from approaches that combine both ideological and material factors—often posed as mutually exclusive sources of foreign policy behavior—situated at different levels of analyses.

Vindicationism is inextricably linked with power: a precondition for the use of intervention or coercion as a mechanism of democratic change is the capability to project political influence and military force. Moral suasion and the power of example are not usually the preferred policy instruments of hegemonic states. But in both the 1890s and the Bush administration, the rise of vindicationism was also associated with underlying ideological changes toward the nature of progress, the U.S. liberal-exceptionalist mission, and the efficacy of U.S. power. Scholars are gradually coming into consensus that both power and ideas interact to produce outcomes of interest in international politics, and these cases demonstrate the utility of this approach in producing a more theoretically sound and empirically comprehensive understanding of this vital dimension of U.S. foreign and security policy.[145]

NOTES

1. "Interview with George Bush, Laura Bush," *CNN Larry King Live*, August 12, 2004.
2. "Remarks by the President at the 20th Anniversary of the National Endowment for Democracy," White House press release, November 6, 2003.
3. Ibid.
4. Robert Kagan, "America as Hegemon," *In the National Interest*, Vol. 2, No. 29 (July 2003), http://www.inthenationalinterest.com. See also Niall Ferguson, "A World without Power," *Foreign Policy*, No. 143 (July/August 2004), p. 32.
5. Jeane Kirkpatrick, *Dictatorships and Double Standards: A Critique of U.S. Policy* (Washington, D.C.: Ethics and Public Policy Center, Georgetown University, 1978), p. 37.
6. Thomas Paine, *The Rights of Man* (New York: Penguin, 1984), p. 34.
7. The concepts of exceptionalism and mission are major themes in the expansive secondary literature on U.S. foreign relations. Although this broad distinction is central to my argument about nationalist ideologies, I use Brands's terminology, both because it is the catchiest and because the academic world does not need yet another set of stylized terms. H.W. Brands, *What America Owes the World: The Struggle for the Soul, of foreign Policy* (Cambridge: Cambridge University Press, 1998). Many authors recognize the distinction identified here and agree on the direction of ideological change, although they often fail to advance clear, systematic explanations. See Arthur Schlesinger Jr., *The Cycles of American History* (Boston: Houghton Mifflin, 1986); Kenneth N. Waltz, *Man, the State, and War* (New York: Columbia University Press, 1959); Walter McDougall, *Promised land, Crusader State: The American Encounter with the World since 1776* (Boston: Houghton Mifflin, 1997); Russell Nye, *This Almost Chosen People: Essays in the History of American Ideas* (East Lansing: Michigan State University Press, 1966); Edward Burns, *The American Idea of Mission: Concepts of National Purpose and Destiny* (New Brunswick, N.J.: Rutgers University Press, 1957); Walter Russell Mead, *Special Providence: American Foreign Policy and How It Changed the World* (New York: Alfred A. Knopf, 2001); Patrick Thaddeus Jackson, "Defending the West: Occidentalism and the Formation of NATO," *Journal of Political Philosophy*, Vol. 11, No. 3 (September 2003), pp. 223–253; and Richard Hofstadter, *The Age of Reform: From Bryan to FDR* (New York: Alfred A. Knopf, 1955).
8. Henry Kissinger, *Diplomacy* (New York: Simon and Schuster, 1994), p. 18.
9. Anthony D. Smith, *Chosen Peoples: Sacred Sources of National Identity* (Oxford: Oxford University Press, 2003), p. 93.
10. Robert Kagan, "Power and Weakness," *Policy Review*, No. 113 (June-July 2002), p. 3.
11. For surveys of this literature, see Gideon Rose "Neoclassical Realism and Theories of Foreign Policy," *World Politics*, Vol. 51, No. 1 (October 1998), pp. 144-172; and Randall L. Schweller, "The Progressivism of Neoclassical Realism," in Colin Elman and Miriam Fendius Elman, eds., *Progress in International Relations Theory; Appraising the Field* (Cambridge, Mass.: MIT Press, 2003).
12. Kenneth N. Waltz, "Structural Realism after the Cold War," in G. John Ikenberry, ed., *America Unrivaled; The Future of the Balance of Power* (Ithaca, N.Y.: Cornell University Press, 2002), p. 51.

13. Thucydides, *The Peloponneskn War,* trans. Steven Lattimore (Indianapolis: Hackctt, 1998), p. 298.

14. Factions within structural realism debate whether states balance against aggressive intentions (a component of "threat") or against power. This debate is critical to competing conceptions of U.S. exceptionalism because vindicationism regards U.S. intentions—and thus power—as inherently benign and nonthreatening.

15. Rose, "Neoclassical Realism and Theories of Foreign Policy," p. 151. The argument that interests expand with power is also introduced in Paul Kennedy, *The Rise and Fall of the Great Powers: Economic Change and Military Conflict from 1500-2000* (New York: Random House, 1987).

16. Robert Gilpin, *War and Change in World Politics* (Cambridge: Cambridge University Press, 1981).

17. Fareed Zakaria, *From Wealth to Power: The Unusual Origins of America's World Role* (Princeton, N.J.: Princeton University Press, 1998).

18. Robert Jervis, "Understanding the Bush Doctrine," *Political Science Quarterly,* Vol. 3, No. 118 (September 2003), pp. 365-388; and Kenneth N. Waltz, *Theory of International Politics* (Reading, Mass.: Addison-Wesley, 1979), chap. 9.

19. This conceptual deficiency in realism, especially with respect to U.S. liberalism, is discussed in the appendix of Tony Smith, America's *Mission: The United States and the Worldwide Struggle for Democracy in the Twentieth Century* (Princeton, N.J.: Princeton University Press, 1994). Sec also see Jeffrey W. Legro and Andrew Moravscik's methodological "two-step," in which certain sets of theories—"epistemic," social-constructivist—explain the sources and perceptions of interests, white rationalist third-image theories—neorealism and ncoliberalism—explain the strategic pursuit of those interests subject to variations in such external constraint as the distribution of material capabilities or information. Lcgro and Moravscik, "Is Anybody Still a Realist?" *International Security,* Vol. 24, No. 2 (Pall 1999), pp. 5-55.

20. I use the term "nationalism" to refer to a national political identity or a quality of national character, and not, as defined by Ernest Gellner, to the "political principle which holds that the political and national unit should be congruent," Gellner, *Nations and Nationalism* (Ithaca, N.Y.: Cornell University Press, 1983), p. 1.

21. Harold Hongju Koh, "Foreword: On American Exceptionalism," *Stanford Law Review,* Vol. 55, No. 5 (May 2003), pp. 1470-1528. Sec also Max Lerner, *America as a Civilization* (New York: Simon and Schuster, 1957); McDougall, *Promised Land, Crusader State,* chap. 2; Seymour Martin Lipset, *American Exceptionalism: A Double-Edged Sword* (New York: W.W. Norton, 1996); and Samuel P. Huntington, *American Politics: The Promise of Disharmony* (Cambridge, Mass.: Belknap, 1981), p. 259.

22. For the purposes of this argument, at issue is not whether the United States is in fact more unique than others, but the extent to which the United States' historical perception of itself as exceptional has influenced foreign policy. Michael Barone, "A Place Like No Other," *U.S. News & World Report,* June 28, 2004, p. 38.

23. Characterizations of American foreign policy as "exceptional" often include dimensions other than the perception of an obligation or interest in the promotion of democracy abroad. For other treatments, see George F. Kennan, *American Diplomacy* (Chicago: University of Chicago Press, 1951); Joseph Lepgold and Timothy McKeown, "Is American Foreign Policy Exceptional? An Empirical Analysis," *Political Science Quarterly,* Vol. 110, No. 3 (Fall 1995), pp. 369-384; and Samuel P. Huntington, "American Ideals versus American Institutions," *Political Science Quarterly,* Vol. 97, No. 1 (Spring 1982), pp. 1-37.

24. According to one historian of the American political tradition, "perhaps no theme has ever dominated the minds of the leaders of this nation to the same extent as the idea that America occupies a unique place and has a special destiny among the nations of the earth." Burns, *The American Idea of Mission.*

25. For specific examples, see Waltz, *Man, the State, the War,* chap. 4; and Smith, *Chosen Peoples.*

26. The term "American Creed" was introduced by Gunnar Myrdal, and borrowed extensively in Huntington. Myrdal, *An American Dilemma: The Negro Problem and Modern Democracy* (New York: Harper and Brothers, 1944); and Huntington, *American Politics.*

27. This argument broadly conforms to a "logic of appropriateness": U.S. political leaders act in terms of what is viewed as normatively appropriate or consistent with a given political identity, in this case defined in terms of the political values of the American Creed. On competing logics of social action, see Thomas Risse, "Constructivism and International Institutions: Toward Conversations across Paradigms," in Ira Katznelson and Helen Milner, eds., *Political Science: The State of the Discipline* (New York: W.W. Norton, 2002).

28. Burns, *The American Idea of Mission,* p. 11.

29. Huntington, *American Politics,* p. 15. On the Puritan influence on U.S. political history, see also Richard Hofstader, *The Progressive Historians: Turner, Beard, Partington* (New York: Alfred A. Knopf, 1968).

30. Quoted in Nye, *This Almost Chosen People,* p. 192.

31. Herman Melville, *White-Jacket: Or, the World in a Man-of-War* (New York: Modern Library, 2002), p. 151.

32. Quoted in Nye, *This Almost Chosen People,* p. 169.

33. Anthony D. Smith, *The Ethnic Origins of Nations* (Oxford: Blackwell, 1986), p. 140. On the civic/ethnic distinction in defining national citizenship, see Rogers Brubaker, *Citizenship and Nationhood in France and Germany* (Cambridge, Mass.: Harvard University Press, 1992). On the ideational origins of U.S. nationalism, see Hans Kohn *American Nationalism: An interpretive Essay* (New York: Macmillan, 1957).

34. On nationalism as a rationalizing source of political cohesion in democracies, see Charles A. Kupchan, *The End of the American Era; U.S. Foreign Policy and the Geopolitics of the Twenty-first Century* (New York: Alfred A. Knopf, 2002), p. 116.

35. Myrdal, *An American Dilemma,* p. 3.

36. Two sets of "causal" claims are employed in the argument thus far: (1) the causal claims or hypotheses that constitute these competing nationalist traditions, and (2) propositions advanced to explain change in U.S. foreign policy, and specifically why one school (i.e., a set of interrelated hypotheses on how to "cause" democracy) became privileged over others.

37. Judith Goldstein and Robert O. Keohane, eds., *Ideas and Foreign Policy: Beliefs, Institutions, and Political Change* (Ithaca, N.Y.: Cornell University Press, 1993). See also Charles A. Kupchan, *The Vulnerability of Empire* (Ithaca, N.Y.: Cornell University Press, 1994).

38. Barry R. Posen, *The Sources of Military Doctrine: France, Germany, and Britain between the World Wars* (Tthaca, N.Y.: Cornell University Press, 1984); and Stephen M. Walt, *The Origins of Alliances* (Ithaca, N.Y.: Cornell University Press, 1987).

39. Mead, *Special Providence,* p. 182.

40. Or as Otto Hintze argues, "Throughout the ages pressures from without have been a determining influence on internal structure." Hintze, "Military Organization and the Organization of the State," in Felix Gilbert, ed., *The Historical Essays of Otto Hintze* (New York: Oxford University Press, 1975), p. 183. For two surveys of this style of argumentation, see Peter Gourevitch, "The Second Image Reversed: The International Sources of Domestic Politics," *International Organization,* Vol. 32, No. 4 (Autumn 1978), pp. 881-912; and Fareed Zakaria, "Realism and Domestic Politics; A Review Essay," *International Security,* Vol. 17, No. 1 (Summer 1992), pp. 177-198.

41. Brands, What *America Owes the World,* p. 2.

42. Huntington, "American Ideals versus American Institutions," p. 25.

43. This argument is made explicitly by Huntington, but is similar to many of the causal mechanisms debated in the democratic peace literature. Huntington, *American Politics,* p. 257.

44. Ibid., p. 4. Sec also Burns, *The American Idea of Mission,* p. 26.

45. Harriet Beecher Stowe, *Oldtown Folks* (Boston: Fields, Osgood, 1869), p. 368.
46. Quoted in Loren Baritz, *City on a Hill: A History of Ideas and Myths in America* (New York: John Wiley and Sons, 1964), p. 13.
47. Baritz, *City on a Hill.*
48. Abraham Lincoln, "Address at Gettysburg, Pennsylvania, November 19, 1863," in Roy P. Easier, ed., *The Collected Works of Abraham Lincoln* (New Brunswick, N.J.: Rutgers University Press, 1953).
49. Washington to Henry Lawrens, November 14,1783, *The Writings of George Washington,* Vol. 10, John Fitzpatrick, ed. (Washington, D.C.: United States Printing Office, 1931–4), p. 256.
50. Schlesinger, *The Cycles of American History,* p. 13.
51. Quoted in ibid., p. 13.
52. Ezra Stiles, *The United States Elevated to Clary and Honor: A Sermon* (1783), in Thomas C. Paterson, ed., *Major Problems in American Foreign Policy,* Vol. 1: *Documents and Essays* (Lexington, Mass.: D.C. Heath, 1995), p. 38. Also quoted in McDougall, *Promised Land, Crusader State,* p. 18.
53. Reinhold Niebuhr, *The Irony of American History* (New York: Scribner, 1952), p. 71.
54. Melville, *White-Jacket,* p. 151.
55. On "optimism" and "pessimism" in international relations, see Waltz, *Man, the State, and War,* pp. 18-19.
56. Thucydides, *The Peloponnesian War,* bk. 1, p. 14.
57. Nye, *This Almost Chosen People,* p. 1.
58. Quoted in ibid., p. 169.
59. Washington, *The Writings of George Washington,* Vol. 13, p. 363. Lest the realist pedigree of this view be doubted, note the striking similarity in language between Washington and the Corcyreans in book 1 and the Mytileans in book 3 of *The Peloponnesian War.*
60. Quoted in Louis Hartz, *The Liberal Tradition in America: An Interpretation of American Political Thought since the Revolution* (New York: I-Iarcouit, Brace, 1955), p. 40.
61. Bernard Bailyn, *The Ideological Origins of the American Revolution* (Cambridge, Mass.: Harvard University Press, 1992). See also Huntington, *American Politics*; and Aaron L. Friedberg, *In the Shadow of the Garrison State: America's Anti-Statism and Its Cold War Grand Strategy* (Princeton, N.J.: Princeton University Press, 2000).
62. Schlesinger, *The Cycles of American History,* p. 7.
63. The founders and the Greek and Roman classics are discussed in ibid., chap. 1; and Mead, *Special Providence,* p. 182.
64. Mead, *Special. Providence,* p. 182; Burns, *The American Idea of Mission,* p. 16; and Brands, *What America Owes the World,* chap. 1.
65. On the effects of these two affairs on U.S. neutrality and unilateralism, see McDougall, *Promised Land, Crusader State,* pp. 30-31.
66. The *Federalist,* No. 8 (New York: Random House, 1941), p. 39.
67. For a broad survey of the foreign policy of the decade, see Robert L. Beisner, *From the Old Diplomacy to the New* (New York: Cromwell, 1975).
68. For an attempt to evaluate competing explanations situated at different levels of analyses, see Peter Trubowitz, Emily O. Goldman, and Edward Rhodes, eds., *The Politics of Strategic Adjustment: Ideas, Institutions, and Interests* (New York: Columbia University Press, 1999).
69. On economic growth in this period, see Samuel P. Hays, *The Response to Industrialism, 1865–1914* (Chicago: University of Chicago Press, 1957).
70. Zakaria, *From Wealth to Power,* p. 46; and Kennedy, *The Rise and Fall of the Great Powers.*
71. Kennan, *American Diplomacy,* p. 17.
72. See Tony Smith, *The Pattern of Imperialism: The United States, Great Britain, and the Late-Industrializing World since 1815* (Cambridge: Cambridge University Press, 1982); and Kennan, *American Diplomacy,* p. 16.

73. Quoted in Kupchan, *The End of the American Era*, p. 175.

74. Smith, *America's Mission*, p. 43.

75. Hofstadter, *The Age of Reform*, p. 5.

76. See William E. Leuchtenberg, "Progressivism and Imperialism: Trie Progressive Movement and American Foreign Policy, 1898-1916," *Mississippi Valley Historical Review*, Vol. 39, No. 3, (December 1952), p. 500; Fred Harrington, "The Anti-Imperialist Movement in the United States, 1890-1900," *Mississippi Valley Historical Review*, Vol. 22, No. 2 (September 1935), pp. 211-239; and McDougall, Promised Land, Crusader State. For an alternative view, see Barton J. Bernstein and Franklin Leib, "Progressive Republican Senators and American Imperialism, 1898-1916: A Reappraisal," in John Silbey, ed., *To Advise and Consent: The United States Congress and Foreign Policy in the Twentieth Century* (Brooklyn, N.Y.: Carson, 1991). Bernstein and Lieb's analysis is limited to Midwestern Republican senators and concedes the broader point that few prominent Progressives joined the anti-imperialist movement in the 1890s.

77. Two excellent accounts of the Social Gospel are Charles Howard Hopkins, *The Rise of the Social Gospel in American Protestantism, 1865–1915* (London; Oxford University Press, 1940); and Robert Handy, ed., *The Social Gospel in America*, 1870-1920 (New York: Oxford University Press, 1966).

78. Quoted in Handy, *The Social Gospel in America*, 1879-1920, p. 10.

79. Robert Abzug, *Cosmos Crumbling: American Reform and the Religious Imagination* (New York: Oxford University Press, 1994); and Timothy Lawrence Smith, *Revivalism and Social Reform: American Protestantism on the Eve of the Civil War* (Baltimore, Md.: Johns Hopkins University Press, 1981). Sabbatarians, for the curious reader, lobbied to make Sunday an officially recognized holy day.

80. Early popularizers of the Social Gospel, especially with regard to the poverty and vice generated by the cities, included Josiah Strong, *Our Country* (Cambridge, Mass.: Belknap, 1963).

81. Smith, *Revivalism and Social Reform*, p. 10.

82. Arthur Link, *Woodrow Wilson: Revolution, War, and Peace* (Arlington Heights, 111.: Harlan Davidson, 1979), p. 6.

83. Quoted in Schlesinger, *The Cycles of American History*, p. 16.

84. Frank Ninkovich refers to this idea as "neo-federalist." Ninkovich, *Modernity and Power: A History of the Domino Theory in the Twentieth Century* (Chicago: University of Chicago Press, 1994), p. 10.

85. This connection is made persuasively in Leuchtenberg, "Progressivism and Imperialism," p. 500.

86. Herbert Croly, *The Promise of American Life* (Cambridge, Mass.: Belknap, 1965), p. 289.

87. Ibid., p. 290.

88. Quoted in Akira Iriye, *From Nationalism to Internationalism*: U.S. *Foreign Policy to 1914* (Boston: Routledge and K. Paul, 1977), p. 323.

89. Theodore Roosevelt, *The Strenuous Life* (1899), in Ernest R. May, ed., *The American Foreign Policy* (New York: George Braziller, 1963), p. 121.

90. Quoted in Ninkovich, *Modernity and Power*, p. 8.

91. For arguments on culture as a constraint, see Peter J. Katzentscin, ed., *The Culture of National Security; Norms and Identity in World Politics* (New York: Columbia University Press, 1996).

92. Kennan, *American Diplomacy*, p. 3

93. Quoted in David Healy, *U.S. Expansionism: The Imperialist Urge in the W90s* (Madison: University of Wisconsin Press, 1970), p. 217.

94. James Mann's *Rise of the Vulcans* offers an example of an interpretation of this core set of beliefs; I am presenting a particular subset as they relate to democracy promotion. Mann, *Rise of the Vulcans: The History of Bush's War Cabinet* (New York: Viking, 2004).

95. See, for example, Kennedy, *The Rise and Fall of Great Powers*; and Kenneth N. Waltz, "The Emerging Structure of International Politics, "*International Security*, Vol. 18, No. 2 (Fall 1993), pp. 44–79.

96. See William C. Wohlforth, "The Stability of a Unipolar World," *International Security*, Vol. 24, No. 1 (Summer 1999), pp. 5-41. On military dominance, see Barry R. Posen, "Command of the Commons: The Military Foundation of U.S. Hegemony, "*International Security*, Vol. 28, No. 1 (Summer 2003), pp. 5-46. On latent U.S. power being revealed after September 11, see Charles Krauthammer, "The Unipolar Moment Revisited, "*National Interest*, No. 70 (Winter 2002/2003), pp. 5-17.

97. Robert Jervis, "The Compulsive Empire," *Foreign Policy*, No. 137 (July/August 2003), p. 82.

98. George W. Bush, *The National Security Strategy of the United States of America* (Washington, D.C.: White House, September 20, 2002), p. 3.

99. George W. Bush, "Remarks Accepting the Presidential Nomination at the Republican National Convention in New York City," *Public Papers of the Presidents*, September 6, 2004.

100. Quoted in Bob Woodward, *Plan of Attack* (New York: Simon and Schuster, 2004), p. 89.

101. Walter Lippman, *U.S. War Aims* (Boston: Little, Brown, 1944).

102. Suzanne Fields, "The Enduring Legacy of Ronald Reagan," *Washington Times*, June 7, 2003, p. A23. On Bush's desire to personally emulate Reagan, see Woodward, *Plan of Attack*.

103. Bush, *The National Security Strategy of the United States of America*, p. 9. On liberal optimism in international politics, see Waltz, *Man, the State, and War*. On liberalism in the Bush doctrine, see Jer-vis, "Understanding the Bush Doctrine," p. 365.

104. "Remarks by the President in Commencement Address to United States Coast Guard Academy," White House press release, May 21, 2003.

105. Michael Gordon, "The Strategy to Secure Traq Did Not Foresee a Second War," *New York Times*, October 19, 2004. On the failure to provide security in Iraq in the months after the military action, see Larry Diamond, "What Went Wrong in Iraq," *Foreign Affairs*, Vol. 83, No. 5 (September/October 2004), pp. 34-57.

106. Quoted in Woodward, *Plan of Attack*, p. 407.

107. Quoted in Lawrence Kaplan, "Springtime for Realism," *New Republic*, June 21, 2004, p. 20.

108. Bush, *The National Security Strategy of the United States of America*, p. 7.

109. "Remarks by the President at the 2002 Graduation Exercise of the United States Military Academy," White House press release, June 1, 2002.

110. Krauthammer, "The Unipolar Moment Revisited," p. 14.

111. Quoted in Robert D. Kaplan, "World of Difference," *New Republic*, March 29, 2004, p. 20.

112. Bush, *The National Security Strategy of the United States of America*, p. 5.

113. Josiah Strong, *Our Country* (Cambridge, Mass.: Belknap, 1963).

114. Jervis, "Understanding the Bush Doctrine"; and Waltz, *Theory of International Politics*, chap. 9.

115. Condoleezza Rice, "Promoting the National Interest," *Foreign Affairs*, Vol. 75, No. 1 (January/February 2000), p. 3.

116. Robert Kagan and William Kristol, "The Present Danger," *National Interest*, No. 59 (Spring 2000), p. 57.

117. Quoted in Woodward, *Plan of Attack*, pp. 251, 308.

118. Ornstein's phrase is similar to what international relations scholars would recognize as bandwagoning. Norman Ornstcin, "Congress Inside Out: High Stakes and an Overloaded Agenda," Roll Call, September 10, 2001. Using a very simple anarchy-hierarchy distinction, however, Kenneth Waltz shows why the effects of "winning" arc different in domestic politics than international politics, and why bandwagoning should be comparatively rare in the latter. See Waltz, *Theory of International Politics*.

119. Quoted in Woodward, *Plan of Attack*, p. 377.

120. Robert lervis, *Systems Effects: Complexity in Political and Social Life* (Princeton, N.J.: Princeton University Press, 1997). See also Walt, *The Origins of Alliances*.

121. This aspect of the 2002 NSS is noted by Jack Snyder, "Imperial Temptations," *National Interest*, No. 77 (Spring 2003), pp. 29-41. Bush, *The National Security Strategy of the United States of America*, p. 3.

122. Quoted in Woodward, *Plan of Attack*, p. 162.
123. Gordon, "The Strategy to Secure Iraq Did, Not Foresee a Second War," p. Al.
124. The document is discussed in Woodward, *Plan of Attack*, p. 328.
125. Jervis, "Understanding the Bush Doctrine," p. 365.
126. Quoted in David Sanger and Thorn Shanker, "Bush Says Regime in Iraq Is No More; Syria Is Penalized," *New York Times*, April "16, 2003.
127. "Excerpts from President Bush's Remarks at the Air Force Academy Graduation Ceremony," *New, York Post*, June 3, 2004, p. 33.
128. Quoted in Martin Indyk, "Iraq War Did Not Force Qadaffi's Hand," *Financial Times*, March 9, 2004, p. 21.
129. Max Bool, "The Bush Doctrine Lives," *Weekly Standard*, February 16, 2004.
130. Woodward, Plan of Attack, p. 81.
131. On this expectation, see Cordon, "The Strategy to Secure Iraq Did Not Foresee a Second War," p. Al; and John Lewis Caddis, *Surprise, Security, and the American Experience* (Cambridge, Mass.: Harvard University Press, 2004).
132. Quoted in James Lindsay and Ivo Daalder, "Shooting First: The Preemptive War Doctrine Has Met an Early Death in Iraq,"*Los Angeles Times*, May 30, 2004.
133. Quoted in Woodward, *Plan of Attack*, p. 41.
134. Norman Podhoretz, "Making the World Safe for Communism," *Commentary*, April 1976, pp. 31-41; and Norman Podhoretz, *The Present Danger: Do We Have the Will to Reverse the Decline of American Power?* (New York: Simon and Schuster, 1980). On the neoconservative belief that U.S. power was never in decline, and the resulting continuity this brought to neoconservative thought from the 1970s to 2001, see Mann, *Rise of the Vulcans. See also* Brands, *What America Owes the World*, p. 268. Andrew Bacevich argues that the belief in "no limits" has become one of the "three no's" in contemporary U.S. foreign policy. See Bacevich, *American Empire: 'The Realities and Consequences of U.S. Diplomacy* (Cambridge, Mass.: Harvard University Press, 2002).
135. For an example of an academic work of this kind, see Robert Kcohane and Joseph Nye, *Power and Interdependence: World Politics in Transition* (Boston: Little, Brown, 1977).
136. For a survey of neoconservative thought in this period, see Mann, *Rise of the Vulcans*.
137. "Remarks by the President at the 2002 Graduation Exercise of the United States Military Academy."
138. Quoted in Woodward, *Plan of Attack*, p. 26.
139. Quoted in G. John Ikenberry, "The End of the Neo-conservative Moment," *Survival*, Vol. 46, No. 1 (Spring 2004), p. 14; and Max Boot, "Iraq War Can Make Up for Earlier U.S. Missteps," *USA Today*, March 25, 2003.
140. According to a recent Gallup poll, 75 percent of respondents say they have a "great deal" of confidence in the military, substantially greater than in Congress, business, unions, and the media. See Suzanne Fields, "The Enduring Legacy of Ronald Reagan," *Washington Times*, June 7, 2003, p. A23.
141. Quoted in Anthony Lewis, "The Court v. Bush," *New York Times*, June 29, 2004, p. 27.
142. Kirkpatrick, *Dictatorships and Double Standards*. For a survey of Kirkpatrick's writings in the 1970s, see John Ehrman, *Rise of Neoconservatism: Intellectuals and Foreign Affairs*, 1945-1994 (New Haven, Conn.: Yale University Press, 1995), pp. 117-121.
143. Jeane Kirkpatrick, "Politics and the New Class," Society, Vol. 16, No. 2 (January-February 1979), p. 48.
144. Quoted in George will, "Politics and Prose in Iraq, *Washington post*, May 24 2004, p. A31.
145. See, for example, Steven G. Brooks and William C. Wohlforth, "Power, Globalization, and the End of the Cold War: Reevaluating a Landmark Case for Ideas," *International Security*, Vol. 25, No- 3 (Winter 2000/01), pp. 5-53; and Peter J. Katzenstcin and Nobuo Okawara, "Japan, Asia-Pacific Security, and the Case for Analytical Eclecticism," *International Security*, Vol. 26, No. 3 (Winter 2001/02), pp. 153-185.

ᖷ PART FIVE ᖷ

Public Opinion, Policy Legitimacy, and Sectional Conflict

These next five essays focus on the influence of the diffuse pressures of public opinion, reigning political images, and societal interests on American foreign policy. As such they share elements of several of the approaches in other sections. They share a general view that periods of American foreign policy are punctuated by crystallized sets of images and publicly held views about the proper direction of American foreign policy. Yet each provides a distinctive analytical cut into these domestic structures and processes.

Michael Roskin focuses on shifting generational views or "paradigms" of foreign policy. Each generation, Roskin argues, carries with it a set of "strategic conventional wisdoms" that are formed by a decisive historical event and that guide public orientations toward policy. The Pearl Harbor paradigm, according to Roskin, was interventionist. This view had many sources but took form in the traumatic events of Pearl Harbor and the Second World War. The paradigm reflected an imagery of the international system and a set of lessons to which American leaders must attend. Most important was the lesson that aggression must be met head on and not appeased. The imagery of Pearl Harbor took deep root and was not dislodged, Roskin argues, until the failures of Vietnam seemingly discredited its interventionist orientation. With Vietnam came a new set of lessons, wrapped in a paradigm of nonintervention. One is left to speculate about the mechanisms by which these changes occur and the lessons become entrenched.

Alexander L. George also focuses on diffuse sets of public views on foreign policy as powerful forces that set the terms of choice within government. George argues that government officials are not free to conduct foreign policy as they choose. Officials can sustain foreign policy only when it is developed within a consensus. Consequently, government officials build support for their policy. In analyzing the importance of domestic support George advances the notion of "policy legitimacy," a measure of the degree to which the president has convinced Congress and the public of the soundness of his policy goals. The legitimation of policy, according to George, requires the president to persuade the public of the feasibility and desirability of that policy. These imperatives of domestic legitimacy set limits on what government officials can propose and sustain in the realm of foreign policy. In invoking the notion of legitimacy, therefore, George has focused on a particular mechanism in which a democratic society exerts an influence on the conduct of foreign policy.

In "Business Versus Public Influence in U.S. Foreign Policy" Lawrence R. Jacobs and Benjamin I. Page ask the critical question: Who most influences U.S. foreign policy? Is it epistemic communities of experts that possess the specialization to objectively analyze an increasingly complex global environment; organized pressure groups and, especially, businesses that seek to advance their own narrow interests; or the mass public which exerts its power on politicians anxious to win their support? Jacobs and Page rely primarily upon multivariate regression analyses to test the independent variables. Their results indicate that business has a strong, consistent, and, at times, lopsided influence upon U.S. foreign policy and tend to confirm the theoretical expectations and case study research of the organized interest group literature in international relations. However, in keeping with calls for multicausal research, these results also suggest that three of the most prominent lines of analysis of foreign policy—the interest group, epistemic community, and public opinion approaches—each have some merit.

Peter Trubowitz looks at the sources of political conflict in America foreign policy. Most analysts look to ideological or institutional cleavages at the national level as the most important sources of conflict over foreign policy. Taking a different approach, Trubowitz looks at geographically based sources of conflict. In an examination of Congressional voting on a variety of foreign policy issues, Trubowitz finds that sectional interests—particularly between the Northeast and South—featured prominently in Congressional debates during the Cold War. At their root, these conflicts were grounded in interregional struggles for political and economic advantage.

John Mearsheimer and Stephen Walt focus on the activities of domestic lobbying groups seeking to influence American foreign policy toward Israel and the Middle East. The authors observe that the United States has given Israel a level of support since the 1970s that is much greater than other states around the world—military, economic, and diplomatic. They argue that this policy of support for Israel cannot be explained simply in terms of traditional understandings of the American national interest or as a response to geopolitical realities. The pattern of American policy can only be fully understood by appreciating the role and activities of domestic pro-Israel pressure groups. Mearsheimer and Walt explore the activities of these groups and the ways that America's distinctively open system provides opportunities for lobbying.

꒛

From Pearl Harbor to Vietnam: Shifting Generational Paradigms and Foreign Policy

Michael Roskin

United States foreign policy can be seen as a succession of strategic conventional wisdoms, or *paradigms,* on whether the country's defense should start on the near or far side of the oceans. An interventionist paradigm favors the latter, a noninterventionist paradigm, the former. This article argues that each elite American generation comes to favor one of these orientations by living through the catastrophe brought on by the application ad absurdum of the opposite paradigm at the hands of the previous elite generation. Thus the bearers of the "Pearl Harbor paradigm" (themselves reacting to the deficiencies of the interwar "isolationism") eventually drove interventionism into the ground in Vietnam, giving rise to a noninterventionist "Vietnam paradigm." These paradigms seem to shift at approximately generational intervals, possibly because it takes that long for the bearers of one orientation, formed by the dramatic experiences of their young adulthood, to come to power and eventually misapply the lessons of their youth.

Recently much foreign-policy discussion has focused on economic interpretation of United States actions, bureaucratic politics and malfunctions, and executive–legislative relations. While such approaches have made interesting contributions to the field, none have been able to gather together seemingly disparate elements of foreign policy into an overall view that explains this behavior over several decades. The reason is that these popular approaches consistently downplay or even ignore the key element to such an overall view: the strategic assumptions held by decision-making elites—that is, who defines what as strategic; why; and when.[1] In other words, these approaches failed to consider that in certain periods United States policy makers deem much of the globe to be worth fighting for, while at other times they regard most of the world with indifference.

THE CONCEPT OF *PARADIGM*

The concepts of *paradigm* and *paradigm shift* are borrowed from Thomas Kuhn, who used them to describe intellectual growth in the natural sciences. Kuhn called paradigms "universally recognized scientific achievements that for a time provide model problems and solutions to a community of practitioners."[2] A paradigm is the basic assumption of a field; acceptance of it is mandatory for practitioners (e.g., those who do not accept the conservation of energy are

Michael Roskin, "From Pearl Harbor to Vietnam: Shifting Generational Paradigms and Foreign Policy." *Political Science Quarterly* 89 (Fall 1974): 563–588. Reprinted with permission.

not physicists; those who do not accept the gas laws are not chemists). Practitioners, having accepted the paradigm, then typically engage in "normal science," that is, the interpretation and detailing of the basic paradigm, which itself is not open to question.[3]

The importance of Kuhn's framework for our purposes is that it is a dynamic view: the paradigms shift. When researchers, operating under their old paradigm, begin to notice that their empirical findings do not come out the way they are supposed to, disquiet enters into the profession. Anomalies or counter-instances crop up in the research and throw the old paradigm into doubt. Then an innovator looks at the data from another angle, reformulates the basic framework, and introduces a new paradigm. Significantly, these innovators tend to be younger men who, "being little committed by prior practice to the traditional rules of normal science, are particularly likely to see that those rules no longer define a playable game and to conceive another set that can replace them."[4] The new paradigm does not triumph immediately and automatically. Now there are two competing, antithetical paradigms; each demands its separate world view. The discussants "are bound partly to talk through each other" because they are looking at the same data from differing angles.[5] The new paradigm makes progress, however, because it claims it "can solve the problems that have led the old one to a crisis."[6] The new paradigm makes particular headway among younger workers. The old practitioners may be beyond conversion; they simply die out. This "paradigm shift" is what Kuhn calls a "scientific revolution," and these "revolutions close with a total victory for one of the two opposing camps."[7]

There is one more point we must include from Kuhn. Which paradigm, the old or the new, is the "truth"? The answer is neither. The new paradigm is at best merely a closer approximation to reality. It seems to explain the data better and offers better paths to future research; it is never the last word. Wide areas of uncertainty remain, especially during the changeover period, when the data can be interpreted ambiguously. It is impossible to say when—or even if—the holders of the old paradigm are completely wrong. The profession merely comes to turn its back on them, ignoring them, leaving them out in the cold.[8]

Kuhn has suggested a theory of the innovation and diffusion of knowledge applicable to all fields, including foreign policy. The crucial difference with foreign-policy paradigms is that they are far less *verifiable* than natural-science paradigms. Students of foreign policy have only the crudest sort of verification procedure: the perception that the old paradigm has given rise to a catastrophe. More subtle perceptions of marginal dysfunctionality tend to go unnoticed (by all but a handful of critics) until the general orientation produces an unmistakable disaster.

How, then, can we adapt the Kuhnian framework to the study of United States foreign policy? The community of practitioners is an elite of persons relevant to foreign policy—both in and out of government, the latter including such opinion leaders as professors and journalists—who structure the debate for wider audiences.[9] While the relationship between mass and elite opinion in foreign policy is well beyond our scope here, most scholarly opinion holds that the mass public has only low or intermittent interest in foreign affairs. One study, for example, found more "isolationism" as one moves down the educational ladder.[10] Foreign aid has never been popular with American voters; only elite opinion sustains it. When the elite ceases to define overseas situations as threats to United States security, the mass public soon loses interest. Major American participation abroad is sustainable only when the elite has been mobilized to support it. Lose this support, and America stays home.

The content of the foreign-policy paradigm varies in detail but is generally reducible to the question of whether overseas areas "matter" to United States security. That is, should the defense of America start on the far or near side of the ocean? The Yale scholar of geopolitics Nicholas Spykman recognized the question as "the oldest issue in American foreign policy" and posed it in 1942 as well as anyone has ever done: "Shall we protect our interests by defense on this side of the water or by active participation in the lands across the oceans?"[11] The former view constitutes what we shall call a "noninterventionist" paradigm; the latter is an "interventionist" paradigm. These antithetical views shift under the impact of catastrophes which seem to prove that the old paradigm was wrong and its adherents mistaken. At that point the previous outsiders (gadflies, radicals, revisionists, etc.) find many of their views accepted as mainstream thinking; their critique becomes the new framework.

Our model resembles Kuhn's but with the important provision that neither old nor new foreign-policy paradigms have much intrinsic validity because neither can be objectively verified in an indeterminate world. Instead of verified, a new foreign-policy paradigm is merely internalized. Counterinstances are ignored; the range of conceivable strategic situations is narrowed to exclude possible alternate paradigms. It may be impossible to distinguish whether this process is emotional or rational, affective or cognitive. The acrimony accompanying foreign-policy paradigm shifts, however, suggests a strong emotional component. Chances are that a member of the American elite who as a young person witnessed the events leading up to Pearl Harbor has developed a very definite orientation to foreign policy, an interventionist one, the assumptions of which are not open for discussion. Similarly, by the early 1970s the interventionist views of Walt Rostow, Dean Rusk, and William Bundy produced mostly irritation (if not outright vituperation) on the part of younger foreign-policy thinkers.

It is here that we add the concept of generation to the Kuhnian model. Political scientists have not looked much at generations in their analyses. Some hold that to separate out a "political generation" is to reify an abstract and nebulous concept. People are born every day and constitute more of a continuum than a segment. The German sociologist Karl Mannheim agreed that generation is a reification, but no more so than the concept of social class, which is indispensable for much modern analysis.[12]

An elite generation freezes upon either an interventionist or noninterventionist paradigm usually after some foreign-policy catastrophe wrought by the application of the opposite paradigm. During a transition period the two paradigms clash. Because they are antithetical, compromise is impossible. The two generations with their different assumptions talk past each other. Eventually the new paradigm wins because it gains more younger adherents, while the advocates of the old paradigm retire and die off. The new paradigm triumphs not so much on an intellectual basis as on an actuarial one.

THE PEARL HARBOR PARADIGM

It may be profitable to look at the foreign-policy paradigm as having a natural life—a birth, a period of growth, and a death. The birth is characterized by a mounting criticism of the old paradigm and then by the conversion of a large portion of the elite to the new paradigm. An event "proves" the old paradigm wrong, as it did to Senator Arthur H. Vandenburg, a staunch isolationist whose turning to interventionism "took firm form on the afternoon of the Pearl

Harbor attack. That day ended isolationism for any realist."[13] In honor of Vandenburg's conversion we can label this interventionist orientation the "Pearl Harbor paradigm."

Pearl Harbor, of course, was merely the culmination of an increasingly heated argument in the interwar period between the dominant noninterventionists and interventionist Cassandras. We could also call the latter view the Munich paradigm, the Ethiopian paradigm, or even the Manchurian paradigm.[14] But the Pearl Harbor attack clinched the interventionists' argument by demonstrating they were "right" in warning that an isolated America was impossible. The isolationists either shut up or quickly changed sides.[15] The handful of holdouts, such as those who charged Roosevelt with dragging the country into war, were by and large simply ignored.

The most clearly visible starting point for the rise of the Pearl Harbor paradigm was Secretary of State Stimson's 1932 "nonrecognition" of Japanese expansion into Manchuria. Thereafter concern slowly grew among the American elite that aggressive powers abroad could eventually threaten America. The growth of this concern among younger persons is important for two reasons: First, people who were in their twenties during the late 1930s were less committed to the then-prevailing noninterventionism of the older generation. Accordingly, more of the younger group were open to formulate a new paradigm—an interventionist one. Second, although some older elite members may have been similarly alarmed at overseas threats, it was mostly the younger generation that would staff foreign-policy positions in future decades.

By the time war broke out in Europe in 1939, elite opinion was starting to split. The formation of two committees expressed this division: the isolationist America First and the increasingly interventionist Committee to Defend America by Aiding the Allies. On December 7, 1941, the interventionists could (and did) say, "I told you so," and then enshrined their argument—permanently, they thought—as the basic assumption of American foreign policy: If we do not nip aggression in the bud, it will eventually grow and involve us. By not stopping aggressors immediately, you encouraged them. Apart from the moral issue of helping a victim of aggression, you are also setting up the first line of defense of your own country. Accordingly, altruism and self-interest merge.

The discredited "isolationists" could only meekly retort that in principle at least, the defense of the United States did not start on the other side of the globe, for that merely guarantees American participation in wars that were not intrinsically hers. The last gasps of the remaining noninterventionism came in the 1951 debate to limit troops in Europe and the 1954 Bricker amendment to restrict executive agreements. Occasional whiffs of preinterventionist views could be sensed in debates over foreign aid.

The interesting aspect of the Pearl Harbor paradigm, however, was its duration long past World War II. The interventionist orientation had been so deeply internalized in the struggle with the isolationists that it did not lapse with the Allied victory. By that time almost all sections of the globe now "mattered" to American security, particularly as a new hostile power—the Soviet Union—seemed bent on territorial and ideological aggrandizement. In the 1930s the fate of East Europe bothered Washington very little, but in the span of a decade East Europe became a matter of urgent American concern.[16] Not only had the Soviets inflicted brutal Hitlerlike dictatorships upon the nations of East Europe, it was taken for granted that they were preparing to do the same to West Europe and other areas. But this time America was smarter and stood prepared to stop aggression. In the span of one decade, 1945–1955, the United States committed itself to the defense of more than seventy nations.

A few quotes might suffice to demonstrate the persistence of the Pearl Harbor paradigm into the Vietnam era. Warning of a "new isolationism," Senator Thomas J. Dodd, in a 1965 floor speech, explained:

The situation in Viet-Nam today bears many resemblances to the situation just before Munich. . . .
  In Viet-Nam today we are again dealing with a faraway land about which we know very little.
  In Viet-Nam today we are again confronted by an incorrigible aggressor, fanatically committed to the destruction of the free world, whose agreements are as worthless as Hitler's. . . .
  If we fail to draw the line in Viet-Nam, in short, we may find ourselves compelled to draw a defense line as far back as Seattle and Alaska, with Hawaii as a solitary out-post in mid-Pacific.[17]

Defense Secretary Robert McNamara, in commenting on Lin Piao's 1965 statement on the universal applicability of "people's war," said, "It is a program of aggression. It is a speech that ranks with Hitler's *Mein Kampf.*"[18]

President Johnson too was immersed in the World War II imagery. In his 1965 Johns Hopkins speech he warned:

The central lesson of our time is that the appetite of aggression is never satisfied. To withdraw from one battlefield means only to prepare for the next. We must say in Southeast Asia—as we did in Europe—in the words of the Bible: "Hitherto shalt thou come, but no further."[19]

In a 1966 speech to NATO parliamentarians, Senator Henry M. Jackson put it this way:

Analogies with the past may be misleading and I would not argue that this is the 30's all over again. But looking back we think, as I am sure many of you do, that it is wise to stop aggression before the aggressor becomes strong and swollen with ambition from small successes. We think the world might have been spared enormous misfortunes if Japan had not been permitted to succeed in Manchuria, or Mussolini in Ethiopia, or Hitler in Czechoslovakia or in the Rhineland. And we think that our sacrifices in this dirty war in little Vietnam will make a dirtier and bigger war less likely.[20]

President Johnson said in a 1966 talk in New Hampshire:

Few people realize that world peace has reached voting age. It has been twenty-one years since that day on the U.S.S. Missouri in Tokyo Bay when World War II came to an end. Perhaps it reflects poorly on our world that men must fight limited wars to keep from fighting larger wars; but that is the condition of the world. . . .
  We are following this policy in Vietnam because we know that the restrained use of power has for twenty-one years prevented the wholesale destruction the world faced in 1914 and again in 1939.[21]

The Pentagon Papers are replete with the World War II analogy. Among these, in a 1966 memo, Walt Rostow explained how his experience as an OSS major plotting German bomb targets taught him the importance of cutting the enemy's POL—petroleum, oil, and lubricants:

With an understanding that simple analogies are dangerous, I nevertheless feel it is quite possible the military effects of a systematic and sustained bombing of POL in North Vietnam may be more prompt and direct than conventional intelligence analysis would suggest.[22]

Rostow seems to have retained a petroleum version of the Pearl Harbor paradigm and to have assumed that Hanoi had *Panzers* and a *Luftwaffe* that could be knocked out.

THE SPECIAL ROLE OF KENNEDY

One member of the foreign-policy elite deserves to be examined at greater length. John F. Kennedy not only internalized what we are calling the Pearl Harbor paradigm, he helped install it.[23] His 1940 best seller, *Why England Slept,* originally written [when] he was twenty-one to twenty-two, was his Harvard senior thesis. The book concerned not only Britain's interwar somnolence in the face of the German threat but posited America in the same position. Kennedy's position at that time, it is interesting to note, was in marked contrast to the isolationism of his father, who was then the United States ambassador to Britain.[24]

The *Why England Slept* of Kennedy's youth laid down a remarkably full-blown view of national security, one that Senator and later President Kennedy retained practically intact. The following were some of the important themes which first appeared in *Why England Slept* and then in his senatorial and presidential speeches:

1. Peace-loving democracy is weak in the face of expansionist totalitarianism.[25]
2. The democratic leader's role is to teach the population that isolated events form an overall pattern of aggression against them.[26]
3. Defense preparedness must be kept up, even if this means increasing defense expenditures.[27]
4. Reliance on a single-weapon defense system is dangerous; a country must have several good defense systems for flexibility.[28]
5. Civil defense measures must be instituted in advance to protect the population in case of war.[29]
6. The nation must be willing actually to go to war in the final crunch; bluffing will not suffice.[30]

In the case of Britain in the late 1930s, argued the young Kennedy, democracy simply did not take the Nazi menace seriously, and British leaders failed to point out the danger and build up defenses. British defense was overconcentrated on the fleet at the expense of the army and most importantly of the air force. Britain's civil defense was weak, particularly in antiaircraft batteries. And finally, British leaders had been so hesitant to actually apply force when needed that Hitler could not take them seriously.

Representative and later Senator Kennedy found these arguments highly applicable to the Eisenhower period, which he often compared to interwar Britain, as in this 1959 speech:

> Twenty-three years ago, in a bitter debate in the House of Commons, Winston Churchill charged the British government with acute blindness to the menace of Nazi Germany, with gross negligence in the maintenance of the island's defenses, and with indifferent, indecisive leadership of British foreign policy and British public opinion. The preceding years of drift and impotency, he said, were "the years the locusts have eaten."
>
> Since January 1953 this nation has passed through a similar period. . . . [31]

America in the 1950s, said Kennedy, refused to see the "global challenge" of Soviet penetration of the Third World. Eisenhower had let United States defense preparedness slide; a "missile gap" had appeared. America must spend more on defense: "Surely our nation's security overrides budgetary considerations. . . . Then why can we not realize that the coming years of the gap present us with a peril more deadly than any wartime danger we have ever known?"[32] The country relied on "massive retaliation" when it needed a flexible response of many options, including counterinsurgency. Kennedy accordingly opposed Republican cuts in our ground troops. And, in a 1959 interview, he emphasized that the United States must be willing to fight for Berlin:

> If we took the view which some Englishmen took, that Prague or the Sudentendeutsch were not worth a war in '38—if we took that view about Berlin, my judgment is that the West Berliners would pass into the communist orbit, and our position in West Germany and our relations with West Germany would receive a fatal blow. . . . They're fighting for New York and Paris when they struggle over Berlin.[33]

One might be tempted to dismiss Senator Kennedy's views as campaign rhetoric. But once in the presidency, Kennedy proceeded to implement them: bigger defense budgets, larger ground forces, "flexible response" (including counterinsurgency), civil defense (especially the 1961 fallout-shelter panic), and finally overt warfare in Southeast Asia. Throughout his presidency, Kennedy and his advisers stuck to the image of the Pearl Harbor paradigm. In his dramatic 1962 television address on the Soviet arms buildup in Cuba, Kennedy used his favorite analogy: "The 1930s taught us a clear lesson: aggressive conduct, if allowed to go unchecked and unchallenged, ultimately leads to war."[34] Vice-President Johnson, in a 1961 memo to Kennedy on Vietnam, wrote:

> The battle against Communism must be joined in South-east Asia with strength and determination to achieve success there—or the United States, inevitably, must surrender the Pacific and take up our defenses on our own shores.[35]

One wonders if Johnson or one of his assistants had read Spykman. Further perusal of the Pentagon Papers shows much the same evaluation of the alleged strategic importance of Vietnam; its fall was defined as a major setback to United States security.[36]

We do not here argue that Vietnam is important or unimportant to the defense of America. That is indeterminate, although within the last decade a considerable portion of elite opinion has switched from the former view to the latter. What interests us is the inability of Kennedy and his advisers to define Southeast Asia as anything but strategic.

Kennedy's age surely contributed to his highly interventionist orientation. He retained what we are calling the Pearl Harbor paradigm as a young man in his early twenties. Eisenhower, by way of contrast, was twenty-seven years older and witnessed the events that led up to American involvement in World War II as a man in his forties. It seems likely, then, that the impact of the events of the late 1930s and early 1940s was far stronger in forming Kennedy's foreign-policy orientation than Eisenhower's.

This perhaps partially explains why the Pearl Harbor paradigm eventually was applied to an extreme and why this process took about a generation. A generation of the United States elite experienced as relatively young people the momentous events leading up to Pearl Harbor. Kennedy was of this generation, which gradually surfaced into public life.[37] Each year there were more members of this generation in positions of foreign-policy leadership. The older generation retired and the proportion of this new generation increased. After about twenty years there were few members of the older generation left in the political machinery. By the time Kennedy assumed the presidency, there were few countervailing views to dilute and moderate a policy of thoroughgoing interventionism. In this sense, we can say that the Pearl Harbor paradigm "blossomed" under Kennedy, who applied it more completely than did Eisenhower.

But while Kennedy was applying the wisdom learned in his youth to its full extent—the Green Berets, the Peace Corps, the Agency for International Development, the Counterinsurgency

Committee—the real world was going its own way, becoming less and less relevant to the mental constructs of American foreign-policy planners. We have then a "dysfunction" growing between policy and reality. On the one hand, we have a foreign orientation essentially frozen since the 1940s, and on the other hand, a world which defied pigeonholing into the compartments of the 1940s.

The most conspicuous indicator of this discrepancy was the persistent American inability to evaluate "communism" as no longer monolithic. Here, as with Kuhn's scientific paradigms, the data can be interpreted ambiguously in transitional periods. One side reads the data as still showing essentially a monolith, the other as a badly fractured movement. But at what point in time did it become unreasonable for United States foreign-policy planners to continue to hold the former view? Scholars had been emphasizing the Sino-Soviet split since the early 1960s,[38] but it was not until the early 1970s—after the trauma of Vietnam had set in—that reality was incorporated into policy. When communism became perceivable as nonmonolithic, under President Nixon, it perforce lost its most threatening attribute. Thus redefined, Indochina was no longer worth evaluating as a strategic prize, and American withdrawal became possible. The paradigm had shifted: Vietnam was no longer part of a gigantic pincer movement enveloping us.

After the Vietnam debacle was over, few voices could be heard advocating a return to "business as usual," that is, to continuing the interventionist paradigm. Nixon introduced a policy markedly different from that of his predecessors. It differed rhetorically in announcing to America's allies that they would have to bear primary responsibility for their defense,[39] and it differed physically in reducing United States ground forces to the point where few were available to send abroad. (Total U.S. armed forces fell from 3.5 million in 1968 to 2.2 million in 1974; especially hard hit were the army and the marines, without whom there can be no overseas intervention.)

Just as Pearl Harbor brought with it a massive and general shift in the foreign-policy orientation of the United States elite, so did Vietnam. Pearl Harbor and Vietnam were the points in time at which critics could say, "I told you so," and win widespread if grudging agreement from the old guard. The Pearl Harbor paradigm, applied for three decades to a world from which it was increasingly alienated, eventually was "shipwrecked" on Vietnam.

THE VIETNAM PARADIGM

What follows? It is not difficult to discern an emerging noninterventionist orientation which can be termed the "Vietnam paradigm." Varying in emphasis and nuance, the bearers of the new view all urge *limitation* of American activity (above all, military activity) overseas, particularly in the Third World. John Kenneth Galbraith, for example, wants

> and even more positive commitment to coexistence with the Communist countries. It means a much more determined effort to get military competition with the Soviets under control. . . . It means abandoning the Sub-Imperial ambitions in the Third World and recognizing instead that there is little we can do to influence political development in this part of the world and less that we need to do.[40]

Arthur Schlesinger, Jr., believes the "lessons of Vietnam" show:

> *First, that everything in the world is not of equal importance to us.* Asia and Africa are of vital importance for Asians and Africans . . . but they are not so important for us. . . .

Second, that we cannot do everything in the world. The universalism of the older generation was spacious in design and noble in intent. Its flaw was that it overcommitted our country—it overcommitted our policy, our resources, and our rhetoric. . . . [41]

The critics of only a few years ago might reflect with satisfaction on how much of their critique (not all, to be sure) has been absorbed by the Nixon doctrine.

A deluge of foreign-policy criticism has appeared in the last several years. If we were to boil down the new conventional wisdom and compare it with the old, it might look like this:[42]

Pearl Harbor Paradigm	Vietnam Paradigm
Communism is a monolithic threat.	Communism is a divided spastic.
If we don't intervene overseas, we may get dragged into a war.	If we do intervene overseas, we are sure to get into a war.
We must nip aggression in the bud.	We are not the world's policeman.
The dominoes are falling. Quick, let's do something!	The dominoes are falling. So what?
United States aid and technology will develop backward countries.	Backward countries will develop themselves or not at all.

The catastrophe that each generation experienced implanted viewpoints which, based on the importance for United States security accorded to overseas events, are flatly antithetical. Rational discussion between the two paradigms tends to be impossible, not for want of "facts" but for how they are structured. The structure, or paradigm, is imparted by a traumatic foreign-policy experience. Without such a trauma the inadequacies of the old paradigm might have gone unnoticed. Unfortunately, the indiscriminate application of one paradigm to increasingly changed circumstances tends to produce just that mishap. Given many interventions, it is likely that one will misfire. The adventures which do not misfire conspicuously—Lebanon, the Congo airlifts, Berlin, the Taiwan Straits, Santo Domingo—can be shrugged off or even used to justify continuing interventionism ("It worked there, didn't it?"). In this manner a foreign-policy paradigm actuates a built-in self-destruct mechanism: its eventual application *ad absurdum* by its elite generation.

THE FOREIGN-POLICY PARADIGMS OF YESTERYEAR

Is the above a comparison of just the two most recent epochs in United States diplomatic history, or might the approach be extended backward in time to validate the generational-paradigm approach as a more general tool of analysis? The author wishes to attempt the latter by dividing American foreign policy into periods on the basis of alternating interventionist and noninterventionist paradigms. To do this it is necessary to ask how the elite of a given period answered Spykman's old question of where the defense of America should start—on the near or far side of the oceans. If the answer is "far," then the lands across the seas "matter" to United States security. If the answer is "near," the lands across the seas "do not matter" so much to the security of the United States. In the former case, we have an interventionist period; in the latter, we have a noninterventionist period.

Let us examine United States diplomatic history, looking at periods first in reverse chronology and then by functional categories. As previously stated, the bearers of the Pearl Harbor paradigm were themselves reacting to what they believed were the gross deficiencies of the interwar "isolationism." The 1920 to 1940 period can be called the "Versailles paradigm"; its bearers were condemned as blind for failing to recognize the obvious threat from abroad in 1939–1941. Who were these people? Prominent among them were senators Borah, Hiram Johnson, Nye, and La Follette, the same "battalion of irreconcilables," who opposed the Versailles Treaty and League Covenant in 1919–1920.[43] For such persons World War II was a conflict the United States must and could—through rigorous application of the Neutrality Acts—avoid. Their great lesson was the aftermath of World War I, which, they believed, had achieved nothing: Europe stayed fractious, and even worse, refused to pay its war debts. American participation in that war had been a mistake. As with the Pearl Harbor paradigm, in their arguments self-interest and morality were intertwined. Versailles had been unfair to various nations (the demands of ethnic groups played a role here); the treaty enshrined the victors in positions of superiority; and the League of Nations's Covenant would then entangle America in the next European crisis. The depth of the interwar bitterness probably was not reached until the 1934–1936 Nye Committee hearings, which, in part, sought to blame munitions manufacturers for United States involvement. Out of the Nye hearings grew the Neutrality Acts of 1935–1937. Like the Pearl Harbor paradigm, the Versailles paradigm seems also to have reached full flowering shortly before its demise, exaggerating its increasing irrelevance to the world situation.

It took the critics of the Versailles paradigm at least half a decade to dislodge it. The "isolationists" fought the growing interventionism every inch of the way. Strong emotions came to the surface. "I could scarcely proceed further without losing my self-control," wrote Secretary of State Cordell Hull of a 1939 confrontation with Senator Borah in which the latter disparaged State Department cables on an impending war in Europe.[44] Other sources said that Hull actually wept at the meeting. It took the catastrophe at Pearl Harbor to squelch the obdurate bearers of the Versailles paradigm.

Was this Versailles paradigm a reaction to a previous orientation—an interventionist one? That there was a previous period, sometimes called imperialistic, from the 1890s extending into the next century cannot be doubted. The problem with labeling the period from 1898 (the Spanish-American War) through 1919 (the aftermath of World War I) an "imperial paradigm" is that the continuity of an interventionist policy between the two wars is not clear. With the Pearl Harbor paradigm we can show a consistent propensity for United States intervention over three decades, but with the 1898–1919 period we have interventions, mostly clustered at the beginning and end. In 1898 the United States occupied Cuba, Puerto Rico, the Philippines, Hawaii, and Wake (and part of Samoa in 1899). Then, mostly relating to World War I, the United States occupied or had troops in Mexico, the Virgin Islands, France, and Russia. In between there were only the relatively minor Caribbean occupations. Thus, if this was an imperial paradigm, it sagged in the middle. It may be further objected that two distinct lines of thought accompanied respectively the beginning and end of this period. The earlier thinking favored unilateral colony grabbing, in recognition of the fact that the great European powers were carving up the globe and leaving America without colonies or areas of influence. The later thinking, accompanying World War I, was much more internationalistic, stressing cooperation rather than unilateralism. Some figures, like Senator Albert J. Beveridge, were imperialists at the turn of the century and isolationists about World War I.[45]

The author agrees that such an imperial paradigm is not nearly so consistent as the later interventionist epoch, the Pearl Harbor paradigm. Nonetheless there is a good deal of unity in the three decades of the 1890s, 1900s, and 1910s, and the period generally was an interventionistic one. In the first place, it was a time of almost continual United States naval growth. Starting with Secretary of the Navy Benjamin Tracy's 1889 plans for a vast American fleet and pushed by Theodore Roosevelt (both as assistant secretary of the navy and as president), the U.S. Navy rose from sixth to fourth place in 1990, to third place in 1906, and to second place (to Britain) in 1907. The naval budget went from $21 million in 1885, to $31 million in 1891, to $79 million in 1902, to $104 million in 1906, and to $137 million in 1909. Wilson, although initially cutting the naval budget somewhat, ended up with a $2.2 billion one in 1919.[46] In respect to naval expenditures then, the imperial paradigm did not "sag in the middle."

Further, although some of the foreign-policy elite of this period moved from unilateral imperialism at the turn of the century to equally unilateral withdrawal from Europe's war, there was also a good deal of consistency in positing a need for a major United States role abroad. Woodrow Wilson, for example, after some uncertainty, endorsed both the war with Spain and the annexation of Hawaii and the Philippines. His motives, to be sure, differed from the imperialists; Wilson wanted to prepare Puerto Rico and the Philippines for self-government.[47] But we are less interested in motive than in general orientation, and in this Wilson was unmistakably an interventionist. Indeed, as president, Wilson "carried out more armed interventions in Latin America than any of his predecessors."[48] In 1898 the twenty-seven-year-old Cordell Hull even raised his own infantry company and went with his men as their captain to Cuba (although they requested the Philippines).[49] Liberalism by no means precludes interventionism, as Waltz has pointed out.[50]

We might even consider the imperial paradigm as a sort of training period for the senior staffers of the later Pearl Harbor paradigm: Congressman Hull as ardent Wilson supporter; Franklin D. Roosevelt as enthusiastic assistant secretary of the navy under Wilson; and Stimson as secretary of war under Taft. This helps explain why the Pearl Harbor period was not staffed exclusively by young converts to the growing interventionism of the late 1930s. There was on hand a much older age cohort who had internalized an interventionist framework some forty years earlier and who were eclipsed by the militant noninterventionism of the 1920s and 1930s. This group formed a countertrend subculture which sat out the interwar isolationism until called back into power for the higher positions during World War II. By the 1950s, however, they had mostly been replaced by the younger interventionists of the Kennedy generation.

Can we discern a period still further back out of which grew the imperial paradigm? The 1870s and 1880s are commonly considered the "nadir of diplomacy." The period was marked by massive indifference to overseas affairs, anglophobia (over Britain's aid to the Confederacy) preoccupation with filling out the presumably self-sufficient United States. We might therefore label this epoch the "Continental paradigm." As with later periods, a minority critique starts in the middle of it on the strategic assumptions of the established orientation. In this case there was a growing strategic insecurity and the efforts of navalists—of whom Admiral Mahan was not the first—to rebuild the decrepit United States Navy. The year 1889 was a turning point; the Harrison administration began to discard the passive, inert policies which had characterized the previous two decades and to start actively making policy for the first time since the Civil War.[51] One need only compare the relatively weak American reactions to the bloodshed of the Cuba uprising of 1868–1878 to the much firmer stand of the 1890s.

It is not necessary to go further back than this. Our principal analytical distinctions—a near or far defense, interventionism or noninterventionism, few or many troops overseas—do not readily apply to nineteenth-century America. The United States was too busy, in a Turnerian sense, with filling out its own frontiers. Further, America had little to fear from Europe or Asia, especially with the British fleet ruling the waves.

COMPARING PARADIGMS

While this division of United States diplomatic history into periods is admittedly an artificial construct, we can compare the periods or the "paradigms" that accompany the periods. (This comparison is summarized in Table 5.1.) The concrete expression of an interventionist or noninterventionist view is the number of United States troops overseas. During the imperial and Pearl Harbor periods America had relatively many troops abroad, and they were abroad not merely because of World Wars I and II, respectively. Long before our entry into World War I, there were American soldiers in Cuba, the Philippines, and throughout the Caribbean, including Mexico. During the intervening Versailles period the troops came home not only from Europe but from the Caribbean as well. Only in Nicaragua and Haiti did United States occupation continue past the 1920s. The Philippines were lightly garrisoned and almost forgotten in the interwar period. During the Pearl Harbor period there were troops overseas not only during World War II but long after it. The United States foreign-policy elite during this time was disposed to consider an overseas defense as the only reasonable American strategy. With President Nixon, this strategy seems to be changing, and there are fewer troops overseas.

Much of United States foreign policy hinges on the relationship between the executive and the legislative branches of government. If the Congress follows the president's lead and delivers what he wants, the United States is then able to engage in interventionist moves. When the Congress, specifically the Senate, tires of such activity and starts resenting strong presidential leadership, the possibilities for intervention are reduced. We would therefore expect to find an assertive Congress during noninterventionist periods, particularly at the beginning of these periods. It is for this reason that we get dramatic showdowns between key senators and the president. Especially important is the Senate Foreign Relations Committee, whose chairmen appear "irascible and contentious" when they engage in limiting executive initiatives in foreign affairs. Ranting anglophobe Charles Sumner defeated President Grant's scheme to annex Santo Domingo in 1870. Henry Cabot Lodge (and William Borah) stopped America's entry into President Wilson's beloved League. J. William Fulbright (and Mike Mansfield) cut down President Nixon's foreign-aid program and tried to put the executive on a leash by means of the 1973 War Powers Bill.

There are also, to be sure, executive–legislative difficulties when the paradigm shifts the other way, from noninterventionist to interventionist, which are perhaps not quite as dramatic because in this case the congressional opponents are the "losers"(see below). From 1898 to 1900 there was the bitter but unsuccessful rear guard of those protesting the war with Spain and the Philippines annexation, such as George F. Hoar and George G. Vest in the Senate and Thomas B. Reed, Speaker of the House.[52] In 1939 to 1941 there was a similar rear guard (discussed earlier), of those demanding United States neutrality. One characteristic of a paradigm shift in either direction, then, is a serious fight between the White House and Capitol Hill over who will have the upper hand in foreign policy. When the paradigm is established, conflict between the two branches subsides because there is relative consensus and the acquiescence of one branch to the other; a spirit of "cooperation" and "bipartisanship" then prevails.

The shift from one paradigm to another also involves a rather clearly identifiable group of "losers"—those whose orientation is repudiated. This is not a happy process and much rancor accompanies the displacement of the bearers of the old paradigm and their consignment to obscurity. The anti-imperialists of 1898–1900 sought to preserve a more limited, continental America. Their arguments—strategic, moral, constitutional, and economic—bear a striking resemblance to some of the arguments used to oppose the Vietnam war.[53] The anti-imperialists were condemned by the interventionists of their day; Theodore Roosevelt called them "simply unhung traitors." The losers of twenty years later, the Wilsonian internationalists, also did not go down without a vituperative fight. The isolationists were the clear and unhappy losers as the Pearl Harbor paradigm replaced the Versailles paradigm. One is not yet certain what to call the present crop of losers, but perhaps "globalists" is a label that will stick.[54] Those who defend the dying paradigm appear as obdurate fools who are unable to come to grips with the new realities and who must therefore be ignored. The losers, who stick with the old paradigm while the new one triumphs, gradually cease to be practitioners.

Another characteristic of noninterventionist periods is the begrudging to friends and allies of United States aid, which flowed rather freely during the preceding interventionist period. The failure of the European powers to pay their World War I debts created both a public and congressional furor in the 1920s and culminated in the 1934 Johnson Act prohibiting debtor nations from raising funds in the United States. The "anticancellationists" helped spread the feeling that America had been cheated by tricky and unreliable ex-partners. In the late 1960s a critique of United States foreign aid developed along similar lines: billions have been wasted; they'll never be repaid; we've been much too generous; the recipients are ungrateful; etc. The interesting point here is that the critique came not only from conservatives, but from liberals who previously spoke in favor of foreign aid.

Arms and munitions appear as a minor but interesting point in noninterventionist periods. Arms sales abroad are viewed with great suspicion, as a possible avenue by which the country could get dragged into foreign wars. The Nye Committee hearings and the ensuing Neutrality Acts in the 1930s were attempts to prevent a repetition of America's gradual entanglement in another European war. It can be argued that precisely such an entanglement was repeated under Roosevelt with "cash and carry," Lend Lease, and the destroyers-for-bases deal with Britain. It indeed led to de facto war in the North Atlantic between the United States and Germany months before Pearl Harbor. But, it is interesting to note, in the interventionist Pearl Harbor period there was practically no regret that the Neutrality Acts had thus been circumvented. The problem of arms sales again flared as the Pearl Harbor paradigm came under question. As a result of a 1967 Senate debate, arms sales by means of Export-Import Bank financing and Pentagon loan guarantees were stopped. Nixon's program to supply military hardware instead of United States troops was severely trimmed in the Senate.

The movement away from interventionism seems also to include the congressional and popular scapegoating of manufacturers of munitions. While Senator Nye had his "merchants of death," Senator Proxmire has his "military-industrial complex." In both cases it was alleged that armaments programs take on a life of their own and weapons makers manipulate public spending to their own advantage. The Nye Committee even "began to attack the war-making potential of the executive branch of the government," records Wayne Cole, and "also began to see the president as part of the compound."[55]

In interventionist periods there is a willingness to enter into arrangements that pledge the country to military action overseas. Admittedly, this was slow in coming during World War I,

Table 5.1 PARADIGMS IN COMPARISON

	Continental 1870s, 1880s	Imperial 1890s–1910s	Versailles 1920s, 1930s	Pearl Harbor 1940s–1960s	Vietnam 1970s–?
General view of foreign areas	"Don't matter"	"Matters"	"Don't matter"	"Matters"	"Don't matter"
View of Europe	Indifference (Anglophobia)	Imitation (Anglophilia)	Irritation	Salvation	Irritation
Losers		Anti-imperialists	Wilsonian internationalists	Isolationists	Globalists
Troops overseas	Almost none	Caribbean, Philippines, China, West Europe, Russia, Mexico	Few in Caribbean, Philippines	Europe, Asia, Latin America, Africa	Decreasing
Congress Funds for overseas	Obstructive None	Cooperative War loans	Obstructive Begrudging of war debts, anticancellationists, Johnson Act	Cooperative Marshall Plan, Point Four, AID, arms-sales credits	Obstructive Begrudging of aid, balance of payments force cutback
Commitments	None	Open Door, Caribbean protectorates, Associated Power in World War I, Philippine defense	Continued Open Door, reduction of Caribbean protectorates	U.N., NATO, SEATO, (CENTO), Congressional resolutions on Formosa, Middle East, Cuba, Berlin, Vietnam	Senate res. 85, War Powers Bill, attempt to repeal resolutions

which the United States entered belatedly and only as an "associate" of the Entente. During the Pearl Harbor period, however, the United States carpeted the globe with commitments.

Following these times of generous pledges have come periods of limiting or discarding commitments. In addition to the already-mentioned League rejection and the Neutrality Acts there was the interesting Ludlow Amendment (shelved in the House in 1937 by a vote of 209–188) to require a national referendum to declare war except for actual invasion. As the Vietnam paradigm took hold there was the National Commitments Resolution (without force of law) in 1969 expressing the sense of the Senate that America should fulfill no commitment without specific legislation. In 1973 a War Powers Bill to permit the president only ninety days to use troops abroad without additional legislation overrode Nixon's veto. Further conflict over commitments seemed inevitable as Senator Mansfield continued his efforts to prune United States forces in Europe.

On a more general level, in the noninterventionist periods there is a lessened interest in Europe and in the interventionist periods a heightened interest. During the Continental period there was aloof indifference to Europe buttressed by a sharp anglophobia in the wake of Britain's aid to the Confederacy. As American leaders adopted imperial views, there was an imitation of Europe (colony grabbing) and some cooperation, as in the Peking expedition in 1900. There was also a marked anglophilia starting in the Spanish-American War. After Versailles there was disgust at European greed and squabbling and regret that America had ever become involved in Europe's war. During the Pearl Harbor period there was the virtual United States occupation of West Europe and an almost crusading American involvement in European recovery, rearmament, and unification. By the early 1970s the devalued dollar and pressure to withdraw our forces marked the beginning of a diminished American role in Europe, a trend that was heightened in 1973 and 1974 by differing United States and European approaches to the Middle East and the petroleum shortage. Again the view surfaced that the Europeans were selfish and hopelessly fractious.

On a more general level still, in the noninterventionist periods the lands abroad "do not matter" much to the United States elite; in the interventionist periods foreign lands "matter" a great deal. (Professors in foreign-area and international studies, as well as of foreign languages, have recently noticed the former view among students.) We may also note that the last three periods each began with a catastrophe of overseas origin. Versailles appeared to demonstrate that American participation in a European war had been futile and a profound mistake. Pearl Harbor appeared to demonstrate that the interwar "isolationism" had been absurd and had led to a disaster. And Vietnam appeared to demonstrate that the long-standing interventionist policy had been "wrong" and had led to a disaster.

CYCLICAL THEORIES REVISITED

The approach to diplomatic history, of course, is not completely new or unique. Several writers have advanced views that United States foreign policy tends to swing like a pendulum (an image used by both President Nixon and Senator Fulbright) from extremes of overinvolvement to underinvolvement. Stanley Hoffmann, for example, discerned "the two *tempi* of America's foreign relations," alternating "from phases of withdrawal (or, when complete withdrawal is impossible, priority to domestic concerns) to phases of dynamic, almost messianic romping on the world stage."[56] Hans Morgenthau saw United States policy moving "back and forth between the extremes of an indiscriminate isolationism and an equally indiscriminate internationalism or globalism."[57]

Getting more specific, historian Dexter Perkins divided American foreign relations into cycles of "relatively pacific feeling," followed by "rising bellicosity and war," followed by "post-war nationalism," and then back to "relatively pacific feeling."[58] Getting even more specific, a behaviorally inclined political scientist, Frank L. Klingberg, using such indicators as naval expenditures, annexations, armed expeditions, diplomatic pressures, and attention paid to foreign matters in presidential speeches and party platforms, discovered alternating phases of "introversion" (averaging twenty-one years) and "extroversion" (averaging twenty-seven years). Klingberg added: "If America's fourth phase of extroversion (which began around 1940) should last as long as the previous extrovert phases, it would not end until well into the 1960s."[59] As social scientists, of course, we do not accept the notion that God plays numbers games with United States foreign policy. The most fruitful approach to this cyclical phenomenon, the author believes, is the generationally linked paradigm, which helps explain both the changes in orientation and their spacing in time.

Other writers have found a roughly generational interval of about twenty-five years between upsurges of world violence. (Klingberg too mentioned generations as one possible explanation for his foreign-policy cycles.) Denton and Phillips suggest what we might term a "forgetting" theory to explain their twenty-five-year cycles of violence: That generation, and particularly its decision makers, that experienced an intensive war tends to remember its horrors and avoid similar conflicts. The following generation of decision makers may forget the horrors and remember the heroism; this generation is more likely to engage in violence.[60] This explanation helps account for our Versailles paradigm, but it is flatly at odds with our Pearl Harbor paradigm, during which a generation, virtually all of whom experienced World War II firsthand, displayed little reluctance to apply force overseas. This generation was of course repelled by the violence of World War II but used it to explain why aggression must be "nipped in the bud" to prevent another large conflagration. Walt Rostow, for example, continued to insist that Vietnam *prevented* a large war. "If we had walked away from Asia or if we walk away from Asia now, the consequences will not be peace," said Rostow in 1971. "The consequence will be a larger war and quite possibly a nuclear war."[61]

This author subscribes to a cyclical theory of United States foreign policy only in the most general terms—namely, that if there are alternating orientations of interventionism and non-interventionism, then logically the former will produce more "action" and this will show up as intermittent peaks in statistical tabulations. The question of cycles falls behind the question of the conventional wisdom of foreign-policy thinkers.

In searching for explanations of any cyclical theory, of course, we cannot rule out purely external factors such as threats or challenges from abroad. It may be that such external forces have impinged upon the United States at roughly generational intervals and that we have merely reacted to them. This then dumps the generation question onto the offending land across the sea. The problem here is that during one epoch American foreign-policy thinkers may largely ignore threats and in another epoch they may take threats very seriously. As we have already considered, the Cuban uprising of the 1870s elicited relatively little response from the United States compared to our response to the Cuban uprising of the 1890s. America paid little attention to East Europe in the 1930s and a great deal of attention in the 1940s and 1950s. In 1948 the Soviet-Yugoslav split was seen as an anomaly; in the 1970s the Sino-Soviet dispute is seen as natural, the almost inevitable collision of two nationalisms. *Quisquid recipitur recipitur secundum modum recipiensis.* The world changes, of course, but it takes a changed set of American attitudes to perceive the new situation.

The problem is one of perception catching up with reality not on a continual and incremental basis, but delayed and in spurts. May we hazard that Vietnam will leave behind it a continuation of this pattern? The immediate impact of Vietnam on United States foreign policy is already apparent: the Senate's restorative revolt, demoralized armed forces, international economic difficulties, and skeptical allies. The longer-term effects may be far deeper. If the above generational-paradigm hypothesis is even approximately correct, we can expect persons who witnessed Vietnam while they were in their twenties to retain a noninterventionist orientation. As the elite of this generation gradually surfaces into policy-relevant positions, we can expect them to implement their views. The most important reactions to Vietnam, then, may be yet to come. We might remember in this regard that the depths of interwar isolationism did not come immediately after Versailles but rather a full decade and a half later, with the Neutrality Acts. Will the foreign-policy elite of the 1980s and 1990s still be slaying their long-dead foes?

NOTES

1. This formulation owes something to John Kenneth Galbraith's 1962 query to President Kennedy apropos of Vietnam: "Incidentally, who is the man in your administration who decides what countries are strategic?" Galbraith, *Ambassador's Journal* (Boston, 1969), p. 311.
2. Thomas S. Kuhn, *The Structure of Scientific Revolutions*, 2d ed. (Chicago, 1970), p. viii.
3. *Ibid.*, pp. 19–20.
4. *Ibid.*, p. 90.
5. *Ibid.*, p. 148.
6. *Ibid.*, p. 153.
7. *Ibid.*, p. 166.
8. *Ibid.*, p. 159.
9. The role of the elite in foreign policy should need little elaboration here. See Gabriel A. Almond, *The American People and Foreign Policy*, 2d ed. (New York, 1960), pp. 138–139; James N. Rosenau, *Public Opinion and Foreign Policy* (New York, 1961), pp. 35–36; James N. Rosenau, *National Leadership and Foreign Policy* (Princeton, N.J., 1963), pp. 6–10.
10. Herbert McCloskey, "Personality and Attitude Correlates of Foreign Policy Orientation," in James N. Rosenau (ed.), *Domestic Sources of Foreign Policy* (New York, 1967), pp. 51–109. As Almond put it: "There is some value in recognizing that an overtly interventionist and 'responsible' United States hides a covertly isolationist longing." Almond, *The American People*, p. 67. An attempt to refute Almond's "instability of mood" theory was marred by having all its data drawn from the peak years of the cold war. William R. Caspary, "The 'Mood Theory': A Study of Public Opinion and Foreign Policy," *American Political Science Review*, LXIV (June 1970), 536–647.
11. Nicholas John Spykman, *America's Strategy in World Politics* (New York, 1942), pp. 5, 7.
12. Karl Mannheim, *Essays on the Sociology of Knowledge*, ed. by Paul Kecskemeti (London, 1952), p. 291. Samuel P. Huntington has recently stressed the importance of generations in American political change. See "Paradigms of American Politics: Beyond the One, the Two, and the Many," *Political Science Quarterly*, 89, no. 1 (March 1974).
13. Arthur H. Vandenburg, Jr. (ed.), *The Private Papers of Senator Vandenburg* (Boston, 1952), p. 1.
14. Paul Seabury and Alvin Drischler called it "the Manchurian assumption" and saw it as the basis for our postwar alliances. Seabury and Drischler, "How to Decommit without Withdrawal Symptoms," *Foreign Policy*, 1 (Winter 1970–1971), 51.
15. It is surprising to learn, for example, that liberal internationalist Chester Bowles served on the national committee of America First. See Wayne S. Cole, *America First: The Battle Against Intervention* (Madison, Wis., 1953), p. 22.

16. Historian Norman Graebner poses the following as the key question in the debate over the origins of the cold war: "Why did the United States after 1939 permit the conquest of eastern Europe by Nazi forces, presumably forever, with scarcely a stir, but refused after 1944 to acknowledge any primary Russian interest or right of hegemony in the same region on the heels of a closely won Russian victory against the German invader?" The shift of foreign-policy paradigms helps answer this question. Graebner, "Cold War Origins and the Continuing Debate: A Review of the Literature," *Journal of Conflict Resolution,* 13 (March 1969), 131.

17. U.S., *Congressional Record,* 89th Cong., 1st Sess. (1965), CXI, Pt. 3, 3350–3351.

18. *New York Times,* October 3, 1965 (supplement), p. 5.

19. U.S., President, *Public Papers of the Presidents of the United States* (Washington, D.C.: Office of the Federal Register, National Archives and Records Service, 1945–19), Lyndon B. Johnson, 1965, p. 395.

20. U.S., Congress, Senate, Committee on Foreign Relations and Committee on Armed Services, *United States Troops in Europe,* Report, 90th Cong., 2d Sess. October 15, 1968 (Washington, D.C., 1968), p. 18.

21. *Public Papers of the Presidents,* Johnson, 1966, Book II, p. 861.

22. *The Pentagon Papers, as Published by the New York Times* (New York, 1971, paper ed.), p. 499.

23. A parallel figure in the field of journalism was Kennedy's friend Joseph Alsop, who also published a book in 1940 that established his views for decades. See Joseph Alsop and Robert Kintner, *American White Paper* (New York, 1940).

24. Such items raise the possibility that some of the paradigm shift may be explicable in terms of father-son conflict on the psychoanalytic plane. But that approach tends to minimize the substantive issue of strategic assumptions, which is the one that concerns us here. The elder Kennedy's isolationism is from Arthur Schlesinger, Jr., *A Thousand Days: John F. Kennedy in the White House* (Greenwich, Conn., 1967, paper ed.), pp. 85, 125.

25. John F. Kennedy, *Why England Slept,* 2d ed. (New York, 1961), p. 222.

26. *Ibid.,* p. 186.

27. *Ibid.,* p. 223.

28. *Ibid.,* p. 171.

29. *Ibid.,* pp. 169–170.

30. *Ibid.,* pp. 229–230.

31. John F. Kennedy, *The Strategy of Peace,* ed. by Allan Nevins (New York, 1960), p. 193.

32. U.S., *Congressional Record,* 85th Cong., 2d Sess. (1958), CIV, 17571.

33. Kennedy, *Strategy of Peace,* p. 213.

34. *Public Papers of the Presidents,* Kennedy, 1962, p. 807.

35. *Pentagon Papers,* p. 128.

36. *Ibid.,* pp. 27, 35–36, 148–149, 284.

37. For a good exposition of this "age-cohort hypothesis," in this case on the attitudes of European youth toward regional integration, see Ronald Inglehart, "An End to European Integration?" *American Political Science Review,* LXI (March 1967), 94–99.

38. See, for example, G. F. Hudson, Richard Lowenthal, and Roderick MacFarquhar, *The Sino-Soviet Dispute* (New York, 1961); Donald S. Zagoria, *The Sino-Soviet Conflict, 1956–1961* (Princeton, N.J., 1962); and Leopold Labedz and G. R. Urban (eds), *The Sino-Soviet Conflict* (London, 1964).

39. The Nixon doctrine was first enunciated on Guam, July 25, 1969, to this effect. See *Public Papers of the Presidents,* Nixon, 1969, p. 552.

40. John Kenneth Galbraith, "The Decline of American Powers," *Esquire,* March 1972, p. 163.

41. Arthur Schlesinger, Jr., "Vietnam and the End of the Age of Superpowers," *Harper's,* March 1969, p. 48.

42. Graham Allison came up with a similar but longer comparison of his foreign-policy "axioms" from interviews with more than a hundred elite young Americans. Allison, "Cool It: The Foreign Policy of Young America," *Foreign Policy,* 1 (Winter 1970–1971), 150–154.

43. Jean-Baptiste Duroselle, *From Wilson to Roosevelt: Foreign Policy of the United States, 1913–1945* (New York, 1968), p. 260.

44. Cordell Hull, *The Memoirs of Cordell Hull* (New York, 1948), Vol. 1, pp. 650–651.

45. Selig Adler, *The Isolationist Impulse: Its Twentieth Century Reaction* (New York, 1966), pp. 28–29.

46. Duroselle, *From Wilson to Roosevelt,* pp. 8–9.

47. Harley Notter, *The Origins of the Foreign Policy of Woodrow Wilson* (New York, 1965), pp. 106–129.

48. Thomas A. Bailey, *A Diplomatic History of American People,* 8th ed. (New York, 1969), p. 553.

49. Hull, *Memoirs,* pp. 33–36.

50. Kenneth N. Waltz, *Man, the State and War: A Theoretical Analysis* (New York, 1959), pp. 95–114.

51. Robert L. Beisner, *From the Old to the New Diplomacy, 1865–1900* (New York, forthcoming 1975).

52. Robert L. Beisner, *Twelve Against Empire: The Anti-Imperialists, 1898–1900* (New York, 1968), pp. 139–164, 203–211.

53. Robert L. Beisner, "1898 and 1968: the Anti-Imperialists and the Doves," *Political Science Quarterly,* LXXXV, no. 2 (June 1970).

54. See, for example, Stephen E. Ambrose, *Rise to Globalism: American Foreign Policy 1938–1970* (Baltimore, 1971); and Gary Porter, "Globalism—The Ideology of Total World Involvement," in Marcus G. Raskin and Bernard B. Fall (eds.), *The Vietnam Reader* (New York, 1965), pp. 322–327.

55. Wayne S. Cole, *An Interpretive History of American Foreign Relations* (Homewood, Ill., 1968), p. 443.

56. Stanley Hoffmann, *Gulliver's Troubles, Or the Setting of American Foreign Policy* (New York, 1969), p. 19.

57. Hans J. Morgenthau, *A New Foreign Policy for the United States* (New York, 1969), p. 15.

58. Dexter Perkins, *The American Approach to Foreign Policy,* 2d ed. (Cambridge, Mass., 1962), pp. 146–147.

59. Frank L. Klingberg, "The Historical Alternation of Moods in American Foreign Policy," *World Politics,* IV (January 1952).

60. Frank H. Denton and Warren Phillips, "Some Patterns in the History of Violence," *Journal of Conflict Resolution,* XII (June 1968), 193.

61. *Washington Post,* July 12, 1971, p. A14.

꒰꒱

Domestic Constraints on Regime Change in U.S. Foreign Policy: The Need for Policy Legitimacy

Alexander L. George

> The acid test of a policy . . . is its ability to obtain domestic support. This has two aspects: the problem of legitimizing a policy within the governmental apparatus . . . and that of harmonizing it with the national experience.[1]

The study of change in the international system must include, of course, attention to the efforts of national actors to create new regimes or to modify existing ones. This chapter focuses upon the role of domestic constraints on the ability of governments to pursue goals of this kind in their foreign policy. The primary objective of the chapter will be to develop an analytical framework suitable for this purpose. The framework will be applied to an analysis of two historical cases in which the United States has attempted to develop a cooperative U.S.–Soviet relationship: first, Franklin D. Roosevelt's effort during World War II to develop a postwar international security system based on cooperation with the Soviet Union; second, the Nixon–Kissinger détente policy of attempting to develop a more constructive relationship with the Soviet Union.

The analysis of these historical cases will be selective and provisional; it is designed to illustrate the utility of the framework for assessing the impact of domestic constraints rather than to produce a definitive scholarly interpretation. For this reason documentation will be minimal.[2]

THE PROBLEM OF DEMOCRATIC CONTROL OF FOREIGN POLICY

No one who reviews the history of U.S. foreign policy since the end of World War II can fail to be impressed with the importance of domestic constraints in the shaping and conduct of that policy. Democratic control of foreign policy is of course indispensable in the U.S. political system. But the forces of public opinion, Congress, the media, and powerful interest groups often make themselves felt in ways that seriously complicate the ability of the president and his advisers to pursue long-range foreign policy objectives in a coherent, consistent manner. It is not surprising that presidents have reacted to these domestic pressures at times by trying to manipulate and control public opinion—as well as to inform and educate the public as best they can.

While efforts to manipulate public opinion cannot be condoned, nonetheless this unhappy experience does point to a fundamental problem that Roosevelt and every president since has faced. This is the problem of obtaining enough legitimacy for his policy towards the Soviet

Alexander L. George, "Domestic Constraints on Regime Change in U.S. Foreign Policy: The Need for Policy Legitimacy,"in Ole Holsti, et al., *Change in the International System,* Boulder, CO: Westview Press, copyright © 1980. Reprinted by permission of Westview Press, Inc. and Alexander L. George.

Union in the eyes of Congress and public opinion so that the forces of democratic control and domestic pressures do not hobble him and prevent him from conducting a coherent, consistent, and reasonably effective long-range policy.

To be able to do so, the president must achieve a fundamental and stable national consensus, one that encompasses enough members of his own administration, of Congress and of the interested public. It is contended here that such a consensus can *not* be achieved and maintained simply by the president adhering scrupulously to constitutional–legal requirements for the conduct of foreign policy, *or* by his following the customary norms for consultation of Congress, *or* by conducting an "open" foreign policy that avoids undue secrecy and deceptive practices, *or* by attempting to play the role of broker mediating and balancing the competing demands and claims on foreign policy advanced by the numerous domestic interest groups.

Neither can the president develop such a consensus merely by invoking "national interest" nor the requirements of "national security." In principle, of course, the criterion of "national interest" should assist the policy maker to cut through the complex, multivalued nature of foreign policy issues and to improve his judgment of the relative importance of different objectives. In practice, however, "national interest" has become so elastic and ambiguous a concept that its role as a guide to foreign policy is highly problematical and controversial. Most thoughtful observers of U.S. foreign policy have long since concluded that the "national interest" concept unfortunately lends itself more readily to being used by our leaders as political rhetoric for *justifying* their decisions and gaining support rather than as an exact, well-defined criterion that enables them to determine what actions and decisions to take. It is symptomatic of the deep crisis of U.S. foreign policy in the past decade that large elements of the public and of Congress are no longer persuaded that foreign policy actions are appropriate merely by the president's invocation of the symbol of "national interest." These skeptical sectors of the public and of Congress have come to view "the national interest" phrase as part of the shopworn political rhetoric that every administration in recent times has employed in order to justify questionable or arbitrary policies and decisions.

If "national interest" does not endow policy with legitimacy, what about a "bipartisan" foreign policy—is that not the way in which a basic consensus on foreign policy can be achieved in a democracy such as the United States? There have been times, it is true, when policy legitimacy has been associated with a bipartisan foreign policy, but it is important not to confuse cause and effect. Bipartisanship is the result, not the cause, of policy legitimacy. If enough members of both parties do not share a sense of the legitimacy of a particular foreign policy, calls for a bipartisan policy and appeals that politics should stop at the water's edge will have little effect except in crisis situations.

How, then, can a broad and stable consensus on behalf of a long-range foreign policy be achieved? The concept of "policy legitimacy" is relevant and useful in this context.[3] A president can achieve legitimacy for his policy only if he succeeds in convincing enough members of his administration, Congress, and the public that he indeed does have a policy and that it is soundly conceived. This requires two things: first, he must convince them that the objectives and goals of his policy are desirable and worth pursuing—in other words that his policy is consistent with fundamental national values and contributes to their enhancement. This is the *normative* or moral component of policy legitimacy.

Second, the president must convince people that he knows how to achieve these desirable long-range objectives. In other words, he must convince them that he understands other national actors and the evolving world situation well enough to enable him to influence the course of events in the desired direction with the means and resources at his disposal. This is the *cognitive* (or knowledge) basis for policy legitimacy.

Thus, policy legitimacy has both a normative-moral component and a cognitive basis. The normative component establishes the *desirability* of the policy; the cognitive component its *feasibility*.

Policy legitimacy is invaluable for the conduct of a long-range foreign policy. If the president gains this kind of understanding and acceptance of his effort to create a new international regime, then the day-to-day actions he takes on behalf of it will become less vulnerable to the many pressures and constraints the various manifestations of "democratic control" would otherwise impose on his ability to pursue that policy in a coherent, consistent manner. In the absence of the fundamental consensus that policy legitimacy creates, it becomes necessary for the president to justify each action to implement the long-range policy on its own merits rather than as part of a larger policy design and strategy. The necessity for ad hoc day-to-day building of consensus under these circumstances makes it virtually impossible for the president to conduct a long-range foreign policy in a coherent, effective manner.

Thus far we have identified the requirements for policy legitimacy in very general terms. In fact, however, the specific operational requirements of normative and cognitive legitimacy will be affected by the marked differences in level of interest and sophistication among individuals and groups. Policy legitimacy must encompass a variety of individuals and groups. Foremost among them are the president and his top foreign policy advisers and officials. It is difficult to imagine them pursuing foreign policy goals that they do not regard as possessing normative and cognitive legitimacy. The bases for their beliefs, however, will not necessarily be communicated fully to all other political actors. In general, as one moves from the highest level of policy making to the mass public, one expects to find a considerable simplification of the set of assertions and beliefs that lend support to the legitimacy of foreign policy. (This important refinement of the analytical framework will not be developed further here, since it will not be utilized in the case studies that follow.)

THE "ARCHITECTURE" OF FOREIGN POLICY

It was noted that in order to establish cognitive legitimacy for his policy, a president must be able to plausibly claim that he and his advisers possess the relevant knowledge and competence needed to choose correct policies and can carry them out effectively. Upon closer examination it is seen that the knowledge evoked in support of a policy consists of several sets of beliefs, each of which supports a different component of the policy in question. It is useful, therefore, to refine the analytical framework that we have presented thus far in order to understand better the policy maker's task of developing policy legitimacy.

Foreign policy that aims at establishing a new international system or regime generally has an internal structure—a set of interrelated components. These are (1) the *design objective* of the policy; (2) the *strategy* employed to achieve it; and (3) the *tactics* utilized in implementing that strategy. The choice of each of these components of the policy must be supported by claims that it is grounded in relevant knowledge. A set of plausible cognitive beliefs must support each of these three components of the policy if it is to acquire what we have been calling "cognitive legitimacy."

By taking the internal structure of policy explicitly into account we add a useful dimension to the concept of policy legitimacy. Now the cognitive component of policy legitimacy is

The "Internal Structure" of Foreign Policy	Supporting Cognitive Assertions and Beliefs
Choice of (1) Design objective	a,b,c,...n
Choice of (2) Strategy	a,b,c...n
Choice of (3) Tactics	a,b,c...n

Figure 5.1 The Problem of Cognitive Legitimacy: The "Internal Structure" of Foreign Policy and Supporting Cognitive Assertions and Beliefs

analytically differentiated in a way that permits a more refined understanding of the task of achieving and maintaining policy legitimacy. The analytical structure of the problem of achieving cognitive legitimacy is depicted in Figure 5.1.

By differentiating in this manner the *functional role* that different cognitive assertions and beliefs play in supporting different parts of the internal structure or "architecture" of a policy, the investigator is in a position to do a number of useful things. First, he can understand better the nature of the task a policy maker faces in attempting to achieve legitimacy for his policy. Thus in order for the policy maker himself to believe that his policy is feasible and to argue this plausibly to others, he has to articulate a set of cognitive beliefs about other national actors whose behavior he seeks to influence and about causal relationships in the issue area in question that will lend support not only to his choice of the design objectives of that policy but also to the strategy and tactics that he employs on its behalf.

Second, the specification of beliefs supporting the internal structure of a complex foreign policy enables the analyst, either at that time or later, to compare these beliefs with the state of scholarly knowledge on these matters. This permits a sharper, better focused evaluation of the validity of the cognitive premises on which different components of a given foreign policy are based.

Third, by keeping in mind the differentiated functional role of cognitive premises, the investigator can more easily refine the description and explanation of pressures for changes in foreign policy that are brought about by interpretations of events that are held to challenge the validity of some of these cognitive premises.

ROOSEVELT'S "GREAT DESIGN," STRATEGY, AND TACTICS

We shall now utilize the analytical framework outlined above to describe the substance of Roosevelt's postwar policy and to indicate how domestic opinion—and the related need for achieving as much policy legitimacy as possible—constrained Roosevelt's policy choices and his ability to achieve them.

We shall consider first Roosevelt's design objective for a postwar security system, what he himself called his Great Design.

To begin with, the very close connection between Roosevelt's wartime policy and his postwar plans should be recalled. Both were quite self-consciously based on Roosevelt's perception—widely shared by his generation—of the "lessons of the past," more specifically the explanations attributed to the various failures of policy after World War I that had led to the rise of totalitarianism and to World War II.[4] Thus, in contrast to the way in which World War I had ended, Roosevelt believed it to be essential this time to completely defeat, disarm, and occupy those aggressor nations that had started World War II. It was also necessary in Roosevelt's view to promote national self-determination more effectively and to prevent future depressions. But above all Roosevelt's planning was dominated by the belief that it was necessary to forestall the possibility that once the war was over, the United States would once again return to an isolationist foreign policy, as it had after World War I.

Thus the postwar objective to which Roosevelt gave the highest priority was to ensure and to legitimize an *internationalist* U.S. postwar foreign policy. We wanted the United States to participate fully, and in fact, to take the lead in efforts to create a workable postwar security system.

To gain public support for his war objectives and to prepare the ground for an internationalist foreign policy thereafter, Roosevelt invoked the nation's traditional idealist impulses and principles. They were written into the Atlantic Charter that he and Churchill agreed to in August 1941 (even before the United States formally entered the conflict) and to which the Russians gave qualified support later.

Thus the principles of the Atlantic Charter provided *normative* legitimacy for Roosevelt's war arms and his hopes for peace. Among the traditional ideals that Roosevelt invoked, one in particular is of interest here. This was the principle of self-determination and independence for all nations. It was this aspect of the normative legitimacy for his policies that was to severely complicate Roosevelt's problems with U.S. public opinion—and President Harry S. Truman's problems later on—when he had to deal with the Russians on matters of territorial settlements and control over Eastern Europe. (We shall return to this later.)

Isolationism had been strong in the United States in the 1930s *before* Pearl Harbor. But once the United States got into the war, U.S. opinion developed strong support for the idea that it should not return to an isolationist position. This shift in public opinion was helpful to Roosevelt's postwar plans, but only up to a point, for in fact those who opposed a return to isolationism were sharply divided over what type of internationalist policy the United States should pursue after the war. Woodrow Wilson's concept of collective security was revived and its supporters, strong in numbers and influence, wanted the United States to take the lead in establishing a new and stronger League of Nations.

Roosevelt himself, however, rejected this idealist approach as impractical and inadequate. He favored an approach that would take power realities into account. In his view it was important that the great powers use their military resources to preserve the peace. This would provide a more reliable way than a league for dealing with any new aggressive states that might emerge after the war. Roosevelt also wanted to establish a more effective postwar system than a new league could provide for preventing dangerous rivalries and conflicts from erupting among Britain, Russia, and the United States once the common enemy had been defeated. But Roosevelt did not wish to risk a battle with the Wilsonian idealists, and so he did not publicly articulate his disagreement with their views. Instead he attempted, with partial success, to use their internationalist viewpoint to help legitimate his own quite different version of an internationalist postwar policy.

Roosevelt's thinking about the requirements of a postwar security system was deeply influenced by his awareness of the situation that would confront the peacemakers once the war against the enemy powers was successfully concluded. The defeat of Nazi Germany and its allies would create an important power vacuum in Central Europe. The question of who and what would fill this vacuum would pose the most serious implications for the vital interests of both the Soviets and the Western powers. If the two sides could not cooperate fairly quickly in finding a mutually acceptable approach for dealing with the vacuum in Europe, then they would inevitably enter into the sharpest competition for control of Central Europe.

The resulting dangers to the peace, it could be foreseen, could be dealt with only within the framework of the existing alliance between the Western powers and the Soviet Union. There would be no other international forums or institutions to bring into play to regulate competition among the victorious powers over Central Europe. Whatever semblance of an international system that had existed in the period between the two world wars had collapsed. What is more, the military alliance between the Western powers and the Soviet Union had been forced on them by circumstances—the common danger of defeat and domination by Nazi Germany and its allies. Once the enemy powers were defeated, all of the long-standing differences in ideology and the historic lack of trust and mutual suspiciousness between the West and the Soviet Union would have an opportunity to emerge once again.

Roosevelt was aware that once the wartime alliance achieved its purpose of defeating Hitler, there would remain only victors and vanquished and no international system that could provide an institutionalized structure and procedures by means of which the Western powers and the Russians could work out a solution to the power vacuum in the center of Europe. Roosevelt, then, was faced with two important and difficult postwar tasks: the need to create the beginnings of a new international system and the necessity of finding a way to prevent dangerous competition to fill the vacuum in Central Europe.

What were the various possibilities available for dealing with these closely related tasks? One possibility was to try to recreate a new balance-of-power system. But the question was, what kind of a balance-of-power system? The history of the last few centuries had seen several significantly different variants of a balance-of-power system.

Roosevelt rejected the kind of balance-of-power system marked by a great deal of competition and conflict among the major powers—the kind of system that had existed during the eighteenth century, that had failed to deter Napoleon from attempting to achieve hegemony, and that had also failed for a number of years to form the kind of coalition needed to bring him down. In Roosevelt's view a highly competitive balance-of-power system of this type for the postwar period would be neither desirable nor feasible. Britain would be too weak by itself to provide a military counterweight to Russia on the European continent. The United States, even with its enormous military power, would not want to or be able to bolster England for the purpose of balancing Soviet pressure in Europe. It must be remembered that Roosevelt operated on the premise—which seemed completely justified at the time—that U.S. public opinion would not tolerate leaving large U.S. military forces in Europe very long once the war ended. So the grim prospect Roosevelt had to contend with, and to avoid if possible, was that the Soviet Union could end up dominating Europe unless the Russians could be brought into a different kind of balance-of-power system.

One way to avoid this dilemma, of course, would have been for the United States and Britain to forego the war objective of inflicting total defeat on Germany and Italy and to settle instead for a negotiated compromise peace with Hitler and Mussolini. But it was most unlikely that this alternative could be made acceptable to U.S. (or British) public opinion. Besides, since the Russians too could have played this game, it would have quickly led to a race between the Western powers and the Russians to see who could first make a separate peace with Hitler in order to bring Germany in on its side of the newly emerging balance of power.

Possibly there was another way of avoiding the dangers that a power vacuum in Europe would pose to a new balance-of-power system. These dangers might be minimized or avoided if the Western powers and the Soviet Union got together and worked out a political division of Europe before the total defeat and occupation of Germany and Italy. But it is difficult to imagine how a political division of Europe between the Russians and the West could be successfully implemented during or immediately after the war, or be made acceptable to the U.S. people. If the thought occurred to Roosevelt, there is little indication that he regarded it as at all a feasible or desirable option. The most that could be done, and was done, was to agree on zones of occupation into which the military forces of the Soviet Union, Britain, and the United States would regroup after the defeat of Nazi Germany. This agreement on military zones of occupation reduced the immediate danger of conflict, but it was neither intended nor expected to eventuate in a political division of Europe; it was not part of a "spheres-of-influence" agreement at that time, even though spheres of influence would emerge later on, based on the occupation zones.

There was still another possibility. If a complete division of Europe between the Western powers and the Soviet Union was deemed impractical or undesirable, the two sides might at least agree to grant each other spheres of influence in parts of Europe, with Germany itself being placed under their joint military occupation. Something of the kind—a partial spheres-of-influence agreement covering Rumania, Hungary, Bulgaria, Italy, Greece, and Yugoslavia—was proposed by Churchill to Stalin at their private meeting in Moscow in October 1944 and accepted by Stalin. But Roosevelt, although initially sympathetic, felt he could not approve such an arrangement.

Roosevelt rejected the model of a highly competitive balance-of-power system and also the idea of attempting to reduce its conflict potential by creating spheres of influence for several reasons. First of all, he doubted—and in this he was undoubtedly right—that U.S. public opinion would agree to U.S. participation in such arrangements, given its historic antipathy to the European balance-of-power system. Besides, for Roosevelt to endorse or participate in a spheres-of-influence agreement would have directly contradicted the principle of self-determination and independence that he had written into the Atlantic Charter. That declaration was the major statement of Allied war aims and major means by which Roosevelt had secured public support for an internationalist postwar foreign policy. For this reason, while Roosevelt was indeed prepared to accept predominant Soviet influence in Eastern Europe, such an outcome had to be legitimized through procedures consistent with the Atlantic Charter.

Besides, Roosevelt did not believe that a competitive balance-of-power system, even one moderated by spheres of influence in Europe, would eliminate rivalry for very long. Any such arrangements would prove to be unstable, and the world would soon become divided into two armed camps—a Western democratic one and a Soviet-led one. An arms race would ensue which at best would result in a dangerous armed truce, and at worst it would lead to another world war. In brief, Roosevelt foresaw the possibility that something like the cold war would emerge—that is, unless some alternative could be devised.

The only alternative, as Roosevelt saw it, was a version of the balance of power modeled on some aspects of the Concert System set up by the European powers in 1815 after defeating Napoleon. To this end Roosevelt hoped that the unity and cooperation of the Allies could be maintained after the defeat of the totalitarian states. This was the option Roosevelt favored from an early stage in the war. He called it his Great Design, and he succeeded in getting Churchill and Stalin to agree to it and to cooperate in trying to bring it about.

The Great Design called for the establishment of a postwar security system in which the United States, Great Britain, the Soviet Union—and hopefully eventually China—would form a consortium of overwhelming power with which to keep the peace. These major powers, forming an executive committee, would consult and cooperate with each other to meet any threat to the peace, either from the defeated powers or any others that might arise to threaten the peace. These four powers would have a virtual monopoly of military power; all other states would be prevented from having military forces that could pose a serious threat to others. Quite appropriately, Roosevelt called this concept the "Four Policemen." It must be noticed that such a system would have violated the principle of the sovereign equality of all states, great or small, and hence it could not be reconciled with the Atlantic Charter.

Turning now to Roosevelt's "Grand Strategy" for achieving his Great Design, the first thing to be noted is that it called for the United States, Great Britain, and the Soviet Union to work out mutually acceptable settlements of the important territorial issues and political problems in Europe. These settlements would be reached through joint consultation and agreement; in other words, through a system of *collective* decision making, not unilateral action by either side. In this respect Roosevelt's Great Design was influenced by the recollection that in 1815, after the European powers finally succeeded in defeating Napoleon, they then formed a Concert System which relied upon frequent meetings of foreign ministers to make joint decisions with regard to keeping the peace, dealing with any threats to it, and resolving any disagreements that might arise among themselves.

Instead of a new balance-of-power system, therefore, Roosevelt sought to create a new Concert System that would maintain the unity and effective cooperation of the victorious Allies after the war as well. And instead of secret agreements and spheres-of-influence, he hoped that new governments would emerge in the occupied states of Europe through procedures and policies that were consistent with the principle of national self-determination and independence.

To this fundamental strategic concept Roosevelt added other elements: reliance on high-level personal diplomacy, confidence-building measures, and conciliation and appeasement of the Soviet Union's legitimate security needs.

As for Roosevelt's *tactics,* the emphasis was on the need to minimize conflict and disagreement in day-to-day relations, the importance of leaning over backwards not to give offense, and the avoidance of behavior that might be interpreted by the Soviets as indicating hostility or lack of sympathy.

Particularly at the level of tactics, but to some extent also at the level of strategy, there were some alternatives to the choices Roosevelt made. Generally speaking, the choice of a design objective—a particular Grand Design for policy—does of course constrain the choice of strategy; and the choice of a particular strategy constrains in turn the choice of tactics. One strategy may be more appropriate for pursuing a given design objective than another, and one set of tactics may be more effective than another. These choices of strategy and tactics are likely to be influenced by the policy maker's beliefs as to the relative efficacy of alternative strategies and tactics. It is entirely possible, therefore, as experience accumulates in attempting to achieve a long-range design-objective, that policy makers will be led to question their initial choice of tactics and/or strategy but without questioning—initially at least—the correctness and legitimacy of the design objective itself.

We have now identified Roosevelt's Grand Design, his Grand Strategy, and his tactics. *Each of them was supported by a set of cognitive beliefs having to do with the characteristics of the Soviets.* These beliefs constituted the knowledge base on which Roosevelt could draw in attempting to gain cognitive legitimacy for his overall postwar plans from members of his administration, Congress, and the public. From available historical materials it is relatively easy to identify the various cognitive beliefs about the Soviets that supported each component of the overall policy.[5]

How well founded were these beliefs about the Soviets on which Roosevelt's postwar policy rested? It must be recognized that the exigencies and pressures of the wartime situation—the need to get along with the Russians in order to ensure the defeat of the enemy powers—no doubt powerfully motivated Roosevelt to develop a somewhat benign, optimistic image of the Soviets. But was that image therefore naive? Was it simply wishful thinking to believe that the Soviets might participate in a cooperative postwar system of some kind?

Roosevelt's hopes and beliefs regarding the Soviets cannot be dismissed so easily as naive. The content of some of Roosevelt's policies and his judgment of the Soviet Union were indeed criticized by some persons at the time. But suffice it to say that the naivete regarding the Soviet Union that Roosevelt has been charged with was much more apparent *after* the failure of his hopes for postwar cooperation with the Russians than before. During the war itself, while Roosevelt was alive and even for a while thereafter, many specialists on the Soviet Union (for example, Charles Bohlen) and other foreign-policy experts, were not at all sure that his policy would fail. Many of the beliefs about the Soviet Union that supported Roosevelt's Grand Design enjoyed a considerable measure of plausibility and support. His policies and the beliefs that supported them were not a hasty improvisation but reflected careful deliberation on his part and on the part of quite a few advisers. Even skeptics about the Soviet Union thought that there was a chance that Soviet leaders would cooperate out of self-interest with Roosevelt's Grand Design. The generally successful wartime collaboration with the Soviets reinforced these hopes, and they were further strengthened by Roosevelt's assessment of Stalin's postwar intentions and the general endorsement he obtained from Stalin of the concept of a cooperative postwar security system.

It should be noted further that despite his generally optimistic personality and outlook, Roosevelt did not hide from himself or others close to him that his image of the Soviets might prove to be defective and that his hopes for postwar cooperation might eventually prove to be unfounded. He realized, in other words, that he was taking a calculated risk, and he remained sensitive to any Soviet actions that threatened the success of his postwar plans or appeared to call into question the validity of the premises on which it was based. Roosevelt was also quick to undertake remedial measures to bring Stalin back into line whenever necessary.

DOMESTIC CONSTRAINTS AFFECTING THE IMPLEMENTATION OF ROOSEVELT'S POSTWAR POLICIES

In addition to the constraints already noted on Roosevelt's choice of a "realist" oriented postwar security system, domestic pressures also hampered his effort to secure and maintain strong legitimacy for his policy. Although he strongly favored the Four Policemen concept, Roosevelt was most cautious in publicizing it. He did not seriously attempt to inform and educate public opinion on the matter because he feared that such an effort would shatter the domestic consensus for an internationalist postwar foreign policy. Roosevelt felt he had to blur the difference between his realistic approach to power and security and the Wilsonian idealists' desire for a system of collective security based on the creation of another stronger League of Nations. Roosevelt did speak about his Four Policemen concept privately with a number of influential opinion leaders. But when he attempted to float a trial balloon to publicize the idea in an interview with a journalist,[6] it triggered a sharply negative reaction at home from the idealists. As a result Roosevelt backed away from further efforts to educate public opinion in order to gain understanding and legitimacy for his Four Policemen concept.

From an early stage in World War II Roosevelt had strongly opposed setting up a new League of Nations after the war. He felt that the task of enforcing the peace would have to be left to the Four Policemen for a number of years. However, once again to avoid political troubles at home, Roosevelt bowed to the pressure of the idealists who wanted the United Nations set up before the war was over. Roosevelt therefore acquiesced when Secretary of State Cordell Hull, who himself was closely identified with the Wilsonian idealists, gradually transformed the Four Policemen idea into what became the Security Council of the United Nations. Roosevelt consoled himself with the thought that it was not the early establishment of the United Nations and the format of the Security Council that were critical but rather that the United States and the Soviet Union should preserve a friendly and cooperative relationship and that they should settle all important issues between them outside the Security Council and work together to maintain peace.

Roosevelt, as suggested earlier, could not approve an old-fashioned spheres- of-influence arrangement in Europe. He feared that it would be perceived by U.S. opinion as another example of how the cynical, immoral European powers periodically got together to make secret agreements to divide up the spoils at the expense of weaker states; and hence as a violation of the principle of national self-determination and independence. Such a development in U.S. opinion, Roosevelt foresaw, could jeopardize his postwar plans right from the beginning. But at the same time Roosevelt recognized that the Soviet Union's legitimate security needs in Eastern Europe would have to be satisfied. Since the Red Army was occupying Eastern Europe and would likely move into Central Europe as well, the Soviet Union could do as it wished there in any case. The United States would not employ force or threats of force to prevent or to dissuade the Soviets from creating friendly regimes and making territorial changes in Eastern Europe. This was understood and accepted even by those of Roosevelt's advisers—including Soviet experts in the State Department—who were most negative in their view of Soviet communism.[7]

From the standpoint of maintaining the U.S. public's support for his postwar policy it was terribly important for Roosevelt first that the Soviet Union should define its security needs in Eastern Europe in *minimal* terms and second that it should go about securing friendly regimes in Eastern Europe in ways that the United States and Britain could agree to and that would not flagrantly conflict with the principles of the Atlantic Charter. What was at stake for Roosevelt was the legitimacy in the eyes of the U.S. public of his entire plan for a postwar security system based on cooperation with the Soviet Union. If Soviet behavior in Eastern Europe was seen by the U.S. public as flagrantly conflicting with the principle of national self-determination and independence, it would create the image of an expansionist Soviet Union— one that could not be trusted.

Roosevelt hoped—perhaps somewhat naively—that the potential conflict between the Soviet Union's security requirements and the principles of the Atlantic Charter could be avoided or minimized in a number of ways. During the war he attempted to persuade Stalin that the complete defeat and disarming of Germany and the arrangements being made to weaken and control postwar Germany would do more to guarantee Soviet security than would Soviet territorial gains and the imposition of tightfisted Soviet control over Eastern Europe.

Roosevelt also attempted to get Stalin to understand the difficulties with U.S. public opinion that would be created should the Soviet Union fail to cooperate in working out territorial settlements and political arrangements in Eastern Europe that did not flagrantly conflict with the commitment to uphold the principle of national self-determination and independence. In effect, Roosevelt was pleading for Stalin to show self-restraint; he hoped that Stalin would cooperate at least to the extent of providing a "cosmetic" facade to the creation of pro-Soviet regimes in Poland and other Eastern European countries. Stalin in fact was disposed to cooperate. Cosmetic solutions were in fact patched up several times. Thus Roosevelt and most of his advisers thought they had achieved that goal at the Yalta Conference in early 1945. But their optimism was quickly shaken by new difficulties with the Russians over interpretation of the Yalta agreements regarding Poland. Within a few months of becoming president, Truman too succeeded in patching up the disagreement over Poland, but once the war was over distrust of Soviet intentions mounted in Congress and among the public. People increasingly interpreted Soviet behavior in Eastern Europe as a harbinger of more ambitious expansionist aims, and it became more difficult to arrest the drift into the cold war.

Roosevelt died before these developments made themselves felt so acutely as to force major changes in his policy towards the Soviet Union. Among the many disadvantages Truman labored under in his effort to make a success of Roosevelt's policy was the reassertion by Congress, once the war ended in the summer of 1945, of its role in foreign policy. Truman was genuinely committed to trying to achieve Roosevelt's Great Design—that is, as best he could given the fact that Roosevelt never took Truman into his confidence and also given the fact that Roosevelt's advisers had various opinions as to how best to deal with the Russians.

Pressures and circumstances of this kind hampered Truman's ability to continue efforts to make Roosevelt's policy succeed, though he certainly tried to do so for a while; eventually, however, Truman was led to move step by step away from that policy to the policy of containment and balance of power associated with the cold war. But only gradually, and it should be noted, with considerable reluctance did Truman replace the image of the Soviets that supported Roosevelt's postwar policy with the quite different set of beliefs about the Soviet Union associated with the cold war.

Several hypotheses help to explain why the transition to containment and cold war was slow and difficult. First, as already noted, the exigencies and situational pressures of the wartime situation provided strong, indeed compelling, incentives for giving credence to evidence that supported the benign, optimistic image of the Soviets. And the generally successful wartime collaboration with the Soviets reinforced hopes that this image was sound and would prove to be stable. But to recognize this fact is by no means to imply that Roosevelt and later Truman were engaged in biased information processing of incoming data on Soviet behavior in order to confirm an existing optimistic image of the Russians. Rather the record shows that incoming information of new Soviet actions was interpreted sometimes as undermining some of the optimistic beliefs on which Roosevelt's policy rested but at other times as reinforcing them, so that there were ups and downs rather than a straight-line steady erosion of the optimistic image of the Soviets.

A second hypothesis helping to account for the gradualness of the transition to the cold war is to be found in the very nature of policy legitimacy. Once a foreign policy is established and achieves a degree of policy legitimacy—both normative and cognitive legitimacy—in the eyes of top policy makers themselves and enough other influential political actors, it is difficult for policy makers to contemplate replacing that policy with one that is radically different.

An entirely new foreign policy will require new normative and/or cognitive legitimation. The uncertainty and expected difficulty of achieving adequate legitimation for a different policy reduces incentives for engaging in policy innovation and strengthens incentives to "save" the existing policy if only via modifications at the margins. *Substantial* erosion in public support for the existing policy and/or effective political pressure by influential critics would appear to be a necessary condition for overcoming the momentum of an established policy and for motivating top policy makers to address seriously the need for a basic overhauling of existing policy.

What this suggests, more specifically in the case at hand, is that disavowal of Roosevelt's policy of cooperation with the Soviet Union carried with it the risk of undermining the basic legitimation of *any* internationalist foreign policy, thereby encouraging a return to isolationism. The two alternative "realist" internationalist foreign policies which Roosevelt had rejected had, as noted earlier, severe disadvantages with regard to public acceptability. In the end Truman rejected both the spheres-of-influence and balance-of-power alternative, choosing instead a somewhat vaguely defined "containment" strategy which he coupled with support for the United Nations. (That the containment strategy and the ensuing cold war could take on some of the characteristics of a balance-of-power system—though bipolar rather than multipolar as in the eighteenth and nineteenth centuries—and eventually lead to a de facto spheres-of-influence arrangement was not clearly foreseen.)

The transition from Roosevelt's policy to containment and the cold war was, as noted earlier, a gradual one. Its relationship to the architecture of Roosevelt's policy is of particular interest. Thus the change started at the level of tactics, worked upwards to strategy, and finally extended to the level of design objectives.

Dissatisfaction with the way in which Roosevelt's policy was working emerged quite early, well before his death, and it focused initially and for some time on the tactics that were being employed. The "kid-gloves" treatment of the Russians was rejected as counterproductive by some advisers and officials, among them Averell Harriman, who was to become particularly influential with Truman's administration. It is true that Truman, quite soon after replacing Roosevelt, adopted a "get-tough" approach to the Russians. But as John Gaddis[8] and others have noted, "getting tough" was initially meant to apply only to a change in tactics in dealing with the Russians. This tactical innovation was to remain for some months part of an effort not to change Roosevelt's Great Design and his strategy but to achieve them more effectively.[9]

In effect Truman *improvised* an alternative to Roosevelt's Great Design over a period of time, working as it were from the bottom up—from tactics to strategy to design objectives—rather than deductively, as Roosevelt had done, from design objectives to strategy to tactics.[10]

As it evolved, the new cold war policy encountered serious difficulties in its ability to gain acceptance both from the standpoint of desirability and feasibility. In striving to attain policy legitimacy with Congress and the public for its cold war policies the Truman administration was led into a considerable rhetorical oversimplification and exaggeration of the Soviet threat, one that rested on a new "devil image" of the Soviets and a new premise to the effect that the U.S.–Soviet conflict was a zero–sum contest. The struggle to maintain policy legitimacy for the cold war led in time to considerable rigidification in the supporting beliefs and an unwillingness of U.S. policy makers to subject them to continual testing that stands in sharp contrast to Roosevelt's and Truman's initial willingness to reassess the policy premises of the earlier policy on the basis of new information.

By way of conclusion several points emerge from this analysis of the difficulties Roosevelt experienced in his efforts to obtain policy legitimacy for his postwar plans. First, U.S. isolationist sentiment was not powerful enough, once the United States got into the war, to prevent or hamper Roosevelt's ability to commit the country to an internationalist postwar policy. Roosevelt, however, was definitely hampered in pursuing the particular internationalist security plan that he favored by the strong idealist wing of the prointernationalist forces in the United States. The idealists felt that World War II provided a second chance to realize Woodrow Wilson's shattered dreams for collective security through a strong League of Nations. Roosevelt, on the other hand, believed this idealist approach to postwar security was naive and that it would not be effective. But in order not to jeopardize domestic support for the war and in order not to risk shattering the internationalist coalition that favored U.S. participation in some kind of postwar security system, Roosevelt shied away from trying to educate public opinion to understand and support his hard-boiled realist approach. Roosevelt felt he could not afford a direct confrontation with the Wilsonian idealists. To consolidate opinion behind U.S. war aims he issued the Atlantic Charter, which restated the country's historic idealist aspirations for national self-determination and equality of nations. And to avoid divisive controversy with the idealists, Roosevelt gradually diluted and modified his Four Policemen concept for postwar security and accepted instead the creation of the United Nations organization much earlier than he had thought desirable.

Thus Roosevelt did secure normative legitimation for an internationalist postwar foreign policy. *But* the means he employed for this purpose—the principles embodied in the Atlantic Charter—severely hampered his ability to design and pursue the particular kind of postwar security system he favored. One is struck, therefore, by the fundamental internal policy contradiction that plagued Roosevelt's efforts to put his Great Design for postwar cooperation with the Soviet Union into practice. For in fact the very national values and aspirations that he appealed to effectively to secure normative legitimation for an internationalist foreign policy served at the same time to impose severe constraints on the strategic flexibility he needed in order to deal with Eastern European issues.

Roosevelt's Grand Strategy called for accommodating the security needs of the Soviet Union in Eastern Europe; but the moral legitimation of his overall policy stood in the way. Roosevelt—and Truman later—found it very difficult to work out arrangements in Eastern Europe that would at the same time satisfy the Russians and not alienate idealist U.S. opinion that thought that thereby the principles of national self-determination and independence were being jeopardized. Roosevelt and for a while Truman as well continued to try to patch up arrangements in Eastern Europe (even "cosmetic" solutions) that would be acceptable to both Russian leaders and U.S. idealists. Their efforts eventually failed as time ran out; the U.S. image of the Soviets hardened and Truman began to improvise an alternative policy toward the Soviets.

The lesson that emerges from this experience is that a foreign policy is vulnerable if, as in this case, the means employed to secure normative legitimation of the policy at home conflict with the requirements of the grand strategy for achieving the design objectives of that policy.

THE NIXON–KISSINGER EFFORT TO SECURE POLICY LEGITIMACY FOR THE DÉTENTE POLICY

We turn now to our second case study, which we shall deal with even more briefly since it is more recent in time and there is less historical data and scholarship on which to draw. After many years of the cold war it is not surprising that the détente policy should be particularly difficult to legitimate well enough to provide U.S. policy makers with a stable fundamental national consensus to enable them to pursue the difficult long-range objectives of détente in a consistent, coherent manner. Such legitimacy as détente enjoyed was brittle to begin with. Moreover, some of the means Nixon and Kissinger employed to strengthen public support for the détente process, even though successful in the short run, as will be noted, entailed special risks. For a variety of reasons, such legitimacy and support as Nixon and Kissinger managed to acquire for the more ambitious of their détente objectives eroded badly well before the end of the two Nixon–Ford administrations.

An answer to the question of why the détente policy was difficult to legitimate and why such legitimacy as it acquired eroded so badly suggests itself if we compare its complex objectives and strategy with the stark simplicity of the cold war. During the cold war the U.S. objective was simply to contain the Soviet Union, without World War III, until some day hopefully the force of Soviet ideology and the forward thrust of Soviet foreign policy would moderate and spend themselves to achieve this long-range objective.

Détente policy, on the other hand, was more ambitious in its objectives and more complicated in its strategy. It aimed at persuading the Russians to mend their ways and to enter into a new "constructive relationship" with the United States. This was what might be called the long-range "grand design objective" of Nixon's détente policy. The development of a new constructive relationship between the two super nuclear powers was to serve as the foundation for a new international system—what Nixon vaguely referred to as "a stable structure of peace." Admittedly, as many commentators noted, what Nixon and Kissinger had in mind in these respects was not clearly conceptualized or spelled out, but it is clear that their détente policy did include the creation of a new U.S.–Soviet regime (or regimes) for security and economic issue areas. In other words, as with Roosevelt's postwar plans, détente too had a long-range system-creating objective which required the development of a friendly, cooperative relationship between the two powers. And once again as in the case of Roosevelt's policy, the image of the Soviets that underlay the détente policy was that of a limited adversary, not that of an implacably hostile foe, as in the cold war image of the Soviets.

The cold war had been easier to legitimate domestically in the United States because it rested on a simple negative stereotype—a devil image of the Soviet leaders. Détente policy, on the other hand, had the more difficult task of getting people to view the Soviets as a limited adversary; but just what that was—neither friend nor foe, something in between—was not easy for many people to understand.

The Grand Strategy for achieving the long-range objectives of détente combined the use of deterrence strategy—a holdover from the cold war era—with various measures of conciliation–accommodation; in other words, a carrot-and-stick approach. The conciliation–accommodation component of deterrence strategy recalled important aspects of Roosevelt's strategy for winning the Soviet leaders over to cooperation in his postwar security system, but some of the underlying cognitive beliefs were different.

The conciliation–accommodation component of détente strategy consisted of various activities that were supposed to weave an increasingly complex and tighter web of incentives and penalties into the evolving U.S.–Soviet relationship. To this end Nixon and Kissinger held out to the Soviets the prospect of a variety of important benefits from détente:

1. Nixon and Kissinger attempted to turn to account Moscow's interest in trade, access to Western credits, grain, and technology.
2. They also indulged the Soviet Union's desire for enhanced international status and recognition as a superpower equal to the United States.

3. They held out the possibility of agreeing to the Soviets' long-standing desire for formal recognition of the territorial changes in Eastern Europe and of the dominant position the Soviet Union had acquired in Eastern Europe.
4. They hoped to further entangle the Soviets in their "web of incentives" and penalties by concluding a détente with Communist China. This, they expected, would strike fear into the hearts of Soviet leaders and motivate them to adopt more moderate and cooperative policies toward the United States.
5. Last but not least in importance, Nixon and Kissinger's web of incentives included negotiations for limiting the arms race and the danger of war.

The strategy of creating a web of incentives had as one of its underlying cognitive premises the belief that it would give the Soviets a strong and continuing stake in the détente process which would lead them to act with restraint in the Third World lest they jeopardize its benefits. As one writer aptly put it, "the strategy was to evolve détente into a new form of containment of the Soviet Union—or better still, *self-containment* on the part of the Russians."[11]

The Nixon–Kissinger strategy included other means as well to promote a new, U.S.–Soviet regime of a more constructive kind. Thus, U.S. leaders urged upon the Russians the necessity of adhering to a new set of norms and rules of conduct for restraining competition and conflict between the two superpowers throughout the world. (The underlying cognitive premise was that a set of norms of sufficient relevance and specificity could be formulated over time. That Soviet and U.S. leaders would not merely pay lip-service to them but also come to constrain their behavior accordingly in order to avoid conflict and promote the longer-range goals and benefits of détente.) These efforts to formulate a set of norms, encouraged by Soviet leaders, culminated in the Basic Principles Agreement signed by Nixon and Brezhnev at their summit meeting in May 1972. This document, which Kissinger heralded at the time as marking the end of the cold war, laid out general rules of conduct: Both governments agreed to cooperate to prevent "the development of situations capable of causing a dangerous exacerbation of their relations" and the possibility of wars into which they might be drawn; to forego efforts to obtain "unilateral advantage" at each other's expense; and to exercise mutual restraint in their relations. Cooperation to prevent the onset of dangerous crises into which they might be drawn was further emphasized in the Agreement on the Prevention of Nuclear War that the two leaders signed the following year. (The multilateral Helsinki Agreement of 1975, it may be noted, also included general crisis-prevention principles.)

This strategy was increasingly denigrated by U.S. critics of détente, who questioned its underlying premise and doubted its practicality. They argued that the Nixon administration was giving Moscow many tangible benefits in return for vague promises of good behavior and that it could offer no more than pious and naive hopes that the Soviets could be bribed into limiting their ambitions and their meddling in the Third World.

What this criticism overlooked was that Nixon and Kissinger did not rely solely on offering bribes and rewards for good behavior. In fact, as already noted, their strategy for inducing restraint on Soviet behavior relied upon continued use of deterrence threats as necessary, as well as positive incentives. If and when the Soviets did not act with restraint in the Third World, Nixon and Kissinger believed and often insisted that the United States must react firmly. And there were quite a few occasions when the Nixon–Ford administrations attempted to do so—i.e., in response to the Syrian tank invasion of Jordan in September 1970, in the Indian-Pakistani war in December 1971, in the case of the construction of a possible Soviet submarine base in Cuba in late 1970, in the Arab–Israeli War of 1973, and in Angola in 1975. In other words, when the "self-containment" Kissinger hoped to induce in Soviet leaders via the détente strategy did not suffice, he felt it was necessary to reinforce it with measures of the kind associated with traditional containment policy and deterrence strategy.

At first glance the strategy of rewards and punishments employed by Nixon and Kissinger bears a striking resemblance to what psychologists call "behavior modification." The Nixon administration in fact was using a carrot-and-stick policy in its effort to induce Soviet leaders to modify certain of their foreign policy behaviors and to resocialize them into new patterns of behavior that would be more consistent with the objectives and modalities of a new regime in U.S.–Soviet relations.

Several questions can be raised about the validity of the cognitive premises that underlay this strategy. In the first place, the effort to resocialize Russian leaders appears to have violated two basic principles of behavior modification. This technique works best when the therapist singles out *specific* items of behavior that are to be changed and indicates the *specific* approved behaviors that are to replace them. Nixon and Kissinger, however, described the behaviors to be eliminated from Soviet foreign policy in general terms and used generalities also to identify the hoped-for changes in Soviet behavior (as in the general principles contained in the Basic Principles Agreement).

Another important principle of behavior modification not sufficiently adhered to in détente strategy has to do with the timing of the reward to the subject. Just when the therapist rewards the subject may be critical in influencing him to modify a particular behavior in the desired direction. In behavior modification a reward is supposed to come *after* the subject behaves as desired; the function of the reward is to reinforce the new behavior. But Kissinger often gave benefits to the Soviets beforehand, i.e, as a bribe to induce Soviet leaders to behave in a generally desired direction.

In any case, whether or not Kissinger applied behavior modification principles correctly in his strategy, what he was trying to accomplish was very ambitious, and this raises another question regarding the feasibility of the strategy and whether still other premises on which it was based were justified. The strategy assumed that the rewards and punishments available to U.S. leaders for modifying Soviet behavior were sufficiently potent for the purpose. But this premise may be questioned. Rather, as some critics of détente held, it may be that Kissinger overestimated the leverage available to him for accomplishing so difficult and ambitious an objective. Perhaps it was overly optimistic to believe—and dangerous to encourage the U.S. public to believe, so as to gain legitimacy for the policy—that the web of incentives and penalties realistically available to the Nixon administration would suffice to create a stake in détente so valuable to Soviet leaders that they would give up opportunities to display their increased power and their efforts to extend their influence in the world. Interestingly, this was among the aspects of détente policy that was most sharply challenged by critics in levying the charge that Kissinger had "oversold" détente.

The legitimacy of détente strategy suffered also because its implementation confused the public. It was perhaps predictable that many members of Congress and the public would fail to grasp the subtleties of a strategy that combined deterrence threats and penalties with efforts at conciliation and bestowal of benefits. If the Soviets behaved so badly on some occasions so as to warrant threats or penalties, why then reward them in other respects? Should there not be more explicit quid pro quos whereby the Soviets would give up something concrete for each benefit we gave them? Criticism of this kind not only eroded the legitimacy of détente policy; it brought increasing pressure to bear on the administration to abandon or at least make significant changes in the strategy employed. The domestic politics of détente within the United States, magnified by Reagan's unexpectedly strong challenge in the Republican presidential primaries, forced the Ford administration to drive harder bargains with Moscow and to apply more exacting standards for acceptable agreements. (And this constraint has applied equally thus far to President Carter's approach to the Soviets.)

But perhaps the worst consequence of the way in which Kissinger applied the complex strategy of conciliation and deterrence was that it tended over time to polarize U.S. public opinion. Both the anti-Soviet hawks and the antiwar doves in this country became dissatisfied with the détente policy for different reasons. And with the passage of time both hawk and dove critics of the détente policy became stronger politically. Thus, when Kissinger bestowed benefits on the Soviets, the anti-Soviet hawks protested. And whenever Kissinger confronted the Soviets—as in the Arab–Israeli War of 1973 and over Angola—the doves sounded the alarm that the administration was about to start down the slippery slope into another Vietnam.

As a result Kissinger found himself caught in an increasingly severe whiplash between hawk and dove critics of his policy. Those members of Congress and the public who did understand and sympathize with the intricate logic and rationale of the dual strategy of conciliation and deterrence and who made up the centrist constituency whose support Kissinger so badly needed to maintain the momentum of the détente process were gradually neutralized by the growing strength and louder voices of hawk and dove critics.

Kissinger's difficulties with his hawkish critics were compounded by other adverse developments that he was unable to control and to which he inadvertently contributed on occasion. These developments included the Soviet leaders' repeated insistence—in part no doubt to quiet the opposition to détente from their own hawks—that détente did not mean that they were betraying their communist ideology and would forego support for "national liberation" movements. U.S. hawks interpreted such Soviet statements as exposing the fallacy of the cognitive premises on which were based Kissinger's aspirations for developing a new constructive relationship with the Soviets. Soviet insistence on defining détente in terms of their own concept of "peaceful coexistence" also revived concern over Soviet intentions. And this concern over the premises of the détente policy was much strengthened by the continuing buildup of Soviet strategic and other military capabilities coupled with the failure of the Strategic Arms Limitations Talks (SALT) negotiations to limit the arms race. Thus the question of Soviet intentions, which has periodically agitated American foreign policy experts and public opinion since the end of World War II, emerged once again as a highly salient and controversial issue.

Uneasiness about Kissinger's conduct of détente strategy was aggravated by the way in which he sometimes expressed his views about growing Soviet power and influence in the world. Kissinger's statements sometimes included unfortunate innuendoes to the effect that the Soviet Union was now the ascendant power and the United States a descending power. This theme was implicit rather than explicit in what Kissinger said, but it struck a highly sensitive chord among Americans who were suffering the many evidences of the decline of U.S. power and hegemony. Kissinger was charged with holding a Spenglerian view of the decline of the West, which of course he denied. But more than one critic detected evidences of pessimism in some of Kissinger's philosophical reflections on the state of the world with regard to the possibility that the West's will to resist expansion of Soviet power and influence was on the decline.

The attribution of such beliefs and predispositions to Kissinger made it all the more plausible to charge him with pursuing détente in a one-sided way, as if he were driven by the feeling that it was imperative for the United States to work out the best deal possible with its mighty adversary before the West grew even weaker. In this regard Kissinger's critics felt that he was underestimating the Soviet Union's economic and political weaknesses, its problems with its Eastern European client states and with Communist parties in the West, and the fact that the Soviet system was not really an appealing model for many developing countries.

For all of these reasons the legitimacy of the détente policy eroded badly, a development that enormously strengthened those various domestic constraints associated with "democratic control" of foreign policy mentioned at the beginning of this chapter. As a result Kissinger's ability to conduct a coherent, effective foreign policy on behalf of the laudable objectives of détente was shattered well before the end of the Ford administration. With the erosion of the stable domestic consensus on behalf of détente, Kissinger could no longer count on minimal public acceptance of the variety of actions that implementation of his détente strategy required. Not only was he no longer given the benefit of the doubt, some of his activities engendered suspicion that they were designed to serve his personal interests or the political fortunes of his administration. His secretive approach to decision making and his diplomatic style did much, of course, to enhance the distrust.

No doubt Kissinger believed that his détente policy fell victim to the public's impatience for quick results and its unreasonable demands for frequent concrete indications that the policy was succeeding. Kissinger might complain with some justification that critics of détente were not justified in expecting that each transaction with the Soviets should give reciprocal advantages to each side; or that the balance sheet should show a profit every month.

Given the ambitious character of the détente objective, which required resocialization of Soviet leaders and their acceptance of the norms of a new regime in U.S.–Soviet relations, it would be only reasonable to assume that considerable time and repeated efforts would be needed to accomplish that goal. In the meantime, before Dr. Kissinger's behavior modification therapy took full effect, one had to expect that the Soviets would occasionally misbehave. But if so, then how could one evaluate whether the strategy was succeeding? Kissinger's critics pointed to instances of Soviet meddling in Third Areas as evidence of the failure and unsound character of the strategy. Kissinger himself could only retort that Soviet behavior would have been perhaps even more aggressive and the confrontations more dangerous had it not been for détente. Neither side could prove its case; but the possibility must be entertained that the critics pronounced the strategy of inducing self-restraints in Soviet foreign policy a failure prematurely.

PUBLIC OPINION AND THE PROBLEM OF EVALUATING FOREIGN POLICY

Any complex long-range foreign policy such as Roosevelt's Grand Design or the Nixon–Kissinger détente policy needs considerable time to achieve its objectives. Such politics cannot be achieved overnight: one summit meeting between the heads of state will not do it; neither will one overall agreement or one decisive action. Nor can one even expect steady progress toward the long-range objective. It is more reasonable to expect occasional ups and downs.

Any long-range policy needs to be evaluated along the way. We expect a president and his administration to engage in objective, well-informed evaluations of the policies they are pursuing. Policy evaluation of Roosevelt's approach to the Russians—and of Nixon's détente policy—involve questions such as the following: Is the long-range concept of a "cooperative" U.S.–Soviet relationship clearly enough defined—that is, does the administration have a clear enough notion of what it is striving to accomplish? Is the *general strategy* the administration is employing to achieve that long-range objective a sound one; and is the strategy working well enough or does it need to be changed in some way? Are the day-to-day *tactics* that are being utilized to implement that strategy well conceived? Are they working or do they need to be changed?

These questions associated with policy evaluation, it may be noted, have to do with the "cognitive legitimacy" of a policy—i.e., the basis for the president's claim that he knows what he is doing; that he understands well enough the nature of the opponent and the forces at work in the world situation, and that he knows how to use the means available to him in order to achieve the long-range objectives of his policy.

The evaluation of an ongoing policy is difficult to begin with from a purely intellectual and analytical standpoint. It is all the more difficult if the monitoring and evaluation of a current policy is unduly influenced by the play of domestic politics.

A president who pursues a long-range foreign policy in a democracy such as ours runs into some formidable problems. In the absence of policy legitimacy the character of U.S. politics, the role of the modern mass media in our political life, and the volatile nature of public opinion combine to subject the president's pursuit of long-range foreign-policy objectives to constant scrutiny and evaluation. As a result the president finds himself forced to defend his long-range policy on a month-to-month—if not also a day-to-day—basis. When this happens, a shortened and often distorted time perspective is then introduced into the already difficult task of evaluating the policy and the related task of deciding whether changes in strategy and tactics are necessary.

One of the characteristics of the U.S. public is its impatience for quick results and its demand for frequent reassurances that a policy is succeeding. This impatience is often fed by and exploited by the mass media and by political opponents of the administration's policy. The result of these domestic political factors is to complicate the ability of a president to pursue a long-range policy with the patience and persistence that is needed. The play of public opinion and politics can distort the difficult task of evaluating the policy; it can erode its legitimacy; it can force changes in that policy before it has had a chance to prove itself.

Faced with the volatile tendencies of U.S. public opinion, a president and his advisers must attempt to carefully control the public's impatience for quick results. They must also offer meaningful assurances that the cognitive premises of their policy goals and of the strategy and tactics employed on their behalf are being subjected to careful, objective evaluation. They must also control their own tendency to pander to the public's demand for quick, dramatic results as a way of making up for the inadequate legitimacy that their policy enjoys. On this score Kissinger and Nixon can be criticized for having pandered to the public's impatience for quick results and its tendency to be impressed by dramatic achievements of a symbolic rather than substantive import. In the early years of détente, Nixon and Kissinger were able to come up with spectacular events that seemed to offer assurance that détente was working— the trips to Peking, the summits with Soviet leaders in Moscow and Washington, the multitude of agreements.[12] But thereby Nixon and Kissinger helped to create a frame of mind and a set of expectations in the public which worked against them later on, when they had no more rabbits to pull out of the hat for the time being. Day-to-day "successes"—whether real successes or contrived public-relations-type successes—are not only a poor substitute for genuine policy legitimacy; they can easily end up helping erode whatever legitimacy has been achieved for a complex, long-range policy such as détente.

ACKNOWLEDGMENTS

Research for this chapter was supported by a grant (number SOC 75–14079) from the National Science Foundation and by the Center for Advanced Study in the Behavioral Sciences, at which the author was a Fellow in 1976–1977. Parts of the chapter were presented earlier in a paper delivered to the Symposium on U.S. Foreign Policy in the Next Decade at the University of Missouri-Saint Louis, April 1977, and in a paper for a conference on approaches to the study of decision making at the Norwegian Institute of International Affairs, Oslo, Norway, August 1977.

NOTES

1. Henry Kissinger, *A World Restored,* (Boston:Houghton Mifflin Co., 1957).
2. In preparing this interpretative essay the author has relied mostly upon secondary sources describing Roosevelt's plans for a postwar security system and the Nixon–Kissinger détente policy.

   Roosevelt's "Great Design" for the postwar period was conveyed by him most explicitly in background interviews with Forrest Davis, who published detailed accounts of Roosevelt's plans and the beliefs supporting them in several articles appearing in the *Saturday Evening Post* "Roosevelt's World Blueprint,"10 April 1943; "What Really Happened at Teheran—I," 13 May 1944; "What Really Happened at Teheran—II," 20 May 1944. [For background and evidence of Roosevelt's later acknowledgment that Davis's articles accurately reflected his views, see John Lewis Gaddis, *The United States and the Origins of the Cold War* (New York: Columbia University Press, 1972), pp. 6, 153.] Detailed secondary accounts of Roosevelt's thinking and plans are to be found in Willard Range, *Franklin D. Roosevelt's World Order* (Athens:University of Georgia Press, 1959); Roland N. Stromberg, *Collective Security and American Foreign Policy* (New York: Praeger Publishers, 1963), see esp. chap. 8; Robert A. Divine, *Roosevelt and World War II* (Baltimore, Md.: Johns Hopkins University Press, 1969); John Lewis Gaddis, *Origins of the Cold War,* Daniel Yergin, *Shattered Peace* (Boston:Houghton Mifflin Co., 1977), esp. chap 2; and Robert Garson, "The Atlantic Alliance, Eastern Europe and the Origins of the Cold War From Pearl Harbor to Yalta," in H. C. Allen and Roger Thompson, eds, *Contrast and Connection* (Columbus: Ohio State University Press, 1976), pp. 296–319.

   For various reasons the Nixon–Kissinger policy of détente is more difficult to reconstruct in terms of the analytical framework ("design objective," "strategy," "tactics") employed in the essay. While Nixon and Kissinger often spoke in general terms regarding their long-range goal of a "new constructive relationship" with the Soviet Union and made cryptic references to a new balance-of-power system, they never disclosed (and perhaps never formulated) a more specific design concept for the international system they hoped to create. The term *détente* itself was a misnomer, since quite obviously the Nixon administration's objectives and strategy went well beyond securing merely a "relaxation of tensions" (which is the traditional definition of détentes and embraced a willingness to engage in substantial "appeasement" (in the pre 1930s nonpejorative sense of the term) and "accommodation" of the Soviet Union in the interest of inducing and socializing this "revolutionary" power into becoming a responsible member of a new, stable international system.

   Perhaps the fullest statement—really, by that time a defense—of the détente policy was provided by Kissinger in his testimony before the U.S. Senate Committee on Foreign Relations, 19 September 1974 ["Détente with the Soviet Union: The Reality of Competition and the Imperative of Cooperation," reprinted in Robert J. Pranger, ed., *Détente and Defense* (Washington, D.C.: American Enterprise Institute for Public Policy Research, 1976), pp. 153–178]. See also earlier statements and speeches by Nixon and Kissinger and in particular the annual reports to the nation: Richard M. Nixon, *U.S. Foreign Policy for the 1970s,* (Washington, D.C.: U.S. Government Printing Office, 1970, 1971, 1972, and 1973); see also Helmut Sonnenfeldt, "The meaning of Détente," *Naval War College Review* 28:1 (Summer 1975).

Among the many published commentaries and critical appraisals of the détente policy, the most useful for present purposes is Stanley Hoffmann, *Primacy or World Order* (New York: McGraw-Hill Book Co., 1978), pp. 33–100, which contains observations regarding the difficulty of gaining legitimacy for the détente policy similar to those offered in the present essay. An important detailed study is the as yet unpublished dissertation by Dan Caldwell, "American-Soviet Détente and the Nixon–Kissinger Grand Design and Grand Strategy" (Ph.D. diss., Department of Political Science, Stanford University, 1978). Among the many other useful commentaries on the Nixon–Kissinger détente policy, see Stephen A. Garrett, "Nixonian Foreign policy: A New Balance of Power—or a Revived Concert?" *Polity* 8 (Spring 1976); Robert Osgood, ed., *America and the World*, vol. 2, *Retreat from Empire? The First Nixon Administration* (Baltimore, Md.: Johns Hopkins University Press, 1973); and B. Thomas Trout, "Legitimating Containment and Détente: A Comparative Analysis: (Paper presented to the Midwest Political Science Association, Chicago, Ill., 19–21 April 1979).

3. The concept of "policy legitimacy" (versus "regime legitimacy") is discussed in a stimulating and insightful way by B. Thomas Trout, "Rhetoric Revisited: Political Legitimation and the Cold War," *International Studies Quarterly* 19:3 (September 1975).

4. For a fuller account see for example John L. Gaddis, *Origins of the Cold War*, chaps. 1, 2.

5. A detailed listing is available from the author upon request.

6. Forrest Davis, "Roosevelt's World Blueprint," *Saturday Evening Post,* 10 April 1943.

7. That the State Department was not an "ideological monolith" in its attitude toward the Soviet Union during and immediately after World War II has been persuasively argued and documented in recent studies. [Cf., for example, Robert L. Messer, "Paths Not Taken: The United States Department of State and Alternatives to Containment, 1945–1946,"*Diplomatic History* 1 (Fall 1977).] Moreover, as Eduard Mark demonstrates, Charles Bohlen and other State Department specialists did not operate on the assumption that there was an ineluctable conflict between the principle of self-determination in Eastern Europe and legitimate Soviet security interests in that area. Instead, they distinguished between different kinds of spheres of influence, arguing that an "open" (versus an "exclusive") Soviet sphere of influence in Eastern Europe was acceptable to and consistent with U.S. interests. See "Charles E. Bohlen and The Acceptable Limits of Soviet Hegemony in Eastern Europe: A Memorandum of 18 October 1945," *Diplomatic History* 2 (Spring 1979). On this point see also Thomas G. Patterson, *On Every Front: The Making of the Cold War* (New York: W. W. Norton & Co., 1979), chap. 3.

8. Gaddis, *Origins of the Cold War,* pp. 198–205.

9. Important changes in Roosevelt's strategy took place later. They included a shift from appeasement to insistence on quid pro quos, and probably of greater significance, a willingness on Truman's part to make important exceptions to Roosevelt's practice of seeking joint decision making among the Great Powers on the major political and territorial questions affecting post-war Europe. Thus Truman, confronted by urgent problems—particularly economic—of governing occupied Germany, which the mechanisms for four-power control could not deal with to his satisfaction, gradually moved toward making unilateral decisions without the Russians and the creation of separate mechanisms for governing the three Western zones of Germany.

10. As John L. Gaddis notes in commenting on Truman's stormy interview with Soviet Foreign Minister Molotov on 23 April 1945, soon after Roosevelt's death—which was perhaps the first example of Truman's new "get-tough" tactics: "to view the new President's confrontation with Molotov as the opening move in a well-planned long-range strategy for dealing with the Soviet Union is to presume a degree of foresight and consistency which simply was not present during the early days of the Truman administration." (*Origins of the Cold War,* pp. 205–206).

11. Leslie Gelb, "The Kissinger Legacy," *N.Y. Times Magazine,* 31 October 1976, italics supplied.

12. The *timing* of the Nixon–Kissinger "spectaculars" may also have opened them to the criticism that détente moves were being used to gain partisan political advantage. For example, the China trip seemed timed to coincide with the 1972 primaries; the SALT Treaty was advantageously signed during the summer of 1972; and the wheat deal, too, coincided with 1972 presidential nomination conventions. (Source: Ole R. Holsti in a personal communication.)

⤳

Business Versus Public Influence in U.S. Foreign Policy

Lawrence R. Jacobs and Benjamin I. Page

Some of the most important debates over U.S. foreign policy focus on who influences government decisions. According to the realist account, government officials design foreign policy to advance the nation's interests in competition with other states in the international system. The process of identifying the national interest is aided, some argue, by experts or "epistemic communities" that possess the specialization to objectively analyze an increasingly complex global environment. An alternative account argues that U.S. foreign policy is driven not by the national interest but rather by organized pressure groups and, especially, businesses in order to advance their own narrow interests. A third account insists that the pressure to win election motivates government officials to tailor foreign policy to the preferences of the mass public.

This chapter examines the relative influence of public opinion, experts, and critical interest groups—organized labor and, especially, business. We begin by reviewing the competing accounts of U.S. foreign policy and then discuss and analyze an unusual body of evidence for evaluating them.

ALTERNATIVE ACCOUNTS OF U.S. FOREIGN POLICY

Three prominent, empirically based interpretations of U.S. foreign policy and what influences it offer what appear to be sharply different predictions.

Neoliberalism and Organized Groups

Many scholars who take a neoliberal approach to international politics emphasize the decisive influence of organized interest groups on foreign policy (e.g. Keohane, 1984). The assumption is that foreign policy is a function of shifting coalitions of multiple and competing political and societal actors. Executive and legislative officials with foreign policy authority bargain with domestic groups that use their members' votes, campaign contributions, threatened or actual capital flight, labor strikes, and other tools to affect the electoral benefits and costs to elected officials of choosing alternative policies (Gourevitch, 1986; Milner, 1988; Rogowski, 1989; Frieden, 1991). For instance, Keohane and Milner (1996) trace targeted government subsidies and trade protections to the influence of well-organized and financed groups; Snyder (1991) attributes defense policy to logrolling coalitions.

Organized labor, and perhaps even more so business corporations, possess critical resources for pressuring policy makers. The ability of labor to strike and to support research and experts on manpower issues as well as its political money, volunteers, millions of voters,

Lawrence R. Jacobs and Benjamin I. Page, "Business Versus Public Influence in U.S. Foreign Policy." An earlier version of this paper was presented at the "Inequality and American Democracy Conference," November 7-8, 2003, Princeton, New Jersey. Reprinted by permission of the authors.

and roots in many congressional districts make it a potentially significant voice in debates about foreign policy. Given its mission to protect the jobs and benefits of its members, "[labor] leaders have spoken out often on foreign affairs" (Galenson, 1986, 62). In addition to addressing foreign policies that affected its bread and butter interests at home, organized labor in the United States was a stalwart supporter of Washington's policies for challenging communism during the Cold War. Labor backed the Vietnam War, increases in defense spending, and various confrontations with the Soviet Union and China. Since the 1980s, labor's support for defense spending waned as the cold war ended and the AFL-CIO saw the influx of civil service and other unions representing white collar, professional and service occupations, challenging the dominance of unions representing blue-collar occupations in building and manufacturing (Lipset, 1986). But it is not clear how much impact labor has actually had. Some analyses of comparative public policy and U.S. foreign policy indicate that labor's influence on American government officials and foreign policy is not significant (e.g. Esping-Anderson, 1990).

Some neoliberal analysts of international politics have singled out business corporations and groups as particularly influential in American foreign policy because of businesses' effects on the economy and their capacity to prompt voters to punish the incumbent political party. "Since political leaders' electoral prospects depend on the state of the economy," Milner (1997) observes, "they must be concerned with those groups that can directly affect the economy" (62). A number of studies have reported the influence of business on specific types of foreign policy: Rogowski (1989) traces government economic policy to powerful domestic economic interests; Trubowitz (1998) points to uneven economic growth and struggles for regional economic advantage to explain U.S. foreign affairs; and Grossman and Helpman (1994 and 1995) link industry lobbying and campaign contributions to international trade relations and, specifically, increased tariffs for politically organized industries. Some argue that pressures on governments to tailor foreign policy to please business have increased over the past three decades with the emergence of an open world economy characterized by rapid international movement of capital and greater exposure to global economic competition (Bates and Lien, 1985; Winters, 1996).

The research suggests that different policy making institutions may vary in their susceptibility to organized pressures. Executive branch officials, who play an especially strong part in foreign policy (particularly national security policy), have been said to focus on identifying collective gains in pursuing the "national interest" and therefore to be somewhat more resistant to organized pressure (Krasner, 1978 and 1972; Art, 1973; Wildavsky, 1991). Organized groups may have been especially influential with Congress, where senators and, especially, Representatives (who are elected in relatively small districts) are acutely responsive to intense demands for concentrated benefits from narrowly-based groups representing constituents and campaign donors (Milner, 1997).

In short, interest-group-oriented scholars suggest that labor and, especially business, should exert strong influence on U.S. foreign policy.

Epistemic Communities and Knowledge-Based Experts

Research on "epistemic communities" has found that the growing complexity and uncertainty of global problems has "led policy makers to turn to new and different channels of advice" and, specifically, to a new "knowledge elite" that is recognized as possessing the technocratic expertise and competence to articulate the objective causes of international problems, the "real" stakes or interests of states affected by those problems, and appropriate policy remedies (Haas, 1992, 12; Nelkin, 1979; Adler and Haas, 1992; Hall, 1989). In the introduction to an influential special volume of *International Organization,* Peter Haas

(1992) explained that the "epistemic community members' professional training, prestige, and reputation for expertise. . . accord them access to the political system and. . . . influence over policy debates" (17). Research in that volume and elsewhere (e.g. Hall, 1989; Nelkin, 1979) suggests that epistemic communities are the intermediaries which transmit the ideas of "networks of knowledge-based experts" into government institutions and influence the substantive content of foreign policies by setting agendas and formulating policy alternatives (Haas, 1992, 2–3; Adler and Haas, 1992).

Epistemic communities exist outside formal government institutions and are drawn from professionals and experts in the academy, think tanks, and other bodies of highly trained specialists in subjects as diverse as economic theory and military technology. These specialists provide critical technical expertise for government officials in the legislative and executive branches to define problems and help form their preferences regarding particular policies.

Research on epistemic communities has two important implications. First, it suggests that experts equip government officials to conduct analyses and reach decisions that can be independent of direct pressures from organized groups or citizens. The scholarship on epistemic communities predicts, then, that business and labor exert at best modest direct influence upon the foreign policy decisions of government officials.

Second, epistemic communities may serve as concrete mechanisms for identifying and addressing a state's objective interests, in the complex global power struggles that classical and structural realists emphasize. Even if objective interests related to inter-state competition, the structure of the international system, and a state's position in that system do constrain states (Waltz, 1959, 1979; Walt, 1987), the definition and identification of such interests in concrete terms is a practical challenge for government officials.[1] Students of epistemic communities argue that realists incorrectly "assume that a state's interests are clear and that the ways in which its interests may be most efficaciously pursued are equally clear" (Haas, 1992, 13–14; Adler and Haas, 1992, 367–9). Instead, they maintain, technical experts are the vehicle for the interpretation of international structures, the identification of the "imperatives" facing the state, and the articulation of state interests in international politics: "[H]uman agency lies at the interstices between systemic conditions, knowledge, and national actions" (Haas, 1992, 2). In short, research on epistemic communities suggests that conditions of uncertainty produce strong incentives for government officials charged with making foreign policy to respond to experts from think tanks, the academy and other reservoirs of highly trained specialists and professionals.

Median Voter Theory and the Influence of Public Opinion

The median voter theory predicts that vote-seeking policy makers will respond strongly to the policy preferences of the mass public. Competition among officeholders and candidates to win elections is expected to motivate them to minimize the distance between their policy stands and the preferences of voters. In the case of unidimensional, two-party competition, both parties should converge at the midpoint of public opinion (Downs, 1957).[2] Empirical evidence of influences by public opinion upon foreign policy has been reported in a large and growing body of research by students of public opinion and policy (Bartels, 1991; Russett, 1990; Wittkopf, 1990; Holsti, 1996; Ostrom and Marra, 1986; Hartley and Russett, 1992; Sobel, 2001; Page and Shapiro, 1983; Monroe, 1979, 1998), as well as by some international relations scholars with broader interests (e.g. Putnam, 1988, 432, 436).

Theory suggests that the general public should have the most impact on highly salient issues that draw intense attention from the media and voters and thereby pose the most direct threat of electoral punishment for unresponsiveness. Presumably, as E.E. Schattschneider (1960) suggests, greater public attention to an issue expands the "scope of conflict" and heightens the risk for government officials who defy their constituents' views. In contrast, narrow, well-organized interests may dominate less visible issues. Some empirical evidence (e.g. Page and Shapiro, 1983, 181) seems to support the prediction of greater public influence with higher salience.

The assumption of government responsiveness to public opinion in median voter theory has informed research on the "democratic peace," which has found a tendency for individual democratic states and, especially, pairs of democratic states to be more pacific on average than non-democratic states (Russett and Oneal, 2001; for review see Elman, 1997, pp. 10–20). One aspect of democratic peace research argues that competitive elections "makes democratic leaders. . . sensitive to public opinion" because politicians either anticipate electoral punishment or they are thrown out of office for being unresponsive: "citizens in a democratic state can influence governmental policy directly, through public opinion, or indirectly, though their representatives."[3]

Tending to confirm the median voter theoretical prediction, quantitative analyses by students of public opinion have found, for example, that 62 percent of U.S. foreign policies *changed* in the same direction as public opinion (Page and Shapiro, 1983, 182), and that congressional-district-level public support for military spending was related to Congress members' votes on military spending bills during the presidency of Ronald Reagan (Bartels, 1991; also see Bartels 2002a and 2002b). Moreover, research based on case studies has reported that public opinion influences U.S. foreign policy by constraining government officials to a range of policies that voters support, removing from consideration broad policy directions that are opposed by the mass public (Sobel, 1991; Russett, 1990).

An ample body of quantitative and qualitative research, then, indicates that U.S. foreign policy and the policy preferences of government officials are substantially influenced by public opinion. Apparently accepting such influence as an empirical fact, a long line of observers including classical realists has urged policy makers *not* to respond to citizens' preferences because of concerns that the general public engaged in "simple moralistic and legalistic" thinking, was detached from the reality of international politics, exhibited unstable shifting "moods," and hungered for "quick results" (Morgenthau, 1973, pp. 135, 146–148; cf. Almond, 1950; Kennan, 1951). Walter Lippmann (1955) warned that following public opinion would create a "morbid derangement of the true functions of power" and produce policies "deadly to the very survival of the state as a free society" (15, 20, 26–27).

Problems with Past Research
Previous research concerning the impact of organized groups, epistemic communities, and public opinion on U.S. foreign policy has produced an impressive body of results that invite diverse expectations regarding who influences government officials. This research also suggests that the characteristics of different government institutions may produce different patterns of influence. For example, members of the House of Representatives, which the Federalist Papers labeled the "people's House" due to their frequent election in small and decentralized districts, were expected to be especially sensitive to public opinion, while officials in the executive branch and Senate were expected to be less responsive due to their insulation from the public by indirect elections and longer terms in office.

Past research has not, however, definitely sorted out the relative impact of different factors upon U.S. foreign policy. This has resulted, at least in part, from two problems related to the scholarly division of labor: omitted variables and lack of comparative testing. Understandably, each of the three main approaches we have reviewed has focused on a set of variables of particular interest to it, rarely investigating and testing competing explanations at the same time. Most studies of public opinion and foreign policy, for example, (including those by the present authors) have failed to include any independent variables *other* than public opinion.

However understandable this strategy may be, it runs the risk that other important influences may be neglected. It may lead each approach to overestimate the importance of its own favorite factors and to offer little or no estimate of the *relative* impact of different possible influences. Also, even excellent case studies that disentangle causal mechanisms and trace processes of policy-making usually leave open the issue of how well they generalize beyond those particular cases.

What is needed, we believe, is *comparative* analysis (based on a large number of diverse cases) of the relative influence upon U.S. foreign policy of these key factors: organized groups (especially business and labor); epistemic communities from think tanks and the academy; and mass public opinion. The present paper offers a first step in that direction.

DATA AND METHODS

We have analyzed a set of data that are uniquely well suited to this purpose, based on eight quadrennial pairs of surveys—conducted from 1974 through 2002—that were sponsored by the Chicago Council on Foreign Relations or CCFR (and, in 2002, also by the German Marshall Fund of the United States) and implemented by the Gallup Organization and Louis Harris and Associates or its later incarnation, Harris Interactive.[4] These surveys provide data on a wide and diverse set of foreign policy preferences of two distinct groups: the general public, and a set of "foreign policy leaders" including important actors that make American policy (government officials in the executive branch, the House of Representatives, and the Senate), members of critical interest groups (especially business and labor), and members of epistemic communities (namely, educators and leaders of private foreign policy organizations or think tanks).[5] Our data come from paired surveys conducted at 8 different time points, for a total of 16 separate surveys.

The paired surveys of the mass public and foreign policy leaders have both strengths and limitations. The government officials and other elites were not randomly selected for interviews; they were chosen from institutional positions involving foreign policy responsibilities or expertise.[6] Nor were the numbers of elites interviewed in any single year very large.[7] The surveys of the general public, though, were based on random, relatively large samples of about 1,550 respondents each.[8]

Despite their limitations, the CCFR data make it possible to conduct what is, so far as we know, the first systematic examination of the relative influences of ordinary citizens, interest groups, and epistemic communities on American government officials across a wide range of foreign policy issues over a lengthy period of time. Data on large numbers of key policy makers are very difficult to obtain (but cf. Holsti and Rosenau, 1984), especially from samples that are comparable over multiple years.[9]

Pooling the Chicago Council surveys for cross-sectional analysis is a promising approach. The samples add up across surveys to 2,916 respondents from all groups of elites and 1,901 respondents from the theoretically crucial groups of leaders from government, business, labor, and experts. The elite samples have the advantage of being drawn in a consistent manner across years, because of continuity in survey organizations and research teams as well as conscious efforts to produce comparable data. In addition, the private and confidential nature of the interviews with respected survey organizations helped to discourage public posturing and encourage relatively candid expression of views.

A crucial advantage of using these survey data is that they permit us to analyze relationships using precise, directly comparable measures between the policy preferences of policy makers and those of the public, members of interest groups, and experts. These measures are based on responses to identical questions asked of the various groups at the same time. Previous researchers have generally lacked such comparable measures and have had to struggle with the question of exactly how close a given policy came to the wishes of particular actors.

Our analyses rest on the assumption that the expressed policy preferences of government officials are reasonable indicators of the foreign policies that they enact or pursue. Although we do not suppose that our data on policy makers' expressed preferences invariably and without exception correspond with actual policy, scrutiny of the data indicates that policy makers' responses have usually reflected the positions and actions of the institutions in which they held office. We believe that the problem of possible slippage between these survey responses and actual foreign policy is outweighed by the enormous advantage of being able to obtain precise, comparable, quantitative measures of the positions of government officials, organized groups, experts, and the public.[10]

Our dependent variables are measured in a simple fashion: the percentage of policy makers (that is, the percentage of all policy makers, or of a subset of policy makers from the administration, the House, or the Senate) who favored or opposed a particular policy alternative in a given survey.[11] We believe that these percentage measures generally reflect the position of the average policy maker on an underlying policy continuum. The percentage that "favors" a particular type of foreign aid, for example, may reflect the *amount* of aid that the average respondent favors.[12]

Our independent variables are measured in the same way: percentages of the general public, or of relevant subsets of elite respondents (of business people, labor leaders, or experts, for example) who favored or opposed the same policy alternative that the policy makers were asked about. Because "Don't know" and "Refuse to answer" responses are more common among the general public than among policy makers, we excluded those responses from the mass public surveys and recomputed percentages without them. This gave us comparable measures of the views of *those with opinions* among elites and the mass public.

The scope and duration of the Chicago Council's parallel studies of elites and the general public enabled us to analyze variations across different institutions (comparing subsets of policy makers from the administration, the House, and the Senate), and variations in levels of issue salience to the public. In addition, we separately examined three broad, exhaustive, and mutually exclusive policy domains: Diplomatic Policy (e.g. relations with other countries and international organizations); Defense Policy (including the recruitment and deployment of troops, military aid, and the development, procurement, and transfer to other countries of military hardware); and Economic Policy (e.g. issues related to trade, tariffs, and the protection and promotion of American jobs and businesses). Diplomatic and Defense policies were asked about most frequently (214 and 209 common items, respectively), followed by Economic policy (144 common items).

Since our aim is to sort out the *independent* impact of each factor and to compare them with each other, we relied primarily upon multivariate regression analyses. The meaningful and intuitively understandable units of measurement involved (percentage points on the familiar zero to 100 scale) led us to focus on unstandardized OLS regression coefficients, which can tell us how many percentage points of change in policy makers' support for a policy are typically associated (controlling for all other factors) with a one-percentage-point increase in support by (for instance) business respondents. A coefficient near zero would signal no influence at all upon policy makers by business, whereas a coefficient near 1.0 would signal very great influence. We conducted these regression analyses for all years combined (the most stable and reliable set of estimates) and for each separate year; for all policy makers combined and for each separate institutional subgroup of policy makers; for all issues together and for each of the three issue categories separately; and for issues grouped according to varying degrees of salience.

We employed three general types of regression models. First, we pooled the data across all eight pairs of surveys into a single cross section and regressed the preferences of policy makers at a given time on those of business people, experts, labor leaders, and ordinary citizens at the same time. The eight surveys of the mass public and eight parallel surveys of foreign policy leaders produced a total of 567 common survey items ascertaining preferences about foreign policy: that is, 567 questions about policy preferences that were asked in the same year, with identical wording, of both citizens and elites.[13] The number of common items varied from a high of 112 in 2002 to a low of 48 in 1986. For each of the 567 common items, then, we obtained measures of the policy preferences of policy makers, the general public, business people, labor leaders, and foreign policy experts, as well as other groups of leaders less relevant to the analysis. This pooled cross-sectional analysis allowed us to estimate the contemporaneous impact on policy makers by members of organized groups (business and labor), experts, and public opinion.

Although the cross-sectional analysis is valuable, we also wanted to examine possible complicating dynamics and causal ambiguities by including one or more variables measured over time. One possible complication is that past government decisions may structure or "lock in" the positions of current government officials. The views of foreign policy makers may be bound or conditioned by past government positions or commitments in treaties or agreements. This kind of self-reinforcing process has been found in the incrementalism of government budget making (Wildavsky, 1975). In short, we needed to design a regression model to incorporate the "inertial" forces of foreign affairs and, to the extent possible, control for them.

Our second type of regression model therefore addresses the potential for incremental, self-reinforcing dynamics by lagging the dependent variable to get at the effects of prior preferences of foreign policy decision makers. What we need are data on the past history of our dependent variables. Fortunately, our data set does allow us to identify many "two-time-period" cases—that is, pairs of identical survey items that were asked in two sequential surveys of both the mass public and elites. We identified 252 sequential pairs, which allow us to conduct regression analyses that lag the dependent variable for one period—using responses to the same policy preference question when it was asked in the survey four years earlier. In such regressions, policy makers' 1978 support for economic foreign aid (for example) is predicted by the policy makers' 1974 views on aid, together with the 1978 preferences of the mass public, business and labor leaders, and experts. This model allows us to examine the impact on policy makers of contemporaneous views of the general public, business and labor leaders, and experts, while taking account of the effects of the past policy preferences of government officials.

Another complicating factor concerns causality. Statistically disentangling whether public opinion and non-governmental elites affect policy makers, or whether the reverse happens—whether policy makers influence the preferences of others—is a daunting challenge. The tracking of temporal sequences (i.e., whether changes in hypothesized independent variables actually precede changes in the dependent variable) and the logic of "Granger causality" (i.e., whether the history of hypothesized independent variables actually adds explanatory power to that of the history of dependent variables) are valuable approaches for assessing the determinants of political phenomenon (see Freeman, 1983).

Our third type of regression model uses the data from sequential pairs of survey questions to conduct two-observation time series analyses. Although the restriction to two time points prevents us from conducting full-scale time series analyses, we can at least begin to get at the logic of causal time asymmetries and Granger causality. For example, in such a regression the 1978 preferences of policy makers concerning foreign economic aid are predicted by the 1974 preferences concerning aid of the public, experts, labor and business leaders, and the policy makers themselves. Since causes generally precede rather than follow effects, this time asymmetry adds to our confidence about causal inferences and indicates whether or not various factors have an impact over time. Incorporating the most recent past history of the independent and dependent variables begins to get at Granger causal logic.

The two-observation time series analyses maximize the potential of our data but are not without limitations. First, because of the four-year intervals between surveys, our lags are relatively long and may not allow us to distinguish the different speeds and effectiveness with which certain groups may exercise influence. For instance, major, internationally oriented business leaders may be able to exercise influence especially quickly because they are highly attuned to policy impacts and have privileged access to policy makers. By contrast, labor leaders may tend to have only delayed influence due to reliance on building up pressure in congressional districts or a national mass constituency. Second, we lack a full account of the history of the independent and dependent variables and therefore cannot conduct full Granger tests. We can only lag our variables one period. Finally, our use of two-observation cases reduces the number of cases available for analysis, which can make it difficult to find statistically significant results.

ANALYZING INFLUENCES ON FOREIGN POLICY MAKERS

We began our analysis by examining bivariate relationships at one point in time between the preferences of all policy makers taken together, and those of the mass public as well as each of the seven distinct clusters of "foreign policy leaders" that the Chicago Council surveys repeatedly interviewed (from business, labor, educators, private foreign policy organizations or think tanks, editors and journalists from the media, special interest groups relevant to foreign policy, and religious officials). All these bivariate relationships were highly significant (at the .01 level) and quite large. The percentage of policy makers preferring a specific policy was most strongly correlated with the percentage preferring the same policy among respondents from the media (r=.94), business (r=.91), foreign policy organizations and think tanks (r=.90), and educators (r=.90). Religious leaders (r=.85) and labor leaders (r=.84) came not far behind, with the general public (r=.77) taking up the rear.

The current preferences of policy makers were almost as strongly correlated (and highly significantly so) with preferences from the *previous time period* for the media (r=.86), business (r=.85), foreign policy organizations and think tanks (r=.84), and educators (r=.83). Religious leaders (r=.78) and labor leaders (r=.81) again came not far behind, while the general public (r=.71) continued to trail the others.

The results for business are consistent with previous research on organized groups, and the findings for think tanks and educators are in line with the analysis of epistemic communities. The relatively low figures for the public are surprising given previous research findings that policy makers are highly responsive. On the other hand, a correlation in the .7 or .8 range cannot be sneered at. It could leave room for an estimate of substantial impact in the context of multivariate analysis.

The high correlations for religious leaders and the media are puzzling. In both cases, there is reason to doubt whether they really have a major, direct impact upon the making of U.S. foreign policy. Few scholars have asserted that they do, and in theoretical terms, any such influence would presumably be primarily channeled through the public. It seems possible that the high correlations are spurious or result from reciprocal relationships. The media, for example, have not often been identified by researchers as a direct influence on policy making, but considerable research does suggest the opposite causal connection—i.e. the influence of government officials upon media that rely upon the officials as news sources (e.g. Sigal, 1973; Gans, 1979; Hallin, 1986; Bennett, 1990 and 1994; Herman and Chomsky, 1988; Nacos et al, 2000, Part I). And the media are often thought of as being affected by, as well as themselves influencing, their audiences, which consist largely of the general public and businesses that take out advertisements.

Not only do the preferences of all the elite groups surveyed by the Chicago Council correlate highly with the preferences of policymakers: they also correlate very highly with each other. Contemporaneous correlations were in the r=.90 to .92 range, and sometimes (as in the case of educators and the media) reached the near-astronomical level (for survey data) of .96; correlations with preferences at the previous time point were also quite high, though generally about a tenth of a point weaker. Substantively, this suggests the existence of something like a "foreign policy establishment," in which policy preferences are largely shared across several different categories of elites engaged in foreign policy, while the general public stands somewhat to the side. (Contemporaneous correlations between the preferences of the public and those of the various elite groups range from .82 and .83—for labor and religious leaders respectively—down to .68 for private foreign policy organizations and think tanks; correlations with responses from the previous time period are similar, though a bit lower.)

The policy preferences of members of this "foreign policy establishment"—especially experts, business people, and policy makers—have consistently differed from those of the general public in some respects. Ordinary Americans, for example, have repeatedly expressed stronger support for multilateral, cooperative foreign policy. The public, more than policy makers and other elites, has favored strengthening the United Nations, working closely with allies, and participating in international treaties and agreements like the Kyoto Agreement on global warming, the International Criminal Court, and the Comprehensive Nuclear Test Ban Treaty. Ordinary Americans have also regularly put a higher priority than elites on domestic-impact aspects of foreign policy, such as protecting Americans' jobs, stopping the inflow of illegal drugs, and reducing illegal immigration (see Rielly 1975, 1979, 1983, 1987, 1991, 1995, and 1999, and Boutin and Page, 2002.)

Methodologically, the high intercorrelations among elite groups augur possible trouble with multicollinearity. Sorting out distinct effects in a precise and reliable fashion is a difficult challenge. In any case, bivariate correlation coefficients are clearly inadequate for estimating the independent impacts of the public and various elite groups upon government officials. To test the hypotheses of interest requires multivariate analyses. We now turn to our three types of regression models: pooled cross-sectional analyses (what we refer to as Model 1); cross-sectional analyses that include a lagged dependent variable (Model 2); and time series analyses that regress the current preferences of policy makers on the preferences of policy makers, public, and non-governmental elites from the previous survey (Model 3).

The Dominance of Business and Experts

Our first step in the cross-sectional multivariate analysis (Model 1) was to estimate what could uncharitably be called a "garbage can" model, with policy makers' foreign policy preferences as the dependent variable and with the preferences of the general public and of each of the CCFR's seven distinct clusters of elites as independent variables. This regression revealed a pattern already hinted at by the bivariate correlations: rather substantial and highly significant coefficients for business (b=.31) and think tanks (b=.22), but a second-tier status for labor (b=.09, significant at only p<.05) and especially the public, which had a near-zero coefficient and apparently no statistically significant effect at all.[14]

Our additional regression models generally confirmed the impression of dominant influence by business. Model 2, which consists of mostly cross-sectional analysis but includes the lagged dependent variable (policy makers at t–1), showed large and highly significant coefficients for business (b=.29). The effects of labor and think tanks about half as strong, and the coefficient for the public failed to reach statistical significance. The estimated effect of the lagged dependent variable was statistically significant, though weak (b=.18). The implication is that, after taking account of policy makers' previous preferences, business continued to exert a substantial contemporaneous effect on government officials: business leaders apparently exert an influence that breaks through the self-reinforcing inertial process of foreign policy making.

Model 3 (which is the time series model that regresses the current preferences of policy makers on the preferences of the public and non-governmental elites from a prior survey) offers some evidence regarding causality that largely fits our earlier findings, but with a new wrinkle. Even with the unusually long lag of four years and the absence of fuller histories of the dependent variables, this model did confirm the influence of business (b=.27) and added new evidence of labor's effect (b=.36). The lagged dependent variable remained significant and substantial (b=.35) and the coefficients for the public, educators, think tanks, the media, and religious groups did not reach statistical significance. According to the logic of time asymmetries and Granger causality, this indicates that business and labor actually do influence the foreign policy preferences of policy makers. These initial results appear to support the notion that business access and resources may facilitate relatively quick impact, while labor exerts pressures over time as it works through decentralized congressional districts.

The "garbage can" models, however, produced, some very odd coefficients,[15] presumably because they ran afoul of two serious methodological problems. First, the cohesiveness of the "foreign policy establishment" did indeed produce extremely high levels of multicollinearity, with VIF coefficients of above 20 for the media and 15 for educators in the cross sectional analysis (a VIF coefficient above 10 is generally considered troubling: see Chatterjee and Price, 1991). Second, the theoretical rationale for the causal structure of the "garbage can" model is highly questionable. For example, this model treats the preferences of media figures as a purely independent variable that directly influences government officials, even though previous research (as noted above) suggests the opposite causal connection, casting a pall of causal ambiguity over the media coefficient. Direct impact by religious leaders is also questionable.

In order to address the methodological flaws of the "garbage can" model we refined the analysis to include only a theoretically solid core of independent variables. We dropped from analysis the media variable (which suffered from high multicollinearity and causal ambiguity), religious leaders (also causally ambiguous), and "special interest groups" (poorly defined and showing little estimated impact).[16] Further, we combined educators with respondents from private foreign policy organizations and think tanks, whose preferences were highly correlated with each other (r=.92) and played essentially the same roles in regressions when entered separately. The result is a single variable for the policy preferences of "experts," which is consistent with research on epistemic communities.

Subsequent regression analyses using refined, parsimonious models yielded results that were considerably more satisfying both substantively and methodologically.

In our first and most important set of refined analyses, the dependent variables were the foreign policy preferences of all policy makers combined, as well as those of the three distinct clusters of government officials in the House of Representatives, the Senate, and the Administration. These analyses included only the four independent variables needed to test the principal theoretical expectations we have discussed: the preferences of the general public, business, labor, and foreign policy experts. Each of these variables, with the possible exceptions of experts and the mass public, can reasonably be treated as exogenous with respect to government decision makers. The policy preferences of business and labor leaders are arguably rooted in economic interests and in well-developed values; they are not likely to vacillate with the particular officials currently holding office. "Experts," on the other hand, may be cultivated and even selected by officials. The foreign policy preferences of the mass public may be influenced by government officials as well; this would lend ambiguity to the interpretation of large coefficients for the public, but (as we will see) no such coefficients have been found. (Estimates of a *lack* of influence are largely free of causal ambiguity.)

As Table 5.2 indicates, our three regression models were rather effective in accounting for the variation in policy makers' preferences: adjusted R-squared values were all high, ranging from .70 to .90. Taken together, the preferences of business, experts, labor and the public account for the bulk of variation in the foreign policy preferences of policy makers, both contemporaneously and over time. This is particularly true for all policy makers together, but nearly as much so for the separate groups.

The strongest and most consistent results in Table 5.2 are the coefficients for business, which suggests that business corporations and associations have a strong—even dominant—impact upon the making of U.S. foreign policy. According to cross sectional analysis (Model 1), when business people change their preferences for a given foreign policy by 10 percentage

Table 5.2 INFLUENCES UPON THE FOREIGN POLICY PREFERENCES OF GOVERNMENT OFFICIALS (BASIC MODELS)

	Dependent Variables											
Independent Variables	All Policy Makers	House	Senate	Adm	All Policy Makers	House	Senate	Adm	All Policy Makers	House	Senate	Adm
Model 1: Pooled Cross Sectional Analysis												
$Public_t$	.03	.10*	.03	-.08								
$Business_t$	.52**	.43**	.43**	.71**								
$Labor_t$	.16**	.19**	.21**	.04								
$Experts_t$	.30**	.28**	.31**	.31**								
Model 2: Analysis with Lagged Dependent Variable												
$Public_t$					-.03	.03	.05	-.10				
$Business_t$					.44**	.29**	.39**	.58**				
$Labor_t$					.16**	.17**	.10	.03				
$Experts_t$					.24**	.31**	.25*	.26**				
$Govt\ Officials_{t-1}$#					.19**	.22**	.24**	.23**				
Model 3: Analysis with Lagged Independent and Dependent Variables Lagged												
$Public_{t-1}$									-.14	-.13	-.12	-.22*
$Business_{t-1}$									.24*	.18	.37**	.46**
$Labor_{t-1}$									.34**	.40**	.33**	.33**
$Experts_{t-1}$									.07	.11	.01	.04
$Govt\ Officials_{t-1}$#									.39**	.34**	.21**	.28**
Adjusted R^2	.88	.86	.72	.82	.90	.89	.78	.83	.80	.79	.70	.72
N	567	482	482	482	252	212	212	212	212	212	212	212

Note: Entries are unstandardized coefficients from OLS regressions, with the percentage of government officials who take a given position as the dependent variable and the percentages of members of each of the listed groups who take that same position as independent variables.

We lagged the preferences of the government officials when they were the dependent variable. For instance, when we used all policy makers in the dependent variable, the preferences of this group of government officials in the previous survey were included as an independent variable.

Level of Significance: * $p < .05$ level, 2-tailed test, ** $p < .01$, 2-tailed test points, policy makers (taken together) respond by changing their preferences about 5 points in the same direction. Business preferences were the strongest predictor within each of the three separate institutional arenas, peaking at a .71 coefficient for administration officials (more than double the only other significant coefficient, that of experts). This result is consistent with the expectations of many international relations scholars who focus on interest groups, but not with the expectations of those who envision an autonomous executive. To the extent that the executive dominates foreign policy, this is especially striking.

Taking account of possible inertial forces in policy making by lagging the dependent variable, Model 2 produces a similar story of business dominance among all policy makers and, especially, administration officials (Table 5.2). The consistently significant and moderately strong coefficients for policy makers lagged one period indicate that the contemporary views of policy makers are indeed influenced or conditioned by the history of already established perspectives. Business leaders are exerting an effect on government officials, then, that is quite apart from whatever influence they had on past policy that carried forward through the self-reinforcing quality of previous decisions.

The Model 3 time series analysis in Table 5.2 provides a critical test of whether the views of business "cause" changes in the foreign policy preferences of policy makers, according to the logic of Granger models. Regressing the preferences of all policy makers (as well as each separate group of officials) on the independent and dependent variables from the prior survey largely confirmed the dominance of business, with one wrinkle. The logic of Granger causality suggests that business leaders are most influential on officials in the Senate and especially the administration, while not exerting any meaningful impact at all on officials in the House of Representatives. This institutional differentiation of business influence is supported by previous research in international relations, which stresses the responsiveness of administration officials to business in order to improve the performance of the economy and the prospects that voters will reward (rather than punish) the president and his party as the electorate retrospectively evaluates incumbent's term in office. The absence of significant business influence on officials in the House seems to contradict expectations, but it may simply mean than the House is more responsive to local, parochial groups than to the major multinational firms included in the CCFR surveys.

Experts appear to be the second strongest contemporaneous influence on policy makers' preferences (Table 5.2, Models 1 and 2). This result, which (to some extent, at least) fits the expectations of researchers on epistemic communities, applied with nearly identical magnitude to all policy makers combined and to those in each of the three institutional settings. But experts did not exert any significant influence at all according to the time series analysis (Model 3), suggesting that their effects are relatively quick and decay quickly—or possibly that the cross-sectional estimates are artifacts of specification error, and experts' preferences are results rather than causes of policy makers' stands.

Labor is estimated to exert contemporaneous influence on foreign policy decision makers, but only weakly (b=.16 for all policy makers in Models 1 and 2), and not consistently across the different clusters of officials. Research on the role of interest groups in the making of U.S. foreign policy generally anticipates just such a modest role for organized labor. What is surprising, though, is that Labor emerges as the second strongest influence in the time series analysis (Model 3), especially among government officials in the House of Representatives. These results offer substantial evidence regarding causal direction: Labor, despite its limited contemporaneous influence, is apparently able—possibly owing to its active presence in states and localities—to apply delayed pressure on government officials and, especially, House members who are particularly sensitive to organized pressure within their decentralized districts.

Perhaps the most surprising finding in this whole set of analyses is the failure of public opinion, even within these reduced and refined models, to show any substantial or consistent influence upon policy makers. The public's preferences had no significant positive coefficient anywhere except for the contemporaneous estimate for officials in the House of Representatives, and even there the estimated impact was quite weak (b=.10) (Model 1). The negative coefficients in the time series analysis (Model 3), if taken seriously, actually indicate that— controlling for the past views of governmental and non-governmental elites—officials tend perversely to move *away* from public opinion. But a more plausible interpretation is that the public simply has no effect at all.

These findings hint at partial confirmation of the Founders' expectations about the House as "the people's" chamber. More importantly, however, they run against the thrust of much past research that has found a substantial impact of public opinion.

The analyses in Table 5.2 are the bedrock of our empirical investigation, but we also used the same set of three regression models to explore possible variations over time and across three different domains of foreign policy—Defense, Diplomacy, and Economic issues. The separate analyses of each of the eight survey years produced results that generally paralleled those for all years combined (as shown in Table 5.2), with some apparently random variation in coefficients due to the small numbers of cases.[17] For the different issue domains, too, the general pattern held: business dominance, contemporaneous but not lagged effects of experts, and delayed effects by labor, with little impact from the public. In the Economic realm, where foreign policy cuts close to home, public opinion appeared to have significant contemporaneous influence on policy makers: a modest coefficient of .17 in Model 1 but a more substantial .36 in Model 2. With regard to Defense policy, Model 1 indicated that business had a particularly strong effect (b=.77) consistent with some previous literature (e.g., Snyder, 1991). But according to Model 2, experts (b=.58) roughly equaled business (b=.49) in effects on Defense policy. Because of the limited number of cases, we are cautious in interpreting these or other issue-specific results.

Searching for Public Influence on Government Officials

Given the surprisingly weak estimates of influence by public opinion (with the partial exception of influence on House members and in economic policy), we were concerned that real public influence might be masked by the inclusion in the analysis of labor leaders, whom we found to have moderate influence on policy makers and whose preferences are fairly strongly correlated with those of the public (r=.82.) In order to give public opinion the best possible opportunity to display effects, we dropped the labor variable and regressed the preferences of policy makers only on the preferences of the general public, business, and experts.

The amount of variance accounted for was virtually the same as in the earlier models, suggesting that the public and labor can indeed be substituted for each other without having much effect on predictive power. But even with these rather generous—and in fact implausible— causal assumptions (namely, that labor leaders have *no* independent impact upon foreign policy at all but are merely proxies for the general public), the estimated influence of public opinion upon the preference of government officials remained, at best, quite modest.

The Model 1 cross sectional analysis that excluded labor produced coefficients for public influence on all policymakers (b=.11), officials in the House (.21) and Senate officials (.12) that were statistically significant and larger than in the earlier analysis. But these remained much smaller than the comparable coefficients for business (.50 for all policy makers, .40 for House officials, .40 for Senate officials) or experts (.40, .41, .34., respectively) And in Model 2 they mostly vanished, with only a small coefficient for public influence on the "people's House" (.12) remaining statistically significant. In Model 3 (our touchstone for "real," over time influence), public opinion had no significant effects at all. Of particular importance, none of the three models indicated any significant public influence upon the administration, the main center for foreign policy decision making.

Analyses across the three different policy domains mostly continued to show the public as a minor influence, with less impact than experts or, especially, business. For diplomatic policies the public had a cross-sectional (Model 1) coefficient of .18, statistically significant but still well behind business' .40; the results were much the same with Model 2; the coefficient for the public was not statistically significant in Model 3. For economic policy, the public matched business (though trailed experts) with a .27 coefficient for Model 1, nearly matched experts with a .41 coefficient in Model 2 (which included the lagged dependent variable), and exerted no significant effect in Model 3 (time series analysis). Again, the public appears to have a somewhat more effective (though still secondary) voice on close-to-home, economic issues.

One additional context in which these generous, labor-excluded models produced estimates of significant influence by the general public involves highly salient issues. We used the percentage of respondents who gave "don't know" survey responses as a measure of *lack* of salience: the higher the level of "don't knows," the lower the salience. We divided our issue cases into four similarly sized groups with varying degrees of salience, and performed the three types of regression analysis separately on each. For none of the three regression models were there significant public coefficients with any of the three lower-salience groups of issues. For the cross-sectional Model 1, however, and for the very highest-salience group of issues (with only 0% to 4% "don't knows,") the public's coefficient was .21, significant at the $p<.001$ level. These findings are consistent with Schattschneider's (1960) framework; the public has little or no influence on issues that are out of the public eye, but some influence when salience is high.

Yet even under the ideal conditions for maximal public influence (a public-friendly model specification and the most salient issues with 4% or less "don't knows"), business was estimated to exert twice as much influence as public opinion (b=.44). Indeed, the estimated influence of the public evaporated altogether (i.e. it became non-significant) when we incorporated the history of policy makers' preferences or the past views of the public, business, experts, and government officials, using Models 2 and 3.

In short, in spite of generous model specifications, the effect of public opinion upon the preferences of foreign policy makers appears to be—at best—quite modest, when critical competing variables are controlled for.[18] These results challenge research that has suggested a strong public impact on foreign policy.

Of course our results do not completely rule out any influence by the general public on U.S. foreign policy. In addition to the effects on the House, highly salient issues, and economic policy that we have noted, the public may have substantial impact on particular foreign policy decisions, such as the highly salient questions of war and peace analyzed in Sobel (2001). We have not explored public effects upon agenda setting, or on the rhetorical packaging policy choices, or on decision makers' anticipations of later, *retrospective* public opinion. (The makers of foreign policy may, for example, work hard to avoid military casualties that tend to provoke electoral punishment; see Mueller, 1973.) It is possible that our use of policy makers' expressed preferences rather than actual policies as dependent variables may lead us to miss some "delegate"-style behavior in which policy makers act against their own inclinations in order to please the public. Finally, methodological factors may conceivably have deflated our estimates of public impact. But it is worth emphasizing that our measurements of public opinion (based on large surveys) are quite good; any attenuation of coefficients due to measurement error should affect elite groups more than the public. And causal ambiguity in model specification is not likely to be a problem: an erroneous finding of *non*-influence by the public is considerably less likely to result from specification bias than is an excessively large estimate of its influence.[19]

All in all, the implications of our findings for previous research connecting public opinion and policy making are sobering.

Indirect Business and Labor Influence through Experts?

The substantial influence of experts suggested by our cross-sectional models, though in line with past analyses of epistemic communities, is subject to doubt about its causal status. Even if one rules out (as our analyses do) the possibility of a consistent reciprocal influence of officials upon experts that may inflate their apparent impact on officials, there remains the question whether the preferences of experts are a truly independent variable or whether they function in an intervening role. In other words, experts might themselves be influenced by business or labor, and in turn transmit the preferences of those groups to officials.

Researchers on epistemic communities sometimes assume that independent, objective analysis by new "knowledge-based elites" guides policy makers; experts are not merely vehicles for pressing officials on behalf of organized interests or others. Yet the widespread funding of think tanks by business—and, to a much lesser extent, by organized labor through such organizations as the Economic Policy Institute (or EPI)—suggests that organized interest groups may sometimes affect who becomes a recognized expert and what such experts say. Thus experts might not be autonomous influences upon policy makers, but instead might—in whole or in part—convey the preferences of others to officials.

Without additional data we cannot hope to definitively untangle these causal complexities. But we already know, from our discussion of the "foreign policy establishment," that the policy preferences of experts are not statistically independent of the preferences of business or labor. They are quite highly correlated: the preferences of think tank respondents, for example, were correlated at r=.90 with the contemporaneous preferences of business and .80 with those of labor.

If we assume one-way causation from business and labor to experts,[20] we can go further and estimate the independent effects of each, through regressions in which experts' preferences are the dependent variable. The results, shown in Table 5.3, are quite striking. The cross-sectional (Model 1) analysis indicates that business had a highly significant and quite large coefficient (b=.61, p<.001), and labor was not far behind (b=.42, p<.001).[21] After taking into account the reinforcing quality of experts' previous views (Model 2), business' estimated effect was nearly twice the magnitude of labor's (b=.48 versus .27). The four-year lag of business views, though, showed no significant effect (Model 3), which suggests that business's influence (if any) is felt relatively quickly.

The results in Table 5.3 suggest that organized groups influence experts, and that this impact is quite substantial. If we set aside the time series findings of no expert effects on

Table 5.3 EFFECTS OF BUSINESS AND LABOR UPON THE FOREIGN POLICY PREFERENCES OF EXPERTS

Independent Variables	Experts as Dependent Variable		
Model 1: Pooled Cross Sectional Analysis			
Labor$_t$	.42**		
Business$_t$	.61**		
Model 2: Analysis with Lagged Dependent Variable			
Labor$_t$		.27**	
Business$_t$		.48**	
Experts$_{t-1}$		.28**	
Model 3: Analysis with Independent and Dependent Variables Lagged			
Labor$_{t-1}$			.19**
Business$_{t-1}$			.03
Experts$_{t-1}$			.70**
Adjusted R^2	.87	.92	.82
N	567	212	212

Note: Entries are unstandardized coefficients from OLS regressions, with the independent and dependent variables measured as the percentage taking the same position on a given issue.

Level of Significance: * p<.05 level, 2-tailed test, ** p<.01, 2-tailed test

policy makers, and accept the cross-sectional estimates of substantial contemporaneous effects, we can go on to estimate indirect effects that business and labor may have upon public officials through their influence on experts. For example, if (as the cross sectional analysis in Table 5.3 indicates) a 1 percentage point increase in business support for some policy generally leads to a .61 percentage point increase in experts' support for that policy, and if (as the cross-sectional analysis in Table 5.2 indicates) such a .61 percentage point increase for experts would then lead to a .183 (.30 × .61) percentage point increase in officials' support, business would obtain a small but not irrelevant increment of indirect clout. This indirect impact of .183 can be added to the direct impact of business upon policy makers (estimated at .52 points in Table 5.2's cross sectional analysis), yielding a total business impact of slightly over .70. That is to say, a 10 percentage point increase in business support for a given policy may lead to a 7 point, rather than 5 point, increase in officials' support for that policy.[22] Similar calculations for labor based on the cross-sectional analysis indicate a .126 indirect effect of labor on officials. Adding that to the direct effect of .16 given in Table 5.2, the total impact of labor (in the cross sectional analysis) is about .29.[23] This suggests that labor may influence foreign policy almost as much by indirect means as it does directly, which underscores its surprising sway in foreign policy given its reputation for ineffectiveness in American politics. Labor's total effect combined with its modest over time role (Table 5.3, Model 3) suggests that it exercises a long-term national influence through experts. Even so, the estimated total effect upon foreign policy of business is more than twice that of labor.

Methodological uncertainties mean that we should not take the magnitudes of these estimates as gospel. Still, they pose a challenge for those who consider the views of experts to be altogether autonomous.

FOREIGN POLICY, THE NATIONAL INTEREST, AND DEMOCRACY

Our analysis using three distinct types of statistical models indicates that business has a strong, consistent, and, at times, lopsided influence upon U.S. foreign policy. The estimates of strong business influence hold up under different statistical models and different political and institutional conditions, and are generally consistent over time. They hold for high- as well as low-salience issues, for a variety of substantive issue areas, and with respect to different institutional groups of policy makers (though especially among administration and Senate officials). They tend to confirm the theoretical expectations and case study research of the organized interest group literature in international relations.

The estimated impacts of experts upon policy makers do not generally match those of business, but they, too, are quite substantial, at least in the cross-sectional rather than time series data. This lends some credence to claims by the analysts of epistemic communities. Our further investigation of who influences experts, however, suggests that organized groups—not just independent, objective evaluations of complex international realities—may color the views of experts. These findings suggest that the foreign policy clout of business and labor may be augmented by an indirect influence upon policy makers that works through experts.

Labor, even taking into account its possible indirect influence, appears to have less impact on U.S. foreign policy than business does. This finding, too, fits with previous work by international relations scholars who focus on organized interest groups. Nonetheless, labor leaders do exert a surprisingly consistently (if secondary) influence on policy makers, especially among members of the House of Representatives and on particular policy areas.

The findings from our cross-sectional analyses as contrasted with the time series analyses (using lagged independent variables) suggest that the influence of business tends to be fairly quick, while labor's influence tends to be delayed and exerted over time as it makes its presence in congressional districts felt. Although labor's effect on foreign policy has been minimized among international relations scholars, our evidence of labor's impact is consistent with recent reevaluations of its nested impact on U.S. social welfare policy (Gottschaulk, 2001).

To our surprise, public opinion—the foreign policy preferences of ordinary citizens—was repeatedly estimated to exert little or no significant influence on government officials. Where the effect of public opinion emerged (namely, very high-salience issues, economic issues, and the House of Representatives), the absolute and relative magnitude of its influence was generally modest. The pattern of *non*-influence by public opinion is generally immune to issues of model specification and causal ambiguity that might affect some of our other results. It seems to contradict the expectations of a large body of previous research.

These findings have several implications for research on international affairs. First, they support the perennial plea (e.g., by Keohane, 1989, and Putnam, 1988) for international relations scholarship to move from mono-causal explanations to multi-causal explanations. Although our evidence suggests that business may exert the most influence on government officials, experts and, to a lesser extent, labor and (occasionally) public opinion also appear to help shape policy makers' views. These results suggest that three of the most prominent lines of analysis of foreign policy—the interest group, epistemic community, and public opinion approaches—each have some merit. But at the same time, each tends to omit critical variables and to avoid systematically examining the relative impact of competing influences. The danger of omitting alternative factors from consideration is that assessments of the importance of particular factors of interest may be inflated. This hazard seems particularly serious for quantitative analyses of the effect of public opinion on foreign policy (cf., however, Ostrom and Marra [1986] and Hartley and Russett [1992], which take steps to be multivariate.)

Second, our results have some troubling normative implications. The apparently weak influence of the public should disappoint those adherents of democratic theory (e.g. Dahl, 1989) who advocate substantial government responsiveness to citizens' preferences. It might initially please classical realist critics of public influence like Lippmann (1955), Morgenthau (1973) and Kennan (1951), who have urged policy makers to resist pressures from what they see as an ill-informed and capricious public. Yet those same critics—and many other observers—would also like to see policy makers rise above the politics of organized interest groups in order to pursue the "national interest," perhaps as identified by independent, objective experts. Our finding of substantial impact upon foreign policy by business—generally greater impact than by experts—suggests that purely technocratic determination of foreign policy does not usually occur. Competing political interests continue to fight over the national interest. Our results suggest that business often wins that competition.

REFERENCES

Adler, Emanuel and Peter Haas. 1992. "Conclusion: Epistemic Communities, World Order, and the Creation of a Reflective Research Program." *International Organization*. 46 (Winter): 367–390.

Almond, Gabriel. 1950. *The American People and Foreign Policy*. New York: Harcourt, Brace.

Art, Robert. 1973. "Bureaucratic Politics and American Foreign Policy: A Critique." *Policy Sciences* 4: 467–90.

Bartels, Larry. 1991. "Constituency Opinion and Congressional Policy Making: The Reagan Defense Buildup." *American Political Science Review* 85: 457–74.

Bartels, Larry. 2002a. "Partisan Politics and the U.S. Income Distribution, 1948–2000." Prepared for presentation at the Annual Meeting of the American Political Science Association, Boston, August 2002.

Bartels, Larry. 2002b. "Partisan Politics and the U.S. Income Distribution, 1948–2000." Paper prepared for the Russell Sage Foundation.

Bates, Robert, and Da-Hsiang Lien. 1985. "A Note on Taxation, Development, and Representative Government." *Politics and Society*. 14: 53–70.

Bennett, W. Lance. 1994. "The Media and the Foreign Policy Process" in *The New politics of American foreign policy* ed. by David Deese. New York: St. Martin's Press.

_____. 1990. "Toward a Theory of Press-State Relations in the United States." *Journal of Communications*. 40 (Spring): 103–25.

Bouton, Marshall M., and Benjamin I. Page (eds). 2002. *Worldviews 2002: American Public Opinion and Foreign Policy*. Chicago: Chicago Council on Foreign Relations.

Burke, Edmund. 1949. "Speech to the Electors of Bristol" in *Burke's Politics, Selected Writings and Speeches* ed. by R. Hoffmann and P Levack. New York: Alfred Knopf.

Chatterjee, Samprit, and Bertram Price. 1991. *Regression Analysis by Example*. 2nd Ed. New York: John Wiley.

Dahl, Robert A. 1989. *Democracy and its Critics.* New Haven: Yale University Press.

_____. 1961. *Who governs? Democracy and power in an American city.* New Haven: Yale University Press.

Doyle, Michael. 1983. "Kant, Liberal Legacies, and Foreign Affairs." *Philosophy and Public Affairs.* 12, no. 3 (Summer): 205–235, and 12, no. 4 (Fall): 323–53.

Downs, Anthony. 1957. *An Economic Theory of Democracy.* New York: Harper and Row.

Elman, Mariam Fendius. 1997. "Introduction: The Need for a Qualitative Test of the Democratic Peace Theory" in *Paths to Peace: Is Democracy the Answer?* Edited by M.F. Elman. Cambridge, MA: MIT Press.

Esping-Andersen, Gøsta. 1990. The Three Worlds of Welfare Capitalism. Princeton, N.J.: Princeton University Press.

Freeman, John. 1983. "Granger Causality and the Time Series Analysis of Political Relationships." *American Journal of Political Science.* 27 (May): 327–58.

Frieden, Jeffry. 1991. "Invested Interests: The Politics of National Economic Policies in a World of Global Finance." *International Organization.* 45: 425–51.

Galenson, Walter. 1986. "The Historical Role of American Trade Unionism" in *Unions in Transition: Entering the Second Century* ed. by Seymour Martin Lipset. San Francisco: Institute for Contemporary Studies.

Gans, Herbert J. 1979. *Deciding What's News.* New York: Random House.

Gottschalk, Marie. 2001. *In the Shadow of the Welfare State* (Ithaca, N.Y.: Cornell University Press).

Gourevitch, Peter. 1986. *Politics in Hard Times.* Ithaca, N.Y: Cornell University Press.

Grossman, Gene, and Ehhanan Helpman. 1995. "Trade Wars and Trade Talks." *Journal of Political Economy.* 103 (August): 675–708.

_____. 1994. "Protection for Sale." *American Economic Review.* 84 (September): 833–850.

Haas, Peter. 1992. "Introduction: Epistemic Communities and International Policy Coordination." *International Organization.* 46 (Winter): 1–35.

Hall, Peter. 1989. *The Political power of economic ideas: Keynesianism across nations.* Princeton: Princeton University Press.

Hallin, Daniel C. 1986. *The "Uncensored War": The Media and Vietnam.* New York: Oxford University Press.

Hartley, Thomas, and Bruce Russett. 1992. "Public Opinion and the Common Defense: Who Governs Military Spending in the United States?" *American Political Science Review.* 86 (December): 905–915.

Herman, Edward and Noam Chomsky. 1988. *Manufacturing consent: The Political Economy of the Mass Media.* New York: Pantheon Books.

Holsti, Oli. 1996. *Public Opinion and American Foreign Policy.* Ann Arbor: University of Michigan Press.

Holsti, Oli, and James N. Rosenau. 1984. *American Leadership in World Affairs: Vietnam and the Breakdown of Consensus.* London: Allen and Unwin.

Kennan, George. 1951. *American Diplomacy, 1900–1950.* (Chicago: University of Chicago Press).

Keohane, Robert. 1989. *International Institutions and State Power.* Boulder, Co: Westview Press.

_____. 1984. *After Hegemony: Cooperation and Discord in the World Political Economy.* Princeton: Princeton University Press.

Keohane, Robert, and Helen Milner, eds. 1996. *Internationalization and Domestic Politics.* Cambridge: Cambridge University Press.

Krasner, Stephen. 1978. *In Defense of the National Interest: Raw Materials, Investments, and U.S. Foreign Policy.* Princeton: Princeton University Press.

_____. 1972. "Are Bureaucracies Important? (Or Allison Wonderland)." *Foreign Policy* 7 (Summer): 159–179.

Lippmann, Walter. 1955. *Essays in the Public Philosophy.* Boston: Little, Brown & Co.

Lipset, Seymour Martin. 1986. *Unions in Transition: Entering the Second Century.* San Francisco: Institute for Contemporary Studies.

Milner, Helen. 1997. *Interests, Institutions, and Information: Domestic Politics and International Relations.* (Princeton, N.J.: Princeton University Press).

_____. 1988. *Resisting Protectionism.* Princeton: Princeton University Press.

Monroe, Alan D. 1979. "Consistency between Public Preferences and National Policy Decisions." *American Politics Quarterly* 7: 3–19.

_____. 1998. "American Public Opinion and Public Policy 1980–1993." *Public Opinion Quarterly* 62: 6–28.

Moravcsik, Andy. 1997. "Taking Preferences Seriously: A Liberal Theory of International Politics." *International Organization.* 51 (Autumn): 513–53.

Morgenthau, Hans. 1973. *Politics Among Nations.* New York: Knopf.

Mueller, John E. 1973. *War, Presidents and Public Opinion.* New York: Wiley.

Nacos, Brigette, Robert Shapiro, and Pierangelo Isernia. 2000. *Decision Making in a Glass House: Mass Media, Public Opinion, and American and European Foreign Policy in the 21st Century.* New York: Rowan and Littlefield Publishers.

Nelkin, Dorothy. 1979. "Scientific Knowledge, Public Policy, and Democracy." *Knowledge, Creation, Diffusion, Utilization.* 1 (September).

Ostrom, Charles W., Jr., and Robin E. Marra. 1986. "U.S. Defense Spending and the Soviet Estimate." *American Political Science Review* 80: 819–41.

Owen, John. 1994. "How Liberalism Produces Democratic Peace." *International Security.* 19 (Fall): 87–125.

Page, Benjamin I., and Robert Y. Shapiro. 1992. *The Rational Public: Fifty Years of Trends in Americans' Policy Preferences.* Chicago: University of Chicago Press.

_____. 1983. "Effects of Public Opinion on Policy." *American Political Science Review.* 77: 175–90.

Peterson, Susan. 1995. "How Democracies Differ: Public Opinion, State Structure, and the Lessons of the Fashoda Crisis." *Security Studies.* 5 (Autumn): 3–37.

Putnam, Robert. 1988. "Diplomacy and Domestic Politics: The Logic of Two-Level Games." *International Organization.* 42 (Summer): 427–60.

Rielly, John. 1975. *American Public Opinion and U.S. Foreign Policy, 1975.* Chicago: Chicago Council on Foreign Relations. Corresponding studies published in 1979, 1983, 1987, 1991, 1995, and 1999.

Rogowski, Ronald. 1989. *Commerce and Coalitions.* Princeton: Princeton University Press.

Rose, Gideon. 1998. "Neoclassical Realism and Theories of Foreign Policy." *World Politics.* 51: 144–72.

Russett, Bruce. 1990. *Controlling the Sword: The Democratic Governance of National Security.* Cambridge: Harvard University Press.

Russett, Bruce. 1996. "Why Democratic Peace?" in *Debating the Democratic Peace* ed. by M. Brown, S. Lynn-Jones, and S. Miller. Cambridge, MA: MIT Press, pp. 82–115.

Russett, Bruce and John Oneal. 2001. *Triangulating Peace: Democracy, Interdependence, and International Organizations.* New York: W.W. Norton & Co.

Sartori, Giovanni. 1987. *The Theory of Democracy Revisited.* Chatham, NJ: Chatham House.

Schattschneider, E.E. 1960. *The Semi-Sovereign People: A Realist's View of Democracy in America.* New York: Holt, Rinehart, and Winston.

Schumpeter, Joseph. 1950. *Capitalism, Socialism, and Democracy.* New York: Harper.

Sigal, Leon V. 1973. *Reporters and Officials: The Organization and Politics of Newsmaking.* Lexington, Mass.: D.C. Heath.

Snyder, Jack. 1991. *Myths of Empire: Domestic Politics and International Ambition.* Ithaca: Cornell University Press.

Sobel, Richard. 2001. *The Impact of Public Opinion on U.S. Foreign Policy Since Vietnam.* New York: Oxford University Press.

Trubowitz, Peter. 1998. *Defining the National Interest: Conflict and Change in American Foreign Policy.* Chicago: University of Chicago Press.

Walt, Stephen M. 1987. *The Origins of Alliances.* Ithaca, N.Y.: Cornell University Press.

Waltz, Kenneth. 1979. *Theory of International Politics.* Reading, MA: Addison-Wesley.

_____. 1959. *Man, the State, and War: A Theoretical Analysis.* New York: Columbia University Press.

Wildavsky, Aaron. 1991. "The Two Presidencies." In *The Two Presidencies: A Quarter Century Assessment.* ed. Steven Shull, 11–25. Chicago: Nelson-Hall Publishers.

_____. 1975. Budgeting: A comparative theory of budgetary processes. Boston: Little, Brown.

Winters, Jeffrey A. 1996. *Power in Motion.* Ithaca: Cornell University Press.

Wittkopf, E. 1990. *Faces of Internationalism: Public Opinion and American Foreign Policy.* Durham, N.C.: Duke University Press.

NOTES

1. Neo-realists devote more attention to the internal effects of domestic politics in the making of foreign policy choices and therefore examine more closely how state policy is formed (cf. Rose, 1998).
2. A number of technical issues affect this prediction. It does not generally hold for competition by more than two parties or in multidimensional issue spaces, and it may be upset if citizens with extreme opinions abstain from voting due to "alienation" from centrist parties.
3. Russett and Oneal, 2001, 274; Peterson, 1995, 10–11; also cf. Russett, 1996, 100. The democratic peace has been attributed not only to the impact of political representation but also to liberal norms that promote non-violent resolution of conflict, international law and shared membership in intergovernmental organizations, and economic interdependence that puts a premium on stable, ongoing commercial relations (Doyle, 1983; Russett and Oneal, 2001; Owen, 1994; Elman, 1997).
4. Gallup conducted the surveys in 1978, 1982, 1986, 1990, 1994, and 1998; Harris conducted them in 1974, and Harris Interactive did so in 2002.
5. Of less interest to the present analysis, the surveys of foreign policy leaders also included respondents from the media, religious leaders, special interest groups relevant to foreign policy, and (in 1974) leaders of minority groups. Moreover, as we discuss below, we created one category of "experts" by combining the distinct groups of "educators" (i.e. faculty who teach in the area of foreign affairs and presidents and chancellors of major universities), "special foreign policy organizations" (i.e. think tanks), and "private foreign policy groups" (i.e. presidents from major foreign policy organizations). In addition to analyzing the impact of this aggregated measure of "experts," we also investigated the separate impact of each of these distinct groups.
6. Senators and Representatives, for example, were chosen (at least through 1990) from the membership of committees and subcommittees related to foreign policy. Administration officials came from the Department of State and from internationally-oriented units of the Commerce, Treasury, Agriculture, and other departments, though rarely from the Department of Defense or the National Security Council. Business respondents were sampled mainly from corporate vice presidents for international affairs, and labor respondents from high level union officials oriented toward foreign

affairs. Experts, as we later analyze them, include "educators" (academics specializing in foreign policy or international relations, as well as some high-level college administrators) and leaders or members of private foreign policy associations and think tanks.

7. The average number interviewed each year was about 76 for government officials, 58 for business, 28 for labor, and 79 for experts, which combines educators with individuals from think tanks. Although the categories of respondents are generally quite stable, the 1974 survey combined officials from the House, Senate, and Administration together, and did not survey think tank members. For the surveys from 1978 to 2002, the average number of government officials from the separate government institutions was the following: 19 from the Senate, 36 from the House, and 23 from the administration.

8. In 2002, 2,862 respondents were interviewed by telephone and 400 were interviewed in person, which made it possible to ensure comparability with the previous in-person surveys. We use the combined telephone and in-person data set. The interviews with the public and leaders were typically conducted in the fall but in 2002 were carried out in June.

9. Holsti and Rosenau (1984) reports an outstanding study of a wide range of U.S. decision makers and foreign policy leaders, including high military officers (unfortunately excluded from the Chicago Council surveys).

10. Even if the correspondence between actual foreign policy and decision makers' expressed preferences is likely to be imperfect, ascertaining the determinants of policy makers' preferences is still of considerable interest so long as those preferences have any substantial impact at all upon policy.

    Another possible concern in using these survey data is that some elite respondents undoubtedly delegated answering the CCFR questionnaires to staff members. We believe that subordinates' responses are generally likely to reflect the views of the superiors who hire, promote, and supervise them.

11. All items were dichotomized, using a quasi-random dichotomizing scheme that alternated the polarity of the responses we tabulated—i.e., whether we tabulated the percentage in "favor," the percentage "oppose[d]," or one of those percentages in some combination with neutral responses. The percentage of relevant respondents making that response or combination of responses was then recorded as the value of the dependent variable on that issue for that given year.

    This randomizing scheme means that the polarity or direction of preferences on different issues does not have a common intuitive meaning. It is not always the case, for example, that higher percentages signal more "liberal" or more "internationalist" responses. But the randomization was necessary in order to ensure substantial variance and to avoid certain statistical biases in the analyses.

12. The precise relationship between (for example) the percentage of respondents favoring an "increase" in foreign aid, and the amount of aid increase favored by the average respondent, is likely to be complex and related to aspects of survey responses and underlying preferences about which we have little information. But our general point is that the percentage of policy makers "favoring" alternative X is likely to track the *amount* of X favored by the average respondent, which is more directly applicable to actual policy and of more central interest.

13. We necessarily deal only with questions asked of both elites and the general public. The public was asked a number of additional questions. We excluded non-policy survey items (that is, questions not related to preferences about future government action), such as those concerning past performance, or U.S. "vital interests," or "feeling thermometer" ratings of American and world leaders.

14. The unstandardized coefficient for the public was −.005, not significant at even the $p<.10$ level.

15. For instance, the Model 1 cross-sectional analysis produced coefficient for educators that was (implausibly) negative: −.22; the coefficient for the media was (also implausibly) a positive .63, higher than that for any other group. Models 2 and 3 produced substantially negative coefficients for educators (−.18) and special interest groups (−.22).

16. The preferences of "special interest groups" (for which we could find no definition in the survey documentation) had a non-significant coefficient of .02 in the cross-sectional analysis of the garbage can model.

17. In most years the coefficient for the public was close to zero, but in 1986 (with particularly few cases) it was an implausibly *negative* −.42. Coefficients for business hovered around .50. Those for labor and experts fluctuated around their combined-years values with no apparent pattern.
18. Given the surprisingly strong findings for labor's influence in Table 5.1 and the possibility that including public opinion may have underestimated its effect, we conducted our 3 regression models for equations that focused on labor, business, and experts as independent variables. The results parallel our earlier findings.
19. Reciprocal effects of government officials upon public opinion, for example, would bias our cross-sectional estimates of the public's influence on officials *upward* rather than downward.
20. We consider the assumption of one-way causation from business and labor to experts to be fairly plausible, because the deeply rooted economic interests of business and labor are likely to make them resistant to others' influence on their foreign policy preferences. Still, groups and individuals may provide financial support for experts in order to get serious advice (i.e. not only to persuade other audiences)—and may therefore sometimes be influenced by them to some degree. To the extent that this occurs, our estimates of effects upon experts will be biased upward.
21. A similar regression of experts' preferences on those of the public as well as business and labor yielded quite similar coefficients for business and labor, but a rather substantial *negative* coefficient (b=−.25) for the public. This casts considerable doubt on the proposition that public preferences positively influence experts' (or that experts' preferences positively affect the publics'). But multicollineary problems preclude taking either the negative sign or the magnitude of the coefficient very seriously.
22. The inclusion of a lagged dependent variable (Model 2) produced estimates of a substantial total business impact upon policy makers of .56: the indirect impact through experts is .115 (.24 × .48) and the direct impact of business upon policy makers is .44 (Table 5.2).
23. In the analysis with a lagged dependent variable (Model 2), labor has a slightly smaller total impact of .22: .06 indirect effect through experts (.24 [Table 5.1] × .27 [Table 5.2]), combined with a direct effect of .16.

༄

Political Conflict and Foreign Policy in the United States: A Geographical Interpretation

Peter Trubowitz

INTRODUCTION

During the quarter-century that followed World War II, American leaders were able to mobilize broad domestic support for their foreign policies. While the conventional wisdom that 'politics stopped at the water's edge' was at best a half-truth, the fact remains that political

Peter Trubowitz, "Political Conflict and Foreign Policy in the United States: A Geographical Interpretation," *Political Geography*, 12, 2 (March 1993): 121–135. Copyright © 1993, with permission from Elsevier.

leaders enjoyed considerable latitude in the making of foreign policy. No one would characterize more recent American foreign policy-making in these terms. From the early 1970s onward, America's leaders experienced great difficulty in articulating a vision of the national interest that inspired broad support in Congress and the polity at large. The foreign policy consensus gave way to bitter and politically divisive conflicts over America's role in the world. Debates took on strongly emotional and symbolic overtones. The Cold War ended, but deep divisions over the ends and means of foreign policy persist. At a time when America's leaders need to make wise choices about the future, doubts remain about their ability to resolve the conflicts that have produced political gridlock and paralysis.

Practitioners, commentators and scholars recognize that American leaders no longer enjoy the freedom or autonomy in managing the nation's foreign policy that they once did. Disagreements arise when it comes to explaining this change. Some analysts locate the source of the problem in the electoral arena, and attribute the change to partisan politics and divided party government (McCormick and Wittkopf, 1990; Winik, 1991). Other observers stress the impact that the dispersion of power in Congress in the 1970s has had on the foreign policy-making process (Destler, 1981; Huntington, 1988; Warburg, 1989). They argue that the breakdown of the seniority system, the proliferation of subcommittees, and the expansion in staff and research resources has made it easier for individual members to pursue their own paths on foreign-policy matters and more difficult for the White House to control Congress. Still others emphasize divisions in élite and mass opinion (Holsti and Rosenau, 1984; Schneider, 1992). Such fragmentation, they contend, makes it harder for national leaders to mobilize consent and act strategically in the international arena.

This paper offers an alternative argument about why consensus-building in the area of foreign policy became more difficult. It is argued that since the early 1970s, conflict over foreign policy has been part-and-parcel of a larger, regionally based struggle for national wealth and power. For over two decades, the fight over America's overseas ambitions and objectives has split the nation along regional lines, pitting the Northeast against the South. Support for the expansive and expensive foreign policy agenda that crystallized after World War II has remained strongest in the South where state and local economies benefit disproportionately from policies that require large federal defense outlays. In the Northeast, where the domestic costs of an expansionist foreign policy now outweigh the benefits, politicians have favored a more restrained and cost-conscious approach to foreign policy. The seemingly intractable divisions over foreign policy are the result of this competition between two regionally-based coalitions which have distinct—and often conflicting—interests.

This argument has two implications for understanding contemporary debates over American foreign policy. The first is that place matters. Sectionalism remains a fundamental feature of American politics, and the politics of foreign policy is no exception. Like other periods in American history when ideological conflicts over foreign policy were shaped by deeper conflicts of interests, today's conflicts between 'liberals' and 'conservatives' over the purposes of American power are fueled by conflicting sectional political imperatives. The second implication follows from this: there is no single national interest. Analysts who assume that America has a unique and discernible national interest, and that this interest should or can determine its relations with other nations, are unable to explain the persistent failure to achieve domestic consensus on international objectives. A regional framework which focuses on the struggle among domestic coalitions for control over the foreign policy agenda reveals how politically-contingent competing definitions of 'the' national interest actually are.

This argument is developed through an analysis of the patterns of regional conflict in the House of Representatives. Using Congress as a proxy for the national polity, the patterns of political alignment over foreign policy are reconstructed from 'key' legislative roll-call votes. The primary empirical task is to demonstrate that the conflicts over foreign policy that first arose in the late 1960s and early 1970s—when the Cold War consensus collapsed—are grounded in a regionally-based struggle that has split the nation's oldest and newest industrial regions into opposing camps. A full explanation of this pattern of regional alignment lies beyond the scope of this paper. For present purposes, a large literature on America's changing geography is drawn on to interpret and explain the pattern of regional competition over foreign policy that is revealed by the data analysis. The conclusion comprises a discussion of the broader implications of the analysis for American foreign policy in the post-Cold War era.

REGIONAL INTERESTS AND FOREIGN POLICY

The geographical diversity of the national economy and the spatially decentralized nature of political representation have made regionalism a distinctive and enduring feature of American political life. Geographical disparities in sectoral concentration, technological advancement and international competitiveness mean that the costs and benefits of public policies are often distributed unequally across the nation. The extreme localism of political representation in the US ensures that these regional differences find political expression at the national level. At the national level, the dispersal of decision-making power and competition between the national parties for regional electoral advantage magnifies the role of regional interests, economic needs and political imperatives in shaping the national agenda. Institutional decentralization provides various channels for elected officials to levy claims on the federal government's resources, initiate or obstruct policy change, and build policy coalitions with political élites from other parts of the country through logrolling, vote-trading, ideological appeals and the like. Regional political competition is the result. This is well understood by political geographers who study the regional bases of political conflict over domestic policy matters.

Regionalism also emerges as a consistent dimension of political competition over foreign policy. Often depicted as contests between competing visions of America's role in the world, conflicts over foreign policy are also conflicts of interest. They have a geographical dimension. To a large extent, this reflects the regionally uneven nature of American involvement in the world economy. During the 1890s, for example, the great debate between the 'imperialists' and the 'continentalists' over overseas expansion pitted the industrial and commercial Northeast against the agrarian South (Hays, 1957; Bensel, 1984; Baack and Ray, 1988). The West played a decisive swing role in the conflict. The Northeast favored a neomercantile strategy combining maritime power, territorial expansion and the bargaining tariff to penetrate and 'capture' underdeveloped markets in Latin America and Asia. The South, in many respects still a colonial appendage of the North, supported a less expansive, *laissez-faire* approach to commercial expansion. Southern interests stressed the advantages of free trade with industrialized nations in Europe and did not require overseas holdings or a large military establishment to achieve its commercial objectives.

A quarter of a century later, conflicting regional imperatives once again shaped debates over foreign policy. At issue this time were the causes of the Great Depression and how America should respond to it. The key question was whether America should assume an active role in promoting global economic recovery and preventing the emergence of closed spheres of influence in Europe and Asia. Politicians who came from parts of the country that had the most to gain from an open, interdependent world economy—the Northeast and South—generally favored policies designed to promote commercial liberalization, global monetary co-operation and collective security (Grassmuck, 1951; Schatz, 1972; Cole, 1983; Frieden, 1988). These 'internationalists' waged a fierce battle against their 'nationalist' rivals from the West. The nationalists, who represented areas of the country that were less competitive in the world economy, called for renewed trade protection and opposed attempts to stabilize global commercial and monetary relations, arguing that such policies granted the White House too much authority in the area of foreign policy and threatened republican ideals at home.

In each of these periods, politicians from different parts of the country sought to equate regional interests with the national interest. Foreign policy issues were debated in terms of their immediate impact on regional prosperity and their longer-range consequences for the social and political arrangements which sustained regional economies. The choices politicians made over foreign policy reflected the fact that decisions over the nation's strategic objectives, market orientation and military posture were not geographically neutral. There were regional winners and regional losers. In each period, politicians who championed a 'strong state' were those best-placed to exercise influence over and benefit from the centralization of power and authority that would accompany an active foreign policy. Competing foreign policy agendas were grounded in interests, and the institutional conflicts that arose between the executive and legislative branches reflected patterns of competition that were grounded in these broader societal conflicts.

Explaining deep and persistent conflict over US foreign policy requires some mapping of the nation's economic geography. Functional position alone, however, is too blunt an instrument to explain fully how regional competition over foreign policy is played out in the national political arena. Party politics also plays a role. American party leaders have a long if inglorious record of playing politics with the national interest (Varg, 1963; Terrill, 1973; Divine, 1974; Nincic, 1992). Within the structures of a two-party system, they have often used foreign policies to mobilize electoral support and marginalize political opponents. During the 1890s, Republican leaders used the lure of new markets in Latin America and Asia to attract agrarian interests in the West to their cause and thus to consolidate Republican hegemony at the national level. In the 1930s, the Democrats used tariff reform to exploit regional tensions within the Republican party and broaden the regional base of the New Deal coalition. These cases underscore the fact that regional foreign policy coalitions are forged in the electoral arena. This means that alternative visions of the national interest are shaped by partisan struggles for political advantage.

SPATIAL ANALYSIS OF HOUSE VOTING

The kind of sectional strife that structured the foreign policy debates of the 1890s and 1930s has not disappeared with time. This paper claims that today's foreign policy conflicts are also structured along regional lines. This proposition is tested by examining how members of the House of Representatives vote on key foreign policy issues from the Nixon through Reagan years. The analysis is based on roll-call votes defined as 'key' votes by groups that monitor political activity in the Congress. These groups are: Americans for Democratic Action, Americans for Constitutional Action, and *Congressional Quarterly*.[1] Each group publishes an annual list of votes on important national issues, foreign as well as domestic. These votes constitute a test of members' policy preferences and their positions on issues whose political significance is unlikely to be lost on elected officials. The data set includes all of the major foreign policy initiatives undertaken by a President that required approval by the House, and votes on all major foreign policy issues that reached the House floor. All of the votes included in the analysis were weighted equally.

The data set was broken down and organized by presidency.[2] For each of the presidencies from Nixon through Reagan, voting similarity or agreement scores were calculated for all pairs of state delegations using a modified version of the pairwise agreement index where state delegations (not individual members) are the unit of analysis.[3] Each state delegation's position on a vote was based on the majority position in the delegation voting yea or nay.[4] The voting index measures the percentage of agreement between state delegations on all of the key foreign policy votes during a presidency. The score is 100 when there is perfect agreement between the majority position of two state delegations; it is 0 if there is perfect disagreement. The number of key votes used to compute the agreement index between delegations varied across presidencies. In part, this reflects differences in the numbers of years Presidents were in office. It also reflects variations in the number of votes selected annually by the various organizations.

Multi-dimensional scaling (MDS) was used to capture the political geography of voting over foreign policy. The basic goal of MDS is to describe the empirical relationships between some set of objects in a space of fixed dimensionality. Others have used this technique to recover patterns in congressional voting (MacRae, 1970; Hoadley, 1980; Easterling, 1987). Here, the simplest, non metric version is used to provide a spatial display of the voting alignments among congressional or state delegations over foreign policy at different points in time. The states (i.e. state delegations) are represented as points in the space, and distance is an analog for similarity (or dissimilarity). The goal is to find the configuration of interpoint distances between state delegations that corresponds as closely as possible to the similarities among the voting behavior of these delegations. Those state delegations which agree most often in voting are closest to each other in the resulting configuration of points. Those which disagree most are farthest apart in the space.

The most important and difficult stage in MDS analysis involves interpretation. First, the quality of a solution, or the fit between the data and the spatial configuration, must be determined. In the program used here, ALSCAL, the quality of a solution is defined by RSQ. Second, the appropriate dimensionality must be determined with respect to RSQ. In principle, a solution can be derived in any number of dimensions, and RSQ will always be higher when a higher dimensionality is allowed. Since MDS works in a space of fixed dimensionality, it is necessary to determine the most appropriate dimensionality, recognizing that there is a trade-off between the quality of fit (high RSQ) and parsimony (a small number of dimensions). Finally, the interpretation involves searching for meaningful patterns, usually defined as clusters or dimensions. While dimensional structure is often emphasized by analysts, it is equally valid to focus on clusters and search for areas or neighborhoods of the space that have meaning associated with other shared characteristics.[5] This is the approach adopted here.

MDS Results

The results of the scaling analysis are summarized in Table 5.4. Configurations were generated in one, two and three dimensions using ALSCAL. The two-dimensional configuration was selected as the best representation of voting patterns in each of the four presidencies.

On average, the two-dimensional solutions account for 94.6 percent of the variance. A third dimension improves the fit by only 1.9 percent on average. (ALSCAL also generates a 'badness of fit' function, known as STRESS, which is also presented in Table 5.4.) The configurations are presented in Figures 15.2–15.5. The vertical and horizontal axes are not labelled and should not be interpreted in terms of two linear, orthogonal dimensions. The configurations

Table 5.4 SUMMARY OF MULTI-DIMENSIONAL SCALING SOLUTIONS

Presidency	RSQ dimensions			STRESS dimensions		
	1	2	3	1	2	3
Nixon	0.843	0.928	0.957	0.233	0.130	0.090
Ford	0.944	0.966	0.979	0.142	0.094	0.067
Carter	0.854	0.924	0.948	0.221	0.133	0.099
Reagan	0.929	0.966	0.974	0.156	0.097	0.077

Source: Derived from recorded roll-call votes in US Congress.

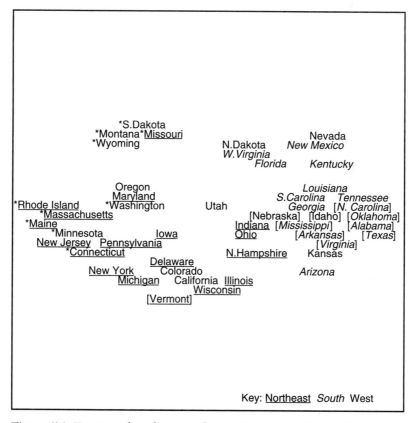

Figure 5.2 Foreign policy alignment during Nixon years. *Source:* derived from multi-dimensional scaling of key roll-call votes in US Congress.

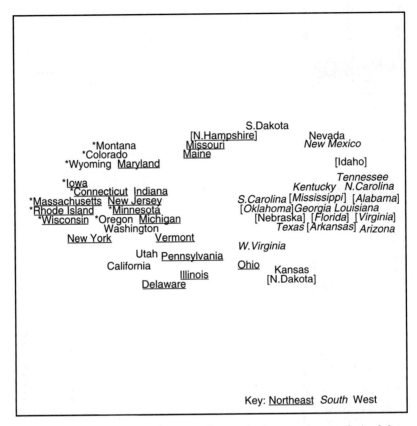

Figure 5.3 Foreign policy alignment during Ford years. *Source:* derived from
multi-dimensional scaling of key roll-call votes in US Congress.

should be interpreted as clusterings of states in a two-dimensional space. A closely grouped
cluster of states indicates a cohesive voting bloc. States from the Northeast are underlined.
Those from the South are in italics. States from the West are in regular typeface. See the
Appendix for a listing of the states in each section.

A visual examination of the MDS configurations reveals that the voting alignment is
regional in nature. In each of the spatial maps, the pattern of alignment is defined by discrete
clusters or blocs of states. While the cohesion of these voting blocks varies over time, it is
apparent that a large proportion of the states consistently cluster on opposite sides of the
configurations. During each of the four administrations, the pattern of alignment breaks down
along north–south lines and falls along lines others have defined as rustbelt–sunbelt,
snowbelt–sunbelt, or core–periphery (Phillips, 1969; Sale, 1975; Weinstein and Firestine,
1978; Bensel, 1984). States from the Northeast tend to cluster together on the left side of the
voting spaces. Most of those from the South coalesce on the right side of the configurations.
By contrast, the pattern of voting among states from the West is much more mixed. Some
states—like California, Oregon and Washington—cluster with those from the Northeast.
Others—like Idaho, Kansas and Nebraska—generally align with states from the South. The
analysis indicates that there is little consensus over foreign policy.

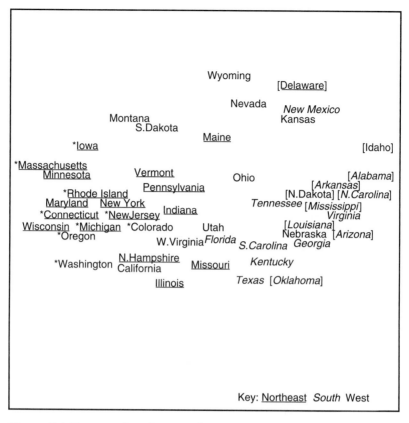

Figure 5.4 Foreign policy alignment during Carter years. *Source:* derived from multi-dimensional scaling of key roll-call votes in US Congress.

Since the Nixon years, the foreign policy agenda in Congress has been dominated by national security issues. While foreign economic policy issues became increasingly important during the Reagan years, the vast majority of the votes in the 1970s and 1980s concerned issues such as defense spending, arms control, war powers, covert operations, military aid, arms sales and overseas alliances. The common and divisive theme that linked these issues was the rising domestic opportunity cost of the *Pax Americana* built after World War II. Critics challenged the *status quo* on two fronts. First, they argued that the ends of American foreign policy outstripped the country's means. Collective energies and resources were being spent unwisely on an expansionist and sometimes misguided foreign policy at the expense of urgent domestic needs and problems. Second, they argued that the method used by national leaders to promote American power overseas threatened republican ideals at home by concentrating political power in the White House.

A number of methods may be used to determine how place-specific these political sentiments are. For present purposes, an index measuring state support for 'strategic retrenchment' was constructed using the votes described above. A vote *against* any of the following was considered a vote in favor of strategic retrenchment: defense spending, foreign aid, arms sales, military bases, overseas alliances, military intervention, international institutions

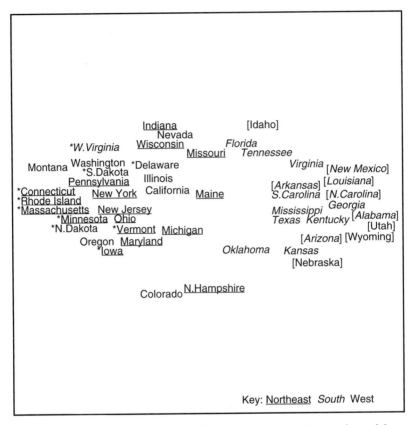

Figure 5.5 Foreign policy alignment during Reagan years. *Source:* derived from multi-dimensional scaling of key roll-call votes in US Congress.

and presidential prerogative in the making of foreign policy. Votes for arms control were treated as a vote in favor of a policy of strategic retrenchment. The position of each member of Congress on these votes was identified. A mean support score for a strategy of retrenchment was calculated by averaging across the votes during each of the four administrations. A state mean was then formed by averaging the scores for all members of a congressional delegation.

In each of the figures, the 10 state delegations that scored highest on the index are marked with an asterisk. The 10 congressional delegations that scored lowest on the index are in brackets. Support for a policy of strategic retrenchment is clearly strongest among states that cluster on the left side of the voting space. Since the early 1970s, this coalition has lobbied for cuts in the defense budget, reductions in America's military presence overseas, and limits on presidential prerogative in the making of foreign policy (e.g. war powers, covert operations, executive agreements). Many of these states are located in the Northeast. A few are from the West. By contrast, states that cluster on the right side of the voting spaces have favored a more expansive and expensive conception of the nation's strategic interests, one that has placed a premium on military power. Most of those states that have strongly opposed efforts to scale-back America's role in world affairs are from the South.

THE RUSTBELT VERSUS THE SUNBELT

Why did the foreign policy debates of the 1970s and 1980s divide the nation along regional lines? Why did the pattern of regional cleavage that arose in the 1970s persist into the 1980s? This section provides an interpretation that locates the source of this conflict in America's changing geography. Drawing on the work of political and economic geographers, it is argued that the conflicts over foreign policy cannot be viewed in isolation from regionally-based struggles over domestic policy. The declining economic fortunes of the Northeast led politicians from this region to seek ways of reducing the costs of the nation's foreign policies in order to devote greater resources to domestic problems and needs. These efforts to redefine the nation's political priorities intensified existing tensions between the Northeast and South over domestic policy and provided fertile ground for political leaders who sought to exploit this regional cleavage for electoral gain. The failure of American leaders to forge a broad and stable foreign policy consensus is one consequence.

It has been apparent for some time that the national political economy is undergoing a process of regional restructuring. Older centers of industrial production in the Northeast have been losing much of their economic base to other parts of the country (Agnew, 1987; Markusen, 1987). The migration of industries, jobs and people from the manufacturing belt to the sunbelt since the 1960s is one indication of this shift in economic activity. While many states located in the industrial core experienced sluggish growth rates and economic stagnation, many in the South and West became more prosperous and diversified (Rostow, 1977; Norton and Rees, 1979). The process of regional restructuring is reflected in the political arena. Shifts in regional populations have led to shifts in political power at the national level as the Northeast has lost congressional seats to the South and West through reapportionment (Stanley and Niemi, 1990). At the same time, the growing strength of the South and West in the electoral college has made these regions decisive battle grounds in national electoral campaigns.

Analysts identify a number of factors that have contributed to this process. The relative decline of the manufacturing belt has been linked to reductions in transport costs, the diffusion of large-scale, high-technology production, and regional disparities in labor costs, energy prices and local tax rates (Weinstein and Firestine, 1978; Rees, 1983). No less important are the uneven consequences of the erosion of American commercial power in the international economy (Glickman and Glasmeier, 1989; Markusen and Carlson, 1989). Since the 1960s, the manufacturing belt has suffered disproportionately from the migration of American firms overseas and the rise of Western Europe and Japan as industrial competitors. Spatial disparities in federal spending and federal tax policies have also played a role in accelerating, if not encouraging, regional restructuring (Advisory Commission on Intergovernmental Relations, 1980). Federal expenditures and tax policies are often cited as forces that have spurred the growth of sunbelt states while exacerbating economic difficulties in the manufacturing belt.

The erosion of the manufacturing belt's position in both the national economy and the world economy contributed decisively to the emergence of a new and intense debate over the nation's priorities. At the center of this debate lie questions of regional equity or fairness, and specifically, the issue of purported transfers of economic wealth and power from the manufacturing belt to the sunbelt (Dilger, 1982; Bensel, 1984; Markusen, 1987).[6] In the domestic arena, the re-emergence of sectional strife has colored a broad range of issues. In most accounts, the 1960s mark the beginning of this process, when regional divisions found expression in debates over civil rights, entitlement programs and unionization. By the 1970s, the scope of these debates expanded and gained notoriety as politicians from these regions locked horns over rising energy costs, capital flight to the sunbelt, and regional bias in federal tax and spending policies. The pattern of conflict between the manufacturing belt and the sunbelt continued through the 1980s, finding expression in a wide variety of issues ranging from 'deregulation' to 'industrial policy' to the 'Reagan deficit'.

The struggle between the manufacturing belt and the sunbelt was not limited to domestic policy matters. The widespread belief in the Northeast that federal spending and tax policies favored the South and West made the military budget an attractive target for criticism in the 1970s (Bensel, 1984; Malecki and Stark, 1988). In an era when much of the Northeast was experiencing hard economic times, elected officials and interest groups found it politically advantageous to emphasize the domestic opportunity costs of military intervention, military spending and military aid to the Third World (McCormick, 1989). Such concerns figured prominently in the debates over the Vietnam War. In the 1980s, this 'guns versus butter' controversy grew even sharper in response to the Reagan military build-up (Trubowitz and Roberts, 1992; Wirls, 1992). Many of those who opposed the military build-up believed that it disproportionately benefited the South and West. What some viewed as an unintended consequence of the administration's efforts to make America's military presence overseas more visible, others saw as an industrial policy veiled in the garb of national security.

Similar tensions surfaced in the area of foreign economic policy. The growing vulnerability of many of America's key industrial sectors to global competition in the 1970s led to growing disenchantment with free-trade policies in the Northeast. Free trade has proven to be a more attractive economic strategy in the South and West (Sanders, 1986; Wade and Gates, 1990). Conflicting regional interests also appear to have shaped political attitudes toward overseas investment. The rapid expansion of American firms overseas in the 1960s and 1970s penalized areas in the manufacturing belt where a disproportionate share of the nation's unionized work force resided (Gilpin, 1975; Bluestone and Harrison 1982). As early as 1970, labor unions like the AFL–CIO and the UAW began sending out distress signals, pointing to the consequences of 'capital flight' for the nation's traditional manufacturing sectors. In an effort to protect jobs, labor pursued a dual strategy: lobbying for common wage standards at home and tighter controls on the outflow of capital abroad. This strategy has struck a far more responsive chord in the Northeast than it has in the South.

The decline of America's industrial core does not fully explain these conflicts over foreign policy. Sectionally-based conflicts over foreign policy have also been fueled by partisan competition. In the 1970s, as northern Democrats gained greater control over the party's national agenda, party leaders pressed for cuts in the military budget, a larger role for Congress in foreign policy-making, and reductions in the size of US forces overseas. These efforts helped the Democratic party expand its political base in the Northeast. At the same time, however, they exacerbated tensions between the northern and southern wings of the party that had arisen over issues such as civil rights, social welfare and the Vietnam War (Sundquist, 1983; Bensel, 1984; Gillon, 1987; Black and Black, 1987). The emergence of this fault line in the Democratic party became increasingly difficult to paper over as a growing number of political organizations, like the Americans for Democratic Action and the Northeast–Midwest Institute, began to mobilize political and economic interests in the manufacturing belt to redress perceived regional inequities in federal spending, labor costs and energy prices.

This regional schism within the Democratic party provided new political opportunities for a Republican party that was also undergoing change. Over the course of the 1970s, the center of political gravity in the Republican party moved from East to West. The rise of the 'Reagan

Right' in the late 1970s and early 1980s marked the culmination of a process that began in the 1960s with the divisive nomination of Goldwater for President. This process gradually eroded the power of the 'eastern' wing of the Republican party (Reinhard, 1983; Rae, 1989; Himmelstein, 1990). Touting the virtues of *'laissez-faire'*, 'law and order', and a 'strong national defense', the Republican party began to penetrate the once-solid Democratic South. This tactical shift is evident in the so-called southern strategy embraced by every Republican candidate for the White House since Nixon. Like Republicans in the 1890s who used the issue of tariff reform to divide the South and West, Republican party leaders in the current era have used defense policy to exploit regional tensions between the Northeast and South.

CONCLUSION

Since the early 1970s, the conflicts between the manufacturing belt and the sunbelt over national priorities have made it extremely difficult for national leaders to mobilize broad national support for their foreign policies. Like other eras in American history marked by protracted domestic struggles over 'the national interest', issues of foreign policy have been defined and debated in terms of their impact on regional growth, stability and power. This fundamental fact is obscured by accounts which identify ideological or institutional cleavages at the national level as the source of domestic political competition and conflict over the foreign policy agenda. What recedes from view are the regional political imperatives that structure the possibilities for building the clearly dominant and stable coalitions that give political leaders wide latitude in conducting foreign policy. The sectional cleavages of the 1970s and 1980s did not afford national leaders this possibility.

The present study suggests that sectionalism remains a persistent force in American political life, and in the foreign policy arena in particular. Contrary to what is now conventional wisdom among foreign policy analysts, sectionalism is not a relic of the past. The findings also speak to debates among political geographers. Some analysts now argue that the political salience of large macro-level cleavages—North versus South, core versus periphery—is fading (Garreau, 1981; Agnew, 1988; Martis, 1988). This study, however, follows the work of others (Bensel, 1984; Archer, 1988; Earle, 1992) in underscoring the enduring significance of macro-level or sectional cleavages in explaining political behavior (e.g. national elections, congressional voting, social movements) in the American context. Sectionalism may not be as salient a political force today as it was a century ago, but it continues to exert a powerful influence on how politicians interpret and respond to changes in America's position in the world.

This means that sectionalism will shape the politics of American foreign policy in the post-Cold War era. Such forces are already at play in the current debate over the 'peace dividend'. Like the debate over the Reagan military build-up in the 1980s, the debate over the 'military build-down' in the 1990s is breaking down along familiar regional lines. At issue is not just how much to cut the Pentagon's budget but perhaps more importantly, how the savings should be spent (Trubowitz, 1992). The stakes are high. The choices politicians face raise fundamental questions about the distribution of national resources, the locus of political power at the federal level and, last but not least, who will benefit and who will not. At a time when there is little consensus over how to revitalize the American economy, and where foreign policy issues are increasingly entering the political arena as economic issues, domestic political competition over foreign policy is likely to intensify. If the recent past is any guide to the future, debates over foreign policy will continue to be shaped by conflicting sectional interests.

ACKNOWLEDGMENTS

I wish to thank Catherine Boone, John O'Loughlin and anonymous reviewers of *Political Geography* for their comments and suggestions. Erik Devereux provided valuable assistance in the data collection and data analysis. The study was supported by a research fellowship from the Center for International Studies at Princeton University. The roll-call data were provided by the Inter-University Consortium for Political and Social Research. An earlier version of this paper was presented at Princeton's Center for International Studies.

NOTES

1. The author was unable to obtain key votes for the 99th Congress (1985–86) from the Americans for Constitutional Action. For this Congress, the list of votes from *Congressional Quarterly* and the Americans for Democratic Action was supplemented by those used by the *National Journal* in rating legislators.
2. The following time-frames were used to classify the votes by presidency: Nixon (1969–74); Ford (1975–76); Carter (1977–80); Reagan (1981–86). The voting records for the House during the 100th Congress (1987–88) were not available in time for this study.
3. The historical scope of the analysis makes it necessary to use a unit of analysis that is stable over time. States are a logical choice for such purposes. The boundaries of legislative districts change; state boundaries do not. Alaska and Hawaii were not included in the data analysis.
4. Following convention, paired votes and announced positions were treated as formal votes.
5. For a good discussion of this issue see Kruskal and Wish (1978).
6. This controversy gained notoriety in the mid–1970s with the publication of articles in the *New York Times*, *Business Week* and the *National Journal* on the regional flow of federal funds.

REFERENCES

Advisory Commission on Intergovernmental Relations (1980). *Regional Growth: Historic Perspective.* Washington, DC: ACIR.

Agnew, J. (1987). *The United States in the World-Economy: A Regional Geography.* Cambridge: Cambridge University Press.

Agnew, J. (1988). Beyond core and periphery: the myth of regional political-economic restructuring and sectionalism in contemporary American politics. *Political Geography Quarterly* 7, 127–139.

Archer, J. C. (1988). Macrogeographical versus microgeographical cleavages in American presidential elections: 1940–1984. *Political Geography Quarterly* 7, 111–125.

Baack, B. and Ray, E. (1988). Special interests and the nineteenth-century roots of the US military-industrial complex. *Research in Economic History* 11, 153–169.

Bensel, R. F. (1984). *Sectionalism and American Political Development: 1880–1980.* Madison, WI: University of Wisconsin Press.

Black, E. and Black, M. (1987). *Politics and Society in the South.* Cambridge, MA: Harvard University Press.

Bluestone, B. and Harrison, B. (1982). *The Deindustrialization of America: Plant Closings, Community Abandonment, and the Dismantling of Basic Industry.* New York: Basic Books.

Cole, W. S. (1983). *Roosevelt and the Isolationists: 1932–45.* Lincoln, NE: University of Nebraska Press.

Destler, I. M. (1981). Executive–congressional conflict in foreign policy. In *Congress Reconsidered*, 2nd edn. (L. C. Dodd and B. I. Oppenheimer eds.) pp. 342–363. Washington, DC: Congressional Quarterly Press.

Dilger, R. (1982). *The Sunbelt/Snowbelt Controversy: The War Over Federal Funds.* New York: New York University Press.

Divine, R. A. (1974). *Foreign Policy and US Presidential Elections, 1940–1948.* New York: New Viewpoints.

Earle, C. (1992). *Geographical Inquiry and American Historical Problems.* Stanford, CA: Stanford University Press.

Easterling, D. (1987). Political science: using the general Euclidean model to study ideological shifts in the US Senate. In *Multidimensional Scaling: History, Theory, and Applications* (F. Young and R. Hamer eds.) pp. 221–256. London: Lawrence Erlbaum Associates.

Frieden, J. (1988). Sectoral conflict and US foreign economic policy, 1914–1940. *International Organization* 42, 59–90.

Garreau, J. (1981). *The Nine Nations of North America.* Boston, MA: Houghton Mifflin.

Gillon, S. M. (1987). *Politics and Vision: The ADA and American Liberalism, 1947–1985.* Oxford: Oxford University Press.

Gilpin, R. (1975). *US Power and the Multinational Corporation: The Political Economy of Foreign Direct Investment.* New York: Basic Books.

Glickman, N. J. and Glasmeier, A. K. (1989). The international economy and the American South. In *Deindustrialization and Regional Economic Transformation: The Experience of the United States* (L. Rodwin and H. Sazanami eds.) pp. 60–80. Boston, MA: Unwin Hyman.

Grassmuck, G. L. (1951). *Sectional Biases in Congress on Foreign Policy.* Baltimore, MD: Johns Hopkins Press.

Hays, S. P. (1957). *The Response to Industrialism: 1885–1914.* Chicago, IL: University of Chicago Press.

Himmelstein, J. L. (1990). *To the Right: The Transformation of American Conservatism.* Berkeley, CA: University of California Press.

Hoadley, J. (1980). The emergence of political parties in Congress, 1789–1803. *American Political Science Review* 74, 757–779.

Holsti, O. R. and Rosenau, J. N. (1984). *American Leadership in World Affairs: Vietnam and the Breakdown of Consensus.* Boston, MA: Allen and Unwin.

Huntington, S. P. (1988). Foreign policy and the constitution. In *Crisis and Innovation: Constitutional Democracy in America* (F. Krinsky ed.) pp. 77–87. Oxford: Basil Blackwell.

Kruskal, J. B. and Wish, M. (1978). *Multidimensional Scaling.* Beverly Hills, CA: Sage Publications.

MacRae, D., Jr. (1970). *Issues and Parties in Legislative Voting.* New York: Harper and Row.

McCormick, J. M. and Wittkopf, E. R. (1990). Bipartisanship, partisanship, and ideology in congressional–executive foreign policy relations, 1947–1988. *Journal of Politics* 52, 1077–1100.

McCormick, T. J. (1989). *America's Half-Century: United States Foreign Policy in the Cold War.* Baltimore, MD: The Johns Hopkins University Press.

Malecki, E. J. and Stark, L. M. (1988). Regional and industrial variation in defence spending: some American evidence. In *Defence Expenditure and Regional Development* (M. J. Breheny ed.) pp. 67–101. London: Mansell Publishing Ltd.

Markusen, A. R. (1987). *Regions: The Economics and Politics of Territory.* Totowa, NJ: Rowman and Littlefield.

Markusen, A. R. and Carlson, V. (1989). Deindustrialization in the American Midwest: causes and responses. In *Deindustrialization and Regional Economic Transformation: The Experience of the United States* (L. Rodwin and H. Sazanami eds.) pp. 29–59. Boston, MA: Unwin Hyman.

Martis, K. C. (1988). Sectionalism and the United States Congress. *Political Geography Quarterly* 7, 99–109.

Nincic, M. (1992). Democracy and Foreign Policy: The Fallacy of Political Realism. New York: Columbia University Press.

Norton, R. D. and Rees, J. (1979). The product cycle and the spatial decentralization of American manufacturing. Regional Studies 13, 141–151.

Phillips, K. (1969). The Emerging Republican Majority. New York: Doubleday.

Rae, N. (1989). The Decline of Liberal Republicans from 1952 to the Present. Oxford: Oxford University Press.

Rees, J. (1983). Regional economic decentralization processes in the United States and their policy implications. In Contemporary Studies in Sociology, 2 (D. A. Hicks and N. Glickman eds.) pp. 241–278. Greenwich, CT: JAI Press.

Reinhard, D. W. (1983). The Republican Right Since 1945. Lexington, KY: The University Press of Kentucky.

Rostow, W. W. (1977). Regional change in the fifth Kondratieff upswing. In The Rise of the Sunbelt Cities (D. C. Perry and A. J. Watkins eds.) pp. 83–103. Beverly Hills, CA: Sage Publications.

Sale, K. (1975). Power Shift: The Rise of the Southern Rim and its Challenge to the Eastern Establishment. New York: Vintage Books.

Sanders, E. (1986). The regulatory surge of the 1970s in historical perspective. In Public Regulation: New Perspectives on Institutions and Policies (E. E. Bailey ed.) pp. 117–150. Cambridge; MA: The MIT Press.

Schatz, A. W. (1972). The reciprocal trade agreements program and the 'farm vote': 1934–1940. Agricultural History 46, 498–514.

Schneider, W. (1992). The old politics and the new world order. In Eagle in a New World: American Grand Strategy in the Post-Cold War Era (K. Oye, R. J. Lieber and D. Rothchild eds.) pp. 35–68. New York: HarperCollins.

Stanley, H. W. and Niemi, R. G. (1990). Vital Statistics on American Politics, 2nd edn. Washington, DC: Congressional Quarterly Press.

Sundquist, J. L. (1983). Dynamics of the Party System: Alignment and Realignment of Political Parties in the United States. Washington, DC: Brookings Institution.

Terrill, T. E. (1973). The Tariff, Politics, and American Foreign Policy: 1874–1901. Westport, CT: Greenwood Press.

Trubowitz, P. (1992). Déjà vu all over again: regional struggles over America's foreign policy agenda. Paper presented at the American Political Science Association, Chicago, Illinois.

Trubowitz, P. and Roberts, B. E.(1992). Regional interests and the Reagan military build-up. Regional Studies 26, 555–567.

Varg, P. A. (1963). Foreign Policies of the Founding Fathers. Lansing, MI: Michigan State University Press.

Wade, L. L. and Gates, J. B. (1990). A new tariff map of the United States (House of Representatives). Political Geography Quarterly 9, 284–304.

Warburg, G. F. (1989). Conflict and Consensus: The Struggle between Congress and the President over Foreign Policymaking. New York: Harper and Row.

Weinstein, B. L. and Firestine, R. E. (1978). Regional Growth and Decline in the United States. New York: Praeger.

Winik, J. (1991). The quest for bipartisanship: a new beginning for a new world order. The Washington Quarterly 14, 115–130.

Wirls, D. (1992). Build-up: The Politics of Defense in the Reagan Era. Ithaca, NY: Cornell University Press.

APPENDIX

Sectional division of states

NORTHEAST: Connecticut, Delaware, Illinois, Indiana, Iowa, Maine, Maryland, Massachusetts, Michigan, Minnesota, Missouri, New Hampshire, New Jersey, New York, Ohio, Pennsylvania, Rhode Island, Vermont, Wisconsin.

SOUTH: Alabama, Arizona, Arkansas, Florida, Georgia, Kentucky, Louisiana, Mississippi, New Mexico, North Carolina, Oklahoma, South Carolina, Tennessee, Texas, Virginia, West Virginia.

WEST: California, Colorado, Idaho, Kansas, Montana, Oregon, Nebraska, Nevada, North Dakota, South Dakota, Utah, Washington, Wyoming.

$\sim$

The Israel Lobby

John Mearsheimer and Stephen Walt

For the past several decades, and especially since the Six-Day War in 1967, the centrepiece of US Middle Eastern policy has been its relationship with Israel. The combination of unwavering support for Israel and the related effort to spread 'democracy' throughout the region has inflamed Arab and Islamic opinion and jeopardised not only US security but that of much of the rest of the world. This situation has no equal in American political history. Why has the US been willing to set aside its own security and that of many of its allies in order to advance the interests of another state? One might assume that the bond between the two countries was based on shared strategic interests or compelling moral imperatives, but neither explanation can account for the remarkable level of material and diplomatic support that the US provides.

Instead, the thrust of US policy in the region derives almost entirely from domestic politics, and especially the activities of the 'Israel Lobby'. Other special-interest groups have managed to skew foreign policy, but no lobby has managed to divert it as far from what the national interest would suggest, while simultaneously convincing Americans that US interests and those of the other country—in this case, Israel—are essentially identical.

Since the October War in 1973, Washington has provided Israel with a level of support dwarfing that given to any other state. It has been the largest annual recipient of direct economic and military assistance since 1976, and is the largest recipient in total since World War Two, to the tune of well over $140 billion (in 2004 dollars). Israel receives about $3 billion in direct assistance each year, roughly one-fifth of the foreign aid budget, and worth about $500 a year for every Israeli. This largesse is especially striking since Israel is now a wealthy industrial state with a per capita income roughly equal to that of South Korea or Spain.

John Mearsheimer and Stephen Walt, "The Israel Lobby," *London Review of Books*, March 23, 2006. Reprinted by permission.

Other recipients get their money in quarterly installments, but Israel receives its entire appropriation at the beginning of each fiscal year and can thus earn interest on it. Most recipients of aid given for military purposes are required to spend all of it in the U.S., but Israel is allowed to use roughly 25 percent of its allocation to subsidise its own defence industry. It is the only recipient that does not have to account for how the aid is spent, which makes it virtually impossible to prevent the money from being used for purposes the US opposes, such as building settlements on the West Bank. Moreover, the US has provided Israel with nearly $3 billion to develop weapons systems, and given it access to such top-drawer weaponry as Blackhawk helicopters and F-16 jets. Finally, the U.S. gives Israel access to intelligence it denies to its Nato allies and has turned a blind eye to Israel's acquisition of nuclear weapons.

Washington also provides Israel with consistent diplomatic support. Since 1982, the U.S. has vetoed 32 Security Council resolutions critical of Israel, more than the total number of vetoes cast by all the other Security Council members. It blocks the efforts of Arab states to put Israel's nuclear arsenal on the IAEA's agenda. The U.S. comes to the rescue in wartime and takes Israel's side when negotiating peace. The Nixon administration protected it from the threat of Soviet intervention and resupplied it during the October War. Washington was deeply involved in the negotiations that ended that war, as well as in the lengthy 'step-by-step' process that followed, just as it played a key role in the negotiations that preceded and followed the 1993 Oslo Accords. In each case there was occasional friction between US and Israeli officials, but the US consistently supported the Israeli position. One American participant at Camp David in 2000 later said: 'Far too often, we functioned…as Israel's lawyer.' Finally, the Bush administration's ambition to transform the Middle East is at least partly aimed at improving Israel's strategic situation.

This extraordinary generosity might be understandable if Israel were a vital strategic asset or if there were a compelling moral case for US backing. But neither explanation is convincing. One might argue that Israel was an asset during the Cold War. By serving as America's proxy after 1967, it helped contain Soviet expansion in the region and inflicted humiliating defeats on Soviet clients like Egypt and Syria. It occasionally helped protect other US allies (like King Hussein of Jordan) and its military prowess forced Moscow to spend more on backing its own client states. It also provided useful intelligence about Soviet capabilities.

Backing Israel was not cheap, however, and it complicated America's relations with the Arab world. For example, the decision to give $2.2 billion in emergency military aid during the October War triggered an Opec oil embargo that inflicted considerable damage on Western economies. For all that, Israel's armed forces were not in a position to protect US interests in the region. The US could not, for example, rely on Israel when the Iranian Revolution in 1979 raised concerns about the security of oil supplies, and had to create its own Rapid Deployment Force instead.

The first Gulf War revealed the extent to which Israel was becoming a strategic burden. The US could not use Israeli bases without rupturing the anti-Iraq coalition, and had to divert resources (e.g. Patriot missile batteries) to prevent Tel Aviv doing anything that might harm the alliance against Saddam Hussein. History repeated itself in 2003: although Israel was eager for the US to attack Iraq, Bush could not ask it to help without triggering Arab opposition. So Israel stayed on the sidelines once again.

Beginning in the 1990s, and even more after 9/11, US support has been justified by the claim that both states are threatened by terrorist groups originating in the Arab and Muslim world, and by 'rogue states' that back these groups and seek weapons of mass destruction.

This is taken to mean not only that Washington should give Israel a free hand in dealing with the Palestinians and not press it to make concessions until all Palestinian terrorists are imprisoned or dead, but that the US should go after countries like Iran and Syria. Israel is thus seen as a crucial ally in the war on terror, because its enemies are America's enemies. In fact, Israel is a liability in the war on terror and the broader effort to deal with rogue states.

'Terrorism' is not a single adversary, but a tactic employed by a wide array of political groups. The terrorist organisations that threaten Israel do not threaten the United States, except when it intervenes against them (as in Lebanon in 1982). Moreover, Palestinian terrorism is not random violence directed against Israel or 'the West'; it is largely a response to Israel's prolonged campaign to colonise the West Bank and Gaza Strip.

More important, saying that Israel and the US are united by a shared terrorist threat has the causal relationship backwards: the US has a terrorism problem in good part because it is so closely allied with Israel, not the other way around. Support for Israel is not the only source of anti-American terrorism, but it is an important one, and it makes winning the war on terror more difficult. There is no question that many al-Qaida leaders, including Osama bin Laden, are motivated by Israel's presence in Jerusalem and the plight of the Palestinians. Unconditional support for Israel makes it easier for extremists to rally popular support and to attract recruits.

As for so-called rogue states in the Middle East, they are not a dire threat to vital U.S. interests, except inasmuch as they are a threat to Israel. Even if these states acquire nuclear weapons—which is obviously undesirable—neither America nor Israel could be blackmailed, because the blackmailer could not carry out the threat without suffering overwhelming retaliation. The danger of a nuclear handover to terrorists is equally remote, because a rogue state could not be sure the transfer would go undetected or that it would not be blamed and punished afterwards. The relationship with Israel actually makes it harder for the US to deal with these states. Israel's nuclear arsenal is one reason some of its neighbours want nuclear weapons, and threatening them with regime change merely increases that desire.

A final reason to question Israel's strategic value is that it does not behave like a loyal ally. Israeli officials frequently ignore US requests and renege on promises (including pledges to stop building settlements and to refrain from 'targeted assassinations' of Palestinian leaders). Israel has provided sensitive military technology to potential rivals like China, in what the State Department inspector-general called 'a systematic and growing pattern of unauthorised transfers'. According to the General Accounting Office, Israel also 'conducts the most aggressive espionage operations against the US of any ally'. In addition to the case of Jonathan Pollard, who gave Israel large quantities of classified material in the early 1980s (which it reportedly passed on to the Soviet Union in return for more exit visas for Soviet Jews), a new controversy erupted in 2004 when it was revealed that a key Pentagon official called Larry Franklin had passed classified information to an Israeli diplomat. Israel is hardly the only country that spies on the U.S., but its willingness to spy on its principal patron casts further doubt on its strategic value.

Israel's strategic value isn't the only issue. Its backers also argue that it deserves unqualified support because it is weak and surrounded by enemies; it is a democracy; the Jewish people have suffered from past crimes and therefore deserve special treatment; and Israel's conduct has been morally superior to that of its adversaries. On close inspection, none of these arguments is persuasive. There is a strong moral case for supporting Israel's existence, but that is not in jeopardy. Viewed objectively, its past and present conduct offers no moral basis for privileging it over the Palestinians.

Israel is often portrayed as David confronted by Goliath, but the converse is closer to the truth. Contrary to popular belief, the Zionists had larger, better equipped and better led forces during the 1947–49 War of Independence, and the Israel Defence Forces won quick and easy victories against Egypt in 1956 and against Egypt, Jordan and Syria in 1967—all of this before large-scale U.S. aid began flowing. Today, Israel is the strongest military power in the Middle East. Its conventional forces are far superior to those of its neighbours and it is the only state in the region with nuclear weapons. Egypt and Jordan have signed peace treaties with it, and Saudi Arabia has offered to do so. Syria has lost its Soviet patron, Iraq has been devastated by three disastrous wars and Iran is hundreds of miles away. The Palestinians barely have an effective police force, let alone an army that could pose a threat to Israel. According to a 2005 assessment by Tel Aviv University's Jaffee Centre for Strategic Studies, 'the strategic balance decidedly favours Israel, which has continued to widen the qualitative gap between its own military capability and deterrence powers and those of its neighbours.' If backing the underdog were a compelling motive, the United States would be supporting Israel's opponents.

That Israel is a fellow democracy surrounded by hostile dictatorships cannot account for the current level of aid: there are many democracies around the world, but none receives the same lavish support. The U.S. has overthrown democratic governments in the past and supported dictators when this was thought to advance its interests—it has good relations with a number of dictatorships today.

Some aspects of Israeli democracy are at odds with core American values. Unlike the U.S., where people are supposed to enjoy equal rights irrespective of race, religion or ethnicity, Israel was explicitly founded as a Jewish state and citizenship is based on the principle of blood kinship. Given this, it is not surprising that its 1.3 million Arabs are treated as second-class citizens, or that a recent Israeli government commission found that Israel behaves in a 'neglectful and discriminatory' manner towards them. Its democratic status is also undermined by its refusal to grant the Palestinians a viable state of their own or full political rights.

A third justification is the history of Jewish suffering in the Christian West, especially during the Holocaust. Because Jews were persecuted for centuries and could feel safe only in a Jewish homeland, many people now believe that Israel deserves special treatment from the United States. The country's creation was undoubtedly an appropriate response to the long record of crimes against Jews, but it also brought about fresh crimes against a largely innocent third party: the Palestinians.

This was well understood by Israel's early leaders. David Ben-Gurion told Nahum Goldmann, the president of the World Jewish Congress:

> If I were an Arab leader I would never make terms with Israel. That is natural: we have taken their country...We come from Israel, but two thousand years ago, and what is that to them? There has been anti-semitism, the Nazis, Hitler, Auschwitz, but was that their fault? They only see one thing: we have come here and stolen their country. Why should they accept that?

Since then, Israeli leaders have repeatedly sought to deny the Palestinians' national ambitions. When she was prime minister, Golda Meir famously remarked that 'there is no such thing as a Palestinian.' Pressure from extremist violence and Palestinian population growth has forced subsequent Israeli leaders to disengage from the Gaza Strip and consider other territorial compromises, but not even Yitzhak Rabin was willing to offer the Palestinians a viable state. Ehud Barak's purportedly generous offer at Camp David would have given them only a disarmed set of Bantustans under de facto Israeli control. The tragic history of the Jewish people does not obligate the U.S. to help Israel today no matter what it does.

Israel's backers also portray it as a country that has sought peace at every turn and shown great restraint even when provoked. The Arabs, by contrast, are said to have acted with great wickedness. Yet on the ground, Israel's record is not distinguishable from that of its opponents. Ben-Gurion acknowledged that the early Zionists were far from benevolent towards the Palestinian Arabs, who resisted their encroachment—which is hardly surprising, given that the Zionists were trying to create their own state on Arab land. In the same way, the creation of Israel in 1947–48 involved acts of ethnic cleansing, including executions, massacres and rapes by Jews, and Israel's subsequent conduct has often been brutal, belying any claim to moral superiority. Between 1949 and 1956, for example, Israeli security forces killed between 2700 and 5000 Arab infiltrators, the overwhelming majority of them unarmed. The IDF murdered hundreds of Egyptian prisoners of war in both the 1956 and 1967 wars, while in 1967, it expelled between 100,000 and 260,000 Palestinians from the newly conquered West Bank, and drove 80,000 Syrians from the Golan Heights.

During the first intifada, the IDF distributed truncheons to its troops and encouraged them to break the bones of Palestinian protesters. The Swedish branch of Save the Children estimated that '23,600 to 29,900 children required medical treatment for their beating injuries in the first two years of the intifada.' Nearly a third of them were aged ten or under. The response to the second intifada has been even more violent, leading *Ha'aretz* to declare that 'the IDF…is turning into a killing machine whose efficiency is awe-inspiring, yet shocking.' The IDF fired one million bullets in the first days of the uprising. Since then, for every Israeli lost, Israel has killed 3.4 Palestinians, the majority of whom have been innocent bystanders; the ratio of Palestinian to Israeli children killed is even higher (5.7:1). It is also worth bearing in mind that the Zionists relied on terrorist bombs to drive the British from Palestine, and that Yitzhak Shamir, once a terrorist and later prime minister, declared that 'neither Jewish ethics nor Jewish tradition can disqualify terrorism as a means of combat.'

The Palestinian resort to terrorism is wrong but it isn't surprising. The Palestinians believe they have no other way to force Israeli concessions. As Ehud Barak once admitted, had he been born a Palestinian, he 'would have joined a terrorist organisation'.

So if neither strategic nor moral arguments can account for America's support for Israel, how are we to explain it?

The explanation is the unmatched power of the Israel Lobby. We use 'the Lobby' as shorthand for the loose coalition of individuals and organisations who actively work to steer U.S. foreign policy in a pro-Israel direction. This is not meant to suggest that 'the Lobby' is a unified movement with a central leadership, or that individuals within it do not disagree on certain issues. Not all Jewish Americans are part of the Lobby, because Israel is not a salient issue for many of them. In a 2004 survey, for example, roughly 36 percent of American Jews said they were either 'not very' or 'not at all' emotionally attached to Israel.

Jewish Americans also differ on specific Israeli policies. Many of the key organisations in the Lobby, such as the American-Israel Public Affairs Committee (AIPAC) and the Conference of Presidents of Major Jewish Organisations, are run by hardliners who generally support the Likud Party's expansionist policies, including its hostility to the Oslo peace process. The bulk of U.S. Jewry, meanwhile, is more inclined to make concessions to the Palestinians, and a few groups—such as Jewish Voice for Peace—strongly advocate such steps. Despite these differences, moderates and hardliners both favour giving steadfast support to Israel.

Not surprisingly, American Jewish leaders often consult Israeli officials, to make sure that their actions advance Israeli goals. As one activist from a major Jewish organisation wrote, 'it is routine for us to say: "This is our policy on a certain issue, but we must check what the

Israelis think." We as a community do it all the time.' There is a strong prejudice against criticising Israeli policy, and putting pressure on Israel is considered out of order. Edgar Bronfman Sr, the president of the World Jewish Congress, was accused of 'perfidy' when he wrote a letter to President Bush in mid-2003 urging him to persuade Israel to curb construction of its controversial 'security fence'. His critics said that 'it would be obscene at any time for the president of the World Jewish Congress to lobby the president of the United States to resist policies being promoted by the government of Israel.'

Similarly, when the president of the Israel Policy Forum, Seymour Reich, advised Condoleezza Rice in November 2005 to ask Israel to reopen a critical border crossing in the Gaza Strip, his action was denounced as 'irresponsible': 'There is,' his critics said, 'absolutely no room in the Jewish mainstream for actively canvassing against the security-related policies ... of Israel.' Recoiling from these attacks, Reich announced that 'the word "pressure" is not in my vocabulary when it comes to Israel.'

Jewish Americans have set up an impressive array of organisations to influence American foreign policy, of which AIPAC is the most powerful and best known. In 1997, *Fortune* magazine asked members of Congress and their staffs to list the most powerful lobbies in Washington. AIPAC was ranked second behind the American Association of Retired People, but ahead of the AFL-CIO and the National Rifle Association. A *National Journal* study in March 2005 reached a similar conclusion, placing AIPAC in second place (tied with AARP) in the Washington 'muscle rankings'.

The Lobby also includes prominent Christian evangelicals like Gary Bauer, Jerry Falwell, Ralph Reed and Pat Robertson, as well as Dick Armey and Tom DeLay, former majority leaders in the House of Representatives, all of whom believe Israel's rebirth is the fulfilment of biblical prophecy and support its expansionist agenda; to do otherwise, they believe, would be contrary to God's will. Neo-conservative gentiles such as John Bolton; Robert Bartley, the former *Wall Street Journal* editor; William Bennett, the former secretary of education; Jeane Kirkpatrick, the former UN ambassador; and the influential columnist George Will are also steadfast supporters.

The U.S. form of government offers activists many ways of influencing the policy process. Interest groups can lobby elected representatives and members of the executive branch, make campaign contributions, vote in elections, try to mould public opinion etc. They enjoy a disproportionate amount of influence when they are committed to an issue to which the bulk of the population is indifferent. Policymakers will tend to accommodate those who care about the issue, even if their numbers are small, confident that the rest of the population will not penalise them for doing so.

In its basic operations, the Israel Lobby is no different from the farm lobby, steel or textile workers' unions, or other ethnic lobbies. There is nothing improper about American Jews and their Christian allies attempting to sway U.S. policy: the Lobby's activities are not a conspiracy of the sort depicted in tracts like the *Protocols of the Elders of Zion*. For the most part, the individuals and groups that comprise it are only doing what other special interest groups do, but doing it very much better. By contrast, pro-Arab interest groups, in so far as they exist at all, are weak, which makes the Israel Lobby's task even easier.

The Lobby pursues two broad strategies. First, it wields its significant influence in Washington, pressuring both Congress and the executive branch. Whatever an individual lawmaker or policymaker's own views may be, the Lobby tries to make supporting Israel the 'smart' choice. Second, it strives to ensure that public discourse portrays Israel in a positive light, by repeating myths about its founding and by promoting its point of view in policy debates. The goal is to prevent critical comments from getting a fair hearing in the political arena. Controlling the debate is essential to guaranteeing U.S. support, because a candid discussion of U.S.-Israeli relations might lead Americans to favour a different policy.

A key pillar of the Lobby's effectiveness is its influence in Congress, where Israel is virtually immune from criticism. This in itself is remarkable, because Congress rarely shies away from contentious issues. Where Israel is concerned, however, potential critics fall silent. One reason is that some key members are Christian Zionists like Dick Armey, who said in September 2002: 'My No. 1 priority in foreign policy is to protect Israel.' One might think that the No. 1 priority for any congressman would be to protect America. There are also Jewish senators and congressmen who work to ensure that U.S. foreign policy supports Israel's interests.

Another source of the Lobby's power is its use of pro-Israel congressional staffers. As Morris Amitay, a former head of AIPAC, once admitted, 'there are a lot of guys at the working level up here'—on Capitol Hill—'who happen to be Jewish, who are willing... to look at certain issues in terms of their Jewishness... These are all guys who are in a position to make the decision in these areas for those senators... You can get an awful lot done just at the staff level.'

AIPAC itself, however, forms the core of the Lobby's influence in Congress. Its success is due to its ability to reward legislators and congressional candidates who support its agenda, and to punish those who challenge it. Money is critical to U.S. elections (as the scandal over the lobbyist Jack Abramoff's shady dealings reminds us), and AIPAC makes sure that its friends get strong financial support from the many pro-Israel political action committees. Anyone who is seen as hostile to Israel can be sure that AIPAC will direct campaign contributions to his or her political opponents. AIPAC also organises letter-writing campaigns and encourages newspaper editors to endorse pro-Israel candidates.

There is no doubt about the efficacy of these tactics. Here is one example: in the 1984 elections, AIPAC helped defeat Senator Charles Percy from Illinois, who, according to a prominent Lobby figure, had 'displayed insensitivity and even hostility to our concerns'. Thomas Dine, the head of AIPAC at the time, explained what happened: 'All the Jews in America, from coast to coast, gathered to oust Percy. And the American politicians—those who hold public positions now, and those who aspire—got the message.'

AIPAC's influence on Capitol Hill goes even further. According to Douglas Bloomfield, a former AIPAC staff member, 'it is common for members of Congress and their staffs to turn to AIPAC first when they need information, before calling the Library of Congress, the Congressional Research Service, committee staff or administration experts.' More important, he notes that AIPAC is 'often called on to draft speeches, work on legislation, advise on tactics, perform research, collect co-sponsors and marshal votes'.

The bottom line is that AIPAC, a de facto agent for a foreign government, has a stranglehold on Congress, with the result that U.S. policy towards Israel is not debated there, even though that policy has important consequences for the entire world. In other words, one of the three main branches of the government is firmly committed to supporting Israel. As one former Democratic senator, Ernest Hollings, noted on leaving office, 'you can't have an Israeli policy other than what AIPAC gives you around here.' Or as Ariel Sharon once told an American audience, 'when people ask me how they can help Israel, I tell them: "Help AIPAC."'

Thanks in part to the influence Jewish voters have on presidential elections, the Lobby also has significant leverage over the executive branch. Although they make up fewer than 3 percent of the population, they make large campaign donations to candidates from both parties.

The *Washington Post* once estimated that Democratic presidential candidates 'depend on Jewish supporters to supply as much as 60 percent of the money'. And because Jewish voters have high turn-out rates and are concentrated in key states like California, Florida, Illinois, New York and Pennsylvania, presidential candidates go to great lengths not to antagonise them.

Key organisations in the Lobby make it their business to ensure that critics of Israel do not get important foreign policy jobs. Jimmy Carter wanted to make George Ball his first secretary of state, but knew that Ball was seen as critical of Israel and that the Lobby would oppose the appointment. In this way any aspiring policymaker is encouraged to become an overt supporter of Israel, which is why public critics of Israeli policy have become an endangered species in the foreign policy establishment.

When Howard Dean called for the United States to take a more 'even-handed role' in the Arab–Israeli conflict, Senator Joseph Lieberman accused him of selling Israel down the river and said his statement was 'irresponsible'. Virtually all the top Democrats in the House signed a letter criticising Dean's remarks, and the *Chicago Jewish Star* reported that 'anonymous attackers…are clogging the email inboxes of Jewish leaders around the country, warnings— without much evidenced—that Dean would somehow be bad for Israel.'

This worry was absurd; Dean is in fact quite hawkish on Israel: his campaign co-chair was a former AIPAC president, and Dean said his own views on the Middle East more closely reflected those of AIPAC than those of the more moderate Americans for Peace Now. He had merely suggested that to 'bring the sides together', Washington should act as an honest broker. This is hardly a radical idea, but the Lobby doesn't tolerate even-handedness.

During the Clinton administration, Middle Eastern policy was largely shaped by officials with close ties to Israel or to prominent pro-Israel organisations; among them, Martin Indyk, the former deputy director of research at AIPAC and co-founder of the pro-Israel Washington Institute for Near East Policy (WINEP); Dennis Ross, who joined WINEP after leaving government in 2001; and Aaron Miller, who has lived in Israel and often visits the country. These men were among Clinton's closest advisers at the Camp David summit in July 2000. Although all three supported the Oslo peace process and favoured the creation of a Palestinian state, they did so only within the limits of what would be acceptable to Israel. The American delegation took its cues from Ehud Barak, co-ordinated its negotiating positions with Israel in advance, and did not offer independent proposals. Not surprisingly, Palestinian negotiators complained that they were 'negotiating with two Israeli teams–one displaying an Israeli flag, and one an American flag'.

The situation is even more pronounced in the Bush administration, whose ranks have included such fervent advocates of the Israeli cause as Elliot Abrams, John Bolton, Douglas Feith, I. Lewis ('Scooter') Libby, Richard Perle, Paul Wolfowitz and David Wurmser. As we shall see, these officials have consistently pushed for policies favoured by Israel and backed by organisations in the Lobby.

The Lobby doesn't want an open debate, of course, because that might lead Americans to question the level of support they provide. Accordingly, pro-Israel organisations work hard to influence the institutions that do most to shape popular opinion.

The Lobby's perspective prevails in the mainstream media: the debate among Middle East pundits, the journalist Eric Alterman writes, is 'dominated by people who cannot imagine criticising Israel'. He lists 61 'columnists and commentators who can be counted on to support Israel reflexively and without qualification'. Conversely, he found just five pundits who consistently criticise Israeli actions or endorse Arab positions. Newspapers occasionally publish guest op-eds challenging Israeli policy, but the balance of opinion clearly favours the other side. It is hard to imagine any mainstream media outlet in the United States publishing a piece like this one.

'Shamir, Sharon, Bibi—whatever those guys want is pretty much fine by me,' Robert Bartley once remarked. Not surprisingly, his newspaper, the *Wall Street Journal*, along with other prominent papers like the *Chicago Sun-Times* and the *Washington Times*, regularly runs editorials that strongly support Israel. Magazines like *Commentary*, the *New Republic* and the *Weekly Standard* defend Israel at every turn.

Editorial bias is also found in papers like the *New York Times*, which occasionally criticises Israeli policies and sometimes concedes that the Palestinians have legitimate grievances, but is not even-handed. In his memoirs the paper's former executive editor Max Frankel acknowledges the impact his own attitude had on his editorial decisions: 'I was much more deeply devoted to Israel than I dared to assert…Fortified by my knowledge of Israel and my friendships there, I myself wrote most of our Middle East commentaries. As more Arab than Jewish readers recognised, I wrote them from a pro-Israel perspective.'

News reports are more even-handed, in part because reporters strive to be objective, but also because it is difficult to cover events in the Occupied Territories without acknowledging Israel's actions on the ground. To discourage unfavourable reporting, the Lobby organises letter-writing campaigns, demonstrations and boycotts of news outlets whose content it considers anti-Israel. One CNN executive has said that he sometimes gets 6000 email messages in a single day complaining about a story. In May 2003, the pro-Israel Committee for Accurate Middle East Reporting in America (CAMERA) organised demonstrations outside National Public Radio stations in 33 cities; it also tried to persuade contributors to withhold support from NPR until its Middle East coverage becomes more sympathetic to Israel. Boston's NPR station, WBUR, reportedly lost more than $1 million in contributions as a result of these efforts. Further pressure on NPR has come from Israel's friends in Congress, who have asked for an internal audit of its Middle East coverage as well as more oversight.

The Israeli side also dominates the think tanks which play an important role in shaping public debate as well as actual policy. The Lobby created its own think tank in 1985, when Martin Indyk helped to found WINEP. Although WINEP plays down its links to Israel, claiming instead to provide a 'balanced and realistic' perspective on Middle East issues, it is funded and run by individuals deeply committed to advancing Israel's agenda.

The Lobby's influence extends well beyond WINEP, however. Over the past 25 years, pro-Israel forces have established a commanding presence at the American Enterprise Institute, the Brookings Institution, the Center for Security Policy, the Foreign Policy Research Institute, the Heritage Foundation, the Hudson Institute, the Institute for Foreign Policy Analysis and the Jewish Institute for National Security Affairs (JINSA). These think tanks employ few, if any, critics of U.S. support for Israel.

Take the Brookings Institution. For many years, its senior expert on the Middle East was William Quandt, a former NSC official with a well-deserved reputation for even-handedness. Today, Brookings's coverage is conducted through the Saban Center for Middle East Studies, which is financed by Haim Saban, an Israeli-American businessman and ardent Zionist. The centre's director is the ubiquitous Martin Indyk. What was once a non-partisan policy institute is now part of the pro-Israel chorus.

Where the Lobby has had the most difficulty is in stifling debate on university campuses. In the 1990s, when the Oslo peace process was underway, there was only mild criticism of Israel, but it grew stronger with Oslo's collapse and Sharon's access to power, becoming quite vociferous when the IDF reoccupied the West Bank in spring 2002 and employed massive force to subdue the second intifada.

The Lobby moved immediately to 'take back the campuses'. New groups sprang up, like the Caravan for Democracy, which brought Israeli speakers to U.S. colleges. Established groups like the Jewish Council for Public Affairs and Hillel joined in, and a new group, the Israel on Campus Coalition, was formed to co-ordinate the many bodies that now sought to put Israel's case. Finally, AIPAC more than tripled its spending on programmes to monitor university activities and to train young advocates, in order to 'vastly expand the number of students involved on campus...in the national pro-Israel effort'.

The Lobby also monitors what professors write and teach. In September 2002, Martin Kramer and Daniel Pipes, two passionately pro-Israel neoconservatives, established a website (Campus Watch) that posted dossiers on suspect academics and encouraged students to report remarks or behaviour that might be considered hostile to Israel. This transparent attempt to blacklist and intimidate scholars provoked a harsh reaction and Pipes and Kramer later removed the dossiers, but the website still invites students to report 'anti-Israel' activity.

Groups within the Lobby put pressure on particular academics and universities. Columbia has been a frequent target, no doubt because of the presence of the late Edward Said on its faculty. 'One can be sure that any public statement in support of the Palestinian people by the pre-eminent literary critic Edward Said will elicit hundreds of emails, letters and journalistic accounts that call on us to denounce Said and to either sanction or fire him,' Jonathan Cole, its former provost, reported. When Columbia recruited the historian Rashid Khalidi from Chicago, the same thing happened. It was a problem Princeton also faced a few years later when it considered wooing Khalidi away from Columbia.

A classic illustration of the effort to police academia occurred towards the end of 2004, when the David Project produced a film alleging that faculty members of Columbia's Middle East Studies programme were anti-semitic and were intimidating Jewish students who stood up for Israel. Columbia was hauled over the coals, but a faculty committee which was assigned to investigate the charges found no evidence of anti-semitism and the only incident possibly worth noting was that one professor had 'responded heatedly' to a student's question. The committee also discovered that the academics in question had themselves been the target of an overt campaign of intimidation.

Perhaps the most disturbing aspect of all this is the efforts Jewish groups have made to push Congress into establishing mechanisms to monitor what professors say. If they manage to get this passed, universities judged to have an anti-Israel bias would be denied federal funding. Their efforts have not yet succeeded, but they are an indication of the importance placed on controlling debate.

A number of Jewish philanthropists have recently established Israel Studies programmes (in addition to the roughly 130 Jewish Studies programmes already in existence) so as to increase the number of Israel-friendly scholars on campus. In May 2003, NYU announced the establishment of the Taub Center for Israel Studies; similar programmes have been set up at Berkeley, Brandeis and Emory.

Academic administrators emphasise their pedagogical value, but the truth is that they are intended in large part to promote Israel's image. Fred Laffer, the head of the Taub Foundation, makes it clear that his foundation funded the NYU centre to help counter the 'Arabic [sic] point of view' that he thinks is prevalent in NYU's Middle East programmes.

No discussion of the Lobby would be complete without an examination of one of its most powerful weapons: the charge of anti-semitism. Anyone who criticises Israel's actions or argues that pro-Israel groups have significant influence over U.S. Middle Eastern policy—an influence AIPAC celebrates—stands a good chance of being labelled an anti-semite. Indeed, anyone who merely claims that there is an Israel Lobby runs the risk of being charged with anti-semitism, even though the Israeli media refer to America's 'Jewish Lobby'. In other words, the Lobby first boasts of its influence and then attacks anyone who calls attention to it. It's a very effective tactic: anti-semitism is something no one wants to be accused of.

Europeans have been more willing than Americans to criticise Israeli policy, which some people attribute to a resurgence of anti-semitism in Europe. We are 'getting to a point', the U.S. ambassador to the EU said in early 2004, 'where it is as bad as it was in the 1930s'. Measuring anti-semitism is a complicated matter, but the weight of evidence points in the opposite direction. In the spring of 2004, when accusations of European anti-semitism filled the air in America, separate surveys of European public opinion conducted by the U.S.-based Anti-Defamation League and the Pew Research Center for the People and the Press found that it was in fact declining. In the 1930s, by contrast, anti-semitism was not only widespread among Europeans of all classes but considered quite acceptable.

The Lobby and its friends often portray France as the most anti-semitic country in Europe. But in 2003, the head of the French Jewish community said that 'France is not more anti-semitic than America.' According to a recent article in *Ha'aretz*, the French police have reported that anti-semitic incidents declined by almost 50 percent in 2005; and this even though France has the largest Muslim population of any European country. Finally, when a French Jew was murdered in Paris last month by a Muslim gang, tens of thousands of demonstrators poured into the streets to condemn anti-semitism. Jacques Chirac and Dominique de Villepin both attended the victim's memorial service to show their solidarity.

No one would deny that there is anti-semitism among European Muslims, some of it provoked by Israel's conduct towards the Palestinians and some of it straightforwardly racist. But this is a separate matter with little bearing on whether or not Europe today is like Europe in the 1930s. Nor would anyone deny that there are still some virulent autochthonous anti-semites in Europe (as there are in the United States) but their numbers are small and their views are rejected by the vast majority of Europeans.

Israel's advocates, when pressed to go beyond mere assertion, claim that there is a 'new anti-semitism', which they equate with criticism of Israel. In other words, criticise Israeli policy and you are by definition an anti-semite. When the synod of the Church of England recently voted to divest from Caterpillar Inc on the grounds that it manufactures the bulldozers used by the Israelis to demolish Palestinian homes, the Chief Rabbi complained that this would 'have the most adverse repercussions on... Jewish–Christian relations in Britain', while Rabbi Tony Bayfield, the head of the Reform movement, said: 'There is a clear problem of anti-Zionist—verging on anti-semitic—attitudes emerging in the grass-roots, and even in the middle ranks of the Church.' But the Church was guilty merely of protesting against Israeli government policy.

Critics are also accused of holding Israel to an unfair standard or questioning its right to exist. But these are bogus charges too. Western critics of Israel hardly ever question its right to exist: They question its behaviour towards the Palestinians, as do Israelis themselves. Nor is Israel being judged unfairly. Israeli treatment of the Palestinians elicits criticism because it is contrary to widely accepted notions of human rights, to international law and to the principle of national self-determination. And it is hardly the only state that has faced sharp criticism on these grounds.

In the autumn of 2001, and especially in the spring of 2002, the Bush administration tried to reduce anti-American sentiment in the Arab world and undermine support for terrorist groups like al-Qaida by halting Israel's expansionist policies in the Occupied Territories and advocating the creation of a Palestinian state. Bush had very significant means of persuasion at his disposal. He could have threatened to reduce economic and diplomatic support for Israel, and the American people would almost certainly have supported him. A May 2003 poll reported that more than 60 percent of Americans were willing to withhold aid if Israel resisted U.S. pressure to settle the conflict, and that number rose to 70 percent among the 'politically active'. Indeed, 73 percent said that the United States should not favour either side.

Yet the administration failed to change Israeli policy, and Washington ended up backing it. Over time, the administration also adopted Israel's own justifications of its position, so that U.S. rhetoric began to mimic Israeli rhetoric. By February 2003, a *Washington Post* headline summarised the situation: 'Bush and Sharon Nearly Identical on Mideast Policy.' The main reason for this switch was the Lobby.

The story begins in late September 2001, when Bush began urging Sharon to show restraint in the Occupied Territories. He also pressed him to allow Israel's foreign minister, Shimon Peres, to meet with Yasser Arafat, even though he (Bush) was highly critical of Arafat's leadership. Bush even said publicly that he supported the creation of a Palestinian state. Alarmed, Sharon accused him of trying 'to appease the Arabs at our expense', warning that Israel 'will not be Czechoslovakia'.

Bush was reportedly furious at being compared to Chamberlain, and the White House press secretary called Sharon's remarks 'unacceptable'. Sharon offered a pro forma apology, but quickly joined forces with the Lobby to persuade the administration and the American people that the United States and Israel faced a common threat from terrorism. Israeli officials and Lobby representatives insisted that there was no real difference between Arafat and Osama bin Laden: the United States and Israel, they said, should isolate the Palestinians' elected leader and have nothing to do with him.

The Lobby also went to work in Congress. On 16 November, 89 senators sent Bush a letter praising him for refusing to meet with Arafat, but also demanding that the U.S. not restrain Israel from retaliating against the Palestinians; the administration, they wrote, must state publicly that it stood behind Israel. According to the *New York Times*, the letter 'stemmed' from a meeting two weeks before between 'leaders of the American Jewish community and key senators', adding that AIPAC was 'particularly active in providing advice on the letter'.

By late November, relations between Tel Aviv and Washington had improved considerably. This was thanks in part to the Lobby's efforts, but also to America's initial victory in Afghanistan, which reduced the perceived need for Arab support in dealing with al-Qaida. Sharon visited the White House in early December and had a friendly meeting with Bush.

In April 2002 trouble erupted again, after the IDF launched Operation Defensive Shield and resumed control of virtually all the major Palestinian areas on the West Bank. Bush knew that Israel's actions would damage America's image in the Islamic world and undermine the war on terrorism, so he demanded that Sharon 'halt the incursions and begin withdrawal'. He underscored this message two days later, saying he wanted Israel to 'withdraw without delay'. On 7 April, Condoleezza Rice, then Bush's national security adviser, told reporters: "Without delay" means without delay. It means now.' That same day Colin Powell set out for the Middle East to persuade all sides to stop fighting and start negotiating.

Israel and the Lobby swung into action. Pro-Israel officials in the vice-president's office and the Pentagon, as well as neo-conservative pundits like Robert Kagan and William Kristol, put the heat on Powell. They even accused him of having 'virtually obliterated the distinction between terrorists and those fighting terrorists'. Bush himself was being pressed by Jewish leaders and Christian evangelicals. Tom DeLay and Dick Armey were especially outspoken about the need to support Israel, and DeLay and the Senate minority leader, Trent Lott, visited the White House and warned Bush to back off.

The first sign that Bush was caving in came on 11 April—a week after he told Sharon to withdraw his forces—when the White House press secretary said that the president believed Sharon was 'a man of peace'. Bush repeated this statement publicly on Powell's return from his abortive mission, and told reporters that Sharon had responded satisfactorily to his call for a full and immediate withdrawal. Sharon had done no such thing, but Bush was no longer willing to make an issue of it.

Meanwhile, Congress was also moving to back Sharon. On 2 May, it overrode the administration's objections and passed two resolutions reaffirming support for Israel. (The Senate vote was 94 to 2; the House of Representatives version passed 352 to 21.) Both resolutions held that the United States 'stands in solidarity with Israel' and that the two countries were, to quote the House resolution, 'now engaged in a common struggle against terrorism'. The House version also condemned 'the ongoing support and co-ordination of terror by Yasser Arafat', who was portrayed as a central part of the terrorism problem. Both resolutions were drawn up with the help of the Lobby. A few days later, a bipartisan congressional delegation on a fact-finding mission to Israel stated that Sharon should resist U.S. pressure to negotiate with Arafat. On 9 May, a House appropriations subcommittee met to consider giving Israel an extra $200 million to fight terrorism. Powell opposed the package, but the Lobby backed it and Powell lost.

In short, Sharon and the Lobby took on the president of the United States and triumphed. Hemi Shalev, a journalist on the Israeli newspaper *Ma'ariv*, reported that Sharon's aides 'could not hide their satisfaction in view of Powell's failure. Sharon saw the whites of President Bush's eyes, they bragged, and the president blinked first.' But it was Israel's champions in the United States, not Sharon or Israel, that played the key role in defeating Bush.

The situation has changed little since then. The Bush administration refused ever again to have dealings with Arafat. After his death, it embraced the new Palestinian leader, Mahmoud Abbas, but has done little to help him. Sharon continued to develop his plan to impose a unilateral settlement on the Palestinians, based on 'disengagement' from Gaza coupled with continued expansion on the West Bank. By refusing to negotiate with Abbas and making it impossible for him to deliver tangible benefits to the Palestinian people, Sharon's strategy contributed directly to Hamas's electoral victory. With Hamas in power, however, Israel has another excuse not to negotiate. The U.S. administration has supported Sharon's actions (and those of his successor, Ehud Olmert). Bush has even endorsed unilateral Israeli annexations in the Occupied Territories, reversing the stated policy of every president since Lyndon Johnson.

U.S. officials have offered mild criticisms of a few Israeli actions, but have done little to help create a viable Palestinian state. Sharon has Bush 'wrapped around his little finger', the former national security adviser Brent Scowcroft said in October 2004. If Bush tries to distance the U.S. from Israel, or even criticises Israeli actions in the Occupied Territories, he is certain to face the wrath of the Lobby and its supporters in Congress. Democratic presidential candidates understand that these are facts of life, which is the reason John Kerry went to great lengths to display unalloyed support for Israel in 2004, and why Hillary Clinton is doing the same thing today.

Maintaining U.S. support for Israel's policies against the Palestinians is essential as far as the Lobby is concerned, but its ambitions do not stop there. It also wants America to help

Israel remain the dominant regional power. The Israeli government and pro-Israel groups in the United States have worked together to shape the administration's policy towards Iraq, Syria and Iran, as well as its grand scheme for reordering the Middle East.

Pressure from Israel and the Lobby was not the only factor behind the decision to attack Iraq in March 2003, but it was critical. Some Americans believe that this was a war for oil, but there is hardly any direct evidence to support this claim. Instead, the war was motivated in good part by a desire to make Israel more secure. According to Philip Zelikow, a former member of the president's Foreign Intelligence Advisory Board, the executive director of the 9/11 Commission, and now a counsellor to Condoleezza Rice, the 'real threat' from Iraq was not a threat to the United States. The 'unstated threat' was the 'threat against Israel', Zelikow told an audience at the University of Virginia in September 2002. 'The American government,' he added, 'doesn't want to lean too hard on it rhetorically, because it is not a popular sell.'

On 16 August 2002, 11 days before Dick Cheney kicked off the campaign for war with a hardline speech to the Veterans of Foreign Wars, the *Washington Post* reported that 'Israel is urging U.S. officials not to delay a military strike against Iraq's Saddam Hussein.' By this point, according to Sharon, strategic co-ordination between Israel and the U.S. had reached 'unprecedented dimensions', and Israeli intelligence officials had given Washington a variety of alarming reports about Iraq's WMD programmes. As one retired Israeli general later put it, 'Israeli intelligence was a full partner to the picture presented by American and British intelligence regarding Iraq's non-conventional capabilities.'

Israeli leaders were deeply distressed when Bush decided to seek Security Council authorisation for war, and even more worried when Saddam agreed to let UN inspectors back in. 'The campaign against Saddam Hussein is a must,' Shimon Peres told reporters in September 2002. 'Inspections and inspectors are good for decent people, but dishonest people can overcome easily inspections and inspectors.'

At the same time, Ehud Barak wrote a *New York Times* op-ed warning that 'the greatest risk now lies in inaction.' His predecessor as prime minister, Binyamin Netanyahu, published a similar piece in the *Wall Street Journal*, entitled: 'The Case for Toppling Saddam'. 'Today nothing less than dismantling his regime will do,' he declared. 'I believe I speak for the overwhelming majority of Israelis in supporting a pre-emptive strike against Saddam's regime.' Or as *Ha'aretz* reported in February 2003, 'the military and political leadership yearns for war in Iraq.'

As Netanyahu suggested, however, the desire for war was not confined to Israel's leaders. Apart from Kuwait, which Saddam invaded in 1990, Israel was the only country in the world where both politicians and public favoured war. As the journalist Gideon Levy observed at the time, 'Israel is the only country in the West whose leaders support the war unreservedly and where no alternative opinion is voiced.' In fact, Israelis were so gung-ho that their allies in America told them to damp down their rhetoric, or it would look as if the war would be fought on Israel's behalf.

Within the U.S., the main driving force behind the war was a small band of neoconservatives, many with ties to Likud. But leaders of the Lobby's major organisations lent their voices to the campaign. 'As President Bush attempted to sell the...war in Iraq,' the *Forward* reported, 'America's most important Jewish organisations rallied as one to his defence. In statement after statement community leaders stressed the need to rid the world of Saddam Hussein and his weapons of mass destruction.' The editorial goes on to say that 'concern for Israel's safety rightfully factored into the deliberations of the main Jewish groups.'

Although neoconservatives and other Lobby leaders were eager to invade Iraq, the broader American Jewish community was not. Just after the war started, Samuel Freedman reported that 'a compilation of nationwide opinion polls by the Pew Research Center shows that Jews are less supportive of the Iraq war than the population at large, 52 percent to 62 percent.' Clearly, it would be wrong to blame the war in Iraq on 'Jewish influence'. Rather, it was due in large part to the Lobby's influence, especially that of the neoconservatives within it.

The neoconservatives had been determined to topple Saddam even before Bush became president. They caused a stir early in 1998 by publishing two open letters to Clinton, calling for Saddam's removal from power. The signatories, many of whom had close ties to pro-Israel groups like JINSA or WINEP, and who included Elliot Abrams, John Bolton, Douglas Feith, William Kristol, Bernard Lewis, Donald Rumsfeld, Richard Perle and Paul Wolfowitz, had little trouble persuading the Clinton administration to adopt the general goal of ousting Saddam. But they were unable to sell a war to achieve that objective. They were no more able to generate enthusiasm for invading Iraq in the early months of the Bush administration. They needed help to achieve their aim. That help arrived with 9/11. Specifically, the events of that day led Bush and Cheney to reverse course and become strong proponents of a preventive war.

At a key meeting with Bush at Camp David on 15 September, Wolfowitz advocated attacking Iraq before Afghanistan, even though there was no evidence that Saddam was involved in the attacks on the U.S. and bin Laden was known to be in Afghanistan. Bush rejected his advice and chose to go after Afghanistan instead, but war with Iraq was now regarded as a serious possibility and on 21 November the president charged military planners with developing concrete plans for an invasion.

Other neoconservatives were meanwhile at work in the corridors of power. We don't have the full story yet, but scholars like Bernard Lewis of Princeton and Fouad Ajami of Johns Hopkins reportedly played important roles in persuading Cheney that war was the best option, though neoconservatives on his staff—Eric Edelman, John Hannah and Scooter Libby, Cheney's chief of staff and one of the most powerful individuals in the administrations—also played their part. By early 2002 Cheney had persuaded Bush; and with Bush and Cheney on board, war was inevitable.

Outside the administration, neoconservative pundits lost no time in making the case that invading Iraq was essential to winning the war on terrorism. Their efforts were designed partly to keep up the pressure on Bush, and partly to overcome opposition to the war inside and outside the government. On 20 September, a group of prominent neoconservatives and their allies published another open letter: 'Even if evidence does not link Iraq directly to the attack,' it read, 'any strategy aiming at the eradication of terrorism and its sponsors must include a determined effort to remove Saddam Hussein from power in Iraq.' The letter also reminded Bush that 'Israel has been and remains America's staunchest ally against international terrorism.' In the 1 October issue of the *Weekly Standard*, Robert Kagan and William Kristol called for regime change in Iraq as soon as the Taliban was defeated. That same day, Charles Krauthammer argued in the *Washington Post* that after the U.S. was done with Afghanistan, Syria should be next, followed by Iran and Iraq: 'The war on terrorism will conclude in Baghdad,' when we finish off 'the most dangerous terrorist regime in the world'.

This was the beginning of an unrelenting public relations campaign to win support for an invasion of Iraq, a crucial part of which was the manipulation of intelligence in such a way as to make it seem as if Saddam posed an imminent threat. For example, Libby pressured CIA analysts to find evidence supporting the case for war and helped prepare Colin Powell's now discredited briefing to the UN Security Council. Within the Pentagon, the Policy Counterterrorism Evaluation Group was charged with finding links between al-Qaida and Iraq that the intelligence community had supposedly missed. Its two key members were David Wurmser, a hard-core neoconservative, and Michael Maloof, a Lebanese-American with close ties to Perle. Another Pentagon group, the so-called Office of Special Plans, was given the task of uncovering evidence that could be used to sell the war. It was headed by Abram Shulsky, a neoconservative with long-standing ties to Wolfowitz, and its ranks included recruits from pro-Israel think tanks. Both these organisations were created after 9/11 and reported directly to Douglas Feith.

Like virtually all the neoconservatives, Feith is deeply committed to Israel; he also has long-term ties to Likud. He wrote articles in the 1990s supporting the settlements and arguing that Israel should retain the Occupied Territories. More important, along with Perle and Wurmser, he wrote the famous 'Clean Break' report in June 1996 for Netanyahu, who had just become prime minister. Among other things, it recommended that Netanyahu 'focus on removing Saddam Hussein from power in Iraq—an important Israeli strategic objective in its own right'. It also called for Israel to take steps to reorder the entire Middle East. Netanyahu did not follow their advice, but Feith, Perle and Wurmser were soon urging the Bush administration to pursue those same goals. The *Ha'aretz* columnist Akiva Eldar warned that Feith and Perle 'are walking a fine line between their loyalty to American governments...and Israeli interests'.

Wolfowitz is equally committed to Israel. The *Forward* once described him as 'the most hawkishly pro-Israel voice in the administration', and selected him in 2002 as first among 50 notables who 'have consciously pursued Jewish activism'. At about the same time, JINSA gave Wolfowitz its Henry M. Jackson Distinguished Service Award for promoting a strong partnership between Israel and the United States; and the *Jerusalem Post*, describing him as 'devoutly pro-Israel', named him 'Man of the Year' in 2003.

Finally, a brief word is in order about the neoconservatives' prewar support of Ahmed Chalabi, the unscrupulous Iraqi exile who headed the Iraqi National Congress. They backed Chalabi because he had established close ties with Jewish-American groups and had pledged to foster good relations with Israel once he gained power. This was precisely what pro-Israel proponents of regime change wanted to hear. Matthew Berger laid out the essence of the bargain in the *Jewish Journal*: 'The INC saw improved relations as a way to tap Jewish influence in Washington and Jerusalem and to drum up increased support for its cause. For their part, the Jewish groups saw an opportunity to pave the way for better relations between Israel and Iraq, if and when the INC is involved in replacing Saddam Hussein's regime.'

Given the neoconservatives' devotion to Israel, their obsession with Iraq, and their influence in the Bush administration, it isn't surprising that many Americans suspected that the war was designed to further Israeli interests. Last March, Barry Jacobs of the American Jewish Committee acknowledged that the belief that Israel and the neoconservatives had conspired to get the U.S. into a war in Iraq was 'pervasive' in the intelligence community. Yet few people would say so publicly, and most of those who did—including Senator Ernest Hollings and Representative James Moran—were condemned for raising the issue. Michael Kinsley wrote in late 2002 that 'the lack of public discussion about the role of Israel...is the proverbial elephant in the room.' The reason for the reluctance to talk about it, he observed, was fear of being labelled an anti-semite. There is little doubt that Israel and the Lobby were key factors in the decision to go to war. It's a decision the U.S. would have been far less likely to take without their efforts. And the war itself was intended to be only the first step. A front-page headline in the *Wall Street Journal* shortly after the war began says it all: 'President's Dream: Changing Not Just Regime but a Region: A Pro-U.S., Democratic Area Is a Goal that Has Israeli and Neo-Conservative Roots.'

Pro-Israel forces have long been interested in getting the US military more directly involved in the Middle East. But they had limited success during the Cold War, because America acted as an 'off-shore balancer' in the region. Most forces designated for the Middle East, like the Rapid Deployment Force, were kept 'over the horizon' and out of harm's way. The idea was to play local powers off against each other—which is why the Reagan administration supported Saddam against revolutionary Iran during the Iran–Iraq War—in order to maintain a balance favourable to the U.S.

This policy changed after the first Gulf War, when the Clinton administration adopted a strategy of 'dual containment'. Substantial U.S. forces would be stationed in the region in order to contain both Iran and Iraq, instead of one being used to check the other. The father of dual containment was none other than Martin Indyk, who first outlined the strategy in May 1993 at WINEP and then implemented it as director for Near East and South Asian Affairs at the National Security Council.

By the mid-1990s there was considerable dissatisfaction with dual containment, because it made the United States the mortal enemy of two countries that hated each other, and forced Washington to bear the burden of containing both. But it was a strategy the Lobby favoured and worked actively in Congress to preserve. Pressed by AIPAC and other pro-Israel forces, Clinton toughened up the policy in the spring of 1995 by imposing an economic embargo on Iran. But AIPAC and the others wanted more. The result was the 1996 Iran and Libya Sanctions Act, which imposed sanctions on any foreign companies investing more than $40 million to develop petroleum resources in Iran or Libya. As Ze'ev Schiff, the military correspondent of Ha'aretz, noted at the time, 'Israel is but a tiny element in the big scheme, but one should not conclude that it cannot influence those within the Beltway.'

By the late 1990s, however, the neoconservatives were arguing that dual containment was not enough and that regime change in Iraq was essential. By toppling Saddam and turning Iraq into a vibrant democracy, they argued, the U.S. would trigger a far-reaching process of change throughout the Middle East. The same line of thinking was evident in the 'Clean Break' study the neoconservatives wrote for Netanyahu. By 2002, when an invasion of Iraq was on the front-burner, regional transformation was an article of faith in neoconservative circles.

Charles Krauthammer describes this grand scheme as the brainchild of Natan Sharansky, but Israelis across the political spectrum believed that toppling Saddam would alter the Middle East to Israel's advantage. Aluf Benn reported in Ha'aretz (17 February 2003):

Senior IDF officers and those close to Prime Minister Ariel Sharon, such as National Security Adviser Ephraim Halevy, paint a rosy picture of the wonderful future Israel can expect after the war. They envision a domino effect, with the fall of Saddam Hussein followed by that of Israel's other enemies... Along with these leaders will disappear terror and weapons of mass destruction.

Once Baghdad fell in mid-April 2003, Sharon and his lieutenants began urging Washington to target Damascus. On 16 April, Sharon, interviewed in Yedioth Ahronoth, called for the United States to put 'very heavy' pressure on Syria, while Shaul Mofaz, his defence minister, interviewed in Ma'ariv, said: 'We have a long list of issues that we are thinking of demanding of the Syrians and it is appropriate that it should be done through the Americans.' Ephraim Halevy told a WINEP audience that it was now important for the U.S. to get rough with Syria, and the Washington Post reported that Israel was 'fuelling the campaign' against Syria by feeding the U.S. intelligence reports about the actions of Bashar Assad, the Syrian president.

Prominent members of the Lobby made the same arguments. Wolfowitz declared that 'there has got to be regime change in Syria,' and Richard Perle told a journalist that 'a short message, a two-worded message' could be delivered to other hostile regimes in the Middle East: 'You're next.' In early April, WINEP released a bipartisan report stating that Syria 'should not miss the message that countries that pursue Saddam's reckless, irresponsible and defiant behaviour could end up sharing his fate'. On 15 April, Yossi Klein Halevi wrote a piece in the *Los Angeles Times* entitled 'Next, Turn the Screws on Syria', while the following day Zev Chafets wrote an article for the *New York Daily News* entitled 'Terror-Friendly Syria Needs a Change, Too'. Not to be outdone, Lawrence Kaplan wrote in the *New Republic* on 21 April that Assad was a serious threat to America.

Back on Capitol Hill, Congressman Eliot Engel had reintroduced the Syria Accountability and Lebanese Sovereignty Restoration Act. It threatened sanctions against Syria if it did not withdraw from Lebanon, give up its WMD and stop supporting terrorism, and it also called for Syria and Lebanon to take concrete steps to make peace with Israel. This legislation was strongly endorsed by the Lobby—by AIPAC especially—and 'framed', according to the *Jewish Telegraph Agency*, 'by some of Israel's best friends in Congress'. The Bush administration had little enthusiasm for it, but the anti-Syrian act passed overwhelmingly (398 to 4 in the House; 89 to 4 in the Senate), and Bush signed it into law on 12 December 2003.

The administration itself was still divided about the wisdom of targeting Syria. Although the neoconservatives were eager to pick a fight with Damascus, the CIA and the State Department were opposed to the idea. And even after Bush signed the new law, he emphasised that he would go slowly in implementing it. His ambivalence is understandable. First, the Syrian government had not only been providing important intelligence about al-Qaida since 9/11: it had also warned Washington about a planned terrorist attack in the Gulf and given CIA interrogators access to Mohammed Zammar, the alleged recruiter of some of the 9/11 hijackers. Targeting the Assad regime would jeopardise these valuable connections, and thereby undermine the larger war on terrorism.

Second, Syria had not been on bad terms with Washington before the Iraq war (it had even voted for UN Resolution 1441), and was itself no threat to the United States. Playing hardball with it would make the U.S. look like a bully with an insatiable appetite for beating up Arab states. Third, putting Syria on the hit list would give Damascus a powerful incentive to cause trouble in Iraq. Even if one wanted to bring pressure to bear, it made good sense to finish the job in Iraq first. Yet Congress insisted on putting the screws on Damascus, largely in response to pressure from Israeli officials and groups like AIPAC. If there were no Lobby, there would have been no Syria Accountability Act, and U.S. policy towards Damascus would have been more in line with the national interest.

Israelis tend to describe every threat in the starkest terms, but Iran is widely seen as their most dangerous enemy because it is the most likely to acquire nuclear weapons. Virtually all Israelis regard an Islamic country in the Middle East with nuclear weapons as a threat to their existence. 'Iraq is a problem ... But you should understand, if you ask me, today Iran is more dangerous than Iraq,' the defence minister, Binyamin Ben-Eliezer, remarked a month before the Iraq war.

Sharon began pushing the U.S. to confront Iran in November 2002, in an interview in the *Times*. Describing Iran as the 'centre of world terror', and bent on acquiring nuclear weapons, he declared that the Bush administration should put the strong arm on Iran 'the day after' it conquered Iraq. In late April 2003, *Ha'aretz* reported that the Israeli ambassador in Washington was calling for regime change in Iran. The overthrow of Saddam, he noted, was 'not enough'. In his words, America 'has to follow through. We still have great threats of that magnitude coming from Syria, coming from Iran.'

The neoconservatives, too, lost no time in making the case for regime change in Tehran. On 6 May, the AEI cosponsored an all-day conference on Iran with the Foundation for the Defense of Democracies and the Hudson Institute, both champions of Israel. The speakers were all strongly pro-Israel, and many called for the U.S. to replace the Iranian regime with a democracy. As usual, a bevy of articles by prominent neoconservatives made the case for going after Iran. 'The liberation of Iraq was the first great battle for the future of the Middle East...But the next great battle—not, we hope, a military battle—will be for Iran,' William Kristol wrote in the *Weekly Standard* on 12 May.

The administration has responded to the Lobby's pressure by working overtime to shut down Iran's nuclear programme. But Washington has had little success, and Iran seems determined to create a nuclear arsenal. As a result, the Lobby has intensified its pressure. Op-eds and other articles now warn of imminent dangers from a nuclear Iran, caution against any appeasement of a 'terrorist' regime, and hint darkly of preventive action should diplomacy fail. The Lobby is pushing Congress to approve the Iran Freedom Support Act, which would expand existing sanctions. Israeli officials also warn they may take pre-emptive action should Iran continue down the nuclear road, threats partly intended to keep Washington's attention on the issue.

One might argue that Israel and the Lobby have not had much influence on policy towards Iran, because the U.S. has its own reasons for keeping Iran from going nuclear. There is some truth in this, but Iran's nuclear ambitions do not pose a direct threat to the U.S.. If Washington could live with a nuclear Soviet Union, a nuclear China or even a nuclear North Korea, it can live with a nuclear Iran. And that is why the Lobby must keep up constant pressure on politicians to confront Tehran. Iran and the U.S. would hardly be allies if the Lobby did not exist, but U.S. policy would be more temperate and preventive war would not be a serious option.

It is not surprising that Israel and its American supporters want the U.S. to deal with any and all threats to Israel's security. If their efforts to shape U.S. policy succeed, Israel's enemies will be weakened or overthrown, Israel will get a free hand with the Palestinians, and the U.S. will do most of the fighting, dying, rebuilding and paying. But even if the U.S. fails to transform the Middle East and finds itself in conflict with an increasingly radicalised Arab and Islamic world, Israel will end up protected by the world's only superpower. This is not a perfect outcome from the Lobby's point of view, but it is obviously preferable to Washington distancing itself, or using its leverage to force Israel to make peace with the Palestinians.

Can the Lobby's power be curtailed? One.would like to think so, given the Iraq debacle, the obvious need to rebuild America's image in the Arab and Islamic world, and the recent revelations about AIPAC officials passing U.S. government secrets to Israel. One might also think that Arafat's death and the election of the more moderate Mahmoud Abbas would cause Washington to press vigorously and even-handedly for a peace agreement. In short, there are ample grounds for leaders to distance themselves from the Lobby and adopt a Middle East policy more consistent with broader U.S. interests. In particular, using American power to achieve a just peace between Israel and the Palestinians would help advance the cause of democracy in the region.

But that is not going to happen—not soon anyway. AIPAC and its allies (including Christian Zionists) have no serious opponents in the lobbying world. They know it has become more difficult to make Israel's case today, and they are responding by taking on staff and expanding their activities. Besides, American politicians remain acutely sensitive to campaign contributions and other forms of political pressure, and major media outlets are likely to remain sympathetic to Israel no matter what it does.

The Lobby's influence causes trouble on several fronts. It increases the terrorist danger that all states face—including America's European allies. It has made it impossible to end the Israeli—Palestinian conflict, a situation that gives extremists a powerful recruiting tool, increases the pool of potential terrorists and sympathisers, and contributes to Islamic radicalism in Europe and Asia.

Equally worrying, the Lobby's campaign for regime change in Iran and Syria could lead the U.S. to attack those countries, with potentially disastrous effects. We don't need another Iraq. At a minimum, the Lobby's hostility towards Syria and Iran makes it almost impossible for Washington to enlist them in the struggle against al-Qaida and the Iraqi insurgency, where their help is badly needed.

There is a moral dimension here as well. Thanks to the Lobby, the United States has become the de facto enabler of Israeli expansion in the Occupied Territories, making it complicit in the crimes perpetrated against the Palestinians. This situation undercuts Washington's efforts to promote democracy abroad and makes it look hypocritical when it presses other states to respect human rights. U.S. efforts to limit nuclear proliferation appear equally hypocritical given its willingness to accept Israel's nuclear arsenal, which only encourages Iran and others to seek a similar capability.

Besides, the Lobby's campaign to quash debate about Israel is unhealthy for democracy. Silencing sceptics by organising blacklists and boycotts—or by suggesting that critics are anti-semites—violates the principle of open debate on which democracy depends. The inability of Congress to conduct a genuine debate on these important issues paralyses the entire process of democratic deliberation. Israel's backers should be free to make their case and to challenge those who disagree with them, but efforts to stifle debate by intimidation must be roundly condemned.

Finally, the Lobby's influence has been bad for Israel. Its ability to persuade Washington to support an expansionist agenda has discouraged Israel from seizing opportunities—including a peace treaty with Syria and a prompt and full implementation of the Oslo Accords—that wquld have saved Israeli lives and shrunk the ranks of Palestinian extremists. Denying the Palestinians their legitimate political rights certainly has not made Israel more secure, and the long campaign to kill or marginalise a generation of Palestinian leaders has empowered extremist groups like Hamas, and reduced the number of Palestinian leaders who would be willing to accept a fair settlement and able to make it work. Israel itself would probably be better off if the Lobby were less powerful and U.S. policy more even-handed.

There is a ray of hope, however. Although the Lobby remains a powerful force, the adverse effects of its influence are increasingly difficult to hide. Powerful states can maintain flawed policies for quite some time, but reality cannot be ignored for ever. What is needed is a candid discussion of the Lobby's influence and a more open debate about U.S. interests in this vital region. Israel's well-being is one of those interests, but its continued occupation of the West Bank and its broader regional agenda are not. Open debate will expose the limits of the strategic and moral case for one-sided U.S. support and could move the U.S. to a position more consistent with its own national interest, with the interests of the other states in the region, and with Israel's long-term interests as well.

❧ PART SIX ❧

Bureaucratic Politics and Organizational Culture

During the 1970s the role of bureaucracy and organizational process was brought squarely into the study of American foreign policy. The basic insight is straightforward: Foreign-policy officials sit atop huge bureaucracies, and the organizational politics and processes that produce decisions often color those decisions. The study of policy, in other words, cannot be separated from the process of creating it. A huge literature has emerged that extends and critiques the claims of this tradition.

The seminal contribution to this approach is Graham T. Allison's study of the Cuban missile crisis. Most studies of foreign policy, Allison argues, are based on rational models of decision making. Scholars attempt to understand policy in terms of the purposive actions of government; explanation involves reconstructing the rationality of the decision. Alongside this model, Allison places two additional models: bureaucratic politics and organizational process. These models highlight the bureaucratic operations within the "black box" of government. In using these models to reconstruct decision making during the Cuban missile crisis, Allison argues that the additional models help reveal decisions that are less explicable in terms of the rational model.

Stephen Krasner presents an important critique of the literature on bureaucratic politics, questioning the argument that the president is simply a victim of the huge organizations he commands. When the issues are sufficiently important, Krasner argues, top officials can overcome the vagaries of parochial bureaucratic interests and politics. Determining when the president cares enough about a particular policy to act and has the capacity to act as commander and when he lets bureaucratic politics and culture shape policy is an important task.

The essay by Michael Mazarr explores the George W. Bush administration's decision to invade Iraq as a case study of the politics of agenda setting within the executive branch. This framework of explanation focuses on the activities of policy communities and activists who operate—often behind the scenes—both within the government and outside to push specific policy agendas. The influence that these policy communities wield is manifest in their framing of the issues and in the choices that government leaders must confront. Mazarr argues that beginning in the 1990s an anti-Saddam activist group was urging the United States government to take action, waiting for the opportunity to bring their policy agenda to a crisis in when the president must act and is looking for options. The post-9/11 crisis in American foreign policy was such a moment. The explanation that Mazarr brings to the Bush decision on Iraq emphasizes "windows of opportunities" and "focusing events" that drive policy choice.

ᴄᴢ̄⁀ᴘ

Conceptual Models and the Cuban Missile Crisis

Graham T. Allison

The Cuban missile crisis is a seminal event. For thirteen days of October 1962 there was a higher probability that more human lives would end suddenly than ever before in history. Had the worst occurred, the death of 100 million Americans, over 100 million Russians, and millions of Europeans as well would make previous natural calamities and inhumanities appear insignificant. Given the probability of disaster—which President Kennedy estimated as "between 1 out of 3 and even"—our escape seems awesome.[1] This event symbolizes a central if only partially thinkable fact about our existence. That such consequences could follow from the choices and actions of national governments obliges students of government as well as participants in governance to think hard about these problems.

Improved understanding of this crisis depends in part on more information and more probing analyses of available evidence. To contribute to these efforts is part of the purpose of this study. But here the missile crisis serves primarily as grist for a more general investigation. This study proceeds from the premise that marked improvement in our understanding of such events depends critically on more self-consciousness about what observers bring to the analysis. What each analyst sees and judges to be important is a function not only of the evidence about what happened but also of the "conceptual lenses" through which he looks at the evidence. The principal purpose of this essay is to explore some of the fundamental assumptions and categories employed by analysts in thinking about problems of governmental behavior, especially in foreign and military affairs.

The general argument can be summarized in three propositions:

1. Analysts think about problems of foreign and military policy in terms of largely implicit conceptual models that have significant consequences for the content of their thought.[2]

Though the present product of foreign policy analysis is neither systematic nor powerful, if one carefully examines explanations produced by analysts, a number of fundamental similarities emerge. Explanations produced by particular analysts display quite regular, predictable features. This predictability suggests a substructure. These regularities reflect an analyst's assumptions about the character of puzzles, the categories in which problems should be considered, the types of evidence that are relevant, and the determinants of occurrences. The first proposition is that clusters of such related assumptions constitute basic frames of reference or conceptual models in terms of which analysts both ask and answer the question: What happened? Why did the event happen? What will happen?[3] Such assumptions are

Graham T. Allison, "Conceptual Models and the Cuban Missile Crisis," *American Political Science Review*, 63, No. 3 (September 1969): 689–718. Reprinted with permission of Cambridge University Press.

central to the activities of explanation and prediction, for in attempting to explain a particular event, the analyst cannot simply describe the full state of the world leading up to that event. The logic of explanation requires that he single out the relevant, important determinants of the occurrence.[4] Moreover, as the logic of prediction underscores, the analyst must summarize the various determinants as they bear on the event in question. Conceptual models both fix the mesh of the nets that the analyst drags through the material in order to explain a particular action or decision and direct him to cast his net in select ponds, at certain depths, in order to catch the fish he is after.

2. Most analysts explain (and predict) the behavior of national governments in terms of various forms of one basic conceptual model, here entitled the rational policy model (model I).[5]

In terms of this conceptual model, analysts attempt to understand happenings as the more or less purposive acts of unified national governments. For these analysts the point of an explanation is to show how the nation or government could have chosen the action in question, given the strategic problem that it faced. For example in confronting the problem posed by the Soviet installation of missiles in Cuba, rational-policy-model analysts attempt to show how this was a reasonable act from the point of view of the Soviet Union, given Soviet strategic objectives.

3. Two "alternative" conceptual models, here labeled an organizational-process model (model II) and a bureaucratic-politics model (model III) provide a base for improved explanation and prediction.

Although the standard frame of reference has proved useful for many purposes, there is powerful evidence that it must be supplemented, if not supplanted, by frames of reference which focus upon the large organizations and political actors involved in the policy process. Model I's implication that important events have important causes, i.e., that monoliths perform large actions for big reasons, must be balanced by an appreciation of the facts (a) that monoliths are black boxes covering various gears and levers in a highly differentiated decision-making structure, and (b) that large acts are the consequences of innumerable and often conflicting smaller actions by individuals at various levels of bureaucratic organizations in the service of a variety of only partially compatible conceptions of national goals, organizational goals, and political objectives. Recent developments in the field of organization theory provide the foundation for the second model. According to this organizational-process model, what model I categorizes as "acts" and "choices" are instead *outputs* of large organizations functioning according to certain regular patterns of behavior. Faced with the problem of Soviet missiles in Cuba, a model II analyst identifies the relevant organizations and displays the patterns of organizational behavior from which this action emerged. The third model focuses on the internal politics of a government. Happenings in foreign affairs are understood, according to the bureaucratic-politics model, neither as choices nor as outputs. Instead, what happens is categorized as *outcomes* of various overlapping bargaining games among players arranged hierarchically in the national government. In confronting the problem posed by Soviet missiles in Cuba, a model III analyst displays the perceptions, motivations, positions, power, and maneuvers of principal players from which the outcome emerged.[6]

A central metaphor illuminates differences among these models. Foreign policy has often been compared to moves, sequences of moves, and games of chess. If one were limited to observations on a screen upon which moves in the chess game were projected without information as to how the pieces came to be moved, he would assume—as model I does—that an individual chess player was moving the pieces with reference to plans and maneuvers toward the goal of winning the game. But a pattern of moves can be imagined that would lead the serious observer, after watching several games, to consider the hypothesis that the chess player was not a single individual but rather a loose alliance of semi-independent organizations, each of which moved its set of pieces according to standard operating procedures. For example, movement of separate sets of pieces might proceed in turn, each according to a routine, the king's rook, bishop, and their pawns repeatedly attacking the opponent according to a fixed plan. Furthermore, it is conceivable that the pattern of play would suggest to an observer that a number of distinct players, with distinct objectives but shared power over the pieces, were determining the moves as the resultant of collegial bargaining. For example, the black rook's move might contribute to the loss of a black knight with no comparable gain for the black team, but with the black rook becoming the principal guardian of the "palace" on that side of the board.

The space available does not permit full development and support of such a general argument.[7] Rather, the sections that follow simply sketch each conceptual model, articulate it as an analytic paradigm, and apply it to produce an explanation. But each model is applied to the same event: the U.S. blockade of Cuba during the missile crisis. These "alternative explanations" of the same happening illustrate differences among the models—*at work.*[8] A crisis decision by a small group of men in the context of ultimate threat, this is a case of the rational policy model par excellence. The dimensions and factors that models II and III uncover in this case are therefore particularly suggestive. The concluding section of this paper suggests how the three models may be related and how they can be extended to generate predictions.

MODEL I: RATIONAL POLICY
Rational-Policy Model Illustrated

Where is the pinch of the puzzle raised by the *New York Times* over Soviet deployment of an antiballistic missile system?[9] The question, as the *Times* states it, concerns the Soviet Union's objective in allocating such large sums of money for this weapon system while at the same time seeming to pursue a policy of increasing détente. In former President Johnson's words, "the paradox is that this [Soviet deployment of an antiballistic missile system] should be happening at a time when there is abundant evidence that our mutual antagonism is beginning to ease."[10] This question troubles people primarily because Soviet antiballistic missile deployment, and evidence of Soviet actions towards détente, when juxtaposed in our implicit model, produce a question. With reference to what objective could the Soviet government have rationally chosen the simultaneous pursuit of these two courses of actions? This question arises only when the analyst attempts to structure events as purposive choices of consistent actors.

How do analysts attempt to explain the Soviet emplacement of missiles in Cuba? The most widely cited explanation of this occurrence has been produced by two RAND sovietologists, Arnold Horelick and Myron Rush.[11] They conclude that "the introduction of strategic missiles into Cuba was motivated chiefly by the Soviet leaders' desire to overcome . . . the existing large margin of U.S. strategic superiority."[12] How do they reach this conclusion? In Sherlock Holmes' style, they seize several salient characteristics of this action and use these features as criteria against which to test alternative hypotheses about Soviet objectives. For example, the size of the Soviet deployment and the simultaneous emplacement of more expensive, more visible intermediate-range missiles as well as medium-range missiles, it is argued, exclude an explanation of the action in terms of Cuban defense—since that objective could have been secured with a much smaller number of medium-range missiles alone. Their explanation presents an argument for one objective that permits interpretation of the details of Soviet behavior as a value-maximizing choice.

How do analysts account for the coming of the First World War? According to Hans Morgenthau, "the first World War had its origin exclusively in the fear of a disturbance of the European balance of power."[13] In the period preceding World War I, the Triple Alliance precariously balanced the Triple Entente. If either power combination could gain a decisive advantage in the Balkans, it would achieve a decisive advantage in the balance of power. "It was this fear," Morgenthau asserts, "that motivated Austria in July 1914 to settle its accounts with Serbia once and for all, and that induced Germany to support Austria unconditionally. It was the same fear that brought Russia to the support of Serbia, and France to the support of Russia."[14] How is Morgenthau able to resolve this problem so confidently? By imposing on the data a "rational outline."[15] The value of this method, according to Morgenthau, is that "it provides for rational discipline in action and creates astounding continuity in foreign policy which makes American, British, or Russian foreign policy appear as an intelligent, rational continuum . . . regardless of the different motives, preferences, and intellectual and moral qualities of successive statesmen."[16]

Stanley Hoffmann's essay "Restraints and Choices in American Foreign Policy" concentrates, characteristically, on "deep forces": the international system, ideology, and national character—which constitute restraints, limits, and blinders.[17] Only secondarily does he consider decisions. But when explaining particular occurrences, though emphasizing relevant constraints, he focuses on the choices of nations. American behavior in Southeast Asia is explained as a reasonable choice of "downgrading this particular alliance (SEATO) in favor of direct U.S. involvement," given the constraint: "one is bound by one's commitments; one is committed by one's mistakes."[18] More frequently Hoffmann uncovers confusion or contradiction in the nation's choice. For example, U.S. policy towards underdeveloped countries is explained as "schizophrenic."[19] The method employed by Hoffman in producing these explanations as rational (or irrational) decisions, he terms "imaginative reconstruction."[20]

Deterrence is the cardinal problem of the contemporary strategic literature. Thomas Schelling's *Strategy of Conflict* formulates a number of propositions focused upon the dynamics of deterrence in the nuclear age. One of the major propositions concerns the stability of the balance of terror: in a situation of mutual deterrence the probability of nuclear war is reduced not by the "balance" (the sheer equality of the situation) but rather by the *stability* of the balance, i.e., the fact that neither opponent in striking first can destroy the other's ability to strike back.[21] How does Schelling support this proposition? Confidence in the contention stems not from an inductive canvass of a large number of previous cases, but rather from two calculations. In a situation of "balance" but vulnerability, there are values for which a rational opponent could choose to strike first, e.g., to destroy enemy capabilities to retaliate. In a "stable balance," where no matter who strikes first, each has an assured capability to retaliate with unacceptable damage, no rational agent could choose such a course of action (since that choice is effectively equivalent to choosing mutual homicide). Whereas most contemporary strategic thinking is driven *implicitly* by the motor upon which this calculation depends, Schelling explicitly recognizes that strategic theory does assume a model. The foundation of a theory of strategy is, he asserts: "the assumption of rational behavior—not just of intelligent behavior, but of behavior motivated by conscious calculation of advantages, calculation that in turn is based on an explicit and internally consistent value system."[22]

What is striking about these examples from the literature of foreign policy and international relations are the similarities among analysts of various styles when they are called upon to produce explanations. Each assumes that what must be explained is an action, i.e., the realization of some purpose or intention. Each assumes that the actor is the national government. Each assumes that the action is chosen as a calculated response to a strategic problem. For each, explanation consists of showing what goal the government was pursuing in committing the act and how this action was a reasonable choice, given the nation's objectives. This set of assumptions characterizes the rational-policy model. The assertion that model I is the standard frame of reference implies no denial of highly visible differences among the interests of sovietologists, diplomatic historians, international relations theorists, and strategists. Indeed, in most respects differences among the work of Hans Morgenthau, Stanley Hoffmann, and Thomas Schelling could not be more pointed. Appreciation of the extent to which each relies predominantly on model I, however, reveals basic similarities among Morgenthau's method of "rational reenactment," Hoffmann's "imaginative reconstruction," and Schelling's "vicarious problem solving;" family resemblances among Morgenthau's "rational statesman," Hoffmann's "roulette player," and Schelling's "game theorist."[23]

Most contemporary analysts (as well as laymen) proceed predominantly—albeit most often implicitly—in terms of this model when attempting to explain happenings in foreign affairs. Indeed, that occurrences in foreign affairs are the *acts of nations* seems so fundamental to thinking about such problems that this underlying model has rarely been recognized: to explain an occurrence in foreign policy simply means to show how the government could have rationally chosen that action.[24] These brief examples illustrate five uses of the model. To prove that most analysts think largely in terms of the rational policy model is not possible. In this limited space it is not even possible to illustrate the range of employment of the framework. Rather my purpose is to convey to the reader a grasp of the model and a challenge: let the reader examine the literature with which he is most familiar and make his judgment.

The general characterization can be sharpened by articulating the rational-policy model as an "analytic paradigm" in the technical sense developed by Robert K. Merton for sociological analyses.[25] Systematic statement of basic assumptions, concepts, and propositions employed by model I analysts highlights the distinctive thrust of this style of analysis. To articulate a largely implicit framework is of necessity to caricature. But caricature can be instructive.

Rational Policy Paradigm

I. *Basic Unit of Analysis: Policy as National Choice*

Happenings in foreign affairs are conceived as actions chosen by the nation or national government.[26] Governments select the action that will maximize strategic goals and objectives. These "solutions" to strategic problems are the fundamental categories in terms of which the analyst perceives what is to be explained.

II. *Organizing Concepts*

A. NATIONAL ACTOR   The nation or government, conceived as a rational unitary decision maker, is the agent. This actor has one set of specified goals (the equivalent of a consistent utility function), one set of perceived options, and a single estimate of the consequences that follow from each alternative.

B. The Problem   Action is chosen in response to the strategic problem which the nation faces. Threats and opportunities arising in the "international strategic marketplace" move the nation to act.

C. Static Selection   The sum of activity of representatives of the government relevant to a problem constitutes what the nation has chosen as its "solution." Thus the action is conceived as a steady-state choice among alternative outcomes (rather than, for example, a large number of partial choices in a dynamic stream).

D. Action as Rational Choice   The components include:

1. Goals and Objectives   National security and national interests are the principal categories in which strategic goals are conceived. Nations seek security and a range of further objectives. (Analysts rarely translate strategic goals and objectives into an explicit utility function; nevertheless, analysts do focus on major goals and objectives and trade off side effects in an intuitive fashion.)

2. Options   Various courses of action relevant to a strategic problem provide the spectrum of options.

3. Consequences   Enactment of each alternative course of action will produce a series of consequences. The relevant consequences constitute benefits and costs in terms of strategic goals and objectives.

4. Choice   Rational choice is value-maximizing. The rational agent selects the alternative whose consequences rank highest in terms of his goals and objectives.

III. Dominant Inference Pattern

This paradigm leads analysts to rely on the following pattern of inference: if a nation performed a particular action, that nation must have had ends towards which the action constituted an optimal means. The rational policy model's explanatory power stems from this inference pattern. Puzzlement is relieved by revealing the purposive pattern within which the occurrence can be located as a value-maximizing means.

IV. General Propositions

The disgrace of political science is the infrequency with which propositions of any generality are formulated and tested. "Paradigmatic analysis" argues for explicitness about the terms in which analysis proceeds and seriousness about the logic of explanation. Simply to illustrate the kind of propositions on which analysts who employ this model rely, the formulation includes several.

The basic assumption of value-maximizing behavior produces propositions central to most explanations. The general principle can be formulated as follows: the likelihood of any particular action results from a combination of the nation's (1) relevant values and objectives, (2) perceived alternative courses of action, (3) estimates of various sets of consequences (which will follow from each alternative), and (4) net valuation of each set of consequences. This yields two propositions.

a. An increase in the cost of an alternative, i.e., a reduction in the value of the set of consequences which will follow from that action, or a reduction in the probability of attaining fixed consequences, reduces the likelihood of that alternative being chosen.

b. A decrease in the costs of an alternative, i.e., an increase in the value of the set of consequences which will follow from that alternative, or an increase in the probability of attaining fixed consequences, increases the likelihood of that action being chosen.[27]

V. *Specific Propositions*

A. Deterrence   The likelihood of any particular attack results from the factors specified in the general proposition. Combined with factual assertions, this general proposition yields the propositions of the subtheory of deterrence.

1. A stable nuclear balance reduces the likelihood of nuclear attack. This proposition is derived from the general proposition plus the asserted fact that a second-strike capability affects the potential attacker's calculations by increasing the likelihood and the costs of one particular set of consequences which might follow from attack—namely, retaliation.
2. A stable nuclear balance increases the probability of limited war. This proposition is derived from the general proposition plus the asserted fact that though increasing the costs of a nuclear exchange, a stable nuclear balance nevertheless produces a more significant reduction in the probability that such consequences would be chosen in response to a limited war. Thus this set of consequences weighs less heavily in the calculus.

B. Soviet Force Posture   The Soviet Union chooses its force posture (i.e., its weapons and their deployment) as a value-maximizing means of implementing Soviet strategic objectives and military doctrine. A proposition of this sort underlies Secretary of Defense Laird's inference from the fact of two hundred SS-9s (large intercontinental missiles) to the assertion that "the Soviets are going for a first-strike capability, and there's no question about it."[28]

Variants of the Rational-Policy Model

This paradigm exhibits the characteristics of the most refined version of the rational model. The modern literature of strategy employs a model of this sort. Problems and pressures in the "international strategic marketplace" yield probabilities of occurrence. The international actor, which could be any national actor, is simply a value-maximizing mechanism for getting from the strategic problem to the logical solution. But the explanations and predictions produced by most analysts of foreign affairs depend primarily on variants of this "pure" model. The point of each is the same: to place the action within a value-maximizing framework, given certain constraints. Nevertheless, it may be helpful to identify several variants, each of which might be exhibited similarly as a paradigm. The first focuses upon the national actor and his choice in a particular situation, leading analysts to further constrain the goals, alternatives, and consequences considered. Thus, (1) national propensities or personality traits reflected in an "operational code," (2) concern with certain objectives, or (3) special principles of action narrow the "goals" or "alternatives" or "consequences" of the paradigm. For example, the Soviet deployment of ABMs is sometimes explained by reference to the Soviet's "defense-mindedness." Or a particular Soviet action is explained as an instance of a special rule of action in the Bolshevik operational code.[29] A second related cluster of variants focuses on the individual leader or leadership group as the actor whose preference function is maximized and whose personal (or group) characteristics are allowed to modify the alternatives, consequences, and rules of choice. Explanations of the U.S. involvement in Vietnam as a natural consequence of the Kennedy-Johnson administration's axioms of foreign policy rely on this variant. A third more complex variant of the basic model recognizes the existence of several actors within a government, for example, hawks and doves or military and civilians, but attempts to explain (or predict) an occurrence by reference to the objectives of the victorious actor. Thus, for example, some revisionist histories of the cold war recognize the forces of light and the forces of darkness within the U.S. government but explain American actions as a result of goals and perceptions of the victorious forces of darkness.

Each of these forms of the basic paradigm constitutes a formalization of what analysts typically rely upon implicitly. In the transition from implicit conceptual model to explicit paradigm much of the richness of the best employments of this model has been lost. But the purpose in raising loose, implicit conceptual models to an explicit level is to reveal the basic logic of analysts' activity. Perhaps some of the remaining artificiality that surrounds the statement of the paradigm can be erased by noting a number of the standard additions and modifications employed by analysts who proceed *predominantly* within the rational policy model. First, in the course of a document analysts shift from one variant of the basic model to another, occasionally appropriating in an ad hoc fashion aspects of a situation which are logically incompatible with the basic model. Second, in the course of explaining a number of occurrences, analysts sometimes pause over a particular event about which they have a great deal of information and unfold it in such detail that an impression of randomness is created. Third, having employed other assumptions and categories in deriving an explanation or prediction, analysts will present their product in a neat, convincing rational policy model package. (This accommodation is a favorite of members of the intelligence community whose association with the details of a process is considerable but who feel that by putting an occurrence in a larger rational framework, it will be more comprehensible to their audience.) Fourth, in attempting to offer an explanation—particularly in cases where a prediction derived from the basic model has failed—the notion of a "mistake" is invoked. Thus, the failure in the prediction of a "missile gap" is written off as a Soviet mistake in not taking advantage of their opportunity. Both these and other modifications permit model I analysts considerably more variety than the paradigm might suggest. But such accommodations are essentially appendages to the basic logic of these analyses.

The U.S. Blockade of Cuba: A First Cut[30]

The U.S. response to the Soviet Union's emplacement of missiles in Cuba must be understood in strategic terms as simple value-maximizing escalation. American nuclear superiority could be counted on to paralyze Soviet nuclear power; Soviet transgression of the nuclear threshold in response to an American use of lower levels of violence would be wildly irrational, since it would mean virtual destruction of the Soviet Communist system and Russian nation. American local superiority was overwhelming: it could be initiated at a low level while threatening with high credibility an ascending sequence of steps short of the nuclear threshold. All that was required was for the United States to bring to bear its strategic and local superiority in such a way that American determination to see the missiles removed would be demonstrated, while at the same time allowing Moscow time and room to retreat without humiliation. The naval blockade—euphemistically named a quarantine in order to circumvent the niceties of international law—did just that.

The U.S. government's selection of the blockade followed this logic. Apprised of the presence of Soviet missiles in Cuba, the president assembled an executive committee (ExCom) of the National Security Council and directed them to "set aside all other tasks to make a prompt and intense survey of the dangers and all possible courses of action."[31] This group functioned as "fifteen individuals on our own, representing the President and not different departments."[32] As one of the participants recalls, "The remarkable aspect of those meetings was a sense of complete equality."[33] Most of the time during the week that followed was spent canvassing all the possible tracks and weighing the arguments for and against each. Six major categories of action were considered.

1. Do Nothing   U.S. vulnerability to Soviet missiles was no new thing. Since the U.S. already lived under the gun of missiles based in Russia, a Soviet capability to strike from Cuba too made little real difference. The real danger stemmed from the possibility of U.S. overreaction. The U.S. should announce the Soviet action in a calm, casual manner, thereby deflating whatever political capital Khrushchev hoped to make of the missiles.

This argument fails on two counts. First, it grossly underestimates the military importance of the Soviet move. Not only would the Soviet Union's missile capability be doubled and the U.S. early warning system outflanked, the Soviet Union would have an opportunity to reverse the strategic balance by further installations, and indeed, in the longer run, to invest in cheaper, shorter-range rather than more expensive longer-range missiles. Second, the political importance of this move was undeniable. The Soviet Union's act challenged the American president's most solemn warning. If the U.S. failed to respond, no American commitment would be credible.

2. Diplomatic Pressures   Several forms were considered: an appeal to the U.N. or OAS for an inspection team, a secret approach to Khrushchev, and a direct approach to Khrushchev, perhaps at a summit meeting. The United States would demand that the missiles be removed, but the final settlement might include neutralization of Cuba, U.S. withdrawal from the Guantanamo base, and withdrawal of U.S. Jupiter missiles from Turkey or Italy.

Each form of the diplomatic approach had its own drawbacks. To arraign the Soviet Union before the U.N. Security Council held little promise, since the Russians could veto any proposed action. While the diplomats argued, the missiles would become operational. To send a secret emissary to Khrushchev demanding that the missiles be withdrawn would be to pose untenable alternatives. On the one hand, this would invite Khrushchev to seize the diplomatic initiative, perhaps committing himself to strategic retaliation in response to an attack on Cuba. On the other hand, this would tender an ultimatum that no great power could accept. To confront Khrushchev at a summit would guarantee demands for U.S. concessions, and the analogy between U.S. missiles in Turkey and Russian missiles in Cuba could not be erased.

But why not trade U.S. Jupiters in Turkey and Italy, which the president had previously ordered withdrawn, for the missiles in Cuba? The U.S. had chosen to withdraw these missiles in order to replace them with superior, less vulnerable Mediterranean Polaris submarines. But the middle of the crisis was no time for concessions. The offer of such a deal might suggest to the Soviets that the West would yield and thus tempt them to demand more. It would certainly confirm European suspicions about American willingness to sacrifice European interests when the chips were down. Finally, the basic issue should be kept clear. As the president stated in reply to Bertrand Russell, "I think your attention might well be directed to the burglars rather than to those who have caught the burglars."[34]

3. A Secret Approach to Castro   The crisis provided an opportunity to separate Cuba and Soviet Communism by offering Castro the alternatives, "split or fall." But Soviet troops transported, constructed, guarded, and controlled the missiles. Their removal would thus depend on a Soviet decision.

4. Invasion   The United States could take this occasion not only to remove the missiles but also to rid itself of Castro. A navy exercise had long been scheduled in which Marines, ferried from Florida in naval vessels, would liberate the imaginary island of Vieques.[35] Why not simply shift the point of disembarkment? (The Pentagon's foresight in planning this operation would be an appropriate antidote to the CIA's Bay of Pigs!)

Preparations were made for an invasion, but as a last resort. American troops would be forced to confront twenty thousand Soviets in the first cold war case of direct contact between the troops of the super powers. Such brinksmanship courted nuclear disaster, practically guaranteeing an equivalent Soviet move against Berlin.

5. Surgical Air Strike   The missile sites should be removed by a clean, swift conventional attack. This was the effective counteraction which the attempted deception deserved. A surgical strike would remove the missiles and thus eliminate both the danger that the missiles might become operational and the fear that the Soviets would discover the American discovery and act first.

The initial attractiveness of this alternative was dulled by several difficulties. First, could the strike really be "surgical"? The air force could not guarantee destruction of all the missiles.[36] Some might be fired during the attack; some might not have been identified. In order to assure destruction of Soviet and Cuban means of retaliating, what was required was not a surgical but rather a massive attack—of at least five hundred sorties. Second, a surprise air attack would of course kill Russians at the missile sites. Pressures on the Soviet Union to retaliate would be so strong that an attack on Berlin or Turkey was highly probable. Third, the key problem with this program was that of advance warning. Could the President of the United States, with his memory of Pearl Harbor and his vision of future U.S. responsibility, order a "Pearl Harbor in reverse"? For 175 years unannounced Sunday morning attacks had been an anathema to our tradition.[37]

6. Blockade   Indirect military action in the form of a blockade became more attractive as the ExCom dissected the other alternatives. An embargo on military shipments to Cuba enforced by a naval blockade was not without flaws, however. Could the U.S. blockade Cuba without inviting Soviet reprisal in Berlin? The likely solution to joint blockades would be the lifting of both blockades, restoring the new status quo, and allowing the Soviets additional time to complete the missiles. Second, the possible consequences of the blockade resembled the drawbacks which disqualified the air strike. If Soviet ships did not stop, the United States would be forced to fire the first shot, inviting retaliation. Third, a blockade would deny the traditional freedom of the seas demanded by several of our close allies and might be held illegal, in violation of the U.N. charter and international law, unless the United States could obtain a two-thirds vote in the OAS. Finally, how could a blockade be related to the problem, namely, some seventy-five missiles on the island of Cuba, approaching operational readiness daily? A blockade offered the Soviets a spectrum of delaying tactics with which to buy time to complete the missile installations. Was a fait accompli not required?

In spite of these enormous difficulties the blockade had comparative advantages: (1) It was a middle course between inaction and attack, aggressive enough to communicate firmness of intention but nevertheless not so precipitous as a strike. (2) It placed on Khrushchev the burden of choice concerning the next step. He could avoid a direct military clash by keeping his ships away. His was the last clear chance. (3) No possible military confrontation could be more acceptable to the U.S. than a naval engagement in the Caribbean. (4) This move permitted the U.S., by flexing its conventional muscle, to exploit the threat of subsequent nonnuclear steps in each of which the U.S. would have significant superiority.

Particular arguments about advantages and disadvantages were powerful. The explanation of the American choice of the blockade lies in a more general principle, however. As President Kennedy stated in drawing the moral of the crisis:

> Above all, while defending our own vital interests, nuclear powers must avert those confrontations which bring an adversary to a choice of either a humiliating retreat or a nuclear war. To adopt that kind of course in the nuclear age would be evidence only of the bankruptcy of our policy—of a collective death wish for the world.[38]

The blockade was the United States' only real option.

MODEL II: ORGANIZATIONAL PROCESS

For some purposes governmental behavior can be usefully summarized as action chosen by a unitary rational decision maker: centrally controlled, completely informed, and value-maximizing. But this simplification must not be allowed to conceal the fact that a "government" consists of a conglomerate of semifeudal loosely allied organizations, each with a substantial life of its own. Government leaders do sit formally and to some extent in fact on top of this conglomerate. But governments perceive problems through organizational sensors. Governments define alternatives and estimate consequences as organizations process information. Governments act as these organizations enact routines. Government behavior can therefore be understood according to a second conceptual model, less as deliberate choices of leaders and more as *outputs* of large organizations functioning according to standard patterns of behavior.

To be responsive to a broad spectrum of problems, governments consist of large organizations among which primary responsibility for particular areas is divided. Each organization attends to a special set of problems and acts in quasi independence on these problems. But few important problems fall exclusively within the domain of a single organization. Thus government behavior relevant to any important problem reflects the independent output of several organizations, partially coordinated by government leaders. Government leaders can substantially disturb but not substantially control the behavior of these organizations.

To perform complex routines the behavior of large numbers of individuals must be coordinated. Coordination requires standard operating procedures: rules according to which things are done. Assured capability for reliable performance of action that depends upon the behavior of hundreds of persons requires established "programs." Indeed, if the eleven members of a football team are to perform adequately on any particular down, each player must not "do what he thinks needs to be done" or "do what the quarterback tells him to do." Rather each player must perform the maneuvers specified by a previously established play which the quarterback has simply called in this situation.

At any given time a government consists of *existing* organizations, each with a *fixed* set of standard operating procedures and programs. The behavior of these organizations—and consequently of the government—relevant to an issue in any particular instance is therefore determined primarily by routines established in these organizations prior to that instance. But organizations do change. Learning occurs gradually, over time. Dramatic organizational change occurs in response to major crises. Both learning and change are influenced by existing organizational capabilities.

Borrowed from studies of organizations, these loosely formulated propositions amount simply to *tendencies*. Each must be hedged by modifiers like "other things being equal" and "under certain conditions." In particular instances tendencies hold—more or less. In specific situations the relevant question is: more or less? But this is as it should be. For on the one hand, "organizations" are no more homogeneous a class than "solids." When scientists tried to generalize about "solids," they achieved similar results. Solids tend to expand when heated, but some do and some don't. More adequate categorization of the various elements now lumped under the rubric *organizations* is thus required. On the other hand, the behavior of particular organizations seems considerably more complex than the behavior of solids. Additional information about a particular organization is required for further specification of the tendency statements. In spite of these two caveats, the characterization of government action as organizational output differs distinctly from model I. Attempts to understand problems of foreign affairs in terms of this frame of reference should produce quite different explanations.[39]

Organizational Process Paradigm[40]

I.   *Basic Unit of Analysis: Policy as Organizational Output*

The happenings of international politics are in three critical senses outputs of organizational processes. First, the actual occurrences are organizational outputs. For example, Chinese entry into the Korean War—that is, the fact that Chinese soldiers were firing at U.N. soldiers south of the Yalu in 1950—is an organizational action: the action of men who are soldiers in platoons which are in companies, which in turn are in armies, responding as privates to lieutenants who are responsible to captains and so on to the commander, moving into Korea, advancing against enemy troops, and firing according to fixed routines of the Chinese army. Government leaders' decisions trigger organizational routines. Government leaders can trim the edges of this output and exercise some choice in combining outputs. But the mass of behavior is determined by previously established procedures. Second, existing organizational routines for employing present physical capabilities constitute the effective options open to government leaders confronted with any problem. Only the existence of men, equipped and trained as armies and capable of being transported to North Korea, made entry into the Korean War a live option for the Chinese leaders. The fact that fixed programs (equipment, men, and routines which exist at the particular time) exhaust the range of buttons that leaders can push is not always perceived by these leaders. But in every case it is critical for an understanding of what is actually done. Third, organizational outputs structure the situation within the narrow constraints of which leaders must contribute their "decision" concerning an issue. Outputs raise the problem, provide the information, and make the initial moves that color the face of the issue that is turned to the leaders. As Theodore Sorensen has observed: "Presidents rarely, if ever, make decisions—particularly in foreign affairs—in the sense of writing their conclusions on a clean slate . . . The basic decisions, which confine their choices, have all too often been previously made."[41] If one understands the structure of the situation and the face of the issue—which are determined by the organizational outputs—the formal choice of the leaders is frequently anticlimactic.

II. *Organizing Concepts*

A. ORGANIZATIONAL ACTORS   The actor is not a monolithic nation or government but rather a constellation of loosely allied organizations on top of which government leaders sit. This constellation acts only as component organizations perform routines.[42]

B. FACTORED PROBLEMS AND FRACTIONATED POWER   Surveillance of the multiple facets of foreign affairs requires that problems be cut up and parceled out to various organizations. To avoid paralysis, primary power must accompany primary responsibility. But if organizations are permitted to do anything, a large part of what they do will be determined within the organization. Thus each organization perceives problems, processes information, and performs a range of actions in quasi independence (within broad guidelines of national policy). Factored problems and fractionated power are two edges of the same sword. Factoring permits more specialized attention to particular facets of problems than would be possible if government leaders tried to cope with these problems by themselves. But this additional attention must be paid for in the coin of discretion for *what* an organization attends to and *how* organizational responses are programmed.

C. PAROCHIAL PRIORITIES, PERCEPTIONS, AND ISSUES   Primary responsibility for a narrow set of problems encourages organizational parochialism. These tendencies are enhanced by a number of additional factors: (1) selective information available to the organization, (2) recruitment of personnel into the organization, (3) tenure of individuals in the organization, (4) small group pressures within the organization, and (5) distribution of rewards by the organization. Clients (e.g., interest groups), government allies (e.g., congressional committees), and extranational counterparts (e.g., the British Ministry of Defense for the Department of Defense, ISA, or the British Foreign Office for the Department of State, EUR) galvanize this parochialism. Thus organizations develop relatively stable propensities concerning operational priorities, perceptions, and issues.

D. ACTION AS ORGANIZATIONAL OUTPUT   The preeminent feature of organizational activity is its programmed character: the extent to which behavior in any particular case is an enactment of preestablished routines. In producing outputs the activity of each organization is characterized by:

1. GOALS: CONSTRAINTS, DEFINING ACCEPTABLE PERFORMANCE   The operational goals of an organization are seldom revealed by formal mandates. Rather each organization's operational goals emerge as a set of constraints defining acceptable performance. Central among these constraints is organizational health, defined usually in terms of bodies assigned and dollars appropriated. The set of constraints emerges from a mix of expectations and demands of other organizations in the government, statutory authority, demands from citizens and special interest groups, and bargaining within the organization. These constraints represent a quasi resolution of conflict—the constraints are relatively stable, so there is some resolution. But conflict among alternative goals is always latent; hence it is a quasi resolution. Typically the constraints are formulated as imperatives to avoid roughly specified discomforts and disasters.[43]

2. SEQUENTIAL ATTENTION TO GOALS   The existence of conflict among operational constraints is resolved by the device of sequential attention. As a problem arises, the subunits of the organization most concerned with that problem deal with it in terms of the constraints they take to be most important. When the next problem arises, another cluster of sub-units deals with it, focusing on a different set of constraints.

3. STANDARD OPERATING PROCEDURES Organizations perform their "higher" functions, such as attending to problem areas, monitoring information, and preparing relevant responses for likely contingencies, by doing "lower" tasks, for example, preparing bud-gets, producing reports, and developing hardware. Reliable performance of these tasks requires standard operating procedures (hereafter SOPs). Since procedures are "standard," they do not change quickly or easily. Without these standard procedures, it would not be possible to perform certain concerted tasks. But because of standard procedures, organizational behavior in particular instances often appears unduly formalized, slug-gish, or inappropriate.

4. PROGRAMS AND REPERTOIRES Organizations must be capable of performing actions in which the behavior of large numbers of individuals is carefully coordinated. Assured per-formance requires clusters of rehearsed SOPs for producing specific actions, e.g., fighting enemy units or answering an embassy's cable. Each cluster comprises a "program" (in the terms both of drama and computers) which the organization has available for dealing with a situation. The list of programs relevant to a type of activity, e.g., fighting, consti-tutes an organizational repertoire. The number of programs in a repertoire is always quite limited. When properly triggered, organizations execute programs; programs cannot be substantially changed in a particular situation. The more complex the action and the greater the number of individuals involved, the more important are programs and repertoires as determinants of organizational behavior.

5. UNCERTAINTY AVOIDANCE Organizations do not attempt to estimate the probability dis-tribution of future occurrences. Rather, organizations avoid uncertainty. By arranging a *negotiated environment,* organizations regularize the reactions of other actors with whom they have to deal. The primary environment, relations with other organizations that comprise the government, is stabilized by such arrangements as agreed budgetary splits, accepted areas of responsibility, and established conventional practices. The secondary environment, relations with the international world, is stabilized between allies by the establishment of contracts (alliances) and "club relations" (U.S. State and U.K. Foreign Office or U.S. Treasury and U.K. Treasury). Between enemies contracts and accepted conventional practices perform a similar function, for example the rules of the "precarious status quo" which President Kennedy referred to in the missile crisis. Where the international environment cannot be negotiated, organizations deal with remaining uncertainties by establishing a set of *standard scenarios* that constitute the contingencies for which they prepare. For example, the standard scenario for Tactical Air Command of the U.S. air force involves combat with enemy aircraft. Planes are designed and pilots trained to meet this problem. That these preparations are less relevant to more probable contingencies, e.g., provision of close-in ground support in limited wars like Vietnam, has had little impact on the scenario.

6. PROBLEM-DIRECTED SEARCH Where situations cannot be construed as standard, organiza-tions engage in search. The style of search and the solution are largely determined by existing routines. Organizational search for alternative courses of action is problem-oriented: it focuses on the atypical discomfort that must be avoided. It is simple-minded: the neighborhood of the symptom is searched first; then the neighborhood of the current alternative. Patterns of search reveal biases which in turn reflect such factors as specialized training or experience and patterns of communication.

7. ORGANIZATIONAL LEARNING AND CHANGE   The parameters of organizational behavior mostly persist. In response to nonstandard problems organizations search and routines evolve, assimilating new situations. Thus learning and change follow in large part from existing procedures. But marked changes in organizations do sometimes occur. Conditions in which dramatic changes are more likely include: (1) Periods of budgetary feast. Typically, organizations devour budgetary feasts by purchasing additional items on the existing shopping list. Nevertheless, if committed to change, leaders who control the budget can use extra funds to effect changes. (2) Periods of prolonged budgetary famine. Though a single year's famine typically results in few changes in organizational structure but a loss of effectiveness in performing some programs, prolonged famine forces major retrenchment. (3) Dramatic performance failures. Dramatic change occurs (mostly) in response to major disasters. Confronted with an undeniable failure of procedures and repertoires, authorities outside the organization demand change, existing personnel are less resistant to change, and critical members of the organization are replaced by individuals committed to change.

E. CENTRAL COORDINATION AND CONTROL   Action requires decentralization of responsibility and power. But problems lap over the jurisdictions of several organizations. Thus the necessity for decentralization runs headlong into the requirement for coordination. (Advocates of one horn or the other of this dilemma—responsive action entails decentralized power vs. coordinated action requires central control—account for a considerable part of the persistent demand for government reorganization.) Both the necessity for coordination and the centrality of foreign policy to national welfare guarantee the involvement of government leaders in the procedures of the organizations among which problems are divided and power shared. Each organization's propensities and routines can be disturbed by government leaders' intervention. Central direction and persistent control of organizational activity, however, is not possible. The relation among organizations and between organizations and the government leaders depends critically on a number of structural variables, including: (1) the nature of the job, (2) the measures and information available to government leaders, (3) the system of rewards and punishments for organizational members, and (4) the procedures by which human and material resources get committed. For example, to the extent that rewards and punishments for the members of an organization are distributed by higher authorities, these authorities can exercise some control by specifying criteria in terms of which organizational output is to be evaluated. These criteria become constraints within which organizational activity proceeds. But constraint is a crude instrument of control.

Intervention by government leaders does sometimes change the activity of an organization in an intended direction. But instances are fewer than might be expected. As Franklin Roosevelt, the master manipulator of government organizations, remarked:

> The Treasury is so large and far-flung and ingrained in its practices that I find it is almost impossible to get the action and results I want. . . . But the Treasury is not to be compared with the State

Department. You should go through the experience of trying to get any changes in the thinking, policy, and action of the career diplomats and then you'd know what a real problem was. But the Treasury and the State Department put together are nothing compared with the na-a-vy . . . To change anything in the na-a-vy is like punching a feather bed. You punch it with your right and you punch it with your left until you are finally exhausted, and then you find the damn bed just as it was before you started punching.[44]

John Kennedy's experience seems to have been similar: "The State Department," he asserted, "is a bowl full of jelly."[45] And lest the McNamara revolution in the Defense Department seem too striking a counterexample, the navy's recent rejection of McNamara's major intervention in naval weapons procurement, the F-111B, should be studied as an antidote.

F. Decisions of Government Leaders   Organizational persistence does not exclude shifts in governmental behavior. For government leaders sit atop the conglomerate of organizations. Many important issues of governmental action require that these leaders decide what organizations will play out which programs where. Thus stability in the parochialisms and SOPs of individual organizations is consistent with some important shifts in the behavior of governments. The range of these shifts is defined by existing organizational programs.

III. Dominant Inference Pattern

If a nation performs an action of this type today, its organizational components must yesterday have been performing (or have had established routines for performing) an action only marginally different from this action. At any specific point in time, a government consists of an established conglomerate of organizations, each with existing goals, programs, and repertoires. The characteristics of a government's action in any instance follows from those established routines and from the choice of government leaders—on the basis of information and estimates provided by existing routines—among existing programs. The best explanation of an organization's behavior at t is $t - 1$; the prediction of $t + 1$ is t. Model II's explanatory power is achieved by uncovering the organizational routines and repertoires that produced the outputs that comprise the puzzling occurrence.

IV. General Propositions

A number of general propositions have been stated above. In order to illustrate clearly the type of proposition employed by model II analysts, this section formulates several more precisely.

A. Organizational Action   Activity according to SOPs and programs does not constitute far-sighted, flexible adaptation to "the issue" (as it is conceived by the analyst). Detail and nuance of actions by organizations are determined predominantly by organizational routines, not government leaders' directions.

1. SOPs constitute routines for dealing with *standard* situations. Routines allow large numbers of ordinary individuals to deal with numerous instances, day after day, without considerable thought, by responding to basic stimuli. But this regularized capability for adequate performance is purchased at the price of standardization. If the SOPs are appropriate, average performance, i.e., performance averaged over the range of cases, is better than it would be if each instance were approached individually (given fixed talent, timing, and resource constraints). But specific instances, particularly critical

instances that typically do not have "standard" characteristics, are often handled sluggishly or inappropriately.

2. A program, i.e., a complex action chosen from a short list of programs in a repertoire, is rarely tailored to the specific situation in which it is executed. Rather, the program is (at best) the most appropriate of the programs in a previously developed repertoire.

3. Since repertoires are developed by parochial organizations for standard scenarios defined by that organization, programs available for dealing with a particular situation are often ill-suited.

B. LIMITED FLEXIBILITY AND INCREMENTAL CHANGE   Major lines of organizational action are straight, i.e., behavior at one time is marginally different from that behavior at $t - 1$. Simple-minded predictions work best: Behavior at $t + 1$ will be marginally different from behavior at the present time.

1. Organizational budgets change incrementally—both with respect to totals and with respect to intraorganizational splits. Though organizations could divide the money available each year by carving up the pie anew (in the light of changes in objectives or environment), in practice, organizations take last year's budget as a base and adjust incrementally. Predictions that require large budgetary shifts in a single year between organizations or between units within an organization should be hedged.

2. Once undertaken, an organizational investment is not dropped at the point where "objective" costs outweigh benefits. Organizational stakes in adopted projects carry them quite beyond the loss point.

C. ADMINISTRATIVE FEASIBILITY   Adequate explanation, analysis, and prediction must include administrative feasibility as a major dimension. A considerable gap separates what leaders choose (or might rationally have chosen) and what organizations implement.

1. Organizations are blunt instruments. Projects that require several organizations to act with high degrees of precision and coordination are not likely to succeed.

2. Projects that demand that existing organization units depart from their accustomed functions and perform previously unprogrammed tasks are rarely accomplished in their designed form.

3. Government leaders can expect that each organization will do its part in terms of what the organization knows how to do.

4. Government leaders can expect incomplete and distorted information from each organization concerning its part of the problem.

5. Where an assigned piece of a problem is contrary to the existing goals of an organization, resistance to implementation of that piece will be encountered.

V. Specific Propositions

A. DETERRENCE   The probability of nuclear attack is less sensitive to balance and imbalance or stability and instability (as these concepts are employed by model I strategists) than it is to a number of organizational factors. Except for the special case in which the Soviet Union acquires a credible capability to destroy the U.S. with a disarming blow, U.S. superiority or inferiority affects the probability of a nuclear attack less than do a number of organizational factors.

First, if a nuclear attack occurs, it will result from organizational activity: the firing of rockets by members of a missile group. The enemy's *control system,* i.e., physical mechanisms and standard procedures which determine who can launch rockets when, is critical. Second, the enemy's programs for bringing his strategic forces to *alert status* determine probabilities of accidental firing and momentum. At the outbreak of World War I, if the Russian tsar had understood the organizational processes which his order of full mobilization triggered, he would have realized that he had chosen war. Third, organizational repertoires fix the range of effective choice open to enemy leaders. The menu available to Tsar Nicholas in 1914 has two entrees: full mobilization and no mobilization. Partial mobilization was not an organizational option. Fourth, since organizational routines set the chessboard, the training and deployment of troops and nuclear weapons is crucial. Given that the outbreak of hostilities in Berlin is more probable than most scenarios for nuclear war, facts about deployment, training, and tactical nuclear equipment of Soviet troops stationed in East Germany—which will influence the face of the issue seen by Soviet leaders at the outbreak of hostilities and the manner in which choice is implemented—are as critical as the question of "balance."

B. SOVIET FORCE POSTURE   Soviet force posture, i.e., the fact that certain weapons rather than others are procured and deployed, is determined by organizational factors such as the goals and procedures of existing military services and the goals and processes of research and design labs, within budgetary constraints that emerge from the government leader's choices. The frailty of the Soviet air force within the Soviet military establishment seems to have been a crucial element in the Soviet failure to acquire a large bomber force in the 1950s (thereby faulting American intelligence predictions of a "bomber gap"). The fact that missiles were controlled until 1960 in the Soviet Union by the Soviet ground forces, whose goals and procedures reflected no interest in an intercontinental mission, was not irrelevant to the slow Soviet buildup of ICBMs (thereby faulting U.S. intelligence predictions of a "missile gap"). These organizational factors (Soviet ground forces' control of missiles and that service's fixation with European scenarios) make the Soviet deployment of so many MRBMs that European targets could be destroyed three times over more understandable. Recent weapon developments, e.g., the testing of a fractional orbital bombardment system (FOBS) and multiple warheads for the SS-9, very likely reflect the activity and interests of a cluster of Soviet research and development organizations rather than a decision by Soviet leaders to acquire a first-strike weapon system. Careful attention to the organizational components of the Soviet military establishment (strategic rocket forces, navy, air force, ground forces, and national air defense), the missions and weapons systems to which each component is wedded (an independent weapon system assists survival as an independent service), and existing budgetary splits (which probably are relatively stable in the Soviet Union as they tend to be everywhere) offer potential improvements in medium- and longer-term predictions.

The U.S. Blockade of Cuba: A Second Cut

Organizational Intelligence

At 7:00 P.M. on October 22, 1962, President Kennedy disclosed the American discovery of the presence of Soviet strategic missiles in Cuba, declared a "strict quarantine on all offensive military equipment under shipment to Cuba," and demanded that "Chairman Khrushchev halt and eliminate this clandestine, reckless, and provocative threat to world peace."[46] This decision was reached at the pinnacle of the U.S. government after a critical week of deliberation. What initiated that precious week were photographs of Soviet missile sites in Cuba taken on October 14. These pictures might not have been taken until a week later. In that case, the President speculated, "I don't think probably we would have chosen as prudently as we finally did."[47] U.S. leaders might have received this information three weeks earlier—if a U-2 had flown over San Cristobal in the last week of September.[48] What determined the context in which American leaders came to choose the blockade was the discovery of missiles on October 14.

There has been considerable debate over alleged American intelligence failures in the Cuban missile crisis.[49] But what both critics and defenders have neglected is the fact that the discovery took place on October 14, rather than three weeks earlier or a week later, as a consequence of the established routines and procedures of the organizations which constitute the U.S. intelligence community. These organizations were neither more nor less successful than they had been the previous month or were to be in the months to follow.[50]

The notorious "September estimate," approved by the United States Intelligence Board (USIB) on September 19, concluded that the Soviet Union would not introduce offensive missiles into Cuba.[51] No U-2 flight was directed over the western end of Cuba (after September 5) before October 4.[52] No U-2 flew over the western end of Cuba until the flight that discovered the Soviet missiles on October 14.[53] Can these "failures" be accounted for in organizational terms?

On September 19, when USIB met to consider the question of Cuba, the "system" contained the following information: (1) shipping intelligence had noted the arrival in Cuba of two large-hatch Soviet lumber ships, which were riding high in the water; (2) refugee reports of countless sightings of missiles, but also a report that Castro's private pilot, after a night of drinking in Havana, had boasted: "We will fight to the death and perhaps we can win because we have everything, including atomic weapons"; (3) a sighting by a CIA agent of the rear profile of a strategic missile; (4) U-2 photos produced by flights of August 29, September 5, and 17 showing the construction of a number of SAM sites and other defensive missiles.[54] Not all of this information was on the desk of the estimators, however. Shipping intelligence experts noted the fact that large-hatch ships were riding high in the water and spelled out the inference: the ships must be carrying "space-consuming" cargo.[55] These facts were carefully included in the catalogue of intelligence concerning shipping. For experts sensitive to the Soviets' shortage of ships, however, these facts carried no special signal. The refugee report of Castro's private pilot's remark had been received at Opa Locka, Florida, along with vast reams of inaccurate reports generated by the refugee community. This report and a thousand others had to be checked and compared before being sent to Washington. The two weeks required for initial processing could have been shortened by a large increase in resources, but the yield of this source was already quite marginal. The CIA agent's sighting of the rear profile of a strategic missile had occurred on September 12; transmission time from agent sighting to arrival in Washington typically took nine to twelve days. Shortening this transmission time would impose severe cost in terms of danger to subagents, agents, and communication networks.

On the information available, the intelligence chiefs who predicted that the Soviet Union would not introduce offensive missiles into Cuba made a reasonable and defensible judgment.[56] Moreover, in the light of the fact that these organizations were gathering intelligence not only about Cuba but about potential occurrences in all parts of the world, the informational base available to the estimators involved nothing out of the ordinary. Nor, from an organizational perspective, is there anything startling about the gradual accumulation of evidence that led to the formulation of the hypothesis that the Soviets were installing missiles in Cuba and the decision on October 4 to direct a special flight over western Cuba.

The ten-day delay between that decision and the flight is another organizational story.[57] At the October 4 meeting the Defense Department took the opportunity to raise an issue important to its concerns. Given the increased danger that a U-2 would be downed, it would be better if the pilot were an officer in uniform rather than a CIA agent. Thus the air force should assume responsibility for U-2 flights over Cuba. To the contrary the CIA argued that this was an intelligence operation and thus within the CIA's jurisdiction. Moreover, CIA U-2s had been modified in certain ways which gave them advantages over Air Force U-2s in averting Soviet SAMs. Five days passed while the State Department pressed for less risky alternatives such as drones and the air force (in Department of Defense guise) and CIA engaged in territorial disputes. On October 9 a flight plan over San Cristobal was approved by COMOR, but to the CIA's dismay, air force pilots rather than CIA agents would take charge of the mission. At this point details become sketchy, but several members of the intelligence community have speculated that an air force pilot in an air force U-2 attempted a high-altitude overflight on October 9 that "flamed out," i.e., lost power, and thus had to descend in order to restart its engine. A second round between air force and CIA followed, as a result of which air force pilots were trained to fly CIA U-2s. A successful overflight took place on October 14.

This ten-day delay constitutes some form of "failure." In the face of well-founded suspicions concerning offensive Soviet missiles in Cuba that posed a critical threat to the United States's most vital interest, squabbling between organizations whose job it is to produce this information seems entirely inappropriate. But for each of these organizations, the question involved the issue: "*Whose* job was it to be?" Moreover, the issue was not simply which organization would control U-2 flights over Cuba, but rather the broader issue of ownership of U-2 intelligence activities—a very long-standing territorial dispute. Thus though this delay was in one sense a "failure," it was also a nearly inevitable consequence of two facts: many jobs do not fall neatly into precisely defined organizational jurisdictions; and vigorous organizations are imperialistic.

Organizational Options

Deliberations of leaders in ExCom meetings produced broad outlines of alternatives. Details of these alternatives and blueprints for their implementation had to be specified by the organizations that would perform these tasks. These organizational outputs answered the question: What, specifically, *could* be done?

Discussion in the ExCom quickly narrowed the live options to two: an air strike and a blockade. The choice of the blockade instead of the air strike turned on two points: (1) the argument from morality and tradition that the United States could not perpetrate a "Pearl Harbor in reverse"; (2) the belief that a "surgical" air strike was impossible.[58] Whether the United States *might* strike first was a question not of capability but of morality. Whether the United States *could* perform the surgical strike was a factual question concerning capabilities. The majority of the members of the ExCom, including the president, initially preferred the air strike.[59] What effectively foreclosed this option, however, was the fact that the air strike they wanted could not be chosen with high confidence of success.[60] After having tentatively chosen the course of prudence—given that the surgical air strike was not an option—Kennedy reconsidered. On Sunday morning, October 21, he called the air force experts to a special meeting in his living quarters, where he probed once more for the option of a "surgical" air strike.[61] General Walter C. Sweeny, Commander of Tactical Air Forces, asserted again that the air force could guarantee no higher than 90 percent effectiveness in a surgical air strike.[62] That "fact" was false.

The air strike alternative provides a classic case of military estimates. One of the alternatives outlined by the ExCom was named *air strike*. Specification of the details of this alternative was delegated to the air force. Starting from an existing plan for massive U.S. military action against Cuba (prepared for contingencies like a response to a Soviet Berlin grab), air force estimators produced an attack to guarantee success.[63] This plan called for extensive bombardment of all missile sites, storage depots, airports, and in deference to the navy, the artillery batteries opposite the naval base at Guantanamo.[64] Members of the ExCom repeatedly expressed bewilderment at military estimates of the number of sorties required, likely casualties, and collateral damage. But the "surgical" air strike that the political leaders had in mind was never carefully examined during the first week of the crisis. Rather this option was simply excluded on the grounds that since the Soviet MRBMs in Cuba were classified "mobile" in U.S. manuals, extensive bombing was required. During the second week of the crisis careful examination revealed that the missiles were mobile in the sense that small houses are mobile: that is, they could be moved and reassembled in six days. After the missiles were reclassified "movable" and detailed plans for surgical air strikes specified, this action was added to the list of live options for the end of the second week.

Organizational Implementation

ExCom members separated several types of blockade: offensive weapons only, all armaments, and all strategic goods including POL (petroleum, oil, and lubricants). But the "details" of the operation were left to the navy. Before the president announced the blockade on Monday evening, the first stage of the navy's blueprint was in motion, and a problem loomed on the horizon.[65] The navy had a detailed plan for the blockade. The president had several less precise but equally determined notions concerning what should be done, when, and how. For the navy the issue was one of effective implementation of the navy's blockade—without the meddling and interference of political leaders. For the president the problem was to pace and manage events in such a way that the Soviet leaders would have time to see, think, and blink.

A careful reading of available sources uncovers an instructive incident. On Tuesday the British ambassador, Ormsby-Gore, after having attended a briefing on the details of the blockade, suggested to the president that the plan for intercepting Soviet ships far out of reach of Cuban jets did not facilitate Khrushchev's hard decision.[66] Why not make the interception much closer to Cuba and thus give the Russian leader more time? According to the public account and the recollection of a number of individuals involved, Kennedy "agreed immediately, called McNamara, and over emotional navy protest, issued the appropriate instructions."[67] As Sorensen records, "in a sharp clash with the Navy, he made certain his will prevailed."[68] The navy's plan for the blockade was thus changed by drawing the blockade much closer to Cuba.

A serious organizational orientation makes one suspicious of this account. More careful examination of the available evidence confirms these suspicions, though alternative accounts must be somewhat speculative. According to the public chronology, a quarantine drawn close to Cuba became effective on Wednesday morning, the first Soviet ship was contacted on Thursday morning, and the first boarding of a ship occurred on Friday. According to the statement by the Department of Defense, boarding of the *Marcula* by a party from the *John R. Pierce* "took place at 7:50 A.M., E.D.T., 180 miles northeast of Nassau."[69] The *Marcula* had been trailed since about 10:30 the previous evening.[70] Simple calculations suggest that the *Pierce* must have been stationed along the navy's original arc, which extended five hundred miles out to sea from Cape Magsi, Cuba's easternmost tip.[71] The blockade line was *not* moved as the president ordered and the accounts report.

What happened is not entirely clear. One can be certain, however, that Soviet ships passed through the line along which American destroyers had posted themselves before the official "first contact" with the Soviet ship. On October 26 a Soviet tanker arrived in Havana and was honored by a dockside rally for "running the blockade." Photographs of this vessel show the name *Vinnitsa* on the side of the vessel in Cyrillic letters.[72] But according to the official U.S. position, the first tanker to pass through the blockade was the *Bucharest,* which was hailed by the navy on the morning of October 25. Again simple mathematical calculation excludes the possibility that the *Bucharest* and the *Vinnitsa* were the same ship. It seems probable that the navy's resistance to the president's order that the blockade be drawn in closer to Cuba forced him to allow one or several Soviet ships to pass through the blockade after it was officially operative.[73]

This attempt to leash the navy's blockade had a price. On Wednesday morning, October 24, what the president had been awaiting occurred. The eighteen dry cargo ships heading towards the quarantine stopped dead in the water. This was the occasion of Dean Rusk's remark, "We are eyeball to eyeball and I think the other fellow just blinked."[74] But the navy had another interpretation. The ships had simply stopped to pick up Soviet submarine escorts. The president became quite concerned lest the navy—already riled because of presidential meddling in its affairs—blunder into an incident. Sensing the president's fears, McNamara became suspicious of the navy's procedures and routines for making the first interception. Calling on the Chief of Naval Operations in the navy's inner sanctum, the navy flag plot, McNamara put his questions harshly.[75] Who would make the first interception? Were Russian-speaking officers on board? How would submarines be dealt with? At one point McNamara asked Anderson what he would do if a Soviet ship's captain refused to answer questions about his cargo. Picking up the Manual of Navy Regulations, the navy man waved it in McNamara's face and shouted, "It's all in there." To which McNamara replied, "I don't give a damn what John Paul Jones would have done; I want to know what you are going to do, now."[76] The encounter ended on Anderson's remark: "Now, Mr. Secretary, if you and your deputy will go back to your office, the navy will run the blockade."[77]

MODEL III: BUREAUCRATIC POLITICS

The leaders who sit on top of organizations are not a monolithic group. Rather each is in his own right a player in a central competitive game. The name of the game is bureaucratic politics: bargaining along regularized channels among players positioned hierarchically within the government. Government behavior can thus be understood according to a third conceptual model not as organizational outputs but as outcomes of bargaining games. In contrast with model I, the bureaucratic politics model sees no unitary actor but rather many actors as players, who focus not on a single strategic issue but on many diverse intranational problems as well, in terms of no consistent set of strategic objectives but rather according to various conceptions of national, organizational, and personal goals, making government decisions not by rational choice but by the pulling and hauling that is politics.

The apparatus of each national government constitutes a complex arena for the intranational game. Political leaders at the top of this apparatus plus the men who occupy positions on top of the critical organizations form the circle of central players. Ascendancy to this circle assures some independent standing. The necessary decentralization of decisions required for action on the broad range of foreign policy problems guarantees that each player has considerable discretion. Thus power is shared.

The nature of problems of foreign policy permits fundamental disagreement among reasonable men concerning what ought to be done. Analyses yield conflicting recommendations. Separate responsibilities laid on the shoulders of individual personalities encourage differences in perceptions and priorities. But the issues are of first-order importance. What the nation does really matters. A wrong choice could mean irreparable damage. Thus responsible men are obliged to fight for what they are convinced is right.

Men share power. Men differ concerning what must be done. The differences matter. This milieu necessitates that policy be resolved by politics. What the nation does is sometimes the result of the triumph of one group over others. More often, however, different groups pulling in different directions yield a resultant distinct from what anyone intended. What moves the chess pieces is not simply the reasons which support a course of action, nor the routines of organizations which enact an alternative, but the power and skill of proponents and opponents of the action in question.

This characterization captures the thrust of the bureaucratic-politics orientation. If problems of foreign policy arose as discrete issues and decisions were determined one game at a time, this account would suffice. But most issues, e.g., Vietnam or the proliferation of nuclear weapons, emerge piecemeal, over time, one lump in one context, a second in another. Hundreds of issues compete for players' attention every day. Each player is forced to fix upon his issues for that day, fight them on their own terms, and rush on to the next. Thus the character of emerging issues and the pace at which the game is played converge to yield government "decisions" and "actions" as collages. Choices by one player, outcomes of minor games, outcomes of central games, and "foul-ups"—these pieces, when stuck to the same canvas, constitute government behavior relevant to an issue.

The concept of national security policy as political outcome contradicts both public imagery and academic orthodoxy. Issues vital to national security, it is said, are too important to be settled by political games. They must be "above" politics. To accuse someone of "playing politics with national security" is a most serious charge. What public conviction demands, the academic penchant for intellectual elegance reinforces. Internal politics is messy; moreover, according to prevailing doctrine, politicking lacks intellectual content. As such, it constitutes gossip for journalists rather than a subject for serious investigation. Occasional memoirs, anecdotes in historical accounts, and several detailed case studies to the contrary, most of the literature of foreign policy avoids bureaucratic politics. The gap between academic literature and the experience of participants in government is nowhere wider than at this point.

Bureaucratic Politics Paradigm[78]

I. *Basic Unit of Analysis: Policy as Political Outcome*

The decisions and actions of governments are essentially intranational political outcomes: outcomes in the sense that what happens is not chosen as a solution to a problem but rather results from compromise, coalition, competition, and confusion among government officials who see different faces of an issue; political in the sense that the activity from which the outcomes emerge is best characterized as bargaining. Following Wittgenstein's use of the concept of a "game," national behavior in international affairs can be conceived as outcomes of intricate and subtle, simultaneous, overlapping games among players located in positions the hierarchical arrangement of which constitutes the government.[79] These games proceed neither at random nor at leisure. Regular channels structure the game. Deadlines force issues to the attention of busy players. The moves in the chess game are thus to be explained in terms of the bargaining among players with separate and unequal power over particular pieces and with separable objectives in distinguishable subgames.

II. *Organizing Concepts*

A. PLAYERS IN POSITIONS   The actor is neither a unitary nation nor a conglomerate of organizations, but rather a number of individual players. Groups of these players constitute the agent for particular government decisions and actions. Players are men in jobs.

Individuals become players in the national security policy game by occupying a critical position in an administration. For example, in the U.S. government the players include "Chiefs": the President, Secretaries of State, Defense, and Treasury, Director of the CIA, Joint Chiefs of Staff, and, since 1961, the Special Assistant for National Security Affairs;[80] "Staffers": the immediate staff of each Chief; "Indians": the political appointees and permanent government officials within each of the departments and agencies; and *Ad Hoc* Players": actors in the wider government game (especially "Congressional Influentials"), members of the press, spokesmen for important interest groups (especially the "bipartisan foreign policy establishment" in and out of Congress), and surrogates for each of these groups. Other members of the Congress, press, interest groups, and public form concentric circles around the central arena—circles which demarcate the permissive limits within which the game is played.

Positions define what players both may and must do. The advantages and handicaps with which each player can enter and play in various games stems from his position. So does a cluster of obligations for the performance of certain tasks. The two sides of this coin are illustrated by the position of the modern Secretary of State. First, in form and usually in fact, he is the primary repository of political judgment on the political-military issues that are the stuff of contemporary foreign policy; consequently, he is a senior personal advisor to the President. Second, he is the colleague of the President's other senior advisers on the problems of foreign policy, the Secretaries of Defense and Treasury, and the Special Assistant for National Security Affairs. Third, he is the ranking U.S. diplomat for serious negotiation. Fourth, he serves as an Administration voice to Congress, the country, and the world. Finally, he is "Mr. State Department" or "Mr. Foreign Office," "leader of officials, spokesman for their causes, guardian of their interests, judge of their disputes, superintendent of their work, master of their careers."[81] But he is not first one, and then the other. All of these obligations are his simultaneously. His performance in one affects his credit and power in the others. The perspective stemming from the daily work which he must oversee—the cable traffic by which his department maintains relations with other foreign offices—conflicts with the president's requirement that he serve as a generalist and coordinator of contrasting perspectives. The necessity that he be close to the President restricts the extent to which, and the force with which, he can front for his department. When he defers to the Secretary of Defense rather than fighting for his department's position—as he often must—he strains the loyalty of his officialdom. The Secretary's resolution of these conflicts depends not only upon the position, but also upon the player who occupies the position.

For players are also people. Men's metabolisms differ. The core of the bureaucratic politics mix is personality. (How each man manages to stand the heat in his kitchen, each player's basic operating style, and the complementarity or contradiction among personalities and styles in the inner circles are irreducible pieces of the policy blend.) Moreover, each person comes to his position with baggage in tow, including sensitivities to certain issues, commitments to various programs, and personal standing and debts with groups in the society.

B. Parochial Priorities, Perceptions, and Issues   Answers to the questions: "What is the issue?" and "What must be done?" are colored by the position from which the questions are considered. For the factors which encourage organizational parochialism also influence the players who occupy positions on top of (or within) these organizations. To motivate members of his organization, a player must be sensitive to the organization's orientation. The games into which the player can enter and the advantages with which he plays enhance these pressures. Thus propensities of perception stemming from position permit reliable prediction about a player's stances in many cases. But these propensities are filtered through the baggage which players bring to positions. Sensitivity to both the pressures and the baggage is thus required for many predictions.

C. Interests, Stakes, and Power   Games are played to determine outcomes. But outcomes advance and impede each player's conception of the national interest, specific programs to which he is committed, the welfare of his friends, and his personal interests. These overlapping interests constitute the stakes for which games are played. Each player's ability to play successfully depends upon his power. Power, i.e., effective influence on policy outcomes, is an elusive blend of at least three elements: bargaining advantages (drawn from formal authority and obligations, institutional backing, constituents, expertise, and status), skill and will in using bargaining advantages, and other players' perceptions of the first two ingredients. Power wisely invested yields an enhanced reputation for effectiveness. Unsuccessful investment depletes both the stock of capital and the reputation. Thus each player must pick the issues on which he can play with a reasonable probability of success. But no player's power is sufficient to guarantee satisfactory outcomes. Each player's needs and fears run to many other players. What ensues is the most intricate and subtle of games known to man.

D. The Problem and the Problems   "Solutions" to strategic problems are not derived by detached analysts focusing coolly on *the* problem. Instead deadlines and events raise issues in games and demand decisions of busy players in contexts that influence the face the issue wears. The problems for the players are both narrower and broader than *the* strategic problem. For each player focuses not on the total strategic problem but rather on the decision that must be made now. But each decision has critical consequences not only for the strategic problem but for each player's organizational, reputational, and personal stakes. Thus the gap between the problems the player was solving and the problem upon which the analyst focuses is often very wide.

E. Action-Channels   Bargaining games do not proceed randomly. Action-channels, i.e., regularized ways of producing action concerning types of issues, structure the game by preselecting the major players, determining their points of entrance into the game, and distributing particular advantages and disadvantages for each game. Most critically, channels determine "who's got the action," that is, which department's Indians actually do whatever is chosen.

Weapon procurement decisions are made within the annual budgeting process; embassies' demands for action cables are answered according to routines of consultation and clearance from State to Defense and White House; requests for instructions from military groups (concerning assistance all the time, concerning operations during war) are composed by the military in consultation with the Office of the Secretary of Defense, State, and White House; crisis responses are debated among White House, State, Defense, CIA, and ad hoc players; major political speeches, especially by the president but also by other chiefs, are cleared through established channels.

F. ACTION AS POLITICS   Government decisions are made and government actions emerge neither as the calculated choice of a unified group nor as a formal summary of leaders' preferences. Rather the context of shared power but separate judgments concerning important choices determines that politics is the mechanism of choice. Note the *environment* in which the game is played: inordinate uncertainty about what must be done, the necessity that something be done, and crucial consequences of whatever is done. These features force responsible men to become active players. The *pace of the game*—hundreds of issues, numerous games, and multiple channels—compels players to fight to "get others' attention," to make them "see the facts," to assure that they "take the time to think seriously about the broader issue." The *structure of the game*—power shared by individuals with separate responsibilities—validates each player's feeling that "others don't see my problem," and "others must be persuaded to look at the issue from a less parochial perspective." The *rules of the game*—he who hesitates loses his chance to play at that point, and he who is uncertain about his recommendation is overpowered by others who are sure—pressures players to come down on one side of a 51:49 issue and play. The *rewards of the game*—effectiveness, i.e., impact on outcomes, as the immediate measure of performance—encourages hard play. Thus, most players come to fight to "make the government do what is right." The strategies and tactics employed are quite similar to those formalized by theorists of international relations.

G. STREAMS OF OUTCOMES   Important government decisions or actions emerge as collages composed of individual acts, outcomes of minor and major games, and foul-ups. Outcomes which could never have been chosen by an actor and would never have emerged from bargaining in a single game over the issue are fabricated piece by piece. Understanding of the outcome requires that it be disaggregated.

III. Dominant Inference Pattern

If a nation performed an action, that action was the *outcome* of bargaining among individuals and groups within the government. That outcome included *results* achieved by groups committed to a decision or action, *resultants* which emerged from bargaining among groups with quite different positions and *foul-ups*. Model III's explanatory power is achieved by revealing the pulling and hauling of various players, with different perceptions and priorities, focusing on separate problems, which yielded the outcomes that constitute the action in question.

IV. General Propositions

1. ACTION AND INTENTION   Action does not presuppose intention. The sum of behavior of representatives of a government relevant to an issue was rarely intended by any individual or group. Rather, separate individuals with different intentions contributed pieces which compose an outcome distinct from what anyone would have chosen.

2. WHERE YOU STAND DEPENDS ON WHERE YOU SIT[82]   Horizontally, the diverse demands upon each player shape his priorities, perceptions, and issues. For large classes of issues, e.g., budgets and procurement decisions, the stance of a particular player can be predicted with high reliability from information concerning his seat. In the notorious B-36 controversy, no one was surprised by Admiral Radford's testimony that "the B-36 under any theory of war is a bad gamble with national security," as opposed to Air Force Secretary Symington's claim that "a B-36 with an A-bomb can destroy distant objectives which might require ground armies years to take."[83]

3. CHIEFS AND INDIANS   The aphorism "where you stand depends on where you sit" has vertical as well as horizontal application. Vertically, the demands upon the president, chiefs, staffers, and Indians are quite distinct.

The foreign policy issues with which the president can deal are limited primarily by his crowded schedule: the necessity of dealing first with what comes next. His problem is to probe the special face worn by issues that come to his attention, to preserve his leeway until time has clarified the uncertainties, and to assess the relevant risks.

Foreign-policy chiefs deal most often with the hottest issue *de jour*, though they can get the attention of the president and other members of the government for other issues which they judge important. What they cannot guarantee is that "the president will pay the price" or that "the others will get on board." They must build a coalition of the relevant powers that be. They must "give the president confidence" in the right course of action.

Most problems are framed, alternatives specified, and proposals pushed, however, by Indians. Indians fight with Indians of other departments; for example, struggles between International Security Affairs of the Department of Defense and Political-Military of the State Department are a microcosm of the action at higher levels. But the Indian's major problem is how to get the *attention* of chiefs, how to get an issue decided, how to get the government "to do what is right."

In policy making then, the issue looking *down* is options: how to preserve my leeway until time clarifies uncertainties. The issue looking *sideways* is commitment: how to get others committed to my coalition. The issue looking *upwards* is confidence: how to give the boss confidence in doing what must be done. To paraphrase one of Neustadt's assertions which can be applied down the length of the ladder, the essence of a responsible official's task is to induce others to see that what needs to be done is what their own appraisal of their own responsibilities requires them to do in their own interests.

V. *Specific Propositions*

1. DETERRENCE   The probability of nuclear attack depends primarily on the probability of attack emerging as an outcome of the bureaucratic politics of the attacking government. First, which players can decide to launch an attack? Whether the effective power over action is controlled by an individual, a minor game, or the central game is critical. Second, though model I's confidence in nuclear deterrence stems from an assertion that in the end governments will not commit suicide, model III recalls historical precedents. Admiral Yamamoto, who designed the Japanese attack on Pearl Harbor, estimated accurately: "In the first six months to a year of war against the U.S. and England I will run wild, and I will show you an uninterrupted succession of victories; I must also tell you that, should the war be prolonged for two or three years, I have no confidence in our ultimate victory."[84] But Japan attacked. Thus, three questions might be considered. One: could any member of the government solve his problem by attack? What patterns of bargaining could yield attack as an outcome? The major difference between a stable balance of terror and a questionable balance may simply be that in the first case most members of the government appreciate fully the consequences of attack and are thus on guard against the emergence of this outcome. Two: what stream of outcomes might lead to an attack? At what point in that stream is the potential attacker's politics? If members of the U.S. government had been sensitive to the stream of decisions from which the Japanese attack on Pearl Harbor emerged, they would have been aware of a considerable probability of that attack. Three: how might miscalculation and confusion generate foul-ups that yield attack as an outcome? For example, in a crisis or after the beginning of conventional war, what happens to the information available to and the effective power of members of the central game?

The U.S. Blockade of Cuba: A Third Cut

The Politics of Discovery

A series of overlapping bargaining games determined both the date of the discovery of the Soviet missiles and the impact of this discovery on the administration. An explanation of the politics of the discovery is consequently a considerable piece of the explanation of the U.S. blockade.

Cuba was the Kennedy administration's "political Achilles' heel."[85] The months preceding the crisis were also months before the congressional elections, and the Republican Senatorial and Congressional Campaign Committee had announced that Cuba would be "the dominant issue of the 1962 campaign."[86] What the administration billed as a "more positive and indirect approach of isolating Castro from developing, democratic Latin America," Senators Keating, Goldwater, Capehart, Thurmond, and others attacked as a "do-nothing" policy.[87] In statements on the floor of the House and Senate, campaign speeches across the country, and interviews and articles carried by national news media, Cuba—particularly the Soviet program of increased arms aid—served as a stick for stirring the domestic political scene.[88]

These attacks drew blood. Prudence demanded a vigorous reaction. The president decided to meet the issue head on. The administration mounted a forceful campaign of denial designed to discredit critics' claims. The president himself manned the front line of this offensive, though almost all administration officials participated. In his news conference on August 19, President Kennedy attacked as "irresponsible" calls for an invasion of Cuba, stressing rather "the totality of our obligations" and promising to "watch what happens in Cuba with the closest attention."[89] On September 4 he issued a strong statement denying any provocative Soviet action in Cuba.[90] On September 13 he lashed out at "loose talk" calling for an invasion of Cuba.[91] The day before the flight of the U-2 which discovered the missiles, he campaigned in Capehart's Indiana against those "self-appointed generals and admirals who want to send someone else's sons to war."[92]

On Sunday, October 14, just as a U-2 was taking the first pictures of Soviet missiles, McGeorge Bundy was asserting:

> I *know* that there is no present evidence, and I think that there is no present likelihood that the Cuban government and the Soviet government would, in combination, attempt to install a major offensive capability.[93]

In this campaign to puncture the critics' charges, the administration discovered that the public needed positive slogans. Thus Kennedy fell into a tenuous semantic distinction between "offensive" and "defensive" weapons. This distinction originated in his September 4 statement that there was no evidence of "offensive ground to ground missiles" and warned "were it to be otherwise, the gravest issues would arise."[94] His September 13 statement turned on this distinction between "defensive" and "offensive" weapons and announced a firm commitment to action if the Soviet Union attempted to introduce the latter into Cuba.[95] Congressional committees elicited from administration officials testimony which read this distinction and the president's commitment into the *Congressional Record*.[96]

What the president least wanted to hear, the CIA was most hesitant to say plainly. On August 22 John McCone met privately with the president and voiced suspicions that the Soviets were preparing to introduce offensive missiles into Cuba.[97] Kennedy heard this as what it was: the suspicion of a hawk. McCone left Washington for a month's honeymoon on the Riviera. Fretting at Cap Ferrat, he bombarded his deputy, General Marshall Carter, with telegrams, but Carter, knowing that McCone had informed the president of his suspicions and received a cold reception, was reluctant to distribute these telegrams outside the CIA.[98] On September 9 a U-2 "on loan" to the Chinese Nationalists was downed over mainland China.[99] The Committee on Overhead Reconnaissance (COMOR) convened on September 10 with a sense of urgency.[100] Loss of another U-2 might incite world opinion to demand cancellation of U-2 flights. The president's campaign against those who asserted that the Soviets were acting provocatively in Cuba had begun. To risk downing a U-2 over Cuba was to risk chopping off the limb on which the president was sitting. That meeting decided to shy away from the western end of Cuba (where SAMs were becoming operational) and modify the flight pattern of the U-2s in order to reduce the probability that a U-2 would be lost.[101] USIB's unanimous approval of the September estimate reflects similar sensitivities. On September 13 the president had asserted that there were no Soviet offensive missiles in Cuba and committed his administration to act if offensive missiles were discovered. Before congressional committees, administration officials were denying that there was any evidence whatever of offensive missiles in Cuba. The implications of a national intelligence estimate which concluded that the Soviets were introducing offensive missiles into Cuba were not lost on the men who constituted America's highest intelligence assembly.

The October 4 COMOR decision to direct a flight over the western end of Cuba in effect "overturned" the September estimate, but without officially raising that issue. The decision represented McCone's victory, for which he had lobbied with the president before the September 10 decision, in telegrams before the September 19 estimate, and in person after his return to Washington. Though the politics of the intelligence community is closely guarded, several pieces of the story can be told.[102] By September 27 Colonel Wright and others in DIA believed that the Soviet Union was placing missiles in the San Cristobal area.[103] This area was marked suspicious by the CIA on September 29 and certified top priority on October 3. By October 4 McCone had the evidence required to raise the issue officially. The members of COMOR heard McCone's argument but were reluctant to make the hard decision he demanded. The significant probability that a U-2 would be downed made overflight of western Cuba a matter of real concern.[104]

The Politics of Issues

The U-2 photographs presented incontrovertible evidence of Soviet offensive missiles in Cuba. This revelation fell upon politicized players in a complex context. As one high official recalled, Khrushchev had caught us "with our pants down." What each of the central participants saw, and what each did to cover both his own and the administration's nakedness, created the spectrum of issues and answers.

At approximately 9:00 A.M. Tuesday morning, October 16, McGeorge Bundy went to the president's living quarters with the message: "Mr. President, there is now hard photographic evidence that the Russians have offensive missiles in Cuba."[105] Much has been made of Kennedy's "expression of surprise,"[106] but *"surprise"* fails to capture the character of his initial reaction. Rather it was one of startled anger, most adequately conveyed by the exclamation: "He can't do that to *me!*"[107] In terms of the president's attention and priorities at that moment, Khrushchev had chosen the most unhelpful act of all. Kennedy had staked his full presidential authority on the assertion that the Soviets would not place offensive weapons in Cuba. Moreover, Khrushchev had assured the president through the most direct and personal channels that he was aware of the president's domestic political problem and that nothing would be done to exacerbate this problem. The chairman had *lied* to the president. Kennedy's initial reaction entailed action. The missiles must be removed.[108] The alternatives of "doing nothing" or "taking a diplomatic approach" could not have been less relevant to *his* problem.

These two tracks—doing nothing and taking a diplomatic approach—were the solutions advocated by two of his principal advisers. For Secretary of Defense McNamara the missiles raised the specter of nuclear war. He first framed the issue as a straightforward strategic problem. To understand the issue one had to grasp two obvious but difficult points. First, the missiles represented an inevitable occurrence: narrowing of the missile gap. It simply happened sooner rather than later. Second, the United States could accept this occurrence, since its consequences were minor: "seven-to-one missile 'superiority,' one-to-one missile 'equality,' one-to-seven missile 'inferiority'—the three postures are identical." McNamara's statement of this argument at the first meeting of the ExCom was summed up in the phrase "a missile is a missile."[109] "It makes no great difference," he maintained, "whether you are killed by a missile from the Soviet Union or Cuba."[110] The implication was clear. The United States should not initiate a crisis with the Soviet Union, risking a significant probability of nuclear war over an occurrence which had such small strategic implications.

The perceptions of McGeorge Bundy, the president's assistant for national security affairs, are the most difficult of all to reconstruct. There is no question that he initially argued for a diplomatic track.[111] But was Bundy laboring under his acknowledged burden of responsibility in Cuba I? Or was he playing the role of devil's advocate in order to make the president probe his own initial reaction and consider other options?

The president's brother, Robert Kennedy, saw most clearly the political wall against which Khrushchev had backed the president. But he, like McNamara, saw the prospect of nuclear doom. Was Khrushchev going to force the president to an insane act? At the first meeting of the ExCom he scribbled a note, "Now I know how Tojo felt when he was planning Pearl Harbor."[112] From the outset he searched for an alternative that would prevent the air strike.

The initial reaction of Theodore Sorensen, the president's special counsel and "alter ego," fell somewhere between that of the president and his brother. Like the president, Sorensen felt the poignancy of betrayal. If the president had been the architect of the policy which the missiles punctured, Sorensen was the draftsman. Khrushchev's deceitful move demanded a strong countermove. But like Robert Kennedy, Sorensen feared lest the shock and disgrace lead to disaster.

To the Joint Chiefs of Staff the issue was clear. *Now* was the time to do the job for which they had prepared contingency plans. Cuba I had been badly done; Cuba II would not be. The missiles provided the *occasion* to deal with the issue: cleansing the Western Hemisphere of

Castro's communism. As the president recalled on the day the crisis ended, "An invasion would have been a mistake—a wrong use of our power. But the military are mad. They wanted to do this. It's lucky for us that we have McNamara over there."[113]

McCone's perceptions flowed from his confirmed prediction. As the Cassandra of the incident, he argued forcefully that the Soviets had installed the missiles in a daring political probe which the United States must meet with force. The time for an air strike was now.[114]

The Politics of Choice

The process by which the blockade emerged is a story of the most subtle and intricate probing, pulling, and hauling; leading, guiding, and spurring. Reconstruction of this process can only be tentative. Initially the president and most of his advisers wanted the clean surgical air strike. On the first day of the crisis, when informing Stevenson of the missiles, the president mentioned only two alternatives: "I suppose the alternatives are to go in by air and wipe them out or to take other steps to render them inoperable."[115] At the end of the week a sizable minority still favored an air strike. As Robert Kennedy recalled: "The fourteen people involved were very significant. . . . If six of them had been president of the U.S., I think that the world might have been blown up."[116] What prevented the air strike was a fortuitous coincidence of a number of factors—the absence of any one of which might have permitted that option to prevail.

First, McNamara's vision of holocaust set him firmly against the air strike. His initial attempt to frame the issue in strategic terms struck Kennedy as particularly inappropriate. Once McNamara realized that the name of the game was a strong response, however, he and his deputy Gilpatric chose the blockade as a fallback. When the Secretary of Defense—whose department had the action, whose reputation in the cabinet was unequaled, in whom the president demonstrated full confidence—marshalled the arguments for the blockade and refused to be moved, the blockade became a formidable alternative.

Second, Robert Kennedy—the president's closest confidant—was unwilling to see his brother become a "Tojo." His arguments against the air strike on moral grounds struck a chord in the president. Moreover, once his brother had stated these arguments so forcefully, the president could not have chosen his initially preferred course without in effect agreeing to become what RFK had condemned.

The president learned of the missiles on Tuesday morning. On Wednesday morning, in order to mask our discovery from the Russians, the president flew to Connecticut to keep a campaign commitment, leaving RFK as the unofficial chairman of the group. By the time the president returned on Wednesday evening, a critical third piece had been added to the picture. McNamara had presented his argument for the blockade. Robert Kennedy and Sorensen had joined McNamara. A powerful coalition of the advisers in whom the president had the greatest confidence, and with whom his style was most compatible, had emerged.

Fourth, the coalition that had formed behind the president's initial preference gave him reason to pause. *Who* supported the air strike—the Chiefs, McCone, Rusk, Nitze, and Acheson—as much as *how* they supported it, counted. Fifth, a piece of inaccurate information, which no one probed, permitted the blockade advocates to fuel (potential) uncertainties in the president's mind. When the president returned to Washington Wednesday evening, RFK and Sorensen met him at the airport. Sorensen gave the president a four-page memorandum outlining the areas of agreement and disagreement. The strongest argument was that the air strike simply could not be surgical.[117] After a day of prodding and questioning, the air force had asserted that it could not guarantee the success of a surgical air strike limited to the missiles alone.

Thursday evening, the president convened the ExCom at the White House. He declared his tentative choice of the blockade and directed that preparations be made to put it into effect by Monday morning.[118] Though he raised a question about the possibility of a surgical air strike subsequently, he seems to have accepted the experts' opinion that this was no live option.[119] (Acceptance of this estimate suggests that he may have learned the lesson of the Bay of Pigs—"Never rely on experts"—less well than he supposed.)[120] But this information was incorrect. That no one probed this estimate during the first week of the crisis poses an interesting question for further investigation.

A coalition, including the president, thus emerged from the president's initial decision that something had to be done; McNamara, Robert Kennedy, and Sorensen's resistance to the air strike; incompatibility between the president and the air strike advocates; and an inaccurate piece of information.[121]

CONCLUSION

This essay has obviously bitten off more than it has chewed. For further developments and synthesis of these arguments the reader is referred to the larger study.[122] In spite of the limits of space, however, it would be inappropriate to stop without spelling out several implications of the argument and addressing the question of relations among the models and extensions of them to activity beyond explanation.

At a minimum the intended implications of the argument presented here are four. First, formulation of alternative frames of reference and demonstration that different analysts, relying predominantly on different models, produce quite different explanations should encourage the analyst's self-consciousness about the nets he employs. The effect of these "spectacles" in sensitizing him to particular aspects of what is going on—framing the puzzle in one way rather than another, encouraging him to examine the problem in terms of certain categories rather than others, directing him to particular kinds of evidence, and relieving puzzlement by one procedure rather than another—must be recognized and explored.

Second, the argument implies a position on the problem of "the state of the art." While accepting the commonplace characterization of the present condition of foreign-policy analysis—personalistic, noncumulative, and sometimes insightful—this essay rejects both the counsel of despair's justification of this condition as a consequence of the character of the enterprise, and the "new frontiersmen's" demand for *a priori* theorizing on the frontiers and *ad hoc* appropriation of "new techniques."[123] What is required as a first step is noncasual examination of the present product: inspection of existing explanations, articulation of the conceptual models employed in producing them, formulation of the propositions relied upon, specification of the logic of the various intellectual enterprises, and reflection on the questions being asked. Though it is difficult to overemphasize the need for more systematic processing of more data, these preliminary matters of formulating questions with clarity and sensitivity to categories and assumptions so that fruitful acquisition of large quantities of data is possible are still a major hurdle in considering most important problems.

Third, the preliminary, partial paradigms presented here provide a basis for serious reexamination of many problems of foreign and military policy. Model II and model III cuts at problems typically treated in model I terms can permit significant improvements in explanation and prediction.[124] Full model II and III analyses require large amounts of information. But even in cases where the information base is severely limited, improvements are possible.

Consider the problem of predicting Soviet strategic forces. In the mid–1950s, model I style calculations led to predictions that the Soviets would rapidly deploy large numbers of long-range bombers. From a model II perspective both the frailty of the air force within the Soviet military establishment and the budgetary implications of such a build-up would have led analysts to hedge this prediction. Moreover, model II would have pointed to a sure, visible indicator of such a build-up: noisy struggles among the services over major budgetary shifts. In the late 1950s and early 1960s model I calculations led to the prediction of immediate massive Soviet deployment of ICBMs. Again, a model II cut would have reduced this number because in the earlier period strategic rockets were controlled by the Soviet ground forces rather than an independent service, and in the later period this would have necessitated massive shifts in budgetary splits. Today, model I considerations lead many analysts both to recommend that an agreement not to deploy ABMs be a major American objective in upcoming strategic negotiations with the USSR and to predict success. From a model II vantage point the existence of an ongoing Soviet ABM program, the strength of the organization (National Air Defense) that controls ABMs, and the fact that an agreement to stop ABM deployment would force the virtual dismantling of this organization make a viable agreement of this sort much less likely. A model III cut suggests that (a) there must be significant differences among perceptions and priorities of Soviet leaders over strategic negotiations, (b) any agreement will affect some players' power bases, and (c) agreements that do not require extensive cuts in the sources of some major players' power will prove easier to negotiate and more viable.

Fourth, the present formulation of paradigms is simply an initial step. As such it leaves a long list of critical questions unanswered. Given any action, an imaginative analyst should always be able to construct some rationale for the government's choice. By imposing and relaxing constraints on the parameters of rational choice (as in variants of model I) analysts can construct a large number of accounts of any act as a rational choice. But does a statement of reasons why a rational actor would choose an action constitute an explanation of the *occurrence* of that action? How can model I analysis be forced to make more systematic contributions to the question of the determinants of occurrences? Model II's explanation of t in terms of $t - 1$ is explanation. The world is contiguous. But governments sometimes make sharp departures. Can an organizational process model be modified to suggest where change is likely? Attention to organizational change should afford greater understanding of why particular programs and SOPs are maintained by identifiable types of organizations and also how a manager can improve organizational performance. Model III tells a fascinating "story." But its complexity is enormous, the information requirements are often overwhelming, and many of the details of the bargaining may be superfluous. How can such a model be made parsimonious? The three models are obviously not exclusive alternatives. Indeed, the paradigms highlight the partial emphasis of the framework—what each emphasizes and what it leaves out. Each concentrates on one class of variables, in effect relegating other important factors to a ceteris paribus clause. Model I concentrates on "market factors:" pressures and incentives created by the "international strategic marketplace." Models II and III focus on the internal mechanism of the government that chooses in this environment. But can these relations be more fully specified? Adequate synthesis would require a typology of decisions and actions, some of which are more amenable to treatment in terms of one model and some to another. Government behavior is but one cluster of factors relevant to occurrences in foreign affairs. Most students of foreign policy adopt this focus (at least when explaining and predicting). Nevertheless, the dimensions of the chess board, the character of the pieces, and the rules of the game—factors considered by international systems theorists—constitute the context in which the pieces are moved. Can the major variables in the full function of determinants of foreign policy outcomes be identified?

Both the outline of a partial *ad hoc* working synthesis of the models and a sketch of their uses in activities other than explanation can be suggested by generating predictions in terms of each. Strategic surrender is an important problem of international relations and diplomatic history. War termination is a new, developing area of the strategic literature. Both of these interests lead scholars to address a central question: *Why* do nations surrender *when?* Whether implicit in explanations or more explicit in analysis, diplomatic historians and strategists rely upon propositions which can be turned forward to produce predictions. Thus at the risk of being timely—and in error—the present situation (August 1968) offers an interesting test case: Why will North Vietnam surrender when?[125]

In a nutshell, analysis according to model I asserts: nations quit when costs outweigh the benefits. North Vietnam will surrender when she realizes "that continued fighting can only generate additional costs without hope of compensating gains, this expectation being largely the consequence of the previous application of force by the dominant side."[126] U.S. actions can increase or decrease Hanoi's strategic costs. Bombing North Vietnam increases the pain and thus increases the probability of surrender. This proposition and prediction are not without meaning. That—"other things being equal"—nations are more likely to surrender when the strategic cost-benefit balance is negative is true. Nations rarely surrender when they are winning. The proposition specifies a range within which nations surrender. But over this broad range the relevant question is: why do nations surrender?

Models II and III focus upon the government machine through which this fact about the international strategic marketplace must be filtered to produce a surrender. These analysts are considerably less sanguine about the possibility of surrender *at the point* that the cost-benefit calculus turns negative. Never in history (i.e., in none of the five cases I have examined) have nations surrendered at that point. Surrender occurs sometime thereafter. *When* depends on process of organizations and politics of players within these governments—as they are affected by the opposing government. Moreover, the effects of the victorious power's action upon the surrendering nation cannot be adequately summarized as increasing or decreasing strategic costs. Imposing additional costs by bombing a nation may increase the probability of surrender. But it also may reduce it. An appreciation of the impact of the acts of one nation upon another thus requires some understanding of the machine which is being influenced. For more precise prediction, models II and III require considerably more information about the organizations and politics of North Vietnam than is publicly available. On the basis of the limited public information, however, these models can be suggestive.

Model II examines two subproblems. First, to have lost is not sufficient. The government must know that the strategic cost-benefit calculus is negative. But neither the categories nor the indicators of strategic costs and benefits are clear. And the sources of information about both are organizations whose parochial priorities and perceptions do not facilitate accurate information or estimation. Military evaluation of military performance, military estimates of factors like "enemy morale," and military predictions concerning when "the tide will turn" or "the corner will have been turned" are typically distorted. In cases of highly decentralized guerrilla operations, like Vietnam, these problems are exacerbated. Thus strategic costs will be underestimated. Only highly *visible* costs can have direct impact on leaders without being filtered through organizational channels. Second, since organizations define the details of options and execute actions, surrender (and negotiation) is likely to entail considerable bungling in the early stages. No organization can define options or prepare programs for this treasonous act. Thus, early overtures will be uncoordinated with the acts of other organizations, e.g., the fighting forces, creating contradictory "signals" to the victor.

Model III suggests that surrender will not come at the point that strategic costs outweigh benefits, but that it will not wait until the leadership group concludes that the war is lost. Rather the problem is better understood in terms of four additional propositions. First, strong advocates of the war effort, whose careers are closely identified with the war, rarely come to the conclusion that costs outweigh benefits. Second, quite often from the outset of a war, a number of members of the government (particularly those whose responsibilities sensitize them to problems other than war, e.g., economic planners or intelligence experts) are convinced that the war effort is futile. Third, surrender is likely to come as the result of a political shift that enhances the effective power of the latter group (and adds swing members to it). Fourth, the course of the war, particularly actions of the victor, can influence the advantages and disadvantages of players in the loser's government. Thus, North Vietnam will surrender not when its leaders have a change of heart, but when Hanoi has a change of leaders (or a change of effective power within the central circle). How U.S. bombing (or pause), threats, promises, or action in the South affect the game in Hanoi is subtle but nonetheless crucial.

That these three models could be applied to the surrender of governments other than North Vietnam should be obvious. But that exercise is left for the reader.

NOTES

1. Theodore Sorensen, *Kennedy* (New York, 1965), p. 705.
2. In attempting to understand problems of foreign affairs, analysts engage in a number of related, but logically separable enterprises: (a) description, (b) explanation, (c) prediction, (d) evaluation, and (e) recommendation. This essay focuses primarily on explanation (and by implication, prediction).
3. In arguing that explanations proceed in terms of implicit conceptual models, this essay makes no claim that foreign-policy analysts have developed any satisfactory empirically tested theory. In this essay the use of the term *model* without qualifiers should be read *conceptual scheme*.
4. For the purpose of this argument we shall accept Carl G. Hempel's characterization of the logic of explanation: an explanation "answers the question, 'Why did the explanadum-phenomenon occur?' by showing that the phenomenon resulted from particular circumstances, specified in $C_1, C_2, \ldots C_k$, in accordance with laws $L_1, L_2, \ldots L_r$. By pointing this out, the argument shows that given the particular circumstances and the laws in question, the occurrence of the phenomenon was to be *expected*; and it is in this sense that the explanation enables us to understand why the phenomenon occurred." *Aspects of Scientific Explanation* (New York, 1965), p. 337. While various patterns of explanation can be distinguished, *viz.*, Ernest Nagel, *The Structure of Science: Problems in the Logic of Scientific Explanation*, (New York, 1961), satisfactory scientific explanations exhibit this basic logic. Consequently prediction is the converse of explanation.
5. Earlier drafts of this argument have aroused heated arguments concerning proper names for these models. To choose names from ordinary language is to court confusion as well as familiarity. Perhaps it is best to think of these models as I, II, and III.
6. In strict terms the "outcomes" which these three models attempt to explain are essentially actions of national governments, i.e., the sum of activities of all individuals employed by a government relevant to an issue. These models focus not on a state of affairs, i.e., a full description of the world, but upon national decision and implementation. This distinction is stated clearly by Harold and Margaret Sprout, "Environmental Factors on the Study of International Politics," in James Rosenau (ed.), *International Politics and Foreign Policy* (Glencoe, Illinois, 1961), p. 116.

This restriction excludes explanations offered principally in terms of international systems theories. Nevertheless, this restriction is not severe, since few interesting explanations of occurrences in foreign policy have been produced at that level of analysis. According to David Singer, "The nation state—our primary actor in international relations . . . is clearly the traditional focus among Western students and is the one which dominates all of the texts employed in English-speaking colleges and universities." David Singer, "The Level-of-Analysis Problem in International Relations," Klaus Knorr and Sidney Verba (eds.), *The International System* (Princeton, 1961). Similarly, Richard Brody's review of contemporary trends in the study of international relations finds that "scholars have come increasingly to focus on acts of nations. That is, they all focus on the behavior of nations in some respect. Having an interest in accounting for the behavior of nations in common, the prospects for a common frame of reference are enhanced."

7. For further development and support of these arguments see the author's larger study, *Bureaucracy and Policy: Conceptual Models and the Cuban Missile Crisis* (forthcoming). In its abbreviated form the argument must at some points appear overly stark. The limits of space have forced the omission of many reservations and refinements.

8. Each of the three "case snapshots" displays the work of a conceptual model as it is applied to explain the U.S. blockade of Cuba. But these three cuts are primarily exercises in hypothesis generation rather than hypothesis testing. Especially when separated from the larger study, these accounts may be misleading. The sources for these accounts include the full public record plus a large number of interviews with participants in the crisis.

9. *New York Times*, February 18, 1967.

10. *Ibid.*

11. Arnold Horelick and Myron Rush, *Strategic Power and Soviet Foreign Policy* (Chicago, 1965). Based on A. Horelick, "The Cuban Missile Crisis: An Analysis of Soviet Calculations and Behavior," *World Politics* (April 1964).

12. Horelick and Rush, *Strategic Power and Soviet Foreign Policy*, p. 154.

13. Hans Morgenthau, *Politics Among Nations* (3rd ed.; New York, 1960), p. 191.

14. *Ibid.*, p. 192.

15. *Ibid.*, p. 5.

16. *Ibid.*, pp. 5–6.

17. Stanley Hoffmann, *Daedalus* (Fall 1962); reprinted in *The State of War* (New York, 1965).

18. *Ibid.*, p. 171.

19. *Ibid.*, p. 189.

20. Following Robert MacIver; see Stanley Hoffmann, *Contemporary Theory in International Relations* (Englewood Cliffs, 1960), pp. 178–179.

21. Thomas Schelling, *The Strategy of Conflict* (New York, 1960), p. 232. This proposition was formulated earlier by A. Wohlstetter, "The Delicate Balance of Terror," *Foreign Affairs* (January 1959).

22. Schelling, *op. cit.*, p. 4.

23. See Morgenthau, *op. cit.*, p. 5; Hoffmann, *Contemporary Theory*, pp. 178–179; Hoffmann, "Roulette in the Cellar," *The State of War*; Schelling, *op. cit.*

24. The larger study examines several exceptions to this generalization. Sidney Verba's excellent essay "Assumptions of Rationality and Non-Rationality in Models of the International System" is less an exception than it is an approach to a somewhat different problem. Verba focuses upon models of rationality and irrationality of *individual* statesmen: in Knorr and Verba, *The International System.*

25. Robert K. Merton, *Social Theory and Social Structures* (Revised and Enlarged Edition; New York, 1957), pp. 12–16. Considerably weaker than a satisfactory theoretical model, paradigms nevertheless represent a short step in that direction from looser, implicit conceptual models. Neither the concepts nor the relations among the variables are sufficiently specified to yield propositions

deductively. "Paradigmatic Analysis" nevertheless has considerable promise for clarifying and cod-
ifying styles of analysis in political science. Each of the paradigms stated here can be represented
rigorously in mathematical terms. For example, model I lends itself to mathematical formulation
along the lines of Herbert Simon's "Behavioral Theory of Rationality," *Models of Man* (New York,
1957). But this does not solve the most difficult problem of "measurement and estimation."

26. Though a variant of this model could easily be stochastic, this paradigm is stated in nonprobabilistic
terms. In contemporary strategy a stochastic version of this model is sometimes used for predictions; but it is almost impossible to find an explanation of an occurrence in foreign affairs that is
consistently probabilistic.

    Analogies between model I and the concept of explanation developed by R. G. Collingwood,
William Dray, and other revisionists among philosophers concerned with the critical philosophy of
history are not accidental. For a summary of the revisionist position see Maurice Mandelbaum,
"Historical Explanation: The Problem of Covering Laws," *History and Theory* (1960).

27. This model is an analogue of the theory of the rational entrepreneur which has been developed
extensively in economic theories of the firm and the consumer. These two propositions specify the
substitution effect. Refinement of this model and specification of additional general propositions by
translating from the economic theory is straightforward.

28. *New York Times,* March 22, 1969.

29. See Nathan Leites, *A Study of Bolshevism* (Glencoe, Illinois, 1953).

30. As stated in the introduction, this "case snapshot" presents, without editorial commentary, a model
I analyst's explanation of the U.S. blockade. The purpose is to illustrate a strong, characteristic
rational policy model account. This account is (roughly) consistent with prevailing explanations of
these events.

31. Theodore Sorensen, *op. cit.,* p. 675.

32. *Ibid.,* p. 679.

33. *Ibid.,* p. 679.

34. Elie Abel, *The Missile Crisis* (New York, 1966), p. 144.

35. *Ibid.,* p. 102.

36. Sorensen, *op. cit.,* p. 684.

37. *Ibid.,* p. 685. Though this was the formulation of the argument, the facts are not strictly accurate.
Our tradition against surprise attack was rather younger than 175 years. For example President
Theodore Roosevelt applauded Japan's attack on Russia in 1904.

38. *New York Times,* June, 1963.

39. The influence of organizational studies upon the present literature of foreign affairs is minimal.
Specialists in international politics are not students of organization theory. Organization theory has only
recently begun to study organizations as decision makers and has not yet produced behavioral studies
of national security organizations from a decision-making perspective. It seems unlikely, however, that
these gaps will remain unfilled much longer. Considerable progress has been made in the study of the
business firm as an organization. Scholars have begun applying these insights to government organizations, and interest in an organizational perspective is spreading among institutions and individuals
concerned with actual government operations. The "decision making" approach represented by
Richard Snyder, R. Bruck, and B. Sapin, *Foreign Policy Decision-Making* (Glencoe, Illinois, 1962),
incorporates a number of insights from organization theory.

40. The formulation of this paradigm is indebted both to the orientation and insights of Herbert Simon
and to the behavioral model of the firm stated by Richard Cyert and James March, *A Behavioral
Theory of the Firm* (Englewood Cliffs, 1963). Here, however, one is forced to grapple with the less
routine, less quantified functions of the less differentiated elements in government organizations.

41. Theodore Sorensen, "You Get to Walk to Work," *New York Times Magazine,* March 19, 1967.

42. Organizations are not monolithic. The proper level of disaggregation depends upon the objectives
of a piece of analysis. This paradigm is formulated with reference to the major organizations that

constitute the U.S. government. Generalization to the major components of each department and agency should be relatively straightforward.

43. The stability of these constraints is dependent on such factors as rules for promotion and reward, budgeting and accounting procedures, and mundane operating procedures.

44. Marriner Eccles, *Beckoning Frontiers* (New York, 1951), p. 336.

45. Arthur Schlesinger, *A Thousand Days* (Boston, 1965), p. 406.

46. U.S. Department of State, *Bulletin*, XLVII, pp. 715–720.

47. Schlesinger, *op. cit.*, p. 803.

48. Theodore Sorensen, *Kennedy*, p. 675.

49. See U.S. Congress, Senate, Committee on Armed Services, Preparedness Investigation Subcommittee, *Interim Report on Cuban Military Build-up*, 88th Congress, 1st Session, 1963, p. 2; Hanson Baldwin, "Growing Risks of Bureaucratic Intelligence," *The Reporter* (August 15, 1963), 48–50; Roberta Wohlstetter, "Cuba and Pearl Harbor," *Foreign Affairs* (July, 1965), p. 706.

50. U.S. Congress, House of Representatives, Committee on Appropriations, Subcommittee on Department of Defense Appropriations, *Hearings,* 88th Congress, 1st Session, 1963, 25 ff.

51. R. Hilsman, *To Move a Nation* (New York, 1967), pp. 172–173.

52. Department of Defense Appropriations, *Hearings,* p. 67.

53. *Ibid.*, pp. 66–67.

54. For (1) Hilsman, *op. cit.*, p. 186; (2) Abel, *op. cit.*, p. 24; (3) Department of Defense Appropriations, *Hearings,* p. 64; Abel, *op. cit.*, p. 24; (4) Department of Defense Appropriations, *Hearings,* pp. 1–30.

55. The facts here are not entirely clear. This assertion is based on information from (1) "Department of Defense Briefing by the Honorable R. S. McNamara, Secretary of Defense, State Department Auditorium, 5:00 P.M., February 6, 1963." A verbatim transcript of a presentation actually made by General Carroll's assistant, John Hughes; and (2) Hilsman's statement, *op. cit.*, p. 186. But see R. Wohlstetter's interpretation, "Cuba and Pearl Harbor," p. 700.

56. See Hilsman, *op. cit.*, pp. 172–174.

57. Abel, *op. cit.*, pp. 26 ff; Weintal and Bartlett, *Facing the Brink* (New York, 1967), pp. 62 ff; *Cuban Military Build-up;* J. Daniel and J. Hubbell, *Strike in the West* (New York, 1963), pp. 15 ff.

58. Schlesinger, *op. cit.*, p. 804.

59. Sorensen, *Kennedy*, p. 684.

60. *Ibid.*, pp. 684 ff.

61. *Ibid.*, pp. 694–697.

62. *Ibid.*, p. 697; Abel, *op. cit.*, pp. 100–101.

63. Sorensen, *Kennedy*, p. 669.

64. Hilsman, *op. cit.*, p. 204.

65. See Abel, *op. cit.*, pp. 97 ff.

66. Schlesinger, *op. cit.*, p. 818.

67. *Ibid.*

68. Sorensen, *Kennedy*, p. 710.

69. *New York Times*, October 27, 1962.

70. Abel, *op. cit.*, p. 171.

71. For the location of the original arc see Abel, *op. cit.*, p. 141.

72. *Facts on File*, Vol. XXII, 1962, p. 376, published by Facts on File, Inc., New York, yearly.

73. This hypothesis would account for the mystery surrounding Kennedy's explosion at the leak of the stopping of the *Bucharest*. See Hilsman, *op. cit.*, p. 45.

74. Abel, *op. cit.*, p. 153.

75. See *ibid.*, pp. 154 ff.

76. *Ibid.*, p. 156.

77. *Ibid.*

78. This paradigm relies upon the small group of analysts who have begun to fill the gap. My primary source is the model implicit in the work of Richard E. Neustadt, though his concentration on presidential action has been generalized to a concern with policy as the outcome of political bargaining among a number of independent players, the president amounting to no more than a "superpower" among many lesser but considerable powers. As Warner Schilling argues, the substantive problems are of such inordinate difficulty that uncertainties and differences with regard to goals, alternatives, and consequences are inevitable. This necessitates what Roger Hilsman describes as the process of conflict and consensus building. The techniques employed in this process often resemble those used in legislative assemblies, though Samuel Huntington's characterization of the process as "legislative" overemphasizes the equality of participants as opposed to the hierarchy which structures the game. Moreover, whereas for Huntington foreign policy (in contrast to military policy) is set by the executive, this paradigm maintains that the activities which he describes as legislative are characteristic of the process by which foreign policy is made.

79. The theatrical metaphor of stage, roles, and actors is more common than this metaphor of games, positions, and players. Nevertheless, the rigidity connotated by the concept of *role* both in the theatrical sense of actors reciting fixed lines and in the sociological sense of fixed responses to specified social situations makes the concept of games, positions, and players more useful for this analysis of active participants in the determination of national policy. Objections to the terminology on the grounds that *game* connotes nonserious play overlook the concept's application to most serious problems both in Wittgenstein's philosophy and in contemporary game theory. Game theory typically treats more precisely structured games, but Wittgenstein's examination of the "language game" wherein men use words to communicate is quite analogous to this analysis of the less specified game of bureaucratic politics. See Ludwig Wittgenstein, *Philosophical Investigations,* and Thomas Schelling, "What is Game Theory?" in James Charlesworth, *Contemporary Political Analysis.*

80. Inclusion of the President's Special Assistant for National Security Affairs in the tier of "Chiefs" rather than among the "Staffers" involves a debatable choice. In fact he is both super-staffer and near-chief. His position has no statutory authority. He is especially de-pendent upon good relations with the President and the Secretaries of Defense and State. Nevertheless, he stands astride a genuine action-channel. The decision to include this position among the Chiefs reflects my judgment that the Bundy function is becoming institutionalized.

81. Richard E. Neustadt, Testimony, United States Senate, Committee on Government Operations, Subcommittee on National Security Staffing, *Administration of National Security,* March 26, 1963, pp. 82–83.

82. This aphorism was stated first, I think, by Don K. Price.

83. Paul Y. Hammond, "Super Carriers and B-36 Bombers," in Harold Stein (ed.), *American Civil-Military Decisions* (Birmingham, 1963).

84. Roberta Wohlstetter, *Pearl Harbor* (Stanford, 1962), p. 350.

85. Sorensen, *Kennedy,* p. 670.

86. *Ibid.*

87. *Ibid.,* pp. 670 ff.

88. *New York Times,* August, September, 1962.

89. *New York Times,* August 20, 1962.

90. *New York Times,* September 5, 1962.

91. *New York Times,* September 14, 1962.

92. *New York Times,* October 14, 1962.

93. Cited by Abel, *op. cit.,* p. 13.

94. *New York Times,* September 5, 1962.

95. *New York Times,* September 14, 1962.

96. Senate Foreign Relations Committee; Senate Armed Services Committee; House Committee on Appropriation; House Select Committee on Export Control.

97. Abel, *op. cit.*, pp. 17–18. According to McCone he told Kennedy, "The only construction I can put on the material going into Cuba is that the Russians are preparing to introduce offensive missiles." See also Weintal and Bartlett, *op. cit.*, pp. 60–61.

98. Abel, *op. cit.*, p. 23.

99. *New York Times*, September 10, 1962.

100. See Abel, *op. cit.*, pp. 25–26; and Hilsman, *op. cit.*, p. 174.

101. Department of Defense Appropriation, *Hearings,* 69.

102. A basic but somewhat contradictory account of parts of this story emerges in the Department of Defense Appropriations, *Hearings,* 1–70.

103. Department of Defense Appropriations, *Hearings,* 71.

104. The details of the ten days between the October 4 decision and the October 14 flight must be held in abeyance.

105. Abel, *op. cit.*, p. 44.

106. *Ibid.,* pp. 44 ff.

107. See Richard Neustadt, "Afterword," *Presidential Power* (New York, 1964).

108. Sorensen, *Kennedy*, p. 676; Schlesinger, *op. cit.*, p. 801.

109. Hilsman, *op. cit.*, p. 195.

110. *Ibid.*

111. Weintal and Bartlett, *op. cit.*, p. 67; Abel, *op. cit.*, p. 53.

112. Schlesinger, *op. cit.*, p. 803.

113. *Ibid.,* p. 831.

114. Abel, *op. cit.*, p. 186.

115. *Ibid.,* p. 49.

116. Interview, quoted by Ronald Steel, *New York Review of Books,* March 13, 1969, p. 22.

117. Sorensen, *Kennedy,* p. 686.

118. *Ibid.,* p. 691.

119. *Ibid.,* pp. 691–692.

120. Schlesinger, *op. cit.*, p. 296.

121. Space will not permit an account of the path from this coalition to the formal government decision on Saturday and action on Monday.

122. *Bureaucracy and Policy* (forthcoming, 1969).

123. Thus my position is quite distinct from both poles in the recent "great debate" about international relations. While many "traditionalists" of the sort Kaplan attacks adopt the first posture and many "scientists" of the sort attacked by Bull adopt the second, this third posture is relatively neutral with respect to whatever is in substantive dispute. See Hedly Bull, "International Theory: The Case for a Classical Approach," *World Politics* (April, 1966); and Morton Kaplan, "The New Great Debate: Traditionalism vs. Science in International Relations," *World Politics* (October, 1966).

124. A number of problems are now being examined in these terms both in the Bureaucracy Study Group on Bureaucracy and Policy of the Institute of Politics at Harvard University and at the Rand Corporation.

125. In response to several readers' recommendations, what follows is reproduced *verbatim* from the paper delivered at the September 1968 Association meetings (Rand P–3919). The discussion is heavily indebted to Ernest R. May.

126. Richard Snyder, *Deterrence and Defense* (Princeton, 1961), p. 11. For a more general presentation of this position see Paul Kecskemeti, *Strategic Surrender* (New York, 1964).

❧

Are Bureaucracies Important?
(Or Allison Wonderland)

Stephen D. Krasner

Who and what shapes foreign policy? In recent years analyses have increasingly emphasized not rational calculations of the national interest or the political goals of national leaders but rather bureaucratic procedures and bureaucratic politics. Starting with Richard Neustadt's *Presidential Power*, a judicious study of leadership published in 1960, this approach has come to portray the American president as trapped by a permanent government more enemy than ally. Bureaucratic theorists imply that it is exceedingly difficult if not impossible for political leaders to control the organizational web which surrounds them. Important decisions result from numerous smaller actions taken by individuals at different levels in the bureaucracy who have partially incompatible national, bureaucratic, political, and personal objectives. They are not necessarily a reflection of the aims and values of high officials.

Presidential Power was well received by John Kennedy, who read it with interest, recommended it to his associates, and commissioned Neustadt to do a private study of the 1962 Skybolt incident. The approach has been developed and used by a number of scholars—Roger Hilsman, Morton Halperin, Arthur Schlesinger, Richard Barnet, and Graham Allison—some of whom held subcabinet positions during the 1960s. It was the subject of a special conference at the Rand Corporation, a main theme of a course at the Woodrow Wilson School at Princeton, and the subject of a faculty seminar at Harvard. It is the intellectual paradigm which guides the new public policy program in the John F. Kennedy School of Government at Harvard. Analyses of bureaucratic politics have been used to explain alliance behavior during the 1956 Suez crisis and the Skybolt incident, Truman's relations with MacArthur, American policy in Vietnam, and now most thoroughly the Cuban missile crisis in Graham Allison's *Essence of Decision: Explaining the Cuban Missile Crisis*, published in 1971 (Little, Brown & Company). Allison's volume is the elaboration of an earlier and influential article on this subject. With the publication of his book this approach to foreign policy now receives its definitive statement. The bureaucratic interpretation of foreign policy has become the conventional wisdom.

My argument here is that this vision is misleading, dangerous, and compelling: misleading because it obscures the power of the president; dangerous because it undermines the assumptions of democratic politics by relieving high officials of responsibility; and compelling because it offers leaders an excuse for their failures and scholars an opportunity for innumerable reinterpretations and publications.

The contention that the chief executive is trammelled by the permanent government has disturbing implications for any effort to impute responsibility to public officials. A democratic political philosophy assumes that responsibility for the acts of governments can be attributed to elected officials. The charges of these men are embodied in legal statutes. The electorate punishes an erring official by rejecting him at the polls. Punishment is senseless unless high officials are responsible for the acts of government. Elections have some impact only if government, that most complex of modern organizations, can be controlled. If the bureaucratic machine escapes manipulation and direction even by the highest officials, then punishment is illogical. Elections are a farce not because the people suffer from false consciousness, but because public officials are impotent, enmeshed in a bureaucracy so large that the actions of government are not responsive to their will. What sense to vote a man out of office when his successor, regardless of his values, will be trapped in the same web of only incrementally mutable standard operating procedures?

THE RATIONAL-ACTOR MODEL

Conventional analyses that focus on the values and objectives of foreign policy, what Allison calls the rational-actor model, are perfectly coincident with the ethical assumptions of democratic politics. The state is viewed as a rational unified actor. The behavior of states is the outcome of a rational decision-making process. This process has three steps. The options for a given situation are spelled out. The consequences of each option are projected. A choice is made which maximizes the values held by decision makers. The analyst knows what the state did. His objective is to explain why by imputing to decision makers a set of values which are maximized by observed behavior. These values are his explanation of foreign policy.

The citizen, like the analyst, attributes error to either inappropriate values or lack of foresight. Ideally the electorate judges the officeholder by governmental performance, which is assumed to reflect the objectives and perspicacity of political leaders. Poor policy is made by leaders who fail to foresee accurately the consequences of their decisions or attempt to maximize values not held by the electorate. Political appeals, couched in terms of aims and values, are an appropriate guide for voters. For both the analyst who adheres to the rational-actor model and the citizen who decides elections, values are assumed to be the primary determinant of government behavior.

The bureaucratic-politics paradigm points to quite different determinants of policy. Political leaders can only with great difficulty overcome the inertia and self-serving interests of the permanent government. What counts is managerial skill. In *Essence of Decision* Graham Allison maintains that "the central questions of policy analysis are quite different from the kinds of questions analysts have traditionally asked. Indeed, the crucial questions seem to be matters of planning for management." Administrative feasibility, not substance, becomes the central concern.

The paradoxical conclusion—that bureaucratic analysis with its emphasis on policy guidance implies political nonresponsibility—has most clearly been brought out by discussions of American policy in Vietnam. Richard Neustadt on the concluding page of *Alliance Politics,* his most recent book, muses about a conversation he would have had with President Kennedy in the fall of 1963 had tragedy not intervened. "I considered asking whether, in the light of our machine's performance on a British problem, he conceived that it could cope with South Vietnam's. . . . [I]t was a good question, better than I knew. It haunts me still." For adherents of the bureaucratic-politics paradigm Vietnam was a failure of the "machine," a war in Arthur Schlesinger's words "which no president . . . desired or intended."[1] The machine dictated a policy which it could not successfully terminate. The machine, not the cold war ideology and hubris of Kennedy and Johnson, determined American behavior in Vietnam. Vietnam could hardly be a tragedy, for tragedies are made by choice and character, not fate. A knowing electorate would express sympathy, not levy blame. Machines cannot be held responsible for what they do, nor can the men caught in their workings.

The strength of the bureaucratic web has been attributed to two sources: organizational necessity and bureaucratic interest. The costs of coordination and search procedures are so high that complex organizations *must* settle for satisfactory rather than optimal solutions. Bureaucracies have interests defined in terms of budget allocation, autonomy, morale, and scope which they defend in a game of political bargaining and compromise within the executive branch.

The imperatives of organizational behavior limit flexibility. Without a division of labor and the establishment of standard operating procedures it would be impossible for large organizations to begin to fulfill their statutory objectives, that is to perform tasks designed to meet societal needs rather than merely to perpetuate the organization. A division of labor among and within organizations reduces the job of each particular division to manageable proportions. Once this division is made, the complexity confronting an organization or one of its parts is further reduced through the establishment of standard operating procedures. To deal with each problem as if it were *sui generis* would be impossible given limited resources and information-processing capacity and would make intraorganizational coordination extremely difficult. Bureaucracies are then unavoidably rigid; but without the rigidity imposed by division of labor and standard operating procedures, they could hardly begin to function at all.

However, this rigidity inevitably introduces distortions. All of the options to a given problem will not be presented with equal lucidity and conviction unless by some happenstance the organization has worked out its scenarios for that particular problem in advance. It is more likely that the organization will have addressed itself to something *like* the problem with which it is confronted. It has a set of options for such a hypothetical problem, and these options will be presented to deal with the actual issue at hand. Similarly, organizations cannot execute all policy suggestions with equal facility. The development of new standard operating procedures takes time. The procedures which would most faithfully execute a new policy are not likely to have been worked out. The clash between the rigidity of standard operating procedures which are absolutely necessary to achieve coordination among and within large organizations and the flexibility needed to spell out the options and their consequences for a new problem and to execute new policies is inevitable. It cannot be avoided even with the best of intentions of bureaucratic chiefs anxious to faithfully execute the desires of their leaders.

THE COSTS OF COORDINATION

The limitations imposed by the need to simplify and coordinate indicate that the great increase in governmental power accompanying industrialization has not been achieved without some costs in terms of control. Bureaucratic organizations and the material and symbolic resources which they direct have enormously increased the ability of the American president to influence the international environment. He operates, however, within limits set by organizational procedures.

A recognition of the limits imposed by bureaucratic necessities is a useful qualification of the assumption that states always maximize their interest. This does not, however, imply that the analyst should abandon a focus on values or assumptions of rationality. Standard operating procedures are rational given the costs of search procedures and need for coordination. The behavior of states is still determined by values, although foreign policy may reflect satisfactory rather than optimal outcomes.

An emphasis on the procedural limits of large organizations cannot explain nonincremental change. If government policy is an outcome of standard operating procedures, then behavior at time t is only incrementally different from behavior at time $t - 1$. The exceptions to this prediction leap out of events of even the last year—the Nixon visit to China and the new economic policy. Focusing on the needs dictated by organizational complexity is adequate only during periods when policy is altered very little or not at all. To reduce policy makers to nothing more than the caretakers and minor adjustors of standard operating procedures rings hollow in an era rife with debates and changes of the most fundamental kind in America's conception of its objectives and capabilities.

Bureaucratic analysts do not, however, place the burden of their argument on standard operating procedures but on bureaucratic politics. The objectives of officials are dictated by their bureaucratic position. Each bureau has its own interests. The interests which bureaucratic analysts emphasize are not clientalistic ties between government departments and societal groups or special relations with congressional committees. They are, rather, needs dictated by organizational survival and growth—budget allocations, internal morale, and autonomy. Conflicting objectives advocated by different bureau chiefs are reconciled by a political process. Policy results from compromises and bargaining. It does not necessarily reflect the values of the president, let alone of lesser actors.

The clearest expression of the motivational aspects of the bureaucratic politics approach is the by now well-known aphorism—where you stand depends upon where you sit. Decision makers, however, often do not stand where they sit. Sometimes they are not sitting anywhere. This is clearly illustrated by the positions taken by members of the ExCom during the Cuban missile crisis, which Allison elucidates at some length. While the military, in Pavlovian fashion, urged the use of arms, the secretary of defense took a much more pacific position. The wise old men such as Acheson, imported for the occasion, had no bureaucratic position to defend. Two of the most important members of the ExCom, Robert Kennedy and Theodore Sorensen, were loyal to the president, not to some bureaucratic barony. Similarly, in discussions of Vietnam in 1966 and 1967, it was the secretary of defense who advocated diplomacy and the secretary of state who defended the prerogatives of the military. During Skybolt McNamara was attuned to the president's budgetary concerns, not those of the air force.

Allison, the most recent expositor of the bureaucratic-politics approach, realizes the problems which these facts present. In describing motivation he backs off from an exclusive focus on bureaucratic position, arguing instead that decision makers are motivated by national, organizational, group, and personal interests. While maintaining that the "propensities and priorities stemming from position are sufficient to allow analysts to make reliable predictions about a player's stand" (a proposition violated by his own presentation), he also notes that "these propensities are filtered through the baggage that players bring to positions." For both the missile crisis and Vietnam it was the "baggage" of culture and values, not bureaucratic position, which determined the aims of high officials.

Bureaucratic analysis is also inadequate in its description of how policy is made. Its axiomatic assumption is that politics is a game with the preferences of players given and independent. This is not true. The president chooses most of the important players and sets the rules. He selects the men who head the large bureaucracies. These individuals must share his values. Certainly they identify with his beliefs to a greater extent than would a randomly chosen group of candidates. They also feel some personal fealty to the president who has elevated them from positions of corporate or legal to ones of historic significance. While bureau chiefs are undoubtedly torn by conflicting pressures arising either from their need to protect their own bureaucracies or from personal conviction, they must remain the president's men. At some point disagreement results in dismissal. The values which bureau chiefs assign to policy outcomes are not independent. They are related through a perspective shared with the president.

The president also structures the governmental environment in which he acts through his impact on what Allison calls "action-channels." These are decision-making processes which describe the participation of actors and their influence. The most important "action-channel" in the government is the president's ear. The president has a major role in determining who whispers into it. John Kennedy's reliance on his brother, whose bureaucratic position did not afford him any claim to a decision-making role in the missile crisis, is merely an extreme example. By allocating tasks, selecting the White House bureaucracy, and demonstrating special affections, the president also influences "action-channels" at lower levels of the government.

The president has an important impact on bureaucratic interests. Internal morale is partially determined by presidential behavior. The obscurity in which Secretary of State Rogers languished during the China trip affected both State Department morale and recruitment prospects. Through the budget the president has a direct impact on that most vital of bureaucratic interests. While a bureau may use its societal clients and congressional allies to secure desired allocations, it is surely easier with the president's support than without it. The president can delimit or redefine the scope of an organization's activities by transferring tasks or establishing new agencies. Through public statements he can affect attitudes towards members of a particular bureaucracy and their functions.

THE PRESIDENT AS "KING"

The success a bureau enjoys in furthering its interests depends on maintaining the support and affection of the president. The implicit assumption of the bureaucratic-politics approach that departmental and presidential behavior are independent and comparably important is false. Allison, for instance, vacillates between describing the president as one "chief" among several and as a "king" standing above all other men. He describes in great detail the deliberations of the ExCom, implying that Kennedy's decision was in large part determined by its recommendations, and yet notes that during the crisis Kennedy vetoed an ExCom decision to bomb a SAM base after an American U-2 was shot down on October 27. In general bureaucratic analysts ignore the critical effect which the president has in choosing his advisers, establishing their access to decision making, and influencing bureaucratic interests.

All of this is not to deny that bureaucratic interests may sometimes be decisive in the formulation of foreign policy. Some policy options are never presented to the president. Others he deals with only cursorily, not going beyond options presented by the bureaucracy. This will only be the case if presidential interest and attention are absent. The failure of a chief executive to specify policy does not mean that the government takes no action. Individual bureaucracies may initiate policies which suit their own needs and objectives.

The actions of different organizations may work at cross-purposes. The behavior of the state, that is, of some of its official organizations, in the international system appears confused or even contradictory. This is a situation which develops, however, not because of the independent power of government organizations but because of failures by decision makers to assert control.

The ability of bureaucracies to independently establish policies is a function of presidential attention. Presidential attention is a function of presidential values. The chief executive involves himself in those areas which he determines to be important. When the president does devote time and attention to an issue, he can compel the bureaucracy to present him with alternatives. He may do this, as Nixon apparently has, by establishing an organization under his special assistant for national security affairs, whose only bureaucratic interest is maintaining the president's confidence. The president may also rely upon several bureaucracies to secure proposals. The president may even resort to his own knowledge and sense of history to find options which his bureaucracy fails to present. Even when presidential attention is totally absent, bureaus are sensitive to his values. Policies which violate presidential objectives may bring presidential wrath.

While the president is undoubtedly constrained in the implementation of policy by existing bureaucratic procedures, he even has options in this area. As Allison points out, he can choose which agencies will perform what tasks. Programs are fungible and can be broken down into their individual standard operating procedures and recombined. Such exercises take time and effort, but the expenditure of such energies by the president is ultimately a reflection of his own values and not those of the bureaucracy. Within the structure which he has partially created himself he can, if he chooses, further manipulate both the options presented to him and the organizational tools for implementing them.

Neither organizational necessity nor bureaucratic interests are the fundamental determinants of policy. The limits imposed by standard operating procedures as well as the direction of policy are a function of the values of decision makers. The president creates much of the bureaucratic environment which surrounds him through his selection of bureau chiefs, determination of "action-channels," and statutory powers.

THE MISSILE CRISIS

Adherents of the bureaucratic-politics framework have not relied exclusively on general argument. They have attempted to substantiate their contentions with detailed investigations of particular historical events. The most painstaking is Graham Allison's analysis of the Cuban missile crisis in his *Essence of Decision.* In a superlative heuristic exercise Allison attempts to show that critical facts and relationships are ignored by conventional analysis that assumes states are unified rational actors. Only by examining the missile crisis in terms of organizational necessity and bureaucratic interests and politics can the formulation and implementation of policy be understood.

The missile crisis, as Allison notes, is a situation in which conventional analysis would appear most appropriate. The president devoted large amounts of time to policy formulation and implementation. Regular bureaucratic channels were short-circuited by the creation of an executive committee which included representatives of the bipartisan foreign-policy establishment, bureau chiefs, and the president's special aides. The president dealt with details which would normally be left to bureaucratic subordinates. If under such circumstances the president could not effectively control policy formulation and implementation, then the rational-actor model is gravely suspect.

In his analysis of the missile crisis Allison deals with three issues: the American choice of a blockade, the Soviet decision to place MRBMs and IRBMs on Cuba, and the Soviet decision to withdraw the missiles from Cuba. The American decision is given the most detailed attention. Allison notes three ways in which bureaucratic procedures and interests influenced the formulation of American policy: first in the elimination of the nonforcible alternatives; second through the collection of information; third through the standard operating procedures of the air force.

In formulating the U.S. response the ExCom considered six alternatives. These were:

1. Do nothing
2. Diplomatic pressure
3. A secret approach to Castro
4. Invasion
5. A surgical air strike
6. A naval blockade

The approach to Castro was abandoned because he did not have direct control of the missiles. An invasion was eliminated as a first step because it would not have been precluded by any of the other options. Bureaucratic factors were not involved.

The two nonmilitary options of doing nothing and lodging diplomatic protests were also abandoned from the outset because the president was not interested in them. In terms of both domestic and international politics this was the most important decision of the crisis. It was a decision which only the president had authority to make. Allison's case rests on proving that this decision was foreordained by bureaucratic roles. He lists several reasons for Kennedy's elimination of the nonforcible alternatives. Failure to act decisively would undermine the confidence of members of his administration, convince the permanent government that his administration lacked leadership, hurt the Democrats in the forthcoming election, destroy his reputation among members of Congress, create public distrust, encourage American allies and enemies to question American courage, invite a second Bay of Pigs, and feed his own doubts about himself. Allison quotes a statement by Kennedy that he feared impeachment and concludes that the "nonforcible paths—avoiding military measures, resorting instead to diplomacy—could not have been more irrelevant to *his* problems." Thus Allison argues that Kennedy had no choice.

Bureaucratic analysis, what Allison calls in his book the governmental-politics model, implies that any man in the same position would have had no choice. The elimination of passivity and diplomacy was ordained by the office and not by the man.

Such a judgment is essential to the governmental-politics model, for the resort to the "baggage" of values, culture, and psychology which the president carries with him undermines the explanatory and predictive power of the approach. To adopt, however, the view that the office determined Kennedy's action is both to underrate his power and to relieve him of responsibility. The president defines his own role. A different man could have chosen differently. Kennedy's *Profiles in Courage* had precisely dealt with men who had risked losing their political roles because of their "baggage" of values and culture.

Allison's use of the term *intragovernmental balance of power* to describe John Kennedy's elimination of diplomacy and passivity is misleading. The American government is not a balance-of-power system; at the very least it is a loose hierarchical one. Kennedy's judgments of the domestic, international, bureaucratic, and personal ramifications of his choice were determined by *who* he was as well as *what* he was. The central mystery of the crisis remains why Kennedy chose to risk nuclear war over missile placements which he knew did not dramatically alter the strategic balance. The answer to this puzzle can only be found through an examination of values, the central concern of conventional analysis.

The impact of bureaucratic interests and standard operating procedures is reduced then to the choice of the blockade instead of the surgical air strike. Allison places considerable emphasis on intelligence gathering in the determination of this choice. U-2 flights were the most important source of data about Cuba; their information was supplemented by refugee reports, analyses of shipping, and other kinds of intelligence. The timing of the U-2 flights, which Allison argues was determined primarily by bureaucratic struggles, was instrumental in determining Kennedy's decision:

> Had a U-2 flown over the western end of Cuba three weeks earlier, it could have discovered the missiles, giving the administration more time to consider alternatives and to act before the danger of operational missiles in Cuba became a major factor in the equation. Had the missiles not been discovered until two weeks later, the blockade would have been irrelevant, since the Soviet missile shipments would have been completed . . . An explanation of the politics of the discovery is consequently a considerable piece of the explanation of the U.S. blockade.

The delay, however, from September 15 to October 14, when the missiles were discovered reflected presidential values more than bureaucratic politics. The October 14 flight took place ten days after COMOR, the interdepartmental committee which directed the activity of the U-2s, had decided the flights should be made. "This ten-day delay constitutes some form of 'failure,'" Allison contends. It was the result, he argues, of a struggle between the Central Intelligence Agency and the air force over who would control the flights. The air force maintained that the flights over Cuba were sufficiently dangerous to warrant military supervision; the Central Intelligence Agency, anxious to guard its own prerogatives, maintained that its U-2s were technically superior.

However, the ten-day delay after the decision to make a flight over western Cuba was not entirely attributable to bureaucratic bickering. Allison reports an attempt to make a flight on October 9, which failed because the U-2 flamed out. Further delays resulted from bad weather. Thus the inactivity caused by bureaucratic infighting amounted to only five days (October 4 to October 9) once the general decision to make the flight was taken. The other five days' delay caused by engine failure and the weather must be attributed to some higher source than the machinations of the American bureaucracy.

However, there was also a long period of hesitation before October 4. John McCone, director of the Central Intelligence Agency, had indicated to the president on August 22 that he thought there was a strong possibility that the Soviets were preparing to put offensive missiles on Cuba. He did not have firm evidence, and his contentions were met with skepticism in the administration.

INCREASED RISKS

On September 10 COMOR had decided to restrict further U-2 flights over western Cuba. This decision was based upon factors which closely fit the rational-actor model of foreign policy formulation. COMOR decided to halt the flights because the recent installation of

SAMs in western Cuba coupled with the loss of a Nationalist Chinese U-2 increased the probability and costs of a U-2 loss over Cuba. International opinion might force the cancellation of the flights altogether. The absence of information from U-2s would be a national, not simply a bureaucratic, cost. The president had been forcefully attacking the critics of his Cuba policy, arguing that patience and restraint were the best course of action. The loss of a U-2 over Cuba would tend to undermine the president's position. Thus, COMOR's decision on September 10 reflected a sensitivity to the needs and policies of the president rather than the parochial concerns of the permanent government.

The decision on October 4 to allow further flights was taken only after consultation with the president. The timing was determined largely by the wishes of the president. His actions were not circumscribed by decisions made at lower levels of the bureaucracy of which he was not aware. The flights were delayed because of conflicting pressures and risks confronting Kennedy. He was forced to weigh the potential benefits of additional knowledge against the possible losses if a U-2 were shot down.

What if the missiles had not been discovered until after October 14? Allison argues that had the missiles been discovered two weeks later, the blockade would have been irrelevant, since the missile shipments would have been completed. This is true, but only to a limited extent. The blockade was irrelevant even when it was put in place, for there were missiles already on the island. As Allison points out in his rational-actor cut at explaining the crisis, the blockade was both an act preventing the shipment of additional missiles and a signal of American firmness. The missiles already on Cuba were removed because of what the blockade meant and not because of what it did.

An inescapable dilemma confronted the United States. It could not retaliate until the missiles were on the island. Military threats or action required definitive proof. The United States could only justify actions with photographic evidence. It could only take photos after the missiles were on Cuba. The blockade could only be a demonstration of American firmness. Even if the missiles had not been discovered until they were operational, the United States might still have begun its response with a blockade.

Aside from the timing of the discovery of the missiles, Allison argues that the standard operating procedures of the air force affected the decision to blockade rather than to launch a surgical air strike. When the missiles were first discovered, the air force had no specific contingency plans for dealing with such a situation. They did, however, have a plan for a large-scale air strike carried out in conjunction with an invasion of Cuba. The plan called for the air bombardment of many targets. This led to some confusion during the first week of the ExCom's considerations because the air force was talking in terms of an air strike of some five hundred sorties, while there were only some forty known missile sites on Cuba. Before this confusion was clarified, a strong coalition of advisers was backing the blockade.

As a further example of the impact of standard operating procedures, Allison notes that the air force had classified the missiles as mobile. Because this classification assumed that the missiles might be moved immediately before an air strike, the commander of the air force would not guarantee that a surgical air strike would be completely effective. By the end of the first week of the ExCom's deliberations, when Kennedy made his decision for a blockade, the surgical air strike was presented as a "null option." The examination of the strike was not reopened until the following week, when civilian experts found that the missiles were not in fact mobile.

This incident suggests one caveat to Allison's assertion that the missile crisis is a case which discriminates against bureaucratic analysis. In crises, when time is short, the president may have to accept bureaucratic options which could be amended under more leisurely conditions.

NOT ANOTHER PEARL HARBOR

The impact of the air force's standard operating procedures on Kennedy's decision must, however, to some extent remain obscure. It is not likely that either McNamara, who initially called for a diplomatic response, or Robert Kennedy, who was partially concerned with the ethical implications of a surprise air strike, would have changed their recommendations even if the air force had estimated its capacities more optimistically. There were other reasons for choosing the blockade aside from the apparent infeasibility of the air strike. John Kennedy was not anxious to have the Pearl Harbor analogy and applied to the United States. At one of the early meetings of the ExCom his brother had passed a note saying, "I now know how Tojo felt when he was planning Pearl Harbor." The air strike could still be considered even if the blockade failed. A chief executive anxious to keep his options open would find a blockade a more prudent initial course of action.

Even if the air force had stated that a surgical air strike was feasible, this might have been discounted by the president. Kennedy had already experienced unrealistic military estimates. The Bay of Pigs was the most notable example. The United States did not use low-flying photographic reconnaissance until after the president had made his public announcement of the blockade. Prior to the president's speech on October 22, twenty high-altitude U-2 flights were made. After the speech there were eighty-five low-level missions, indicating that the intelligence community was not entirely confident that U-2 flights alone would reveal all of the missile sites. The Soviets might have been camouflaging some missiles on Cuba. Thus, even if the immobility of the missiles had been correctly estimated, it would have been rash to assume that an air strike would have extirpated all of the missiles. There were several reasons, aside from the air force's estimate, for rejecting the surgical strike.

Thus in terms of policy formulation it is not clear that the examples offered by Allison concerning the timing of discovery of the missiles and the standard operating procedures of the air force had a decisive impact on the choice of a blockade over a surgical air strike. The ultimate decisions did rest with the president. The elimination of the nonforcible options was a reflection of Kennedy's values. An explanation of the Cuban missile crisis which fails to explain policy in terms of the values of the chief decision maker must inevitably lose sight of the forest for the trees.

The most chilling passages in *Essence of Decision* are concerned not with the formulation of policy but with its implementation. In carrying out the blockade the limitations on the president's ability to control events become painfully clear. Kennedy did keep extraordinarily close tabs on the workings of the blockade. The first Russian ship to reach the blockade was allowed to pass through without being intercepted on direct orders from the president. Kennedy felt it would be wise to allow Khrushchev more time. The president overrode the ExCom's decision to fire on a Cuban SAM base after a U-2 was shot down on October 27. A spy ship similar to the *Pueblo* was patrolling perilously close to Cuba and was ordered to move farther out to sea.

Despite concerted presidential attention coupled with an awareness of the necessity of watching minute details which would normally be left to lower levels of the bureaucracy, the president still had exceptional difficulty in controlling events. Kennedy personally ordered the navy to pull in the blockade from eight hundred miles to five hundred miles to give Khrushchev additional time in which to make his decision. Allison suggests that the ships were not drawn in. The navy, being both anxious to guard its prerogatives and confronted with the difficulty of moving large numbers of ships over millions of square miles of ocean, failed to promptly execute a presidential directive.

There were several random events which might have changed the outcome of the crisis. The navy used the blockade to test its antisubmarine operations. It was forcing Soviet submarines to surface at a time when the president and his advisers were unaware that contact with Russian ships had been made. A U-2 accidentally strayed over Siberia on October 22. Any one of these events, and perhaps others still unknown, could have triggered escalatory actions by the Russians.

Taken together, they strongly indicate how much caution is necessary when a random event may have costly consequences. A nation like a drunk staggering on a cliff should stay far from the edge. The only conclusion which can be drawn from the inability of the chief executive to fully control the implementation of a policy in which he was intensely interested and to which he devoted virtually all of his time for an extended period is that the risks were even greater than the president knew. Allison is more convincing on the problems concerned with policy implementation than on questions relating to policy formulation. Neither bureaucratic interests nor organizational procedures explain the positions taken by members of the ExCom, the elimination of passivity and diplomacy, or the choice of a blockade instead of an air strike.

CONCLUSION

A glimpse at almost any one of the major problems confronting American society indicates that a reformulation and clarification of objectives, not better control and direction of the bureaucracy, is critical. Conceptions of man and society long accepted are being undermined. The environmentalists present a fundamental challenge to the assumption that man can control and stand above nature, an assumption rooted both in the successes of technology and industrialization and Judeo-Christian assertions of man's exceptionalism. The nation's failure to formulate a consistent crime policy reflects in part an inability to decide whether criminals are freely willing rational men subject to determinations of guilt or innocence or the victims of socioeconomic conditions or psychological circumstances over which they have no control. The economy manages to defy accepted economic precepts by sustaining relatively high inflation and unemployment at the same time. Public officials and economists question the wisdom of economic growth. Conflicts exist over what the objectives of the nation should be and what its capacities are. On a whole range of social issues the society is torn between attributing problems to individual inadequacies and social injustice.

None of these issues can be decided just by improving managerial techniques. Before the niceties of bureaucratic implementation are investigated, it is necessary to know what objectives are being sought. Objectives are ultimately a reflection of values, of beliefs concerning what man and society ought to be. The failure of the American government to take decisive action in a number of critical areas reflects not so much the inertia of a large bureaucratic machine as a confusion over values which afflicts the society in general and its leaders in particular. It is in such circumstances too comforting to attribute failure to organizational inertia, although nothing could be more convenient for political leaders who having either not formulated any policy or advocated bad policies can blame their failures on the governmental structure. Both psychologically and politically, leaders may find it advantageous to have others think of them as ineffectual rather than evil. But the facts are otherwise—particularly in foreign policy. There the choices—and the responsibility—rest squarely with the president.

NOTE

1. Quoted in Daniel Ellsberg, "The Quagmire Myth and the Stalemate Machine," *Public Policy* (Spring 1971): 218.

ↀ

The Iraq War and Agenda Setting

Michael J. Mazarr
U.S. National War College

This essay takes concepts from early examples of a literature that is seldom used in foreign policy analysis—the literature on agenda setting in the U.S. government—and applies it to the case study of the U.S. decision to launch Operation Iraqi Freedom in 2003. After a brief case history, the essay examines various core themes in the agenda-setting framework, and finds that concepts such as policy communities, focusing events, and policy windows can help explain the U.S. decision to go to war. The purpose of the essay is not to advance the current state of agenda-setting research, whose focus is usually not on explaining decision-making processes within the executive branch; the purpose, instead, is to revive an older framework of analysis from the agenda-setting field and demonstrate its utility in examining foreign policy behavior. The essay suggests that the agenda-setting literature could offer similar insights to many other examples of foreign policy decision making, and concludes by suggesting a handful of broader lessons of the agenda-setting paradigm for the analysis of national behavior.

The U.S. decision to intervene in Iraq was, in the view of some observers, the result of a classic groupthink process. To others, it stemmed from one or another cognitive error—perhaps wishful thinking, or cognitive dissonance, or bad analogies. A more traditional way to view the decision would be in rational actor terms: President George W. Bush and his key aides defined their objectives, considered alternatives, weighed the risks and benefits of each, and selected the option that maximized benefits and minimized risks. To the extent that the decision to invade has been studied at all, the results tend to imply one of these well-known theories to

Author's note: Michael Mazarr is professor of national security strategy at the U.S. National War College in Washington, DC, and an adjunct professor in the security studies program at Georgetown University. The views expressed here are his own and do not reflect the policy or position of the U.S. Department of Defense or the National Defense University.

Michael J. Mazarr, "The Iraq War and Agenda Setting," *Foreign Policy Analysis* 3(1): 1–23. Reprinted by permission of John Wiley & Sons.

explain the choice—theories such as groupthink, groupthink, cognitive errors, or pure rational action. But one much less frequently used concept—the literature on agenda setting—offers at least as much insight into the question of why the United States launched Operation Iraqi Freedom (OIF), and may be useful in cases well beyond the Iraq War in explaining national security choices.

This essay's goal is not to advance the state of research on key debates in the agenda-setting literature. That insightful and by now quite extensive literature has come a long way from the contributions of the sources I will rely upon—but its focus is most often on domestic politics, and especially agenda-setting within the Congress.[1] Another area of agenda-setting focus, and the one that deals most often with foreign policy, is in the area of the media's effect on agendas.[2] My purpose is to look back to some of the original writings in this field, to revive an older and more general framework of analysis, and to demonstrate its utility in examining a part of the governmental foreign policy process that is seldom the focus of agenda setting works: the executive branch. My argument is not that the framework outlined here applies to all decision-making situations, or that, alone, it can explain the decision to invade Iraq. It does, however, throw such a useful light on the OIF decision that it may well be useful in assessing other decisions as well. As I will stress, truly accurate portraits of national-level decision making can only be drawn using a variety of frameworks and perspectives.[3] The agenda-setting approach is one among a number of insightful approaches that can aid analysis.[4]

THE DECISION TO ATTACK IRAQ

For a decade before the election of George W. Bush as President, many of the men and women who would become his top foreign policy advisers argued for several major propositions. Two of the leading ones were that American power ought to be vigorously asserted to bring order to a potentially disintegrating post-Cold War world, and that Saddam Hussein had to be removed from power. The first of these goals had been on the minds of key Republican foreign policy leaders for nearly a decade: the writer James Mann contends that the Iraq war can be found in the 1992 Defense Policy Guidance (DPG), drafted at the tail end of the first Bush administration. "The underlying rationale" for OIF "was both broader and more abstract: The war was carried out in pursuit of a larger vision of using America's overwhelming military superiority to shape the future," he contends (Mann 2004b).

Mann explains that the author of the first DPG draft was not, as commonly reported, Paul Wolfowitz, but Zalmay Khalilzad—later a main player on U.S. Iraq policy. The most enthusiastic early reader was then-Secretary of Defense Richard Cheney. And a second version of the report, allegedly "toned down" after the first draft had been publicly revealed, in fact preserved—and in some ways even extended—the core ideas of American dominance offered in the first draft. In fact, a continued argument for U.S. power could have been expected, because the official given responsibility for editing and revising the draft was I. Lewis ("Scooter") Libby, then serving as principal deputy undersecretary of defense for strategy. Rather than walking away from the idea of American predominance, Mann writes, "Libby's rewrite encompassed a more breathtaking vision. The United States would buildup its military capabilities to such an extent that there could never be a rival." It also built up the suggestion that the United States would "act to ensure events moved in ways favorable to U.S. interests"—an early statement of what was to become the preemption doctrine in the second Bush administration. When the draft was done, Defense Secretary Cheney "took ownership of it," according to Khalilzad.

Mann draws a number of lessons from the episode. One is that an especially crucial player in the second Bush administration—Richard Cheney—was a bold, aggressive thinker years before 9/11. A persuasive analysis in *The New Republic* by Spencer Ackerman and Franklin Foer (2003:17–18) agrees: They describe, for example, Cheney's unsuccessful battle in the first Bush administration to shift U.S. Soviet policy away from Mikhail Gorbachev and toward an effort to collapse a tottering Soviet Union and promote democracy. Their sources pointed to a willingness, even then, on Cheney's part to "circumvent the typical bureaucratic channels to gain advantage over his rivals." In retrospect, Cheney probably felt he had been right about the Soviet Union: Gorbachev did not survive; Yeltsin, for whom Cheney had urged support, had arisen to power in Russia and proved a friendly, if unsteady, interlocutor; and the Soviet Union had collapsed in a wave of democratic reforms. If Dick Cheney learned a lesson from the event, it was probably to trust his instincts, to favor rollback rather than incrementalism, to scoff at those who saw all problems as "intractable," and to favor bold moves.

The importance of expressions of American power to many men who would become senior officials in the second Bush administration was joined by, and closely related to, a second foreign policy preoccupation: that Saddam Hussein must be driven from power. During the first Gulf War, Hussein had revealed aggressive regional ambitions; afterwards, U.S. intelligence found him to have been much closer to a nuclear arsenal than had been thought. This episode seems to have cemented several beliefs on the parts of key members of the U.S. national security policy community: that Saddam would do anything to obtain weapons of mass destruction; that he was skilled in concealing his WMD programs from inspectors; that U.S. intelligence tended to underplay, rather than exaggerate, emerging threats; and that no scenario would safeguard U.S. interests short of regime change (Mann 2004a: 182-183, 234–238). Even as of May 1991, therefore, President George H. W. Bush had signed a presidential order authorizing the CIA to spend over a hundred million dollars on various covert operations to "create the conditions for [the] removal of Saddam Hussein from power" (Mayer 2004:61). Dealing with Saddam would directly support the first goal, of restoring American credibility: George Packer (2005:36) suggests that the conservatives saw Iraq "as a test case for their ideas about American power and world leadership."

During the 1990s, a group of dedicated anti-Saddam activists emerged, largely outside government (because most of them were Republicans), who worked together to understand and promote the issue—and who would later assume senior policy positions in the administration of George W. Bush. This group kept abreast of developments in Iraq; spoke to Iraqi exile groups and leaders; published articles and op-eds on the Iraq issue; held conferences and informal meetings on the subject; lobbied members of the administration and Congress to get tougher on Saddam; and fed key information about Saddam's behavior to U.S. and international news media. By the late 1990s, they had become convinced that U.S. policy toward Iraq—and its twin pillars of economic sanctions and no-fry-zones—was collapsing, that time was on Saddam's side.[5] Their policy recommendations centered largely around plans—such as one developed by leading Iraqi exiles, including Ahmed Chalabi—that envisioned a Bay of Pigs-style regime change option (Mayer 2004:58–72). Chalabi made his case in the draft plan called "End Game" by claiming that "The time for the plan is now. Iraq is on the verge of spontaneous combustion. It only needs a trigger to set off a chain of events that will lead to the overthrow of Saddam" (Hersh 2001:58).[6]

In February 1998, this group of anti-Saddam activists sent President Clinton a letter recommending that regime change in Iraq become a major foreign policy priority.[7] The letter claimed that Saddam possessed weapons of mass destruction, and charged that the existing policy of containment was "bound to erode," and "only a determined program to change the regime in Baghdad will bring the Iraqi crisis to a satisfactory conclusion." Iraq "is ripe for a broad-based insurrection," the letter contended. "We must exploit this opportunity." Signatories of the letter included a host of people who would become senior officials in or advisers to the Bush administration, the defining core of the group of anti-Saddam activists: Richard Perle, Douglas Feith, Paul Wolfowitz, Elliot Abrams, Richard Armitage, John Bolton, Paula Dobrianski, Zalmay Khalilzad, Peter Rodman, Donald Rumsfeld, David Wurmser, and Dov Zakheim.

In October 1998, partly under the prodding of this same group, Congress passed the Iraq Liberation Act.[8] It provided for assistance to radio and television broadcasting into Iraq, $97 million in military assistance to "democratic opposition organizations," and humanitarian assistance to Iraqis living in liberated areas. That November, President Clinton stated that containment of Saddam was insufficient, and committed the United States to regime change. In January 1999, Secretary of State Madeline Albright took this message throughout the Middle East—bringing with her on the trip State's "special representative for transition in Iraq," an official charged with developing a strategy to "create the environment and pressures inside Iraq" to overthrow Saddam Hussein (Perlex 1999:A3). Little practical actions came of these statements, however, and even as the Iraq Liberation Act was passing in the Congress, Secretary of Defense William Cohen tempered expectations by saying that Clinton "was not calling for the overthrow of Saddam Hussein" (Loeb 1998:A17). As it became clear that the Clinton administration was not interested in near-term regime change, Chalabi and others turned more of their attention to the anti-Saddam policy activists outside government (Mayer 2004:64–65).

During the campaign, both Bush and Cheney threatened to take action in Iraq. "If I found in any way, shape, or form that he was developing weapons of mass destruction," Bush said, "I'd take 'em out"—a reference, he quickly claimed, to the weapons, not to Hussein himself (Lancaster 2000). In a later television appearance, Bush quipped: "I will tell you this: If we catch him developing weapons of mass destruction in any way, shape, or form, I'll deal with him in a way that he won't like." Cheney, when asked about the "take 'em out" quote, said that "If in fact Saddam Hussein were taking steps to try to rebuild nuclear capacity or weapons of mass destruction, we'd have to give very serious consideration to military action to stop that activity" (Lemann 2001:34).

A number of quiet, largely behind-the-scenes clues also hinted that they planned a greater emphasis on Saddam Hussein's regime. One account, from June of 2000, suggests that an adviser to Bush mentioned during a briefing session that "we ought to have been rid of Saddam Hussein a long time ago," and implied that candidate Bush agreed with the sentiment (Lancaster 2000:A1).[9]

Bush Administration Enters Office

Once George W. Bush was elected, key members of the new administration quickly turned their attention to Iraq. In January 2001, even before Bush had been inaugurated, Vice President-Elect Cheney reportedly asked outgoing Secretary of Defense William Cohen to brief President-Elect Bush, He did not, however, want the "routine, canned, round-the-world tour," according to Bob Woodward's account; instead, he "wanted a serious discussion about Iraq and different options.... Topic A should be Iraq" (Woodward 2004:9).

On January 30, 2001, the new Bush national security team held its first NSC meeting. This session is recounted at length in the Ron Suskind book on former Treasury Secretary Paul O'Neill, *The Price of Loyalty*. O'Neill describes a session heavily focused on Iraq at which Secretary of Defense Rumsfeld, President Bush, and others seemed intent on taking action soon. O'Neill contends that the next NSC meeting, on February I, also focused on Iraq (Suskind 2004:73-74, 85–86). My own interviews did not support O'Neill's version of events: others who participated in these meetings, or spoke directly to participants in them, describe a much less focused discussion, and certainly not one that implied any near-term intention to take on Iraq directly. What was clear to many in the administration was that sanctions were collapsing, that Saddam was growing stronger by the year, and that U.S. policy badly needed attention (Interviewee 7). What a new policy would become, however, was far from clear; and no one with whom I spoke read the meeting as an indication that George Bush was anxious to go after Saddam (Interviewees 3, 15).

These early questions and discussions morphed into an administration-wide debate about the future of sanctions against Iraq, proposals for new models of "smart sanctions," and dialogue about various plans to move against Saddam short of an all-out U.S. attack. At both the principals' and deputies' levels, options were examined that included coups and support for opposition or insurgent groups within Iraq. The broad goal was to put more pressure on Saddam Hussein, but beyond that there was little consensus of what precisely the United States should do or how far it should go. But there was little urgency to the debates, no clear goal, a fragmented policy process, no focusing event to rally policy change, and— apart from a decision on a revised sanctions program—the result was inaction. One report suggests that the "process swiftly became bogged down in bitter interagency disagreements" and "remained stuck" in "gridlock" until September 11 (Burrough et al. 2004:234; Interviewees 3, 4, 9, 11, 15).

Planning did continue, however. Between May 31 and July 26, 2001, the deputies committee met several times to discuss options for how to push Saddam's regime toward collapse. Their resulting proposal, called "A Liberation Strategy," seems to have been a cobbled-together set of initiatives—increased support for opposition groups, tighter economic sanctions, more intrusive weapons inspections, more muscular use of no-fly-zones, and other U.S. military presence in the country—designed to make Saddam more uncomfortable and his people more tempted to revolt (Woodward 2004:21). But it did not envisage direct U.S. military action, and little immediate result came of the plan.

Aftermath of September 11

There is little question that the attacks of September 11, 2001 brought a new urgency, and readiness to take bigger risks, to the administration's thinking on Iraq. Unsurprisingly, given all that had gone before, some administration officials reportedly began thinking about Iraq just hours after the attacks. On September 11 itself, for example, one aide to Secretary of Defense Rumsfeld made notes suggesting "that Rumsfeld had mused about whether to 'hit S. H. at same time—not only UBL.' Rumsfeld also asked for analysis to be done about the possible connection between Iraq and Osama bin Laden (Woodward 2004:25). That same evening, President Bush made the decision to focus the U.S. response to the attacks both on terrorists and on "those who harbor them" (Woodward 2002:30). For advocated of action against Iraq, the invitation to push Saddam Hussein front-and-center in the U.S, answer to 9/11 may have become irresistible.

The most detailed account of key events on the 12th and 13th of September comes from former senior NSC staffer Richard Clarke. On the 12th, Clarke writes that he confronted "a series of discussions about Iraq." Deputy Secretary of Defense Paul Wolfowitz argued that the Al-Qaeda attack could not have been launched without help, probably Iraqi help. Eventually, the group settled on an Afghanistan-first approach—but it was clear to everyone that a "broader war on terrorism" was brewing that was likely to draw in other countries (Clarke 2004:30–31).[10] On the evening of September 12, President Bush pulled Clarke and two of his aides into a small conference room. "Look," Clarke quotes the president as saying. "I Know you have a lot to do and all . . . but I want you, as soon as you can, to go back over everything, everything. See if Saddam did this. See if he's linked in any way." After Clarke said there was no evidence of Iraqi support for Al-Qaeda, Bush said, "Look into Iraq, Saddam," and left (Clarke 2004:32).

Meanwhile, in those first days, senior Defense Department officials turned immediately to Iraq as well. Between September 11 and 15, Deputy Secretary of Defense Paul Wolfowitz and Undersecretary Douglas Feith wrote several memos urging action against Saddam Hussein; on the 13th, Feith sent a classified fax to Third Army headquarters in Atlanta directing planners there to develop a plan for seizing Iraq's southern oil fields—a concept closely tied to the long-standing plans for exile-based operations—within 72 hours. By the Camp David meetings on the 15th, the Defense Department arrived with an official proposal for taking on three initial targets in the war on terror: Al-Qaeda, the Taliban in Afghanistan, and Saddam Hussein's Iraq—and not necessarily in that order (Gordon and Trainor 2006:16, 19–20; Interviewee 9).

On September 15, during those Camp David sessions, Wolfowitz took the opportunity to push Iraq again, arguing that taking down Saddam would be easier than uprooting the Taliban (Woodward 2002:83–84). The group decided to defer a direct confrontation with Iraq—but all agreed that the question would recur, and President Bush specifically stated his belief that Iraq was somehow involved in the 9/11 attacks (Woodward 2002:91, 99). On September 16, Bush told National Security Advisor Condoleeza Rice that "We won't do Iraq now, we're putting Iraq off. But eventually we'll have to return to that question" (Woodward 2004:25–26). Different participants left the meeting with different interpretations: State officials believed they had effectively quashed the discussion of going after Iraq; Defense Department officials thought they had essentially won—the President had agreed that Iraq could be a target; the question was only timing (Interviewees 3, 4, 9, and 11). Paul Wolfowitz would later say that, "To the extent it was a debate about tactics and timing, the President clearly came down on the side of Afghanistan first. To the extent it was a debate about strategy and what the larger goal was, it is at least clear with 20/20 hindsight that the President came down on the side of the larger goal" (Wolfowitz 2003).

On September 17, President Bush signed an order for war in Afghanistan—an order that also asked for military plans for going to war in Iraq. On the 18th and 19th, the Defense Policy Board met to discuss Iraq and hear the comments of Ahmed Chalabi, who talked of Iraq as a breeding ground for terrorists and promised that overthrowing Saddam would not be difficult. Policy Board chief Richard Perle would later tell *Vanity Fair* that Secretary of Defense Rumsfeld "was getting confirmation of his own instincts . . . He seemed neither surprised nor discomfited by the idea of taking action against Iraq" (Burrough et al. 2004:236; another account of this meeting can be found in Mayer 2004:70–71).

For Vice President Cheney, the attacks—according to a variety of knowledgeable sources in public reports, and also according to his own public statements—would seem to have accelerated his commitment to radical, pro-democracy reorientation of the Middle East. Just as he advocated a decade earlier for abandoning incremental measures and taking a sledge hammer to the problem of the Soviet Union, so now he came out in full force for a similar strategy toward the seemingly intractable problems of the Arab and Islamic worlds. One report quotes a "friend" of Cheney's as saying that the Vice President now believed that "what you had to do was transform the Middle East" (Ackerman and Foer 2003:20; Interviewee 14).

On November 21, 2001, after a National Security Council meeting, President Bush pulled Rumsfeld aside, and told him to update his war plans for Iraq (Woodward 2004:1–3). There is every indication, as one account puts it—quoting senior officials close to the president— that Bush "understood instantly after September 11 that Iraq would be the next major step in the global war against terrorism, and that he made up his mind" to deal with Saddam Hussein "within days, if not hours, of that fateful day" (Kessler 2003:A1). All accounts are agreed that the president continued to hope that war could be avoided, but was at the same time determined to remove Hussein from power. On December 28, 2001, U.S. Central Command chief General Tommy Franks provided a detailed briefing on possible Iraq war plans to the president at his Crawford ranch (Woodward 2004:52–64). "Is this good enough to win?" the president asked Franks, and Bush recalls Franks replying that it was. Bush told Woodward "we weren't ready to execute then," but that he left the meeting "with two things on his mind: 'Saddam's a threat. This is an option'" (Woodward 2004:66).

Another press report, this one from the fall of 2002, quoted sources in the U.S. government as suggesting that a de facto regime change decision was made in late 2001. "President Bush's determination to oust Iraq's Saddam Hussein by military force if necessary was set last fall without a formal decision-making meeting or the intelligence assessment that customarily precedes such a momentous decision," suggests the USA Today article, co-written by the paper's senior defense and intelligence reporters. The debate after that time, their sources contended, "has been about the means to accomplish that end." Condoleeza Rice admitted that "There wasn't a flash moment. There's no decision meeting. But Iraq had been on the radar screen—that it was a danger and that it was something you were going to have to deal with eventually" (Diamond et al. 2002).

Recently revealed documents from the United Kingdom have shed additional light on the decision process during early 2002. In anticipation of a visit by British Prime Minister Tony Blair to Crawford in April, Blair's foreign policy adviser David Manning visited Washington and reported back to Blair on his findings. Condoleeza Rice's "enthusiasm for regime change," he wrote in a March 14, 2002 memo—is "undimmed. But there were some signs, since we last spoke, of greater awareness of the practical difficulties and political risks" (Manning 2002). On Sunday, March 17, Paul Wolfowitz lunched with British Ambassador Sir Christopher Meyer. According to the confidential memo, that Meyer wrote to London about the meeting, the trend toward war was obvious, with Wolfowitz arguing for a focus on Saddam Hussein's atrocities as the rationale and scorning the idea of a military coup to topple Saddam. The Iraqi generals all "had blood on their hands," Wolfowitz reportedly said. "The important thing was to try to have Saddam replaced by something like a functioning democracy" (Meyer 2002, 2005).

A month after that conversation, on July 23, 2002, the British Cabinet met with Prime Minister Tony Blair to discuss the emerging Iraqi war plan and U.S. policy. Present at the meeting were such principals as the defense secretary, Geoffrey Hoon; the foreign secretary, Jack Straw; the head of MI6, Sir Richard Dearlove (code-named "C"); Tony Blair's chief of staff, Jonathan Powell; and several others. In the main, these men were reporting back to one another on what they had heard from their contacts in Washington. The "memo" is actually an official set of notes recounting what was said at the meeting. The most famous passage refers to a comment from Dearlove:

> C reported on his recent talks in Washington. There was a perceptible shift in attitude. Military action was now seen as inevitable. Bush wanted to remove Saddam, through military action, justified by the conjunction of terrorism and WMD. But the intelligence and facts were being fixed around the policy. The NSC had no patience with the UN route, and no enthusiasm for publishing material on the Iraqi regime's record. There was little discussion in Washington of the aftermath after military action.

The discussion then turned to a detailed recounting of specific invasion scenarios, confirming the notion that everyone in the room fully expected that war was in-evitable. It "seemed clear" to Foreign Secretary Straw, according to the notes, that "Bush had made up his mind to take military action, even if the timing was not yet decided" (Rycroft 2002).

In April, during an interview with the ITV television network from England, Bush said, "I made up my mind that Saddam needs to go . . . The policy of my government is that he goes." When asked how he planned to attain this goal, Bush replied: "Wait and see" (Woodward 2004:119–120). At about the same time, Richard Haass, then director of policy planning at the State Department, went to see National Security Advisor Condoleeza Rice. "I raised this issue about were we really sure that we wanted to put Iraq front and center at this point," Haass said later. "And she said, essentially, that decision's been made, don't waste your breath. And that was early July" (Lemann 2003:39).

By September 1, 2002, President Bush was telling Cabinet members that he wanted a congressional resolution authorizing force. On September 26, Bush spoke with 18 House members in the White House. "If we use force, it will be fierce and swift and fast," he said. On October 10 and 11, 2002, the use of force resolution passed the Congress. After achieving one United Nations resolution and sustaining growing frustration with later UN debates and IAEA inspections, just after New Year's 2003, Bush met privately with Rice and said the inspections were not working. "We're going to have to go to war," he told her. On March 20, 2003, the first strike of the war on Iraq signaled the beginning of OIF (Woodward 2004:188–189, 254).

EXPLAINING THE DECISION: AN AGENDA-SETTING FRAMEWORK

The literature on agenda setting offers a fresh perspective on decisions like the Iraq war, in part by offering a way to meld the impact of systemic effects and the beliefs and actions of individual decision-makers. Authors who popularized this notion twenty or more years ago set out to explain how, why, and when specific ideas move from concepts to active priorities. In this essay, I will build largely around the framework developed by John Kingdon in *Agendas, Alternatives, and Public Policies* (Kingdon 1984), with references to other agenda-setting works where appropriate.[11]

The basic question at issue for those who focus on agenda-setting processes is "How does an idea's time come?" (Kingdon 1984:1). The agenda-setting literature is concerned with how issues get onto and move up the agenda, but by extension, it is asking the same question posed by international relations and decision-making theories: why do nation-states make the decisions they do? Kingdon explicitly follows the concept offered in the famous essay 1972 "A Garbage Can Model of Organizational Choice" by Michael Cohen, James March, and Johan Olsen. They argued that the policy environment is "a collection of choices looking for problems, issues and feelings looking for decision situations in which they might be aired, solutions looking for issues to which they might be the answer, and decision makers looking for work" (Cohen, March, and Olsen 1972:2). Kingdon (92) describes this as an "organized anarchy" of policy problems, solutions, and advocates, and aims in his framework to describe how policies emerge from it.[12]

Note immediately how different the starting point of agenda setting is from traditional theories of international relations or decision making. Those traditions tend to assume a more linear, orderly world of discrete groups of senior-level national decision makers confronting problems and deciding, influenced by whatever factors are being emphasized by the theory (anarchy, cognitive flaws, socially constructed norms). An agenda-setting approach views national decisions as arising from a more complex, swirling interplay of issues, context, politics, policy advocates, and events.

Kingdon (1984:92–93) describes three separate streams of thinking and action within this organized anarchy: problem recognition; the formation and refining of policy proposals; and politics. These three streams, he contends, "come together at critical times. A problem is recognized, a solution is available, the political climate makes the time right for change, and the constraints do not prohibit action." It is when the three streams come together—partly as a product of events, partly under the influence of policy entrepreneurs who are trying to bring them together—that national policy is made.[13] An agenda-setting framework, then, suggests that nations make policy—make decisions, take action, "behave" in certain ways—when a fortuitous combination of problems, options, events, and policy advocates comes together to spring an idea free from the gridlock of the political process.

This, as I will argue, is precisely the story of the Iraq war. Each piece of the agenda-setting puzzle can be found mirrored in the people and events that led to OIF.

BACKGROUND TO AGENDAS: POLICY COMMUNITIES

Kingdon describes a number of specific steps or elements of the process, and the first one is his notion of "policy communities." Within the organized anarchy of the policy world exist various incubators of new ideas. These can be policy-makers, think tanks, commissions, members of Congress, universities, individual scholars, and other sources.[14] The groups discuss and refine ideas, discarding some and developing others, and a group of specialists concerned with a particular issue develops recognized expertise, interacts with one another, and builds ideas for public policies. Such groups tend to be belief- and idea-driven, rather than interest-driven. Kingdon sees these groups as having an important influence in the first two of his three streams of public policy—the identification of problems and the nomination of policy solutions.

Defining Policy Communities

Policy communities share similar ideas, outlooks, and perspectives (although for ideological or other reasons, they will differ on what policies they support). They are "a bit like academic disciplines, each with their own theories, ideas, preoccupations, and fads" (Kingdon 1984:134). Importantly, then, policy communities are not mere objective experts. They develop belief systems, operational codes, theories, and agendas; they are subject to the same cognitive and social psychological and group dynamics that affect decision makers.[15] The agenda-setting, epistemic community, and policy domain literatures all emphasize the importance of shared *causal beliefs* to such communities: they agree on the basic reasons *why* problems are arising, and from shared views of causation develop shared proposals for policy responses.

Finally, Kingdon emphasizes the broad strategy adopted by policy communities for promoting their ideas, and the resulting way in which the policy process ends up settling upon specific actions. The process does not work in a linear fashion in terms of problem identification leading to option generation producing choice. Instead, advocates from within the policy community develop their ideas "and then wait for problems to come along to which they can attach their solutions" (Kingdon 1984:93–94). The result is that "advocacy of solutions often precedes the highlighting of problems to which they become attached. Agendas are not first set and then alternatives generated; instead, alternatives must be advocated for a long period before a short-run opportunity presents itself on an agenda" (Kingdon 1984:215; see also Polsby 1984:157).

Policy Communities, Groupthink, and Social Construction

Among other possible insights, the concept of the policy community offers a new way to conceptualize the traditional notion of "groupthink." The groupthink model examines cases when a deep and thorough process of rational decision-making gives way to distorted decisions because of the group processes involved (see Janis 1982). Decision-makers in a group setting that is highly cohesive, insulated, and informal in its decision procedures can come to value the group itself more than the quality of its analysis. When this happens, they will crave belongingness over all else and engage in furious concurrence-seeking. The result will be a tendency for quick and ill-considered agreement, a refusal to voice personal doubts, a quashing of independent opinion, an emerging sense of the moral and intellectual superiority of the group leading to a sense of invulnerability, and the demonization of anyone who criticizes the group's favored analysis or policies.

All of these ills flow from the same source—the desire for concurrence.[16] Members need the group, and to preserve it they defend the purity and single-mindedness of its deliberations. Groupthink does not refer to a situation in which people simply agree with one another; for groupthink to be in evidence, a need for cohesion must hang over the proceedings as the primary motivation for concurrence. Seen as members of policy or epistemic communities, however, these experts' views emerge as the product of a combination of shared beliefs and more subtle conformity pressures, rather than a desperate drive for concurrence. The motive force is not membership, but long-incubated similarities in beliefs and worldviews produced by the interactions, research, debate, and mutual conformity pressures of a policy community.[17]

The role of policy communities also allows us to reconceptualize the way in which socially constructed norms work their way into national behavior. The route from the broad process of social construction to established policy has always been somewhat vague; many different norms are in evidence in most societies at any given time, different crowds of decision-makers reflect different norms, and it seems difficult to pin down a specific chain of causation from society-wide construction of norms to national behavior, when we know that various groups *within* societies disagree violently about what behavior is best for the state.[18] If, on the other hand, we refocus the lens onto specific policy communities and their belief systems, the social construction model works quite well: the processes it describes are at work within such communities; these processes generate worldviews and beliefs; and on the basis of those worldviews and beliefs, the policy communities join the swirling crowd of groups and individuals competing to influence national behavior. Some sociological literature on policy domains emphasizes the degree to which the domains themselves are "socially constructed by those active in politics" (Burstein 1991:328), and the most consistently active and relevant to national behavior are influential policy communities.

As beliefs and norms get socially constructed, the role of "causal stories" becomes terribly important. There is good psychological evidence that human beings respond to stories more than they do objective evidence or rational argumentation. Consciously and unconsciously, the factors and people responsible for the social construction of ideas use this receptivity. As one scholar has explained it, "A key element in defining something as a public issue seems to be the development of a 'causal story' purporting to explain how a group comes to experience harm and to show who is to blame and must take responsibility" (Burstein 1991:331–332). When policy proposals can be defended in the context of a meaningful story, their chances for acceptance are greatly improved.

Policy Communities and the Iraq War

The group of anti-Saddam activists who urged stronger measures against Iraq constituted a form of policy community that matches closely the basic idea put forward in the agenda-setting literature. The policy community on this issue was smaller, less technically expert, and more ideologically sell-defined than the broader concept at work in the agenda-setting framework. Nonetheless, the essential role of the community in this policy process mirrors that laid out in the agenda-setting literature: the anti-Saddam activists discussed issues, generated and circulated knowledge, and established themselves—at least within the newly elected Bush administration—as the source of competence on a key policy decision. In Kingdon's terms, this certainly counts as a tightly knit community, one that nurtured common view—especially causal stories about the source of instability and risk in the Middle East.[19]

These particular individuals ended up in key positions of power, it seems, by a combination of intent and happenstance. Some officials who favored the aggressive reassertion of American power recruited like-minded friends into government. Some people sounded out for major jobs (such as former senator Dan Coats for secretary of defense) demurred, leading to the selection of senior officials who became key players in the drive to war (Donald Rumsfeld). The commitment to the destruction of Saddam Hussein's regime does not seem to have been a precondition for being named to the administration of George W. Bush; indeed, had just a few positions been filled differently—for example, a Coats/Richard Armitage team at Defense—President Bush might have received starkly different advice after 9/11. President Bush seems to have chosen Condoleeza Rice based on an evolving relationship of mutual respect and because he valued her advice—not because he had the sense she would be overshadowed by more experienced and powerful bureaucratic players in a debate on Iraq. And of course, Vice President Cheney—chosen for a host of reasons, with his anti-Saddam bona fides probably not among the leading ones, if they were mentioned at all—emerged as a leader of the anti-Saddam policy community in a manner that few outside his inner circle may have expected in 2000. The Iraq case, then, arguably suggests that a decisive policy community can emerge in a given administration without that result having been intended or expected by anyone.

This policy community then lurked beside the stream of events with ready-made options, waiting for an appropriate problem or issue or crisis to come along to which they could attach their pet project. Such a perspective helps to explain the seemingly odd connection: why, as Iraq plainly had little or nothing to do with 9/11 (and when U.S. officials were told as much, in very unambiguous terms, immediately after the terrorist attacks), did advocates of action persist in making the connection? Some have raised dark conspiracy theories, but the agenda-setting framework offers a somewhat more pedestrian explanation: the anti-Saddam activists adopted this approach because *that is what policy communities do*. It fits a natural and well-established pattern of policy advocates who are, as Kingdon explains, less interested in solving specific problems than they are in attaching their long-incubated and deeply felt pet project to problems as they arise (Kingdon 1984:129). Some former senior officials confirmed this broad view of events after 9/11: advocates of confronting Iraq were "using the 9/11 situation to promote their Iraq preferences," said one (Interviewee 3). Immediately after September 11, "Paul Wolfowitz was interested" in going after Iraq, said another; "Paul took his shot, because thats how you do it." Wolfowitz's advocacy "wasn't surprising to me at all. It represented intelligent people of excellent bureaucratic skills using an opportunity to press their agenda" (Interviewee 4).[20]

To be clear, recognizing that the Iraq decision process fits such a well-established pattern is not to endorse that process, or to suggest that it is a good way to make public policy. It is one thing to use the policy window of a health-care bill to attach a favored provision on child welfare clinics; it is another thing entirely to use an attack by one enemy to justify a long-harbored desire to destroy a different adversary. Advocates of war with Iraq intentionally used the post-9/11 atmosphere to promote a policy option in which they fervently believed, but even people sympathetic to their goal must recognize the costs of such a procedural approach. Because the upshot was that the United States decided to go to war in a manner that—as the advocates well recognized—would keep their pet proposal immune from the usual public debate and private, governmental analysis, which is, after all, appropriate for such a momentous decision of statecraft. The result was an ill-considered, ill-planned operation.

The Iraq case also reinforces the suggestion of the agenda-setting literature to reframe our concept of groupthink. Anti-Saddam policy communities—think-tank experts, commissions, special lobbying projects—had been honing the notion of removing Saddam Hussein from power for years. In the case of Iraq, these communities played a number of critical roles. By creating self-selecting forums for dialogue and by circulating confirming evidence about Saddam Hussein's continuing aggressiveness and pursuit of weapons of mass destruction, the communities served to reinforce the view of their participants. A mutual confirmation bias was at work, in which members of these policy communities continually reaffirmed the core tenets of their thinking about Iraq, raising those tenets to the level of accepted faith. In terms of both beliefs and policy options, then, the conservative policy communities on the Iraq issue came to think similarly, reinforce the similarity of their thought, encourage one another in similar views, and suggest implicit social sanctions for those who strayed from the group's accepted consensus.[21] And indeed, the powerful residual effect of these communities on the beliefs of their members is perhaps the single best explanation for the administration's approach to intelligence about Iraq. Policy communities (especially tightly bound ones) can thus have the effect of intensifying the cognitive effects already well underway in human decision-making settings—effects such as confirmation bias. The result, in the Iraq case, was a crimped, casual decision process in which vast assumptions were allowed to slide by without notice or debate. When an option is worked out in advance and slipped into policy during a crisis, this case suggests, it will not be subject to sufficiently rigorous debate. Advocates believe they have already thought the problem through.

ROLE OF THE FOCUSING EVENT AND POLICY WINDOWS

With policy communities laboring to develop and market policy ideas, a second step in the agenda-setting framework then enters the picture: the focusing event. Events play a major role in agenda setting by creating opportunities for advocates from policy communities to pursue well-established beliefs and to promote well-developed policy alternatives.

Defining Focusing Events

Kingdon emphasizes that the slow accumulation of indicators of trouble will not necessarily generate action.[22] His agenda-setting framework points toward sudden breaks from established policy rather than slow, incremental shifts. Event substantial evidence of a growing threat can be ignored, his model suggests, unless energized by a focusing event to break the policy world out of its inertia and create an opening for advocates to champion a new idea. A focusing event does not need to be world-shaking, but it must be a significant enough development that it both calls for and justifies a policy response (Kingdon 1984:95–105). Some of them, however, are intensely powerful: "Sometimes crises come along that simply bowl over everything standing in the way of prominence on the agenda" (Kingdon 1984:101).

Focusing events represent a subset of a larger phenomenon that Kingdon (1984:174–177) describes as a "policy window." Ideas developed within policy communities will generally lie dormant for years, until such time as such a window opens: a crisis occurs; a new president gets elected who is interested in an issue; and a foreign government makes an unprecedented offer. Policy ideas do not migrate into the implementation phase accidentally, but make the trip through such a window of opportunity, when the time is ripe for change. Policy windows do not remain open for long—but when one does open, "solutions flock to it" (Kingdon 1984:185), as policy advocates rush to try to attach their favored policy to the opportunity represented by the window. One lesson of Kingdon's analysis is that policymakers often do not think up new options when windows open; these opportunities are so unpredictable, and remain open for such short periods, that policymakers can only turn to policy communities for ready-made options rather than think up entirely new ones.[23] This magnifies the importance of policy communities in generating national behavior: they are the cultivators and purveyors of only detailed options for government action that will be considered by senior leaders.

A focusing event or policy window has the result of joining the three streams of policy—problem recognition, development of policy options, and politics—in a way that makes change possible. Indeed, Kingdon stresses that a focusing event in and of itself is not enough to generate policy; without existing indicators of trouble that are perceived to come to fruition in the focusing event, and without preexisting policy ideas and advocates ready to jump on the opportunity of the event, nothing will happen (Kingdon 1984:103). In the same context, Kingdon distinguishes between "problems" and "conditions." Conditions are merely situations that the policy world believes it has to put up with—facts of life that cannot be changed. Conditions morph into problems when "we come to believe that we should do *something* about them"; obviously, then, there are "great stakes" in defining the two categories, and placing various issues in one as opposed to another (Kingdon 1984:103, 115; emphasis mine).[24]

Critically, then, the same process of social construction and meaning-making that we found to be underway in policy communities in general continues and indeed intensifies under the glare of a focusing event. Events, one scholar explains, "have little meaning by themselves; they are given meaning by groups utilizing particular interpretive frameworks and may affect politics only when groups are ideologically and organizationally prepared to take advantage of them" (Polsby 1984:168–169; Burstein 1991:335). A nation's response to a focusing event is strongly influenced by the socially constructed beliefs, norms, worldviews, and policy options developed by the policy community that happens to be activated by the event.

Focusing Events and Iraq

This particular case study benefits from an obvious and intensely powerful focusing event: the terrorist attacks of September 11, 2001. But the similarity to the agenda-setting framework does not begin and end there; in other, more specific ways, events with regard to Iraq both before and after 9/11 follow the script outlined in the agenda-setting literature.

The first part of that script contends that gradually accumulating evidence of a problem will not in itself cause a major policy change without some form of a more pointed focusing event. This was the story of the Iraq issue before 9/11: the same evidence about weapons of mass destruction and terrorist ties existed on 9/10 as on 9/13, but no one in the U.S. government was talking about invasion. As we saw, the policy entrepreneurs who would later attach their project to the fallout from 9/11 had been making a more limited argument for stronger U.S. support of opposition groups; but this was going nowhere in the interagency process, and there is little reason to believe that the Bush administration would have adopted radically tougher policies toward Saddam Hussein's Iraq without a focusing event to latch onto. But of course 9/11 did occur, and it then became the focusing event onto which the anti-Saddam activists attached their projects.

This mechanism—of pre-existing policy ideas latching onto focusing events, even if the match between them is unclear—helps to explain another element of bad assumptions and poor planning that took place in OIF, the refusal to engage in more detailed long-range planning for post-war contingencies. The model that the anti-Saddam activists had been developing for years was not one of a U.S. invasion—it was based on rebel groups in Iraq, built around Kurds and Shi'ites toppling Saddam with some U.S. help, and then governing the country. How that governance would take place no one really defined, but then the stakes for U.S. planners were smaller when Iraqis would be the ones doing it. While the failure to plan more rigorously once the option shifted to a U.S. invasion seems senseless in retrospect, when seen through an agenda-setting lens, such thinking makes perfect sense: U.S. *officials were applying a pre-existing policy idea to the opportunity offered by a focusing event*—and in that pre-existing idea, in which Iraqis would have run the post-war phase, such assumptions made reasonable sense. The problem was not that U.S. officials were ignorant of post-war complications; the problem was that they had spent years incubating a policy option—Iraqi rebellions against Saddam supported, but not led or aided on the ground, by the United States—that had embedded a certain way of looking at the post-war phase deep into their thought process. Part of the problem may have been that anti-Saddam activists could not break out of the mental map that told them the post-war phase would take care of itself.

But the Iraq case also signals the dangers of such analytical outcomes, the problems with an opportunistic model of policy formation. As Polsby (1984:169) explains, a crisis can offer an opportunity for those with ready-made solutions to get them enacted, "but it cannot make the policy actually work afterward." Policy advocates thus "have to be reasonably confident of the efficacy of the alternatives they propose—or they may get what they "want" and find it was not worth getting."

ROLE OF THE POLICY ENTREPRENEUR

When a focusing event or policy window creates an opportunity to change national behavior, the person or persons who then make this happen are the "policy entrepreneurs"—advocates determined, for one reason or another, to fight inertia, the bureaucracy, opposing interests, and anything else in their way to get the idea through the window and into law or policy. Policy entrepreneurs are active all the time, not only when window's of opportunity are opportunity are open. But they also act as judges of ripeness and work to push the hardest when they perceive such a policy window to be open.

Defining the Policy Entrepreneur

Policy entrepreneurs are people willing to "invest their resources—time, energy, reputation, and sometimes money—in the hope of a future return" (Kingdon 1984:129; Polsby 1984:55, 173–174). That return could come in the form of the adoption of policies or promotion of values they support, satisfaction for being a part of the governmental policy-making machinery, personal advancement, or other benefits. They are highly motivated advocates lying in wait in and around government, on the lookout for policy windows and focusing events to justify their pet projects.

Kingdon makes clear (1984:47; see also Cobb and Elder 1983:89–90) that elected officials exercise the most influence in the process, and it is a natural extension to claim that the most effective and powerful policy entrepreneurs will be senior government officials. As one essay on epistemic communities put it: "To the extent to which an epistemic community consolidates bureaucratic power within national administrations and international secretaries, it stands to institutionalize its influence and insinuate its views into broader international politics" (Haass 1992:4; cf. also 23). The qualities of policy entrepreneurs include being able to claim a hearing from senior officials, through positional authority, expertise, or interest-group power; being known for one's connections and political skill; and, above all, persistence (Kingdon 1984:189–190).[25]

Policy entrepreneurs regularly engage, Kingdon argues, in a long-term process of "softening up" to lay the day-to-day groundwork for the ultimate acceptance of their idea once a window happens to open. Their targets in this process can include the general public, the "specialized" public, and policy communities (and I would add, other officials throughout government who will have a voice in the interagency process). He describes specific mechanisms used for softening up to include introducing legislation, giving speeches, creating commissions and generating blue-ribbon panel reports, and floating trial balloons (Kingdon 1984:135–136; for a related list, see also Adler 1992:140–142). Policy entrepreneurs, then, can be seen as the human embodiment of the social construction of policy, the personification of the stories that policy communities tell (Burstein 1991:332).

Policy Entrepreneurs and the Iraq War

The role of the policy entrepreneur was pronounced in the U.S. decision to conduct OIF. More even than other cases amenable to an agenda-setting framework, the Iraq example seems highly dependent on the role of entrepreneurs—specific, key individuals, mostly within government, who (as the framework would suggest) favored long-established policy options and used the focusing event of 9/11 to advance them.[26]

Paul Wolfowitz emerges as a key policy entrepreneur. Already pushing, according to many accounts, for strong and-Saddam policy before 9/11, several sources concur that he began urging President Bush to think about an Iraq-Al-Qaeda connection in the days after September 11. Another strong entrepreneurial figure, according to many reports, appears to have been Vice President Cheney. Below their level, a variety of other officials in the Defense Department, the Vice President's office, and elsewhere in government endorsed and pushed the recommendation to deal decisively with the problem of Saddam Hussein's Iraq. Outside government, others, most notably including pundit and Defense Policy Board head Richard Perle and Iraqi exile Ahmad Chalabi, argued for the same course. But it was the role of key government officials— and their ability, in paraphrasing Haass' conclusion, to "institutionalize their influence and insinuate their views into policy"—that was decisive in this case. These policy entrepreneurs had, as suggested in Kingdon's model, been engaged in a "softening up" process for years, in precisely the ways Kingdon would expect—publishing articles, holding conferences, promoting legislation, lobbying officials, and more. In this case, of course, the role of Vice President Cheney as an entrepreneur has been well discussed—as had been the challenge such an energetic vice presidential role poses for an interagency process more commonly built around debates between appointed cabinet officials.

Interestingly, in the Iraq case, the most important policy entrepreneur may well have been the figure that veterans of the U.S. government routinely describe as the "only real policy maker in the executive branch": the president himself. Evidence in the case study strongly suggests that George W. Bush did not have to be hauled into advocacy for OIF; he harbored such inclinations from the beginning, and quickly began sending signals that removing Saddam Hussein from power was a serious option. Because of the way the U.S. executive branch is such a president-centric system, the way that it responds so powerfully and diligently to the slightest policy hints from the president, Bush's leanings may have exercised a decisive effect. A fascinating question that begs further thought is what happens when a president becomes policy entrepreneur, the policy-community-member-in-chief; a tentative answer suggested by this case is that the natural checks and balances within the executive branch, of varying perspectives and bureaucratic standoffs, tend to melt away—as does rigorous debate, questioning of assumptions, and careful planning. "Once the President decides," one former senior government official told me, "then the only thing anyone cares about is making what he wants happen" (Interviewee 4). The result, though, can be a bad process. "I don't fault the policy entrepreneurs for being entrepreneurial and pressing their case," another official said. "What I fault is that it was so easy for them to win, and that the decision-making was so unsystematic" (Interviewee 3).

Criteria for Ideas to Succeed

Kingdon also offers some thoughts about which ideas survive once pushed forward by policy entrepreneurs, ideas that shed further light on the process that led to OIF.

At one point, he suggests three basic criteria for ideas to survive and prosper in the policy stream: technical feasibility, value acceptability, and anticipation of future constraints (Kingdon 1984:138–146).[27] In the Iraq case, there is little question about the second criterion: invading Iraq supported numerous values important to senior decision-makers, from removing Saddam Hussein from power to demonstrating U.S. military strength and resolve. As for the other two criteria, however, while they were at work in the Iraq decision, they were only considered in ways that have proven to be tragically incomplete. The planning process, for example, examined the technical feasibility of the *initial military campaign* in great detail, and from that extrapolated to the feasibility of the complete operation, through post-conflict stabilization to occupation and the creation of a new government. The technical feasibility of post-conflict reconstruction was never assessed in any rigorous way at the principals' level; several interviewees told me that the president's entire formal briefing time on postwar Iraq amounted to a single, one-hour presentation. Meanwhile, close consideration of possible future constraints was side-tracked by the assumption that the invasion would not produce a long, drawn-out, costly occupation. These examples demonstrate the ways in which an analytical tool such as the agenda-setting framework must be completed by other perspectives—in this case, the literature on cognitive dynamics, which helps explain how theoretically objective criteria like an appreciation of future constraints can be filtered through wishful thinking, cognitive dissonance, or bad analogies.

Another point that Kingdon makes about policy making viewed through an agenda-setting lens is that it is not incremental. A gradual process of idea-generation, softening up, and coalition building goes go on within policy communities, but this is more properly viewed as background noise to policy. Actual decisions—national behavior—emerge when a policy window opens long enough to let some of that noise through, and the moment feels to the participants like a sudden coalescing of the opinion: people in government "'speak of a growing realization,' an 'increasing feeling'… and 'coming to a conclusion'"(1984:147). There are no new policy ideas, Kingdon suggests; existing ones merely cluster around policy windows, trying to get through. When a policy window does open, then, the policy it helps usher into being will generally be a recombination of long-proposed ideas rather than something tailored to the situation. This paradigm leads kingdom to another conclusion: the crucial factor when a policy window opens is not what policy ideas might conceivably meet the needs it creates, but what "available alternative" is lying around, waiting to be applied. Well-developed available alternatives can elbow aside "equally worthy" concepts that do not happen to have "available, worked-out proposal attached" (1984:150).

Paul Light (1999:193-194) emphasizes similarly that, because of time and attention constraints on senior decision-makers, the search for policy alternatives is generally "simpleminded"—that is, "limited to the 'neighborhood of the current alternatives.'" Neither new and innovative ideas, nor detailed assessments of the proposals loitering in the "neighborhood," are called for. And, again stressing the importance of the president as policy entrepreneur, Light contends that this policy search will be "biased" in whatever direction the executive branch thinks the president wants to go. "If a President is interested in large-scale initiatives," Light contends, "the search will produce large-scale initiatives."

All of this mirrors the Iraq case quite closely. After years of broad worry about Saddam Hussein's Iraq and some planning, never put into action, to support a military coup or exile-based insurrections, 9/11 led to a "growing realization" that Saddam would have to be dealt with. More importantly, dealing decisively with Iraq was one or the few "available alternatives" for responding to a major terrorist attack: there was no global counterterrorism strategy lying on a shelf, waiting to be dusted off. As time has made clear, moreover, fighting terrorism is an enormously complicated, nuanced, self-contradictory task dial does not lend itself to simple policy solutions of the sort entrepreneurs can shove through a policy window on short notice. Again, one possible interpretation of Bush's state of mind after his December 28, 2001 CENTCOM briefing on the war plan, for example, is that it furnished precisely the sort of "available alternative" he was looking for—an available, acceptable option assembled by a general who had just won a surprisingly easy conflict in Afghanistan. The danger, of course, was that such thinking closed out the numerous other factors, from world opinion to non-military aspects of postwar planning, that would play a decisive role in determining the fate of the Iraq mission writ large.

It is striking how little outside advice Bush sought, how few tough questions were asked of knowledgeable observers. He admitted to Woodward that he simply never asked Powell whether the Secretary of State thought attacking Iraq was the right thing to do. Rumsfeld himself said, "Whether there was ever a formal moment when he asked me, 'Do I think he should go to war,' I can't recall it" (Woodward 2004:416). As Richard Clarke has written, "I doubt that anyone ever had the chance to make the case to [President Bush] that attacking Iraq would actually make America less secure... Certainly he did not hear that from the small circle of advisers who alone are the people whose views he respects and trusts" (Clarke 2004:244). Again, this behavior makes perfect sense from an agenda-setting perspective: when a policy window opens, available alternatives are not likely to be subjected to laborious rethinking. Entrepreneurs are trying to push them through, and policymakers have too little time to be deliberate.

Also in this case, the system was clearly responding to hints from its chief entrepreneur—President Bush—about what be wanted. His very early suggestion that the United States was now "at war" against terrorism encouraged Defense Department officials, rushing back to Washington in the immediate aftermath of 9/11, to view their task in a certain way (Burroughs et al. 2004:234). His numerous comments about Iraq in the days after 9/13 left little doubt that he was sympathetic to a case for removing Saddam Hussein.

OIF thus occurred in part because a policy window opened, and going after Saddam Hussein was one of the few available alternatives ready for policy entrepreneurs to take up and act upon. Again, though, as I stressed in the section on social construction, it is important to think or these processes as being at work on specific groups, communities, or movements, rather than on all players in the policy world. Invading Iraq seemed an available alternative to the anti-Saddam policy community, which counted among its members many senior officials of the Bush administration as well as supportive members of the broader national security community. It is not likely that it would have seemed so attractive, as a ready-made available alternative, to a Gore administration, or a McCain administration, or even a George H. W. Bush administration. When the agenda-setting framework speaks of considerations like feasibility, value acceptability, or available alternatives, those things take on real life *as seen by specific groups of people at specific moments in history*: groups with socially constructed beliefs and norms, human cognitive limitations, the pressure of group dynamics, and so on. It is only in a set of overlapping frameworks—agenda-setting, social construction, cognitive dynamics, group dynamics, beliefs, and ideas—that we can begin to capture the full richness of national behavior.

CONCLUSION: A USEFUL MODEL FOR FOREIGN POLICY ANALYSIS

If the Iraq case is any guide, the agenda-setting model offers a useful template for evaluating how and why national security and foreign policy decisions get made. The decision to embark upon OIF matches very closely the agenda-setting framework: at the beginning of the Bush administration, the beliefs and options nurtured by the policy communities—as the agenda-setting literature would suggest—joined a swirling policy environment. However, as that literature also suggests, even powerful preexisting beliefs and clear options need further situational help to mature into established policy, and a hawkish view on Iraq did not get this help at first. The Al-Qaeda attacks and subsequent declaration of a Global War on Terror furnished a classic policy window—an opportunity for advocates, their beliefs, and proposals developed in policy communities, to get access to the president and other senior leaders and make a persuasive case for action. As explained above, many other, more discrete insights of the agenda-setting literature are borne out in the Iraq decision-making case.

Applying agenda-setting to the Iraq case can also generate broader insights on theories and frameworks commonly used in foreign policy analysis. A tentative list of such insights might include the following:

- *Absent any one of the four major factors outlined in the model, a policy idea might never come to fruition.* Without impassioned policy entrepreneurs in the Bush administration who favored the liberation of Iraq—had President Bush been getting advice from Jim Baker, Lawrence Eagleburger, and Brent Scowcroft, in other words, rather than Wolfowitz and Cheney—there may have been no critical mass of opinion favoring an attack. Had a relevant policy community connected to the levers of power not both developed the idea and nurtured a group of analysts passionately committed to it, the option may have seemed too unfinished to implement. And of course, without the attacks of September 11, President Bush may not have been able to generate—or seen the political viability of generating, or indeed the substantive need to generate—public support for the idea.
- *Finding the true origins of policy is elusive.* Policy communities can work an issue indefinitely until a policy window opens. Many individuals contribute to the creation and development of a policy idea. Policy entrepreneurs are needed to take an idea from its slumber in the policy community into the consciousness of government officials. A propitious event is needed to create a policy window. Given all of these (and many other) factors involved in finally bringing a policy idea to fruition, it becomes impossible to track down a simple or single origin. This conclusion is not friendly toward monocausal theories that posit a single major variable in explaining national behavior.
- *An agenda-setting perspective does not necessarily imply strong public participation in foreign policy decisions. In fact, it may suggest the opposite.* Some of the earliest works in the agenda-setting field came from political scientists concerned with issues of participation, and the degree of "true" democracy in the U.S. system (Schattschneider 1960; Cobb and Elder 1971). Despite worries that an agenda-setting avenue to decisions would intensify narrow, elite control of policy, at least one early verdict was optimistic: the broad agenda-setting process, drawing in groups outside government and generating a debate on issues, "makes allowances for continuing mass involvement" (Cobb and Elder 1971:912). This may be true for domestic issues and issues involving the Congress

and a broad array of interest groups, but in the more rarified world of foreign policy—if the OIF case is any guide—an agenda-setting framework applied to decisions by the executive branch suggests the possibility for decisions of the greatest national import to be determined by extraordinarily small numbers of people.[28]

- Factors such as power considerations and structural dynamics may be part of the background noise in the policy community, but they do not explain behavior (Haass 1992:4). Behavior emerges, not from a simple linkage between ideas about the international system—such as classical realism's emphasis on power-seeking—and policy, but from a much more complicated set of intermediary tumblers that must be engaged for the lock of policy to be opened. The agenda-setting framework helps us to understand more properly the role of the factors suggested by international relations theory: structural dynamics, power considerations, the role of institutions and regimes, avid similar notions are part of the input—contextual, normative, belief-system—to policy communities and policy entrepreneurs. They are pieces of the puzzle, not the puzzle itself.

- *Social construction is very much at work, but on a community-by-community, issue-by-issue basis*. It is not a generic, societal, or state-based process as *sometimes* suggested—or at least not only that, and on national security issues, not primarily that. "States" possess no singular, unified norms, beliefs, values, or operational codes that are brought to bear on policy issues. Various groups of policy-makers and policy-influencers—policy communities—have different versions of sometimes conflicting, sometimes overlapping norms and beliefs. Depending on who is in power, which policy community is ascendant at the moment, which focusing events create what policy windows for which issues, the policy proposals generated by these norms and beliefs work their way into national behavior.

- The reality of the agenda-setting technique reinforces the importance of checks and balances in the decision to go to war. If it is true that policy entrepreneurs in *the* executive branch will use policy windows to push forward pet projects—even including decisions to go to war—the role of the Congress in overseeing and checking the actions of the executive becomes even more important. Once the executive branch is in the grip of a set of devoted policy entrepreneurs, only the legislature will be able to mandate a more thorough debate—something that the U.S. Congress manifestly failed to do in 2002–2003.

In sum, the literature on agenda setting is an oft-ignored tool that can furnish important insights into the making of national security and foreign policy decisions. Students of such processes would benefit from a closer knowledge of this literature.

REFERENCES

ACKERMAN. SPENDER, AND FRANKLIN FOER, (2003) The Radical: What Dick Cheney Really Believes. *The New Republic*, December 1 and 8.

ADLER. EMANUEL. (1992) The Emergence of Cooperation: National Epistemic Communities and the International Evolution of the Idea of Nuclear Arms Control. *International Organization* 46: 101–145.

ANDRADE, LYDIA, AND GARY YOUNG. (1996) Presidential Agenda Setting: Influences on the Emphasis of Foreign Policy. *Political Research Quarterly* 49:591–605.

BAER, ROBERT (2002) *See No Evil: The True Story of a Ground Soldier in the CIA's War on Terrorism.* New York: Crown.

BUX, HANS. (2004) *Disarming Iraq.* New York: Pantheon Books.

BURROUGH, BRYAN, EVGENJA PERETZ. DAVID ROSE, AND DAVID WISE. (2004) Path to War. *Vanity Fair*, May.

BURSTEIN. PAUL. (1991) Policy Domains: Organization, Culture, and Policy Outcomes. *Annual Review of Sociology* 17:327–350.

BYMAN, DANIEL, KENNETH POLLACK, AND GIDEON ROSE. (1999) The Rollback Fantasy. *Foreign Affairs* 78:24–41.

CAMPBELL, COLIN. (2004) Unrestrained Ideological Entrepreneurship in the Bush II Advisory System: An Explanation of the Response to 9/11 and the Decision to Seek Regime Change in Iraq. In *The George W. Busk Presidency: Appraisals and Prospects*, edited by Colin Campbell and Bert A. Rockman. Washington, DC: Congressional Quarterly Press.

CLARKE, RICHARD. (2004) *Against All Enemies*, New York: Free Press.

COBB. ROGER W., AND CHARLES D. ELDER. (1971) The Politics of Agenda-Building: An Alternative Perspective for Modern Democratic Theory. *The Journal of Politics* 33:892–915.

COBB. ROGER W., AND CHARLES D. ELDER. (1983) *Participation in American Politics: The Dynamics of Agenda-Building.* 2nd edition. Baltimore: Johns Hopkins University Press.

COBB, ROGER, JEANNIE K. ROSS, AND MARC H. ROSS. (1976) Agenda Building as a Comparative Political Process. *The American Political Science Review* 70:125–138.

COHEN, JEFFREY E. (1995) Presidential Rhetoric and the Public Agenda. *American Journal of Political Science* 39:87–107.

COHEN, MICHAEL D., JAMES G. MARCH, AND JOHAN P OLSEN, (1972) A Garbage can Model of Organizational Choice. *Administrative Science Quarterly* 17:1–25.

COOK, ROBIN. (2004) *Point of Departure: Diaries from the Front Bench.* London: Pocket Books.

COOK, FAY LOMAX, TOM R. TYLER, EDWARD G. GOETZ, MARGARET T. GORDON, DAVID POTESS, DONNA R.LEFF AND HARVEY L. MOLOTCH. (1983) Media and Agenda Setting: Effects on the Public, Interest Group Leaders, Policy Makers, and Policy. *The Public Opinion Quarterly* 47:16–35.

DIAMOND, JOHN, JUDY KEEN. DAVID MONIZ. SUSAN PACE, AND BARBARA SLAVON, (2002) Iraq Course Set from Tight White House Circle. *USA Today*, September 11. Available from http://www.usatoday.com/news/ world/2002–09–10-iraq-iraq-war_x.htm

EAVEY, CHERYL L., AND GARY J. MILLER. (1984) Bureaucratic Agenda control: Imposition or Bargaining? *The American Political Science Review* 78:719–733.

EDWARDS, GEORGE C., AND B. DAN WOOD. (1999) Who Influences Whom? The President, Congress, and the Media. *The American Political Science Review* 93:327–344.

FINNEMORE, MARTHA. (1996) *National Interests in International* Society. Ithaca: Cornell University Press.

GADDIS. JOHN LEWIS. (2002) *The Landscape of History: How Historians Map the Past.* New York: Oxford University Press.

GORDON, MICHAEL R., AND BERNARD E. TRAINOR. (2006) *Cobra II: The Inside Story of the Invasion and Occupation of Iraq.* New York: Pantheon Books.

HAASS. PETER M. (1992) Introduction: Epistemic Communities and International Policy Coordination. International *Organization* 10:1–35.

HART. PAUL T. (1990) *Groupthink in Government: A Study of Small Groups and Policy Failure.* Baltimore: Johns Hopkins University Press.

HERSH, SEYMOUR. (2001) The Iraq Hawks: Can Their Plan Work? *The New Yorker*, December 24 and 31.

JANIS, IRVING. (1982) *Groupthink: Psychological Studies of Policy Decisions and Fiascoes.* New York: Houghton Mifflin.

KESSLER, GLENN. (2003) U.S. Decision on Iraq Has Puzzling Past. *Washington Post*, January 12.

KINGDOM, JOHN. (1984) *Agendas, Alternatives, and Public Policies*. New York: HarperCollins.

KOSICKL GERALD M. (1993) Problems and Opportunities in Agenda Setting Research. *Journal of Communications* 43:100–128.

LANCASTER. JOHN. (2000) In Saddam's Future, A Harder U.S Line, *Washington Post,* June 3.

LEMANN, NICHOLAS. (2001) The Iraq Factor. *The New Yorker*, January 22.

LEMANN, NICHOLAS. (2003) How It Came to War. *The New Yorker*, March 31.

LIGHT PALE. C. (1999) *The Presidents Agenda: Domestic Policy Choice from Kennedy to Clinton*. 3rd edition. Baltimore: Johns Hopkins University Press.

LOEB, VERNON. (1998) Saddam's Iraqi Foes Heartened by Clinton. *Washington Post*, November 16.

MANHEIM, JAROL B. (1986) A Model of Agenda Dynamics. *Communication Yearbook* 499–516.

MANN. JAMES. (2004a) *Rise of the Vulcans: The History of Bush's War Cabinet*. New York: Viking.

MANN. JAMES. (2004b) The True Rationale? It's a Decade Old. *Washington Post*, March 7, 2004.

MANNING, DAVID. (2002) Prime Minister: Your Trip to the U.S.. British Government memo, March 14. Available from http://www.downingstreetmcmo.com

MAYER, JANE. (2004) The Manipulator. *The New Yorker*, June 7

MCCOMBS, MAXWELL E., AND DONALD L. SHAW. (1972) The Agenda-Setting Function of Mass Media. *Public Opinion Quarterly* 36:176–184.

MENDELSON, SARAH. (1993) Internal Battles and External Wars: Politics, Learning, and the Soviet Withdrawal from Afghanistan. *World Politics* 45:327–360.

MEYER. CHRISTOPHER. (2005) How Britain Failed to Cheek Bush in the Run Up to War. *The Guardian*, November 7.

MEYER, CHRISTOPHER. (2002) "Confidential and Personal Memo" to Sir David Manning. British Embassy, Washington, March 18. Available from http://www.downingstreetmemo.com

MUFSON. STEVEN. (2000) A World View of His Own: On Foreign Policy, Bush Parts Ways With Father. *The Washington Post*, August 11.

PACKER, GEORGK. (2005) *The Assassin's Gate: America in Iraq*. New York: Farrar, Straus and Giroux.

PEAKS, JEFFREY S. (2001) Presidential Agenda Setting in Foreign Policy. *Political Research* Quarterly 34:69–86.

PERLEZ, JANE. (1999) Albright Introduces a New Phrase to Promote Hussein's Ouster. *New York Times*, January 29.

POLSBY, NATHAN W. (1984) *Political Innovation in America: The Politics of Initiation*. New Haven: Yale University Press.

ROCHEFORT DAVID A., AND ROGER W. COBB, EDS. (1994) *The Politics of Problem* Definition: *Shaping the Policy Agenda*. Lawrence: University Press of Kansas.

RYCROFT MATTHEW. (2002) Iraqi Prime Minister's Meeting, 23 July. Secret and Strictly Personal U.K. government memorandum. Available from http://www.downingstreetmemo.com

SCHATTVSCHNEIDER, ELMER E. (1960) *The Semi-Sovereign People*. New York: Holt; Rinehart and Winston.

SEIB, GERALD. (2000) Campaign Query: Who Will Act to Oust Saddam? *The Wall Street journal*, June 28.

SINCIAIR. BARBARA DECKARD. (1985) Agenda Control and Policy Success: Ronald Reagan and the 97th House. *Legislative Studies Quarterly* 10:291–314.

SUSKIND. RON. (2004) *The Price of Loyalty: George W. Bush, the White House, and the Education of Paul O'Neill*. New York: Simon and Schuster.

TAYLOR, ANDREW J. (1998) Domestic Agenda Setting, 1947–1994. *Legislative Studies Quarterly* 23: 373–397.

VAN BELLE, DOUG. (1993) Domestic Imperatives and Rational Models of Foreign Policy Decision Making. In *The Limits of State Autonomy: Societal Groups and Foreign Policy Formulation Chapter*, edited by D. Skid move arid V. Hudson. Boulder: Westview Press.

VAN BELLE. DOUG. (2000) New York Times and Network TV News Coverage of Foreign Disasters: The Significance of the Insignificant Variables. *Journalism and Mass Communication* Quarterly 77:50–70.

WALKER, JACK L. (1377) Setting the Agenda in the U.S. Senate: A Theory of Problem Selection. *British journal of Political Science* 7:423–445.

WENDT, ALEXANDER. (1992) Anarchy is What States Make of It: The Social Construction of Power Politics. *International Organization* 46:391–425.

WOLFOWITZ. PAUL. (2003) Interview with *Vanity Fair* magazine, May 9, 2003. Department of Defense transcript of interview. Available from http://www.dod.goy/transcripts/2003/tr20030509-depsecdef0223.html

WOODWARD, BOB. (2002) *Bush at War*. New York: Simon and Schuster.

WOODWARD, BOB. (2004) *Plan of Attack-*. New York: Simon and Schuster.

NOTES

1. See, for example, Walker (1977), Sinclair (1985). Taylor (1998), and Edwards and Wood (1999). Other areas of specific focus include the work of Eavey on bureaucratic control of agendas (see, for e.g., Eavey and Miller 1984), and the role of presidential rhetoric on public agendas (see Cohen 1995).

2. See, for example. McCombs and Shaw (1972), Cook et at (1983), Manheim (1986), Kosicki (1993), and Van Belle (1993, 2000).

3. John Lewis Gaddis (2002) makes an excellent extended argument on this score: see, especially chapters 4 and 5.

4. In the research for this continuing project, I have conducted interviews with a number of former senior government officials, from working level to cabinet level in the administration of George W. Bush, to supplement the numerous published sources of information on the Iraq war. My agreement with the interview subjects was for anonymity, and so they wall be cited only by number.

5. This process was well underway by 2000. Even Hans Blix (2004:53–54; Interviewee 13) stresses this fact in his book, noting the "sanctions fatigue" that was afflicting leading powers at the time, the popular outrage at the effects of the sanctions. Baghdad was becoming filled with businessmen; the oil-for-food program was enriching Saddam and strengthening his hold on power—ironically, creating just the sort of kleplocracy that would prove unable to function as an effective government, thus consigning Iraqi infrastructure to a gradual decline, requiring vast new investments to rescue something U.S. planners did not recognize until it was too late.

6. Former CIA case officer Robert Baer reports being briefed on the End Game plan in August 1994, by which time, according to Baer. It had been "well shopped around Washington" (Baer 2002:188). See also Gordon and Trainor (2006:12–13). For an early critique of such strategies, see Byman, Pollack, and Rose (1999) These concepts became an initial basis for post-9/11 Iraq planning, but once CENTCOM was fully engaged, they were dropped; Interviewees 5, 6, 7, 9.

7. A good, although skeptical, account of the group and the text of its letter can be found at www.disinfopedia.org.

8. The Iraq Liberation Act, PL 105–338, October 31, 1998; available in full text, among other places, at: http#news.findlaw.com/hdocs/docs/iraq/libact103198.pdf#search = 'The %20Iraq%20 Liberation%20Act'.

9. During the election, several newspaper and magazine analyses predicted that a Bush administration would deal more forcefully with Iraq (Mufson 2000:A1). Condoleeza Rice was quoted in June 2000 as saying that "regime changes is necessary," without laying out a specific timetable (Seib 2000:A24).

10. Bob Woodward (2002:49) describes what must be the same meeting in nearly identical terms.

11. There is, of course, no single agenda-setting framework shared among all authors. Paul Light (19999:3) warns that "much of the contemporary confusion in the study of agenda-building stems from the attempt to define an ordered process where one does not necessarily exist." Each author in this field uses a different framework; Polsby's (1984) model, foe example, differs from Kingdon's. Polsby's "Type A" or "acute" innovation more nearly matches the framework offered by Kingdon, and its analytical claims. Various writers stress that the sort of agenda-setting process at work will depend upon the character of the issue (Cobb and Elder 19873:14: Polsby 1964:146–149). One of the earliest treatments was Schattschneider (1960). But many core themes exist among the various works, and the major categories I use seem to find support in most treatments.

12. Light (1999:199) prefers a behavior model to the "organized anarchy" notion because he sees a "semblance of organization and staff order" that deny an anarchic policy context. I do not see the two ideas as mutually exclusive, however: order is present, and political leaders take into account factors such as coalitions, bargaining, strategic considerations, and numerous other factors. These things, and more, will help determine which ideas survive until a policy window opens, and they do presume rational intent and organizational skill on the part of leaders. But the dynamics of the framework 1 use here can still be present even assuming such logical thought about policy: the objection does not deny, for example, that in the heat of a response to a focusing event, policymakers will cast around for quickly available solutions.

13. Polsby (1984:99; of also 173) sees policy as two parallel processes. "One process invents an alternative, nurtures it, floats it into the subculture of decision-makers; another process searches for ideas, finds them, renovates them for immediate use, and exploits them politically." When the two processes merge, policy happens. Elsewhere (1984:100), he refers to three "forces" in the policy process: group interests, the intellectual beliefs of policy makers, and the knowledge of subject-matter experts. The ideas are very similar to Kingdon's even if the particulars differ.

14. Light (1999:82–1031 points to a broader array of sources of new policy ideas.

15. The concept of "epistemic communities" shares much in common with that of policy communities. One survey article has described epistemic communities as "networks of knowledge-based experts" with shared beliefs, which play an important role especially when uncertainty requires interpretive judgment to make policy (Haass 1992:2–4). Another concept related to policy communities is the idea of "policy domains"—in many ways the same idea, just looked at through the prism of the issue area rather than the group of people who cluster around it (Burstein 1991:328). Domains on different issues are relatively independent of one another, and the combination of all issue areas generating attention and policy at a given time could be seen as the governmental agenda, in Kingdon's terms.

16. A superb reassessment of groupthink that looks closely at the concurrence mechanism is Hart (1990).

17. Polsby, too, asks whether agreement within a policy community was always the result of groupthink. or was it simply agreement among like-minded analysts? The concludes (1984:76–77) that "evidence of 'groupthink' is hard to pin down," while what he calles "consensus formation" is "of overwhelming importance in enabling legislation." The literature on epistemic communities makes the same point; see, for example, Haass (1992:20).

18. In a key article in the literature, Alexander Wendt (1992) refers occasionally to "actors" and "people," but focuses on the norms as viewed by states. Martha Finnemore's (1996) excellent constructivist study refers repeatedly to "states" and society-level norm construction.

19. For a critical assessment of how: these ideas came to be accepted by a self-reinforcing group of "hawkish" Democrats, see Berman (2005). One could contend that the policy community on this issue was broader than the most committed anti-Saddam activists—it also included many in the national security community who were directly supportive, or accepting, of the idea of unseating Hussein.

20. Similar sentiments were expressed by British official Robin Cook in his diary, which became famous upon being published in the U.K.: anti-Saddam activists "were already focused on Iraq" before 9/11, he belied, and they saw in 9/11 "a catalyst for securing their goals for American foreign policy" Cook (2004:49).

21. Polsby's (1984:75–911) account of U.S. aid to Greece and Turkey early in the Cold War emphasizes that rapid policy innovations are more likely when the "major participants in the development [of policy] are more or less in agreement about the nature of the problem to be faced." He calls this common worldview a "subcultural framework," and one was certainly at work among the Iraqi policy community.

22. Other words on agenda-setting are equally strong in their emphasis on events as keys to policy action. See, for example, Andrade and Young (1996), Peake (2001:70–71), and Cobb and Elder (1983:84–85), who term the same notion "triggering devices." It should be stressed, though, that other agenda-selling models treat more seriously the incremental rise of issues to prominence: both Polsby and Light's approaches tend to emphasize that avenue more than does Kingdon's. All agree, however, that the role of a crisis in springing loose long-incubated ideas is at least *one* possible route to policy.

23. Polsby (1984:168) agrees. A crisis "evokes search behavior from decision-makers." Looking for "well-worked-out alternatives" that seem to "meet their needs." which will then be "pressed into service" whether or not they represent a precise fit. Sometimes, "the need to act is so great that measures are enacted even when no remotely sensible alternatives are available"; such moments represent "a set of opportunities for those who are prepared" in other words, those who have "ready-made alternatives."

24. The literature on epistemic communities also emphasizes the connection between such communities and the forcing function of events. Once a focusing event has occurred, policymakers call on policy communities to play a number of specific roles. Policy communities can help policymakers understand the cause and effect relationships involved in the event. They can identify various courses of action in response, and the likely consequences of each. They can describe the interrelationships among the new event and other problems or issues on the governmental agenda. They can help outline the state's national interests, and of course formulate detailed policy proposals (Haass 1992:15).

25. Mendelson (1993:338–339), writing about the role of epistemic communities in the Gorbachev foreign policy revolution, stresses that the leadership style of the most senior decision makers—and a leader's need, to engage policy communities—can crucially affect the degree of policy community influence on policy. Leadership style is thus another piece of the policy puzzle. The mutual dependence of policy makers and policy entrepreneurs is also highlighted in Polsby (1984:171).

26. One reference that discusses the notion of "unrestrained ideological entrepreneurship" in the Bush administration, and ties it loosely to Kingdon's template, is Campbell 2004.

27. For similar lists, see Cobb and Elder (1883:112–124), Rochefort and Cobb (1994:15–22), and Light (1999:136–153).

28. Of the three models of agenda-setting offered by one analysis (Cobb, Ross, and Ross [1976]), for example—two of which ("outside initiatives" stemming from groups outside government, and "mobilization" in which government officials mobilize outside support) point to mass participation the third model, "inside initiative," most aptly describes this case. It describes a situation in which a small number of government officials can set an agenda without any meaningful outside participation.

❧ PART SEVEN ❧

Perceptions, Personality, and Social Psychology

The following four essays are concerned with the cognitive and social psychological limitations and patterns of decision making in foreign policy. Rather than focusing on societal or bureaucratic constraints on policy making, these writers focus on the role of the individual making choices. In a trail-blazing essay Robert Jervis presents a series of hypotheses that specify types of misperception in foreign-policy decision making. Decision makers tend to fit incoming information into existing theories and images. Furthermore, decision makers tend to be closed to new information and to resist new theories or expectations. Jervis also explores the sources of these theories or images of other actors and the international system. Further hypotheses are developed about the way decision makers misperceive opposing actors and their processes of decision making. Taken together, Jervis presents a complex array of cognitive biases that decision makers are prone to exhibiting and that constitute an interlocking web of misperceptions in foreign policy.

Philip Tetlock and Charles McGuire present a more general statement of the cognitive approach to foreign policy. What unites their approach is a set of assumptions about foreign-policy decision makers and their environment; the environment is overflowing with information and policy makers must inevitably deal with problems of incomplete and unreliable information. The central research question is to understand the "cognitive strategies" that policy makers rely on to make sense of their environment.

Yuen Foong Khong looks at one particularly powerful device that policy makers often use to make sense of the foreign policy circumstances they confront—the historical analogy. He argues that analogies are attractive to foreign policy officials for a variety of reasons: They make a new situation look familiar, they provide a normative assessment of the situation, they provide a convenient path to policy action, and they suggest what might happen in the future.

Winter and his associates explore the way political personalities can be described and predictions developed about the impact of personality on foreign policy. Former President George H. W. Bush and Soviet President Mikhail Gorbachev, who presided over the two superpowers at the end of the Cold War, provide the case studies for this type of analysis. The authors acknowledge that personality is not always a significant variable in the conduct of foreign policy—FDR's response to the Japanese attack on Pearl Harbor in 1941 had more to do with the structure of the situation than his own personality biases. But the authors argue that critical moments do occur when a leader's own personal history and psychological predispositions matter.

Hypotheses on Misperception

Robert Jervis

In determining how he will behave, an actor must try to predict how others will act and how their actions will affect his values. The actor must therefore develop an image of others and of their intentions. This image may, however, turn out to be an inaccurate one; the actor may for a number of reasons misperceive both others' actions and their intentions. In this research note I wish to discuss the types of misperceptions of other states' intentions which states tend to make. The concept of intention is complex, but here we can consider it to comprise the ways in which the state feels it will act in a wide range of future contingencies. These ways of acting usually are not specific and well developed plans. For many reasons a national or individual actor may not know how he will act under given conditions, but this problem cannot be dealt with here.

PREVIOUS TREATMENTS OF PERCEPTION IN INTERNATIONAL RELATIONS

Although diplomatic historians have discussed misperception in their treatments of specific events, students of international relations have generally ignored this topic. However, two sets of scholars have applied content analysis to the documents that flowed within and between governments in the six weeks preceding World War I. But the data have been put into quantitative form in a way that does not produce accurate measures of perceptions and intentions and that makes it impossible to gather useful evidence on misperception.[1]

The second group of theorists who have explicitly dealt with general questions of misperception in international relations consists of those, like Charles Osgood, Amitai Etzioni, and to a lesser extent Kenneth Boulding and J. David Singer, who have analyzed the cold war in terms of a spiral of misperception.[2] This approach grows partly out of the mathematical theories of L. F. Richardson[3] and partly out of findings of social and cognitive psychology, many of which will be discussed in this research note.

These authors state their case in general if not universal terms but do not provide many historical cases that are satisfactorily explained by their theories. Furthermore, they do not deal with any of the numerous instances that contradict their notion of the self-defeating aspects of the use of power. They ignore the fact that states are not individuals and that the findings of psychology can be applied to organizations only with great care. Most important, their theoretical analysis is for the most part of reduced value because it seems largely to be a product of their assumption that the Soviet Union is a basically status-quo power whose apparently aggressive behavior is a product of fear of the West. Yet they supply little or no evidence

Robert Jervis, "Hypotheses on Misperception," *World Politics* 20, No. 3 (April 1968): 454–479. Reprinted with permission of Cambridge University Press.

to support this view. Indeed, the explanation for the differences of opinion between the spiral theorists and the proponents of deterrence lies not in differing general views of international relations, differing values, and morality,[4] or differing methods of analysis,[5] but in differing perceptions of Soviet intentions.

THEORIES—NECESSARY AND DANGEROUS

Despite the limitations of their approach, these writers have touched on a vital problem that has not been given systematic treatment by theorists of international relations. The evidence from both psychology and history overwhelmingly supports the view (which may be labeled hypothesis 1) that decision makers tend to fit incoming information into their existing theories and images. Indeed, their theories and images play a large part in determining what they notice. In other words, actors tend to perceive what they expect. Furthermore (hypothesis 1a), a theory will have greater impact on an actor's interpretation of data (a) the greater the ambiguity of the data and (b) the higher the degree of confidence with which the actor holds the theory.[6]

For many purposes we can use the concept of differing levels of perceptual thresholds to deal with the fact that it takes more, and more unambiguous, information for an actor to recognize an unexpected phenomenon than an expected one. An experiment by Bruner and Postman determined "that the recognition threshold for . . . incongruous playing cards (those with suits and colors reversed) is significantly higher than the threshold for normal cards."[7] Not only are people able to identify normal (and therefore expected) cards more quickly and easily than incongruous (and therefore unexpected) ones, but also they may at first take incongruous cards for normal ones.

However, we should not assume, as the spiral theorists often do, that it is necessarily irrational for actors to adjust incoming information to fit more closely their existing beliefs and images. (*Irrational* here describes acting under pressures that the actor would not admit as legitimate if he were conscious of them.) Abelson and Rosenberg label as "psycho-logic" the pressure to create a "balanced" cognitive structure—i.e., one in which "all relations among 'good elements' [in one's attitude structure] are positive (or null), all relations among 'bad elements' are positive (or null), and all relations between good and bad elements are negative (or null)." They correctly show that the "reasoning [this involves] would mortify a logician."[8] But those who have tried to apply this and similar cognitive theories to international relations have usually overlooked the fact that in many cases there are important logical links between the elements and the processes they describe which cannot be called "psycho-logic." (I am here using the term *logical* not in the narrow sense of drawing only those conclusions that follow necessarily from the premises, but rather in the sense of conforming to generally agreed-upon rules for the treating of evidence.) For example, Osgood claims that psycho-logic is displayed when the Soviets praise a man or a proposal and people in the West react by distrusting the object of this praise.[9] But if a person believes that the Russians are aggressive, it is logical for him to be suspicious of their moves. When we say that a decision maker "dislikes" another state, this usually means that he believes that that other state has policies conflicting with those of his nation. Reasoning and experience indicate to the decision maker that the "disliked" state is apt to harm his state's interests. Thus in these cases there is no need to invoke "psycho-logic," and it cannot be claimed that the cases demonstrate the substitution of "emotional consistency for rational consistency."[10]

The question of the relations among particular beliefs and cognitions can often be seen as part of the general topic of the relation of incoming bits of information to the receivers' already-established images. The need to fit data into a wider framework of beliefs, even if doing so does not seem to do justice to individual facts, is not, or at least is not only, a psychological drive that decreases the accuracy of our perceptions of the world, but is "essential to the logic of inquiry."[11] Facts can be interpreted and indeed identified only with the aid of hypotheses and theories. Pure empiricism is impossible, and it would be unwise to revise theories in the light of every bit of information that does not easily conform to them.[12] No hypothesis can be expected to account for all the evidence, and if a prevailing view is supported by many theories and by a large pool of findings, it should not be quickly altered. Too little rigidity can be as bad as too much.[13]

This is as true in the building of social and physical science as it is in policy making.[14] While it is terribly difficult to know when a finding throws serious doubt on accepted theories and should be followed up and when instead it was caused by experimental mistakes or minor errors in the theory, it is clear that scientists would make no progress if they followed Thomas Huxley's injunction to "sit down before fact as a mere child, be prepared to give up every preconceived notion, follow humbly wherever nature leads, or you will learn nothing."[15]

As Michael Polanyi explains, "It is true enough that the scientist must be prepared to submit at any moment to the adverse verdict of observational evidence. But not blindly. . . . There is always the possibility that as in [the cases of the periodic system of elements and the quantum theory of light], a deviation may not affect the essential correctness of a proposition. . . . The process of explaining away deviations is in fact quite indispensable to the daily routine of research," even though this may lead to the missing of a great discovery.[16] For example, in 1795 the astronomer Lalande did not follow up observations that contradicted the prevailing hypotheses and could have led him to discover the planet Neptune.[17]

Yet we should not be too quick to condemn such behavior. As Thomas Kuhn has noted, "There is no such thing as research without counterinstances."[18] If a set of basic theories—what Kuhn calls a paradigm—has been able to account for a mass of data, it should not be lightly trifled with. As Kuhn puts it: "Life-long resistance, particularly from those whose productive careers have committed them to an older tradition of normal science [i.e., science within the accepted paradigm], is not a violation of scientific standards but an index to the nature of scientific research itself. The source of resistance is the assurance that the older paradigm will ultimately solve all its problems, that nature can be shoved into the box the paradigm provides. Inevitably, at times of revolution, that assurance seems stubborn and pigheaded as indeed it sometimes becomes. But it is also something more. That same assurance is what makes normal science or puzzle-solving science possible."[19]

Thus it is important to see that the dilemma of how "open" to be to new information is one that inevitably plagues any attempt at understanding in any field. Instances in which evidence seems to be ignored or twisted to fit the existing theory can often be explained by this dilemma instead of by illogical or nonlogical psychological pressures toward consistency. This is especially true of decision makers' attempts to estimate the intentions of other states, since they must constantly take account of the danger that the other state is trying to deceive them.

The theoretical framework discussed thus far, together with an examination of many cases, suggests hypothesis 2: scholars and decision makers are apt to err by being too wedded to the established view and too closed to new information, as opposed to being too willing to alter their theories.[20] Another way of making this point is to argue that actors tend to establish their theories and expectations prematurely. In politics, of course, this is often necessary because of the need for action. But experimental evidence indicates that the same tendency also occurs on the unconscious level. Bruner and Postman found that "perhaps the greatest single barrier to the recognition of incongruous stimuli is the tendency for perceptual hypotheses to fixate after receiving a minimum of confirmation. . . . Once there had occurred in these cases a partial confirmation of the hypothesis . . . it seemed that nothing could change the subject's report."[21]

However, when we apply these and other findings to politics and discuss kinds of misperception, we should not quickly apply the label of cognitive distortion. We should proceed cautiously for two related reasons. The first is that the evidence available to decision makers almost always permits several interpretations. It should be noted that there are cases of visual perception in which different stimuli can produce exactly the same pattern on an observer's retina. Thus for an observer using one eye the same pattern would be produced by a sphere the size of a golf ball which was quite close to the observer, by a baseball-sized sphere that was further away, or by a basketball-sized sphere still further away. Without other clues the observer cannot possibly determine which of these stimuli he is presented with, and we would not want to call his incorrect perceptions examples of distortion. Such cases, relatively rare in visual perception, are frequent in international relations. The evidence available to decision makers is almost always very ambiguous, since accurate clues to others' intentions are surrounded by noise[22] and deception. In most cases, no matter how long, deeply, and "objectively" the evidence is analyzed, people can differ in their interpretations, and there are no general rules to indicate who is correct.

The second reason to avoid the label of cognitive distortion is that the distinction between perception and judgment, obscure enough in individual psychology, is almost absent in the making of inferences in international politics. Decision makers who reject information that contradicts their views—or who develop complex interpretations of it—often do so consciously and explicitly. Since the evidence available contains contradictory information, to make any inferences requires that much information be ignored or given interpretations that will seem tortuous to those who hold a different position.

Indeed, if we consider only the evidence available to a decision maker at the time of decision, the view later proved incorrect may be supported by as much evidence as the correct one—or even by more. Scholars have often been too unsympathetic with the people who were proved wrong. On closer examination it is frequently difficult to point to differences between those who were right and those who were wrong with respect to their openness to new information and willingness to modify their views. Winston Churchill, for example, did not open-mindedly view each Nazi action to see if the explanations provided by the appeasers accounted for the data better than his own beliefs. Instead, like Chamberlain, he fitted each bit of ambiguous information into his own hypotheses. That he was correct should not lead us to overlook the fact that his methods of analysis and use of theory to produce cognitive consistency did not basically differ from those of the appeasers.[23]

A consideration of the importance of expectations in influencing perception also indicates that the widespread belief in the prevalence of "wishful thinking" may be incorrect, or at least may be based on inadequate data. The psychological literature on the interaction between affect and perception is immense and cannot be treated here, but it should be noted that phenomena that at first were considered strong evidence for the impact of affect on perception often can be better treated as demonstrating the influence of expectations.[24] Thus, in international relations, cases like the United States' misestimation of the political climate in Cuba in April 1961, which may seem at first glance to have been instances of wishful thinking, may instead be more adequately explained by the theories held by the decision makers (e.g., Communist governments are unpopular). Of course desires may have an impact on perception by influencing expectations, but since so many other factors affect expectations, the net influence of desires may not be great.

There is evidence from both psychology[25] and international relations that when expectations and desires clash, expectations seem to be more important. The United States would like to believe that North Vietnam is about to negotiate or that the USSR is ready to give up what the United States believes is its goal of world domination, but ambiguous evidence is seen to confirm the opposite conclusion, which conforms to the United States' expectations. Actors are apt to be especially sensitive to evidence of grave danger if they think they can take action to protect themselves against the menace once it has been detected.

SAFEGUARDS

Can anything then be said to scholars and decision makers other than "Avoid being either too open or too closed, but be especially aware of the latter danger"? Although decision makers will always be faced with ambiguous and confusing evidence and will be forced to make inferences about others which will often be inaccurate, a number of safeguards may be suggested which could enable them to minimize their errors. First and most obvious, decision makers should be aware that they do not make "unbiased" interpretations of each new bit of incoming information, but rather are inevitably heavily influenced by the theories they expect to be verified. They should know that what may appear to them as a self-evident and unambiguous inference often seems so only because of their preexisting beliefs. To someone with a different theory the same data may appear to be unimportant or to support another explanation. Thus many events provide less independent support for the decision makers' images than they may at first realize. Knowledge of this should lead decision makers to examine more closely evidence that others believe contradicts their views.

Second, decision makers should see if their attitudes contain consistent or supporting beliefs that are not logically linked. These may be examples of true psycho-logic. While it is not logically surprising, nor is it evidence of psychological pressures, to find that people who believe that Russia is aggressive are very suspicious of any Soviet move, other kinds of consistency are more suspect. For example, most people who feel that it is important for the United States to win the war in Vietnam also feel that a meaningful victory is possible. And most people who feel defeat would neither endanger U.S. national security nor be costly in terms of other values also feel that we cannot win. Although there are important logical linkages between the two parts of each of these views (especially through theories of guerrilla warfare), they do not seem strong enough to explain the degree to which the opinions are correlated. Similarly, in Finland in the winter of 1939, those who felt that grave consequences would follow Finnish agreement to give Russia a military base also believed that the Soviets would withdraw their demand if Finland stood firm. And those who felt that concessions would not lead to loss of major values also believed that Russia would fight if need be.[26] In this country those who favored a nuclear test ban tended to argue that fallout was very harmful, that only limited improvements in technology would flow from further testing, and that a test ban would increase the chances for peace and security. Those who opposed the test ban were apt to disagree on all three points. This does not mean, of course, that the people holding such sets of supporting views were necessarily wrong in any one element. The Finns who wanted to make concessions to the USSR were probably correct in both parts of their argument. But decision makers should be suspicious if they hold a position in which elements that are not logically connected support the same conclusion. This condition is psychologically comfortable and makes decisions easier to reach (since competing values do not have to be balanced off against each other). The chances are thus considerable that at least part of the reason why a person holds some of these views is related to psychology and not to the substance of the evidence.

Decision makers should also be aware that actors who suddenly find themselves having an important shared interest with other actors have a tendency to overestimate the degree of common interest involved. This tendency is especially strong for those actors (e.g., the United States, at least before 1950) whose beliefs about international relations and morality imply that they can cooperate only with "good" states and that with those states there will be no major conflicts. On the other hand, states that have either a tradition of limited cooperation with others (e.g., Britain) or a strongly held theory that differentiates occasional from permanent allies[27] (e.g., the Soviet Union) find it easier to resist this tendency and need not devote special efforts to combating its danger.

A third safeguard for decision makers would be to make their assumptions, beliefs, and the predictions that follow from them as explicit as possible. An actor should try to determine, before events occur, what evidence would count for and against his theories. By knowing what to expect he would know what to be surprised by, and surprise could indicate to that actor that his beliefs needed reevaluation.[28]

A fourth safeguard is more complex. The decision maker should try to prevent individuals and organizations from letting their main task, political future, and identity become tied to specific theories and images of other actors.[29] If this occurs, subgoals originally sought for their contribution to higher ends will take on value of their own, and information indicating possible alternative routes to the original goals will not be carefully considered. For example, the U.S. Forest Service was unable to carry out its original purpose as effectively when it began to see its distinctive competence not in promoting the best use of lands and forests but rather in preventing all types of forest fires.[30]

Organizations that claim to be unbiased may not realize the extent to which their definition of their role has become involved with certain beliefs about the world. Allen Dulles is a victim of this lack of understanding when he says, "I grant that we are all creatures of prejudice, including CIA officials, but by entrusting intelligence coordination to our central intelligence service, which is excluded from policy making and is married to no particular military hardware, we can avoid to the greatest possible extent the bending of facts obtained through intelligence to suit a particular occupational viewpoint."[31] This statement overlooks the fact that the CIA has developed a certain view of international relations and of the cold war which maximizes the importance of its information gathering, espionage, and subversive activities. Since the CIA would lose its unique place in the government if it were decided that the "back alleys" of world politics were no longer vital to U.S. security, it is not surprising that the organization interprets information in a way that stresses the continued need for its techniques.

Fifth, decision makers should realize the validity and implications of Roberta Wohlstetter's argument that "a willingness to play with material from different angles and in the context of unpopular as well as popular hypotheses is an essential ingredient of a good detective, whether the end is the solution of a crime or an intelligence estimate."[32] However, it is often difficult psychologically and politically for any one person to do this. Since a decision maker usually cannot get "unbiased" treatments of data, he should instead seek to structure conflicting biases into the decision-making process. The decision maker, in other words, should have devil's advocates around. Just as, as Neustadt points out,[33] the decision maker will want to create conflicts among his subordinates in order to make appropriate choices, so he will also want to ensure that incoming information is examined from many different perspectives with many different hypotheses in mind. To some extent this kind of examination will be done automatically through the divergence of goals, training, experience, and information that exists in any large organization. But in many cases this divergence will not be sufficient. The views of those analyzing the data will still be too homogeneous, and the decision maker will have to go out of his way not only to cultivate but to create differing viewpoints.

While all that would be needed would be to have some people examining the data trying to validate unpopular hypotheses, it would probably be more effective if they actually believed and had a stake in the views they were trying to support. If in 1941 someone had had the task of proving the view that Japan would attack Pearl Harbor, the government might have been less surprised by the attack. And only a person who was out to show that Russia would take objectively great risks would have been apt to note that several ships with especially large hatches going to Cuba were riding high in the water, indicating the presence of a bulky but light cargo that was not likely to be anything other than strategic missiles. And many people who doubt the wisdom of the administration's Vietnam policy would be somewhat reassured if there were people in the government who searched the statements and actions of both sides in an effort to prove that North Vietnam was willing to negotiate and that the official interpretation of such moves as the communist activities during the Tet truce of 1967 was incorrect.

Of course all these safeguards involve costs. They would divert resources from other tasks and would increase internal dissension. Determining whether these costs would be worth the gains would depend on a detailed analysis of how the suggested safeguards might be implemented. Even if they were adopted by a government, of course, they would not eliminate the chance of misperception. However, the safeguards would make it more likely that national decision makers would make conscious choices about the way data were interpreted rather than merely assuming that they can be seen in only one way and can mean only one thing. Statesmen would thus be reminded of alternative images of others just as they are constantly reminded of alternative policies.

These safeguards are partly based on hypothesis 3: actors can more easily assimilate into their established image of another actor information contradicting that image if the information is transmitted and considered bit by bit than if it comes all at once. In the former case each piece of discrepant data can be coped with as it arrives and each of the conflicts with the prevailing view will be small enough to go unnoticed, to be dismissed as unimportant, or to necessitate at most a slight modification of the image (e.g., addition of exceptions to the rule). When the information arrives in a block, the contradiction between it and the prevailing view is apt to be much clearer and the probability of major cognitive reorganization will be higher.

SOURCES OF CONCEPTS

An actor's perceptual thresholds—and thus the images that ambiguous information is apt to produce—are influenced by what he has experienced and learned about.[34] If one actor is to perceive that another fits in a given category he must first have, or develop, a concept for that category. We can usefully distinguish three levels at which a concept can be present or absent. First, the concept can be completely missing. The actor's cognitive structure may not include anything corresponding to the phenomenon he is encountering. This situation can occur not only in science fiction but also in a world of rapid change or in the meeting of two dissimilar systems. Thus China's image of the Western world was extremely inaccurate in the mid-nineteenth century, her learning was very slow, and her responses were woefully inadequate. The West was spared a similar struggle only because it had the power to reshape the system it encountered. Once the actor clearly sees one instance of the new phenomenon, he is apt to recognize it much more quickly in the future.[35] Second, the actor can know about a concept but not believe that it reflects an actual phenomenon. Thus communist and Western decision makers are each aware of the other's explanation of how his system functions but do not think that the concept corresponds to reality. Communist elites, furthermore, deny that anything *could* correspond to the democracies' description of themselves. Third, the actor may hold a concept but not believe that another actor fills it at the present moment. Thus the British and French statesmen of the 1930s held a concept of states with unlimited ambitions. They realized that Napoleons were possible, but they did not think Hitler belonged in that category. Hypothesis 4 distinguishes these three cases: misperception is most difficult to correct in the case of a missing concept and least difficult to correct in the case of a recognized but presumably unfilled concept. All other things being equal (e.g., the degree to which the concept is central to the actor's cognitive structure), the first case requires more cognitive reorganization than does the second, and the second requires more reorganization than the third.

However, this hypothesis does not mean that learning will necessarily be slowest in the first case, for if the phenomena are totally new, the actor may make such grossly inappropriate responses that he will quickly acquire information clearly indicating that he is faced with something he does not understand. And the sooner the actor realizes that things are not—or may not be—what they seem, the sooner he is apt to correct his image.[36]

Three main sources contribute to decision makers' concepts of international relations and of other states and influence the level of their perceptual thresholds for various phenomena. First, an actor's beliefs about his own domestic political system are apt to be important. In some cases, like that of the USSR, the decision makers' concepts are tied to an ideology that explicitly provides a frame of reference for viewing foreign affairs. Even where this is not the case, experience with his own system will partly determine what the actor is familiar with and what he is apt to perceive in others. Louis Hartz claims, "It is the absence of the experience of social revolution which is at the heart of the whole American dilemma. . . . In a whole series of specific ways it enters into our difficulty of communication with the rest of the world. We find it difficult to understand Europe's 'social question.' . . . We are not familiar with the deeper social struggles of Asia and hence tend to interpret even reactionary regimes as 'democratic.' "[37] Similarly, George Kennan argues that in World War I the Allied powers, and especially America, could not understand the bitterness and violence of others' internal conflicts: ". . . The inability of the Allied statesmen to picture to themselves the passions of the Russian civil war [was partly caused by the fact that] we represent . . . a society in which the manifestations of evil have been carefully buried and sublimated in the social behavior of people, as in their very consciousness. For this reason, probably, despite our widely traveled and outwardly cosmopolitan lives, the mainsprings of political behavior in such a country as Russia tend to remain concealed from our vision."[38]

Second, concepts will be supplied by the actor's previous experiences. An experiment from another field illustrates this. Dearborn and Simon presented business executives from various divisions (e.g., sales, accounting, production) with the same hypothetical data and asked them for an analysis and recommendations from the standpoint of what would be best for the company as a whole. The executives' views heavily reflected their departmental perspectives.[39] William W. Kaufmann shows how the perceptions of Ambassador Joseph Kennedy were affected by his past: "As befitted a former chairman of the Securities Exchange and Maritime Commissions, his primary interest lay in economic matters. . . . The revolutionary character of the Nazi regime was not a phenomenon that he could easily grasp. . . . It was far simpler, and more in accord with his own premises, to explain German aggressiveness in economic terms. The Third Reich was dissatisfied, authoritarian, and expansive largely because her economy was unsound."[40] Similarly it has been argued that Chamberlain was slow to recognize Hitler's intentions partly because of the limiting nature of his personal background and business experiences.[41] The impact of training and experience seems to be demonstrated when the background of the appeasers is compared to that of their opponents. One difference stands out: "A substantially higher percentage of the anti-appeasers (irrespective of class origins) had the kind of knowledge which comes from close acquaintance, mainly professional, with foreign affairs."[42] Since members of the diplomatic corps are responsible for meeting threats to the nation's security before these grow to major proportions, and since they have learned about cases in which aggressive states were not recognized as such until very late, they may be prone to interpret ambiguous data as showing that others are aggressive. It should be stressed that we cannot say that the professionals of the 1930s were more apt to make accurate judgments of other states. Rather, they may have been more sensitive to the chance that others were aggressive. They would then rarely take an aggressor for a status-quo power, but would more often make the opposite error.[43] Thus in the years before World War I the permanent officials in the British Foreign Office overestimated German aggressiveness.[44]

A parallel demonstration in psychology of the impact of training on perception is presented by an experiment in which ambiguous pictures were shown to both advanced and beginning police-administration students. The advanced group perceived more violence in the pictures than did the beginners. The probable explanation is that "the law enforcer may come to accept crime as a familiar personal experience, one which he himself is not surprised to encounter. The acceptance of crime as a familiar experience in turn increases the ability or readiness to perceive violence where clues to it are potentially available."[45] This experiment lends weight to the view that the British diplomats' sensitivity to aggressive states was not totally a product of personnel selection procedures.

A third source of concepts, which frequently will be the most directly relevant to a decision maker's perception of international relations, is international history. As Henry Kissinger points out, one reason why statesmen were so slow to recognize the threat posed by Napoleon was that previous events had accustomed them only to actors who wanted to modify the existing system, not overthrow it.[46] The other side of the coin is even more striking: historical traumas can heavily influence future perceptions. They can either establish a state's image of the other state involved or can be used as analogies. An example of the former case is provided by the fact that for at least ten years after the Franco-Prussian War most of Europe's statesmen felt that Bismarck had aggressive plans when in fact his main goal was to protect the status quo. Of course the evidence was ambiguous. The post-1871 Bismarckian maneuvers, which were designed to keep peace, looked not unlike the pre-1871 maneuvers designed to set the stage for war. But that the post-1871 maneuvers were seen as indicating aggressive plans is largely attributable to the impact of Bismarck's earlier actions on the statesmen's image of him.

A state's previous unfortunate experience with a type of danger can sensitize it to other examples of that danger. While this sensitivity may lead the state to avoid the mistake it committed in the past, it may also lead it mistakenly to believe that the present situation is like the past one. Santayana's maxim could be turned around: "Those who remember the past are condemned to make the opposite mistakes." As Paul Kecskemeti shows, both defenders and critics of the unconditional surrender plan of the Second World War thought in terms of the conditions of World War I.[47] Annette Baker Fox found that the Scandinavian countries' neutrality policies in World War II were strongly influenced by their experiences in the previous war, even though vital aspects of the two situations were different. Thus "Norway's success [during the First World War] in remaining nonbelligerent though pro-Allied gave the Norwegians confidence that their country could again stay out of war."[48] And the lesson drawn from the unfortunate results of this policy was an important factor in Norway's decision to join NATO.

The application of the Munich analogy to various contemporary events has been much commented on, and I do not wish to argue the substantive points at stake. But it seems clear that the probabilities that any state is facing an aggressor who has to be met by force are not altered by the career of Hitler and the history of the 1930s. Similarly the probability of an aggressor's announcing his plans is not increased (if anything, it is decreased) by the fact that Hitler wrote *Mein Kampf.* Yet decision makers are more sensitive to these possibilities, and thus more apt to perceive ambiguous evidence as indicating they apply to a given case, than they would have been had there been no Nazi Germany.

Historical analogies often precede, rather than follow, a careful analysis of a situation (e.g., Truman's initial reaction to the news of the invasion of South Korea was to think of the Japanese invasion of Manchuria). Noting this precedence, however, does not show us which of many analogies will come to a decision maker's mind. Truman could have thought of nineteenth-century European wars that were of no interest to the United States. Several factors having nothing to do with the event under consideration influence what analogies a decision maker is apt to make. One factor is the number of cases similar to the analogy with which the decision maker is familiar. Another is the importance of the past event to the political system of which the decision maker is a part. The more times such an event occurred and the greater its consequences were, the more a decision maker will be sensitive to the particular danger involved and the more he will be apt to see ambiguous stimuli as indicating another instance of this kind of event. A third factor is the degree of the decision maker's personal involvement in the past case—in time, energy, ego, and position. The last-mentioned variable will affect not only the event's impact on the decision maker's cognitive structure, but also the way he perceives the event and the lesson he draws. Someone who was involved in getting troops into South Korea after the attack will remember the Korean War differently from someone who was involved in considering the possible use of nuclear weapons or in deciding what messages should be sent to the Chinese. Greater personal involvement will usually give the event greater impact, especially if the decision maker's own views were validated by the event. One need not accept a total application of learning theory to nations to believe that "nothing fails like success."[49] It also seems likely that if many critics argued at the time that the decision maker was wrong, he will be even more apt to see other situations in terms of the original event. For example, because Anthony Eden left the government on account of his views and was later shown to have been correct, he probably was more apt to see as Hitlers other leaders with whom he had conflicts (e.g., Nasser). A fourth factor is the degree to which the analogy is compatible with the rest of his belief system. A fifth is the absence of alternative concepts and analogies. Individuals and states vary in the amount of direct or indirect political experience they have had which can provide different ways of interpreting data. Decision makers who are aware of multiple possibilities of states' intentions may be less likely to seize on an analogy prematurely. The perception of citizens of nations like the United States, which have relatively little history of international politics, may be more apt to be heavily influenced by the few major international events that have been important to their country.

The first three factors indicate that an event is more apt to shape present perceptions if it occurred in the recent rather than the remote past. If it occurred recently, the statesman will then know about it at first hand even if he was not involved in the making of policy at the time. Thus if generals are prepared to fight the last war, diplomats may be prepared to avoid the last war. Part of the Anglo-French reaction to Hitler can be explained by the prevailing beliefs that the First World War was to a large extent caused by misunderstandings and could have been avoided by farsighted and nonbelligerent diplomacy. And part of the Western perception of Russia and China can be explained by the view that appeasement was an inappropriate response to Hitler.[50]

THE EVOKED SET

The way people perceive data is influenced not only by their cognitive structure and theories about other actors but also by what they are concerned with at the time they receive the information. Information is evaluated in light of the small part of the person's memory that is presently active—the "evoked set." My perceptions of the dark streets I pass walking home from the movies will be different if the film I saw had dealt with spies than if it had been a comedy. If I am working on aiding a country's education system and I hear someone talk about the need for economic development in that state, I am apt to think he is concerned with education, whereas if I had been working on, say, trying to achieve political stability in that country, I would have placed his remarks in that framework.[51]

Thus hypothesis 5 states that when messages are sent from a different background of concerns and information than is possessed by the receiver, misunderstanding is likely. Person A and person B will read the same message quite differently if A has seen several related messages that B does not know about. This difference will be compounded if, as is frequently the case, A and B each assume that the other has the same background he does. This means that misperception can occur even when deception is neither intended nor expected. Thus Roberta Wohlstetter found not only that different parts of the United States government had different perceptions of data about Japan's intentions and messages partly because they saw the incoming information in very different contexts, but also that officers in the field misunderstood warnings from Washington: "Washington advised General Short [in Pearl Harbor] on November 27 to expect 'hostile action' at any moment, by which it meant 'attack on American possessions from without,' but General Short understood this phrase to mean 'sabotage.'"[52] Washington did not realize the extent to which Pearl Harbor considered the danger of sabotage to be primary, and furthermore it incorrectly believed that General Short had received the intercepts of the secret Japanese diplomatic messages available in Washington which indicated that surprise attack was a distinct possibility. Another implication of this hypothesis is that if important information is known to only part of the government of state A and part of the government of state B, international messages may be misunderstood by those parts of the receiver's government that do not match, in the information they have, the part of the sender's government that dispatched the message.[53]

Two additional hypotheses can be drawn from the problems of those sending messages. Hypothesis 6 states that when people spend a great deal of time drawing up a plan or making a decision, they tend to think that the message about it they wish to convey will be clear to the receiver.[54] Since they are aware of what is to them the important pattern in their actions, they often feel that the pattern will be equally obvious to others, and they overlook the degree to which the message is apparent to them only because they know what to look for. Those who have not participated in the endless meetings may not understand what information the sender is trying to convey. George Quester has shown how the German and to a lesser extent the British desire to maintain target limits on bombing in the first eighteen months of World War II was undermined partly by the fact that each side knew the limits it was seeking and its own reasons for any apparent "exceptions" (e.g., the German attack on Rotterdam) and incorrectly felt that these limits and reasons were equally clear to the other side.[55]

Hypothesis 7 holds that actors often do not realize that actions intended to project a given image may not have the desired effect because the actions themselves do not turn out as planned. Thus even without appreciable impact of different cognitive structures and backgrounds, an action may convey an unwanted message. For example, a country's representatives may not follow instructions and so may give others impressions contrary to those the home government wished to convey. The efforts of Washington and Berlin to settle their dispute over Samoa in the late 1880s were complicated by the provocative behavior of their agents on the spot. These agents not only increased the intensity of the local conflict but led the decision makers to become more suspicious of the other state because they tended to assume that their agents were obeying instructions and that the actions of the other side represented official policy. In such cases both sides will believe that the other is reading hostility into a policy of theirs which is friendly. Similarly, Quester's study shows that the attempt to limit bombing referred to above failed partly because neither side was able to bomb as accurately as it thought it could and thus did not realize the physical effects of its actions.[56]

FURTHER HYPOTHESES FROM THE PERSPECTIVE OF THE PERCEIVER

From the perspective of the perceiver several other hypotheses seem to hold. Hypothesis 8 is that there is an overall tendency for decision makers to see other states as more hostile than they are.[57] There seem to be more cases of statesmen incorrectly believing others are planning major acts against their interest than of statesmen being lulled by a potential aggressor. There are many reasons for this which are too complex to be treated here (e.g., some parts of the bureaucracy feel it is their responsibility to be suspicious of all other states; decision makers often feel they are "playing it safe" to believe and act as though the other state were hostile in questionable cases; and often, when people do not feel they are a threat to others, they find it difficult to believe that others may see them as a threat). It should be noted, however, that decision makers whose perceptions are described by this hypothesis would not necessarily further their own values by trying to correct for this tendency. The values of possible outcomes as well as their probabilities must be considered, and it may be that the probability of an unnecessary arms-tension cycle arising out of misperceptions, multiplied by the costs of such a cycle, may seem less to decision makers than the probability of incorrectly believing another state is friendly, multiplied by the costs of this eventuality.

Hypothesis 9 states that actors tend to see the behavior of others as more centralized, disciplined, and coordinated than it is. This hypothesis holds true in related ways. Frequently too many complex events are squeezed into a perceived pattern. Actors are hesitant to admit or even see that particular incidents cannot be explained by their theories.[58] Those events not caused by factors that are important parts of the perceiver's image are often seen as though they were. Further, actors see others as more internally united than they in fact are and generally overestimate the degree to which others are following a coherent policy. The degree to which the other side's policies are the product of internal bargaining,[59] internal misunderstandings, or subordinates' not following instructions is underestimated. This is the case partly because actors tend to be unfamiliar with the details of another state's policy-making processes. Seeing only the finished product, they find it simpler to try to construct a rational explanation for the policies, even though they know that such an analysis could not explain their own policies.[60]

Familiarity also accounts for hypothesis 10: because a state gets most of its information about the other state's policies from the other's foreign office, it tends to take the foreign office's position for the stand of the other government as a whole. In many cases this perception will be an accurate one, but when the other government is divided or when the other foreign office is acting without specific authorization, misperception may result. For example, part of the reason why in 1918 Allied governments incorrectly thought "that the Japanese were preparing to take action [in Siberia], if need be, with agreement with the British and French alone, disregarding the absence of American consent,"[61] was that Allied ambassadors had talked mostly with Foreign Minister Motono, who was among the minority of the Japanese favoring this policy. Similarly, America's NATO allies may have gained an inaccurate picture of the degree to which the American government was committed to the MLF because they had greatest contact with parts of the government that strongly favored the MLF. And states that tried to get information about Nazi foreign policy from German diplomats were often misled because these officials were generally ignorant of or out of sympathy with Hitler's plans. The Germans and the Japanese sometimes purposely misinformed their own ambassadors in order to deceive their enemies more effectively.

Hypothesis 11 states that actors tend to overestimate the degree to which others are acting in response to what they themselves do when the others behave in accordance with the actor's desires; but when the behavior of the other is undesired, it is usually seen as derived from internal forces. If the *effect* of another's action is to injure or threaten the first side, the first side is apt to believe that such was the other's *purpose*. An example of the first part of the hypothesis is provided by Kennan's account of the activities of official and unofficial American representatives who protested to the new Bolshevik government against several of its actions. When the Soviets changed their position, these representatives felt it was largely because of their influence.[62] This sort of interpretation can be explained not only by the fact that it is gratifying to the individual making it, but also, taking the other side of the coin mentioned in hypothesis 9, by the fact that the actor is most familiar with his own input into the other's decision and has less knowledge of other influences. The second part of hypothesis 11 is illustrated by the tendency of actors to believe that the hostile behavior of others is to be explained by the other side's motives and not by its reaction to the first side. Thus Chamberlain did not see that Hitler's behavior was related in part to his belief that the British were weak. More common is the failure to see that the other side is reacting out of fear of the first side, which can lead to self-fulfilling prophecies and spirals of misperception and hostility.

This difficulty is often compounded by an implication of hypothesis 12: when actors have intentions that they do not try to conceal from others, they tend to assume that others accurately perceive these intentions. Only rarely do they believe that others may be reacting to a much less favorable image of themselves than they think they are projecting.[63]

For state A to understand how state B perceives A's policy is often difficult because such understanding may involve a conflict with A's image of itself. Raymond Sontag argues that Anglo-German relations before World War I deteriorated partly because "the British did not like to think of themselves as selfish or unwilling to tolerate 'legitimate' German expansion. The Germans did not like to think of themselves as aggressive or unwilling to recognize 'legitimate' British vested interest."[64]

Hypothesis 13 suggests that if it is hard for an actor to believe that the other can see him as a menace, it is often even harder for him to see that issues important to him are not important to others. While he may know that another actor is on an opposing team, it may be more difficult for him to realize that the other is playing an entirely different game. This is especially true when the game he is playing seems vital to him.[65]

The final hypothesis, hypothesis 14, is as follows: actors tend to overlook the fact that evidence consistent with their theories may also be consistent with other views. When choosing between two theories, we have to pay attention only to data that cannot be accounted for by one of the theories. But it is common to find people claiming as proof of their theories data that could also support alternative views. This phenomenon is related to the point made earlier that any single bit of information can be interpreted only within a framework of hypotheses and theories. And while it is true that "we may without a vicious circularity accept some datum as a fact because it conforms to the very law for which it counts as another confirming instance, and reject an allegation of fact because it is already excluded by law,"[66] we should be careful lest we forget that a piece of information seems in many cases to confirm a certain hypothesis only because we already believe that hypothesis to be correct and that the information can with as much validity support a different hypothesis. For example, one of the reasons why the German attack on Norway took both that country and England by surprise, even though they had detected German ships moving toward Norway, was that they expected not an attack but an attempt by the Germans to break through the British blockade and reach the Atlantic. The initial course of the ships was consistent with either plan, but the British and Norwegians took this course to mean that their predictions were being borne out.[67] This is not to imply that the interpretation made was foolish, but only that the decision makers should have been aware that the evidence was also consistent with an invasion and should have had a bit less confidence in their views.

The longer the ships would have to travel the same route, whether they were going to one or another of two destinations, the more information would be needed to determine their plans. Taken as a metaphor, this incident applies generally to the treatment of evidence. Thus as long as Hitler made demands for control only of ethnically German areas, his actions could be explained either by the hypothesis that he had unlimited ambitions or by the hypothesis that he wanted to unite all the Germans. But actions against non-Germans (e.g., the takeover of Czechoslovakia in March 1938) could not be accounted for by the latter hypothesis. And it was this action that convinced the appeasers that Hitler had to be stopped. It is interesting to speculate on what the British reaction would have been had Hitler left Czechoslovakia alone for a while and instead made demands on Poland similar to those he eventually made in the summer of 1939. The two paths would then still not have diverged, and further misperception could have occurred.

NOTES

1. See for example Ole Holsti, Robert North, and Richard Brody, "Perception and Action in the 1914 Crisis," in J. David Singer, ed., *Quantitative International Politics* (New York, 1968). For a fuller discussion of the Stanford content analysis studies and the general problems of quantification, see my "The Costs of the Quantitative Study of International Relations," in Klaus Knorr and James N. Rosenau, eds., *Contending Approaches to International Politics* (forthcoming).

2. See, for example, Osgood, *An Alternative to War or Surrender* (Urbana, 1962); Etzioni, *The Hard Way to Peace* (New York, 1962); Boulding, "National Images and International Systems," *Journal of Conflict Resolution,* III (June 1959), 120–31; and Singer, *Deterrence, Arms Control, and Disarmament* (Columbus, 1962).

3. *Statistics of Deadly Quarrels* (Pittsburgh, 1960) and *Arms and Insecurity* (Chicago, 1960). For non-mathematicians a fine summary of Richardson's work is Anatol Rapoport's "L. F. Richardson's Mathematical Theory of War," *Journal of Conflict Resolution,* I (September 1957), 249–99.

4. See Philip Green, *Deadly Logic* (Columbus, 1966); Green, "Method and Substance in the Arms Debate," *World Politics,* XVI (July 1964), 642–67; and Robert A. Levine, "Fact and Morals in the Arms Debate," *World Politics,* XIV (January 1962), 239–58.

5. See Anatol Rapoport, *Strategy and Conscience* (New York, 1964).

6. Floyd Allport, *Theories of Perception and the Concept of Structure* (New York, 1955), 382; Ole Holsti, "Cognitive Dynamics and Images of the Enemy," in David Finlay, Ole Holsti, and Richard Fagen, *Enemies in Politics* (Chicago, 1967), 70.

7. Jerome Bruner and Leo Postman, "On the Perceptions of Incongruity: A Paradigm," in Jerome Bruner and David Krech, eds., *Perception and Personality* (Durham, N.C., 1949), 210.

8. Robert Abelson and Milton Rosenberg, "Symbolic Psycho-logic," *Behavioral Science,* III (January 1958), 4–5.

9. p. 27.

10. *Ibid.,* 26.

11. I have borrowed this phrase from Abraham Kaplan, who uses it in a different but related context in *The Conduct of Inquiry* (San Francisco, 1964), 86.

12. The spiral theorists are not the only ones to ignore the limits of empiricism. Roger Hilsman found that most consumers and producers of intelligence felt that intelligence should not deal with hypotheses but should only provide the policy makers with "all the facts" (*Strategic Intelligence and National Decisions* [Glencoe, 1956], 46). The close interdependence between hypotheses and facts is overlooked partly because of the tendency to identify "hypotheses" with "policy preferences."

13. Karl Deutsch interestingly discusses a related question when he argues, "Autonomy . . . requires both intake from the present and recall from memory, and selfhood can be seen in just this continuous balancing of a limited present and a limited past. . . . No further self-determination is possible if either openness or memory is lost. . . . To the extent that [systems cease to be able to take in new information], they approach the behavior of a bullet or torpedo: their future action becomes almost completely determined by their past. On the other hand, a person without memory, an organization without values or policy . . . —all these no longer steer, but drift: their behavior depends little on their past and almost wholly on their present. Driftwood and the bullet are thus each the epitome of another kind of loss of self-control . . ." (*Nationalism and Social Communication* [Cambridge, Mass., 1954], 167–68). Also see Deutsch's *The Nerves of Government* (New York, 1963), 98–109, 200–256. A physicist makes a similar argument: "It is clear that if one is too attached to one's preconceived

model, one will miss all radical discoveries. It is amazing to what degree one may fail to register mentally an observation which does not fit the initial image. . . . On the other hand, if one is too open-minded and pursues every hitherto-unknown phenomenon, one is almost certain to lose oneself in trivia" (Martin Deutsch, "Evidence and Inference in Nuclear Research," in Daniel Lerner, ed., *Evidence and Inference* [Glencoe, 1958], 102).

14. Raymond Bauer, "Problems of Perception and the Relations Between the U.S. and the Soviet Union," *Journal of Conflict Resolution*, V (September 1961), 223–29.

15. Quoted in W. I. B. Beveridge, *The Art of Scientific Investigation*, 3rd ed. (London, 1957), 50.

16. *Science, Faith, and Society* (Chicago, 1964), 31. For a further discussion of this problem, see *ibid.*, 16, 26–41, 90–94; Polanyi, *Personal Knowledge* (London, 1958), 8–15, 30, 143–68, 269–98, 310–11; Thomas Kuhn, *The Structure of Scientific Revolution* (Chicago, 1964); Kuhn, "The Function of Dogma in Scientific Research," in A. C. Crombie, ed., *Scientific Change* (New York, 1963), 344–69; the comments on Kuhn's paper by Hall, Polanyi, and Toulmin, and Kuhn's reply, *ibid.*, 370–95. For a related discussion of these points from a different perspective, see Norman Storer, *The Social System of Science* (New York, 1960), 116–22.

17. "He found that the position of one star relative to others . . . had shifted. Lalande was a good astronomer and knew that such a shift was unreasonable. He crossed out his first observation, put a question mark next to the second observation, and let the matter go" (Jerome Bruner, Jacqueline Goodnow, and George Austin, *A Study of Thinking* [New York, 1962], 105).

18. *The Structure of Scientific Revolution*, 79.

19. *Ibid.*, 150–51.

20. Requirements of effective political leadership may lead decision makers to voice fewer doubts than they have about existing policies and images, but this constraint can only partially explain this phenomenon. Similar calculations of political strategy may contribute to several of the hypotheses discussed below.

21. p. 221. Similarly, in experiments dealing with his subjects' perception of other people, Charles Dailey found that "premature judgment appears to make new data harder to assimilate than when the observer withholds judgment until all data are seen. It seems probable . . . that the observer mistakes his own inferences for facts" ("The Effects of Premature Conclusion Upon the Acquisition of Understanding of a Person," *Journal of Psychology*, XXX [January 1952], 149–50). For other theory and evidence on this point, see Bruner, "On Perceptual Readiness," *Psychological Review*, LXIV (March 1957), 123–52; Gerald Davidson, "The Negative Effects of Early Exposure to Suboptimal Visual Stimuli," *Journal of Personality*, XXXII (June 1964), 278–95; Albert Myers, "An Experimental Analysis of a Tactical Blunder," *Journal of Abnormal and Social Psychology*, LXIX (November 1964), 493–98; and Dale Wyatt and Donald Campbell, "On the Liability of Stereotype or Hypothesis," *Journal of Abnormal and Social Psychology*, XLIV (October 1950), 496–500. It should be noted that this tendency makes "incremental" decision making more likely (David Braybrooke and Charles Lindblom, *A Strategy of Decision* [New York, 1963]), but the results of this process may lead the actor further from his goals.

22. For a use of this concept in political communication, see Roberta Wohlstetter, *Pearl Harbor* (Stanford, 1962).

23. Similarly, Robert Coulondre, the French ambassador to Berlin in 1939, was one of the few diplomats to appreciate the Nazi threat. Partly because of his earlier service in the USSR, "he was painfully sensitive to the threat of a Berlin-Moscow agreement. He noted with foreboding that Hitler had not attacked Russia in his *Reichstag* address of April 28. . . . So it went all spring and summer, the ambassador relaying each new evidence of the impending diplomatic revolution and adding to his admonitions his pleas for decisive counteraction" (Franklin Ford and Carl Schorske, "The Voice in the Wilderness: Robert Coulondre," in Gordon Craig and Felix Gilbert, eds., *The Diplomats*, Vol. III [New York, 1963] 573–74). His hypotheses were correct, but it is difficult to detect differences between the way he and those ambassadors who were incorrect, like Neville Henderson, selectively

noted and interpreted information. However, to the extent that the fear of war influenced the appeasers' perceptions of Hitler's intentions, the appeasers' views did have an element of psychologic that was not present in their opponents' position.

24. See for example Donald Campbell, "Systematic Error on the Part of Human Links in Communications Systems," *Information and Control*, I (1958), 346–50; and Leo Postman, "The Experimental Analysis of Motivational Factors in Perception," in Judson S. Brown, ed., *Current Theory and Research in Motivation* (Lincoln, Neb., 1953), 59–108.

25. Dale Wyatt and Donald Campbell, "A Study of Interviewer Bias as Related to Interviewer's Expectations and Own Opinions," *International Journal of Opinion and Attitude Research,* IV (Spring 1950), 77–83.

26. Max Jacobson, *The Diplomacy of the Winter War* (Cambridge, Mass., 1961), 136–39.

27. Raymond Aron, *Peace and War* (Garden City, 1966), 29.

28. C. F. Kuhn, *The Structure of Scientific Revolution,* 65. A fairly high degree of knowledge is needed before one can state precise expectations. One indication of the lack of international-relations theory is that most of us are not sure what "naturally" flows from our theories and what constitutes either "puzzles" to be further explored with the paradigm or "anomalies" that cast doubt on the basic theories.

29. See Philip Selznick, *Leadership in Administration* (Evanston, 1957).

30. Ashley Schiff, *Fire and Water: Scientific Heresy in the Forest Service* (Cambridge, Mass., 1962). Despite its title, this book is a fascinating and valuable study.

31. *The Craft of Intelligence* (New York, 1963), 53.

32. p. 302. See Beveridge, 93, for a discussion of the idea that the scientist should keep in mind as many hypotheses as possible when conducting and analyzing experiments.

33. *Presidential Power* (New York, 1960).

34. Most psychologists argue that this influence also holds for perception of shapes. For data showing that people in different societies differ in respect to their predisposition to experience certain optical illusions and for a convincing argument that this difference can be explained by the societies' different physical environments, which have led their people to develop different patterns of drawing inferences from ambiguous visual cues, see Marshall Segall, Donald Campbell, and Melville Herskovits, *The Influence of Culture on Visual Perceptions* (Indianapolis, 1966).

35. Thus when Bruner and Postman's subjects first were presented with incongruous playing cards (i.e., cards in which symbols and colors of the suits were not matching, producing red spades or black diamonds), long exposure times were necessary for correct identification. But once a subject correctly perceived the card and added this type of card to his repertoire of categories, he was able to identify other incongruous cards much more quickly. For an analogous example—in this case changes in the analysis of aerial reconnaissance photographs of an enemy's secret weapons-testing facilities produced by the belief that a previously unknown object may be present—see David Irving, *The Mare's Nest* (Boston, 1964), 66–67, 274–75.

36. Bruner and Postman, 220.

37. *The Liberal Tradition in America* (New York, 1955), 306.

38. *Russia and the West Under Lenin and Stalin* (New York, 1962), 142–43.

39. DeWitt Dearborn and Herbert Simon, "Selective Perception: A Note on the Departmental Identification of Executives," *Sociometry,* XXI (June 1958), 140–44.

40. "Two American Ambassadors: Bullitt and Kennedy," in Craig and Gilbert, 358–59.

41. Hugh Trevor-Roper puts this point well: "Brought up as a business man, successful in municipal politics, [Chamberlain's] outlook was entirely parochial. Educated Conservative aristocrats like Churchill, Eden, and Cranborne, whose families had long been used to political responsibility, had seen revolution and revolutionary leaders before, in their own history, and understood them correctly; but the Chamberlains, who had run from radical imperialism to timid conservatism in a generation of life in Birmingham, had no such understanding of history or the world: to them the

scope of human politics was limited by their own parochial horizons, and Neville Chamberlain could not believe that Hitler was fundamentally different from himself. If Chamberlain wanted peace, so must Hitler" ("Munich—Its Lessons Ten Years Later," in Francis Loewenheim, ed., *Peace or Appeasement?* [Boston, 1965], 152–53). For a similar view see A. L. Rowse, *Appeasement* (New York, 1963), 117.

But Donald Lammers points out that the views of many prominent British public figures in the 1930s do not fit this generalization (*Explaining Munich* [Stanford, 1966], 13–140). Furthermore, arguments that stress the importance of the experiences and views of the actors' ancestors do not explain the links by which these influence the actors themselves. Presumably Churchill and Chamberlain read the same history books in school and had the same basic information about Britain's past role in the world. Thus what has to be demonstrated is that in their homes aristocrats like Churchill learned different things about politics and human nature than did middle-class people like Chamberlain and that these experiences had a significant impact. Alternatively, it could be argued that the patterns of child-rearing prevalent among the aristocracy influenced the children's personalities in a way that made them more likely to see others as aggressive.

42. *Ibid.*, 15.

43. During a debate on appeasement in the House of Commons, Harold Nicolson declared, "I know that those of us who believe in the traditions of our policy, . . . who believe that one great function of this country is to maintain moral standards in Europe, to maintain a settled pattern of international relations, not to make friends with people who are demonstrably evil . . . —I know that those who hold such beliefs are accused of possessing the Foreign Office mind. I thank God that I possess the Foreign Office mind" (quoted in Martin Gilbert, *The Roots of Appeasement* [New York, 1966], 187). But the qualities Nicolson mentions and applauds may be related to a more basic attribute of "the Foreign Office mind"—suspiciousness.

44. George Monger, *The End of Isolation* (London, 1963). I am also indebted to Frederick Collignon for his unpublished manuscript and several conversations on this point.

45. Hans Toch and Richard Schulte, "Readiness to Perceive Violence as a Result of Police Training," *British Journal of Psychology*, LII (November 1961), 392 (original italics omitted). It should be stressed that one cannot say whether or not the advanced police students perceived the pictures "accurately." The point is that their training predisposed them to see violence in ambiguous situations. Whether on balance they would make fewer perceptual errors and better decisions is very hard to determine. For an experiment showing that training can lead people to "recognize" an expected stimulus even when that stimulus is in fact not shown, see Israel Goldiamond and William F. Hawkins, "Vexierversuch: The Log Relationship Between Word-Frequency and Recognition Obtained in the Absence of Stimulus Words," *Journal of Experimental Psychology*, LVI (December 1958), 457–63.

46. *A World Restored* (New York, 1964), 2–3.

47. *Strategic Surrender* (New York, 1964), 215–41.

48. *The Power of Small States* (Chicago, 1959), 81.

49. William Inge, *Outspoken Essays*, First Series (London, 1923), 88.

50. Of course, analogies themselves are not "unmoved movers." The interpretation of past events is not automatic and is informed by general views of international relations and complex judgments. And just as beliefs about the past influence the present, views about the present influence interpretations of history. It is difficult to determine the degree to which the United States' interpretation of the reasons it went to war in 1917 influenced American foreign policy in the 1920s and 1930s and how much the isolationism of that period influenced the histories of the war.

51. For some psychological experiments on this subject see Jerome Bruner and A. Leigh Minturn, "Perceptual Identification and Perceptual Organization," *Journal of General Psychology*, LIII (July 1955), 22–28; Seymour Feshbach and Robert Singer, "The Effects of Fear Arousal and Suppression of Fear Upon Social Perception," *Journal of Abnormal and Social Psychology*, LV (November 1957), 283–88; and Elsa Sippoal, "A Group Study of Some Effects of Preparatory Sets," *Psychology*

Monographs, XLVI, No. 210 (1935), 27–28. For a general discussion of the importance of the per-ceiver's evoked set, see Postman, 87.

52. pp. 73–74.

53. For example, Roger Hilsman points out, "Those who knew of the peripheral reconnaissance flights that probed Soviet air defenses during the Eisenhower administration and the U-2 flights over the Soviet Union itself . . . were better able to understand some of the things the Soviets were saying and doing than people who did not know of these activities" (*To Move a Nation* [Garden City, 1967], 66). But it is also possible that those who knew about the U-2 flights at times misinterpreted Soviet messages by incorrectly believing that the sender was influenced by, or at least knew of, these flights.

54. I am grateful to Thomas Schelling for discussion on this point.

55. *Deterrence Before Hiroshima* (New York, 1966), 105–22.

56. *Ibid.*

57. For a slightly different formulation of this view, see Holsti, 27.

58. The Soviets consciously hold an extreme version of this view and seem to believe that nothing is accidental. See the discussion in Nathan Leites, *A Study of Bolshevism* (Glencoe, 1953), 67–73.

59. A. W. Marshall criticizes Western explanations of Soviet military posture for failing to take this into account. See his "Problems of Estimating Military Power," a paper presented at the 1966 Annual Meeting of the American Political Science Association, 16.

60. It has also been noted that in labor-management disputes both sides may be apt to believe incor-rectly that the other is controlled from above, either from the international union office or from the company's central headquarters (Robert Blake, Herbert Shepard, and Jane Mouton, *Managing Intergroup Conflict in Industry* [Houston, 1964], 182). It has been further noted that both Democratic and Republican members of the House tend to see the other party as the one that is more disciplined and united (Charles Clapp, *The Congressman* [Washington, 1963], 17–19).

61. George Kennan, *Russia Leaves the War* (New York, 1967), 484.

62. *Ibid.,* 404, 408, 500.

63. Herbert Butterfield notes that these assumptions can contribute to the spiral of "Hobbesian fear. . . . You yourself may vividly feel the terrible fear that you have of the other party, but you can-not enter into the other man's counterfear or even understand why he should be particularly ner-vous. For you know that you yourself mean him no harm and that you want nothing from him save guarantees for your own safety; and it is never possible for you to realize or remember properly that since he cannot see the inside of your mind, he can never have the same assurance of your intentions that you have" (*History and Human Conflict* [London, 1951], 20).

64. *European Diplomatic History 1871–1932* (New York, 1933), 125. It takes great mental effort to realize that actions which seem only the natural consequence of defending your vital interests can look to others as though you are refusing them any chance of increasing their influence. In rebutting the famous Crowe "balance of power" memorandum of 1907, which justified a policy of "contain-ing" Germany on the grounds that she was a threat to British national security, Sanderson, a former permanent undersecretary in the Foreign Office, wrote, "It has sometimes seemed to me that to a foreigner reading our press the British Empire must appear in the light of some huge giant sprawl-ing all over the globe, with gouty fingers and toes stretching in every direction, which cannot be approached without eliciting a scream" (quoted in Monger, 315). But few other Englishmen could be convinced that others might see them this way.

65. George Kennan makes clear that in 1918 this kind of difficulty was partly responsible for the inabil-ity of either the Allies or the new Bolshevik government to understand the motivations of the other side: "There is . . . nothing in nature more egocentric than the embattled democracy. . . . It . . . tends to attach to its own cause an absolute value which distorts its own vision of everything else. . . . It will readily be seen that people who have got themselves into this frame of mind have little under-standing for the issues of any contest other than the one in which they are involved. The idea of

people wasting time and substance on any *other* issue seems to them preposterous" (*Russia and the West,* 11–12).

66. Kaplan, 89.

67. Johan Jorgen Holst, "Surprise, Signals, and Reaction: The Attack on Norway," *Cooperation and Conflict,* No. 1 (1966), 34. The Germans made a similar mistake in November 1942 when they interpreted the presence of an Allied convoy in the Mediterranean as confirming their belief that Malta would be resupplied. They thus were taken by surprise when landings took place in North Africa (William Langer, *Our Vichy Gamble* [New York, 1966], 365).

&

Cognitive Perspectives on Foreign Policy*

Philip E. Tetlock and Charles B. McGuire, Jr.

The last fifteen years have witnessed an impressive expansion of cognitive research on foreign policy—on both methodological and theoretical fronts. On the methodological front, investigators have shown skill in drawing insights from a variety of research techniques, including laboratory experiments (reviewed by Holsti and George, 1975; Jervis, 1976); historical case studies (George and Smoke, 1974; Janis, 1982; Lebow, 1981); content analyses of archival documents (Axelrod, 1976; Falkowski, 1979; Hermann, 1980a, 1980b; Tetlock, 1983c), interview and questionnaire studies (Bonham, Shapiro, and Trumble, 1979; Heradstveit, 1974, 1981); and computer simulations of belief systems (Abelson, 1968; Anderson and Thorson, 1982). There are, moreover, numerous examples of multimethod convergence in the research literature: investigators from different methodological traditions have often arrived at strikingly similar conclusions concerning the roles that cognitive variables play in the foreign policymaking process. The theoretical diversity is equally impressive and healthy. In developing hypotheses linking cognitive and foreign policy variables, investigators have drawn upon a variety of intellectual traditions, including work on attribution theory (Heradstveit, 1981; Jervis, 1976; Tetlock, 1983b); cognitive-consistency theory (Jervis, 1976); behavioral decision theory (Fischhoff, 1983; Jervis, 1982); the effects of stress on information processing (Holsti and George, 1975; Janis and Mann, 1977; Suedfeld and Tetlock, 1977), organizational principles underlying political belief systems (George, 1969; Holsti, 1977; Walker, 1983); and individual differences in cognitive styles (Bonham and Shapiro, 1977; Hermann, 1980a; Tetlock, 1981, 1983a, 1984). Each of these approaches has borne at least some empirical fruit.

We believe careful appraisal is now needed of what has been accomplished and of the directions in which theoretical and empirical work appears to be developing. We have divided

Philip E. Tetlock and Charles B. McGuire, Jr., "Cognitive Perspectives on Foreign Policy." Excerpted from S. Long, ed., *Political Behavior Annual* (Boulder, CO: Westview Press, 1985). Reprinted by permission of the author.

our review chapter into four sections: "The Cognitive Research Program in Foreign Policy," "Representational Research," "Process Research," and "Conclusions."

THE COGNITIVE RESEARCH PROGRAM IN FOREIGN POLICY

Cognitive research on foreign policy can be viewed as an incipient research program. The hard core of the cognitive research program is difficult to specify with confidence. (What fundamental assumptions do the overwhelming majority of investigators who work at this level of analysis share?) We believe, however, that the hard core consists of two key assumptions which deserve to be spelled out in detail:

1. The international environment imposes heavy information-processing demands upon policymakers. It is very difficult to identify the best or utility-maximizing solutions to most foreign policy problems. Policymakers must deal with incomplete and unreliable information on the intentions and capabilities of other states. The range of response options is indeterminate. The problem consequences of each option are shrouded in uncertainty. Policymakers must choose among options that vary on many, seemingly incommensurable value dimensions (e.g., economic interests, international prestige, domestic political advantages, human rights, even lives). Finally, to compound the difficulty of the task, policymakers must sometimes work under intense stress and time pressure.

2. Policymakers (like all human beings) are limited-capacity information processors who resort to simplifying strategies to deal with the complexity, uncertainty, and painful trade-offs with which the world confronts them (cf. Abelson and Levi, in press; Einhorn and Hogarth, 1981; George, 1980; Jervis, 1976; Nisbett and Ross, 1980; Simon, 1957; Taylor and Fiske, 1984). The foreign policy of a nation addresses itself, not to the external world per se, but to the simplified image of the external world constructed in the minds of those who make policy decisions (Axelrod, 1976; George, 1980; Holsti, 1976; Jervis, 1976). Policymakers may behave "rationally" (attempt to maximize expected utility) but only within the context of their simplified subjective representations of reality.

Implicit in these hard-core assumptions is the central research objective of the cognitive research program: to understand *the cognitive strategies that policymakers rely upon to construct and maintain their simplified images of the environment*. We find it useful to distinguish two basic types of cognitive strategies, both of which have received substantial attention: (a) reliance on cognitive or knowledge structures that provide frameworks for assimilating new information and choosing among policy options (belief systems, operational codes, cognitive maps, scripts); (b) reliance on low-effort judgmental and choice heuristics that permit policymakers to make up their minds quickly and with confidence in the correctness of their positions (e.g., "satisficing" decision rules, the availability, representativeness, and anchoring heuristics).

These two (by no means mutually exclusive) coping strategies correspond closely to the distinction cognitive psychologists have drawn between declarative knowledge (first category) and procedural knowledge (second category) of mental functioning (cf. Anderson, 1978, 1980). Research on declarative knowledge in the foreign policy domain—which we call representational research—is concerned with clarifying *what* policymakers think. What assumptions do they make about themselves, other states, the relationships among states, the goals or values underlying foreign policy, and the types of policies most instrumental to attaining those goals or values? Can typologies or taxonomies of foreign policy belief systems be developed? To what extent and in what ways do policymakers' initial beliefs or assumptions guide—even dominate—the interpretation of new evidence and the making of new decisions? The best-known examples of representational research are studies of the operational codes and cognitive maps of political elites (Axelrod, 1976; George, 1969, 1980; Heradstveit, 1981; Holsti, 1977). Research on procedural knowledge—which we call process research—is concerned with identifying abstract (content-free) laws of cognitive functioning that focus on *how* policymakers think about issues (the intellectual roots of process research can be directly traced to experimental cognitive and social psychology). The best-known examples of process research are studies of perception and misperception in international relations: the rules or heuristics that policymakers use in seeking causal explanations for the behavior of other states, in drawing lessons from history or in choosing among courses of action (cf. George, 1980; Jervis, 1976, 1982; Tetlock, 1983b).

Reasonable challenges can be raised to the hard-core premises of the program. One can question, for instance, the causal importance of policymakers' cognitions about the environment. Correlations between cognitions and actions are not sufficient to establish causality. The beliefs, perceptions, and values that people express may merely be justifications for policies they have already adopted as a result of other processes (e.g., psychodynamic needs and conflicts, bureaucratic role demands, domestic political pressures, international exigencies).

REPRESENTATIONAL RESEARCH

Psychologists and political scientists have invented an intimidatingly long list of terms to describe the cognitive structures that perceivers rely upon in encoding new information. These terms include "scripts" (Abelson, 1981; Schank and Abelson, 1977); "operational codes" (George, 1969; Holsti, 1977); "cognitive maps" (Axelrod, 1976); "stereotypes" (Allport, 1954; Hamilton, 1979); "frames" (Minsky, 1975); "nuclear scenes" (Tompkins, 1979); "prototypes" (Cantor and Mischel, 1979); as well as the more traditional and inclusive term "schemas" (Nisbett and Ross, 1980). We do not propose a detailed classification of all possible cognitive structures in this chapter (for preliminary efforts in this area see Nisbett and Ross, 1980; Schank and Abelson, 1977; Taylor and Fiske, 1984). Our goals are more modest. We shall focus only on cognitive research specifically concerned with foreign policy. Within that domain, we further restrict our attention to two issues likely to be central to future theoretical developments in the field:

1. What theoretical and methodological tools are at our disposal to describe the cognitive structures that influence foreign policy?
2. To what extent is information processing in the foreign policy domain theory-driven (dominated by existing cognitive structures) as opposed to data-driven (responsive to external reality)?

Describing Foreign Policy Belief Systems

In principle, people can subscribe to an infinite variety of images of their own states, of other states, and of the relationships among states. We use the term "idiographic representational research" to describe case studies which present detailed descriptions of the foreign policy belief systems of individual decision makers. We use the term "nomothetic representational" research to describe studies in which the primary goal is the development and testing of general theoretical statements that apply to large populations of individuals. The focus thus shifts from the uniqueness of particular policymakers to underlying similarities or themes that permit cross-individual and cross-situational comparisons. We discuss three lines of nomothetic representational research: the work on operational codes, cognitive mapping, and personality correlates of foreign policy belief systems.

Operational Code Research

Operational codes impose badly needed cognitive order and stability on an ambiguous and complex international environment (George, 1969). They do so in multiple ways: by providing norms, standards, and guidelines that influence (but do not unilaterally determine) decision makers' choices of strategy and tactics in dealings with other nations. George proposed that the essence of an operational code can be captured in its answers to a number of "philosophical" questions concerning the "nature of the political universe" and a number of "instrumental" questions concerning the types of policies most likely to achieve important objectives (see also Holsti, 1977).

Operational codes are organized hierarchically such that central or core beliefs exert more influence on peripheral beliefs than vice versa. One strong "belief candidate" for a central organizing role in operational codes is whether the decision maker believes the political universe to be essentially one of conflict or one of harmony (Holsti, 1977). People who view the world in Hobbesian, zero-sum terms (a war of all against all) are likely to differ on a variety of belief dimensions from those who see the world as potentially harmonious. These two groups will tend to appraise the motives and goals of opponents differently and disagree on the best strategies for pursuing policy goals. Another strong candidate for a central organizing role in operational codes is the decision-maker's belief concerning the root causes of international conflict. People who attribute conflict to different root causes (e.g., human nature, attributes of nations, the international system) will tend to have different views on the likelihood of, and necessary conditions for, long-term peace.

Tetlock (1983b) notes that both sides seem to possess an unlimited capacity to view international events in ways that support their initial positions ("aggressive" Soviet acts can always be construed as defensive responses to external threats; "conciliatory" Soviet acts can always be construed as deceptive maneuvers designed to weaken Western resolve). This is consistent with the "principle of least resistance" in the attitude change literature (McGuire, in press). Those beliefs most likely to "give in" to contradictory evidence are beliefs that have the fewest connections to other beliefs in the cognitive system.

Cognitive Mapping

Cognitive mapping is a methodological technique for capturing the causal structure of policy-makers' cognitive representations of policy domains (Axelrod, 1976). Cognitive maps consist of two key elements: concept variables, which are represented as points, and causal beliefs linking the concepts, represented as arrows between points. A concept variable is defined simply: something that can take on different values (e.g., defense spending, American national security, balance of trade). Causal beliefs exist whenever decision makers believe that change in one concept variable leads to change in another variable.

Axelrod and other investigators have constructed a number of cognitive maps based on detailed content analyses of archival documents (e.g., Hitler-Chamberlain negotiations at Munich, the British Far Eastern Committee deliberations on Persia) and interviews with policymakers (e.g., State Department officials, energy experts). These studies demonstrate, at minimum, that: (1) cognitive mapping can be done with acceptable levels of intercoder reliability; (2) policymaking deliberations are saturated with causal arguments and that maps of these deliberations tend to be large and elaborate (in the sense that many different concept variables are causally connected with each other). (See Axelrod, 1976; Bonham and Shapiro, 1976; Bonham, Shapiro, and Trumble, 1979; Levi and Tetlock, 1980; Ross, 1976.)

Systematic analysis of cognitive maps has, however, provided more than descriptive information; it has also deepened our understanding of the cognitive bases of foreign policy. For instance, although cognitive maps are large and causally elaborate, they also tend to be simple, in that maps do not usually include trade-off relationships. Preferred policies usually have only positive consequences; rejected policies, only negative ones (cf. Jervis, 1976). This obviously makes decision making much easier; competing, difficult-to-quantify values do not have to be weighed against each other. Maps also rarely include reciprocal causal relationships (feedback loops) among variables: causality flows in only one direction. Axelrod summarizes the cognitive portrait of the decision-maker that emerges from his work in this way:

> one who has more beliefs than he can handle, who employs a simplified image of the policy environment that is structurally easy to operate with, and who then acts rationally within the context of his simplified image. (1976)

Our confidence in this summary portrait is reinforced by the very similar conclusions that have emerged from laboratory research on judgment and decision making (Abelson and Levi, in press; Einhorn and Hogarth, 1981; Kahneman, Slovic, and Tversky, 1981).

Individual Difference Research on Belief Systems

Even the most prominent advocate of the realist school of international politics—Henry Kissinger—concedes that foreign policymakers "work in darkness"; they make choices not only without knowledge of the future but usually even without adequate knowledge of what is happening in the present (Kissinger, 1979). This "structural uncertainty" (Steinbruner, 1974) of foreign policy problems has led many analysts to propose an analogy between international politics and projective tests used in personality assessment: the international scene, in much the same way as a good projective test, evokes different psychologically important response themes from national leaders. Foreign policy belief systems do not emerge in a psychological vacuum; they emerge as plausible self-expressive responses to the situations in which policymakers find themselves (Etheredge, 1978). From this standpoint, it is essential to study the personality background or context out of which belief systems evolve.

Evidence on relations between personality and foreign policy preferences comes from the full range of methodological sources, including laboratory experiments, surveys, content analyses of archival documents, expert ratings of policymakers, and case studies (Christiansen, 1959; Eckhardt and Lentz, 1967; Etheredge, 1978; Lasswell, 1930; McClosky, 1967; Terhune, 1970; Tetlock, 1981; Tetlock, Crosby, and Crosby, 1981). The similarity in results across methodologies is, moreover, impressive.

These lines of research remind us that foreign policy belief systems do not exist in isolation from broader dimensions of individual differences in interpersonal style, cognitive style, and basic motivational variables. To paraphrase Lasswell (1930), foreign policy beliefs may sometimes serve as rationalizations for psychological needs and tendencies that have been displaced onto the international scene. A critical challenge for future theory will be to resolve the tension between purely cognitive analyses of foreign policy (which grant "functional autonomy" to belief systems) and motivational analyses of foreign policy (which view belief systems as subservient to other psychological variables and systems).

A Comment on Theory-Driven versus Data-Driven Processing

We turn from the nature of foreign policy belief systems to the impact of belief systems on the policymaking process. A casual reader of the literature might easily walk away with the impression that foreign policy is overwhelmingly "theory-driven" (i.e., that the preconceptions policymakers bring to decision-making situations are much more important determinants of the actions taken than is the objective evidence). Both experimental and case study evidence appear to support this conclusion. The laboratory evidence comes from multiple sources, including research on primary effects in impression formation, the resistance of political attitudes and stereotypes to change (Hamilton, 1979; Lord, Ross, and Lepper, 1979); rigidity or set effects in problem solving (Luchins, 1942); and the persistence of causal attributions even after the discrediting of the information on which the attributions were initially based (Nisbett and Ross, 1980). The evidence from actual foreign policy settings comes most importantly from the pioneering work of Jervis (1976). He notes that the historical record contains many references to government leaders who have treated belief-supportive information uncritically while simultaneously searching for all possible flaws in belief-challenging information.

We need to be careful, however, in discussing the theory-driven nature of foreign policy. Reliance on prior beliefs and expectations is not irrational per se (one would expect it from a "good Bayesian"); it becomes irrational only when perseverance and denial dominate openness and flexibility. Cognitive models of foreign policy—like cognitive models generally—must acknowledge the coexistence of theory-driven and data-driven processing. Each is necessary; neither will suffice alone (see Bennett, 1981).

PROCESS RESEARCH

The previous section examined representational research on the beliefs and assumptions decision makers bring to policy problems and on the impact of those beliefs and assumptions on foreign policy. In this section, we focus on the rules or procedures that people may use in making policy decisions: the rules vary widely in form, in complexity, and in the "mental effort" required for their execution (Newell and Simon, 1972; Payne, 1982).

In practice, however, the laboratory and field evidence of the last ten years indicates that people do not rely equally on effort-demanding and top-of-the-head procedural rules. People appear to be "cognitive misers"—effort savers who show a marked preference for simple, low-effort heuristics that permit them to make up their minds quickly, easily, and with confidence in the correctness of the stands they have taken (see Abelson and Levi, in press; Einhorn and Hogarth, 1981; Fischhoff, 1981; Nisbett and Ross, 1980; Taylor and Fiske, 1984).

This "cognitive miser" theme helps to unify research on cognitive processes in foreign policy. We examine here five lines of research: work on the fundamental attribution error, extracting lessons from history, avoidance of value trade-offs, the policy-freezing effects of commitment, and crisis decision making. In each case, the cognitive miser image of the decision maker serves as leitmotif: policymakers often seem unwilling or unable to perform the demanding information-processing tasks required by normative models of judgment and choice.

The "Fundamental Attribution Error"

The fundamental attribution error has been described as a pervasive bias in social perception (Jones, 1979; Nisbett and Ross, 1980; Ross, 1977). Numerous experiments indicate that, in explaining the actions of others, people systematically underestimate the importance of external or situational causes of behavior and overestimate the importance of internal or dispositional causes (Kelley and Michela, 1980; Jones, 1979; Nisbett and Ross, 1980). The most influential explanation for the fundamental attribution error focuses on people's tendency to rely on low-effort judgmental heuristics (as opposed to more demanding procedural rules) in interpreting events. Jones (1979), for instance, argues that in many settings the most cognitively available (first-to-come-to-mind) explanation for behavior is some intrinsic property or disposition of the person who performed the behavior.

Do the laboratory studies describe judgmental processes that also operate in foreign policy settings? Our answer is a tentative yes. Two important qualifications should, however, be noted. First, the natural unit of causal analysis for foreign policymakers is often the nation-state, not the individual human actor used in laboratory experiments. With this caveat, though, much seems to fall into place. Jervis (1976) argues that policymakers tend to see the behavior of other states as more centralized, planned, and coordinated than it is. He notes, for instance, a number of historical situations in which national leaders have ascribed far too much significance to movements of military forces that were routine, accidental, or responses to immediate situational variables (e.g., the North Vietnamese interpretation of reduced American air attacks on Hanoi and Haiphong in 1966 as support for a peace initiative, not a reaction to inclement weather). Jervis also notes historical situations in which policymakers have seriously overestimated the internal coherence of the foreign policies of states. National policies are not always the result of long-term planning; sometimes they are reactions to immediate opportunities or setbacks or the products of miscalculation, miscommunication, bureaucratic infighting, or domestic political pressures. Observers often attribute Machiavellian intentions to policies that are the cumulative result of many unrelated causes (e.g., the Allies exaggerated the coordination among German, Italian, and Japanese moves in the late 1930s and early 1940s; the Soviets saw the failure of the Western powers to invade France in 1943 as part of a well-calculated effort to make the Soviet Union bear the brunt of the war against Nazi Germany).

A second qualification is also, however, necessary to our discussion of the fundamental attribution error. As with belief perseverance, we should refrain from strong normative judgments. We rarely know the true causes of the behavior of other states. In a world in which policymakers are motivated to make or misrepresent their intentions (Heuer, 1981), the truth tends to emerge slowly and rarely completely.

Extracting Lessons from History

Analogical reasoning can be defined as "the transfer of knowledge from one situation to another by a process of mapping—finding a set of one-to-one correspondences (often incomplete) between aspects of one body of information and other" (Gick and Holyoak, 1983, p. 2). Many psychologists regard analogical reasoning as fundamental to human intelligence and problem solving (e.g., Newell and Simon, 1972; Sternberg, 1982). People try to categorize and structure unfamiliar problems in terms of familiar ones.

Students of foreign policy have also paid attention to analogical reasoning—in particular, to how policymakers use historical precedents to justify current policies (George, 1980; Jervis,

1976; May, 1973). Case studies of foreign policy decisions are filled with references to policymakers who were determined to profit from what they think were the lessons of the past (e.g., Stanley Baldwin, Adolf Hitler, Harry Truman, Charles de Gaulle, John F. Kennedy, Lyndon Johnson). For instance, when the Korean War broke out unexpectedly in 1950, Harry Truman perceived parallels with totalitarian aggression in the 1930s and quickly concluded that the North Korean invasion had to be repelled (Paige, 1968). Similarly, Lyndon Johnson's fear of "another Castro" shaped his perceptions of the unrest in the Dominican Republic in 1965 and his judgment of the need for American intervention (Lowenthal, 1972).

There is nothing wrong with trying to learn from the past. Unfortunately, policymakers often draw simplistic, superficial, and biased lessons from history. Various lines of evidence are revealing in this connection:

1. One's political perspective heavily colors the conclusions one draws from history. In a survey of American opinion leaders, Holsti and Rosenau (1979) examined the lessons that supporters and opponents of American involvement drew from the Vietnam War. Prominent lessons for hawks were that the Soviet Union is expansionist and that the United States should avoid graduated escalation and honor alliance commitments. Prominent lessons for doves were that the United States should avoid guerrilla wars (e.g., Angola), that the press is more truthful on foreign policy than the administration, and the civilian leaders should be wary of military advice. Interestingly, *no one lesson* appeared on both the hawk and dove lists (cf. Zimmerman and Axelrod, 1981).

2. If contending states learn anything from one crisis experience to the next, it may be simply to become more belligerent in their dealings with adversaries. Lessons of history are often assimilated into Realpolitik belief systems that emphasize the importance of resolve and toughness when "vital interests" are at stake (Leng, 1983).

3. Policymakers rarely consider a broad range of historical analogies before deciding which one best fits the problem confronting them. They rely on the most salient or cognitively available precedent (usually a precedent that policymakers have experienced at firsthand or that occurred early in their adult lives).

4. Policymakers often draw sweeping generalizations from preferred historical analogies and are insensitive to differences between these analogies and current situations (history, after all, never repeats itself exactly). One rarely hears policymakers, privately or publicly, conceding the partial relevance of several analogies to a problem and then attempting to draw contingent rather than universal generalizations. For example, instead of "If a military buildup (or appeasement), then a nuclear holocaust," one could ask, "Under what conditions will one or the other policy increase or decrease the likelihood of war?"

Avoidance of Value Trade-Offs

In many decision-making situations, there are no clear right or wrong answers. Each policy option has both positive and negative features (e.g., lower inflation is accompanied by higher unemployment; greater military strength is accompanied by greater budget deficits). Available experimental and historical evidence indicates that decision makers find trade-offs unpleasant and tend to avoid them (Abelson and Levi, in press; Einhorn and Hogarth, 1981; Gallhofer and Saris, 1979; George, 1980; Jervis, 1976; Slovic, 1975; Steinbruner, 1974). Trade-offs are unpleasant for cognitive reasons (it is very difficult to "net out" the positive and negative features of alternatives—What common units can be used to compare the value of human lives and one's national credibility as an ally?) and for motivational reasons (it is very difficult to justify to oneself and to others that one has sacrificed one basic value in favor of another). To avoid trade-offs, decision makers rely on a variety of "noncompensatory choice heuristics" (Montgomery and Svenson, 1976). For instance, according to Tversky's (1972) elimination-by-aspects rule, people compare response alternatives on one value dimension at a time, with the values being selected with a probability proportional to their perceived importance. All alternatives not having satisfactory loadings on the first (most important) value are eliminated. A second value is then selected with a probability proportional to its importance, and the process continues until only one option remains.

Experimental data have repeatedly demonstrated the importance of noncompensatory choice heuristics in decision making (Bettman, 1979; Montgomery and Svenson, 1976; Payne, 1976; Tversky, 1972; Wallsten, 1980). In the words of Hammond and Mumpower (1979): "We are not accustomed to presenting the rationale for the choice between values. . . . When our values conflict, we retreat to a singular emphasis on our favorite value."

Research in foreign policy settings supports this generalization. As already noted, cognitive maps of policymaking deliberations make few references to value trade-offs (i.e., policy options typically are not seen as having contradictory effects on "utility"). Similarly, Jervis (1976) has used the term "belief system overkill" to describe the tendency of policymakers in historical situations to avoid trade-offs by generating a plethora of logically independent reasons in support of the stands they have taken. Jervis (1976, p. 137) describes the phenomenon in this way: "decision-makers do not simultaneously estimate how a policy will affect many values. Instead, they look at only one or two most salient values. As they come to favor a policy that seems best on these restricted dimensions, they alter their earlier beliefs and establish new ones so that as many reasons as possible support their choice." (See also George, 1980).

The Freezing Effects of Commitment

Once people have committed themselves to a course of action, they find it very difficult to retreat from that commitment. These "attitude-freezing" effects of commitment have been studied extensively in experimental social psychology and organizational behavior (e.g., Deutsch and Gerard, 1955; Helmreich and Collins, 1968; Janis and Mann, 1977; Kiesler, 1971; Staw, 1980). Public announcement of an attitudinal position increases later resistance to persuasive attacks on the attitude and motivates people to generate cognitions supportive of the attitude. The more irreversible the commitment, the stronger the effects tend to be (Janis and Mann, 1977; Staw, 1980). The most influential explanation for these findings is in terms of cognitive dissonance theory (Festinger, 1964). People seek to justify their commitments (and their self-images as rational, moral beings) by portraying actions they have freely chosen as reasonable and fair.

In addition to the laboratory evidence, many foreign policy examples exist of the "freezing" effects of commitment on the attitudes of national leaders. Jervis (1976) has offered the most comprehensive analysis of such effects. He identifies many plausible examples, including: the unwillingness of the pre-World War II Japanese government to compromise the gains achieved as a result of its large military losses in China, President Wilson's abandonment of his serious reservations about entering World War I after making the crucial decision, and the reluctance of American officials committed to the Diem regime in South Vietnam to acknowledge the regime's shortcomings. To some extent, such postcommitment bolstering of decisions is adaptive (little would be accomplished if we abandoned commitments in the face of the first setback). Postcommitment bolstering becomes "irrational" only when the desire of decision makers to justify their commitments (and to recoup "sunk costs"—Staw, 1980) blinds them to alternative policies with higher expected payoffs. Assessing exactly when postcommitment bolstering becomes irrational is, of course, a tricky judgment call.

Crisis Decision Making

Policymakers fall prey to the previously discussed biases and errors even under favorable information-processing conditions. Policymakers do not, however, always work under favorable conditions. They must sometimes function in highly stressful crisis environments in which they need to analyze large amounts of ambiguous and inconsistent evidence under severe time pressure, always with the knowledge that miscalculations may have serious consequences for their own careers and vital national interests (Brecher, 1979; C. Hermann, 1969; Holsti, Brody, and North, 1969; Holsti and George, 1975; Lebow, 1981).

Converging evidence—from laboratory experiments and simulations, historical case studies, and content analyses of decision makers' statements—supports this "disruptive-stress" hypothesis. The experimental literature on the effects of stress is enormous (for reviews, see Janis and Mann, 1977; Staw, Sandelands, and Dutton, 1981). There is basic agreement, though, that high levels of stress reduce the complexity and quality of information processing. The impairment includes a lessened likelihood of accurately identifying and discriminating among unfamiliar stimuli (Postman and Bruner, 1948); rigid reliance on old, now inappropriate problem-solving strategies (Cowen, 1952); reduced search for new information (Schroder, Driver, and Streufert 1967); and heightened intolerance for inconsistent evidence (Streufert and Streufert, 1978).

Case studies and content analyses of historical records point to similar conclusions. As crises intensify, particularly crises that culminate in war, images of environment and policy options appear to simplify and rigidify. Policymakers are more likely to ignore alternative interpretations of events, to attend to a restricted range of options, and to view possible outcomes of the conflict in terms of absolute victory or defeat (C. Hermann, 1972; Holsti, 1972; Holsti and George, 1975; Lebow, 1981; Raphael, 1982; Suedfeld and Tetlock, 1977; Tetlock, 1979, 1983b, 1983c).

Simplification effects are not, however, an automatic reaction to international crises (see Tanter, 1978, for a detailed review). We need a theory—similar to the Janis and Mann (1977) conflict model of decision making—that allows for the possibility that threats to important values do not always disrupt, and sometimes even facilitate, complex information processing. The effects of crises may depend on many factors: individual difference variables (self-image as effective coper, track record of performance in previous crises) and situational variables (the reversibility and severity of existing threats).

CONCLUDING REMARKS

How successful has the cognitive research program been? Many positive signs exist. There is no shortage of theoretical speculation and hypotheses on how cognitive variables influence foreign policy. Considerable research has been done. There are impressive indications of multimethod convergence in the work to date. A cumulative body of knowledge appears to be developing. Perhaps most important, the research program continues to be "heuristically provocative" in the sense of suggesting new avenues of empirical and theoretical exploration.

But all is not well within the cognitive research program. Current theory is seriously fragmented. Consensus is lacking on the extent to which and the ways in which cognitive variables influence foreign policy. Contradictory examples can be identified for most, if not all, of the theoretical generalizations offered earlier on the role that cognitive variables play in foreign policy. Consider the following claims:

- Policymakers are too slow in revising their initial impressions of an event.
- Policymakers overestimate the importance of long-term planning and underestimate the importance of chance and immediate situational pressures as causes of the behavior of other states.
- Policymakers avoid difficult value trade-offs.
- Policymakers draw simple and biased lessons from history.
- Policymakers rigidly defend and bolster past commitments.
- Policymakers analyze information in especially simplistic and superficial ways under high-stress crisis conditions.

Although the preponderance of the evidence is consistent with the above generalizations, the exceptions cannot be glibly dismissed. One can point to laboratory and historical situations in which the generalizations do not hold up well (e.g., Abelson and Levi, in press; Janis, 1982; Jervis, 1976; Maoz, 1981; McAllister, Mitchell, and Beach, 1979; Payne, 1982; Tetlock, 1983b).

The cognitive research program must ultimately come to grips with these anomalies. We believe a viable cognitive theory will have to take the form of a "contingency theory" of political information processing—one that acknowledges the capacity of people to adopt different modes of information processing in response to changing circumstances. From a contingency theory perspective, the search for immutable laws of cognitive functioning is misguided (Jenkins, 1981; McAllister et al., 1979; Payne, 1982; Tetlock, 1984). The appropriate question is not "What kind of machine is the human information processor?" but rather "What kinds of machines do people become when confronted with particular types of tasks in particular types of environments?" No single cognitive portrait of the policymaker is possible. Under some conditions, people rely on complex information-processing rules that approximate those prescribed by normative models of judgment and choice. Under other conditions, policymakers rely on simple top-of-the-head rules that minimize mental effort and strain. The major objective of the positive heuristic of the research program should not be to arrive at a global characterization of the information processor; rather, it should be to identify the personality and situational boundary conditions for the applicability of different characterizations of the information processor.

REFERENCES

Abelson, R. P. (1968). "Psychological Implication." In R. P. Abelson et al., eds., *Theories of Cognitive Consistency: A Sourcebook.* Chicago: Rand-McNally.

——— (1973). "The Structure of Decision." In R. C. Schank, and K. M. Colby, eds., *Computer Models of Thought and Language.* San Francisco: Freeman.

——— (1981). "Psychological Status of the Script Concept." *American Psychologist* 36: 715–29.

Abelson, R. P., and Levi, A. (3d ed., in press). "Decision-Making and Decision Theory." In G. Lindzey and E. Aronson, eds., *Handbook of Social Psychology.* Reading, MA: Addison-Wesley.

Allison, G. (1972). *Essence of Decision.* Boston: Little, Brown.

Aliport, G. W. (1943). "The Ego in Contemporary Psychology," *Psychological Review* 50: 451–78.

———— (1954). *The Nature of Prejudice.* Garden City, NY: Doubleday/Anchor.

Anderson, J. (1976). *Language, Memory and Thought.* Hillsdale, NJ: Erlbaum.

———— (1978). "Arguments Concerning Representations for Mental Imagery." *Psychological Review* 85: 249–77.

———— (1980). *Cognitive Psychology and Its Implications.* San Francisco: Freeman.

Anderson, P. A., and Thorson, S. J. (1982). "Systems Simulation: Artificial Intelligence Based Simulations of Foreign Policy Decision Making." *Behavioral Science* 27: 176–93.

Axelrod, R. (1976). *Structure of Decision.* Princeton: Princeton University Press.

Bennett, W. L. (1981). "Perception and Cognition: An Information Processing Framework for Politics." In S. Long, ed., *Handbook of Political Behavior.* NY: Plenum.

Bellman, J. R. (1979). *An Information Processing Theory of Consumer Choice.* Reading, MA: Addison-Wesley.

Bonham, G. M., and Shapiro, M. J. (1976). "Explanation of the Unexpected: The Syrian Intervention in Jordan in 1970." In R. P. Axelrod, ed., *Structure of Decision.* Princeton: Princeton University Press.

———— (1977). "Foreign Policy Decision Making in Finland and Austria: The Application of a Cognitive Process Model." In G. M. Bonham and M. J. Shapiro, eds., *Thought and Action in Foreign Policy.* Basel: Birkhauser Verlag.

Bonham, G. M.; Shapiro, M.; and Trumble, T. (1979). "The October War: Changes in Cognitive Orientation Toward the Middle East Conflict." *International Studies Quarterly* 23: 3–44.

Brecher, M. (1979). "State Behavior in a Crisis: A Model." *Journal of Conflict Resolution* 23: 446–80.

Cantor, N., and Mischel, W. (1979). "Prototypes in Person Perception." In L. Berkowitz, ed., *Advances in Experimental Social Psychology.* Vol. 2, NY: Academic Press.

Cantril, H. (1967). *The Human Dimension: Experiences in Policy Research.* New Brunswick: Rutgers University Press.

Christiansen, B. (1959). *Attitudes Toward Foreign Affairs as a Function of Personality.* Oslo: Oslo University Press.

Converse, P. E. (1964). "The Nature of Belief Systems in Mass Publics." In D. Apter, ed., *Ideology and Discontent.* NY: The Free Press.

Cowen, E. L. (1952). "Stress Reduction and Problem Solving Rigidity." *Journal of Consulting Psychology* 16: 425–28.

Deutsch, M., and Gerard, H. (1955). "A Study of Normative and Informational Social Influences upon Individual Judgment." *Journal of Abnormal and Social Psychology* 15: 629–36.

Dollard, J.; Doob, L.; Miller, N.; Mowrer, O. H.; and Sears, R. (1939). *Frustration and Aggression.* New Haven: Yale University Press.

Eckhardt, W., and Lentz, T. (1967). "Factors of War/Peace Attitudes." *Peace Research Reviews* 1: 1–22.

Einhorn, H., and Hogarth, R. M. (1981). "Behavioral Decision Theory." *Annual Review of Psychology* 31: 53–88.

Etheredge, L. S. (1978). *A World of Men: The Private Sources of American Foreign Policy.* Cambridge: MIT Press.

———— (1981). "Government Learning: An Overview." In S. Long, ed., *Handbook of Political Behavior.* NY: Plenum.

Falkowski, L. S., ed. (1979). *Psychological Models in International Politics.* Boulder, CO: Westview Press.

Feifer, G. (February 1981). "Russian Disorders: The Sick Man of Europe." *Harpers*. pp. 41–55.

Festinger, L. (1964). *Conflict, Decision and Dissonance.* Stanford: Stanford University Press.

Fischhoff, B. (1975). "Hindsight and Foresight: The Effects of Outcome Knowledge on Judgment Under Uncertainty." *Journal of Experimental Psychology: Human Perception and Performance* 1: 288–99.

———— (1981). "For Those Condemned to Study the Past: Heuristics and Biases in Hindsight." In D. Kahneman, P. Slovic, and A. Tversky, eds., *Judgment Under Uncertainty.* Cambridge: Cambridge University Press.

———— (1983). "Strategic Policy Preferences: A Behavioral Decision Theory Perspective." *Journal of Social Issues* 39: 133–60.

Gallhofer, I. N., and Saris, W. E. (1979). "Strategy Choices of Foreign Policy-Makers." *Journal of Conflict Resolution* 23: 425–45.

George, A. L. (1969). "The 'Operational Code': A Neglected Approach to the Study of Political Leaders and Decision-Making." *International Studies Quarterly* 13: 190–222.

———— (1980). *Presidential Decisionmaking in Foreign Policy: The Effective Use of Information and Advice.* Boulder, CO: Westview Press.

George, A. L., and Smoke, R. (1974). *Deterrence in American Foreign Policy: Theory and Practice.* NY: Columbia University Press.

Gick, M., and Holyoak, K. (1983). "Schema Induction and Analogical Transfer." *Cognitive Psychology* 15: 1–38.

Hamilton, D. (1979). "A Cognitive-Attributional Analysis of Stereotyping." In L. Berkowitz, ed., *Advances in Experimental Social Psychology.* Vol. 12. NY: Academic Press.

Hammond, D., and Mumpower, J. (1979). "Risks and Safeguards in the Formation of Social Policy." *Knowledge: Creation, Diffusion, Utilization* 1: 245–58.

Helmreich, R., and Collins, B. (1968). "Studies in Forced Compliance: Commitment and Magnitude of Inducement to Comply as Determinants of Opinion Change." *Journal of Personality and Social Psychology* 10: 75–81.

Heradstveit, D. (1974). *Arab and Israeli Elite Perceptions.* Oslo: Universitatforlaget.

———— (1981). *The Arab-Israeli Conflict: Psychological Obstacles to Peace.* Oslo: Universitatforlaget.

Hermann, C. (1969). *Crises in Foreign Policy.* Indianapolis: Bobbs-Merrill.

———— (1972). *International Crises: Insights from Behavioral Research.* NY: The Free Press.

Hermann, M. G. (1980a). "Assessing the Personalities of Soviet Politburo Members." *Personality and Social Psychology Bulletin* 6: 332–52.

———— (1980b). "Explaining Foreign Policy Behavior Using the Personal Characteristics of Political Leaders." *International Studies Quarterly* 24: 7–46.

Heuer, R. (1981). "Strategic Deception and Counter-Deception." *International Studies Quarterly* 25: 294–327.

Hitch, C., and McKean, R. (1965). *The Economics of Defense in the Nuclear Age.* NY: Atheneum.

Holsti, O. R. (1972). *Crisis Escalation War.* Montreal: McGill-Queen's University Press.

———— (1976). "Foreign Policy Formation Viewed Cognitively." In R. Axelrod, ed., *Structure of Decision.* Princeton: Princeton University Press.

———— (1977). "The 'Operational Code' as an Approach to the Analysis of Belief Systems." *Final Report to the National Science Foundation.* Grant No. SOC 75–15368. Duke University.

Holsti, O. R.; Brody, R. A.; and North, R. C. (1969). "The Management of International Crisis: Affect and Action in American-Soviet Relations: " In D. G. Pruitt and R. C. Snyder, eds., *Theory and Research on the Causes of War.* Englewood Cliffs, NJ: Prentice-Hall.

Holsti, O. R., and George, A. L. (1975). "Effects of Stress Upon Foreign Policymaking." In C. P. Cotter, ed., *Political Science Annual*. Indianapolis: Bobbs-Merrill.

Holsti, O. R., and Rosenau, J. (1979). "Vietnam, Consensus, and the Belief Systems of American Leaders." *World Politics* 32: 1–56.

Janis, I. (2d ed., 1982), *Groupthink*. Boston: Houghton Mifflin.

Janis, I., and Mann, L. (1977). *Decision Making*. NY: The Free Press.

Jenkins, J. (1981). "Can We Have a Fruitful Cognitive Psychology?" In J. H. Flowers, ed., *Nebraska Symposium on Motivation*. Lincoln: University of Nebraska Press.

Jervis, R. (1976). *Perception and Misperception in International Politics*. Princeton: Princeton University Press.

——— (1982). "Perception and Misperception in International Politics: An Updating of the Analysis." Paper presented at the Annual Meeting of the International Society of Political Psychology, Washington, D.C., June 24–27, 1982.

Jones, E. E. (1979). "The Rocky Road from Acts to Dispositions." *American Psychologist* 34: 107–17.

Kahn, H. (1961). *On Thermonuclear War*. Princeton: Princeton University Press.

Kahneman, D.; Slovic, P.; and Tversky, A., eds. (1981). *Judgment Under Uncertainty: Heuristics and Biases*. Cambridge: Cambridge University Press.

Kaiser, R. (1981). "U.S.-Soviet Relations: Goodbye to Detente." *Foreign Affairs*. Special issue, "America and the World, 1980" 59 (3): 500–21.

Kelley, H. H., and Michela, J. (1980). "Attribution Theory and Research." *Annual Review of Psychology* 31: 457–501.

Kiesler, C., ed. (1971). *The Psychology of Commitment*. NY: Academic Press.

Kissinger, H. A. (1979). *White House Years*. NY: Knopf.

Lakatos, I. (1970). "Falsification and the Methodology of Scientific Research Programs." In I. Lakatos and A. Musgrave, eds., *Criticism and the Growth of Knowledge*. Cambridge: Cambridge University Press.

Lasswell, H. (1930). *Psychopathology and Politics*. Chicago: University of Chicago Press.

Lebow, R. N. (1981). *Between Peace and War*. Baltimore: Johns Hopkins University Press.

Leng, R. J. (1983). "When Will They Ever Learn?: Coercive Bargaining in Recurrent Crises." *Journal of Conflict Resolution* 27: 379–419.

Levi, A., and Tetlock, P. E. (1980). "A Cognitive Analysis of the Japanese Decision to Go to War." *Journal of Conflict Resolution* 24: 195–212.

Lord, C.; Ross, L.; and Lepper, M. (1979). "Biased Assimilation and Attitude Polarization: The Effects of Prior Theory on Subsequently Considered Evidence." *Journal of Personality and Social Psychology* 37: 2098–2108.

Lowenthal, A. F. (1972). *The Dominican Intervention*. Cambridge: Harvard University Press.

Luchins, A. S. (1942). "Mechanization in Problem-Solving: The Effects of Einstellung." *Psychological Monographs* 54: 1–95.

Lyons, E. (1954). *Our Secret Allies*. NY: Duell, Sloan and Pearce.

Maoz, Z. (1981). "The Decision to Raid Entebbe." *Journal of Conflict Resolution* 25: 677–707.

May, E. (1973). *Lessons of the Past*. NY: Oxford University Press.

McAllister, P. W.; Mitchell, T. R.; and Beach, L. R. (1979). "The Contingency Model for the Selection of Decision Strategies: An Empirical Test of the Effects of Significance, Accountability, and Reversibility." *Organizational Behavior and Human Performance* 24: 228–44.

McClosky, H. (1967). "Personality and Attitude Correlates of Foreign Policy Orientation." In J. N. Rosenau, ed., *Domestic Sources of Foreign Policy*. NY: The Free Press.

McGuire, W. J. (3d ed., in press). "The Nature of Attitudes and Attitude Change." In G. Lindzey and E. Aronson, eds., *Handbook of Social Psychology.* Reading, MA: Addison-Wesley.

Minsky, M. (1975). "A Framework for Representing Knowledge." In P. H. Winston, ed., *Psychology of Computer Vision.* NY: McGraw-Hill.

Montgomery, H., and Svenson, O. (1976). "On Decision Rules and Information Processing Strategies for Choice Among Multiattribute Alternatives." *Scandinavian Journal of Psychology* 17: 283–91.

Newell, A., and Simon, H. A. (1972). *Human Problem Solving.* Englewood Cliffs, NJ: Prentice-Hall.

Niebuhr, R. (1960). *Moral Man and Immoral Society.* NY: Scribner's.

Nisbett, R., and Ross, L. (1980). *Human Inference: Strategies and Shortcomings of Social Judgment.* Englewood Cliffs, NJ: Prentice-Hall.

Paige, G. D. (1968). *The Korean Decision.* NY: The Free Press.

Payne, J. W. (1976). "Task Complexity and Contingent Processing in Decision-Making: An Information Search and Protocol Analysis." *Organizational Behavior and Human Performance* 16: 366–87.

——— (1982). "Contingent Decision Behavior." *Psychological Bulletin* 92: 382–402.

Postman, L., and Bruner, J. S. (1948). "Perception Under Stress." *Psychological Review* 55: 314–23.

Putnam, R. (1971). *The Beliefs of Politicians.* New Haven: Yale University Press.

Raphael, T. D. (1982). "Integrative Complexity Theory and Forecasting International Crises: Berlin 1946–1962." *Journal of Conflict Resolution* 26: 423–50.

Ross, L. (1977). "The Intuitive Psychologist and His Shortcomings: Distortions in the Attribution Process." In L. Berkowitz, ed., *Advances in Experimental Social Psychology.* Vol. 10, NY: Academic Press.

Ross, S. (1976). "Complexity and the Presidency: Gouverneur Morris in the Constitutional Convention." In R. Axelrod, ed., *Structure of Decision.* Princeton: Princeton University Press.

Schank, R. C., and Abelson, R. P. (1977). *Scripts, Plans, Goals and Understanding: An Inquiry into Human Knowledge Structures.* Hillsdale, NJ: Erlbaum.

Schelling, T. (1963). *The Strategy of Conflict.* Cambridge: Harvard University Press.

Schroder, H. M.; Driver, M.; and Streufert, S. (1967). *Human Information Processing.* NY: Holt, Rinehart, and Winston.

Simon, H. A. (1957). *Models of Man: Social and Rational.* NY: Wiley.

Slovic, P. (1975). "Choice Between Equally Valued Alternatives." *Journal of Experimental Psychology: Human Perception and Performance* 1: 280–87.

Staw, B. M. (1980). "Rationality and Justification in Organizational Life." In B. M. Staw and L. Cummings, eds., *Research in Organizational Behavior.* Vol. 2. Greenwich, CT: JAI Press.

Staw, B. M.; Sandelands, L. E.; and Dutton, J. E. (1981). "Threat-Rigidity Effects in Organizational Behavior: A Multilevel Analysis." *Administrative Science Quarterly* 26: 501–24.

Steinbruner, J. (1974). *The Cybernetic Theory of Decision.* Princeton: Princeton University Press.

Steinbruner, J., and Carter, B. (1975). "The Organizational Dimension of the Strategic Posture: The Case for Reform." *Daedalus* (Summer) Issued as Vol. 4, No. 3, of *The Proceedings of the American Academy of Arts and Sciences.*

Sternberg, R. J. (1982). *Handbook of Human Intelligence.* NY: Cambridge University Press.

Streufert, S., and Streufert, S. (1978). *Behavior in the Complex Environment.* Washington, D.C.: Winston and Sons.

Suedfeld, P., and Tetlock, P. E. (1977). "Integrative Complexity of Communications in International Crises." *Journal of Conflict Resolution* 21: 168–78.

Tanter, R. (1978). "International Crisis Behavior: An Appraisal of the Literature." In M. Brecher, ed., *Studies of Crisis Behavior.* New Brunswick, NJ: Transaction.

Taylor, S., and Fiske, S. (1984). *Social Cognition.* Reading, MA: Addison-Wesley.

Terhune, K. (1970). "The Effects of Personality on Cooperation and Conflict." In R. G. Swingle, ed., *The Structure of Conflict.* NY: Academic Press.

Tetlock, P. E. (1979). "Identifying Victims of Groupthink from Public Statements of Decision Makers." *Journal of Personality and Social Psychology* 37: 1314–24.

———— (1981). "Personality and Isolationism: Content Analysis of Senatorial Speeches." *Journal of Personality and Social Psychology* 41: 737–43.

———— (1983a). "Accountability and Complexity of Thought." *Journal of Personality and Social Psychology* 45: 74–83.

———— (1983b). "Policy-Makers' Images of International Conflict." *Journal of Social Issues* 39: 67–86.

———— (1983c). "Psychological Research on Foreign Policy: A Methodological Overview." In L. Wheeler, ed., *Review of Personality and Social Psychology.* Vol. 4, Beverly Hills, CA: Sage.

———— (1984). "Accountability: The Neglected Social Context of Judgment and Choice." In B. Staw and L. Cummings, eds., *Research in Organizational Behavior.* Vol. 6, Greenwich, CT: JAI Press.

Tetlock, P. E.; Crosby, F.; and Crosby, T. (1981). "Political Psychobiography." *Micropolitics* 1: 193–213.

Tompkins, S. S. (1979). "Script Theory: Differential Magnification of Affects." In H. E. Howe and R. A. Dienstbier, eds., *Nebraska Symposium on Motivation.* Vol. 26. Lincoln: University of Nebraska Press.

Tuchman, B. (1962). *The Guns of August.* NY: Macmillan.

Tversky, A. (1972). "Elimination by Aspects: A Theory of Choice." *Psychological Review* 79: 281–99.

Walker, S. (1983). "The Motivational Foundations of Political Belief Systems: A Re-analysis of the Operational Code Construct." *International Studies Quarterly* 27: 179–201.

Wallsten, T. (1980). "Processes and Models to Describe Choice and Inference." In T. Wallsten, ed., *Cognitive Processes in Choice and Behavior.* Hillsdale, NJ: Erlbaum.

White, R. K. (1965). "Soviet Perceptions of the U.S. and the U.S.S.R." In H. C. Kelman, ed., *International Behavior.* NY: Holt, Rinehart, and Winston.

———— (1969). "Three Not-so-Obvious Contributions of Psychology to Peace." Lewin Memorial Address, *Journal of Social Issues* 25 (4): 23–29.

———— (rev. ed., 1970). *Nobody Wanted War: Misperception in Vietnam and Other Wars.* NY: The Free Press.

———— (1977). "Misperception in the Arab-Israeli Conflict." *Journal of Social Issues* 33 (1): 190–221.

Wohlstetter, A. (1959). "The Delicate Balance of Terror." *Foreign Affairs* 37: 211–35.

Zimmerman, W., and Axelrod, R. P. (1981). "The Lessons of Vietnam and Soviet Foreign Policy." *World Politics* 34: 1–24.

Seduction by Analogy in Vietnam: The Malaya and Korea Analogies

Yuen Foong Khong

At the beginning of Herzog's *Aguirre the Wrath of God,* a troop of Spanish conquistadors is seen debating about whether to continue the dangerous search for El Dorado. The leader of the expedition urged the troop to turn back but lost out to his assistant Aguirre, who, through argument and intimidation, persuaded the entourage to continue. Aguirre invoked the Mexico analogy twice—Cortez founded Mexico against all odds and survived to reap the fortune—to bolster his argument. What he and his entourage did not know was that El Dorado, that "Lost City of Gold," was a fiction invented by the weak Peruvians to trick them. There was no El Dorado. Only death and destruction awaited them.

Analogies have not played quite so decisive a role in convincing America's leaders to fight communism in Greece, Korea, or Vietnam. But they did inform the thinking of successive Presidents, Secretaries, Undersecretaries and others who formulated America's post-war foreign policy. As Paul Kattenburg, former chairman of the Interdepartmental Working Group on Vietnam in the early 1960's, puts it, "Reasoning by historical analogy became a virtual ritual in the United States under Secretaries of State Acheson (1949–52), Dulles (1953–58) and Rusk (1961–68). . . ." (1980, p. 98). Dean Acheson, for example, helped convince Congressional leaders to support Truman's request for $400 million in aid to Greece and Turkey in 1947 by emphasizing the drastic consequences of abdicating this responsibility: like apples in a barrel infected by one rotten one, he prophesized, the corruption of Greece would infect Iran and everything east. Truman's decision to defend South Korea in 1950 was strongly influenced by the lessons of the past. He saw North Korea's actions as analogous to those of Hitler's, Mussolini's, and Japan's in the 1930s. These events taught that failure to check aggression early on only brought about a world war later (May, 1973, pp. 80–83). If the stakes were so high and the prevention of world war so worthy a goal, it should not come as a surprise that Truman approved MacArthur's march North to roll back totalitarianism (álá Germany and Japan) in the fall of 1950. Four years later, Eisenhower invoked the same analogies to persuade Churchill to join America to prevent the fall of Dien Bien Phu:

> If I may refer again to history; we failed to halt Hirohito, Mussolini, and Hitler by not acting in unit and in time. That marked the beginning of many years of stark tragedy and desperate peril. May it not be that our nations have learned something from that lesson? . . . (cited in Pentagon Papers, 1971, v. 1, p. 99)

Yuen Foong Khong, "Seduction by Analogy in Vietnam: The Malaya and Korea Analogies," in *Institutions and Leadership: Prospects for the Future,* Kenneth Thompson, ed.. Copyright © 1987 University Press of America. Reprinted by permission.

Churchill rejected the analogy; he feared that joint intervention by the United States and Britain "might well bring the world to the verge of a major war" (cited in Schlesinger, 1966, p.7). John F. Kennedy saw great similarities between Malaya and Vietnam—the New Villages of Malaya became Strategic Hamlets in Vietnam, the major difference being the New Villages worked whereas the Strategic Hamlets did not. In meetings with his advisers, Lyndon Johnson repeatedly voiced worries about Chinese intervention álá Korea if the United States pushed Hanoi too hard; United States intelligence then guessed and we now know that it was improbable that the Chinese would have intervened short of a United States invasion of North Vietnam (Pentagon Papers, v. 4, p. 63; Karnow, 1983, pp. 329, 452–53). More recent and even more dubious uses of analogies include seeing the Nicaraguan contras as the "moral equal of our Founding Fathers," as well as the claim that failure to aid the contras is tantamount to a Munich-like "self-defeating appeasement."

What makes historical analogies so attractive, despite their obvious limitations? I want to argue that historical analogies possess four properties which make them especially endearing to policy makers. One, they explain a new situation to us in terms we are familiar with. This is the "what is" or descriptive property of the analogy. Two, they provide a normative assessment of the situation. This is the "what ought to be" aspect. Three, analogies also prescribe a strategy to get from "what is" to "what ought to be." This is the prescriptive component of the analogy. Four, analogies also suggest what is likely to occur in the future. In other words, they also have predictive abilities. Not all historical analogies exhibit all four characteristics; when they do, however, they become especially potent, and perhaps in the last analysis, mischievous.

I hope to make the above points by examining two of the most important analogies used by policy makers in thinking about Vietnam: Malaya and Korea. Malaya and Korea have also been chosen because they succeed one another as the most important analogies: Malaya being especially relevant from 1961–63, Korea for the crucial years of 1964–66. The structural properties of these two analogies only partially illuminate why they were so popular despite being so imprecise; I am aware that there are cognitive, psychological and historical reasons which also account for their attractiveness. Cognitive explanations, for example, will stress the information processing value of analogies—they allow the policy maker to simplify and assess the vast amount of information out there. Historical-psychological explanations, on the other hand, will stress the degree to which direct experience with the events of the 1930s or 50s conditions policy makers to see future events along those lines. I deal with the cognitive and historical explanations in my research-in-progress; the focus in this paper shall be on the structural properties of analogies.

MALAYA AND THE NEW INSURGENCIES

John F. Kennedy and his New Frontiersmen came into office convinced that China and the Soviet Union formed a monolithic bloc bent on expanding the area under their control. Only containment by the United States—especially in Greece, Turkey and most of all, Korea—have kept the communists at bay. Despite the failure to "integrate" South Korea into the communist bloc, China and the Soviet Union remained inherently expansionist. Their new strategy, however, relied neither on missiles nor conventional troops. "Non-nuclear wars, and sub-limited or guerrilla warfare," Kennedy believed, "have since 1945 constituted the most active and constant threat to Free World security" (Public Papers, 1961, p. 229). National Security Action Memorandum 132, signed by Kennedy in February 1962, reiterated this theme. Kennedy directed Fowler Hamilton, the Administrator of the Agency for International Development, to "give utmost attention and emphasis to programs designed to counter Communist indirect aggression, which I regard as a grave threat during the 1960s" (Pentagon Papers, 1971, v. 2, p. 666). The key word here is indirect, for it was this new communist strategy which called for an appropriate U.S. response.

Kennedy's address to the graduating class of the U.S. Military Academy in the spring of 1962 is worth quoting at length because it spelled out his beliefs more concretely:

> Korea has not been the only battle ground since the end of the Second World War. Men have fought and died in Malaya, in Greece, in the Philippines, in Algeria and Cuba, and Cyprus and almost continuously on the Indo-China Peninsula. No nuclear weapons have been fired. No massive nuclear retaliation has been considered appropriate. This is another type of war, new in its intensity, ancient in its origin—war by guerrillas, subversives, insurgents, assassins, war by ambush instead of by combat; by infiltration, instead of aggression, seeking victory by eroding and exhausting the enemy instead of engaging him. It requires in those situations where we must counter it . . . a whole new kind of strategy, a wholly different kind of force, and therefore a new and wholly different kind of military training (Public Papers, 1962, p. 453).

Quite apart from the problem of telling the new graduates that their training might have been obsolete, this speech exemplified the thinking of the New Frontiersmen. The historian Ernest May found it surprising that documents of the Vietnam debate in 1961 contained few references to the Korean analogy whereas documents of 1964 contained many (May, 1973, p. 96). The diagnosis implied in the above speech explains this "surprise": Malaya, Greece, the Philippines, not Korea, were the models for thinking about Vietnam in the early 1960s. The Korea analogy illustrated the aggressive tendencies of communist regimes well but it had one shortcoming. In 1950, North Korea attempted a conventional invasion of the South; the U.S. U.N. response was also conventional. In 1961–62, the situation in Vietnam was different. Ngo Dinh Diem's South Vietnam was not threatened by an outright invasion of regular North Vietnamese units but by communist guerrillas who were mostly Southerners. Malaya and the other "indirect aggression" analogies were more useful in explaining the new kind of war brewing in South Vietnam and in thinking about the appropriate response to such threats.

The parallels between Malaya and Vietnam are striking. A British colony until 1957, Malaya was occupied by the Japanese during the Second World War. The Malayan Communist Party, reorganized as the Malayan People's Anti-Japanese Army (MPAJA) was the only domestic group to cooperate with the British to mount an armed resistance against the Japanese. MPAJA members, mostly ethnic Chinese, mounted guerrilla operations against the Japanese army. Although they succeeded in making life difficult for the Japanese, they were unable to dislodge them.

The MPAJA, however, attracted a substantial number of recruits and with their anti-imperialists credentials enhanced towards the end of the war, they emerged as a viable contender for power after Japan's surrender. Unlike Ho Chi Minh's Communist Party which took over Hanoi in the aftermath of Japan's defeat, the communists in Malaya did not or were unable to take over. While they did enjoy some support from Chinese peasants and workers, they did not really command the support of most Malays, the majority group in Malaya. When the British returned to Malaya, they quickly and ruthlessly surpressed the communist and the urban organizations (e.g. trade unions) controlled by them. Fighting for their political survival and also reasoning that they did not fight against an imperialist power only to bring back another, the Malayan Communist Party launched a major insurrection in 1948. The insurrection began with the ambush-murder of three European rubber estate managers; assassinations of government officials, terrorizing of uncooperative peasants—the kind of violence which Kennedy alluded to above—were common. The conflict dragged on for twelve years but in the end the guerrillas lost (Short, 1975).

Robert K. G. Thompson is the man most often credited for defeating the guerrillas in Malaya. Initially, the British saw the insurrection as a military problem. They launched large-scale military operations and bombed suspected jungle bases. Two years later, they were worse off than when they began (Hilsman, p. 429). Thompson concluded that so long as the guerrillas had the support—voluntary or involuntary—of the peasants, it was impossible to defeat them. He came up with the idea of "New Villages," secure hamlets where the peasants were isolated from the guerrillas. Civic action teams would visit to provide simple government services and the police would train the peasants in the use of firearms and win their confidence so that the communist sympathizers could be identified. The switch from a "search and destroy" strategy to a "clear and hold" strategy contributed greatly to the successful containment of communism in Malaya.

The Malaya analogy is helpful in making sense of the war in South Vietnam. Those familiar with the case of Malaya can identify similar forces at work: a legitimate government, supported by the majority, is threatened by local communist insurgents bent on seizing power at the behest of China and the Soviet Union. Related to, but distinct from, this description is a normative assessment of the parties in conflict in Malaya-South Vietnam: the cause of the guerrillas is unjust, as are the means—infiltration, assassination, terror—they employ. As such, the guerrillas ought to be defeated in South Vietnam as they were defeated in Malaya.

But the Malaya analogy does more than designate the end of defeating the communist guerrillas as good. It also prescribes a morally acceptable means of countering indirect aggression. By morally acceptable I mean a proportional response. In moral discourse, it is not enough to have a moral end, the means chosen to realize that end must also not incur disproportionate costs relative to the benefits conferred by achieving the end. In other words, a just end can be tarnished by unjust—i.e., disproportionate—means.

The proportional response suggested by the Malaya analogy is the construction of New Villages to physically isolate the guerrilla's potential supporters from the guerrillas. As conceived and executed by Robert K. G. Thompson in Malaya, this response to guerrilla insurgency passes the proportionality test because it leaves the rest of the population in peace and the costs of relocation are imposed on likely supporters. Weighed against the end of preserving a government supported by the majority, the costs do not appear disproportionate. The Kennedy administration encouraged Diem to follow this strategy and provided much of the material (Strategic Hamlet Kits) and money necessary to construct the Strategic Hamlets. It is of course not possible to say that Kennedy and his advisers (especially Roger Hilsman) believed in the Strategic Hamlet program because it was morally sound but it is possible to say that the Malaya analogy did not prescribe a strategy which might have exacted disproportionate costs. The idea of proportional response, with or without its moral dimension, would have appealed to the Kennedy administration. It fitted right in with the strategy of "flexible response," the attempt by Kennedy and his advisers to tailor the amount of force the U.S. should apply to the requirements of any given situation.

The Malaya analogy went beyond prescribing a proportional response, it also suggested that such a response could work. Again, in moral discourse, effectiveness is a critical consideration. Pursuing the most noble goal does not make one's actions morally sound if they are unlikely to achieve the goals. The Malaya analogy predicts a high probability of success: if the problem in Vietnam is like the problem in Malaya and if the New Villages worked in Malaya, then they or their equivalent—the Strategic Hamlets—are likely to work in South Vietnam as well. Thus Roger Hilsman, Assistant Secretary for Far Eastern Affairs, believed that the best way to "pull the teeth of the Viet Cong terrorist campaign" was not by killing them but by protecting the peasants in Strategic Hamlets. "[T]his technique," according to Hilsman, "was used successfully in Malaya against the Communist movement there" (*Department of State Bulletin*, July 8, 1963, p. 44). By suggesting that the prescribed means is able to attain the desired end (defeating the communist guerrillas), the predictive component of the Malaya analogy reinforces the normative weight of Kennedy's policy towards South Vietnam.

KOREA AND THE CHANGING CHARACTER OF THE VIETNAM WAR

By 1965 Malaya was no longer the dominant analogy. Its place was taken by the Korea analogy. The descriptive, normative, prescriptive and predictive elements found in the Malaya analogy are also present in the Korea analogy.

The Korea analogy was invoked primarily to show that the war in Vietnam was a war of aggression by the North against the South. This is in contrast to the Malaya analogy, which, while implying external support, saw the war primarily in terms of Southern guerrillas fighting against the army of South Vietnam (ARVN). The Korean analogy emphasized the more prominent role, if not the direct participation, of North Vietnamese soldiers. Thus Secretary of State Dean Rusk equated the infiltration of North Vietnamese material and men into South Vietnam with the overt aggression of North Korea against South Korea (*DOSB*, June 28, 1965, p. 1032). Lyndon Johnson did the same in his public speeches as well as his private conversations. Years after the he made the fateful decisions of 1965, Johnson admonished Doris Kearns, his biographer, for seeing the Vietnam conflict as a civil war:

> How . . . can you . . . say that South Vietnam is not a separate country with a traditionally recognized boundary? . . . Oh sure, there were some Koreans in both North and South Korea who believed their country was one country, yet was there any doubt that North Korean aggression took place? (Kearns, 1976, p. 328)

For William Bundy, perhaps the most consistent proponent of the Korea analogy, Korea forced the relearning of the lessons of the 1930s—"aggression of any sort must be met early and head-on or it will be met later and in tougher circumstances" (*DOSB*, February 8, 1965, p. 168). Adlai Stevenson's United Nation address titled "Aggression from the North" best captures the Johnson administration's position. Stevenson, reversing Kennedy's slighting of the Korea analogy, questioned the relevance of the Malaya, Greece and Philippine analogies and went on to emphasize the parallel between Vietnam and Korea: "North Vietnam's commitment to seize control of the South is no less total than was the commitment of the regime in North Korea in 1950" (*DOSB*, March 22 1965, p. 404).

What is interesting about the descriptive component of the Korea analogy is that it does provide a better description of "what is" in 1964–66. By the fall of 1964, the U.S. was finding "more and more 'bona fide' North Vietnamese soldiers among the infiltrees" (Pentagon Papers,

v. 3, p. 207). An estimated ten thousand North Vietnamese troops went South in 1964 (Pentagon Papers, v. 3, p. 207; Cf. Karnow, 1983, p. 334). As the perceived and actual nature of the war changed from guerrilla warfare to a mixture of guerrilla as well as conventional assaults, there was also a shift from reliance on the Malaya to the Korea analogy. Both the Malaya and Korea analogies explained the nature of the Vietnam conflict in terms we are familiar with; the Korea analogy, however, captured the changing nature of the conflict more successfully.

If one accepts the description of the North-South relationship—i.e., a case of the North trying to conquer the South—given by the Korea analogy, the actions of the North clearly become unjustifiable. Regardless of how it is put, the normative invocation is clear: aggression ought to be stopped, South Vietnam should not be allowed to fall, the United States ought to come to the help of the South.

The Korea analogy does more than merely invoke these normative ends, it also prescribes the means to realize them: through the introduction of U.S. troops. I am not claiming that when policy makers relied on the Korea analogy throughout 1965 in thinking about Vietnam, they were decisively influenced by the Korean strategy of using U.S. troops to halt aggression. However, if one believes that the problem in Vietnam is like the problem in Korea 1950, one is likely to consider quite seriously the ready-made answer supplied by the Korea analogy, namely, the introduction of U.S. troops. In this sense, the introduction of U.S. ground forces as the appropriate response is part and parcel of the Korea analogy.

Like the Malaya analogy, the Korea analogy also prescribed a proportional response. That is, if one accepts the description, provided by the Korea analogy, that the North was attacking the South. Introducing U.S. troops is proportional in the sense that it falls short of more drastic measures (e.g., invading North Vietnam or using nuclear weapons, see Pentagon Papers, v. 3, p. 623) and it is a step beyond merely advising and training the ARVN. If Kennedy's interest in not replying with overwhelming force had to do with the dictates of flexible response and the attempt to calibrate force to meet a given threat, Johnson's reluctance to consider a vastly disproportionate response had to do with the fear of bringing about a general war.

Evidence of Johnson's concern about proportionality can be found in a crucial meeting he had with his Joint Chiefs in July 1965, a few days before his decision to grant McNamara's request for 100 thousand combat troops. Johnson probed the JCS for North Vietnamese and Chinese reactions to the proposed U.S. action. The President was worried: "If we come in with hundreds of thousands of men and billions of dollars, won't this cause China and Russia to come in?" General Johnson, Army Chief of Staff, replied that they would not, to which Johnson retorted: "MacArthur didn't think they would come in either" (cited in Berman, 1982, pp. 117–18). It is well known that Johnson was always careful about not going beyond like MacArthur did. Consequently the use of nuclear weapons, the invasion of North Vietnam, destruction of the latter's dyke system and bombing the North Vietnamese civilians were never even proposed (Gelb and Betts, 1979, pp. 264–65).

Beyond proportionality is the issue of likelihood of success. Here again, the Korea analogy, like the Malaya, and virtually all analogies used in thinking about Vietnam, predicts a high probability of success. If the problem in Korea and Vietnam are essentially similar, it stands to reason that the strategy which proved ultimately successful in Korea, namely U.S. intervention, will also be successful in Vietnam. And probability of success, we have argued earlier, adds moral weight to the policy. By providing an optimistic prediction of the likely outcome of introducing U.S. troops, the Korea analogy makes this policy prescription all the more attractive.

MALAYA, KOREA AND VIETNAM: THE IGNORED DIFFERENCES

Having explored the features of the Malaya and Korea analogies which made them attractive to policy makers, it is necessary to point out that there were those who were suspicious of these analogies, in part and in whole. General L.L. Lemnitzer, Chairman of the Joint Chiefs of Staff in the first two years of Kennedy's administration, was highly skeptical of the Malaya analogy. In a memorandum to General Maxwell Taylor, Kennedy's handpicked personal adviser and soon-to-be successor to Lemnitzer, the latter complained that "The success of the counter-terrorist police organization in Malaya has had considerable impact" on the Kennedy administration's approach to Vietnam. Given the "considerable impact" of the Malaya analogy, General Lemnitzer felt obliged to point out its defects. He pointed to five "major differences between the situations in Malaya and South Vietnam." His analysis is prescient and important enough to be cited in full:

1. Malayan borders were far more controllable in that Thailand cooperated in refusing the Communists an operational safe haven.
2. The racial characteristics of the Chinese insurgents in Malaya made identification and segregation a relatively simple matter as compared to the situation in Vietnam where the Viet Cong cannot be distinguished from the loyal citizen.
3. The scarcity of food in Malaya versus the relative plenty in South Vietnam made the denial of food to the Communist guerrillas a far more important and readily usable weapon in Malaya.
4. Most importantly, in Malaya the British were in actual command, with all of the obvious advantages this entails, and used highly trained Commonwealth troops.
5. Finally, it took the British nearly 12 years to defeat an insurgency which was less strong than the one in South Vietnam. (Pentagon Papers, v. 2, p. 650).

Lemnitzer's critique of the Malaya analogy is interesting because it appreciated the on-the-ground differences between Malaya and South Vietnam. He took issue with the description, prescription and prediction provided by the Malaya analogy. The latter implied that sanctuaries for the guerrillas was not a major issue, Lemnitzer believed that such a description did not conform to the situation in South Vietnam, where the guerrillas could have "safe haven[s]" in Laos and Cambodia. Lemnitzer also found the prescription—emphasis on counter-terrorist police and hence political measures instead of emphasis on military measures—suggested the Malaya analogy wanting. He preferred the Philippine experience, where "the military framework used was highly successful" (Pentagon Papers, v. 2, p. 650). Finally, Lemnitzer was less sanguine about the prediction of eventual success than Kennedy's civilian advisers. The implication of Lemnitzer's analysis was that the Vietnamese communists would be hard to beat.

History proved Lemnitzer right. Even with American troops and command, the National Liberation Front could not be subdued. Uncontrollable borders, namely sanctuaries and infiltration routes in Laos and Cambodia, also partially explain the difficulty. So does the difficulty of distinguishing loyal from disloyal peasants in Vietnam. There was also the character of the government being helped, a crucial difference omitted in Lemnitzer's analysis. Malaya had a relatively stable and popular government both as a British colony and as a newly independent country; it was apparent even by 1961 that the South Vietnamese government was neither popular nor stable. Within the Diem regime, there was constant infighting and jockeying for power, so much so that the only principals Diem could trust were his brothers and their wives; without, Diem did not encourage the setting up of institutions which could have channeled the political participation of the religious sects, nationalist political parties, and students.

The other interesting point about Lemnitzer's critique is that it was ignored. The Kennedy administration continued to believe in the relevance of the Malaya analogy. Thus in April 1963, U. Alexis Johnson, Deputy Under Secretary of State suggested that the post war insurgencies in Burma, Indonesia, Malaya, Indochina, and the Philippines were coordinated by China but singled out Malaya as the struggle which "provided valuable lessons which are now being applied in Viet-Nam" (*DOSB*, April 29, 1963, p. 636). Similarly, Roger Hilsman, Kennedy's major adviser on communist insurgencies, claimed that the best way to defeat the Viet Cong was not by killing them but by protecting them in strategic hamlets, a "technique used successfully in Malaya against the Communist movement there." (*DOSB*, July 8, 1963, p. 44).

The Strategic Hamlet program failed. Formally initiated as "Operation SUNRISE" in Bin Duong Province in early 1962, it died with the Ngos in late 1963. The failure of the strategic hamlet does not necessarily mean that the error lay in misapplying the lessons of Malaya to Vietnam but it does make the analogy suspect. It is, however, always necessary to point out the differences which account for the dissimilar outcomes. General Lemnitzer's memorandum— written in late 1961—is a first step in this direction. To be sure Lemnitzer was not addressing himself to the Strategic Hamlet program, but his observations, if correct, could help explain why a similar program was successful in Malaya but not in Vietnam.

The Korea analogy, on the other hand, found its antagonist in George Ball, Under Secretary of State. In an October 1964 memorandum to Dean Rusk, Robert McNamara, and McGeorge Bundy, Ball sought to question "the assumptions of our Viet-Nam policy," before deciding in "the next few weeks" between a number of options, including bombing North Vietnam and introducing substantial U.S. ground forces in South Vietnam (Ball, *Atlantic Monthly*, July 1972, p. 36). Ball wrote:

> . . . I want to emphasize one key point at the outset: The problem of South Viet-Nam is *sui generis*. South Vietnam is not Korea, and in making fundamental decisions it would be a mistake for us to rely too heavily on the Korean analogy (Ball, *Atlantic Monthly*, 1972, p. 37).

Ball, like Lemnitzer, found five differences. Most of them, in this memorandum at least, dealt with the descriptive deficiencies of the Korean analogy: the U.S. had a clear United Nations mandate in Korea but not in South Vietnam; fifty-three other countries provided troops to fight in Korea while the U.S. was "going it alone" in Vietnam. More importantly, Syngman Rhee's government was stable and enjoyed wide support whereas South Vietnam was characterized by "governmental chaos." Perhaps the most important difference Ball identified was over the nature of the war: the Korean War was a classical case of invasion whereas in South Vietnam "there has been no invasion—only slow infiltration. . . . The Viet Cong insurgency does have substantial indigenous support" (Ball, 1972, p. 37). Whether Ball intended it or not, and I think he intended it, spelling out these differences raises questions about the normative assessment as well as the predictions provided by the Korean analogy. If the insurgency enjoyed substantial support and if the South Vietnamese government was incompetent, should and could the South Vietnamese regime be preserved?

Ball received better treatment from his superiors than Lemnitzer did from his. After reading the memorandum, Rusk, McNamara, and Bundy debated the arguments with Ball on two successive Saturday afternoons (Atlantic Monthly, July 1972, p. 33). Ball failed to convince his superiors. The lessons of Korea continued to haunt the principal policy makers, almost to a man. Johnson could not forget "the withdrawal of our forces from South Korea and then our immediate reaction to the Communist aggression of 1950" and he worried about "repeating the same sharp reversal" in Vietnam (Johnson, 1971, p. 152). For Dean Rusk, the war in Vietnam, like Korea, was not a civil war but a case of aggression of one state against another across national boundaries. William Bundy argued that it took a war to beat back aggression in Korea and that it might take another to beat back the North Vietnamese and Chinese in Southeast Asia (*DOSB*, June 21, 1965).

If in retrospect some of Lyman Lemnitzer's and George Ball's objections to the Malaya and Korea analogy seem prescient and sound, one needs to remember that their advice was heard but not taken. This was so partly because the descriptive, normative, prescriptive and predictive components of the respective analogies combined to form an internally consistent and remarkably wholesome way to look at Vietnam. Together with the cognitive and historical-psychological reasons alluded to earlier but not discussed in this paper, these structural properties of historical analogies help explain why policy makers hold on to their analogies despite warnings about their limitations.

REFERENCES

Ball, George. "Top Secret: The Prophecy the President Rejected." *Atlantic Monthly,* July 1972.

Berman, Larry. *Planning A Tragedy.* New York: W. W. Norton, 1982.

Gelb, Leslie, and Betts, Richard. *The Irony of Vietnam: The System Worked.* Washington D.C.: Brookings, 1979.

Hilsman, Roger. *To Move A Nation.* New York: Doubleday, 1967.

Karnow, Stanley. *Vietnam: A History.* New York: Viking, 1983.

Kattenburg, Paul. *The Vietnam Trauma.* New Jersey: Transaction, 1980.

Kearns, Doris. *Lyndon Johnson and the American Dream.* New York: Harper and Row, 1976.

May, Ernest. *Lessons of the Past: The Use and Misuse of History in American Foreign Policy.* New York: Oxford, 1973.

The Pentagon Papers: The Defense Department History of United States Decision Making on Vietnam. Senator Gravel edition. v. 1–4. Boston: Beacon Press, 1971.

Public Papers of the Presidents: John F. Kennedy.

Public Papers of the Presidents: Lyndon B. Johnson.

Schlesinger, Arthur. *The Bitter Heritage: Vietnam and American Democracy 1941–1966.* Boston: Houghton Mifflin, 1966.

Short, Anthony. *The Communist Insurrection in Malaya 1948–1960.* London: Frederick Muller, 1975.

United States Department of State. *Department of State Bulletin.* 1961–1966.

◈

The Personalities of Bush and Gorbachev Measured at a Distance: Procedures, Portraits, and Policy

David G. Winter,[1] Margaret G. Hermann,[2]
Walter Weintraub,[3] and Stephen G. Walker[4]

INTRODUCTION

In recent months, internal developments within the Soviet Union, and between the Soviet Union and the United States, have raised the possibility of a new era in relations between the superpowers. In 1981, for example, who would have predicted that Ronald Reagan would cap his presidency, against the background of the Statue of Liberty, by exchanging smiles, handshakes, and waves with the leader of the Soviet Union? Or that newspaper headlines would speak of genuinely contested elections within the USSR (even mentioning the familiar democratic electoral paraphernalia of "exit polls"?) With the inauguration of George Bush, each country now has a leader of whom much is expected, yet about whom surprisingly little is known. What is George Bush really like? And who is the "real" Mikhail Gorbachev? How should we interpret their actions? What can we expect when they come together to negotiate?

ON STUDYING BUSH AND GORBACHEV

The Leader as "Projective Screen"

So far, each leader's actions, and even the "manifest" or policy content of their words, are an ambiguous stimulus (not unlike a Rorschach inkblot) in which different observers can read their own interpretations. With his hand initially extended to Congress in cooperation (after a negative campaign filled with innuendo), President Bush has confused liberal opponents and troubled his conservative supporters (Dionne, 1989). Yet in the first 18 months, Bush's administration seemed off to a slow start in terms of defining policy and filling positions, and echos of innuendo still emanated from the Republican National Committee. Events seem to confirm the words of *Time* magazine back during the campaign: "Many who know him find it difficult to imagine what he would do [as president]. . . . Could Bush show the decisiveness, the moral authority and necessary sense of command to guide the country . . . ?"

In the case of Gorbachev, opinion and analysis have been even more sharply divided. Many students of Soviet politics suggest that Gorbachev has chosen peace over socialism—"cooperation

David G. Winter et al., "The Personalities of Bush and Gorbachev Measured at a Distance: Procedures, Portraits, and Policy," *Political Psychology*, Vol. 12, No. 2 (1991). Reprinted by permission of Blackwell Publishing.

with the West over the search for unilateral advantage" (Holloway, 1989, pp. 67, 70); "not the struggle between classes but the common plight of man" (Legvold, 1989, p. 85). In sharp contrast, however, are the words of columnist William Safire (1989): "They're [Soviet leaders] all headed the same way—toward fixing the Soviet economy until it becomes strong enough to feed itself and afford the arms to dominate its neighbors." Richard Nixon's analysis runs along similar lines. Beneath the "fashionably tailored suits, the polished manners and the smooth touch in personal encounters," he suggests, the "new Gorbachev" is mainly motivated toward such familiar Soviet goals: "to erode the strength of the [NATO] alliance" and "to lull the West into a false sense of security," thus to create "a stronger Soviet Union and an expanding Soviet empire" (Nixon, 1989, pp. 207, 211, 218). Vice-President Quayle echoes Nixon's doubts: "For although the Soviet leadership professes to adhere to 'new thinking,' it is still quite capable of 'old thinking,' as well" (1989, p. 6). One columnist reached even argued bluntly that "Gorbachev is on [a] power trip" (Charen, 1990). Finally, as we write, a respected authority on Soviet matters concluded that Gorbachev "is in truth a puzzling and enigmatic figure, and is becoming more so as his troubles deepen" (Shulman, 1990, p. 5).

Thus although Bush's career in government service spans several decades, and although Gorbachev has been in office for 6 years, we do not have consensus in the West about the "real" personalities of the two men—their motives, beliefs, operational codes, self-concept, and styles. (They are not unique in this respect. Previous behavior and the manifest content of campaign rhetoric are often of little use in forecasting American presidential behavior, as students of the surprising administrations of Chester Arthur, Harry Truman, and Lyndon Johnson can attest.)

The Importance of Leaders' Personalities

Are the answers to these questions important? Obviously personality is not the only predictor of political behavior, and sometimes it is not even a major predictor. (On December 8, 1941, for example, Franklin D. Roosevelt's personality was largely irrelevant to whether the United States declared war on Japan.) Whatever Bush's and Gorbachev's personalities, their political behavior will be strongly shaped and constrained by situational factors such as budget deficits and economic-organization difficulties, respectively. Still, conditions in both countries do embody many of Greenstein's (1969, chap. 2) classic criteria for identifying occasions when personalities of single actors can have an important influence on events: (1) First, Gorbachev and Bush occupy strategic locations in their respective political systems; (2) The present situation contains many new or ambiguous elements and is open to restructuring; (3) Internally and internationally, opposed forces are delicately balanced; (4) The important issues and problems demand active effort rather than routine role performance.

Thus in the 1990s we have, as it were, an equation in two unknowns. Perhaps psychological interpretations of the personalities of both leaders, drawing on systematic theory and research, could guide our understanding of events and even suggest answers to questions of policy. Yet we lack direct access to either leader, and so analysis and interpretation must be carried out at a distance. We intend this paper as a first step. Though drawn from diverse disciplines, each of the present authors is experienced in studying personality at a distance. We have applied our individual techniques to the study of Bush and Gorbachev, using both a common data set and individually selected additional materials. Drawing on the rather striking convergence of our separate results, we then construct personality profiles for both leaders. We conclude with some predictions and suggest a few broad policy implications.

We are acutely aware of the perils of prediction. What we write, during a time of nationalist fer-ment in the Baltic republics and negotiations for German unification, will appear in print only after many months. We run the risk of being dramatically wrong. [Indeed, the final draft of this paper was finished in June 1990, when the Iraqi invasion of Kuwait was only a gleam in Saddam Hussein's eye; and revisions were completed even as one columnist pronounced that "the Gorbachev era ends"; see Rosenthal (1990).] Yet if personality assessment at a distance is worth doing, it is worth doing boldly—suggesting answers that go beyond the obvious, to questions that are important.

ASSESSING PERSONALITY AT A DISTANCE

How can psychologists assess the motives of people whom they have never met and cannot study directly? In recent years, personality researchers have developed a variety of objective methods of measuring motives and other personality characteristics "at a distance," through systematic content analysis of speeches, interviews, and other spontaneous verbal material (Hermann, 1977, 1980a, 1980b, 1987; Walker, 1983; Weintraub, 1981, 1989; Winter, 1991; Winter and Stewart, 1977). These techniques have often been used in aggregate studies of political leaders—for example, in predicting foreign policy orientation or propensity for violence (Hermann, 1980a,b; Winter, 1980). Sometimes, though, at-a-distance techniques have been used to construct systematic portraits of particular leaders: Hermann assessed the motives and other personal characteristics of Ronald Reagan (1983) and Syrian leader Hafez Al-Assad (1988); Walker (1986) analyzed Woodrow Wilson's operational code; Weintraub (1989) studied the verbal behavior of seven recent American presidents; and Winter and Carlson (1988) used the motive scores of Richard Nixon's first inaugural address to resolve several paradoxes of his political career, while seeking validation of these scores from a system-atic review of Nixon's public and private life.

When prepared speeches and even "spontaneous" interview responses are scored for any psychological characteristic, skeptical readers often ask whether the resulting scores reflect the motives or other characteristics of the leader or of the speechwriters, or whether the scores are affected by efforts at positive self-presentation (even disinformation). Of course, speechwriters are generally selected for their ability to express what the leader wants to say, especially in the case of important speeches. In most cases, American presidents are involved in the preparation of important speeches [see Safire (1975, pp. 24, 25, 529, 530) and Price (1980, pp. 42–50) regarding Richard Nixon; and Noonan (1990, pp. 68–92, 186–200) regard-ing Reagan].

Using more spontaneous interview material may reduce (though it does not fully elimi-nate) this problem. Yet in a larger sense, it may not matter whether the source was the leader or a speechwriter, or whether the speeches reflect "real personality" or self-presentation. Whatever their status, they exist as, are taken as, and have effects as the leader's words.

The major assumption of the present at-a-distance study, then, is that a leader's words and the scores based on them are a reasonable guide to the speaker's personality. More specifically, we assume that the personality variables we have measured, using the procedures we have followed, are sufficiently robust to override any effects of authorship, impression manage-ment, disinformation, and ego defensiveness. We further assume that the effects of the particular topics discussed and the situation in which the leader speaks are adequately con-trolled by the comparison groups that we have used for interpreting the raw scores we obtained (see below). Obviously, these assumptions are debatable; but for us their usefulness rests on the pragmatic criterion of whether the scores are useful in predicting or interpreting interesting and significant political behavior and outcomes.

In the present paper, we apply our various techniques to a comparative study of Bush and Gorbachev. We then suggest some likely trends, opportunities, issues, problems, and pitfalls confronting each leader, both separately and in joint interaction.

PERSONALITY VARIABLES ASSESSED

Taken together, our methods cover quite a range of personality variables, including the major personality domains of motivation, cognition, styles, and traits and defenses, drawn from many different personality theories. In this section, we introduce each variable, describing its theoretical antecedents and how it is measured in verbal behavior, indicating who was responsible for its measurement in the present study, and noting the major references in the personality and political psychology literature. Table 7.1 summarizes this information.

Motives

Motivation involves goals and goal-directed actions. Drawing on the classic theoretical insights of Freud (1915–1917/1961–1963), Jung (1910), and Murray (1938), personality psychologists have in recent decades developed methods of measuring several important human motives through content analysis of fantasy productions of other imaginative verbal material (see Atkinson, 1958). The *achievement motive* involves a concern for excellence and unique accomplishment, and is associated with restless activity, moderate risk-taking, using feedback or knowledge of results, and entrepreneurial activity (see McClelland, 1961). The *affiliation motive* involves a concern for close relations with others. Sometimes it predicts interpersonal warmth and self-disclosure, but under conditions of threat or stress, it can produce a "prickly," defensive orientation to others (see Boyatzis, 1973; McAdams, 1982). The *power motive*, a concern for impact and prestige, leads both to formal social power and also to profligate, impulsive actions such as aggression, drinking, and taking extreme risks (see Winter, 1973; Winter and Stewart, 1978). These three motives are selected from Murray's (1938) comprehensive taxonomy as involving some of the most common and important human goals and concerns. In the present study, power and affiliation motives were scored in two different ways: (a) by Hermann's computer-based adaptation of the original scoring systems, which focuses particularly on verb phrases, and (b) by Winter's (1991) integrated "running text" scoring system, which was also used to score achievement motivation.

Beliefs and Styles

These variables, scored by Hermann, reflect some of the most widely studied beliefs and dimensions of cognitive and interpersonal style, as emphasized in the personality theories of Kelly (1955), Rotter (1990), Rogers (1959) and others. *Nationalism* (or ethnocentrism), a belief in the superiority of one's own group or nation and the inferiority of others, and *distrust*, or suspicion of other people and institutions, are two key belief and stylistic components of authoritarianism, arguably the single most studied personality variable (see Adorno et al., 1950; Brown, 1965, chap. 10; Meloen et al., 1988; and Tucker, 1965).

Table 7.1   MAJOR PERSONALITY VARIABLES ASSESSED AT A DISTANCE
FOR BUSH AND GORBACHEV

Variable	Scoring description and major references
Motives (Hermann, 1987; Winter, 1991)	
Achievement	Concern with excellence, success in competition, or unique accomplishment.
Affiliation	Concern with warm, friendly relationships; friendly, convivial activity; nurturant help.
Power	Concern with impact or effect on others, prestige, or reputation.
Beliefs and styles (Hermann, 1980, 1987)	
Beliefs	
Nationalism	Identification with or favorable reference to own nation; nonidentification with or unfavorable reference to other nations.
Events controllable	Accepts responsibility for planning or initiating action.
Self-confidence	Self seen as instigator of activity, authority figure, or recipient of positive feedback.
Cognitive and interpersonal styles	
Conceptual complexity	Ratio of high complexity words to low complexity words.
Distrust	Doubts, misgivings, or expectation of harm from groups not identified with.
Task emphasis	Ratio of task words to interpersonal words.
Operational code (George, 1969; Walker, 1983, 1990)	
Self-attributions	
Friendly/hostile	Political life seen as harmonious vs. conflicted; relationship with opponents seen as friendly vs. hostile.
Optimistic/pessimistic	Optimism vs. pessimism about realizing values and aspirations.
High/low control	History seen as shaped by people vs. chance.
Comprehensive/limited goals	Articulates goals that are comprehensive and long-range vs. piecemeal and limited.
Self-scripts	
Methods of reaching goals	Verbal (promises, threats) versus action (reward, sanctions); politics (rewards, promises) vs. conflict (sanctions, threats); positive (appeals for support, gives support) vs. negative (resists, opposes).
Verbal style (reflecting traits and defenses) (Weintraub 1981, chap. 2; 1989, chap. 1)	
I/we ratio	Ratio of "I" pronouns to "we" pronouns.
Expression of feeling	Self-described as experiencing some feeling.
Evaluators	Judgments of good/bad, useful/useless, right/wrong, correct/incorrect, proper/improper, pleasant/unpleasant, and exclamations of opinion.
Direct references to audience	Direct references to the audience, the situation, or the physical surroundings.
Adverbial intensifiers	Adverbs that increase the force of a statement.
Rhetorical questions	Questions meant to arouse and engage the audience.
Retractors	Partial or complete retraction of an immediately preceeding statement.
Negatives	All negating words such as "not,""no,""never,""nobody," "nothing,"etc.
Explainers	Reasons or justifications for actions; causal connections.
Qualifiers	Expressions of uncertainty, modifiers that weaken assertions, and phrases contributing vagueness or looseness.
Creative expressions	Novel words or combinations of words; metaphors.

Belief in the Controllability of Events

This belief captures the ancient distinction between will and fate as determinants of outcomes, as in the famous words of Cassius to Brutus, in Shakespeare's Julius Caesar (I, ii, 140–141):

> The fault, dear Brutus, is not in our stars
> But in ourselves, that we are underlings.

In modern personality research, this belief has been variously conceptualized as internal versus external locus of control (Strickland, 1977) and more recently as facilitating versus debilitating attributional style (Weiner, 1980; Zullow et al., 1989). Among leaders, the belief that events can be controlled is associated with effective action and adaptation.

Self-Confidence

The sense that one is both effective and loved reflects self-esteem and related aspects of the self-concept. Its theoretical roots go back to the psychoanalytic concept of narcissism. Ziller et al. (1977) have demonstrated its importance in leader behavior. Self-confident leaders tend to be active rather than reactive; however, leaders who are less self-confident may be better listeners and more responsive to others.

Conceptual Complexity

Conceptual complexity, or the ability to differentiate aspects or dimensions of the environment, derives from Kelly's theory of personality (1955; see also Bieri. 1961; and Ziller et al., 1977). As a cognitive style, it is negatively related to the "intolerance of ambiguity" (black-and-white thinking) component of authoritarianism. Among leaders, high nationalism and distrust and low conceptual complexity are associated with an aggressive, autocratic, and often simplistic political style.

Task Versus Social-Emotional Emphasis

This variable reflects two different kinds of leadership or interpersonal style, derived from early social psychological studies of experimental small groups [Bales (1958), see Byars (1973) for an extension of this distinction to specifically political material].[5] Task-focused leaders have an "agenda," whether relating to economic affairs or national security. Social-emotional leaders, lower in task emphasis, are more attuned to the subtle nuances, interpersonal structures, and shifting alignments of the political process.

Overall Personality Orientations

Recently Hermann (1987) has elaborated a series of six broad "orientations," each consisting of different combinations of the motivational and cognitive variables that she had previously studied as separate variables. For example, the "expansionist" orientation involves controlling more territory, resources, and people. It involves a combination of power motivation, nationalism and distrust, belief that events can be controlled, self-confidence, and a strong task emphasis. In contrast, the "developmental" orientation (composed of affiliation motivation, nationalism, cognitive complexity, self-confidence, and an interpersonal emphasis) involves improvement (with the help of other countries) rather than expansion. Table 7.2 lists these orientations along with their component variables.

Table 7.2   PERSONALITY ORIENTATIONS AND THEIR COMPONENT VARIABLES[a]

Orientation	Definition	Component variables
Expansionist	Interest in gaining control over more territory, resources, or people	Power motivation Nationalism Belief in own ability to control events Self-confidence Distrust Task emphasis
Active independent	Interest in participating in the international community, but on one's own terms and without engendering a dependent relationship with another country	Affiliation motivation Nationalism Belief in own ability to control events Cognitive complexity Self-confidence Task emphasis
Influential	Interest in having an impact on other nations' foreign policy behavior, in playing a leadership role in regional or international affairs	Power Motivation Belief in own ability to control events Cognitive complexity Self-confidence Interpersonal emphasis
Mediator/Integrator	Concern with reconciling differences between other nations, with resolving problems in the international arena	Affiliation motivation Belief in own ability to control events Cognitive complexity Interpersonal emphasis
Opportunist	Interest in taking advantage of present circumstances, in dealing effectively with the demands and opportunities of the moment, in being expedient	Cognitive complexity Interpersonal emphasis
Developmental	Commitment to continued improvement of one's own nation with the best help available from other countries or international organizations	Affiliation motivation Nationalism Cognitive complexity Self-confidence Interpersonal emphasis

[a]Source: Adapted from Hermann (1987, pp. 170–173)

Operational Codes and "Self-Scripts"

In contrast to the broad, abstract cognitive elements discussed above, which are drawn from psychological theories of personality, the concept of operational code was developed by political scientists to describe structures of specifically political beliefs. Originated by Leites (1951), the operational code construct has been developed by George (1969), Holsti (1970), and later Walker (1983, 1990). As reformulated by George, a political leader's operational code beliefs can be described as the "answers" (phrased as a choice from among two or more alternatives) to a series of philosophical and instrumental questions such as the following: What is the essential nature of political life (friendly or hostile)? What are the prospects for realizing one's fundamental political aspirations? How much control can one have over history? How can political goals be pursued effectively? What is the best timing? What is the usefulness of different means?

In the present study, Walker conceptualized the answers to George's philosophical questions as a series of "self-attributions" describing the individual's relationship to the political universe (friendly versus hostile, optimistic versus pessimistic, high versus low control, and comprehensive versus limited goals), and conceptualized the answers to the instrumental questions as a series of "selfscripts" (promises, rewards, threats, sanctions, appeals, giving support, opposition and resistance). Specific self-attributions and self-scripts coded in the present study are shown in Table 7.1. Taken together, these two kinds of codes act as cognitive heuristics, mediating or filtering the day-to-day flow of information about the situation and other political actors. Because the operational code construct is currently undergoing development and refinement (see Walker, 1990), the specific variables actually coded for Bush and Gorbachev are slightly different and the Gorbachev coding is more elaborate, as will be seen in Table 7.7. For example, the Bush coding emphasized his view of the political universe, while the later Gorbachev coding focused more on his view of self, or how the self was located in relation to that political universe.

Traits and Defenses

Traits are the everyday language of personality description: the enduring ways in which people interact with others and appear to them, as described in the writings of Jung (1921/1971), Eysenck (see Eysenck and Eysenck, 1985), and Allport (1961), among others. On the basis of numerous clinical experimental studies and at-a-distance research, Weintraub (1981, 1986, 1989) has measured several features of verbal style that are indicators of different traits and their characteristic defensive styles (as originally developed in the theoretical work of Anna Freud, 1946). Table 7.3 shows how the different verbal style measures, described in Table 7.1, are combined to assess these traits and defenses (see Weintraub, 1989, pp. 95–102).

Recent personality research (see Eysenck and Eysenck, 1985; Norman, 1963) suggests that many of these traits can be further grouped into two major factors: introversion-extraversion and stability-neuroticism.

A Common Theoretical Conception of Personality

While we each have our own conceptions of personality, the present study reflects a shared theoretical view of personality that is eclectic and diverse, with special emphases on (a) motives or goals, (b) adaptive or defensive transformations of these goals, and (c) cognitive characteristics or "algorithms" that filter or process information from the environment.

SELECTING MATERIAL TO BE SCORED

All four methods of assessing personality at a distance are based on content analysis of verbal material, typically transcripts of speeches and press conference responses. In an effort to provide common databases for the present study, the second author assembled two collections of documents: (a) For Bush, there were transcripts of his "stump speech," several television interviews, and the New Hampshire Republican candidates' debate, all from the 1988 presidential election campaign. Comparison materials were available from the two other major candidates, Michael Dukakis and Jesse Jackson. (b) For Gorbachev, there were transcripts of

Table 7.3 COMPONENT VERBAL STYLE FEATURES OF TRAITS AND DEFENSE

Trait or Defense	Component Features of Verbal Behavior
Interpersonal style	
Engaging (vs. aloof)	Direct references
	Rhetorical questions
Passivity	Frequency of "me"
Oppositional	Negatives
Emotional style	
Emotional expressiveness	High I/we ratio
	Low nonpersonal references
	Expressions of feeling
	Evaluators
	Adverbial intensifiers
	Direct references
	Rhetorical questions
Anxiety	Negatives
	Explainers
	Qualifiers
Depression	High I/we ratio
	Low nonpersonal references
	Direct references
Anger	Negatives
	Frequency of "I" and "we"
Sensitivity to criticism	Adverbial intensifiers
	Negatives
	Evaluators
Decision-making style	
Decisiveness	High ratio of (I + we)/me
Dogmatic	Low qualifiers, low retractors
Impulsive	Low or moderate qualifiers, high retractors
Paranoid	High qualifiers, low retractors
Obsessive	High qualifiers, high retractors

20 speeches and 27 interviews during the period December 10, 1984 through December 7, 1988. These two collections are referred to as the "standard samples."

The methods employed by each author, however, vary in the kinds and amounts of verbal material they customarily use, in the ways this material is analyzed, and in the nature and amount of material from other persons needed for making comparisons. Motive imagery scores, for example, are usually standardized within a sample of similar material from as many as 30 other people. In the present study, therefore, some authors selected from the standard samples and added extra material in ways that reflected their customary procedures. Table 7.4 summarizes the materials used to score each category of personality variables.

In measuring Bush's motives, Winter used two sources: (a) scores from the October 12, 1987, speech announcing his candidacy for president, interpreted in comparison to similar speeches by 13 other major 1988 candidates (see Winter, 1988); and (b) his January 20, 1989 Inaugural Address, interpreted in comparison to all previous first inaugural addresses from George Washington through Ronald Reagan (see Winter, 1987, Table 7.1; 1990). Gorbachev's

Table 7.4 MATERIALS USED TO SCORE AND COMPARE PERSONALITY VARIABLES

	Material Used For	
Variable	Scoring	Comparison
Bush Motives	(a) Standard campaign sample (MGH)	(a) 1988 Standard campaign sample; also sample of 53 world leaders
	(b) Candidacy announcement speech (DGW)	(b) Other 1988 announcement speeches
	(c) Inaugural address (DGW)	(c) Other inaugurals
Beliefs and styles	Standard campaign sample	Standard campaign sample; also sample of 53 world leaders
Operational code	Foreign policy statements from standard campaign sample	Foreign policy statements from standard campaign sample
Traits and defenses	Selections from standard campaign sample	Selections from standard campaign sample; also selections from recent U.S. presidents
Gorbachev Motives	(a) Standard sample (MGH)	(a) Sample of 53 world leaders
	(b) Selected interviews from standard sample (DGW)	(b) Interviews from 22 world leaders
	(c) First "report" to CPSU Congress (DGW)	(c) Similar reports by Lenin through Brezhnev
Beliefs and styles	Standard sample	Sample of 53 world leaders
Operational code	Selected paragraphs from standard sample	No explicit comparison
Traits and defenses	Selections from standard sample	Selections from recent U.S. presidents; also (implicitly) selections from other Slavic leaders

motive scores were also based on two sources: (a) From the standard sample, four interviews from the period April–October 1985 (his first year in office), and two interviews from December 1987–June 1988, by which time the main lines of his policy were established, were scored. These were interpreted in comparison to scores from similar interviews with 22 world leaders (see Winter, 1990). (b) To compare Gorbachev with previous Soviet leaders, his first speech ("report") to a Congress of the Communist Party of the Soviet Union, after assuming the position of General Secretary, was scored along with equivalent speeches by Lenin, Stalin, Khrushchev, and Brezhnev.[6]

Hermann measured beliefs, cognitive, and interpersonal styles, and affiliation and power motivation from the full standard samples. Bush's raw scores were interpreted in comparison with those of Dukakis and Jackson; Gorbachev's, in comparison with those of a sample of 53 world leaders. [See Hermann (1980b) for a detailed description of this sample.]

Walker measured Bush's operational code by examining campaign statements on foreign policy topics such as the Middle East, South Africa, U.S.-Soviet relations and arms control, and communist insurgency in the Western Hemisphere; as compared to similar statements by Dukakis and Jackson (providing at least an ordinal comparison). For Gorbachev, he examined a random subset of 107 paragraphs (stratified by occasion and topic) from the standard sample. Gorbachev's scores were directly interpreted without comparisons to others because at the time this latter coding was done each element of self-attribution or self-script had been elaborated into a pair of binary alternatives (see Walker, 1990).

Weintraub scored traits and defenses from a 6000-word subset of the standard sample for Bush, and from six interviews of the standard sample for Gorbachev. In both cases, scores were interpreted by comparison with those of seven postwar U.S. presidents (see Weintraub, 1989); Bush was also compared with Dukakis and Jackson, and Gorbachev with a sample of Slavic political leaders.

Methodological Issues

We intend this study as an approach to the goal of a standardized taxonomy for describing personality at a distance. Obviously the variation in materials used across (and sometimes within) each of the authors of this study means that this goal is not yet realized. While such variation creates a certain methodological "looseness" and possible difficulties, we believe that the convergence of results across methods and materials is sufficiently robust in the present case.

Two more specific methodological issues need to be addressed. Procedures for assessing interscorer reliability vary across the different techniques (see the references listed in Table 7.1 for details). For the motive, belief, and style variables, category agreement between scorers and experts and among scorers is usually calculated formally, with a standard of 0.85 or higher required for all variables [see Winter (1973, p. 248) for details of category agreement calculation]. While the verbal-style measures of traits are objectively defined (see Weintraub, 1989; pp. 11–16), formal measures of interscorer agreement are not routinely calculated. Operational code analysis involves more holistic interpretation of the speaker's entire line of argument. No formal measures of inter-scorer agreement are calculated.

The Gorbachev material, of course, had been translated from Russian into English (in some interviews, by way of some other intermediate language). Previous research (Hermann, 1980a, p. 352, n. 2; Winter, 1973, pp. 92–93) suggests that little bias on these scoring systems is introduced by this translation process.

RESULTS

Tables 7.5 through 7.8 present the results of the scoring and analysis of data for each of the main domains and variables of personality described in Tables 7.1 through 7.4. For each variable, the tables give scores both in raw form and then in comparison to the appropriate other groups, as discussed above. We will proceed domain by domain, presenting results, drawing conclusions and making predictions on the basis of previous research. In the final selection, we will bring all of our results, conclusions, and predictions together into integrated personality portraits of Bush and Gorbachev.

Motives

Table 7.5 presents motive scores for Bush and Gorbachev. Affiliation and power motives were measured in two different ways (Hermann's and Winter's procedures), using different samples of interviews and speeches, and making comparisons to several different groups of other

Table 7.5   MOTIVES OF BUSH AND GORBACHEV

Motive	Study	Bush Speech or Comp[a]	Bush Score Raw[b]	Bush Score Comparison[c]	Gorbachev Speech or Comp[a]	Gorbachev Score Raw[b]	Gorbachev Score Comparison[c]
Achievement	DGW	ACS	8.76	61	SS	3.82	59
	DGW	IA	7.85	58	CPSU	5.45	60
Mean				60 H			60 H
SD				1.5			0.5
Affiliation	MGH	WL	0.18	66	WL	0.20	68
		C88		53	PBM		58
	DGW	ACS	4.04	62	SS	3.91	69
		IA	10.81	83	CPSU	1.27	50
Mean				66 H			61 H
SD				10.9			7.8
Power	MGH	WL	0.44	72	WL	0.50	77
		C88		48	BPM		38
	DGW	ACS	8.76	51	SS	5.15	47
		IA	6.92	53	CPSU	1.88	39
Mean				56 M			50 M
SD				9.4			15.8

[a] Speech and/or comparison group for this score: For MGH analysis: SS = Standard sample; WL = Compared to 53 world leaders; BPM = Compared to Brezhnev-era Politburo members; C88 = compared to 1988 candidates. For DGW analysis: ACS = Announcement of candidacy speech (compared to other 1988 candidates); IA = Inaugural address (compared to other first inaugural addresses); SS = Standard sample (compared to 22 other world leaders); CPSU = First report after assuming leadershp to a Communist Party Congress (compared to first reports of other leaders).

[b] Proportion of verb phrases scored for imagery in MGH analysis; images per 1000 words in DGW analysis.

[c] Standard score (based on comparison group as in note a); M = 50, SD = 10. For averaged scores, H = high (one SD or more above comparison mean); M = medium (within SD of comparison mean).

political leaders. To facilitate comparisons of these different estimates, Table 7.5 presents the means and standard deviations for all estimates of each motive. Despite the differences of method, the results suggest reasonably clear and consistent motive profiles for each leader. Bush scores high in the achievement and affiliation motives, but only a little above average in power. (Compared with other Americans—1988 candidates or previous presidents—he is average; compared with leaders from other countries, he is high.) Gorbachev's motive profile— high achievement, high affiliation, and average power—is remarkably similar. As with Bush, the power comparison score depends on the comparison group used. Compared with other Soviet leaders, Gorbachev is low in power motivation; but compared with other world leaders, he is average (Winter) or high (Hermann).[7] This suggests that as a group, Soviet and American leaders may be more power-motivated than the world average.

Comparison to Other United States Presidents and Other World Leaders

Winter (1976, 1988) suggested that achievement, affiliation, and power motives could be conceptualized as three orthogonal dimensions, and that the more similar the motive profiles of any two leaders, the less the Pythagorean distance between the two "points" representing the motive scores of those leaders. By this criterion,[8] Bush and Gorbachev are very similar to each other, and each is more similar to Richard Nixon than to any other United States president. Compared to other world leaders (see Winter, 1990), Gorbachev most closely resembles King Hussein of Jordan, Enrico Berlinguer (leader of the Italian Communist party from 1972 until his death in 1984), Argentine general (later president from 1976 to 1981) Jorge Videla, and Brazilian general (later president from 1974 to 1979) Ernesto Giesel. He is *least* like Ayatollah Khomeini and SWAPO leader Sam Nujoma.

What is the use of such comparisons? Characterizing Bush as a "preppy Nixon" or Mikhail Gorbachev as a "socialist Nixon" may be an entertaining statistical game, but do these comparisons have any broader practical purpose? Similarities of motive profile may draw our attention to deeper similarities of style and performance. Thus Gorbachev, like Nixon, extricated his country from a disastrous "third world" war, and sought rapproachement with long-standing enemies. Like Hussein and Berlinguer, and in contrast to Khomeini, Gorbachev is charting a pragmatic course of realistic compromise through the minefields of militant ideological-theological dispute. Like Nixon, Bush reacts negatively to personalized criticism; also like Nixon, he walks a narrow line between suspicion and the desire to negotiate arms reduction.

These comparisons may also alert us to possible problems and dangers. Would Bush and Gorbachev, like Nixon, be vulnerable to scandal? And if their remarkable flexibility ever fails them, would they rigidly dig in to support a failing line of policy? Thus generals Videla and Geisel both set out to dismantle constricting bureaucracies and expand economic growth; but intractable problems, dissatisfaction, and opposition eventually led them toward authoritarian solutions—"dirty wars" against their own people if not outright attacks on a foreign enemy.

Predictions Based on Motive Scores

In terms of previous at-a-distance research on motives (see Terhune, 1968a, 1968b; Winter, 1980, 1991), the motive profiles of Bush and Gorbachev suggest that they will be *rationally cooperative* (high achievement and affiliation), interested in maximizing joint outcomes rather than exploiting the other (low power). They will *seek arms limitation agreements* (high affiliation) and will be *unlikely or use aggression* in the pursuit of policy (average power). On the other hand, they are sensitive to the nuances of friendship-versus-rejection (high affiliation). Under stress they may become prickly and defensive, especially if they perceive the other side as threatening or exploitative. If backed into an extreme corner in this way, they might even strike out with ill-conceived and inchoate hostility.

Beliefs and Styles

Table 7.6 presents scores for the cognitive variables measured by Hermann's techniques. Again, the results vary somewhat according to which comparison groups are used. Considering the world leaders' comparison scores (which are based on the larger sample), Bush and Gorbachev both score high in nationalism, distrust, and conceptual complexity.[9] Their high complexity scores suggest that Bush and Gorbachev are both able to differentiate among alternative principles, policies, and points of view, and then to integrate these disparate elements into complex higher-order generalizations. Bush and Gorbachev both have strongly nationalist orientations and tend to distrust others. (This distrust may be a sign of the prickly defensiveness that affiliation-motivated people display when they are in uncomfortable situations.) In most people, suspicious nationalism goes along with simplistic,

Table 7.6   BELIEFS AND STYLES OF BUSH AND GORBACHEV

Variable	Bush			Gorbachev		
		Comparison Scores[b]			Comparison Scores[b]	
	Raw score[a]	World leaders	1988 candidates	Raw score[a]	World leaders	Brezhnev Politburo members
Beliefs						
Nationalism	0.40	76 H	50 M	0.38	74 H	37 L
Events controllable	0.33	35 L	48 M	0.42	41 M	42 M
Self-confidence	0.60	31 L	48 M	0.84	48 M	75 H
Styles						
Conceptual complexity	0.54	64 H	48 M	0.54	64 H	74 H
Distrust	0.29	59 M	49 M	0.39	66 H	69 H
Task emphasis	0.47	37 L	47 M	0.61	48 M	20 L

[a] Proportion of time during which a characteristic that could have been exhibited was in fact exhibited.

[b] Standardized score (based on comparison group noted at the top of the column); M = 50, SD = 10. H = relatively high (one SD or more above comparison mean; M = medium (within one SD of comparison mean); L = relatively low (one SD or more below comparison mean).

black-or-white thinking [see Brown (1963, chap. 10) on these cognitions as features of the authoritarian personality]. In Bush and Gorbachev, however, these tendencies should be mitigated by their high conceptual complexity. Thus they may be able to defuse competitive, "patriotic" issues by making subtle distinctions and complex integrations—in short, by intellectualization.

Gorbachev's average scores on the belief that events are controllable, self-confidence, and task emphasis all suggest a leader who is reasonably capable of sustained, optimistic work. (For a Soviet leader, however, Gorbachev gives much greater emphasis to the interpersonal dimension of leadership than to task issues.) Bush's low scores on these three variables, in contrast, suggest a slightly more interpersonally focused leader, who is vulnerable to fatalistic drift (or distraction through affiliative conviviality), at least under stress.

Overall Personality Orientations

Scores on these cognitive variables (as well as scores on their affiliation and power motives) combine to suggest that Gorbachev has a *developmental orientation* to the political process. Previous research (see Hermann, 1987) shows that leaders with this orientation are intent on improving their nations, either economically or militarily, or both. But because they are uncertain that they or their nations can govern events, they are constantly trying to see what others can do to help them and through persuasion to get these others to be of aid. With constant vigilance, such leaders seek out those who appear able to shape events; indeed, they often seem aware of potentially rewarding relationships before most other actors in the international or domestic political system become aware.

Developmentally oriented leaders engage in "controlled dependence": they use others but do not become symbiotic with these others, nor do they try to control or dominate others. Through an attitude of friendliness and collaboration, they make others feel good but do so while committing only a moderate amount of their own resources. By taking the initiative, leaders with this orientation perceive they can work with others to create opportunities for themselves. The ultimate goal is improvement of the condition of the nation, and like a "dog with a bone," these leaders keep maneuvering their governments toward actions that will have some payoff toward that goal. They are not very tolerant of problems or events that take away from this ultimate goal, or of people who do not "pull their weight" in working toward the regime's goal.

Bush also has many aspects of the developmental orientation; but his primary political orientation is that of *integrator* or consensus-builder, concerned with morale and the cohesiveness of the groups with which he works (see Hermann, 1989). Leaders with this orientation see themselves as agents of the people, reflecting their needs and wishes, reconciling differences, and minimizing conflict. They are reactive, working on the policies and programs that their followers want addressed. As an integrator or mediator, Bush would seek to forge compromise and consensus among his constituents, letting them define the agenda rather than imposing one himself. For this orientation, the "best" policy is that which brings together the broadest base of support. Thus these leaders are driven by popularity ratings. For developmental leaders, in contrast, the "best" policy is whatever will solve the problem and improve the condition of the nation. They are driven by vision, thus, in the process, by the need for information, and finally by results.

Operational Codes

Table 7.7 gives the operational code characterizations of each leader. As an incrementalist with limited goals, Bush sees the world as potentially dangerous, calling for a variety of responses but initially emphasizing the paths of conflict (threats, sanctions), In a world perceived to be less dangerous and more friendly, Gorbachev has a comprehensive perspective and goals. While he can take either the path of politics (praise, reward) or the path of conflict, his choice of response emphasizes positive reactions rather than negative ones and words rather than action. In simplest terms, Bush employs *specific threats,* while Gorbachev is more likely to make broader *exhortations to virtue.* Both leaders express an optimistic sense of being able to control foreign policy outcomes.

Traits

Table 7.8 presents the scores on the verbal characteristics that Weintraub (1981, 1989) uses to construct trait ratings. Both Bush and Gorbachev have an engaging interpersonal style (high direct references and rhetorical questions). Bush's higher scores on negatives and "me" pronouns, however, suggest that his engaging style is tinged with oppositional and passive tendencies. In terms of emotional style, Bush and Gorbachev are both highly expressive, but in different ways. Bush shows personally expressive verbal characteristics (high I/we ratio, expressions of feeling, and low nonpersonal references). Gorbachev's expressivity, in contrast, is based on less personal verbal characteristics that suggest intensification and thus perhaps calculation (evaluators, adverbial intensifiers, direct references, and rhetorical questions). Gorbachev thus appears to engage in controlled expression of feelings; he is, in short, an accomplished actor-politician.

Neither Bush nor Gorbachev is especially high in anxiety (average negatives, explainers, and qualifiers), but Bush is perhaps prone to depression (high I/we ratio, direct references, low

Table 7.7   OPERATIONAL CODES OF BUSH AND GORBACHEV[a]

Component	Bush Characterization	Gorbachev Characterization
Self-attributions		
Friendly/hostile	Dangerous (potentially hostile relations with others; varied kinds of opponents)	Friendly (13:0)[b]
Optimistic/pessimistic	Optimistic	Optimistic (9:1)
High/low control	High control	Moderately high control (5:2)
Comprehensive/limited	Limited goals	Comprehensive goals (8:0)
Self-script		
Methods of reaching goals	Conflict	Mixed politics/conflict (9:8); Positive vs. negative (15:5); Verbal vs. action (12:5)

[a] *Note:* The conceptualizations and measurement of some variables were slightly different for Bush and Gorbachev; see text.

[b] Ratio of frequency of first alternative to frequency of second alternative.

Table 7.8   TRAITS AND DEFENSES OF BUSH AND GORBACHEV

Variable	Postwar U.S. Presidents Raw score[a]	Bush Raw score[a]	Comparisons[b] C88	USP	Gorbachev Raw score[a]	Comparison[b] USP
Use of "I"	25.0	47.8	H	H	11.8	L
Use of "we"	18.0	10.4	L	L	19.3	M
I/we ratio	1.4	4.6	H	H	0.6	L
Use of "me"	2.0	3.5	H	H	0.9	L
Expressions of feeling	3.0	4.0	H	M	1.8	L
Evaluators	9.0	15.0	M	H	12.4	H
Direct references to audience	2.0	4.2	H	H	3.1	M
Adverbial intensifiers	13.0	12.9	M	M	21.4	H
Rhetorical questions	1.0	2.5	H	H	2.5	H
Retractors	7.0	10.9	H	M	7.4	M
Negatives	12.0	1.52	M	M	13.1	M
Explainers	5.0	3.5	L	L	5.1	M
Qualifiers	11.0	9.0	M	M	6.3	L
Nonpersonal references	750.0	543.5	L	L	854.1	L
Creative expressions	2.0	4.0	M	M	1.3	L

[a] Frequency per 1000 words.

[b] Comparison groups: C88 = 1988 candidates; USP = postwar U.S. presidents.

nonpersonal references). Both leaders are especially sensitive to criticism (high negatives and evaluators, and for Gorbachev, high adverbial intensifiers). In such cases, Bush is especially likely to show anger (high I, we, and negatives), while Gorbachev, in contrast, tends to take control of the challenge (frequent interruptions and direct engagement).

In terms of decision style, Bush appears rather impulsive (low qualifiers and high retractors). Sometimes leaders with this pattern can become paralyzed with indecision in crisis situations. Gorbachev shows a more balanced flexibility (moderate retractors). His low qualifiers score may suggest impulsive tendencies, although this may be in part an artifact of using some interviews in which he answered previously submitted questions. Bush scores moderate on creativity, while Gorbachev scores low. This suggests that Gorbachev draws on others for new ideas and solutions to problems.

Overall, both leaders are engaging, expressive, and perhaps impulsive and prone to anger. Neither is anxious, although Bush may be depressed on occasion. In terms of the broader factors of introversion-extraversion and neuroticism-stability, each leader could therefore be classified as a stable extravert, with Gorbachev a little more so and Bush a little less so on both dimensions.

DISCUSSION: PERSONALITY PORTRAITS, PREDICTIONS, AND POLICY

Personality Portraits of Bush and Gorbachev

Table 7.9 draws together the scores presented in the last section into brief personality portraits of Bush and Gorbachev. Both are motivated primarily for achievement and affiliation—for standards of excellence, improvement, and innovation, as well as for friendly cooperation— rather than for impact, power, and exploitation. At heart, both are somewhat suspicious and nationalistic, characteristics which under threat could be defensively exacerbated by their high affiliation motives. Under most circumstances, however, both are able to recognize and deal with complexity, which keeps their suspicious nationalism under control.

Bush expresses his own emotions openly. He may be somewhat unpredictable, with episodes of impulsive behavior alternating with periods of depression and drift. In these circumstances, his conflict self-script may be engaged. Gorbachev is also expressive, but in a more calculated way. With greater emotional control, he is optimistic and capable of sustained effort, involving mostly positive verbal self-scripts that balance politics and conflict. Both leaders are reasonably stable extroverts.

Gorbachev, with his developmental orientation, is concerned with solving national problems and seeking national improvement; to accomplish this he would seek out information and approach others for help. While Bush shares some of the characteristics of this developmental orientation, his stronger integrator/mediator orientation would lead him more to reconciling the feelings and opinions of others than to shaping his own agenda.

Predicting Political Outcomes

Cooperation

Considering these portraits in the light of previous at-a-distance research on political leaders, we can characterize both Bush and Gorbachev as leaders who want to be *peacemakers, concerned with development and not prone to seek political ends through violence and war.*

Table 7.9 PERSONALITY PORTRAITS OF BUSH AND GORBACHEV

Personality Domain	Bush	Gorbachev
Motives	Achievement and affiliation; only moderate power	Achievement and affiliation; low to moderate power
Beliefs	Distrustful nationalist, but high on cognitive complexity	Distrustful nationalist, but high on cognitive complexity
	Events only seen as partly controllable	Events seen as controllable
	Low self-confidence	High self-confidence
Style	Tends to emphasize people rather than task	Tends to emphasize people and task
Operational code	Sees world as dangerous	Sees world as friendly
	Sets limited goals	Sets comprehensive goals
	Uses conflict	Uses politics (positive words) as well as conflict
Traits	Emotionally expressive	Emotionally expressive, in a calculated way
	Not anxious	Not anxious
	Vulnerable to depression, indecision	Not vulnerable to depression
	Sensitive to criticism	Sensitive to criticism
	Reacts with anger	Reacts by taking control of situation
	Impulsive	Somewhat impulsive
	Reasonably stable extrovert	Stable extrovert
Overall	*Integrator/mediator orientation (with secondary developmental/ improvement orientation)*	*Developmental/improvement orientation*

They are likely to pursue interdependent rather than independent foreign policies. This conclusion is supported by their motive profiles, their cognitions or beliefs, and their patterns of traits.

With respect to Gorbachev, this analysis supports the "cooperative" view put forward by Holloway (1989) and Legvold (1989), rather than the traditionalist interpretations by Nixon, Quayle, and others quoted at the beginning of this paper.

Much of the Bush presidential record supports a similarly cooperative view. An apparent exception, such as the December 1989 invasion of Panama, would on this interpretation be understood as an expression of Bush's impulsivity rather than any enduring desire for power and conquest. Actually, the whole sequence of Bush's inaction during the October 1989 attempted coup in Panama and his invasion two months later may reflect his alternating tendencies toward passive drift and impulsive action. Our results are also consistent with phrases used by Duffy (1989, pp. 16, 22) to describe Bush's style: "very loyal to people, more than to ideas" and "reactive" (high affiliation motive) "gambles . . . only after carefully researching the odds," "lack of ideological conviction," and "regards almost anything . . . as negotiable" (high achievement motive); and "working his will among fellow [leaders] rather than through appeals to pubic opinion" (high affiliation motive, only moderate power motive).

Negotiation

Given this predisposition toward cooperation, what will happen when Bush and Gorbachev actually negotiate with each other? Of course, high-level negotiations are carefully orchestrated by policy planning staffs, with only limited scope for any effects of leaders' personalities. Nevertheless, it is interesting to extrapolate from several laboratory studies of motivation and negotiation behavior (see Schnackers and Kleinbeck, 1975; Terhune, 1968a, b) in order to estimate what these limited, marginal effects might be.

Under almost all bargaining conditions, achievement-motivated people are consistently the most cooperative negotiators. In international-relations simulation games, they have the highest ratio of cooperative acts to conflict acts. They are low in "military effort"; and while they may lie in simulation game "newspapers," they are likely to tell the truth in direct messages. These tendencies would be reinforced by their overall "developmental" orientations. (Power-motivated people, in contrast, are the most exploitative and conflict-prone.) Extrapolating (perhaps excessively) from these laboratory studies, then, we may expect that *Bush and Gorbachev will be predisposed by their personality dispositions toward cooperative negotiations for mutual advantage and toward maximizing joint outcomes.* Affiliation motivation, on the other hand, plays a much more variable role in negotiation, depending on the degree of threat in the "payoff matrix" and the perceived similarity of the counterplayer. Under low threat, and when surrounding others are similar in attitude and friendly in style (i.e., "friends"), affiliation-motivated people are genuinely warm and cooperative. Under higher threat, or when faced with strangers or dissimilar, unfriendly others ("enemies"), they can become suspicious and defensive, perhaps reflecting their fear of rejection, as well as their nationalistic distrust and sensitivity to criticism.

Achievement and affiliation-motivated negotiators tend to articulate "strategic" and "mutual" reasons (rather than "greed") for their choices. They tend to view their partner as a "cooperator" or "fellow worker" rather than a "competitor," "yielder," or "gambler"—but with also occasional negative overtones of "opportunist."

Finally, their overall orientations of developmental (Gorbachev) and mediator (Bush) seem almost perfect foils for each other: Bush seeks a broader consensus; Gorbachev is willing to give that consensus in exchange for developmental help.

Change and Reform

Both leaders are faced with rapidly changing international and (for Gorbachev especially) domestic situations, creating a need for reforms and new policies. Their high achievement motive scores suggest both an opportunity and a possible problem. First, the evidence from laboratory and field studies suggests that people high in achievement motivation are more *likely to change policies that are not working.* For example, achievement-motivated people are more likely to pick up new information and, as a result, to modify their performance on the basis of results [Sinha and Mehta (1972); see also the general discussion in McClelland (1961, pp. 231–233, and 1985, pp. 237–238, 247–249)]. An earlier political example would be the dramatic changes introduced by achievement motivated Richard Nixon in American foreign policy (the opening to China and detente with the Soviet Union) and domestic policy (the "New Economic Policy" of 1971). This *capacity for conceptual breakthrough* seems evident in Gorbachev's words and deeds since 1985.

Among 20th-century American presidents, however, achievement motivation is significantly correlated with Barber's (1977) classification of "active-negative"[10]—that is, showing *under stress a self-defeating "rigidification"* or reluctance to give up an obviously failing policy. Barber's examples include Wilson, Hoover, Johnson, and Nixon, each of whom scored high in achievement motivation. Jimmy Carter, also high in achievement motivation, showed a similar pattern of rigidification and "malaise." These five leaders certainly did not lack the capacity for vision—that is, the ability to size up situations and forecast consequences.

Yet if these five leaders had the vision associated with achievement motivation, why did they sometimes ignore the gathering signs of failure, rigidly pursuing discredited policies? I suggest that their rigidity can be explained by their *sense of limited control over policy implementation.* Actual policy change involves the political process: compromising on a "less-than-the-best" alternative (in Simon's terms, "satisficing" rather than "optimizing"); repeated negotiating to secure approval from diffuse and decentralized groups; and delegating authority to people of doubtful competence, whom one did not choose and may not trust. Taken together, these steps all reflect the leader's limited control over policy implementation.

To leaders high in achievement motivation but low in power motivation, such lack of personal control over the achievement process would be aversive because they naturally tend to assume personal responsibility for outcomes.[11] To preserve a sense of personal control over outcomes, therefore, they may do one of three things: (1) make demagogic appeals to "the people" over the heads of "the politicians" (as did Wilson), (2) take ethical shortcuts (as did Nixon), or (3) become too deeply involved in minor details or "micromanaging" (as did Carter). Their perspective becomes foreshortened, their frustration mounts, and they become trapped. On the basis of their motive scores, *the problems of frustration and the temptations to popular demagoguery, shortcuts or micromanagement* might be potential problems for Bush and Gorbachev.

Political visions, once articulated, can only be achieved through the political process, success at which is likely to call for power motivation. To a power-motivated leader, building alliances through compromise, negotiating, calculating support, and careful monitoring of delegated authority are the very stuff of power—pleasures in themselves rather than painful distractions from a larger vision. If leaders scoring low or average in power motivation cannot be expected to enjoy these necessary functions, perhaps they can delegate them to a more power-motivated lieutenant. In that case, it becomes important to assess the motives of those around Bush and Gorbachev—people such as James Baker and Aleksandr Yakovlev, whom Legvold has termed "Gorbachev's alter ego" (1989, p. 85).

Another part of the political process involves articulating a political vision to the people. Initially, this involves arousing popular enthusiasm. But no vision is achieved overnight; and so leaders must sustain popular energy, bridging the inevitable times of deprivation and difficulty with continued commitment and sacrifice. These are the situations that call for charismatic leaders—Franklin Roosevelt and Churchill are vivid historical examples—whose high power motives lead them to seek impact on others, as part of "expansionist" or "influential" orientations (see Table 7.2).

Considering the situations and leadership orientations of Bush and Gorbachev, then, we might speculate that any serious future erosion of consensus, or continuing difficulty and failure of development goals, could set the conditions for the emergence of alternative, power-motivated leaders who are better able to articulate (in Bush's words) "the vision thing" and thereby arouse popular enthusiasm and kindle popular energy. In history, the danger of charisma is that enthusiasm, once aroused, often overflows its visionary channels and spills over into aggression toward others.

Policy Implications

Perhaps it is always important to structure negotiations so that both parties like each other. *In negotiations between two affiliation-motivated leaders (each prone to distrust and nationalism), however, it becomes especially critical to ensure that initial impressions are favorable:* (1) that the other is perceived as similar, and (2) that agreements on minor matters be used to build the impression of broader underlying agreement that will generate further momentum. For this reason it is probably wise to proceed slowly and cautiously. On each side, the reason for caution is not so much the question of whether the other side is "really" trustworthy, but rather whether they will be *perceived* as trustworthy. Ironically, these policy prescriptions for affiliation-motivated leaders in negotiation are aptly reflected in the advisory words of Richard Nixon—another leader very high in the affiliation motive, and known for being prickly and defensive in the presence of his "enemies"—whose doubts about Gorbachev were quoted at the beginning of this paper:

> The people of the United States and the people of the Soviet Union can be friends. *Because of our profound differences, the governments of our two nations cannot be friends. . . .* Gorbachev's historic challenge is to implement reforms that will *remove those differences* (1989, p. 219, emphasis added).

Given the importance of these symbolic first steps, and the constant mutual potential for prickly defensiveness, some early 1989 exchanges in the U.S. Soviet dialogue seem unfortunate. In May, for example, defense secretary Cheney predicted, on television, that Gorbachev "would ultimately fail; that is to say, that he will not be able to reform the Soviet economy. . . . And when that happens, he's likely to be replaced by somebody who will be far more hostile. . . ." ("Rethinking a gloomy view," 1989.) Two weeks later, presidential spokesperson Fitzwater described a Gorbachev weapons reduction proposal as "throwing out, in a kind of drugstore cowboy fashion, one arms control proposal after another" (Hoffman, 1989, p. A30).

On the other hand, an incident from the 1989 Malta summit meeting illustrates a more positive way of dealing with sensitivities of this sort (see Maynes, 1990). On the first day of the summit, Gorbachev complained about Bush's repeated statements that changes within the Soviet Union represented an acceptance of "western" democratic values. Democracy, Gorbachev argued, is a "universal" value; Bush's use of "western" had overtones that were humiliating both to himself and to the Soviet people. Bush replied that he had never thought about this; since that time, he has omitted the adjective "western" when speaking of "democratic values."

Since both leaders have the capacity for conceptualizing and articulating change, but also have possible problems with implementing that change, each leader would do well to cultivate implementation "back-up," in the form of associates whose power motivation would enable them to enjoy the political process in its own terms and for its own sake. Ideally, these associates should be immune from distrustful nationalism, be deliberative instead of impulsive, and be decisive (for Bush) and creative (for Gorbachev).

SUMMARY

Based on previous research with other political leaders and laboratory studies of ordinary people, there is reason to be optimistic about the impact of the personalities of Bush and Gorbachev on world peace and international cooperation, at least between the superpowers.

Their motives seem benign. Their political orientations seem complementary—almost ideally so. To get the reconciliation, integration and wider consensus that he seeks, Bush seems willing to give the development help that Gorbachev wants and needs. Their beliefs and operational codes are largely compatible, with any problems (such as nationalism, or a low sense that events are controllable) being overcome by their traits and cognitive and interpersonal styles.

The biggest problem for both leaders is likely to be a sense of frustration and possible malaise if new ideas, structural reforms, and emerging reconciliations become bogged down in the mire of political opposition. Given the situation of the Soviet economy and nationalities, these are likely to be especially acute problems for Gorbachev, although long-term United States economic vulnerabilities could pose the same problem for Bush. In those circumstances, their personalities could make them vulnerable to frustration and depression; in an extreme case, even to impulsive and inchoate violence. Moreover, their low power motivation, in combination with latent sensitivity and distrust, could jeopardize their continuation in office.

So far at least, the 1989 and 1990 summit meetings between Bush and Gorbachev support the analyses suggested in this paper, demonstrating that with a positive start and especially strong efforts to minimize the mutual sense of threat, negotiations can proceed cooperatively toward a new structure of superpower peace.

ACKNOWLEDGMENTS

This paper is based on two symposia in which all four authors participated: "Assessing the personality characteristics of the current presidential candidates," at the July 1988 annual meeting of the International Society of Political Psychology, and "How Gorbachev's personality shapes Soviet foreign policy behavior," at the March 1989 annual meeting of the International Studies Association.

REFERENCES

Adorno, T. W., Frenkel-Brunswik, E., Levinson, D. J., and Sanford, R. N. (1950). *The authoritarian personality.* New York: Harper.

Allport, G. W. (1961). *Pattern and growth in personality.* New York: Holt, Rinehart, & Winston.

Atkinson, J. W. (Ed.). (1958). *Motives in fantasy, action, and society.* Princeton, NJ: Van Nostrand.

Bales, R. F. (1958). Task roles and social roles in problem-solving groups. In E. E. Maccoby, T. M. Newcomb, and E. L. Hartley (Eds.), *Readings in social psychology* (3rd ed., pp. 437–447). New York: Holt, Rinehart, & Winston.

Barber, J. D. (1977). *Presidential character: Predicting Performance in the White House.* 2nd ed. Englewood Cliffs, NJ: Prentice-Hall.

Bieri, J. (1961). Complexity-simplicity as a personality variable in cognitive and preferential behavior. In D. W. Fiske and S. R. Maddi (Eds.), *Functions of varied experience* (pp. 355–379). Homewood, IL: Dorsey.

Boyatzis, R. (1973). Affiliation motivation. In D. C. McClelland & R. S. Steele (Eds.), *Human motivation* (pp. 252–276). Morristown, NJ: General Learning Press.

Brown, R. W. (1965). *Social psychology.* New York: Free Press.

Byars, R. S. (1973). Small-group theory and shifting styles of political leadership. *Comparative Political Studies, 5,* 443–469.

Charen, M. (1990, February 13). Gorbachev is on power trip. *Ann Arbor News,* p. All.

Dionne, E. J., Jr. (1989, May 14). Conservatives find Bush troubling. *New York Times,* section I, p. 24.

Duffy, M. (1989, August 21). Mr. Consensus. *Time,* 134, 16–22.

Eysenck, H. J., and Eysenck, M. W. (1985). *Personality and individual differences: A natural science approach.* New York: Plenum.

Freud, A. (1946). *The ego and the mechanisms of defense.* New York: International Universities Press.

Freud, S. (1961–1963). *Introductory lectures on psychoanalysis.* In J. Strachey (Ed.), *Standard edition of the complete psychological works of Sigmund Freud* (Vol. 15,16). London: Hogarth Press. (Original work published 1915–1917)

George, A. L. (1969). The "operational code: " A neglected approach to the study of political leaders and decision-making. *International Studies Quarterly* 13, 190–222.

Greenstein, F. 1. (1969). *Personality and politics.* Chicago: Markham.

Hermann, M. G. (Ed.) (1977). *A psychological examination of political leaders.* New York: Free Press.

Hermann, M. G. (1980a). Assessing the personalities of Soviet Politburo members. *Personality and Social Psychology Bulletin,* 6, 332–352.

Hermann, M. G. (1980b). Explaining foreign policy behavior using the personal characteristics of political leaders. *International Studies Quarterly,* 24, 7–46.

Hermann, M. G. (1983). Assessing personality at a distance: A portrait of Ronald Reagan. *Mershon Center Quarterly Report,* 7(6). Columbus, OH: Mershon Center of the Ohio State University.

Hermann, M. G. (1987). Assessing the foreign policy role orientations of sub-Saharan African leaders. In S. G. Walker (Ed.), *Role theory and foreign policy analysis* (pp. 161–198). Durham, NC: Duke University Press.

Hermann, M. G. (1988). Syria's Hafez Al-Assad. In B. Kellerman and J. Rubin (Eds.), *Leadership and negotiation in the Middle East* (pp. 70–95). New York: Praeger.

Hermann, M. G. (1989, Spring). Defining the Bush presidential style. *Mershon Memo.* Columbus OH: Ohio State University.

Hoffman, D. (1989, May 17). Gorbachev's gambits challenged. *Washington Post,* p. A1, A30.

Holloway, D. (1989). Gorbachev's new thinking. *Foreign Affairs,* 68(1), 66–81.

Holsti, O. (1970). The "Operational Code" approach to the study of political leaders: John Foster Dulles's philosophical and instrumental beliefs. *Canadian Journal of Political Science,* 3, 123–157.

Jervis, R. (1976). *Perception and misperception in international politics.* Princeton, NJ: Princeton University Press.

Jung, C. J. (1910). The association method. *American Journal of Psychology,* 21, 219–240.

Jung, C. J. (1971). *Psychological types.* In *The connected works of. C. J. Jung* (Vol. 6). Princeton, NJ: Princeton University Press. (Original work published 1921)

Kelly, G. A. (1955). *A theory of personality.* New York: Norton.

Legvold, R. (1989). The revolution in Soviet foreign policy. *Foreign Affairs.* 68, 82–98.

Leites, N. (1951). *The operational code of the Politburo.* New York: McGraw-Hill.

McAdams, D. P. (1982). Intimacy motivation. In A. 1. Stewart, (Ed.), *Motivation and society* (pp. 133–171). San Francisco: Jossey-Bass.

McClelland, D. C. (1961). *The achieving society.* Princeton, NJ: Van Nostrand.

Maynes, C. W. (1990). America without the Cold War. *Foreign Policy,* 78, 3–26.

Meloen, J. D., Hagendoom, L., Raaijmakers, Q., and Visser, L. (1988). Authoritarianism and the revival of political racism: Reassessment in the Netherlands of the reliability and validity of the concept of authoritarianism by Adorno *et al., Political Psychology,* 9, 413–429.

Murray, H. A. (1938). *Explorations in personality.* New York: Oxford University Press.

Nixon, R. M. (1989). American foreign policy: The Bush agenda. *Foreign Affairs.* 68, 199–219.

Noonan, P. (1990). *Present at the revolution.* New York: Random House.

Norman, W. (1963). Toward an adequate taxonomy of personality attributes: Replicated factor structure in peer nomination personality ratings. *Journal of Abnormal and Social Psychology,* 60, 574–583.

Parsons, T., and Bales, R. F. (1955). *Family: Socialization and interaction process.* Glencoe, IL: Free Press.

Price, R. (1977). *With Nixon.* New York: Viking Press.

Quayle, J. D. (1989, June 9). Text of remarks by the Vice President at the Conference on Atlantic Community. Washington, DC: Office of the Vice President.

Rethinking a gloomy view on perestroika. (1989, May 2). *New York Times,* p. I.

Rogers, C. R. (1959). A theory of therapy, personality, and interpersonal relationships, as developed in the client-centered framework. In S. Koch (Ed.), *Psychology: A study of a science,* Vol. 3. (pp. 184–256). New York: McGraw-Hill.

Rosenthal, A. M. (1990, September 21). The Gorbachev era ends. *New York Times,* p. A13.

Rotter, J. B. (1990). Internal versus external control of reinforcement: A case history of a variable. *American Psychologist,* 45, 489–493.

Safire, W. (1975). *Before the fall: An inside view of the pre-Watergate White House.* New York: Belmont Tower Books.

Safire, W. (1989, March 27). *Taking the crabby view of the grinning Russkies. New York Times,* section I, p. 17.

Schmitt, D. (1990, July). *Measuring the motives of Soviet leaders and Soviet society: Congruence created or congruence reflected?* Paper presented at the annual meeting of the International Society of Political Psychology, Washington. D.C.

Schnackers, U., and Kleinbeck, U. (1975). Machmotiv und machtthematisches Verhalten in einem Verhandlungsspiel [Power motivation and power-related behavior in a bargaining game]. *Archiv für Psychologie,* 127, 300–319.

Shulman, M. D. (1990, June 17). How well do we know this man? Review of D. Doder and L. Branson, *Gorbochev: Heretic in the Kremlin. New York Times Book Review,* p. 5.

Sinha, B. P., and Mehta, P. (1972). Farmers' need for achievement and change-proneness in acquisition of information from a farm telecast. *Rural Sociology,* 37, 417–427.

Strickland, B. (1977). Internal-external control of reinforcement. In T. Blass. (Ed.), *Personality variables in social behavior* (pp. 219–279). Hillsdale, NJ: Erlbaum.

Terhune, K. W. (1968a). Motives, situation, and interpersonal conflict within prisoners' dilemma. *Journal of Personality and Social Psychology Monograph Supplement,* 8, part 2.

Terhune, K. W. (1968b). Studies of motives, cooperation, and conflict within laboratory microcosms. *Buffalo Studies,* 4, 29–58.

Tetlock, P. E., and Boettger, R. (1989). Cognitive and rhetorical styles of traditionalist and reformist Soviet politicians: A content analysis study. *Political Psychology,* 10, 209–232.

Tucker, R. C. (1965). The dictator and totalitarianism. *World Politics,* 17, 55–83.

Walker, S. (1983). The motivational foundations of political belief systems: A re-analysis of the operational code construct. *International Studies Quarterly,* 27, 179–201.

Walker, S. (1986, July). *Woodrow Wilson's operational code.* Paper presented at the meeting of the International Society of Political Psychology, Amsterdam.

Walker, S. (1990). The evolution of operational code analysis. *Political Psychology,* 11. 403–418.

Weiner, B. (1980). *Human motivation.* New York: Holt, Rinehart, and Winston.

Weintraub, W. (1981). *Verbal behavior: Adaptation and psychopathology.* New York: Springer.

Weintraub, W. (1986). Personality profiles of American presidents as revealed in their public statements: The presidential news conferences of Jimmy Carter and Ronald Reagan. *Political Psychology, 7,* 285–295.

Weintraub, W. (1989). *Verbal behavior in everyday life.* New York: Springer.

Winter, D. G. (1973). *The power motive.* New York: Free Press.

Winter, D. G. (1979). *Psychological characteristics of selected world leaders assessed at a distance.* Unpublished paper, Wesleyan University.

Winter, D. G. (1980). Measuring the motive patterns of southern Africa political leaders at a distance. *Political Psychology, 2,* 75–85.

Winter, D. G. (1987). Leader appeal, leader performance, and the motive profiles of leaders and followers: A study of American presidents and elections. *Journal of Personality and Social Psychology, 52,* 196–202.

Winter, D. G. (1988, July). What makes Jesse run? [Motives of the 1988 candidates]. *Psychology Today,* pp. 20ff.

Winter, D. G. (1990). *Inventory of motive scores of persons, groups, and societies measured at a distance.* Ann Arbor: University of Michigan Department of Psychology.

Winter, D. G. (1991). Measuring personality at a distance: Development of an integrated system for scoring motives in running text. In A. J. Stewart, J. M. Healy, Jr., and D. J. Ozer, (Eds.), *Perspectives in personality: Approaches to understanding lives.* London: Jessica Kingsley.

Winter, D. G., and Carlson, L. (1988). Using motive scores in the psychobiographical study of an individual: The case of Richard Nixon. *Journal of Personality, 56,* 75–102.

Winter, D. G., and Stewart, A. J. (1977). Content analysis as a method of studying political leaders. In M. G. Hermann (Ed.), *A psychological examination of political leaders* (pp. 27–61). New York: Free Press.

Winter, D. G., and Stewart, A. J (1978). The power motive. In H. London, and J. Exner (Eds.), *Dimensions of personality* (pp. 391–447). New York: Wiley.

Ziller, R. C., Stone, W. F., Jackson, R. M., and Terbovic, N. J. (1977). Self-other orientations and political behavior. In M. G. Hermann (Ed.), *A psychological examination of political leaders* (pp. 176–204). New York: Free Press.

Zullow, H. M., Oettingen, G., Peterson, C., and Seligman, M. E. P. (1988). Pessimistic explanatory style in the historical record: CAVing LBJ, presidential candidates, and East versus West Berlin. *American Psychologist, 43,* 673–682.

NOTES

1. Department of Psychology. University of Michigan. Ann Arbor, Michigan 48109.
2. Mershon Center, Ohio State University. Columbus, Ohio 43201.
3. Department of Psychiatry, University of Maryland School of Medicine. Baltimore, Maryland 21201.
4. Department of Political Science. Arizona State University. Tempe, Arizona 85281.
5. Parsons and Bales (1955) suggest that these two kinds of leaders reflect the even more basic distinction between "instrumental" and "expressive" functions.
6. We are grateful to David Schmidt (1990) for assembling this speech material, and to Janet E. Malley for scoring it. Malenkov, Andropov, and Chernenko were not included because they did not, as party leaders, give such a speech to a CPSU Congress. It is difficult to know whether Stalin's 1924 "Organizational Report," and even more, Lenin's 1918 "Political Report," can be properly compared with the later reports, which were given in a much different organizational setting and political

climate. For standardization purposes, however. they were included because it was desirable to use as large a sample as possible.

7. One final source of data can be used to estimate Gorbachev's motive profile. His December 7, 1988, speech to the United Nations, when compared with the average of John F. Kennedy's two United Nations addresses, shows similar achievement and affiliation motivation levels, and a much lower power motive. Compared with other American presidents, Kennedy's Inaugural Address was about average in achievement and very high in affiliation and power (see Winter, 1987). Assuming that Kennedy's UN speeches were really similar to his inaugural (for which we have standardized scores), this would at least suggest that Gorbachev is relatively high in affiliation and low in power.

8. These comparisons were made using Bush's inaugural scores and Gorbachev's interview scores ("IA" and "SS," respectively, in Table 7.4).

9. Tetlock and Boettger (1989) found that Gorbachev scores high on a different but related measure of integrative complexity. Tetlock also found (personal communication) that Bush scored low during his vice-presidential years, but has increased to moderate as president.

10. Barber (1977) argues the reverse: that active-negative presidents are power-driven, while active-positives want to achieve. Since his analysis refers to manifest actions and results, rather than to latent motives, there is no necessary conflict with the present results. In addition, Barber's use of "achievement" and "power" motives is probably different from the scoring definitions.

11. To illustrate: In response to the disarmingly simple question, "Why not the best?" that Jimmy Carter used as the title of his campaign autobiography, a seasoned politician can suggest several "realpolitik" answers: (1) because members of Congress, foreign leaders, and others with veto power may have different ideas about what *is* "best;" (2) because "the best" might not benefit powerful constituencies; (3) because getting to "the best" may involve delays and detours—a "Pilgrim's Progress" through the quagmire of politics; (4) because "the best" costs too much; and (5) because reaching "the best" requires reliance on lower-level officials who are themselves far from being "the best."

❧ PART EIGHT ❧

American Foreign Policy After the Bush Administration

This last section explores the current debate over the future direction of American foreign policy. The essay by Barry Posen makes the case for a sharp limit on American global strategic commitments and activities. Posen argues that the internationalist aspirations of both neoconservatives and liberals are not premised on realistic assessments of American power and their policies lead to dangers and mistakes. Posen advocates a strategy of "restraint" which entails eschewing efforts at global domination and hegemonic leadership in favor of a more modest agenda of national security.

G. John Ikenberry offers a liberal internationalist agenda for post-Bush foreign policy. The Bush administration's unilateralist orientation had the effect of eroding the institutional foundations upon which the United States exercised leadership in the postwar era. New policy challenges are emerging that require more intensive forms of international cooperation. The United States is uniquely positioned to bring countries together and rebuild the governance institutions of the global system. Liberal order building involves strengthening the frameworks of cooperation and stand-by capacities of allied states to cope with the diffuse, shifting, and uncertain security threats of the 21st century.

Derek Chollet and Tod Lindberg make the case for a values-based American foreign policy. In their view, the United States needs to remain a moral beacon for the world. This foreign policy is not only faithful to American ideas, it also advances the nation's interests. The Bush administration may have failed in specific policy areas but its emphasis on liberty and democracy should remain at the cutting edge of American leadership.

Robert Kagan sees a coming era of conflict between the Western democracies and rising "autocratic" challengers—most notably China and Russia. Americans may think that the end of the Cold War has ushered in an era of liberal dominance—a sort of "end of history" in which ideological challenges to Western liberal democracy vanish. But Kagan argues that this optimistic assessment of great power politics and the directionality of history is wrong. China and Russia may be capitalist states but they are nonetheless authoritarian states that are hostile to American-led liberal international order. Kagan argues that the United States needs to strengthen cooperation among the democracies and prepare for a growing divide between the West and the rising autocratic great powers.

ᔛ

The Case for Restraint

Barry R. Posen

Since the end of the Cold War, the American foreign policy establishment has gradually con-verged on a grand strategy for the United States. Republican and Democratic foreign policy experts now disagree little about the threats the United States faces and the remedies it should pursue. Despite the present consensus and the very great power of the United States, which mutes the consequences of even Iraq-scale blunders, a reconsideration of U.S. grand strategy seems inevitable as the costs of the current consensus mount—which they will. The current consensus strategy is unsustainable.

If we understand properly the current foreign policy consensus and review the four key forces affecting U.S. grand strategy, the contours of an alternative strategy will emerge. The alternative, a grand strategy of "restraint," recommends policies dramatically different from those to which we have grown accustomed not just since the end of the Cold War, but since its beginning.[1] The United States needs to be more reticent about the use of military force; more modest about the scope for political transformation within and among countries; and more distant politically and militarily from traditional allies. We thus face a choice between habit and sentiment on the one side, realism, and rationality on the other.

THE CONSENSUS

A state's grand strategy is its foreign policy elite's theory about how to produce national secu-rity. Security has traditionally encompassed the preservation of a nation's physical safety, the country's sovereignty and its territorial integrity, and its power position—the last being the necessary means to the first three. States have traditionally been willing to risk the safety of their people to protect sovereignty, territorial integrity, and power position. A grand strategy enumerates and prioritizes threats and adduces political and military remedies for them. A grand strategy also explains why some threats attain a certain priority, and why and how the remedies proposed could work.

Democratic and Republican strategists alike hold that the most imminent threats today are threats to U.S. safety. Terrorism, basically Islamist in origin, is the key problem. It is caused by something that is wrong with Arab society in particular, but also the societies of other Islamic countries such as Pakistan, Iran, and Afghanistan. "Rogue" states—with interests and forms of government different from our own, a willingness to use force and, in the worst case, an inclination to acquire nuclear weapons—are a closely related threat because they may assist terrorists. "Failed" states, and the identity politics that travels with them, are also a serious threat: They produce or nurture terrorists, and they produce human rights violations, refugees

---

Barry R. Posen, "The Case for Restraint," *The American Interest*, November/December 2007. Reprinted by permission.

and crime. Declining U.S. global influence relative to the rise of one or more peer competitors sometimes is recognized as an overarching threat, but this is construed to be a more distant problem.

Based on this threat analysis, the consensus therefore supports a U.S. grand strategy of international activism. The United States must remain the strongest military power in the world by a wide margin. It should be willing to use force—even preventively, if need be—on a range of issues. The United States should directly manage regional security relationships in any corner of the world that matters strategically, which seems increasingly to be every corner of the world. The risk that nuclear weapons could fall into the hands of violent non-state actors is so great that the United States should be willing to take extraordinary measures to keep suspicions countries possibly or even potentially in league with such actors from acquiring these weapons. Beyond uses of force, the United States should endeavor to change other societies so that they look more like ours. A world of democracies would be the safest for us, and we should be willing to pay considerable costs to produce such a world.

The key conceptual difference between the two political parties lies in attitudes toward international institutions: Democrats like and trust them; Republicans do not. Republicans accuse Democrats of a willingness to sacrifice U.S. sovereignty to these organizations. This is not the case. Democrats think that the great power of the United States will permit it to write the rules and dominate the outcomes in international institutions, thus producing a net gain in U.S. influence. Democrats accuse Republicans of not understanding this, especially of failing to appreciate the value of international legitimacy.

The Iraq war, meanwhile, has mainly produced only tactical arguments between the two parties. The most sustained critiques of the Bush Administration have centered on two issues: The poor quality of the intelligence on Iraq's weapons of mass destruction programs, and whether this was a result of honest error or political manipulation; and the Administration's bungling of the occupation and reconstruction efforts, and the subsequent counterinsurgency campaign. Though some Democratic Party leaders believe the war was launched on false pretenses, its current presidential front-runner, Hillary Clinton, has not repudiated her original support for the war. Though some Democratic Senators and Congressmen voted against the 2002 resolution permitting the use of force against Iraq, few party leaders argue forthrightly that Iraq could have and should have been contained and deterred rather than invaded, even had the intelligence on Iraq's weapons programs been correct. Advocates of a policy of containment and deterrence toward a potentially nuclear Iran are even harder to find.

Nor do Democrats assert that nation-, state-, and democracy-building in Iraq were always fools' errands; instead, they argue that it could and should have been done better. Even now, policy analysts connected to the Democratic Party offer implausible and internally contradictory schemes to get the United States out of Iraq while keeping the United States in Iraq.[2] We do not have a debate on the deep foundations of grand strategy in the U.S. mainstream today. Instead, we loudly dispute only those matters that lie close to the surface.

FOUR FACTS

Since the Cold War ended, the United States has been affected by four important facts: the great concentration of capability in the United States relative to other consequential powers, a condition often shorthanded as "unipolarity"; the re-emergence of identity politics, especially amalgams of religion and ethno-nationalism, as the key ideational foundations of modern domestic and, to a lesser extent, international political conflict; the diffusion of power—especially military power—to nominally weak states and to non-state actors alike; and, finally, globalization.

These four facts each have discrete effects on the international environment, but they also interact. The consequences of their interaction have been costly to the United States and will likely continue to be so. Put simply, the great power of the United States has proved a constant temptation to action for policymakers, even as the other three factors have combined to increase the costs of U.S. action.

Unipolarity. By almost every reasonable measure the United States emerged from the Cold War as one of the most powerful states in history. Its population exceeded that of any other great or middle power except China and India, and has continued to grow. Its GDP was (and remains) two or three times that of its closest economic competitor. Even after post-Cold War reductions, U.S. military spending exceeded the combined defense budgets of most of the other large powers in the world; today it exceeds the defense spending of the rest of the entire world combined. U.S. military technology sets the world standard; its strategic nuclear and conventional forces are peerless. The United States had (and retains) command of the global commons—the sea, the air and space—and U.S. technical capabilities for intelligence collection far eclipse those of any other state. (Indeed, the U.S. intelligence budget alone has roughly equaled the *entire* defense budgets of Britain or France, two of the world's most capable military powers, and the only Ones other than the United States with any global reach.)

The United States also enjoyed (and still enjoys) a favorable geographical position—with weak and friendly neighbors to the north and south, oceans to the east and west. The Cold War network of global alliances, coupled with massive investments in strategic lift, gave the U.S. military the ability to put large forces almost anywhere there is a coastline. In 1991, five U.S. divisions reached Saudi Arabia in four months, and nearly ten in six months.

Additionally, the collapse of Soviet power, and the all-but-rhetorical abandonment of communist principles of economic, social and political organization in China, left Western elites, especially in the United States, with a feeling of ideological triumph. Democracy and capitalism had won the great ideological struggle of the 20 century, and it was easy to suppose that all that was left were mopping-up operations. Other nation-states would easily find their way to our way: History, if it wasn't "over," was certainly on our side.

These enormous strengths masked certain weaknesses, however, U.S. active ground forces have been relatively small since conscription was abandoned at the end of the Vietnam War.

The all-volunteer ground forces of the United States shrunk quickly from their end-of-Cold War peak of nearly a million, reaching 470,000 in the Army and a bit under 170,000 in the Marines in 2001. By comparison, the United States had 440,000 soldiers and marines in Vietnam in 1969, out of a total personnel strength of nearly two million.

Even with the 92,000-soldier increase now pledged by Republicans and Democrats alike, U.S. ground forces will remain small. It is difficult to maintain more than a third of a professional ground force in combat at any one time without suffering acute retention, recruitment and training problems. The United States now has roughly half of its forces deployed, and this is widely understood to be unsustainable. The demands of the Iraq war have essentially swallowed the Army and Marines over the past five years, and other possible U.S. adversaries dwarf Iraq in population—Iran is nearly three times as populous, Pakistan nearly six times.

The U.S. national security establishment, to include the intelligence agencies and the State Department, also remains short of individuals who understand other countries and their cultures. It lacks sufficient numbers of analysts, diplomats, advisors, and intelligence agents for the array of global engagement opportunities it has taken up. It also seems to lack the domestic political capacity to generate sufficient non-military material resources to support its foreign policy. Whether foreign economic assistance is money well spent or not, the United States has a difficult time generating these funds. In a more general sense, the American public has been trained by its politicians to be chary of taxes. So the U.S. government has financed much of its security effort since September 11, 2001 with borrowed money. Even obvious security-related taxes, such as a tax on gasoline to discourage consumption and thus help wean the United States off imported oil, find no political sponsors.

Identity Politics

Aside from Saddam Hussein's attempted smash-and-grab robbery of Kuwait, the most troublesome conflicts of the post-Cold War world have been internal and have centered on identity politics. For the U.S. military this included Desert Storm's unhappy postscript in the Kurdish and Shi'a rebellions in northern and southern Iraq, respectively, and civil wars in Somalia, Bosnia, and Kosovo. The United States eschewed military intervention to stop the Rwanda genocide, but those in the Clinton Administration who made this decision all regret it deeply, and most critics of this policy believe with unwarranted certainty that such an intervention would have been easy and successful.

The U.S. approach to all of these conflicts bore certain similarities rooted in U.S. liberalism, which exalts in the rational calculating individual and thus underestimates the power of group loyalty. The United States was usually surprised by one or more of the following: the outbreak of conflict itself, the extent of group ambitions, the ferocity of the violence, the intensity of group loyalties, and the cost and duration of any U.S. military intervention. This myopia crossed party lines: Most Republican security strategists have been as confounded by the bloody, stubborn, and resilient identity politics of Iraq as the Clinton Administration was in Somalia, Rwanda, Bosnia, and Kosovo.

But why? Academic disputes aside, there is enough of an historical pattern of association between identity politics and violence that U.S. policymakers should know to take nationalism and religion seriously, both as immediate causes of violence and as key ingredients sustaining military capability and armed resistance—particularly in periods of political and economic insecurity,

The Diffusion of Power

The diffusion of power, especially of military capacity, is the third important trend of the last twenty years. Though the United States faces few if any plausible competitors in the open oceans or space, or even in the air at medium and high altitudes, states and groups have learned how to tilt with the Americans using the advantages of their home turf. Ruthless, committed and skilled Somalis, Iraqis, Afghans and miscellaneous al-Qaeda fighters have fought U.S. forces directly; they seldom "win," but they do make the Americans pay. Somali, Iraqi and al-Qaeda air-defense gunners have shot down dozens of U.S. helicopters, mainly with heavy machine guns and rocket-propelled grenades. Serb SAM operators using mainly 1970s technology shot down few U.S. aircraft, but so complicated U.S. air operations that most Serb ground forces in Kosovo survived the 1999 air campaign.

At the same time, the ability to manufacture such relatively low-tech weapons has spread. Simple long-range artillery rockets and more complex anti-ship missiles manufactured in Iran turned up in the hands of Hizballah in the summer 2006 war with Israel. According to the U.S. government, components of "Explosively Formed Penetrators" (EFPs), off-route, anti-armored-vehicle mines discovered in Iraq were manufactured and supplied by Iran—which surely has more sophisticated versions of the same weapons on the other side of the border. Iran is also one of the world's largest producers of new warheads for the ubiquitous Soviet-designed RPG-7 rocket-propelled grenade launcher. More ominously, Iranian arms exporters now offer night-vision devices for sale. If they work, a presumed U.S. area of great tactical superiority in infantry combat will soon wane.

More important than the proliferation of moderately sophisticated conventional weapons is the apparent spread of military expertise. The combination of good-enough conventional weapons, large numbers of committed young men, proven tactics and competent training, cleverly adapted to urban, suburban, and rural environments that favor infantry, has inflicted meaningful combat costs on high-technology U.S. ground forces. Costs get even higher if the United States or other Western forces intend to settle into other countries to reform their politics, and are thus forced into long counterinsurgency campaigns.

Globalization

Globalization is the final trend complicating U.S. foreign and security policy. I define globalization as the spread of capitalism across the globe along with the intensification of international trade and the diffusion of manufacturing, investment and finance. Globalization is enabled by the crumbling of old political barriers and by the continuing improvements in all modes of transportation for goods and people. The IT revolution, too, has made low-cost, high-bandwidth communications possible on a global scale.

Globalization has largely been embraced by U.S. business and political elites as a good thing. Certainly it offers economic opportunity to many formerly excluded from most of the benefits of modernity, and it seems to explain the vast abatement in acute poverty over the past dozen years. Bur all this opportunity and change come with a cost, and not for the first time.

The intensification of industrial capitalism in the late 19th century mobilized large numbers of people for politics by disrupting their traditional ways of life, drawing them into cities, subjecting them to the new insecurities of industrial capitalism, and exposing them to regular, intense political communication. Globalization is now having similar effects in many heretofore unperturbed parts of the world. Those socially mobilized for politics in the late 19th century became vulnerable to the appeals of nationalists, communists and fascists, all of whom offered simple and powerful ideologies of solidarity and inclusion in times of economic and political uncertainty. Estimates of population growth and urbanization over the next several decades suggest that the developing world will see a steady supply of urbanized citizens at the lower end of the income scale. Most will experience acute economic and personal insecurity at the same time that modern technology opens them to intense mass communications, and simultaneously permits small independent groups to communicate directly with large numbers of people. These individuals will seek political protection and participation, and will be vulnerable to political mobilization on the basis of identity politics. The governments of many developing countries are bound to have a hard time keeping up with these demands, so that political entrepreneurs will find fertile ground for appeals based on the resurrection of supposedly traditional values.

Globalization adds some new complications to these old processes. The intensity of international trade and investment makes it easy for political entrepreneurs to blame foreigners for local problems. The enhanced ability to communicate and travel makes it possible for like-minded groups in different countries to find each other, and to organize and cooperate.

To the generic problems posed by globalization must be added the peculiar tinder of the Arab world. There pan-Arab and Islamic identities overlap in 22 countries with a combined population of more than 200 million. Population growth and urbanization proceed apace but economic growth lags, and the political organization of these countries leaves vast numbers bereft of any sense of control over their destinies. The oil wealth of some Arab countries, compared with the poverty of others, fuels resentment. Oil and gas also bring the interests and presence of the great powers to the region, especially the United States. The emergence of an economically and militarily successful Westernized Jewish liberal democracy—Israel—in their midst serves both as a focus of identity politics and a reminder of the extent of Arab political failure in the postwar independence era. Macro-level economic and technological forces and specifically regional characteristics thus combine to create fertile ground in the Arab world for extremists hostile to existing international political and economic systems.

These four facts have interacted to draw the United States into costly national security policies that produce new problems faster than they can solve old ones. The great concentration of power in the United States skews the American security-policy debate toward activism. If the global distribution of power were more equal, U.S. policymakers would have to be more cautious about the projects they choose. The existence of a peer competitor would inject into the U.S. policy debate a persistent question: Will this project help or hurt our ability to deter or contain X? Moreover, it is tempting to imagine that with this much power, the United States could organize a safe world, once and for all—where the United States would remain the acknowledged military and ideological leader.

Whatever else it may achieve, U.S. activism is bound to discomfit other states. The great preponderance of U.S. power makes direct opposition to the United States difficult and dangerous, but other states are doing what they can to put themselves in a better position. Some fear U.S. freedom of action, worry about the possibility of being drawn into policies inimical to their interests, and so wish to distance themselves from the United States—even as they free-ride within the broader U.S. security umbrella. The European Union has gradually strengthened its military capabilities so that it can get along without the United States if it must. Others fear that U.S. policies will harm their interests indirectly, and look for ways to concert their power, as Russia and China have done in the Shanghai Cooperation Organization. Still others expect U.S. attentions to be directed straight at them, and so they seek to improve their abilities to deter U.S. military action or fight the United States directly if they must. North Korea and Iran pursue nuclear weapons for those purposes. Iran also has developed a conventional capability to inflict costs on U.S. forces in the Gulf and has been implicated in inflicting such costs in Iraq. To the extent that the United States continues its current activist policy path, these reactions will continue and will slowly increase the costs of future U.S. activism. They will also reduce the propensity of others to share these costs.

American activism also interacts with globalization to provoke negative reactions to the United States. Insofar as the U.S. economy is the largest and most dynamic in the world, the forces associated with globalization—trade, global supply chains, investment, travel and communications—are often associated with the United States by those experiencing the downside consequences. Not only does an activist foreign and security policy make the United States the most obvious unkind face of globalization, political entrepreneurs in the developing world will find it expedient to attribute the difficulties experienced by their target populations to the actions of the United States. When U.S. activism turns to direct military intervention in the affairs of other countries, local political leaders can rely on the most elemental of forces: nationalism.

Increased opportunities for travel and communications have enabled transnational groups, particularly al-Qaeda, to organize against the United States. They can mobilize people politically without one-to-one contact. Given populations of hundreds of millions, these organizations do not need a high conversion rate to sustain themselves. They need only produce sympathy on a large enough scale to provide an environment from which relatively modest material and human resources can be collected.

Al-Qaeda and other similar, but less ambitious, groups have also professionalized the training of their soldiers and terrorist operatives. They learn from one another, adapt to local circumstances, and profit from the more general availability of weaponry. The ease of international travel and trade allows human and material resources to be shifted rapidly from place to place. This turns U.S. interventions into opportunities for transnational anti-system groups like al-Qaeda to assist local resistance movements and to harness the power of nationalism and politicized religion to their more diffuse but still distinctly anti-American agenda.

The activist U.S. grand strategy currently preferred by the national security establishment in both patties thus has a classically tragic quality about it. Enabled by its great power, and fearful of the negative energies and possibilities engendered by globalization, the United States has tried to get its arms around the problem: It has essentially sought more control. But the very act of seeking more control injects negative energy into global politics as quickly as it finds enemies to vanquish. It prompts states to balance against U.S. power however they can, and it prompts peoples to imagine that the United States is the source of all their troubles.

Iraq should therefore be seen not as a singular debacle, but as a harbinger of costs to come. There is enough capacity and motivation out in the world to increase significantly the costs of any U.S. effort to manage global politics directly. Public support for this policy may wane before profligacy so diminishes U.S. power that it becomes unsustainable. But it would be unwise to count on it.

A STRATEGY OF RESTRAINT

If more activism has not produced better policy, what is to be done? The United States should try doing less: It should pursue a grand strategy of restraint. Less is not nothing, however, meaning in essence that the United States should conceive ways to *shape* rather than to *control* international politics.

We can well afford to think this way because extant threats to the United States are not threats to U.S. sovereignty. The country is in no danger of conquest or intimidation from those more powerful. U.S. territorial integrity is secure. The power position of the United States is excellent; any power position that allows a country to even think about running the world ought to provide ample capability for defense. Protecting this power position is an important goal, but direct action is the wrong way to go about it. If regional powers grow strong enough to threaten their neighbors—and perhaps ultimately threaten the United States—local actors will wish to balance that power. The United States should preserve an ability to help out if necessary, but it should be stingy in this regard. Others should get organized and dig into their own pockets before the United States shows up to help. U.S. command of the sea, air and space enables such assistance, but, coupled with a favorable geographic position, it also permits the United States to wait. This capability should cast a stabilizing shadow in any case.

Today the most imminent U.S. security problem has to do not with conquest or intimidation but safety. Here, at least, the consensus view is correct. The main discrete threat is al-Qaeda, but if the foregoing analysis is right, there are deeper forces feeding that organization than its interpretation of religious texts. These forces could give rise to other violent organizations. In other words, al-Qaeda is not *the* problem, but a particularly threatening example of a condition of global disorder and disaffection capable of giving rise to numerous such groups, Islamist, and otherwise. This condition is the problem, which American power and actions over the years have done a good deal, albeit inadvertently, to cause, but cannot now easily or by themselves redress.

This threat should not be minimized, but neither should it be exaggerated. Al-Qaeda is ruthless, persistent and creative. It and other groups yet to form will retain the ability to kill tens and hundreds if not occasionally thousands with materials already at hand. This will not bring down the United States, however, and it would be wise to stop suggesting to these groups that it can. If such groups get their hands on a nuclear weapon and use it, our costs obviously go much higher, but even then the United States would still go on. Its soldiers and agents will hunt down the perpetrators and whoever helped them, no matter how long it takes. Public repetition of this promise may assist in deterrence, and a single effective execution after the fact may contribute to the deterrence of subsequent attacks. That is obvious, but still unsettling. Discomfort with punishment after the fact leads policy makers to consider preventive war against new nuclear weapons states for fear that they will give nuclear weapons to terrorists, or simply lose them. But a rich and capable country that asks its citizens to commit hundreds of billions of dollars annually to defense ought to be able to come up with a better answer than an open-ended series of costly preventive wars.

Two strategies have been suggested to take on al-Qaeda. The Bush Administration has pursued the first: an expansive strategy of direct offensive action. Its priorities, however, have been bizarre. It appropriately first went after al-Qaeda and its immediate friends in Afghanistan, but before finishing the job quickly turned to Saddam Hussein and Iraq, dubious future allies of al-Qaeda. By the U.S. intelligence community's own admission, the respite allowed al-Qaeda to recover.

Moreover, the United States has squandered one relatively constant factor that should work in its favor. Al-Qaeda's very nature condemns it to theatrical terrorist attacks against innocent people, and such attacks have a way of alienating potential supporters. By overstressing offensive action in Iraq, and in particular by occupying an Arab country, the United States has added credence to the al-Qaeda story in the Arab world, and done a terrible job of telling its own.

After September 11, I suggested a second strategy—more defensive than offensive and more precisely directed at al-Qaeda.[3] We should seek to draw as many other states as possible into the effort, while avoiding adding new facts to the jihadi narrative. The United States needs to reduce, not increase, its presence within the abode of Islam. The U.S. military should abandon permanent and semi-permanent land bases in Arab countries, and generally lower the profile of its military and security cooperation with Arab states. The fight against al-Qaeda should continue, but it should be conducted in the world of intelligence. Cooperation with foreign intelligence and police agencies comes first, but the U.S. intelligence community may need to engage in direct action from time to time. To the extent that the United States has interests in the Arab world that can only be pursued with old-fashioned military power, such as the possible need to defend Arab states from Iranian expansionism, the United States should rely on its massive power-projection capabilities. The U.S. military should be "over the horizon."

Politically, the United States needs projects in the developing world that are consistent with U.S. values and that permit the United States to look like the "good guy." Three steps commend themselves. First, the United States should build on the experience of Operation Unified Assistance, which provided prompt relief to victims of the Indian Ocean tsunami of December 26, 2004. The remarkable power-projection capability of the U.S. military provides an inherent capability to get into many major natural disaster areas "first with the most." Assistance rendered by the U.S. military in the early desperate days after the disaster brought fairly dramatic political results, not least in Indonesia. Disasters happen, and the United States can gain significant political respect for helping victims dig out of them. And in contrast to peacekeeping and peace-enforcement operations, which for many have the same purpose, natural-disaster relief has a natural exit strategy.

Second, instead of focusing on the export of democracy, which we lack sufficient cause-effect knowledge to accomplish in any case, let us recommend practices that will allow others to find their own way to democracy—or at least to more benign forms of government. The United States should therefore make itself a voice for the rule of law, for press freedom and for the rights of collective bargaining, not just or mainly for democracy.

Third, the United States should be willing to assist in humanitarian interventions, but under reasonable guidelines. The most important guideline is to avoid overselling the prospective results to the American people. When the United States is about to engage in armed philanthropy, it should not disguise the effort as the pursuit of a security interest. If the latter is required to sell the policy, then the policy is already in trouble. Once characterized as a security interest, the U.S. Congress and the public expect that the United States will lead the fight; that decisive military means will be employed; and that victory will be achieved—all of which raises U.S. military and political costs. Instead, the United States should only engage in armed philanthropy in coalitions, operating under some kind of regional or international political mandate. The United States should not insist on leadership; indeed, it should avoid it whenever possible. On the whole, too, the United States should offer logistical rather than direct combat assets.

The United States must also develop a more measured view of the risks of nuclear proliferation. Without the promiscuous use of preventive war, it will not be possible to stop all possible new nuclear weapons programs. Nuclear weapons are no longer mysterious, but neither are they easy to get. It is costly and technically difficult to produce fissionable material in quantities sufficient for nuclear weapons, and only a few countries can do it. It has taken a good bit of time for those smaller states who wished to develop nuclear weapons to get them. Though an imperfect regime, the Nuclear Non-Proliferation Treaty and the International

Atomic Energy Agency do provide obstacles to the development of nuclear weapons, and some early warning that mischief is afoot. Good intelligence work can provide more warning, and well-crafted intelligence operations could presumably slow the diffusion of nuclear know-how, and even the progress of national nuclear programs, if need be.

It is worthwhile to keep proliferation relatively costly and slow because other states require time to adapt to such events, and extra time would be useful to explain to new nuclear powers the rules of the game they are entering. U.S. policy makers feel compelled to trumpet that all options, including force, are on the table when dealing with "rogue" state proliferators. True enough: The United States is a great military power and on vital security matters its forces can never be off the table. But preventive war must never become either a casual or a default policy choice. It has serious and probably enduring political costs, which the United States need not incur. Deterrence is still a better-strategy.

The United States is a great nuclear power and should remain so. Against possible new nuclear powers such as North Korea or Iran, U.S. capabilities are superior in every way. In contrast to the Cold War competition with the Soviet Union, where neither country would have survived a nuclear exchange, it is clear which nation would survive such an exchange between the United States and North Korea or Iran. Indeed, these states should be made to worry that they will be vulnerable to preemptive nuclear attacks by the United States in the unhappy event that they attempt to make nuclear threats over important issues. Similarly, new nuclear states ought not to be encouraged through loose talk to believe that they can give nuclear weapons to others to use on the United States and somehow free themselves of the risks of U.S. retaliation. Clear deterrent statements and strong nuclear forces are preferable to preventive war, because deterrence is both a more credible and more sustainable policy.

ENCOURAGE RESPONSIBILITY

Finally, U.S. security guarantees and security assistance tend to relieve others of the need to do more to ensure their own security, and they often ironically enable others to pursue policies that are unhelpful to the United States. The United States should stop offering such guarantees and assistance. A U.S. strategy of restraint must include a coherent, integrated and patient effort to encourage its long-time wards to look after themselves. If others do more, this will not only save U.S. resources, it will increase the political salience of other countries in the often bitter discourse over globalization. If other consequential powers benefit as much from globalization as does the United States, they should share ownership of its political costs. If others need to pay more for their security, they will think harder about their choices.

Virtually all existing U.S. international relationships need to be rethought in this light. Policy changes must be implemented as a package to produce the desired effect, but it would not be prudent to launch these policies overnight. A governing rule should be *not* to shift positions so rapidly or decisively that altered regional politics open windows of vulnerability or opportunity that either tempt or compel military action. Three examples will serve to suggest the magnitude of the changes I have in mind: NATO, Israel and Japan.

The effort to preserve and expand NATO, a project aimed at ensuring U.S. power and influence in Eurasia, enabled the excessive draw-down of some European military capabilities, notably those of Germany and Italy, and deflected possible improvements in European and EU military capacities. This also has had the effect of allowing EU members to postpone decisions about how to integrate Turkey into Europe: They can merely consign this task to NATO and the United States. The United States should develop a ten-year plan to turn NATO into a more traditional political alliance. During this decade, U.S. forces should gradually withdraw from all military headquarters and commands in Europe, which could migrate to the EU if Europeans still find them useful.

U.S. military assistance to Israel makes the occupation of the territories relatively inexpensive for Israeli political leaders, and implicates the United States in the deed. This may not be "central" to U.S. problems in the Arab world, as so many insist, but it certainly does not help. The United States should therefore develop a ten-year plan to reduce U.S. government direct financial assistance to Israel to zero. Israel is now a prosperous country that happens to be surrounded by military powers lacking any capacity to conquer it. Two of these countries, Egypt and Jordan, have peace treaties with Israel, and the rest have no possible superpower patron to back them with new supplies of modern conventional offensive weapons. Israel has to decide on the merits, and within its own sovereign capacities, how much the occupied territories matter to its security, and how to allocate security spending accordingly.

Israel is not an enemy of the United States and will not become one: friendly relations should continue. Israel should be permitted to purchase spare parts for existing U.S. military equipment and new military equipment to the extent necessary to ensure a regional military balance conducive to peace. To ensure that the reduction of military assistance to Israel is perceived as fair in American politics, and to ensure against the creation of any windows of vulnerability or opportunity, U.S. assistance to Egypt should be put on the same diet, with due allowance for Egypt's comparative poverty. The United States should also practice restraint in all its arms sales to the region and encourage others to do the same. If other states attempt to disrupt the regional military balance, the United States can reconsider these decisions, and should make clear that it would not hesitate to do so.

The United States also needs to reconsider its security relationship with Japan. The current relationship allows Japan to avoid the domestic political debate necessary to determine a new role for itself in Asia. In particular, it allows Japan to avoid coming to terms with its own past and relieves it of the necessity to develop diplo-matic strategies to make it more "alliance worthy" in Asia. The modalities of a change in the alliance with Japan are trickier than they are in Europe because Asia is a more unsettled place due to China's rapid economic expansion and concomitant military improvements. Nevertheless, change is in order.

Since the end of the Cold War 16 years ago, Bill Clinton and George W. Bush have been running an experiment with U.S. grand strategy. The theory to be tested has been this: Very good intentions, plus very great power, plus action can transform both international policies and the domestic politics of other states in ways that are advantageous to the United States, and at costs it can afford. The evidence is in: The experiment has failed. Transformation is unachievable, and costs are high.

The United States needs now to test a different grand strategy: It should conceive its security interests narrowly, use its military power stingily, pursue its enemies quietly but persistently; share responsibilities and costs more equitably, watch and wait mote patiently. Let's do this for 16 years and see if the outcomes aren't better.

Francis Fukuyama

I find myself agreeing with Barry Posen's outline for a strategy of "restraint" much more than I expected. We are at an important juncture in the history of American foreign policy, at the denouement of a disastrous war that has undermined American prestige and poisoned our relations with much of the world. There are many efforts to define a "not-Bush" foreign policy, but Posen is right that both Democrats and Republicans are stuck in frameworks left over from the Cold War, and that the present situation begs for a more radical rethinking of many of the premises on which U.S. foreign policy has been based. While I agree with much of the logic of his analysis, however, his specific suggestions for how to implement "restraint" in policy are very unrealistic and need to be reformulated if they are to carry weight in the policy debate.

The central driver of American policy since September 11, 2001 is an overestimation of the threat posed both by al-Qaeda, and by rogue state proliferators like Iraq, Iran and North Korea. These two kinds of threats were, incidentally, quite distinct, but were deliberately amalgamated in the Bush Administration's effort to sell the Iraq war. Posen hits it exactly right in saying that while both of them pose serious problems, they do not pose the kind of apocalyptic challenges to our way of life that earlier totalitarian threats did. We answered the post-September 11 question—"Why do they hate us?"—too readily with the response that they "hate us for what we are," or they "hate freedom." In fact, a great deal of anti-Americanism in the Middle East is generated by the way we have inserted ourselves into that region, and it will die down if we assume a lower profile.

The four factors Posen cites as changing the nature of the environment we face—unipolarity, identity politics, the diffusion of power and globalization—all make, as he argues, the present world rather different from that of the 1914-89 period. And he is indubitably right about the underlying point, that America is not nearly as powerful as it thinks it is, and therefore is unlikely to succeed in its ambitious plans to transform global politics through a hyper-activist policy.

I would emphasize, perhaps, a somewhat different set of factors than the military ones Posen cites. One of the things that makes the arc from North Africa through the Middle East and on into Central Asia so difficult to deal with is not just identity politics and the diffusion of military power, but state weakness in places like Palestine, Lebanon, Sudan, Somalia, Iraq, Afghanistan and Pakistan. State weakness means that conventional military power, which was the coin of the realm in 20th century power politics, is much less usable. We cannot coerce these states into doing things they are incapable of doing, like cracking down on armed militias, sealing borders or chasing terrorists in a way that would be possible with strong states. What we need is stronger and more capable governments, but for now we have few tools or usable concepts for how to get them. So even if the United States had significantly larger military forces, it would still be unable to use them effectively to achieve the political goals it sets for itself.

Globalization also works differently than Posen suggests. As Josef Joffe noted in *Überpower* (2006), the countries that have most successfully integrated into the global economy (for example, China and India) are among the least anti-American countries in the world. It is

Francis Fukuyama *is Bernard I. Schwartz Professor of International Political Economy at the Paul H, Nitze School of Advanced International Studies, Johns Hopkins University, and chairman of the editorial hoard of* The American Interest.

those that get left behind by globalization, or those that can't cope with globalization's substantial political challenges, that feel the most resentful. It is above all the lack of reciprocity in levels of influence between the United States and much of the rest of the world that creates a high level of structural anti-Americanism, a fact we need to get used to, for it's not going away anytime soon.

Two of Posen's specific suggestions for how to implement "restraint" seem to me particularly unrealistic. Ending all aid to Israel over a ten-year period is a political non-starter. Whether one could justify this in theory is irrelevant; it simply isn't going to happen, and particularly will not happen if not put in the context of some conditionality that links aid to progress in the peace process.

The second problematic analysis concerns Japan. It is the nationalist Right in Japan that argues that the United States is an unreliable ally. Reducing our commitment to them will not force them to come to terms with historical issues; it will drive them to acquire nuclear weapons and adopt a much more confrontational posture with regard to Korea and China.

"Restraint" in current circumstances can also be interpreted very differently from the Posen approach. Restraint may mean no big destabilizing shifts in American behavior. The United States has undermined political order in an important part of the world over the past few years because it was overly activist in a clumsy and incompetent way. While we can afford to pull back in Iraq and other places, we risk destabilizing the world if we move too quickly to reduce our core international commitments. It might be fine to think in terms of ten-year adjustment periods, but not to announce them in advance.

Josef Joffe

Barry Posen's essay essentially boils down JLJ to a grand strategy of nuclear isolationism. Nuclear weapons are indeed an isolationist's dream. As Robert W. Tucker correctly noted a quarter century ago: As long as they are "deployed only in the direct defense of the homeland, they confer a physical security that is virtually complete, and that the loss of allies cannot alter."

But for a great power, alas, there is more to security than just the physical ability to stave off invasion and defeat. Great powers seek order beyond their borders, and rightly so, because they have other vital interests. Protecting critical allies is such a vital interest. First, because it preserves influence. Second, precisely because U.S. guarantees relieve allies of the need to protect themselves, such "extended security" builds regional order by inhibiting intra-area rivalry and arms-racing. We don't really want an unrestrained arms race between China and Japan in the Pacific, do we? Or between Israel and Egypt.

Another vital interest grows from a precautionary principle. Posen not only wants to retract the U.S. umbrella from Japan and Germany, or from Israel and Egypt; he also wants the United States to quit the Middle East. This requires faith in a sanguine assumption: that this region stretching from Beirut to Kandahar is capable of balancing itself. It never has been able to do so, as the strife-torn post-Ottoman history of this area demonstrates. It has always required an outside balancer.

Nor is the Middle East like Vietnam or Somalia, which could be safely abandoned. It is the strategic arena of the 21st century, replete with allies who must be sheltered and enemies

Josef Joffe *is publisher-editor of the German news weekly Die Zeit and a member of the executive committee of the AI editorial board. He is also a fellow of Stanford University's Hoover Institution.*

who must be chastened. Hence, whatever the fate of the U.S. presence in Iraq, bases will have to be kept: informal ones like Haifa, formal ones like Qatar, Oman and Kuwait. In fact, in the penultimate moment of truth with Iran, all of Israel will be one big stationary aircraft carrier for the United States. Let's add a "minor" item like oil and gas—strategic resources par excellence, whose flow will not be regulated by market forces alone, as the Russians and Chinese so well understand.

So "hands off" and "over the horizon"—Great Britain's historical recipe, plus nukes—will not add up to a post-Iraq grand strategy, Especially since Britain's behind was twice saved by the United States—when Albion so grievously miscalculated the European balance of power in the first and third decades of the century. But who will save the American posterior once the chickens of aloofness come home to roost? A great power must carry great burdens, or it stops being one.

Walter Russell Mead

Barry Posen puts his fingers on some of the classic and enduring tensions in American foreign policy and makes a strong, Jeffersonian case for a grand strategy based on restraint. However, given the multiplicity of actors in the American foreign policy process and the conflicting perspectives and interests that they bring to the political process, it seems unlikely to me that his vision will prevail. American policy is likely to remain more interventionist than Posen would like, in part because too many Americans have too many convictions and interests that seek a more engaged and activist America. In part, too, American policy is likely to remain more activist and engaged because developments in a tumultuous world will cry out for American engagement.

That engagement will not always be wise or well planned. We will often not like the consequences of the engagements we undertake, either. But from the early 20th century when the British world system began to fray at the edges, the pattern of world history has been that the United States, despite the hunger of many of its citizens and of its foreign policy intellectuals for a quiet life, has been drawn over and over again into a series of engagements because the consequences of disengagement seem unacceptable.

That is likely to remain the case in coming decades, particularly so in Asia. In a short paper, Posen cannot present a full picture of his views on the unfolding Asian order, but his recommendation (that the United States "reconsider its security relationship with Japan") covers only a very short stretch of a very large waterfront. Responding to the rising power of China and India (or responding to the failure of one or both to rise and to stabilize) is a big job. A new Asian framework has to be created, and while the United States neither can nor should seek to control this development, Asia is unlikely to find a stable geopolitical framework without a great deal of American engagement: political, military and economic.

It is likely that U.S. involvement with Africa will also deepen in coming decades. Energy needs and investments will entangle the United States with the fate of Nigeria and other West African states; the rise of African Christianity and the growing political, cultural and moral ties between American Christians and their African counterparts is likely to add to the strong currents that already favor deeper American commitment to the economic, social and political development of this emerging but still troubled continent.

Walter Russell Mead *is the Henry A. Kissinger Senior Fellow for U.S. Foreign Policy at the Council on Foreign Relations and a member of the executive committee of the AT editorial board.*

The engagement of the American people with the rest of the world is going to continue to deepen and grow. Economic, religious, humanitarian, social and political engagements and commitments made by American business, American religious groups, secular civil society organizations, and the need for closer intergovernmental coordination over a variety of transnational issues continually press American foreign policy toward a closer engagement than Jeffersonians want; this is unlikely to change any time soon.

Niall Ferguson

Those of who have been attempting for some years to have a "debate on the deep foundations of [American] grand strategy," not only in the academy but also in the press and on television, have evidently been wasting our energy. According to Barry Posen, this debate has remained outside "the U.S. mainstream today." If by the "mainstream" he means *The Oprah Winfrey Show*, he may well be right. But I, for one, have been writing about the limits of American power since before September 11, 2001 in the *New York Times,* the *Los Angeles Times* and the *Wall Street Journal*, not to mention *The Atlantic* and the *New Republic*. It would be easy to list at least a dozen other writers who have addressed the mismatch between the goals of American foreign policy and the means at the disposal of any administration, and who have suggested alternative strategies. Few, if any, have failed to recommend restraint in some form or another.

Where Posen is certainly right is that the current crop of leading American politicians are reluctant to debate grand strategy. Just as it was mandatory during the Cold War for those seeking elective office to denounce Soviet Communism, so too, since the terrorist attacks of September 11, 2001, has it been politically risky to question the proposition that the United States faces an existential threat from Islamist terrorism, and from "rogue" and "failed" states that supposedly sponsor them.

There is, however, an exception whom Posen overlooks. At least one candidate for the presidency has urged Americans to "get back to the place we were, where terrorists are not the focus of our lives, but they're a nuisance" comparable with prostitution, illegal gambling and other forms of organized crime. He says his aim is "to reduce it" to a level where it isn't on the rise, "isn't threatening peoples lives every day, and isn't threatening the fabric of your life." If he were elected, he insists he would do a better job of cutting off financing, exposing terrorist groups, working cooperatively across the globe, improving our intelligence capabilities nationally and internationally, training our military and deploying them differently, specializing in special forces and special ops, working with allies and, most importantly, "restoring America's reputation as a country that listens, is sensitive, brings people to our side, is the seeker of peace, not war, and that uses our high moral ground and high-level values to augment us in the war on terror, not to diminish us." If all that sounds rather familiar to readers of Barry Posen's piece, it is because it is essentially Posen's prescription. The candidate in question is of course John Kerry. And all the quotations above are taken from an interview he gave to Matt Bai less than a month before the 2004 election.[4] No prizes for guessing why no current presidential candidate is using that kind of language: Appeals to pragmatism failed last time around.

Posen asserts that there is a cross-party consensus in favor of "a U.S. grand strategy of international activism." Democrats, he suggests, differ from Republicans only with respect to

---

Niall Ferguson *is Laurence A. Tisch Professor of History at Harvard University and a senior fellow of Stanford University's Hoover Institution.*

tactics. Indeed, he follows Andrew Bacevich in tracing this consensus back to before 9/11.[5] Ever since the end of the Cold War, he argues, the United States has been trying to "transform both international politics and the domestic politics of other states in ways that are advantageous to the United States." He shares my own view, advanced more than three years ago, that American leaders have exaggerated the power they wield by attaching too much importance to their unrivalled economic and military resources. In *Colossus: The Rise and Fall of the American Empire* (2004), I pointed to three deficits that fundamentally limited the resources the United States could actually deploy on regime-changing or nation-building campaigns: the financial deficit, the manpower deficit and the electorate's attention deficit. Posen makes similar points. He is certainly not the first to announce the passing of the "unipolar" moment.

Nor is he the first analyst to suggest new external checks on American power. Posen cites four. First, the explosive (and to many Americans incomprehensible) "re-emergence of identity politics, especially amalgams of religion and ethno-nationalism" in countries like Somalia, Rwanda, Bosnia, Kosovo and Iraq. Second, the return of "symmetrical warfare" with the dissemination of weapons like "Explosively Formed Penetrator" (EFP) mines or rocket-propelled grenade launchers, which have greatly increased the vulnerability of American forces engaged in patrolling activities. Third, the effect of globalization in creating "a steady supply of urbanized citizens at the lower end of the income scale" who will be "vulnerable to political mobilization on the basis of identity politics." And fourth, the backlash against American activism even among traditional allies, which is eroding the international legitimacy of the United States. Note that this last external check is itself a consequence of defective American strategy.

So much for the American predicament. What of Posen's alternative grand strategy based on American self-restraint? The terms he uses are themselves revealing. The United States needs to be more "reticent" about its use of military force, more "modest" about its political goals overseas, more "distant" from traditional allies, and more "stingy" in its aid policies. Good luck to the presidential candidate who laces his next foreign policy speech with those adjectives: "My fellow Americans, I want, to make this great country of ours more reticent, modest, distant and stingy!"

Let us, however, leave aside this quintessentially academic and operationally useless rhetoric. What exactly does Posen want the United States to do? I count six concrete recommendations. The United States should:

• Abandon the Bush Doctrine of "preemption," which in the case of Iraq has been a policy of preventive war. Posen argues that this applies even in cases of nuclear proliferation. By implication, he sees preventive war as an inferior option to deterrence, though he does not make clear how exactly a nuclear-armed Iran would be deterred, least of all if his second recommendation were to be implemented.

• Reduce U.S. military presence in the Middle East ("the abode of Islam") by abandoning "its permanent and semi-permanent land bases in Arab countries." Posen does not say so, but he appears to imply the abandonment of all these bases, not just the ones in Iraq, but also those in, for example, Qatar. It is not clear what would be left of Central Command after such a drastic retreat. Note that this would represent a break with the policy not just of the last two Presidents, but with that of the last 12.

• Ramp up efforts to provide relief in the wake of natural disasters, exemplified by Operation Unified Assistance after the Indian Ocean tsunami of December 26, 2004. No doubt the American military did some good in the wake of the tsunami, but Posen needs to explain why a government that so miserably bungled the aftermath of Hurricane Katrina less than a year later should be expected to be consistently effective in the wake of natural disasters.

• Assist in humanitarian military interventions only "under reasonable guidelines" and "in coalitions, operating under some kind of regional or international political mandate." Does Posen mean that he would favor sending American troops to Darfur at the same time as he is withdrawing them from other "abodes of Islam?" He does not say.

• Promote not democracy abroad but "the rule of law, press freedom and the rights of collective bargaining." Here again I am experiencing cognitive dissonance. The government that sought systematically to evade the Geneva Conventions in order to detain indefinitely and torture suspected terrorists as an upholder of the rule of law?

• Stop offering "U.S. security guarantees and security assistance, [which] tend to relieve others of the need to do more to ensure their own security." This is in fact the most important of all Posen's recommendations, though he saves it until last. He envisages radical diminution of American support for other members of NATO. Over the next ten years, he writes, the United States "should gradually withdraw from all military headquarters and commands in Europe." In the same timeframe it should "reduce U.S. government direct financial assistance to Israel to zero," as well as reducing (though not wholly eliminating) assistance to Egypt. And it should "reconsider its security relationship with Japan," whatever that means. Again, this represents a break with traditional policy so radical that it would impress even Noam Chomsky, to say nothing of Osama bin Laden (who would, indeed, find little here to object to).

Posen, in other words, has proceeded from relatively familiar premises (the limits of American "hyperpower") to some quite fantastic policy recommendations, which are perhaps best summed up as a cross between isolationism and humanitarianism. Only slightly less fantastic than his vision of an American military retreat from the Middle East, Europe and East Asia is Posen's notion that it could be sold to the American electorate—just six years after they were the targets of the single largest terrorist attack in history—in the language of self-effacement. Coming from a man who wants to restart mainstream debate on American grand strategy, that is pretty rich.

Owen Harries

I am in general agreement with the case Barry Posen makes for a grand strategy of restraint for the United States. It is a case that, in a more piecemeal way, I have been trying to make for the last decade and a half. Indeed, in the mid-1990s it even led me to offer a very qualified appreciation of the Clinton Administration's conduct of foreign policy, on the ground that, bereft of serious purpose as it was and subordinated to a domestic agenda, it inadvertently provided a counter to the dangers associated with excessive idealism and optimism at a time when American power made anything seem possible.

Things briefly looked promising when George W. Bush fought his first election campaign talking about the need to be more "humble," assuming that what he meant by that odd choice of word was the need for more prudence and modesty in dealing with the world. Whether or not he was serious, we shall never know, for September 11 intervened. By March 2002, a full year before the invasion of Iraq, I had concluded that the foreign policy significance of that terrible event was likely to be that

Owen Harries *is a fellow of both the Lowy Institute for International Policy and the Centre for Independent Studies in Sydney.*

it forced America decisively along a course of action that—by emphasizing her military dominance, by requiring her to use her vast power conspicuously, by making restraint and moderation virtually impossible, and by making unilateralism an increasing feature of American behavior—is bound to generate widespread and increased criticism and hostility towards her. That may turn out to be the real tragedy of September 11.[6]

Actually, things were to turn out even worse than that, as I had not anticipated either the full unleashing of America's Utopian hopes represented by the Bush Doctrine or the display of gross incompetence in implementation that was to follow.

Posen lists four important facts as bearing on the question of the future of U.S. grand strategy: unipolarity, identity politics, the diffusion of power and globalization. It seems to me that a fifth must be added: American exceptionalism, the deeply and widely held belief that it is the destiny and mission of the United States to reshape the world in its image. Recent events have undoubtedly dealt this belief a blow, but it is surely much too important a component of the American makeup for it not to recover and to be a continuing important factor in shaping the strategic outlook of the country that still possesses unmatched power. We can plead for restraint and prudence, and hope that in the aftermath of the Iraq fiasco that pleading will have some effect. But it would be unrealistic to expect a crucial element of self-belief and self-definition to perish or be abandoned, and we should give thought to how, and to what extent, it can be accommodated and channeled in ways that are compatible with a grand strategy of restraint.

Posen's analysis proceeds in terms of power factors, which is right and proper. But a cluster of terms which is highly relevant to any consideration of strategy plays little or no part in his analysis: terms like authority, legitimacy, respect, prestige. Much has been made of the growth of a violent anti-Americanism in the last few years, but a superpower can handle a lot of hostility and hatred. What is much more serious for it is a loss of authority and legitimacy, and there is no doubt that the United States has suffered significantly in this respect in the Bush years, both because of its heavy-handedness and its incompetence. (The failure of the can-do country to cope even with the effect of a hurricane on one of its great cities has suggested a weakness that goes beyond Iraq.)

In this respect I suggest that it would be useful to consider Posen's article along with that by Pierre Hassner in the July/August 2007 issue of this magazine. Hassner maintains that while "American power is vast and may yet grow by many measures . . . the legitimacy of that power is waning, and with it the authority of America's word and its model." Hassner may be mistaken, or at least premature, in maintaining that the "de-Westernization of authority structures on a global scale" is well underway, but I think he is right about a significant decline in the U.S. authority.

If so, it is a cause of concern not only for Americans but for the international system. For, as there is no other candidate in sight to provide leadership, we run the danger of being left with a leaderless world at a time when international problems are mounting: the need for new and effective rules for globalization; global warming; mass uncontrolled human migration; nuclear proliferation, extending to weak states with poor security and control systems; and, of course, terrorism, which is real enough, however much its dimensions may often be exaggerated. The only conceivable alternative to American leadership would be some sort of concert of powers; but as the creation and functioning of such a body would itself require American initiative and acquiescence, the challenge remains: to fashion a policy of restraint that is not also a policy of abdication.

I agree with the specific proposals Posen makes concerning NATO and Israel at the end of his article.

G. John Ikenberry

The Iraq war will be rendered all the more tragic if it leads America to pull back from its European and Asian security partnerships and its leadership in maintaining the institutional bases of global order—but this is precisely what Barry Posen proposes. One can applaud his arguments for a less-is-more approach to the Middle East and the problem of Islamic radicalism, which are based on a more plausible theory of terrorism and modern Arab history than the shifting theses offered by the Bush Administration. However, this argument is only loosely related to his broader call for a grand strategy of "restraint," and this is deeply problematic.

Posen makes four mistakes. First, he conflates all the various types of "activist" grand strategies and sees all of them as equally misguided. In fact, liberal and neoconservative strategies offer profoundly different visions of international order. If neoconservatives want to employ American power to *control* the international system, liberal internationalists want to use American power to *shape* it through the provisioning of rules and institutions.

Second, in conflating these alternatives, Posen misses the same point that his neoconservative rivals miss namely, that America can best pursue its global interests with a functioning governance system that facilitates cooperation in world politics. Posen acknowledges the importance of such governance mechanisms when he talks about the need for a revived Non-Proliferation Treaty and other security regimes. Indeed, the world is thirsting today for a revived system of rules and tools for collective action. Posen notes the troubling way in which the world has pushed back in the face of the unbridled exercise of American power, but it is precisely Washington's commitment to rules and institutions or governance that reduces the incentives for these soft balancing moves.

Hence Posen's third mistake is that he narrowly associates "restraint" with the retraction of America's security commitments in Europe and Asia. The argument he makes is that these alliance partnerships create a moral hazard. Relying on American commitments, other countries shirk their responsibilities, while the United States finds itself intervening everywhere and getting into trouble. But these alliances—as well as America's commitment to a wider array of multilateral institutions—are actually an essential tool for the establishment of American Strategic restraint. These institutions provide mechanisms for other countries to engage Washington, and they establish constraints and obligations that at least partly inhibit American unilateralism. The lesson of the Iraq war is not for America to "come home," but to tie itself more tightly to its allies. Yes, there are dangers that this extended security system will provide opportunities for strategic blunders and overextension. But the solution is better collective decision-making, not the wholesale scrapping of the postwar system.

Finally, to pull back from a liberal internationalist grand strategy is to lose the opportunity to lay down the institutional foundations for a global order that serves American interests in future years, when it is likely to be relatively less powerful. Think of it as investing in the future. We should be working at this moment to shape the global system so that the institutional legacies of today's actions put the United States in the best position possible to secure its interests when the wheel of power turns and other countries loom larger. This requires activism, of a certain sort.

G. John Ikenberry *is Albert G. Milbank Professor of Politics and International Affairs at Princeton University.*

Lilia Shevtsova

"Bravo!" Vladimir Putin or any representative of the Russian elite would say were they to read Barry Posen's recommendations. For an elite that has been fighting what it considers American preponderance, Washington's adoption of "a grand strategy of restraint" would be a dream come true. The Kremlin would applaud the United States for scaling back its global commitments and especially for being "more modest about the scope for political transformation within and among countries." The Russian policy elite would be supported by a chorus of other authoritarian leaders who have always been ardent supporters of realism, demanding that the United States "accept us as we are."

A call for restraint would make sense, first, if the crisis of the U.S. global role were really a product of its excessive "activism" and, second, if a *realpolitik* approach could successfully create a benevolent international environment (at least for America). But I doubt either is the case. In the first case, it's not the amount of activity that matters, but the soundness of the strategic vision animating it. Activism bereft of sound strategic vision often has unintended consequences, Iraq being of course the clearest example. As for the second case, one need only consider that the relationship between Washington and Moscow has been based on realism for the past eight years and has bottomed out as a consequence.

Now the grand architect of *realpolitik* himself, Henry Kissinger, says in analyzing the reasons behind the "estrangement" between Russia and America, "A major challenge is the degree to which Russia's internal evolution should affect U.S.-Russia relations."[1] By admitting that Russian domestic politics is a factor in U.S.-Russian relations, Kissinger appears to be writing an epitaph on the gravestone of American realism. And Posen's contention that U.S. activism is defined in large part by democracy promotion efforts is, simply put, a myth.

In the interest of both the United States and the global community, America does indeed need to reconsider its unilateralism, its doctrine of preemption and its denigration of international institutions. I also support Posen's call for Washington "to be more reticent about the use of military force." However, calling for restraint in democracy promotion efforts is ill-considered—even despite the fact that they have on occasion done more harm than good.

Again, it is not the "quantity" of action that counts, but the quality of the vision guiding those actions. The world needs a bold but viable new framework to deal with new global threats, and America in particular needs to reinvigorate the idea of liberal democracy and link it to the idea of global justice. We need to define a new global mission, and there are two nations in the world whose historical characters predispose them to such missionary activity: America and Russia.

We saw this predisposition at work during the last half of the 20th century. Russia's mission to spread communism across the world failed. The project that U.S. statesmen undertook in 1945, on the other hand, not only helped Europe achieve sustainable peace but also made liberal democracy "the only game in town." Yes, today's America is bogged down in Iraq, and its aims are viewed skeptically, if not with hostility, by most of the world. But if America is not ready to take on the new global challenges, who will?

I doubt that the European Union could fill the vacuum. As a rule, conglomerates like the EU are not driven by a mission. The optimal solution would be for America and the EU to

---

Lilia Shevtsova *is senior associate of the Carnegie Endowment for International Peace.*

undertake a new project together, but only America can take the lead in such a project—a mission that would need to follow de Gaulle's axiom: *"Regarder loin et viser haut"* ("Look far and aim high").

Looking far and aiming high is of course the antithesis of restraint. If it turns out that Americans prefer restraint to a new, multilateral global mission, as Posen argues, that would mean the end of U.S. preponderance. You can't lead by retreating. This might not end up being a tragedy for the world, but in a time of world disorder, and absent any other great power worthy of a global role, is that a risk we should take?

Stephen D. Krasner

The transformation in American strategic thinking that took place after 9/11 amounted to a judgment by some that the nexus of failed, repressive and rogue states, on the one hand, and globalization, transnational terrorism, radical Islamic ideology and easier accessibility to WMD, on the other, posed an existential threat to international security and global development. We know that the ambitions of al-Qaeda are limitless; we do not know exactly what al-Qaeda's capabilities are or might be. The worst-case scenario is dire: nuclear bombs in Los Angeles, London, Berlin and Tokyo.

Would such an event bring an end to the United States, the United Kingdom, Germany or Japan? No. But it would transform the way in which these states organized their societies, depress global economic growth, and put an end to the conventional rules of sovereignty that have, for better and worse, guided international politics for the few centuries. What might such an "end" lead to? Ungoverned spaces would be occupied. The global financial system, which transfers of billions of dollars daily, would be more tightly controlled to prevent the funding of radical Islamist activities. The Middle East oil fields would be seized by more powerful states, or perhaps declared to be part of the common heritage of mankind with revenues contributed to international financial institutions. This would be a much messier and more dangerous world.

There is no way to confidently assign probabilities to this scenario, or to one less horrific but still likely to catalyze significant political regression, such as the use of dirty nuclear bombs or multiple attacks with chemical or biological agents. But stranger things than mega-terrorist attacks have happened in the last century. The rise and collapse of the Soviet Union, Nazi control of Germany, two world wars and the Holocaust, the tens of millions killed by the policies of Stalin and Mao, and the rapid democratization of central Europe under the tutelage of the European Union were all bizarre and improbable events.

In the face of the prospect of radical upheaval, Barry Posen argues that the appropriate way to address the challenges facing the United States is through a policy of restraint that would scale back alliances, use force more reticently, and be more modest about the possibilities for political transformation within and among countries. I am skeptical.

The benefits of scaling back alliances, the clearest implications of Posen's conception of strategic restraint, are outweighed by the risks. A more modest NATO might inspire greater

Stephen D. Krasner *is the Graham H. Stuart Professor of International Relations at Stanford University, senior fellow at the Freeman Spogli Institute and senior fellow by courtesy at the Hoover Institution*

security commitments from Europe, but it might not. A weaker U.S. position in Asia might lead Japan to engage its neighbors, or it might aggravate the security dilemma and precipitate an arms race. The United States could be more pointed with regard to Israeli occupation policies, but distancing itself from Israel would signal a lack of American support that would make major war more likely, not less.

The harder issues for the United States are not the future of its alliances but the appropriate use of military force, and the extent to which the United States, with its allies, can change domestic authority structures in other countries. External actors can promote political change, including even transformations to liberal democracy. Central Europe's movement from communism to liberal democracy, a transformation that could not have taken place without the incentives, procedures and promise offered by the European Union, is the most successful example of democracy promotion even seen. American military intervention in the Caribbean and Central America in the 1980s and 1990s did contribute to more open and accountable regimes in several countries, if not ideal liberal democratic ones. And, of course, there are always the examples of Japan and Germany.

It is hard to promote movement toward liberal democracy, however, and there have been many failures as well as some successes. Organizational forms are relatively easy to transfer, but the substance and culture of institutions are not. Every liberal democracy has followed its own trajectory, and even the United States, perhaps the most successful political regime in history, has had a very bumpy ride that has included a civil war.

Supporting freedom, openness and democracy is like a venture capital investment. Information is imperfect. Contingencies matter. Leadership can be crucial. We know in general that incentives are better than bribes, that domestic allies are essential, that past experience with democracy helps, that it is better to be richer than poorer, that military force can sometimes precipitate lasting change. But we do not know with certainty what devices or combinations of devices will bring success in a particular place.

Given the threat posed by the nexus of failed and repressive states, globalization, and the diffusion of military power to non-state as well as state actors, is restraint really the optimal U.S. strategy? Leaving aside the ambiguity of what restraint means, let me offer another slogan: opportunism or, better yet, flexibility.

The United States and other liberal democracies need an array of instruments to promote movement toward more open, liberal and accountable regimes. They also need, of course, conventional intelligence sharing and policing to combat domestic as well as transnational terrorist threats. Policy cannot just be about elections and democracy in some narrow sense. It must also involve, as Posen recognizes, the protection of human rights, the promotion of civil society, support for more open media and the rule of law. Economic openness offers powerful incentives. Trade agreements are not just about trade; they involve changing domestic institutions in partner countries in ways that can enhance American security.

I make no claim for opportunism or flexibility as a grand strategy. Like restraint, these terms are little more than slogans. They do not have the kind of heuristic power needed for framing a genuine grand strategy. It is not from any lack of effort that six years after 9/11 we still have no consensus about grand strategy. An effective grand strategy must be based on a shared conception of the nature of the challenge, and that is something we lack. Restraint is a strategy for those who believe that U.S. activism itself is the problem, not for those who believe otherwise.

Wang Jisi

The Posen essay is a rare masterpiece in the rich literature on U.S. grand strategy since the end of the Cold War. Without deviating from the leading U.S. ideology, it proposes an alternative strategy—a strategy of restraint. I wish his ideas could be developed into a consensus in America's foreign and security policy establishments, but I doubt they will.

I imagine that a vast majority of political elites around the world, particularly since the unpopular decision to launch the Iraq war, would welcome a United States that would restrain its use of military power. Osama bin Laden, al-Qaeda and the Taliban, for their part, would be happier to see an even more overstretched U.S. power, such as would result from new American military operations against Iran or North Korea, all in addition to the U.S. Army being bogged down in Iraq.

Unfortunately, many Americans remain blind to what is so obvious to others. As Posen illustrates, mainstream American strategic culture is based on the conviction that this nation's "very good intentions, plus very great power, plus action" can transform global politics at costs it can afford. No one should be surprised that in the coming election year American presidential candidates will compete for advocating a "can do" foreign policy; calling for a "strategy of restraint" would make no politician attractive.

Indeed, Posen's argument neither appeals to many Americans nor meets the "iron logic of power." An American may ask, "If we have good intentions, and our power is unparalleled, why shouldn't we be more proactive?" That is why I fear Posen's good advice will not be heeded in the United States.

What could be added to Posen's reasoning is that most people outside of the United States do not view U.S. actions as being as well intended as Americans believe them to be. The perception gap is huge. American self-righteousness and presumptuousness, seen even in the eyes of its friends and admirers, is as harmful to U.S. interests as unwelcome U.S. actions. When U.S. material power is at its peak, Americans should be reminded of Lord Acton's familiar quotation, "Power tends to corrupt, and absolute power corrupts absolutely. Great men are seldom good men." To many others in the world, Americans are great men but not-so-good men, and that's why they should be self-restrained. Otherwise, they will eventually be constrained by others.

Posen's analysis suggests a latent question that shouldn't go unexamined: If the United States carries out a strategy of restraint in focusing on counter-terrorism, will it help or hurt its ability to deter or contain a possible peer competitor in the future? Looking around other great powers, this competitor or challenger is likely to be China.

A careful reader of Chinese official pronouncements will find that Beijing has reduced sharply its "anti-hegemony" (a code word for U.S. supremacy) rhetoric since 9/11, and has defined its international surroundings as generally benign. If the United States continues to be the dominant superpower (as is portrayed in China's official media) when China's strategic surroundings are still benign, does it mean that the United States is a benign power to China? Not necessarily. To be sure, China feels more secure when the United States regards terrorism as its most imminent threat. But if Washington predetermines that China as a future adversary should be deterred or contained when terrorism is no longer the main problem to U.S. safety, Beijing will have to take precautionary measures to prepare for confronting America.

Wang Jisi *is dean of the School of International Studies, Peking University, China.*

Consequently, a strategy of restraint today—even relative restraint—will help case China's guardedness and encourage it to be a more responsible player in global affairs.

James Q. Wilson

Barry Posen believes that the United States should follow a policy of restraint instead of activism. By "restraint" he means a defensive rather than offensive strategy in which the United States would avoid playing a leadership role, rely on intelligence operations rather than military force, withdraw troops from many overseas bases and count on deterrence for protection.

I believe that Posen's argument is either unclear or wrong. It is vague to say that restraint should have been our policy since the beginning of the Cold War because he fails to discuss American military activities since that time, leaving us uncertain as to what he means. Which of the following should we not have done: Fight in Korea and Vietnam? Use a naval blockade to induce the withdrawal of Soviet missiles from Cuba? Force Iraq to withdraw from Kuwait? Send troops to Haiti in an effort to block a dictatorial regime? Overthrow a Marxist regime in Guatemala? Seize Manuel Noriega in Panama?

It is wrong to assert that our general policy should lead us to defer to others, supply logistical aid rather than use military force, avoid preemptive strikes in areas that tolerate Islamic radicals, not supply guarantees and assistance to allies, and counter al-Qaeda with intelligence operations rather than invasions. Doing these things would leave the world unprotected and confirm Osama Union that the *mujaheddin* threw out of Afghanistan.

Indeed, when we look at the last forty years, America has relentlessly, until the overthrow of the Taliban in Afghanistan, followed a policy of restraint. The Shah was overthrown in Iran, 241 Marines were killed in Lebanon, a CIA station chief was tortured and murdered there, the ship *Achille Lauro* was hijacked and an American was killed, Pan Am Flight 103 was blown up over Scotland, a bomb was detonated under the World Trade Center, two of our Embassies were destroyed in Africa, the USS *Cole* was attacked in Yemen, and American soldiers were murdered in Somalia. When these and other attacks, all carried out by Islamic radicals, occurred, the United States did nothing except occasionally to lob a few cruise missiles into some empty buildings. By 1998, bin Laden had drawn the right conclusion. In an interview, he described the American military as a "paper tiger" who "after a few blows ran in defeat."

The notion that these attacks could be handled by intelligence officers is laughable. I commend to Posen the new book by Tim Wiener, *Legacy of Ashes* (2007), about the failure of most covert operations undertaken by the CIA.

At the end of his proposal, Posen suggests that we eliminate all aid to Israel because it is surrounded by "military powers lacking any capacity to conquer it." Lacking any capacity? Is he counting Iran after it acquires a nuclear weapon? Or even without that, he says little about the roughly $1.8 billion in aid we give Egypt every year—aid that, if continued, will make Egypt stronger by the time power there is seized by the Muslim Brotherhood.

When President George W. Bush clarified our commitment to preventive attacks—a policy that had in fact been in effect long before he took office—he said that "the war on terror will not be won on the defensive" because "time is not on our side." This does not mean that we should intervene everywhere, but only where an intervention will make a decisive difference. Afghanistan was one such case, Iraq is another.

James Q. Wilson *is Ronald Reagan Professor of Public Policy at Pepperdine University.*

The struggle in Iraq has been costly, and it will not stop soon. But we have gained a great deal: We ended a regime that had in the past built and used—and if left alone would again have built and used—weapons of mass destruction; that invaded two neighboring countries; that murdered its own people with chemical weapons and summary executions; that provided aid to the families of terrorists; and that, if left alone, would have brought Kuwait and Saudi Arabia to heel. This was only possible because we exercised leadership and did not wait, with restraint, for others to pass yet another meaningless Security Council resolution.

Bronislaw Geremek

Barry Posen's essay very well defines what ought to be abandoned in U.S. foreign policy. But the new grand strategy he would put in its place requires a few cautionary remarks.

First, it is very important that a "strategy of restraint" not develop into a "strategy of retreat." Renouncing excessive activism does not have to mean playing a passive role in world politics. When Washington wisely and willingly practices multilateralism, overcoming its propensity to act arrogantly as a "hyperpower," it will win back the world's confidence. Posen rightly cites U.S. actions to help the December 2004 tsunami victims as an outstanding example of the right way to act.

Second, the United States must reappraise its policy toward the European Union. In short, it must make the EU its main partner on the global stage. NATO cannot take on this role—not in its present form and not in what Posen calls a "more traditional political alliance." There may come a day when the United States, the EU and perhaps India will be able to come together, as the world's greatest democratic powers, to manage global disorder without being perceived as new imperial powers. Such an alliance for peace and order would not preclude American military forces based on European territory, but it would require a broader co-operative security philosophy. It makes sense that the EU takes on the responsibility primarily within the European Balkans, beginning with Kosovo, and that it offer its skills and experience beyond, as well. But such narrowing of the American political scope as Posen seems to suggest does not take account of the unavoidable U.S. responsibility for the "World Balkans"—the vast arc of danger and disorder from Central Asia to the Middle East and North Africa.

Third, as Posen suggests, one cannot successfully export democracy or impose it on the rest of the world. We must forget about trying to use foreign policy to accelerate "the end of history." Let us rather think humbly, along with Kant and Tocqueville, about devising a minimum democratic framework for a global order: the rule of law, freedom of the press and freedom of association. Some believe that even striving for such a minimalist democratic framework is a bridge too far for U.S. foreign policy. I think, and 1 hope, that it is not.

C. Raja Mohan

Barry Posen's eminently sensible proposal for "restraint" as U.S. grand strategy need not be construed, as he presents it, as a radical departure from America's present engagement with the world. Indeed, a shift toward more modest political goals is already evident in Asia,

Bronislaw Geremek *holds the Chair of European Civilisation at the College of Europe in Warsaw and is former Foreign Minister of Poland.*
C. Raja Mohan *is professor of South Asian studies at the S. Rajaratnam School of International Studies, Nanyang Technological University, Singapore, and a foreign affairs columnist for the Indian Express in New Delhi.*

where China is emerging as a potential peer competitor. The Bush Administration, however, does not get enough credit in a polarized Washington obsessed with the Middle East for beginning a re-orientation of U.S. strategy in Asia—arguably a more important region in the longer run.

In the past few years, for example, the United States has strongly encouraged Japan to take larger political and military responsibilities, and this encouragement has found a receptive audience. The new nationalists in Tokyo are straining at the leash to reclaim Japans "rightful place" in Asia. Today it is Tokyo, not Washington, that has taken the lead in calling on Asian democracies to act in concert. Unlike the liberals of the Clinton Administration, too, President Bush has not hectored the world's largest democracy, India, on human rights and the Kashmir dispute with Pakistan. Recognizing the importance of assisting India's rise as a great power, Bush has been willing to debunk the non-proliferation ideology and accommodate India into the global nuclear order. He has also embarked on a course of strategic outreach toward Vietnam and Indonesia.

All these nations have strong motivations of their own to balance China, regardless of the nature of the foreign policy debate in Washington and fluctuations in Sino-American relations. The Bush Administration has been wise enough to understand this, and to leverage local interests to its own benefit. The problem, of course, is that good news does not travel well. American achievements in Asia barely feed into current U.S. debates on grand strategy.

Nor has the history of U.S. policy in Asia seemed to garner much attention. But consider: The threat to U.S. security from the ideology of violent political Islam is not very different from the one once posed by international communism in Asia. This threat was ultimately defeated not by military force, but by manipulating its internal contradictions. A variety of factions in Asia—including nationalist and conservative groups—had reasons of their own to oppose communism. Divisions among the communist powers and the inevitable fragmentation of the international Left helped the United States recover ground in Asia. Similarly, exploiting existing divisions within political Islam, letting regional contradictions unfold, managing regional balances of power, and assisting friendly states to defend shared interests in the Middle East are sensible alternatives to the current, costly U.S. attempts to single-handedly control and direct the evolution of the Middle East.

Anxious debate in the United States over the construction of a new global order reveals the post-Cold War narcissism of the American elite. It does not necessarily enlighten us on how the world might actually look in coming years. Despite a long political tradition of ideological grandstanding and bouts of international activism, America is also blessed with an innate sense of pragmatism. As its margin for error steadily shrinks amidst a global redistribution of power, and a recognition dawns that the United States cannot play god by resolving every single problem in the world, restraint is bound to emerge as a natural course for U.S. grand strategy.

The rest of the world, meanwhile, has not held its breath to see which way the United States goes. Having become acutely sensitive to the depth and breadth of U.S. power over many decades, most nations are now adept at coping with it—taking advantage where they can, going around it where they must, and avoiding a direct confrontation at all costs. A more relaxed America that unburdens itself from the presumed mandate to run the world, that is focused on doing less and that is more prepared to work with partners, might find that it can accomplish more.

Ruth Wedgwood

Barry Posen is always interesting, but sometimes he is flat wrong. In preaching a grand strategy of "restraint," he may strike a chord with members of Congress, the press and the public who have grown weary of the burdens imposed by the war in Iraq and the American role in international security. But his prescriptions on how to ration our power are not practical.

To be sure, our ground forces need replenishment. Both political parties indulged the foolhardy decision of the 1990s to shrink the American military and wizen the capabilities of the intelligence community. Delighted at defeating Soviet Communism, we wishfully supposed that archaic ideologies would no longer seduce men away from the advantages of cooperation. Praising the attractions of soft power, democratic peace and the rule of law, we forgot that we might need a legion of diplomats, soldiers, intelligence agents and intellectuals who could treat with the Arab world in its own language and with comprehension of its culture. American universities added to the brew with a disdain for issues of national security and condescension toward regional studies, hatching a monolingual generation of Americans who are (apart from émigrés) unable to join the conversation that is so badly needed with the Arab and Islamic worlds.

Looking forward, the United States can speak in a softer voice and seek to act through the United Nations whenever the political stars (including Russia and China) can be brought into alignment. We should call on all members of the United Nations to contribute to the reconstruction of Iraq through UN humanitarian and relief agencies. The new UN Secretary-General has restored a working relationship with Washington, and appreciates that some quadrants (such as Northeast Asia) face real security dilemmas. In Europe, the refreshing pragmatism of Nicolas Sarkozy and Angela Merkel may renew NATO's common spirit. And if European allies make good on their Prague pledge to invest at least 2 percent of GDP in military capability, NATO might be able to handle robust peacekeeping missions in more than one area, in contrast to the present circumstance in which peacekeeping in Afghanistan is the outer limit.

None of this, however, means that we can walk away from our commitments to Japan and Israel, as Posen suggests. American power is still an irreducible necessity. At a time when North Korea is bracketing Japan with missile tests, an "over the horizon" posture is likely to be mistaken as a dangerous withdrawal of support. Occasional flashes of lucidity on the part of Pyongyang may be aided by Chinese pressure, but they are also promoted by the ability of the United States to flow forces into the region in the event of any conflict. American bases in Japan are also important as a logistical guarantee in the face of a South Korean regime that is, at times, intimidated by the North.

As for Israel, it is odd to posit that this small state faces no serious threat at a time when Syria is allied with Iran, and Hizballah is rearming in southern Lebanon, boasting that its Tehran-provided rocket technology can reach as far as Tel Aviv. Iran's drive for a nuclear weapon has renewed existential doubts about Israel's capacity to sustain itself against conventional threats that are linked to a nuclear sponsor.

Posen is right in saying that it has been provocative, to some Muslims, to have American ground forces stationed in the Middle East. Yet so long as Saddam remained in power, keeping

Ruth Wedgwood *is a member of the Hoover Task Force on National Security and Law. The views expressed are her own.*

forces in Kuwait and Saudi Arabia was bound to continue. In the current conflict, a rapid American exit would leave the Iraqi people vulnerable to the brutal opportunism of al-Qaeda, spoiling any fledgling *modus vivendi* between Shi'a and Sunni factions, as we saw after al-Qaeda's bombing of the Samarra mosque. Heading for the door would invite Iran to seek control of the eastern half of the country, with likely intervention by Sunni states and a possible regional war. The siren song of the Internet will solicit young recruits to al-Qaeda's perverse form of radicalism by arguing, with some reason, that the United States has lost its staying power and nerve. We can honor and lament the sacrifice of the young men and women of the American armed forces without losing sight of the strategic objectives for which they have fought.

Finally, on the critical question of nuclear terrorism and rogue states, deterrence will not work. No, al-Qaeda cannot "occupy" the United States, but with a nuclear attack it could inflict immense damage to our economy, culture, self-confidence and willingness to engage in any international role. It is wishful to suppose that deterrence, rather than prevention, is sufficient here. There may be procedures to determine a "return address" of a bomb's uranium, but those procedures do not announce where, amid the international commerce of rogue regimes, uranium passed from a government to a terrorist actor. It is surely better to take energetic steps to keep nuclear weapons out of the hands of radical governments, not least that of Iran.

We should try to persuade other countries that there is a grandeur in the prospect of a growing economy, where young people can flourish, with opportunities for political participation. We should praise our allies for their contributions to international security. But we should not suppose, in this moment above all, that the United States can take a busman's holiday.

Itamar Rabinovich

Barry Posen's advocacy of a grand strategy of "restraint" for the United States may well resonate loudly throughout West Wing corridors, come January 2009. Whether out of a desire: to adopt a radically different national security policy or because they are the intellectual products of policy analysts and experts, at least some elements of Posen's argument will be included in a new administration's foreign and national security policy. My purpose here is not to address the doctrine of "restraint" or its underlying ideas and principles; it is to point to the troubling way in which Posen translates them into policy recommendations in one crucial part of the world.

By Posen's own light, the Arab world and the Middle East present the major threats to a relatively safe United States—"Terrorism, basically Islamist in origin," "rogue states [including Iran]," failed states." This is surely correct, and Posen is also right to draw two specific conclusions: no more wars like the bungled war in Iraq, and no more attempts to impose Western-style democracy upon reluctant Arab states.

His other policy recommendations, however, are deeply troubling. Posen tacitly accepts (if not explicitly) a nuclear Iran. He hopes to deter Iran, without a credible threat to use force, by means of a diplomatic panacea: a ten-year plan to reduce direct U.S. assistance to Israel; balancing U.S. military sales and aid between Israel and Egypt in order to deny Israel a military edge; and all of the above as part of an effort to persuade Jerusalem to give up the occupied territories.

Itamar Rabinovich, *former president of Tel Aviv University, is currently a visiting professor at the John F. Kennedy School of Government, Harvard University, and a visiting fellow at the Brookings Institution.*

This neither makes sense nor suffices as U.S. policy for the Middle East as it is now. A nuclear Iran will not start by attacking Israel or Europe with nuclear weapons; it will use them as a shield for a more aggressive policy of direct and indirect attack on several U.S. allies (such as Saudi Arabia and the other oil producers in the Gulf, which Posen never mentions). These states, in the face of U.S. "restraint," will see no alternative to making their peace with the devil. Furthermore, the way to persuade Israel to give up territory is to enhance its military power, not reduce it.

From now to January 2009 and beyond, identity politics, terrorism and proliferation in the Middle East are likely to produce new challenges and burdens. "Restraint," Posen-style, will not be able to cope with them.

NOTES

1. Eugene Gholz, Daryl G. Press and I larvey M. Sapolsky, "Come Home America: The Strategy of Restraint in the Face of Temptation." *International Security (Spring 1997).*
2. See James N. Miller and Shawn W. Brimley, *Phased Transition: A Responsible Way Forward and Out of Iraq,* Center for a New American Security, June 2007. Under this plan, 60,000 or more U.S. soldiers would still be in Iraq in January 2009, and the last ones would not leave until the end of 2012.
3. Posen, "The Struggle Against Terrorism, Grand Strategy, Strategy, and Tactics," *International Security* (Winter 2001-02).
4. 'Bai, "Kerry's Undeclared War," *New York Times Magazine*, October 10, 2004.
5. Bacevich, *American Empire: The Realities and Consequences of U.S. Diplomacy* (Harvard University Press, 2002).
6. "American pie losing its flavour," *The Age* (Australia), April 4, 2002.
7. Kissinger, "The icon and the eagle," *International Herald Tribune*, March 20, 2007.

Liberal Order Building

G. John Ikenberry

In the twenty-first century, America confronts a complex array of security challenges—diffuse, shifting, and uncertain. But it does not face the sort of singular geopolitical threat that it did with the Fascist and Communist powers of the last century. Indeed, compared with the dark days of the 1930s or the cold war, America lives in an extraordinarily benign security environment, and it possesses an extraordinary opportunity to shape its security environment for the long term. It is the dominant global power, unchecked by a coalition of balancing states or a superpower wielding a rival universalistic ideology. Most of the great powers are democracies and tried to the United States through formal alliances and informal partnerships. State power

G. John Ikenberry, "Liberal Order Building" from *To Lead the World: American Strategy after the Bush Doctrine,* ed. by Melvyn P. Leffl er and Jeffrey W. Legro, p. 84–108. Reprinted by permission.

is ultimately based on sustained economic growth— and no major state today can modernize without integrating into the globalized capitalist system; that is, if you want to be a world power, you will need to join the World Trade Organization (WTO). What made the Fascist and Communist threats of the twentieth century so profound was not only the danger of territorial aggression but also the fact that these great power challengers embodied rival political-economic systems that could generate growth, attract global allies, and create counterbalancing geopolitical blocs. America has no such global challengers today.

The most serious threat to U.S. national security enemy but the erosion of the institutional found that the United States has commanded for half a century and through which it has pursued its interests and national security. Am and authority within the global system are in serious crisis—and this puts American national security at risk. The grand strategy America needs to pursue in the years ahead is one aimed not at a particular threat but rather at restoring its role as the recognized and legitimate leader of the system and at rebuilding the institutions and partnerships on which this leadership position is based. America's global position is in crisis, but it is a crisis that is largely of its own making, and one that can be overcome in a way that leaves the United States in a stronger position to meet the diffuse, shifting, and uncertain threats of the twenty-first century.

The grand strategy I am proposing can be called "liberal order building." It is essentially a twenty-first-century version of the strategy that the United States pursued after World War II in the shadow of the cold war—a strategy that produced the liberal hegemonic order that has provided the framework for the Western and global system ever since. This is a strategy in which the United States leads the way in the creation and operation of a loose rule-based international order. The United States provides public goods and solves global collective action problems, American "rule" is established through the provisioning of international rules and institutions and its willingness to operate within them. American power is put in the service of an agreed-on system of Western-oriented global governance. American power is made acceptable to the world because it is embedded in these agreed-on rules and institutions. The system itself leverages resources and fosters cooperation that makes the actual functioning of the order one that solves problems, creates stability, and allows democracy and capitalism to flourish. Liberal order building is America's distinctive contribution to world politics—and it is a grand strategy that the country should return to in the post-Bush era.

The Bush administration did not embrace the logic of liberal hegemonic rule or support the rules and institutions on which it is based—and America is now paying the price in an extraordinary decline in its authority, credibility?, prestige, and the ready support of other states. Along the way, the Bush administration has made America less rather than more secure, and its ruinous foreign policy is fast becoming an icon of grand strategic failure.

If America is smart and plays its foreign policy "cards" right, it is not fanciful to think that the United States can still be in twenty years at the center of a "one world" system defined in terms of open markets, democratic community, cooperative security, and rule-based order. This is a future that can be contrasted with less desirable alternatives that echo through the past—great power balancing orders, regional blocs, or bipolar rivalries. The United States should seek to consolidate a global order in which other countries bandwagon rather than balance against it—and in which it remains at the center of a prosperous and secure demo era tic-capita list order that in turn provides the architecture and axis points around which the wider global system turns. But to reestablish this desired world order, the United make a radical break with Bush foreign policy and basic governance institutions of the system—investing in alliances, partnerships, multilateral institutions, special relationship, great power concerts, cooperative security pacts, and democratic security communities.

It is useful to distinguish between two types of grand strategies—positional and milieu oriented. A "positional" grand strategy is one in which a great power seeks to counter, undercut, contain, and limit the power and threats of a specific challenger state or group of states: Nazi Germany, imperial Japan, the Soviet bloc, and perhaps—in the future—Greater China. A "milieu" grand strategy is one in which a great power does not target a specific state but seeks to structure its general international environment in ways that are congenial with its long-term security. This might entail building the infrastructure of international cooperation, promoting trade and democracy in various regions of the world, or establishing partnerships that might be useful for various contingencies. The point I want to make is that under conditions of unipolarity, in a world of diffuse threats, and with pervasive uncertainty over what the specific security challenges will be in the future, this milieu-basic approach to grand strategy is needed.

This chapter makes five arguments. I start with an argument about the character of America's security environment in the decades to come. The United States does not confront a first-order security threat as it has in the past. It faces a variety of decentralized, complex, and deeply rooted threats. It does not face a singular threat—a great power or violent global movement—that deserves primacy in the organization of national security. The temptation is to prioritize the marshaling of American resources against a threat such as jihadist terrorism or rogue states, but this is both an intellectual and political mistake. If the world of the twenty-first century were a town, the security threats faced by its leading citizens would not be organized crime or a violent assault by a radical mob on city hall. It would be a breakdown of law enforcement and social services in the face of constantly changing and ultimately uncertain vagaries of criminality, nature, and circumstance.

Second, these more diffuse, shifting, and uncertain threats require a different sort of grand strategy than those aimed at countering a specific enemy such as a rival great power or a radical terrorist group. Rather, the United States needs to lead in the re-creation of the global architecture of governance, rebuilding its leadership position and the institutional frameworks through which it pursues its interests and cooperates with others to provide security. Above all, it needs to create resources and capacities for the collective confrontation of a wide array of dangers and challenges. That is, America needs a grand strategy of "multitasking"—creating shared capacities to respond to a wide variety of contingencies. In the twenty-first-century threat environment, a premium will be placed on mechanisms for collective action and sustained commitments to problem solving.

Third, America does have a legacy of liberal order building—it knows how to do it, and doing it in the past has made America strong and secure. It needs to rediscover and renew this strategy of liberal order building. During the decades after World War II, the United States did not just fight the cold war, but it also created a liberal international order of multilayered pacts and partnerships that served to open markets, bind democracies together, and create a transregional security community. The United States provided security, championed mutually agreed-on rules and institutions, and led in the management of an open world economy. In return, other states affiliated with and supported the United States as it led the larger order. It was an American-led hegemonic order with liberal characteristics. There is still no alternative model of international order that is better suited to American interests or stable global governance.

Fourth, American foreign policy in the past six years has severely eroded America's global position—and endangered its ability to lead and to facilitate collective action. This "crisis" of

American authority is perhaps the most serious threat to the ability of the United States to secure itself in the decades ahead. The proximate cause of this crisis is the Bush administration's failure to operate within America's own postwar liberal hegemonic order. But there are deep shifts in the global system that make it harder for the United States to act as it did in the past—as a global provider of goods and a liberal hegemon willing to both restrain and commit itself. Unipolariry and the erosion of norms of state sovereignty—among other long-term shifts—make the American pursuit of a liberal order-building strategy both more difficult and more essential.

Fifth, the new agenda for liberal order building involves an array of efforts to strengthen and rebuild a global architecture. These initiatives include building a "protective infrastructure" for preventing and responding to socioeconomic catastrophe, renewing the cold war-era alliances, reforming the United Nations (UN), and creating new multilateral mechanisms for cooperation in East Asia and among democracies. In the background, the United States will need to renegotiate and renew its grand bargains with Europe and East Asia. In these bargains, the United States will need to signal a new willingness to restrain and commit its power, to accommodate rising states, and to operate within reconfigured and agreed-on global rules and institutions.

My point is that America needs to develop a post-post-9/11 grand strategy. It is not enough simply to fight the "global war on terror" (or GWOT). Instead, we need to return to basics—to a focus on the logic and organization of global order and governance. The United States does not need to fight an enemy so much as construct a political order that can function to protect the United States from lots of enemies and to solve collective action problems necessary to prevent the rise of new enemies. We do not need a GWOT 2.0. What we need is a PATC 2.0. PATC stands for *Present at the Creation,* which is the title of Dean Acheson's famous memoir in which he describes how he and his colleagues built the postwar American-led system. My point is that we need to think about international order building today with the same ambition and imagination as Acheson and other postwar architects did with PATC 1.0.

THREATS, CHALLENGES, AND OPPORTUNITIES

Grand strategy is, as Barry Posen argues, "a state's theory about how it can best cause security for itself." As such, it is an exercise in public worrying about the future—and doing something about it. Looking into the future, what should America be most worried about? Grand strategy is a set of coordinated and sustained policies designed to address these prioritized national worries.

Some observers argue that American grand strategy should be organized around the confrontation with a specific enemy, as it was during the cold war Jihadist terrorism, in particular, is offered as this premier global threat to which all else should be subordinated and directed. The Bush administration, of course, has made this the centerpiece of its grand strategy—describing a "long war" against terrorism, a generational struggle akin to the cold war. In the most evocative versions of this thesis, the United States is engaged in a war against "jihadist terrorism," "militant Islam," or "Islamofascists" who are the heirs of the Fascist and Communist threats of the part century—wielding a totalitarian political ideology and seeking our violent destruction. We face the prospect of a twilight war with an evil foe while Western civilization hangs in the balance.

But it is not altogether clear that fighting Islamic terrorism is the preeminent security challenge of the coming decades. Various are the threats that America faces. Global warming, health pandemics, nuclear proliferation, jihadist terrorism, energy scarcity—these and other dangers loom on the horizon. Any of these threats could endanger American lives and way of life either directly or indirectly by destabilizing the global system on which American security and prosperity depend. Pandemics and global warming are not threats wielded by human hands, but their consequences could be equally devastating. Highly infectious disease has the potential to kill millions of people. Global warming threatens to trigger waves of environmental migration and food shortages and to further destabilize weak and poor states around the world. The world is also on the cusp of a new round of nuclear proliferation, putting mankind's deadliest weapons in the hands of unstable and hostile states. Terrorist networks offer a new specter of nonstate transnational violence. The point is that none of these threats is, in itself, so singularly preeminent that it deserves to be the centerpiece of American grand strategy in the way that anti-Fascism and anti-Communism did in an earlier era.[2]

What is more, these various threats are interconnected, and it is the possibility of their interactive effects that multiplies the dangers. This point is stressed by Thomas Homer-Dixon: "It's the convergence of stresses that's especially treacherous and makes synchronous failure a possibility as never before. In coming years, our societies won't face one or two major challenges at once, as usually happened in the past. Instead, they'll face an alarming variety of problems—likely including oil shortages, climate change, economic instability, and mega terrorism—all at the same time." The danger is that several of these threats will materialize simultaneously and interact to generate greater violence and instability: "What happens, for example, if together or in quick succession the world has to deal with a sudden shift in climate that sharply cuts food production in Europe and Asia, a severe oil price increase that sends economies tumbling around the world, and a string of major terrorist attacks on several Western capital cities?"[3] The global order itself would be put at risk, as well as the foundations of American national security.

We can add to these worries the rise of China and, more generally, the rise of Asia. It is worth recalling that China was the preoccupation of the American national security community in the years before the September 11, 2001, terrorist attacks. China's rapid economic growth and assertive regional diplomacy are already transforming East Asia, and Beijing's geopolitical influence is growing. The United States has no experience managing a relationship with a country that is potentially its principal economic and security rival. It is unclear, and probably unknowable, how China's intentions and ambitions will evolve as it becomes more powerful. We do know, however, that the rise and decline of great powers—and the problem of "power transitions"—can trigger conflict, security competition, and war. The point here is that, in the long run, the way that China rises up in the world could have a more profound impact on American national security than incremental shifts up or down in the fortunes of international terrorist groups.[4]

The larger point is—and it is a critical assumption here—that today the United States confronts an unusually diverse and diffuse array of threats and challenges. When we try to imagine what the premier threat to the United States will be in 2015 or 2020, it is not easy to say with any confidence that it will be X, or Y, or Z. Moreover, even if we could identify X, or Y, or Z as the premier threat around which all others turn, it is very likely that it will be complex and interlinked with lots of other international moving parts. Global pandemics are connected to failed states, homeland security, international public health capacities, and so forth. Terrorism is related to the Middle East peace process, economic and political development, nonproliferation, intelligence cooperation, European social and immigration policy, and so forth. The rise of China is related to alliance cooperation, energy security, and democracy promotion, the WTO, management of the world economy, and so forth. So again we are back to renewing and rebuilding the architecture of global governance and frameworks of cooperation to allow the United States to marshal resources and tackle problems along a wide and shifting spectrum of possibilities.

In a world of multiple threats and uncertainty about their relative significance in the decades to come, it is useful to think of grand strategy as an "investment" problem. Where do you invest your and take actions so as to maximize your ability to be positioned to confront tomorrow's unknowns? Grand strategy is about se about diversifying risks and avoiding surprises.

This is where the pursuit of a milieu-based grand strategy is attractive. The objective is to shape the international environment to maximize your capacities to protect the nation from uncertain, diffuse, and shifting threats. You engage in liberal order building. This means investment in international cooperative frameworks—that is, rules, institutions, partnerships, networks, standby capacities, social knowledge, and so forth—in which the United States operates. To build international order is to increase the global stock of "social capital," which is the term Pierre Bourdieu, Robert Putnam, and others have used to define the actual and potential resources and capacities within a political community, manifest in and through its networks of social relations, that are available for solving collective problems. Taken together, liberal order building involves investing in the enhancement of global social capital so as to create capacities to solve problem that left unattended, will threaten national security.

AMERICA AND LIBERAL ORDER BUILDING

To pursue a milieu strategy- of liberal order building is to return to the type of grand strategy that America pursued in the 1940s and onward with great success. It is useful to recall the logic and accomplishments of this quintessentially American grand strategy. In fact, in the postwar era the United States did not just fight a global war against Soviet Communism, It also built a liberal international order. This order was not just the by-product of the pursuit of containment. It sprang from ideas and a logic of order that are deeply rooted in the American experience. It is an international order that generated power, wealth, stability, and security—all of which allowed the West to prevail in the cold war.

This postwar liberal order was built around a set of ideas, institutions, bargains, democratic community, and American hegemonic power. It is on this foundation that a renewed strategy of liberal order building must be based.

In comparison with the doctrine of containment, the ideas and policies of American postwar liberal order building were more diffuse and wide ranging. It was less obvious that the liberal order-building agenda was a "grand strategy" designed to advance American security interests. But in other respects it was the more enduring American project, one that was aimed at creating international order that would be open, stable, and friendly and that solved the problems of the 1930s—the economic breakdown and competing geopolitical blocs that paved the way for world war. The challenge was not merely to deter or contain the power of the Soviet Union but to lay the foundation for an international order that would allow the United States to thrive. This impulse—to build a stable and open international system that advantaged America—existed before, during, and after the cold war. Even at the moment when the cold war gathered force, the grand strategic interest in building such an order was appreciated. Indeed, one recalls that National Security Council Report 68 (NSC-68) laid out a doctrine of containment, but it also articulated a rationale for building a positive international order.

The United States needs, it said, to "build a healthy international community," which "we would probably do even if there were no international threat." The United States needs a "world environment in which the American system can survive and flourish."[5]

The vision of an American-led liberal international order was expressed in a sequence of declarations and agreements. The first was the Atlantic Charter of 1941, which spelled out a view of what the Atlantic and the wider world order would look like if the Allies won the war. This agreement was followed by the Bretton Woods agreements of 1944, the Marshall Plan in 1947, and the Atlantic pact in 1949. Together these agreements provided a framework for a radical reorganization of relations among the Atlantic democracies. The emerging cold war gave this Western-oriented agenda some urgency, and the American Congress was more willing to provide resources and approve international agreements because of the threats of Communist expansion lurking on the horizon. But the vision of a new order among the Western democracies predated the cold war, and even if the Soviet Union had slipped into history', some sort of Western order—open, institutionalized, American-led—would have been built.

Between 1944 and 1951, American leaders engaged in the most intensive institution building the world had ever seen—global, regional, security, economic, and political. The UN, Bretton Woods, the General Agreements on Tariffs and Trade (GATT), the North Atlantic Treaty Organization (NATO), and the U.S.–Japan alliance were all undertook costly obligations to aid Greece and Turkey and reconstruct Western Europe. It helped rebuild the economies of Germany and Japan. It fought the Korean War, putting paid to America's hegemonic presence in East Asia. With the Atlantic Charter, the UN Charter, and the Universal Declaration of Human Rights, it articulated a new vision of a progressive international community. In all these ways, the United States took the lead in fashioning a world of multilateral rules, institutions, open markets, democratic community, and regional partnerships—and it put itself at the center of it all.[6]

This was an extra ordinary and unprecedented undertaking for a major state. It marked the triumph of American inter 1919 and interwar failures. It signaled the creation of a new type of international order, fusing together new forms of liberalism, internationalism, and national security. It heralded the beginning of the "long peace"—the longest period of modern history without war between the great powers. It laid the foundation for the greatest world economic boom in history. This liberal international order is in crisis today, and it needs to be reimagined and rebuilt. But in almost all important respects, we still live in the world created during these hyperactive postwar years of liberal international order building.

The core idea of this liberal international order was that the United States would need to actively shape its security environment, creating a stable, open and friendly geopolitical space across Europe and Asia.[7] This required making commitments, building institutions, forging partnerships, acquiring clients, and providing liberal hegemonic leadership. In doing this, several ideas informed the substantive character of the emerging order. One idea was a basic commitment to economic openness among the regions. That is, capitalism would be organized internationally and or imperial lines. In many ways, this is what World War II was fought over. Germany and Japan each built their states around the military domination of their respective regions, Soviet Russia was an imperial continental power, and Great Britain had the imperial preference system. American interests were deeply committed to an open world economy—and an open world economy would tie together friends and former enemies.

A second idea behind liberal international order was that the new arrangements would need to be managed through international institutions and agreements. This was certainly the view of the economic officials who gathered in Bretton Woods in 1944. Governments would need to play a more direct supervisory role in stabilizing- and managing economic order. New forms of intergovernmental cooperation would need to be invented. The democratic countries would enmesh themselves in a dense array of intergovernmental networks and loose rule-based institutional relationships. In doing so, the United Stares committed itself to exercising power through these regional and global institutions. This was a great innovation in international order: the United States and its partners would create permanent governance institutions (ones that they themselves would dominate) to provide ongoing streams of cooperation needed to manage growing realms of complex interdependence.

A third idea was a progressive social bargain. If the United States and its partners were to uphold a global system of open markets, they would need to make commitments to economic growth, development, and social protections. This was the social bargain. There are losers in a system of open markets, but winners win more—so some of those winnings must be used for social protection and adjustment. Likewise, if the United States wants other countries to buy into this open order, it will need to help and support those states in establishing the sorts of Western social support structures that will allow for a stable and emerging democracy to coexist with open trade and investment.

Finally, there is the idea of cooperation security, or "security cobinding," In this liberal vision of international order, the United States will remain connected in close alliance with other democratic countries. NATO and the U.S.–Japan alliance are at the core of this alliance system, and these security pacts will be expanded and strengthened. This is a very important departure from past security arrangements—the United States would be connected to the other major democracies to create a single security system. Such a system would ensure that the democratic great powers would not go back to the dangerous game of strategy rivalry and power politics. It helped, of course, to have an emerging cold war to generate this cooperative security arrangement. But a security relationship between the United States and its allies was implicit in other elements of liberal order. A cooperative security order—embodied in formal alliance institutions—ensured that the power of the United States would be rendered more predictable. Power would be caged in institutions, thereby making American power more reliable and connected to Europe and East Asia.

With the end of the cold war, the American alliance system has seemed less vital to some people. What is forgotten, however, is that the postwar security pacts have always been about more than simply deterrence and containment of Soviet Communism. The alliances have also performed the function of providing "political architecture" for the policy community that bridges Europe, North America, and East Asia. The alliances provide mechanisms for each side to send signals of restraint and commitment. They provide institutional channels to "do business" across the advanced industrial world. They keep the United States engaged in Europe and Asia, and they allow leaders in Europe and East Asia to be engaged in and connected to Washington.

In the background, this American-led order is built on two historic bargains that the United States has made with its European and East Asian partners. One is a realist bargain and grows out of cold war grand strategy. The United States provides its European partners access to American markets, technology, and supplies within an open world economy. In return, these countries agree to be reliable partners who provide diplomatic, economic, and logistical support for the United States as it leads the wider Western postwar order. The result has been to tie America and its partners together—to make peace "indivisible" across the

Atlantic and Pacific. Binding security ties also provide channels for consultation and joint decision making.

The other is a liberal bargain that addresses the uncertainties of American preeminent power. East Asian and European states agree to work with the United States and operate within an agreed-on political-economic system. In return, the United States opens itself up and binds itself to its partners. In effect, the United States builds an institutionalized coalition of partners and reinforces the stability of these long-term mutually beneficial relations by making itself more "user friendly"—that is, by playing by the rules and creating ongoing political processes with these other states that facilitate consultation and joint decision making. The United States makes its power sage for the world and, in return, Europe and East Asia—and the wider world—agree to live within this liberal international system. The institutional structure of the order provides mechanisms for conveying reassurance and signals of restraint and commitment on the part of the United States, embedding American hegemonic power inside of a community of democracies.

Out of these ideas, institutions, and bargain has come a liberal hegemonic order that has been at the center of world politics for over half a century. It is an order that is not simply organized around the decentralized cooperation of like-minded democracies—although it is premised on a convergence of interests and values among the democratic capitalist great powers. It is an engineered political order that reconciles power and hierarchy with cooperation and legitimacy.

The resulting order is liberal hegemony, not empire. It is a political order in which the United States is first among equals, but it is not an imperial system. The United States dominates the order, but that domination is made relatively acceptable to other states by the liberal features of this order: the United States supports and operates within an agreed-on array of rules and institutions; the United States legitimates its leadership through the provision of public goods; and other states in the order have access to and "voice opportunities" within it—that is, there are reciprocal processes of communication and influence.

THE CRISIS OF AMERICAN LIBERAL HEGEMONY

This postwar system of global governance—organized around a set of ideas, institutions, bargains, democratic community, and American hegemonic power—is now in trouble. So too is America's position within it. This is a problem because in a world of shifting, diffuse, and uncertain threats, the United States needs to lead and operate within a strengthened—rather than weakened—liberal order.

This liberal hegemonic order is in crisis in several ways. It is a crisis, most immediately, of America's global position as manifest in Bush administration foreign policy. The credibility, respect, and authority of the United States as the leader of the global system has been radically diminished in recent years.[8] America has a legitimacy problem. There is a basic disconnect between the way the Bush administration wants the world to be run and the way other states and peoples want the world to be run. This is the most visible aspect of the crisis. Moreover, the postwar institutions through which America has traditionally operated are in crisis, or at least they have become severely weakened in recent years. The UN, NATO, the International Monetary Fund (IMF), the World Bank, and even the WTO are all searching for missions and authority The rise of new powers, particularly in Asia, is also putting pressure on these old postwar institutions to reform their membership and governance arrangements.[9] The institutional mechanisms of the system are not functioning very effectively or responding to emerging new demands. Finally, the deeper foundations of liberal international order have also been called into question. These are questions about how to reconcile rule-based order with a variety of new world historical developments—the rise of unipolariry, eroded state sovereignty, democratic legitimacy, and new sorts of security threats.

The immediate source of crisis is the Bush administration itself, which signaled from the beginning that it did not want to operate within the old postwar liberal order. This was signaled early in the administration by its resistance to a wide array of multilateral agreements, including the Kyoto Protocol on Climate Change, the Rome Statute of the International Criminal Court (ICC), the Germ Weapons Convention, and the Programme of Action on Illicit Trade in Small and Light Arms. It also unilaterally with drew from the 1970 Anti-Ballistic Missile (ABM) treaty, which many experts regard as the cornerstone of modern arms control agreements. Unilateralism, of course, is not a new feature of American foreign policy. In every historical era, the United States has shown a willingness rules, ignore allies, and use military force on it today's unilateralism as practiced by the Bush administration as something much more sweeping—not an occasional ad hoc policy decision but a new strategic orientation, or what one pundit calls the "new unilateralism."[10]

The most systematic rejection of the old lo the 2002 National Security Doctrine and the Iraq war, articulation a vision of America as a unipolar state positioned above and beyond the rules and institutions of the global system, providing security and enforcing order. It was a strategy of global rule in which the United States would remain a military power in a class by itself, thereby "making destabilizing arms races pointless and limiting rivalry to trade and other pursuits"[11] American preeminent power would, in effect, put an end to five centuries of great power rivalry. In doing so, it would take the lead in identifying and attacking threats—preemptively if necessary. America was providing the ultimate global public good. In return, the United States would ask to be less encumbered by rules and institutions of the old order. It would not sign the land troops were uniquely at risk in war zones around the world. It would not sign the ICC treaty because Americans would prosecutions. In effect, America would step forward and solve the problem of for Hobbes—it would be the world's Leviathan.

But in the hands of the Bush administration, America was to become a conservative Leviathan. That is, the Bush architects if grand strategy brought a conservative discourse about order to the unipolar moments rather than the traditional liberal discourse. This is crucial. At the earlier moments of American order building—after 1919, 1945, and 1989—American officials by the large invoked liberal ideas about order. These liberal ideas included, first, that the exercise of American power was consistent with, and indeed advanced by, strengthening the rule-based fabric of international community; second, that institutions and rules were integral tools of American power; and, third, that international legitimacy mattered in the conduct of U.S. foreign policy. As noted earlier, these ideas reinforced an American conviction that a loose multilateral order was the best vehicle for the advancement of American interests. What the Bush administration did was introduce a conservative discourse on international order. These ideas included, first national community that the United States had to build or adjust to; second, that rules and institutions were constraints on the United States; and, third, that legitimacy begins and ends at home—there is no "global test" for American foreign policy.[12]

The leading edge of this new conception of America's role and rule in the world concerned the use of force. The Bush administration's security doctrine was new and sweeping. The United States announced a right to use force anywhere in the world against "terrorists with global reach." It would do so largely outside the traditional alliance system through coalitions of the willing. The United States would take "anticipatory action" when it, by itself, determined that the use of force was necessary. Because these actions would be taken to oppose terrorists or overthrow despotic regimes, they would be self-legitimating. Countries were either "with us or against us"—or, as Bush announced, "no nation can be neutral in this conflict." Moreover, this new global security situation was essentially permanent—it "was not just a temporary emergency. There could be no final victory or peace settlement in this new war, so there would be no return to normalcy."[13]

The point is that the Bush administration was, in effect, announcing unilaterally the new rules of the global security order. It was not seeking a new global consensus on the terms of international order and change, and it was not renegotiating old bargains. The United States was imposing the rules of the new global order, rules that would be ratified not by the support of others but by the lurking presence of American power. This grand strategic move was a more profound shift than is generally appreciated. The Bush administration was not simply acting "a little bit more unilaterally" than previous administrations. In rhetoric, doctrine, and ultimately in the Iraq war, the United States was articulating a new logic of global order. The old liberal hegemonic rules, institutions, and bargains were now quaint artifacts of an earlier and less threatening era.

In the background, longer term shifts in the global system provided the permissive circumstances for the Bush administration's big doctrinal move. The shift from cold war bipolarity to American unipolarity has triggered a geopolitical adjustment process that runs through the 1990s and continues today. Unipolarity has given the United States more discretionary resources—and without a peer competitor or a great power-balancing coalition arrayed around it, the external constraints on American action are reduced. But with the end of the cold war, other states are not so much dependent on the United States for protection, and a unifying common threat has been eliminated. So old bargains, alliance partnerships, and shared strategic visions are thrown into question. At the very least, the shift in power advantages in favor of the United States would help explain why it might want to renegotiate older rules and institutions.

But more profoundly, unipolarity may be creating conditions that reduce the willingness of the United States to support and operate within a loosely rule-based order. If America is less dependent on other states for its own security, then it has reduced incentives restraints entailed in alliances and multilateral agreements. Incentives also increase for other states to free-ride on a unipolar America. Under these circumstances, the United States may indeed the past—or, in the absence of willing partners, its own willingness to provide hegemonic leadership may decline.[14]

The erosion of international norms of state sovereignty is also putting pressure on the old liberal hegemonic order. This is the quiet revolution in world politics: the rise of rights within the international community to intervene within states to protect individuals against the abuses of their own governments. The contingent character of sovereignty was pushed further after 9/11 in the intervention in Afghanistan, in which outside military force, used to topple a regime that actively protected terrorist attackers, was seen as an acceptable act of self-defense. But the erosion of state sovereignty has not been accompanied by the rise of new norms about how sovereignty-transgressing interventions should proceed. The "international community" has the right to act inside troubled and threatening states—but who precisely is the international community? The problem is made worse by the rise of unipolarity. Only the United

States really has the military power to engage systematically in large-scale uses of force around the world. The UN has no troops or military capacity of its own. The problem of establishing legitimate international authority grows.

The shift in the "security problem" away from great power war to transnational dangers such as terrorism disease, and insecurity generated within weak states also compounds the problem of legitimate authority inherent in the rise of unipolarity. If intervention into the affairs of weak and hostile states in troubled regions of the world is the new security frontier, the problems of who speaks for the international community and of the establishment of legitimate rules on the use of force multiply. America's unipolar military capabilities are both in demand and deeply controversial.

So the rise of unipolarity brought with it a shift in the underlying logic of order and rule in world politics. In a bipolar or multipolar system, powerful states "rule" in the process of leading a coalition of states in balancing against other states. When the system shifts to unipolarity, this logic of rule disappears. Power is no longer based on balancing and equilibrium but on the predominance of one state. This is new and different—and potentially threatening to weaker and secondary states. As a result, the power of the leading state is thrown into the full light of day. Unipolar power itself becomes a "problem" in world politics. As John Lewis Gaddis argues, American power during the cold war was accepted by other states because there was "something worse" over the horizon.[15] With the rise of unipolarity, that "something worse" disappears.

American power and a functioning global governance system have become disconnected. In the past, the United States provided global "services"—such as security protection and support for open markets—that made other states willing to work with rather than resist American power. The public goods provision tended to make it worthwhile for these states to endure the day-to-day irritations of American foreign policy. But the trade-off seems to have shifted. Today, the United States appears to be providing fewer public goods, whereas at the same time the irritations associated with American dominance appear to be growing.

THE NEW AGENDA OF LIBERAL ORDER BUILDING

If American grand strategy is to be organized around liberal order building, what are the specific objectives, and what is the policy agenda?

As we have seen, there are several objectives that such a strategy might seek to accomplish. The first is to build a stronger "protective infrastructure" of international capacities to confront an array of shifting, diffuse, and uncertain threats and catastrophes—this is, in effect, creating an infrastructure of global social services. The second is the rebuilding of a system of cooperative security, reestablishing the primacy of America's alliances for strategic cooperation and the projection of force. The third is the reform of global institutions that support collective action and multilateral management of globalization—such as the UN and multilateral economic institutions—creating greater institutional capacities for international decision making and the provision of public goods. The fourth is to create new institutions and reform old ones so that rising states—particularly China, but also India and other emerging powers—can more easily be embedded in the existing global system rather than operating as dissatisfied revisionist states on the outside. Finally, through all these efforts, the United States needs to endeavor to reestablish its hegemonic legitimacy—a preeminent objective that must be pursued with policies and a doctrine that signal America's commitment to rule-based order.[16]

Given these goals, the agenda of institutional order building would include the following.

First, the United States needs to lead in the building of an enhanced "protective infrastructure" that helps prevent the emergence of threats and limits the damage if they do materialize.[17] Many of the threats mentioned earlier manifest as socioeconomic backwardness and failure that generate regional and international instability and conflict. These are the sorts of threats that are likely to arise with the coming of global warning and epidemic disease. What is needed here is institutional cooperation to strengthen the capacity of governments and the international community to prevent epidemics, food shortages, or mass migrations that create global upheaval—or to mitigate the effects of these upheavals if they, in fact, occur.

It is useful to think of a strengthened protective infrastructure as investment in global social services, much as cities and states invest in such services. It typically is money well spent. Education, health programs, shelters, social services—these are vital components of stable and well-functioning communities. The international system already has a great deal of this infrastructure—institutions and networks that promote cooperation over public health, refugees, and emergency aid. But in the twenty-first century, as the scale and scope of potential problems grow, investments in these preventive and management capacities will also need to grow. Early warning systems, protocols for emergency operations, standby capacities, and so forth—these are the stuff of a protective global infrastructure.

Second, the United States should recommit to and rebuild its security alliances. The idea would be to update the old bargains that lie behind these security pacts. In NATO—but also in the Ease Asia bilateral partnerships—the United States agrees to provide security protection to the other states and bring its partners into the process of decision making over the use of force. In return, these partners agree to work with the United States, providing manpower, logistics, and other types of support in wider theaters of action. The United States gives up some autonomy in strategic decision making—although it is a more informal than legally binding restraint—and in exchange it gets cooperation and political support. The United States also remains "first among equals" within these organizations, and it retains leadership of the unified military command. The updating of these alliance bargains would involve widening the regional or global missions in which the alliance operates and making new compromises over the distribution of formal rights and responsibilities."[18]

There are several reasons why the renewal of security partnerships is critical to liberal order building. One is that security alliances involve relatively well-defined, specific, and limited commitments, and this is attractive for both the leading military power and its partners. States know what they are getting into and what the limits are on their obligations and liabilities. Another is that alliances provide institutional mechanisms that allow accommodations for disparities of power among partners within the alliance. Alliances do not embody universal rules and norms that apply equally to all parties. NATO, at least, is a multilateral body with formal and informal rules and norms of operation that both accommodate the most powerful state and provides roles and rights for others. Another virtue of renewing the alliances is that they have been institutional bodies that are useful as "political architecture" across the advanced democratic world. The alliances provide channels of communication and joint decision making that spill over into the wider realms of international relations. They are also institutions with grand histories and records of accomplishment. The United States is a unipolar military power, but it still has incentives to share the costs of security protection and to find ways to legitimate the use of its power. The postwar alliances—renewed and reorganized—are an attractive tool for these purposes.

Robert Kagan has argued that to regain its lost legitimacy, the United States needs to return to its postwar bargain: giving some Europeans voice over American policy in exchange for their support. The United States, Kagan points out, "should try to fulfill its part of the transatlantic bargain by granting Europeans some influence over the exercise of its power—provided that, in return, Europeans wield that influence wisely."[19] This is the logic that informed American security cooperation with its European and East Asian partners during the cold war. It is a logic that can be renewed today to help make unipolarity more acceptable.

Third, the United States needs encompassing global institutions that foster and legitimate collective action. The first move here should be to reform the United Nations, starting with the expansion of the permanent membership on the Security Council. Several plans have been proposed. All of them entail new members—such as Germany, Japan, India, Brazil, South Africa, and others—and reformed voting procedures. Almost all of the candidates for permanent membership are mature or rising democracies. The goal, of course, is to make them stakeholders in the United Nations and thereby strengthen the primacy of the United Nations as a vehicle for global collective action. There really is no substitute for the legitimacy that the United Nations can offer to emergency actions—humanitarian interventions, economic sanctions, use of force against terrorists, and so forth. Public support in advanced democracies grows rapidly when their governments can stand behind a United Nations-sanctioned action.

The other step is to create a "concert of democracies." The idea would not be to establish a substitute body for the United Nations—which some advocates of a concert or league suggest—but simply to provide another international forum where democracies can discuss common goals and reinforce cooperation. Proposals exist for various types of groupings of democracies, some informal and consultative and others more formal and task oriented.[20]

The experience of the last century suggests that the United States is more likely to make institutional commitments and bind itself to other states if those countries are democracies. This is true for both practical and normative reasons. Because liberal democracies are governed by the rule of law and open to scrutiny, it is easier to establish the credibility of their promises and to develop long-term commitments. But the values and identities that democracies share also make it easier for them to affiliate and build cooperative relations. These shared identities were probably more strongly felt during the cold war when the United States was part of a larger "free world." Institutionalized cooperation between the United States and its European and East Asian partners is surely driven by shared interests, but it is reinforced by shared values and common principles of government. American leaders find it easier to rally domestic support for costly commitments and agreements abroad when the goal is to help other democracies and to strengthen the community of democracies.

Fourth, the process of order building must include the embedding of rising states. The rise of China—and Greater Asia—is perhaps the seminal drama of our time. In the decades to come, america's unipolar power will give way to a more bipolar, multipolar, or decentralized distribution of power. China will most likely be a dominant state, and the United States will need to yield to it in various ways. The national security question for America to ask today is: What sorts of investments in global institutional architecture do we want to make now so that the coming power so that the coming power shifts will adversely affect us the least? That is, what sorts of institutional arrangements do we want to have in place to protect our interests when we are less powerful? This is a sort of neo-Rawlsian question that should inform American strategic decision making.

The answer to this neo-Rawlsian question would seem to be twofold. One is that the United States should try to embed the foundations of the Western-oriented international system so deeply that China has overwhelming incentives to integrate into it rather than to oppose and overturn it. Those American strategists who fear a rising China the most should be ultra-ambitious liberal institution builders. The United States should compose its differences with Europe and renew joint commitments to alliance and multilateral global governance, The more that China faces not just the United States but a united West, the better. The more that China faces not must a united West but the entire Organization for Economic Cooperation and Development (OECD) world of capitalist democracies, the better. This is not to argue that China should face a grand counterbalancing alliance against it. Rather, China should face a complex and deeply integrated global system—one that is so encompassing and deeply entrenched that China essentially has no choice but to join it and seek to prosper within it. Indeed, the United States should take advantage of one of the great virtues of liberal hegemony, namely, that it is easy to join and hard to overturn. The layers of institutions and channels of access provide relatively easy entry points for China to join the existing international order.[21] is precisely the wrong historical moment for the United States to be uprooting and disassembling its own liberal hegemonic order.

In a version of this argument, Timothy Garten Ash has suggested that the United States and Europe have about twenty years more to control the levers of global governance before they will need to cede power to China and other rising states. His point is that the two Western powers need to take the long view, develop a common strategic vision, and redouble commitment to Atlantic cooperation.[22]

The second answer to the neo-Rawlsian question is to encourage the building of a regional East Asian security order that will provide a framework for managing the coming power shifts. The idea is not to block China's entry into the regional order but to help shape its terms, looking for opportunities to strike strategic bargains at various moments along the shifting power trajectories and encroaching geopolitical spheres. The big bargain that the United States will want to strike with China is this: to accommodate a rising China by offering it status and position within the regional order in return for Beijing's accepting and accommodating Washington's core strategic interests, which include remaining a dominant security provider within East Asia.

In striking this strategic bargain, the United States will also want to try to build multilateral institutional arrangements in East Asia that will tie down and bind China to the wider region. China has already grasped the utility of this strategy in recent years, and it is now actively seeking to reassure and co-opt its neighbors by offering to embed itself in regional institutions such as the Association of Southeast Asian Nations (ASEAN) Plus Three and the East Asia Summit. This is, of course, precisely what the United States did in the decades after World War II, building and operating within layers of regional and global economic, political, and security institutions—thereby making itself more predictable and approachable and reducing the incentives that other states would otherwise have to resist or undermine the United States by building countervailing coalitions.

The challenge for the United States is to encourage China to continue along this pathway, allaying worries about its growing power by binding itself to its neighbors and the region itself. But to do this, there will need to be a more formal and articulated regional security organization established into which China can integrate. Such an organization need not have the features of an alliance system—the countries in the region are not ready for this. But what is needed is a security organization that has at its center a treaty of nonaggression and mechanisms for periodic consultation.

Fifth and finally, a liberal internationalist "public philosophy" should be reclaimed. When American officials after World War II championed the building of a rule-based postwar order, they articulated a distinctive internationalist vision of order that has faded in recent decades. It was a vision that entailed a synthesis of liberal and realist ideas about economic and national security and the sources of stable and peaceful order. These ideas, drawn from the experiences in the 1940s with the New Deal and in the previous decades of war and depression, led American leaders to associate the national interest with the building of a managed and institutionalized global system. What is needed today is a renewed public philosophy of liberal internationalism that can inform American elites as they make trade-offs between sovereignty and institutional cooperation.

What American elites need to do today is recover this public philosophy of internationalism. The restraint and the commitment of U.S. power went hand in hand. Global rules and institutions advanced America's national interest rather than threatened it. The alternative public philosophies that circulate today—philosophies that champion American unilateralism and disentanglement from global rules and institutions—are not meeting with great success. So an opening exists for America's postwar vision of internationalism to be updated and rearticulated today.

CONCLUSION

In his memoir on American diplomacy at the end of the cold war, former Secretary of State James Baker recalled the thinking of his predecessors from the 1940s: "Men like Truman and Acheson were above all, though we sometimes forget it, institution builders. They created NATO and the other security organizations that eventually won the Cold War. They fostered the economic institutions . . . that brought unparalleled prosperity . . . At a time of similar opportunity and risk, I believed we should take a leaf from their book."[23] In proposing a post-Bush grand strategy of liberal order building, I am urging the return to this same global strategy, updated to the security environment of the twenty-first century.

The United States needs to plan for a future of sprawling and shifting threats. This means pursuing a milieu-based grand strategy, building international frameworks of cooperation to deal with multiple and evolving contingencies. To build a grand strategy around one threat is to miss the importance of the others, as well as to miss the dangerous connections between these threats. This is not to belittle the al Qaeda threat. But the point is that it is important for the United States to pull back and invest in the creation of an international environment to handle, well, come what may.

The good news is that the United States is fabulously good at pursuing a milieu-based grand strategy. The Bush administration sought a radical break with the postwar American approach to order but it failed—and failed spectacularly. It sought to construct global order around American unipolar rule, asserting new rights to use force while reducing the country's exposure to multilateral rules and institutions, America's strategic position has weakened as a result, and the institutions that have leveraged and legitimated its power have eroded. If America wants to remain at the center of an open world system—one that is friendly and cooperative and capable of generating collective action in pursuit of diverse and shifting security challenges—it will need to return to its tradition of liberal order building.

For the most part, the great powers in the modern era have pursued "positional" grand strategies. They have identified rivals and enemies and organized their foreign policy accordingly. Across the historical eras, the results have been various sorts of balances of power and imperial systems. Once in a while, a state can dare to ask slightly loftier questions about the organization of the international system. Here the questions are metaquestions about political order itself. These are essentially "constitutional" questions about the first principles and organizational logic of the global system. The great powers collectively addressed these questions after 1815, and the United States and its allies did it again after the world wars. Today, the United States can once again ask these constitutional-like questions. What sort of global governance order would the United States like to see in operation in, say, 2020 or 2030? If we are uncertain today about what precisely will worry us tomorrow, what sort of mechanisms of governance would we like to see established to deal with these unknowns? If all we know is that the security threats of tomorrow will be shifting, diffuse, and uncertain, we should want to create a flexible and capable political system that can meet and defeat a lot of complex threats.

We do know that growing globalization and the diffusion of technologies of violence will make it necessary to develop a complex protective infrastructure drat will support global efforts at intelligence, monitoring, inspections, and enforcement. We will need the International Atomic Energy Agency on steroids. We also know that new states will be rising and wanting to share or compete for leadership, so there is an incentive today to get the rules and institutions embedded for the future. Under conditions of intensifying globalization, the opportunity costs of not coordinating national policies grow relative to the costs of lost autonomy associated with making binding agreements. So when we look into the future, we do know that there will be a growing premium attached to institutionalized forms of cooperation. The governance structures that pass for international politics today will need to be rebuilt and made much more complex and encompassing in the decades ahead.

Looking into this brave new world, the United States will find itself needing to share power and to rely in part on others to ensure its security. It will not be able to depend on unipolar power or airtight borders. To operate in this coming world, the United States will need—more than anything else—authority and respect as a global leader. It has lost that authority and respect in recent years. In committing itself to a grand strategy of liberal order building, it can begin the process of gaining it back.

NOTES

1. *Barry Posen, Sources of Military Doctrine* (Ithaca, NY: Cornell University Press, 1983), 13.
2. This is our judgment in the Final Report of the Princeton Project on National Security. See G. John Ikenberry and Anne-Marie Slaughter, *Forging a World of Liberty: under Law* (Princeton, NJ: Woodrow Wilson School of International and Public Affairs, 2006).
3. Thomas Homer-Dixon, *The Upside of Down: Catastrophe, Creativity, and the Renewal of Civilization* (Washington, DC: Island Press, 2006), 16–17.
4. This argument is advanced in Francis Fukuyama and G. John Ikenberry, "Report of the Grand Strategic Choices Working Group" (Princeton Project on National Security, Princeton University, 2005).
5. NSC-68 as published in Ernest May, ed., *American Cold War Strategy: Interpreting NSC-68* (New York: St. Martin's, 1993), 40.

6. I sketch this logic of liberal hegemony in G. John Ikenberry, *After Victory: Institutions, Strategic Restraint, and the Rebuilding of Order after Major War* (Princeton, NJ: Princeton University Press, 2001).

7. See Melvyn P. Leffler, *A Preponderance of Power: National Security, the Truman Administration, and the Cold War* (Stanford, CA: Stanford University Press, 1992), chapter 2.

8. Recent opinion polls from around the world reveal this changed reality. In a summary of these results, the report indicates: "A multinational poll finds that publics around the world reject the idea that the United States should play the role of preeminent world leader. Most publics say the United States plays the role of world policeman more than it should, fails to take their country's interests into account and cannot be trusted to act responsibly." The Chicago Council on Global Affairs and WorldPublicOpinion.org, "World Publics Reject U.S. Role as the World Leader" (April 18, 2007), http://www.thechicagocouncil.org/media_press_room_detail.php?press_release_id=62.

9. See G. John Ikenberry, "A Weakened World," *Prospect* (UK) (November 2005): 30–33.

10. Charles Krauthammer, "The New Unilateralism," Washington Post, June 8, 2001.

11. President George W. Bush, 2002 West Point commencement speech (June 1, 2002), http://www.whitehouse.gov/news/releases/2002/06/20020601–3.html.

12. G. John Ikenberry, "Why Bush Foreign Policy Fails," unpublished paper (2005).

13. These features of the Bush doctrine are discussed in Ian Shapiro, *Containment: Rebuilding a Strategy against Global Terror* (Princeton, NJ: Princeton University Press, 2007).

14. See Robert Jervis, "The Remaking of a Unipolar World," *Washington Quarterly* 29, no. 2 (2006): 7–19; and G. John Ikenberry, "Global Security Trap," *Democracy: A Journal of Ideas* 1, no. 2 (September 2006).

15. John Lewis Gaddis, *Surprise, Security and the American Experience* (Cambridge, MA: Harvard University Press, 2004), 66–67.

16. This section builds on Ikenberry and Slaughter, *Forging a World of Liberty under Law*. The case for global order built around "multi-multilateralism" is made in Francis Fukuyama, *America at the Crossroads: Democracy, Power, and the Neoconservative Legacy* (New Haven, CT: Yale University Press, 2007).

17. See Ikenberry and Slaughter, *Forging a World of Liberty under Law*, 10.

18. The case for renewal of NATO is made in Ikenberry and Slaughter, *Forging a World of Liberty under Law*.

19. Robert Kagan, "America's Crisis of Legitimacy," Foreign Affairs 83, no. 2 (March 2004): 86.

20. For proposals to create a concert of democracies, see Ikenberry and Slaughter, *Forging a World of Liberty under Law*; Ivo Daalder and James Lindsey, "Democracies of the World Unite," *The American Interest* (January–February 2007), http://www.the-american-interestcorn/ai2/artide.cfm?Id=2i9&MId=6; and Tod Lindberg, "The Treaty of the Democratic Peace," *Weekly Standard* (February 12, 2007): 19–24,

21. See G. John Ikenberry, "The Rise of China, Power Transitions, and Western Order," in *China's Ascent: Power, Security, and the Future of International Politics*, ed. Robert S. Ross and Zhu Feng (Ithaca, NY: Cornell University Press, 2008).

22. Timothy Garten Ash, *Free World: America, Europe, and the Surprising Future of the West* (New York: Random House, 2004).

23. James A. Baker, *The Politics of Diplomacy: Revolution, War, and Peace, 1989–1992* (New York: Putnam, 1995), 605–606.

᠀

A Moral Core for U.S. Foreign Policy: Is Idealism Dead?

By Derek Chollet and Tod Lindberg

Is idealism dead? Should the promotion of American values of liberalism, democracy, human rights, and rule of law be a core element of U.S. foreign policy? Where to strike the balance between principles and interests is—one of the most enduring debates about America 's role in the world. But since September 11, this question has become intensely contested and deeply controversial. It has emerged as one of the central divides between the political right and left—in large part because of the history of the past seven years, the Bush administration's rhetoric, its strong association with the "freedom agenda," and its actions justified at least in part by democracy promotion (namely the war in Iraq). Yet it is also becoming a sharper division *within* each end of the political spectrum.

Of course, the choice between realism and idealism is a false one: U.S. foreign policy must be firmly rooted in both national interests and values. But now, after two successive presidents of opposite political parties (Bill Clinton and George W. Bush) have argued that spreading American values is itself a vital interest, there is growing skepticism in many quarters about whether trying to do so is worth significant costs, or even a true interest of the United States at all. Facts matter, and after several difficult years of pursuing a foreign policy framed as a fight for American values, more are wondering whether the sacrifice is worth it. In the view of many policymakers, politicians, analysts, and average citizens, the time has come to have a more realistic foreign policy—scaling back the United States' global ambitions, respecting the limits to America's capabilities and will, recognizing and embracing the constraints of the international system, and maintaining a healthy skepticism about the broad applicability of American values.

But if the values agenda has been discredited among many on both the left and the right and a greater realism is the preferred alternative, what would such a strategy look like? Moving beyond the slogans, would a truly values-free foreign policy really secure U.S. interests, strengthen U.S. power, and draw the sustained support of the American people? We think not. American values are an indispensable component of the U.S. role in the world— they are a key part of what unites the United States to allies in Europe and elsewhere and distinguishes the United States from countries like China. Instead of dividing conservatives and liberals, American values in foreign policy can in fact translate into a moral core that both sides can rally around. In the current political environment, as we approach the first post-9/11, post-Bush election, building such a policy bridge will be difficult. But given the stakes, it is imperative.

Derek Chollet and Tod Lindberg, "A Moral Core for U.S. Foreign Policy," *Policy Review*, Dec. 2007 and Jan. 2008. Reprinted by permission.

SKEPTICISM ON THE LEFT

The emphasis placed on promoting liberal values internationally has drawn increasing hostility among traditional liberals and within the Democratic Party. Many of those who once embraced the proud liberal tradition of Woodrow Wilson, Franklin D. Roosevelt, and John F. Kennedy find themselves questioning their assumptions. And for those liberals who still embrace the importance of values, their numbers are fewer. According to a June 2006 poll commissioned by the German Marshall Fund of the United States, only 35 percent of Democrats said that the United States should "help establish democracy in other countries"—whereas 64 percent of Republicans responded favorably.[1]

This skepticism is driven by several factors. First, and most fundamental, is the fact that this approach is so closely identified with President Bush and his administration 's policies. In the wake of 9/11, Bush tapped into many common (and bipartisan) themes about the enduring importance of American values, but his vision is infused with a religiosity that leaves many liberals nervous. Yet even when he got his rhetoric right—for example, many liberals admired statements like his November 2003 speech at the National Endowment for Democracy—the means he chose to implement policies, such as the war in Iraq, have proven very costly. The result now is that for many on the left, efforts to pursue policies largely rooted in values, especially democracy promotion, have become discredited and are increasingly unpopular politically.

For some liberals, the political difficulty of supporting a values-based foreign policy stems from a second factor: the structural incentives of the current political environment. Because an unpopular president has so closely identified his policies with the promotion of values, liberals are driven to oppose him. In fact, the president's leadership style has offered very little in return, even to those liberals who might agree with him. So for many on the left, if Bush is for it, they must be against it—even if this means embracing the dognitive dissonance of turning away from long-held beliefs and traditions. For many liberals, it has become politically incorrect to admit it when Bush has actually gotten something right. With Democrats in control of the U.S. Congress these incentives of opposition are now also institutional. This creates a dynamic similar to that of the aftermath of the 1994 congressional elections, when the new Republican majority turned increasingly inward in opposition to the internationalism of the Clinton administration. Whereas the Bush team came into office in 2001 with an "ABC" policy—anything but Clinton—the Democratic Congress today, and a possible Democratic president in 2009, will be tempted to do exactly the same: anything but Bush.

But liberal skepticism is more than structural or institutional—it is also internal to the debates among different camps within liberal politics. The history of the past seven years—and the consequences of a policy perceived as driven more by values than interest—has been sobering for a number of left-leaning members of the foreign policy establishment. Many supported the 2003 invasion of Iraq for the same reasons that they supported confronting Saddam Hussein during the Clinton years. And many applauded President Bush when he talked about the importance of democracy promotion. Yet now that the costs of such policies are apparent—whether in terms of political capital, U.S. global prestige, or blood and treasure—many in the foreign policy elite have become more cautious, scaling back ambitions and endorsing more realistic goals. For many mainstream foreign policy liberals, the downfall of Britain's Tony Blair—who championed values-based concepts like "humanitarian intervention" during the late 1990s—is a stark warning about the costs of embracing such policies too tightly.

The intellectual and political disconnect between the liberal establishment and the liberal grassroots activists is growing, especially over U.S. foreign policy and the purpose and use of American power. The convulsions within the political left that began in the late 1990s—illustrated by the rise of the antiglobalization movement and division over the Clinton administration's military interventions in Bosnia, Kosovo, and its 1998 air strikes against Iraq—have only become more severe and divisive. To be sure, this reflects anger with President Bush. But it is more than that. When it comes to national security issues, the left has become splintered in a way not seen since the 1970s, when Vietnam split the Democratic party and ruined the post-World War II liberal establishment. A similar dynamic is at work today as a new generation of liberal activists (fueled by the power of the blogosphere) rages not just against Bush, but against a Democratic foreign policy establishment they perceive as aiding and abetting the Bush agenda—central to which is the promotion of American values. If this divide deepens, it will become very difficult for Democratic leaders to embrace explicitly values-centered policies even if they want to.

WARINESS ON THE RIGHT

The growing discomfort with the promotion of American values in foreign policy is felt not only by those on the left. Increasingly, conservatives are having second thoughts about the extent to which U.S. foreign policy should be driven by ideology and the promotion of values ahead of interests. Since the Bush administration still dominates conservative politics, the right remains more strongly identified with the values agenda, and the wariness among conservatives is more muted than among liberals. But the recent rise of "realists"—as illustrated by the personnel changes at the Defense Department and the U.S. Mission to the United Nations, greater pragmatism at the State Department, and the return to prominence of figures like former Secretary of State James Baker and Brent Scowcroft—has been heralded as a rebalancing away from what many argue were the ideological excesses of the president's first four years in office. Like liberals, conservatives are contemplating their future beyond the Bush presidency—and this debate will only intensify as the focus turns from the current administration to the one that will take office in January 2009.

In several respects, the factors driving conservatives' frustrations with the values agenda mirror the frustrations on the left. The first issue is a practical one: The American people's deepening disillusionment with the Bush administration's policies is raising the political costs of supporting the Bush agenda. Bush's unpopularity makes supporting his policies risky. Put another way, the president's success at branding his administration's actions as part of a values-based policy is directly related to the political efficacy of supporting it. When it was seen as working, the bandwagon was enthusiastic and big, but the more it is perceived as a failure, many of the president's political allies are more than happy to let him ride alone.

Like liberals, conservatives also face a structural challenge that will only increase as the 2008 election draws closer. Any Republican presidential nominee will seek to differentiate himself from his predecessor. And since more conservatives are reading the Bush years as a caution against an ambitious, values-based foreign policy, stressing realism might be the way to distinguish oneself. In this sense, one can foresee a replay of the early 1990s, when the lesson drawn from George H. W. Bush's electoral defeat in 1992—that his presidency was too focused on foreign affairs at the expense of domestic issues—caused many conservatives to move away not only from a values-based policy but from internationalism itself.

Moreover, the events of the past several years, especially the war in Iraq, have thrown much of the conservative foreign policy establishment into a crisis of confidence. Like many establishment liberals, conservatives in and out of government are questioning not only the capabilities required to implement values-promoting policies (and whether the United States can ever develop such capabilities), but the underlying assumptions of the policy itself. Such self-doubt is especially acute because many of the officials so closely identified with these policies were once heralded for their national security experience and acumen. Expectations were high, so the results of their time in office—a major crisis for America's role in the world—have been sobering.

The neoconservatives, those most closely identified with a foreign policy based on promoting American values and bold interventionism—have come in for the most criticism, and not just from the left. The internal split reemerging within conservatism over ideals is the fourth driver of wariness. During the 1990s, neoconservatives saw themselves as insurgents, agitating against both the creeping isolationism within the Republican party and what they considered the feckless policies of the Clinton team (even if most neoconservatives agreed on actions like intervention in the Balkans). But for several years after 9/11, their agenda wielded great influence over the direction of the Bush administration's policy, especially its focus on spreading American values. Six years later, neoconservatives again find themselves largely on the outside looking in as many mainstream Republicans seek a return to the kinds of policies then-Governor Bush articulated during the 2000 presidential campaign: a foreign policy based on humility, skepticism about the United States' interests in "nation-building," and the limited applicability of American values to regions like the Middle East.

So for political and intellectual reasons, the role of values in foreign policy is now in retreat domestically—liberals are increasingly skeptical, and conservatives have deep doubts. One must also note the suspicion (or worse) with which many in other countries view a values-based U.S. foreign policy. In the first place, many around the world are disinclined to take Americans at their word on the principles they claim to be promoting. They hear rhetoric of principle as nothing more than a cover for the raw assertion of American power. Some world leaders hear the rhetoric of democracy promotion and take it seriously and for that very reason regard it as dangerous, a threat to their own claims of legitimacy. One could probably break this category down further, into those hostile to any threat to their personal prerogatives on the one hand and, on the other, those generally sympathetic to liberalization but worried that too-hasty movement in that direction might tear their societies apart.

Finally, the promotion of American values opens the United States to charges of hypocrisy: Does American conduct actually live up to the values America espouses? Many have found the United States's actions wanting in areas ranging from Guantanamo and Abu Ghraib to the U.S. relationship with Pakistan and the House of Saud and would urge that the United States tone down its complaints about others until it removes the log in its own eye. By these lights, the promotion of American values should begin at home (a view that also has purchase both on the left side of American public opinion and, to a degree, on the libertarian right).

THE "ACIREMA" WORLD

But if a foreign policy that promotes American values is the problem, what is the solution? In considering this question, it might be helpful to ask: What would U.S. foreign policy actually look like if it were somehow stripped of its "values" component? It's worth trying to conjure such a vision, not only as an intellectual exercise, but also because there is no quicker way to see exactly why such a policy would be a nonstarter for the United States.

As a point of departure, we might look to the assumptions about the character of the international system embraced by scholars in the "neorealist" school of international relations, on the grounds that neorealists regard such considerations as morality as largely epiphenomenal in explaining the behavior of states. Since one key neorealist assumption is that the internal characteristics of states don't matter (or matter much), we find a more or less explicit attempt to write moral considerations out of the rules of statecraft. What they posit, then, is an anarchical international system—no authority higher than the state. Each state wishes to be entirely free to make its own judgments about the conduct of its internal affairs. These judgments, insofar as they implicate events outside the state's territory and thus beyond its uncontested authority, yield a set of national interests in relation to other states. Because any state's supreme vital interest is self-preservation, each state's first priority is to ensure its security. The only means of achieving security is self-help. Unfortunately, the actions states take in pursuit of their own security and national interests tend to bring them into conflict with other states. Some structural configurations of the international system are more conducive to peace and stability than others, but no structure is impervious to internal stresses that may cause it to collapse or change convulsively as states act in pursuit of security under shifting perceptions of national interest.

How might this abstract description of state action in the international system translate into policy choices for a state in the position in which the United States finds itself today? For purposes of our investigation, we will call this state "Acirema," which is "America" spelled backwards. We do this for two reasons. First, by speculating in accordance with this "values-free" scenario, we do not want to be taken to be proposing what follows as a genuine alternative to U.S. policy; on the contrary, the speculation shows how far removed from the realm of possibility and desirability such a neorealist scenario would be. Second, "Acirema" strikes us as capturing just how radical an inversion of American priorities and traditions the pursuit of such a values-free policy would be.

In the first place, Acirema is the dominant military power in the world, and it would certainly make sense to try to maintain that dominance. This is not a judgment alien to existing U.S. policy: The Bush administration's 2002 National Security Strategy (NSS) pledged not to allow a "peer competitor" to its military power to emerge. The Bush NSS, however, justified this policy as a way to encourage peaceful relations among states. State-on-state conflict—for example, the attempt to conquer territory by force—would be discouraged by overwhelming U.S. power. But it is by no means clear, from a values-free perspective, why Acirema should be attached to a principle of peaceful relations among states and the illegitimacy of aggressive war or conquest. True, Acirema does not want to be attacked and would seek to maintain sufficient power to deter and if necessary defeat any potential aggressor. But why Acirema would care if Iran attacked Iraq, or China attacked Russia, or France attacked Germany is entirely a question of whether Acirema's aims would best be served by peace or war between any given two states.

Acirema would pursue an overall strategy of maintaining its dominance. Again, this is not foreign to current U.S. grand strategy. But the United States has welcomed and encouraged modernization, economic growth, and globalization not only in order to enrich Americans, but also according to a theory that greater trade flows and economic interdependence make for a more peaceful international environment and are good in themselves. Neither of the latter two justifications would matter to Acirema.

There is danger in an Acireman policy that encourages other states to become rich: With riches comes the capacity to develop military power that in turn might challenge Acirema, or covertly to fund challenges and challengers. Acireman policymakers would want to examine the trade-off between the economic benefits of an open trading system and the potential danger in allowing others to enrich themselves, thus potentially increasing their power. An Asian economic flu might be a bad thing, but it might also be a good thing.

China's modernization might yield cheap goods, but if the price is a more formidable military challenge to Acirema, the price might be too high. The best way to deal with China's self-professed desire for a "peaceful rise" might be to disregard the rhetoric of peaceability and act to prevent the rise. Acirema might want to identify potential vulnerabilities in the Chinese economy and try to exploit them to undermine Chinese economic growth. The collapse of central authority in China would be destabilizing—but primarily for the Chinese, who might then be too preoccupied with their internal turmoil to pose a threat.

More generally, the stability Acirema would seek would be the stability of its own position. The stability of other states and relations among other states is of concern only insofar as it impinges on the stability of the Acireman position. Indeed, a subsidiary strategy of preserving dominance might be to maintain a *fragile* international stability, one in which all other states felt themselves to be constantly at *risk* from instability without actually sliding into it with a potentially adverse effect on Acirema.

Under this scenario, one would have to reject engagement in the Middle East, except with regard to securing Acireman energy needs. To the extent that support for Israel arouses hostility from Israel's neighbors, Acirema should cease such support unless Israel is capable of providing a benefit to Acirema sufficient to offset the damage—a tall order. Meanwhile, however, it is not solely Acireman support for Israel that antagonizes certain elements in the Middle East, and to the extent that funding for these elements comes from governments that have grown wealthy from oil revenues, it may be best to go directly to the source and deprive the funders of the revenue. Acirema might seize and hold sufficient oilfields to see to its needs and then destroy the capacity of others to exploit the resources on their territory.

In the event that the negative repercussions of such a move might be deemed too costly, then Acireman disengagement from the region might work—provided accompanied by an unambiguous warning from Acirema to states in the region about the unacceptability of funding terrorists, their ideological supporters, and their sympathizers. Acirema would have to make clear that regime elimination awaits any states that fail to accept that their continued oil revenue depends on their refraining from harboring, funding, or supporting anti-Acireman terrorism. The credibility of such a policy would likely require a demonstration. A policy of regime elimination would differ from "regime change" in its rejection of Colin Powell's "Pottery Barn" principle: You break it, you own it. On the contrary, any state foolish enough to provoke Acirema to forcibly remove its regime, with all the risk and expense that would entail for Aciremans, would be on its own to sort out what comes next. Acirema wouldn't care, though it would certainly hope that whatever regime emerged had learned a lesson from the experience of the toppling of its predecessor.

The policy of Acirema toward Israel is a specific case of what would be a more general revision in alliance policy. The essential question for Acirema with regard to any ally is whether Acireman security is improved, on net, as a result of the alliance. The notion of an alliance as an all-purpose mechanism for securing the cooperation of others in mutual pursuit of security objectives would need to be reassessed. What, specifically, is the value of "cooperation"?

Needless to say, Acirema will harbor no prejudice in favor of cooperation or multilateralism, instead asking whether cooperative or multilateral means would bring a benefit that Acirema cannot obtain on its own. Acirema need not be especially concerned with the opinions of states that lack the capacity to make a difference. There will be no free-riding on the provision of security, because Acirema will not enter into alliance relationships except with partners whose tangible assets improve Acireman security.

Needless to say, any assistance Acirema would choose to provide to other states would be tightly tied to the tangible benefit received, either economically or in terms of security. The notion of "humanitarian" aid or "humanitarian" intervention of any kind is self-evidently meaningless to a foreign policy free of moral consideration. Acirema might have a concern with averting refugee flows toward its shores, but only if the cost of action abroad to prevent the flows exceeds the cost of turning away those attempting to enter.

Local disputes in faraway places would not necessarily bother Acirema. There is nothing historically unusual about violent contests for power within states, and Acirema would not worry overmuch about the outbreak of such conflicts. They have disadvantages in terms of disrupting commerce, but they have advantages as well in that those engaged in fierce local conflict are unlikely to have the surplus capacity to threaten Acireman national interests. Even intense local conflict, with civilian deaths running to hundreds of thousands, would have to be assessed through the prism of whether it poses any sort of threat to Acirema that might warrant intervention.

It is difficult to see what gain Acirema might get from raising the issue of "human rights" with other states. Doing so would come at the cost of pressing other, more useful demands upon weaker states and would needlessly complicate relations with stronger states. There might be advantages to be gained from fomenting internal dissension and rebellion within stronger states in accordance with a general strategy of fragile stability, and this provocation might be couched in terms of "human rights" in the event that doing so would be efficacious. But the use of "human rights" would be entirely instrumental, and Acirema would have to refrain from establishing any sentimental bonds with those it was encouraging, since the likelihood is that the state in which they are rebelling will move to crush them if the crisis becomes serious, and of course Acirema would have no reason to assist them at that point.

The strongest states will be those with nuclear weapons, and the impulse of states to acquire them would undoubtedly be very strong. Needless to say, Acirema would have to be very wary of states already possessing substantial nuclear arsenals. Freedom of action against Russia, China, Great Britain, France, and Israel would accordingly be constrained. As for those newly seeking to acquire the technology of atomic weapons, Acirema might choose to acquiesce, provided it was confident that its own arsenal was deterring any aggression against Acirema. This might be true of some but not all states. On the other hand, possession of a nuclear deterrent by another state might embolden that state to act against the national interests of Acirema. It might be necessary to take preemptive action to establish that mere possession of a few nuclear weapons is not sufficient to deter or coerce Acirema. Acirema might have to launch a nuclear attack first. Of course, there would be some risk of nuclear counterattack if the other state had the means to deliver its nuclear weapons. On the other hand, Acirema could withstand such a small strike, whereas its antagonist would be obliterated.

Yes, we have wandered into the bizarro territory of *Dr. Stangelove*, and the scenario described above is both monstrous to contemplate and impossible to envision actually coming to pass. But why is that? In the first place, can anyone—liberal or conservative—plausibly imagine the United States electing a president on such a callous "Acirema First" platform? Patrick Buchanan tried a slightly attenuated version of the Acirema project and was unable to win the Republican nomination, let alone seriously contest the general election. During the 2000 election, the platform of Ralph Nader's Green Party shared many aspects of the Acireman program but garnered little support (yet just enough to help determine the outcome). The closest a Democratic presidential nominee has ever come to the Acirema agenda is probably George McGovern's disastrous 1972 campaign, in which his slogan "Come home, America" was taken as a call for broad-based disengagement and dramatic reduction of defense spending, not just an immediate end to the Vietnam War.

Disband, NATO abandon Israel, destabilize China, welcome wars when useful, disregard genocide, and wage preemptive nuclear war? While such views are consistently found in certain small segments of the political spectrum, there is, thankfully, no plausible passageway from America to Acirema.

Some have claimed—and the 2002 National Security Strategy and other statements of President Bush flirt with—the notion that U.S. values and interests are quite closely aligned or can be so. Such an argument effectively dodges the question of which should take precedence. And indeed, it may be that "failed states" are something the United States should take action to prevent because of the potential for danger where no one is adequately in charge. We disagree on the relative magnitude of the danger there.[2] We agree, however, that U.S. action to prevent the failure of states is morally good. The point is that without the moral frame of reference, one could imagine having a debate about whether the collapse of a state into civil war, warlordism, and genocide is good or bad for the United States—and that such a debate would remain imaginary, because it can never occur in the real world.

Moreover, it is a conceit that this "values-free" *machtpolitik* or *realpolitik* is truly free of moral considerations. Even the proposition "look out for No.1" has a moral aspect. Why should you look out for No. 1? Because you place a value on No. 1 and think it is morally good to seek the benefit of No. 1. Indeed, there may have been a time in human history—perhaps in Hobbes's state of nature, the "war of all against all"—when moral considerations, though hardly absent, involved calculations no more complicated than this.

But the United States was founded not as a "values-free" rational calculator of what's good for No. 1, but as a nation embodying certain values or principles that justified rebellion against its lawful sovereign. While, to this day, the United States has been accused (often with justification) of failing to live up to the values of the Declaration of Independence, the United States has never been able to or seriously attempted to expunge those values from all consideration in the conduct of domestic or foreign policy. This seems unlikely to change. And rightly or wrongly, Americans demand consideration for those principles not simply because they are "ours"—and no one has the right to interfere in our affairs by telling us anything different—but because of our belief that they are true.

TOWARD A NEW CONSENSUS ON PRINCIPLES

While the place of American values in foreign policy endures, questions remain about how such policies should be implemented and how the inevitable trade-offs should be managed, especially in the current political environment. The Bush legacy casts a long shadow. During the past several years, intellectuals and policy analysts have offered numerous grand strategies as a corrective to Bush, rebalancing foreign policy between realism and idealism. Some stress one perspective more than the other, and they usually combine some version of both words in their titles: Francis Fukuyama offers "Realistic Wilsonianism," Robert Wright proposes "Progressive Realism," John Hulsman and Anatol Lieven describe "Ethical Realism," Charles Krauthammer espouses "Democratic Realism," James Baker explains "Pragmatic Idealism," and John Ikenberry and Charles Kupchan outline "Liberal Realism" (we could go on).

Instead of adding yet another grand strategy slogan into the mix, we believe that it is more important to describe a set of principles and priorities that should guide U.S. foreign relations in the challenging years ahead. Below we outline six principles, each rooted in American ideals and serving American interests. This is not an exhaustive list, yet it shows that it is possible to construct a common agenda between liberals and conservatives that is firmly built upon a commitment to uphold—and promote—values.

Standing against the conquest of territory by force. The United States must continue to uphold one of tie most basic norms of international relations: preventing and, when necessary, reversing the conquest of territory across an international border by military force. While support for this principle may seem self-evident—after all, it is at the heart of the UN Charter and the underlying rationale of the world's most important security organization, NATO—it is in fact a value that the United States must choose to defend. As made clear by the alternative Acirema world described earlier, a great power like the United States could decide that upholding this norm is too costly or outside the bounds of its core national interests. We believe that since preventing territorial conquest by force remains a keystone of the international system and a driver of its enduring stability, this must remain a core value of U.S. foreign policy.

Such a commitment entails certain responsibilities around the world and, fundamentally, demands an interventionist foreign policy—preferably as an active partner through international institutions, but if necessary alone. The means that are required will depend on the specific situation and the other U.S. interests at stake, such as alliance or other security or political relationships and the potential for wider violence. Yet the full range of tools—from diplomacy to sanctions and political isolation to military force—must always be available.

Sometimes this might require active diplomacy to prevent one state from threatening another with force, such as the United States' repeated efforts in recent years to reduce tensions between India and Pakistan. Other instances will require U.S. leadership to try to negotiate an end to conflicts after they have broken out. For example, this is what the Clinton administration did when it hammered out the Dayton Peace Accords in 1995, reversing Slobodan Milosevic's aggression against the newly independent Bosnia. And on some (arid hopefully rare) occasions, the United States will have to use military force to reverse aggression, as George H. W. Bush did in 1991 when he created and led a UN-sanctioned international coalition to kick Iraq out of Kuwait. Today, looking into the future and the probability of a smaller American presence in Iraq, the commitment to territorial integrity will be critical insurance against potential incursions by neighbors such as Iran.

Of course, another way of describing this is that by valuing the protection of territorial integrity from threats of force, we are valuing the defense of sovereignty. That's correct to an extent, but we do recognize that under certain circumstances this value can be trumped by other values, such as the responsibility to defend the rights and lives of people living within another state's territory. We discuss this in greater detail below, but suffice it to say that the United States should not allow any leader to hide behind one value (the right not to be invaded) in order to violate another (his people's right not to be brutalized).

Defending liberal regimes. The United States should be prepared and willing to help any and all democratic governments that come under challenge internationally or from internal antidemocratic elements seeking to overturn liberal political and social order and the rule of law. This is a basic principle of *democratic solidarity*, according to which the most secure, established, and stable liberal democracies, the United States above all, should acknowledge a responsibility to come to the assistance of democratic governments that are threatened, that have yet to become fully consolidated and mature, or are subject to forces of internal instability.

Liberal democracy, in the view of most of those who govern themselves according to its principles, is not merely a matter of sovereign choice—just one among many options. Rather, citizens of democracies tend to regard their form of government as the *right* or best choice, at least for them; they would not consider trading their form of government for autocratic or totalitarian or theocratic government and would rightly consider any force in favor of such a change in governance as a serious threat, one to be challenged and defeated—*not* by whatever means necessary, such as abandonment of liberal principles for the sake of security, but by any means legitimate *within* the horizon of liberal principles.

If citizens of democracies view their system as the right or best choice for themselves, those citizens and that state ought to be willing to acknowledge the rightness of the choice of liberal democracy among the citizens of other states. They have a stake not only in their own domestic political arrangements, but in their view of the rightness of liberal democracy, which does not end at their borders. A threat to liberal democracy elsewhere is accordingly a challenge and one to which any democratic states with the means to do so should be willing to meet head on.

The United States has a number of alliances with democratic states, including several with allies that were not democratic when the alliance relationship began but became so, perhaps partly as a result of the security provided by the United States. These alliance commitments remain fully in force, but they are only a beginning. The United States must recognize that it will not sit idly by as nondemocratic states try to undermine or even overturn democracies or fragile liberalizing states. On the contrary, the United States should step up, together with other democratic states, to provide all the support or assistance possible.

The correct response when a powerful nondemocratic state tries to coerce a weaker democratic state—as Russia has tried with Ukraine and especially Georgia—is not to temporize out of deference to the power of the strong but to speak up unequivocally in defense of democracy under threat. To stand aloof or to appease the stronger power would be to embolden antidemocratic forces, and not just locally. Some argued that extending the NATO alliance to the Baltic States was foolish because of the military difficulty of defending Estonia, Latvia, and Lithuania against attack and because extending the Atlantic Alliance onto the territory of the former Soviet Union would unnecessarily antagonize Russia. We strongly disagreed at the time and believe we were correct. In our view, the newly won freedom of the Baltic nations and the establishment of liberal democratic governments there *already* created obligations for the United States and NATO countries. NATO accession did not create but ratified and codified that obligation toward these peoples. The process was exemplary in warding off any urge to interfere with and disrupt democratic development and consolidation there—and elsewhere in Central and Eastern Europe, in our view.

A principle of democratic solidarity is not only good in itself; it makes external threats to democratic governments less likely by demonstrating that making such threats will have adverse *global* consequences for anyone inclined to pursue such a course. It would be a mistake to view the principle of democratic solidarity as a military doctrine; its main components are political, diplomatic, and social.

There are some instances in which democratic solidarity comes with conditions. For example, U.S. willingness to defend Taiwan against Chinese attack depends on Taipei's not taking the provocative step of a declaration of independence—to which China would respond militarily, according to Beijing's declaratory policy. This is a reasonable codicil given local circumstances. There may be others (though Taiwan is arguably the most neuralgic of such at present). An absolute *military* doctrine of democratic solidarity would create moral hazard, since a state might conclude it could act as provocatively as it wished in response to local circumstances and still receive the backing of the United States and other democratic states. That is not the deal. Such a state, by taking action other democratic states would regard as unreasonable, would itself be breaking from democratic solidarity. But with such nuances always in mind, a principle of democratic solidarity should guide U.S. policy, and the United States should encourage other democratic states to embrace it.

Promoting liberal governance. If a principle of democratic solidarity makes sense at the level of state-to-state relations, it also makes sense for the United States in relation to people working toward liberalization and democracy in their own societies. This is not likely to be especially controversial as a matter of principle among democratic allies. Opinion surveys in Europe, for example, show large majorities in favor of promotion of democracy by peaceful means.[3] And it seems likely that a substantial part of the lingering opposition is a product of concern that democracy will not be liberal, but rather will bring to power illiberal elements. Our discussion should be understood to refer to the promotion of liberal democracy, in which the two components are a liberal social order based on principles of freedom and minority rights as well as popularly elected governments followed by peaceful transfer of power.

Nevertheless, it cannot be denied that a principle of democratic solidarity—even if broadly accepted by and among, and in application to, democratic states facing external threats or internal challenge, and even if accepted as the rightness of supporting development of liberal democracy in principle—will surely be controversial when considered in application to supporters of democracy in nondemocratic states.

We think that the United States should, as far as possible, provide whatever help aspiring democrats and liberalizers seek. The United States should also encourage similar support among fellow democratic states—an extension of democratic solidarity. But considerations of prudence, national interests (such as access to energy resources), and *force majeure* will inevitably weigh into such decisions.

What we propose is the imperative of *balancing prudential considerations and principle*. It is not enough to take note of Saudi oil fields and declare, therefore, that Saudi Arabia is off limits for criticism and promotion of reform of its extraordinarily repressive regime. Similarly, China is big, powerful, rising—and undemocratic (indeed, increasingly openly antidemocratic). We must deal with the fact that China is a vast and increasingly powerful country; it would be madness to try to deny it. But we must also deal with the fact that China is undemocratic.

The United States can and must pursue dual-track policies in such cases, as Francis Fukuyama and Michael McFaul argue.[4] One track will address exigency, the other the moral case. On the moral track, rather than a one-size-fits-all model of democracy promotion, we propose a method, a way of thinking about and acting on the problem that does not pretend to a greater degree of generality than is appropriate. The objective, in each country in which liberal democracy has yet to take hold or take hold fully, is to identify *next steps*. What is the next plausible step for the expansion of the liberal and democratic space? Conversely, what is the next plausible step for the constriction of the space in which authoritarians or antidemocratic elements operate? The United States should then work vigorously to promote the next step, applying pressure for reform against the authoritarian element (typically, the government) and assistance to the democratic element to help achieve measurable progress. Once the next-step objective has been achieved, the United States must immediately move on to the *next* next step. Pressure and assistance must not let up following interim successes; on the contrary, it should increase.

We agree that the key failure of the Bush administration's democracy promotion policy in Egypt, for example, was overeagerness to claim credit for progress in response to small positive steps. Yes, it was consequential that the Mubarak government decided to allow other parties to compete in a presidential election. But it was hardly the birth of liberal democracy on the Nile Delta. Mubarak deserved congratulations for taking the step he took—followed without pause by the demand that he take the next step of moving toward a free and fair election.

With this next-step policy of constant pressure to expand the liberal space while contracting the authoritarian space, the United States will be in a position to say it is keeping faith with the forces of democracy and liberalization in every country, even in the face of inevitable practical constraints.

Enforcing the "responsibility to protect." Liberal democracy, in which people choose their leaders in free and fair elections and in which political and human rights are secure, including for minorities, stands at the pinnacle of human political achievement. For some states, such as the United States, the most urgent political task lies in helping others achieve this great end while being ever mindful of and seeking to address the imperfections of its own governance. For others, the consolidation of transition to democratic governance is the key political task, and it can often be one of life and death, as the assassination of reformist Serbian Prime Minister Zoran Djindjic or the dioxin poisoning of Orange Revolution leader Viktor Yushchenko in Ukraine both demonstrate. For still others, the political challenge is to pry open any space at all for the opposition in an authoritarian country.

But for the worst off of all, such as the Tutsi minority in Rwanda or the Kurds of Saddam Hussein's Iraq, the essential political challenge is survival—against the wishes of the government or the mob in whose midst they have the misfortune to live. Surely, it cannot be right to embrace a principle of democratic solidarity and democracy promotion for those relatively high on the social ladder while offering nothing to those in greatest peril of losing the most basic human right: the right to live.

At the United Nations' 2005 World Summit in New York, the world's leaders embraced for the first time the doctrine of the "responsibility to protect." It holds, briefly, that with sovereign rights come sovereign responsibility, and the primary responsibility of a government is to protect the people who live within its territory. In the event that a government is unable or unwilling to provide protection for its people from would-be perpetrators of genocide or mass killing and ethnic cleansing—or worse, is complicit in such crimes against humanity—the international community must take upon itself the responsibility to protect. No government that fails to protect its people may legitimately assert a right to noninterference in its internal affairs.

The responsibility to protect is a transformational concept in international relations. Previously, the victims of the worst sort of war crimes and human rights abuses on a mass scale had no recourse, trapped as they were behind a curtain of sovereign right. The adoption of the responsibility to protect grants them an appeal to the international community.

This is often construed solely through the prism of military intervention, and in some cases, the only way to stop determined genocidaires may be by force. But it is wrong to think that military means are the first or main recourse. The international community needs to take active measures in terms of monitoring and applying diplomatic and other forms of pressure (such as sanctions, diplomatic isolation, and negotiations) to avert mass killings and ethnic cleansing whenever possible.

Of course, there is much dispute over how the "international community" may act. We agree that the United Nations Security Council is the best venue, not because we think that the United Nations is the only path to legality and legitimacy, but because so many other states take this view, and their wishes deserve respect. However, in the event the Security Council fails to take timely and effective action as a human rights catastrophe unfolds, the United States must not stand on the sidelines. In the case of Kosovo, when the Security Council was blocked, NATO stepped up to take decisive action, thereby preventing a genocide. Some still question the legality of that action. We take the concern seriously coming from those who were willing to act; we do not take it seriously coming from those who were prepared to let hundreds of thousands fall prey to ethnic cleansing and genocide. When necessary, the United States must lead or be willing to join others to mobilize an effective response to mass killing and widespread repression.

Addressing global hardship. As the world's most powerful country, the United States has the capability to help address the challenges stemming from poverty, hunger, disease, and lack of opportunity for billions of people in the developing world. We believe that leadership in these areas is not just something the United States can do—it is what the United States *must* do.

While these issues were once only considered "humanitarian" or "soft"—implying that they are always elective or secondary—there are instrumental reasons why the United States s' should focus on them. If one accepts the argument" (and we do) that threats emanating from weak or failed states can endanger U.S. national security, then it is in America's interest to help these states stabilize. Some describe this as part of "draining the swamp" of desperation and hardship that radical jihadists and other extremists thrive in by reducing extreme poverty and replacing the extreme fundamentalism taught in some madrassas with basic education. As evidence of the growing consensus on the relationship between these issues and national security, the Bush administration justifies many of its efforts along these lines—and when it is criticized, it is usually for not doing enough.

But U.S. leadership in these areas is about more than protecting security. America's actions in the world are a powerful demonstration of what it wants to accomplish with its power and the values it wishes to uphold. In this sense, the United States should embrace humanitarianism and not consider it optional or of minor importance. To do so is both the smart and the morally right thing to do for our security.

This is also an area where there is significant common ground between the political right and left. Liberals have long argued that addressing issues like poverty and disease need to be a core part of U.S. foreign policy. Many conservatives have as well, especially among the evangelical community (as exemplified by the work of Franklin Graham and Rick Warren). Spurred in part by evangelical advocates, the Bush administration has made positive strides in this direction, increasing assistance to Africa by 67 percent and boosting spending for programs to fight HIV/AIDS. Meanwhile, three of the major Democratic candidates for president have talked about the importance of fighting global poverty and making a major push to improve education throughout the developing world.

Looking ahead, both conservatives and liberals should embrace an agenda centered on stronger American leadership in these areas—in fact, one valid criticism of recent U.S. policy is that it too often cedes the initiative to others. For example, greater resources should be put behind combating poverty and disease, and there should be a broad recognition that free trade is critical to helping the developing world advance economically. And we should consider fundamental reforms in the way the U.S. government is organized to implement such policies, including ideas like establishing a Department of Global Development (along the lines of that in the United Kingdom) and replacing the Foreign Assistance Act.

Strengthening alliances and institutions. Any discussion of implementing the principles outlined above begs a fundamental question about means: How should the United States work with other countries? Throughout American history, the subject of whether the United States should tie itself to the fate of others abroad—or work with others to solve problems—has been hotly contested. This has been especially true since the end of tine Cold War and the apogee of U.S. primacy, when we really didn't *need* others to solve a lot of problems. While this tugging between unilateralism and multilateralism is often seen as concerned solely with efficacy and instrumentality—sometimes it is better for us to share the burden, sometimes not—we believe that it is in fact a debate about what kind of global power America should be and what kind of international system we should support. It is not about instruments; it is about principles.

As Ivo Daalder and Robert Kagan argue, it is important for U.S. policies to be seen as legitimate both in the eyes of the American people and in the eyes of the the world.[5] That is a value that other countries—certainly Acirema—might not necessarily care about. America does and should. But the question is how best to uphold this value and what institutions (whether existing or new) or multilateral arrangements are the best means to do so. As discussed earlier, when it comes to implementing values-based policies like defending liberal regimes or enforcing the responsibility to protect, working through alliances and international institutions should be as important to the United States (at least as something to aspire to) as it is to others.

The challenge has been that for many conservatives and liberals, the unilateral vs. multilateral discourse has framed these ideas as an either/or choice. The right has focused too much on the constraints of multilateralism and maintaining U.S. freedom of action. We agree that the United States always reserves the right to act alone if the circumstances require, but this should not be the preferred option. In this sense, the Bush administration's substance and style—exemplified by its "with us or against us" statements or rhetoric about preemption—have prompted international skepticism about whether the United States genuinely wants institutions like the United Nations to function or even exist at all.

Yet too many liberals slide into the opposite problem; upholding multilateralism for its own sake. This has only intensified during the Bush years, when support for the United States around the world has reached alarming lows. If the United States is unpopular, some believe that it must be solely our fault and make no judgment about the behavior of our allies. The remedy among many on the left seems to us to be overly simplistic: defer at all times to the collective decisions of institutions. This confuses the reality that international organizations are stages, not actors. They are simply groupings of other sovereign states, and while organizations can help facilitate decisions for states, they cannot make choices for them. They can neither prevent internal disagreements nor force free riders and buck passers to act.

Recently we've seen signs of greater nuance in the unilateral/multilateral debate between left and right. For example, in his second term President Bush began working through institutions like the UN Security Council to deal with problems like Iran and Darfur, and with an ad hoc coalition to negotiate with North Korea. Even his rhetoric is softening: when asked recently what he has learned from his European partners, he said, "I have come to realize that other countries do rely upon the United Nations, and I respect that a lot. So there's an area, for example, where I have been taught a lesson by my allies and friends."[6] And among liberals, there is greater recognition that the multilateral route often can frustrate rather than facilitate action. For example, the longer the Security Council's divisions prevent strong action to end the genocide in Darfur, the louder the calls become for a NATO response or even unilateral U.S. military intervention.

This bolsters our belief that a new concensus can be formed in support of seeking the broadest possible coalition to pursue U.S. foreign policy goals. This means working through alliances and institutions, but also ensuring that these organizations work. The United States should have high expectations of its alliances, and in turn it should have high expectations of its allies. It should be an active and energetic partner, recognizing that getting something done through a coalition often requires the same kind of daily politicking, strong-arming, logrolling, and handholding used every day in working with the U.S. Congress. And while the United States should seek to make existing institutions like the United Nations and NATO stronger and more effective, it should also work to build other organizations like the Alliance of Democracies.

THE MORAL CORE

The conclusion we come to is that while an idealistic foreign policy has become harder to defend politically, it is possible to construct a forward-looking, values-based agenda that both liberals and conservatives can support. In fact, such an approach should garner more than just passive support—the policies presented above can actually serve as part of the foundation for U.S. foreign policy in the years ahead. Neither sentimental nor coldly aloof, these values comprise the core of the rules-based, liberal international order that the United States should aspire to achieve. This is about more than what we want; it is about who we are.

Yet because the political incentives against an approach to foreign policy that promotes American values remain so powerful, as we described at the outset, such a policy will not emerge on its own. Even with greater clarity about what values we want to uphold and promote, difficult questions will remain about how to do so. There will always be debates about acceptable costs and the trade-offs involved. So success will require sustained attention and steadfast leadership. With both, the American people will rise to the challenge.

NOTES

1. *Transatlantic Trends 2006*, German Marshall Fund of the United States (2006), 16.
2. Lindberg tends to the view that failed states pose a problem mainly for those directly affected, who have their hands full trying to survive the local crisis. Chollet is more concerned about spillover effects and broader destabilization.

3. *Transatlantic Trends* 2006, German Marshall Fund of the United States.
4. Francis Fukuyama and Michael McFaul, "Should Democracy Be Promoted or Demoted?" in Derek Chollet, Tod Lindberg, and David Shorr, eds., *Bridging the Foreign Policy Divide* (Routledge 2007), Chap. 9.
5. Ivo Daalder and Robert Kagan, "America and the Use of Force: Sources of Legitimacy," in Chollet et al., *Bridging trie Foreign Policy Divide*, Chap. 1.
6. See Bush press conference with German Chancellor Angela Merkel (January 4, 2007).

$\mathcal{B}$

End of Dreams, Return of History

By Robert Kagan

The world has become normal again. The years immediately following the end of the Cold War offered a tantalizing glimpse at a new kind of international order, with nations growing together or disappearing altogether, ideological conflicts melting away, cultures intermingling through increasingly free commerce and communications. But that was a mirage, the hopeful anticipation of a liberal, democratic world that wanted to believe the end of the Cold War did not end just one strategic and ideological conflict but all strategic and ideological conflict. People and their leaders longed for "a world transformed."[1] Today the nations of the West still cling to that vision. Evidence to the contrary—the turn toward autocracy in Russia or the growing military ambitions of China—is either dismissed as a temporary aberration or denied entirely.

The world has not been transformed, however. Nations remains as strong as ever, and so too the nationalist ambitions, the passions, and the competition among nations that have shaped history. The is still "unipolar," with the United States remaining the only super-power. But international competition among great powers has returned, with the United States, Russia, China, Europe, Japan, India, Iran, and others vying for regional predomi-nance. Struggles for honor and status and influence in the world have once again become key features of the international scene. Ideologically, it is a time not of convergence but of divergence. The competition between liberalism and absolutism has reemerged, with the nations of the world increasingly lining up, as in the past, along ideological lines. Finally, there is the fault line between modernity and tradition, the violent struggle of Islamic fun-damentalists against the modern powers and the secular cultures that, in their view, have penetrated and polluted their Islamic world.

CREATING AND SUSTAINING THE UNIPOLAR WORLD

How will the United States deal with such a world? Today there is much discussion of the so-called Bush Doctrine and what may follow it. Many prefer to believe the world is in turmoil not because it is in turmoil but because Bush made it so by destroying the new hopeful era.

Robert Kagan, "End of Dreams, Return of History," *Policy Review*, August/Sept. 2007, p. 17–44. Reprinted by permission.

And when Bush leaves, it can return once again to the way it was. Having glimpsed the mirage once, people naturally want to see it and believe in it again.

The first illusion, however, is that Bush really changed anything. Historians will long debate the decision to go to war in Iraq, but what they are least likely to conclude is that the intervention was wildly out of character for the United States. Since the end of World War II at least, American presidents of both parties have pursued a fairly consistent approach to the world. They have regarded the United States as the "indispensable nation"[2] and the "locomotive at the head of mankind."[3] They have amassed power and influence and deployed them in ever-widening arcs around the globe on behalf of interests, ideals, and ambitions, both tangible and intangible. Since 1945 Americans have insisted on acquiring and maintaining military supremacy, a "preponderance of power" in the world rather than a balance of power with other nations. They have operated on the ideological conviction that liberal democracy is the only legitimate form of government and that other forms of government are not only illegitimate but transitory. They have declared their readiness to "support free peoples who are resisting attempted subjugation" by forces of oppression, to "pay any price, bear any burden" to defend freedom, to seek "democratic enlargement" in the world, and to work for the "end of tyranny."[4] They have been impatient with the status quo. They have seen America as a catalyst for change in human affairs, and they have employed the strategies and tactics of "maximalism," seeking revolutionary rather than gradual solutions to problems. Therefore, they have often been at odds with the more cautious approaches of their allies.[5]

When people talk about a Bush Doctrine, they generally refer to three sets of principles—the idea of preemptive or preventive military action; the promotion of democracy and "regime change"; and a diplomacy tending toward "unilateralism," a willingness to act without the sanction of international bodies such as the United Nations Security Council or the unanimous approval of its allies.[6] It is worth asking not only whether past administrations acted differently but also which of these any future administration, regardless of party, would promise to abjure in its conduct of foreign policy. As scholars from Melvyn P. Leffler to John Lewis Gaddis have shown, the idea of preemptive or preventive action is hardly a novel concept in American foreign policy.[7] And as policymakers and philosophers from Henry Kissinger to Michael Walzer have agreed, it is impossible in the present era to renounce such actions *a priori*.[8] As for "regime change," there is not a single administration in the past half-century that has not attempted to engineer changes of regime in various parts of the world, from Eisenhower's CIA-inspired coups in Iran and Guatemala and his planned overthrow of Fidel Castro, which John F. Kennedy attempted to carry out, to George Herbert Walker Bush's invasion of Panama to Bill Clinton's actions in Haiti and Bosnia. And if by unilateralism we mean an unwillingness to be constrain by the disapproval of the UN Security Council, by some of the NATO allies, by the OAS, or by any other international body, which presidents of the past allowed themselves to be so constrained?[9]

These qualities of American foreign policy reflect not one man or one party or one circle of thinkers. They spring from the nation's historical experience and are a characteristic American response to international circumstances. They are underpinned, on the one hand, by old beliefs and ambitions and, on the other hand, by power. So long as Americans elect leaders who believe it is the role of the United States to improve the world and bring about the "ultimate good,"[10] and so long as American power in all its forms is sufficient to shape the behavior of others, the broad direction of American foreign policy is unlikely to change, absent some dramatic—indeed, genuinely revolutionary—effort by a future administration.

These American traditions, together with historical events beyond Americans' control, have catapulted the United States to a position of pre-eminence in the world. Since the end of the Cold War and the emergence of this "unipolar" world, there has been much anticipation of the end of unipolarity and the rise of a multipolar world in which the United States is no longer the predominant power, Not only realist theorists but others both inside and outside the United States have long argued the theoretical and practical unsustainability, not to mention undesirability, of a world with only one superpower. Mainstream realist theory has assumed that other powers must inevitably band together to balance against the superpower. Others expected the post-Cold War era to be characterized by the primacy of geoeconomics over geopolitics and foresaw a multipolar world with the economic giants of Europe, India, Japan, and China rivaling the United States. Finally, in the wake of the Iraq War and with hostility to the United States, as measured in public opinion polls, apparently at an all-time high, there has been a widespread assumption that the American position in the world must finally be eroding.

Yet American predominance in the main categories of power persists as a key feature of the international system. The enormous and productive American economy remains at the center of the international economic system. American democratic principles are shared by over a hundred nations. The American military is not only the largest but the only one capable of projecting force into distant theaters. Chinese strategists, who spend a great deal of time thinking about these things, see the world not as multipolar but as characterized by "one superpower, many great powers," and this configuration seems likely to persist into the future absent either a catastrophic blow to American power or a decision by the United States to diminish its power and international influence voluntarily.[11]

The anticipated global balancing has for the most part not occurred. Russia and China certainly share a common and openly expressed goal of checking American hegemony. They have created at least one institution, the Shanghai Cooperation Organization, aimed at resisting American influence in Central Asia, and China is the only power in the world, other than the United States, engaged in a long-term military buildup. But Sino-Russian hostility to American predominance has not yet produced a concerted and cooperative effort at balancing. China's buildup is driven at least as much by its own long-term ambitions as by a desire to balance the United States. Russia has been using its vast reserves of oil and natural gas as a lever to compensate for the lack of military power, but it either cannot or does not want to increase its military capability sufficiently to begin counterbalancing the United States. Overall, Russian military power remains in decline. In addition, the two powers do not trust one another. They are traditional rivals, and the rise of China inspires at least as much nervousness in Russia as it does in the United States. At the moment, moreover, China is less abrasively confrontational with the United States. Its dependence on the American market and foreign investment and its perception that the United States remains a potentially formidable adversary mitigate against an openly confrontational approach.

In any case, China and Russia cannot balance the United States without at least some help from Europe, Japan, India, or at least some of the other advanced, democratic nations. But those powerful players are not joining the effort. Europe has rejected the option of making itself a counterweight to American power. This is true even among the older members of the European Union, where neither France, Germany, Italy, nor Spain proposes such counterbalancing, despite a public opinion hostile to the Bush administration. Now that the EU has expanded to include the nations of Central and Eastern Europe, who fear threats from the east, not from the west, the prospect of a unified Europe counterbalancing the United States is practically nil. As for Japan and India, the clear trend in recent years has been toward closer strategic cooperation with the United States.

If anything, the most notable balancing over the past decade has been aimed not at the American superpower but at the two large powers: China and Russia. In Asia and the Pacific, Japan, Australia, and even South Korea and the nations of Southeast Asia have all engaged in "hedging" against a rising China. This has led them to seek closer relations with Washington, especially in the case of Japan and Australia. India has also drawn closer to the United States and is clearly engaged in balancing against China. Russia's efforts to increase its influence over what it regards as its "near abroad," meanwhile, have produced tensions and negative reactions in the Baltics and other parts of Eastern Europe Because these nations are now members of the European Union, this has also complicated EU-Russian relations. On balance, traditional allies of the United States in East Asia and in Europe, while their publics may be more anti-American than in the past, nevertheless pursue policies that reflect more concern about the powerful states in their midst than about the United States.[12] This has provided a cushion against hostile public opinion and offers a foundation on which to strengthen American relations with these countries after the departure of Bush.

The Iraq War has not had the effect expected by many. Although there are reasonable-sounding theories as to why America's position should be eroding as a result of global opposition to the war and the unpopularity of the current administration, there has been little measurable change in the actual policies of nations, other than their reluctance to assist the United States in Iraq. In 2003 those who claimed the U.S. global position was eroding pointed to electoral results in some friendly countries: the election of Schröder in Germany, the defeat of Aznar's party in Spain, and the election of Lula in Brazil.[13] But if elections are the test, other more recent votes around the world have put relatively pro-American leaders in power in Berlin, Paris, Tokyo, Canberra, and Ottawa. As for Russia and China, their hostility to the United States predates the Iraq War and, indeed, the Bush administration. Russia turned most sharply anti-American in the late 1990s partly as a consequence of NATO enlargement. Both were far more upset and angered by the American intervention in Kosovo than by the invasion of Iraq. Both began complaining about American hegemonism and unilateralism and calling for a multipolar order during the Clinton years. Chinese rhetoric has been, if anything, more tempered during the Bush years, in part because the Chinese have seen September 11 and American preoccupation with terrorism as a welcome distraction from America's other preoccupation, the "China threat."

The world's failure to balance against the superpower is the more striking because the United States, notwithstanding its difficult interventions in Iraq and Afghanistan, continues to expand its power and military reach and shows no sign of slowing this expansion even after the 2008 elections. The American defense budget has surpassed $500 billion per year, not including supplemental spending totaling over $100 billion on Iraq and Afghanistan. This level of spending is sustainable, moreover, both economically and politically.[14] As the American military budget rises, so does the number of overseas American military bases. Since September 11, 2001, the United States has built or expanded bases in Afghanistan, Kyrgyzstan, Pakistan, Tajikistan, and Uzbekistan in Central Asia; in Bulgaria, Georgia, Hungary, Poland, and Romania in Europe; and in the Philippines, Djibouti, Oman, and Qatar. Two decades ago, hostility to the American military presence began forcing the United States out of the Philippines and seemed to be undermining support for American bases in Japan. Today, the

Philippines is rethinking that decision, and the furor in Japan has subsided. In places like South Korea and Germany, it is American plans to reduce the U.S. military presence that stir controversy, not what one would expect if there was a widespread fear or hatred of overween- ing American power. Overall, there is no shortage of other countries willing to host U.S. forces, a good indication that much of the world continues to tolerate and even lend support to American geopolitical primacy if only as a protection against more worrying foes.[15]

Predominance is not the same thing as omnipotence. Just because the United States has more power than everyone else does not mean it can impose its will on everyone else. American predominance in the early years after the Second World War did not prevent the North Korean invasion of the South, a communist victory in China, the Soviet acquisition of the hydrogen bomb, or the consolidation of the Soviet empire in Eastern Europe—all far greater strategic setbacks than anything the United States has yet suffered or is likely to suffer in Iraq and Afghanistan. Nor does predominance mean the United States will succeed in all its endeavors, any more than it did six decades ago.

By the same token, foreign policy failures do not necessarily undermine predominance. Some have suggested that failure in Iraq would mean the end of predominance and unipolarity. But a superpower can lose a war—in Vietnam or in Iraq—without ceasing to be a superpower if the fundamental international conditions continue to support its predominance. So long as the United States remains at the center of the international economy and the predominant military power, so long as the American public continues to support American predominance as it has consistently for six decades, and so long as potential challengers inspire more fear than sympathy among their neighbors, the structure of the international system should remain as the Chinese describe it: one superpower and many great powers.

This is a good thing, and it should continue to be a primary goal of American foreign policy to perpetuate this relatively benign international configuration of power. The unipolar order with the United States as the predominant power is unavoidably riddled with flaws and contradictions. It inspires fears and jealousies. The United States is not immune to error, like all other nations, and because of its size and importance in the international system those errors are magnified and take on greater significance than the errors of less powerful nations. Compared to the ideal Kantian international order, in which all the world's powers would be peace-loving equals, conducting themselves wisely, prudently, and in strict obeisance to inter- national law, the unipolar system is both dangerous and unjust. Compared to any plausible alternative in the real world, however, it is relatively stable and less likely to produce a major war between great powers. It is also comparatively benevolent, from a liberal perspective, for it is more conducive to the principles of economic and political liberalism that Americans and many others value.

American predominance does not stand in the way of progress toward a better world, therefore. It stands in the way of regression toward a more dangerous world. The choice is not between an American-dominated order and a world that looks like the European Union. The future international order will be shaped by those who have the power to shape it. The leaders of a post-American world will not meet in Brussels but in Beijing, Moscow, and Washington.

THE RETURN OF GREAT POWERS AND GREAT GAMES

If the world is marked by the persistence of unipolarity, it is nevertheless also being shaped by the reemergence of competitive national ambitions of the kind that have shaped human affairs from time immemorial. During the Cold War, this historical tendency of great powers to jostle with one another for status and influence as well as for wealth and power was largely suppressed by the two superpowers and their rigid bipolar order. Since the end of the Cold War, the United States has not been powerful enough, and probably could never be powerful enough, to suppress by itself the normal ambitions of nations. This does not mean the world has returned to multipolarity, since none of the large powers is in range of competing with the superpower for global influence. Nevertheless, several large powers are now competing for regional predominance, both with the United States and with each other.

National ambition drives China's foreign policy today, and although it is tempered by prudence and the desire to appear as unthreatening as possible to the rest of the world, the Chinese are powerfully motivated to return their nation to what they regard as its traditional position as the preeminent power in East Asia. They do not share a European, postmodern view that power is passé, hence their now two-decades-long military buildup and modernization. Like the Americans, they believe power, including military power, is a good thing to have and that it is better to have more of it than less. Perhaps more significant is the Chinese perception, also shared by Americans, that status and honor, and not just wealth and security, are important for a nation.

Japan, meanwhile, which in the past could have been counted as an aspiring postmodern power—with its pacifist constitution and low defense spending—now appears embarked on a more traditional national course. Partly this is in reaction to the rising power of China and concerns about North Korea's nuclear weapons. But it is also driven by Japan's own national ambition to be a leader in East Asia or at least not to play second fiddle or "little brother" to China. China and Japan are now in a competitive quest with each trying to augment its own status and power and to prevent the other's rise to predominance, and this competition has a military and strategic as well as an economic and political component. Their competition is such that a nation like South Korea, with a long unhappy history as a pawn between the two powers, is once again worrying both about a "greater China" and about the return of Japanese nationalism. As Aaron Friedberg commented, the East Asian future looks more like Europe's past than its present. But it also looks like Asia's past.

Russian foreign policy, too, looks more like something from the nineteenth century. It is being driven by a typical, and typically Russian, blend of national resentment and ambition. A postmodern Russia simply seeking integration into the new European order, the Russia of Andrei Kozyrev, would not be troubled by the eastward enlargement of the EU and NATO, would not insist on predominant influence over its "near abroad," and would not use its natural resources as means of gaining geopolitical leverage and enhancing Russia's international status in an attempt to regain the lost glories of the Soviet empire and Peter the Great. But Russia, like China and Japan, is moved by more traditional great-power considerations, including the pursuit of those valuable if intangible national interests: honor and respect. Although Russian leaders complain about threats to their security from NATO and the United States, the Russian sense of insecurity has more to do with resentment and national identity man with plausible external military threats.[16] Russia's complaint today is not with this or that weapons system. It is the entire post-Cold War settlement of the 1990s that Russia resents and wants to revise. But that does not make insecurity less a factor in Russia's relations with the world; indeed, it makes finding compromise with the Russians all the more difficult.

One could add others to this list of great powers with traditional rather than postmodern aspirations. India's regional ambitions are more muted, or are focused most intently on

Pakistan, but it is clearly engaged in competition with China for dominance in the Indian Ocean and sees itself, correctly, as an emerging great power on the world scene. In the Middle East there is Iran, which mingles religious fervor with a historical sense of superiority and leadership in its region.[17] Its nuclear program is as much about the desire for regional hegemony as about defending Iranian territory from attack by the United States.

Even the European Union, in its way, expresses a pan-European national ambition to play a significant role in the world, and it has become the vehicle for channeling German, French, and British ambitions in what Europeans regard as a safe supranational direction. Europeans seek honor and respect, too, but of a postmodern variety. The honor they seek is to occupy the moral high ground in the world, to exercise moral authority, to wield political and economic influence as an antidote to militarism, to be the keeper of the global conscience, and to be recognized and admired by others for playing this role.

Islam is not a nation, but many Muslims express a kind of religious nationalism, and the leaders of radical Islam, including al Qaeda, do seek to establish a theocratic nation or confederation of nations that would encompass a wide swath of the Middle East and beyond. Like national movements elsewhere, Islamists have a yearning for respect, including self-respect, and a desire for honor. Their national identity has been molded in defiance against stronger and often oppressive outside powers, and also by memories of ancient superiority over those same powers. China had its "century of humiliation." Islamists have more than a century of humiliation to look back on, a humiliation of which Israel has become the living symbol, which is partly why even Muslims who are neither radical nor fundamentalist proffer their sympathy and even their support to violent extremists who can turn the tables on the dominant liberal West, and particularly on a dominant America which implanted and still feeds the Israeli cancer in their midst.

Finally, there is the United States itself. As a matter of national policy stretching back across numerous administrations, Democratic and Republican, liberal and conservative, Americans have insisted on preserving regional predominance in East Asia; the Middle East; the Western Hemisphere; until recently, Europe; and now, increasingly, Central Asia. This was its goal after the Second World War, and since the end of the Cold War, beginning with the first Bush administration and continuing through the Clinton years, the United States did not retract but expanded its influence eastward across Europe and into the Middle East, Central Asia and the Caucasus. Even as it maintains its position as the predominant global power, it is also engaged in hegemonic competitions in these regions with China in East and Central Asia, with Iran in the Middle East and Central Asia, and with Russia in Eastern Europe, Central Asia, and the Caucasus. The United States, too, is more of a traditional than a postmodern power, and though Americans are loath to acknowledge it, they generally prefer their global place as "No. 1" and are equally loath to relinquish it. Once having entered a region, whether for practical or idealistic reasons, they are remarkably slow to withdraw from it until they believe they have substantially transformed it in their own image. They profess indifference to the world and claim they just want to be left alone even as they seek daily to shape the behavior of billions of people around the globe.

The jostling for status and influence among these ambitious nations and would-be nations is a second defining feature of the new post-Cold War international system. Nationalism in all its forms is back, if it ever went away, and so is international competition for power, influence, honor, and status. American predominance prevents these rivalries from intensifying—its regional as well as its global predominance. Were the United States to diminish its influence in the regions where it is currently the strongest power, the other nations would settle disputes as great and lesser powers have done in the past; sometimes through diplomacy and accommodation but often through confrontation and wars of varying scope, intensity, and destructive-ness. One novel aspect of such a multipolar world is that most of these powers would possess nuclear weapons. That could make wars between them less likely, or it could simply make them more catastrophic.

It is easy but also dangerous to underestimate the role the United States plays in providing a measure of stability in the world even as it also disrupts stability. For instance, the United States is the dominant naval power everywhere, such that other nations cannot compete with it even in their home waters. They either happily or grudgingly allow the United States Navy to be the guarantor of international waterways and trade routes, of international access to markets and raw materials such as oil. Even when the United States engages in a war, it is able to play its role as guardian of the waterways. In a more genuinely multipolar world, however, it would not. Nations would compete for naval dominance at least in their own regions and possibly beyond. Conflict between nations would involve struggles on the oceans as well as on land. Armed embargos, of the kind used in World War I and other major conflicts, would disrupt trade flows in a way that is now impossible.

Such order as exists in the world rests not merely on the goodwill of peoples but on a foundation provided by American power. Even the European Union, that great geopolitical miracle, owes its founding to American power, for without it the European nations after World War II would never have felt secure enough to reintegrate Germany. Most Europeans recoil at the thought, but even today Europe's stability depends on the guarantee, however distant and one hopes unnecessary, that the United States could step in to check any dangerous development on the continent. In a genuinely multipolar world, that would not be possible without renewing the danger of world war.

People who believe greater equality among nations would be preferable to the present American predominance often succumb to a basic logical fallacy. They believe the order the world enjoys today exists independently of American power. They imagine that in a world where American power was diminished, the aspects of international order that they like would remain in place. But that's not the way it works. International order does not rest on ideas and institutions. It is shaped by configurations of power. The international order we know today reflects the distribution of power in the world since World War II, and especially since the end of the Cold War. A different configuration of power, a multipolar world in which the poles were Russia, China, the United States, India, and Europe, would produce its own kind of order, with different rules and norms reflecting the interests of the powerful states that would have a hand in shaping it. Would that international order be an improvement? Perhaps for Beijing and Moscow it would. But it is doubtful that it would suit the tastes of enlightenment liberals in the United States and Europe.

The current order, of course, is not only far from perfect but also offers no guarantee against major conflict among the world's great powers. Even under the umbrella of unipolarity, regional conflicts involving the large powers may erupt. War could erupt between China and Taiwan and draw in both the United States and Japan. War could erupt between Russia and Georgia, forcing the United States and its European allies to decide whether to intervene or suffer the consequences of a Russian victory. Conflict between India and Pakistan remains possible, as does conflict between Iran and Israel or other Middle Eastern states. These, too, could draw in other great powers, including the United States.

Such conflicts may be unavoidable no matter what policies the United States pursues. But they are more likely to erupt if the United States weakens or withdraws from its positions of regional dominance. This is especially true in East Asia, where most nations agree that a reliable American power has a stabilizing and pacific effect on the region. That is certainly the view of most of China's neighbors. But even China, which seeks gradually to supplant the United States as the dominant power in the region, faces the dilemma that an American withdrawal could unleash an ambitious, independent, nationalist Japan.

In Europe, too, the departure of the United States from the scene—even if it remained the world's most powerful nation—could be destabilizing. It could tempt Russia to an even more overbearing and potentially forceful approach to unruly nations on its periphery. Although some realist theorists seem to imagine that the disappearance of the Soviet Union put an end to the possibility of confrontation between Russia and the West, and therefore to the need for a permanent American role in Europe, history suggests that conflicts in Europe involving Russia are possible even without Soviet communism. If the United States withdrew from Europe—if it adopted what some call a strategy of "offshore balancing"—this could in time increase the likelihood of conflict involving Russia and its near neighbors, which could in turn draw the United States back in under unfavorable circumstances.

It is also optimistic to imagine that a retrenchment of the American position in the Middle East and the assumption of a more passive, "offshore" role would lead to greater stability there. The vital interest the United States has in access to oil and the role it plays in keeping access open to other nations in Europe and Asia make it unlikely that American leaders could or would stand back and hope for the best while the powers in the region battle it out. Nor would a more "even-handed" policy toward Israel, which some see as the magic key to unlocking peace, stability, and comity in the Middle East, obviate the need to come to Israel's aid if its security became threatened. That commitment, paired with the American commitment to protect strategic oil supplies for most of the world, practically ensures a heavy American military presence in the region, both on the seas and on the ground.

The subtraction of American power from any region would not end conflict but would simply change the equation. In the Middle East, competition for influence among powers both inside and outside the region has raged for at least two centuries. The rise of Islamic fundamentalism doesn't change this. It only adds a new and more threatening dimension to the competition, which neither a sudden end to the conflict between Israel and the Palestinians nor an immediate American withdrawal from Iraq would change. The alternative to American predominance in the region is not balance and peace. It is further competition. The region and the states within it remain relatively weak. A diminution of American influence would not be followed by a diminution of other external influences. One could expect deeper involvement by both China and Russia, if only to secure their interests.[18] And one could also expect the more powerful states of the region, particularly Iran, to expand and fill the vacuum. It is doubtful that any American administration would voluntarily take actions that could shift the balance of power in the Middle East further toward Russia, China, or Iran. The world hasn't changed that much. An American withdrawal from Iraq will not return things to "normal" or to a new kind of stability in the region. It will produce a new instability, one likely to draw the United States back in again.

The alternative to American regional predominance in the Middle East and elsewhere is not a new regional stability. In an era of burgeoning nationalism, the future is likely to be one of intensified competition among nations and nationalist movements. Difficult as it may be to extend American pre dominance into the future, no one should imagine that a reduction of American power or a retraction of American influence and global involvement will provide an easier path.

LIBERALISM AND AUTOCRACY

Complicating the equation and adding to the stakes is that the return to the international competition of ambitious nations has been accompanied by a return to global ideological competition. More precisely, the two-centuries-old struggle between political liberalism and autocracy has reemerged as a third defining characteristic of the present era.

The Cold War may have caused us to forget that the more enduring ideological conflict since the Enlightenment has not been between capitalism and communism but between liberalism and autocracy. That was the issue that divided the United States from much of Europe in the late eighteenth and early nineteenth centuries, and it divided Europe itself through much of the nineteenth century and into the twentieth. The assumption that the death of communism would bring an end to disagreements about the proper form of government and society seemed more plausible in the 1990s, when both Russia and China were thought to be moving toward political as well as economic liberalism. Such a development would have produced a remarkable ideological convergence among all the great powers of the world and heralded a genuinely new era in human development.

But those expectations have proved misplaced. China has not liberalized but has shored up its autocratic government. Russia has turned away from imperfect liberalism decisively toward autocracy. Of the world's great powers today, therefore, two of the largest, with over a billion and a half people, have governments that are committed to autocratic rule and seem to have the ability to sustain themselves in power for the foreseeable future with apparent popular approval.

Many assume that Russian and Chinese leaders do not believe in anything, and therefore they cannot be said to represent an ideology, but that is mistaken. The rulers of China and Russia do have a set of beliefs that guide them in both domestic and foreign policy. They believe autocracy is better for their nations than democracy. They believe it offers order and stability and the possibility of prosperity. They believe that for their large, fractious nations, a strong government is essential to prevent chaos and collapse. They believe democracy is not the answer and that they are serving the best interests of their peoples by holding and wielding power the way they do. This is not a novel or, from a historical perspective, even a disreputable idea. The European monarchies of the seventeenth, eighteenth, and nineteenth centuries were thoroughly convinced of the superiority of their form of government. They disdained democracy as the rule of the licentious and greedy mob. Only in the past half-century has liberalism gained widespread popularity around the world, and even today some American thinkers exalt "liberal autocracy" over what they, too, disdain as "illiberal democracy." If two of the world's largest powers share a common commitment to autocratic government, autocracy is not dead as an ideology. The autocratic tradition has a long and distinguished past, and it is not as obvious as it once seemed that it has no future.

The foreign policies of such states necessarily reflect the nature and interests of their governments. In the age of monarchy, foreign policy served the interests of the monarchy. In the age of religious conflict, it served the interests of the church. In the modern era, democracies have pursued foreign policies to make the world safe for democracy. And autocracies pursue foreign policies aimed at making the world safe, if not for all autocracies, at least for their own continued rule. Today the competition between them, along with the struggle of radical Islamists to make the world safe for their vision of Islamic theocracy, has become a defining feature of the international scene.

The differences between the two camps appear on many issues of lesser strategic importance—China's willingness to provide economic and political support to certain African dictatorships that liberal governments in Europe and the United States find odious, for instance. But they are also shaping international relations at a more fundamental level. Contrary to expectations at the end of the Cold War, the question of "regime" or "polity" is once again becoming a main subject of international relations.

The world looks very different from Moscow and Beijing than it does from Washington, London, Berlin, and Paris. In Europe and the United States, the liberal world cheered on the "color revolutions" in Ukraine, Georgia, and Kyrgyzstan and saw in them the natural unfolding of humanity's political evolution. In Russia and China, these events were viewed as Western-funded, CIA-inspired coups that furthered the geopolitical hegemony America and its (subservient) European allies. The two autocratic powers responded similarly to NATO's intervention in Kosovo in 1999, and not only because China's embassy was bombed by an American warplane and Russia's slavic orthodox allies in Serbia were on the receiving end of the NATO onslaught. What the liberal "West" considered a moral act, a "humanitarian" intervention, leaders and analysts in Moscow and Beijing saw as unlawful and self-interested aggression. Indeed, since they do not share the liberal West's liberalism, how could they have seen it any other way?

What is more, the allied intervention in Kosovo *was* unlawful, at least according to centuries of international law and the UN Charter. It was undertaken without authorization by the UN Security Council and against a sovereign nation that had committed no act of aggression beyond its borders. Americans and Europeans went to war in service of what they regarded as a "higher law" of liberal morality. For those who do not share this liberal morality, however, such acts are merely lawless, destructive of the traditional safeguards of national sovereignty.

Of course, it is precisely toward a less rigid conception of national sovereignty that the liberal world of Europe and the United States would like to go. It is their conception of progress and a beneficial evolution of international legal principles, Ideas that are becoming common currency in Europe and the United States—limited sovereignty, "the responsibility to protect," a "voluntary sovereignty waiver"—all aim to provide liberal nations the right to intervene in the affairs of nonliberal nations. The Chinese and Russians and the leaders of other autocracies cannot welcome this kind of progress. Nor is it surprising that China and Russia have become the world's leading defenders of the Westphalian order of states, with its insistence upon the inviolable sovereign equality of all nations.

This is more than a dispute over the niceties of international law. It concerns the fundamental legitimacy of governments, which at the end of the day is a matter of life and death. Autocrats can hardly be expected to aid in legitimizing an evolution in the international system toward "limited sovereignty" and "the responsibility to protect." For even if the people and governments pushing this evolution do not believe they are establishing the predicate for international interventions against Russia and China, the leaders of those nations have no choice but to contemplate the possibility and to try to shield themselves. China, after all, has been a victim of international sanctions imposed by the U.S.-led liberal world, and for killing far fewer people than the governments of Sudan or Zimbabwe. Nor do China's rulers forget that if the liberal world had had its way in 1989, they would now be out of office, probably imprisoned, possibly dead.

Because autocratic governments have a vital interest in disputing liberal principles of interventionism, they will often resist efforts by the liberal international community to put pressure on other autocracies around the world. Many in the United States and Europe have begun to complain about Chinese policies that provide unfettered aid to dictatorships in Africa and Asia, thereby undermining American and European efforts to press for reforms in countries such as Zimbabwe and Burma. To ask one dictatorship to aid in the undermining of another dictatorship, however, is asking a great deal. Chinese leaders will always be extremely reluctant to impose sanctions on autocrats when they themselves remain subject to sanctions for their own autocratic behavior. They may bend occasionally so as to avoid too-close association with what the West calls "rogue regimes." But the thrust of their foreign policy will be to support an international order that places a high value on national sovereignty.

Neither Russia nor China has any interest in assisting liberal nations in their crusade against autocracies around the world. Moreover, they can see their comparative advantage over the West when it comes to gaining influence with African, Asian, or Latin American governments that can provide access to oil and other vital natural resources or that, in the case of Burma, are strategically located. Moscow knows it can have more influence with governments in Kazakhstan and Turkmenistan because, unlike the liberal West, it can unreservedly support their regimes. And the more autocracies there are in the world, the less isolated Beijing and Moscow will be in international forums such as the United Nations. The more dictatorships there are, the more global resistance they will offer against the liberal West's efforts to place limits on sovereignty in the interest of advancing liberalism.

The general effect of the rise of these two large autocratic powers, therefore, will be to increase the likelihood that autocracy will spread in some parts of the world. This is not because Russia and China are evangelists for autocracy or want to set off a worldwide autocratic revolution. It is not the Cold War redux. It is more like the nineteenth century redux. Then, the absolutist rulers of Russia and Austria shored up fellow autocracies—in France, for instance—and used force to suppress liberal movements in Germany, Italy, Poland, and Spain. China and Russia may not go that far, at least not yet. But Ukraine has already been a battleground between forces supported by the liberal West and forces supported by Russia. The great-power autocracies will inevitably offer support and friendship to those who feel besieged by the United States and other liberal nations. This in itself will strengthen the hand of autocracy in the world. Autocrats and would-be autocrats will know they can again find powerful allies and patrons, something that was not as true in the 1990s.

Moreover, China and (to a much lesser extent) Russia provide a model for successful autocracy, a way to create wealth and stability without political liberalization. This is hardly novel, of course. Hugo Chavez did not need China to show him the possibilities of successful autocracy, least of all in Latin America. In the 1970s, autocratic regimes such as Pinochet's Chile, the shah's Iran, and Suharto's Indonesia also demonstrated that economic success could come without political liberalization. But through the 1980s and 1990s the autocratic model seemed less attractive as dictatorships of both right and left fell before the liberal tide. That tide has not yet turned in the other direction, but the future may bring a return to a global competition between different forms of government, with the world's great powers on opposite sides.

This has implications for international institutions and for American foreign policy. It is no longer possible to speak of an "international community." The term suggests agreement on international norms of behavior, an international morality, even an international conscience. The idea of such a community took hold in the 1990s, at a time when the general assumption was that the movement of Russia and China toward western liberalism was producing a global commonality of thinking about human affairs. But by the late 1990s it was already clear that the international community lacked a foundation of common understanding. This was exposed most blatantly in the war over Kosovo, which divided the liberal West from both Russia and China and from many other non-European nations. Today it is apparent on the issue of Sudan and Darfur. In the future, incidents that expose the hollowness of the term "international community" will likely proliferate.

As for the United Nations Security Council, after a brief awakening from the Cold War coma, it has fallen back to its former condition of near-paralysis. The agile diplomacy of France and the tactical caution of China have at times obscured the fact that the Security Council on most major issues is clearly divided between the autocracies and the democracies, with the latter systematically pressing for sanctions and other punitive actions against Iran, North Korea, Sudan, and other autocracies and the former just as systematically resisting and attempting to weaken the effect of such actions. This is a rut that is likely to deepen in the coming years. It will hinder, as it has already hindered, international efforts to provide assistance in humanitarian crises such as Darfur. It will also obstruct American and allied efforts to impose pressure and punishments on nations seeking nuclear and other weapons of mass destruction, as it has already done in the cases of Iran and North Korea.

The problem goes beyond the Security Council. Efforts to achieve any international consensus in any   little Sense of forum are going to be more and more difficult because of the widening gap between liberal and autocratic governments. The current divisions between the United States and its European allies that have garnered so much attention in recent years are going to be overtaken by more fundamental ideological divisions, and especially by growing tensions between the democratic transatlantic alliance and Russia.

The divisions will be all the sharper where ideological fault lines coincide with those caused by competitive national ambitions. It may be largely accidental that two of the world's more nationalistic powers are also the two leading autocracies, but this fact will have immense geopolitical significance.

Under these circumstances, calls for a new "concert" of nations in which Russia, China, the United States, Europe, and other great powers operate under some kind of international condominium are unlikely to succeed. The early nineteenth-century "concert of Europe" operated under the umbrella of a common morality and shared principles of government. It aimed not only at the preservation of a European peace but also, and more importantly, at the maintenance of a monarchical and aristocratic order against the liberal and radical challenges presented by the French and American revolutions and their echoes elsewhere in Europe. The conceit gradually broke down under the strains of popular nationalism, fueled in part by the rise of liberalism.

Today there is little sense of shared morality and common political principle among the great powers. Quite the contrary: There is suspicion, growing hostility, and the well-grounded view on the part of the autocracies that the democracies, whatever they say, would welcome their overthrow. Any concert among them would be built on a shaky foundation likely to collapse at the first serious test.

American foreign policy should be attuned to these ideological distinctions and recognize their relevance to the most important strategic questions. It is folly to expect China to help undermine a brutal regime in Khartoum or to be surprised if Russia rattles its saber at pro-Western democratic governments near its borders. There will be a tendency toward solidarity among the world's autocracies, as well as among the world's democracies.

For all these reasons, the United States should pursue policies designed both to promote democracy and to strengthen cooperation among the democracies. It should join with other democracies to erect new international institutions that both reflect and enhance their shared principles and goals. One possibility might be to establish a global concert or league of democratic states, perhaps informally at first but with the aim of holding regular meetings and consultations on the issues of the day. Such an institution could bring together Asian nations such as Japan, Australia, and India with the European nations—two sets of democracies that have comparatively little to do with each other outside the realms of trade and finance. The institution would complement, not replace, the United Nations, the G-8, and other global forums. But it would at the very least signal a commitment to the democratic idea, and in time it could become a means of pooling the resources of democratic nations to address a number of issues that cannot be addressed at the United Nations. If successful, it could come to be an organization capable of bestowing legitimacy on actions that liberal nations deem necessary but autocratic nations refuse to countenance—as NATO conferred legitimacy on the conflict in Kosovo even though Russia was opposed.

Some will claim that such an organization will only create divisions in the world. But those divisions are already there. The question now is whether there is any way to pursue American interests and liberal democratic ends despite them.

Others will worry that European democracies are either unwilling or unable to share the burden in pursuing common goals with the United States. That may be true. But there is still reason to hope that an effort to reinvigorate democratic solidarity may increase European willingness to take on such burdens, especially when it coincides with the increasingly autocratic and belligerent behavior of Russia and the continuing rise of autocratic China.

In such an international environment the United States should continue, as it has in the past, to prefer democracy over autocracy and to use its influence to promote the former when opportunities arise. This is more than just a matter of moral preference, although Americans often cannot avoid expressing and acting on that preference. But in a world where autocracies increasingly look for allies in fellow autocracies, the democracies will want to do the same. The United States should discourage moves toward autocracy in democratic nations, both by punishing steps that undo democratic institutions and by providing support to those institutions and individuals who favor democratic principles. It should isolate autocratic governments when possible while encouraging internal pressure for democratic reform. History suggests that external influences, especially by the global superpower, have a positive if not determinative influence on the political course nations take. The United States should express support for democracy in word and deed without expecting immediate success. It should support the development of liberal institutions and practices, understanding that elections alone do not guarantee a steady liberal democratic course. But neither should Americans lose sight of the centrality of free and fair elections for both democracy and true liberalism.

The United States need not engage in a blind crusade on behalf of democracy everywhere at all times, nor need it seek a violent confrontation with the autocratic powers. For one thing, all the world's great powers share some important common interests, especially in the economic realm. Nor can an intelligent foreign policy ever be guided solely by one set of principles. Promoting democracy cannot and should not be the only goal of American foreign policy, any more than can producing wealth, fighting terrorism, preventing the spread of nuclear weapons, or any other national goal or ambition. There will be times when promoting democracy will have to take a back seat to other objectives. The job of statesmen is to determine when. But democracy should be as highly valued as the others, for it is, like them, of strategic importance. As the hard-headed Dean Acheson put it, Americans "are children of freedom" and "cannot be safe except in an environment of freedom."[19]

The emphasis on democracy, liberalism, and human rights has strategic relevance in part because it plays to American strengths and exposes the weaknesses of the autocratic powers. It is easy to look at China and Russia today and believe they are simply getting stronger and stronger. But one should not overlook their fragility. These autocratic regimes may be stronger than they were in the past in terms of wealth and global influence. But they do still live in a predominantly liberal era. That means they face an unavoidable problem of legitimacy. They are not like the autocracies of nineteenth-century Europe, which still enjoyed a historical legitimacy derived partly from the fact that the world had known nothing but autocracy for centuries.

To be an autocrat today is to be constantly concerned that the powerful forces of liberalism, backed by a collection of rich, advanced nations, including the world's only superpower, will erode or undermine the controls necessary to stay in power. Today's autocracies struggle to create a new kind of legitimacy, and it is no easy task. The Chinese leaders race forward with their economy in fear that any slowing will be their undoing. They fitfully stamp out signs of political opposition partly because they live in fear of repeating the Soviet experience. Having watched the Soviet Union succumb to the liberal West, thanks to what they regard as Mikhail Gorbachev's weakness and mistakes, they are determined neither to show weakness nor to make the same mistakes.

Vladimir Putin shares both their contempt for Gorbachev and their commitment to the lessons learned from his downfall. In a nice historical irony, fitfully Stamp put the Russian leader, in order to avoid a Russian dénouement, is trying to adopt a Chinese model of , modern autocracy, using oil and gas wealth instead of entrepreneurship to buy off the Russian elite as he consolidates power in the name of stability and nationalism. In both countries, the renewed international competition among ambitious nations is helpful in this respect. It allows the governments to charge dissidents and would-be democrats as fifth-columnists for American hegemony. In Russia's case, it has been easy for Putin to tarnish liberal democrats by associating them in the popular mind with past policies of accommodation and even subservience to the United States and the West.

Nevertheless, the Chinese are not just pretending when they claim their deep internal problems make them hesitant to pursue a more adventurous foreign policy. Leaders in Beijing rightly fear they are riding a tiger at home, and they fear external support for a political opposition more than they fear foreign invasion. Even promoting nationalism as a means of enhancing legitimacy is a dangerous business, since in Chinese history nationalist movements have evolved into revolutionary movements.

The Russian regime is also vulnerable to pressures from within and without, for unlike China, Russia still maintains the trappings of democracy. It would not be easy for a Russian leader simply to abandon all pretense and assume the role of tsar. Elections must still be held, even if they are unfair or are merely referendums on the selection of the leadership. This provides an opportunity for dissidents within and liberals on the outside to preserve the possibility of a return to democratic governance in Russia. It certainly would be a strategic error to allow Putin and any possible successor to strengthen their grip on power without outside pressures for reform, for the consolidation of autocracy at home will free the Russian leadership to pursue greater nationalist ambitions abroad. In these and other autocracies, including Iran, promoting democracy and human rights exacerbates internal political contradictions and can have the effect of blunting external ambitions as leaders tend to more dangerous threats from within.

In most of the world today—in Asia, Europe, Latin America, and even Africa—the idea of supporting democracy against autocracy is not very controversial, though there are heated debates over precisely how to do it. The issue becomes more complicated when one turns to the Middle East, where some observers believe the Arab people are simply not ready for democracy and where the prospect of electoral victories by Islamist movements seems to some the worst possible outcome. Should the United States and others promote democracy in the Middle East too?

Part of the answer comes if one turns the question around and asks: Should the United States support autocracy in the Middle East? That is the only other choice, after all. There is no neutral stance on such matters. The United States is either supporting an autocracy, through aid, recognition, amicable diplomatic relations, and regular economic intercourse, or it is using its manifold influence in varying degrees to push for democratic reform. The number of American thinkers who believe that the United States should simply support Middle Eastern autocrats and not push for change at all is small, and the number of policymakers and politicians who support that view is even smaller. After September 11, 2001, most observers agreed that American support for autocratic regimes in Egypt and Saudi Arabia was the "principal source of resentment" of the terrorists who launched the attack on the United States and that, therefore, a policy of simply supporting autocrats in those and other Middle Eastern countries would be a mistake.[20]

The main questions, then, are really a matter of tactics and timing. But no matter whether one prefers faster or slower, harder or softer, there will always be the risk that pressure of any kind will produce a victory for radical Islamists. Is that a risk worth taking? A similar question arose constantly during the Cold War, when American liberals called on the United States to stop supporting Third World dictators and American conservatives and neoconservatives warned that the dictators would be replaced by pro-Soviet communists. Sometimes this proved true. But other times such efforts produced moderate democratic governments that were pro-American. The lesson of the Reagan years, when pro-American and reasonably democratic governments replaced right-wing dictatorships in El Salvador, Guatemala, the Philippines, and South Korea, to name just a few, was that the risk was, on balance, worth taking.

It may be worth taking again in the Middle East, and not only as a strategy of democracy promotion but as part of a larger effort to address the issue of Islamic radicalism by accelerating and intensifying its confrontation with the modern, globalized world.

MODERNIZATION, GLOBALIZATION, ISLAM, AND THEIR DISCONTENTS

The islamists struggle against the powerful and often impersonal forces of modernization, capitalism, and globalization is another significant fact of life in the world today. Much of this fight has been peaceful, but some of it has been violent and now, oddly, poses by far the greatest threat of a catastrophic attack on the mainland of the United States.

It is odd because the struggle between modernization and globalization, on the one hand, and traditionalism, on the other, is largely a sideshow on the international stage. The future is more likely to be dominated by the struggle among the great powers and between the great ideologies of liberalism and autocracy than by the effort of some radical Islamists to restore an imagined past of piety. But of course that struggle has taken on a new and frightening dimension. Normally, when old and less technologically advanced civilizations have confronted more advanced civilizations, their inadequate weapons have reflected their backwardness. Today, the radical proponents of Islamic traditionalism, though they abhor the modern world, are nevertheless not only using the ancient methods of assassination and suicidal attacks, but also have deployed the weapons of the modern world against it. Modernization and globalization inflamed their rebellion and also armed them for the fight.

It is a lonely and ultimately desperate fight, for in the struggle between tradition and modernization, tradition cannot win—though traditional forces armed with modern technology can put up a good fight. All the world's rich and powerful nations have more or less embraced the economic, technological, and even social aspects of modernization and globalization. All have embraced, albeit with varying degrees of complaint and resistance, the free flow of goods, finances, and services, and the intermingling of cultures and lifestyles that characterize the modern world. Increasingly, their people watch the same television shows, listen to the same music, and go to the same movies. And along with this dominant modern culture they have accepted, even as they may also deplore, the essential characteristics of a modern morality and aesthetics: the sexual as well as political and economic liberation of women, the weakening of church authority and the strengthening of secularism, the existence of what used to be called the counterculture, free expression in the arts (if not in politics), which includes the freedom to commit blasphemy and to lampoon symbols of faith, authority, and morality—these and all the countless effects of liberalism and capitalism unleashed and unchecked by the constraining hand of tradition, a powerful church, or a moralistic and domineering government. The Chinese have learned that while it is possible to have capitalism without political liberalization, it is much harder to have capitalism without cultural liberalization.

Today radical Islamists are the last holdout against these powerful forces of globalization and modernization. They seek to carve out a part of the world where they can be left alone, shielded from what they regard as the soul-destroying licentiousness of unchecked liberalism and capitalism. The tragedy for them is that their goal is impossible to achieve. Neither the United States nor the other great powers will turn over control of the Middle East to these fundamentalist forces, if only because the region is of such vital strategic importance to the rest of the world. The outside powers have strong internal allies as well, including the majority of the populations of the Middle East who have been willing and even eager to make peace with modernity. Nor is it conceivable in this modern world that a people can wall themselves off from modernity even if the majority wanted to. Could the great Islamic theocracy that al Qaeda and others hope to erect ever completely block out the sights and sounds of the rest of the world and thereby shield their people from the temptations of modernity? The mullahs have not even succeeded at doing that in Iran. The project is fantastic.

The world is thus faced with the prospect of a protracted struggle in which the goals of the extreme Islamists can never be satisfied because neither the United States nor anyone else has the ability to give them what they want. The West is quite simply not capable of retreating as far as the Islamic extremists require.

If retreat is impossible, perhaps the best course is to advance. Of the many bad options in confronting this immensely dangerous problem, the best may be to hasten the process of modernization in the Islamic world: more modernization, more globalization, faster. This would require greater efforts to support and expand capitalism and the free market in Arab countries, as many have already recommended, as well as efforts to increase public access to the modern world through television and the Internet. Nor should it be considered a setback if these modern communication tools are also used to organize radical extremism. That is unavoidable so long as the radical Islamist backlash persists, which it will for some time.

Finally, the liberal world should continue to promote political modernization and liberalization; support human rights, Including the rights of women; and use its influence to support repeated elections that may, if nothing else, continually shift power from the few to the many. This, too, will produce setbacks. It will provide a channel for popular resentments to express themselves and for radical Islamism itself to take power. But perhaps this phase is as unavoidable as the present conflict. Perhaps the sooner it is begun, the sooner a new phase can take its place.[21]

Throughout all these efforts, whose success is by no means guaranteed and certainly not any time soon, the United States and others will have to persist in fighting what is, in fact, quite accurately called "the war on terrorism." Now and probably for the coming decades, organized terrorist groups will seek to strike at the United States, and at modernity itself, when and where they can. This war will not and cannot be the totality of America's worldwide strategy. It can be only a piece of it. But given the high stakes, it must be prosecuted ruthlessly, effectively, and for as long as the threat persists. This will sometimes require military interventions when, as in Afghanistan, states either cannot or will not deny the terrorists a base. That aspect of the "war on terror" is certainly not going away. One need only contemplate the American popular response should a terrorist group explode a nuclear weapon on American soil. No president of any party or ideological coloration will be able to resist the demands of the American people for retaliation and revenge, and not only against the terrorists but against any nation that aided or harbored them. Nor, one suspects, will the American people disapprove when a president takes preemptive action to forestall such a possibility—assuming the action is not bungled.

The United States will not have many eager partners in this fight. For although in the struggle between modernization and tradition, the United States, Russia, China, Europe, and the other great powers are roughly on the same side, the things that divide them from each other—the competing national ambitions and ideological differences—will inevitably blunt their ability or their willingness to cooperate in the military aspects of a fight against radical Islamic terrorism. Europeans have been and will continue to be less than enthusiastic about what they emphatically do not call "the war on terror." And it will be tempting for Russian and Chinese leaders to enjoy the spectacle of the United States bogged down in a fight with al Qaeda and other violent Islamist groups in the Middle East, just as it is tempting to let American power in that region be checked by a nuclear-armed Iran. Unfortunately, the willingness of the autocrats in Moscow and Beijing to run interference for their fellow autocrats in Pyongyang, Tehran, and Khartoum increases the chance that the connection between terrorists and nuclear weapons will eventually be made.

THE END OF GRAND EXPECTATIONS

When the Cold War ended, it was possible to imagine that the world had been utterly changed: the end of international competition, the end of geopolitics, the end of history. When in the first decade after the Cold War people began describing the new era of "globalization," the common expectation was that the phenomenon of instantaneous global communications, the free flow of goods and services, the rapid transmission of ideas and information, and the intermingling and blending of cultures would further knit together a world that had already just patched up the great ideological and geopolitical tears of the previous century. "Globalization" was to the late twentieth century what "sweet commerce" was to the late eighteenth—an anticipated balm for a war-weary world.

In the 1990s serious thinkers predicted the end of wars and military confrontations among great powers. European "postmodernism" seemed to be the future: the abandonment of power politics in favor of international institutions capable of managing the disagreements among nations. Even today, there are those who believe the world is moving along the same path as the European Union. John Ikenberry recently described the post-Cold War era, the decade of the 1990s, as a liberal paradise:

> The Cold War ended, democracy and markets flourished around the world, globalization was enshringd as a progressive historical force, and ideology nationalism and war were at a low ebb. NAFTA, APEC, and the WTO signaled a strengthening of the rules and institutions of the world economy, NATO was expanded and the U.S.–Japan alliance was renewed. Russia became a quasi-member of the West and China was a "strategic partner" with Washington. Clinton's grand strategy of building post-Cold War order around expanding markets, democracy, and institutions was the triumphant embodiment of the liberal vision of international order.[22]

Perhaps it was these grand expectations of a new era for humankind that helped spur the anger and outrage at American policies of the past decade. It is not that those policies are in themselves so different, or in any way out of character for the United States. It is that to many people in Europe and even in the United States, they have seemed jarringly out of place in a world that was supposed to have moved on.

As we now know, however, both nationalism and ideology were already making their comeback in the 1990s. Russia had ceased to be and no longer desired to be a "quasi-member" of the West, and partly because of NATO enlargement. China was already on its present trajectory and had already determined that American hegemony was a threat to its ambitions. The forces of radical Islam had already begun their jihad, globalization had already caused a backlash around the world, and the juggernaut of democracy had already stalled and begun to tip precariously.

After the Second World War, another moment in history when hopes for a new kind of international order were rampant, Hans Morgenthau warned idealists against imagining that at some point "the final curtain would fall and the game of power politics would no longer be played." But the world struggle continued then, and it continues today. Six decades ago American leaders believed the United States had the unique ability and the unique responsibility to use its power to prevent a slide back to the circumstances that produced two world wars and innumerable national calamities. Although much has changed since then, America's responsibility has not.

NOTES

1. This was the title chosen by former President George H. W. Bush and his national security adviser Brent Scowcroft, for their account of American foreign policy at the end of the Cold War.
2. Second Inaugural Address of William J. Clinton (January 20, 1997).
3. Dean Acheson, quoted in Robert L. Beisner, *Dean Acheson: A Life in the Cold War* (Oxford University Press, 2006), 372.
4. The quotations are of course from Harry Truman, John F. Kennedy, Bill Clinton, and George W. Bush.
5. See Stephen Sestanovich, "American Maximalism," *National Interest* (Spring 2005).
6. Critics obviously don't mean that the Bush administration literally acts alone, since even in Iraq the United States had a number of allies. It had more partners in that war than the administration of George H.W. Bush had in its invasion of Panama and than Bill Clinton had in his intervention in Haiti. "Unilateralism" apparently is a relative term and depends for its interpretation on circumstances.
7. Melvyn P. Leffler, "9/11 and American Foreign Policy," *Diplomatic History*, 29:3 (June 2005); John Lewis Gaddis, *Surprise, Security, and the American Experience* (Harvard University Press, 2005).
8. In "Walzer's view, traditional legal arguments against preventive war look "different when the danger is posed by weapons of mass destruction, which are developed in secret, and which might be used suddenly, without warning, with catastrophic results." Not only might preventive action be "legitimate" under such circumstances, but so would "unilateral action" without a Security Council authorization. The "refusal of a U.N. majority to act forcefully" is not "a good reason for ruling out the use of force by any member state that can use it effectively." Michael Walzer, "The Hard Questions: Lone Ranger," *New Republic* (April 27, 1998). Kissinger's argument is similar. See Henry Kissinger, "Iraq Poses Most Consequential Foreign-Policy Decision for Bush," *Los Angeles Times* (August 8, 2002).
9. To review the behavior of the most recent administrations: The Reagan administration sought no international authorization for its covert war against the Sandinistas or its arming of guerrillas in Angola and Afghanistan, and it sought neither un nor OAS support for the invasion of Grenada. The first Bush administration invaded Panama without un authorization and would have gone to war with Iraq without authorization if Russia had vetoed. The Clinton administration intervened in Haiti without UN authorization, bombed Iraq over the objection of un Security Council permanent members, and went to war in Kosovo without UN authorization.
10. Remarks of Senator Barack Obama to the Chicago Council on Global Affairs (April 23, 2007).
11. Rosalie Chen, "China Perceives America: Perspectives of International Relations Experts," *Journal of Contemporary China* 12:35 (May 2003).
12. This is what William Wohlforth predicted almost a decade ago. See William C. Wohlforth, "The Stability of a Unipolar World," *International* Security 24:1 (Summer 1999).
13. See, for instance, G. John Ikenberry, "Strategic Reactions to American Preeminence: Great Power Politics in the Age of Unipolarity," working group paper prepared for the National Intelligence Council (July 2003).
14. American defense spending remains historically low as a percentage of CDP, at about 4 percent. In the Reagan years, it reached nearly 8 percent. During the early years of the Cold War, it was well over 15 percent. Nor is the size of the defense budget a political issue, even among Democrats. Both Barack Obama nd Hillary Clinton currently call for increases in the size of U.S. ground forces, for instance—a huge additional expense.
15. For the most thorough discussion of worldwide trends that run counter to the prediction of balancing, see Keir A. Lieber and Gerard Alexander, "Waiting For Balancing: Why the World Is Not Pushing Back," *International Security* 30:1 (Summer 2005).

16. A recent editorial in the *Economist* ("Pining for the Cold War," May 14, 2007) artfully provides the view of the world as seen from Moscow, that "Russia is a strong, sovereign and prosperous country, surrounded by enemies and traitors who are bent on undermining its geopolitical power. Upstarts such as Estonia and Poland are trying to spoil Russia's far more important relationships with proper European countries, such as Germany or France. The freshly-baked European Union (EU) members act on the instructions of America, a hypocritical and arrogant dictator of the world order, which pretends to be a democracy but in fact is closer to the Third Reich."

17. "Whether the U.S. likes it or not, Iran is a major regional power with great political and spiritual influence. It is in the United States' interests to accept Iran's influence as a reality, though it may be a bitter pill to swallow, and to stop leveling accusations against the Islamic Republic based on prejudices." *Tehran Times* (May 15, 2007).

18. It would be pleasant to imagine deeper European involvement as well. But that seems unlikely, given Europe's general weakness and its internal problems with Islam.

19. Beisner, Acheson, 152

20. Samantha Power, "U.S. Democracy Promotion: Failure or Folly?" remarks to the Pell Center for International Relations and Public Policy (April 10, 2006).

21. See, for instance, Reuel Marc Gerecht, The Islamic Paradox (AEI Press, 2004).

22. G. John Ikenberry, "Liberal International Theory in the Wake of 9/11 and American Unipolarity," paper prepared for seminar on "IR Theory, Unipolarity and September 11th—Five Years On," NUPI, Oslo, Norway (February 3-4, 2006).